INTERNATIONAL ENVIRONMENTAL LAW

A PROBLEM-ORIENTED COURSEBOOK

Fourth Edition

■ ■ ■

Jonathan C. Carlson
Professor of Law
Victor and Carol Alvarez Fellow in Law
The University of Iowa

Sir Geoffrey W.R. Palmer, P.C., K.C.M.G., A.C., Q.C.
Barrister
Distinguished Fellow Victoria University of Wellington
Faculty of Law and Centre for Public Law
Global Affiliated Professor, The University of Iowa College of Law

AMERICAN CASEBOOK SERIES®

444 Cedar Street, Suite 700
St. Paul, MN 55101
1-877-888-1330

Printed in the United States of America

ISBN: 978-1-68328-785-8

INTERNATIONAL ENVIRONMENTAL LAW

A PROBLEM-ORIENTED COURSEBOOK

Fourth Edition

■ ■ ■

Jonathan C. Carlson
Professor of Law
Victor and Carol Alvarez Fellow in Law
The University of Iowa

Sir Geoffrey W.R. Palmer, P.C., K.C.M.G., A.C., Q.C.
Barrister
Distinguished Fellow Victoria University of Wellington
Faculty of Law and Centre for Public Law
Global Affiliated Professor, The University of Iowa College of Law

AMERICAN CASEBOOK SERIES®

444 Cedar Street, Suite 700
St. Paul, MN 55101
1-877-888-1330

Printed in the United States of America

ISBN: 978-1-68328-785-8

We are the planet, fully as much as its water, earth, fire and air are the planet, and if the planet survives, it will only be through heroism. Not occasional heroism, a remarkable instance of it here and there, but constant heroism, systematic heroism, heroism as governing principle.

—Russell Banks
Continental Drift 40 (1985)

We dedicate this book

*to our spouses, our children, and to their spouses
and children—our grandchildren
(in alphabetical order)*

Aadi	*Gwendoline*	*Russell*
Adam	*Helena*	*Ruth*
Andrew	*Jeremy*	*Shelby*
Bernard	*Margaret*	*Susan*
Kate	*Matthew*	*Ursula*
	Rebekah	

*to all other children and grandchildren
present and future*

*and to our dear departed colleague
Burns H. Weston (1933–2015)*

PREFACE

The environment affects us all and influences all human activities that take place here on Earth. Yet often it seems that we humans are heedless of that fact, as we continue to foul our nest and destroy the resources that support our civilizations with little regard for the consequences of our actions. As this book is going to press, two examples are prominent in the news.

First, a recent report from the Intergovernmental Science-Policy Platform on Biodiversity and Ecosystem Services (IPBES) revealed that the current global decline in biodiversity is more dramatic and more dangerous than at any time in human history. According to Sir Robert Watson, IPBES Chair, the data present "an ominous picture." "The health of ecosystems on which we and all other species depend is deteriorating more rapidly than ever. We are eroding the very foundations of our economies, livelihoods, food security, health and quality of life worldwide."

Second, there is climate change. We have known for decades that our behavior is causing changes in the composition of the atmosphere that will adversely affect climate across the planet. Diplomats have worked for decades to develop solutions to the problem. Yet the latest evidence shows that CO_2 concentrations in the atmosphere are higher than ever, that the planet is warming faster than ever, and that annual global greenhouse gas emissions hit an all-time high in 2018. Far from changing our behavior to address the problem, we continue to act in ways that make the future bleak for our grandchildren.

The global community seems to lack the political will and determination to tackle and solve these problems. While substantial commitment was present in earlier years, particularly around the time of the United Nations Conference on Environment and Development in 1992 at Rio de Janeiro, attention is now focused elsewhere. The first edition of this book appeared two years after that conference. It was a time of optimism and hope, although progress at Rio did not match the magnitude of the problem.

It is twenty-five years since the first edition of this book appeared in 1994. The way we see it, the prospects for the health of our global environment have dimmed since then. It seems to us that the years since Rio have by and large been wasted. There have been significant achievements—the improvement in the condition of the hole in the ozone layer is one of the most obvious—but our overall progress in solving environmental problems must receive a failing grade. We have had a reasonably constant stream of treaties and declarations that have added to an already thick wad of international environmental instruments that cover in total something approaching 2,000 pages. But hard questions must be asked. Have they made a difference or a sufficient difference?

The condition of the international legal order seems to us not fit for purpose when it comes to dealing with the global environmental challenge. The incubus of outdated ideas about state sovereignty too often prevents progressive and necessary outcomes in a multitude of international environmental negotiations. The frustration, the waste of time and resources, and the spinning of wheels that these negotiations involve should not be underestimated. These failures are attributable directly to the structural weaknesses of the international legal framework. A new global legal regime bringing the virtues of the rule of law to protect the international environment seems as remote now as it was when the first edition of this book appeared.

We put forward this view not in some fit of impatient crusading zeal. We do so, rather, on the basis of a sober, realistic assessment of where the world is at, in terms of both theory and practice. The authors of this coursebook believe that humankind's destruction and defilement of the natural environment is seriously endangering the continuation of life on this planet. We are in desperate need of rational ecological governance. If the international legal order does not adapt to meet this need, the consequences for the planet will be serious and long-lasting.

Lawyers can help in this regard. The essence of the task of the international environmental lawyer is to marry the techniques and modalities of public international law and apply them to the environmental problems we face. Success requires the ability to navigate a complex matrix of scientific, political, social, economic, and ethical considerations. Our goal in producing a coursebook that teaches international environmental law through the problem method is therefore two-fold. First, we hope to inspire students to become serious and passionate about using international law to solve these global problems, for there will be no solutions without international law. Second, we hope to equip students with the critical-thinking and problem-solving skills that will allow them to use the tools of international law when those tools work and to develop new principles and norms of international law when new law is necessary to make real progress.

* * *

This fourth edition of our coursebook is a mix of old and new. We have retained the problem orientation of the first three editions of the book and most of the problems in the book will be familiar to previous users. We continue to believe that the problem-oriented approach has great pedagogical value. The exercise of identifying and framing issues in factual context, organizing and evaluating relevant law and policy, and applying

that law and policy to the facts not only hones analytical skills but kindles student interest and enthusiasm far more effectively—and efficiently—than doctrinal exposition.

With that in mind, we have dramatically restructured the first part of the book. We have largely eliminated the extensive theoretical and doctrinal exposition on international law that characterized the first five chapters of earlier editions. In place of those chapters we have substituted four new chapters that aim to introduce students to this subject by showing how international law has been used and developed by states in various real-world contexts.

Chapter One focuses on the long-running dispute over whaling in the Southern Ocean, dramatized in the reality television series *Whale Wars*. Many of our students are familiar with the television show and are excited by the opportunity to learn about the legal and policy disputes surrounding the whaling issue. To set the stage for a close examination of the whaling issue, the chapter begins with expositions on international dispute settlement and the sources of international law, followed by a short review of the Bering Sea Fur Seal Arbitration, a case that can be used to teach much about both the sources of international law and international dispute settlement processes.

Chapter Two tells the story of the *Rainbow Warrior* incident. It allows continued exploration of international dispute settlement techniques and includes, at the end, a short review of the application of international law in domestic legal systems.

Chapter Three is entirely new. It uses the stories of the Trail Smelter Arbitration and the negotiation of the Convention on Long-range Transboundary Air Pollution to illustrate how international law impacts, and is impacted by, efforts to solve international problems. It places special emphasis on the *sic utere* principle and the doctrine of State Responsibility.

Chapter Four concludes the restructured Part I by examining the historical development of international environmental law.

Part II of the book is much the same as in previous editions. The biggest change is that we have reorganized the problems. We encourage users to teach those problems that they prefer and in the order that they prefer. There are many options, and each user must pick an approach with which she is comfortable. We begin Part II with chapters on protection of the atmosphere and protection of the oceans because those are arenas in which international law has been relatively successful. We believe it can be helpful to expose students to some international law success stories before confronting those environmental challenges (e.g. climate change and biodiversity protection) that remain unresolved despite the proliferation of international efforts to address them.

We know that these significant changes will require past users of the book (ourselves included!) to make considerably greater adjustments than are usually needed when a new edition of a book is published. We hope, however, that the changes we've made will generate sufficiently increased student excitement for the material, and sufficiently improved student learning outcomes, that faculty will consider any increased preparation time to be time well spent.

JONATHAN C. CARLSON
IOWA CITY, IOWA

SIR GEOFFREY W.R. PALMER
WELLINGTON, NEW ZEALAND

May 2019

FIVE NOTES ON EDITORIAL MATTERS

First, as in our prior editions, the texts of treaties and other legal documents referenced in this coursebook are found largely in a separate *Supplement of Basic Documents to International Environmental Law* that we have prepared to provide the comprehensive coverage of them that would be otherwise impossible without it. References in our coursebook to "Basic Documents" are references to that supplement.

Second, footnotes are numbered consecutively throughout each chapter. Most of the footnotes in the book are our own. Occasionally we have retained original footnotes from a reading used in the coursebook. Our footnotes and original footnotes are distinguishable by context and content.

Third, we have used references such as "North," "South," "developing countries," "Third World," and the like. While these terms do not adequately reflect the complexity of our world, they are necessary for reasons of convenience.

Fourth, we have not altered the words of writers whose language implies that only men are international lawyers, judges, diplomats, politicians, or other actors in the international legal process. We urge the reader to take a critical view and recognize that the language used by writers reflects the fact that international law itself has developed in a lop-sided, gendered way. We apologize in advance if in any instance our own language inadvertently continues to reflect that problem.

Finally, we have eliminated most footnotes and internal citations from readings without explicitly reflecting the omission. Where text has been omitted we use ". . ." to indicate omissions within paragraphs and * * * to indicate more substantial omissions of a paragraph or more.

ACKNOWLEDGMENTS

We are greatly indebted to a large number of generous people who gave invaluably to the realization of this fourth edition. There of course can be no full accounting of our indebtedness, but as much as possible we seek to recognize these people and extend to them our most heartfelt thanks.

Those student research assistants who gave generously of themselves, typically above and beyond the call of duty and always with curiosity, wisdom, and good humor, are (in alphabetical order): Katherine Birchok, Luke Cole, Bernadette Nelson, Emma Russ, and Daniel Strawhun. In New Zealand the research assistant was Scarlet Roberts. We are grateful, as well, to Gerard van Bohemen, Philippa Brakes, and Monica Medina for their input into issues related to whaling. Their thoughtful comments and observations have made Chapter One better than it otherwise would have been. The authors are, of course, entirely responsible for any inaccuracies or problems that remain. The New Zealand Ministry of Foreign Affairs and Trade were helpful on this issue and a number of other matters.

For dedication and skill, we thank Professor Carlson's secretarial assistant, Mary Sleichter at The University of Iowa, and Sir Geoffrey Palmer's executive assistant, Sarah Jenner.

We are grateful as well to Dean Kevin Washburn of The University of Iowa College of Law and his predecessor Gail Agrawal, each of whom supported this work with research assistant salaries for several years. Professor Mark Hickford, Dean of the Faculty of Law at the Victoria University of Wellington, was supportive and helpful in many ways, particularly with the provision of support facilities.

A special thank you also to the ever helpful and gracious professionals at West Academic, most especially Megan Putler, who extended herself above and beyond the norm in helping bring this volume to fruition.

Finally, as the following pages bear ample witness, we are indebted to many authors and publishers for permission to reprint materials used in this coursebook. We acknowledge with appreciation the permission granted to reprint copyright material by the following authors and publishers:

Adam D. K. Abelkop, for permission to reprint from Adam D. K. Abelkop & Jonathan C. Carlson, *Reining in Phaëthon's Chariot: Principles for the Governance of Geoengineering,* 21 TRANSNAT'L L. & CONTEMP. PROBLS. 763 (2013).

American Society of International Law, for permission to reprint from Michael Glennon, *Has International Law Failed the Elephant Michael,* 84 AM. J. INT'L L. 1–4, 10–18, 20–23, 26–28, 30–33 (1990); Sir Geoffrey

Palmer, *New Ways To Make International Environmental Law*, 86 AM. J. INT'L L. 259, 262–63 (1992); Animal Law Review, for permission to reprint from Sam B. Edwards III, *Legal Trade in African Elephant Ivory: Buy Ivory to Save the Elephant?*, 7 ANIMAL LAW 119, 128–131 (2001).

Donald K. Anton, for permission to reprint from Donald K. Anton. *"Treaty Congestion" in Contemporary International Environmental Law*, ANU College of Law Research Paper No. 12-05 (2012)

Arizona Law Review, for permission to reprint from George Frisvold & Kelly Day-Rubenstein, *Biosprospecting and Biodiversity Conservation: What Happens When Discoveries Are Made*, 50 ARIZ. L. REV. 545, 546–54 (2008).

Abou Bamba, Kim Diana Connolly, and Royal C. Gardner, for permission to reprint from Royal C. Gardner, Kim Diana Connolly, & Abou Bamba, *African Wetlands of International Importance: Assessment of Benefits Associated With Designations Under the RAMSAR Convention*, 21 GEO. INT'L ENVTL. L. REV. 257, 258–64, 285–90 (2009).

Paula Barrios, for permission to reprint from Paula Barrios, *The Rotterdam Convention on Hazardous Chemicals: A Meaningful Step Toward Environmental Protection*, 16 GEO. INT'L ENVTL. L. REV. 679–82, 697–99, 700–01, 725–33, 739–42, 762 (2004).

Reed Boland, for permission to reprint from Reed Boland, *The Environment, Population and Women's Human Rights*, 27 ENVTL. L. 1137, 1142–54 (1997);

Boston University International Law Journal, for permission to reprint from John B. Heppes & Eric J. McFadden, *The Convention on International Trade in Endangered Species of Wild Fauna and Flora: Improving the Prospects for Preserving Our Biological Heritage*, 5 BOSTON U. INT'L L.J. 229, 229–32 (1987).

Vicki Breazeale and Sustainable Development Law and Policy, for permission to reprint from Vicki Breazeale, *Introduction: A Perspective on Sustainable Pathways Toward Preservation of Biodiversity*, 10 SUSTAINABLE DEV. L. & POL'Y 2 (2010).

Frances Cairncross, for permission to reprint from FRANCES CAIRNCROSS, COSTING THE EARTH-THE CHALLENGE FOR GOVERNMENTS, THE OPPORTUNITIES FOR BUSINESS 131–41 (1993).

Cardozo Journal of International and Comparative Law, for permission to reprint from Paul J. Heald, *The Rhetoric of Biopiracy,* 11 CARDOZO J. INT'L & COMP. L. 519 (2003).

Colorado Journal of International Environmental Law & Policy, for permission to reprint from Rachelle Adam, *Missing the 2010*

Biodiversity Target: A Wake-up Call for the Convention on Biodiversity?, 21 COLO. J. INT'L ENVTL. L. & POL'Y 123, 133–38, 140–41, 145 (2010); Gabriel E. Eckstein, *Commentary on the U.N. International Law Commission's Draft Articles on the Law of Transboundary Aquifers*, 18 COLO. J. INT'L ENVTL. L. & POL'Y 537, 537–38, 553–56, 560–68, 570–73 (2007); Jonathan Lautze & Mark Giordano, *Equity in Transboundary Water Law: Valuable Paradigm or Merely Semantics?*, 17 COLO. J. INT'L ENVTL. L & POL'Y 89, 90–1, 94–5, 98, 110–11 (2006).

Columbia Journal of Environmental Law, for permission to reprint from John Charles Kunich, *Losing Nemo: the Mass Extinction Now Threatening the World's Ocean Hotspots,* 30 COLUM. J. ENVT'L L. 1, 66–69 (2005); David Ring, *Sustainability Dynamics: Land-Based Marine Pollution and Development Priorities in the Island States of the Commonwealth Caribbean*, 22 COLUM. J. ENVTL. L. 65, 73, 78–79, 81–98, 112–13 (1997).

Columbia Journal of Asian Law for permission to reprint under Creative Commons Attribution (CC-BY) License [https://creativecommons.org/licenses/by/4.0/] from Lisa B. Gregory, *Examining the Economic Component of China's One-Child Family Policy Under International Law: Your Money or Your Life*, 6 J. CHINESE L. 45, 60–78 (1992).

Convention on Biological Diversity Secretariat, for permission to reprint from *Executive Summary,* GLOBAL BIODIVERSITY OUTLOOK (GBO) 3 (2010).

Kyle W. Danish, for permission to reprint from Kyle W. Danish, *International Environmental Law and the Bottom-Up Approach: A Review of the Desertification Convention,* 3 IND. J. GLOBAL LEGAL STUD. 133 (1995).

Mario Del Baglivo, for permission to reprint from Mario Del Baglivo, *CITES at the Crossroad: New Ivory Sales and Sleeping Giants,* 14 FORDHAM ENVTL. L. J. 279, 279–280, 285–301 (2003).

Joseph W. Dellapenna, for permission to reprint from Joseph W. Dellapenna, *International Water Law in a Climate of Disruption,* 17 MICH. ST. J. INT'L L. 43, 68–71, 72–75 (2008).

Denver Journal of International Law and Policy, for permission to reprint from Alexandre Kiss, *State Responsibility and Liability for Nuclear Damage,* 35 DENV. J. INT'L L. & POLICY 67, 77–78 (2006); John E. Noyes, *Book Review: Places of Refuge for Ships,* 37 DENV. J. INT'L L. & POL'Y 135, 135–36, 137–38 (2008).

John C. Dernbach, for permission to reprint from John C. Dernbach, *Achieving Early and Substantial Greenhouse Gas Reductions Under a*

Post-Kyoto Agreement, 20 GEO. INT'L ENVTL. L. REV. 573–74, 582, 594–97, 599–603 (2008).

Gabriel Eckstein, for permission to reprint from Gabriel E. Eckstein, *Commentary on the U.N. International Law Commission's Draft Articles on the Law of Transboundary Aquifers,* 18 COLO. J. INT'L ENVTL. L. & POL'Y 537, 537–38, 553–56, 560–68, 570–73 (2007).

Hilal Elver, for permission to reprint from Hilal Elver, *Palestinian/Israeli Water Conflict and Implementation of International Water Law Principles,* 28 HASTINGS INT'L & COMP. L. REV. 421, 435–37, 441–43 (2005).

Environmental Law, for permission to reprint from Reed Boland, *The Environment, Population and Women's Human Rights,* 27 ENVTL. L. 1137, 1142–54 (1997).

Gareth Evans, for permission to reprint from Gareth Evans, INCORRIGIBLE OPTIMIST: A POLITICAL MEMOIR (Melbourne University Press, 2017).

Vincent J. Foley and Christopher R. Nolan, for permission to reprint from Vincent J. Foley & Christopher R. Nolan, *The Erika Judgment—Environmental Liability and Places of Refuge: A Sea Change in Civil and Criminal Responsibility that the Maritime Community Must Heed,* 33 TUL. MAR. L. J. 41, 42–46, 65–72 (2008).

Fordham Environmental Law Journal, for permission to reprint from Mario Del Baglivo, *CITES at the Crossroad: New Ivory Sales and Sleeping Giants,* 14 FORDHAM ENVTL. L. J. 279, 279–280, 285–301 (2003).

Fordham International Law Journal, for permission to reprint from Paolo Galizzi, *From Stockholm to New York, Via Rio and Johannesburg: Has the Environment Lost Its Way on the Global Agenda,* 29 FORDHAM INT'L L. J. 952, 952–53, 962–63, 966, 971–76, 984–87, 988–97, 1001 (2006).

Paolo Galizzi, for permission to reprint from Paolo Galizzi, *From Stockholm to New York, Via Rio and Johannesburg: Has the Environment Lost Its Way on the Global Agenda,* 29 FORDHAM INT'L L. J. 952, 952–53, 962–63, 966, 971–76, 984–87, 988–97, 1001 (2006).

Georgetown University Law Center, for permission to reprint from Stephen C. McCaffrey and Kate J. Neville, *Small Capacity and Big Responsibilities: Financial and Legal Implications of a Human Right to Water for Developing Countries,* 21 GEO. INT'L ENVTL. L. REV. 679, 681–85, 693, 696, 700–02 (2009).

Georgia Journal of International and Comparative Law, for permission to reprint from Daniel Bodansky, *Introduction: Climate Change and Human Rights: Unpacking the Issues,* 38 GEORGIA J. OF INT'L & COMP. L. 511, 516–19 (2010); Devereaux F. McClatchey, *Chernobyl and*

Sandoz One Decade Later: The Evolution of State Responsibility for International Disasters, 1986–1996, 25 GA. J. INT'L & COMP. L. 659, 673–75, 676–78, 680 (1996).

Mark Giordano and Jonathan Lautze, for permission to reprint from Jonathan Lautze & Mark Giordano, *Equity in Transboundary Water Law: Valuable Paradigm or Merely Semantics?*, 17 COLO. J. INT'L ENVTL. L & POL'Y 89, 90–1, 94–5, 98, 110–11 (2006).

Lisa B. Gregory, for permission to reprint Lisa B. Gregory, *Examining the Economic Component of China's One-Child Family Policy Under International Law: Your Money or Your Life*, 6 J. CHINESE L. 45, 60–78 (1992).

Harvard Business School Press, for permission to reprint from FRANCES CAIRNCROSS, COSTING THE EARTH-THE CHALLENGE FOR GOVERNMENTS, THE OPPORTUNITIES FOR BUSINESS 131–41 (1993).

Paul Heald, for permission to reprint from Paul J. Heald, *The Rhetoric of Biopiracy,* 11 CARDOZO J. INT'L & COMP. L. 519 (2003).

Indiana Journal of Global Legal Studies, for permission to reprint from Kyle W. Danish, *International Environmental Law and the Bottom-Up Approach: A Review of the Desertification Convention*, 3 IND. J. GLOBAL LEGAL STUD. 133 (1997).

Intergovernmental Panel on Climate Change, for permission to reprint from CLIMATE CHANGE 2014: SYNTHESIS REPORT (2007).

International Institute for Environment and Development, for permission to reprint from CED HESSE AND SUE CAVANNA, MODERN AND MOBILE: THE FUTURE OF LIVESTOCK PRODUCTION IN AFRICA'S DRYLANDS 15, 19, 37, 40, 47, 84 (IIED 2010).

International Law Society of the Golden State School of Law, for permission to reprint from Andrea Marcus, *Transboundary Toxic Waste Disposal: Understanding the Gravity of the Problem and Addressing the Issue Through the Human Rights Commission*, 1 INT'L DIMENSIONS 11–13 (1997).

International Maritime Organization, for permission to reprint from GESAMP (IMO/FAO/UNESCO/WMO/IAEA/UN/UNEP Joint Group of Experts on the Scientific Aspects of Marine Pollution), A SEA OF TROUBLES 1–3, 5–9, 14–15, 21 (2001); IMPLICATIONS OF THE UNITED NATIONS CONVENTION ON THE LAW OF THE SEA FOR THE INTERNATIONAL MARITIME ORGANIZATION 8–10, 12–, 50–52, IMO Doc LEG/MISC.6 (2008), accessed from http://www.imo.org.

Island Press, for permission to reprint from Uriel Safriel & Azfar Adeel (lead authors), *Dryland Systems,* in ECOSYSTEMS AND HUMAN WELL-

BEING: CURRENT STATES & TRENDS by the Millennium Ecosystem Assessment.

Dr. Odette Jankowitsch, for permission to reprint from Odette Jankowitsch-Prevor, *The Convention on Nuclear Safety,* in INTERNATIONAL NUCLEAR LAW IN THE POST-CHERNOBYL PERIOD 155 (OECD 2006).

Journal of Land Use & Environmental Law, for permission to reprint from Dale D. Goble, *What are Slugs Good For? Ecosystem Services and the Conservation of Biodiversity,* 22 J. LAND USE & ENVTL. L. 411, 412, 422–424 (2007).

John H. Knox, for permission to reprint from John H. Knox, *Climate Change and Human Rights Law,* 50 VA. J. INT'L. L. 163, 165–66, 189–93, 195–96, 201–13 (2009).

Joseph LaDou, for permission to reprint from Joseph LaDou, et al., *The Case for a Global Ban on Asbestos,* 118 ENVIRON. HEALTH PERSPECT. [doi: 10.1289/ehp.1002285] (2010).

Libreria Editrice Vaticana, for permission to reprint from Pope Francis's Encyclical Letter *Laudato Si. On Care for Our Common Home* (2015).

Andrea Marcus, for permission to reprint from Andrea Marcus, *Transboundary Toxic Waste Disposal: Understanding the Gravity of the Problem and Addressing the Issue Through the Human Rights Commission,* 1 INT'L DIMENSIONS 11–13 (1997).

Thomas O. McGarity, for permission to reprint from Pep Fuller & Thomas O. McGarity, *Beyond the Dirty Dozen: the Bush Administration's Cautious Approach to Listing New Persistent Organic Pollutants and the Future of the Stockholm Convention,* 28 WM. & MARY ENVTL L. & POL. REV. 1, 1–9 (2003).

Stephen C. McCaffrey and Kate J. Neville, for permission to reprint from Stephen C. McCaffrey and Kate J. Neville, *Small Capacity and Big Responsibilities: Financial and Legal Implications of a Human Right to Water for Developing Countries,* 21 GEO. INT'L ENVTL. L. REV. 679, 681–85, 693, 696, 700–02 (2009).

David Mulliken, Christine Rolph and Jennifer Zambone, for permission to reprint from David L. Mulliken, Jennifer D. Zambone, & Christine G. Rolph, *DDT: A Persistent Lifesaver,* 19 NAT. RES. & ENVT. 3 (Spring 2005).

New York University Law Review, for permission to reprint from Monica J. Washington, *Note, The practice of Peer Review in the International Nuclear Safety Regime,* 72 N.Y.U. L. REV. 430, 432–36, 442–45, 452–55 (1997).

Christopher R. Nolan and Vincent J. Foley, for permission to reprint from Vincent J. Foley & Christopher R. Nolan, *The Erika Judgment—Environmental Liability and Places of Refuge: A Sea Change in Civil and Criminal Responsibility that the Maritime Community Must Heed*, 33 TUL. MAR. L. J. 41, 42–46, 65–72 (2008).

OECD, for permission to reprint Norbert Pelzer, *Learning the Hard Way: Did the Lessons Taught by the Chernobyl Nuclear Accident Contribute to Improving Nuclear Law?*, in INTERNATIONAL LAW IN THE POST-CHERNOBYL PERIOD (2006).

General Secretariat of the Organization of American States, for permission to reprint from Edith Brown Weiss, *Environmental Disasters in International Law*, ANN. JUR. INTERAM. 141, 145–50 (1986).

Science Shop Wageningen UR, for permission to reprint from Kooistra, K.J., Pyburn, R., Termorshuizen, A.J. 2006. The sustainability of cotton. Consequences for man and environment, Science Shop Wageningen University & Research Centre. Report 223. ISBN: 90–6754–90–8585–000–2.

Southeastern Environmental Law Journal, for permission to reprint from Don Mayer, *The Precautionary Principle and International Efforts to Ban DDT*, 9 S.C. ENVTL L. J. 135, 142–151 (2002).

A. Dan Tarlock, for permission to reprint from A. Dan Tarlock, *Four Challenges for International Water Law*, 23 TUL. ENVTL. L. J. 369, 371, 375, 377–78, 383–84, 385–88, 396–98, 402–03, 404–08 (2010).

Texas International Law Journal, for permission to reprint from John Warren Kindt & Samuel Pyeatt Menefee, *The Vexing Problem of Ozone Depletion in International Law and Policy*, 24 TEX. INT'L L. J. 261, 262–67, 277–282 (1989).

Ramesh Thakur, for permission to reprint from *Asia-Pacific and Global Nuclear Orders in the Second Nuclear Age,* APLN-CNND, PB 21 (July 2016).

United Kingdom National Archives, for permission to reprint from STERN REVIEW: THE ECONOMICS OF CLIMATE CHANGE (2006) under U.K. Open Government License, version 2.

United Nations, for permission to reprint from *Large Scale Pelagic Driftnet Fishing and Its Impact on the Living Marine Resources of the World's Oceans and Seas: Report of the Secretary General*, UN GAOR, 45th Sess., Agenda Item 79, 26–33, UN Doc. A/45/663 (1990); *Oceans and the Law of the Sea: Report of the Secretary General*, UN GAOR., 60th Sess., Agenda Item 79, UN Doc. A/60/63/Add.1 (2005).

United Nations Conference on Trade and Development, for permission to reprint from Aaron Cosbey, DEVELOPING COUNTRY INTERESTS IN

CLIMATE CHANGE ACTION AND THE IMPLICATIONS FOR A POST-2012 CLIMATE CHANGE REGIME, UN Doc UNCTAD/DITC/BCC/2009/2 at 6, 9–15 (2009); Atul Kaushik, *Protecting Traditional Knowledge, Innovations and Practices: The Indian Experience* in PROTECTING AND PROMOTING TRADITIONAL KNOWLEDGE: SYSTEMS, NATIONAL EXPERIENCES AND INTERNATIONAL DIMENSIONS 85, 85–89 (Sophia Twarog & Promila Kapoor, eds., 2004), UN Doc UNCTAD/DITC/TED/10 (2004).

United Nations Environment Programme, for permission to reprint from THE EMISSIONS GAP REPORT 2014; THE EMISSIONS GAP REPORT 2017; GLOBAL ENVIRONMENT OUTLOOK-5: ENVIRONMENT FOR THE FUTURE WE WANT(2012); WASTE CRIME-WASTE RISKS: GAPS IN MEETING THE GLOBAL WASTE CHALLENGE. A UNEP RAPID RESPONSE ASSESSMENT (2015).

United Nations Framework Convention on Climate Change Secretariat, for permission to reprint from UNITING ON CLIMATE: A GUIDE TO THE CLIMATE CHANGE CONVENTION AND THE KYOTO PROTOCOL (2007).

United States Army War College, for permission to reprint from Colonel Elizabeth M. Damonte, *National Security Strategy: What About the Environment?*, US ARMY WAR COLLEGE STRATEGY RESEARCH PROJECT 3–6 (15 March 2006).

University of Michigan and William C. Burns, for permission to reprint from William C. Burns, *The International Convention to Combat Desertification: Drawing a Line in the Sand?*, 16 MICH. J. INT'L L. 831 (1995).

University of Pennsylvania Law Review, for permission to reprint from Alan Carlin, *Global Climate Change Control: Is There a Better Strategy Than Reducing Greenhouse Gas Emissions?*, 166 U. PA. L. REV. 1401, 1486–88 (2007).

Viking Books, an imprint of Penguin Publishing Group, a division of Penguin Random House LLC, for permission to reprint from Jared Diamond, COLLAPSE: HOW SOCIETIES CHOOSE TO FAIL OR SUCCEED 486–496 & 498 (2005).

Virginia Journal of International Law and John H. Knox, for permission to reprint from John H. Knox, Climate Change and Human Rights, 50 VA. J. INT'L. L. 163, 165–66, 189–93, 195–96, 201–13 (2009).

World Bank (International Bank for Reconstruction and Development), for permission to reprint from *World Bank Safeguard Policies* at http://go.worldbank.org/QL7ZYN48M0.

TABLE OF ABBREVIATIONS

The following abbreviations are used in this coursebook. Other abbreviations are explained in the text. Except for minor clarifying alterations, additional abbreviations within citations are given according to *A Uniform System of Citation* (20th ed. 2015).

A	United Nations General Assembly
A.J.I.L., AJIL	American Journal of International Law
App.	Appendix
ASEAN	Association of South-East Asian Nations
ATCM	Antarctic Treaty Consultative Meeting
ATCP	Antarctic Treaty Consultative Parties
ATS, ATCA	Alien Tort Statute (US), Alien Tort Claims Act (US)
ATS	Antarctic Treaty System
ATSCM	Special Consultative Meeting of Antarctic Treaty Parties
BAU	Business as usual
B.Y.B.I.L., BYBIL	British Yearbook of International Law
CBD	Convention on Biological Diversity
CCAMLR	Commission for the Conservation of Antarctic Marine Living Resources
CDM	Clean Development Mechanism
CHM	Common Heritage of Mankind
CIL	Customary international law
CITES	Convention on International Trade in Endangered Species of Wild Fauna and Flora
CL	Civil liability
CLOS	Convention on the Law of the Sea (also UNCLOS)
CLRTAP	Convention on Long-range Transboundary Air Pollution
CMS	Convention on the Conservation of Migratory Species of Wild Animals
CONF, Conf	Conference

CRAMRA	Convention for the Regulation of Antarctic Mineral Resource Activities
Doc., Doc	Document
E	United Nations Economic and Social Council
E.C.E., ECE	Economic Commission for Europe (also UNECE)
ECHR	European Court of Human Rights
E.E.C., EEC	European Economic Community
EEZ	Exclusive Economic Zone
EIA	Environmental Impact Assessment
E.J.I.L., EJIL	European Journal of International Law
EMEP	Cooperative programme for monitoring and evaluation of the long range transmission of air pollutants in Europe
E.U., EU	European Union
E.Y.B.	European Yearbook
FAO	Food and Agriculture Organisation of the United Nations
FCCC	Framework Convention on Climate Change
FDI	Foreign direct investment
FOC	Flag of Convenience
FTA	Free trade agreement
G.A., GA	United Nations General Assembly
GAOR	General Assembly Official Records
G.A.T.T., GATT	General Agreement on Tariffs and Trade
GESAMP	Joint Group of Experts on the Scientific Aspects of Marine Environmental Pollution
GHG	Greenhouse gas
GMO	Genetically modified organism
Hague Receuil	Receuil des Cours (of the Hague Academy of International Law)
H.I.L.J., HILJ	Harvard International Law Journal
I.A.E.A., IAEA	International Atomic Energy Agency
IBRD	International Bank for Reconstruction and Development

I.C.J., ICJ	International Court of Justice, including official Reports of Judgments, Advisory Opinions and Orders of the Court
I.C.L.Q., ICLQ	International and Comparative Law Quarterly
IEL	International environmental law
IGO	Intergovernmental organization
I.L.A., ILA	International Law Association, Reports of Annual Conferences of the International Law Association
I.L.C., ILC	International Law Commission
I.L.M., ILM	International Legal Materials
I.L.R., ILR	International Law Reports
I.M.C.O., IMCO	Inter-Governmental Maritime Consultative Organisation
I.M.O., IMO	International Maritime Organisation
INC	Intergovernmental negotiating committee
IO	International organization
IPCC	Intergovernmental Panel on Climate Change
IRPTC	International Register of Potentially Toxic Chemicals
IRS	Indoor Residual Spraying
IUCN	International Union for Conservation of Nature
IUU	Illegal, unreported, and unregulated
LBMP	Land-based marine pollution
Leg.	Legal, Legislation
LOS	Law of the Sea
LULUCF	Land use, land use change, and forestry
LRTAP	Long-range transboundary air pollution
MARPOL	International Convention for the Prevention of Pollution from Ships
MEA	Multilateral environmental agreement
Mtg.	Meeting
NGO	Nongovernmental organization
NNWS	Non-nuclear-weapon states

NPT	Non-proliferation Treaty
No.	Number
N.R.J.	Natural Resources Journal
NWS	Nuclear-weapon states
O.A.S. Off. Rec.	Organisation of American States Official Records
O.A.U., OAU	Organisation of African Unity
ODS	Ozone-depleting substances
OEA/Ser.	Organizacion Estados Americanos Series (Organisation of American States Series)
O.E.C.D., OECD	Organisation for Economic Co-operation and Development
Off.	Official
O.J.E.C., OJEC	Official Journal of the European Communities
O.J.E.U., OJEU	Official Journal of the European Union
P.C.I.J.	Permanent Court of International Justice: Reports
PIC	Prior Informed Consent
PPM	Parts per million
PSSA	Particularly sensitive sea area
Pt., pt.	Part
Proc., A.S.I.L.	Proceedings of the American Society of International Law
REDD	Reducing Emissions from Deforestation and Forest Degradation in Developing Countries
RES, Res.	Resolution
Rev.	Revision, Revised
S	United Nations Security Council
Ser.	Series
Sess.	Session
SIDS	Small Island Developing States
SOLAS	International Convention on the Safety of Life at Sea
SPS	WTO Agreement on Sanitary and Phytosanitary Measures

Stat.	U.S. Statutes at Large
Supp.	Supplement
TBT	WTO Agreement on Technical Barriers to Trade
T.I.A.S., TIAS	U.S. Treaties and Other International Acts Series
T.L.C.P., TLCP	Transnational Law and Contemporary Problems
Transact. Grot. Soc'y	Transactions of the Grotius Society
U.K., UK	United Kingdom
U.N., UN	United Nations
UNCCD	United Nations Convention to Combat Desertification
UNCED	United Nations Conference on Environment and Development
UNCLOS	United Nations Convention on the Law of the Sea
UNCTAD	United Nations Conference on Trade and Development
UNECE	United Nations Economic Commission for Europe
UNESCO	United Nations Educational Scientific and Cultural Organization
U.N.E.P., UNEP	United Nations Environment Programme
U.N.G.A., UNGA	United Nations General Assembly
U.N. GAOR	United Nations General Assembly Official Record
UNFCCC	United Nations Framework Convention on Climate Change
U.N.J.Y.B.	United Nations Juridical Yearbook
UN-REDD	United Nations Collaborative Programme on Reducing Emissions from Deforestation and Forest Degradation in Developing Countries
U.N.R.I.A.A., UNRIAA	United Nations Reports of International Arbitral Awards
UNSC	United Nations Security Council
U.N.T.S., UNTS	United Nations Treaty Series

U.S., US	United States
U.S.T., UST	U.S. Treaties
Weston & Carlson	International Law and World Order: Basic Documents (Burns H. Weston & Jonathan C. Carlson ed., 5 vols, 1994–)
WCED	World Commission on Environment and Development
WHC	World Heritage Convention
WHO	World Health Organization
WSSD	World Summit on Sustainable Development
W.T.O., WTO	World Trade Organization
WWF	World Wildlife Fund
Y.B.U.N., YBUN	Yearbook of the United Nations
Y.J.I.L., YJIL	Yale Journal of International Law

SUMMARY OF CONTENTS

PART TWO. CHALLENGES IN ADDRESSING EARTH'S MOST PRESSING ENVIRONMENTAL THREATS

TABLE OF CONTENTS

TABLE OF ARBITRAL AND JUDICIAL DECISIONS

The principal cases are in bold type.

TABLE OF TREATIES AND OTHER INSTRUMENTS

INTERNATIONAL ENVIRONMENTAL LAW

A PROBLEM-ORIENTED COURSEBOOK

Fourth Edition

PART ONE

INTERNATIONAL LAW AND THE GLOBAL ENVIRONMENT

■ ■ ■

INTRODUCTION

The world faces a wide range of serious environmental problems. Some of these problems are primarily local in their impact and require mainly local solutions. For example, when local cities and factories pollute a river that is located entirely within the territory of a particular country, the pollution is unlikely to be a matter of particular international concern.[1] However, there are many situations in which environmental problems have obvious international dimensions. For example, formulating and implementing an adequate response to dangerous global phenomena like climate change and the depletion of the ozone layer requires coordinated action by many states. Even local environmental deterioration can be a matter of international concern when it is caused by behavior in other countries (e.g., transboundary pollution) or exacerbated by international trade (e.g., unsafe local disposal of hazardous wastes shipped from abroad; local slaughter of endangered species for sale in international markets). Adequate solutions to such problems can rarely be achieved without international cooperation.

When environmental problems require international action or attract international concern, international law inevitably enters the picture. The international legal system provides a set of tools on which nations rely in dealing with their shared problems, including environmental problems. These tools include: established political/diplomatic arenas (like the United Nations General Assembly) in which problems can be debated and discussed and possible solutions identified; recognized processes for formulating principles and rules to guide nation-state behavior and for transforming those norms into binding legal commitments (e.g., the process for making treaties); and techniques for resolving disputes among individual nation-states.

In Part One of this coursebook (chapters 1–4), we introduce you to the toolbox of international legal processes, principles, and rules that nation-

[1] However, concern for the suffering of people affected by the pollution may generate international attention and pressure, especially if the relevant government is indifferent to that suffering or incapable of responding to it effectively.

states use to resolve their disputes and address shared environmental problems. These materials also provide an overview of the historical development of international environmental law and the political forces and policy perspectives that have shaped that development. In Part Two of the coursebook, we examine particular areas of international environmental law through the study of hypothetical problems. Although the fact patterns are hypothetical, we have tried to make them as true to life as possible. We hope thereby to encourage you to think about the complex webs of fact, law, and policy that typically confront international law decision-making in the "real world." We ask you to study problems because we believe that problem-solving requires the exercise of important legal skills (e.g., issue-spotting, synthesis, creative thinking) and is thereby much more important in the legal learning experience than the mere assimilation of disembodied knowledge.

Before we leap into our study of international law, however, we think it is desirable to begin with a few readings on the state of the global environment. If you are like us, your reasons for studying international *environmental* law have quite a lot to do with your desire to learn how law and legal processes can contribute to the resolution of environmental problems. So a quick review of those problems and their international dimensions seems in order.

GLOBAL ENVIRONMENT OUTLOOK-5: ENVIRONMENT FOR THE FUTURE WE WANT

UNITED NATIONS ENVIRONMENT PROGRAMME
xviii, 5, 32, 66, 98–99, 134, 170, 195–96 (2012)

The Earth System Context

The Earth System provides the basis for all human societies and their economic activities. People need clean air to breathe, safe water to drink, healthy food to eat, energy to produce and transport goods, and natural resources that provide the raw materials for all these services. However, the 7 billion humans alive today are collectively exploiting the Earth's resources at accelerating rates and intensities that surpass the capacity of its systems to absorb wastes and neutralize the adverse effects on the environment. In fact, the depletion or degradation of several key resources has already constrained conventional development in some parts of the world.

* * *

Drivers [of Environmental Change]

The last 100 years was characterized by exceptional growth both in the human population and in the size of the global economy, with the population quadrupling to 7 billion and global economic output, expressed as gross domestic product (GDP), increasing about 20-fold. This expansion has been accompanied by fundamental changes in the scale, intensity and character of society's relationship with the natural world. In tracking and analysing these transformations, a new understanding of the complexities of the Earth's biophysical systems has been developed.

* * *

[This report] identifies two major drivers [of environmental change]—population and economic development—that influence cross-cutting dynamic patterns and generate complex systemic interactions. For example, the pressure of supplying food, feed and fibre to growing urban centres threatens biodiversity, a pressure then exacerbated by climate change.

Pressures can include resource extraction, land-use change and the modification and movement of organisms. For example, as economic growth and the demand for agricultural products rise, so does the conversion of land for agricultural purposes, as well as the use of agrochemicals. Similarly, market demands, trade and globalization patterns can lead to the inadvertent transport of invasive species that may wreak havoc on the natural ecosystems they newly inhabit.

* * *

Population growth and economic development are seen as ubiquitous drivers of environmental change with particular facets exerting pressure: energy, transport, urbanization and globalization. While this list may not be exhaustive, it is useful. Understanding the growth in these drivers and the connections between them will go a long way to address their collective impact and find possible solutions, thereby preserving the environmental benefits on which human societies and economies depend.

* * *

Atmosphere

Substances emitted to the atmosphere as a result of human activities are a challenge to both the environment and development: millions of people die prematurely each year from indoor and outdoor air pollution; ozone-depleting substances (ODS) have thinned the ozone layer and created seasonal holes in the stratospheric ozone layer over polar regions; and climate change is happening now, and atmospheric concentrations of greenhouse gases and other substances that affect climate continue to increase. Climate change threatens, amongst other things, food security and biodiversity, and it is likely to increase storm damage on all parts of the globe. People in many of the developing regions are especially vulnerable.

* * *

Land

Changing climate patterns, economic globalization, population growth, increasing use of natural resources and rapid urbanization are putting pressure on terrestrial ecosystems as never before, and virtually all of them are under stress. Biophysical limits on what is available for human use are real and there are strong signals that these limits are close to being reached or have already been exceeded. Even so, the fact that some areas show recent gains in forested area or land reclamation suggests that declines are not inevitable, and indeed that recovery may be possible—even though original ecosystem functions may be modified or pressure on ecosystems may shift elsewhere.

Growing demands for food, feed, fuel, fibre and raw materials create local and distant pressures for land-use change. The cascade of outcomes resulting from these demands is complicated by urbanization and globalization, which separate the production of goods from their consumption over vast distances. The central question is how these demands can be met—or managed—in ways that recognize the joint imperatives of human well-being and environmental sustainability. Addressing this requires careful examination of the social relations and biophysical processes involved in managing terrestrial ecosystems, setting priorities for policies and policy instruments, and considering the likely distribution of implications, both positive and negative.

* * *

Water

. . . Human water demands, with only limited improvements in efficiency, are increasing and are already unsustainable in many regions. Nevertheless, potential exists for efficiency gains: irrigation efficiency, for example, could be increased by approximately one-third simply by implementing existing technology. At the local level, integrated demand and supply strategies are critical. At a river-basin level, more efficient and fair water allocation systems are needed. More broadly, virtual water trade can ease water demands in some locations.

. . . Freshwater and marine ecosystem services are critical to human development and integral to the transition to a green economy. Inadequately articulated objectives and lack of data, however, make it difficult to evaluate progress in meeting environmental water requirements. Better strategies and tools are needed for efficient, equitable water allocation between users, including the environment. Full implementation of international commitments and enforcement of legally binding agreements, and due consideration of customary water-use arrangements, will facilitate sustainable human and ecosystem use.

Reducing both point and non-point pollution is imperative to improve ecosystem health and provide safe water for humans. Substantial achievements in reducing some pollutants have occurred since 1992, although many water bodies are still affected, and many new contaminants have poorly understood effects. Treating municipal and industrial wastewater is achievable with existing technology, but requires better regulatory oversight, infrastructure investment and capacity building, especially in developing countries. Integrated land-water management and stakeholder participation are necessary to reduce non-point pollution of both freshwater and marine systems.

Improved water supply and sanitation is probably the single most cost-effective means of reducing water-related death and disease globally. Although the Millennium Development Goal (MDG) target on water supply was met in 2010, more than 600 million people will still lack access to safe drinking water in 2015. The MDG target on sanitation is unlikely to be met, with 2.5 billion people currently without improved sanitation facilities; poor rural populations are most affected. Meeting the water supply and sanitation MDGs would reduce the water-related global disease burden by about 10 per cent. Increased investment in infrastructure, capacity building and regulation are needed, and the participation of women is crucial for water management and the prevention of waterborne disease.

Climate-sensitive policies across all water-related sectors are essential to address extreme events and increased climatic variability. Floods and droughts still cause losses of billions of dollars annually. Climate change is altering the hydrologic cycle, threatening freshwater and marine ecosystems as well as human water security in many regions. Open oceans play a major role in regulating global climate and weather patterns, with climate change impacts manifested in warmer surface waters and rising sea levels. Ocean warming and acidification threaten tropical coral reef ecosystems, with rapid contraction predicted by 2050. Mitigation and adaptation to climate change impacts must be considered within the context of other drivers and pressures. Those related to energy production are likely to require trade-offs between human energy needs, water demands and ecosystem protection.

The pace of increasing demands on freshwater and ocean resources must be matched by improved governance. Freshwater systems integrate human activities and land management across nations and regions. The open oceans are a major global commons and require effective international cooperation and governance. Most human and environmental water problems result from inadequate governance involving policy, institutional, financial and/or stakeholder issues. Integrated management approaches for addressing these constraints require time and resources to be successful. They need enhanced integration of policies and institutions between sectors and governance levels, implementation and enforcement of relevant agreements and goals, improved monitoring and resolution of transboundary issues. Good governance, including stakeholder and private sector participation and gender considerations, is critical to increasing societal and environmental resilience and sustainability.

* * *

Biodiversity

The pressure on biodiversity continues to increase.

Habitat loss and degradation from agriculture and infrastructure development, overexploitation, pollution and invasive alien species remain the predominant threats. Climate change is increasing in importance and will have profound impacts, particularly in combination with other threats. Greater integration of policies and institutional responses, including effective engagement of local communities, is required to stop and reverse current trends. The world lost over 100 million hectares of forest from 2000 to 2005, and has lost 20 per cent of its seagrass and mangrove habitats since 1970 and 1980 respectively. In some regions, 95 per cent of wetlands have been lost. The condition of coral reefs globally has declined by 38 per cent since 1980. Two-thirds of the world's largest rivers are now moderately to severely fragmented by dams and reservoirs.

The state of global biodiversity is continuing to decline, with substantial and ongoing losses of populations, species and habitats. For instance, vertebrate populations have declined on average by 30 per cent since 1970, and up to two-thirds of species in some taxa are now threatened with extinction. Declines are most rapid in the tropics, in freshwater habitats and for marine species utilized by humans. Conversion and degradation of natural habitats is ongoing, with some having experienced declines of 20 per cent since 1980. Limited successes, such as saving particular species from extinction, reversing the decline of some populations, and restoring some habitats, are outweighed by continuing declines.

The benefits humans obtain from biodiversity are at risk. Conversion of natural habitats to large-scale, commercial agriculture has resulted in net benefits for human well-being. However, this has often been accompanied by reductions in other services, such as carbon sequestration and flood regulation. Continuing ecological degradation, unsustainable levels of consumption and inequities in sharing of the benefits from biodiversity threaten the improvements in human well-being and health that have been achieved in recent decades.

* * *

Chemicals and Waste

More than 248 000 chemical products are commercially available and subject to regulatory and inventory systems. Chemicals provide valuable benefits to humanity including in agriculture, medicine, industrial manufacturing, energy extraction and generation, and public health and disease vector control. Chemicals play an important role in achieving developmental and social goals, especially for improving maternal health, reducing child mortality and ensuring food security, and advances in their production and management have increased their safe application. Nonetheless, because of their intrinsic hazardous properties, some pose risks to the environment and human health. Simultaneous exposure to many chemicals—the cocktail or synergistic effect—is likely to exacerbate the impacts.

Chemicals are released at many steps in their life cycle, from the extraction of raw materials, through production chains, transport and consumption, to final waste disposal. They are distributed through indoor environments, food and drinking water, and through soils, rivers and lakes. Certain long-lived chemicals such as persistent organic pollutants (POPs) and heavy metals are transported globally, reaching otherwise pristine environments such as rain forests, deep oceans or polar regions, and can quickly pass along the food chain, bio-accumulating to cause toxic effects in humans and wildlife.

Products derived from chemicals often become hazardous wastes in their end-of-life phase, generating additional pollution risks that can devalue their initial benefits and counteract development advantages. Pollution from dumping and uncontrolled open burning is common, and is even increasing in some parts of the world, though some progress has been made in recent decades. The causes of mismanagement often lie in such factors as deficiencies in institutional and regulatory frameworks. Such shortcomings also have an impact on the growing transboundary movement of hazardous wastes from developed to developing countries, where compliance, monitoring and enforcement of regulations tend to be weak, and the financial and technical capacity to implement improved waste management practices is limited. This leads to a risk of rapidly increasing exposure for greater portions of the population and to related, often serious, health problems, in particular for women and children.

Broadly, a two-speed situation exists, with developed countries generally having comprehensive systems for chemical and hazardous waste management, while developing countries generally do not. Developing countries and economies in transition struggle with basic landfill co-disposal of many types of wastes, with little capacity for their separation and sound management.

While many developing countries have ratified the multilateral environmental agreements on chemicals and wastes—such as the Basel Convention on the Control of Transboundary Movement of Hazardous Wastes and their Disposal (Basel Convention 1989)—these are not always transposed into national legislation in a comprehensive manner. In addition, given the cross-sectoral nature of the issue, the regulation and management of chemicals in most developing countries is spread over several ministries—including agriculture, industry, labour, environment and health—and between several agencies within each ministry.

In most countries, it is the poorest members of the population that are at particular risk of exposure. This may be due to occupational exposure, poor living conditions, lack of access to clean water and food, domestic proximity to polluting activities, or a lack of knowledge about the detrimental impacts of chemicals—or a combination of these factors.

Radioactive contamination is another source of potential environmental and health hazards, both from controlled emissions and waste management, and from accidental release. The controlled release of radionuclides to the atmospheric and aquatic environments may occur as authorized effluent discharge, while uncontrolled release may occur as a result of accidents and at legacy sites left by nuclear weapons testing. The management and disposal of radioactive waste from industry, research and medicine, as well as from nuclear power, is relevant to almost all countries, requiring different approaches according to the volume, radioactivity and other properties of the waste.

* * *

An Earth System Perspective

A system is a collection of component parts that interact with one another within a defined boundary. The Earth System is a complex social-environmental system, including the vast collection of interacting physical, chemical, biological and social components and processes that determine the state and evolution of the planet and life on it. The biophysical components of the Earth System are often referred to as spheres: atmosphere, biosphere, hydrosphere and geosphere. They provide environmental processes that regulate the functioning of the Earth, such as the climate system, the ecological services generated by the living biosphere, including food production, and natural resources like fossil fuels and minerals. Humans are an integral part of the Earth System. All spheres include countless subsystems and levels of organization. The interactions within and between these spheres are complex and the predictability of future states of the Earth System is limited.

Unprecedented changes

Some experts suggest that the Earth has entered a new geological epoch, the Anthropocene. The word was coined by Nobel Laureate Paul Crutzen to capture the idea that humans are now overwhelming the forces of nature. An implication of entering the Anthropocene would be the leaving of the Holocene, the interglacial period that has provided humanity, over the past 10,000 years, with extraordinarily good living conditions, enabling the development of modern societies and a world with 7 billion people.

Crutzen (2002) suggests that the Industrial Revolution 250 years ago saw the beginning of the Anthropocene. The unprecedented rise in human population since the early 19th century, from less than a billion to 7 billion at present, is inherent to the Anthropocene as it unfolds. Many societal changes have accompanied this proliferation of the human population, such as increased consumption of natural resources and an enormous expansion of dependence on fossil fuels.

The Earth System demonstrates complexity in its natural variability independently of, and previous to, human influence. . . . [However,] current concentrations of atmospheric CO2 are well outside the range of the past, having risen from 310 parts per million (ppm) in 1950 to 391 ppm in 2011 (NOAA 2011), with half the total rise in atmospheric CO2 since the pre-industrial era having occurred in the last 30 years (Steffen et al. 2007).

Biodiversity, the variety of life on Earth, has evolved over the last 3.8 billion years or so of the planet's approximately 5-billion-year history. Five major extinction events have been recorded over this period, but, unlike the previous events—which were due to natural upheavals and planetary change—the current loss of biodiversity is mainly due to human activities and is often referred to as the sixth global extinction. According to the Global Biodiversity Outlook 3, the abundance of some vertebrate populations fell by nearly one-third on average between 1970 and 2006 and continues to fall globally. Many biologists consider that coming decades will see the loss of large numbers of species, increasing the risk of abrupt change in landscapes and seascape. Fewer scientists appear to have recognized that, in the longer term, these extinctions will alter not only biological diversity but also the evolutionary processes by which diversity is generated.

COLLAPSE: HOW SOCIETIES CHOOSE TO FAIL OR SUCCEED

JARED DIAMOND
486–96, 498 (2005)[2]

It seems to me that the most serious environmental problems facing past and present societies fall into a dozen groups. . . . The first four of the 12 consist of destruction or losses of natural resources; the next three involve ceilings on natural resources; the three after that consist of harmful things that we produce or move around; and the last two are population issues. Let's begin with the natural resources that we are destroying or losing: natural habitats, wild food sources, biological diversity, and soil.

1. At an accelerating rate, we are destroying natural habitats or else converting them to human-made habitats, such as cities and villages, farmlands and pastures, roads, and golf courses. The natural habitats whose losses have provoked the most discussion are forests, wetlands, coral reefs, and the ocean bottom. As I mentioned in the preceding chapter, more than half of the world's original area of forest has already been converted to other uses, and at present conversion rates one-quarter of the forests that remain will become converted within the next half-century. Those losses of forests, represent losses for us humans, especially because forests provide us with timber and other raw materials, and because they provide us with so-called ecosystem services such as protecting our watersheds, protecting soil against erosion, constituting essential steps in the water cycle that generates much of our rainfall, and providing habitat for most terrestrial plant and animal species. . . .

Other valuable natural habitats besides forests are also being destroyed. An even larger fraction of the world's original wetlands than of its forests has already been destroyed, damaged, or converted. Consequences for us arise from wetlands' importance in maintaining the quality of our water supplies and the existence of commercially important freshwater fisheries, while even ocean fisheries depend on mangrove wetlands to provide habitat for the juvenile phase of many fish species. About one-third of the world's coral reefs—the oceanic equivalent of tropical rainforests, because they are home to a disproportionate fraction of the ocean's species—have already been severely damaged. If current trends continue, about half of the remaining reefs would be lost by the year 2030. . . .

2. Wild foods, especially fish and to a lesser extent shellfish, contribute a large fraction of the protein consumed by humans. In effect, this is protein that we obtain for free (other than the cost of catching and transporting the fish), and that reduces our needs for animal protein that we have to grow ourselves in the form of domestic livestock. About two

---

billion people, most of them poor, depend on the oceans for protein. If wild fish stocks were managed appropriately, the stock levels could be maintained, and they could be harvested perpetually. Unfortunately, the problem known as the tragedy of the commons has regularly undone efforts to manage fisheries sustainably, and the great majority of valuable fisheries already either have collapsed or are in steep decline. . . .

* * *

3. A significant fraction of wild species, populations, and genetic diversity has already been lost and at present rates a large fraction of what remains will be lost within the next half-century. . . .

* * *

4. Soils of farmlands used for growing crops are being carried away by water and wind erosion at rates between 10 and 40 times the rates of soil formation, and between 50 and 10,000 times soil erosion rates on forested land. . . .

Other types of soil damage caused by human agricultural practices include salinization . . .; losses of soil fertility, because farming removes nutrients much more rapidly than they are restored by weathering of the underlying rock; and soil acidification in some areas, or its converse, alkalinization, in other areas. All of these types of harmful impacts have resulted in a fraction of the world's farmland variously estimated at between 20% and 80% having become severely damaged, during an era in which increasing human population has caused us to need more farmland rather than less farmland. . . .

5. The world's energy sources, especially for industrial societies, are fossil fuels: oil, natural gas, and coal. While there has been much discussion about how many big oil and gas fields remain to be discovered, and while coal reserves are believed to be large, the prevalent view is that known and likely reserves of readily accessible oil and natural gas will last for a few more decades. . . . [F]urther reserves will be deeper underground, dirtier, increasingly expensive to extract or process, or will involve higher environmental costs. . . .

6. Most of the world's freshwater in rivers and lakes is already being utilized for irrigation, domestic and industrial water, and in situ uses such as boat transportation corridors, fisheries, and recreation. Rivers and lakes that are not already utilized are mostly far from major population centers and likely users, such as in Northwestern Australia, Siberia, and Iceland. Throughout the world, freshwater underground aquifers are being depleted at rates faster than they are being naturally replenished, so that they will eventually dwindle. . . .

7. . . . Given the rate of increase of human population, and especially of population impact (see point 12 below), since 1986, we are

projected to be utilizing most of the world's terrestrial photosynthetic capacity by the middle of this century. That is, most energy fixed from sunlight will be used for human purposes, and little will be left over to support the growth of natural plant communities, such as natural forests. . . .

8. The chemical industry and many other industries manufacture or release into the air, soil, oceans, lakes, and rivers many toxic chemicals, some of them "unnatural" and synthesized only by humans, others present naturally in tiny concentrations (e.g., mercury) or else synthesized by living things but synthesized and released by humans in quantities much larger than natural ones (e.g., hormones). . . . Often in very low concentrations, they variously cause birth defects, mental retardation, and temporary or permanent damage to our immune and reproductive systems. Some of them act as endocrine disruptors, i.e., they interfere with our reproductive systems by mimicking or blocking effects of our own sex hormones. . . .

* * *

9. The term "alien species" refers to species that we transfer, intentionally or inadvertently, from a place where they are native to another place where they are not native. Some alien species are obviously valuable to us as crops, domestic animals, and landscaping. But others devastate populations of native species with which they come in contact, either by preying on, parasitizing, infecting, or outcompeting them. . . . There are by now literally hundreds of cases in which alien species have caused one-time or annually recurring damages of hundreds of millions of dollars or even billions of dollars. . . .

10. Human activities produce gases that escape into the atmosphere, where they either damage the protective ozone layer (as do formerly widespread refrigerator coolants) or else act as greenhouse gases that absorb sunlight and thereby lead to global warming. . . .

11. The world's human population is growing. More people require more food, space, water, energy, and other resources. Rates and even the direction of human population change vary greatly around the world, with the highest rates of population growth (4% per year or higher) in some Third World countries, low rates of growth (1% per year or less) in some First World countries such as Italy and Japan, and negative rates of growth (i.e., decreasing populations) in countries facing major public health crises, such as Russia and AIDS-affected African countries. Everybody agrees that the world population is increasing, but that its annual percentage rate of increase is not as high as it was a decade or two ago. However, there is still disagreement about whether the world's population will stabilize at some value above its present level (double the present population?), and (if so) how many years (30 years? 50 years?) it will take for population to reach that level, or whether population will continue to grow.

* * *

12. What really counts is not the number of people alone, but their impact on the environment. If most of the world's 6 billion people today were in cryogenic storage and neither eating, breathing, nor metabolizing, that large population would cause no environmental problems. Instead, our numbers pose problems insofar as we consume resources and generate wastes. That per-capita impact—the resources consumed, and the wastes put out, by each person—varies greatly around the world, being highest in the First World and lowest in the Third World. On the average, each citizen of the U.S., western Europe, and Japan consumes 32 times more resources such as fossil fuels, and puts out 32 times more wastes, than do inhabitants of the Third World.

* * *

There are many "optimists" who argue that the world could support double its human population, and who consider only the increase in human numbers and not the average increase in per-capita impact. But I have not met anyone who seriously argues that the world could support 12 times its current impact, although an increase of that factor would result from all Third World inhabitants adopting First World living standards. . . . Even if the people of China alone achieved a First World living standard while everyone else's living standard remained constant, that would double our human impact on the world. . . .

People in the Third World aspire to First World living standards. . . . Third World citizens are encouraged in that aspiration by First World and United Nations development agencies, which hold out to them the prospect of achieving their dream if they will only adopt the right policies, like balancing their national budgets, investing in education and infrastructure, and so on.

But no one in First World governments is willing to acknowledge the dream's impossibility: the unsustainability of a world in which the Third World's large population were to reach and maintain current First World living standards. . . .

* * *

Our world society is presently on a non-sustainable course, and any of [the] problems of non-sustainability . . . summarized [herein] would suffice to limit our lifestyle within the next several decades. They are like time bombs with fuses of less than 50 years.

ENCYCLICAL LETTER *LAUDATO SI.* ON CARE FOR OUR COMMON HOME[3]

POPE FRANCIS
24 May 2015

19. Following a period of irrational confidence in progress and human abilities, some sectors of society are now adopting a more critical approach. We see increasing sensitivity to the environment and the need to protect nature, along with a growing concern, both genuine and distressing, for what is happening to our planet. Let us review, however cursorily, those questions which are troubling us today and which we can no longer sweep under the carpet. Our goal is not to amass information or to satisfy curiosity, but rather to become painfully aware, to dare to turn what is happening to the world into our own personal suffering and thus to discover what each of us can do about it.

I. Pollution and climate change

Pollution, waste and the throwaway culture

20. Some forms of pollution are part of people's daily experience. Exposure to atmospheric pollutants produces a broad spectrum of health hazards, especially for the poor, and causes millions of premature deaths. People take sick, for example, from breathing high levels of smoke from fuels used in cooking or heating. There is also pollution that affects everyone, caused by transport, industrial fumes, substances which contribute to the acidification of soil and water, fertilizers, insecticides, fungicides, herbicides and agrotoxins in general. . . .

21. Account must also be taken of the pollution produced by residue, including dangerous waste present in different areas. Each year hundreds of millions of tons of waste are generated, much of it non-biodegradable, highly toxic and radioactive, from homes and businesses, from construction and demolition sites, from clinical, electronic and industrial sources. The earth, our home, is beginning to look more and more like an immense pile of filth. In many parts of the planet, the elderly lament that once beautiful landscapes are now covered with rubbish. Industrial waste and chemical products utilized in cities and agricultural areas can lead to bioaccumulation in the organisms of the local population, even when levels of toxins in those places are low. Frequently no measures are taken until after people's health has been irreversibly affected. . . .

* * *

Climate as a common good

23. The climate is a common good, belonging to all and meant for all. At the global level, it is a complex system linked to many of the essential

[3] 8 Libreria Editrice Vaticana.

conditions for human life. A very solid scientific consensus indicates that we are presently witnessing a disturbing warming of the climatic system. In recent decades this warming has been accompanied by a constant rise in the sea level and, it would appear, by an increase of extreme weather events, even if a scientifically determinable cause cannot be assigned to each particular phenomenon. . . . The problem is aggravated by a model of development based on the intensive use of fossil fuels, which is at the heart of the worldwide energy system. Another determining factor has been an increase in changed uses of the soil, principally deforestation for agricultural purposes.

24. . . . If present trends continue, this century may well witness extraordinary climate change and an unprecedented destruction of ecosystems, with serious consequences for all of us. A rise in the sea level, for example, can create extremely serious situations, if we consider that a quarter of the world's population lives on the coast or nearby, and that the majority of our megacities are situated in coastal areas.

* * *

II. The issue of water

27. Other indicators of the present situation have to do with the depletion of natural resources. We all know that it is not possible to sustain the present level of consumption in developed countries and wealthier sectors of society, where the habit of wasting and discarding has reached unprecedented levels. The exploitation of the planet has already exceeded acceptable limits and we still have not solved the problem of poverty.

28. Fresh drinking water is an issue of primary importance, since it is indispensable for human life and for supporting terrestrial and aquatic ecosystems. Sources of fresh water are necessary for health care, agriculture and industry. Water supplies used to be relatively constant, but now in many places demand exceeds the sustainable supply, with dramatic consequences in the short and long term. Large cities dependent on significant supplies of water have experienced periods of shortage, and at critical moments these have not always been administered with sufficient oversight and impartiality. Water poverty especially affects Africa where large sectors of the population have no access to safe drinking water or experience droughts which impede agricultural production. Some countries have areas rich in water while others endure drastic scarcity.

29. One particularly serious problem is the quality of water available to the poor. Every day, unsafe water results in many deaths and the spread of water-related diseases, including those caused by microorganisms and chemical substances. Dysentery and cholera, linked to inadequate hygiene and water supplies, are a significant cause of suffering and of infant mortality. Underground water sources in many places are threatened by the pollution produced in certain mining, farming and industrial activities,

especially in countries lacking adequate regulation or controls. It is not only a question of industrial waste. Detergents and chemical products, commonly used in many places of the world, continue to pour into our rivers, lakes and seas.

* * *

31. Greater scarcity of water will lead to an increase in the cost of food and the various products which depend on its use. Some studies warn that an acute water shortage may occur within a few decades unless urgent action is taken. The environmental repercussions could affect billions of people; it is also conceivable that the control of water by large multinational businesses may become a major source of conflict in this century.

III. Loss of biodiversity

32. The earth's resources are also being plundered because of short-sighted approaches to the economy, commerce and production. The loss of forests and woodlands entails the loss of species which may constitute extremely important resources in the future, not only for food but also for curing disease and other uses. Different species contain genes which could be key resources in years ahead for meeting human needs and regulating environmental problems.

33. It is not enough, however, to think of different species merely as potential "resources" to be exploited, while overlooking the fact that they have value in themselves. Each year sees the disappearance of thousands of plant and animal species which we will never know, which our children will never see, because they have been lost forever. The great majority become extinct for reasons related to human activity. Because of us, thousands of species will no longer give glory to God by their very existence, nor convey their message to us. We have no such right.

34. It may well disturb us to learn of the extinction of mammals or birds, since they are more visible. But the good functioning of ecosystems also requires fungi, algae, worms, insects, reptiles and an innumerable variety of microorganisms. Some less numerous species, although generally unseen, nonetheless play a critical role in maintaining the equilibrium of a particular place. . . .

* * *

36. Caring for ecosystems demands far-sightedness, since no one looking for quick and easy profit is truly interested in their preservation. But the cost of the damage caused by such selfish lack of concern is much greater than the economic benefits to be obtained. Where certain species are destroyed or seriously harmed, the values involved are incalculable. We can be silent witnesses to terrible injustices if we think that we can obtain

significant benefits by making the rest of humanity, present and future, pay the extremely high costs of environmental deterioration.

37. . . . Certain places need greater protection because of their immense importance for the global ecosystem, or because they represent important water reserves and thus safeguard other forms of life.

38. Let us mention, for example, those richly biodiverse lungs of our planet which are the Amazon and the Congo basins, or the great aquifers and glaciers. We know how important these are for the entire earth and for the future of humanity. The ecosystems of tropical forests possess an enormously complex biodiversity which is almost impossible to appreciate fully, yet when these forests are burned down or levelled for purposes of cultivation, within the space of a few years countless species are lost and the areas frequently become arid wastelands. A delicate balance has to be maintained when speaking about these places, for we cannot overlook the huge global economic interests which, under the guise of protecting them, can undermine the sovereignty of individual nations. . . .

* * *

40. Oceans not only contain the bulk of our planet's water supply, but also most of the immense variety of living creatures, many of them still unknown to us and threatened for various reasons. What is more, marine life in rivers, lakes, seas and oceans, which feeds a great part of the world's population, is affected by uncontrolled fishing, leading to a drastic depletion of certain species. Selective forms of fishing which discard much of what they collect continue unabated. Particularly threatened are marine organisms which we tend to overlook, like some forms of plankton; they represent a significant element in the ocean food chain, and species used for our food ultimately depend on them.

41. In tropical and subtropical seas, we find coral reefs comparable to the great forests on dry land, for they shelter approximately a million species, including fish, crabs, molluscs, sponges and algae. Many of the world's coral reefs are already barren or in a state of constant decline. . . .

42. Greater investment needs to be made in research aimed at understanding more fully the functioning of ecosystems and adequately analyzing the different variables associated with any significant modification of the environment. Because all creatures are connected, each must be cherished with love and respect, for all of us as living creatures are dependent on one another. Each area is responsible for the care of this family. This will require undertaking a careful inventory of the species which it hosts, with a view to developing programmes and strategies of protection with particular care for safeguarding species heading towards extinction.

IV. Decline in the quality of human life and the breakdown of society

43. Human beings too are creatures of this world, enjoying a right to life and happiness, and endowed with unique dignity. So we cannot fail to consider the effects on people's lives of environmental deterioration, current models of development and the throwaway culture.

DISCUSSION NOTES/QUESTIONS

1. Since the 1970s at least, there has been an ongoing debate between those who see our environmental problems as a symptom of our over-exploitation of the resources of the planet, and those who believe that sensible environmental management, advances in existing technology, and future discoveries can generate constantly rising standards of living for a growing global population while simultaneously permitting continual improvements in environmental conditions.

Those who believe we are approaching the limits of the planet's "carrying capacity" argue that we must fundamentally alter our mindset in order to overcome our environmental problems. Economist Herman Daly warned that our assumption that economic growth is the solution to most economic ills (e.g., poverty, unemployment, environmental degradation) is erroneous and that we must develop "new ways of thinking":

> [T]he facts are plain and uncontestable: the biosphere is finite, nongrowing, closed (except for the constant input of solar energy), and constrained by the laws of thermodynamics. Any subsystem, such as the economy, must at some point cease growing and adapt itself to a dynamic equilibrium, something like a steady state.

Herman E. Daly, *Economics in a Full World,* in Ecological Economics and Sustainable Development: Selected Essays of Herman Daly 12–13 (2007).

This perspective was first presented to the international community in a 1972 report commissioned by the Club of Rome (an international group of business persons and scientists) and entitled *Limits to Growth.* That report predicted that world growth trends in "population, industrialization, pollution, food production, and resource depletion" would need to be curtailed to avoid economic and ecological collapse within a century. Several of the lead authors of that report, writing 20 years later, said their conclusions were "still valid":

> 1. Human use of many essential resources and generation of many kinds of pollutants have already surpassed rates that are physically sustainable. Without significant reductions in material and energy flows, there will be in the coming decades an uncontrolled decline in per capita food output, energy use, and industrial production.
>
> 2. This decline is not inevitable. To avoid it two changes are necessary. The first is a comprehensive revision of policies and practices that perpetuate growth in material consumption and in

> population. The second is a rapid, drastic increase in the efficiency with which materials and energy are used.
>
> 3. A sustainable society is still technically and economically possible. It could be much more desirable than a society that tries to solve its problems by constant expansion. The transition to a sustainable society requires a careful balance between long-term and short-term goals and an emphasis on sufficiency, equity, and quality of life rather than on quantity of output. It requires more than productivity and more than technology; it also requires maturity, compassion, and wisdom.

Donella H. Meadows, Dennis L. Meadows & Jørgen Randers, Beyond the Limits: Confronting Global Collapse, Envisioning a Sustainable Future xv (1992).

Overcoming the challenge of unsustainability, according to some, will require even more fundamental changes than altering our attitude toward "growth in material consumption" or improving our technology to make more efficient use of natural resources:

> Profound changes will be needed to sustain natural and human communities—changes in public policy and changes in individual and social behavior. . . .
>
> Many of our deepest thinkers and many of those most familiar with the scale of the challenges we face have concluded that the transitions required can be achieved only in the context of what I will call the rise of a new consciousness. For some, it is a spiritual awakening—a transformation of the human heart. For others it is a more intellection process of coming to see the world anew and deeply embracing the emerging ethic of the environment and the old ethic of what it means to love thy neighbor as thyself. But for all it involves major cultural change and a reorientation of what society values and prizes most highly."

James Gustave Speth, The Bridge at the Edge of the World 199–200 (2008).

Are you persuaded by any of the arguments summarized in this note? Which, if any, of the principal readings in this Introduction make similar arguments or adopt a similar perspective?

2. As mentioned in Note 1, there are many commentators who adopt a less gloomy view about our environmental problems, believing that it is possible to continually grow the global economy and improve people's material circumstances while simultaneously improving the condition of the environment. Two of the more famous proponents of this perspective are the late Julian Simon, an economist, and the Danish statistician, Bjørn Lomborg. Both point to the fact that, over time, "in almost every respect important to humanity, the trends [concerning the state of the environment and the availability of natural resources] have been improving, not deteriorating," despite the constant increase in human population. Julian Simon, *There is No*

Environmental, Population or Resource Crisis, in Living in the Environment: An Introduction to Environmental Science 29, 29–31 (George Tyler Miller, Jr. ed., 7th ed. 1992).

Simon's analysis was mirrored and extended by Bjørn Lomborg in his controversial 2001 book, The Skeptical Environmentalist. Like Simon, Lomborg concluded that things are getting better, that there is no environmental crisis, and that the continued pursuit of economic development and material well-being will invariably be for the good of humans and the planet. Writing against what he calls "the Litany that doomsday is nigh," Lomborg argues that the opposite is true. Our industrialized society has "given us a life that is so much better [than the lives of previous humans] that we at last have enough time and resources to consider how we want to make the most of life"; and, he says, the benefits of industrialization are gradually being spread across the world. Moreover, our ability to handle past environmental problems and improve life (air is cleaner in most western cities than it was 100 years ago) is proof that environmental threats will be managed. We do not need to change our way of life. Lomborg writes:

> [O]ur food production will continue to give more people more and cheaper food. We will not lose our forests; we will not run out of energy, raw materials or water. We have reduced atmospheric pollution in the cities of the developed world and have good reason to believe that this will also be achieved in the developing world. Our oceans have not been defiled, our rivers have become cleaner and support more life, and although the nutrient influx has increased in many coastal waters like the Gulf of Mexico, this does not constitute a major problem—in fact, benefits generally outweigh costs. Nor is waste a particularly big problem. The total US waste throughout the twenty-first century could be deposited in a single square landfill, less than 18 miles on the side—or 26 percent of Woodward County, Oklahoma.
>
> Acid rain did not kill off our forests, our species are not dying out as many have claimed, with half of them disappearing over the next 50 years—the figure is likely to be about 0.7 percent. The problem of the ozone layer has been more or less solved. The current outlook on the development of global warming does not indicate a catastrophe—rather, there is good reason to believe that our energy consumption will change towards renewable energy sources way before the end of the century. Indeed, the catastrophe seems rather in spending our resources unwisely on curbing present carbon emissions at high costs instead of helping the developing countries and increasing non-fossil fuel research. And finally, our chemical worries and fear of pesticides are misplaced and counterproductive. First, phasing out pesticides will probably waste resources and actually cause more cancer. Second, the main causes of cancer are not chemicals but our own lifestyle.

Lomborg, The Skeptical Environmentalist: Measuring the Real State of the World 329–30 (2001).

Neither Simon nor Lomborg contend that environmental law is unnecessary. Indeed, many of the improvements Lomborg mentions (e.g., an end to acid rain) are due to the development of legal solutions to the problem and, in particular, to the adoption of international legal rules that imposed limits on pollution (*see* Chapter 3). But clearly, those who embrace the Simon/Lomborg perspective are likely to advocate for legal rules for controlling environmental degradation that differ from the legal solutions likely to be supported by proponents of the limits-to-growth perspective.

Are you persuaded by any of the arguments summarized in this note? Which, if any, of the principal readings in this Introduction make similar arguments or adopt a similar perspective?

3. At the beginning of this chapter, we suggested that some environmental problems are "primarily local in their impact" and require "mainly local" solutions, while effective solutions to other problems are not possible without some international action to address the problem. The second half of that statement is unlikely to be contested by most people. There are, indeed, environmental problems that are transnational (transboundary pollution) or global (depletion of the ozone layer) in their scope and require international solutions. Similarly, where international behavior exacerbates an environmental problem (e.g., as the trade in elephant ivory exacerbates the problem of elephant poaching in sub-Saharan Africa), few would contest the desirability of international law to deal with the international dimension of the problem.

But is the first part of our statement correct? Are there environmental problems that are "primarily local in their impact" or that require "mainly local" solutions?

4. There are at least four bases on which one might argue that environmental problems are everyone's problem and should be addressed by action at an international level, even if a particular problem seems local in its origin and impact. First, one might take a "small Earth" perspective, according to which environmental threats in any location are threats to the Earth's ecological system, and thus a concern of all.

A second common argument is that even local environmental problems have roots in the global economy (and in free trade policies adopted internationally) and thus are problems for which the international community is responsible, even if the problem manifests itself only locally. Consider the problem of air and water pollution in Mexico. Even if the pollution remains within Mexican borders, many would say it is not exclusively a local problem because, in all probability, the factories generating the pollution are doing so to produce goods for sale in the United States and Canada. In effect, U.S. consumers are exporting their pollution problem to Mexico, and the U.S. therefore has some responsibility to help Mexico address the problem. *See, e.g.,*

Lori Wallach & Patrick Woodall, Whose Trade Organization?: A Comprehensive Guide to the WTO 19–50 (2004); Corey L. Lofdahl, Environmental Impacts of Globalization and Trade (2002).

Others who view local environmental degradation as a matter of international concern take a moral perspective. For example, Pope Francis argues that human suffering from environmental degradation should be a concern of humans everywhere, regardless of where that suffering occurs. Similarly, many human rights advocates argue that individuals, regardless of where they live, are entitled to live in a clean and healthy environment and that protecting that right is an essential component of the international community's commitment to the protection of human rights. *See generally* Human Rights Approaches to Environmental Protection (Alan E. Boyle & Michael R. Anderson eds. 1996); Peter Singer, One World: The Ethics of Globalization (2nd Ed. 2004).

Finally, even when environmental problems seem purely local in nature, some commentators are attentive to the unexpected ways in which environmental problems might become international peace and security problems if not adequately addressed.

> The scope of environmental issues that affect the national well-being of the United States is immense. Resource availability, in particular, is a critical national security issue, neglect of which at the strategic level is potentially dangerous. . . . Today, much of the danger lies in the exacerbation of already poor human conditions in regions where some form of environmental degradation exists due to resource mismanagement or destruction.
>
> * * *
>
> When the government in a country or region cannot attend to the conditions that deprive its populace of food, water, and basic survival resources, the people can become desperate for any source of relief. This provides the fertile ground for instability and anarchy, and thus a threat to the security of the region and anyone who may interact with the region. In this age of globalization, all regions are interconnected. So, what threatens the stability of one region, affects all. Likewise, the conditions that create that instability affect all and can threaten their well-being and security as well.

Colonel Elizabeth M. Damonte, *National Security Strategy: What About the Environment?,* U.S. Army War College Strategy Research Project 3–6 (15 March 2006). *See also* Colin P. Kelley, et al., *Climate Change in the Fertile Crescent and Implications of the Recent Syrian Drought,* 112 Proceedings of the National Academy of Science 3241 (2015) (arguing that drought in Syria caused "massive agricultural failures and livestock mortality," with resulting severe social impacts that led directly to the onset of the Syrian civil war.)

What is your view: should the international community (and international law) concern itself primarily (or exclusively) with environmental problems with an obvious transnational or global dimension, or are all severe environmental problems, regardless of their location, appropriate for international attention?

5. If apparently local environmental problems are nonetheless appropriate for international attention, what form should international action take when a particular environmental problem is not the result of transboundary pollution and has no transboundary impact? Is it appropriate for the international community to provide money and technology to poorer countries to help them solve their local problems? To require poor countries to address those problems themselves (e.g., by imposing trade restrictions on products produced in developing countries if the production methods are environmentally harmful)? To accept large numbers of immigrants from poor countries, thus relieving the environmental stress caused by over-population?

If a poorer country were asked to take actions that protect its local environment (or that protect the global environment from local actions), would it be justified in linking any action it took to adequate levels of foreign assistance to pay for that action? For example, if Brazil were asked to stop clear-cutting in the Amazon rainforest, would it be entitled to link any changes in its environmental policies to changes it wished to see in rich country policies regarding sovereign debt, technology transfer, intellectual property protection, or trade?

6. We have suggested that international law and the international legal system provide a set of tools for addressing environmental problems. You will study some of those tools in the next few chapters. As you do, you should consider how you might use those tools in different legal practice settings. For example, if you work for a national government, how would international law affect your choice of means to resolve a dispute with another country over transboundary pollution? If you worked for a nongovernmental organization dedicated to environmental protection, how could international laws and processes be used by your organization to facilitate social change and move policy in your preferred direction? If you worked for a for-profit corporation concerned about excessive or unnecessary environmentally-related regulations in various countries, or about competition from businesses operating in regulation-free locations, how could international law and legal processes help your client?

One point of asking you to think about these questions is to help you discover an important truth: international environmental law is an intensely practical subject although sometimes it does not appear so. The real world practicality of the subject flows from the fact that political leaders, diplomats, public servants, business leaders and advisers, and civil society all now find themselves enmeshed in international environmental issues for significant portions of their working lives. This tendency follows the increasing globalization of business and commerce, and it is fed by the fact that no nation alone can address and solve problems that require concerted collaborative action from several or many states.

7. Although the essence of the task of the international environmental lawyer is to marry the techniques and modalities of public international law and apply them to environmental problems, it is useful to appreciate that international environmental law comprises law *plus*—and the plus draws from many academic disciplines other than law. Those disciplines have important contributions to make when it comes to analyzing both the problems and solutions. Virtually all of the sciences are engaged: biology, chemistry, geology, and physics, and atmospheric science, ecology, genetics, mathematics, and meteorology; also geography, a discipline that spans both natural and social sciences. Even engineers who deal with earthquakes are looking increasingly to social science research to understand how to handle the human problems that arise when assisting people whose homes have been destroyed by earthquake. Philosophy, ethics, feminism, anthropology—all offer insights that are valuable in international environmental law.

8. Economics and the role of the market in the allocation of resources is of particular importance in the international environmental law arena. Unbridled exploitation of natural resources can have profound and adverse environmental effects. Frequently the environmental costs imposed by this exploitation are externalized, and export of the costs to countries other than one's own is an issue that now arises often. The "polluter pays" principle is firmly enough established and so is the "precautionary" principle, but often they are avoided or evaded. Special interests can and do "screw the scrum" as they say in rugby, allowing subsidies for particular activities that may be environmentally deleterious.

When it comes to environmental issues, the market fails to capture many of the values and contributions that are at play. Ecosystems provide many services to all of us, but of which we are almost oblivious, in major part because of the difficulty in dealing with them in market transactions—forests that reduce soil erosion as well as capture carbon, lakes that provide us with recreation, bees that pollinate crops and fruit trees, and shell fish that filter water pollution. Mountains and beaches provide many benefits both sporting and spiritual. How does the market cope with these?

9. Battalions of scientists and economists, with their splendid but worrying diversity of views, are required to analyze the right questions; but the making of decisions to rectify the problems is required as well, and here is located the often missing link to resolving environmental problems. Scientists may be able to identify the problems, economists to evaluate and identify cost-effective solutions, and lawyers to craft legal documents embodying those solutions. But still, real action is wanting. Why?

Politics is the key—if politics is the art of the possible then the global environment seems to be testing us beyond the collective means at our disposal. A famous political scientist, Professor Harold Lasswell, once stated, in a rather anthropocentric view of politics, that it was all about who got what, when, where, and how. And if that is the case, as it certainly seems to be at least in the liberal democracies of the world, then who guards the environment?

For good or ill, then, the international environmental lawyer must be a master of law and legal processes, a student of science and economics, and—if real solutions to our problems are to be implemented in the real world—a practitioner of the political arts. The journey upon which this book takes both teacher and student touches all these fields. It is sometimes a demanding voyage, but we find it fascinating and hope you will as well.

CHAPTER ONE

ADJUDICATING SOUTHERN OCEAN WHALING: CULTURAL CONFLICT AND THE LIMITS OF INTERNATIONAL LAW

■ ■ ■

A. INTRODUCTION

In this chapter we aim to achieve five objectives.

First, we attempt to provide you with a general overview of the international legal system. We begin with a brief examination of the processes existing in the international system for resolving disputes in a peaceful manner. We then examine the sources of the international law that may (or may not) be used to resolve those disputes. You should read these materials with care. A solid understanding of international dispute settlement and of the sources of international law is an important prerequisite to the study and practice of international environmental law.

Second, we want to show you international dispute settlement in action. International law usually involves disputes between nations, and it often also involves disputes over the content of customary international law or the interpretation of environmental treaty obligations. Dispute resolution differs greatly in the international sphere from the methods that are used in domestic jurisdictions. In the domestic sphere, when voluntary dispute settlement efforts fail, one person can compel another to appear in front of a court and the dispute is resolved by a judgment of the court. In the international sphere, nations often cannot be compelled to answer a claim in an international court against their will. Moreover, even when they do agree to appear in an international court or arbitral tribunal, the judgment issued may not succeed in bringing the dispute to an end.

We examine first the *Bering Sea Fur Seals Arbitration*. In that case, the United States claimed a legal right to protect a population of fur seals from over-exploitation. The arbitral tribunal ruled against the United States, but the disputing parties eventually reached an amicable agreement with a favorable outcome for the fur seals.

By contrast, in the case considered at the end of this chapter, the International Court of Justice ruled that Japan's research whaling program in the Southern Ocean was inconsistent with its whale-protection obligations under the 1946 International Convention for the Regulation of

Whaling **(Basic Document 5.17)**. Australia, after years of seeking an end to Japanese whaling, won an apparently great victory. But, following the Court's decision, nothing much changed. Japan continued to whale in the Southern Ocean in more or less the same fashion as before. Worse, in December 2018, four years after the ICJ's decision, Japan announced that it was withdrawing completely from the International Whaling Convention. Australia's success before the ICJ now seems likely to prove a Pyrrhic victory from the whales' point of view, although only time will tell. The point is: going to court can have unexpected results in the international sphere that are not duplicated in domestic legal systems.

Our third goal in this chapter is to seek to illustrate, from the real-life example of the International Whaling Convention, how multilateral international treaties work and how the international organizations created by those treaties behave and sometimes change their emphasis over time. Treaties are the most important source of international environmental law, and there has been a proliferation of international organizations established to carry out the objectives and rules of those treaties. The whaling example illustrates just how complex the political and legal issues can become, particularly when states develop fundamentally different views about how the treaty regime should operate.

Fourth, we hope to demonstrate with the real world examples in this chapter the vital role that negotiation plays in the international sphere. Most diplomats spend most of their time negotiating. In multilateral arenas these processes are infinitely complex and often frustrating. But anyone who works in international environmental law must secure knowledge of the techniques of what is called in the most influential book on the subject "Getting to Yes".[1]

Finally, we want to introduce you to the passion and emotion that surrounds many international environmental issues, particularly on a subject like whales. The weight of public opinion and the activities of Non-Government Organizations (NGOs) can place heavy constraints on nation-states in their negotiations. Just as pressure groups can influence domestic policy, so too can they influence state behavior and decision-making in the international arena. This may surprise you, but it is a reality of international politics and an important driver of international environmental law.

B. INTERNATIONAL DISPUTE SETTLEMENT

We begin with the settlement of disputes, because usually a dispute is the reason lawyers are called in. There are a wide range of methods and processes commonly employed to aid in the resolution of disputes in any

---

[1] Roger Fisher, William Ury and Bruce Patton, *Getting to Yes: Negotiating an Agreement Without Giving In* (3rd ed. 2012).

context. Each differs slightly in its approach and in the autonomy it gives participant parties, and each has varying strengths that may make it optimal in one situation but not another.

The most common methods of dispute resolution employed in the international sphere are those set out expressly in Article 33(1) of the Charter of the United Nations **(Basic Document 1.1)**. The Charter of the United Nations has as one of its central purposes the requirement, set out in Article 2(3), that all members are to settle their international disputes by peaceful means. Provisions relating to the pacific settlement of disputes appear in Chapter VI of the Charter. Article 33(1) imposes a specific legal principle on member states and sets out the various methods that may be employed for the peaceful resolution of inter-state disputes at the international level. It provides:

> The parties to any dispute, the continuance of which is likely to endanger the maintenance of international peace and security, shall, first of all, seek a solution by negotiation, enquiry, mediation, conciliation, arbitration, judicial settlement, resort to regional agencies or arrangements, or other peaceful means of their own choice.

All of these methods—negotiation, enquiry, mediation, conciliation, arbitration, judicial settlement and regional agencies—are used to varying degrees in international practice when seeking to resolve disputes between states. This can be through the direct invocation of Article 33 or through one of the many dispute settlement clauses written into treaties.[2]

Thus, it is necessary when operating in the international sphere to understand the range of settlement processes which may be engaged in seeking the resolution of a dispute.

When seeking to resolve a dispute, whether in the realm of international environmental law or elsewhere, it is an important ingredient of preparation to think carefully about what precisely the dispute is about. How the subject matter of a dispute is framed or characterized and the avenues, both legal and political, available to resolve it can be critical. The framing often determines the law that applies to the dispute. An example that resonates is the *Southern Bluefin Tuna* case.[3] There it was necessary to decide early whether there was a dispute about the interpretation of the United Nations Convention on the Law of the Sea (UNCLOS) **(Basic Document 3.4)** or whether it was a dispute that revolved around the interpretation of the Southern Bluefin Tuna

[2] Also note that these methods are also frequently used at the international level by non-state actors, particularly in private international law. However, our main focus at the moment is states.

[3] Southern Bluefin Tuna, Australia and New Zealand v Japan, Award on Jurisdiction and Admissibility, 2000, 13 R.I.A.A. 1, decided by Arbitral Tribunal constituted under the UNCLOS.

Convention.[4] This decision was a key factor in determining whether jurisdiction existed for the case to be heard.

The range of methods with which to arrive at a resolution of the dispute is extensive—from negotiation to adjudication and every modern method of dispute settlement in between.[5] Each of the enumerated methods has its own features, its own literature and its own practice. What follows is a description of each of the methods of dispute settlement set out in Article 33 of the United Nations Charter, as well as an account of how they are used in the international context between states.

Negotiation

Negotiations are the standard fare of diplomacy and usually the first step.[6] Negotiation covers different categories of dispute. New law is made in treaties that are negotiated. Disputes, both bi-lateral and multi-lateral, are also settled by negotiation. States like negotiations because they remain in the driver's seat in a manner that they do not in third-party adjudication. But to negotiate is not necessarily to reach an agreement, even though that is the aim.

One trouble with negotiations is that they often go on for a lengthy period because not resolving the dispute now is often better from a political point of view than concluding there has been a complete failure to resolve it. But negotiation can be quick if there is a will and it is certainly flexible. Of course negotiations have to be conducted in good faith, but there is a large degree of elasticity about what may or may not constitute good faith in the particular circumstances, and that issue can itself become the subject of dispute. Allegations of bad faith are frequently made in the authors' experience but not often followed through on. Obviously bilateral negotiations are different from multilateral ones; group dynamics play an important role in the latter category. In the international sphere negotiations between states are usually conducted through diplomatic channels by diplomats. Negotiations can be organized and structured in many different ways, depending on the nature of the issues. When negotiations fail to bring an end to a dispute over a lengthy period, then resort can be had to other dispute settlement methods. Remember, not all

---

[4] United Nations Convention on the Law of the Sea, Dec. 10, 1982, 1833 U.N.T.S. 397; Convention for the Conservation of Southern Bluefin Tuna, May 10, 1993, 1819 U.N.T.S. 359.

[5] J.G. Merrills, International Dispute Settlement (5th ed. 2011); Francesco Orrego Vicuna, International Dispute Settlement in an Evolving Global Society: Constitutionalization Accessibility Privatization (2004); Duncan French, International Law and Dispute Settlement: New Problems and Techniques (2010); and H. Lauterpacht (ed.) and L. Oppenheim, International Law, a Treatise (1952), in particular vol 2, Disputes, War and Neutrality at 3–120 is still worthy of examination.

[6] One old but useful reference is Harold Nicholson, Diplomacy (3rd ed., 1964). *See also* Jean-Robert Lequey-Feilleuz, The Dynamics of Diplomacy (2009). An extensive and useful bibliography is set out at 369–389.

disputes between nations can be solved. A negotiated resolution requires finding a solution that both sides believe is more advantageous to them than maintaining the *status quo*.

Inquiry

Inquiry, mediation, and conciliation are all related. The Hague Conventions for the Pacific Settlement of International Disputes in 1899 and 1907 devised Commissions of Inquiry, the functions of which were to investigate the facts of a dispute and make a report setting them out.[7] The report is not intended to be binding. It is left up to the parties to decide what to do with it. Under the Hague rules, a Commission of Inquiry would be set up on each occasion where a dispute arose, by agreement between the nations involved.[8] This method was famously used in the *Dogger Bank* case between Great Britain and Russia where a dispute arose as a result of an attack by Russian warships on British fishing vessels in the North Sea.[9] Such an arrangement is open under the provision relating to Inquiry in Article 33. Where there are factual issues in a dispute, such a procedure may help ascertain what the true situation is. To avoid the consequences of a stalemated negotiation, bringing in a third party can help open up the issues between the parties and bring them to a resolution. Yet the occasions upon which such a formal tribunal can be successfully used seem to have been limited despite the comparatively old age of the method. Further, it involves nations having to account for their behavior to some degree, which they often do not relish.

Mediation

Mediation may be regarded as a method that has a more active third-party involvement; a third party is present not to adjudicate on the dispute but to try and help the parties reach agreement. This can be done in a number of ways. Their job is to promote a solution and the process of arriving at one may go through various iterations. Mediators can put up proposals to the parties. They can cajole. They can help the parties see reason and encourage a rational approach. They can attempt to instill a sense of fairness in the parties. They can point out weaknesses in the approach of each side. As a dispute settlement method, it is highly flexible

---

7 For the text of these treaties *see* Yale Law School, Lillian Goldman Law Library *The Avalon Project*, available at http://avalon.law.yale.edu/subject_menus/lawwar.asp.

8 There is an issue of orthography in relation to the terms 'Enquiry' and 'Inquiry'. A useful distinction exists between enquire and inquire, although some authors use these two terms interchangeably. Enquire is best used to mean 'to ask' in general contexts, while inquire is reserved to mean 'to make a formal investigation'. We have standardized the spelling to 'inquiry'. The international practice is variable. *The American Heritage Dictionary* (3rd ed. 1992) at 613 states that 'inquiry' is a variant of 'enquiry'.

9 *The Dogger Bank Case (G.B. v. Russ.)*, The Hague Court Reports 403 (James B. Scott ed., Carnegie Endowment for International Peace, 1916).

and is not inhibited by legal structures surrounding it. But finding acceptable mediators to deal with disputes between nation states is frequently difficult. In disputes between two states sometimes a third state may act as a mediator. Success depends on the parties ultimately reaching agreement. The mediator cannot impose a solution.

Conciliation

Conciliation sits between mediation and arbitration and contains elements of both. Apart from the reference to conciliation in Article 33 of the U.N. Charter, dispute settlement by conciliation is provided for in both the Vienna Convention on the Law of Treaties **(Basic Document 1.14)** and the Vienna Convention on Succession of States in respect of Treaties.[10] In 1995, the General Assembly adopted Model Rules for the Conciliation of Disputes between States with the goal of improving traditional practices in this arena.[11]

Procedures for establishing and administering a conciliation vary. But the Annex to the Vienna Convention on the Law of Treaties provides a fairly typical set of rules. Under the process set out in that Convention, a party involved in particular kinds of disputes may request conciliation of that dispute.[12] When such a request is made, the matter is referred to a conciliation commission that is constituted by appointing four conciliators, one each from the states in dispute and the others drawn from a list maintained by the Secretary-General not of the nationality of the disputing states. Those four appoint a fifth who is the chair. The Commission decides for itself on the procedures it will follow, but it must "hear the parties, examine the claims and objections, and make proposals to the parties with a view to reaching an amicable settlement of the dispute." The Convention establishes timelines for a conciliation commission's action, and provides expressly that the factual and legal conclusions of commissions "shall not be binding upon the parties and shall have no other character than that of recommendations."

Conciliation is not these days popular for bilateral disputes, but there are a number of multilateral treaties that provide for it as one method by which to approach a dispute. For example, the Vienna Convention for the Protection of the Ozone Layer **(Basic Document 2.7)** provides that a conciliation commission shall be created upon the request of one of the parties to a dispute.[13] A commission established under this provision is

[10] Vienna Convention on the Law of Treaties, May 23, 1969, 1155 U.N.T.S. 331; Vienna Convention on Succession of States in Respect of Treaties, Aug. 23, 1978, 1946 U.N.T.S. 3.

[11] G.A. Res. 50/50, Annex (Dec. 11, 1995).

[12] Vienna Convention on the Law of Treaties art. 66 and Annex, May 23, 1969, 1155 U.N.T.S. 331.

[13] Vienna Convention for the Protection of the Ozone Layer art. 11(5), Mar. 22, 1985, 26 I.L.M. 1529.

directed to render a final and recommendatory award that the parties must consider in good faith. There is also provision for conciliation in Annex V(1) of the United Nations Convention on the Law of the Sea **(Basic Document 3.4).**[14] And, of course, a procedure for conciliation can be set up between contending states whenever there is a will to do so.

Arbitration

Arbitration is a formal and binding method of adjudication applying the law. Arbitral proceedings are usually held in private, thus making arbitration more attractive to political leaders than adjudication in a court. Arbitrators are usually appointed by the parties, but they are not subject to orders as to what to decide. Arbitration can be more flexible than adjudication in the sense that it is possible for the parties to frame the issues to be decided and the procedure to be followed to a greater degree than with adjudication in a court.

There are a wide variety of arbitral forums in which environmental claims may be pursued by and against states. For example, the Permanent Court of Arbitration (PCA), which was established in 1899 as "the first global mechanisms for the settlement of inter-State disputes,"[15] is identified in several multilateral environmental treaties as a preferred forum for dispute settlement. The PCA has established special rules for the arbitration and conciliation of environmental disputes that "provide the most comprehensive set of environmentally tailored dispute resolution procedural rules presently available."[16]

Environmental issues are also frequently arbitrated in the context of investor-state disputes. Such disputes generally involve claims by foreign investors that a state's environmental regulations unlawfully harmed their investment. Many international investment and trade agreements call for these disputes to be arbitrated under the auspices and rules of the World Bank's International Centre for the Settlement of Investment Disputes (ICSID), on an *ad hoc* basis using UNCITRAL rules,[17] or following the rules of the Arbitration Institute of the Stockholm Chamber of Commerce.

Private arbitration is a widely used dispute settlement technique for international commercial disputes. Sometimes these disputes involve environmental issues. States often act as commercial contracting parties, and so may be involved in such arbitrations. There are many private

---

14 United Nations Convention on the Law of the Sea, Dec. 10, 1982, 1833 U.N.T.S. 397.

15 Alexandre-Charles Kiss, *Environmental Disputes and the Permanent Court of Arbitration*, 16 Hague Y.B. Int'l L. 41, 41 (2003).

16 Permanent Court of Arbitration, *Environmental Dispute Resolution*, https://pca-cpa.org/en/services/arbitration-services/environmental-dispute-resolution/ (last visited March 18, 2019).

17 *See* for example the United Nations Commission on International Trade Law Arbitration Rules available at www.uncitral.org/pdf/english/texts/arbitration/arb-rules-2013/UNCITRAL-Arbitration-Rules-2013-e.pdf.

commercial arbitration organizations. Private commercial arbitrations most frequently proceed according to the rules of the sponsoring organization or pursuant to UNCITRAL rules.[18]

Judicial Settlement

The International Court of Justice[19]

The 1922 Covenant of the League of Nations provided for the establishment of a Permanent Court of International Justice [PCIJ], with competence to "hear and determine any dispute of an international character which the parties thereto submit to it."[20] Any state that became a Member of the League agreed to submit to "arbitration or judicial settlement" any dispute with another member that was suitable for such resolution and that could not be settled by diplomatic means.[21] Unresolved disputes that were not taken to arbitration or adjudication were subject to mandatory conciliation by the League of Nations Council.[22] From its establishment in 1922 until its dissolution in 1964, the PCIJ handled 29 contentious cases.

The United Nations Charter replaced the PCIJ with the International Court of Justice (ICJ). The ICJ was established as the principal judicial organ of the United Nations,[23] and all Members of the United Nations are "*ipso facto* parties to the Statute of the International Court of Justice."[24] Today, 193 states are party to, and bound by, the Court's Statute **(Basic Document 1.2)**.

The Court's function is "to decide in accordance with international law such disputes as are submitted to it." The Court's decision in a contentious case is binding only on the parties to the case.[25] The Court has no power to compel a state to comply with a decision against it. However, each member of the U.N. "undertakes to comply" with the decision of the Court in any case to which the member is a party, and a failure to comply could lead to enforcement action by the Security Council.[26]

---

[18] Important private organizations include: the American Arbitration Association, the London Court of International Arbitration, the Arbitration Institute of the Stockholm Chamber of Commerce, the ICC International Court of Arbitration, and the recently created Japan International Dispute Resolution Center.

[19] *See generally* Shabtai Rosenne, *The Law and Practice of the International Court of Justice 1920–2005* (4th ed. 2006) (4 volumes).

[20] Covenant of the League of Nations, art. 14.

[21] Covenant of the League of Nations, art. 13.

[22] Covenant of the League of Nations, art. 15.

[23] Charter of the United Nations, arts. 7 & 93.

[24] Charter of the United Nations, art. 93.

[25] Statute of the International Court of Justice, art. 59.

[26] Charter of the United Nations, art. 94.

The U.N. Charter also authorizes the General Assembly and the Security Council to request an advisory opinion from the Court on "any legal question."[27] Advisory opinions of the Court are, of course, advisory, and neither the U.N. Charter nor the Court's Statute make any provision for their enforcement.

The jurisdiction of the ICJ

Although all members of the United Nations are parties to the Statute of the ICJ, this does not mean that all members of the United Nations are subject to the jurisdiction of the Court! Some nations argued strongly at the time of the foundation of the United Nations that the Court should have compulsory jurisdiction in respect to all member states, but they were defeated by the permanent members of the Security Council.[28] Instead, the Court's jurisdiction in contentious cases is based upon the consent of the contesting states.

There are three ways in which states can consent to the Court's jurisdiction. First, states can give their consent to ICJ adjudication on a case-by-case basis, pursuant to a special agreement known as a "*compromis*." Second, a state may agree in advance that disputes that arise under a particular treaty will be subject to ICJ decision-making. Finally, a state might decide to accept the Court's compulsory jurisdiction by affirmatively declaring, per Article 36(2) of the Court's Statute (the so-called 'optional clause'), that it "recognize[s the Court's jurisdiction] as compulsory *ipso facto* and without special agreement, in relation to any other state accepting the same obligation."

Only 66 states have accepted the compulsory jurisdiction of the Court under the optional clause.[29] Among the permanent members of the U.N. Security Council, only the United Kingdom accepts the compulsory jurisdiction of the Court. Russia and China have never accepted the jurisdiction of the Court either under the optional clause or by special agreement. The United States terminated its acceptance of the compulsory jurisdiction effective 1986 in the aftermath of a decision of the Court in a case Nicaragua brought against the United States for military and para-military activities, particularly the laying of mines in Nicaraguan ports.[30]

---

[27] United Nations Charter, art. 96. In addition, the General Assembly may authorize other U.N. bodies to request advisory opinions "on legal questions arising within the scope of their activities." *Id.*

[28] *United Nations Conference on International Organization, Report of the New Zealand Delegation* 9 External Affairs Publication No. 11, 103004 (1945).

[29] This number is derived from the International Court of Justice list of declarations from nations recognizing the compulsory jurisdiction of the ICJ, available on the ICJ website at www.icj-cij.org/jurisdiction/index.php?p1=5&p2=1&p3=3.

[30] Military and Paramilitary Activities in and Against Nicaragua (Nicar. v. U.S.) (Jurisdiction), 1984 I.C.J. 392; Military and Paramilitary Activities in and Against Nicaragua (Nicar. v. U.S.) (Merits), 1986 I.C.J. 14 (June 27). *Statement of the Legal Adviser of the State Department, Abraham D. Sofaer to Senate Foreign Relations Committee 4 December 1985* 86 Department of State Bulletin 67 (No. 2106, Jan. 1986).

France terminated its acceptance of the compulsory jurisdiction in the wake of the *Nuclear Tests* cases.[31]

Hundreds of treaties in force provide for the possibility of resolution of disputes by the ICJ.[32] But in most cases, referral to the ICJ is option, not compulsory. If a treaty does provide for mandatory submission of disputes to the ICJ, it generally does so in a separate protocol that is binding only on states that consent to it or in a provision of the treaty that allows states to choose ICJ dispute settlement but does not require that choice. In short, the jurisdiction of the Court is essentially consensual. States are not obliged to accept the compulsory jurisdiction of the Court, and most do not. But many nevertheless accept it for particular disputes by special agreement, and the ICJ has decided a number of important cases involving issues of international environmental law.[33]

Other adjudicative tribunals

The World Trade Organization has a sophisticated mechanism for resolving disputes that culminates in a binding decision by the WTO Appellate Body, an independent group of judges with expertise in trade matters. The Appellate Body has decided a number of trade disputes in which issues of environmental protection have played a central role.[34]

The United Nations Convention on the Law of the Sea (UNCLOS) **(Basic Document 3.4)** has extensive provisions aimed at protecting the oceanic environment.[35] Where disputes arise over the "interpretation and application" of these or other provisions, the Convention generally provides for mandatory and binding judicial or arbitral adjudication of the issues.[36] The parties must first attempt to settle a dispute through negotiation, mediation, conciliation, and similar peaceful consensual means. If the matter is not so resolved, any party to the dispute can insist that it be resolved pursuant to some form of binding adjudication. The precise form depends on the parties' prior agreements and stipulations. Where the parties have agreed to do so, a dispute may be submitted for judicial

---

[31] Nuclear Tests Case (Austl. v. France) (Judgment), 1974 I.C.J. 253; (N.Z. v. France) (Judgment), 1974 I.C.J. 457.

[32] *See* International Court of Justice, *Treaties*, https://www.icj-cij.org/en/treaties (last visited March 18, 2019).

[33] *See, e.g.*, Nuclear Tests Case (Austl. v. France) (Judgment), 1974 I.C.J. 253; (N.Z. v. France) (Judgment), 1974 I.C.J. 457 (20 December); The Gabčíkovo-Nagymaros Project (Hung. v. Slov.), 1997 ICJ 7 (September 25); Pulp Mills on the River Uruguay (Arg. v. Urg.), 2010 ICJ 14 (20 April); Whaling in the Antarctic (Austl. V. Japan, N.Z. intervening), 2014 ICJ 226 (31 March); Certain Activities Carried Out by Nicaragua in the Border Area (Costa Rica v. Nicaragua), 2018 ICJ, No. 150 (February 2) (decision on compensation).

[34] *See, e.g., Appellate Body Report, Australia—Measures Affecting the Importation of Apples from New Zealand,* WT/DS367/AB/R (7 December 2010), available at http://www.wto.org/english/tratop_e/dispu_e/cases_e/ds367_e.htm. *See generally* Problem 12-1, *supra*.

[35] *See* Chapter Six, *supra*.

[36] United Nations Convention on the Law of the Sea arts. 286–290, Dec. 10, 1982, 1833 U.N.T.S. 397. *See also* Louis B Sohn. *Settlement of Disputes Arising out of the Law of the Sea Conversation*, 12 San Diego L. Rev. 495 (1975).

resolution to the International Court of Justice or the International Tribunal for the Law of the Sea. If the parties cannot agree on a form of binding adjudication, then the dispute is submitted to binding arbitration pursuant to Annex VII of the Convention.[37]

Finally, human rights courts are increasingly called upon to adjudicate environmental issues that have a human rights dimension.[38] The European Court of Human Rights has decided a number of such cases.[39] Environmental claims have also been brought before the American Court of Human Rights.[40]

As the previous discussion demonstrates, the range of methods available for settling international disputes is wide and each has its own strengths and weaknesses. It all depends upon the particular circumstances of the dispute at hand as to which method will be chosen by the states involved. The internal and external political ramifications of the dispute will weigh heavily upon the minds of government decision-makers, and the avoidance of political embarrassment is always high on their agenda. As the author of the leading text on international dispute settlement put it in the conclusion to his book:[41]

> The peaceful settlement of international disputes is the most critical issue of our time. Although human rights, the environment, and economic and financial issues, among other matters, present challenges which must be addressed if our planet is to have a future, the problems which these subjects pose are always going to generate an abundance of international disputes. However, the use of force in certain disputes could result in the destruction of civilization. Even without such nuclear nightmares, it is clear that the destructiveness of modern warfare is such as to inflict suffering on an unprecedented scale. And, leaving aside for a moment the terrible risks associated with force, for states, as for individuals, a persistent failure to resolve disputes leads only to wasted effort and antagonism.

---

[37] *Id.* There are some exceptions to these obligations. Articles 297 and 298 completely exempt certain kinds of dispute from compulsory arbitration. For certain other categories of cases, the parties can agree to a form of arbitration that is binding as to factual matters only. *See* article 287(d) and *Annex VIII.*

[38] *See* Problem 9-3, *supra.*

[39] *See* European Court of Human Rights, *Factsheet—Environment and the ECHR* (March 2019).

[40] *See, e.g.,* Inter-American Court of Human Rights, *Advisory Opinion on the Environment and Human Rights*, Advisory Opinion OC-23/18, Inter-Am. Ct. H.R. (ser.A) No. 23 (Nov. 15, 2017).

[41] J.G. Merrills, *International Dispute Settlement* 308–309 (5th ed. 2011).

DISCUSSION NOTES/QUESTIONS

1. As you will learn in the next section of this chapter, the two most important sources of international law are international customary law and international treaties. When a dispute arises under international customary law, the disputing states are obligated to "seek a solution by negotiation, enquiry, mediation, conciliation, arbitration, judicial settlement, resort to regional agencies or arrangements, or other peaceful means of their own choice."[42] Except in the relatively unusual case where the disputants have accepted the compulsory jurisdiction of the ICJ, there is no obligation to resolve the dispute through adjudication, nor is there any obligation to submit to any particular method of dispute settlement. By contrast, when a dispute involves the interpretation or application of a treaty, the treaty itself may specify the available methods of dispute settlement, and it may require some form of binding adjudication, as is the case with the United Nations Convention on the Law of the Sea.

Many multilateral environmental treaties contain dispute settlement provisions that permit the parties to agree in advance to compulsory dispute settlement but do not require them to do so. Article 27 of the Convention on Biological Diversity **(Basic Document 5.6)** fits a typical pattern: the parties may accept binding arbitration or ICJ adjudication as compulsory. If they do not do so, a dispute that cannot be resolved by agreement must be submitted to conciliation. The conciliation commission is directed to render a "proposal for resolution of the dispute," which is non-binding but which the parties must "consider in good faith."[43]

Other multilateral environmental treaties do not provide for any formal method of dispute resolution. For example, the Convention on Long-range Transboundary Air Pollution **(Basic Document 2.1)** says only that the parties should "seek a solution" to disputes "by negotiation or by any other method of dispute settlement" acceptable to them.[44] The Montreal Protocol on Substances that Deplete the Ozone Layer imposes strict rules regulating the production and consumption of ozone-depleting substances, yet it has no provisions on dispute settlement. Instead, it authorizes the Parties to adopt "procedures and institutional mechanisms for determining non-compliance" and for the "treatment of Parties found to be in non-compliance."[45] The Parties have

---

[42] Charter of the United Nations, art. 33. *See also*

[43] Convention on Biological Diversity, art. 27 & Annex II, Part 2, June 5, 1992, 1760 UNTS 79 **(Basic Document 5.6)**. Similar provisions appear in the following treaties: Vienna Convention for the Protection of the Ozone Layer, art. 11, March 22, 1985, 1513 U.N.T.S. 293 **(Basic Document 2.7)**; United Nations Framework Convention on Climate Change, art. 14, May 9, 1992, 1771 U.N.T.S. 107 **(Basic Document 2.4)**; Rotterdam Convention on the Prior Informed Consent Procedure for Certain Hazardous Chemicals and Pesticides in International Trade, art. 20, Sept. 10, 1998, 2244 U.N.T.S. 337 **(Basic Document 4.1)**; Stockholm Convention on Persistent Organic Pollutants, art. 18, May 22, 2001, 2256 U.N.T.S. 119 **(Basic Document 4.2)**.

[44] Convention on Long-range Transboundary Air Pollution, art. 13, Nov. 13, 1979, 1302 U.N.T.S. 217 **(Basic Document 2.1)**.

[45] Montreal Protocol on Substances that Deplete the Ozone Layer, art. 8, Sept. 16, 1987, 1522 U.N.T.S. 3 **(Basic Document 2.8)**.

adopted a non-compliance procedure that is intended to be non-confrontational and oriented toward helping parties to implement their obligations.[46] The strongest action that can be taken is the adoption by the Meeting of the Parties of "recommendations."

Why do you think states are reluctant to accept adjudication or other binding forms of third-party decision-making as a means of resolving disputes under environmental treaties?

2. What is true of environmental treaties is equally true in other areas of international law: states for the most part have been reluctant to submit their legal disputes to the Court. As the late Oscar Schachter wrote of international adjudication generally:[47]

> Litigation is uncertain, time consuming, troublesome. Political officials do not want to lose control of a case that they might resolve by negotiation or political pressures. Diplomats naturally prefer diplomacy; political leaders value persuasion, manoeuvre and flexibility. They often prefer to "play it by ear," making their rules to fit the circumstances rather than submit to pre-existing rules. Political forums, such as the United Nations, are often more attractive, especially to those likely to get wide support for political reasons. We need only compare the large number of disputes brought to the United Nations with the few submitted to adjudication. One could go on with other reasons. States do not want to risk losing a case when the stakes are high or be troubled with litigation in minor matters. An international tribunal may not inspire confidence, especially when some judges are seen as "political" or hostile. There is apprehension that the law is too malleable or fragmentary to sustain "true" judicial decisions. In some situations, the legal issues are viewed as but one element in a complex political situation and consequently it is considered unwise or futile to deal with them separately. Finally we note the underlying perception of many governments that law essentially supports the *status quo* and that courts are [not] responsive to demands for justice or change.

3. Should states be more willing to submit their international disputes to judicial settlement? Would increased resort to international adjudication help to develop and strengthen international environmental law? Consider in these respects the following extract from Daniel G. Parton, *Increasing the Effectiveness of the International Court*, 18 Harv. Int'l. L. J. 559, 561 (1977), identifying three functions of the World Court specifically that can be said to characterize international adjudication generally:

---

[46] Report of the Tenth Meeting of the Parties to the Montreal Protocol on Substances that Deplete the Ozone Law, U.N. Doc. UNEP/OzL.Pro. 10/9 (Annex II).

[47] Oscar Schachter, *International Law in Theory and Practice—General Course in Public International Law*, 178 Recueil 9, 208 (1982–V).

> The effectiveness of the International Court, like that of any international institution, must be examined in terms of the purpose and functions of the Court. At the risk of over-simplification, three functions of the International Court might be distinguished. First, the Court functions as a vehicle for the peaceful settlement of international disputes. Second, in articulating international law and applying that law to disputes before it, the Court exerts a major influence on the progressive development of international law. Third, in carrying out its dispute settlement and law development roles, the Court must balance claims for legal change against claims for the enforcement of established rights under traditional international law. . . . [S]ubject to many intense differences of views as to their proper exercise, the three functions just stated would probably enjoy wide acceptance as a framework within which to define the Court's role and measure its effectiveness.

In your view, are any of these functions important for the effectiveness of international environmental law? Why?[48]

4. Any international lawyer ought to have a basic understanding of the International Court's jurisdiction and the means by which states can invoke it.

To begin with, only states may be parties to a contentious action before the Court. This means that, in contentious proceedings, international organizations, including the United Nations, do not have access to the Court's procedures, nor do private parties. Claims originating in wrongs to private parties can be heard by the Court, however, if the injured party's state chooses to raise a claim based on that wrong.

In addition, states must satisfy certain conditions to be entitled to appear before the Court. Any state that is a party to the Statute of the Court is, by that fact, entitled to appear before it. Members of the United Nations are automatically parties to the Statute of the Court. A non-UN member can become party to the Statute of the Court if it meets certain conditions set down by the UN General Assembly on the recommendation of the Security Council. And states that are neither members of the UN nor of the Court's Statute can obtain the right to appear before the Court if they accept the Court's jurisdiction and agree to comply with its decision in all or a particular class of dispute.

As noted earlier, the Court can hear a case only if the parties have consented to the Court's jurisdiction, which they may do by special agreement, by ratification of a treaty that provides for ICJ decision-making, or by acceptance of the Court's compulsory jurisdiction.

---

[48] For elaboration on these and related themes, *see* Richard B. Bilder, *International Dispute Settlement and the Role of International Adjudication*, 1 Emory J. Int'l Dispute Resolution 131 (1987). *See also* Richard B. Bilder, *An Overview of International Dispute Settlement*, 1 Emory J. Int'l Dispute Resolution 1 (1986); John G. Merrills, International Dispute Settlement (3d ed. 1998); Onuma Yasuaki, *Is the International Court of Justice and Emperor without Clothes?*, 8 Int'l Leg. Theory 1 (2002).

5. The law concerning the Court's compulsory jurisdiction is somewhat complicated. Article 36(2) of the Court's Statute provides in relevant part:

> (2) The states party to the present Statute may at any time declare that they recognize as compulsory ipso facto and without special agreement, in relation to any other state accepting the same obligation, the jurisdiction of the Court in all legal disputes concerning:
>
> (a) the interpretation of a treaty;
>
> (b) any question of international law;
>
> (c) the existence of any fact which, if established, would constitute a breach of an international obligation;
>
> (d) the nature or extent of the reparation to be made for the breach of an international obligation.

Although many states have made declarations of acceptance of that jurisdiction, not all declarations of acceptance are identical in content or effect. Some of these declarations of acceptance have been made "unconditionally"—for example, Costa Rica's declaration of acceptance. Others are made subject to some limitation, as in the case of the current Australian declaration of acceptance, which includes the reservation that

> This declaration does not apply to:
>
> (a) any dispute in regard to which the parties thereto have agreed or shall agree to have recourse to some other method of peaceful settlement;
>
> (b) any dispute concerning or relating to the delimitation of maritime zones, including the territorial sea, the exclusive economic zone, and the continental shelf, or arising out of, concerning, or relating to the exploitation of any disputed area of or adjacent to any such maritime zone pending its delimitation;
>
> (c) any dispute in respect of which any other party to the dispute has accepted the compulsory jurisdiction of the Court only in relation to or for the purpose of the dispute; or where the acceptance of the Court's compulsory jurisdiction on behalf of any other party to the dispute was deposited less than 12 months prior to the filing of the application bringing the dispute before the Court.

Canada's declaration of acceptance contains a clause similar to that found in Australia's declaration but also excludes from ICJ jurisdiction disputes with other members of the Commonwealth, "disputes with regard to questions which by international law fall exclusively within the jurisdiction of Canada," and disputes with respect to conservation and management measures taken by Canada with respect to fishing in the northwest Atlantic.[49]

---

[49] For discussion of the issue of reservations to the ICJ Statute, see Stanimir A. Alexandrov, *Accepting the Compulsory Jurisdiction of the International Court of Justice with Reservations: An*

When a state accepts the Court's compulsory jurisdiction with limitations, those limitations can also be invoked against that state. In other words, compulsory jurisdiction is subject to a requirement of reciprocity. States accept the compulsory jurisdiction of the Court with respect to disputes with other states insofar as those other states accept "the same obligation." Thus, if one state says that it will not accept the Court's compulsory jurisdiction over a particular kind of dispute, it cannot then seek to bring a case involving that kind of dispute against another state based on that state's unlimited acceptance of the Court's jurisdiction.

6. In its declaration of acceptance of the compulsory jurisdiction of the Court in 1946, the United States provided that its declaration of acceptance "shall not apply to . . . disputes with regard to matters which are essentially within the domestic jurisdiction of the United States of America *as determined by the United States of America. . . .*" Declaration by the President of the United States of America, 14 Aug 46, respecting recognition by the United States of America of the compulsory jurisdiction of the International Court of Justice, 61 Stat. 1218, TIAS. No. 1598, 4 Bevans 140, 1 UNTS 9. Popularly known as the "Connally Amendment," after Senator Tom Connally of Texas (Chairman of the Senate Foreign Relations Committee when the Declaration was adopted), this language was for many years severely criticized by proponents of a stronger World Court. They lamented both the fact that other states could invoke the language against the United States in accordance with the reciprocity doctrine. They also censured the language for its self-judging and self-serving character. In the words of former Vice-President Hubert Humphrey, the amendment "hampered the effectiveness of the Court [while rendering] little advantage and much embarrassment to this country."[50]

The wisdom of the restriction in the U.S. declaration is today a moot point. On 26 November 1984, the Court determined that it had jurisdiction to adjudicate claims brought by Nicaragua alleging violations of international law by the United States in the aftermath of the Sandinista Revolution. *See Military and Paramilitary Activities in and Against* (Nicar. v. U.S.) (Jurisdiction and Admissibility of the Application), 1984 ICJ 392 (November 26). Following the ICJ's assertion of jurisdiction, the United States refused to further participate in the case. On 7 October 1985, the United States terminated its Article 36(2) declaration. *See* Letter to UN Secretary-General Concerning Termination of Acceptance of Compulsory Jurisdiction of the International Court of Justice (7 Oct. 1985), 86 Dep't State Bull. 67 (1986). This withdrawal of the United States from the World Court's compulsory jurisdiction and the Court's 26 November 1984 jurisdictional ruling prompted a heated debate among international lawyers.[51]

Overview of Practice with a Focus on Recent Trends and Cases, 1 Leiden J. Int'l L. 89 (2001); John G. Merrills, *The Optional Clause Revisited*, 65 B.Y.B.I.L. 197 (1993).

[50] Hubert H. Humphrey, *The United States, the World Court and the Connally Amendment*, 11 Va. J. Int'l. L. 310, 311 (1971).

[51] *See, e.g.*, Herbert W. Briggs, *Nicaragua v. United States: Jurisdiction and Admissibility*, 79 A.J.I.L. 373 (1985); Anthony A. D'Amato, *Comment: Modifying US Acceptance of the*

A similar story occurred with respect to United States acceptance of the Court's jurisdiction under the Optional Protocol to the Vienna Convention on Consular Relations concerning the Compulsory Settlement of Disputes. In 1969, the United States ratified the Optional Protocol, which provides in article I that "disputes arising out of the interpretation or application of the Convention shall lie within the compulsory jurisdiction of the International Court of Justice."[52] Following losses in a series of ICJ cases concerning the treatment of foreign citizens arrested by U.S. law-enforcement officials,[53] the United States withdrew from the Optional Protocol.[54]

7. Do you agree with the position taken by the United States government toward submitting to the compulsory jurisdiction of the ICJ, whether under the optional clause or pursuant to separate treaty agreements? How might it affect the work of the World Court in the future? Imagine yourself as a lawyer in the Office of the Legal Adviser of the US Department of State. Would you, in this capacity, recommend that the United States re-accept the Court's compulsory jurisdiction or would you argue against it? How would you feel about US participation in treaties that require parties to agree to submit to the Court's jurisdiction? Does it depend on the nature of the treaty? Would you support acceptance of the Court's jurisdiction to resolve disputes over the treatment of foreign investment? Disputes over the environment? Disputes over issues relating to national security and the use of military force?[55]

8. The ICJ generally discharges its duties as a full court, but it does have the power to form permanent or temporary "chambers" of fewer than all the judges to resolve particular cases. A chambers can hear a case only with the consent of the parties. A "Chamber for Environmental Matters" was formed

---

Compulsory Jurisdiction of the World Court, 79 AJIL. 385 (1985); Monroe Leigh, *Comment: Military and Paramilitary Activities In and Against Nicaragua v. United States of America*, 79 AJIL 442 (1985); John Norton Moore, *The Case: Political Questions Before the International Court of Justice*, 27 Va. J. Int'l L. 459 (1987); W. Michael Reisman, *Has the International Court Exceeded Its Jurisdiction?*, 80 AJIL 128 (1986). *See also* US Decision to Withdraw from the International Court of Justice: Hearing Before the Subcomm. on Human Rights and International Organizations of the House Comm. on Foreign Aff., 99th Cong., 1st Sess. (1985) (especially statements by Abraham D. Sofaer, Legal Adviser, Department of State; Professor Richard N. Gardner, Columbia University School of Law; and Professor Burns H. Weston, Independent Commission on Respect for International Law and The University of Iowa College of Law).

[52] Optional Protocol to the Vienna Convention on Consular Relations concerning the Compulsory Settlement of Disputes, art. I, April 24, 1963, 596 U.N.T.S. 487.

[53] Vienna Convention on Consular Relations (Para. v. U.S.), Order of 9 April 1998, 1998 I.C.J. 248 (provisional measures); LaGrand Case (Ger. V. U.S.), 2001 ICJ 466 (June 27); Avena and Other Mexican Nationals (Mex. V. U.S.), 2004 I.C.J. 12 (Mar. 31).

[54] *See* Letter from U.S. Secretary of State Condoleezza Rice to U.N. Secretary General Kofi Annan (March 7, 2005), *reprinted* in Digest of United States Practice in International Law 2005 at 30–31 (2006).

[55] *See* The United States and the Compulsory Jurisdiction of the International Court of Justice (A. Arend ed., 1986); Anthony A. D'Amato, *Modifying US Acceptance of the Compulsory Jurisdiction of the World Court*, 79 AJIL 385 (1985); Louis B. Sohn, *Suggestions for the Limited Acceptance of Compulsory Jurisdiction of the International Court of Justice by the United States*, 18 Ga. J. Int'l & Comp. L. 1 (1988); The United States and the Compulsory Jurisdiction of the International Court of Justice (A. Arend ed., 1986); Shigeru Oda, *The Compulsory Jurisdiction of the International Court of Justice: A Myth—A Statistical Analysis of Contentious Cases*, 49 ICLQ 251 (2000).

by the Court in 1993, but no state ever requested that a case be heard by it, and the Chamber was discontinued in 2006. By contrast, an *ad hoc* chamber was created in 1982 in the case concerning the *Delimitation of the Maritime Boundary in the Gulf of Maine Area* between Canada and the United States, and five more *ad hoc* chambers have been created since then. What would be the advantages of a chambers procedure? What would be the disadvantages?

9. Although international organizations cannot be parties to disputes before the ICJ, the Court does have legal competence, under Article 65 of its Statute, to render Advisory Opinions at the request of an international institution that is authorized to make such requests. Authorized institutions include the UN General Assembly. Interested states may make submissions to the Court. Requests for Advisory Opinions are often controversial, however, either because the question posed is highly contested (*e.g.*, Legality of the Threat or Use of Nuclear Weapons, 1996 ICJ 225) or because the request is perceived as an indirect way of obtaining a ruling on what is properly a contentious case that cannot be litigated because the relevant parties have not accepted the jurisdiction of the ICJ (*e.g.*, Legal Consequences of the Construction of a Wall in the Occupied Palestinian Territory 2004 ICJ No. 131). For discussion, see Kenneth Keith, *The Advisory Jurisdiction of the International Court of Justice: Some Comparative Reflections* 17 Austl. Y.B.I.L. 39 (1996).

10. The International Court of Justice is not the only permanently constituted international tribunal. Except for the ICJ, however, all have limited subject-matter jurisdiction: the International Tribunal for the Law of the Sea, the International Criminal Court, the Court of Justice of the European Communities, the Benelux Court of Justice, the European Court of Human Rights, the Inter-American Court of Human Rights, and an emerging African Court of Human Rights. Would the world benefit from an array of courts of general jurisdiction? How might this be accomplished?

As noted earlier, the Court's decisions are binding only on the parties to a dispute. There is no doctrine of *stare decisis* in international law. Moreover, as you'll see in the next section of this chapter, judicial decisions are not themselves "law" in the international system, although they provide a "subsidiary means for the determination of rules of law."[56]

Given this limited formal role for judicial decisions as a source of international law, what would be their utility in the development of international law? Do you think that courts would have a tendency to follow their prior decisions, even though they have no obligation to do so? Do you think that states would be inclined to rely on judicial pronouncements about the meaning of treaties or the content of customary law, even absent any obligation to do so? For a discussion of the power of judicial precedent, even in the absence of any formal obligation to adhere to it, *see generally* Anne Scully-Hill & Hans Mahncke, *The Emergence of the Doctrine of Stare Decisis in the*

[56] Statute of the International Court of Justice, art. 38(1)(d).

World Trade Organization Dispute Settlement System, 36 Legal Issues of Econ. Integ. 133 (2009).

11. What are the consequences of not having effective means for judicial resolution of disputes? Professor Lung-chu Chen writes that he has "reluctantly concluded that absent effective machinery for collective law enforcement under the present world conditions, self-help, even involving military force, remains permissible as a measure of last resort, subject to the rigorous requirements of necessity and proportionality." Lung-chu Chen, An Introduction to Contemporary International Law 365 (2nd ed. 2000). Do you agree/disagree with this conclusion? What theory of world order lies behind this analysis? What problems does it raise? *See* Mary-Ellen O'Connell, *Controlling Countermeasures, in* International Responsibility Today: Essays in Memory of Oscar Schachter 49 (M. Ragazzi ed., 2005).

12. A different form of adjudication may be found in various "peoples' tribunals" organized by civil society to respond to the limited formal mechanisms in international law. The first such tribunal was initiated by Bertrand Russell in 1967 to hear evidence on alleged United States aggression and war crimes in Vietnam. The French existentialist philosopher, Jean-Paul Sartre, was its chair. More recently peoples' tribunals have been formed to deal with issues such as environmental damage, corporate responsibility for crimes against humanity, Japanese treatment of Korean "comfort women" during World War II and the legality of the invasion of Iraq in 2003.[57] What are the advantages and limitations of these developments?[58]

13. Both the IMF and the World Bank use their control over access to financial resources to induce recipients to comply with policies preferred by those organizations. The World Bank requires its clients to comply with certain policies concerning the environmental and social impact of Bank-funded projects. The IMF requires compliance by funded states with certain economic and trade policies that the IMF believes will promote long-term economic growth in the recipient state. The IMF is frequently accused of infringing the sovereignty of states that borrow from it. The World Bank, on the other hand, is more frequently praised for the conditions it imposes on its lending. Why the difference?

C. THE SOURCES OF INTERNATIONAL LAW

Already it will be clear to students that international law comprises a different type of jurisprudence from domestic common law or statute law. Some introduction to the sources of international law and how they differ from those of domestic law would be useful now.

[57] For discussion of some of these tribunals and their public impact *see* Yves Beigbeder, Judging War Criminals: The Politics of International Justice 137–140 (1999); Christine Chinkin, *Women's International Tribunal on Japanese Military Sexual Slavery,* 95 A.J.I.L. 335 (2001).

[58] For pertinent related discussion focusing on the peoples' tribunal known as the International Court of Environmental Arbitration and Conciliation, *see* Ole W. Pedersen, *An International Environmental Court and International Legalism,* 24 J. Envtl. L. 547 (2012).

Because the nature of international law is different from domestic law, it should come as no surprise to students of international law that its sources are different too. The most authoritative statement of the sources of international law is to be found in Article 38 of the Statute of the International Court of Justice 1945 **(Basic Document 1.2)**, which states that the Court is to apply international law to the disputes submitted to it, and goes on to define the sources of those rules. These are:

- international treaties or conventions, whether general or particular, establishing rules expressly recognized by the contesting states;
- international custom, as evidence of a general practice accepted as law;
- general principles of law recognized by civilized nations; and
- judicial decisions and the teachings of the most highly qualified experts of the various nations, as subsidiary means for the determination of rules of law.

To these should be added (though they are not mentioned in the ICJ Statute):

- declarations, statements, and other material known as 'soft' international law.[59]

International Treaties

Treaties are the most important source of international law. They are the main instruments by which international norms and rules are developed and international matters are regulated. There are many different types of treaty. Some treaties establish undertakings that are contractual in nature; others make new law and establish the norms of complete legal regimes.[60] Multilateral treaties have many nations as parties and, indeed, the most important treaties in the environmental arena are multilateral treaties to which nearly every nation in the world has adhered.[61] But the vast majority of treaties currently in force in the world are bilateral agreements, some of which can be very important to environmental lawyers.[62]

The negotiation of treaties can be a difficult business. Multilateral conventions are usually negotiated in complicated international

---

[59] *See*, for example, Malcolm N. Shaw, International Law 107–112 (6th ed. 2008).

[60] Andrew Clapham Brierly, The Law of Nations 302 (7th ed. 2012).

[61] *See, e.g.*, United Nations Framework Agreement on Climate Change **(Basic Document 2.4)**, Montreal Protocol on Substances that Deplete the Ozone Layer **(Basic Document 2.8)**, United Nations Convention on the Law of the Sea **(Basic Document 3.4)**.

[62] *See, e.g.*, Treaty between the United States of America and Mexico on the Utilization of Waters of the Colorado and Tijuana Rivers and of the Rio Grande, Feb. 3, 1944, T.S. No. 994.

conferences, in which, often, repeated meetings are held over a number of years, with steering committees and drafting committees, plenary sessions, and rapporteurs. At such meetings, informal negotiations are often as important as the formal sessions in hammering out compromises and language. Particularly when there are many nations involved, there is often a tendency to use language in the treaty that covers issues in an ambiguous manner in order to try and get the broadest agreement possible. As noted below, no treaty will bind a state without its consent. Thus, in order to ensure as wide an acceptance as possible, the negotiating parties aim to develop a text that can be adopted by consensus. This can add an element of searching for "the lowest common denominator" to treaty negotiations. While this may seem an unfortunate lowering of ambition, there is little point in negotiating a text that only a few states will be able to ratify and be bound by. Especially in the environmental arena, where problems often cannot be solved without near universal participation, widespread agreement with negotiated texts is important.

In many countries, including the United States, treaties cannot become binding until they receive the approval of a legislative body. In the cases of the United States, treaties must be made "with the advice and consent" of the Senate. The need to gain such approval is constantly on the minds of negotiators and is a further factor leading to the negotiation of ambiguous or weak treaty language.[63]

The creation and development of treaty law in a particular arena can take years. The treaty text must first be negotiated and adopted. It is then usually necessary to secure ratification of the treaty which, in countries where legislative approval is necessary, may itself require lengthy discussion and negotiation. The treaty will only enter into force when sufficient ratifications have been secured. This process can sometimes be so slow and time-consuming that events overtake the convention. Such was the fate of the Convention on the Regulation of Antarctic Mineral Resource Activities.[64] Negotiations on the convention began in about 1982 and it was agreed in 1988. But, in the end, efforts were outstripped by public opinion and the Convention went unratified because of the widespread conviction that its provisions did not sufficiently protect the Antarctic environment. A different agreement was subsequently negotiated.[65]

---

[63] U.S. practice allows the President to negotiate and ratify certain kinds of international agreements without Senate approval. *See* American Law Institute, Restatement of the Law Third: The Foreign Relations Law of the United States § 303 (1987).

[64] Convention on the Regulation of Antarctic Mineral Resource Activities, Jun. 2, 1988 (not in force).

[65] Protocol on Environmental Protection to the Antarctic Treaty, Oct. 4, 1991, [1998] A.T.S. 6.

A brief overview of the law of treaties

A "treaty," as defined in the Vienna Convention on the Law of Treaties (VCLT) **(Basic Document 1.14)**, is "an international agreement concluded between States in written form and governed by international law."[66] Treaties go under a variety of names, including treaty, convention, protocol, agreement, arrangement, statute, exchange of notes, final act. Regardless of the name of the agreement, it will be subject to certain fundamental rules concerning its conclusion, its effectiveness, its interpretation, and its termination. The law on these matters is well stated in the VCLT, many of the provisions of which are restatements of pre-existing customary international law or have been so widely followed in practice as to now be considered part of customary international law. Students are urged to review the text of the VCLT at this time and study it with some care. Special attention should be paid to Articles 11, 24, 26–27, 31–32, and 34–36.

There are several rules of treaty law that are of particular importance to the student of international environmental law. First, *no state is legally bound by the provisions of an international agreement unless it consents to be bound by that agreement and the agreement enters into legal force.*[67] In the case of multilateral treaties, a state's consent is generally given by its formal "ratification" or "acceptance" of the treaty. The head of state (or another authorized official) will submit a document indicating its acceptance of the obligations of the treaty to the government or international organization that is identified in the treaty as the depositary. In treaty law parlance, the ratifying or accepting state will *deposit* its *instrument of ratification or acceptance*, thus confirming that it intends to be bound by the agreement. Whether a ratifying state will be bound by the treaty depends on whether the treaty "enters into force." Most multilateral treaties provide that they will not "enter into force" (i.e. become legally binding) until a certain number of states have ratified the treaty. Environmental treaties often require, in addition, that the ratifying states be states that, collectively, are responsible for a majority of the activity (e.g., emissions of greenhouse gases) that the treaty seeks to control.

A second fundamental rule is the rule of *pacta sunt servanda:* "every treaty in force is binding upon the parties to it and must be performed by

---

66 Vienna Convention on the Law of Treaties, art. 2, May 23, 1969, 1155 U.N.T.S. 331 [hereinafter VCLT]. The Vienna Convention does not address the binding effect of agreements between states and international organization or among international organizations, although international practice clearly allows for the existence and legal effectiveness of such agreements. *See* Ian Brownlie, Principles of Public International Law 648 (6th ed. 2003). The Vienna Convention also does not cover agreements "not in written form," although it is careful to specify that the omission "shall not affect the legal force of such agreements." Vienna Convention, art. 3.

67 VCLT, arts. 24 & 34. It is possible for treaty rules to be (or become) rules of customary international law, in which case they could bind states that are not party to the treaty. *See* North Sea Continental Shelf Cases (F.R.G. v. Den.) (F.R.G. v. Neth.), 1969 I.C.J. 3 at paras. 70–81. In that case, however, it is the customary law that binds non-party states, not the treaty itself.

them in good faith."[68] To put the point another way, a treaty has binding force and ought to be observed, whether or not there are effective enforcement mechanisms. Moreover, the fact that a party's internal law is inconsistent with the treaty is no excuse for a party's "failure to perform a treaty."[69] By consenting to a treaty, states agree to take the steps required to comply with the treaty, including modifying their internal law when that is necessary.

A third set of fundamental rules has to do with the interpretation of treaties. The starting point for the interpretation of a treaty is the text of that treaty. That text should be interpreted "in accordance with the ordinary meaning to be given to the terms of the treaty in their context and in the light of its object and purpose."[70] For that purpose, the context of a treaty includes its preamble, its annexes, and any agreements or instruments made or accepted by all parties in connection with the conclusion of the treaty. Note, however, that the documented "preparatory work" or *travaux preparatoire* leading up to the treaty (what one might call the "legislative history" of the agreement) is *not to be considered in interpreting the agreement* except under circumstances where the ordinary principles of interpretation lead to interpretations that are "ambiguous," "obscure," "manifestly absurd," or "unreasonable."[71] On the other hand, it is perfectly appropriate to interpret the treaty in light of subsequent agreements or practices that indicate the parties' understanding as to its meaning and in light of other rules of international law applicable to relations between the parties.[72]

The Vienna Convention and customary international law both include rules for the termination of treaties. Many of these rules resemble rules that one finds in domestic contract law. Hence, a party may revoke its consent to a treaty under certain narrowly defined circumstances, including when its consent was the product of mistake of fact,[73] fraud,[74] coercion or corruption of the state's representative,[75] or forcible coercion of the state itself.[76] A treaty may be terminated by a party when another party commits a material breach of the agreement,[77] when there is a "supervening impossibility of performance,"[78] or when an unforeseen "fundamental change of circumstances" has occurred that would radically

[68] VCLT, art. 26.

[69] VCLT, art. 27.

[70] VCLT, art. 31(1).

[71] VCLT, art. 32.

[72] VCLT, art. 31(3).

[73] VCLT, art. 48.

[74] VCLT, art. 49.

[75] VCLT, art. 50–51.

[76] VCLT, art. 52.

[77] VCLT, art. 60.

[78] VCLT, art. 61.

transform the extent of the state's performance obligations under the treaty.[79] States may also withdraw from treaties by agreement with the other parties, when the treaty expressly allows withdrawal, or when a right to withdrawal may be implied from the conduct of the parties or the nature of the treaty.[80]

Customary International Law

Customary international law is entirely different from treaty law. As treaties have proliferated, customary international law is perhaps not as important as it once was. However, in many ways, it remains the bedrock of the system. Treaty regimes are not exhaustive and there continue to be areas that are not regulated by treaties, making customary international law essential for ensuring there are no gaps.

It is, however, difficult to ascertain the precise content of customary international law. Not all custom in the international arena amounts to customary international law. According to the International Law Commission, establishing the existence of a rule of customary international law "requires establishing the existence of two constituent elements: a general practice, and acceptance of that practice as law (*opinio juris*)."[81] Other commentators have expressed the test slightly differently, identifying the following required elements of customary law:[82]

1. the same practice by a number of states in regard to a particular situation;
2. the continuation of the practice over time;
3. a belief that the practice is required by the prevailing international law (*opinio juris*); and
4. general acquiescence in the practice by other states.

Whether the test is broken down into two elements, four elements, or some other number, there is broad agreement among states and commentators that customary international law exists when a) there is widespread adherence by states to a particular practice and b) there is a general recognition among states that the relevant practice is obligatory as a matter of law.

The existence of customary law allows international law to evolve over time, to respond to new challenges. It also allows states to use the various

[79] VCLT, art. 62.

[80] VCLT, arts. 54–59.

[81] International Law Commission, Draft Conclusions on Identification of Customary International Law, with commentaries, Report of the International Law Commission on the Work of its Seventieth Session, U.N. Doc. A/73/10 at 124 (introduction to commentaries on Part Two of the Draft Conclusions).

[82] James Crawford *Brownlie's Principles of Public International Law* 23 (8th ed. 2012).

tools and forums of international diplomacy to articulate principles and rules that they hope will be widely enough followed in practice to enter the corpus of international law. Two of the most difficult issues in determining whether a customary international rule exist are a) determining whether a widely followed state practice is supported by *opinio juris*—a belief that the practice is obligatory as a matter of law, and b) determining whether apparent statements of legal rules (e.g., expressions of *opinio juris*) are actually backed up by sufficient state practice to be considered part of customary international law. In practical terms, this means that lawyerly skills are important to the identification of rules of customary international law—those who argue for the existence of a rule of customary international law must be able to persuasively marshall evidence of state practice and *opinio juris*, and those who oppose recognition of a rule must be able to explain why those elements are not satisfied.

Students are encouraged at this point to read with care the International Law Commissions Draft Conclusions on Identification of Customary International Law **(Basic Document 1.19)**. They provide an excellent introduction to how international lawyers go about the task of ascertaining the existence and content of rules of customary international law. In 2018, the U.N. General Assembly took note of the Draft Conclusions and encouraged their use as a guide to the identification of customary international law.[83]

There are often important connections between customary international law and treaties. In some cases, treaties are intended to codify customary international law, synthesizing existing customary international law rules into treaty obligations. This was the case with many of the provisions of United Nations Convention on the Law of the Sea. It was also true of portions of the Vienna Convention on the Law of Treaties. In some ways, this eases the job of lawyers. If a treaty provision is widely viewed as codifying customary international law, there may be no need to engage in elaborate proofs that the rule is, in fact, part of customary international law. On the other hand, determining which treaty rules are accepted as reflecting pre-existing custom can be challenging.

Even when the rules in a treaty are not considered part of customary international law at the time the treaty is adopted, they can evolve into customary international law if they are widely followed and come to be regarded as binding even on non-party states, i.e., if the elements of practice and *opinio juris* are present.[84] Again, the law of the sea provides an example. The law of the sea is one of the oldest branches of international law, and it was entirely customary for centuries. Today, however, it has been heavily modified and virtually taken over by treaty law in the form of

[83] G.A. Res. 73/203, & 4 (Dec. 20, 2018).

[84] *See* North Sea Continental Shelf Cases (F.R.G. v. Den.)(F.R.G. v. Neth.), 1969 I.C.J. 3 at paras. 70–81.

the United Nations Convention on the Law of the Sea **(Basic Document 3.4)**, which was signed in 1982 and which entered into force in 1994. Adherence to that treaty and respect for its rules is so widespread that many of its important innovations (including the right of states to exercise control of the natural resources in a 200-mile exclusive economic zone adjacent to their coasts) are now widely accepted to be part of customary international law and applicable even to states (such as the United States) which have refused to ratify the Convention.

A third important connection between treaties and customary international law is that treaties are often the means by which states fulfill their customary international law obligations. For example, states have long had a customary law duty to cooperate in the exploitation of ocean fisheries in order to protect against over-harvesting of target species. That obligation is most frequently carried out through the negotiation of bilateral or multilateral agreements governing the use of the fishery.[85] Where the existence of a customary international rule is debated, agreements aimed at fulfilling the obligations of the rule may be taken as evidence of state practice, *opinio juris,* or both.

Recognized General Principles of Law

The scope of "general principles of law recognized by civilized nations" as set out in Article 38 of the Statute of the ICJ is unclear, and there is considerable debate and controversy about what is meant by this source of international law. For example, some jurists argue that it affirms that pre-existing principles and norms (Natural Law) underlie international law and can be used to decide cases before the Court even when treaty norms and customary law are silent on a critical issue. Others believe that the reference to "general principles" adds little to other sources of international law and only allows the application of alternative norms that are clearly based on the consent of states, although that consent may be expressed in some fashion other than through adherence to a treaty or development of a customary law rule. Some newer states are suspicious that the phrase "recognized by *civilized* nations" is designed to discriminate against them.

Probably the most common conception of "general principles of law" is that they are those broad legal principles (as opposed to detailed rules) that are common to well-developed domestic legal systems in the world.[86] Given the variety of legal systems in the world, the search for such principles may not be an easy one. However, there are certain general legal principles that run through many legal systems, and commonalities prevail within types of legal orders, such as the common law and civil law systems. We have already mentioned the principle of *pacta sunt servanda* (agreements should

---

85 *See* Chapter 6, *supra.*

86 James Crawford *Brownlie's Principles of Public International Law* 34–37 (8th ed. 2012).

be honored in good faith), which is a recognized general principle of law. Others include the principle of good faith and the principle of *res judicata.*

One fruitful place to look for general principles that might be appropriate for application on the international plane is in the decision of disputes in federal systems between sub-federal entities (e.g., U.S. states or Canadian provinces) and between sub-federal entities and the federal government. Such decisions are useful material for consideration under this head because they may rest on broadly stated principles designed for application in disputes between co-equal sovereigns.[87]

Judicial Decisions and Teachings

Little needs to be said here about this source of international law: judicial decisions and the teachings of the most highly qualified publicists or experts. These are subsidiary means for determining the rules of international law. But it should be said that there is a vast quantity of published writing on international law in many languages and it is of greater influence in the international system than is scholarly commentary in our own domestic common law legal systems, where decided cases have much greater authority.

As noted previously, judicial decisions have no binding force in the international legal system except between the parties and in respect of that particular case.[88] In other words, the system of precedent that is so important in a common law domestic legal system has no place in the theory of international law. However, in practice, decisions are of considerable value to later cases in the international system.[89] Lawyers advising in international environmental law need to consult the case law diligently.

"Soft" International Law

There is an emerging species of international law known as "soft" law.[90] "Hard" law in the international arena comes mainly from custom or treaties. Custom takes time and, often, a lot of state practice before it

---

[87] *See, e.g.*, the decision of the panel in the Trail Smelter Arbitration, excerpted in Chapter Three, *supra.*

[88] Regarding decisions of the ICJ, *see* Article 59 of the Statute of the International Court of Justice.

[89] *See* Malcolm N. Shaw *International Law* 109–113 (6th ed. 2008). At 110, Shaw states "the Court has striven to follow its previous judgments and insert a measure of certainty within the process so that while the doctrine of precedent as it is known in the common law, whereby rulings of certain courts must be followed by other courts, does not exist in international law, one still finds that states in disputes and textbook writers quote judgments of the Permanent Court and the International Court of Justice as authoritative decisions." Similarly, judges at other international courts and tribunals have shown themselves reluctant, in most instances, to reach decisions conflicting with those made earlier and have striven for consistency in the law.

[90] *See* Andrew Clapham Brierly *The Law of Nations* 74–77 (7th ed. 2012).

hardens into a legally enforceable rule. Treaties take a long time to negotiate and nations tend to shy away from the specificity they often involve. A much more politically attractive approach is the soft law option.

"Soft law" comprises non-binding high-level instruments and documents, such as declarations, recommendations, guidelines, codes of practice or statements of principle that are carefully drafted and seem to rely upon the language of obligation. They usually emanate from inter-state meetings, such as high-level international conferences or meetings of international bodies, such as the UN General Assembly. What is important about these instruments is not so much the form in which they appear as the manner in which their content is expressed. Frequently what is expressed is a series of policy statements and declarations of values and intentions. The Declaration of the United Nations Conference on the Human Environment 1972 ("Stockholm Declaration") **(Basic Document 1.21)** and the Rio Declaration on Environment and Development 1992 ("Rio Declaration") **(Basic Document 1.30)** are good examples.

We believe that this phenomenon is increasingly used because it is so politically convenient. Resort to soft law leaves large amounts of discretion to states. The language is usually aspirational rather than prescriptive, meaning both that states are not required to behave in a certain manner (although they are encouraged to do so) and that third-party adjudication would be impossible even if it were provided for. This makes it easier for states to sign up.

The use of soft law instruments has substantial advantages. All politicians know the value of ambiguity, and soft law is frequently drafted with studied ambiguity. While such an approach may have deceptive elements and may create wrong impressions, it can also serve to secure agreement where it might not otherwise be achieved. Importantly, soft law instruments can change the international political thinking on and attitudes towards an issue, particularly when they are controversial or politically difficult. Soft law instruments alter the circumstances in which an issue is considered; they cause opinion to coalesce. These changes can be a very important catalyst in later securing an agreement with a harder edge. Soft law solutions can, therefore, be useful steps on a longer journey.

Soft law is where international law and international politics combine to build new norms. The Helsinki Declaration on the Protection of the Ozone Layer 1989 is such an instrument.[91] Its purpose was to ensure that the London meeting in 1990 could agree on hard amendments to the Montreal Protocol; the consensus expressed at Helsinki was undoubtedly helpful in that respect.

---

[91] Helsinki Declaration on the Protection of the Ozone Layer, May 2, 1989, 28 I.L.M. 335.

The ability to reach agreement through soft law instruments also promotes very valuable feelings of international comity and cooperation. Since political leaders and countries must continue dealing with one another, it is better that those dealings be based on agreement than on disagreement—and soft law solutions produce agreement.

Finally, statements of principles or rules that first appear in soft-law instruments may, over time, come to be regarded as reflecting principles or rules of customary international law. However, to establish that such a process has, in fact, occurred, one must be prepared to establish the existence of the two elements of customary international law: i) a general state practice ii) engaged in with the belief that it is legally obligatory. The articulation of a norm in General Assembly resolution or in a conference declaration may be of importance, but it does not in and of itself create international law.

D. THE BERING SEA FUR SEALS ARBITRATION

Putting together both the material on dispute settlement and the material on the sources of international law, we now want to show them at work in an example that is one of the earliest examples of an environmental issue being subjected to international arbitration. The plight of seals in the Bering Sea in the 1890s has some analogies to the fate of whales that is the subject of the rest of the chapter. Man has always captured animals and used them. The legal regulation of that practice often raises issues of international law where the wildlife is migratory and beyond the exclusive territorial control of one nation.

BERING SEA FUR SEALS ARBITRATION (GB V US) (1893)

1 Moore's Int'l Arb. Awards 755

[*Eds.*—After acquiring the Alaska territory by purchase from Russia in 1867, the United States adopted legislation aimed at protecting populations of fur-bearing animals, including fur-seals, from over-exploitation. Acting pursuant to this legislation, the U.S. seized several British vessels that were engaged in the hunting and killing of seals on the high seas, at least 60 miles from the nearest U.S.-owned land. The seals being hunted by the British vessels were known to make their home on the Pribilof Islands, within U.S. territory, and evidence suggested that pelagic sealing by the British and others was decimating the seal herd.

Britain protested the seizures and, after a long period of negotiation, the two countries agreed to submit the dispute to arbitration.

Five specific questions were submitted for arbitration. The following excerpts concern the fifth and final question whether the United States had "any right, and, if so, what right, of protection or property in the fur-seals frequenting the islands of the Unites States in the Behring Sea when such seals are found outside the ordinary 3-mile limit?"]

Excerpts from the Written Argument of the United States[92]

The controversy to be determined arises between two different nations, and it has been submitted to the judgment of a tribunal composed, in part, of the citizens of several other nations. It is immediately obvious that it must be adjudged upon principles and rules which both nations and all the Arbitrators alike acknowledge; that is to say, those which are dictated by that *general standard of justice* upon which civilized nations are agreed; and this is *international law*. Just as, in municipal societies, municipal law, aside from legislative enactments, is to be found in the general standard of justice which is acknowledged by the members of each particular state, so, in the large society of nations, international law is to be found in the general standard of justice acknowledged by the members of that society.

* * *

Some writers have been inclined to question the propriety of designating as law that body of principles and rules which it is asserted are binding upon nations, for the reason that there is no common superior power which may be appealed to for their enforcement. But this is a superficial view. . . . The public opinion the civilized world is a power to which all nations are forced to submit. No nation can afford to take up arms in defence of an assertion which is pronounced by that opinion to be erroneous. . . .

* * *

[A]lthough the actual practice and usages of nations are the best evidence of what is agreed upon as the law of nations, it is not the only evidence. These prove what nations have *in fact* agreed to as binding law. But, in the absence of evidence to the contrary, nations are to be *presumed* to agree upon what natural and universal justice dictates. It is upon the basis of this presumption that municipal law is from time to time developed and enlarged by the decisions of judicial tribunals and jurists which make up the unwritten municipal jurisprudence. Sovereign states are presumed to have sanctioned as law the general principles of justice, and this constitutes the authority of municipal tribunals to declare the law in cases where legislation is silent. . . . So also in international law, if a case arises for which the practice and usages of nations have furnished no rule, an international tribunal like the present is not to infer that no rule exists. The consent of nations is to be presumed in favor of the dictates of natural justice, and that source never fails to supply a rule. . . .

---

92 IX Fur Seal Arbitration 2–8 (Government Printing Office, Washington, 1895).

* * *

The [United States position] is that the United States have, by reason of the nature and habits of the seals and their ownership of the breeding grounds to which the herds resort . . . a property interest in those herds as well while they are in the high seas as upon the land.

* * *

The position taken on the part of Great Britain is [that the seals] do not belong to any nations or to any men; that they are *res communes*, or, *res nullius*; in other words, that they are *not the subject* of property, and are consequently open to pursuit and capture on the high seas by the citizens of any nation. This position is based upon the assertion that they belong to the class of wild animals, animals *feræ naturæ*, and that these are not the subject of ownership. . . .

* * *

Inasmuch as the present controversy upon this point is one between nations, . . . [t]he rule of decision must be found in international law. . . . But the question whether a particular thing is the subject of property, as between nations, is substantially the same as the question whether the same thing is property between individuals in a particular nation. Now, it so happens that . . . the municipal jurisprudence of all nations, proceeding upon the law of nature, is everywhere in substantial accord upon the question what things are the subject of property. That jurisprudence, therefore, so far as it is consentaneous, may be invoked in this controversy, as directly evidencing the law of nature, and, therefore, of nations.

* * *

[T]he *essential facts* which, according to [the] doctrines [of municipal law], render animals commonly designated as wild, the subjects of property not only while in the actual custody of their masters but also when temporarily absent therefrom, are that the *care and industry of man* acting upon a *natural disposition* of the animals to *return* to a place of wonted resort, secures their *voluntary* and *habitual return to his custody* and *power*, so as to enable him to *deal with them in a similar manner*, and to obtain from them *similar benefits*, as in the case of *domestic* animals. They are thus for all the purposes of *property* assimilated to domestic animals. It is the *nature and habits* of the animal, which enable man, by the practice of *art, care, and industry*, to bring about these *useful results* that constitute the foundation upon which the law makes its award of property, and extends to this product of human industry the protection of ownership. This species of property is well described as property *per industriam*.

The Alaskan fur-seals are a typical instance for the application of this doctrine. They are by the imperious and unchangeable instincts of their nature impelled to return from their wanderings to the *same place*; they are defenseless against man, and in returning to the same place voluntarily subject themselves to his power, and enable him to treat them in the same way and to obtain from them the same benefits as maybe had in the case of domestic animals. They thus become the subjects of ordinary husbandry as much as sheep or any other cattle. All that is needed to secure this return, is the exercise of care and industry on the part of the human owner of the place of resort. He must *abstain* from killing or repelling them when they seek to return to it, and must invite and cherish such return. He must defend them against all enemies by land or sea. And in making his selections for slaughter, he must disturb them as little as possible and take *males* only. All these conditions are perfectly supplied by the United States, and their title is thus fully substantiated.

* * *

[*Eds.*—The United States then proceeded to argue that the fundamental principles supporting the institution of private property justified a conclusion of U.S. ownership in this situation. In particular, the U.S. argued that the institution of private property served to preserve social "order and peace" by satisfying the "desire of human nature for exclusive ownership" and that property ownership encouraged the "progress and advancement" of society by encouraging individual effort through the reward of ownership of what is produced. But, said the U.S., these principles make clear that ownership is only for social purposes and property is ultimately held in trust for all—that fact—that property is an institution created by the law of nature to serve social purposes—was especially salient in supporting its claim to the ownership of the seals.]

* * *

But what is the extent of the dominion which is thus given by the law of nature to the owner of property? This question has much importance in the present discussion and deserves deliberate consideration.

* * *

First. No possessor of property, whether an individual man, or a nation, has an absolute title to it. His title is coupled with a trust for the benefit of mankind.

Second. The title is further limited. The things themselves are not given to him, but only the *usufruct* or *increase*. He is but the custodian of the stock, or principal thing, holding it in trust for the present and future generations of man.

The first of these propositions is stated in the language employed by one of the highest authorities on the law of nature and nations. Says Puffendorf, "God gave the world, not to this, nor to that man, but to the human race in general." The bounties of nature are gifts not so much to those whose situation enables them to gather them but to these who need them for *use*. And Locke, "God gave the world to men in common." If it be asked how this gift in common can be reconciled with the exclusive possession which the institution of property gives to particular nations and particular men, the answer is by the instrumentality of commerce which springs into existence with the beginnings of civilization as a part of the order of nature. . . . Every bounty of nature, however, it may be gathered by this, or that man, will eventually find its way, through the instrumentality of commerce, to those who want it for its inherent qualities. . . . But for commerce, and the exchanges effected by it, the greatest part of the wealth of the world would be wasted, or unimproved. . . .

[I]t follows that, by the law of nature, every nation, so far as it possesses the fruits of the earth in a measure more than sufficient to satisfy its own needs, is, in the truest sense, a *trustee* of the surplus for the benefit of those in other parts of the world who need them, and are willing to give in exchange for them the products of their own labor; and the truth of this conclusion and of the views from which it is drawn will be found fully confirmed by a glance at the approved usages of nations. . . . [C]ommerce is obligatory upon all nations, . . . no nation is permitted to secluded itself from the rest of mankind and interdict all commerce with foreign nations. Temporary prohibitions of commerce for special reasons of necessity are, indeed, allowed; but they must not be made permanent.

. . . The instances in history are rare in which nations have exhibited unwillingness to engage in commercial intercourse; but they . . . have sometimes actually occurred. Such a refusal is generally believed to have been the real, though it was not avowed, cause of the war waged by Great Britain against China in 1840.

For the purposes of further illustration, . . . [l]et it be supposed that some particular region from which alone a commodity deemed necessary by man everywhere, such as Peruvian bark, could be procured, was within the exclusive dominion of a particular power and that it should absolutely prohibit the exportation of the commodity; could there be any well-founded doubt that other nations would be justified, under the law of nature, in compelling that nation by arms to permit free commerce in such a commodity?

And this trust, of which we are speaking, is not limited to that surplus of a nation's production which is not needed for its own wants, but extends to its means and capabilities for production. No nation has, by the law of nature, a right to destroy its sources and means of production or leave them unimproved. None has the right to convert any portion of the earth into a waste or desolation, or to permit any part which may be made fruitful to remain a waste. To destroy the source from which any human blessing flows is not merely an error, it is a *crime*. And the wrong is not limited by the boundaries of nations, but is inflicted upon those to whom the blessing would be useful wherever they may dwell. And those to whom the wrong is done have the right to redress it.

Let the case of the article of India rubber be . . . taken for an illustration, and let it be supposed that the nation which held the fields from which the world obtained its chief supply should destroy its plantations and refuse to continue the cultivation, can it be doubted that other nations would, by the law of nature, be justified in taking possession by force of the territory of the recent Power and establishing over it a governmental authority which would assure a continuance of the cultivation? And what would this be but a removal of the unfaithful trustee, and the appointment of one who would perform the trust?

It is, indeed, upon this ground, and this ground alone, that the conquest by civilized nations of countries occupied by savages has been, or can be, defended. The great nations of Europe took possession by force and divided among themselves the great continents of North and South America. Great Britain has incorporated into her extensive empire vast territories in India, and Australia by force, and against the will of their original inhabitants. She is now, with France and Germany as rivals, endeavoring to establish and extend her dominion in the savage regions of Africa. The United States, from time to time, expel the native tribes of Indians from their homes to make room for their own people. These acts of the most civilized and Christian nations are inexcusable robberies, unless they can be defended, under the law of nature, by the argument that these uncivilized countries were the gifts of nature to man, and that their inhabitants refused, or were unable, to perform that great trust, imposed upon all nations, to make the capacities of the countries which they hold subservient to the needs of man. And this argument is a sufficient defense, not indeed for the thousand excesses which have stained these conquests, but for the conquests themselves.

The second proposition above advanced, namely, that the title which nature bestows upon man to her gifts is of the *usufruct* only, is, indeed, but a corollary from that which has just been discussed, or rather a part of it, for in saying that the gift is not to this nation or that, but to all mankind, all generations, future as well as present, are intended. The earth was designed as the permanent abode of man through ceaseless generations. Each generation, as it appears upon the scene, is entitled only to use the fair inheritance. It is against the law of nature that any waste should be committed to the disadvantage of the succeeding tenants. . . .

The obligation not to invade the stock of the provision made by nature for the support of human life is [especially] imposed upon *civilized* societies, for the danger proceeds almost wholly from them. It is commerce, the fruit of civilization, . . . that subjects the production of each part of the globe to the demands of every other part, and thus threatens, unless the tendency is counteracted by efficient husbandry, to encroach upon the sources of supply. . . . [W]ith the advance of civilization, the increase in population, and the multiplication of wants, a peril of overconsumption arises, and along with it a development of that prudential wisdom which seeks to avert the danger.

The great and principal instrumentality designed to counteract this threatening tendency is the institution of *private individual property*, which, by holding out to every man the promise that he shall have the exclusive possession and enjoyment of any increase in the products of nature which he may effect by his care, labor, and abstinence, brings into play the powerful motive of self-interest, stimulates the exertion in every direction of all his faculties, both of mind and body, and thus leads to a prodigiously increased production of the fruits of the earth.

* * *

The inquiry which has thus been prosecuted into the grounds and reasons upon which the institution of property stands fully substantiates, it is believed, the main proposition with which it began, namely, that *where any useful animals so far subject themselves to the control of particular men as to enable them exclusively to cultivate such animals and obtain the annual increase for the supply of human wants, and at the same time preserve the stock, they have a property interest in them*. And this conclusion, deducible from the broad and general doctrines of the law of nature, is confirmed by the actual fact as exhibited in the usages and laws of all civilized states. Wherever a useful animal exhibits in its nature and habits this quality, it must be denominated and treated as the subject of property and as well between nations as between individual men. . . .

In the added light thrown by this inquiry into the foundations of the institution of property the case of the fur-seal can no longer be open to doubt, if it ever was. It is a typical instance. Polygamous in its nature, compelled to breed upon the land, and confined to that element for half the year, gentle and confiding in its disposition, nearly defenseless against attack, it seems almost to implore the protection of man, and to offer to him as reward that superfluity of increase which is not needed for the continuance of the race. Its own habits go very far to effect a separation of this superfluity, leaving little to be done by man to make it complete. The selections for slaughter are easily made without disturbance or inquiry to the herd. The return of the herd to the same spot to submit to renewed drafts is assured by the most imperious instincts and necessities of the animal's nature. During the entire period of all absences the *animus revertendi* is ever present. The conditions are, as observed by the eminent naturalist, Prof. Huxley, *ideal*. All that is needed to make the full extent of the blessing to mankind available is the exercise on the one hand of care, self-denial, and industry on the part of man at the breeding places, and, on the other, exemption from the destructive pursuit at sea. The first requisite is supplied. A rich reward is offered for, and will certainly assure, the exercise of art and industry upon the land. All that is demanded from the law is that exemption from destructive pursuit on the sea which the award of a property interest will insure.

* * *

Excerpts From the Arbitral Award

. . . We, the said Baron de Courcel, Lord Hannen, Sir John Thompson, Marquis Visconti Venosta and Mr. Gregers Gram, being a majority of the said arbitrators, do decide and determine that the United States has not any right of protection or property in the fur-seals frequenting the islands of the United States in the Behring Sea, when such seals are found outside the ordinary three-mile limit.

Excerpt From Comments of Alphonse de Courcel, President of the Tribunal

We have felt obliged to maintain intact the fundamental principles of that august law of nations, which extends itself like the vault of heaven above all countries, and which borrows the laws of nature herself to protect the peoples of the earth, one against another, by inculcating in them the dictates of mutual goodwill.

Excerpt From Comments of Senator Morgan

[Justice Harlan] and I [the arbitrators appointed by the United States] concurred in the view that the treaty [for arbitration of this case] presented [the question of the right of the U.S. to protect the seals] in its broadest aspect [including the question of the equity of the situation]. Our honorable colleagues, however, did not so construe the scope of the duty prescribed to the Tribunal by the treaty. They considered that these questions of the right of property and protection in respect of the fur-seals were to be decided upon the existing state of the law, and, finding no existing precedent in the international law, they did not feel warranted in creating one.

As the rights claimed by the United States could only be supported by international law, in their estimation, and inasmuch as that law is silent on the subject, they felt that under the treaty they could find no legal foundation for the rights claimed that extended beyond the limits of the territorial jurisdiction of the United States.

Excerpts from Separate Opinion of Mr. Justice Harlan

The only possible objection that can be urged against the claim of ownership of these fur seal animals by the United States is the general rule that animals *ferae naturae* are not subject to individual ownership. But . . . an exception to this rule . . . is everywhere recognized, which admits of individual ownership of useful wild animals, the supply of which is limited, and which, by reason of their nature and habits, and the control or power which man may acquire over them, are susceptible of ownership, that is, are capable of exclusive appropriation. All of these conditions are fulfilled in the case of the Pribilof fur seals. It is not denied that they are useful animals, or that the supply is limited. The experience of the past proves that the race can be easily exterminated if man is allowed to hunt and slaughter them wherever they may be found, on the land or in the high seas. It is equally beyond dispute that they may be exclusively appropriated, because they come, at stated periods to the islands of the United States, where they remain under such control that the increase can be obtained for the benefit of the world without any injurious diminution of the stock.

The reason why the doctrines to which I have adverted have been taught more directly and fully in municipal jurisprudence [than in international law] is that questions of property more frequently arise between individuals. . . . [B]ut where the same grounds and reasons exist for the recognition of property, as between nations, that are found in . . . municipal law, [the writers on international law] have conceded national ownership. Illustrations of this rule are the cases of pearl and other oyster beds, coral reefs, etc., situates on the sea outside of territorial waters, in some instances thirty or more miles. These gifts of nature are exhaustible, and would be soon exhausted if treated as *res nullius*, and left open to the indiscriminate enjoyment of the people of all nations. They cannot well be enjoyed unless they are under particular control, so that the product may be taken at the right season and in limited amounts. In other words, they require the sort of care, restraint, and self-denial which is induced only by a recognition of property in those who bestow such care, and practice such restraint and self-denial.

* * *

That the United States, by its ownership of Pribilof Islands, is in a condition to reap the benefit of these animals, and preserve the race, and that no other nation, by any action it may alone take can accomplish these beneficial results, and that the preservation of the race does not admit of their being taken at any other place than at their breeding grounds, are conclusive reasons why the law should recognize its claim of property.

* * *

If the claim of the United States to own these fur seals rests, in law, upon a sound foundation, the next inquiry is whether it may protect its property? There can be but one answer to this question. . . . No one questions its right to afford protection . . . while the seals are on its islands, and while they are within territorial waters. That right—if the United States *owns* the seals—is not lost while they are temporarily absent in the high seas. . . .

[Do British citizens have a right to hunt these animals on the high seas, free of interference from the United States?] [N]o individual can be said to have a *right*, under international law, to *exterminate a race* of valuable animals, for the sake simply of the temporary profit realized from such practices. . . .

* * *

[T]he mind instantly recoils from the suggestion that [the destruction of these animals, for temporary gain, by methods that are inhuman and barbarous, and which will surely result in the speedy extermination of the entire race is] in the exercise of a *right* protected by the law of nations, and must be submitted to by the United States. . . .

* * *

With entire truth, therefore, it may be said that the extermination of this race of animals by the destructive methods of pelagic sealing, involving necessarily the killing in vast numbers of female seals heavy with young or nursing their pups, or impregnated, is a crime against the law of nature, and consequently without any sanction whatever in the law of nations. That law, indeed, recognizes the freedom of the seas for the people of all nations, and no nations have stood more firmly by that doctrine or are more interested in its enforcement than Great Britain and the United States. But I have not found in any treatise upon international law, or in the judgment of any court, a hint even that this doctrine confers upon individuals or associations a *right* to employ methods for the taking of useful animals found in the high seas which will exterminate the race, when all know . . . that such animals may be readily taken at their breeding grounds, and not elsewhere, by methods that regularly give their increase for man's use without at all impairing or diminishing the stock. One method results in the extermination of the race, whereby the object of its creation is entirely defeated; the other results in its preservation, whereby that object is secured. It is inconceivable that the law of nations gives or recognizes the right to employ the former. . . .

DISCUSSION NOTES/QUESTIONS

1. Consider the traditional norms regarding the taking of wild animals in ocean waters:

a. The territorial jurisdiction of the United States extended only three miles beyond the coast of the Pribilof Islands. The United States had seized the British Canadian sealing vessels on the high seas, 60 miles from U.S. land, where it had no jurisdictional authority.

b. Because the seals were wild animals, they were traditionally treated as belonging to no one, *res nullius,* and hence the property of whoever captured them, at least when they were on the high seas and beyond the jurisdiction of any nation.

2. The United States sought to avoid the international legal limits on its sovereign authority by arguing that it was the owner of all Alaskan fur seals originating on the Pribilof Islands.

a. On what source of international law did it base its argument? Did it contend that treaty law gave it ownership? Customary law?

b. At one point in its argument, the United States seems to concede that there is no evidence that nations have explicitly agreed to the conception of property for which it argues, including no "actual practice" or "usage" to support it. Yet it claims that "in international law," even if "the practice and usages of nations have furnished no rule," still a tribunal can always find an applicable rule. What is the source of this law that exists even in the absence of practice, usage, or express agreement? Can you fit this analysis into the "sources of law" identified in Article 38 of the Statute of the International Court of Justice?

3. The United States argued that all nations have a duty to preserve natural resources, including living resources, because they hold or own resources only "in trust for the [benefit of] present and future generations of man," including for the benefit of other nations.

a. How does this argument help the US support its claim to ownership of the Pribiloff seals?

b. How does the US use this claim that all ownership is "in trust for present and future generations" to support international trade and the use of force to open international borders to trade?

c. How does the US use this argument to justify imperialism and the conquering of native peoples by people of European descent?

d. Can you endorse the principle that natural resources are held in trust for the benefit of "present and future generations" of humankind when that principle is used to provide a rationale for imperialism and the oppression of poorer nations by rich nations? Can the principle that natural resources are held in trust for "present and future generations" be supported without endorsing the interpretation given to it by the United States in 1893? Is it consistent with the modern view that all nations have the right to "permanent sovereignty over their natural wealth and resources"?[93]

e. Article 30 of the Charter of Economic Rights and Duties of States **(Basic Document 7.3)** says that all States have the responsibility to protect, preserve and enhance the environment "for the present and future generations." Is this an adoption of the principle urged by the United States nearly 100 years earlier?

4. The arbitration agreement directed the Arbitral Tribunal to formulate regulations for the protection of fur seals in the event that the U.S. claim to exclusive jurisdiction was denied. Thus, following its ruling against the United States, the Tribunal issued regulations that severely restricted hunting of fur seals by both Britain and United States in areas surrounding the Pribilof Islands and in high seas areas.

Unfortunately, the regulations were generally ineffective. Worse, sealers from other nations, particularly Japan, began killing large numbers of seals in the waters surrounding the Pribilof Islands. Generally these pelagic sealers operated beyond the three-mile limit and, according to the legal principles endorsed in the Tribunal's ruling, there was nothing either the United States or Great Britain could do to stop the continued decimation of the herd.

In 1897, Japan, Russia, and the United States met in Washington and agreed to ban pelagic sealing temporarily if Britain would also do so, but Britain refused. Diplomatic efforts continued over the next several years as the plight of the seals worsened. Finally, in 1911, with seal populations down to fewer than 100,000 animals (from an estimated high of 4,000,000), an agreement was reached among Japan, Great Britain, Russia and the United States.

All four countries agreed to ban pelagic sealing, and to allow killing of seals only on land (where the kill could be limited to certain adult male seals and managed to allow growth in the herds). All agreed to share a certain percentage of the seal skins obtained from hunts on their own territories with the other three countries. The United States agreed to make an immediate cash payment to Great Britain and Japan as compensation for giving up their rights to seal on the high seas. *See generally* Thomas A. Bailey, *The North Pacific Sealing Convention of 1911,* IV Pacific Historical Review 1 (1935). The Convention was promptly ratified by all four powers and is widely considered to have succeeded in ensuring the survival of the North Pacific fur seal. Populations grew rapidly once pelagic sealing was outlawed, even though commercial exploitation continued through land-based hunts.

5. Commercial hunting of seals in the 18th, 19th, and early 20th centuries caused huge declines in seal populations, prompting national and international efforts to protect pinnipeds (as seals, sea lions, and walruses are scientifically known) in many areas of the world. Today, one species of seal is

---

[93] G.A. Res. 1803 on Permanent Sovereignty over Natural Resources, & 1 (Dec. 14, 1962) **(Basic Document 1.20)**.

extinct and five others are listed as endangered. However, though the commercial seal hunt continues today in many areas of the world, the regulatory efforts of nations have resulted in significant protection for many seal populations.

E. TO PRESERVE WHALES OR TO SLAUGHTER THEM?

At the Stockholm Conference in 1972, where the United States proposed a moratorium on commercial whaling, chants of "Save the Whales" rang throughout the army of activists camped out in a suburb of Stockholm, and whales became the symbol and rallying cry of a new global environmental consciousness.

Ten years after Stockholm, the International Whaling Commission finally adopted the global whaling moratorium sought by the United States. Activists were jubilant over what appeared to be a major victory for the global environmental movement.

But was it? Ask yourself that question again at the end of this chapter.

Whales

The world has at least 80 species of cetaceans (whales), including dolphins and porpoises, divided into baleen (filter-feeding) whales and toothed whales. There are 13 species of baleen whales, ranging in size from the pygmy right whales (21 feet) to the blue whale (88 feet). They include the fin, bowhead, humpback, northern right, southern right, gray, sei, two species of minke, and two or possibly three species of Bryde's whale. All of these whales are listed as "great whales" by the International Whaling Commission (IWC).

Toothed whales number 69–73 species (including sperm, orca, pilot, beluga, and narwhal), around 20 species of beaked whales, and 46 species of dolphins and porpoises. Among toothed whales, only the sperm whale is listed by the IWC as a great whale (despite the fact that some toothed whales, such as Baird's beaked whale, are bigger than the 30-foot-long minke whales, which are considered great whales).

The blue whale, a baleen whale, is the biggest animal on earth. The immensity of the creature is hard to grasp in the abstract, but some relevant numbers might be evocative. For example, a female blue whale killed in the Antarctic in 1928 weighed 150 tons, or 330,000 pounds. This made her by far the largest animal ever known to have lived on earth during its entire 4600-million-year history, far bigger than any dinosaur. A normal adult blue whale's heart alone weighs two tons, and a small child could crawl through its aorta. A nursing mother produces 113 gallons of milk a day. During the feeding season in the Southern Ocean, an adult blue will consume up to 11,000 pounds of krill a day.[94] Blue whales also produce loud noises—188 decibels—louder than a jumbo jet taking off. They can swim at twenty knots, which made it possible for them to avoid capture from sailing ships in the early days of whaling; with the advent of steam power and chaser boats, they were outpaced. Between 1920 and 1965, 350,000 blue whales were slaughtered, almost to the point of extinction. There are believed to be around 2,000 in the Southern Hemisphere now.

Many species of cetaceans have not been significantly threatened by commercial exploitation (although they can face significant threats of other sorts). The large or "great" whales, however, have been commercially hunted by Europeans for centuries, with the result that some species were extinct in the North Atlantic by the early 1700s. As great whale numbers in Europe plummeted, and as whaling technology improved, whalers opened new whaling grounds around the world and commercial whaling became a global business. The remainder of this introductory essay tells the story of large whales, the whaling industry, and the international efforts to stop the unsustainable exploitation of these magnificent animals.

A Brief History of Whaling

People have ruthlessly exploited marine mammals for thousands of years, but it has been only since the development of industrial society, with its expanded markets and more efficient means of capture and destruction, that this exploitation has threatened the survival of these animals.

Whaling played an important role in the early history of many countries, particularly the United States. The whalers of Nantucket, New Bedford, and other parts of New England developed a large industry that was described for posterity in that classic of American literature, Herman Melville's *Moby Dick*, first published in 1851. Moby Dick was a great white sperm whale that had become an object of superstition among whalers. Captain Ahab lost a leg trying to capture it and was determined to gain vengeance. He concentrated upon that task with an obsession. In the end of the novel, the whale triumphs, killing Ahab and sinking the whale ship itself as well as all the boats.[95]

Melville's masterpiece paints a fascinating, and not inaccurate, picture of the American whaling industry in the early 1800s. There is much interesting detail in *Moby Dick* about the varieties of whales, the methods of killing them, and the processing of them once killed. The book gives a sense of the importance and sophistication of the industry, as well as the

---

[94] Krill is a tiny crustacean particularly abundant in the Antarctic.

[95] Remarkable as the story of the book is, it appears to have been based on real events. *See* Thomas Nickerson, Owen Chase and others, The Loss of the Ship Essex-Sunk by a Whale (Penguin Classic, 2000) and Nathaniel Philbrick, In the heart of the Sea: the Tragedy of the Whale Ship Essex (2000). *See generally* Eric Jay Dolin, Leviathan: The History of Whaling in America (2007). A recent and highly acclaimed British book is Philip Hoare, Leviathan, or the whale (2009).

bravery and adventurousness of the men who engaged in it. In the end, though, it is a romance, and the power of the human side of the story should not obscure the fact that the industry eventually brought devastation to populations of whales across the globe.

Commercial whaling was big business in early 19th century New England. Between 1835 and 1846, about 600 ships were engaged in whale hunting. The main purpose of killing whales was to secure the oil, but every other part of the whale was used as well. The products that were made from various bits of whale included:

- lamp oil (from sperm oil)
- margarine and cooking oil (from whale oil)
- candles, soaps, cosmetics and perfumes (from sperm oil)
- corsets and umbrellas (from whalebone)
- whale-meat for human consumption[96]
- animal feed (from meat meal)
- fertilizer (from bone meal)

The American industry began a long period of decline after the discovery of oil in Pennsylvania in 1859.[97]

In its heyday, the whaling industry was global in its reach. Indeed, 19th century whalers from the United States and elsewhere concentrated their efforts on sperm whales in the South Pacific, far from their home ports. For example, over 700 whaling ships, many of them American, visited Russell, New Zealand, in 1840. And, of course, this huge and global whaling enterprise was completely unregulated.

The Americans, Dutch, and English had the largest whaling industries at various times, but the Norwegians eventually became the biggest

---

96 The whaling industry does not appear to have secured much revenue from the eating of whale meat, although the early Basque whalers made the salted meat popular in Europe. In more modern times it was eaten in war time in a number of countries. There is also some use of it for animal food. But human consumption of whale meat, now the predominant reason for the taking of whales, is no longer a major industry around the world. Japan is one of three nations which continues to whale in large part for human consumption. Japan's position on taking whales is defended on the basis that Japanese people have been eating whale meat for many years, that it is part of Japanese culture, and is necessary for food security so should continue to be used as a source of food. Yasuo Lino and Dan Goodman "Japan's Position in the International Whaling Commission" in *The Future of Cetaceans in a Changing World* 3, 7–8 (William C.G. Burns and Alexander Gillespie eds., 2003).

97 All of the products that used to be derived from whale oil are now made from alternative sources, such as petroleum and vegetable oils. Candles and lamp oil are not in such demand since the invention of electricity and can be made from other materials in any event. The one product for which there is no substitute is whale meat, and this is still extensively eaten in Iceland, Japan, and Norway. It is also eaten by aboriginal people for subsistence in a number of places in the world. *See* Key Centre for Polymer Colloids, established and supported under the Australia Research Council's Research Centre Program, Module 9.5.1–Replacing Natural Products *see* www.kcpc.usyd.edu.au/discovery/9.5.1/9.5.1_whale.html (last visited on 21 September 2005).

whalers of all. It was a Norwegian who invented the harpoon gun in 1864, a technology that moved the odds against the whales. It consisted of a cannon that fired a barbed harpoon with an explosive head. When fired accurately, the harpoon would become firmly attached to the body of the whale and then the explosive charge would go off, inflicting a wound that the whaler hoped would soon be fatal. The whale would be hauled in by winch alongside the vessel and pumped full of air to keep it afloat. At the same time that these innovations made it easier to capture whales, the development of the factory ship—an enormous self-sufficient vessel onto which a captured whale is loaded—made it easier to process them. A blue whale could be flensed, dismembered, butchered, and pressure-cooked to produce oils and various meals in about 45 minutes on a factory ship.

The history of whaling can be summed up as a repeated pattern of over-exploitation of a targeted species followed by a collapse of the stocks, with whalers then moving on to other species or other areas.[98] Something akin to commercial whaling started in about 1100 AD, when Basques hunted "right" whales in the Bay of Biscay and eventually wiped them out. The Basque whalers then moved to other areas of the North Atlantic, and the English, Dutch, and French joined the industry. With the diligent application of modern technology, the whaling business was industrialized, and commercial whalers sought more whales than ever before. As numbers of large whales in the North Atlantic declined, the industry moved to the South Atlantic and South Pacific. And as whale numbers in these areas declined, the whalers were forced even farther south, into the inhospitable waters of the Antarctic, which, by the 20th century, had become the most prolific grounds for taking whales.

The International Whaling Convention

The failure of the whaling industry to conduct its operations in a sustainable manner led to growing recognition in the 20th century of the need to regulate the industry. Whales are migratory, a factor that complicates their protection because the measures of no coastal state alone can control or regulate the stocks. Hence, nations began to search for international solutions to the problem of over-exploitation of whales. The issues were considered at a meeting of the League of Nations in 1929, and in 1931 a Convention on the Regulation of Whaling was negotiated. This Convention prohibited altogether the taking of Right whales, but as an effective means of regulating the industry, the agreement achieved very little. Germany and Japan did not join and they were whaling nations. Only 22 countries did join. Thus, the Convention was rewritten in 1937, and

[98] Being market driven, it can be characterized also as an enclosure or privatization of the oceanic biodiversity commons.

there were Protocols adopted to it in 1938 and 1945,[99] but these efforts did not attract broad enough participation, and, in late 1946, a new International Convention for the Regulation of Whaling (ICRW) was signed in Washington, D.C. **(Basic Document 5.17)** by 15 whaling nations.[100]

In contrast to the previous efforts, the ICRW was successful in the sense that most whaling nations joined. The Convention was in force by late 1948, and participants included all the leading whaling nations. Pursuant to Article III of the Convention, the Contracting Parties established the International Whaling Commission (IWC). Each Contracting Party is entitled to appoint one member of the Commission, and each Commission member has a single vote. The Commission carries out the most important provisions of the Convention, including the adoption of amendments to the Convention's Schedule, which establishes rules regarding "the conservation and utilization of whale resources."[101]

Unfortunately, success in securing adherents to the ICRW did not equate to success in preventing the over-exploitation of whales. The annual quotas set by the IWC, pursuant to its authority under the ICRW, did not stop the mass killing, and many whale populations continued to decline at dangerous rates.

The Moratorium on Commercial Whaling

A committee of the 1972 UN (Stockholm) Conference on the Human Environment was charged with reporting on the condition of global whale stocks, and it reached an alarming conclusion: whale stocks were near collapse in many areas of the globe and a ten-year moratorium on commercial whaling was necessary to allow their recovery. The Committee's suggestion was adopted by the Stockholm Conference in its Recommendation 33, which called upon concerned governments, acting through the IWC, to adopt a moratorium on commercial whaling.

Efforts to push the moratorium proposal through the IWC were at first unsuccessful. The U.S. offered a moratorium proposal in 1973, but it was rejected by the IWC's Technical Committee, partly in response to an opinion from the IWC Scientific Committee that "a blanket moratorium on whaling could not be justified scientifically, since prudent management required regulation of the stocks."[102] But anti-whaling forces responded to

---

[99] For citations, *see* 5 International Law and World Order: Basic Documents, App. II (Burns H. Weston & Jonathan C. Carlson eds., 1994—).

[100] International Convention for the Regulation of Whaling, Dec. 2, 1946, 161 U.N.T.S. 72; The membership of the International Whaling Commission in 2017 was 89 countries.

[101] *Id.* at art. V.

[102] Chairman's Report of the Twenty-Fourth Meeting, 24 Rep. Int'l Whaling Comm'n 24 (1973). For more detailed discussions of these events, *see* A.W. Harris, *The Best Scientific Evidence Available: The Whaling Moratorium and Divergent Interpretations of Science*, 29 Wm. & Mary Envtl. L. & Pol'y Rev. 375 (2005); Robert Buron, The Life and Death of Whales (2d ed. 1980).

the deadlock at the IWC by recruiting non-whaling states to join the IWC in order to vote against commercial whaling. By 1982, the anti-whaling forces had a solid majority of IWC members, and the moratorium was adopted. Commercial whaling was to be phased out and eliminated by 1986. The moratorium was imposed for an indefinite period, subject to periodic review by the Commission.[103]

The moratorium was not before time. Failure to regulate the taking of whales had led to the collapse of many whale stocks and the endangerment of a number of species. Unbridled exploitation was not restrained by the organization set up for the purpose until it was almost too late. Professor Edward O. Wilson of Harvard University described what happened in *The Future of Life*.[104] He stated that destroying natural resources without careful analysis in the manner that the IWC permitted up until the moratorium was a mistake.

> [Such a policy] suffers the same delusion as the one that destroyed the whaling industry. As harvesting and processing techniques were improved, the annual catch of whales rose, and the industry flourished. But the whale populations declined in equal measure until they were depleted. Several species, including the blue whale, the largest animal species in the history of the earth, came close to extinction. Whereupon most whaling was called to a halt.[105]

Professor Wilson went on to point out that "the dollars-and-cents value of a dead blue whale" is based "only on the measures relevant to the existing market—that is, on the going price per unit weight of whale oil and meat." This does not reflect other values that the continued survival of the species may have to "science, medicine and aesthetics, in dimensions and magnitudes still unforeseen. What was the value of the blue whale in AD 1000? Close to zero. What will be its value in AD 3000? Essentially limitless, plus the gratitude of the generation then alive to those who, in their wisdom save the whale from extinction."[106]

The adoption of the commercial whaling moratorium did not bring an end to whaling. This is for several reasons. First, Article V of the

[103] The IWC's moratorium on commercial whaling did not eliminate all whaling. As noted earlier, the ICRW allows nations to engage in scientific research whaling, and Japan maintains a large program of this sort despite calls for its abandonment and claims that it serves primarily to maintain a whaling industry pending removal of the moratorium. The IWC also permits subsistence whaling by aboriginal groups following their traditional practices. The meaning and scope of the exception for this "aboriginal whaling" is also subject to debate and controversy. Finally, some whaling nations have exercised their international legal rights in a way that excepts them from the moratorium. Some have simply withdrawn from the ICRW; Iceland, which withdrew in 1992, rejoined in 2002, but subject to a reservation to the moratorium.

[104] Edward O. Wilson, The Future of Life (2002).

[105] Edward O. Wilson, *The Future of Life* 26–27 (2002).

[106] Id. at 113.

Convention permits any member state to opt out of new regulations simply by objecting to the amendment to the Convention's Schedule that is required to give such regulations legal effect. Norway continues lawfully to engage in commercial whaling because it followed the opt-out procedure and promptly objected to the moratorium. Iceland, which did not opt-out of the moratorium, found a different path to avoid it. Iceland withdrew from the Convention completely. It then rejoined with the reservation that it would not honor the moratorium, and so it also engages in commercial whaling without being in violation of its treaty obligations. Both Norway and Iceland engage in whaling only within their own Exclusive Economic Zones.

Some states that are bound by the moratorium take advantage of the IWC's special treatment of "aboriginal subsistence whaling" to permit whaling within their borders. Aboriginal subsistence whaling (whaling that is part of the traditional culture of native peoples) is not considered commercial whaling, and the IWC regularly authorizes limited catches of whales by native peoples in Denmark (Greenland), Russia (Chukotka), the United States (Alaska and Washington State), and St. Vincent and the Grenadines.

Finally, of particular note, Article VIII of the Convention provides:[107]

> Notwithstanding anything contained in this Convention, any Contracting Government may grant to any of its nationals a special permit authorizing that national to kill, take and treat whales for purposes of scientific research subject to such restrictions as to number and subject to such other conditions as the Contracting Government thinks fit, and the killing, taking, and treating of whales in accordance with the provisions of this Article shall be exempt from the operation of this Convention. Each Contracting Government shall report at once to the Commission all such authorizations which it has granted. Each Contracting Government may at any time revoke any such special permit which it has granted.
>
> Any whales taken under these special permits shall so far as practicable be processed and the proceeds shall be dealt with in accordance with directions issued by the Government by which the permit was granted.
>
> Each Contracting Government shall transmit to such body as may be designed by the Commission, in so far as practicable, and at intervals of not more than one year, scientific information available to that Government with respect to whales and whaling,

[107] International Convention for the Regulation of Whaling art. VIII, Nov. 10, 1948, 161 U.N.T.S. 72.

> including the results of research conducted pursuant to paragraph 1 of this Article and to Article IV.
>
> Recognizing that continuous collection and analysis of biological data in connection with the operations of factory ships and land stations are indispensable to sound and constructive management of the whale fisheries, the Contracting Governments will take all practicable measures to obtain such data.

This "scientific whaling" or "research whaling" exception is the loophole under which Japan operated a whaling program of commercial magnitude for many years. For example, in the 2009–2010 season as reported to the IWC, 1,867 whales were killed—825 under Special Permit research whaling under Article VIII, 690 under reservation (these are caught mainly by Norway), 336 under indigenous subsistence whaling, and 16 under illegal whaling reported to the Commission by South Korea.[108] The extent of Japan's research whaling, and whether it was really research or just commercial whaling in disguise, was a matter of frequent contention at the IWC.[109]

Despite the continued existence of whaling, the IWC reports that the status of whale stocks is generally improving. Although two species of great whales have low enough population levels to be considered in danger of extinction, the populations of many species are healthy and even increasing.[110] Indeed, the Southern Ocean population of minke whales, a commercially important species, is measured in the hundreds of thousands. It is this fact that has led Japan, Iceland, Norway and others to call for an end to the moratorium and a resumption of commercial whaling, subject to appropriate regulations to protect against renewed over-exploitation of the animals.

The IWC: A "Conservationist" or "Preservationist" Organization?[111]

The argument for a resumption of commercial whaling is straightforward. Japan points out that the purpose of the Convention, as

---

[108] International Whaling Commission *Chair's Summary of the Report of the 62nd Annual Meeting* (2010) (Annex).

[109] As explained in detail later in this chapter, the International Court of Justice concluded in 2014 that Japan's research whaling operation did not satisfy the requirements of Article VIII. Japan responded by altering the terms of its program and urging the IWC to consider a resumption of limited commercial whaling. When its effort to secure changes in IWC policies failed in late 2018, Japan announced its withdrawal from the International Convention on the Regulation of Whaling. On July 1, 2019, it resumed commercial whaling in its territorial waters and exclusive economic zone.

[110] *See* International Whaling Commission, Status of Whales, https://iwc.int/index.php?cID=status (last visited March 19, 2019).

[111] The distinction between conservation and preservation dates at least to the turn of the 20th Century when the mountaineer and naturalist John Muir clashed with Gifford Pinchot, first head of the U.S. Forest Service, over the management of public lands in the United States. Pinchot

expressed in its preamble, is "to provide for the proper conservation of whale stocks and thus make possible the orderly development of the whaling industry."[112] So long as whales can be taken commercially without threatening the sustainability of whale stocks, such action should be allowed. Indeed, they contend, the purpose of whale conservation is to allow "the orderly development of the [commercial] whaling industry." This position is supported at the IWC by a wide range of developing countries from Africa and the Caribbean. They argue that natural resources like whales should be exploited and utilized if that can be achieved in a sustainable manner. There is no justification, they say, to treat whales any differently than any other resource in this regard.

Those who support continuing the moratorium fall roughly into two camps. On the one hand, there are those who do not believe that we yet know enough about the numbers of whales or the factors that affect their survival to assess accurately the consequences of renewed whaling. Moreover, they worry that the international mechanisms for policing renewed commercial whaling would prove to be inadequate. In the 1990s, for example, it was discovered that the Soviet Union dramatically understated the number of whales killed by its fleet during the 1950s and 1960s, and did so without detection by the IWC. There is genuine concern any renewal of commercial whaling will be unmanageable and could have disastrous consequences for some whale stocks.

Alongside those pragmatic voices are a number of states that object to whaling on ethical grounds and argue that only a ban on whaling can "provide for the proper conservation of whale stocks," as required by the treaty. Some anti-whaling advocates would oppose commercial whaling even if it were undeniably sustainable. "Whales are a vanguard species in the environmental movement because of their intelligence, beauty, and communal lifestyle. The fact that they are considered to be a consumable resource by some ignites passionate debate about ethics, human and animal rights, cultural preservation, cultural relativism, and resource utilization."[113] These whaling opponents argue that the Convention's goal of "orderly development of the whaling industry" can be achieved through non-lethal activities, like whale watching.

---

favored managed conservation, in which the lands would be available to the public for recreational purposes, but also could be used for mining, logging, and similar exploitive uses. Muir favored preserving lands and forbidding any industrial exploitation of their resources. In the United States, Muir's preservationist vision is reflected in the National Parks, while Pinchot's conservationist approach is taken with respect to the management of public lands such as National Forests. *See* Robert Westover, *Conservation versus Preservation?*, USDA website, https://www.usda.gov/media/blog/2016/03/22/conservation-versus-preservation (last accessed April 11, 2019).

[112] International Convention for the Regulation of Whaling preambular paragraph 7, Nov. 10, 1948, 161 U.N.T.S. 72.

[113] Howard Schiffman, *The International Whaling Commission: Challenges from Within and Without*, 10 I.L.S.A. J. Int'l & Comp. L. 367, 370 (2004).

DISCUSSION NOTES/QUESTIONS

1. Assuming that commercial whaling could be policed and limited in a way that ensured its sustainability, would you support a lifting of the IWC moratorium? Do you think that continuing the moratorium is consistent with the purpose of the Convention? Do you accept the argument that rules to promote whale watching (e.g., by ensuring an abundance of whales) constitute rules promoting the "orderly development of the whaling industry?" Is this what was meant by the "whaling industry" in 1946 when the Convention was adopted? Can the meaning of that phrase evolve over time to deal with the reality that, today, whale watching may actually be a more important and more lucrative industry than commercial whaling?

2. Putting whale watching aside, are there any other reasons not to allow the commercial exploitation of whales. Is the "intelligence, beauty, and communal lifestyle" of whales a justification for an international rule outlawing the traditional practices of the Japanese and other whale-consuming peoples?

Some of the countries (e.g., Australia and New Zealand) that oppose a resumption of commercial whaling at the IWC have large meat industries of their own. They were called on by Japan to explain why the killing of sheep, cattle and particularly the culling of wild kangaroos was different from killing whales. Often the response argued that there was, and still is, no humane way to kill a large whale. Is that a sufficient response, in your view? What other responses would you make?

3. Many people, particularly those living in the relative affluence of western societies, believe that whales are unique animals that should not be regarded as resources to be harvested, even as a source of food for human consumption. Documentation of their large brains and gentle and family-oriented behavior is advanced as evidence of intelligence at least equivalent to our own. Emphasis on the aesthetic and sentient values ascribed to whales is the focus of whale watching and educational programs. However, others coming from a background or tradition where hunting is regarded as a normal method of acquiring food find such attitudes difficult to accept. Additionally, in a new century in which there are increasing demands for food to meet the needs of burgeoning human populations, is it justifiable to deliberately deny the use of a particular resource because of one, albeit dominant, cultural approach? It is here that the differing viewpoints, beliefs, and traditions of the peoples and nations comprising the IWC come into conflict.

4. Certain coastal communities in Japan that are prevented from whaling by the commercial whaling moratorium have societal and cultural structures and traditions similar to communities that are allowed to continue hunting whales for subsistence purposes under the aboriginal subsistence hunting exception. Japan has often tried, without success, to secure approval for limited coastal whaling under that exception. What is the justification for allowing some communities to pursue their traditional whaling practices while denying that privilege to others? What distinction warrants allowing Alaskan

natives in the United States to continue their traditional whale hunts while denying that right to the residents of coastal communities in Japan that have an equally venerable whaling tradition?

5. As noted earlier, the ICRW has a number of structural problems that prevent it from being fully effective. First, states can avoid its regulations by making a timely objection to them. Second, even if a state were fully governed by regulations limiting its commercial whaling, it could avoid those regulations by utilizing the research whaling exception under Article VIII.

Those problems are compounded by the fact that the IWC does not have power to enforce its regulations or punish violations. Enforcement is the exclusive province of the member states. The Convention does not specify the types of measures that should be adopted to ensure compliance. The IWC can only make recommendations to member states regarding issues of enforcement.

The historical record of compliance with IWC regulations is not good. As noted earlier, IWC efforts to regulate the commercial take of whales in the 1950s-1970s largely failed, and recent efforts to ensure the humane treatment of hunted whales have not been a particular success. It needs to be asked whether lessons from past mistakes have been learned sufficiently to warrant a lifting of the moratorium. It is easy to imagine circumstances in which the resumption of commercial whaling could lead to the same excesses that occurred before. The singular and unhappy history of whaling in the world indicates a need for caution. Past damage inflicted on whale stocks is far from restored. Whales are slow breeders. A moratorium that is now 30 years old may not seem sufficient. Neither does there seem to be any pressing human need to kill whales.

Such considerations lead some member nations to say that there must be changes to the enforcement provisions of the Convention before there is a resumption of commercial whaling. Do you agree? If enforcement is so difficult, why do most nations comply entirely with the commercial whaling moratorium? Why wouldn't they comply with more lenient, but still rigorous, restrictions? Indeed, we live in a much more environmentally conscientious global society than the one that existed in the 1950s. Should we assume that nations will willingly repeat the environmental excesses of that era if they are given the chance to do so?

6. The ICRW lacks any compulsory dispute settlement mechanism. There are a large number of issues on which the parties to the Convention disagree, and which will require resolution if commercial whaling is allowed. For example, one increasingly important disagreement is over what animals fall within the competence of the Convention. A number of member nations take the view that all cetaceans (including dolphins and porpoises) are covered by the Convention. The Japanese Government takes the opposite position. Both cannot be right.

What type of dispute settlement provision would you recommend be inserted in the IWRC? Mandatory adjudication or arbitration? Mandatory fact-finding by a conciliation commission? Only voluntary methods?

Should the IWC itself be given the power to adopt binding interpretations of the Convention's provisions? Currently, changes to the Convention's Schedule require a 75% vote by the Commission? What vote should be required to adopt interpretations of the Convention provisions?

7. One criticism that has been made of the whaling regime is that any nation can join the International Convention for the Regulation of Whaling and become a voting member of the IWC. It matters not whether the nation has any historic connection with whaling or even if it is a landlocked state. Several landlocked states now belong, including Mongolia and San Marino.

In many cases nations appear to have joined at the behest of states or interest groups deeply engaged in the debate over whether whales should be exploited and killed or conserved. Allegations have been made that environmental NGOs have used financial incentives to encourage particular countries to join the IWC and appoint an NGO representative as the country's IWC commissioner. Japan, for its part, has been accused of using promises of aid to induce many small and undeveloped countries to join the IWC and vote in Japan's favor. This raises questions about the ability of the IWC to make sound decisions based on science and conservation rather than politics. It is said that these nations have very little interest in the actual issues presented for resolution by the IWC, and that the body more often resembles a fractious parliamentary forum rather than a responsible international organization.

What would you do about this problem? Should membership of the IWRC be limited in some way? On what basis would you deny any particular nation a say in the use or preservation of a resource (whales) that can be said to be an interest common to all nations and the world in general? Would you exclude all landlocked nations? All nations with no history of whaling? All nations with no populations of whales in their coastal waters?

8. Looking more broadly, an important weakness with the Convention is that it does not address significant threats to cetaceans other than commercial and aboriginal whaling. For example, cetaceans are increasingly by-caught, i.e., getting fatally entangled in nets used to fish for other species. Every year over 300,000 dolphins, porpoises, and whales are estimated to be killed in this way. Indeed, there are some who suspect some nets may be deliberately set in order to trap whales. Rather than being assessed and then released, these whales may be killed and their meat then sold on the local market.

In 2001, the Japanese Fisheries Ministry changed a domestic law (first passed in 1990) relating to whales accidentally by-caught in fishing nets. The original law required that fishermen should attempt to release by-caught whales, if they were still alive. If the by-caught whale was dead, then the law instructed the fishermen either to bury the carcass or to consume the meat locally. The amended law, however, permits unlimited numbers of whales caught in nets to be killed. The meat can then be sold, as long as the fishermen responsible send a DNA sample to the authorities for registration.

This change in the law heralded, in the first year, a four-fold increase in the number of minke whales by-caught in nets and reported as killed around the coast of Japan. Before the new law was implemented, an average of 20 minke whales were caught in "trap nets" annually. During the first year that the law was changed, the number of minke whales that were by-caught in trap nets increased dramatically to 79, nearly 4 times the previous annual average. In subsequent years the number of minke whales caught in nets has continued to rise steadily.

9. The Convention also has not been applied to protect small cetaceans. Though it is very difficult to estimate the total number of small cetaceans that are killed in annual hunts around the globe, the numbers are undoubtedly substantial. Many of these hunts are completely unregulated (in terms of the numbers killed and the killing methods used) and many go unreported. Japan is believed to kill tens of thousands of dolphin and porpoises every year.

10. Those states that are seeking to overcome the impasse over the moratorium on commercial whaling hope to "move the IWC away from bickering over the current management of whaling and shift its focus toward whale conservation. . . ."[114] If such a move could be made, the IWC might be able to begin to discuss such issues as protection of small cetaceans and assessment of "the long-term threats [to whales] of climate change, entanglements, ship strikes, and pollution." To date, serious efforts to address these issues have not occurred, despite the fact that they may pose a greater threat to whales than whaling, largely because of the ongoing dispute over the commercial whaling moratorium.

The Ongoing Diplomatic Struggle

IWC annual meetings have been paralyzed for many years by the chasm between those who want to preserve whales and those who want to kill them and use them. The bitterness of debates surrounding the commercial whaling moratorium is partly a reflection of the fundamental nature of the philosophical conflict between those who wish to exploit whales and those who object to whaling on ethical grounds.

The ban on commercial whaling that was originally intended to be temporary has remained in force with no realistic possibility of its removal, much to the chagrin of the whaling countries—Japan, Norway and Iceland. As noted earlier in this chapter, all three of them have found a way around the moratorium, but none are happy with the IWC's apparent determination that commercial whaling shall never again be lawful.

[114] Geoffrey Palmer, Notes Prepared for An Address to New Zealand Institute of International Affairs, *Negotiations at the International Whaling Commission* (16 August 2010).

For their part, the nations that support the moratorium were angry and offended by Japan's use of the Article VIII research whaling exception to continue to take large numbers of whales from the Southern Ocean. Every year about the time the Japanese fleet set out for the Southern Ocean, the like-minded group within the ICJ which opposes whaling organized a diplomatic *demarche*—protest—to the Japanese Government about the scientific whaling. Drafting and coordinating that was a lot of work, indicating the depth of feeling on these issues.

The fights at the IWC are rancorous, and the organization does not behave like an international organization. It has been described as more like an unruly Parliament.[115] Resort is often had to procedural tactics and hard debating to advance a nation's particular interests.

An Effort at Reform

States have divided into roughly three main groups with respect to IWC reform. Some nations do not think any whales should be killed under any circumstances and that any reform should entail permanent continuation of the moratorium, the establishment of whale sanctuaries in various parts of the world, and the elimination of the research whaling exception. Japan and other nations argue that whaling is fine as long it is based on the principle of sustainable use and that some limited quantity of commercial whaling should be authorized. Still other nations take the position that commercial whaling might be acceptable, but only if the Convention were made readily enforceable and provisions were in place for the policing of whaling. Among these groups, none has had the 75 per cent majority required to change the rules.

Following an intense recruitment campaign for the 2006 meeting in the Caribbean, the pro-whaling forces were able to secure a resolution known as the St. Kitts Declaration—passed by a single vote—that called for a return to commercial whaling insofar as it could be done in a "controlled and sustainable" fashion.[116] This result showed that the pro-whaling and pro-whales forces in the Commission were almost equally balanced, which meant that the Commission faced the prospect of prolonged deadlock if things did not change.

In response to the St. Kitts Declaration, a heavy diplomatic effort was made by the United States, in partnership with New Zealand, to reform the IWC. In the months and years that followed the Declaration, intense and contentious negotiations occurred concerning the future of the IWC. Professional diplomats were called in to offer advice on how the IWC could

---

[115] Geoffrey Palmer *Whales and Humans: How whaling went from being a major industry to a leading environmental issue then landed Japan in the International Court of Justice for the first time*, (2015) 13 N.Z. Y.B. Int'l L. 1, 6.

[116] International Whaling Commission *Chair's Summary of the 58th Annual Meeting* (2006) [St Kitts Declaration].

mend its ways and lower the political temperature. An informal Pew process organized by NGOs running on a parallel track provided impetus, and processes were put in place to try and reach a way through the impasse. At the 2008 IWC meeting a 33-nation "Small Working Group" was established to work through the issues.

At the 2009 plenary meeting in Madeira, Portugal, it was decided to go ahead on a different tack. A smaller Support Group was established. It had many meetings and produced a substantial amount of text on the basis that nothing is agreed until everything is agreed. The group had a long meeting in Santiago, Chile, then more meetings in Seattle, Honolulu, and Washington. Consensus was not reached, although it came tantalizingly close.

The compromise proposal was to create a 10-year interim period of stability during which no major decisions would be made that would require nations to change their philosophical or legal position on research whaling, commercial whaling or whaling under reservation. At the same time, the proposal would have brought all whaling under full IWC control, and the proposal was designed to ensure that catch limits would be set at levels "significantly below the current limits and scientifically determined to be sustainable over the period."[117] The central idea was that the IWC would gain control again over the number of whales that would be killed and it would not be in the hands of nations issuing their own special permits.

The number of whales to be killed by Japan in the Southern Ocean was a crucial sticking point. Because no compromise could be found on this point, the group wound up its activities in April 2010 without preparing a formal proposal for consideration by the IWC. The Chair and Vice Chair of the IWC sought to move things forward by offering their own "Proposed Consensus Decision to Improve the Conservation of Whales" for consideration at the IWC's June 2010 meeting at Agadir, Morocco.[118]

The Chair's document as it was offered comprised all the work done by the Support Group, but the Chair and Vice Chair also filled in the blanks about the total number of whales that could be killed under the arrangements. The total number of whales under all forms of whaling they proposed to be killed was 1,819, including 400 Antarctic minke whales. This was a number that the whaling countries would have ultimately

---

[117] *Proposed Consensus Decision to Improve the Conservation of Whales from the Chair and Vice-Chair of the Commission* IWC/62/7 (April 28, 2010) presented to IWC members in advance of the 62nd meeting.

[118] G.A. Res. 46/215, Large-Scale Pelagic Driftnet Fishing and Its Impact on the Living Marine Resources of the World's Oceans and Seas (Dec. 20, 1991).

agreed to. Moreover, the whole proposal would have resulted in a substantial reduction of the total number of whales then being killed.[119]

It was hoped the proposal would move the IWC away from bickering over the current management of whaling and shift its focus toward whale conservation and assessing the long-term threats of climate change, entanglements, ship strikes, and pollution. Proponents also argued that it was important to understand what the proposal did not do. It did not lift the moratorium. It legitimized Japan's whaling, but it left discussion of the continuation of the moratorium for a later period.

The proposal's endorsement of continued whaling, even at a lower level, was deeply unpopular with whale preservationists, especially those in Australia who had been promised by the Labor Government in its election campaign that Australia would seek to end Antarctic whaling by taking Japan to court. In a calculated move aimed at ensuring the defeat of the reform efforts, Australia filed a legal proceeding against Japan in the International Court of Justice shortly before the Agadir meeting. The action had the desired effect—compromise became nearly impossible. In his memoir, Peter Garrett, Australia's Minister for the Environment during the critical period, makes it plain that Australia's determined strategy was to litigate and ensure the compromise proposal did not succeed.[120] A substantial diplomatic campaign was waged by Australia to bring about that result. For its part, Japan resisted cutting its take in the Southern Ocean by the requisite amount, and that resistance also hindered the reform effort. In the end, the effort failed, although it came close.

Instead of compromising on institutional reform, Australia preferred litigation.

WHALING IN THE ANTARCTIC (AUSTL. V. JAPAN; N.Z. INTERVENING)

2014 ICJ 226 (Mar. 31)

I. Jurisdiction of the Court

30. In the present case Australia contends that Japan has breached certain obligations under the [International Convention on the Regulations of Whaling] by issuing special permits to take whales within the framework of [a research program known as] JARPA II. Japan maintains that its activities are lawful because the special permits are issued for "purposes of

[119] The Chairs argued that compromise was necessary, and that the proposal actually would lead to better results for whale conservation than continuation of the moratorium. Indeed, during the years of the moratorium the total take of whales by Japan, Norway, and Iceland had grown from 300 whales in 1990 to 750 in 1995 to 1,700 in 2005. In the year of the Agadir meeting, the three countries had plans to kill more than 3,000 whales.

[120] Peter Garrett, *Big Blue Sky: A Memoir* 375–390 (2015).

scientific research", as provided by Article VIII of the ICRW. The Court will first examine whether it has jurisdiction over the dispute.

31. Australia invokes as the basis of the Court's jurisdiction the declarations made by both Parties under Article 36, paragraph 2, of the Court's Statute. Australia's declaration of 22 March 2002 reads in relevant part as follows:

"The Government of Australia declares that it recognizes as compulsory ipso facto and without special agreement, in relation to any other State accepting the same obligation, the jurisdiction of the International Court of Justice in conformity with paragraph 2 of Article 36 of the Statute of the Court, until such time as notice may be given to the Secretary-General of the United Nations withdrawing this declaration. This declaration is effective immediately.

This declaration does not apply to: . . .

(b) any dispute concerning or relating to the delimitation of maritime zones, including the territorial sea, the exclusive economic zone and the continental shelf, or arising out of, concerning, or relating to the exploitation of any disputed area of or adjacent to any such maritime zone pending its delimitation."

Japan's declaration of 9 July 2007 reads in relevant part as follows:

"Japan recognizes as compulsory ipso facto and without special agreement, in relation to any other State accepting the same obligation and on condition of reciprocity, the jurisdiction of the International Court of Justice, over all disputes arising on and after 15 September 1958 with regard to situations or facts subsequent to the same date and being not settled by other means of peaceful settlement."

32. Japan contests the jurisdiction of the Court over the dispute submitted by Australia with regard to JARPA II, arguing that it falls within Australia's reservation (b), which it invokes on the basis of reciprocity. While acknowledging that this dispute does not concern or relate to the delimitation of maritime zones, Japan maintains that it is a dispute "arising out of, concerning, or relating to the exploitation of any disputed area of or adjacent to any such maritime zone pending its delimitation".

* * *

36. The Court recalls that, when interpreting a declaration accepting its compulsory jurisdiction, it "must seek the interpretation which is in harmony with a natural and reasonable way of reading the text, having due regard to the intention" of the declaring State (Anglo-Iranian Oil Co. (United Kingdom v. Iran), Preliminary Objection, Judgment, I.C.J. Reports 1952, p. 104). The Court noted in the Fisheries Jurisdiction case that it had

"not hesitated to place a certain emphasis on the intention of the depositing State" (Fisheries Jurisdiction (Spain v. Canada), Jurisdiction of the Court, Judgment, I.C.J. Reports 1998, p. 454, para. 48). The Court further observed that "[t]he intention of a reserving State may be deduced not only from the text of the relevant clause, but also from the context in which the clause is to be read, and an examination of evidence regarding the circumstances of its preparation and the purposes intended to be served" (ibid., p. 454, para. 49).

37. Reservation (b) contained in Australia's declaration (see paragraph 31 above) refers to disputes concerning "the delimitation of maritime zones" or to those "arising out of, concerning, or relating to the exploitation of any disputed area of or adjacent to any such maritime zone pending its delimitation". The wording of the second part of the reservation is closely linked to that of the first part. The reservation thus has to be read as a unity. The disputes to which the reservation refers must either concern maritime delimitation in an area where there are overlapping claims or the exploitation of such an area or of an area adjacent thereto. The existence of a dispute concerning maritime delimitation between the Parties is required according to both parts of the reservation.

38. The meaning which results from the text of the reservation is confirmed by the intention stated by Australia when it made its declaration accepting the compulsory jurisdiction of the Court. According to a press release issued by the Attorney-General and the Minister for Foreign Affairs of Australia on 25 March 2002, the reservation excluded "disputes involv[ing] maritime boundary delimitation or disputes concerning the exploitation of an area in dispute or adjacent to an area in dispute". The same statement is contained in the National Interest Analysis submitted by the Attorney-General to Parliament on 18 June 2002, which referred to "maritime boundary disputes" as the object of the reservation. Thus, the reservation was intended to cover, apart from disputes concerning the delimitation of maritime zones, those relating to the exploitation of an area in respect of which a dispute on delimitation exists, or of a maritime area adjacent to such an area. The condition of a dispute between the parties to the case concerning delimitation of the maritime zones in question was clearly implied.

39. Both Parties acknowledge that the dispute before the Court is not a dispute about maritime delimitation. The question remains whether JARPA II involves the exploitation of an area which is the subject of a dispute relating to delimitation or of an area adjacent to it.

Part of the whaling activities envisaged in JARPA II take place in the maritime zone claimed by Australia as relating to the asserted Australian Antarctic Territory or in an adjacent area. Moreover, the taking of whales, especially in considerable numbers, could be viewed as a form of exploitation of a maritime area even if this occurs according to a programme for scientific research. However, while Japan has contested Australia's maritime claims generated by the asserted Australian Antarctic Territory, it does not claim to have any sovereign rights in those areas. The fact that Japan questions those maritime entitlements does not render the delimitation of these maritime areas under dispute as between the Parties. As the Court stated in the *Territorial and Maritime Dispute* case, "the task of delimitation consists in resolving the overlapping claims by drawing a line of separation between the maritime areas concerned" (Territorial and Maritime Dispute (Nicaragua v. Colombia), Judgment, I.C.J. Reports 2012 (II), pp. 674–675, para. 141). There are no overlapping claims of the Parties to the present proceedings which may render reservation (b) applicable.

40. Moreover, it is significant that Australia alleges that Japan has breached certain obligations under the ICRW and does not contend that JARPA II is unlawful because the whaling activities envisaged in the programme take place in the maritime zones over which Australia asserts sovereign rights or in adjacent areas. The nature and extent of the claimed maritime zones are therefore immaterial to the present dispute, which is about whether or not Japan's activities are compatible with its obligations under the ICRW.

41. The Court therefore concludes that Japan's objection to the Court's jurisdiction cannot be upheld.

II. Alleged Violations of International Obligations Under the Convention

1. *Introduction*

A. *General overview of the Convention*

42. The present proceedings concern the interpretation of the International Convention for the Regulation of Whaling and the question whether special permits granted for JARPA II are for purposes of scientific research within the meaning of Article VIII, paragraph 1, of the Convention. Before examining the relevant issues, the Court finds it useful to provide a general overview of the Convention and its origins.

43. The ICRW was preceded by two multilateral treaties relating to whaling. The Convention for the Regulation of Whaling, adopted in 1931, was prompted by concerns over the sustainability of the whaling industry. This industry had increased dramatically following the advent of factory ships and other technological innovations that made it possible to conduct extensive whaling in areas far from land stations, including in the waters off Antarctica. The 1931 Convention prohibited the killing of certain categories of whales and required whaling operations by vessels of States

parties to be licensed, but failed to address the increase in overall catch levels.

This increase in catch levels and a concurrent decline in the price of whale oil led to the adoption of the 1937 International Agreement for the Regulation of Whaling. The preamble of this Agreement expressed the desire of the States parties "to secure the prosperity of the whaling industry and, for that purpose, to maintain the stock of whales". The treaty prohibited the taking of certain categories of whales, designated seasons for different types of whaling, closed certain geographic areas to whaling and imposed further regulations on the industry. As had already been the case under the 1931 Convention, States parties were required to collect from all the whales taken certain biological information which, together with other statistical data, was to be transmitted to the International Bureau for Whaling Statistics in Norway. The Agreement also provided for the issuance by a "Contracting Government . . . to any of its nationals [of] a special permit authorising that national to kill, take and treat whales for purposes of scientific research". Three Protocols to the 1937 Agreement subsequently placed some additional restrictions on whaling activities.

44. In 1946, an international conference on whaling was convened on the initiative of the United States. The aims of the conference, as described by Mr. Dean Acheson, then Acting Secretary of State of the United States, in his opening address, were "to provide for the coordination and codification of existant regulations" and to establish an "effective administrative machinery for the modification of these regulations from time to time in the future as conditions may require". The conference adopted, on 2 December 1946, the International Convention for the Regulation of Whaling, the only authentic text of which is in the English language. The Convention entered into force for Australia on 10 November 1948 and for Japan on 21 April 1951. New Zealand deposited its instrument of ratification on 2 August 1949, but gave notice of withdrawal on 3 October 1968; it adhered again to the Convention with effect from 15 June 1976.

45. In contrast to the 1931 and 1937 treaties, the text of the ICRW does not contain substantive provisions regulating the conservation of whale stocks or the management of the whaling industry. These are to be found in the Schedule, which "forms an integral part" of the Convention, as is stated in Article I, paragraph 1, of the latter. The Schedule is subject to amendments, to be adopted by the IWC. This Commission, established under Article III, paragraph 1, of the Convention, is given a significant role in the regulation of whaling. It is "composed of one member from each Contracting Government". The adoption by the Commission of amendments to the Schedule requires a three-fourths majority of votes cast (Art. III, para. 2). An amendment becomes binding on a State party unless it presents an objection, in which case the amendment does not become

effective in respect of that State until the objection is withdrawn. The Commission has amended the Schedule many times. The functions conferred on the Commission have made the Convention an evolving instrument.

Among the objects of possible amendments, Article V, paragraph 1, of the Convention lists "fixing (a) protected and unprotected species . . . (c) open and closed waters, including the designation of sanctuary areas . . . (e) time, methods, and intensity of whaling (including the maximum catch of whales to be taken in any one season), (f) types and specifications of gear and apparatus and appliances which may be used". Amendments to the Schedule "shall be such as are necessary to carry out the objectives and purposes of this Convention and to provide for the conservation, development, and optimum utilization of the whale resources" and "shall be based on scientific findings" (Art. V, para. 2).

46. Article VI of the Convention states that "[t]he Commission may from time to time make recommendations to any or all Contracting Governments on any matters which relate to whales or whaling and to the objectives and purposes of this Convention". These recommendations, which take the form of resolutions, are not binding. However, when they are adopted by consensus or by a unanimous vote, they may be relevant for the interpretation of the Convention or its Schedule.

47. In 1950, the Commission established a Scientific Committee (hereinafter the "Scientific Committee" or "Committee"). The Committee is composed primarily of scientists nominated by the States parties. However, advisers from intergovernmental organizations and scientists who have not been nominated by States parties may be invited to participate in a non-voting capacity.

The Scientific Committee assists the Commission in discharging its functions, in particular those relating to "studies and investigations relating to whales and whaling" (Article IV of the Convention). It analyses information available to States parties "with respect to whales and whaling" and submitted by them in compliance with their obligations under Article VIII, paragraph 3, of the Convention. It contributes to making "scientific findings" on the basis of which amendments to the Schedule may be adopted by the Commission (Art. V, para. 2 (b)). According to paragraph 30 of the Schedule, adopted in 1979, the Scientific Committee reviews and comments on special permits before they are issued by States parties to their nationals for purposes of scientific research under Article VIII, paragraph 1, of the Convention. The Scientific Committee has not been empowered to make any binding assessment in this regard. It communicates to the Commission its views on programmes for scientific research, including the views of individual members, in the form of reports or recommendations. However, when there is a division of opinion, the Committee generally refrains from formally adopting the majority view.

Since the mid-1980s, the Scientific Committee has conducted its review of special permits on the basis of "Guidelines" issued or endorsed by the Commission. At the time that JARPA II was proposed in 2005, the applicable Guidelines had been collected in a document entitled "Annex Y: Guidelines for the Review of Scientific Permit Proposals" (hereinafter "Annex Y"). The current Guidelines, which were elaborated by the Scientific Committee and endorsed by the Commission in 2008 (and then further revised in 2012), are set forth in a document entitled "Annex P: Process for the Review of Special Permit Proposals and Research Results from Existing and Completed Permits" (hereinafter "Annex P").

B. Claims by Australia and response by Japan

48. Australia alleges that JARPA II is not a programme for purposes of scientific research within the meaning of Article VIII of the Convention. In Australia's view, it follows from this that Japan has breached and continues to breach certain of its obligations under the Schedule to the ICRW. Australia's claims concern compliance with the following substantive obligations: (1) the obligation to respect the moratorium setting zero catch limits for the killing of whales from all stocks for commercial purposes (para. 10 (e)); (2) the obligation not to undertake commercial whaling of fin whales in the Southern Ocean Sanctuary (para. 7 (b)); and (3) the obligation to observe the moratorium on the taking, killing or treating of whales, except minke whales, by factory ships or whale catchers attached to factory ships (para. 10 (d)). Moreover, according to Australia's final submissions, when authorizing JARPA II, Japan also failed to comply with the procedural requirements set out in paragraph 30 of the Schedule for proposed scientific permits.

49. Japan contests all the alleged breaches. With regard to the substantive obligations under the Schedule, Japan argues that none of the obligations invoked by Australia applies to JARPA II, because this programme has been undertaken for purposes of scientific research and is therefore covered by the exemption provided for in Article VIII, paragraph 1, of the Convention. Japan also contends that there has been no breach of the procedural requirements stated in paragraph 30 of the Schedule.

50. The issues concerning the interpretation and application of Article VIII of the Convention are central to the present case and will be examined first.

2. Interpretation of Article VIII, paragraph 1, of the Convention

A. The function of Article VIII

51. Article VIII, paragraph 1, of the Convention reads as follows:

"Notwithstanding anything contained in this Convention any Contracting Government may grant to any of its nationals a special permit authorizing that national to kill, take and treat whales for purposes of scientific research subject to such restrictions as to number and subject to such other conditions as the Contracting Government thinks fit, and the killing, taking, and treating of whales in accordance with the provisions of this Article shall be exempt from the operation of this Convention. Each Contracting Government shall report at once to the Commission all such authorizations which it has granted. Each Contracting Government may at any time revoke any such special permit which it has granted."

* * *

55. The Court notes that Article VIII is an integral part of the Convention. It therefore has to be interpreted in light of the object and purpose of the Convention and taking into account other provisions of the Convention, including the Schedule. However, since Article VIII, paragraph 1, specifies that "the killing, taking, and treating of whales in accordance with the provisions of this Article shall be exempt from the operation of this Convention", whaling conducted under a special permit which meets the conditions of Article VIII is not subject to the obligations under the Schedule concerning the moratorium on the catching of whales for commercial purposes, the prohibition of commercial whaling in the Southern Ocean Sanctuary and the moratorium relating to factory ships.

B. The relationship between Article VIII and the object and purpose of the Convention

56. The preamble of the ICRW indicates that the Convention pursues the purpose of ensuring the conservation of all species of whales while allowing for their sustainable exploitation. Thus, the first preambular paragraph recognizes "the interest of the nations of the world in safeguarding for future generations the great natural resources represented by the whale stocks". In the same vein, the second paragraph of the preamble expresses the desire "to protect all species of whales from further over-fishing", and the fifth paragraph stresses the need "to give an interval for recovery to certain species now depleted in numbers". However, the preamble also refers to the exploitation of whales, noting in the third paragraph that "increases in the size of whale stocks will permit increases in the number of whales which may be captured without endangering these natural resources", and adding in the fourth paragraph that "it is in the common interest to achieve the optimum level of whale stocks as rapidly as possible without causing widespread economic and nutritional distress"

and in the fifth that "whaling operations should be confined to those species best able to sustain exploitation". The objectives of the ICRW are further indicated in the final paragraph of the preamble, which states that the Contracting Parties "decided to conclude a convention to provide for the proper conservation of whale stocks and thus make possible the orderly development of the whaling industry". Amendments to the Schedule and recommendations by the IWC may put an emphasis on one or the other objective pursued by the Convention, but cannot alter its object and purpose.

57. In order to buttress their arguments concerning the interpretation of Article VIII, paragraph 1, Australia and Japan have respectively emphasized conservation and sustainable exploitation as the object and purpose of the Convention in the light of which the provision should be interpreted. According to Australia, Article VIII, paragraph 1, should be interpreted restrictively because it allows the taking of whales, thus providing an exception to the general rules of the Convention which give effect to its object and purpose of conservation. New Zealand also calls for "a restrictive rather than an expansive interpretation of the conditions in which a Contracting Government may issue a Special Permit under Article VIII", in order not to undermine "the system of collective regulation under the Convention". This approach is contested by Japan, which argues in particular that the power to authorize the taking of whales for purposes of scientific research should be viewed in the context of the freedom to engage in whaling enjoyed by States under customary international law.

58. Taking into account the preamble and other relevant provisions of the Convention referred to above, the Court observes that neither a restrictive nor an expansive interpretation of Article VIII is justified. The Court notes that programmes for purposes of scientific research should foster scientific knowledge; they may pursue an aim other than either conservation or sustainable exploitation of whale stocks. This is also reflected in the Guidelines issued by the IWC for the review of scientific permit proposals by the Scientific Committee. In particular, the Guidelines initially applicable to JARPA II, Annex Y, referred not only to programmes that "contribute information essential for rational management of the stock" or those that are relevant for "conduct[ing] the comprehensive assessment" of the moratorium on commercial whaling, but also those responding to "other critically important research needs". The current Guidelines, Annex P, list three broad categories of objectives. Besides programmes aimed at "improv[ing] the conservation and management of whale stocks", they envisage programmes which have as an objective to "improve the conservation and management of other living marine resources or the ecosystem of which the whale stocks are an integral part" and those directed at "test[ing] hypotheses not directly related to the management of living marine resources".

C. The issuance of special permits

59. Japan notes that, according to Article VIII, paragraph 1, the State of nationality of the person or entity requesting a special permit for purposes of scientific research is the only State that is competent under the Convention to issue the permit. According to Japan, that State is in the best position to evaluate a programme intended for purposes of scientific research submitted by one of its nationals. In this regard it enjoys discretion, which could be defined as a "margin of appreciation". Japan argues that this discretion is emphasized by the part of the paragraph which specifies that the State of nationality may grant a permit "subject to such restrictions as to number and subject to such other conditions as the Contracting Government thinks fit".

60. According to Australia, while the State of nationality of the requesting entity has been given the power to authorize whaling for purposes of scientific research under Article VIII, this does not imply that the authorizing State has the discretion to determine whether a special permit for the killing, taking and treating of whales falls within the scope of Article VIII, paragraph 1. The requirements for granting a special permit set out in the Convention provide a standard of an objective nature to which the State of nationality has to conform. New Zealand also considers that Article VIII states "an objective requirement", not "something to be determined by the granting Contracting Government".

61. The Court considers that Article VIII gives discretion to a State party to the ICRW to reject the request for a special permit or to specify the conditions under which a permit will be granted. However, whether the killing, taking and treating of whales pursuant to a requested special permit is for purposes of scientific research cannot depend simply on that State's perception.

D. The standard of review

62. The Court now turns to the standard that it will apply in reviewing the grant of a special permit authorizing the killing, taking and treating of whales on the basis of Article VIII, paragraph 1, of the Convention.

* * *

67. When reviewing the grant of a special permit authorizing the killing, taking and treating of whales, the Court will assess, first, whether the programme under which these activities occur involves scientific research. Secondly, the Court will consider if the killing, taking and treating of whales is "for purposes of" scientific research by examining whether, in the use of lethal methods, the programme's design and implementation are reasonable in relation to achieving its stated objectives. This standard of review is an objective one. Relevant elements

of a programme's design and implementation are set forth below (see paragraph 88).

68. In this regard, the Court notes that the dispute before it arises from a decision by a State party to the ICRW to grant special permits under Article VIII of that treaty. Inherent in such a decision is the determination by the State party that the programme's use of lethal methods is for purposes of scientific research. It follows that the Court will look to the authorizing State, which has granted special permits, to explain the objective basis for its determination.

69. The Court observes that, in applying the above standard of review, it is not called upon to resolve matters of scientific or whaling policy. The Court is aware that members of the international community hold divergent views about the appropriate policy towards whales and whaling, but it is not for the Court to settle these differences. The Court's task is only to ascertain whether the special permits granted in relation to JARPA II fall within the scope of Article VIII, paragraph 1, of the ICRW.

E. Meaning of the phrase "for purposes of scientific research"

70. The Parties address two closely related aspects of the interpretation of Article VIII the meaning of the terms "scientific research" and "for purposes of" in the phrase "for purposes of scientific research". Australia analysed the meaning of these terms separately and observed that these two elements are cumulative. Japan did not contest this approach to the analysis of the provision.

71. In the view of the Court, the two elements of the phrase "for purposes of scientific research" are cumulative. As a result, even if a whaling programme involves scientific research, the killing, taking and treating of whales pursuant to such a programme does not fall within Article VIII unless these activities are "for purposes of" scientific research.

* * *

(a) The term "scientific research"

73. At the outset, the Court notes that the term "scientific research" is not defined in the Convention.

* * *

78. As to the use of lethal methods, Australia asserts that Article VIII, paragraph 1, authorizes the granting of special permits to kill, take and treat whales only when non-lethal methods are not available, invoking the views of the experts it called, as well as certain IWC resolutions and Guidelines. For example, Australia refers to Resolution 1986–2 (which recommends that when considering a proposed special permit, a State party should take into account whether "the objectives of the research are not practically and scientifically feasible through non-lethal research

techniques") and to Annex P (which provides that special permit proposals should assess why non-lethal methods or analyses of existing data "have been considered to be insufficient"). Both of these instruments were approved by consensus. Australia also points to Resolution 1995–9, which was not adopted by consensus, and which recommends that the killing of whales "should only be permitted in exceptional circumstances where the questions address critically important issues which cannot be answered by the analysis of existing data and/or use of non-lethal research techniques".

79. Australia claims that IWC resolutions must inform the Court's interpretation of Article VIII because they comprise "subsequent agreement between the parties regarding the interpretation of the treaty" and "subsequent practice in the application of the treaty which establishes the agreement of the parties regarding its interpretation", within the meaning of subparagraphs (a) and (b), respectively, of paragraph 3 of Article 31 of the Vienna Convention on the Law of Treaties.

80. Japan disagrees with the assertion that special permits authorizing lethal methods may be issued under Article VIII only if non-lethal methods are not available, calling attention to the fact that Article VIII authorizes the granting of permits for the killing of whales and thus expressly contemplates lethal methods. . . .

* * *

82. The Court observes that, as a matter of scientific opinion, the experts called by the Parties agreed that lethal methods can have a place in scientific research, while not necessarily agreeing on the conditions for their use. Their conclusions as scientists, however, must be distinguished from the interpretation of the Convention, which is the task of this Court.

83. Article VIII expressly contemplates the use of lethal methods, and the Court is of the view that Australia and New Zealand overstate the legal significance of the recommendatory resolutions and Guidelines on which they rely. First, many IWC resolutions were adopted without the support of all States parties to the Convention and, in particular, without the concurrence of Japan. Thus, such instruments cannot be regarded as subsequent agreement to an interpretation of Article VIII, nor as subsequent practice establishing an agreement of the parties regarding the interpretation of the treaty within the meaning of subparagraphs (a) and (b), respectively, of paragraph (3) of Article 31 of the Vienna Convention on the Law of Treaties.

Secondly, as a matter of substance, the relevant resolutions and Guidelines that have been approved by consensus call upon States parties to take into account whether research objectives can practically and scientifically be achieved by using non-lethal research methods, but they do not establish a requirement that lethal methods be used only when other methods are not available.

* * *

86. Taking into account these observations, the Court is not persuaded that activities must satisfy the four criteria advanced by Australia in order to constitute "scientific research" in the context of Article VIII. As formulated by Australia, these criteria appear largely to reflect what one of the experts that it called regards as well-conceived scientific research, rather than serving as an interpretation of the term as used in the Convention. Nor does the Court consider it necessary to devise alternative criteria or to offer a general definition of "scientific research".

(b) The meaning of the term "for purposes of" in Article VIII, paragraph 1

87. The Court turns next to the second element of the phrase "for purposes of scientific research", namely the meaning of the term "for purposes of".

88. The stated research objectives of a programme are the foundation of a programme's design, but the Court need not pass judgment on the scientific merit or importance of those objectives in order to assess the purpose of the killing of whales under such a programme. Nor is it for the Court to decide whether the design and implementation of a programme are the best possible means of achieving its stated objectives.

In order to ascertain whether a programme's use of lethal methods is for purposes of scientific research, the Court will consider whether the elements of a programme's design and implementation are reasonable in relation to its stated scientific objectives (see paragraph 67 above). As shown by the arguments of the Parties, such elements may include: decisions regarding the use of lethal methods; the scale of the programme's use of lethal sampling; the methodology used to select sample sizes; a comparison of the target sample sizes and the actual take; the time frame associated with a programme; the programme's scientific output; and the degree to which a programme co-ordinates its activities with related research projects (see paragraphs 129–132; 149; 158–159; 203–205; 214–222 below).

* * *

94. As the Parties and the intervening State accept, Article VIII, paragraph 2, permits the processing and sale of whale meat incidental to the killing of whales pursuant to the grant of a special permit under Article VIII, paragraph 1.

In the Court's view, the fact that a programme involves the sale of whale meat and the use of proceeds to fund research is not sufficient, taken alone, to cause a special permit to fall outside Article VIII. Other elements would have to be examined, such as the scale of a programme's use of lethal sampling, which might suggest that the whaling is for purposes other than scientific research. In particular, a State party may not, in order to fund the research for which a special permit has been granted, use lethal sampling on a greater scale than is otherwise reasonable in relation to achieving the programme's stated objectives.

95. Secondly, Australia asserts that a State's pursuit of goals that extend beyond scientific objectives would demonstrate that a special permit granted in respect of such a programme does not fall within Article VIII. In Australia's view, for example, the pursuit of policy goals such as providing employment or maintaining a whaling infrastructure would indicate that the killing of whales is not for purposes of scientific research.

* * *

97. The Court observes that a State often seeks to accomplish more than one goal when it pursues a particular policy. Moreover, an objective test of whether a programme is for purposes of scientific research does not turn on the intentions of individual government officials, but rather on whether the design and implementation of a programme are reasonable in relation to achieving the stated research objectives. Accordingly, the Court considers that whether particular government officials may have motivations that go beyond scientific research does not preclude a conclusion that a programme is for purposes of scientific research within the meaning of Article VIII. At the same time, such motivations cannot justify the granting of a special permit for a programme that uses lethal sampling on a larger scale than is reasonable in relation to achieving the programme's stated research objectives. The research objectives alone must be sufficient to justify the programme as designed and implemented.

3. JARPA II in light of Article VIII of the Convention

98. The Court will now apply the approach set forth in the preceding section to enquire into whether, based on the evidence, the design and implementation of JARPA II are reasonable in relation to achieving its stated objectives.

* * *

(i) Research objectives

113. The JARPA II Research Plan identifies four research objectives: (1) Monitoring of the Antarctic ecosystem; (2) Modelling competition among whale species and future management objectives; (3) Elucidation of temporal and spatial changes in stock structure; and (4) Improving the management procedure for Antarctic minke whale stocks.

* * *

B. Whether the design and implementation of JARPA II are reasonable in relation to achieving the programme's stated research objectives

127. The Court observes that the JARPA II Research Plan describes areas of inquiry that correspond to four research objectives and presents a programme of activities that involves the systematic collection and analysis of data by scientific personnel. The research objectives come within the research categories identified by the Scientific Committee in Annexes Y and P (see paragraph 58 above). Based on the information before it, the Court thus finds that the JARPA II activities involving the lethal sampling of whales can broadly be characterized as "scientific research". There is no need therefore, in the context of this case, to examine generally the concept of "scientific research". Accordingly, the Court's examination of the evidence with respect to JARPA II will focus on whether the killing, taking and treating of whales in pursuance of JARPA II is for purposes of scientific research and thus may be authorized by special permits granted under Article VIII, paragraph 1, of the Convention. To this end and in light of the applicable standard of review (see paragraph 67 above), the Court will examine whether the design and implementation of JARPA II are reasonable in relation to achieving the programme's stated research objectives, taking into account the elements identified above (see paragraph 88).

(a) Japan's decisions regarding the use of lethal methods

* * *

135. Taking into account the evidence indicating that non-lethal alternatives are not feasible, at least for the collection of certain data, and given that the value and reliability of such data are a matter of scientific opinion, the Court finds no basis to conclude that the use of lethal methods is per se unreasonable in the context of JARPA II. Instead, it is necessary to look more closely at the details of Japan's decisions regarding the use of lethal methods in JARPA II, discussed immediately below, and the scale of their use in the programme, to which the Court will turn at paragraph 145 below.

* * *

(iii) Comparison of sample size to actual take

199. There is a significant gap between the JARPA II target sample sizes and the actual number of whales that have been killed in the implementation of the programme. The Parties disagree as to the reasons for this gap and the conclusions that the Court should draw from it.

200. The Court recalls that, for both fin whales and humpback whales, the target sample size is 50 whales, following a two-year feasibility study

during which the target for humpback whales was zero and the target for fin whales was ten.

201. As to actual take, the evidence before the Court indicates that a total of 18 fin whales have been killed over the first seven seasons of JARPA II, including ten fin whales during the programme's first year when the feasibility of taking larger whales was under study. In subsequent years, zero to three fin whales have been taken annually. No humpback whales have been killed under JARPA II. Japan recounts that after deciding initially not to sample humpback whales during the first two years of JARPA II, it "suspended" the sampling of humpback whales as of 2007. The Court observes, however, that the permits issued for JARPA II since 2007 continue to authorize the take of humpback whales.

202. Notwithstanding the target sample size for minke whales of 850 (plus or minus 10 per cent), the actual take of minke whales under JARPA II has fluctuated from year to year. During the 2005–2006 season, Japan caught 853 minke whales, a number within the targeted range. Actual take has fallen short of the JARPA II sample size target in all subsequent years. On average, approximately 450 minke whales have been killed in each year. The evidence before the Court indicates that 170 minke whales were killed in the 2010–2011 season and that 103 minke whales were killed in the 2012–2013 season.

203. As to the reasons for the gap between target sample sizes and actual take, Japan states that it decided not to take any humpback whales in response to a request by the then-Chair of the IWC. With respect to fin whales, Japan points to sabotage activities by anti-whaling non-governmental organizations, noting in particular the Sea Shepherd Conservation Society, and to the inability of the main JARPA II research vessel, the Nisshin Maru, to pull on board larger whales. As to minke whales, Japan offers two reasons that actual sample sizes have been smaller than targets: a fire on board the Nisshin Maru in the 2006–2007 season and the aforementioned sabotage activities.

* * *

(d) Conclusion regarding the application of Article VIII, paragraph 1, to JARPA II

223. In light of the standard of review set forth above (see paragraph 67), and having considered the evidence with regard to the design and implementation of JARPA II and the arguments of the Parties, it is now for the Court to conclude whether the killing, taking and treating of whales under the special permits granted in connection with JARPA II is "for purposes of scientific research" under Article VIII of the Convention.

224. The Court finds that the use of lethal sampling per se is not unreasonable in relation to the research objectives of JARPA II. However,

as compared to JARPA, the scale of lethal sampling in JARPA II is far more extensive with regard to Antarctic minke whales, and the programme includes the lethal sampling of two additional whale species. Japan states that this expansion is required by the new research objectives of JARPA II, in particular, the objectives relating to ecosystem research and the construction of a model of multi-species competition. In the view of the Court, however, the target sample sizes in JARPA II are not reasonable in relation to achieving the programme's objectives.

225. First, the broad objectives of JARPA and JARPA II overlap considerably. To the extent that the objectives are different, the evidence does not reveal how those differences lead to the considerable increase in the scale of lethal sampling in the JARPA II Research Plan. Secondly, the sample sizes for fin and humpback whales are too small to provide the information that is necessary to pursue the JARPA II research objectives based on Japan's own calculations, and the programme's design appears to prevent random sampling of fin whales. Thirdly, the process used to determine the sample size for minke whales lacks transparency, as the experts called by each of the Parties agreed. In particular, the Court notes the absence of complete explanations in the JARPA II Research Plan for the underlying decisions that led to setting the sample size at 850 minke whales (plus or minus 10 per cent) each year. Fourthly, some evidence suggests that the programme could have been adjusted to achieve a far smaller sample size, and Japan does not explain why this was not done. The evidence before the Court further suggests that little attention was given to the possibility of using non-lethal research methods more extensively to achieve the JARPA II objectives and that funding considerations, rather than strictly scientific criteria, played a role in the programme's design.

226. These problems with the design of JARPA II must also be considered in light of its implementation. First, no humpback whales have been taken, and Japan cites non-scientific reasons for this. Secondly, the take of fin whales is only a small fraction of the number that the JARPA II Research Plan prescribes. Thirdly, the actual take of minke whales has also been far lower than the annual target sample size in all but one season. Despite these gaps between the Research Plan and the programme's implementation, Japan has maintained its reliance on the JARPA II research objectives—most notably, ecosystem research and the goal of constructing a model of multi-species competition—to justify both the use and extent of lethal sampling prescribed by the JARPA II Research Plan for all three species. Neither JARPA II's objectives nor its methods have been revised or adapted to take account of the actual number of whales taken. Nor has Japan explained how those research objectives remain viable given the decision to use six-year and 12-year research periods for different species, coupled with the apparent decision to abandon the lethal

sampling of humpback whales entirely and to take very few fin whales. Other aspects of JARPA II also cast doubt on its characterization as a programme for purposes of scientific research, such as its open-ended time frame, its limited scientific output to date, and the absence of significant co-operation between JARPA II and other related research projects.

227. Taken as a whole, the Court considers that JARPA II involves activities that can broadly be characterized as scientific research (see paragraph 127 above), but that the evidence does not establish that the programme's design and implementation are reasonable in relation to achieving its stated objectives. The Court concludes that the special permits granted by Japan for the killing, taking and treating of whales in connection with JARPA II are not "for purposes of scientific research" pursuant to Article VIII, paragraph 1, of the Convention.

DISSENTING OPINION OF JUDGE BENNOUNA

To my great regret, I have had to vote against points 2, 3, 4, 5 and 7 of the Judgment's operative paragraph, since I do not agree with the majority's interpretation of the relevant provisions of the International Convention for the Regulation of Whaling of 2 December 1946 (hereinafter the "Convention") and of the Schedule annexed thereto (hereinafter the "Schedule").

I regret, in particular, that the majority has failed to adhere to the methods of interpretation envisaged by the Vienna Convention on the Law of Treaties (Arts. 31 and 32), which have the status of customary law, and has consequently failed to confine itself to a strictly legal analysis of the Parties' obligations. I know that the issue of whaling is one that carries a heavy emotional and cultural charge, nourished over the centuries by literature, mythology and religious writings. This background was indeed evoked before the Court, but the judges, while they cannot ignore it, are bound, by virtue of their function, to ensure that it does not impinge in any way on their strictly legal analysis. The best way for the Court to contribute to the promotion of co-operation between the States concerned is to do justice by applying international law, in accordance with its Statute.

Unfortunately, the approach adopted by the majority remains somewhat "impressionistic", inasmuch as it rests essentially on queries, doubts and suspicions, based on a selection of indicators from among the mass of reports and scientific studies.

The Convention was adopted in 1946, in a context very different from that in which the Court is called upon to interpret and apply it today. The consumption of whale meat has fallen dramatically, so as to have become negligible, and the whaling industry has declined accordingly. The fact nonetheless remains that, when interpreting a provision of the Convention, the Court is bound to take account of the objectives set out in its preamble, in particular the conservation and sustainable development of whale stocks. The Court cannot content itself with stating that "neither a restrictive nor an expansive interpretation of Article VIII is justified", and that programmes for purposes of scientific research "may pursue an aim other than either conservation or sustainable exploitation of whale stocks" (Judgment, paragraph 58). But we are not concerned here with the issue of whether the interpretation should be "restrictive" or "expansive", but rather with determining "the ordinary meaning to be given to the terms of the treaty in their context and in the light of its object and purpose" (Vienna Convention, Art. 31, para. 1).

What the Court has to do is to confront Article VIII, as an integral part of the Convention, with the latter's object and purpose, and to ask itself whether, in light of its ordinary meaning, the research programme, in this case JARPA II, is fully covered by this provision.

Furthermore, Article VIII must be analysed in the context of the other provisions of the Convention and of its Schedule, as amended since its adoption. Under that article, any State party may "grant to any of its nationals a special permit authorizing that national to kill, take and treat whales for purposes of scientific research", subject to such conditions as it "thinks fit". In so doing, the State in question is not required to comply with the other provisions of the Convention, in particular those relating to commercial whaling. At the time when the Convention was adopted, the only concern was to regulate and not to prohibit this category of whaling. And it was for that reason that the power given to a State party to grant permits "for scientific research" was a very wide one, since commercial whaling was regulated by the Convention and subject to compliance with the latter's objectives. As long as it remained within the framework of scientific research, the Government concerned was free to decide on the use to be made of the proceeds from the sale of killed and processed whales. It is implicit that any proceeds from the sale of such whales must be allocated to the objective of scientific research, which lies at the heart of Article VIII, and which justifies the exemption of the State party concerned from all of the other obligations relating to the regulation of commercial whaling.

* * *

The wide normative power which Article VIII . . . gives to States parties in issuing permits is offset by the supervision exercised by the central body established by the Convention, namely the International Whaling Commission (Convention, Art. III) (hereinafter the "Commission"), assisted by the Scientific Committee. Thus, under the terms of paragraph 3 of Article VIII, the State concerned "shall transmit to such body as may be designated by the Commission, in so far as practicable, and at intervals of not more than one year, scientific information available to that Government with respect to whales and whaling, including the results of research conducted pursuant to paragraph 1 of this Article and to Article IV".

The Judgment recognizes that Japan has complied with its procedural obligations in relation to the Commission and to the Scientific Committee, in particular by submitting proposals of special permits prior to their grant, as required under paragraph 30 of the Schedule.

* * *

The Court begins by declining to establish a definition of the notion of "scientific research", of which there is not one in the Convention. As regards the definition proposed by the experts, the Court considers that it is not applicable in the present case (Judgment, paragraph 86). However, immediately afterwards, the Court undertakes an analysis of the meaning of the phrase "for purposes of scientific research" (Judgment, paragraph 87), which might be regarded as something of a paradox. In effect, the Court seeks to determine the purpose of a given activity without having first clarified what that activity consists of. This is a perilous exercise, all the more so since what it turns out to consist in is a discussion of whether the design and implementation of the programme "are reasonable in relation to its stated scientific objectives" (Judgment, paragraph 88).

It becomes apparent, reading the Court's subsequent reasoning, that in reality it fails to apply the test of correspondence between the programme's objectives, on the one hand, and its design and implementation on the other. Thus the Judgment (in paragraphs 135 to 156) essentially undertakes a comparison between JARPA and JARPA II, in order to conclude that the latter has not been conducted "for purposes of scientific research". And this is said to be because the programme has utilized lethal methods, when it could have had greater recourse to non-lethal methods. However, nowhere does the majority demonstrate the existence of a requirement on the State concerned to give priority to non-lethal methods in the conduct of scientific research.

The Court seeks to remedy the lack of such an obligation by invoking (Judgment, paragraph 144) the inadequacy of Japan's analysis of non-lethal methods, and its failure to give due regard to IWC resolutions and Guidelines, despite the fact that, by their nature, these are not binding upon that State. We may well ask ourselves how a legal obligation can derive from the inadequacy of an analysis, or from a failure to have regard to acts of international bodies which carry no normative force in relation to those to whom they are addressed.

In my view, a State is perfectly entitled, for purposes of scientific research, to eschew the use of non-lethal methods if it considers them too costly and, if need be, to fund the costs of research out of the proceeds from the sale of the whales taken and processed.

* * *

I would add that the position taken by the majority is not only unfounded in law, but has failed to take account of the spirit of the Convention, which aims at strengthening co-operation between States parties for the purposes of managing a shared resource. The Commission and the Scientific Committee play a key role in this regard. In particular, they are required to conduct periodic examinations of the special permits granted by States parties and to comment thereon, including on aspects which might be improved. Moreover, they performed this task in relation to JARPA, as is shown by the list of resolutions adopted by the Commission. As things stand at present, JARPA II underwent a prior examination in 2005, and its periodic examination is currently under way. The results are due to be published shortly. In other words, neither the Commission nor the Scientific Committee has yet had the opportunity to pass judgement on the implementation of JARPA II. In engaging in an evaluation of the programme, the Court has, in a sense, substituted itself for these two bodies.

In order to strengthen the object and purpose of the Convention, it is clearly desirable that States parties should act within the institutional framework established by the latter. That would probably be the best way of strengthening multilateral co-operation between States parties in defence of their common interest—as the preamble to the Convention emphasizes—and of enabling them to arrive at an authentic interpretation of the Convention.

(Other dissenting and concurring opinions omitted.)

DISCUSSION NOTES/QUESTIONS ON THE CASE

1. The early portion of the opinion deals with the issue of the Court's jurisdiction. This is particularly important to study because it is an issue that comes up in many ICJ judgments. Both Australia and Japan had made declarations under the optional clause, when accepting the jurisdiction of the Court under Article 36(2) of the Statute of the ICJ **(Basic Document 1.2)**. One state party before the court can take advantage of the exceptions of the other party contained in the declaration of its acceptance of the Court's jurisdiction. Such arguments can be highly complex and often international adjudication deals with complicated issues of jurisdiction before the substance. Do you agree with the Court's resolution of the issue?

2. There is important scientific analysis in this judgment, yet the court says it is not deciding matters of science. Is this convincing? Environmental cases frequently involve disputed issues of science. How should international adjudicators deal with such issues. Should the state parties to the litigation call scientific evidence before the court or should the court commission its own

scientific experts? Could scientists be appointed to sit with the Judges in appropriate cases?

3. Did the Court apply a proper approach to the science involved in this case? Consider this conclusion:[121]

> While the ICJ ultimately found in favour of Australia, it did so in a relatively cautious way, largely avoiding some of the more fundamental questions about legal-scientific obligations. In particular the Court sidestepped defining 'scientific research' or 'science' for the purposes of treaty law while implicitly applying selective scientific criteria to determine legal legitimacy. Hence, while the decision marks a move towards more rigour and rationality in the application of legal-scientific obligations, there is some cause to question just how broadly it has advanced international treaty law in this area.

Do you think there is merit in this statement?

4. Can the judgment be regarded as a victory for environmental conservation efforts for whales?

5. How strong do you think the dissent is?

6. How would you advise the Japanese Government in light of the decision? Should they stop whaling in the Southern Ocean or can they continue consistent with the judgment?

7. Japanese scholars have subjected the judgment to criticism. In a Symposium in Kobe, including overseas and Japanese scholars, some of the Japanese scholars were disposed to take a negative view of the ICJ judgment, to criticise its reasoning and question the treaty interpretation. The judgment was said to be "a challenge for international law scholars . . . because of its laconic legal reasoning . . . ."[122] Criticisms were made of "clever" litigation "tactics" in relation to New Zealand's decision to intervene formally rather than as a party, which meant Australia was not deprived of an ad hoc Judge as would have occurred had it become a full party to the litigation given that New Zealand had a judge on the ICJ, Judge Keith, who was a permanent member of the Court.[123] It was also said that there was hidden "anti-whaling sentiment in the Court,"[124] and that it was "policy-oriented litigation by the anti-whaling countries of Australia and New Zealand."[125] Is this fair criticism and why?

---

[121] Brendan Gogarty, *Conceptions and (Mis)conceptions of Science in International Treaties; the ICJ Whaling Case in Context*, 7 Y.B. of Polar L. 607, 622 (2015).

[122] Akiho Shibata, *ICRW as an Evolving Instrument: Potential Broader Implications of the Whaling Judgment*, Jap. Y.B. Int'l L. 298, 298 (2015).

[123] Shigeki Sakamoto, *ICJ Judgment in the Antarctic: Its significance and Implications—The Whaling in the Antarctic from a Japanese Perspective*, 58 Jap. Y.B. Int'l L. 247, 249 (2015).

[124] Id. at 251.

[125] Id. at 271.

You may wish to examine Penelope Ridings, *The Intervention Procedure in Whaling in the Antarctic: A Threat to Bilateralism?*, 32 Austl. Y.B. Int'l L. 97 (2015).

Aftermath of the Case

The decision of the ICJ in the case, announced on 31 March 2014, gave hope to those nations that oppose whaling. In addition, the judgment contained surprisingly good news not only for the whales, but also for international environmental law in general.[126] The decision was in many ways remarkable and may presage a new approach for the Court in such cases. It is an approach reminiscent of strict-scrutiny judicial review in domestic law rather than the traditional deference to states that has been the more usual stance of the ICJ when applying international law. In this case the Court showed essentially no deference to Japan at all, in Japan's first-ever case before the Court.

The decision exhibits substantial judicial statecraft. While finding against Japan, the Court deliberately fell short of finding that its whaling had no scientific character and was purely "commercial" rather than "scientific." The width of Article VIII is remarkable and if interpreted broadly has the capacity to render the rest of the Convention nugatory. If all nations that belong to the IWC used Article VIII to take unlimited numbers of whales, no regulation would exist. Japan argued for such an interpretation, telling the Court that Article VIII was an exemption from the Convention that gave a large "margin of appreciation" to states.

In its construction of Article VIII, the Court declined to apply either a restrictive or expansive interpretation to Article VIII. It made the point, however, that Article VIII was not an exemption from the Convention, but an "integral part" of it that had to be interpreted consistently with the Convention's other provisions. It held that the two elements of the phrase "for purposes of scientific research" were cumulative. Thus "even if a whaling program involves scientific research, the killing, taking and treating of whales pursuant to such a program does not fall within Article VIII unless these activities are 'for the purposes' of scientific research."[127] The essence of the Court's determination was that the special permits fell outside Article VIII because they were not "for the purposes of scientific research" as that article required.[128]

There was science in Japan's program but there were other features as well, indicating mixed motivations—although that was not necessarily

[126] Whaling in the Antarctic (Austl. v. Japan: N.Z. intervening) Judgment, 2014 I.C.J. 226 (Mar. 31), (hereinafter referred to as "Judgment").

[127] Id. at [72].

[128] The court's decision is carefully dissected by two of New Zealand's counsel in Elana Geddis and Penelope Ridings, *Whaling in the Antarctic: Some Reflections by Counsel*, (2013) 11 N.Z. Y.B. Int'l L. 143.

fatal. An assessment of whether whaling is "for purposes of scientific research," said the Court, does not turn on the intentions of individual government officials but "rather on whether the design and implementation of a program are reasonable in relation to achieving the stated research objectives."[129] That in turn depends upon the standard of review to be adopted.

On the standard of review, the court held the test was an objective one, taking into account elements of the program's design and implementation such as the scale of lethal sampling, the timeframe of the program, and its scientific output.[130] Research objectives alone must be sufficient to justify the program as designed and implemented.[131] The Court was clear that it would look to the state that had issued a scientific permit under Article VIII to "explain the objective basis for its determination"[132]—essentially placing the onus on Japan.

The standard of review applied by the Court is demanding and rigorous. If applied to the multitude of multilateral international environmental conventions in existence, the wiggle room for states that they have traditionally thought they enjoy will be curtailed. Scientists, environmentalists, and NGOs will be greatly encouraged by this decision.

The Court subjected JARPA II to close scrutiny and found it wanting. The reasons that led the Court to hold that the programme was not "for the purposes of" scientific research lay in Japan's failure to provide adequate scientific analysis to the Court on critical elements. The lengthy and technical scientific arguments will be summarized only. They turned on an assessment of the design and implementation of JARPA II in light of its stated objectives.

The four objectives of JARPA II were to:

- Monitor elements of the Antarctic ecosystem (e.g., whale abundance, prey density, the effects of contaminants on cetaceans, and cetacean habitat),
- Model competition among whale species and the impact on future management objectives, including exploring the krill hypothesis and why some species of whale had increased and others decreased.
- Study stock structures and shifts in stock boundaries.

[129] Whaling in the Antarctic (Austl. v. Japan: N.Z. intervening) (Judgment), 2014 I.C.J. 226, [97] (Mar. 31).

[130] Id. at [67] and [97].

[131] Id. at [97].

[132] Id. at [68].

- Explore improvements to the management procedure for Antarctic minke whales.

The court accepted that those objectives were broadly speaking "scientific" but found that the design and implementation of JARPA II were not reasonable to achieve them. The main deficiencies lay in two areas: the use of lethal methods for research and the sample size.

In relation to the decision to use lethal methods for research when other means were available for many elements of the programme, Japan provided no scientific evidence to the Court about the feasibility of non-lethal methods or that it had seriously considered the issue. The Court was impressed by the fact that smaller takes of minke whales may have been possible if non-lethal research methods were employed.

In considering the sample sizes, the Court proceeded to compare JARPA with JARPA II, much to the detriment of the latter. The issue was whether the increased sample sizes were "reasonable" to achieve the research objectives. The court found that they were not for a number of reasons. There was no substantial difference between the research objectives of JARPA and JARPA II to justify the increase. Japan had set the JARPA II sample sizes before a review of the JARPA programme had been completed, lending support to the view that the sample sizes were not driven by science. The Court was particularly unconvinced by the evidence about the sample sizes for fin and humpback whales. Japan's scientific expert from Norway conceded that statistically relevant information would not be secured from the sample sizes adopted for these species. On the minke sample size, the Court held that the evidence provided scant analysis and justification for the underlying decisions to generate the overall sample size. Further, there were significant gaps between the target samples and actual numbers of whales killed—suggesting that the target samples were larger than required to meet the objectives of the programme. The Court concluded there were doubts whether the target sample of 50 fin and humpback whales and 850 minke whales was reasonable in relation to achieving the stated goals.

The Court also commented on JARPA II's open-ended timeframe, the lack of cooperation between this and other research programmes, and the very low number of scientific publications resulting from Japan's "research." Taking all of the evidence together, the Court found that JARPA II was not conducted "for purposes of scientific research". It did not fall within the provisions of Article VIII, so Japan's whaling activities were regulated by the ordinary rules of the Schedule to the Convention—including the whaling moratorium.

Winning on the Issue and Losing on the Substance

This case amounted to a comprehensive, and unexpected, forensic defeat for Japan. The legal theories available at international law to attack Japan's whaling program, such as abuse of right, were problematic. Usual methods of treaty interpretation could have easily led to a different conclusion. Many believed that Australia had no chance of a victory. Many were surprised and delighted when that view turned out to be wrong.[133]

In the immediate aftermath of the decision, Japan appeared willing to comply. It revamped its research whaling program and presented a new plan in November 2014 to the IWC for taking 333 minke whales in the Southern Ocean from the 2015–2016 season onwards for 12 years.[134] But its new plan met with a somewhat hostile reaction from the expert panel established to review its proposals,[135] a reaction that was mirrored by the Scientific Committee when it reviewed the expert panel's analysis. Making matters worse from Japan's perspective, the biennial meeting of the IWC in September 2014 had passed a resolution recommending that no new special permits for the taking of whales should be issued until the Scientific Community had reviewed the proposals and determined that lethal methods were necessary to achieving the research objectives.[136]

---

[133] Geoffrey Palmer, *A Victory for the Whales*, N.Z. L. J. 124 (2014).

[134] This new proposal, NEWRWP-A, was discussed by the Second Sydney Panel of Independent Experts "Summary of Findings: Second Sydney Panel of Independent Experts—the conformity with international law of Japan's proposed scientific whaling in the Antarctic Ocean ("NEWREP-A")" (paper published following Second Sydney Panel of Independent Experts, Sydney, November 2015).

[135] International Whaling Commission *Report of the Expert Panel to review the proposal by Japan for NEWREP-A, 7–10* SC/66A/REP/6 (February 2015, Tokyo).

[136] The operative portions of the first part of the IWC Resolution 201405 are as follows:

> 1. Instructs the Scientific Committee, in its review of new and existing special permit research programmes, to provide advice to the Commission on: whether the design and implementation of the programme, including sample sizes, are reasonable in relation to achieving the programme's stated research objectives;
>
> (a) whether the elements of the research that rely on lethally obtained data are likely to lead to improvements in the conservation and management of whales;
>
> (b) whether the objectives of the research could be achieved by non-lethal means or whether there are reasonably equivalent objectives that could be achieved non-lethally;
>
> (c) whether the scale of lethal sampling is reasonable in relation to the programme's stated research objectives, and non-lethal alternatives are not feasible to either replace or reduce the scale of lethal sampling proposed; and
>
> (d) such other matters as the Scientific Committee considers relevant to the programme, having regard to the decision of the International Court of Justice, including the methodology used to select sample sizes, a comparison of the target sample sizes and the actual take, the timeframe associated with a programme, the programme's scientific output; and the degree to which a programme coordinates its activities with related research projects.

The resolution went on request that no further special permits for the take of whales are issued under existing research programmes until the Scientific Committee had reviewed the research programme.

Ultimately, however, Australia's apparent victory before the ICJ evaporated. In October 2015, apparently in response to the IWC's pushback against its new research program, Japan filed a new declaration concerning its acceptance of the compulsory jurisdiction of the ICJ. The purpose of the new declaration was to ensure that Japan's research whaling activities could not in the future be challenged in that court. Thus, the new declaration excludes from the Court's jurisdiction "any dispute arising out of, concerning, or relating to research on, or conservation, management or exploitation of, living resources of the sea."[137]

Worse, on December 26, 2018, Japan notified the United States (as depositary) of Japan's complete withdrawal from the International Convention for the Regulation of Whaling, effective as of June 30, 2019.[138] As of mid-2019, Japan will be able to whale without regard to the IWC moratorium and without facing any obligation to report its activities to the IWC. Indeed, on July 1, 2019, Japan authorized its whalers to resume commercial whaling in its exclusive economic zone. While Japan has announced that it plans, for now, to whale only within its EEZ,[139] such whaling in the North Pacific may, in fact, threaten populations of whales that are less abundant and less resilient than those of the Southern Ocean. And, of course, there is no guarantee that Japan will ultimately confine its whaling to its coastal regions.

The future of the IWC, and the future of the whales, remain very much in doubt.

DISCUSSION NOTES/QUESTIONS

1. Japan has threatened for years to set up a rival organization of nations to support sustainable whaling. Do you think it is likely to do so now that it has left the IWC? What will that mean for the IWC? Could the IWC enforce its ban on whaling in the Southern Ocean against Japan or any other non-IWC member?

2. What lesson do you draw from the current situation? Was litigation an appropriate diplomatic strategy or did it simply ensure that no compromise would ever be reached? Consider the following observation by an experienced international lawyer and a former member of the International Law Commission, Bill Mansfield:[140]

---

[137] International Court of Justice "Declarations Recognizing the Jurisdiction of the Court as Compulsory" (6 October 2015) www.icj-cij.org.

[138] *See* United States State Department, Status of International Convention for the Regulation of Whaling, note 4, https://www.state.gov/documents/organization/191051.pdf (last visited January 31, 2019).

[139] *See* Linda Sieg, et al., *Japan to resume commercial whaling after pulling out of IWC*, Reuters, Dec. 26, 2018.

[140] Bill Mansfield, *Peaceful Settlement of International Disputes: Litigation or Negotiation—Some Practical Considerations*, 14(2) Otago L. Rev. 1 (2016).

> A key question that did not seem to receive much consideration [before the case was filed], at least in the media, was whether the initiation of litigation would make it more or less difficult politically for the Japanese Government to forego or significantly reduce its scientific programme. I, for one, argued publicly that taking a case to the ICJ would not only be ineffective, it would be counterproductive. My main argument was that, at the time, the economics and the politics surrounding the Japanese whaling programme were not working in favour of the Japanese Fisheries Agency (JFA) and the interests it represented and reflected. Therefore the diplomatic negotiations aimed at finding some form of phase-out solution had a reasonably good prospect of bringing an eventual end to whaling in the southern ocean, albeit not as quickly as many would have liked.

A basic point to be considered when deciding to litigate in the international arena is to consider wider strategic considerations, the strength of the legal case being only one factor to be weighed. Here is what Bill Mansfield says on that issue:

> [B]efore deciding on state-to-state litigation as the preferred course, some of the questions that can usefully be asked include the following:
>
> (a) will the introduction of legal principle and legal argument into the dispute help or hinder its resolution?
>
> (b) will the issuing of proceedings help or hinder at this particular point in time?
>
> (c) will the nature of the decision sought, and its timing, contribute to the resolution of the dispute?
>
> (d) if some other states, or the wider international community, have an interest in the substantive matters at issue will the proceedings contribute to an outcome that takes account of that interest and attracts their support?
>
> (e) will the proceedings and the outcome mean the parties are better equipped to resolve future issues that arise in the same context?
>
> (f) will the parties be more or less disposed to use third party assistance in resolving future difficulties?

3. Following Japan's decision to restrict its acceptance of the ICJ's jurisdiction, legal experts, some of whom had been instrumental in persuading Australia to bring its case, met in November 2015 in Sydney to review what could be done.[141] The group took the view that Japan's new research programme was not reasonable and not consistent with Japan's international

[141] Second Sydney Panel of Independent Experts "Summary of Findings: Second Sydney Panel of Independent Experts—the conformity with international law of Japan's proposed scientific whaling in the Antarctic Ocean ("NEWREP-A")" (paper published following Second Sydney Panel of Independent Experts, Sydney, November 2015).

obligations. They suggested that it may be possible to argue that if Japan proceeded with the programme—as it did—that Japan may be in breach of some provisions of the United Nations Convention on the Law of the Sea.

The possibility that Japan may be held in violation of UNCLOS seems unrealistic and remote. And, now that Japan has withdrawn from the IWRC, it would seem that any legal claims against it must rest on the UNCLOS provisions about marine mammals, which are vague and general. In addition, those provisions seem to contemplate that the IWC is the regulator, which might permit an argument that IWC regulations apply even to non-party states. But that argument is unlikely to succeed.

In light of Japan's new reservation to the ICJ's jurisdiction, future cases on whaling by Japan before the Court will be difficult from a practical point of view and impossible in most circumstances. In light of its withdrawal from the IWC, the legal constraints on its conduct are much diminished. Furthermore, the authors can detect no willingness on the part of the two governments most closely involved—Australia and New Zealand—to resume litigious activity on the issue. It would seem that diplomacy is now the only option?

4. What does the outcome of the case say about Japan's commitment to international law and, more broadly, about the ability to maintain and develop a rule-based international order?

Japan began to encounter international law after the expedition of Commodore Matthew Perry in 1854.[142] There had been a suspicion, naturally enough, that international law might be a scheme to favor western nations and unequal treaty relations. But Japan began to interact much more with other nations and accepted international law without questioning its legitimacy. Japan adhered to the international rules of war in the Sino-Japanese war of 1894–95, and has had a Japanese Association of International Law since 1897.[143] After the First World War, Japan became a member of the League of Nations and Judge Oda of Japan was elected to the first panel of Judges of the Permanent Court of International Justice.

Obviously, when Japan later left the League and embarked upon an imperial programme founded on the use of force, Japan deviated from international legal norms in a major way. It turned over a new leaf after the Second World War and was accepted as a member of the United Nations in 1956. Two years later, Japan accepted with little qualification the jurisdiction of the International Court of Justice "as compulsory *ipso facto*."

Japanese judges have sat on the ICJ between 1961 and 1970 and from 1976 to the present. Running through Japanese professional legal thought has been "a positive attitude to international adjudication."[144]

---

[142] Kanae Taijudo, *Some reflections on Japan's practice of international law during a dozen eventful decades*, 69 Am. Soc. Int'l L. Proc. 64 (1975).

[143] Id. at 67.

[144] Kanae Taijudo, *Some reflections on Japan's practice of international law during a dozen eventful decades*, 69 Am. Soc. Int'l L. Proc. 64, 68 (1975).

The issue arises how deep and how sincere the commitment to international legal norms on the part of Japan is when it withdraws its acceptance of the Court's jurisdiction on the subject matter of a case that it lost—its first case before the Court. If a matter as relatively trivial in geopolitical terms as whaling cannot be settled by adjudication, one might wonder what matters can be. On 29 September 2015, Japan's Prime Minister told the General Assembly in the general debate that:[145]

> The Rule of Law and the principles of equality before the law are values Japan respects more highly than anything else.

One week later, on 6 October, his Government deposited its new declaration limiting its acceptance of ICJ jurisdiction.

On the other hand, Japan continues to advocate for the ICJ. The Permanent Representative of Japan on 15 February 2016 in a debate at the UN strongly advocated more use of the Court by nations and encouraged them to accept its compulsory jurisdiction:[146]

> The ICJ has played a constructive role in the field of peaceful settlement of international disputes for seven decades by resolving 150 cases. In this context, I wish to repeat the plea of my government that more Member States accept the compulsory jurisdiction of the International Court of Justice.

The contrast between the actions of Japan in relation to the whaling case and its rhetorical support for the Court is difficult to reconcile.[147] Either Japan believes in the rule of international law, or it does not. Japan was unwilling to comply with the ICJ's judgment in the Whaling Case because Japan could not defend the number of whales it intended to take on a proper scientific basis in conformity with the sampling issues and the non-lethal issues outlined in the judgment. Its whaling programme in the Northern Pacific (JARPN II) was also vulnerable to challenge.

5. The irony of this story is that Japan had offered something better (for the whales) at the IWC negotiations in 2009–2010. All this litigation and anti-rule-of-law fallout could likely have been avoided, and IWC control over the number of whales killed could have been secured, had Australia not campaigned so vigorously to prevent a compromise. In retrospect, would

[145] Statement by His Excellency Shinzo Abe, Prime Minister of Japan, at the 70th Session of the UN General Assembly (Sept. 29, 2015).

[146] Statement by His Honorable Motohide Yoshikawa, Permanent Representative to the United Nations, at the Security Council Ministerial Open Debate on "the Respect of the Principles and Purposes of the Charter of the United Nations as Key Elements for the Maintenance of International Peace and Security" (Febr. 15, 2016).

[147] Japan has suggested that it is prepared to accept the jurisdiction of the International Tribunal of the Law of the Sea (ITLOS) on whaling disputes. Articles 64, 65 and 119 and 120 of UNCLOS have potential application to cetaceans. Japan may be more comfortable in ITLOS because of the relative weakness of UNCLOS's substantive provisions and because of the potential limits on ITLOS authority in cases of this sort. *See generally* Southern Blue Fin Tuna Cases (Austl. v. Japan and N.Z. v. Japan), Order of 27 August 1999, 1999 ITLOS Rpts. 280.

Australia have done better to accept the compromise offered at Agadir in June 2010?

At the time Australia rejected diplomatic compromise, it was facing unrelenting pressure from environmental groups adamantly opposed to all whaling. The Australian government's election had been secured in part based on its promise to "sue Japan." It did not feel that it could back down from that promise or accept any outcome that allowed Japan to continue a practice that Australia considered to be nothing more than commercial whaling in disguise.

What does this suggest to you about the role of civil society in advancing international law? Do you consider that anti-whaling advocacy has been a positive force or a negative force in this story? Without it, do you think any progress toward whale protection could be made at all? Is it possible that the Australian government became so much the servant of a civil society group with a narrow point of view that it lost sight of the broader legal and diplomatic ramifications of its decisions?

CHAPTER TWO

THE RAINBOW WARRIOR INCIDENT: NEGOTIATING ABOUT STATE TERRORISM AND ENVIRONMENTAL ACTIVISM IN THE SHADOW OF INTERNATIONAL LAW

■ ■ ■

In the first chapter of this book the dispute involved a multilateral treaty that established an international organization. In this chapter we concentrate on a bilateral dispute between two nations: France, a permanent member of the Security Council, and New Zealand, a small nation in the South Pacific. Obviously big differences exist between the conduct of multilateral and bilateral diplomacy. Considerable creativity is necessary in order to find a way through that resolves the dispute and allows both nations to put it behind them. The background to this dispute concerned nuclear weapons testing in French Polynesia. The environmental implications of this testing were front and center of the dispute, and it was those issues that inflamed public opinion over a long period of time in New Zealand, leading that country to adopt a nuclear-free policy. France, on the other hand, was committed to its *force du frappe* policy so it could remain a big player in the world and enjoy a nuclear deterrent of its own.

Three other issues of importance flow from the dispute set out here. First, centrally involved here were the activities of an international nongovernmental organization, Greenpeace. It is necessary to contemplate the importance of NGOs in international environmental law. They were very active in the whaling dispute as you will recall. NGOs bring pressure to bear on governments by working on the public opinion of their citizens. Frequently they are very effective. Sometimes, indeed, there is a real question of who is determining policy, the government or the NGO. But whether any particular NGO's interest is congruent with the public interest is a question worth considering, as political agitation by NGOs is never far away in many international environmental disputes.

Second, the application of international law in the domestic sphere and the relationship between international law and domestic law is not a simple subject. Different legal systems take different approaches to it. We explore that issue, with special attention to the approaches taken in New Zealand and the United States, at the end of the chapter.

Third, as is obvious from the manner in which this dispute is presented, the pressures on foreign office legal advisers are heavy and extraordinarily demanding. The manner in which the international and domestic spheres relate to one another is hard enough, but add big public controversy with inflamed public opinion and the politics of settling the dispute tends to become unmanageable. The challenges exceed those that fall upon lawyers who practice in the domestic sphere alone.

A. THE RAINBOW WARRIOR INCIDENT

In 1978, with funds provided by the Dutch branch of the World Wildlife Fund,[1] a 27-year-old converted research trawler that once fished the North Sea under the name *Sir William Hardy* was purchased from the British Ministry of Agriculture by Greenpeace International, a world-wide environmentalist and anti-nuclear nongovernmental organization (NGO),[2] and promptly renamed the *Rainbow Warrior* after a legend of questionable Native American origin.[3] Registered in the United Kingdom and crewed by men and women of deliberately diverse nationality, the *Rainbow Warrior* was to become the flagship of Greenpeace's small fleet of four vessels that, in the next few years, would protest commercial whaling operations in Iceland, Spain, and Peru; the slaughter of harp seal pups on the icepacks of Canada; the dumping of nuclear waste in the North Atlantic; chemical dumping and offshore oil and gas development in the United States; and illegal Russian whaling off the coast of Siberia.

On July 10, 1985, while docked at Marsden Wharf in Auckland Harbor, midst New Zealand's largest city, the *Rainbow Warrior* blew up and sank shortly before midnight. Sporting a "Nuclear Free Pacific" banner across its bridge at the time, the *Warrior* had been dispatched to the South Pacific

---

1 As its name suggests, the World Wildlife Fund (WWF), founded in 1961 and based in Switzerland, is a worldwide nongovernmental organization dedicated to the preservation of biodiversity and the health of ecological systems by protecting natural areas and wildlife populations, promoting the sustainable use of natural resources, and encouraging efficient resource and energy use and the maximum reduction of pollution.

2 Greenpeace is especially known for its derring-do efforts to protect and enhance the natural environment.

3 In Richard Shears & Isobelle Gidley, The Rainbow Warrior Affair 21 (1986), the legend is recounted as follows:

> A North American legend tells how a Cree grandmother known as Eye of Fire looked into the future and saw poisoned fish in the rivers, deer dropping dead in the forests, birds plummeting from the skies. The sea was black and the sun did not shine. The Indian race would come close to losing its spirit, but, unlike other creatures of the earth, they would not succumb entirely to the White Man's technology which had brought such desecration. They would gather together all the races of the world under a rainbow, and the group would be taught how to revere Mother Earth. Then these warriors of the Rainbow would set out to educate others on how their world could be saved.

According to Michael King, Death of the Rainbow Warrior 9 n. (1986), however, "there is no such Indian legend." King writes: "The story is an interpolation of Indian ideas worked into a millennial vision by a European and an eskimo writer, Vinson Brown and William Willoya . . . [in] *Warriors of the Rainbow* (1962)." *Id.*

to express solidarity with New Zealand's closing of its ports to nuclear-propelled and weapons-carrying ships and, in addition, to protest French nuclear testing at France's Mururoa atoll. At first, uncertainty prevailed as to what caused the explosions that tore two holes in the *Warrior's* side and simultaneously killed, as a result of drowning, Fernando Periera, a 34-year-old Portuguese-born Dutch citizen and photographer who had joined the crew only a few weeks earlier. It was not long, however, before the truth became known: the *Rainbow Warrior* was sunk by two high-explosive devices attached in the middle of the night by special agents under official orders from the military intelligence service of the Government of France, the *Directorat-Général de Sécurité Extérieur* (DGSE). Angered by fifteen years of Greenpeace "campaigns of disparagement and indeed hostile action against French nuclear tests,"[4] including several attempts "to have vessels penetrate into the waters prohibited to navigation which surround Mururoa atoll,"[5] France wanted no further interference with its nuclear testing program in French Polynesia.

The principal facts are now well documented.[6]

In March 1985, French Admiral Henri Fages, director of the French nuclear testing sites on Mururoa, communicated to French defense minister Charles Hernu about the possibility of the *Rainbow Warrior* and other small boats disrupting French nuclear tests, and on March 4, Minister of Defense Hernu ordered increased intelligence-gathering in respect of Greenpeace so as to prepare for any actions that Greenpeace might be contemplating. Shortly thereafter, on April 22, Christine Gabon, a French army officer posted to the DGSE, arrived in Auckland, assumed the pseudonym of Frederique Bonlieu, represented herself as a sailor-scientist, and began working undercover in the local Greenpeace office. Remaining in New Zealand until May 24, she regularly photographed Auckland's wharves and surrounding coastal areas, relayed the photographs to Paris, and simultaneously gathered and transmitted information on automobile, boat, and diving equipment rentals.

In Paris, meanwhile, plans were in the making for neutralizing Greenpeace, among them a plan to sink the *Warrior*. With the information

4 United Nations Secretary-General, Ruling on the *Rainbow Warrior* Affair Between France and New Zealand (July 6, 1986), *reprinted in* 26 I.L.M. 1346, 1349 (1987).

5 *Id.*

6 *See generally, e.g.*, Richard Bernstein, *Greenpeace Attack: Memo in March, Death in July*, N.Y. Times, 18 Sept. 1985, at A12, col. 3; King, *supra* note 3; David Robie, Eyes of Fire: The Last Voyage of the *Rainbow Warrior* (1987); Shears & I. Gidley, *supra* note 3; The Sunday Times Insight Team, *Rainbow Warrior* (1986); C. Chatterjee, *The Rainbow Warrior Arbitration Between New Zealand and France*, 9 J. Int'l Arb. 17 (Mar. 1992); Roger Clark, State Terrorism: Some Lessons from the Sinking of the "Rainbow Warrior," 20 Rutgers L. J. 393 (1989); J. Scott Davidson, *The Rainbow Warrior Arbitration Concerning the Treatment of French Agents Mafart and Prieur*, 40 ICLQ. 446 (1991); Geoffrey Palmer, *Settlement of International Disputes: The "Rainbow Warrior" Affair*, 15 Commonwealth L. Bull. 585 (1989); Michael Pugh, *Legal Aspects of the Rainbow Warrior Affair*, 36 ICLQ. 655 (1987); Jodi Wexler, *The Rainbow Warrior Affair: State and Agent Responsibility for Authorized Violations of International Law*, 5 B.U. Int'l L. J. 389 (1987).

provided by Christine Gabon and with an emergency fund under the discretion of the French prime minister's office, the plan was put into action when several DGSE agents chartered a French-built yacht then in New Caledonia, the *Ouvéa*, to transport explosives and other equipment to New Zealand. Another DGSE agent, Gerard Andries, was reported by the British Secret Service to have bought an inflatable dinghy and an outboard engine in the name of a bogus Belgian diving company.

In June 1985, eight DGSE agents arrived aboard the *Ouvéa* in Parengaranga, a remote New Zealand harbor with no customs office, and slowly navigated their way to Whangarei where, after hiding their cargo of explosives and other equipment along the way, they passed through customs. At the same time, two other DGSE agents—Major Alain Mafart and Captain Dominique Prieur—arrived in Auckland, posed on false passports as a married Swiss couple, and hired a camper van to travel around New Zealand. On July 9, the *Ouvéa* and its DGSE crew left New Zealand for Norfolk Island, Australia, and arrived there, speedily, a mere three days later. On July 10, at 9:30 PM (New Zealand time), members of the Auckland Outboard Motoring Club, keeping watch for thieves at Auckland's Waitemata Harbor, spotted what turns out to have been Major Mafart and Captain Prieur picking up a man dressed in a wet suit who, moments before, had been observed dumping an engine into the ocean and beaching a dinghy. About two and a half hours later, two detonations sank the *Rainbow Warrior* at Marsden's Wharf in Auckland Harbor.

The immediate aftermath of this sinking is quickly summarized. On the basis of mounting evidence linking them to the *Rainbow Warrior* bombing, Major Mafart and Captain Prieur were soon arrested and charged with murder and arson under New Zealand law.[7] The *Ouvéa* and its crew, though also found linked to the sinking of the *Warrior*, escaped arrest at Australia's Norfolk Island because of a delay in executing arrest warrants from New Zealand, continued on their voyage, and subsequently vanished.[8] And the French government, despite increasing evidence to the contrary, insisted that it played no role in, and therefore was not responsible for, the *Warrior's* demise.[9]

Until, that is, it became embarrassing and counterproductive to continue in this fashion. New Zealand sent the file of investigations completed by the police to the French Foreign Office. Denial ceased to be credible. The French government conceded that DGSE agents had

---

[7] For example, Dominique Prieur, alias Sophie Turenge, made the mistake of calling a Paris number reserved for emergency calls to the DGSE when allowed a phone call during questioning.

[8] A French submarine was in the area of the *Ouvéa's* last reported position, and it is speculated that the yacht was sunk and its DGSE crew picked up by the submarine. *See* Shears & Gidley, *supra* note 3, at 131.

[9] France stated that its agents were in New Zealand only to carry out surveillance and that there was no evidence that they are involved in anything more. Indeed, the French government produced an official report to this effect.

participated in the bombing, although all the while insisting that the agents had exceeded their authority. Simultaneously, French President François Mitterand ordered France's armed forces to prevent any further attempt to enter French territorial waters where nuclear tests were scheduled—"by force if necessary," he said.[10]

Political reality, however, demanded more. On September 19, 1985, French defense minister Hernu submitted his resignation to French Prime Minister Laurent Fabius. Pierre Lacoste, head of the DGSE, was fired for refusing to answer questions about the *Warrior*. On September 22, Prime Minister Fabius himself issued a communiqué finally admitting that the DGSE agents had been ordered to sabotage the ship. And, on the same day, French foreign minister Roland Dumas indicated that France was ready to make reparations to New Zealand for the consequences of the action.

The amount of reparations actually suggested, however, was less than the "millions" to which New Zealand claimed it was entitled, and the issue was further complicated by France's request for the extradition of agents Mafart and Prieur, contending that New Zealand had no right to hold onto and imprison them because they had acted under superior orders. Additionally, there was no way that New Zealand could seek vindication of its claims before the International Court of Justice at The Hague (popularly known as the "World Court").[11] A decade earlier, following its refusal to appear in 1974 World Court proceedings brought by Australia and New Zealand to protest its atmospheric testing of nuclear weapons at Mururoa,[12] France had terminated its acceptance of the Court's compulsory jurisdiction, and thus would not likely be taken before the World Court against its will again, although New Zealand unsuccessfully sought to resume the 1974 case before the International Court of Justice in 1995.

But we are getting ahead of the story. Imagine that it is late August 1985, not yet two months since the death and destruction at Marsden Wharf. Imagine, too, that you are a relatively new lawyer in the Legal Division of New Zealand's Ministry of Foreign Affairs,[13] with experience primarily in the law of private international investment and trade. You and your colleagues are familiar with Greenpeace's campaigns against the French nuclear testing program, and none of you doubts that France had good reason to expect that the *Rainbow Warrior* would seek to disrupt France's 1985 schedule of tests at Mururoa. But all of you know, also, that the French action was contrary to New Zealand law at least, and that for

---

[10] *France to Block Pacific Protests*, NY Times, 19 Aug. 1985, at A1, col. 3.

[11] *See* Chapter 1, *supra*, for discussion about the International Court of Justice.

[12] *See* Nuclear Tests Cases (Austl. v. Fr.), 1974 ICJ 253; (N.Z. v. Fr.), 1974 I.C.J. 457; *Request for an Examination of the Situation*, 1995 ICJ 288.

[13] New Zealand's Ministry of Foreign Affairs was subsequently renamed the "Ministry of External Relations and Trade" and now is known as the "Ministry of Foreign Affairs and Trade."

this reason, if for no other, France should not go unpunished. Indeed, you personally have already begun to assist in the prosecution of Major Mafart and Captain Prieur for murder and arson under New Zealand law (an effort that was later to be rewarded, as it turns out, by a November 4 plea of "guilty" to manslaughter and to wilful damage to a ship by means of an explosive by the two French agents, as well as by a November 22 sentence to ten years imprisonment for each agent on each count by the Chief Justice of New Zealand in the High Court at Auckland). But when the Head of the Ministry's Legal Division, your boss or supervisor, Mr. Colin Keating, asks you for advice on what *international* legal action he should recommend to his superiors, you ask for time to formulate a thoroughly considered reply. You are of course mindful that physical possession of Major Mafart and Captain Prieur gives New Zealand valuable leverage in its increasingly tense negotiations with France. But you are mindful, too, of a complex history between France and New Zealand over the question of nuclear testing, a history that might have bearing on what you should advise.

Accordingly, you decide first to review all the facts as known and revealed to you so far. Your training tells you that legal issues, whether national or international in character, cannot be precisely identified and framed until their full contexts are properly chronicled.

France, you note, has a continuing colonial presence in the South Pacific, as evidenced by New Caledonia, Wallis and Futuna, and French Polynesia, a vast archipelagic sea territory in which is located the Mururoa atoll where France began atmospheric nuclear testing in September 1966. Prior thereto, France had tested its nuclear devices in Algeria. But Algerian independence from France in 1962, coupled with dissatisfaction with the Algerian site because of the Saharan winds that carried radioactive debris into Europe, caused France to find a new testing ground.

Another consequence of France's presence in the South Pacific, you discover, is its participation in the proposed Convention for the Protection of the Natural Resources and Environment of the South Pacific Region **[Basic Document 3.7]**, a treaty then being hammered out by the South Pacific Forum[14] and including as probable parties the United Kingdom and the United States in addition to France and the Forum countries. This proposed "SPREP" Convention, you note, prohibits the dumping of all

[14] The Pacific Forum, with a Secretariat in Suva, Fiji, and a Fisheries Agency at Honiara in the Solomon Islands, a regional organization of fifteen States, has been mutually supportive and effective in presenting to the world beyond a common point of view on a variety of issues, including self-determination for the Kanak people of New Caledonia, a range of environmental issues, and, not least, nuclear testing by France in the Pacific. The Forum has an annual meeting of Heads of Government and is run in accordance with the policies adopted at the annual meeting. Run in a more-or-less informal manner according to what is known as "the Pacific way," it is nonetheless a cohesive and effective organization. Its members are Australia, the Cook Islands, the Federated States of Micronesia, Fiji, Kiribati, the Marshall Islands, Nauru, New Zealand, Niue, Palau, Papua New Guinea, the Solomon Islands, Tonga, Tuvalu, Vanuatu, and Western Samoa. Many are now threatened with extinction by sea level rise as a consequence of climate change.

radioactive waste at sea in the region and requires the State Parties to prevent regional pollution from nuclear testing. The opinion among the Pacific nations has tended to be that nuclear testing is not safe and should be stopped; if it is as safe as the French government claims it is, they say, then it should be carried out in France. But despite substantial political pressure over the years, you observe, France has adamantly resisted. France's *force du frappe* policy is an essential dimension of independent-minded French domestic and foreign policy, with nuclear testing viewed as necessary to keep up with the other nuclear powers.[15]

Of course, this French view is not shared by your government or that of Australia, or at least not since 1972 when Labor governments were elected in both Australia and New Zealand. Indeed, New Zealand, with logistical support from the Australian navy, had sent a frigate to France's Mururoa atoll with a cabinet minister aboard to signal, dramatically, its opposition to France's atmospheric nuclear testing program. It was, as it happens, a futile effort, as was also, in the opinion of many, Australia's and New Zealand's subsequent effort to stop France's South Pacific nuclear testing program via proceedings before the International Court of Justice.[16] Claiming that radioactive fallout from the Mururoa tests violated their territorial sovereignty, Australia and New Zealand asked the Court to declare France's Mururoa tests illegal under international law. But instead of reaching the merits, the Court ruled that the case had been rendered moot by virtue of the fact that France had ceased testing during the proceedings and that, via an official press statement declaring that it would conduct no further atmospheric tests, it had made a promise to which it was legally bound.

But that was almost eleven years ago in 1972, you observe, and since then much has happened. A year ago, you note, in July 1984, a Labor Government was elected in New Zealand, one that had campaigned on a strong anti-nuclear policy that later brought the new government into conflict with the United States over port visits of U.S. naval vessels because nuclear-armed ships, of which the United States had many, were unacceptable in New Zealand under the new policy. The United States took the view that the alliance relationship it had with Australia and New Zealand, set out in the 1951 ANZUS Treaty,[17] required New Zealand, as a matter of treaty obligation, to admit without hesitation or exception all ships of the United States Navy. New Zealand argued contrariwise: there was no reference to nuclear weapons in the Treaty; the New Zealand policy was not therefore inconsistent with the letter of the Treaty; there was no

[15] France's *force de frappe* policy, which asserts an independent but relatively small nuclear defense posture capable of deterring all attacks on France, was proclaimed by French President Charles DeGaulle when he pulled France out of NATO in 1966.

[16] *See supra* note 12.

[17] Security Treaty Between Australia, New Zealand, and the United States of America, 1 Sept. 1951, 131 UNTS 83.

need for deployment of nuclear weapons in the South Pacific; it was, indeed, sound policy to keep the area free of nuclear weapons; this sentiment was widely shared in the region, as evidenced by the 1985 South Pacific Nuclear Free Zone Treaty **[Basic Document 7.21]** prohibiting the deployment of nuclear weapons on land in the region, which the South Pacific Forum had just negotiated and was about to conclude; the Nuclear Free Zone Treaty contained no provision dealing with port visits; it therefore left this matter to each State Party's discretion (and thereby allowed Australia, parenthetically, to become a party while at the same time permitting it to berth U.S. Navy ships as it saw fit).

In any event, with nuclear weapons regarded as abhorrent by the majority of New Zealand's voters, and with anti-American (as well as anti-French) sentiment consequently running high, New Zealand's new Labor Government was not about to succumb to pressure to change its ports-visit policy. To the contrary, it denied entry to an American ship because the ship was considered too "ambiguous" vis-à-vis the presence or absence of nuclear weapons on board; and, following unsuccessful negotiations with the United States to find a way out of the diplomatic impasse, it moved quickly to adopt promised legislation that would convert into domestic law the obligations it had undertaken in the 1985 South Pacific Nuclear Free Zone Treaty and that would otherwise implement its nuclear-free stance. The legislation provides, *inter alia*, that "[t]he Prime Minister may only grant approval for entry into the internal waters of New Zealand by foreign warships if the Prime Minister is satisfied that the warships will not be carrying any nuclear explosive device upon their entry into the internal waters of New Zealand."[18] The United States, you have heard, is now threatening to suspend its obligations toward New Zealand under the ANZUS Pact[19] (something the United States later did in fact, in 1986, arguing that New Zealand had basically withdrawn from the alliance by virtue of its anti-nuclear stance[20]). And in the meanwhile, of course, France continues its underground nuclear testing program at Mururoa, insisting upon its sovereign territorial right to do so.

All of which serves to remind you that nuclear questions are an important aspect of South Pacific environmental politics and that it is against this background that Mr. Keating, your supervisor, has asked you to prepare a memorandum indicating your opinion about the international legal "pros" and "cons" relative to the sinking of the *Rainbow Warrior* and to the underground nuclear testing that France insists upon continuing at Mururoa. And he wants it yesterday! Deputy Prime Minister Geoffrey

---

18 New Zealand Nuclear Free Zone, Disarmament and Arms Control Act 1987, NZ Statutes 1987 No. 86.

19 *Supra* note 17.

20 "[W]e part as friends . . .," said then US Secretary of State George Shultz. Joint Press Conference by U.S. Secretaries Shultz and Weinberger and Australian Ministers Hayden and Beazley, San Francisco, California, 11 Aug. 1986.

Palmer, he tells you, is to address the United Nations General Assembly at the end of September, and on that occasion to meet with French foreign minister M. Roland Dumas, prepared to argue that the doctrine of superior orders (invoked by France to bring about Major Mafart's and Captain Prieur's extradition) is not a defense under New Zealand's criminal law, eager to protest France's continued nuclear testing at Mururoa, and determined to demand reparations. You are informed, too, that France may impede imports of lamb and other New Zealand products to France specifically and to the European Community generally if it does not get its way.

And so, the questions come tumbling forth.

Is New Zealand required by international law to grant Mafart's and Prieur's extradition? Or may it exercise its own discretion and allow its domestic (i.e., internal) law to take its course? If the latter, are there any treaties or other sources of international law—e.g., customary international law—that limit the extent to which it can punish Mafart and Prieur? If New Zealand is allowed or does allow its own law to take its course, what are the risks, legal and otherwise? Can France lawfully threaten retaliatory economic sanctions? Impose them? If so, according to what authority and to what extent? If not, why not? Is it bound by international law not to do so? Can the international legal system prevent it from doing so?

What about the *Rainbow Warrior* incident itself? Was it not a form of international terrorism and is not international terrorism prohibited under international law? Is espionage unlawful under international law? Sabotage? Regardless, is New Zealand entitled under international law to insist upon a formal French apology for the actions France took against the *Rainbow Warrior*? Is the French government responsible for the acts of its DGSE agents? If so, according to what theory? To whom and to what extent? If not, why not? What about the doctrine of superior orders? Was it not rejected at Nuremberg in the trial of the Nazi war criminals following World War II, and does not the judgment at Nuremberg constitute legally binding precedent? In any event, can New Zealand, under international law, legally demand reparations from France for the damage done? If so, what damages may be assessed? Property damages? Damages for the death of Fernando Periera? Penal damages for arguable violations of the U.N. Charter **[Basic Document 1.2]**? Other damages? If any of these, in what amount or according to what valuation criteria? Criteria established by French law? New Zealand law? International law?

Perhaps most importantly, what legal significance attaches, if any, to France's continuing underground nuclear testing at its Mururoa atoll?[21]

---

[21] It being 1985, it is premature for you to consult the World Court's 1996 advisory opinion on the *Legality of the Threat or Use of Nuclear Weapons*, 1996 I.C.J. 226. However, we, your authors/editors, are possessed of formidable clairvoyance, and thus urge you to read this future

Does it violate the 1986 Convention for the Protection of the Natural Resources and Environment of the South Pacific Region **[Basic Document 3.7]**? The 1985 South Pacific Nuclear Free Zone Treaty **[Basic Document 7.21]**? Any other source of international environmental law? If so, is New Zealand legally entitled to bring a claim for damages against France in this connection also? Would it be smart tactics for New Zealand to make a claim directly to the French government and to indicate the compensatory damages to which it would be entitled? If so, how should these damages be measured and according to what law? If not, why not? If a remedy of damages is unlikely, can New Zealand at least get a legal order forbidding France from continuing its Mururoa nuclear testing, which appears to be in defiance of the people of the South Pacific and their natural environment?

And, by the way, where does Greenpeace fit into all of this? Does it have standing to challenge France under international law in relation to the *Rainbow Warrior* incident? In relation to France's nuclear testing program at Mururoa? Or, alternatively, does New Zealand have standing to represent Greenpeace's interests in either of these connections? If so, according to what authority? If not, why not—and what, then, is Greenpeace left to do?

Finally, supposing France does have legal liability, what can be done about it? The application of international law doctrines, principles, and rules is indispensable to their counting as law. Unless they are applied to some degree, signaling an intention if not always a capacity to make them fully effective or controlling, they remain essentially aspirational or hortatory exercises—*moral* prescriptions, perhaps, but not *legal* ones. What hope does tiny New Zealand have of holding mighty France to account?

B. THE APPLICATION OF INTERNATIONAL LAW IN THE CASE OF THE *RAINBOW WARRIOR*

It is now early October 1985, about two weeks since you completed your legal memorandum concerning New Zealand's rights vis-a-vis the prosecution of Major Alain Mafart and Captain Dominique Prieur, the sinking of the *Rainbow Warrior,* and France's continuing underground testing of nuclear weapons at its Mururoa atoll. In that memorandum, you advised your boss, Mr. Colin Keating, Head of the Legal Division of New Zealand's Ministry of Foreign Affairs, that nothing in international law precluded New Zealand from prosecuting the French special agents under New Zealand law; that New Zealand, on the basis of the Law of State Responsibility as reflected in part in the International Law Commission's

opinion. For commentary thereon, see Burns H. Weston, *Nuclear Weapons and the World Court: Ambiguity's Consensus*, 7 Transnat'l L. & Contemp. Probs. 371 (1997).

Draft Articles on the Responsibility of States for Internationally Wrongful Acts **[Basic Document 1.15]**,[22] has firm international legal grounds for demanding compensatory and penal damages from France for its sabotage of the *Rainbow Warrior;* and that France's Mururoa nuclear weapons tests arguably breach international law. However, although you are quite certain of New Zealand's right to try the French agents and of France's responsibility for their activities, you advise Mr. Keating that you are much less confident that France's nuclear tests are illegal. For one thing, France is not a party to the 1985 South Pacific Nuclear Free Zone Treaty **[Basic Document 7.21]**. In addition, the evidence of a customary norm against underground nuclear tests is not nearly as strong as you would wish.

Your phone rings. It is Mr. Keating. After thanking you for your helpful memorandum, he brings you up to date on developments. First, the Ministry has chosen not to press New Zealand's case against France's nuclear testing, a decision made partly because of your advice and partly because France had terminated its acceptance of the compulsory jurisdiction of the International Court of Justice some years earlier and therefore could not be brought before the World Court against its will.

Second, Mr. Keating tells you that Deputy Prime Minister Palmer has run into heavy resistance in his *Rainbow Warrior* negotiations with the French foreign minister, Roland Dumas. France, you are told, admits its responsibility under international law for the *Rainbow Warrior* incident, but it remains adamant that Major Mafart and Captain Prieur should be immediately released and returned to France. In particular, it rejects New Zealand's claim of the right to prosecute French agents in New Zealand courts for their violations of New Zealand law. The French government, it appears, is of the view that its special agents had acted under official orders, that it had formally assumed responsibility for the consequence of those orders, and that therefore Mafart and Prieur could not be held personally accountable and should be promptly released. Drawing upon the nineteenth century *Caroline* incident between Great Britain and the United States,[23] France argues a doctrine of "superior orders" pursuant to which State responsibility replaced agent responsibility.

---

[22] Of course, the *Rainbow Warrior* incident pre-dated the International Law Commission's work on the law of state responsibility, but the ILC Articles mostly restate the principles and rules of state responsibility that were in effect at that time as a matter of customary law. For a discussion of the basic principles of the Law of State Responsibility, *see* Chapter 3, part B, *infra.*

[23] In the aftermath of the infamous *Caroline* incident, a British citizen, McLeod, was charged by a New York court with murder as a result of his alleged participation in the destruction of *The Caroline,* a United States vessel, when it was anchored on United States territory. The defendant was eventually acquitted by the court for want of evidence, but his detention was the subject of much diplomatic disputation between the governments. The British accepted responsibility for the destruction of the *Caroline* by persons in its service and, on that ground, demanded McLeod's release. The U.S. Secretary of State, Daniel Webster, expressed his agreement with the proposition that, under the "principles of public law and the general usage of civilized State," individuals involved in a "public transaction, authorized and undertaken by the British authorities," ought not to be held "personally responsible, in the ordinary tribunals of law, for their participation in it."

However, Mr. Keating tells you, the New Zealand government is unwilling to deport Major Mafart and Captain Prieur from New Zealand so long as judicial proceedings against them are in progress. Such an act would be seen by many as an improper interference by the government with the judiciary, and the release of the defendants to France would be hugely unpopular politically. Moreover, the release of the agents to France would result in their complete immunity from punishment for their conduct.[24] Consequently, the decision has been made to continue the prosecution of the French agents under New Zealand law and to continue to negotiate with France. The French, for their part, are making veiled and not-so-veiled threats of trade retaliation against New Zealand. Moreover, they are unwilling to meet New Zealand's demands for compensatory and penal damages relative to the sinking of the *Rainbow Warrior* (even though admitting responsibility for the incident) as long as their agents are in New Zealand's custody.

A few weeks after your conversation with Mr. Keating, on 4 November 1985, both French agents pleaded guilty to manslaughter and willful damage to a ship by means of an explosive. On 22 November, each defendant was sentenced to ten years' imprisonment on each count by the Chief Justice of New Zealand in the High Court of Auckland.[25]

The matter rested there for several months, with negotiations between the two governments sputtering on until 19 May 1986, when, to protest France's threat of retaliatory sanctions against the importation of New Zealand butter and lamb, New Zealand broke off its talks with France altogether. New Zealand complained to France and to the European Communities Trade Commission, which, in turn, upheld New Zealand's complaint. All of which served to embarrass the French government to a considerable degree; and in due course, with "L'Affaire Greenpeace" becoming a major issue in upcoming French elections, France began to seek a face-saving way out.

Not surprisingly, your phone rings again. This time Mr. Keating instructs you to revisit your legal arguments regarding all aspects of the *Rainbow Warrior* incident and, additionally, to canvass all the possibilities for their application in the context of a third-party conciliation or arbitration of some sort—which, he says, looks likely. The Prime Minister of The Netherlands, he tells you, has offered to mediate between Paris and Wellington, and there is a good possibility that his mediation could lead

---

Daniel Bryant Talmadge, Review of the opinion of Judge Cowen of the Supreme Court of the State of New York on the Case of Alexander McLeod 27 (1841). *See also* II John Bassett Moore, A Digest of International Law 409 (1906).

[24] Under New Zealand law, acting pursuant to superior orders is not a defense to homicide. Under the French Penal Code, however, "when the homicide, wounding, or striking are ordered by law or lawfully ordered authority, no felony or misdemeanor has been committed." Code Penal § III, art. 327 (Fr.).

[25] *See* 74 ILR 241 (1987).

quickly to an agreement on the means for settling the *Rainbow Warrior* dispute once and for all.

And, so, you again return to your review of international legal processes, this time with emphasis upon the application (or enforcement) of international law. Naturally, questions abound. Through exactly what mechanisms of international decision-making might the many issues arising out of the *Rainbow Warrior* incident be resolved? Inasmuch as the International Court of Justice does not appear to be within reach because of France's withdrawal from its compulsory jurisdiction, what is available? The United Nations General Assembly? The Security Council? Some other decision-making institution?

You sense from France's renewed willingness to negotiate that there is a real opportunity to resolve the *Rainbow Warrior* dispute expeditiously. You quickly learn from your further review of the international law treatise you withdrew from the Legal Division's law library that France's unwillingness to subject itself to the jurisdiction of the ICJ does not mean that law will necessarily be irrelevant to the resolution of the dispute. To the contrary, you discover that formal judicial resolution of international legal issues is relatively rare, and that international law is more frequently invoked by States in the context of other processes, both non-adjudicative and adjudicative (e.g., negotiations, good offices, mediation, conciliation, and arbitration), through which States seek peacefully to resolve their disputes.[26] After consideration of the options, and recognizing that negotiations appear to have reached an impasse, you recommend to your superiors that the entire dispute be submitted for final determination, by way of *conciliation*, to U.N. Secretary-General Perez de Cuellar, a former professor of international law. Your superiors like the idea, and it is subsequently agreed between them and their French counterparts, to ask Secretary-General de Cuellar to hear the dispute. On 19 June 1986, the Secretary-General informs Paris and Wellington that he is willing to undertake the task, and two weeks later, on July 5, he issues his ruling. It is reproduced here in major part, complete with the legal memoranda (or briefs) prepared by New Zealand and France.

---

[26] "Viewed comprehensively," writes Professor Chen, "[the] application [of law] may embrace the following sequential features: exploration of potentially relevant facts, including the precipitating events and their larger context; exploration of potentially relevant policies; identification of significant facts; determination of the authoritative policies applicable; making of the decision, including the projection of future relations between the parties; enforcement; and review." Lung-chu Chen, An Introduction to Contemporary International Law 376 (1989).

RULING OF THE SECRETARY-GENERAL OF THE UNITED NATIONS PERTAINING TO THE DIFFERENCES BETWEEN FRANCE AND NEW ZEALAND ARISING FROM THE RAINBOW WARRIOR AFFAIR

Reprinted in 26 ILM 1346 (1987) and 74 ILR 256 (1987)

I invited the two Governments to submit written statements of their positions to me. Arrangements were made for copies of each side's submission to be made available to the other. The statements are set out below.

MEMORANDUM OF THE GOVERNMENT OF NEW ZEALAND TO THE SECRETARY-GENERAL OF THE UNITED NATIONS

This memorandum is submitted pursuant to the agreement of 19 June 1986 between New Zealand and France that all of the problems between them arising from the Rainbow Warrior affair would be submitted to the Secretary-General of the United Nations for a binding ruling.

* * *

The Facts

On 10 July 1985 a civilian vessel the "Rainbow Warrior" was sunk at its moorings in Auckland Harbour, New Zealand, as a result of extensive damage caused by two high explosive devices. One person, a Netherlands citizen, Mr. Fernando Pereira, was killed as a direct result of this action.

The attack against the "Rainbow Warrior" was carried out under official orders by a team of agents from the Directorate General of External Security, an agency of the French Government. The team of agents had previously made covert and illegal entries into New Zealand. A communique issued on 22 September 1985 by the then Prime Minister of France confirms France's responsibility for this action. A copy is attached as Annex A.[27]

On 12 July 1985 two members of the French team of agents were interviewed by the New Zealand Police and subsequently arrested. They were Major Alain Mafart and Captain Dominique Prieur of the French Armed Forces. On 4 November 1985 Mafart and Prieur pleaded guilty in the District Court in Auckland to charges of manslaughter and wilful damage to a ship by means of an explosive.

Under New Zealand law the crime of manslaughter is culpable homicide and is subject to a maximum punishment of life imprisonment. Wilful damage to a ship by means of an explosive is a crime punishable by a maximum penalty of 14 years' imprisonment.

[27] Annex A and all subsequent annexes are omitted here.

On 22 November 1985, Mafart and Prieur were each sentenced by the Chief of Justice of New Zealand to a term of 10 years' imprisonment.

A copy of the Chief Justice's statement delivered in the High Court is available if required.

The affair was formally brought to the attention of the United Nations by the Deputy Prime Minister of New Zealand, the Rt. Hon. Geoffrey Palmer, in his statement to the General Assembly on 24 September 1985 (UN Document A/40/PV.7 of 24 September).

Attempts to resolve the dispute by negotiation began in September 1985 following a meeting in New York between the New Zealand Deputy Prime Minister and the then French Minister of External Relations. Despite a number of meetings it did not prove possible to reach a settlement.

The Violation of International Law

The position of the New Zealand Government was first formally set out in a Diplomatic Note dated 6 September 1985 from the New Zealand Embassy in Paris to the French Ministry of External Relations. . . .

The attack against the "Rainbow Warrior" was indisputably a serious violation of basic norms of international law. More specifically, it involved a serious violation of New Zealand sovereignty and of the Charter of the United Nations.

These violations were neither accidental nor technical. International law and New Zealand's sovereignty were violated deliberately and contemptuously. There is no room for doubt that the attack was both authorised and funded at a high level. The purpose of the operation was to prepare the ground for and to execute a criminal act of violence against property in New Zealand. This was done without regard for innocent civilians. That purpose was achieved and one of its consequences was the death of an innocent civilian.

Responsibility

The international legal responsibility of the French Government was engaged at every stage of this affair and not merely in its authorisation and initiation. In a letter of 8 August 1985 from the President of the French Republic to the Prime Minister of New Zealand . . . it was stated that the incident was "a criminal attack committed on your territory and which cannot for any reason be excused". It is also stated that "I intend that this affair be treated with the greatest severity and that your country be able to count on France's full collaboration". In an exchange of letters of the same date with the French Prime Minister, the President of France spoke of the guilty being "severely punished". . . .

Reparation Sought by New Zealand

New Zealand seeks redress as follows:

(A) Apology

The Government of New Zealand is entitled, in accordance with international law, to a formal and unqualified apology for the violation of its sovereignty and its rights under international law.

(B) Compensation

The sinking of the "Rainbow Warrior" led to a deep and genuine sense of public outrage in New Zealand. It was the first time in New Zealand history that an act of international violence was committed by the armed forces of a foreign state in New Zealand territory. The sense of outrage was magnified by reason of the fact that the state responsible was a traditionally close friend and ally.

The consequent Police investigation became the largest single investigation into criminal activity that has ever taken place in New Zealand. Substantial costs were incurred by various agencies of Government including:

–the New Zealand Police

–the Department of Justice

–the Ministry of Defence

–the Ministry of Foreign Affairs

–the Department of Scientific and Industrial Research

–the Security Intelligence Service

–the Solicitor-General

–the Auckland Harbour Board.

New Zealand is entitled under international law to reimbursement by France of all costs which are a direct result of France's unlawful acts. Details of these costs are available.

New Zealand is also entitled to compensation for the violation of sovereignty and the affront and insult that involved. The sum awarded under this heading should take account of the fact that France has refused to extradite or prosecute other persons in France responsible for carrying out the illegal and criminal act of 10 July 1985.

In respect of all the damage it has suffered, as outlined above, New Zealand (which is in no way at fault in any aspect of the affair) believes that the compensation to which it is entitled should be no less than US$9 million.

Damage to the Vessel and Compensation in Respect of the Death of its Crewman

The vessel, the "Rainbow Warrior", was not a New Zealand ship and the dead crewman was a Netherlands citizen. New Zealand is therefore unable to assert formal standing to claim on behalf of either Greenpeace or the dead crewman. New Zealand has, however, expressed strongly to France its concern that both Greenpeace and the family of the dead man should receive fair compensation.

During the bilateral negotiations with France, New Zealand indicated that a settlement with New Zealand would only be possible if adequate compensation had been paid or if there were reasonable and binding arrangements in place that assured that this would be done.

Trade Matters

By its own action and statements the Government of France has introduced trade matters into the dispute. As to the past, certain restrictive measures affecting New Zealand exports to France, which were the subject of a complaint by the Government of New Zealand to the OECD [Organization for European Cooperation and Development] and also the subject of a complaint by New Zealand to the Director-General of GATT [General Agreement on Tariffs and Trade] and a request on 7 March 1986 for consultations under Article XXII:I of the GATT, were withdrawn prior to the agreement to seek the Secretary-General's ruling. They call for no further comment. As to the future, a matter of very great concern to New Zealand is the threat made by the French External Trade Minister, M. Noir, on 3 April 1986 and reported by Reuters on 4 April 1986 . . . that France might seek to link the present dispute to the question of access for New Zealand butter to the European Community. This question is due for consideration by the Council of the European Communities before 1 August 1986. M. Noir told French Radio that a total ban of New Zealand butter imports was in contemplation by France.

New Zealand has not introduced trade issues into this dispute. It has, however, no choice but to seek protection against such threats to its vital economic interests. Accordingly, New Zealand seeks a ruling that will prevent France from opposing continuing imports of New Zealand butter into the United Kingdom in 1987 and 1988 at levels proposed by the Commission of the European Communities in so far as these do not exceed those mentioned in Document COM(83)574 of 6 October 1983, that is to say, 77,000 tonnes in 1987 and 75,000 tonnes in 1988.

New Zealand also seeks a ruling that will prevent France from taking any measures which might impair the implementation of the agreement between New Zealand and the EEC on Trade in Mutton Lamb and Goatmeat which entered into force on 20 October 1980 (as complemented by the exchange of letters of 12 July 1984). (New Zealand Treaty Series 1980, No. 13).

The French Agents in Prison in New Zealand

There is an important constitutional principle in New Zealand, (as in most other democratic countries), which restrains the executive branch of government from interfering for political or other purposes in judicial matters.

Decisions in New Zealand about prosecutions are not taken by Ministers and the Courts rightly accept no political interference in their consideration of cases before them.

It was for this reason that New Zealand repeatedly informed in the early stages of the negotiations that were held that it was not open for the New Zealand Government to agree, or even negotiate, about the two prisoners in New Zealand while the cases were before the courts. This principle was steadfastly maintained by New Zealand. After the conviction and sentencing of the agents, it was acknowledged that there is power under New Zealand law for the deportation of convicted foreign prisoners. It was pointed out, however, that the New Zealand Government was wholly unwilling to exercise that power in circumstances that would give the prisoners their freedom in return for an acknowledgment by France of responsibility under international law and payment of compensation. That remains the case.

New Zealand does not accept that military personnel acting under official orders are exempt from personal responsibility for criminal acts. "Superior orders" is not a defence in New Zealand law, nor is it a defence in the legal systems of most countries. It is certainly not a defence in international law, as was clearly established in the judgements of the Nuremberg Tribunal and the post-Nuremberg war crimes trials.

Under New Zealand law the two prisoners would not be eligible to be released on parole until they had served at least 5 years. New Zealand could not countenance the release to freedom after a token sentence of persons convicted of serious crimes. This would undermine the New Zealand judicial system. It is essential to the integrity of any judicial system that persons convicted of similar offences be treated similarly.

In the course of the bilateral negotiations with France, New Zealand was ready to explore possibilities for the prisoners serving their sentences outside New Zealand.

But it has been, and remains, essential to the New Zealand position that there should be no release to freedom, that any transfer should be to custody, and that there should be a means of verifying that.

Enforcement

New Zealand is committed to the settlement of international disputes by judicial means and insisted, throughout the bilateral negotiations, that any settlement of this matter with France must contain provision for compulsory and legally binding adjudication.

New Zealand therefore requests the Secretary-General to include in his rulings provision for binding adjudication of any dispute relating to the interpretation or application of all his findings.

MEMORANDUM OF THE GOVERNMENT OF THE FRENCH REPUBLIC TO THE SECRETARY-GENERAL OF THE UNITED NATIONS

1. Following the appeal made to France and New Zealand on 31 May 1986 by the Netherlands Prime Minister, the two countries decided to submit all problems between them arising from the "Rainbow Warrior" incident to the Secretary-General of the United Nations and agreed to abide by his ruling. The agreement was announced simultaneously in Paris and in Wellington on 19 June 1986. The Secretary-General was willing to accept responsibility for this task. . . . The purpose of this Memorandum is to set out the viewpoint of the French Government.

The Facts

2. For many years, France has organised underground nuclear tests on the atoll of Mururoa in French Polynesia. These are essential for the modernisation of its defence. Following visits by French and foreign scientists, in particular in 1983 and 1984, it was established that these tests have no real consequences for the environment.

The "Greenpeace" movement has nevertheless pursued, for more than 15 years, campaigns of disparagement and indeed hostile action against the French nuclear tests. To this end, it has on several occasions attempted to have vessels penetrate into the waters prohibited to navigation which surround Mururoa Atoll. The National Navy has obviously opposed these illegal attempts, particularly in 1973 and 1982. The "Greenpeace" movement again planned to provoke similar incidents in 1985 by sending several vessels, including the "Rainbow Warrior", into the neighbourhood of the French Pacific Nuclear Testing Centre.

This operation could not be carried out in accordance with the original plans due to the fact that on 10 July 1985 the "Rainbow Warrior" was destroyed at its moorings in the Port of Auckland by two explosive devices. The loss of the ship through sinking was to involve the death of a crewman of the "Rainbow Warrior", Mr. Fernando Pereira.

3. The French authorities sought to throw light on this incident. As early as 8 August 1985, as the New Zealand Government recalls, the President of the French Republic assured New Zealand of French

cooperation in this respect. Indeed, the New Zealand authorities had on 30 July requested the assistance of the French authorities in the context of the enquiry pursued by the New Zealand Police. This assistance was granted even though no agreement on mutual criminal judicial assistance existed between the two states.

Following investigations carried out in both countries and especially in France, the then French Prime Minister specifically stated on 22 September 1985 that the "Rainbow Warrior" had been "sunk under orders by agents of the Directorate-General of External Security" (DGSE). The French Minister of Defence then offered his resignation and the Director-General of the DGSE was dismissed. On the same day, the French Minister of External Relations stated to the New Zealand Prime Minister that "The French Government is of course prepared to take responsibility for reparations for the harm of various sorts resulting from this occurrence" . . . . He informed him moreover that the French Prime Minister was "deeply grieved that this affair should have had consequences for relations between France and New Zealand". Finally, Mr. Roland Dumas said that he was prepared, as Mr. David Lange had suggested, to meet Mr. Geoffrey Palmer, the New Zealand Deputy Prime Minister, in New York at the time of the General Assembly of the United Nations, "in order to examine on a state to state basis the conditions under which this affair could be settled".

This meeting took place on 23 and 25 September 1985 and the two Ministers "began to discuss possible courses in order to find out solutions to the problems arising from the 'Rainbow Warrior' incident". Then they agreed that "representatives of the two Governments would meet . . . on this subject". In spite of a certain number of meetings, these discussions were unable to reach a successful conclusion.

4. Meanwhile, in fact, two of the agents belonging to the French team involved in the incident, Major Mafart and Captain Prieur, had been arrested in New Zealand, then sentenced on 23 November 1985 by the New Zealand Chief Justice to ten years' imprisonment. The French Government could obviously not remain indifferent to the fate of these officers and no settlement with New Zealand was possible without the release of the persons concerned. The New Zealand Government having refused to consider such release, the matters in dispute between the two countries could not be settled by negotiation and it was in these circumstances that the decision was taken to have recourse to the mediation of the Secretary-General of the United Nations.

The Violation of International Law and France's Responsibility

5. The attack against the "Rainbow Warrior" originates in the illegal actions of the "Greenpeace" organisation. It could not moreover be understood without recalling the interventions of certain New Zealand authorities in French internal affairs, especially with respect to the nuclear

tests conducted on Mururoa. These interventions all the more aroused French public opinion as they proceeded from a country which, as the New Zealand Memorandum properly stresses, was traditionally a close friend and ally.

The French Government nevertheless recognises that the attack carried out against the "Rainbow Warrior" took place in violation of the territorial sovereignty of New Zealand and that it was therefore committed in violation of international law. New Zealand consequently has a right to compensation for the harm which it directly suffered from that attack.

Reparation Sought by New Zealand

A. Apologies

6. The violation of New Zealand territory by France did not in itself cause any material damage to New Zealand. On the other hand it may be admitted that it has caused it moral damage which, according to international law, may be compensated by the offer of regrets or apologies.

The Government of New Zealand requests the French Government to offer it such apologies. The French Government is prepared to make compensation in this manner for the moral damage suffered by New Zealand and the French Prime Minister is ready, therefore, to address to the New Zealand Prime Minister a formal and unconditional letter of apology for the attack carried out on 10 July 1985.

B. Compensation

7. The request for compensation presented by New Zealand also appears to be justified in its principle, and the French Government is prepared to pay to the New Zealand Government a global, lump-sum indemnity compensating for all the damage suffered directly by New Zealand. The sum of US$9 million put forward by the New Zealand side, however, appears in this perspective altogether excessive.

In the first instance, the indemnity owing could only compensate for the damages suffered by New Zealand (and not those suffered by the family of Mr. Fernando Pereira or by the "Greenpeace" organisation which will be dealt with below). On this point, moreover, the two Governments are in full agreement.

In the second instance, it could concern only the material damage suffered by New Zealand. In fact, according to constant legal precedent, in inter-state relations moral damage is compensated by the solemn recording of a breach of international law (in this sense the award brought down between France and Italy by the Permanent Court of Arbitration on 6 May 1913 in the Carthage and Manouba cases—Reports of International Arbitral Awards—Volume XI p. 450 and p. 464 and the Judgement brought down by the International Court of Justice on 9 April 1949 in the Corfu

Channel case—Compendium of Decisions of the Court 1949 pp. 25, 26 and 36). This being the case, the formal and unconditional offer of apologies by France compensates for the moral damage suffered by New Zealand and this damage could not in addition be the object of a pecuniary compensation.

Equally, and even if it were envisaged to proceed differently it would be appropriate to take account in the evaluation of possible moral damage of the overall context of the affair and the grievances which France could for its part have harboured with respect to New Zealand.

There remains, therefore, only the material damage suffered by the New Zealand State as a result of the attack: clearing of the Port of Auckland, expenses arising from the Police enquiry, the trial of Major Mafart and Captain Prieur and their detention.

The French Government is prepared to reimburse New Zealand for these expenses and for its part New Zealand has declared itself prepared to furnish the details of them to the Secretary-General.

Nonetheless, France assesses that in total a compensation of US$4 million would be a lavish calculation and that the figure of US$9 million put forward by New Zealand is altogether exaggerated in character.

Damage to the Vessel and Compensation for the Death of a Member of Its Crew

8. The New Zealand Government, while recognising that because of the nationality of Mr. Pereira and that of the vessel "Rainbow Warrior" it is not in a position to assert formal standing to claim on behalf of individuals who have suffered harm in the wake of the events of 10 July 1985, has taken a close interest in compensation for them.

The French Government has paid to the relatives of Mr. Fernando Pereira indemnities which have been accepted by them. Mrs. Van den Boomen, common-law wife of the person concerned, has received, in addition to the indemnity of 30,000 Guilders paid by the insurers (and reimbursed to the latter by France), sums of 650,000 Francs for herself and 1,500,000 Francs for the two children who are minors, Paul and Marelle. Two sums of 75,000 Francs in compensation have in addition been paid to the father and mother of Mr. Fernando Pereira.

Furthermore, a compromise was reached on 19 December 1985 between the French State and the "Stichting Greenpeace Council" acting in its own name and in the name of the organisations affiliated to Greenpeace and of the owner and operators of the vessel "Rainbow Warrior". The two parties committed themselves, under this compromise, to pursue negotiations in good faith aimed at fixing by mutual agreement the amount of the damages which the French State will agree to pay. It has, in addition, been provided that, failing agreement on this amount, the matter would be submitted to an arbitral tribunal of three members. "Responsibility for calamity . . . not being in dispute, . . . the arbitrators who are appointed will have as their task to pronounce on the only point remaining at issue between the parties, namely the question of the amount of damages which the State will have to pay".

Since it was not possible to bring the negotiation aiming at fixing this amount to a successful conclusion, each of the parties has designated an arbitrator, namely Professor Terre for France and Judge Woodhouse for Greenpeace. Unless there is agreement between the arbitrators on a third arbitrator, it will fall to the President of the Federal Swiss Court to designate the latter.

Finally, it has been agreed that the judgement brought down by the tribunal will be binding and the French State has committed itself to execute it in six months.

The measures thus taken both as far as the family of Mr. Fernando Pereira and the Greenpeace organisation are concerned, appear in these circumstances equitable and consequently seem to meet the concerns of the New Zealand Government.

<u>Situation of Major Mafart and Captain Prieur</u>

9. The French Government considers that a settlement which is equitable and principled implies the immediate release of Major Mafart and Captain Prieur. The New Zealand Government refuses this. It considers that the persons concerned should serve their sentence under the same conditions as any person found guilty in New Zealand of comparable offences and that any transfer from New Zealand could only be to custody.

The French Government wishes to observe in the first place that the New Zealand Government has the necessary legal means to carry out the deportation of Major Mafart and Captain Prieur by virtue of Section 22 of the New Zealand Immigration Act 1964. What is more, in his statement on 22 November 1985, the New Zealand Chief Justice, after having rejected a request for a recommendation for deportation, specifically declared that: "adequate powers exist for the Minister to act under that section of the Immigration Act and, if he so decides, to order deportation. I regard it as appropriate in the circumstances of this case that any question of deportation of the defendants should be considered by the Minister in accordance with the provisions of the Act."

On the other hand and conversely, the French Government could not ensure the execution in France of the prison sentences pronounced by the New Zealand court. Indeed, as is the case in any democratic country, a person could be imprisoned in France only by virtue of a decision taken by a French judge or in application of an international convention on the transfer of sentenced offenders (such as that concluded in the framework of the Council of Europe on 21 March 1983). Now France and New Zealand are not bound by any convention of this type and no sentence has been pronounced in France against the two officers concerned. Moreover, and taking into account that these persons acted under orders, they could not be subjected to fresh criminal prosecution after their transfer into the hands of the French authorities (cf. Article 327 of the French Penal Code).

Thus the New Zealand Government can deport Major Mafart and Captain Prieur to France, but, conversely, France could not imprison them.

In these circumstances, the French Government considers that, both for reasons of law and in order to restore the traditional friendly relations between the two countries, it behooves the New Zealand Government to release the two officers.

Trade Matters

10. The New Zealand Government claims that the French Government has introduced certain trade matters into the dispute and seeks to benefit from various guarantees in this regard.

It is a fact that the competent French services have been led during recent months to carry out various checks on certain New Zealand exports (especially as regards lambs' brains) with a view to ensuring that such goods (often difficult to preserve) meet the requirements, particularly in the veterinary and phytosanitary fields, of the applicable national and Community regulations. These checks had no connection with the dispute now submitted to the Secretary-General. In any case, they have now been terminated. In these circumstances, the French Government fails to understand why the New Zealand Government presents requests of a commercial nature in this affair. Anxious not to mix these various questions, the French Government is nevertheless prepared to reassure the New Zealand Government in this regard.

In fact, France does not intend to oppose in the Council of the Communities the continuation of imports of New Zealand butter to the United Kingdom in 1987 and 1988 at the levels which the Commission of the European Communities will propose, provided, of course, that these levels will not exceed those proposed by the Commission in 1983.

As the New Zealand Memorandum recalls, there currently exists, furthermore, an Agreement between New Zealand and the European Economic Community on Trade in Mutton, Lamb and Goatmeat which entered into force on 20 October 1980 (as complemented by the Exchange of Letters of 12 July 1984). France obviously does not intend to take any steps which might interfere with the implementation of that Agreement.

Arbitration

11. The New Zealand Government requests the Secretary-General to include in his decision a provision concerning compulsory settlement of any dispute which may arise between the two countries on the interpretation or implementation of the conclusions at which he arrives.

The French Government is not opposed to a compulsory arbitration procedure being put in place for the settlement of the disputes in question. Traditionally in favour of such procedures and having frequently had recourse to them in recent years, it relies on this point on the wisdom of the Secretary-General.

* * *

After I had received these written statements of the New Zealand and French Positions, I then made contact, through diplomatic channels, with each of the two Governments. I did so in order to satisfy myself that I had a full and complete understanding of their respective positions and to be sure that I am able to produce a ruling on all aspects of the affair which in terms of the agreement announced in Paris, Wellington and New York on 19 June, is both equitable and principled.

RULING

1. Apology

New Zealand seeks an apology. France is prepared to give one. My ruling is that the Prime Minister of France should convey to the Prime Minister of New Zealand a formal and unqualified apology for the attack, contrary to international law, on the "Rainbow Warrior" by French service agents which took place on 10 July 1985.

2. Compensation

New Zealand seeks compensation for the wrong done to it and France is ready to pay some compensation. The two sides, however, are some distance apart on quantum. New Zealand has said that the figure should not be less than US Dollars 9 million, France that it should not be more than US Dollars 4 million. My ruling is that the French Government should pay the sum of US Dollars 7 million to the Government of New Zealand as compensation for all the damage it has suffered.

3. The Two French Service Agents

It is on this issue that the two Governments plainly had the greatest difficulty in their attempts to negotiate a solution to the whole issue on a bilateral basis before they took the decision to refer the matter to me.

The French Government seeks the immediate return of the two officers. It underlines that their imprisonment in New Zealand is not justified, taking into account in particular the fact that they acted under military orders and that France is ready to give an apology and to pay compensation to New Zealand for the damage suffered.

The New Zealand position is that the sinking of the "Rainbow Warrior" involved not only a breach of international law but also the commission of a serious crime in New Zealand for which the two officers received a lengthy sentence from a New Zealand court. The New Zealand side states that their release to freedom would undermine the integrity of the New Zealand judicial system. In the course of bilateral negotiations with France, New Zealand was ready to explore possibilities for the prisoners serving their sentences outside New Zealand.

But it has been, and remains, essential to the New Zealand position that there should be no release to freedom, that any transfer should be to custody, and that there should be a means of verifying that.

The French response to that is that there is no basis either in international law or in French law on which the two could serve out any portion of their New Zealand sentence in France, and that they could not be subjected to new criminal proceedings after a transfer into French hands.

On this point, if I am to fulfil my mandate adequately, I must find a solution in respect of the two officers which both respects and reconciles these conflicting positions.

My ruling is as follows:

(a) The Government of New Zealand should transfer Major Alain Mafart and Captain Dominique Prieur to the French military authorities. Immediately thereafter, Major Mafart and Captain Prieur should be transferred to a French military facility on an isolated island outside of Europe for a period of three years.

(b) They should be prohibited from leaving the island for any reason, except with the mutual consent of the two Governments. They should be isolated during their assignment on the island from persons other than military or associated personnel and immediate family and friends. They should be prohibited from any contact with the press or other media whether in person or in writing or in any other manner. These conditions should be strictly complied with and appropriate action should be taken under the rules governing military discipline to enforce them.

(c) The French Government should every three months convey to the New Zealand Government and to the Secretary-General of the United Nations, through diplomatic channels, full reports on the situation of Major Mafart and Captain Prieur in terms of the two preceding paragraphs in order to allow the New Zealand Government to be sure that they are being implemented.

(d) If the New Zealand Government so requests, a visit to the French military facility in question may be made, by mutual agreement by the two Governments, by an agreed third party.

(e) I have sought information on French military facilities outside Europe. On the basis of that information, I believe that the transfer of Major Mafart and Captain Prieur to the French military facility on the isolated island of Hao in French Polynesia would best facilitate the enforcement of the conditions which I have laid down in paragraphs (a) to (d) above. My ruling is that should be their destination immediately after their transfer.

4. Trade Issues

The New Zealand Government has taken the position that trade issues have been imported into the affair as a result of French action, either taken or in prospect. The French Government denies that, but it has indicated that it is willing to give some undertakings relating to trade, as sought by the New Zealand Government. I therefore rule that France should:

(a) Not oppose continuing imports of New Zealand butter into the United Kingdom in 1987 and 1988 at levels proposed by the Commission of the European Communities in so far as these do not exceed those mentioned in document COM(83)574 of 6 October 1983 that is to say, 77,000 tonnes in 1987 and 75,000 tonnes in 1988; and

(b) Not take measures that might impair the implementation of the agreement between New Zealand and the European Economic Community on Trade in Mutton, Lamb and Goatmeat which entered into force on 20 October 1980 (as complemented by the exchange of letters of 12 July 1984).

5. Arbitration

The New Zealand Government has argued that a mechanism should exist to ensure that any differences that may arise about the implementation of the agreements concluded as a result of my ruling can be referred for binding decision to an arbitral tribunal. The Government of France is not averse to that. My ruling is that an agreement to that effect should be concluded and provide that any dispute concerning the interpretation or application of the other agreements, which it has not been possible to resolve through the diplomatic channel, shall, at the request of either of the two Governments, be submitted to an arbitral tribunal under the following conditions:

(a) Each Government shall designate a member of the tribunal within 30 days of the date of the delivery by either Government to the other of a written request for arbitration of the dispute, and the two Governments shall, within 60 days of that date, appoint a third member of the tribunal who shall be its chairman;

(b) If, within the times prescribed, either Government fails to designate a member of the tribunal or the third member is not agreed, the Secretary-General of the United Nations shall be requested to make the necessary appointment after consultations with the two Governments by choosing the member or members of the tribunal;

(c) A majority of the members of the tribunal shall constitute a quorum and all decisions shall be made by a majority vote;

(d) The decisions of the tribunal, including all things concerning its constitution, procedure and jurisdiction, shall be binding on the two Governments.

6. The two Governments should conclude and bring into force as soon as possible binding agreements incorporating all of the above rulings. These agreements should provide that the undertaking relating to an apology, the payment of compensation and the transfer of Major Mafart and Captain Prieur should be implemented at the latest on 25 July 1986.

7. On one matter I find no need to make a ruling. New Zealand, in its written statement of position, has expressed concern regarding compensation for the family of the individual whose life was lost in the incident and for Greenpeace. The French statement of position contains an account of the compensation arrangements that have been made; I understand that those assurances constitute the response that New Zealand was seeking.

And so, it seemed, the unhappy saga of the *Rainbow Warrior* was at an end. Despite heavy domestic criticism of the transfer of Major Mafart and Captain Prieur to French custody on the island of Hao on 23 July 1986, you and your colleagues are relieved. No less than the Secretary-General of the United Nations—an international lawyer—had determined essentially to ratify New Zealand's claims of French malfeasance contrary to international law, and, to your satisfaction and that of your colleagues, your government and the French government, in accordance with Paragraph 6 of the Secretary-General's ruling, concluded in Paris, on 9 July 1986, by exchange of letters, three agreements incorporating the provisions of that ruling,[28] all elements of which were implemented.

A job well done![29]

---

28 The agreements are reproduced in 74 ILR 274–77 (1987).

29 The strategy of submitting a dispute to the Secretary-General of the United Nations is an unusual one, but it is necessary to understand that in the world of international diplomacy things are not always what they seem. Behind the scenes, France and New Zealand negotiated most of the Secretary-General's ruling in advance. The reasons were essentially two. First, domestic opinion in both countries was highly charged on the issue. A bilaterally negotiated settlement that was in no way insulated by the imprimatur of a respected third party might well have made both countries subject to severe political criticism domestically. Second, politically sensitive or

But, alas, the case of the *Rainbow Warrior* was *not* at an end. Several months short of two years after being committed to Hao for three years' imprisonment in accordance with U.N. Secretary-General Perez de Cuellar's conciliatory ruling, special agents Mafart and Prieur, at the initiative of the French government, were released forever from Hao and repatriated to France *without* New Zealand's consent, *contrary* to the Secretary-General's ruling. And for the year, until the establishment of an *ad hoc* international arbitral tribunal to resolve their differences, the two countries argued back and forth over the meaning of their first 9 July 1986 agreement, which related to the situation of the two French officers, each of whose circumstances were only superficially different.

Alain Mafart's health, it appears, had deteriorated on Hao. On 1 December 1987, the French Ministry of Defense was advised that Major Mafart "poses the etiological and therapeutic problem of stabbing abdominal pains" which required "an emergency return to a hospital in mainland France";[30] and on December 12, New Zealand's permission for Mafart's evacuation was sought, with the French Ambassador to New Zealand instructed to stress that "the only means of transport immediately available between Hao to Paris was the military aircraft leaving Sunday morning [13 December]."[31] In response, by *note verbale* delivered within four hours of the French request, New Zealand indicated its concern simultaneously for Major Mafart's health and for the jurisdictional risks posed by this proposal, stating that it preferred, instead, "a suitably qualified New Zealand military doctor" to examine the prisoner, with "the necessary clearance for a military flight to Hao for this purpose."[32] The French government, in turn, refused this counter-proposal. "For imperative reasons of national security," it said in quick reply, "access to this [Hao military] base is strictly regulated and is prohibited to foreign aircraft."[33] The French government did, however, simultaneously offer "to allow Major Mafart to be examined, as soon as he arrives in mainland France, by a

---

otherwise delicate matters often are better dealt with via closed diplomacy. The media and politics obtrude substantially when it is known that intergovernmental negotiations are taking place; and, so, negotiations were conducted in secret, for the most part in Switzerland.

On the other hand, almost all of the elements of the Secretary-General's ruling that were put before him by France and New Zealand were in fact agreed to between the two governments and endorsed by the Secretary-General. Also, the Secretary-General did decide for himself on the amount of compensation to be paid by France to New Zealand. The Secretary-General's authority and neutrality doubtless made it easier for the governments of both nations to save face in ways that were important to each.

[30] Letter from Dr. Maurel to the French Ministry of Defense (Dec. 10, 1987), *as quoted in* New Zealand v. France, Int'l Arb. Award, 30 April 1990 at 14, *reprinted in* XX Reports of International Arbitral Awards 215–284 [hereinafter "Int'l Arb. Award"].

[31] Int'l Arb. Award at 14.

[32] Note Verbale of 12 Dec. 1987, *as quoted in* Int'l Arb. Award at 14.

[33] Telegram from the French Ministry of Foreign Affairs via the French Ambassador in Wellington to the New Zealand Ministry of Foreign Affairs (Dec. 13, 1987), *as quoted in* Int'l Arb. Award at 15.

physician designated by New Zealand."[34] But this counter-counterproposal was seen by New Zealand as no less jurisdictionally risky than the first, and so it put forward two new alternatives: to fly a New Zealand medical doctor to Papeete on the French island of Tahiti by a New Zealand military aircraft and then onward to Hao by a French military aircraft; or, if France preferred, to fly a New Zealand medical doctor to Papeete by a commercial airliner and then onward to Hao by a French military aircraft. On December 14, however, contending that these options would create a delay "absolutely incompatible with the urgency [of the medical circumstances],"[35] Major Mafart was flown to Paris and medically examined and treated there, without New Zealand's consent. On the same day, Dr. R. S. Croxson, a New Zealand doctor residing in London was sent to examine Mafart, and he shortly reported that, though Mafart was in need of help that was unavailable on Hao, "it is . . . highly arguable whether an emergency evacuation as opposed to a planned urgent evacuation was necessary."[36] All of which led, as one might expect, to many detailed recriminations and representations between the two governments, including, first, a subsequent 12 February 1988 report by Dr. Croxson that "[t]here was no evidence produced to show that Commander Mafart had an impending obstruction at the time he was evacuated from Hao and [that] certainly if he had, he should have been airlifted to the nearest general surgical center, which we believe exists in Tahiti," adding that "[it] would have been dangerous to have flown him to Paris";[37] and, second, a rejection by New Zealand of a suggestion that its sending of Dr. Croxson to Paris could be construed as acceptance of Major Mafart's evacuation from Hao. In any event, in the end, Major Mafart never was returned to Hao. For medical reasons, said the French government, Mafart was to remain in France. In time, he was returned to military duty and promoted.

The situation of Dominique Prieur, who was accompanied on Hao by her husband, was driven first by medical necessity and later by the impending death of her father. On 3 May 1988, she was reported to be six weeks pregnant and in need of special care because of her thirty-nine years of age, her gynecological history, and the fact that the child she bore would be her first. It also was reported that the medical facilities on Hao were unable to provide the medical examinations and care her pregnancy required. This time, however, France did not object to a New Zealand military doctor traveling to Hao, and the next day, 4 May, it was agreed that Dr. Bernard Brenner should travel to Hao via Tahiti the next morning,

---

[34] *Id.*

[35] Note from the French Ambassador to New Zealand to the New Zealand Ministry of Foreign Affairs (Dec. 14, 1987), *as quoted in* Int'l Arb. Award at 16.

[36] Report of Dr. R.S. Croxson to the New Zealand authorities (Dec. 14, 1987), *as quoted in* Int'l Arb. Award at 20.

[37] Report of Dr. R.S. Croxson to the New Zealand authorities (Feb. 12, 1988), *as quoted in* Int'l Arb. Award at 30.

5 May. But on 5 May, before Dr. Brenner could make the journey (he and his interpreter were delayed by one day by a French airline pilots' strike), France informed New Zealand of a new development, namely, that Captain Prieur's father in Paris was dying of cancer and that her presence by his bedside was urgently needed—a situation which led, as by now one might expect, to further exchanges between the two governments. Included among these exchanges were both an understanding that, in the interest of time, Dr. Brenner could be flown by New Zealand military aircraft directly from Auckland to Hao and an understanding that a New Zealand doctor could contact the doctors treating Captain Prieur's father to verify the urgency of his condition. It appeared, in other words, that the two governments were moving toward a satisfactory solution. But at 10:30 p.m. on 5 May (Paris time), ostensibly because New Zealand could not deliver Dr. Brenner to Hao within a three or four hours time limit set by France but at a time immediately preceding French presidential elections, the French government informed New Zealand that "for obvious humanitarian reasons,"[38] Captain Prieur "will . . . depart immediately for Paris"[39] and on 6 May this repatriation was effectuated. Captain Prieur arrived in Paris the evening of 6 May, without New Zealand's consent. Her father died on 16 May. She never was returned to Hao.

On 22 September 1988, in accordance with the U.N. Secretary-General's ruling (*supra*) and the associated agreements with France, New Zealand requested the convening of an international arbitral panel to resolve with France what could not be resolved through diplomacy.[40] An international arbitral tribunal was constituted pursuant to the parties 9 July 1986 agreement,[41] with Sir Kenneth Keith designated by New

---

[38] Int'l Arb. Award at 34.

[39] *Id.*

[40] On 22 September 1988, the New Zealand government presented to the French Ministry of Foreign Affairs a note requesting arbitration, as follows:

> Extensive efforts have been made in the intervening months to resolve this dispute through the diplomatic channel. The Government of New Zealand greatly regrets the fact that constructive proposals to this end which it advanced on 10 August 1988 met no satisfactory response from the French Government. The New Zealand Government is therefore forced to the conclusion that all reasonable efforts to resolve this dispute have been exhausted. The Embassy is therefore instructed to advise that the Government of New Zealand hereby requests, in accordance with the Ruling of the Secretary-General of the United Nations and the Agreement of 9 July 1986 between New Zealand and France, that the dispute be submitted to an arbitral tribunal.

[41] The terms of the original arbitration agreement were contained in a letter from the Prime Minister of France to the New Zealand Government. The letter read, in relevant part:

> On the basis of [the Secretary-General's] ruling, I have the honour further to propose that any dispute concerning the interpretation or application of either of these two Agreements which it has not been possible to resolve through the diplomatic channel shall, at the request of either of our two Governments, be submitted to an Arbitral Tribunal under the following conditions:
>
> (a) each Government shall designate a member of the Tribunal within 30 days of the date of the delivery by either Government to the other of a written request for arbitration of the dispute, and the two Governments shall, within 60 days of that date, appoint a third member of the Tribunal who shall be its Chairman;

Zealand, M. Jean-Denis Bredin designated by France, and Dr. Eduardo Jiménez de Aréchaga, a Uruguayan and former Judge and President of the International Court of Justice, appointed by the two governments as Chairman of the tribunal. A Supplementary Agreement (or *compromis)* concerning the operation of that Tribunal was adopted on 14 February 1989.[42] The Tribunal began proceedings on 8 May 1989 in New York.

In its memorial to the tribunal, New Zealand contended that France had committed six separate breaches of the international obligations it had

---

(b) if, within the times prescribed, either Government fails to designate a member of the Tribunal or the third member is not agreed the Secretary-General of the United Nations shall be requested to make the necessary appointment after consultations with the two Governments by choosing the member or members of the Tribunal;

(c) a majority of the members of the Tribunal shall constitute a quorum and all decisions shall be made by a majority vote;

(d) the decisions of the Tribunal, including all rulings concerning its constitution, procedure and jurisdiction, shall be binding on the two Governments.

If the foregoing is acceptable to the Government of New Zealand, I would propose that the present letter and your response to it to that effect should constitute an agreement between our two Governments with effect from today's date.

The New Zealand Government accepted the terms in the letter and the Agreement was concluded that day.

42 The Supplementary Agreement reads, in part, as follows:

ARTICLE 1

1. Subject to paragraphs 2, 3, and 4 of this Article, the composition of the Tribunal shall remain unchanged through the period in which it is exercising its functions.

2. In the event that either the arbitrator designated by the Government of New Zealand or the arbitrator designated by the Government of French Republic is, for any reason, unable or unwilling to act as such, the vacancy may be filled by the Government which designated that arbitrator.

3. The proceedings of the Tribunal shall be suspended during a period of twenty days from the date on which the Tribunal has acknowledged such a vacancy. If at the end of that period the arbitrator has not been replaced by the Government which designated him the proceedings of the Tribunal shall nonetheless resume.

4. In the event that the Chairman of the Tribunal is, for any reason, unable or unwilling to act as such, he shall be replaced by agreement between the two Governments. If the two Governments are unable to agree within a period of forty days from the date on which the Tribunal has acknowledged such a vacancy, the Secretary-General of the United Nations shall be requested to make the necessary appointment after consultations with the two Governments. The proceedings of the Tribunal shall be suspended until such time as the vacancy has been filled.

ARTICLE 2

The decisions of the Tribunal shall be made on the basis of the Agreements concluded between the Government of New Zealand and the Government of the French Republic by Exchanges of Letters on 9 July 1986, this Agreement and the applicable rules and principles of international law.

ARTICLE 7

1. On completion of the proceedings, the Tribunal shall render its award as soon as possible and shall forward a copy of the award, signed by the Chairman and Registrar of the Tribunal, to the two Agents.

2. The award shall state in full the reasons for the conclusions reached.

ARTICLE 9

Any dispute between the two Governments as to the implementation of the award may, at the request of either Government, be referred to the Tribunal for clarification within three months after the date of receipt of the award by its Agent.

assumed in the first of its 9 July 1986 agreements with New Zealand, three each in respect of Major Mafart and Captain Prieur: first, by failing to seek in good faith New Zealand's consent to the removal of the two agents from Hao; second, by actually removing the two agents from Hao without New Zealand's consent; and, third, by failing to return the two agents to Hao. For these breaches, New Zealand requested relief in the form of both a public condemnation of the French government and an order of specific performance for the return of the two agents to Hao.

For its part, France acknowledged that it did not obtain New Zealand's prior consent, but it nevertheless maintained that the necessity of the transfers under very special and urgent circumstances caused neither the repatriations of Major Mafart and Captain Prieur nor their non-return to Hao to bear any trace of illegality under the first 9 July 1986 agreement or the rules and principles of general international law. It also contended that, in any event, its obligation to keep Major Mafart and Captain Prieur on Hao did not extend beyond 22 July 1989, the expiration date of the first 9 July 1986 agreement.

On 30 April 1990, after reviewing the facts in the case and after deciding the applicability of the customary (international) Law of State Responsibility to them, the international arbitral tribunal surveyed briefly the Law of State Responsibility relative to "circumstances that preclude wrongfulness" (*force majeure, distress, and necessity*) and concluded that[43]

> three conditions would be required to justify the conduct followed by France in respect to Major Mafart and Captain Prieur:
>
> 1) [T]he existence of very exceptional circumstances of extreme urgency involving medical or other considerations of an elementary nature, provided always that a prompt recognition of the existence of those exceptional circumstances is subsequently obtained from the other interested party or is clearly demonstrated.
>
> 2) The reestablishment of the original situation of compliance with the assignment in Hao as soon as the reasons of emergency invoked to justify the repatriation had disappeared.
>
> 3) The existence of a good faith effort to try to obtain the consent of New Zealand in terms of the 1986 Agreement.

Then, after lengthy discussion in which it applied these and kindred international law rules to the intricate cases of both Major Mafart and

[43] Int'l Arb. Award, at 49.

Captain Prieur as well as to the relief requested by New Zealand, the tribunal held as follows:[44]

THE ARBITRAL TRIBUNAL

1) by a majority declares that the French Republic did not breach its obligations to New Zealand by removing Major Mafart from the island of Hao on 13 December 1987;[45]

2) declares that the French Republic committed a material and continuing breach of its obligations to New Zealand by failing to order the return of Major Mafart to the island of Hao as from 12 February 1988;

3) declares that the French Republic committed a material breach of its obligations to New Zealand by not endeavouring in good faith to obtain on 5 May 1988 New Zealand's consent to Captain Prieur's leaving the island of Hao;

4) declares that as a consequence the French Republic committed a material breach of its obligations to New Zealand by removing Captain Prieur from the island of Hao on 5 and 6 May 1988;

5) declares that the French Republic committed a material and continuing breach of its obligations to New Zealand by failing to order the return of Captain Prieur to the island of Hao;

6) by a majority declares that the obligations of the French Republic requiring the stay of Major Mafart and Captain Prieur on the island of Hao ended on 22 July 1989;[46]

7) as a consequence declares that it cannot accept the requests of New Zealand for a declaration and an order that Major Mafart and Captain Prieur return to the island of Hao;

8) declares that the condemnation of the French Republic for its breaches of its treaty obligations to New Zealand, made public by the decision of the Tribunal, constitutes in the circumstances appropriate satisfaction for the legal and moral damage caused to New Zealand;

9) in the light of the above decisions, recommends that the Governments of the French Republic and of New Zealand set up a fund to promote close and friendly relations between the

[44] *Id.* at 72–73.

[45] In a separate opinion, the New Zealand arbitrator, Sir Kenneth Keith, indicated his disagreement with his two colleagues regarding the lawfulness of the removal of Major Mafart from the island of Hao. *See* Separate Opinion of Sir Kenneth Keith, Int'l Arb. Award, at 75–78.

[46] In a separate opinion, the New Zealand arbitrator, Sir Kenneth Keith, indicated his disagreement with his two colleagues regarding the duration of the period the two agents were to stay on Hao. *See* Separate Opinion of Sir Kenneth Keith, Int'l Arb. Award, at 78–85.

citizens of the two countries, and that the Government of the French Republic make an initial contribution equivalent to US $2 million to that fund.

Thus concluded an unfortunate, protracted, and bitter international dispute which had its origins in a concern for the global environment.[47] Much can be learned from it about international law and politics, including, as we have seen, the manner in which international law is applied, as well as how it is prescribed.

DISCUSSION NOTES/QUESTIONS

1. Was the case of the *Rainbow Warrior* a victory for international law or did France "get away with it?" Was it a case of a big, powerful nation being able to treat a smaller, less powerful nation as it wished? Was it a case of might makes right? In sum, does it prove or disprove that there is such a thing as international law? How? How not?

2. Why did France and New Zealand decide to submit the *Rainbow Warrior* dispute for settlement, first, by the U.N. Secretary-General and, second, by the *ad hoc* international arbitral tribunal? Surely France could have just refused. If she had, what could New Zealand have done about it? Would you be surprised to learn that most of the Secretary-General's ruling had been secretly negotiated by France and New Zealand in advance? If they had already reached agreement on what to do, why did France and New Zealand need the Secretary-General's involvement? Sir Geoffrey Palmer suggests that this was "an example of political people using third-party adjudication . . . to soften and ameliorate the political problems that they would otherwise have." What would those problems have been in this case? *See* Geoffrey Palmer, *Adjudication, Politics and International Law*, 17 Temple Int'l & Comp. L. J. 523, 526 (2003).

3. What about special agents Mafart and Prieur? Were they not just doing their job and following orders? Should superior orders have been a

[47] Well, almost concluded. Approximately eight years and three months after the sinking of the *Rainbow Warrior* and about three and one-half years after the arbitral decision and award, a seemingly final chapter was reported. *See* Graham Barrett, *France: Passion Sank Ship, Book Claims-Rainbow Warrior,* The Age (Melbourne), 11 Oct. 1993, at 9. This newspaper account explained: "The Rainbow Warrior affair has returned to haunt France with a disclosure that the minister who ordered the Greenpeace vessel to be sunk in Auckland harbor had been in the grip of romantic passion at the time." A biography of Mr. Charles Hernu, former French Defense Minister, revealed that Mr. Hernu was "madly in love with a younger woman" at the time of the Rainbow Warrior incident and so distracted that aides said he "appeared to lose touch with reality." When intelligence officials informed Mr. Hernu "of the Rainbow Warrior's imminent departure for Mururoa Atoll," they suggested three possible actions: disable the ship by damaging its propeller or putting sugar in its fuel tank, spike food in the galley to make the crew sick, or blow up and sink the vessel." To the shock of aides, "Mr. Hernu, apparently anxious to get on with his love life," immediately accepted the third option and "breezed out of the room." Just a few days afterward, the Rainbow Warrior was resting on the bottom of Auckland Harbor, and France "was embroiled in a diplomatic scandal that brought the nation and its eccentric intelligence services into considerable disrepute."

The news report concluded: "Mr. Hernu died three years ago. The French President, Mr. Francois Mitterand, who as head of state carries ultimate responsibility for matters of foreign policy and defence, is still trying to distance himself from the dirty deed."

defense for them? Where did the rule against the defense of superior orders come from?

4. What about Greenpeace? Should it have been part of the proceedings? In fact, in a separate arbitration, Greenpeace was awarded damages against France, and the family of Mr. Pereira was compensated.

5. How might the *Rainbow Warrior* dispute have been better handled or resolved? How might such a dispute be avoided in the future?

6. Now more than thirty years after the bombing in Auckland Habour how are relations between France and New Zealand? Sir Geoffrey Palmer, on a visit to France in 2015, made inquiries. Here is what he found:

> I called at the New Zealand Embassy when I was in Paris in April 2015 to inquire whether there were any lasting effects from the Rainbow Warrior saga on the relationship between France and New Zealand. Ambassador James Kember reported that relations were in good heart. There were high levels of engagement between the countries—on the commemorations of the First World War and because of our current Security Council membership. France values co-operation with New Zealand on such issues as disaster relief in the Pacific.
>
> I think it is fair to say that while the Rainbow Warrior chapter between France and New Zealand is closed, it has not been forgotten. Despite the unusual methods of settling the dispute that necessarily had to be adopted, the dispute has been successfully resolved and leaves now hardly a mark on the New Zealand body politic nor its diplomacy. From the point of view of New Zealand it can be said that principles important to the political health of small states were vindicated and the principles of international law upheld. If the case was a game changer it was in the innovative methods used to resolve it. Although it is hard to imagine another dispute for which the same methods could be used.
>
> I conclude that New Zealand could not reasonably have expected to have achieved more than it did in this whole saga. International law was twice vindicated to uphold New Zealand's rights, once by negotiations and with the assistance of the United Nations Secretary-General and on the second occasion by arbitration. The matter is behind us now, but we should not forget what a heavy test it was for New Zealand and how wickedly difficult was the resolution.

Geoffrey Palmer, *The Rainbow Warrior—Thirty Years Later,* 2015 NZLJ 324, 325 (2015).

7. What do you think would be the answer to the same question from the French point of view?

8. How could France have been forced to settle the dispute? What would have happened if it had not been willing to do so?

9. Was this an example of shaming, reputational damage and embarrassment that allowed the dispute to be settled?

C. THE APPLICATION OF INTERNATIONAL LAW ON THE NATIONAL PLANE

When the New Zealand government elected to prosecute French special agents Alain Mafart and Dominique Prieur for their nighttime sabotage of the *Rainbow Warrior* on 10 July 1985, it had, in theory, two strategic choices: it could, per France's request, deport the two agents to France in hopes of trial there.[48] But that would entail the risk that no trial would take place or that the French courts would allow the defense of superior orders and thereby permit the two agents to go unpunished. Alternatively, with Mafart and Prieur captive and therefore subject to personal jurisdiction in New Zealand, it could prosecute in New Zealand and, likely as not, risk little or nothing at all. The choice was of course clear and, as we have seen, vindicated.

As it turns out, the choice of law to be applied by the New Zealand courts was clear as well. Major Mafart and Captain Prieur had already pleaded guilty to criminal wrongdoing by the time the case came before the courts; all that was left was their sentencing. France was in no mood to risk further public embarrassment by raising a defense under international law which it likely would lose, so it acceded to the application of New Zealand law.

But assume that Major Mafart and Captain Prieur had not pleaded guilty to criminal wrongdoing and that they, with the support of the French government, had decided to challenge their prosecution in the New Zealand courts by mounting a defense based on international as well as New Zealand law. What then? Would the New Zealand courts have accepted the application of international law within New Zealand? If so, how and to what extent? Would international law have been seen as superior to New Zealand law and allowed to override it in whole or in part? What, precisely, would have been the relation of international law to New Zealand's internal or domestic law?

These are not idle questions. As it happens, international law comes up very often in national decision-making arenas, being commonly resorted to, albeit in varying degree, for the actual *rules of decision* in domestic litigation and settlement. This is increasingly true in the environmental realm. As one international environmental law scholar observed already forty years ago:

> As far as national tribunals are concerned . . ., there is some indication of an emerging trend towards a widening of their

[48] New Zealand has no extradition treaty with France.

> portals in transnational environmental matters. When an incident has caused oil pollution damage in the territory (including territorial sea) of a particular state or states (wherever the escape or discharge responsible may have occurred), the International Convention on Civil Liability for Oil Pollution Damage stipulates that actions for compensation may only be brought in the courts of the damaged state(s); it does additionally, however, commit each contracting state to "ensure that its Courts possess the necessary jurisdiction to entertain such actions for compensation." With regard to any kind of transnational environmental nuisance or damage, Denmark, Finland, Norway, and Sweden have provided for access of each other's nationals to their courts. More specifically, they have agreed that any person who is or may be affected by a nuisance caused by environmentally harmful activities or is seeking compensation for damage caused by such activities in another contracting state shall have the right to bring before the appropriate Court or Administrative Authority of that State the question of the permissibility of such activities, including the question of measures to prevent damage, and to appeal against the decision of the Court or the Administrative Authority to the same extent and on the same terms as, legal entity of the State in which the activities are being carried out.
>
> Without an explicit international agreement, a Canadian citizen and a Canadian environmental organization were early permitted to intervene in litigation in US courts under the National Environmental Policy Act of 1969 to ensure representation of their own separate interests.[49]

Jan Schneider, World Public Order of the Environment: Towards an International Ecological Law and Organization 91 (1979).

In any event, to the extent that national courts do decide cases of international consequence, it may be said that they act as agents of the international legal order. If international law were relevant only in foreign offices, intergovernmental organizations, and third-party decision-making arenas such as the International Court of Justice, then, though the subject still would be deserving of serious study, it would be confined to limited amounts of conflict resolution across national boundaries.

Thus, in the resort to international law in domestic law systems we find a vast extension of the influence of international law. Therefore, before we plunge into the problems in Part II of this Coursebook, we here present

[49] Wilderness Society v. Morton, 463 F.2d 1261 (D.C. Cir. 1972).

material concerning the incorporation of international law as a basis for decision in national courts.

As James Crawford had observed, "the relationship between international and national law is often presented as a clash at a level of high theory, usually between 'dualism' and 'monism'."[50] *Dualists* take the position that the international legal system and national legal systems are entirely separate bodies of law. Thus, international law cannot become part of the national legal system—cannot, for example, be applied as a rule of decision in national courts—unless the political authorities of a state take some action to *transform* the international legal rule into a domestic legal rule. For example, the parliament or legislature of a nation might adopt an international rule as domestic law. But, for a dualist, international law will not be applicable in the domestic system until some such act of transformation occurs.

A *monist* on the other hand, "postulates that national and international law form one single legal order."[51] Once a state has accepted (or otherwise become bound by) an international legal rule, a monist would argue that the courts of that state should directly apply the international rule without the need for any separate legislative or executive action making it a part of the domestic legal system.

As Crawford observes:

> [N]either theory offers an adequate account of the *practice* of international and national courts . . . . Each legal system has . . . its own approach . . . [and] each system reserves to itself the authority to determine [the role of international law in domestic legal decision-making].[52]

Insofar as the international community is concerned, the important question is whether a state has complied with its international obligations. The state's chosen method of ensuring that its international commitments are honored is relatively unimportant.

> The domestic instruments that the State employs to perform its international obligations are a matter of indifference to international law. It may employ statute or administrative official or judicial control. It may directly incorporate international law into the local system, or it may incorporate only treaties and not customary law.[53]

---

[50] James Crawford, Brownlie's Principles of Public International Law 48 (7th ed. 2012)

[51] *Id.*

[52] *Id.* at 49–50.

[53] Edwin A. Borchard, The Relation Between International Law and Municipal Law, 27 Va. L. Rev. 137, 140 (1940).

In other words, each nation decides for itself how it will comply with its international legal obligations. In particular, each nation decides whether its courts can enforce its international law obligations on their own or whether there must be some act (e.g., legislation) by which an international obligation is "transformed" into domestic law before the courts can enforce it. But, it is important to note, even if a nation fails to authorize its courts to enforce its international legal obligations, that nation is still responsible on the international plane if those obligations are violated (by a court decision or otherwise). Thus, if New Zealand had an international legal duty to release the French agents to France upon France's acceptance of responsibility, New Zealand would be answerable to France for its failure to do so, even if New Zealand's courts were not bound under domestic law to accept or apply that international rule.

In the remainder of this chapter we briefly review the approach to these issues taken in New Zealand and in the United States. In the material that follows, you should pay particular attention to the following two issues:

- Under what circumstances will the courts of each country apply rules from treaties as the applicable law in cases before them (assuming, of course, the relevance of the treaty rule in question)?
- Under what circumstances will the courts of each country apply rules of customary international law as the applicable law in cases before them?

1. NEW ZEALAND'S "DUALIST" SYSTEM

The *dualist approach* to the relationship between national and international law, manifest in the United Kingdom and elsewhere in The Commonwealth where the common law prevails, is illustrated by New Zealand law, which we invoke here to answer several of the questions we have raised in connection with the *Rainbow Warrior* affair. We quote from a report of New Zealand's Legislation Advisory Committee adopted as an official government policy by the New Zealand cabinet.[54]

LEGISLATIVE CHANGE: GUIDELINES ON PROCESS AND CONTENT, APPENDIX E, PARA. 44 (REV. ED. 1991)

International law and practice make it clear that various representatives of the state . . . have authority to negotiate and adopt or

[54] In 2015, the Legislation Advisory Committee was replaced by a Legislation Design and Advisory Committee. The Guidelines document from which we quote has also been replaced. We have retained this excerpt from the 1991 document because of its excellent discussion of the relationship between domestic and international law in New Zealand's legal system.

authenticate the text of [a] treaty. Other officials may also be given specific authority to undertake a negotiation or to agree to a treaty text.

These functions are executive functions. The Privy Council made that clear in 1937 in a Canadian case from which it is convenient to quote . . .:

> It will be essential to keep in mind the distinction between (1) the formation, and (2) the performance, of the obligations constituted by a treaty, using that word as comprising any agreement between two or more sovereign States. Within the British Empire there is a well-established rule that the making of a treaty is an executive act, while the performance of its obligations, if they entail alteration of the existing domestic law, requires legislative action. If the national executive, the government of the day, decide to incur the obligations of a treaty which involve alteration of law they have to run the risk of obtaining the assent of Parliament to the necessary statute or statutes. To make themselves as secure as possible they will often in such cases before final ratification seek to obtain from Parliament an expression of approval. But it has never been suggested, and it is not the law, that such an expression of approval operates as law, or that in law it precludes the assenting Parliament, or any subsequent Parliament, from refusing to give its sanction to any legislative proposals that may subsequently be brought before it. . . . Once [obligations undertaken in treaties] are created, while they bind the State as against the other contracting parties, Parliament may refuse to perform them and so leave the State in default. In a unitary State[55] whose Legislation possesses unlimited powers the problem is simple. Parliament will either fulfil or not treaty obligations imposed upon the State by its executive. The nature of the obligations does not affect the complete authority of the Legislature to make them law if it so chooses. (*Attorney-General for Canada v Attorney-General for Ontario* [1937] AC 326, 347–348).

* * *

This question [of how treaties are given effect in New Zealand] arises at two levels, the international and the national. . . . So far as national implementation is concerned, the passage . . . quoted from the Privy Council in the Canadian case provides the starting point. While the government can enter into treaties it cannot, by that action alone, change the rights and duties of individuals or of the state under the law of New Zealand. If such changes are called for then legislation will be necessary.

---

55 *E.g.*, New Zealand, in contrast to a federated state such as the United States.

Many treaties do not have a direct impact on the rights and duties of individuals. They can operate without legislative support. The obligations arising under alliances or the Charter of the United Nations provide an example. For the most part those obligations are met through the powers which the government has under the prerogative and the common law to administer its foreign relations and to deploy its armed forces. . . .

In a second category of cases, New Zealand law will already conform, or largely so, with the treaty to which the government is proposing to become a party. That view was taken for instance of the International Covenants on Civil and Political Rights and on Economic, Social and Cultural Rights. . . .

In the third case, New Zealand law is not in compliance with the proposed treaty obligations. Legislative action will have to be taken. It might be taken by the executive under delegated authority if Parliament has conferred that authority (as with UN sanctions or in the case of extradition and double taxation agreements for instance), or the action might have to be taken by Parliament.

* * *

Legislative provisions giving effect to treaty obligations can take one of two broad forms. They might be more or less conspicuously woven into the texture of existing legislation. That is so for instance of that part of international criminal law which can be found in the Crimes Act 1961. . . .

The second method is more direct. The particular treaty provisions are set out and are given the force of law in New Zealand. Legislation relating to extradition, double taxation, and diplomatic and consular privileges and immunities uses that method for instance. . . .

Even if a treaty is not given force by legislation, it might nevertheless have significance in the operation of our legal system. For instance:[56]

(a) The treaty might be declaratory of customary international law on a particular topic . . . and customary international law *is* part of the law of New Zealand.

(b) Courts will if possible interpret statutes consistently with international obligations. But if the statute plainly contradicts the treaty, that interpretative course is not available.

There are three points to note about this discussion. First, treaties are not directly binding on New Zealand courts, even if the treaty purports to

[56] In the following two instances, New Zealand (and other Commonwealth countries) may be seen to borrow from the monist tradition, allowing the incorporation of customary international law directly into the local common law without requiring an enabling act of Parliament.

regulate the rights and duties of individuals. There must be some legislative action to implement the treaty (which may include administrative action by the government pursuant to delegated legislative powers). Second, the New Zealand government has some inherent authority (e.g., command over its armed forces) which it may use to carry out its international legal obligations in that arena of government action. Finally, New Zealand courts treat customary international law as "part of the law of New Zealand" and, accordingly, they can and do use customary international law as the rule of decision in appropriate cases. This is a reflection of a broader tradition among common-law countries that treats customary international law as part of the "common law."[57]

2. THE APPROACH IN THE UNITED STATES

In this section we will devote considerable space to addressing the approach followed in the United States to the adoption and implementation of international law. It is important to recognize, however, that our coverage of this topic will be superficial. Entire law school courses are devoted to the creation and enforcement of international law in the legal system of the United States, and thousands upon thousands of pages have been written on the subject. We can only highlight a few key concepts.[58]

(a) The Negotiation and Ratification of Treaties

Article II of the Constitution says that the President holds the "[p]ower, by and with the Advice and Consent of the Senate, to make Treaties, provided two thirds of the Senators present concur . . . ." In practice, this means that the President (or, more probably, his or her representatives in the foreign service) negotiates agreements with foreign nations or bodies. At the conclusion of those negotiations, a treaty is often "signed," but it will not yet be binding on the United States.[59] The treaty is next presented to the Senate, which may reject it or approve it with a two-thirds majority. This is typically the extent of the Senate's contribution of "advice and consent"—senators themselves have little to do with negotiating the terms of treaties. However, the Senate often places conditions on its advice and consent through RUDs—an acronym that stands for "reservations, understandings, and declarations." RUDs might be included for several reasons: to reject portions of the treaty that are inconsistent with the Constitution; for political reasons; to define

---

[57] In many jurisdictions that follow the common law, its rules (including any incorporated rules of customary international law) are only applicable insofar as there is no statute that displaces them.

[58] For a thorough analysis, *see* Curtis A. Bradley, International Law in the U.S. Legal System (2nd ed. 2015).

[59] There are exceptions to these rules for international treaties that are entered into by the President as "executive agreements."

ambiguous terms; or to declare that a treaty is not self-executing (see section b, *infra*).

Although it is common to speak of the Senate as "ratifying" a treaty, that is not what the Senate does. The Senate gives its consent to the President's ratification of the treaty. Once the Senate has consented to the treaty, it becomes the President's responsibility to complete the process of "making" the treaty, usually by depositing an instrument of ratification on behalf of the United States with the country or organization named as treaty depositary. The President's ratification of the treaty will be subject to whatever conditions the Senate has imposed on that ratification and, indeed, the President might add conditions of his own. The conditions expressed in the instrument of ratification may or may not be valid and enforceable under international law. The United States will be a party to the treaty once the instrument is deposited and not before.

It is important to note that ratification of a treaty is a process that is distinct from the negotiation and signing of a treaty. Although the states that negotiate a treaty could agree that it takes effect on signature, usually they do not. Hence, states do not ordinarily become bound by a treaty unless they ratify it.[60] In newspaper reporting, and even in judicial opinions, one commonly reads statements that assert that the United States is a party to a treaty because it has signed the treaty. Such statements are usually incorrect. In most cases, especially where multilateral treaties are concerned, the United States will a party to a treaty only if it has ratified the treaty; its signature alone is not enough.

For a variety of reasons, the United States might sign a treaty that it never ratifies and never accepts as an international legal obligation. Sometimes a treaty will be negotiated but not presented to the Senate, perhaps because it will not fare well with the members of that body. The President might wait for political will to turn more favorable, at which time the treaty will be presented for legislative approval. Or a new President might not approve of a treaty negotiated by his or her predecessor and refuse to present it for the Senate for its approval. Moreover, even if a treaty is approved by the Senate, the President is not required to ratify and may refuse to do so. Sometimes this is because the President does not believe the United States can comply with the treaty and does not wish to accept an international obligation unless it can be honored. Sometimes a new President simply disagrees with the treaty and refuses to ratify despite the Senate's approval.

---

[60] Under international law, the term "ratification" is generally used to refer to the process of consenting to a treaty after a state has signed it. Other terms (e.g., acceptance or approval) refer to consent expressed by states that never signed the treaty. Here, we use the term "ratification" to refer generically to a state's expression of consent to be bound by a treaty as distinguished from its simple signing of a treaty.

(b) The Effect of Treaties in the Domestic Legal System

When a treaty is properly "made" by the President with the advice and consent of the Senate, Article VI(2) of the United States Constitution provides for the treaty's effectiveness in the following terms:

> This Constitution, and the Laws of the United States which shall be made in Pursuance thereof; and all Treaties made, or which shall be made, under the Authority of the United States, shall be the supreme Law of the Land; and the Judges in every State shall be bound thereby, any Thing in the Constitution or Laws of any State to the Contrary notwithstanding.

This provision seems to adopt the following approach to the application of international treaties as "law" in United States courts: i) they are automatically part of "the supreme Law of the Land" and applicable in court; ii) they therefore prevail over contrary state law;[61] and iii) they are not superior to other federal law,[62] by implication from the fact that the clause makes no distinction among "this Constitution, and the Laws of the United States which shall be made in Pursuance thereof; and all Treaties made, or which shall be made, under the Authority of the United States."

In practice, however, Article VI has not been read literally by the Supreme Court. Instead, the Court has said that not all "treaties," even when approved by the Senate and ratified by the President, count as "law." According to the Court's *non-self-execution doctrine,* a treaty is enforceable as "the supreme law of the land" only when the treaty provision is "self-executing"—when it "operates of itself, without the aid of any legislative provision." But when the provisions of the treaty "import a contract, when either of the parties engages to perform a particular act," then the treaty is deemed unenforceable without supporting legislation. Such a treaty is "non-self-executing" and "the legislature must execute the contract before it can become a rule for the Court." Foster v. Neilson, 27. U.S. (2 Pet.) 253, 314 (1829).[63] In other words, despite the seemingly absolute language of

---

[61] Interpreting this language for the first time in 1796, the Court decided that a Virginia law requiring debts owed to British creditors to be paid to the State of Virginia was nullified by a provision in the 1783 Paris Peace Treaty without the need for Congress to pass any implementing legislation. *Ware v. Hylton,* 3 Dall. 199, 220–21, 1 L.Ed. 568 (1796).

[62] Federal legislation and Senate-approved treaties have been treated by the Court as legally equivalent sources of law. In the event of an apparent conflict between a treaty obligation and federal legislation, a court will first attempt to construe the provisions to avoid the conflict. *See, e.g.,* Cook v. United States, 288 U.S. 102 (1933) ("A treaty will not be deemed to have been abrogated or modified by a later statute unless such purpose on the part of Congress has been clearly expressed.") If conflict is inevitable, the law that is later in time will prevail. *See, e.g.,* Whitney v. Robertson, 124 U.S. 190 (1888) ("The duty of the courts is to construe and give effect to the latest expression of the sovereign will.").

[63] The treaty at issue in *Foster v. Nielson* provided that the United States would recognize land grants previously made by Spain to private individuals in territory ceded by Spain to the United States. The precise language, in English, was that such land grants "shall be ratified and confirmed." The Court held that this language was not self-executing and that a claim to land

the Constitution, some treaties create no judicially enforceable legal rights absent Congressional legislation to implement those treaties.

Determining whether a treaty is self-executing or non-self-executing is no simple task,[64] and judicial opinions traditionally identified a number of factors relevant to the inquiry whether the courts should directly apply the treaty or leave the matter of treaty implementation to legislative action. Justice Breyer summarized this traditional approach (in a dissenting opinion[65]) as follows:

> [When determining whether a treaty provision is self-executing or not], this Court has found the provision's subject matter of particular importance. Does the treaty provision declare peace? Does it promise not to engage in hostilities? If so, it addresses itself to the political branches. Alternatively, does it concern the adjudication of traditional private legal rights such as rights to own property, to conduct a business, or to obtain civil tort recovery? If so, it may well address itself to the Judiciary. Enforcing such rights and setting their boundaries is the bread-and-butter work of the courts.
>
> One might also ask whether the treaty provision confers specific, detailed individual legal rights. Does it set forth definite standards that judges can readily enforce? Other things being equal, where rights are specific and readily enforceable, the treaty provision more likely 'addresses ' the judiciary. . . .
>
> Alternatively, would direct enforcement require the courts to create a new cause of action? Would such enforcement engender constitutional controversy? Would it create constitutionally undesirable conflict with the other branches?

In *Medellin v. Texas*,[66] a majority of the Supreme Court rejected the traditional approach to self-execution analysis, arguing that it was unacceptably "indeterminate." Instead, the Court said, one must focus on the particular language of the treaty and ask a simple question: do "the textual provisions [of the treaty] indicate that the President and Senate intended for the agreement to have domestic effect?"[67] Although it is not

---

based on a Spanish land grant would not be recognized because Congress had not "ratified and confirmed" it.

[64] In fact, the conclusion that the treaty provision at issue in *Foster v. Nielson* was non-self-executing was overturned by the Supreme Court four years later, in in *U.S. v. Percheman*, 32 U.S. 51, 89 (1833). In Percheman, the Court reviewed the Spanish-language version of the treaty, which said (as translated) that Spanish land grants "shall remain ratified and confirmed." Construing this Spanish version and the English version together, the Court concluded that the English text in question meant, in fact, that the Spanish land grants "'shall be ratified and confirmed,' *by force of the instrument itself*" and without the need for further legislation.

[65] *Medellin v. Texas*, 552 U.S. 491, 549–550 (2008) (Breyer, J., dissenting).

[66] 552 U.S. 491 (2008).

[67] *Id.* at 519.

necessary that the treaty "provide for self-execution in so many talismanic words," a treaty provision is nonetheless self-executing only when its "terms reflect a determination by the President who negotiated it and the Senate that confirmed it that the treaty has domestic effect."[68] How, exactly, intent will or won't be inferred from treaty language is not clearly explained in *Medellin*, and one might expect that factors such as those mentioned by Justice Breyer will inevitably influence judicial determinations of the intentions of Congress and the President regarding judicial treaty enforcement.

In addition to holding that courts could not directly enforce a non-self-executing treaty against contrary state law, *Medellin* held that the President was similarly constrained. The President has "an array of political and diplomatic means" for enforcing international obligations, but he cannot force U.S. States to comply with our international obligations when the relevant treaty provision is non-self-executing. To the contrary, a non-self-executing treaty is simply not "law" within the meaning of the Constitution, and the President cannot execute it against the States unless and until Congress transforms it into domestic law.[69]

In reaching this conclusion, the Court moved a long way in the direction of overruling several prior precedents that held that the President sometimes has inherent authority to enforce the provisions of non-self-executing international agreements.[70] Those cases, said the Court, should be understood only as an affirmation of the President's power "to settle foreign claims pursuant to an executive agreement," a "narrow and strictly limited" power that is a "gloss" on Executive Power and based on a "pervasive" history of "congressional acquiescence." There is no inherent Presidential power to enforce non-self-executing treaties.[71]

This does not mean, of course, that a President could not implement a non-self-executing treaty by exercising other powers delegated to him by Congress or granted to him by the Constitution. Thus, a President might carry out the terms of a mutual defense treaty by exercising his power as Commander in Chief. Or the President might implement an environmental treaty by exercising authority granted to him under federal environmental laws. In short, "the President may comply with the treaty's obligation by . . . means [that] are consistent with the Constitution. But he may not rely upon a non-self-executing treaty to 'establish binding rules of decision that preempt contrary state law.' "[72]

---

[68] *Id.* at 521.

[69] *Id.* at 525.

[70] *See, e.g., United States v. Pink*, 315 U.S. 203 (1942); *United States v. Belmont*, 301 U.S. 324 (1937); *Dames & Moore v. Regan*, 453 U.S. 654 (1981).

[71] *Id. at* 530–32.

[72] *Id.* at 530.

Thus, in the United States, there are three ways in which the provisions of treaties ratified by the United States might become domestic law enforceable in domestic courts:

1. Those treaties will be directly enforceable in court if the terms of the treaty create private rights and the President and the ratifying Senate intended those provisions to be self-executing.

2. Congress could pass legislation to implement a non-self-executing treaty.[73]

3. Even if Congress does not act to implement a treaty, the President might be able to implement that treaty through the exercise of some constitutionally granted presidential power or through the exercise of powers delegated to the Executive Branch by other Congressional legislation.

(c) Executive Agreements Not Approved by the Senate

U.S. Presidents enter many international agreements without involving the Senate. Sometimes the President has inherent power under the Constitution to enter an agreement (e.g., an agreement to exchange ambassadors with another country). Such agreements are called "sole executive agreements." In other circumstances, a treaty may give the United States the power to enter into agreements with other countries and the President, as the "sole organ" of the United States in its dealings with other countries, is charged with exercising that treaty power on behalf of the United States.[74] These are sometimes called "treaty executive agreements." In still other circumstances, executive agreements are entered by the President pursuant to a prior or subsequent Congressional authorization. These are so-called "congressional-executive agreements." Congressional-executive agreements are typically used when the President negotiates trade agreements with other countries.[75]

---

[73] The Court has long held that the President (with Senate approval) can make a treaties on any subject. It has also held that Congress can pass legislation to implement those treaties, even if Congress would otherwise lack constitutional authority to legislate on the subject matter of the treaty in question. *See Missouri v. Holland,* 252 U.S. 416 (1920). Recently, however, some members of the Court have challenged that conclusion, suggesting that the Treaty Power (and Congress's power to implement treaties) is limited and that the Court may need to step in to draw a line between "matters of international intercourse" (which can be properly addressed using the Treaty Power) and "matters of purely domestic regulation" (which cannot). *See Bond v. United States,* 572 U.S. 844, 896 (2014) (Thomas, J., concurring).

[74] For example, the Convention on the Organization for Economic Co-Operation and Development provides that the Organization may "take decisions which . . . shall be binding on all the Members." To be bound, however, a Member must ordinarily vote in favor of the decision. This, in effect, means that decisions constitute international agreements binding on OECD Member States. The U.S. vote in the OECD is determined by the executive branch.

[75] Because trade agreements involve tariffs—a form of taxation—they implicate the constitutional requirement that "All Bills for raising Revenue shall originate in the House of Representatives." Thus, one reason for negotiating and implementing trade agreements through

The domestic legal effect of executive agreements depends on the nature of the agreement and on what branch of government has implemented it. The Supreme Court has held in several cases that sole executive agreements entered by the President are judicially enforceable and can preempt state law.[76] But, as noted earlier, *Medellin* interpreted those cases very narrowly. When Congress approves an executive agreement, it will often specify whether, and to what extent, the terms of that agreement enter into domestic law.[77] After *Medellin,* it is probably fair to say that executive agreements cannot create domestic law of their own force: they will be enforceable in domestic courts i) to the extent that the President is able to implement them by exercising authority delegated by Congress or a constitutionally based presidential power, or ii) to the extent that Congress expressly provides for an agreement's implementation through legislation.

President Obama entered, and ratified, the Paris Agreement on Climate Change as a sole executive agreement. He did not seek or receive Senate approval of the agreement. Nor did he seek approval of the Congress as a whole. Many of his opponents regarded his action as a usurpation of power, and his authority to enter a binding international agreement without Senate ratification or Congressional approval was hotly debated. He was nevertheless able to give the agreement "legal teeth under domestic law" by relying on his regulatory authority under the Clean Air Act.[78] When he came into office, President Trump announced that the United States would withdraw from the Paris Agreement, and the Trump Administration immediately began taking steps to dismantle the regulatory rules that had been adopted to implement U.S. commitments under that agreement.

(d) Customary International Law in the Courts

The question of the status of customary international law in the legal system of the United States is even more complicated than the question of the status of treaties and executive agreements. At the time the Constitution was adopted, the "law of nations" was considered to be part of the common law and enforceable by courts in appropriate cases.[79] This view

a legislative process that includes the House of Representatives, rather than through the Senate-only treaty process, is to mitigate the risk of constitutional challenge to such agreements.

[76] *See, e.g., American Ins. Assn. v. Garamendi,* 539 U.S. 396 (2003), and cases cited in note 66, *supra.*

[77] *See, e.g.,* North American Free Trade Agreement Implementation Act, Pub. L. 103–182, §§ 101 & 102, 19 U.S.C. §§ 3311–3312.

[78] *See* Curtis A. Bradley & Jack L. Goldsmith, *Presidential Control Over International Law,* 131 Harv. L. Rev. 1201, 1248–52 (2018).

[79] Stewart Jay, *The Status of the Law of Nations in Early American Law,* 42 Vand. L. Rev. 819 (1989).

was expressed most famously by the Supreme Court in *The Paquete Habana:*

> International law is part of our law, and must be ascertained and administered by the courts of justice of appropriate jurisdiction, as often as questions of right depending upon it are duly presented for their determination. For this purpose, where there is no treaty, and no controlling executive or legislative act or judicial decision, resort must be had to the customs and usages of civilized nations . . . .[80]

The legal status of customary international law under this view was that of "general common law." As such, it was inferior to legislation, as the Court observed, or even to a contrary "controlling executive . . . act or judicial decision." In addition, it was not considered part of federal law and thus did not preempt contrary state law or provide a basis for federal question jurisdiction.[81]

After the Supreme Court's decision in *Erie R.R. Co. v. Tompkins*,[82] the precise domestic legal status of customary international law became a matter of some doubt. *Erie* declared that federal courts sitting in diversity could apply the law set out in "the Federal Constitution or . . . Acts of Congress." Otherwise, their obligation was to apply the law of a particular state to decide cases before them. There was no such thing as "federal general common law" that a federal court could apply in preference to state law. When a case required the application of common law rules, federal courts were to be bound by the common law as articulated by the courts of the state in which the case was being heard.

Whether *Erie's* reject of a "general federal common law" also applied to customary international law was not entirely clear. Some courts concluded that federal courts were, indeed, bound by state court decisions concerning the content of customary international law.[83] But that conclusion struck many as utterly contrary to the Constitution's investiture of foreign affairs authority in the federal government.[84]

Eventually, the Supreme Court began to recognize the existence of pockets of "federal common law," and customary international law came to be treated by many scholars and courts as a branch of the "federal common

---

[80] 175 U.S. 677, 700 (1900).

[81] *See* Curtis A. Bradley & Jack L. Goldsmith, *Customary Law as Federal Common Law: A Critique of the Modern Position*, 110 Harv. L. Rev. 815, 822–25 (1997).

[82] 304 U.S. 64 (1938).

[83] *See Bergman v. De Sieyes*, 170 F.2d 360 (2nd Cir. 1948) (holding that state court interpretations of customary international law are binding on federal courts).

[84] *See, e.g.*, Philip C. Jessup, *The Doctrine of Erie Railroad v. Tompkins Applied to International Law*, 33 Am. J. Int'l L. 740 (1939).

law."[85] However, treating customary international law as full-fledged "federal common law" carries major implications that are unpalatable to many observers—e.g., that customary international law (as federal common law) is supreme over state law, that federal question jurisdiction could be based on a claim brought under customary international law, that customary international law (as federal common law) could trump prior-in-time federal statutes, and even that the President is bound to adhere to customary international law (as federal common law). For that reason, courts and commentators have never fully endorsed the view that customary international law is "federal common law" with legal effects on a par with other recognized branches of federal common law.[86]

Today, there are at least two situations in which it is generally accepted that customary international law will provide the rule of decision for a federal court (in the absence of a contrary federal statute). The first situation is when a current or former foreign government official who has been sued in U.S. courts invokes the law of foreign official immunity. The Supreme Court has held that such claims must be resolved under the common law and, to date, most courts hold that the common law incorporates the norms of customary international law.[87]

The second situation in which federal courts[88] regularly apply customary international law is in actions under the Alien Tort Statute (ATS). The ATS gives federal courts jurisdiction over "any civil action by an alien for a tort only, committed in violation of the law of nations or a treaty of the United States."[89] Beginning in the 1980s, plaintiffs brought a slew of cases against a variety of defendants alleging that the particular defendant in the case had violated customary international law and thereby injured the plaintiff.[90] Generally these cases involved claims based on international human rights law, but some major cases also raised claims based on international environmental law.[91]

---

85 *See, e.g., Filartiga v. Pena-Irala*, 630 F.2d 876, 885 (2nd Cir. 1980) ("the law of nations . . . has always been part of the federal common law"). *See also* Bradley & Goldsmith, *supra* note 81, at 827–37. This acceptance of customary international law as part of federal common law did not happen quickly or without the presence of disputing voices.

86 *Bradley & Goldsmith, supra* note 81, at 827–37.

87 *See Samantar v. Yousuf*, 560 U.S. 305 (2010) (common law of foreign official immunity applies); *Yousuf v. Samantar*, 699 F.3d 763 (4th Cir. 2012) (questions of foreign official immunity "turn upon principles of customary international law"). The State Department has consistently taken the view that the courts should follow its decisions about which foreign officials deserve immunity and which do not.

88 Theoretically, if customary international law is part of the common law, state courts could also apply it in cases properly brought before them.

89 28 U.S.C. § 1350.

90 *See, e.g,. Filartiga v. Pena-Irala*, 630 F.2d 876, 885 (2nd Cir. 1980).

91 *See, e.g., Sarei v. Rio Tinto, PLC*, 671 F.3d 736 (9th Cir. 2011), *cert. granted and judgment vacated by Rio Tinto PLC v. Sarei*, 569 U.S. 945 (2013). *See also Institute of Cetacean Research v. Sea Shepherd Conservation Society*, 725 F.3d 940 (9th Cir. 2013) (holding that anti-whaling organization engaged in acts of piracy under customary international law when it interfered with

A series of Supreme Court cases has severely restricted the ability of plaintiffs to bring ATS claims based on alleged violations of customary international law. First, in *Sosa v. Alvarez-Machain*, the Court ruled that not all claims of violations of customary international law are cognizable under the ATS. Federal courts should recognize a cause of action for violation of customary international law only when the customary norm in question is "accepted by the civilized world and defined with a specificity comparable to the features of the 18th-century paradigms we have recognized."[92] The norm must be "specific, universal, and obligatory."[93] The Court cautioned strongly against judicial activism or creativity—unless a customary international law rule was widely accepted and specific and clear in its content, judicial recognition of a cause of action for violation of the rule would "imping[e] on the discretion of the Legislative and Executive Branches in managing foreign affairs."[94]

In 2013, the Supreme Court erected a further hurdle to ATS actions by holding that the statute did not have extraterritorial reach.[95] Where "all the relevant conduct takes place outside the United States," it would be inappropriate in most cases to allow a cause of action based on the ATS to proceed. Because asserting jurisdiction over conduct abroad based on a claimed violation of international law would risk "triggering . . . serious foreign policy consequences," the courts should not assert such jurisdiction absent a clearer directive from the political branches than is contained in the ATS. The Court left open the possibility that claims might "touch and concern the territory of the United States . . . with sufficient force" to warrant hearing them. But the thrust of the Court's opinion was to disallow tort claims based on violations of international law occurring outside the United States.

The final blow to those hoping to hold businesses accountable for activities that violated international environmental law norms came in 2018, with the Court's decision in *Jesner v. Arab Bank, PLC.*[96] In *Jesner,* individuals injured by terrorist acts committed overseas sought damages from a bank that they alleged had financed the terrorist activities through transactions processed at its branch in New York. Applying the rule in *Sosa* that ATS actions must rest on an international norm that is "specific, universal, and obligatory," the Court held that there is no such "international-law norm imposing liability on corporations for acts of their

---

navigation and activities of whaling ships and granting preliminary injunction against organization's activity).

[92] *Sosa v. Alvarez-Machain*, 542 U.S. 692 (2004). The 18th-century paradigms referred to by the court were customary law rules concerning offenses against ambassadors, violations of grants of safe conduct, acts of piracy, and the capture of prizes.

[93] 542 U.S. at 732.

[94] *Id.* at 727.

[95] *Kiobel v. Royal Dutch Petroleum Co.*, 569 U.S. 108 (2013).

[96] *Jesner v. Arab Bank, PLC*, 138 S.Ct. 1386 (2018).

employees that contravene fundamental human rights." In reaching this decision, the Court relied heavily on the view that the policy decision—whether "to extend ATS liability to foreign corporations"—was a matter for Congress to resolve.[97]

(e) Customary International Law and Federal Legislation

Congress can, if it wishes, incorporate customary international law into U.S. law through the adoption of appropriate legislation to that effect. This depends, of course, on Congress having the authority to adopt such legislation but, in most cases, this is likely. The Constitution expressly gives Congress the ability to "define and punish Piracies and Felonies committed on the high Seas, and Offences against the Law of Nations."[98] More importantly, customary international law typically touches upon matters (e.g., interstate relations, protection of the oceanic environment, and the conduct of hostilities) that are of national importance. Many provisions of the Constitution, including the necessary and proper clause, give Congress powers to legislate that could be used to incorporate customary international law rules into the domestic legal system in these situations. Just as there are many cases in which Congress has passed legislation implementing treaty law, so too has Congress frequently incorporated international customary law norms into domestic legislation.[99]

Finally, the *Charming Betsy* canon instructs courts to endeavor to interpret federal statutes in a manner consistent with international law, including customary international law.[100] The strength of this rule, however, is debatable. Some courts have opined that it "bears [only] on a limited range of cases" and only when Congress's intent is ambiguous. Where Congress has legislated in a way that clearly permits actions contrary to international law, these courts conclude that a narrow construction of the statute is unwarranted.[101]

---

[97] *Id.* at 1403.

[98] United States Constitution, article I, § 8, cl. 10.

[99] *See, e.g.*, Foreign Sovereign Immunities Act, 28 U.S.C. §§ 1602, et seq.; 33 U.S.C. § 1912 (action taken to respond to pollution from ships in U.S. waters must be taken "in accordance with international law"); 33 U.S.C. § 1509 (rules governing vessel movements and similar matters must be adopted consistently with "recognized principles of international law"); 18 U.S.C. § 1651 (whoever commits "the crime of piracy *as defined by the law of nations*" is subject to life imprisonment); Coast Guard rules on marine environmental protection and other matters are "subject to recognized principles of international law."

[100] *See Murray v. Schooner Charming Betsy*, 6 U.S. (2 Cranch) 64, 118 (1804) ("an act of Congress ought never to be construed to violate the law of nations if any other possible construction remains").

[101] *See, e.g., Serra v. Lapin*, 600 F.3d 1101 (9th Cir. 2010) (Congress passed a statute giving the Attorney General discretion in a matter, and that precludes judicial examination of the consistency of the Attorney General's actions with international law). *But see Ma v. Reno*, 208 F.3d 815 (9th Cir. 2000), *reaffirmed and amended after remand*, 257 F.3d 1095 (9th Cir. 2001) (refusing

DISCUSSION NOTES/QUESTIONS

1. International law can be applied in the domestic legal system in a number of ways, and potentially by any branch of government. Thus, in the United States at least, the courts have the authority to enforce and apply self-executing treaties and, under certain circumstances, they also will enforce and apply customary international law. Congress, for its part, can pass legislation incorporating treaty or customary norms into domestic law, or an administrative agency might use its rule-making authority to implement international norms. The President will sometimes have inherent power to implement an international legal commitments directly or by proclamation.

2. Which approaches to the domestic implementation of international law are likely to be most effective with respect to international environmental law? Consider the provisions of a complex environmental agreement like the Montreal Protocol on Substances that Deplete the Ozone Layer **(Basic Document 2.8)**: this agreement requires nations to phase-out the use of specified ozone-depleting substances over time. What implementation techniques would you recommend?

From time to time, the Parties to the Montreal Protocol make decisions concerning the maximum quantity of a particular ozone-depleting substance that can be produced in a given year under certain exemptions in the treaty. What's the best approach to implementation and enforcement of such decisions? New US legislation? Amended US regulations? A court order? A presidential decree? *See* Problem 5-2, *infra*.

What about a broad international environmental principle, like the principle of sustainable development? How should it be implemented in US law? What would it mean to implement it?

3. Not all states have to grapple with the issue of whether a treaty is self-executing or non-self-executing. As demonstrated by the readings on New Zealand law, the rule in some states (especially common law jurisdictions) is that a treaty must be adopted through legislation before it can have full domestic effect. This rule and a number of narrow exceptions to it are discussed in James Crawford & William R. Edeson, *International Law and Australian Law*, in International Law in Australia 71 (Kevin W. Ryan ed., 2d ed. 1994). *See also* Fluid States: International Law in National legal Systems (Hilary Charlesworth, Madlaine Chiam, Devika Hovell & George Williams eds., 2005). For useful comparative coverage of this issue, see Martin Dixon & Robert McCorquodale, Cases and Materials on International Law 140–45 (2d ed. 1995).

4. Generally, in the United States at least, statutes later in time repeal earlier statutes that address the same subject-matter. What is the theory or rationale behind this "last-in-time" rule, and should it apply as between treaties and statutes? Is it ever appropriate for the President or the Senate, as

---

to construe statutory language authorizing the INS to detain an alien "beyond the removal period" as authorizing indefinite detention because such a rule might violate international law).

the treaty-makers in the United States, to alter the will of Congress by concluding a self-executing treaty that provides for different rules?

5. Putting aside the current state of the law in the United States, what *should* be the role of domestic courts in the application of international law? Do national courts bear the responsibility to hold their own governments accountable for violations of international law? Would it be beneficial or harmful to have domestic courts issuing rulings on the content of international law when the meaning of the international norms is uncertain?

In this connection, consider the comments of Richard A. Falk, The Role of Domestic Courts in the International Legal Order xi–xii (1964):

> Two sets of considerations dominate my interpretation of the proper role for domestic courts to play. First, international law exists in a social system that possesses weak central institutions. As a result, international tribunals are not consistently or conveniently available to resolve most disputes involving questions of international law. Domestic courts can help to overcome this structural weakness in the international legal system. Also, since no international institution is endowed with legislative competence, it is difficult to change old rules in response to changes in the composition and character of international society. If international law is to develop into a universal basis of order, then it is necessary that divergent attitudes toward the content of law be treated with respect. The older states must put forth a special effort to broaden international law enough to make it compatible with the values of [the formerly colonized and other newer] states. It is of no value to insist upon the old rules developed when all of the active international actors accepted *laissez-faire* economics at home and imperialism abroad. Domestic courts in the older states can help adapt international law to the modern world by developing principles that express tolerance for diverse social and economic systems.
>
> Second, domestic courts must struggle to become their own masters in international law cases. The executive must not be allowed, and must certainly not be invited, to control the outcome of judicial proceedings by alleging precedence of foreign policy considerations. The courts are not good vehicles for the promotion of foreign policy; moreover, the independence of courts from national political control is essential if international legal order is to be upheld and developed. A legal tradition depends upon the autonomy of its method and the saliency of its governing principles. Only an independent judiciary can establish a tradition.

Do you agree with Falk? Is his approach realistic? Are domestic courts ever likely to achieve the independence from national policies and values that Falk advocates? If so, how? If courts are not going to make an independent assessment and application of international law, should they stay completely out of international cases? Or is their role, rather, to implement the Executive

Branch's international policy decisions, applying international law when the Executive Branch approves and dismissing the case when it does not? Should the courts make their own interpretation of international law, or is that also an Executive Branch prerogative?

6. In the end, does it matter whether international law is directly applicable in domestic courts or not? Is it a matter of indifference whether international law is enforced by domestic courts or through international processes of state responsibility? Which approach would give greater effect to international law? Which approach would give more control to domestic officials? Which approach do you prefer? Why?

7. No one doubts that the US Congress can, if it wishes, pass legislation that is based on international legal standards and that makes international legal norms part of domestic law. The well-known "fast track" procedure for the adoption and approval of international trade agreements is structured to ensure that the legal commitments made by the United States in an international trade agreement are incorporated into domestic law simultaneously with Congress's approval of the trade agreement. As a result, international trade rules and parallel provisions in US domestic law are often nearly identical in content.

The same approach has been used with environmental treaties. For example, portions of the US Endangered Species Act were adopted, in part, to ensure that US domestic law would be consistent with US international obligations under the 1973 Convention on International Trade in Endangered Species of Wild Fauna and Flora (CITES) **[Basic Document 5.3]**.

Legislative adoption of international norms may not even be necessary. In the modern administrative state, federal agencies have a great deal of power to make rules governing a broad range of private activities. So long as there has been a constitutional delegation of power to an administrative agency, that agency can exercise its rule-making authority to incorporate international legal standards into its rules and therefore into domestic law. Thus, for example, when a new species of plant or animal is added to the list of endangered species under CITES, there is no need for new legislation to ensure protection of that species in the US. Instead, the governing administrative agency simply amends its rules to bring the US endangered species list into conformity with the international list.

But some questions arise. First, if a US agency refuses to amend its regulations to ensure that US domestic law will be in conformity with the country's international legal commitments, could it be forced by a court to make the necessary change? Also, is the administrative agency bound by the international law in question, and who would have standing to insist that it follow that law? Second, if the agency is considering changing its rules to ensure that they are consistent with US international legal commitments, does it need to give prior notice of that change so that citizens who oppose compliance with the international rules can register their objections? Does the agency need to justify regulatory changes on any basis other than "the changes are required by international law?" If international law mandates regulatory changes that reduce environmental protection, would the agency still be justified in making the change? None of these questions has been definitively answered in US law. *See* Problem 5-2, *infra*.

CHAPTER THREE

ADDRESSING TRANSBOUNDARY ENVIRONMENTAL HARM

■ ■ ■

A. THE OBLIGATION TO AVOID CAUSING TRANSBOUNDARY HARM

In 1926, Mr. J.H. Stroh, a landowner and farmer in the Columbia River valley in Washington State, complained to Consolidated Mining and Smelting Company of Canada about the damage to his property allegedly caused by sulfur dioxide fumes emitted from Consolidated's lead and zinc smelter located near Trail, British Columbia. Mr. Stroh's complaint was followed by additional complaints from other U.S. farmers and landowners. The company undertook an investigation after which it paid damages to settle many of the claims. The next year more complaints were made and additional settlements paid. In 1928, a group called the Citizens' Protective Association was formed with the goal of finding a permanent solution to the problem. Members of the Association were forbidden from settling claims with Consolidated without the prior written consent of the Association's Board. After formation of the Citizens' Protection Association, there were no further settlement agreements between Consolidated and individual landowners or farmers.

Meanwhile, the United States government had entered into diplomatic discussions with the Canadian government about the pollution problem. The United States proposed that the matter should be referred to the International Joint Commission [IJC], a body created by the US-Canadian Boundary Waters Treaty of 1909 **(Basic Document 3.16)** and composed of six members, three appointed by each country. Although the IJC's primary responsibility is for transboundary water issues, article 9 of the Boundary Waters Treaty permits the US and Canadian governments to refer to the Commission "any other questions or matters of difference" arising in the border area. Canada agreed with the U.S. government's proposed referral, and the matter was submitted to the Commission on August 7, 1928.

The Commission studied the matter for more than 2½ years. Each government had appointed its own team of scientists to conduct research aimed at evaluating the extent and impact of the pollution, and the Commission reviewed the reports prepared by those scientists. The

Commission also employed its own independent experts to perform an overall evaluation of the situation, based on the available scientific information, including the information provided by the government scientists. In addition, the Commission held hearings to receive information from individuals affected by the pollution as well as from Consolidated. After gathering all this information and considering the legal and factual arguments made by each government, the Commission issued a unanimous report at the end of February, 1931.

The Commission recommended that Canada pay the United States $350,000 as an indemnity for all damages caused by SO2 emissions from the Trail Smelter occurring at any time up to and including January 1, 1932. The Commission also recommended that Consolidated be required to "proceed as expeditiously as may be reasonably possible" to complete certain emission-reduction plans that were underway, and that Consolidated should also be required to take any other action necessary "to reduce the amount and concentration of SO2 fumes drifting from its said plant into the United States until it has reduced the amount by some means to a point where it will do no damage in the United States." If further damage occurred despite such efforts, the Commission indicated that such damage should be compensated, although it also indicated that "any future indemnity will arise only if and when these conditions and recommendations [concerning Consolidated's obligation to implement pollution-control measures] are not complied with and fully met."

Crucially, the Commission specified that "damage" for the purpose of its decision meant only "such damage as the Governments of the United States and Canada may deem appreciable." Moreover, with respect to Consolidated's obligation to reduce emissions to a level where they would "do no damage in the United States," the Commission defined "damage" as not including "occasional damage that may be caused by SO2 fumes being carried across the international boundary in air pockets or by reason of unusual atmospheric conditions."

It eventually became clear that the United States was unwilling to accept the Commission's report and recommendations, largely because of the Commission's limited definition of "damage." Consequently, after several more years of discussion and negotiation, the United States and Canada agreed to submit the matter to binding arbitration.[1]

The agreement to arbitrate began by providing that Canada would pay the U.S. $350,000, as recommended by the International Joint Commission, for all damage caused in the United States by emissions from the Trail Smelter prior to January 1, 1932. The Convention then provided for the creation of an arbitral tribunal and the selection of the arbitrators.

---

[1] *See* Convention between Canada and the United States Relating to Certain Complaints Arising from the Operation of the Smelter at Trail, B.C., Can.-U.S., April 15, 1935.

Finally, in articles III and IV, the Parties identified the matters in dispute and the law to be applied. Those provisions provided, in full, as follows:

> Article III
>
> The Tribunal shall finally decide the questions, hereinafter referred to as "the Questions," set forth hereunder, namely:
>
> (1) Whether damage caused by the Trail Smelter in the State of Washington has occurred since the first day of January, 1932, and, if so, what indemnity should be paid therefore?
>
> (2) In the event of the answer to the first part of the preceding Question being in the affirmative, whether the Trail Smelter should be required to refrain from causing damage in the State of Washington in the future and, if so, to what extent?
>
> (3) In the light of the answer to the preceding Question, what measures or regime, if any, should be adopted or maintained by the Trail Smelter?
>
> (4) What indemnity or compensation, if any, should be paid on account of any decision or decisions rendered by the Tribunal pursuant to the next two preceding Questions?
>
> Article IV
>
> The Tribunal shall apply the law and practice followed in dealing with cognate questions in the United States of America as well as International Law and Practice, and shall give consideration to the desire of the High Contracting Parties to reach a solution just to all parties concerned.

TRAIL SMELTER ARBITRATION (CAN. V. U.S.) FINAL DECISION (11 MARCH 1941)

3 UNRIAA 1938

PART ONE

. . . The Columbia River has its source in the Dominion of Canada. At a place in British Columbia named Trail, it flows past a smelter located in a gorge, where zinc and lead are smelted in large quantities. From Trail, its course is easterly and then it swings in a long curve to the international boundary line, at which point it is running in a southwesterly direction; and its course south of the boundary continues in that general direction. The distance from Trail to the boundary line is about seven miles as the crow flies or about eleven miles, following the course of the river (and possibly a slightly shorter distance by following the contour of the valley). At Trail and continuing down to the boundary and for a considerable distance below the boundary, mountains rise on either side of the river in slopes of various angles to heights ranging from 3,000 to 4,500 feet above sea-level, or between 1,500 to 3,000 feet above the river. The width of the valley proper is between one and two miles. On both sides of the river are a series of bench lands at various heights.

* * *

In 1896, a smelter was started under American auspices near the locality known as Trail, B.C. In 1906, the Consolidated Mining and Smelting Company of Canada, Limited, obtained a charter of incorporation from the Canadian authorities, and that company acquired the smelter plant at Trail as it then existed. Since that time, the Canadian company, without interruption, has operated the Smelter, and from time to time has greatly added to the plant until it has become one of the best and largest equipped smelting plants on the American continent. In 1925 and 1927, two stacks of the plant were erected to 409 feet in height and the Smelter greatly increased its daily smelting of zinc and lead ores. This increased production resulted in more sulphur dioxide fumes and higher concentrations being emitted into the air. In 1916, about 5,000 tons of sulphur per month were emitted; in 1924, about 4,700 tons; in 1926, about 9,000 tons—an amount which rose near to 10,000 tons per month in 1930. In other words, about 300–350 tons of sulphur were being emitted daily in 1930.

* * *

The subject of fumigations and damage claimed to result from them was referred by the two Governments on August 7, 1928, to the International Joint Commission, United States and Canada, under Article IX of the Convention of January 11, 1909, between the United States and Great Britain. . . . The International Joint Commission . . . rendered a unanimous report which need not be considered in detail.

After outlining the plans of the Trail Smelter for extracting sulphur from the fumes, the report recommended (Part I, Paragraphs (a) and (c)) that "the company be required to proceed as expeditiously as may be reasonably possible with the works above referred to and also to erect with due dispatch such further sulphuric acid units and take such further or other action as may be necessary, if any, to reduce the amount and concentration of SO2 fumes drifting from its said plant into the United States until it has reduced the amount by some means to a point where it will do no damage in the United States".

The same Part I, Paragraph (g) gave a definition of "damage":

> The word "damage", as used in this document shall mean and include such damage as the Governments of the United States and Canada may deem appreciable, and for the purposes of paragraphs (a) and (c) hereof, shall not include occasional damage that may be caused by SO2 fumes being carried across the

> international boundary in air pockets or by reason of unusual atmospheric conditions. Provided, however, that any damage in the State of Washington howsoever caused by said fumes on or after January 1, 1932, shall be the subject of indemnity by the company to any interests so damaged. . . .

Paragraph 2 read, in part, as follows:

> In view of the anticipated reduction in sulphur fumes discharged from the smelter at Trail during the present year, as hereinafter referred to, the Commission therefore has deemed it advisable to determine the amount of indemnity that will compensate United States interests in respect to such fumes, up to and including the first day of January, 1932. The Commission finds and determines that all past damages and all damages up to and including the first day of January next, is the sum of $350,000. Said sum, however, shall not include any damage occurring after January 1, 1932.

This report failed to secure the acceptance of both Governments. A sum of $350,000 has, however, been paid by the Dominion of Canada to the United States.

Two years after the filing of the above report, the United States Government, on February 17, 1933, made representations to the Canadian Government that existing conditions were entirely unsatisfactory and that damage was still occurring and diplomatic negotiations were entered into which resulted in the signing of the present Convention.

The Consolidated Mining and Smelting Company of Canada, Limited, proceeded after 1930 to make certain changes and additions in its plant, with the intention and purpose of lessening the sulphur contents of the fumes, and in an attempt to lessen injurious fumigations, a new system of control over the emission of fumes during the crop growing season came into operation about 1934. To the three sulphuric acid plants in operation since 1932, two others have recently been added. The total capacity is now of 600 tons of sulphuric acid per day, permitting, if these units could run continually at capacity, the fixing of approximately 200 tons of sulphur per day. In addition, from 1936, units for the production of elemental sulphur have been put into operation. There are at present three such units with a total capacity of 140 tons of sulphur per day. The capacity of absorption of sulphur dioxide is now 600 tons of sulphur dioxide per day (300 tons from the zinc plant gases and 300 tons from the lead plant gases). As a result, the maximum possible recovery of sulphur dioxide, with all units in full operation has been brought to a figure which is about equal to the amount of that gas produced by smelting operations at the plant in 1939. However, the normal shutdown of operating units for repairs, the power supply, ammonia available, and the general market situation are factors which influence the amount of sulphur dioxide treated.

* * *

The tons of sulphur emitted into the air from the Trail Smelter fell from about 10,000 tons per month in 1930 to about 7,200 tons in 1931 and 3,400 tons in 1932 as a result both of sulphur dioxide beginning to be absorbed and of depressed business conditions. As depression receded, this monthly average rose in 1933 to 4,000 tons, in 1934 to nearly 6,300 tons and in 1935 to 6,800 tons. In 1936, however, it had fallen to 5,600 tons; in 1937, it further fell to 4,850 tons; in 1938, still further to 4,230 tons to reach 3,250 tons in 1939. It rose again, however, to 3,875 tons in 1940.

* * *

PART TWO

The first question under Article III of the Convention is: "(1) Whether damage caused by the Trail Smelter in the State of Washington has occurred since the first day of January, 1932, and, if so, what indemnity should be paid therefor."

[The Tribunal considered possible damages over two time periods: January 2, 1932—October 1, 1937 and October 2, 1937—October 1, 1940. With respect to the first period, the United States had made a claim for damages of $2.1 million. In an earlier decision, issued on 16 April 1938, the Tribunal rejected most of the items of damage claimed by the United States. It awarded damages of only $78,000 for the nearly five-year period, largely vindicating Canada's claim that the steps taken by the Trail Smelter had, in fact, significantly reduced the amount of damage being caused in the United States.

As for the period running from October 1, 1937—October 1, 1940, the Tribunal, after reviewing a large amount of data and the several scientific reports, concluded that no damages had been proved at all. It explained:]

The Tribunal has examined carefully the records of all fumigations specifically alleged by the United States as having caused or been likely to cause damage, as well as the records of all other fumigations which may be considered likely to have caused damage. In connection with each such instance, it has taken into detailed consideration, with a view of determining the fact or probability of damage, the length of the fumigation, the intensity of concentration, the combination of length and intensity, the frequency of fumigation, the time of day of occurrence, the conditions of humidity or drouth, the season of the year, the altitude and geographical locations of place subjected to fumigation, the reports as to personal surveys and investigations and all other pertinent factors. As a result, it has come to the conclusion that the United States has failed to prove that any fumigation between October 1, 1937, and October 1, 1940, has caused injury to crops, trees or otherwise.

* * *

PART THREE

The second question under Article III of the Convention is as follows: In the event of the answer to the first part of the preceding question being in the affirmative, whether the Trail Smelter should be required to refrain from causing damage in the State of Washington in the future and, if so, to what extent?

Damage has occurred since January 1, 1932, as fully set forth in the previous decision. To that extent, the first part of the preceding question has thus been answered in the affirmative.

As has been said above, the report of the International Joint Commission (1 (g)) contained a definition of the word "damage" excluding "occasional damage that may be caused by SO2 fumes being carried across the international boundary in air pockets or by reason of unusual atmospheric conditions", as far, at least, as the duty of the Smelter to reduce the presence of that gas in the air was concerned.

The correspondence between the two Governments during the interval between that report and the conclusion of the Convention shows that the problem thus raised was what parties had primarily in mind in drafting Question No. 2. Whilst Canada wished for the adoption of the report, the United States stated that it could not acquiesce in the proposal to limit consideration of damage to damage as defined in the report (letter of the Minister of the United States of America at Ottawa to the Secretary of State for External Affairs of the Dominion of Canada, January 30, 1934). The view was expressed that "so long as fumigations occur in the State of Washington with such frequency, duration and intensity as to cause injury", the conditions afforded "grounds of complaint on the part of the United States, regardless of the remedial works . . . . and regardless of the effect of those works" (same letter).

The first problem which arises is whether the question should be answered on the basis of the law followed in the United States or on the basis of international law. The Tribunal, however, finds that this problem need not be solved here as the law followed in the United States in dealing with the quasi-sovereign rights of the States of the Union, in the matter of air pollution, whilst more definite, is in conformity with the general rules of international law.

Particularly in reaching its conclusions as regards this question as well as the next, the Tribunal has given consideration to the desire of the high contracting parties "to reach a solution just to all parties concerned". As Professor Eagleton puts in (Responsibility of States in International

Law, 1928, p. 80): "A State owes at all times a duty to protect other States against injurious acts by individuals from within its jurisdiction." A great number of such general pronouncements by leading authorities concerning the duty of a State to respect other States and their territory have been presented to the Tribunal. These and many others have been carefully examined. International decisions, in various matters, from the Alabama case onward, and also earlier ones, are based on the same general principle, and, indeed, this principle, as such, has not been questioned by Canada. But the real difficulty often arises rather when it comes to determine what, *pro subjecta materie*, is deemed to constitute an injurious act.

A case concerning, as the present one does, territorial relations, decided by the Federal Court of Switzerland between the Cantons of Soleure and Argovia, may serve to illustrate the relativity of the rule. Soleure brought a suit against her sister State to enjoin use of a shooting establishment which endangered her territory. The court, in granting the injunction, said: "This right (sovereignty) excludes.... not only the usurpation and exercise of sovereign rights (of another State) .... but also an actual encroachment which might prejudice the natural use of the territory and the free movement of its inhabitants." As a result of the decision, Argovia made plans for the improvement of the existing installations. These, however, were considered as insufficient protection by Soleure. The Canton of Argovia then moved the Federal Court to decree that the shooting be again permitted after completion of the projected improvements. This motion was granted. "The demand of the Government of Soleure", said the court, "that all endangerment be absolutely abolished apparently goes too far." The court found that all risk whatever had not been eliminated, as the region was flat and absolutely safe shooting ranges were only found in mountain valleys; that there was a federal duty for the communes to provide facilities for military target practice and that "no more precautions may be demanded for shooting ranges near the boundaries of two Cantons than are required for shooting ranges in the interior of a Canton."

No case of air pollution dealt with by an international tribunal has been brought to the attention of the Tribunal nor does the Tribunal know of any such case. The nearest analogy is that of water pollution. But, here also, no decision of an international tribunal has been cited or has been found.

There are, however, as regards both air pollution and water pollution, certain decisions of the Supreme Court of the United States which may legitimately be taken as a guide in this field of international law. for it is reasonable to follow by analogy, in international cases, precedents established by that court in dealing with controversies between States of the Union or with other controversies concerning the quasi-sovereign rights of such States, where no contrary rule prevails in international law and no reason for rejecting such precedents can be adduced from the limitations of sovereignty inherent in the Constitution of the United States.

In the suit of the State of Missouri v. the State of Illinois (200 U.S. 496, 521) concerning the pollution, within the boundaries of Illinois, of the Illinois River, an affluent of the Mississippi flowing into the latter where it forms the boundary between that State and Missouri, an injunction was refused. "Before this court ought to intervene", said the court, "the case should be of serious magnitude, clearly and fully proved, and the principle to be applied should be one which the court is prepared deliberately to maintain against all considerations on the other side." The court found that the practice complained of was general along the shores of the Mississippi River at that time, that it was followed by Missouri itself and that thus a standard was set up by the defendant which the claimant was entitled to invoke.

* * *

In the more recent suit of the State of New York against the State of New Jersey, concerning the pollution of New York Bay, the injunction was also refused for lack of proof, some experts believing that the plans which were in dispute would result in the presence of "offensive odors and unsightly deposits," other equally reliable experts testifying that they were confidently of the opinion that the waters would be sufficiently purified. The court, referring to Missouri v. Illinois, said: ". . . the burden upon the State of New York of sustaining the allegations of its bill is much greater than that imposed upon a complainant in an ordinary suit between private parties. Before this court can be moved to exercise its extraordinary power under the Constitution to control the conduct of one State at the suit of another, the threatened invasion of rights must be of serious magnitude and it must be established by clear and convincing evidence."

What the Supreme Court says there of its power under the Constitution equally applies to the extraordinary power granted this Tribunal under the Convention. What is true between States of the Union is, at least, equally true concerning the relations between the United States and the Dominion of Canada.

* * *

In the matter of air pollution itself, the leading decisions are those of the Supreme Court in the State of Georgia v. Tennessee Copper Company and Ducktown Sulphur, Copper and Iron Company, Limited. Although dealing with a suit against private companies, the decisions were on questions cognate to those here at issue. Georgia stated that it had in vain sought relief from the State of Tennessee, on whose territory the smelters were located, and the court defined the nature of the suit by saying: "This is a suit by a State for an injury to it in its capacity of quasi-sovereign. In that capacity, the State has an interest independent of and behind the titles of its citizens, in all the earth and air within its domain." On the question whether an injunction should be granted or not, the court said:

> It (the State) has the last word as to whether its mountains shall be stripped of their forests and its inhabitants shall breathe pure air. . . . It is not lightly to be presumed to give up quasi-sovereign rights for pay and . . . . if that be its choice, it may insist that an infraction of them shall be stopped. This court has not quite the same freedom to balance the harm that will be done by an injunction against that of which the plaintiff complains, that it would have in deciding between two subjects of a single political power. Without excluding the considerations that equity always takes into account. . . . it is a fair and reasonable demand on the part of a sovereign that the air over its territory should not be polluted on a great scale by sulphurous acid gas, that the forests on its mountains, be they better or worse, and whatever domestic destruction they may have suffered, should not be further destroyed or threatened by the act of persons beyond its control, that the crops and orchards on its hills should not be endangered from the same source. . . . Whether Georgia, by insisting upon this claim, is doing more harm than good to her own citizens, is for her to determine. The possible disaster to those outside the State must be accepted as a consequence of her standing upon her extreme rights.

Later on, however, when the court actually framed an injunction, . . . they did not go beyond a decree "adequate to diminish materially the present probability of damage to its (Georgia's) citizens".

Great progress in the control of fumes has been made by science in the last few years and this progress should be taken into account. The Tribunal, therefore, finds that the above decisions, taken as a whole, constitute an adequate basis for its conclusions, namely, that, under the principles of international law, as well as of the law of the United States, no State has the right to use or permit the use of its territory in such a manner as to cause injury by fumes in or to the territory of another or the properties or persons therein, when the case is of serious consequence and the injury is established by clear and convincing evidence.

The decisions of the Supreme Court of the United States which are the basis of these conclusions are decisions in equity and a solution inspired by them, together with the régime hereinafter prescribed, will, in the opinion of the Tribunal, be "just to all parties concerned", as long, at least, as the present conditions in the Columbia River Valley continue to prevail.

Considering the circumstances of the case, the Tribunal holds that the Dominion of Canada is responsible in international law for the conduct of the Trail Smelter. Apart from the undertakings in the Convention, it is, therefore, the duty of the Government of the Dominion of Canada to see to it that this conduct should be in conformity with the obligation of the Dominion under international law as herein determined.

The Tribunal, therefore, answers Question No. 2 as follows: (2) So long as the present conditions in the Columbia River Valley prevail, the Trail Smelter shall be required to refrain from causing any damage through fumes in the State of Washington; the damage herein referred to and its extent being such as would be recoverable under the decisions of the courts of the United States in suits between private individuals. The indemnity for such damage should be fixed in such manner as the Governments, acting under Article XI of the Convention, should agree upon.

PART FOUR

The third question under Article III of the Convention is as follows: "In the light of the answer to the preceding question, what measures or régime, if any, should be adopted and maintained by the Trail Smelter?"

Answering this question in the light of the preceding one, since the Tribunal has, in its previous decision, found that damage caused by the Trail Smelter has occurred in the State of Washington since January 1, 1932, and since the Tribunal is of opinion that damage may occur in the future unless the operations of the Smelter shall be subject to some control, in order to avoid damage occurring, the Tribunal now decides that a régime or measure of control shall be applied to the operations of the Smelter and shall remain in full force unless and until modified in accordance with the provisions hereinafter set forth in Section 3, Paragraph VI of the present part of this decision.

* * *

[*Eds.* Relying heavily on expert advice, the Tribunal imposed science-based requirements, involving both the use of pollution control equipment and the time and manner of operation of the smelter, regulating the emission of sulphur dioxide from the Trail Smelter. The regulations were intended "to prevent the occurrence of sulphur dioxide in the atmosphere in amounts, both as to concentration, duration and frequency, capable of causing damage in the State of Washington. . . ."]

PART FIVE

The fourth question under Article III of the Convention is as follows: What indemnity or compensation, if any, should be paid on account of any decision or decisions rendered by the Tribunal pursuant to the next two preceding Questions?

The Tribunal is of the opinion that the prescribed régime will probably remove the causes of the present controversy and, as said before, will probably result in preventing any damage of a material nature occurring in the State of Washington in the future.

But since the desirable and expected result of the régime or measure of control hereby required to be adopted and maintained by the Smelter may not occur, and since in its answer to Question No. 2, the Tribunal has required the Smelter to refrain from causing damage in the State of Washington in the future, as set forth therein, the Tribunal answers Question No. 4 and decides that on account of decisions rendered by the Tribunal in its answers to Question No. 2 and Question No. 3 there shall be paid as follows: (a) if any damage as defined under Question No. 2 shall have occurred since October 1, 1940, or shall occur in the future, whether through failure on the part of the Smelter to comply with the regulations herein prescribed or notwithstanding the maintenance of the régime, an indemnity shall be paid for such damage. . . .

DISCUSSION NOTES/QUESTIONS

1. Both Canada and the United States agreed that, "a State owes at all times a duty to protect other States against injurious acts by individuals from within its jurisdiction."[2] However, the precise scope of that duty in the context of transboundary pollution was unclear. Was Canada only required to take reasonable steps to limit the amount and impact of SO_2 emissions from the Trail smelter (i.e., exercise due diligence to limit transboundary harm)? Or did Canada have an obligation to shut down the Trail smelter completely if it could not be operated in a way that protected the United States from suffering any pollution whatsoever? How had the International Judicial Commission answered these questions? How did the arbitral Tribunal answer them?

2. In 2001, the International Law Commission articulated the international legal obligation to prevent transboundary environmental harm in qualified terms: "The State of origin shall take all *appropriate measures* to prevent *significant* transboundary harm *or* at any event to *minimize the risk* thereof." Int'l Law Comm'n, Draft Articles on Prevention of Transboundary Harm from Hazardous Activities, article 3, Report on the Work of Its Fifty-Third Session, U.N. Doc. A/56/10, at 146–148 (2001) (emphasis added) **(Basic Document 1.16)**. Similarly, ICJ Judge ad hoc Sir Garfield Barwick has noted that "there are doubtless uses of territory by a State which are of such a nature that the consequences for another State and its territory and environment of such a use must be accepted by that other State. It may very well be that a line is to be drawn between depositions and intrusions which are lawful and must

[2] *Quoting* Clyde Eagleton, The Responsibility of States in International Law 80 (1928). This is sometimes called the *sic utere* principle, referring to the maxim *sic utere tuo ut alienum non laedas*—use your own property in such a manner that you do not injure the property of another. Lauterpacht suggested that a State that commits or permits acts within its border that are injurious to other States or to the world at large is subject to having its right to internal sovereignty curtailed on grounds of "abuse of right." H. Lauterpacht, The Function of Law in the International Community 286–87 (1933).

be borne and those which are unlawful." *Nuclear Test Cases* (N.Z. v. Fr.), 1974 I.C.J 253 (dissenting opinion).

Where should the line between unlawful and lawful pollution be drawn, and what factors should be considered in the analysis? At the time of the Tribunal's decision, Canada was already involved in World War II, and the metal produced by the Trail Smelter was important to the war effort. The Tribunal did not discuss those facts. Should it have done so? In determining whether to restrict productive activity in one country that causes pollution damage in another, should a decision maker consider the benefits to the polluting country as well as the costs to the country suffering the pollution?

3. The International Court of Justice has repeatedly affirmed the customary law obligation of a State to ensure that activities within its jurisdiction do not cause injury to other States. In the *Corfu Channel Case (United Kingdom v. Albania),* 1949 I.C.J 39 (1949), the International Court of Justice had to determine whether Albania was responsible to Britain for damage and loss of life caused when British vessels, exercising their right of passage through an international strait, hit a mine placed in Albanian territorial waters by unknown persons. Finding Albania liable, the Court concluded that Albania must have known of the presence of the mines and that this knowledge imposed upon it a duty to warn the British vessels, a duty based, in part, on "every State's obligation not to allow knowingly its territory to be used for acts contrary to the rights of other States." In its advisory opinion on the *Legality of the Threat or Use of Nuclear Weapons,* 1996 I.C.J 226 (1996), the Court applied the principle to the environmental context, stating that "[t]he existence of the general obligation of States to ensure that activities within their jurisdiction and control respect the environment of other States or of areas beyond national control is now part of the corpus of international law relating to the environment." More recently, in *Pulp Mills on the River Uruguay*, 2010 I.C.J. 14 (2010), the Court cited both *Corfu Channel* and the *Nuclear Weapons* advisory opinion in concluding that every State is "obliged to use all the means at its disposal in order to avoid activities which take place in its territory, or in any area under its jurisdiction, causing significant damage to the environment of another State." (The *Pulp Mills* decision is discussed at greater length following these notes.)

4. In its initial investigation of the Trail Smelter situation, the International Joint Commission had sought and received a report from two independent experts who wrote as follows:

> [T]he Trail smelter is a very important institution, serving a great economic purpose in developing and distributing earth values that would otherwise lie lost to mankind . . . . [T]he smelter is in a logical position, in that it is situated within and delivers its fumes down a valley that is comparatively unproductive, where the best timber has been logged off, to be followed by destructive fires at intervals. . . . It is also true that the farms [affected by the pollution] are small and not very productive. . . . It is true too that the Consolidated had

> manifested a commendable anxiety to settle for damages done, and, where settlement has been made, we are inclined to regard them as reasonable.
>
> [But] we do not think that any remedy, based upon actual physical damage appraisal, fully meets the situation. . . . These very modest holdings are the homes of a people whom we early described as kindly and courteous who, in the main, are convinced that they are being imposed upon, who are convinced, mistakenly we think, that smelter fumes furnish the prime cause of the decadence of their profession of farming in this valley. All we have said, and we could have said much more, as a tribute to the great enterprise embodied by the Trail smelter, does not give this great organization any right to 'park their smelter fumes upon other peoples' property without paying rent,' an expression used by one of the landholders. . . . There is a feeling of trespass, a definite mental hazard, that is a feature of the undesirable occupancy just as much as physical damage caused. . . . Our appraisal of recompense due will be found to have been guided by this factor as well as that of actual crop damage.

The International Joint Commission was obviously influenced by this report, recommending damages (which Canada ultimately paid) in an amount that included the expert's assessment of both the physical damage caused as well as compensation for the farmers' "feeling of trespass." Was that appropriate?

If, as the experts' report to the International Joint Commission intimated, a cost-benefit assessment of the situation would clearly favor continued operation of the smelter, was it appropriate to award damages to the United States at all? Or was this a situation where the operation of the Trail smelter was such a valuable use of Canadian territory that, as Judge Barwick might have said (*see* note 2), the "consequences for . . . its territory and environment . . . must be accepted" by the United States?

5. Problems of transboundary environmental harm implicate the sovereign rights of <u>both</u> countries involved in such disputes. On the one hand, "the deposition" of pollutants emitted in one country on the territory of another is "an infringement of [the affected country's] right to territorial and . . . decisional sovereignty [and a] breach of its undoubted sovereign right to territorial integrity." *Nuclear Test Cases, supra* (Judge Barwick, dissenting). On the other hand, the polluting nation surely has the sovereign right to use its own territory for its own purposes and in its own interests, including by mining and smelting ore to produce valuable metals. As expressed by the U.N. General Assembly, "Every State has and shall freely exercise full permanent sovereignty, including possession, use and disposal, over all its wealth, natural resources and economic activities." G.A. Res. 3281, Charter of Economic Rights and Duties of States, article 2 (Dec. 12, 1974) **(Basic Document 7.3)**.

An absolutist interpretation of a nation's territorial sovereignty—the sovereign right to exploit one's own resources in one's own best interests—

would imply that any efforts to restrict transboundary pollution is illegitimate if it interferes with another State's ability effectively to pursue its own economic development according to its own policies: "No State may use or encourage the use of economic, political or any other type of measures to coerce another State in order to obtain from it the subordination of the exercise of its sovereign rights." *Id.* at article 32. On the other hand, an absolutist interpretation of a nation's right to territorial integrity—right to be free of territorial incursions by others—would plainly be destructive of the territorial sovereignty of other States if applied to prohibit all activities that lead to any sort of transboundary pollution.

Does the rule stated in the *Trail Smelter* decision resolve the potential conflict between territorial sovereignty and territorial integrity in a reasonable way? What about the rule as it was restated by the International Law Commission? By the International Court of Justice in the *Pulp Mills* decision? Are these rules consistent with the notion that each State has the sovereign right to exploit its natural resources according to its own policies? If the rules are applied to resolve disputes over transboundary pollution, does their application amount to "coercing" the polluting state to "subordinate" its "sovereign rights" in favor of the State that is suffering the pollution?

Does your answer to any of the questions above depend on whether the polluting State is rich or poor? Does it depend on whether the State that is suffering pollution is rich or poor?

6. Consolidated Mining, the owner of the Trail smelter, had attempted to settle the claims of the American landowners by paying damages. But that was a temporary solution that had to be repeated regularly as new damages occurred. At the time of the dispute, the usual permanent remedy in such situations was for the polluter to purchase the injured landowner's land or to acquire a smoke easement from the landowner. Sometimes such arrangements were reached through voluntary transactions and sometimes the polluting company would use state condemnation proceedings to seek to force the landowner to sell it the land or an easement. Consolidated claimed that neither of these avenues to a permanent solution was open to it because the law of the State of Washington forbade foreign persons from holding any legal interest in land in the state.

PULP MILLS ON THE RIVER URUGUAY (ARG. V. URU.)

2010 I.C.J 14 (Apr. 20)

[*Eds.* Argentina brought an action complaining that Uruguay's construction of two pulp mills on the River Uruguay had been authorized and conducted in violation of an agreement between the two countries concerning use of the River (the "1975 Statute") and would, or had, caused environmental damage.]

I. LEGAL FRAMEWORK AND FACTS OF THE CASE

25. The dispute before the Court has arisen in connection with the planned construction authorized by Uruguay of one pulp mill and the construction and commissioning of another, also authorized by Uruguay, on the River Uruguay. . . .

26. The boundary between Argentina and Uruguay in the River Uruguay is defined by the bilateral Treaty entered into for that purpose at Montevideo on 7 April 1961 . . . Article 7 [of the Treaty] provides for the establishment by the parties of a "régime for the use of the river" covering various subjects, including the conservation of living resources and the prevention of water pollution of the river. . . .

27. The "régime for the use of the river" contemplated in Article 7 of the 1961 Treaty was established through the 1975 Statute. . . . Article 1 of the 1975 Statute states that the parties adopted it "in order to establish the joint machinery necessary for the optimum and rational utilization of the River Uruguay, in strict observance of the rights and obligations arising from treaties and other international agreements in force for each of the parties". . . . The 1975 Statute sets up the Administrative Commission of the River Uruguay (hereinafter "CARU"). . . .

* * *

65. . . . In interpreting the terms of the 1975 Statute, the Court will have recourse to the customary rules on treaty interpretation as reflected in Article 31 of the Vienna Convention **[Basic Document 1.14]**. Accordingly the 1975 Statute is to be "interpreted in good faith in accordance with the ordinary meaning to be given to the terms of the [Statute] in their context and in light of its object and purpose". That interpretation will also take into account, together with the context, "any relevant rules of international law applicable in the relations between the parties."

* * *

101. The Court points out that the principle of prevention, as a customary rule, has its origins in the due diligence that is required of a State in its territory. It is "every State's obligation not to allow knowingly its territory to be used for acts contrary to the rights of other States" (Corfu Channel (United Kingdom v. Albania), Merits, Judgment, I.C.J. Reports 1949, p. 22). A State is thus obliged to use all the means at its disposal in order to avoid activities which take place in its territory, or in any area under its jurisdiction, causing significant damage to the environment of another State. This Court has established that this obligation "is now part of the corpus of international law relating to the environment" (Legality of the Threat or Use of Nuclear Weapons, Advisory Opinion, I.C.J. Reports 1996 (I), p. 242, para. 29).

* * *

The obligation to prevent pollution and preserve the aquatic environment (Article 41)

190. Article 41 provides that:

> Without prejudice to the functions assigned to the Commission in this respect, the parties undertake:
>
> (a) to protect and preserve the aquatic environment and, in particular, to prevent its pollution, by prescribing appropriate rules and [adopting appropriate] measures in accordance with applicable international agreements and in keeping, where relevant, with the guidelines and recommendations of international technical bodies; . . .

* * *

191. Argentina claims that by allowing the discharge of additional nutrients into a river that is eutrophic and suffers from reverse flow and stagnation, Uruguay violated the obligation to prevent pollution, as it failed to prescribe appropriate measures in relation to the Orion (Botnia) mill. . . . . It maintains that the 1975 Statute prohibits any pollution which is prejudicial to the protection and preservation of the aquatic environment or which alters the ecological balance of the river. Argentina further argues that the obligation to prevent pollution of the river is an obligation of result and extends not only to protecting the aquatic environment proper, but also to any reasonable and legitimate use of the river, including tourism and other recreational uses.

192. Uruguay contends that the obligation laid down in Article 41 (a) of the 1975 Statute to "prevent . . . pollution" does not involve a prohibition on all discharges into the river. It is only those that exceed the standards jointly agreed by the Parties within CARU in accordance with their international obligations, and that therefore have harmful effects, which can be characterized as "pollution" under Article 40 of the 1975 Statute. Uruguay also maintains that Article 41 creates an obligation of conduct, and not of result, but that it actually matters little since Uruguay has complied with its duty to prevent pollution by requiring the plant to meet best available technology ("BAT") standards.

193. Before turning to the analysis of Article 41, the Court recalls that:

> "The existence of the general obligation of States to ensure that activities within their jurisdiction and control respect the environment of other States or of areas beyond national control is now part of the corpus of international law relating to the environment." (Legality of the Threat or Use of Nuclear Weapons, Advisory Opinion, I.C.J. Reports 1996 (I), pp. 241–242, para. 29.)

* * *

195.... First, in the view of the Court, Article 41 makes a clear distinction between regulatory functions entrusted to CARU under the 1975 Statute, which are dealt with in Article 56 of the Statute, and the obligation it imposes on the Parties to adopt rules and measures individually to "protect and preserve the aquatic environment and, in particular, to prevent its pollution". Thus, the obligation assumed by the Parties under Article 41, which is distinct from those under Articles 36 and 56 of the 1975 Statute, is to adopt appropriate rules and measures within the framework of their respective domestic legal systems to protect and preserve the aquatic environment and to prevent pollution. This conclusion is supported by the wording of paragraphs (b) and (c) of Article 41, which refer to the need not to reduce the technical requirements and severity of the penalties already in force in the respective legislation of the Parties as well as the need to inform each other of the rules to be promulgated so as to establish equivalent rules in their legal systems.

196. Secondly, it is the opinion of the Court that a simple reading of the text of Article 41 indicates that it is the rules and measures that are to be prescribed by the Parties in their respective legal systems which must be "in accordance with applicable international agreements" and "in keeping, where relevant, with the guidelines and recommendations of international technical bodies."

197. Thirdly, the obligation to "preserve the aquatic environment, and in particular to prevent pollution by prescribing appropriate rules and measures" is an obligation to act with due diligence in respect of all activities which take place under the jurisdiction and control of each party. It is an obligation, which entails not only the adoption of appropriate rules and measures, but also a certain level of vigilance in their enforcement and the exercise of administrative control applicable to public and private operators, such as the monitoring of activities undertaken by such operators, to safeguard the rights of the other party. The responsibility of a party to the 1975 Statute would therefore be engaged if it was shown that it had failed to act diligently and thus take all appropriate measures to enforce its relevant regulations on a public or private operator under its jurisdiction. The obligation of due diligence under Article 41 (a) in the adoption and enforcement of appropriate rules and measures is further reinforced by the requirement that such rules and measures must be "in accordance with applicable international agreements" and "in keeping, where relevant, with the guidelines and recommendations of international technical bodies". This requirement has the advantage of ensuring that the rules and measures adopted by the parties both have to conform to applicable international agreements and to take account of internationally agreed technical standards.

198. Finally, the scope of the obligation to prevent pollution must be determined in light of the definition of pollution given in Article 40 of the 1975 Statute. Article 40 provides that: "For the purposes of this Statute, pollution shall mean the direct or indirect introduction by man into the aquatic environment of substances or energy which have harmful effects." The term "harmful effects" is defined in the CARU Digest as:

> "any alteration of the water quality that prevents or hinders any legitimate use of the water, that causes deleterious effects or harm to living resources, risks to human health, or a threat to water activities including fishing or reduction of recreational activities" (Title I, Chapter I, Section. 2, Article 1 (c) of the Digest (E3)).

* * *

265. [After reviewing in depth Argentina's claims that Uruguay had failed to conduct an adequate environmental impact assessment and that the projects would cause unacceptable pollution and ecological damage, the Court concluded:] . . . [T]here is no conclusive evidence in the record to show that Uruguay has not acted with the requisite degree of due diligence or that the discharges of effluent from the Orion (Botnia) mill have had deleterious effects or caused harm to living resources or to the quality of the water or the ecological balance of the river since it started its operations in November 2007. Consequently, on the basis of the evidence submitted to it, the Court concludes that Uruguay has not breached its obligations under Article 41.

DISCUSSION NOTES/QUESTIONS

1. What is the difference between an obligation of due diligence and an obligation of result? According to the International Court of Justice, which type of obligation is the obligation to avoid transboundary harm? Is that conclusion consistent with the arbitral tribunal's decision in the *Trail Smelter* case?

2. What constitutes the exercise of "due diligence" to avoid transboundary pollution? In determining whether Uruguay had exercised "due diligence," the ICJ considered international standards relating to environmental protection, including the obligation to conduct an environmental impact assessment when engaged in behavior that might adversely affect the environment of other states.

3. In this case, although it cited customary norms, the ICJ was applying a treaty obligation. Does that affect the significance of the decision with respect to our understanding the meaning of the customary obligation to avoid transboundary harm?

4. Suppose it could be demonstrated that greenhouse gas emissions by the United States are directly responsible for a certain proportion of the global warming that is predicted to occur between now and the year 2030. Suppose also that reasonable estimates of the harm caused by that global warming to

other countries could be made. Would the US be in violation of its obligation not to cause transboundary harm if it does not immediately cease greenhouse gas emissions? Would gradual emissions reductions be enough, even if they were inadequate to prevent significant climate-change-related harm? Would it matter whether the U.S. was or was not cooperating with international efforts to reduce greenhouse gas emissions, even if reduction efforts did not prevent harmful global warming? How should damages be apportioned among the U.S. and other polluters?

Base your answers to these questions on the *Trail Smelter* decision, the International Law Commission's statement of the *sic utere* principle (*see* discussion note 2 following the *Trail Smelter* decision), and the *Pulp Mills* decision.

If it is impractical to apply the *sic utere* principle to impose damages liability on states for global problems like climate change, does the principle nonetheless have importance as states consider how to address such problems?

5. The *Trail Smelter* and *Pulp Mills* decisions dealt with harm caused by one state to the territory of another state. But what about environmental harm caused to areas of the planet that are not within any state's jurisdiction? Do states have an obligation to limit such harm, just as they have an obligation to limit harm caused to the territory of neighboring states? Beginning with the 1972 Stockholm Declaration **(Basic Document 1.21)**, the international community has endorsed a broad concept of transboundary harm that includes harm to commons areas:

> States have, in accordance with the Charter of the United Nations and the principles of international law, the sovereign right to exploit their own resources pursuant to their own environmental policies, and the responsibility to ensure that activities within their jurisdiction or control do not cause damage to the environment of other States *or of areas beyond the limits of national jurisdiction.*

See U.N. Conference on the Human Environment, Stockholm Declaration, principle 21, U.N. Doc. A/CONF.48/14/Rev.1/3 (June 16, 1972) (emphasis added). The same basic formula has since been repeated in many U.N. conference declarations, U.N. General Assembly resolutions, and multilateral environmental agreements.

6. In paragraph 101 of its *Pulp Mills* opinion, the ICJ refers to a customary "principle of prevention," which it seems to equate with the customary-law obligation to avoid causing transboundary harm. According to one prominent commentator, however, the obligation to avoid transboundary harm and the obligation to prevent pollution differ in important ways:

> First, the [obligation to avoid transboundary harm arises] from application of respect for the principle of sovereignty, whereas the preventive principle seeks to minimize environmental damage as an objective in itself. This difference of underlying rationale relates to the second distinction: under the preventive principle, a state may be

> under an obligation to prevent damage to the environment within its own jurisdiction. . . .

Philippe Sands, Principles of International Environmental Law (2003).

Assuming these are distinct principles and that the principle of prevention (as described by Professor Sands) is not yet well established as a rule of customary international law, would you support the promulgation of international instruments and practices aimed at more clearly establishing a separate obligation of prevention as a part of the corpus of international environmental law?

B. TRANSBOUNDARY HARM AND THE DOCTRINE OF STATE RESPONSIBILITY

In the *Rainbow Warrior* incident, France admitted that its agents had violated international law through their bombing of the *Rainbow Warrior,* and France accepted "state responsibility" for that behavior. Canada also agreed that it was responsible for some of the damage caused by the Trail smelter to property in the United States. Under international law, such an admission of responsibility carries significant consequences. We here consider briefly the core principles of the Law of State Responsibility.

FACTORY AT CHORZÓW (MERITS) (GER V. POL)

1928 P.C.I.J, Series A, No. 17 at 29, 47 (Sept. 13)

[T]he application [in this case] is designed to obtain, in favour of Germany, reparation the amount of which is determined by the damage suffered by [two German companies as a result of Poland's unlawful seizure of the factory at Chorzów.] Three fundamental questions arise:

(1) The existence of the obligation to make reparation.

(2) The existence of the damage which must serve as a basis for the calculation of the amount of the indemnity.

(3) The extent of this damage.

As regards the first point, the Court observes that it is a principle of international law, and even a general conception of law, that any breach of an engagement involves an obligation to make reparation. In Judgment No. 8 . . . the Court has already said that reparation is the indispensable complement of a failure to apply a convention, and there is no necessity for this to be stated in the convention itself. The existence of the principle establishing the obligation to make reparation, as an element of positive international law, has moreover never been disputed in the course of the[se] proceedings. . . .

* * *

The existence of a damage to be made good being recognized by the respondent Party as regards the Bayerische, and the objections raised by the same Party against the existence of any damage that would justify compensation to the Oberschlesische being set aside, the Court must now lay down the guiding principles according to which the amount of compensation due may be determined.

* * *

The essential principle contained in the actual notion of an illegal act—a principle which seems to be established by international practice and in particular by the decisions of arbitral tribunals—is that reparation must, as far as possible, wipe out all the consequences of the illegal act and reestablish the situation which would, in all probability, have existed if that act had not been committed. Restitution in kind, or, if this is not possible, payment of a sum corresponding to the value which a restitution in kind would bear; the award, if need be, of damages for loss sustained which would not be covered by restitution in kind or payment in place of it—such are the principles which should serve to determine the amount of compensation due for an act contrary to international law.

DRAFT ARTICLES ON THE RESPONSIBILITY OF STATES FOR INTERNATIONALLY WRONGFUL ACTS, ARTS. 1–2

Report of the International Law Commission on the Work of its Fifty-third Session U.N. Doc. A/56/10, at 43 (2001) (Basic Document 1.15)

Article 1

Responsibility of a State for its internationally wrongful acts

Every internationally wrongful act of a State entails the international responsibility of that State.

Article 2

Elements of an internationally wrongful act of a State

There is an internationally wrongful act of a State when conduct consisting of an action or omission:

(a) Is attributable to the State under international law; and

(b) Constitutes a breach of an international obligation of the State.

UNITED STATES DIPLOMATIC AND CONSULAR STAFF IN TEHRAN (US V. IRAN)

1980 I.C.J 3, at 28–30, 32–36, 41–42 (May 24)

[*Eds.*—Student militants had seized the US embassy in Tehran, Iran. Instead of taking action to free the US personnel held hostage in the embassy, the Iranian government declined to act against the students and, eventually, even endorsed their actions. At the time of this ICJ decision, the embassy and its personnel were still in the hands of the militants. The question for the Court was whether the Government of Iran bore state responsibility for the actions of the students, who were acting as private citizens.]

58. No suggestion has been made that the militants, when they executed their attack on the Embassy, had any form of official status as recognized "agents" or organs of the Iranian State. Their conduct in mounting the attack, overrunning the Embassy and seizing its inmates as hostages cannot, therefore, be regarded as imputable to that State on that basis. Their conduct might be considered as itself directly imputable to the Iranian State only if it were established that, in fact, on the occasion in question the militants acted on behalf of the State, having been charged by some competent organ of the Iranian State to carry out a specific operation. The information before the Court does not, however, suffice to establish with the requisite certainty the existence at that time of such a link between the militants and any competent organ of the State.

* * *

61. The conclusion . . . that the initiation of the attack on the United States Embassy on 4 November 1979 . . . cannot be considered as in itself imputable to the Iranian State does not mean that Iran is, in consequence, free of any responsibility in regard to those attacks; for its own conduct was in conflict with its international obligations. By a number of provisions of the Vienna Conventions of 1961 and 1963, Iran was placed under the most categorical obligations, as a receiving State, to take appropriate steps to ensure the protection of the United States Embassy and Consulates, their staffs, their archives, their means of communication and the freedom of movement of the members of their staffs.

* * *

67. [The] inaction of the Iranian Government [i.e. its failure to act to end the student militants' occupation of the U.S. embassy] by itself constituted clear and serious violation of Iran's obligations to the United States under the provisions of Article 22, paragraph 2, and Articles 24, 25, 26, 27 and 29 of the 1961 Vienna Convention on Diplomatic Relations, and Articles 5 and 36 of the 1963 Vienna Convention on Consular Relations.

* * *

69 .... The occupation having taken place and the diplomatic and consular personnel of the United States' mission having been taken hostage, the action required of the Iranian Government by the Vienna Conventions and by general international law was manifest. Its plain duty was at once to make every effort, and to take every appropriate step, to bring these flagrant infringements of the inviolability of the premises, archives and diplomatic and consular staff of the United States Embassy

to a speedy end, . . . and in general to re-establish the status quo and to offer reparation for the damage.

DRAFT ARTICLES ON THE RESPONSIBILITY OF STATES FOR INTERNATIONALLY WRONGFUL ACTS, ARTS. 30–37

Report of the International Law Commission on the Work of its Fifty-third Session U.N. Doc. A/56/10, at 51–52 (2001) (Basic Document 1.15)

Article 30
Cessation and non-repetition

The State responsible for the internationally wrongful act is under an obligation:

(a) To cease that act, if it is continuing;

(b) To offer appropriate assurances and guarantees of non-repetition, if circumstances so require.

Article 31
Reparation

1. The responsible State is under an obligation to make full reparation for the injury caused by the internationally wrongful act.

2. Injury includes any damage, whether material or moral, caused by the internationally wrongful act of a State.

* * *

Article 34
Forms of reparation

Full reparation for the injury caused by the internationally wrongful act shall take the form of restitution, compensation and satisfaction, either singly or in combination, in accordance with the provisions of this chapter.

Article 35
Restitution

A State responsible for an internationally wrongful act is under an obligation to make restitution, that is, to re-establish the situation which existed before the wrongful act was committed, provided and to the extent that restitution:

(a) Is not materially impossible;

(b) Does not involve a burden out of all proportion to the benefit deriving from restitution instead of compensation.

Article 36
Compensation

1. The State responsible for an internationally wrongful act is under an obligation to compensate for the damage caused thereby, insofar as such damage is not made good by restitution.

2. The compensation shall cover any financially assessable damage including loss of profits insofar as it is established.

Article 37
Satisfaction

1. The State responsible for an internationally wrongful act is under an obligation to give satisfaction for the injury caused by that act insofar as it cannot be made good by restitution or compensation.

2. Satisfaction may consist in an acknowledgement of the breach, an expression of regret, a formal apology or another appropriate modality.

3. Satisfaction shall not be out of proportion to the injury and may not take a form humiliating to the responsible State.

PULP MILLS ON THE RIVER URUGUAY (ARG. V. URU.)

2010 I.C.J 14 (Apr. 20)

[*Eds.*—As set forth in the previous excerpt from this opinion, the International Court of Justice concluded that Uruguay did not breach its substantive international legal obligations to Argentina with respect to the prevention of transboundary harm. However, the ICJ concluded that Uruguay had violated its procedural international law obligations by authorizing construction of pulp mills and a port terminal without following notification and negotiation processes provided for by the treaty between the countries. "Consequently, Uruguay disregarded the whole of the co-operation mechanism provided for in Articles 7 to 12 of the 1975 Statute."

The question for the Court then became a question of remedy. During the pendency of the litigation, Uruguay had proceeded with construction of one of the pulp mills. If, as the Court concluded, Uruguay had violated its legal obligations in authorizing and permitting the construction of the pulp mill, would it now be required to tear down the mill?]

267. Having concluded that Uruguay breached its procedural obligations under the 1975 Statute . . . , it is for the Court to draw the conclusions following from these internationally wrongful acts giving rise to Uruguay's international responsibility and to determine what that responsibility entails.

270. . . . Argentina contends that Uruguay is under an obligation to "re-establish on the ground and in legal terms the situation that existed before [the] internationally wrongful acts were committed". To this end, the Orion (Botnia) mill should be dismantled. According to Argentina, *restitutio in integrum* is the primary form of reparation for internationally wrongful acts. Relying on Article 35 of the International Law Commission's Draft Articles on the Responsibility of States for Internationally Wrongful Acts, Argentina maintains that restitution takes precedence over all other forms of reparation except where it is "materially impossible" or involves "a burden out of all proportion to the benefit deriving from restitution instead of compensation". It asserts that dismantling the mill is not materially impossible and would not create for the Respondent State a burden out of all proportion, since the Respondent has

> "maintained that construction of the mills would not amount to a *fait accompli* liable to prejudice Argentina's rights and that it was for Uruguay alone to decide whether to proceed with construction and thereby assume the risk of having to dismantle the mills in the event of an adverse decision by the Court,"

as the Court noted in its Order on Argentina's request for the indication of provisional measures in this case. Argentina adds that whether or not restitution is disproportionate must be determined at the latest as of the filing of the Application instituting proceedings, since as from that time Uruguay, knowing of Argentina's request to have the work halted and the status quo ante re-established, could not have been unaware of the risk it ran in proceeding with construction of the disputed mill.

* * *

273. The Court recalls that customary international law provides for restitution as one form of reparation for injury, restitution being the re-establishment of the situation which existed before occurrence of the wrongful act. The Court further recalls that, where restitution is materially impossible or involves a burden out of all proportion to the benefit deriving from it, reparation takes the form of compensation or satisfaction, or even both.

274. Like other forms of reparation, restitution must be appropriate to the injury suffered, taking into account the nature of the wrongful act having caused it. As the Court has made clear,

> [w]hat constitutes 'reparation in an adequate form' clearly varies depending upon the concrete circumstances surrounding each case and the precise nature and scope of the injury, since the question has to be examined from the viewpoint of what is the 'reparation in an adequate form' that corresponds to the injury

(Avena and Other Mexican Nationals (Mexico v. United States of America), Judgment, I.C.J. Reports 2004 (I), p. 59, para. 119).

275.... [C]onstruction of [the Orion (Botnia) mill] began before negotiations had come to an end, in breach of the procedural obligations laid down in the 1975 Statute. [However], ... the operation of the Orion (Botnia) mill has not resulted in the breach of substantive obligations laid down in the 1975 Statute.... As Uruguay was not barred from proceeding with the construction and operation of the Orion (Botnia) mill after the expiration of the period for negotiation and as it breached no substantive obligation under the 1975 Statute, ordering the dismantling of the mill would not, in the view of the Court, constitute an appropriate remedy for the breach of procedural obligations.

276. As Uruguay has not breached substantive obligations arising under the 1975 Statute, the Court is likewise unable, for the same reasons, to uphold Argentina's claim in respect of compensation for alleged injuries suffered in various economic sectors, specifically tourism and agriculture.

* * *

282. For these reasons, the Court ... finds that the Eastern Republic of Uruguay has breached its procedural obligations under Articles 7 to 12 of the 1975 Statute of the River Uruguay and that the declaration by the Court of this breach constitutes appropriate satisfaction;....

CERTAIN ACTIVITIES CARRIED OUT BY NICARAGUA IN THE BORDER AREA (COSTA RICA V. NICAR.)

2018 I.C.J No. 150 (Feb. 2)

[*Eds.* Costa Rica and Nicaragua disputed the location of the border between them, and Nicaragua's army moved into territory claimed by Costa Rica. Costa Rica brought this action to determine the location of the border and to recover damages for harm caused to Costa Rican territory by the Nicaraguan military's construction projects. The Court ruled that the disputed territory in question belonged to Costa Rica, and that Costa Rica was entitled to compensation for the "material damage" caused by Nicaragua, including environmental damage.]

41. The Court has not previously adjudicated a claim for compensation for environmental damage. However, it is consistent with the principles of international law governing the consequences of internationally wrongful acts, including the principle of full reparation, to hold that compensation is due for damage caused to the environment, in and of itself, in addition to expenses incurred by an injured State as a consequence of such damage. The Parties also agree on this point.

42. The Court is therefore of the view that damage to the environment, and the consequent impairment or loss of the ability of the environment to provide goods and services, is compensable under international law. Such compensation may include indemnification for the impairment or loss of environmental goods and services in the period prior to recovery and payment for the restoration of the damaged environment.

* * *

78. The Court considers, for the reasons specified below, that it is appropriate to approach the valuation of environmental damage from the perspective of the ecosystem as a whole, by adopting an overall assessment of the impairment or loss of environmental goods and services prior to recovery, rather than attributing values to specific categories of environmental goods and services and estimating recovery periods for each of them.

[*Eds.* The Court awarded Costa Rica damages of $120,000 to compensate for impairment of the value of environmental goods and services and $2,708 to cover the cost of necessary restoration measures.]

DISCUSSION NOTES/QUESTIONS

1. Did the Court grant an adequate remedy in the *Pulp Mills* case? If not, what would have been a more appropriate remedy? In the absence of any evidence of actual harm, would it be appropriate to order Uruguay to tear down the pulp mill? In the absence of evidence of harm would damages be appropriate? What about reimbursement to Argentina for costs incurred in determining whether pollution from the pulp mill was damaging the river? What about reimbursement to Argentina for its litigation costs?

2. In calculating the "impairment or loss of environmental goods and services" caused by alleged harm, what environmental goods and services should count? Costa Rica claimed more than $2 million in damages from the loss of "standing timber; other raw materials (fibre and energy); gas regulation and air quality; natural hazards mitigation; soil formation and erosion control; and biodiversity, in terms of habitat and nursery." Some of these items have ascertainable market values; others do not. How would you determine the value, for example, of the carbon dioxide that would have been absorbed by a tree that is no longer standing? The value of several acres of lost habitat in an otherwise intact rain forest? In the end, the Court's award was a small fraction of Costa Rica's request.

3. The International Law Commission's Articles on Responsibility of States for Internationally Wrongful Acts **(Basic Document 1.15)** include provisions that are widely viewed as reflecting established customary international law, as well as provisions that are understood to include elements aimed at "progressive development" of the law. The provisions quoted

previously are among those that are considered to be accurate restatements of established customary international law.

4. How does one state make a claim against another state based on principles of state responsibility? Many such claims are made, initially at least, through a process of unilateral determination and reciprocal response, usually in the diplomatic arena. This, for example, was how New Zealand presented its claim for compensation to France—by means of a demand presented through diplomatic channels. *See* Chapter 2, *supra*. Eventually, New Zealand's claim for compensation was upheld by the UN Secretary General, but in many cases, international legal principles of state responsibility are implemented entirely through negotiations in the diplomatic arena.

Such claims can also be raised and resolved in judicial or arbitral tribunals, as the *Trail Smelter* decision and the three cases in this section demonstrate. The effectiveness of judicial assessments of state responsibility depends in the first instance on the willingness of the parties to consent to the jurisdiction of a court or arbitral tribunal. It also depends on the parties' subsequent compliance with whatever order is issued by the tribunal.

Finally, state-responsibility law can also be applied by intergovernmental organizations. Following Iraq's invasion of Kuwait, for example, the UN Security Council declared that Iraq bore state responsibility for "any direct loss, including environmental damage and the depletion of natural resources' caused as a result of its unlawful action." *See* Security Council Resolution 687 (1991). The UN Compensation Commission was established to review claims, with payments made from a fund established by a tax on Iraqi oil revenues. *See* Olufemi Elias, *The UN Compensation Commission and Liability for the Costs of Monitoring and Assessment of Environmental Damage*, in Issues of State Responsibility before International Judicial Institutions (Malgosia Fitzmaurice & Dan Sarooshi, eds. 2004).

5. Does a state always have a state-responsibility-based obligation to compensate for transboundary harm? Consider the following scenario:

> An accident in a privately-owned chemical factory in Patria results in a chemical spill into a river that flows into Xandia. The polluted water causes a massive fish kill in Xandia. In addition, Xandian cities along the river are unable to use the water for several days. All this has caused great hardship to Xandian's population. In addition, the Xandian government has spent several million dollars in its clean-up effort.
>
> For its part, Patria has reasonably strict environmental regulations in place that are designed to protect against such accidents. Moreover, it inspects factories regularly to ensure compliance with those regulations. Patria was also seriously injured by the chemical spill, and it intends to hold the company liable for cleanup, although no one yet knows exactly why this chemical spill happened.

Evaluate Patria's obligations to Xandia under the doctrine of state responsibility. Patria has responsibility toward Xandia only if it violated its international legal obligations. Assuming it had no treaty obligation to Xandia, did Patria violate the customary obligation regarding the avoidance of transboundary harm?

6. Under customary international law, when a state seeks compensation from another state based on harm done to the injured state's nationals (as opposed to direct harm to the state itself), there is a rule that the injured private persons or businesses must exhaust available legal remedies in the injury-causing State before their home state may espouse their claim diplomatically. *See generally* Ian Brownlie, Principles of Public International Law 472 (2003).

In the *Trail Smelter* arbitration, the American plaintiffs could have brought nuisance claims against the Trail smelter in Canadian courts but did not do so. In its briefing to the arbitral tribunal, Canada took note of this failure to use available remedies, but it did not insist on exhaustion of those remedies as a precondition to its international responsibility. Why do you think Canada agreed to arbitrate and to accept responsibility for actionable harm without requiring the injured Americans to pursue their claims in Canadian courts? As you think about this, consider whether a judicial action in Canada could have brought a permanent end to the matter or resulted in the kind of solution authored by the arbitral tribunal.

C. TRAIL SMELTER *REDUX*: USING NATIONAL LEGAL PROCESSES TO ADDRESS TRANSBOUNDARY ENVIRONMENTAL PROBLEMS

In its submissions during the *Trail Smelter* arbitration in the 1930s, the United States had claimed that "the Trail Smelter disposes of slag in such a manner that it reaches the Columbia River and enters the United States in that stream." As a result, said the United States, the "waters of the Columbia River in Stevens County are injuriously affected." Canada contended that water pollution damage was not within the scope of the arbitration. In the end, the Tribunal didn't resolve the issue because the United States did not produce any evidence from which a finding of damage to the Columbia River could be made.[3]

Sixty years later, in 1999, the Confederated Tribes of the Colville Reservation (the "Tribes") petitioned the U.S. Environmental Protection Agency to conduct an assessment of hazardous substance pollution of the Columbia River from the Grand Coulee Dam to the Canadian border. The EPA conducted a preliminary study and concluded that the relevant portion of the Columbia River was polluted by contaminants "including, but not limited to, heavy metals such as arsenic, cadmium, copper, lead,

[3] Decision of April 16, 1938, 33 UNRIAA 1911, 1931–32.

mercury and zinc." The Trail smelter had been dumping slag into the Columbia River until 1995, and the EPA determined that its discharges of slag and other contaminants were one principal cause of the contamination of the river.

The EPA entered negotiations with Teck Cominco Metals, Ltd. (the current owner of the Trail smelter) seeking Teck's agreement to conduct a Remedial Investigation/Feasibility Study for cleanup of the affected portions of the river. The negotiations were not initially successful, and the EPA issued a Unilateral Administrative Order (UAO) directing Teck Cominco to conduct the study. Teck refused to comply with the order, "arguing that as it discharged its wastes in Trail, B.C., it was not subject to United States environmental law." Pakootas v. Teck Cominco Metals, Ltd., 2016 WL 4258929, *2 (August 12, 2016).

Extensive litigation followed. The litigation was initiated in 2004 by two members of the Colville Tribes, suing in their personal capacity, and by the Tribes themselves. Suit was brought in the United States District Court for the Eastern District of Washington. The original action was aimed at forcing Teck to comply with the EPA's order that it conduct a Remedial Investigation/Feasibility Study for cleanup. After Teck entered an agreement with the EPA to conduct such a study (which is ongoing at this writing), the focus shifted to securing from the court a declaration that Teck was responsible for the contamination in the Columbia River and an award to the Tribes of their costs of investigating and litigating the matter.

Teck argued that the applicable U.S. environmental law, the Comprehensive Environmental Response and Liability Act (CERCLA), did not apply extraterritorially and therefore could not apply to impose liability on Teck for discharges it had made in British Columbia. Moreover, Teck argued that United States law should not be applied to impose liability on Teck for conduct that, under Canadian law, was perfectly lawful. The district court rejected those arguments and, on appeal, the 9th Circuit ruled that CERCLA could apply to Teck because, although it discharges its waste in Canada, the hazardous chemicals were released from the waste after it reached the United States and, accordingly, the law was being applied to conduct that occurred within the territory of the United States.

PAKOOTAS V. TECK COMINCO METALS, LTD.

452 F. 3d 1066 (9th Cir. 2006), *cert. denied,* 552 U.S. 1095 (2008)

[*Eds.* After finding that the entire upper Columbia River area from the Grand Coulee Dam to the border was a CERCLA "facility" and a hazardous waste site, the court observed:]

A significant amount of slag has accumulated and adversely affects the surface water, ground water, sediments, and biological resources of the Upper Columbia River and Lake Roosevelt. Technical evidence shows that the Trail Smelter is the predominant source of contamination at the Site. The physical and chemical decay of slag is an ongoing process that releases arsenic, cadmium, copper, zinc, and lead into the environment, causing harm to human health and the environment.

* * *

. . . CERCLA imposes liability for the cleanup of [hazardous waste] sites where there is a release or threatened release of hazardous substances into the environment. . . . Here, several events could potentially be characterized as releases. First, there is the discharge of waste from the Trail Smelter into the Columbia River in Canada. Second, there is the discharge or escape of the slag from Canada when the Columbia River enters the United States. And third, there is the leaching of heavy metals and other hazardous substances from the slag into the environment at the Site. Although each of these events can be characterized as a release, CERCLA liability does not attach unless the "release" is from a CERCLA facility.

* * *

Pakootas has alleged that the leaching of hazardous substances from the slag that is in the Site is a CERCLA release, and Teck has not argued that the slag's interaction with the water and sediment of the Upper Columbia River is not a release within the intendment of CERCLA. Our precedents establish that the passive migration of hazardous substances into the environment from where hazardous substances have come to be located is a release under CERCLA. . . . We hold that the leaching of hazardous substances from the slag at the Site is a CERCLA release. That release—a release into the United States from a facility in the United States—is entirely domestic.

* * *

Here, the operative event creating a liability under CERCLA is the release or threatened release of a hazardous substance. Arranging for disposal of such substances, in and of itself, does not trigger CERCLA liability, nor does actual disposal of hazardous substances. A release must occur or be threatened before CERCLA is triggered. A party that "arranged for disposal" of a hazardous substance . . . does not become liable under CERCLA until there is an actual or threatened release of that substance into the environment. . . . Further, disposal activities that were legal when conducted can nevertheless give rise to liability . . . if there is an actual or threatened release of such hazardous substances into the environment.

The location where a party arranged for disposal or disposed of hazardous substances is not controlling for purposes of assessing whether CERCLA is being applied extraterritorially, because CERCLA imposes liability for releases or threatened releases of hazardous substances, and not merely for disposal or arranging for disposal of such substances. Because the actual or threatened release of hazardous substances triggers CERCLA liability, and because the actual or threatened release here, the leaching of hazardous substances from slag that settled at the Site, took place in the United States, this case involves a domestic application of CERCLA.

In conclusion, we hold that the district court correctly denied Teck's motion to dismiss Pakootas's complaint. . . . Applying CERCLA to the Site, as defined by the Order issued by the EPA, is a domestic application of CERCLA. The argument that this case presents an extraterritorial application of CERCLA fails because CERCLA liability does not attach until there is an actual or threatened release of hazardous substances into the environment; the suit concerns actual or threatened releases of heavy metals and other hazardous substances into the Upper Columbia River Site within the United States. We reject Teck's argument that it is not liable. . . .

Teck filed a petition for certiorari with the United States Supreme Court. The Government of Canada filed an amicus curiae brief in support of Teck, urging the Supreme Court to take the case and reverse the decisions below.

GOVERNMENT OF CANADA'S AMICUS CURIAE BRIEF PAKOOTAS V. TECK COMINCO METALS, LTD.

2005 WL 2175370 (June 10, 2005)

. . . This case raises serious issues of comity, interference by United States courts and agencies in the internal affairs of Canada, and compliance with the rule of national treatment applicable under customary international law. Contrary to the district court's pronouncement, the Government of Canada believes that it has a unique legal position and viewpoint of which this Court should be aware in deciding this appeal.

The 5,525-mile border between Canada and the United States includes more than 150 lakes and rivers, making issues of transboundary water pollution—including the proper means of resolving disputes over claims of pollution—a matter of recurring and special importance to the Government of Canada. In addition to its broader interest in such disputes, the Government of Canada has a specific interest in this case, where the district court has admittedly engaged in extraterritorial application of United States law, in a case of first impression. It has done so, not at the request of the United States . . ., but at the behest of two private litigants. The district court order thus allows private citizens to proceed with a suit aimed at forcing a corporate person, resident in Canada, to conduct a study in Canada, and to pay for that study.

The district court's order was issued despite Canada's having proposed alternative means of resolving the issues raised by plaintiffs, in the form of a Memorandum of Understanding Respecting the Investigation of Contamination in the Upper Columbia River/Lake Roosevelt Area between Canada and the United States, or a proceeding between the two governments under Article IX of the Treaty Relating to Boundary Waters between the United States and Canada, Jan. 11, 1909, U.S.-Gr. Brit., 36 Stat. 2448, CUS 312 ("Boundary Waters Treaty") **[Basic Document 3.16]**. Canada's proposals follow well-established precedents for resolving transborder environmental disputes between the countries diplomatically. In contrast, the district court order departs from past practice and sets a new precedent of favoring resort to lawsuits in domestic courts, under domestic law, over government-to-government, non-judicial resolutions.

The Government of Canada has a strong interest in preserving from interference, by private litigation in United States courts, its sovereign right to regulate Canadian persons and companies operating in Canada. If the district court's order is upheld, the decision will have repercussions for numerous Canadian businesses operating along or near the Canadian-United States border by purporting to make them directly subject to CERCLA, regardless of Canadian law. It would also raise issues regarding the susceptibility to United States laws of other Canadian businesses whose conduct in Canada may have effects in the United States.

The Canadian Government also has a compelling interest in preserving the viability of diplomatic mechanisms for resolving disputes with the United States over boundary issues; these mechanisms include a valid treaty to which Canada and the United States are parties and other internationally recognized procedures available to both countries. Regardless of the particular method of resolution, Canada has a vital sovereign interest in having this dispute settled through diplomatic measures, rather than by adjudication in the domestic courts of the United States.

* * *

Traditionally, Canada and the United States have worked cooperatively to solve transboundary environmental issues through bilateral negotiations or the Boundary Waters Treaty, which plainly applies in this case. The Treaty created the IJC, which has had a long, successful history of operation. Not only was the IJC created for the specific purpose of resolving disputes such as the one underlying this case, but the Commission has, over time, maintained consistent credibility with Canada and the United States.

The longstanding practice of the two countries has been to deal with environmental issues of concern through diplomatic means. The ongoing Canadian-United States cooperation regarding environmental issues is evidenced by the 1972 Agreement on Great Lakes Water Quality, Apr. 15, 1972, U.S.-Can., 23 U.S.T. 301, CTS 1978/20. Canada and the United States have also entered into the Agreement Concerning the Transboundary Movement of Hazardous Waste, Oct. 28, 1986, Can.-U.S., T.I.A.S. No. 11,099, CTS 1986/39, and the Canada-United States Joint Inland Pollution Contingency Plan, July 25, 1994, U.S.-Can.,8 to address spills and other environmental emergencies along the Canada-United States border. Canada and the United States each implemented the Convention for the Protection of Migratory Birds, Aug. 16, 1916, U.S.-Gr. Brit. (for Canada), 39 Stat. 1702, CUS 465, and the Agreement on Air Quality, Mar. 13, 1991, U.S.-Can., 30 I.L.M. 676, CTS 1991/3.9 Both countries are also parties to the Bilateral Agreement on Shellfish Sanitation, Mar. 4, 1948, U.S.-Can., T.I.A.S. No. 1747, CTS 1948/10.

These treaties, and a long history of bilateral cooperation, underscore the unique potency of non-judicial resolution of the issues before this court. Moreover, the Boundary Waters Treaty directly addresses the issues raised by plaintiffs. . . .

In these circumstances, for this Court to allow the case to proceed under CERCLA, in United States courts, displacing the procedures that both Canada and the United States have endorsed in the past, and which Canada has proposed in this instance, constitutes a clear violation of the rules of comity. ""The United States should not . . . conduct foreign policy through the U.S. court system." . . .

* * *

. . . Canada has an interest in regulating, and does regulate, the smelter and refinery activities of the Trail facility at issue here, at both the federal and provincial levels of government. Canada has comprehensive environmental protection legislation. . . . The federal government, through the Fisheries Act, imposes a number of obligations on the Trail facility respecting discharges to fish habitat (in this case, the Columbia River). For example, the federal government used the Fisheries Act in 1996 to require the Trail facility to cease discharges of slag.

Concurrent regulatory pressure by the provincial government has resulted in substantially reduced discharges of specific contaminants. Canada continues to work through the provincial permit system to improve the effluent quality by further lowering the permit limits.

Here, where the issues raised by plaintiffs are susceptible of resolution bilaterally between Canada and the United States, and where such methods of resolution have been proposed by Canada, it was unnecessary and inappropriate for the district court to construe CERCLA to interfere with Canada's domestic affairs, including Canada's domestic regulatory regime.

* * *

As set out in the principal brief of Teck Cominco, United States companies charged with violations of CERCLA may rely on United States environmental permits as defenses, but these permits are not available to non-residents such as Teck Cominco. Canadian environmental permits are not recognized as a defense under CERCLA, regardless of any similarity between Canadian and United States regulation.

The application of CERCLA to Teck Cominco thus violates the international obligation of national treatment. *See* Borchard, supra, at 101 (Foreign governments' willingness to permit local courts in other states to exercise jurisdiction over their citizens abroad is predicated, inter alia, upon "[t]he existence of regular courts and of laws assuring to the alien the administration of civilized justice, on terms of equality with nationals.").

This discrimination against Canadian companies may be exacerbated by CERCLA's adoption of the principle of joint and several liability; United States entities contributing to the pollution at a site may be able to assert a "federally permitted release" defense not available to a non-resident, leaving the foreign entity to face sole or disproportionate liability despite others' contributions to the pollution. In such a situation, applying CERCLA would, in effect, set a zero-release limit in Canada, while permitting releases by United States companies. . . .

As noted above, the Supreme Court declined to hear the case, so the case proceeded forward. The next issue for decision was whether the federal district court in Washington could exercise personal jurisdiction over Teck Cominco. The court held that it could.

PAKOOTAS V. TECK COMINCO METALS, LTD.

2012 WL 6546088, 76 ERC 1310 (U.S. Dist. Ct., E.D. Washington 2012)

In cases sounding in tort, as here, courts [determine whether there is personal jurisdiction by inquiring] whether a defendant "purposefully direct[s] his activities at the forum state, applying an 'effects' test that focuses on the forum in which the defendant's actions were felt, whether or not the actions themselves occurred within the forum." The relevant "actions" here are Teck's disposal of waste into the Columbia River . . . having "effects" in the UCR [Upper Columbia River] Site located in the United States. These "actions" create personal jurisdiction, while the "effects"—releases of hazardous substances from the waste create liability under CERCLA.

The [*Calder*] "effects" test . . . requires that the defendant must have: "(1) committed an intentional act; (2) expressly aimed at the forum state, (3) causing harm that the defendant knows is likely to be suffered in the forum state."

An "intentional act" has a specialized, limited meaning in the context of the *Calder* effects test. "We construe 'intent' in the context of the 'intentional act' test as referring to an intent to perform an actual, physical act in the real world, rather than an intent to accomplish a result or consequence of that act." Teck intentionally disposed of waste into the Columbia River, thereby satisfying the first element of the Calder effects test.

. . . Teck dumped waste in the Columbia River, intending to take advantage of the natural transport mechanism the river offered, with knowledge its waste would repose in Washington State. Teck knew that repose of its waste in Washington State was a natural consequence of river disposal. Teck persisted in river disposal well past its acknowledgment that its waste reposed in Washington State. Such conduct is "expressly aimed" at Washington State and satisfies the second element of the *Calder* effects test. Teck's actions do not amount to untargeted negligence with effects in the Washington State. Teck's intentional actions were specifically targeted at Washington State. . . .

The third element of the *Calder* effects test requires that the defendant's conduct cause harm which the defendant knows is likely to be suffered in the forum state, interpreted as foreseeability that harm resulting from defendant's conduct would occur in the forum state. . . . The harm Teck caused in the forum state was foreseeable. It was foreseeable that the effects of Teck's discarding of waste would be felt in the United States in Washington State.

Teck knew its disposal of hazardous waste into the UCR was likely to cause harm. It was told by the Canadian government that its slag was toxic to fish and leached hazardous metals. It acknowledged its effluent settled to sediments in the UCR and that its slag leached hazardous metals into the aquatic environment, yet persisted with river disposal.

* * *

Teck Cominco settled with the EPA and agreed to pay for a study of environmental contamination in the upper Columbia River. That study is ongoing at this writing. *See* www.ucr-rifs.com (last visited June 27, 2019). Teck is also funding cleanup at several residences where the ground has been contaminated by heavy metals. In 2016, the district court ordered Teck to pay over $8.2 million to the Colville Tribes to cover the costs they incurred to investigate and litigate Teck's liability. These costs were mostly in the form of expert witness fees, attorneys' fees, and other litigation expenses.

DISCUSSION NOTES/QUESTIONS

1. Was it appropriate for the United States to apply its law to hold Teck Cominco responsible for the pollution in the upper Columbia River? As Canada pointed out in its brief to the Supreme Court, American firms that contributed to pollution of the upper Columbia would have no responsibility under CERCLA if those firms had possessed federal permits for the release. In lieu of CERCLA liability, they would face liability under "existing law," primarily weak, common law remedies. *See* CERCLA '101(10), 42 U.S.C. '9601(10). Teck Cominco, on the other hand, which polluted pursuant to Canadian-issued permits, had no such immunity from CERCLA. Worse, because it was a major contributor to pollution in the upper Columbia area, it was 'jointly and severally liable' for the cleanup, meaning it had to pay for all the damage, not just for its proportionate share. Contribution from other polluters might be available, except that most of them would be exempt from CERCLA liability pursuant to the provision just noted. Is this fair? Does it bother you? Would a diplomatic solution have been a better way to go, as Canada argued?

2. Canadian actors have also invoked U.S. environmental laws to secure favorable action in transboundary environmental disputes. For example, in 2002, Manitoba sued the Secretary of the U.S. Department of Interior claiming that Interior had not complied with the National Environmental Policy Act (NEPA) when it approved a project in North Dakota to transfer water from the Missouri river basin to the Souris river basin. The Souris river basin ultimately drains into the Hudson Bay (in Canada), and Manitoba claimed that the water transfer created a risk of introducing alien and invasive species into the Hudson Bay system. A federal court rejected the Bureau of Reclamation's finding that the project would have "No Significant Impact" as "preposterous," and ordered the Bureau to produce a full Environmental Impact Statement. In the meantime, the court enjoined completion of the water transfer project. *See Province of Manitoba v. Salazar,* 926 F.Supp.2d 189 (2013). The Bureau completed a NEPA analysis that would allow the project to proceed. That analysis was immediately challenged in court by Manitoba. In the meantime, the DC Circuit ordered a modification of the lower court's injunction to allow design work to begin on a water treatment plant needed for the project. *See Government of Province of Manitoba v. Zinke,* 849 F.3d 1111 (DC Cir. 2017).

3. Is litigation in U.S. courts the best way to resolve these cross-border disputes? Can Canadian interests get full and fair consideration in U.S. courts? To the extent that the issues must be weighed and evaluated by U.S. administrative agencies headed by political appointees, can foreign interests expect full and fair consideration of their concerns and points of view? Would

you expect U.S. citizens who complained about pollution by a Canadian corporation to receive a fair hearing if they lodged that complaint in a Canadian court?

4. Would it be better if the United States made more use of the International Joint Commission and the procedures for dispute resolution established by the Boundary Waters Treaty of 1909 **(Basic Document 3.16)**? As one U.S.-based commentator observes, "[t]he International Joint Commission continues to enjoy a well-deserved reputation for objective work supported by the best available science and free of political biases." Noah Hall, *Bilateral Breakdown: U.S.-Canada Pollution Disputes,* 21 Nat. Resources & Env't 18 (2006). Wouldn't the International Joint Commission provide a faster, fairer, and less expensive means for resolving such disputes? *See* John H. Knox, *The Boundary Waters Treaty: Ahead of Its Time, and Ours,* 54 Wayne L. Rev. 1591 (2008).

5. Suppose the U.S. government thought that the Teck Cominco matter should have been resolved through the procedure provided for in the Boundary Waters Treaty of 1909. The court case against Teck Cominco was brought by private parties acting under the citizen suit provisions of CERCLA. Could the government have persuaded the court to dismiss or stay the litigation while proceedings were held before the International Joint Commission? *Compare Ungaro-Benages v. Dresdner Bank AG,* 379 F.3d 1227 (11th Cir. 2004) (court abstains from deciding case brought by U.S. citizens under state law when an "adequate alternative forum," supported by the U.S. government, was available in Germany) *with Pravin Banker Assocs. V. Banco Popular Del Peru,* 109 F.3d 850 (2nd Cir. 1997) (refusing to abstain in action to force foreign bank to pay on defaulted loans despite ongoing negotiations between U.S. government and Peruvian government to restructure Peru's commercial debts).

6. In 1979, the Canadian Bar Association and the American Bar Association recommended that their governments adopt and ratify a "Draft Treaty on a Regime of Equal Access and Remedy in Cases of Transfrontier Pollution." One aim of the treaty was to make it easier for persons injured by transboundary pollution to secure a remedy in the polluter's jurisdiction by guaranteeing those injured persons judicial access and remedies equal to that provided by each country to its own citizens. The treaty envisioned, therefore, that polluters would be sued by foreign victims in the polluter's home country under local laws. Is that a better solution than allowing an action against the polluter in the victim's country and applying that country's law to the polluter, as was done in *Teck Cominco*? *See generally* Joel A. Gallob, *Birth of the North American Transboundary Environmental Plaintiff: Transboundary Pollution and the 1979 Draft Treaty for Equal Access and Remedy,* 18 Harv. Envtl. L. Rev. 85 (1991). The proposed Canadian-American treaty on access to justice was never adopted.

An "access to justice" approach to dealing with harm from transboundary pollution has been favorably received outside of North America. "Access to justice" is the primary theme of the 1972 Convention on the Protection of the Environment Between Denmark, Finland, Norway and Sweden, 19 February 1974, 1092 U.N.T.S. 279 (entered into force, October 5, 1976). In 1977, building on earlier recommendations, the members of the Organization for Economic Cooperation and Development (OECD) (which includes the United States and Canada) unanimously endorsed a set of principles aimed at promoting establishment among the industrialized countries of "a regime of equal right of access and non-discrimination in matters of transfrontier pollution." OECD Council Recommendation for the Implementation of a Regime of Equal Right of Access and Non-Discrimination in Relation to Transfrontier Pollution, May 17, 1977, 19777 OECD C(77)28. In 1998, the concept of "equal access" received fuller and broader development with the adoption of Aarhus Convention on Access to Information, Public Participation in Decision-Making and Access to Justice in Environmental Matters, June 25, 1998, 2161 UNTS 447. As of June 27, 2019, 46 countries and the European Union were party to this convention, which entered into force on October 30, 2001. Neither the United States nor Canada has yet joined.

What are the strengths and weaknesses of an "equal access to justice" approach to transboundary air pollution?

For general discussions of the use of domestic legal remedies to address transboundary pollution in the North American context, *see* Jack Tuholske and Mark Foster, *Solving Transboundary Pollution Disputes Locally: Success in the Crown of the Continent,* 92 Oregon L. Rev. 649 (2014); Bret Benedict, Comment and Casenote, *Transnational Pollution and the Efficacy of International and Domestic Dispute Resolutions Among the NAFTA Countries,* 15 L. & Bus. Rev. Am. 863 (2009). *See also* Noah D. Hall, *The Evolving Role of Citizens in United States-Canadian International Environmental Law Compliance,* 24 Pace Envtl. L. Rev. 131 (2007).

D. THE CONVENTION ON LONG-RANGE TRANSBOUNDARY AIR POLLUTION

The story of the Convention on Long-Range Transboundary Air Pollution (CLRTAP) **(Basic Document 2.1)** is very much a story about "acid rain" and the efforts of the Nordic nations to persuade the rest of Europe that acid rain was a significant problem, that it was caused by transboundary air pollution, and that international action was needed to address the problem. The CLRTAP story provides insight into the complexity of international law-making processes (in this case, treaty-making) and illustrates how seemingly unrelated issues (acid rain, on the one hand, and Cold War politics, on the other) can impact each other and shape the development of international solutions to shared problems. We tell the story here, in brief. Fuller accounts can be found in the readings cited in the footnote at the bottom of the page.[4]

1. ACID RAIN

Acid rain is the popular name given to precipitation that is significantly more acidic than ordinary rainwater. Acid rain has a number of deleterious effects. It corrodes metals, paint and stone, and can cause significant damage to buildings, roads, bridges, and statues. It can acidify lakes and streams, preventing fish eggs from hatching and even killing adult fish. It leaches nutrients from soil, harming plant life. It also leaches nutrients directly from the leaves of trees, weakening their ability to survive.

Although there are natural events that might contribute to acidic precipitation (e.g., volcanic emissions of SO_2), acid rain is mainly associated with the burning of fossil fuels for energy. Unless pollution control technology is in place, the burning of fossil fuels releases sulfur dioxide (SO_2) and nitrous oxides (NO_x) into the atmosphere. Those chemicals then react with other atmospheric chemicals to form sulfuric acid and nitric acid. The sulfuric and nitric acids subsequently return to the earth as a component of rainwater or other precipitation: hence, "acid rain." Today the term "acid rain" refers to all kinds of deposition of acid from the atmosphere to the ground, including in rain, snow, fog, hail, or even acidic dust.

2. IDENTIFYING THE PROBLEM

A British scientist described the causes and effects of acid rain in 1872.[5] The association between acid rain and the long-range transport of air pollutants was scientifically identified in 1955, 80 years later.[6] In the 1960s, scientists in Norway and Sweden discovered that freshwater lakes and streams in the region were becoming increasingly acid and that this acidification was having deleterious effects on aquatic life in the region. But although concern about freshwater acidification was growing, the earlier science on acid rain did not attract much attention until the late 1960s, when Svante Oden, a Swedish scientist, linked the two phenomena.

Oden combined data from a wide-ranging study of precipitation chemistry that had begun in the 1940s with data from more recent studies

---

[4] Thomas Gehring, Dynamic International Regimes: Institutions for International Environmental Governance 63–193 (1994); Jutta Brunnée, Acid Rain and Ozone Layer Depletion: International Law and Regulation 143–221 (1988); Gregory S. Wetstone, *A History of the Acid Rain Issue* in Science for Public Policy 163–96 (Harvey Brooks & Chester L Cooper, eds. 1987); Gregory S. Wetstone & Armin Rosencranz, Acid Rain in Europe and North America: National Responses to an International Problem 131–155 (1983).

[5] R.A. Smith, Air and Rain: The Beginnings of a Chemical Climatology (1872).

[6] *See* Wetstone, *supra* note 4, at 164–65.

of surface water chemistry. The precipitation data came from a precipitation-monitoring network that spanned much of Europe. Data from that network showed that pollutants emitted in one part of Europe could travel hundreds of miles before being deposited in another part of Europe. Combining that information with data from a network that studied surface-water chemistry in Scandinavia, Oden concluded "that acid precipitation from distant industrial emissions was acidifying fresh water systems."[7] In other words, the Nordic problem with acidifying lakes and streams was caused by pollution from other countries, a source beyond local control. In October 1967, Oden published his conclusions in a popular Swedish newspaper, informing the public that "acid precipitation from distant industrial emissions was acidifying fresh water ecosystems, leaching toxic metals from soils into surface waters, and leading to dramatic declines in fish populations."[8] A few months later, Oden published similar findings in a scientific journal.

Needless to say, Oden's analysis and conclusions attracted much public attention. Though Wetstone reports that the scientific community reacted "with skepticism" and that the Swedish government "was unconvinced" and "declined to continue funding Oden's research," subsequent events suggest that Oden's work had an immediate impact on government policy.[9] Within weeks of publication of his conclusions, the Swedish government began lobbying for international action on environmental problems, including acid rain. Norway, too, began to take the first steps in what became a decade-long lobbying effort culminating in the negotiation and ratification of the LRTAP Convention and, a few years later, its Protocol on the Reduction of Sulphur Emissions or Their Transboundary Fluxes.

3. BUILDING AN INTERNATIONAL CONSENSUS

At the United Nations. On December 13, 1967, Sweden proposed to the United Nations General Assembly that the United Nations sponsor a conference "on the extremely complex problems related to the human environment," including the "serious and ever-increasing inconvenience and dangers * * * caused by air pollution, water pollution, sulphur fall-out, waste, etc."[10] In May 1968, Sweden's Permanent Representative to the UN pressed this request at meetings of the United Nations Economic and Social Council, calling for a conference that would "create a basis for comprehensive consideration with the United Nations of the problems of human environment," one goal of which would be to identify problems "that

---

7 *Id.* at 165.

8 *Id.*

9 *Id.*

10 Verbatim Records of the United Nations General Assembly, 13 December 1967, UN Doc A/PV.1629, p. 14–15 (statement of Mr. Billner, Sweden).

can only be solved through international co-operation and agreement * * *, particularly those that have to be dealt with as a matter of urgency if irreparable damage is to be avoided."[11]

Sweden's proposal was ultimately accepted by the United Nations General Assembly in 1969 and, three years later, the first United Nations Conference on the Human Environment was held in Stockholm, Sweden, from June 5th to June 16th, 1972. Prior to the conference, Sweden circulated a report identifying acid rain as a serious problem and long-distance movement of industrial pollutants as its cause.[12]

Although the Stockholm Conference did not result in the adoption of any binding international agreements, it did identify goals and principles to guide future international action on environmental problems generally and transboundary pollution more specifically. In particular, the declaration of principles adopted at the end of the conference included this famous endorsement of the *sic utere* principle as applied to environmental matters:

> States have, in accordance with the Charter of the United Nations and the principles of international law, the sovereign right to exploit their own resources pursuant to their own environmental policies, and the responsibility to insure that activities within their jurisdiction or control do not cause damage to the environment of other States or areas beyond the limits of national jurisdiction.[13]

In addition, several recommendations included in the Action Plan adopted by the Conference called upon governments to increase the study of pollutants and their effects and to share scientific research and information about pollution-control technology. The Action Plan urged "the identification of pollutants of international significance," the creation of "appropriate intergovernmental, expert bodies" to assess the risks posed by those pollutants, and "international cooperation for pollution control."[14] However, these recommendations were in general terms. Sweden's attempt to focus particular attention on acid rain was met with resistance, and the Conference outcomes did not specifically address the problem.

---

[11] Letter of 20 May 1968 with supporting memorandum, from Permanent Representative of Sweden to the United Nations Economic and Social Council, *reproduced* in United Nations Economic and Social Council, 44th Sess., *Consideration of the Provisional Agenda for the Forty-fifth Session,* U.N. Doc. E/4466/Add.1 (22 May 1968).

[12] Swedish Preparatory Committee for the United Nations Conference on the Human Environment, Air Pollution Across National Boundaries: The Impact on the Environment of sulfur in Air and Precipitation (1971). *See also* Walter Sullivan, *U.N. Parley Told of Sulfur 'Rains,'* New York Times, June 12, 1972, p. 12.

[13] U.N. Conference on the Human Environment, *Stockholm Declaration,* principle 21, U.N. Doc. A/CONF.48/14/Rev.1, at 5 (June 16, 1972) **(Basic Document 1.21)**.

[14] Report of the United National Conference on the Human Environment, Stockholm, 5–16 June 1972, Recommendations 72, 84–85, U.N. Doc. A/CONF.48/14/Rev.1 at 20–22 (1972).

In the OECD. The Organization for Economic Cooperation and Development (OECD) is an organization of industrialized countries that studies and makes recommendations on issues of concern to its members. In some cases, the OECD will issue binding decisions or propose the adoption of binding international agreements on particular issues.

At the urging of Norway and Sweden, the OECD began studying the problem of acid rain in 1969. The first step taken was to call a meeting of experts to study the evidence of acid precipitation that had been gathered by Scandinavian scientists. That was followed, in 1970, by a study of air pollution from stationary sources burning fossil fuels, and, in 1972, by establishment of the Co-Operative Technical Programme to Measure the Long-Range Transport of Air Pollutants. This latter program gathered data from eleven participating nations in an effort to determine the extent to which sulfur emissions were "exported" from emitting countries and "imported" into other countries in the form of acid deposition.

The OECD reported the results of the long-range-transport study in 1977. Its findings "offered the first independent verification of Scandinavian charges that imported air pollution was the primary source of sulfuric air pollution in Sweden and Norway."[15] But the study also showed that the same was true in several other European countries: the bulk of the observed acid deposition in those countries was also from foreign sources. This led the OECD staff to the conclusion that air pollution in the European airshed was an international problem that should be addressed by national actions that were "integrated internationally."[16] It also led other net importers of pollutants to support the push for international action being led by Sweden and Norway.

Other OECD members, however, were not convinced. The United Kingdom, in particular, while acknowledging (after long denial) that sulfur emitted in the UK could reach Scandinavia, continued to deny that acid rain caused serious problems or that the UK was responsible for any problems that did exist. A 1977 editorial in the UK publication *Nature*, reacting to the OECD report, described the impact of acid rain in Scandinavia as "a million-dollar problem" with a "billion-dollar solution" and argued that some solution other than "removing pollution at source" must be found.[17] Germany had a similar view, as did several other European nations.

The OECD continued to work on the acid rain problem only for four more years. In 1978, it completed a study that concluded that "sulfur emissions could be substantially reduced in both Europe and North America without serious economic repercussions," and it offered guidance

---

[15] Harvey Brooks & Chester L. Cooper, Science for Public Policy 168 (1987).

[16] *Id.*

[17] Opinion, *Million-dollar problem—billion-dollar solution?*, 268 Nature 89 (July 14, 1977),

on how to achieve that result.[18] In 1981, it produced a report on *The Costs and Benefits of Sulphur Oxide Control.*[19] Although the authors of that study had originally argued that the benefits of emissions reductions would exceed the costs, attacks on the reliability of their data and on their analytic method led them to abandon any effort to reach conclusions and presented the study as simply "illustrative" of "how pollution control costs and benefits could be compared."

While the debate over the costs-and-benefits study was underway, the OECD decided to phase out its work on long-range transboundary pollution. It is not clear whether this was because the area was taken over by the UNECE (see below) or because of political pressure from the United States and other industrialized nations who were unhappy with the results of the OECD's work.[20]

Meanwhile, at the UNECE. The United Nations Economic Commission for Europe [UNECE] was established in 1947 to assist in the post-war economic reconstruction of Europe. Its original membership included the United States, Canada, and all European countries from both sides of the Iron Curtain. As a result, it became the main arena for cooperation between the capitalist states of Western Europe on the one hand and the communist states of Eastern Europe on the other.

In 1969, the UNECE created a Working Party on Air Pollution Problems. In 1971, it convened a high-level group of Senior Advisers to the UNECE Governments on Environmental Matters, and the Working Party on Air Pollution became a subsidiary organization of the Group of Senior Advisers.

One of the main responsibilities of the newly-formed Senior Advisers group was to prepare materials on the environment for the 1975 Conference on Security and Co-operation in Europe, a European meeting that was aimed at reducing conflict and enhancing cooperation between the capitalist states of Western Europe and the communist bloc in the East. The Nordic countries pressed hard for action on environmental issues. Although no agreement on substantive environmental standards was reached, the Helsinki Accords (a declaration adopted at the end of the conference) included a section on environmental cooperation which called for international cooperation on "control of air pollution," with a specific recommendation for the development of a program "for the monitoring and evaluation of the long-range transport of air pollutants." The program was

---

[18] Gregory S. Wetstone & Armin Rosencranz, *supra* note 4, at 137, *citing* OECD, *Clean Fuel Supply* 5 (1978).

[19] OECD, The Costs and Benefits of Sulphur Oxide Control (1981).

[20] Wetstone & Rosencranz, *supra* note 4, at 139.

to be based upon a proposal prepared by a group of experts convened by the Norwegian Institute of Air Research in 1974.[21]

The Western countries had resisted the socialist countries' call for a new permanent international organization to implement the Helsinki Accords. A compromise was reached in which certain existing international organizations would be charged with implementation of particular parts of the Accords. The task of carrying through on the environmental commitments was assigned to UNECE, a move that made sense given the role of the Senior Advisers in the development of the environmental provisions of the Accords.

UNECE moved almost immediately to establish a monitoring program. The UNECE Air Pollution Working Group and the group of Senior Advisers had established a task force charged with study of the long-range movement of air pollutants, and, in 1976, the task force proposed what is now known as the Cooperative Programme for Monitoring and Evaluation of the Long-range Transmission of Air Pollutants in Europe (EMEP). A Steering Body was created to run EMEP, and it held its first session in August 1977. EMEP later became a central feature of the CLRTAP regime.

Monitoring transboundary movements of air pollutants is one thing; doing something about the pollution is something else. The Nordic countries were determined that the latter should occur, and here they took full advantage of Cold War politics to move matters from talk to action.

Following the Helsinki Conference, the Soviet Union and the socialist countries called for additional high-level diplomatic conferences with the West. But the Helsinki participants were split on the issue. Some nations welcomed the Soviet initiative. Others, like the United States and key European Community countries, resisted, primarily for political reasons: among other things, they were concerned that closer relations with the socialist countries would legitimate those governments and hinder the effectiveness of the West's calls for improvements in the human-rights records of those countries. So, while not outright rejecting the idea of further conferences in the future, the West argued that it would be inappropriate to hold conferences on the vaguely defined subjects proposed by the Soviet Union.

At the 1977 UNECE meeting, the debate over the possibility of high-level conferences found the Western industrialized nations agreeing in principle to holding such conferences so long as several preconditions were met: i) any such conference would need to be carefully prepared and have the possibility of resulting in important decisions; ii) the conference would

[21] Final Act of the Conference on Security and Co-operation in Europe, adopted by the Conference on Security and Co-operation in Europe, at Helsinki, Finland, 1 August 1979, 14 I.L.M. 1292 (1975).

have to be held within the framework of the UNECE; and iii) the conference would have to address a topic of concern to the entire European region.

This response provided an opening for the Nordic countries. Immediately they argued that long-range transboundary air pollution, and especially SO_2 pollution, was a matter of region-wide concern. Moreover, they pointed out that substantial work had already been done on the subject within the UNECE and that, with additional preparatory work, it would be possible to reach substantive decisions at a conference on the topic.[22] Eventually, "an open coalition between Eastern and Nordic countries emerged," with the Eastern countries seeking further high-level diplomatic conferences with the West and the Nordic countries arguing that protection of the environment in general, and the problem of transboundary air pollution in particular, were appropriately specific topics for such a conference. By the end of the 1977 UNECE meeting, "the impression prevailed that a high-level meeting on the environment could take place late in 1978,"[23] although it was not clear that it would necessarily focus on transboundary air pollution. Moreover, the UNECE did not actually call for or schedule a meeting—the matter was left for decision in 1978.

Between the UNECE meeting in 1977 and the meeting in 1978, the Senior Advisers group had extensive discussions of possible topics for a high-level meeting on the environment. Transboundary air pollution emerged as one of the topics that nearly every country could agree upon, although opinions varied widely about the possible outcome of a conference on the subject. Norway argued that the conference should be aimed at adopting a treaty on transboundary air pollution that included serious commitments on the reduction of SO_2 pollution. The United Kingdom, on the other hand, initially resisted the idea that transboundary air pollution was a proper subject for the conference, but eventually accepted discussion of the topic, and even the possibility of a framework convention on the subject, but with less focus on international control of SO_2 pollution and more focus on exchange of information, research, dispute settlement, and equal access to national courts for the private resolution of transboundary pollution disputes.

At the 1978 meeting of the UNECE, however, planning for the high-level conference hit a snag. Disappointed with the outcome of a recent meeting with the socialist countries in Belgrade, the United States and other Western countries renewed their opposition to holding additional high-level conferences with the Soviet bloc under UNECE auspices. The Soviet Union, however, insisted that the UNECE should call such a conference for the end of 1978, as tacitly agreed in 1977. The Nordic

[22] Gehring, *supra* note 4, at 95–96.

[23] *Id.* at 97.

countries struck a middle ground that served their objective of obtaining meaningful agreement on the acid rain problem. On the one hand, they sided with the West: the proposed conference should not be held at the end of 1978. But they took this position for environmental reasons: more time was needed to negotiate an outcome document that would involve real progress on the problem of transboundary air pollution. On the other hand, they agreed with the Soviet Union that the time was right to commit to a high-level conference on the environment in general, and transboundary air pollution specifically.

The resulting compromise resolution adopted at the 1978 UNECE meeting called for "further and detailed work by the Senior Advisers" to "prepare important decisions, including the possible forms of appropriate agreements that would be adopted at a high-level meeting." The Resolution suggested that a "successful conclusion" of the preparatory work would allow a high-level meeting to be held in 1979. It also identified topics for discussion in the context of negotiations over transboundary air pollution, including policies to combat polluting emissions, cooperation in research and development of SO_2-control technologies, further enhancement of the EMEP program, exchange of information, and dispute settlement.[24] "The Nordic countries [had] succeeded in transferring political dynamics generated by a Soviet initiative into progress on substantive aspects of concern to them."[25]

4. NEGOTIATION OF THE CONVENTION

Following the 1978 Commission resolution, negotiation of the content of the agreements to be adopted at the expected 1979 conference began in earnest under the purview of the Senior Advisers group. The Nordic countries submitted a draft convention, along with a plan for adoption of annexes that would require states to take specific steps to reduce particular air pollutants or, at least, the transboundary movement of those pollutants. This became the basis for many months of negotiations, during which the main point of disagreement was whether the negotiating countries were prepared to make a binding commitment to reduce their emissions of sulfur dioxide. The Nordic countries, of course, believed that such a commitment was essential, given their conviction that their freshwater acidification problems were caused by pollutants generated in other European states. Several major polluters, including the United States, Germany, and the United Kingdom, resisted the adoption of any binding obligation on emissions reduction. The desire for success led, again, to compromise: the outcome of the high-level conference would be a *legally-binding* document on transboundary air pollution—a convention, as the Nordic countries

[24] ECE Resolution 1(XXXIII), Annual Report of the Economic Commission for Europe on its Thirty-Third Session, U.N. Doc. E/1978/47 at 108–111 (1978).

[25] Gehring, *supra* note 4, at 103.

wished; but the convention would have no binding commitments on pollution reduction—such commitments, if any, would be agreed in protocols adopted at a later date.

With drafts agreed and compromises made, a High-Level Meeting on the Protection of the Environment was convened in Geneva from November 13–15, 1979. The meeting adopted by acclamation a Convention on Long-range Transboundary Air Pollution **(Basic Document 2.1)**, which was signed by 32 states before the meeting was over. As the following excerpts illustrate, the Convention provides, at best, a 'framework' for action to abate transboundary air pollution. The Convention's preamble reiterates the "responsibility" of states to avoid transboundary harm. Article 2 provides that Contracting Parties to the Convention "shall endeavor" to combat "long-range transboundary air pollution." But there are no specific pollution-reduction obligations in the agreement. Rather, it calls for research, the exchange of information, monitoring, and consultation. It creates a governing body and a secretariat with the view that they will work to promote further, potentially more meaningful steps, to reduce pollution, if needed. In a resolution adopted contemporaneously with the Convention, the attendees at the meeting expressed their desire "to develop without delay further co-operation in problem areas within the scope of the Convention," and, in particular, "to bring closer together their policies and strategies for combating air pollution." That was the closest the High-Level Meeting came to endorsing action to reduce SO_2 emissions or otherwise take meaningful steps to reduce transboundary air pollution.

CONVENTION ON LONG-RANGE TRANSBOUNDARY AIR POLLUTION

Adopted on 13 Nov. 1979; Entered into Force, 16 Mar. 1983
1302 U.N.T.S. 217 (Basic Document 2.1)

The Parties to the present Convention,

* * *

Cognizant of the references in the chapter on environment of the Final Act of the Conference on Security and Co-operation in Europe calling for co-operation to control air pollution and its effects, including long-range transport of air pollutants,

* * *

Considering the pertinent provisions of the Declaration of the United Nations Conference on the Human Environment, and in particular principle 21, which expresses the common conviction that States have, in accordance with the Charter of the United Nations and the principles of international law, the sovereign right to exploit their own resources pursuant to their own environmental policies, and the responsibility to ensure that activities within their jurisdiction or control do not cause damage to the environment of other States or of areas beyond the limits of natural jurisdiction,

Recognizing the existence of possible adverse effects, in the short and long term, of air pollution including transboundary air pollution,

Concerned that a rise in the level of emissions of air pollutants within the region as forecast may increase such adverse effects,

Recognizing the need to study the implications of the long-range transport of air pollutants and the need to seek solutions for the problems identified,

Affirming their willingness to reinforce active international co-operation to develop appropriate national policies and by means of exchange of information, consultation, research and monitoring, to co-ordinate national action for combating air pollution including long-range transboundary air pollution,

Have agreed as follows:

* * *

FUNDAMENTAL PRINCIPLES

Article 2

The Contracting Parties, taking due account of the facts and problems involved, are determined to protect man and his environment against air pollution and shall endeavour to limit and, as far as possible, gradually reduce and prevent air pollution including long-range transboundary air pollution.

Article 3

The Contracting Parties, within the framework of the present Convention, shall by means of exchanges of information, consultation, research and monitoring, develop without undue delay policies and strategies which shall serve as a means of combating the discharge of air pollutants, taking into account efforts already made at national and international levels.

* * *

EXECUTIVE BODY

Article 10

1. The representatives of the Contracting Parties shall, within the framework of the Senior Advisers to ECE Governments on Environmental Problems, constitute the Executive Body of the present Convention, and shall meet at least annually in that capacity.

2. The Executive Body shall:

(a) review the implementation of the present Convention;

(b) establish, as appropriate, working groups to consider matters related to the implementation and development of the present Convention and to this end to prepare appropriate studies and other documentation and to submit recommendations to be considered by the Executive Body;

(c) fulfil such other functions as may be appropriate under the provisions of the present Convention.

3. The Executive Body shall utilize the Steering Body for the EMEP to play an integral part in the operation of the present Convention, in particular with regard to data collection and scientific co-operation.

4. The Executive Body, in discharging its functions, shall, when it deems appropriate, also make use of information from other relevant international organizations.

SECRETARIAT

Article 11

The Executive Secretary of the Economic Commission for Europe shall carry out, for the Executive Body, the following secretariat functions:

(a) to convene and prepare the meetings of the Executive Body;

(b) to transmit to the Contracting Parties reports and other information received in accordance with the provisions of the present Convention;

(c) to discharge the functions assigned by the Executive Body.

After reading these provisions of the LRTAP Convention, you would be forgiven for thinking that the Nordic countries had won the battle (they secured action on long-range transboundary pollution in the form of a binding legal document), but lost the war (the agreement did little or nothing to actually solve the problem they were seeking to solve). But such an assessment would be too pessimistic. Within a few years, an agreement on reductions in SO_2 emissions was in place, negotiated within the framework of CLRTAP.

5. REDUCING SULPHUR EMISSIONS

The Nordic countries hoped that the Convention would be the first step in a fairly rapid process that would lead to effective international action to reduce SO_2 emissions in Europe. But by the end of 1981 (two years after its adoption), only 12 states had ratified the Convention and 24 ratifications were required for the Convention to enter into force.

To help speed up ratification, Sweden invited all the signatories of the Convention to attend a conference in Stockholm in June 1982 that would address "acidification of the environment." More than 100 scientists joined diplomats from 21 countries and several international organizations in reviewing the accumulating evidence about the impact of acid rain. The outcome of the conference was dramatic:

> For the first time, a major industrial nation—a major polluter—joined the Scandinavian side in its views about the seriousness of the acidification problem. Until recently, West Germany vigorously defended the idea that not enough was known about the problem to warrant control actions. Now the West German government has adopted a diametrically opposite view and announced a new policy of reducing SO2 emissions by 50%. . . .
>
> What persuaded [Germany] to abandon [its] previous position[ ] were disturbing revelations linking acid deposition . . . to 'crown dieback' in [West German] forests. . . .[26]

Switzerland shared West Germany's change of heart and suddenly the Scandinavian countries had two significant allies on their side in the battle against transboundary pollution.

By the end of 1982 a sufficient number of States had ratified the Convention for it to enter into force in March 1983. Immediately thereafter, at the first meeting of the Convention's Executive Body, the Nordic countries submitted a proposal aimed at securing a 30 percent reduction of sulfur emissions, or transboundary fluxes of those emissions, over a 10-year period. Although the European Community opposed any binding commitment of this sort, West Germany broke with its EC partners and supported the Nordic proposal. What's more, West Germany argued that studies of transboundary movements of NO_X and heavy metals should also be initiated under the auspices of CLRTAP.[27]

No action on these proposals was taken at the 1982 Executive Body meeting, but the political ball had begun rolling. Over the next two years, the number of States supporting the proposed 30 percent reduction grew from eight to 21. Although the Soviet Union was reportedly an early supporter, its commitment strengthened when a group of Russian scientists reported that acid rain caused by sulfur emissions in Western and Central Europe was adversely affecting over 350,000 square miles of Soviet territory.[28]

---

[26] *1982 Stockholm Conference on Acidification of the Environment: Through a glass selectively—or some governments saw what they wanted to see,* 17 Environ. Sci. Technol. 15A (1983).

[27] Gehring, *supra* note 4, at 142.

[28] Theodore Shabad, *Acid Rain Reported Over Soviet Union,* New York Times (April 24, 1984).

At its second meeting in September 1984, the CLRTAP Executive Body authorized negotiations on an SO_2 instrument and created a Working Group to prepare a draft. Negotiations were arduous and intense, but successful. At its third session, in July 1985, the Executive Body adopted a protocol that endorsed the 30% reduction target through provisions that imposed binding pollution-reduction commitments on states that chose to join the protocol.

PROTOCOL TO THE 1979 CONVENTION ON LONG-RANGE TRANSBOUNDARY AIR POLLUTION ON THE REDUCTION OF SULPHUR EMISSIONS OR THEIR TRANSBOUNDARY FLUXES BY AT LEAST 30 PER CENT

Adopted on 8 July 1985; Entered into Force, 2 Sept. 1987
1480 U.N.T.S. 215

The Parties,

Determined to implement the Convention on Long-range Transboundary Air Pollution,

* * *

Have agreed as follows:

* * *

Article 2
BASIC PROVISIONS

The Parties shall reduce their national annual sulphur emissions or their transboundary fluxes by at least 30 per cent as soon as possible and at the latest by 1993, using 1980 levels as the basis for calculation of reductions.

Article 3
FURTHER REDUCTIONS

The Parties recognize the need for each of them to study at the national level the necessity for further reductions, beyond those referred to in article 2, of sulphur emissions or their transboundary fluxes when environmental conditions warrant.

Article 4
REPORTING OF ANNUAL EMISSIONS

Each Party shall provide annually to the Executive Body its levels of national annual sulphur emissions, and the basis upon which they have been calculated.

* * *

Article 6

NATIONAL PROGRAMMES, POLICIES AND STRATEGIES

The Parties shall, within the framework of the Convention, develop without undue delay national programmes, policies and strategies which shall serve as a means of reducing sulphur emissions or their transboundary fluxes, by at least 30 per cent as soon as possible and at the latest by 1993, and shall report thereon as well as on progress towards achieving the goal to the Executive Body.

DISCUSSION NOTES/QUESTIONS

1. Having read about the *Trail Smelter* arbitration and the *sic utere* principle of international law, you might wonder why Norway and Sweden did not pursue some sort of international litigation against the main polluters responsible for their acid rain problem. Gregory Wetstone and Armin Rosencranz, two early commentators on CLRTAP, noted that a solution to the acid rain problem would require "major modifications in the energy and pollution control policies of industrialized nations." They explained that a treaty was necessary to achieve this goal because the then-existing principles of international law, including the *sic utere* principle, did not provide an adequate basis for securing such far-reaching changes in governmental behavior.

> First, the principles are not sufficiently defined to support ready application to specific controversies. General statements concerning the duty of nations to avoid actions adversely affecting the environment of other nations are not responsive to the difficult questions concerning precisely what types of conduct are acceptable.... Second, ... there is presently no effective mechanism for enforcement of international legal doctrines.... Third, the present international legal framework does not effectively foster preventive action.... Finally, ... [even if nations consented to arbitration, the "demanding causation" requirement of the Trail Smelter decision would be hard to satisfy where injury is caused by multiple sources of pollution from multiple countries.] [T]he intricacies of the long-range transport phenomenon confound the assignment of responsibility for transboundary environmental effects.

Gregory S. Wetstone & Armin Rosencranz, Acid Rain in Europe and North America: National Responses to an International Problem 158–59 (1983).

Do you agree with this assessment? If you agree, were there nonetheless ways in which existing international law and legal processes (the "international legal framework" in place at the time) shaped the negotiated solution to the problem?

2. Today, acid rain is not nearly as serious a problem in Europe as it was in the 1960s and 1970s. This is primarily because government regulations

have led to a dramatic decline in human emissions of SO_2 and NO_x from the burning of fossil fuels. In many cases, these regulations were adopted in direct response to the mandates imposed by the Convention on Long-range Transboundary Air Pollution and its protocols. Indeed, the Convention is one of the great success stories of international environmental law, and those successes go well beyond addressing the acid rain problem in Europe. Acting within the framework of the Convention, UNECE members have adopted eight separate protocols addressing a variety of transboundary pollution problems and requiring ratifying States to control emissions of SO_2, NO_x, volatile organic compounds, persistent organic pollutants, ammonia, and heavy metals.

3. In some ways, the situation that Norway and Sweden found themselves in with respect to the problem of acid rain was similar to New Zealand's situation in its dealings with France over the *Rainbow Warrior* incident. In both cases, small nations had been, or were being, harmed by the actions of much larger and more powerful nations. In both cases, that harm was attributable to behavior that infringed the territorial sovereignty of the smaller nation. But, of course, in the *Rainbow Warrior* case, the legal violation was clearer, there was a single incident to be addressed, and France accepted its responsibility once the facts were proved. Norway and Sweden, by contrast, initially faced great reluctance by leading polluters like the United Kingdom and West Germany to accept that they were causing harm, that the harm was serious, or that they had any responsibility to stop it.

What were the factors that ultimately led to successful resolution of the problem? How important was the skill of the Scandinavian diplomats in taking advantage of Cold War politics to get their issue on the international agenda? How important was the presentation of scientific proof linking damage in Scandinavia to emissions from the United Kingdom and other European states? How important was the discovery that other European states were also suffering harm from acid rain? What other factors mattered?

4. You have seen in this and previous chapters that the application and development of international law goes forward in a variety of different legal and legislative arenas, some characterized by third-party decision-making (e.g., arbitration and adjudication), and some not.

> The ***adjudicative arena,*** including, in addition to litigation before international arbitral tribunals and international judicial bodies, the submission of disputes to third-party decision-makers for non-binding resolution (as in the case of the *Rainbow Warrior* and the early effort to settle the Trail Smelter dispute by referral to the International Joint Commission).
>
> The ***diplomatic arena***, typically on a foreign office-to-foreign office basis, utilizing both persuasive (e.g., fact-finding, negotiation, reporting) techniques and coercive (e.g., economic, military) instruments of policy, in routine and exceptional circumstances alike;

The ***parliamentary-diplomatic arena,*** through recourse to formal conferences, both official and unofficial (e.g., the 1972 United Nations Conference on the Human Environment in Stockholm);

The ***parliamentary arena,*** in legislative and quasi-legislative assemblies on the global, regional, and national levels (as in such institutions as the United Nations Security Council or General Assembly, the International Whaling Commission, the UNECE Commission, the Executive Body of CLRTAP, the European Parliament, and the Congress of the United States); and

The ***executive arena*** via the secretariats of such international governmental organizations as the United Nations, the European Council, the UNECE, and NATO.

Based on your study so far, in which of these arenas are states likely to make the most progress in addressing international environmental problems? Does your answer depend on the particular problem being addressed? Does it depend on your assumptions about the nature of international environmental problems in general? (We suggest you reconsider your answers to these questions after studying the material in Chapter 4.)

CHAPTER FOUR

DEVELOPING GLOBAL ENVIRONMENTAL PRINCIPLES AND POLICIES

■ ■ ■

The first three chapters of this book introduced you to the international legal system by examining several specific international disputes and the processes and rules that were used to resolve those disputes. In this final introductory chapter, we step back from detailed examination of particular disputes and offer a broader overview of international environmental law, with a particular focus on the principles that have emerged to guide international environmental policymaking.

The principles of international environmental law have developed over many decades as states have interacted to resolve environmental disputes and address environmental problems. Some of these law-generating interactions have occurred through traditional dispute-settlement and treaty-making processes such as those illustrated in Chapters 1–3. In addition, states have used nonbinding declarations or decisions—adopted in arenas such as the United Nations General Assembly, international treaty organizations, and international conferences—to articulate principles and rules to guide their behavior in environmental matters. Although the legal character of norms developed in these nontraditional ways has been the subject of considerable debate, there is no doubt that many principles originally stated in nonbinding political declarations have become accepted as part of the corpus of international environmental law.

This chapter is organized chronologically so that you can see the important changes that have occurred over time. But you should note that there is also continuity. Although new principles and new legal processes have emerged in this arena, they have supplemented, not replaced, traditional norms and traditional ways of doing diplomatic business.

A. TRADITIONAL INTERNATIONAL LAW AND THE ENVIRONMENT

Environmental issues have been addressed through international law for hundreds of years. The earliest "environmental" treaty reported by the International Environmental Agreements Database Project is a 1351 treaty between England and Castile that dealt, in part, with marine fisheries. Until the early 20th century, most treaties dealing with nature were adopted to resolve disputes about access to marine resources and to protect against over-exploitation of those resources. To the extent that those treaties reflected any sort of overarching environmental policy, it was likely to be a 'conservationist' policy—nature was protected not for its own sake but because of its value to the humans who made use of it.

The conservationist perspective was on full display in the Bering Sea Fur Seals controversy: the U.S. plea for authority to protect against over-exploitation of the seals was premised entirely on the usefulness of the seals to humankind. A conservationist ethic similarly motivated the 1900 Convention for the Preservation of Wild Animals, Birds and Fish in Africa and the 1902 Convention for the Protection of Birds Useful to Agriculture. Each of those agreements carefully distinguished "useful" animals from others, providing significant protection primarily to animals that were seen as directly important to human well-being.

During the latter part of the 19th century and the first half of the 20th century, a preservationist ethic began to gain currency among persons concerned with nature protection, and that ethic duly found its way into policy. At the international level, a preservationist focus is found in two major nature protection treaties negotiated just prior to World War II. The 1933 London Convention Relative to the Preservation of Fauna and Flora in the Natural State is one example. Aimed at nature protection in Africa, the London Convention of 1933 called for the creation of national parks and nature preserves and for the protection of endangered species without regard to their human usefulness. The 1940 Convention on Nature Protection and Wildlife Preservation in the Western Hemisphere likewise aimed at the establishment of national parks and nature reserves across the western hemisphere in order to protect all native species from extinction, as well as to preserve areas of "aesthetic, historic or scientific interest" and to ensure the maintenance of some regions of the hemisphere in their strictly natural, "primitive" condition.

However, as you learned from the material on whaling in Chapter 1, it would be error to think that preservationist policies dominated international treaties in the 20th century or even that they prevail today. The 1946 International Convention on the Regulation of Whaling was motivated by a conservationist, not preservationist, policy. And today, although preservationists have managed to impose a ban on commercial whaling and appear to have the upper hand on the International Whaling Commission, there remain many nations that would prefer to allow the commercial exploitation of whales so long as the killing does not exceed levels that are sustainable.

The 20th century also saw the emergence of international action addressed to pollution and other environmental issues unrelated to the conservation of animal and plant species.[1] The 1909 Boundary Waters Treaty between the U.S. and Canada had provisions aimed at reducing conflicts over the use of transboundary waters, including conflicts arising from pollution of those waters. A 1911 Declaration by the Institute of International Law sought to formulate rules to regulate the non-navigational uses of international rivers, including a strict ban on pollution: "all alterations injurious to the water, the emptying therein of injurious matter (from factories, etc.) is forbidden." A 1933 Declaration by the Seventh International Conference of American States included a similar admonition that states should avoid "alterations" of shared watercourses when such alterations "may prove injurious" to other states using the same river. Transboundary air pollution was the subject of the famous Trail Smelter arbitration discussed in Chapter 3.

The first international convention aimed at preventing oceanic oil pollution was adopted in 1954. It was followed by many more conventions dealing with various aspects of the same subject.

The 1950s and 1960s also saw the adoption of several conventions aimed at minimizing (or insuring against) the risks posed by the development of nuclear energy. While not all of these agreements were ratified, most entered into force shortly after their adoption.

These efforts to deal with emerging environmental problems occurred against a backdrop of customary law rules that shaped state responses to those problems. For example, customary law facilitated the adoption of agreements on environmental matters by providing widely accepted processes for entering treaties and establishing rules for their interpretation and enforcement. Customary law also provided the mechanisms for resolving bilateral disputes and the default rules that would apply if dispute settlement failed. In 1973, Professor Ian Brownlie identified "three sets of rules" of "major relevance" to environmental protection and the resolution of environmental disputes:

> First, the rules relating to state responsibility have a logic and vitality not to be despised or taken for granted. Secondly, the territorial sovereignty of States has a double impact. It provides a basis for individualist use and enjoyment of resources without setting any high standards of environmental protection. However, it also provides a basis for imposition of State responsibility on a sovereign State causing, maintaining, or failing to control a source of nuisance to other States. Thirdly, the concept of the freedom of the seas ... contains elements of reasonable user and non-exhaustive enjoyment which approach standards for

[1] For a useful overview of important environmental treaties adopted in the first three quarters of the 20th century, *see* E.D. Brown, *The Conventional Law of the Environment,* 13 Nat. Resources 203 (1973).

> environmental protection, although they are primarily based upon the concept of successful sharing rather than conservation in itself.[2]

To the rules mentioned by Professor Brownlie, one should add the duty to cooperate for the peaceful resolution of international disputes and the related duty to fulfil international obligations in good faith.[3]

None of these rules is specifically tailored for environmental protection or aimed at environmental problems in particular. As Professor Brownlie observed, traditional "general international law (or customary law) contains no rules or standards related to the protection of the environment as such." Nonetheless, general customary law has played a significant role in the resolution of international environmental disputes. The next three cases are illustrative. In addition, you may wish to review the excerpts from the *Bering Sea Fur Seals Arbitration* in Chapter 1 and the *Trail Smelter Arbitration* in Chapter 3.

NORTH ATLANTIC COAST FISHERIES CASE (GB V. US)

Permanent Court of Arbitration, The Hague (7 September 1910)
11 UNRIAA 173

[*Eds.*—In the 1783 Treaty of Peace between Great Britain and the United States, Britain agreed to allow U.S. inhabitants to continue to fish in the coastal fisheries of Newfoundland, Labrador, and other parts of the North Atlantic coast of Canada. Following the War of 1812, which Britain viewed as abrogating the 1783 Treaty, the United States and Great Britain entered a new treaty—the 1818 Treaty of Commerce—which again affirmed the right of U.S. citizens to fish in British Canadian waters. But the parties did not fully agree about the meaning of the relevant treaty provisions, and the scope of U.S. fishing rights in British Canadian waters was contested for over 80 years. In 1905, the dispute intensified after Newfoundland adopted severely restrictive fisheries legislation intended to protect fish stocks from depletion. The United States and Great Britain submitted their dispute to arbitration in January 1909. The Arbitral Tribunal issued its award on 7 September 1910.

A central question in the arbitration was whether the fishing rights granted to the United States by the 1818 Treaty of Commerce were subject to regulation by the territorial sovereign (or its political subunits) or whether the grant of fishing rights to the United States was an abrogation of British sovereignty sufficient to preclude Great Britain (or

---

[2] Ian Brownlie, *A Survey of International Customary Rules of Environmental Protection*, 13 Nat. Resources J. 179, 179 (1973).

[3] *See, e.g.*, G.A. Res. 2625, *Declaration on Principles of International Law Concerning Friendly Relations and Co-operation Among States in Accordance with the Chart of the United Nations*, principles 4 & 7 (Oct. 24, 1970).

Newfoundland) from imposing fishing restrictions on U.S. fishermen without the consent of the United States.]

Excerpts from the Award of the Arbitrators

[By] Article I of the Convention signed at London on the 20th day of October, 1818, between Great Britain and the United States, it was agreed as follows:

> [T]he Inhabitants of the . . . United States shall have forever, in common with the Subjects of His Britannic Majesty, the Liberty to take Fish of every kind on . . . the Southern Coast of Newfoundland . . . , the Western and Northern Coast of Newfoundland, . . . and . . . the Southern Coast of Labrador. . . .

It is contended on the part of the United States that the exercise of such liberty is not subject to limitations or restraints by Great Britain, Canada, or Newfoundland in the form of municipal laws, ordinances, or regulations . . . unless [the] appropriateness, necessity, reasonableness, and fairness [of such regulations] [is] determined by the United States and Great Britain by common accord and the United States concurs in [the] enforcement [of such regulations].

* * *

The Treaty of 1818 contains no explicit disposition in regard to the right of regulation, reasonable or otherwise; it neither reserves that right in express terms, nor refers to it in any way. It is therefore incumbent on this Tribunal to answer the [question of Britain's right of regulation] by interpreting the general terms of Article I of the Treaty, and more especially the words 'the inhabitants of the United States shall have, forever, in common with the subjects of His Britannic Majesty, the liberty to take fish of every kind'. . . .

* * *

[T]he right to regulate the liberties conferred by the Treaty of 1818 is an attribute of sovereignty, and as such must be held to reside in the territorial sovereign, unless the contrary be provided[.] [O]ne of the essential elements of sovereignty is that it is to be exercised within territorial limits, and that, failing proof to the contrary, the territory is co-terminous with the Sovereignty[.] [I]t follows that the burden of [proving] that the right to regulate does not reside independently in Great Britain, the territorial Sovereign[,] must fall on the United States. And for the purpose of sustaining this burden, the United States have put forward the [contention that:]

> the liberties of fishery granted to the United States constitute an International servitude in their favour over the territory of Great Britain, thereby involving a derogation from the sovereignty of

Great Britain, the servient State, and that therefore Great Britain is deprived, by reason of the grant, of its independent right to regulate the fishery.

The Tribunal is unable to agree with this contention:. . . .

[T]he doctrine of international servitude in the sense which is now sought to be attributed to it originated in the peculiar and now obsolete conditions prevailing in the Holy Roman Empire of which the *domini terrae* were not fully sovereigns; they holding territory under the Roman Empire, subject at least theoretically, and in some respects also practically, to the Courts of that Empire. . . . [I]n contradistinction to this quasi-sovereignty with its incoherent attributes acquired at various times, by various means, and not impaired in its character by being incomplete in any one respect or by being limited in favour of another territory and its possessor, the modern State, and particularly Great Britain, has never admitted partition of sovereignty, owing to the constitution of a modern State requiring essential sovereignty and independence[.]

Because this doctrine [of international servitude is] but little suited to the principle of sovereignty which prevails in States under a system of constitutional government such as Great Britain and the United States, and to the present international relations of Sovereign States, [it] has found little, if any, support from modern publicists. It could therefore in the general interest of the Community of Nations, and of the Parties to this Treaty, be affirmed by this Tribunal only on the express evidence of an International contract[.]

[E]ven if these liberties of fishery constituted an International servitude, the servitude would derogate from the sovereignty of the servient State only in so far as the exercise of the rights of sovereignty by the servient State would be contrary to the exercise of the servitude right by the dominant State. . . . [I]t is evident that, though every regulation of the fishery is to some extent a limitation, as it puts limits to the exercise of the fishery at will, yet such regulations as are reasonable and made for the purpose of securing and preserving the fishery and its exercise for the common benefit, are clearly to be distinguished from those restrictions and 'molestations', the annulment of which was the purpose of the American demands . . . in 1782, and such regulations consequently cannot be held to be inconsistent with a servitude.

* * *

[*Eds.*—The United States next argued that it should be recognized as having a right to participate in the formulation of any regulations affecting the fisheries and that no regulations could go into effect without its consent. The tribunal also rejected this contention.]

The recognition of a concurrent right of consent to the United States would affect the independence of Great Britain, which would become dependent on the Government of the United States for the exercise of its sovereign right of regulation, and, considering that such a co-dominium would be contrary to the constitution of both sovereign States[,] the burden of proof is imposed on the United States to show that the independence of Great Britain was thus impaired by international contract in 1818 and that a co-dominium was created.

For the purpose of such proof it is contended by the United States:

> . . . That a concurrent right to co-operate in the making and enforcement of regulations is the only possible and proper security to their inhabitants for the enjoyment of their liberties of fishery, and that such a right must be held to be implied in the grant of those liberties by the Treaty under interpretation.

The Tribunal is unable to accede to this claim. . .:

[E]very State has to execute the obligations incurred by Treaty *bona fide*, and is urged thereto by the ordinary sanctions of International Law in regard to observance of Treaty obligations. Such sanctions are, for instance, appeal to public opinion, publication of correspondence, censure by Parliamentary vote, demand for arbitration with the odium attendant on a refusal to arbitrate, rupture of relations, reprisal, etc. But no reason has been shown why this Treaty, in this respect, should be considered as different from every other Treaty under which the right of a State to regulate the action of foreigners admitted by it on its territory is recognized[.]

* * *

[I]f the consent of the United States were requisite for the fishery a general veto would be accorded them, the full exercise of which would be socially subversive and would lead to the consequence of an unregulatable fishery . . . [.]

In any event, Great Britain, as the local sovereign, has the duty of preserving and protecting the fisheries. In so far as it is necessary for that purpose, Great Britain is not only entitled, but obliged, to provide for the protection and preservation of the fisheries; always remembering that the exercise of this right of legislation is limited by the obligation to execute the Treaty in good faith. This has been admitted by counsel and recognized by Great Britain in limiting the right of regulation to that of reasonable regulation. The inherent defect of this limitation of reasonableness, without any sanction except in diplomatic remonstrance, has been supplied by the submission to arbitral award as to existing regulations in accordance with Arts. II and III of the Special Agreement, and as to further regulation by the obligation to submit their reasonableness to an arbitral test in accordance with Art. IV of the Agreement.

* * *

[T]he right to make reasonable regulations, not inconsistent with the obligations of the Treaty, which is all that is claimed by Great Britain, for a fishery which both Parties admit requires regulation for its preservation, is not a restriction of or an invasion of the liberty granted to the inhabitants of the United States. . . .

DISCUSSION NOTES/QUESTIONS

1. Both the *Fur Seals Arbitration* (*see* Chapter 1) and the *North Atlantic Coast Fisheries Arbitration* involved efforts by a nation-state to protect certain populations of wild animals that lived within its territory from over-exploitation. In both cases, the nation sought to protect the animals by regulating the activities of persons hunting or fishing for those animals, regardless of the nationality of those persons. In the *Fur Seals Arbitration,* the United States was denied the right unilaterally to regulate the killing of the Bering Sea fur seals, even though there was overwhelming evidence that regulation was necessary to the long-term survival of the species. In the *North Atlantic Coast Fisheries Arbitration,* on the other hand, Great Britain was allowed to regulate fishing on a unilateral basis, even though it had agreed by treaty to give nationals of the United States the "liberty to fish" in the waters in question. What key jurisdictional facts explain the difference in result in these two cases?

2. Britain had granted U.S. fishermen the "liberty" to take fish in some of the coastal waters of British Canada. But it then claimed the right to restrict that liberty without first consulting the United States.

   a. The tribunal says that Britain can, in fact, regulate fishing by U.S. citizens without violating their "liberty" to fish. Can you explain that conclusion? What if the regulations banned fishing during certain times? What if they banned fishing for an entire season?

   b. The United States argued that the treaty gave it an "international servitude" over waters that were otherwise within British dominion. The tribunal concludes that the notion of an "international servitude" was a legally sensible doctrine for European nations during the Holy Roman Empire, but was not a legally appropriate doctrine for the modern international community (i.e., after the Treaty of Westphalia). What changed?

   c. The United States also argued that it had a co-dominion with Britain over these waters. Why was this claim rejected?

3. The 1959 Antarctic Treaty (*see* Chapter 1) suspends all territorial claims to the continent of Antarctica and gives the "Consulting Parties" to the

Treaty effective control over the continent of Antarctica. Similarly, the United Nations Convention on the Law of the Sea declares that the "sea-bed and ocean floor and subsoil thereof, beyond the limits of national jurisdiction," and the resources thereof are "the common heritage of mankind" and not subject to appropriation except under terms set by an international body. In effect, one could say that both Antarctica and the deep seabed are today subject to a type of co-dominion governance. Could the concept of "co-dominion" be applied to non-territorial environmental assets like fisheries, the atmosphere, or the earth's biodiversity?

4. The tribunal says that Britain's right to regulate is limited to "reasonable regulation." What is the source of that limitation? What does the tribunal mean when it says that "inherent defect of this limitation of reasonableness, without any sanction except in diplomatic remonstrance," has been corrected "by the submission to arbitral award" of issues involving reasonableness? What is the "inherent defect" of the reasonableness limitation? Do you agree that it is solved by submission of the issue to arbitration? Isn't the effectiveness of the arbitral award itself subject to an "inherent defect"—that the only sanction for non-compliance is "diplomatic remonstrance?" If so, what does arbitration add?

5. The tribunal says that Britain's sovereign control over fisheries within its borders carries "the duty of preserving and protecting the fisheries." To whom is the duty owed? If Britain failed to enact strict enough regulations, could the United States demand that it do more?

LAKE LANOUX ARBITRATION (FRANCE V. SPAIN) FINAL DECISION (16 NOVEMBER 1957)

12 UNRIAA 281

[*Eds.*—Lake Lanoux is located in France on the southern slope of the Pyrenees Mountains. The lake is fed by streams located entirely in French territory. The Font-Vive stream flows out of Lake Lanoux and is one of the headwaters of the River Carol. The river Carol, in turn, flows through French territory for about 25 kilometres before entering Spain.

The Lake Lanoux Arbitration concerned a dispute between France and Spain over a plan by France to build a hydroelectric power plant that would require diverting the waters of Lake Lanoux toward the River Ariège. The French and Spanish first began discussing French plans for diversion of Lake Lanoux's waters in 1917. They intermittently negotiated about the matter for the next 35 years. During the course of these negotiations, France modified its plans on several occasions in response to Spanish concerns. Spain, however, rejected all the French proposals.

France finally decided to proceed without Spain's consent. Under the plan that France adopted, Lake Lanoux waters would be diverted to feed a hydroelectric power plant and then discharged into the River Ariège. As a result of the diversion, those waters would no longer reach the River Carol. However, to ensure that the River Carol continued to receive a volume of water equal to the volume it had previously received from Lake Lanoux, France proposed to build a tunnel to carry waters of the River Ariège to the River Carol in a quantity sufficient to replace the waters lost from Lake Lanoux.

Spain objected to this plan, and the Arbitration ensued. A central issue in the arbitration was whether France's actions were in violation of several bilateral treaties France and Spain had entered in the 1860s concerning the Franco-Spanish border region. Those treaties included the following provisions relating to the control and enjoyment of waters of common use between the two countries:

> *"Control and Enjoyment of Waters of Common User between the Two Countries"*
>
> *"Article* 8: All standing and flowing waters, whether they are in the private or public domain, are subject to the sovereignty of the State in which they are located, and therefore to that State's legislation, except for the modifications agreed upon between the two Governments.
>
> "Flowing waters change jurisdiction at the moment when they pass from one country to the other, and when the watercourses constitute a boundary, each State exercises its jurisdiction up to the middle of the flow.
>
> *"Article 9:* For watercourses which flow from one Country to the other, or which constitute a boundary, each Government recognizes, subject to the exercise of a right of verification when appropriate, the legality of irrigations, of works and of enjoyment for domestic use currently existing in the other State, by virtue of concession, title or prescription, with the reservation that only that volume of water necessary to satisfy actual needs will be used, that abuses must be eliminated, and that this recognition will in no way injure the respective rights of the Governments to authorize works of public utility, on condition that proper compensation is paid.
>
> *"Article 10:* If, after having satisfied the actual needs of users recognized on each side respectively as regular, there remains at low tide water available where the frontier is crossed, such water will be shared in advance between the two countries, in proportion to the areas of the irrigable lands belonging to the immediate respective riparian owners, *minus* land already irrigated.
>
> *"Article 11*: When in one of the two States it is proposed to construct works or to grant new concessions which might change

the course or the volume of a watercourse of which the lower or opposite part is being used by the riparian owners of the other country, prior notice will be given to the highest administrative authority of the Department or of the Province to which such riparian owners are subject by the corresponding authority in the jurisdiction where such schemes are proposed, so that, if they might threaten the rights of the riparian owners of the adjoining Sovereignty, a claim may be lodged in due time with the competent authorities, and thus the interests that may be involved on both sides will be safeguarded. If the work and concessions are to take place in a *Commune* contiguous to the border, the engineers of the other Country will have the option, upon proper notice given to them reasonably in advance, of agreeing to inspect the site with those in charge of it.

"*Article* 12: The downstream lands are obliged to receive from the higher lands of the neighbouring country the waters which flow naturally therefrom together with what they carry without the hand of man having contributed thereto. There may be constructed neither a dam, nor any obstacle capable of harming the upper riparian owners, to whom it is likewise forbidden to do anything which might increase the burdens attached to the servitude of the downstream lands.]

Excerpts from the Award of the Arbitrators

1. The public works envisaged in the French scheme are wholly situate in France; the most important part if not the whole of the effects of such works will be felt in French territory; they would concern waters which Article 8 of the Additional Act submits to French territorial sovereignty:

> "Article 8. All standing and flowing waters, whether they are in the private or public domain, are subject to the sovereignty of the State in which they are located, and therefore to that State's legislation, except for the modifications agreed upon between the two Governments. * * *"

This text itself imposes a reservation on the principle of territorial sovereignty ("except for the modifications agreed upon between the two Governments"); some provisions of the Treaty and of the Additional Act of 1866 contain the most important of these modifications; there may be others.

It has been contended before the Tribunal that these modifications should be strictly construed because they are in derogation of sovereignty. The Tribunal could not recognize such an absolute rule of construction. Territorial sovereignty plays the part of a presumption. It must bend before all international obligations, whatever their origin, but only before such obligations.

* * *

3. The present dispute can be reduced to two fundamental questions:

> (A) Do the works for utilizing the waters of Lake Lanoux in the conditions laid down in the French scheme . . . constitute an infringement of the rights of Spain recognized by [Articles 9, 10 and 11 of the governing treaties]?
>
> (B) [Do the treaties make] the execution of the said works . . . subject to a prior agreement between the two Governments. . . ?

As to question (A):

* * *

6. [Because France will replace all diverted waters with an equivalent volume of water from the River Ariege,] none of the guaranteed users [under Article 9] will suffer in his enjoyment of the waters;. . . . [Furthermore, Article 10 is not applicable because], at the lowest water level, the volume of the surplus waters of the Carol, at the boundary, will at no time suffer a diminution; it may even, by virtue of the minimum guarantee given by France, benefit by an increase in volume assured by the [diversion of the] waters of the Ariege [into the Carol]. . . .

It could have been argued that the works would bring about an ultimate pollution of the waters of the Carol or that the returned waters would have a chemical composition or a temperature or some other characteristic which could injure Spanish interests. Spain could then have claimed that her rights had been impaired in violation of the Additional Act. Neither in the *dossier* nor in the pleadings in this case is there any trace of such an allegation.

* * *

7. The Spanish Government takes its stand on a different ground. In the arbitration *Compromis* it had already alleged that the French scheme "modifies the natural conditions of the hydrographic basin of Lake Lanoux by diverting its waters into the Ariège and thus making the restoration of the waters of the Carol physically dependent on human will, which would involve the *de facto* preponderance of one Party in place of the equality of the two Parties as provided by the Treaty of Bayonne of May 26, 1866, and by the Additional Act of the same date.

* * *

8. [Protection of the natural] unity of a basin is sanctioned at the juridical level only to the extent that it corresponds to human realities. The water which by nature constitutes a fungible item may be the object of a

restitution which does not change its qualities in regard to human needs. A diversion with restitution, such as that envisaged by the French project, does not change a state of affairs organized for the working of the requirements of social life.

The state of modern technology leads to more and more frequent justifications of the fact that waters used for the production of electric energy should not be returned to their natural course. Water is taken higher and higher up and it is carried ever farther, and in so doing it is sometimes diverted to another river basin, in the same State or in another country within the same federation, or even in a third State. Within federations, the judicial decisions have recognized the validity of this last practice *(Wyoming v. Colorado* . . . [259 U.S. 419]). . . .

The Tribunal therefore is of opinion that the diversion with restitution as envisaged in the French scheme and proposals is not contrary to the Treaty and to the Additional Act of 1866.

9. [The] Spanish Government has [also] contested the legitimacy of the works carried out on the territory of [France] [on the grounds that] the works are of such a nature as to permit that State, albeit in violation of its international pledges, to bring pressure to bear on the other signatory. . . . Spain considers that France has not the right to bring about, by works of public utility, the physical possibility of cutting off the flow of [water to Spain]. . . .

[T]he proposals of the French Government which form an integral part of its project carry "the assurance that in no case will it impair the régime thus established." . . . It cannot be alleged that, despite this pledge, Spain would not have a sufficient guarantee, for there is a general and well-established principle of law according to which bad faith is not presumed. . . .

* * *

As to question (B):

10. In the *Compromis,* the Spanish Government had already declared that, in its opinion, the French scheme required for its execution "the previous agreement of both Governments, in the absence of which the country making the proposal is not at liberty to undertake the works".

* * *

11. . . . To admit that jurisdiction in a certain field can no longer be exercised except on the condition of, or by way of, an agreement between two States, is to place an essential restriction on the sovereignty of a State, and such restriction could only be admitted if there were clear and convincing evidence. Without doubt, international practice does reveal some special cases in which this hypothesis has become reality; thus,

sometimes two States exercise conjointly jurisdiction over certain territories (joint ownership, *co-imperixm*, or *condominium);* likewise, in certain international arrangements, the representatives of States exercise conjointly a certain jurisdiction in the name of those States or in the name of organizations. But these cases are exceptional, and international judicial decisions are slow to recognize their existence, especially when they impair the territorial sovereignty of a State, as would be the case in the present matter.

* * *

13. The Spanish Government endeavoured to establish [that] current positive international law [requires agreement of all co-riparians before modification of a watercourse is permitted]. * * * In fact, States are today perfectly conscious of the importance of the conflicting interests brought into play by the industrial use of international rivers, and of the necessity to reconcile them by mutual concessions. The only way to arrive at such compromises of interests is to conclude agreements on an increasingly comprehensive basis. International practice reflects the conviction that States ought to strive to conclude such agreements: there would thus appear to be an obligation to accept in good faith all communications and contracts which could, by a broad comparison of interests and by reciprocal good will, provide States with the best conditions for concluding agreements. . . .

But . . . [a] rule that States may utilize the hydraulic power of international watercourses only on condition of a *prior* agreement between the interested States cannot be established as a custom, even less as a general principle of law.

* * *

14. As between Spain and France, the existence of a rule requiring prior agreement for the development of the water resources of an international watercourse can therefore result only from a Treaty. . . .

* * *

[*Eds.*—The Tribunal then examined the language of the Treaty and found that it did not support Spain's argument about the need for a prior agreement. The Tribunal observed, in particular, that the text of Article 11 imposed only an obligation to provide notice and information and, it explained, "if the contracting Parties had wished to establish the necessity for a prior agreement, they would not have confined themselves to mentioning in Article 11 only the obligation to give notice."]

[16.] [The idea that France cannot act without Spain's agreement] is in contradiction with the most general principles of international law. It is for each State to evaluate in a reasonable manner and in good faith the situations and the rules which will involve it in controversies; its evaluation may be in contradiction with that of another State; in that case, should a dispute arise the Parties normally seek to resolve it by negotiation or, alternatively, by submitting to the authority of a third party; but one of them is never obliged to suspend the exercise of its jurisdiction because of the dispute except when it assumes an obligation to do so. . . .

23. In the present case, the Spanish Government reproaches the French Government for not having based the development scheme for the waters of Lake Lanoux on a foundation of absolute equality * * *. According to the Spanish Government, the French Government refused to take into consideration schemes which, in the opinion of the Spanish Government, would have involved a very small sacrifice of French interests and great advantages for the Spanish rural economy. . . .

On a theoretical basis the Spanish argument is unacceptable to the Tribunal, for Spain tends to put rights and simple interests on the same plane. . . .

* * *

France is entitled to exercise her rights; she cannot ignore Spanish interests.

Spain is entitled to demand that her rights be respected and that her interests be taken into consideration.

As a matter of form, the upstream State has, procedurally, a right of initiative; it is not obliged to associate the downstream State in the elaboration of its schemes. If, in the course of discussions, the downstream State submits schemes to it, the upstream State must examine them, but it has the right to give preference to the solution contained in its own scheme provided that it takes into consideration in a reasonable manner the interests of the State.

24. In the case of Lake Lanoux, France has maintained to the end the solution which consists in diverting the waters of the Carol to the Ariege with full restitution. By making this choice France is only making use of a right; the development works of Lake Lanoux are on French territory, the financing of and responsibility for the enterprise fall upon France, and France alone is the judge of works of public utility which are to be executed on her own territory, save for the provisions of Articles 9 and 10 of the Additional Act, which, however, the French scheme does not infringe.

On her side, Spain cannot invoke a right to insist on a development of Lake Lanoux based on the needs of Spanish agriculture. . . . [S]he can only urge her interests in order to obtain, within the framework of the scheme decided upon by France, terms which reasonably safeguard them.

It remains to be established whether this requirement had been fulfilled.

In whatever fashion one regards the course of dealings covering the period 1917–1954, it is beyond doubt that the French position became very flexible and even transformed. From a promise of compensation but without restoration of diverted water, it passed to a partial restoration; then . . . to complete restoration. . . .

* * *

When one examines the question of whether France, either in the course of the dealings or in her proposals, has taken Spanish interests into sufficient consideration, it must be stressed how closely linked together are the obligation to take into consideration, in the course of negotiations, adverse interests and the obligation to give a reasonable place to these interests in the solution finally adopted. A State which has conducted negotiations with understanding and good faith in accordance with Article 11 of the Additional Act is not relieved from giving a reasonable place to adverse interests in the solution it adopts simply because the conversations have been interrupted even though owing to the intransigence of its partner. Conversely, in determining the manner in which a scheme has taken into consideration the interests involved, the way in which negotiations have developed, the total number of the interests which have been presented, the price which each Party was ready to pay to have those interests safeguarded, are all essential factors in establishing, with regard to the obligations set out in Article II of the Additional Act, the merits of that scheme.

Having regard to all the circumstances of the case, set out above, the Tribunal is of opinion that the French scheme complies with the obligations of Article 11 of the Additional Act.

DISCUSSION NOTES/QUESTIONS

1. Do you think France complied with its customary and treaty obligations to cooperate with Spain and fulfilled those obligations "in good faith?" Did France's efforts to fulfil its legal duties, including its duty to cooperate, result in any significant alterations in its plan for diversion of the waters of Lake Lanoux?

2. The issues raised in this proceeding were very similar to the issues raised in the North Atlantic Coast Fisheries case. The issues were also resolved in a similar way. In both cases, the Tribunal held i) that a territorial sovereign is entitled to regulate the use of natural resources within its territory, ii) that treaty commitments toward another sovereign that used the resource did not mean that the territorial sovereign was required to obtain the agreement of those other sovereigns before taking actions affecting the resource, and iii) that

the territorial sovereign must, however, take the interests of the other user into account when making decisions about the resource.

In Lake Lanoux, does the Tribunal view these conclusions as flowing exclusively from the provisions of the applicable treaties, or do these results also follow from customary law?

3. The principle of territorial sovereignty is invoked in both cases as relevant to the interpretation of treaties. What role does it play in each case?

FISHERIES JURISDICTION CASE (UNITED KINGDOM V. ICELAND) (MERITS)

1974 I.C.J 3 (July 25)

[*Eds.*—In 1961, Iceland and the United Kingdom entered a treaty in which the United Kingdom agreed to respect Iceland's claim of a 12-mile exclusive fishery zone extending from its coast. Iceland indicated that it intended to seek further extensions of its exclusive fisheries jurisdiction, but it agreed that any disputes with the United Kingdom over such extensions would be referred to the International Court of Justice "at the request of either party."

In 1972, Iceland took steps to extend its exclusive fishery zone to 50 nautical miles beyond its coast and to prohibit British vessels from fishing in the area. The United Kingdom brought the matter to the International Court of Justice, as provided for in the 1961 agreement. Iceland contested the Court's jurisdiction and refused to participate. Finding that it had jurisdiction, the Court issued its final judgment in the United Kingdom's favor on 25 July 1974.]

Excerpts from the Judgment of the Court

11. In the course of the written proceedings, the following submissions were presented on behalf of the Government of the United Kingdom [the Applicant]:. . .

> ". . . the Government of the United Kingdom submit to the Court that the Court should adjudge and declare:
>
> (a) that the claim by Iceland to be entitled to a zone of exclusive fisheries jurisdiction extending 50 nautical miles from baselines around the Coast of Iceland is without foundation in international law and is invalid;
>
> (b) that, as against the United Kingdom, Iceland is not entitled unilaterally to assert an exclusive fisheries jurisdiction beyond the limits agreed to in the Exchange of Notes of 1961;
>
> (c) that Iceland is not entitled unilaterally to exclude British fishing vessels from the area of the high seas beyond the limits

agreed to in the Exchange of Notes of 1961 or unilaterally to impose restrictions on the activities of such vessels in that area."

* * *

50. The Geneva Convention on the High Seas of 1958, which was adopted "as generally declaratory of established principles of international law," defines in Article 1 the term "high seas" as "all parts of the sea that are not included in the territorial sea or in the internal waters of a State." Article 2 then declares that "The high seas being open to all nations, no State may validly purport to subject any part of them to its sovereignty" and goes on to provide that the freedom of the high seas comprises, *inter alia*, both for coastal and non-coastal States, freedom of navigation and freedom of fishing. The freedoms of the high seas are however made subject to the consideration that they "shall be exercised by all States with reasonable regard to the interests of other States in their exercise of the freedom of the high seas."

51. . . . The question of the breadth of the territorial sea and that of the extent of the coastal State's fishery jurisdiction were left unsettled at the 1958 Conference.

52. The 1960 Conference failed by one vote to adopt a text governing the two questions of the breadth of the territorial sea and the extent of fishery rights. However, after that Conference the law evolved through the practice of States on the basis of the debates and near-agreements at the Conference.

* * *

58. State practice on the subject of fisheries reveals an increasing and widespread acceptance of the concept of preferential rights for coastal States, particularly in favour of countries or territories in a situation of special dependence on coastal fisheries. Both the 1958 Resolution and the 1960 joint amendment concerning preferential rights were approved by a large majority of the Conferences, thus showing overwhelming support for the idea that in certain special situations it was fair to recognize that the coastal State had preferential fishing rights. After these Conferences, the preferential rights of the coastal State were recognized in various bilateral and multilateral international agreements. . . .

59. There can be no doubt of the exceptional dependence of Iceland on its fisheries. . . .

60. The preferential rights of the coastal State come into play only at the moment when an intensification in the exploitation of fishery resources makes it imperative to introduce some system of catch-limitation and sharing of those resources, to preserve the fish stocks in the interests of their rational and economic exploitation. This situation appears to have been reached in the present case. In regard to the two main demersal

species concerned—cod and haddock—the Applicant has shown itself aware of the need for a catch-limitation which has become indispensable in view of the establishment of catch-limitations in other regions of the North Atlantic. If a system of catch-limitation were not established in the Icelandic area, the fishing effort displaced from those other regions might well be directed towards the unprotected grounds in that area.

* * *

62. [However,] the concept of preferential rights is not compatible with [Iceland's effort to exclude] all fishing activities of other States. A coastal State entitled to preferential rights is not free, unilaterally and according to its own uncontrolled discretion, to determine the extent of those rights. The characterization of the coastal State's rights as preferential implies a certain priority, but cannot imply the extinction of the concurrent rights of other States, and particularly of a State which, like the Applicant, has for many years been engaged in fishing in the waters in question, such fishing activity being important to the economy of the country concerned. The coastal State has to take into account and pay regard to the position of such other States, particularly when they have established an economic dependence on the same fishing grounds.

* * *

66. Considerations similar to those which have prompted the recognition of the preferential rights of the coastal State in a special situation apply when coastal populations in other fishing States are also dependent on certain fishing grounds. In both instances the economic dependence and the livelihood of whole communities are affected. Not only do the same considerations apply, but the same interest in conservation exists. In this respect the Applicant has recognized that the conservation and efficient exploitation of the fish stocks in the Iceland area are of importance not only to Iceland but also to the United Kingdom.

67. The provisions of the Icelandic Regulations of 14 July 1972 and the manner of their implementation disregard the fishing rights of the Applicant. Iceland's unilateral action thus constitutes an infringement of the principle enshrined in Article 2 of the 1958 Geneva Convention on the High Seas which requires that all States, including coastal States, in exercising their freedom of fishing, pay reasonable regard to the interests of other States. It also disregards the rights of the Applicant as they result from the Exchange of Notes of 1961. The Applicant is therefore justified in asking the Court to give all necessary protection to its own rights, while at the same time agreeing to recognize Iceland's preferential position. Accordingly, the Court is bound to conclude that the Icelandic Regulations of 14 July 1972 establishing a zone of exclusive fisheries jurisdiction extending to 50 nautical miles from baselines around the Coast of Iceland, are not opposable to the United Kingdom, and the latter is under no

obligation to accept the unilateral termination by Iceland of United Kingdom fishery rights in the area.

* * *

69. It follows from the reasoning of the Court in this case that in order to reach an equitable solution of the present dispute it is necessary that the preferential fishing rights of Iceland, as a State specially dependent on coastal fisheries, be reconciled with the traditional fishing rights of the Applicant.

* * *

72. [B]oth States have an obligation to take full account of each other's rights and of any fishery conservation measures the necessity of which is shown to exist in those waters. It is one of the advances in maritime international law, resulting from the intensification of fishing, that the former *laissez faire* treatment of the living resources of the sea in the high seas has been replaced by a recognition of a duty to have due regard to the rights of other States and the needs of conservation for the benefit of all. Consequently, both Parties have the obligation to keep under review the fishery resources in the disputed waters and to examine together, in the light of scientific and other available information, the measures required for the conservation and development, and equitable exploitation, of those resources. . . .

73. The most appropriate method for the solution of the dispute is clearly that of negotiation. Its objective should be the delimitation of the rights and interests of the Parties, the preferential rights of the coastal State on the one hand and the rights of the Applicant on the other, to balance and regulate equitably questions such as those of catch-limitation, share allocations and "related restrictions concerning areas closed to fishing, number and type of vessels allowed and forms of control of the agreed provisions". This necessitates detailed scientific knowledge of the fishing grounds. It is obvious that the relevant information and expertise would be mainly in the possession of the Parties. . . .

74. It is implicit in the concept of preferential rights that negotiations are required in order to define or delimit the extent of those rights, as was already recognized in the 1958 Geneva Resolution on Special Situations relating to Coastal Fisheries, which constituted the starting point of the law on the subject. This Resolution provides for the establishment, through collaboration between the coastal State and any other State fishing in the area, of agreed measures to secure just treatment of the special situation.

75. The obligation to negotiate thus flows from the very nature of the respective rights of the Parties; to direct them to negotiate is therefore a proper exercise of the judicial function in this case. This also corresponds to the Principles and provisions of the Charter of the United Nations

concerning peaceful settlement of disputes. As the Court stated in the North Sea Continental Shelf cases:

> ". . . this obligation merely constitutes a special application of a principle which underlies all international relations, and which is moreover recognized in Article 33 of the Charter of the United Nations as one of the methods for the peaceful settlement of international disputes" . . . .

78. In the fresh negotiations which are to take place on the basis of the present Judgment, the Parties will have the benefit of the above appraisal of their respective rights, and of certain guidelines defining their scope. The task before them will be to conduct their negotiations on the basis that each must in good faith pay reasonable regard to the legal rights of the other in the waters around Iceland outside the 12-mile limit, thus bringing about an equitable apportionment of the fishing resources based on the facts of the particular situation, and having regard to the interests of other States which have established fishing rights in the area. It is not a matter of finding simply an equitable solution, but an equitable solution derived from the applicable law. As the Court stated in the North Sea Continental Shelf cases:

> ". . . it is not a question of applying equity simply as a matter of abstract justice, but of applying a rule of law which itself requires the application of equitable principles."

DISCUSSION NOTES/QUESTIONS

1. In reaching its decision in this case, the International Court of Justice concluded that the traditional 'laizzez faire' approach to access to high seas fisheries had been displaced by new customary law rules. What are those rules? What evidence of state practice or *opinio juris* does the Court rely on to support its conclusion that such rules exist?

2. In the 1893 Bering Sea Fur Seals arbitration (Chapter 2), the Tribunal ruled that the United States could not lawfully prevent British Canadian sealers from killing seals on the high seas, even if the sealing threatened the extinction of the species in question. But Britain and the United States had agreed that they would abide by any Regulations recommended by the Tribunal as necessary for protection of the seals. The Tribunal responded by directing both states to adhere to a strict set of restrictions on the taking of fur seals, including a prohibition on the hunting of such seals "within a zone of sixty miles around the Pribilov Islands." After announcing those "Regulations," Alphonse de Courcel, the President of the Tribunal, commented as follows:

> This part of our work inaugurates great innovation. Hitherto the nations were agreed to leave out of special legislation the vast domain of the seas, as in times of old, according to the poets, the earth itself was common to all men, who gathered its fruits at their will, without

> limitation or control. . . . The sea, however, like the earth, has become small for men, who, like the hero Alexander, and no less ardent for labor than he was for glory, feel confined in a world too narrow. Our work is a first attempt at a sharing of the products of the ocean, which has hitherto been undivided, and at applying a rule to things which escaped every other law but that of the first occupant. If this attempt succeeds, it will doubtless be followed by numerous imitations, until the entire planet—until the waters as well as the continents—will have become the subject of a careful partition.

3. The 1982 United Nations Convention on the Law of the Sea (UNCLOS) **(Basic Document 3.4)** affirmed the "right" of all states "for their nationals to engage in fishing on the high seas." However, UNCLOS also recognized that fishing states have "the duty to take, or to cooperate with other States in taking" measures "necessary for the conservation of the living resources of the high seas." UNCLOS also gave coastal states authority to regulate fishing in an exclusive economic zone extending 200 miles from their coasts. Finally, UNCLOS suggested that states fishing on the high seas should have regard for the interests of coastal states in fish stocks that straddle, or migrate between, the high seas and the coastal state's EEZ.

Do you think that the provisions of UNCLOS satisfy de Courcel's hope for a more careful partition aimed at the "sharing of the products of the ocean?" If not, what else needs to be done? For more on the protection of high-seas fisheries, *see* Chapter 6.

B. THE DEVELOPMENT OF INTERNATIONAL ENVIRONMENTAL LAW: THE STOCKHOLM CONFERENCE AND BEYOND

The 1972 United Nations Conference on the Human Environment, held in Stockholm, was the first attempt by nation-states, acting at a global level, to articulate priorities, policies, and norms relating to environmental protection. Moreover, unlike earlier conferences at which environmental issues were addressed, the Stockholm conference did not focus on any particular environmental issue. It was concerned with "the protection and improvement of the human environment" as a whole—with "water, air, earth and living beings;" with "the ecological balance of the biosphere;" and with the "depletion of irreplaceable resources."

It is fair to say that modern international environmental law began at Stockholm. But Stockholm was only a beginning. In the nearly 50 years since that conference, the goals and principles articulated in the Stockholm Declaration have been restated, refined, elaborated, modified and supplemented. These developments have occurred in the context of state efforts to resolve environmental disputes, to clarify their legal duties in the environmental arena, and to develop meaningful and effective responses to particular environmental problems, especially those of global scope.

Subsection 1 of this part reproduces a substantial portion of the 1972 Stockholm Declaration.

Subsection 2 focuses on the post-Stockholm efforts of states to articulate, in the words of the Declaration, "a common outlook and . . . common principles to inspire and guide the peoples of the world in the preservation and enhancement of the human environment."[4] We reproduce excerpts from important documents adopted by state and non-state actors as they worked to articulate norms suitable for guiding efforts to address the perceived global environmental crisis.[5] These excerpts are organized under particular subject-matter headings. Our purpose is to highlight, in particular, new principles of special relevance to environmental protection.

Subsection 3 briefly reviews the burst of environmental treaty making that occurred in the 30 years following the Stockholm Conference. Subsection 4 introduces the important concept of "sustainable development." Finally, subsection 5 provides excerpts from several cases that illustrate how international adjudication of environmental issues has been impacted by post-Stockholm developments in the law.

1. THE STOCKHOLM DECLARATION

STOCKHOLM DECLARATION OF THE UNITED NATIONS CONFERENCE ON THE HUMAN ENVIRONMENT

Adopted by the UN Conference on the Human Environment, 16 June 1972
U.N. Doc A/CONF.48/14/Rev.1 at 3 (1972) (Basic Document 1.21)

The United Nations Conference on the Human Environment. . .,

I

Proclaims That:

* * *

2. The protection and improvement of the human environment is a major issue which affects the well-being of peoples and economic development throughout the world; it is the urgent desire of the peoples of the whole world and the duty of all Governments.

* * *

4. In the developing countries most of the environmental problems are caused by under-development. Millions continue to live far below the minimum levels required for a decent human existence, deprived of adequate food and clothing, shelter and education, health and sanitation. Therefore, the developing countries must direct their efforts to

[4] U.N. Conference on the Human Environment, *Stockholm Declaration,* U.N. Doc. A/CONF.48/14/Rev.1 (June 16, 1972).

[5] Complete versions of these documents are available in the Documents Supplement.

development, bearing in mind their priorities and the need to safeguard and improve the environment.

* * *

6. . . . To defend and improve the human environment for present and future generations has become an imperative goal for mankind—a goal to be pursued together with, and in harmony with, the established and fundamental goals of peace and of world-wide economic and social development.

* * *

II

Principles

Principle 1

Man has the fundamental right to freedom, equality and adequate conditions of life, in an environment of a quality that permits a life of dignity and well-being, and he bears a solemn responsibility to protect and improve the environment for present and future generations. . . .

Principle 2

The natural resources of the earth including the air, water, land, flora and fauna and especially representative samples of natural ecosystems must be safeguarded for the benefit of present and future generations through careful planning or management, as appropriate.

* * *

Principle 6

The discharge of toxic substances or of other substances and the release of heat, in such quantities or concentrations as to exceed the capacity of the environment to render them harmless, must be halted in order to ensure that serious or irreversible damage is not inflicted upon ecosystems. The just struggle of the peoples of all countries against pollution should be supported.

* * *

Principle 8

Economic and social development is essential for ensuring a favourable living and working environment for man and for creating conditions on earth that are necessary for the improvement of the quality of life.

* * *

Principle 12

Resources should be made available to preserve and improve the environment, taking into account the circumstances and particular requirements of developing countries and any costs which may emanate from their incorporating environmental safeguards into their development planning and the need for making available to them, upon their request, additional international technical and financial assistance for this purpose.

Principle 13

In order to achieve a more rational management of resources and thus to improve the environment, State should adopt an integrated and co-ordinated approach to their development planning so as to ensure that development is compatible with the need to protect and improve the human environment for the benefit for their population.

* * *

Principle 16

Demographic policies, which are without prejudice to basic human rights and which are deemed appropriate by Governments concerned, should be applied in those regions where the rate of population growth or excessive population concentrations are likely to have adverse effects on the environment or development, or where low population density may prevent improvement of the human environment and impede development.

* * *

Principle 20

Scientific research and development in the context of environmental problems, both national and multinational, must be promoted in all countries, especially the developing countries. In this connection, the free flow of up-to-date scientific information and transfer of experience must be supported and assisted, to facilitate the solution of environmental problems; environmental technologies should be made available to developing countries on terms which would encourage their wide dissemination without constituting an economic burden on the developing countries.

Principle 21

States have, in accordance with the Charter of the United Nations and the principles of international law, the sovereign right to exploit their own resources pursuant to their own environmental policies, and the responsibility to ensure that activities within their jurisdiction or control do not cause damage to the environment of other States or of areas beyond the limits of national jurisdiction.

* * *

Principle 23

Without prejudice to such criteria as may be agreed upon by the international community, or to standards which will have to be determined nationally, it will be essential in all cases to consider the systems of values prevailing in each country, and the extent of the applicability of standards which are valid for the most advanced countries but which may be inappropriate and of unwarranted social cost for the developing countries.

Principle 24

International matters concerning the protection and improvement of the environment should be handled in a co-operative spirit by all countries, big or small, on an equal footing. Co-operation through multilateral or bilateral arrangements or other appropriate means is essential to effectively control, prevent, reduce and eliminate adverse environmental effects resulting from activities conducted in all spheres, in such a way that due account is taken of the sovereignty and interests of all States.

* * *

DISCUSSION NOTES/QUESTIONS

1. The events at Stockholm in 1972 provided an early preview of how international environment law would develop in the coming years. The Declaration, of course, contained many principles that were further developed by subsequent state practice in the environmental arena. But the Conference itself had political features that profoundly influenced later events.

First, several developing states initially threatened to boycott the Stockholm Conference. The reasons they gave then remain salient today and, in fact, are a major theme of international environmental law. The developing countries feared that the environmental concerns of the developed powers would distract attention from the desperate need to address the problems of poverty and underdevelopment. As the price of their participation, they insisted that their economic development must be recognized as being as important as environmental protection. They insisted also that they could not be expected to make major efforts toward environmental protection without financial support from richer countries. Hence, paragraph 4 of the Declaration recognized that "the developing countries must direct their efforts to development," and paragraph 7 called upon the international community "to raise resources to support the developing countries in carrying out their responsibilities in this field." Today, resolving the tension between environmental protection and the economic development of poorer countries remains a major challenge for international environmental law.

A second noteworthy political development at Stockholm was the emergence of civil society as an important factor in international environmental negotiations. Maurice Strong, Secretary General of the Conference, actively encouraged the participation of representatives of non-governmental organizations as members of national delegations at the Conference. He also encouraged NGOs to organize a parallel "People's Forum" to run alongside the Conference. Over 10,000 people, including organized environmental groups, literally camped near the Conference site, using the techniques of protest, demonstrations, and educational dialogue to promote an environmental agenda. At the same time, a smaller group of scientists, some of whom were participants in the UNECE's group of Senior Advisers to the UNECE Governments on Environmental Matters, worked to push participating governments for meaningful action to address the planet's environmental challenges.

Representatives of civil society have become a permanent fixture at international meetings and conferences. At the Rio Conference in 1992, nearly 1600 NGOs were represented. Tens of thousands of civil society delegates have attended the Conferences of the Parties to the UN Framework Convention on Climate Change, and thousands of scientists participate in the work of the Intergovernmental Panel on Climate Change. The phenomenon is not limited to the environmental arena. There has been a general "explosion in the number of civil society organizations seeking to influence national and international policy making and implementation" in every arena of international cooperation. Laura Pedraza-FariZa, *Conceptions of Civil Society in International Lawmaking and Implementation: A Theoretical Framework,* 34 Mich. J. Int'l. L. 605, 606 (2013).

2. The Stockholm Conference led directly to the creation of the United Nations Environment Programme (UNEP) by the UN General Assembly in December 1972.[6] UNEP played an important role in the development of international environmental law after Stockholm. By 1990, it had "negotiated and obtained adoption of nearly thirty binding multilateral instruments,. . . as well as ten sets of nonbinding environmental law guidelines and principles." In addition, "UNEP serves as secretariat to a number of environmental conventions, offers technical assistance to developing countries in the formulation of environmental legislation, and publishes a set of reference texts for international environmental law scholars and practitioners." Carol A. Petsonk, *The Role of the United Nations Environment Programme (UNEP) in the Development of International Environmental Law,* 5 Am. Univ. Int'l L. Rev. 351, 352–53 (1990).

From 1972–2014, UNEP was led by a Governing Council elected by the General Assembly and including representatives from each region of the world. Membership in the Governing Council was limited, but in 2012, the UN General Assembly determined that the Governing Council should be open to all UN member states. Subsequent to that decision, the Governing Council was renamed the "United Nations Environment Assembly" (UNEA). The first meeting of the UNEA was held in 2014. Today, the UNEA is very much a universal organization. All 193 UN Member states are members of the UN

[6] G.A. Res. 2997, *Resolution on the Institutional and Financial Arrangements for International Environmental Co-operation,* (Dec. 15, 1972).

Environmental Assembly. In addition, over 400 organizations are accredited by the UNEA and have observer status at UNEA meetings. These 400 organizations represent a range of interests including businesses, environmental NGOs, the scientific community, local governments and worker organizations.

3. In 1992, twenty years after the Stockholm Conference, the United Nations convened another conference on the environment, held in Rio de Janeiro, Brazil. As its name—the United Nations Conference on Environment and Development (UNCED)—implies, the Rio Conference aimed to treat development as a global concern at least equivalent to environmental protection. Five important documents were adopted at the Conference. Conference participants adopted both a declaration of principles (Rio Declaration on Environment and Development) and a lengthy plan identifying objectives and recommending cooperative actions to be taken on a wide variety of environmental and developmental issues (Agenda 21). In addition, participants adopted a Statement of Forest Principles. The United Nations Framework Convention on Climate Change and the Convention on Biological Diversity were both opened for signature at Rio.

To ensure "the integration of environment and development issues and to examine the progress in" its implementation, Agenda 21 included a recommendation for the establishment of a new organization, the Commission on Sustainable Development, to operate under the auspices of the United Nations Economic and Social Council. In December 1992, the U.N. General Assembly directed the Economic and Social Council to establish the new body.[7] The Commission on Sustainable Development did not replace UNEP, but it is probably fair to see its creation as a reflection of the belief of some developing nations that UNEP's focus was too strongly on environmental protection and that organized international action on environmental issues was paying insufficient attention to the development side of the equation.

4. Many of the principles articulated in the Stockholm Declaration fall into a category of norm that has been called "soft international law" or simply "soft law." Soft law has been defined to include norms that are characterized by "the intended vagueness of the obligations [they impose] or the weakness of [their] commands." Joseph Gold, *Strengthening the Soft International Law of Exchange Arrangements,* 77 AJIL 443, 443 (1983). Declarations by the participants in international conferences, such as the Stockholm Declaration, are generally considered by the participants as non-binding and aspirational in character. Nevertheless, such norms are said to have a legal character, despite their non-binding nature, because there is "an expectation that the states accepting [them] will take their content seriously and will give them some measure of respect." *Id.* International consent to the norm gives it an authoritative basis, and the expectation that it will be taken seriously communicates an intention that state behavior should alter in response to the

---

7 G.A. Res. 47/191, *Resolution on Institutional Arrangements to Follow Up the United Nations Conference on Environment and Development,* (Dec. 22, 1992).

norm. Thus, although the norm is not binding, it has legal import—it is "soft law." *See* Jonathan C. Carlson, *Hunger, Agricultural Trade Liberalization, and Soft International Law*, 70 Iowa L. R. 1187, 1200–09 (1985).

Soft law is a "part of the contemporary law-making process" at the international level and has played an important role in the development of international environmental law. Pierre-Marie Dupuy, *Soft Law and the International Law of the Environment,* 12 Mich. J. Int'l L. 420, 420 (1991). As Professor Dupuy describes it, "*repetition* is a very important factor in the international environmental 'soft' law-making process." Once articulated, some norms are repeated and cross-referenced by different international authorities.

> [This] recurrent invocation of the same rules formulated in one way or another at the universal, regional and more restricted levels, all tend progressively to develop and establish a common international understanding. As a result of this process, conduct and behavior which would have been considered challenges to State sovereignty twenty years ago are now accepted within the mainstream.

Id. at 424–25. *See also* Anthea Elizabeth Roberts, *Traditional and Modern Approaches to Customary International Law: A Reconciliation*, 95 AJIL 757 (2001) (discussing the role played in the formation of customary international law by general statements of norms or rules and articulations of international values).

Some commentators have expressed grave reservations about the widespread use of so-called soft law in environmental matters. One of their concerns is that soft law may serve as a tool that allows governments to create "only apparent commitments," with the intention of deceiving the public into believing that a problem is being addressed internationally when, in fact, it is not. *See* Alberto Szekely, *A Commentary on the Softening of International Environmental Law,* 91 ASIL Proc. 234, 235 (1997). Other commentators note that soft law has several advantages: "It can serve to secure agreement where agreement may otherwise not be achieved," it "promotes feelings of international comity and cooperation," and it can "change the political thinking on an issue," thus serving as a "catalyst in securing an agreement with a harder edge later." Sir Geoffrey W.R. Palmer, *New Ways to Make International Environmental Law,* 87 AJIL 259, 269–70 (1992). Finally, nonbinding commitments raise the level of international ambition significantly above what could reasonably be achieved through a binding agreement, and thus are an effective way to set "the broad direction and pace for cooperation" on environmental problems. David G. Victor, *The Use and Effectiveness of Nonbinding Instruments in the Management of Complex International Environmental Problems,* 91 ASIL Proc. 241, 243, 247–48 (1997).

The process of developing international law is a political process, and shared values and understandings can impact that process, whether those values are articulated in "soft law" or otherwise. Nonetheless, not every nonbinding statement of a norm or value will ultimately become a customary rule or find expression in a binding document. As you read the following materials (and, indeed, all the remaining material in this book), you should consider the extent to which norms and principles originally articulated in nonbinding statements like the Stockholm Declaration eventually find their way into the provisions of treaties and/or are reflected in the approach that the international community takes to particular problems.

2. PRINCIPLES OF INTERNATIONAL ENVIRONMENTAL LAW

This section omits materials specific to the obligation to avoid transboundary harm and the doctrine of state responsibility, both of which are covered at length in Chapter 3. We begin with materials on sovereignty and on the duty of states to cooperate in the resolution of international problems. Although these concepts have also been discussed earlier, we think their centrality to the international legal system makes it appropriate to include them as a starting point here. The materials then cover a number of principles of special relevance in the environmental context.

(a) The Concept of Sovereignty

CHARTER OF THE UNITED NATIONS, ART. 2(1), (4) & (7)

Concluded, 26 June 1945. Entered into Force, 24 Oct. 1945.
1976 YBUN 1043, 59 Stat 1031, TS 993 (Basic Document 1.1)

Article 2

The Organization and its Members . . . shall act in accordance with the following Principles.

1. The Organization is based on the principle of the sovereign equality of all its Members.

* * *

4. All Members shall refrain in their international relations from the threat or use of force against the territorial integrity or political independence of any state, or in any other manner inconsistent with the Purposes of the United Nations.

* * *

7. Nothing contained in the present Charter shall authorize the United Nations to intervene in matters which are essentially within the domestic jurisdiction of any state or shall require the Members to submit such matters to settlement under the present Charter; but this principle shall not prejudice the application of enforcement measures under Chapter VII.

CORFU CHANNEL CASE (UK V. ALB)

1949 I.C.J. 39, 43 (Apr. 9)

(Individual opinion of Judge Alvarez)

By sovereignty, we understand the whole body of rights and attributes which a State possesses in its territory, to the exclusion of all other States, and also in its relations with other States. Sovereignty confers rights upon States and imposes obligations on them.

* * *

. . . We can no longer regard sovereignty as an absolute and individual right of every State, as used to be done under the old law founded on the individualist regime, according to which States were only bound by the rules which they had accepted. Today, owing to social interdependence and to the predominance of the general interest, the States are bound by many rules which have not been ordered by their will. The sovereignty of States has now become an *institution*, an *international social function* of a psychological character, which has to be exercised in accordance with the new international law.

CHARTER OF ECONOMIC RIGHTS AND DUTIES OF STATES, ARTS. 2, 3, 7, 30 & 32

Adopted by the UN General Assembly, 12 December 1974
G.A. Res. 3281 (Dec. 12, 1974) (Basic Document 7.3)

Article 2

1. Every State has and shall freely exercise full permanent sovereignty, including possession, use and disposal, over all its wealth, natural resources and economic activities.

* * *

Article 3

In the exploitation of natural resources shared by two or more countries, each State must co-operate on the basis of a system of information and prior consultations in order to achieve optimum use of such resources without causing damage to the legitimate interest of others.

* * *

Article 7

Every State has the primary responsibility to promote the economic, social and cultural development of its people. To this end, each State has the right and the responsibility to choose its means and goals of development, fully to mobilize and use its resources.

* * *

Article 30

The protection, preservation and enhancement of the environment for the present and future generations is the responsibility of all States. All States shall endeavour to establish their own environmental and developmental policies in conformity with such responsibility. The environmental policies of all States should enhance and not adversely affect the present and future development potential of developing countries. All States have the responsibility to ensure that activities within their jurisdiction or control do not cause damage to the environment of other States or of areas beyond the limits of national jurisdiction. All States should co-operate in evolving international norms and regulations in the field of the environment.

* * *

Article 32

No State may use or encourage the use of economic, political or any other type of measures to coerce another State in order to obtain from it the subordination of the exercise of its sovereign rights.

DISCUSSION NOTES/QUESTIONS

1. What does it mean to say that a state is sovereign? Professor Louis Henkin wrote that "the essential quality of statehood in a state system is the autonomy of each state. State autonomy suggests that a state is not subject to any external authority unless it has voluntarily consented to such authority." Would Judge Alvarez (*Corfu Channel* case) agree? Can a newly formed state be bound by customary law rules to which it has not explicitly consented? If it is bound, would that be because, by joining the international system as a state, it has implicitly consented to all existing customary rules of that system? Or is it because states are bound by widely accepted international norms whether they have consented to them or not?

2. What *obligations* does the concept of sovereignty impose on states? Does it impose at least the obligation to respect the sovereignty of other states? Or does sovereignty mean that a state has no obligation to respect any other state's sovereignty unless it consents to do so?

3. The principle of permanent sovereignty over natural resources was vigorously asserted by developing nations in the 1960s as a legal justification for decisions to nationalize (or otherwise regulate) foreign-owned businesses engaged in the exploitation of natural resources in those countries. The principles also provided a legal basis for resisting efforts by industrialized country governments to interfere with those decisions through military action or economic coercion. In Resolution 1803, the UN General Assembly affirmed the right of nations to utilize their natural resources "in the interest of their national development and of the well-being of the people of the State

concerned," thus implicitly denying any obligation to give primacy to the interests of foreign-based owners of those resources. Resolution 1803 also condemned "violence" (presumably by the investors' home countries) against nations that exercised their sovereign rights as "contrary to the spirit and principles" of the UN Charter. *See* G.A. Res. 1803, (Dec. 14, 1962). *See generally* Burns H. Weston, *The Charter of Economic Rights and Duties of States and the Deprivation of Foreign Owned Wealth*, 75 AJIL 437 (1981).

4. In the Charter of Economic Rights and Duties of States, the principle of permanent sovereignty is reiterated, as is the corollary principle that states should not be "coerced" by other states in order to modify their decisions about resource use. But the Charter acknowledges that the right of permanent sovereignty comes with corresponding duties, including the duty to protect the environment for the benefit of future generations and the obligation to ensure that local activities do not "cause damage to the environment of other States or of areas beyond the limits of national jurisdiction."

5. How should one resolve conflicts between a state's right to use its natural resources "in the interest of [its] national development" and the state's obligation to avoid causing harm to the environment of other states? Suppose, for example, that a developing nation with substantial coal reserves wishes to build several coal-burning power plants in order to provide the energy needed to power new factories and deliver electricity to rural communities, actions that will greatly assist economic development in that nation. Suppose, also, that the proposed power plants will cause substantial transboundary pollution and, in addition, add significantly to atmospheric greenhouse gas concentrations (the primary cause of global warming). Is the developing nation entitled to prioritize its development interests over the environmental interests of its neighbors and, indeed, of the world? If it does choose to prioritize its own interests in a way that causes substantial harm to others, can other states legitimately respond with economic, diplomatic, or military sanctions?

6. Leave aside the problem of transboundary pollution and consider the situation when a nation-state contains resources within its borders that are important to other nations. Does it retain full autonomy with respect to the exploitation of those resources? Or should (does) international law impose limits? Suppose, for example, that a developing nation's agricultural development plan called for the nearly complete destruction of a rain forest that serves as a repository of a substantial amount of the world's carbon?

(b) The Duty to Cooperate and the Obligation to Act in Good Faith

CHARTER OF THE UNITED NATIONS, ART. 1(3)

Concluded, 26 June 1945. Entered into Force, 24 Oct. 1945
1976 YBUN 1043, 59 Stat 1031, TS 993 (Basic Document 1.1)

The Purposes of the United Nations are:

* * *

3. To achieve international co-operation in solving international problems of an economic, social, cultural, or humanitarian character. . . .

VIENNA CONVENTION ON THE LAW OF TREATIES, ART. 26

Concluded, 23 May 1969. Entered into Force, 27 Jan. 1980
1155 UNTS 331 (Basic Document 1.14)

Every treaty in force is binding upon the parties to it and must be performed by them in good faith.

DECLARATION ON PRINCIPLES OF INTERNATIONAL LAW CONCERNING FRIENDLY RELATIONS AND CO-OPERATION AMONG STATES IN ACCORDANCE WITH THE CHARTER OF THE UNITED NATIONS, PRINCIPLES 2, 4, & 7

Adopted by the UN General Assembly, 24 October 1970
G.A. Res. 2625, (Oct. 24,1970)

Every State shall settle its international disputes with other States by peaceful means, in such a manner that international peace and security, and justice, are not endangered.

* * *

States have the duty to co-operate with one another . . . in the various spheres of international relations, in order to maintain international peace and security and to promote international economic stability and progress, the general welfare of nations and international co-operation. . . .

States should co-operate in the economic, social and cultural fields as well as in the field of science and technology and for the promotion of international cultural and educational progress.

* * *

Every State has the duty to fulfil in good faith its obligations under the generally recognized principles and rules of international law.

Every State has the duty to fulfil in good faith its obligations under international agreements valid under the generally recognized principles and rules of international law.

RIO DECLARATION ON ENVIRONMENT AND DEVELOPMENT, PRINCIPLE 7

Adopted by consensus by the UN Conference on Environment and Development, 14 June 1992
U.N. Doc. A/CONF.151/26/Rev.1 (Vol. I), annex I (1992) (Basic Document 1.30)

States shall cooperate in a spirit of global partnership to conserve, protect and restore the health and integrity of the Earth's ecosystem. . . .

UNEP DRAFT PRINCIPLES OF CONDUCT IN THE FIELD OF THE ENVIRONMENT FOR GUIDANCE OF STATES IN THE CONSERVATION AND HARMONIOUS UTILIZATION OF NATURAL RESOURCES SHARED BY TWO OR MORE STATES, PRINCIPLES 1 AND 2

Adopted by the UN Environment Programme Governing Council, 19 May 1978
U.N. Doc. UNEP/IG12/2 (1978) (Basic Document 1.24)

Principle 1

It is necessary for States to co-operate in the field of the environment concerning the conservation and harmonious utilization of natural resources shared by two or more States. Accordingly, it is necessary that . . . States co-operate with a view to controlling, preventing, reducing or eliminating adverse environmental effects which may result from the utilization of such resources. Such co-operation is to take place on an equal footing and taking into account the sovereignty, rights and interests of the States concerned.

Principle 2

. . . States sharing such natural resources should endeavor to conclude bilateral or multilateral agreements between or among themselves in order to secure specific regulation of their conduct in this respect. . . .

DISCUSSION NOTES/QUESTIONS

1. The duty to cooperate in the resolution of international problems, and the related principles of good faith and good-neighborliness, are important components of both general international law and international environmental law. One finds these duties constantly reaffirmed in treaties, conference declarations, arbitral awards, and judicial decisions. But are these obligations anything more than empty words? What do these principles mean? Is actual nation-state behavior likely to be altered by recognition of these principles?

2. Can you imagine, for example, a situation in which an obligation to cooperate would cause sovereign states to engage in meaningful cooperation

when they would not otherwise do so? Or is the obligation to cooperate likely to be realized only in those circumstances in which cooperation would be beneficial to each side (and thus pursued by the relevant actors even in the absence of any obligation)?

3. What about the duty to perform international obligations (including treaty obligations) in good faith? What does this mean? If you consider it to be a meaningless obligation, then why does one find a similar duty in domestic contract law? The Uniform Commercial Code, for example, provides that "every contract or duty within this Act imposes an obligation of good faith in its performance or enforcement." U.C.C. § 1–304. Is the principle of good faith as meaningless when expressed domestically as when it is expressed internationally? If not, is it as meaningful when expressed internationally as when it is expressed domestically?

(c) Intergenerational Equity

RESOLUTION ON HISTORICAL RESPONSIBILITY OF STATES FOR THE PRESERVATION OF NATURE FOR PRESENT AND FUTURE GENERATIONS

Adopted by the UN General Assembly, 30 October 1980
G.A. Res. 3548 (Oct. 30, 1980) (Basic Document 1.25)

The General Assembly, * * *

Determined to preserve nature as a prerequisite for the normal life of man,

1. *Proclaims* the historical responsibility of States for the preservation of nature for present and future generations * * *.

WORLD CHARTER FOR NATURE, PREAMBLE, CLAUSE 3

Adopted by the UN General Assembly, 28 October 1982
G.A. Res. 37/7 (Annex) (Oct. 28, 1982) (Basic Document 1.27)

Reaffirming that man must acquire the knowledge to maintain and enhance his ability to use natural resources in a manner which ensures the reservation of the species and ecosystems for the benefit of present and future generations.

LEGAL PRINCIPLES FOR ENVIRONMENTAL PROTECTION AND SUSTAINABLE DEVELOPMENT, ARTICLE 2

Adopted by the WCED Experts Group on Environmental Law, 18–20 June 1986
U.N. Doc. WCED/86/23/Add.1 (1986) (Basic Document 1.28)

Article 2

Conservation for present and future generations

States shall ensure that the environment and natural resources are conserved and used for the benefit of present and future generations.

RIO DECLARATION ON ENVIRONMENT AND DEVELOPMENT, PRINCIPLE 3

Adopted by consensus by the UN Conference on Environment and Development, 14 June 1992
U.N. Doc. A/CONF.151/26/Rev.1 (Vol. I), annex I (1992) (Basic Document 1.30)

Principle 3

The right to development must be fulfilled so as to equitably meet developmental and environmental needs of present and future generations.

DISCUSSION NOTES/QUESTIONS

1. What does it mean to "equitably" meet the needs of future generations? Must environmental assets be preserved? Or is it possible that the non-sustainable consumption of environmental assets could provide developmental gains that are far in excess of the costs of environmental degradation? Indeed, haven't most developed countries achieved their current standards of living by significantly degrading their environmental assets—cutting their forests, damming and polluting their waterways, fouling their air, and dramatically reducing populations of native species? If so, was this an "equitable" way to achieve development? Was it unfair to future generations, or will they benefit by living richer and more comfortable lives as a result?

2. In this regard, consider the argument of the United States in the 1893 *Bering Sea Fur Seals Arbitration*:

> No possessor of property, whether an individual . . . or a nation, has an absolute title to it. His title is coupled with a trust for the benefit of mankind. * * * [And] in saying that the gift [of nature] is not to this nation or that, but to mankind, all generations, future as well as present, are intended. . . .

According to the United States, because resources are held in trust for present and future generations, nations are not entitled to complete autonomy with respect to their use of the resources in their charge. Nations that do not share surplus resources with others can be made to do so by force; and nations or peoples that use more than the surplus of renewable resources can be forced to conserve.

> No nation has, by the law of nature, a right to destroy its sources and means of production or leave them unimproved. None has the right to convert any portion of the earth into a waste or desolation, or to permit any part which may be made fruitful to remain a waste. To destroy the sources from which any human blessing flows is not merely an error, it is a *crime*. And the wrong is not limited by the boundaries of nations, but is inflicted upon those to whom the blessing would be useful wherever they may dwell. And those to whom the wrong is done have the right to redress it.

Do you agree? If you do agree, then what is left of the principle of territorial sovereignty over natural resources? Is a nation's right to exploit its natural resources subject always to the requirement that the exploitation be sustainable? Or are their situations where "equitable" treatment of future generations will allow significant degradation of natural resources in the interest of development and enhanced economic wellbeing?

3. The conservation of resources "for the benefit of present and future generations" is mentioned in the preamble of the Convention on Biological Diversity **(Basic Document 5.6)**. It is also mentioned in the preamble of the United Nations Framework Convention on Climate Change and is one of the principles articulated in Article 3(1) of that same Convention. Several regional seas conventions similarly reference the need to protect the environment for the benefit of present and future generations in their preambles or substantive provisions. The United Nations Convention on the Protection and Use of Transboundary Watercourses and International Lakes provides, in article 2, that "Water resources shall be managed so that the needs of the present generation are met without compromising the ability of future generations to meet their own needs."

(d) The Principle of Prevention

UNEP GOVERNING COUNCIL DRAFT PRINCIPLES OF CONDUCT IN THE FIELD OF THE ENVIRONMENT FOR GUIDANCE OF STATES IN THE CONSERVATION AND HARMONIOUS UTILIZATION OF NATURAL RESOURCES SHARED BY TWO OR MORE STATES, PRINCIPLE 1

Adopted by the UNEP Governing Council, 19 May 1978
U.N. Doc. UNEP/IG 12/1 (1978) (Basic Document 1.24)

It is necessary for States to co-operate in the field of the environment concerning the conservation and harmonious utilization of natural resources shared by two or more States. Accordingly, it is necessary that consistent with the concept of equitable utilization of shared natural resources, States co-operate with a view to controlling, preventing, reducing or eliminating adverse environmental effects which may result from the utilization of such resources. . . .

WORLD CHARTER FOR NATURE, PRINCIPLE 11

Adopted by the UN General Assembly, 28 October 1982
G.A. Res. 37/7 (Annex) (Oct. 28, 1982) (Basic Document 1.27)

11. Activities which might have an impact on nature shall be controlled, and the best available technologies that minimize significant risks to nature or other adverse effects shall be used; in particular:

(a) Activities which are likely to cause irreversible damage to nature shall be avoided;. . . .

IUCN COMMISSION ON ENVIRONMENTAL LAW, DRAFT INTERNATIONAL COVENANT ON ENVIRONMENT AND DEVELOPMENT, ART. 6 & CMT.

IUCN Environmental Policy and Law Paper No. 31 Rev. 2 (3d ed. 2004)

Article 6. Prevention

Protection of the environment is better achieved by preventing environmental harm than by endeavouring to remedy or compensate for such harm.

Commentary

Article 6 expresses a principle fundamental to environmental protection, the preventive approach, which is applicable to all actors wherever the consequences of their actions may be felt. It restates an ecological fact that preventive efforts are always preferable to remedial actions that may be attempted after harm has occurred. Not only is harm irreversible in many cases, but ex post facto action is usually more expensive and less effective than preventive measures. Experience reveals that preventive measures are most efficient when aimed at the sources of environmental harm, particularly those causing pollution, rather than at establishing quality standards for the affected environmental milieu. This is especially true where there are diffuse and cumulative sources.

The preventive approach requires each Party [to the Draft Covenant] to exercise due diligence, i.e., to act reasonably and in good faith and to regulate public and private activities subject to its jurisdiction or control that are potentially harmful to any part of the environment. The principle does not include a minimum threshold of harm, because the obligation is one of conduct (due diligence), not of result. Thus, the principle does not impose an absolute duty to prevent all harm, making the State a guarantor, but rather an obligation on each State to minimize detrimental consequences of permissible activities through regulation. . . .

DISCUSSION NOTES/QUESTIONS

1. What is the relationship between the principle of prevention and the obligation not to cause transboundary harm? According to Philippe Sands, Principles of International Environmental Law 246 (2d ed. 2003), they are "closely related" but differ in two fundamental ways. First, the obligation not to cause transboundary harm arises "from the application of respect for the principle of sovereignty, whereas the preventive principle seeks to minimize environmental damage as an objective in itself." Second, "under the preventive principle, a state may be under an obligation to prevent damage to the environment within its own jurisdiction, including by means of appropriate regulatory, administrative and other measures."

2. Does the view that states have a legal obligation to prevent environmental harm within their jurisdictions depend on an assumption that harm to any part of the global environment will eventually have transboundary effects and perhaps contribute to significant global environmental damage, even if we cannot currently prove the existence of such damage? Or would a state have an obligation to prevent serious environmental harm within its jurisdiction even if there is no possibility of the damage being felt elsewhere at some future time?

3. If a state has an obligation to prevent environmental harm even where there is no possibility of a transboundary impact, what is the rationale for such an obligation? One could argue, perhaps, that "nature as a whole warrants respect," and "every form of life is unique and is to be safeguarded independent of its value to humanity." *See* IUCN, *Draft Covenant on Environment and Development*, Article 2. But is an obligation to protect nature from environmental harm for its own sake consistent with the Rio Declaration **(Basic Document 1.30)**, which states in Article 1 that "human beings are at the centre of concerns for sustainable development," and in Article 2 that "States have . . . the sovereign right to exploit their own resources pursuant to their own environmental and developmental policies. . ."?

4. Alternatively, perhaps the reason states must take action to prevent even purely internal environmental harm is precisely because each state has an obligation to ensure that its citizens (present and future) can enjoy a clean environment and a "healthy and productive life in harmony with nature." Rio Declaration, Article 1. Indeed, some commentators argue that there is at least a limited human right to a clean environment that states should respect and protect. *See, e.g.,* Burns H. Weston, *Climate Change, Human Rights, and Intergenerational Justice*, 9 Vt. J. Envtl. L. 375 (2008). For extended discussion of the human rights approaches to environmental harm, see the readings in Problem 9-3, *infra.*

5. If the obligation to take preventive action is somehow derivative of the human right to a clean environment, then what should be done if there is a collision between the desire for economic development and the desire for environmental protection? Isn't development also a right? Who is the appropriate decision-maker when the right to development and the right to a

clean environment come into conflict? Assuming no transboundary impact, would the "preventive principle" be an appropriate basis upon which an *international* adjudicative body could make a decision to order a halt to an economic development project (e.g., the building of a hydroelectric dam) that threatened purely internal environmental harm? Would it be an appropriate basis for an international funding agency to refuse funding for such a project?

(e) The Precautionary Principle

UNEP GOVERNING COUNCIL DECISION 15/27 ON THE PRECAUTIONARY APPROACH TO MARINE POLLUTION, INCLUDING WASTE-DUMPING AT SEA

Adopted, 25 May 1989
U.N. Doc. UNEP/GC/DEC/15/27

The Governing Council, aware of the threat to the marine environment from a variety of polluting sources, aware of the need to protect marine biological diversity,

Recognizing that waiting for scientific proof regarding the impact of pollutants discharged into the marine environment may result in irreversible damage to the marine environment and in human suffering,

* * *

Noting that the Second International Conference on the Protection of the North Sea held in London from 24 to 25 November 1987, adopted the "principle of precautionary action" and that some other Governments have adopted and begun to implement preventive policies for the safety of human health and the environment,

. . . Recommends that all Governments adopt the "principle of precautionary action" as the basis of their policy with regard to the prevention and elimination of marine pollution;. . . .

RIO DECLARATION ON ENVIRONMENT AND DEVELOPMENT, PRINCIPLE 15

Adopted by consensus by the UN Conference on Environment and Development, 14 June 1992
U.N. Doc. A/CONF.151/26/Rev.1 (Vol. I), annex I (1992) (Basic Document 1.30)

In order to protect the environment, the precautionary approach shall be widely applied by States according to their capabilities. Where there are threats of serious or irreversible damage, lack of full scientific certainty shall not be used as a reason for postponing cost-effective measures to prevent environmental degradation.

DISCUSSION NOTES/QUESTIONS

1. The precautionary principle has been adopted in many international treaties, including in several treaties aimed at global environmental problems. For example, Article 3(3) of the United Nations Framework Convention on Climate Change **(Basic Document 2.4)** provides that:

> The Parties should take precautionary measures to anticipate, prevent or minimize the causes of climate change and mitigate its adverse effects. Where there are threats of serious or irreversible damage, lack of full scientific certainty should not be used as a reason for postponing such measures, taking into account that policies and measures to deal with climate change should be cost-effective so as to ensure global benefits at the lowest possible cost. . . ."

Sometimes this policy is described as the "precautionary principle," sometimes it is described as the "precautionary approach," and sometimes it is not labeled at all. Does it matter what one calls it? *See, e.g.,* Bamako Convention on the Ban of Import into Africa and the Control of Transboundary Movement and Management of Hazardous Wastes within Africa, 29 Jan. 1991, art. 4(3)(f) **(Basic Document 4.8)** (using both the phrase "precautionary approach" and the phrase "precautionary principle"); Convention on the Protection and Use of Transboundary Watercourses and International Lakes, 17 March 1992, art. 2(5)(a), 1936 UNTS 269 (calling upon parties to be guided by the "precautionary principle" when taking measures to prevent transboundary harm); Convention on Biological Diversity, 5 June 1992, preamble (expressing the policy that "lack of full scientific certainty should not be used as a reason for postponing measures" to avoid serious threats, but not labelling it as a principle or approach); Fish Stocks Agreement, 4 Aug 1995, art. 6, 2167 UNTS 3 (requiring the application of a "precautionary approach" to the management of shared fisheries); Cartagena Protocol on Biosafety, 29 January 2000, preamble and art. 1, 2226 UNTS 208 (adopting "precautionary approach.")

2. The United States has resisted use of the phrase "precautionary principle" and has argued, instead, that any reference to precaution in international agreements should be limited to the adoption of a "precautionary approach" to environmental problems. Why? In *The United States and International Environmental Law: Living with an Elephant,* 15 EJIL 617–49 (2004), Professor Jutta Brunnée suggests that the U.S. position is motivated by a desire to limit the impact of precaution in "international legal processes." By insisting on the identification of precaution as an "approach" only, the United States reduces the likelihood that it will acquire a legally-binding character. Professor Brunnée explains:

> Whereas a non-binding precautionary principle [created by endorsement of a "precautionary approach"] may shape international regimes or even influence interpretative processes, a customary rule [created by endorsement of an internationally binding precautionary principle] would be actionable through WTO or other dispute settlement processes. It could qualify the requirement of science-

> based justification for [trade-restricting environmental measures], upon which the United States insists internationally. . . .

Do you understand the argument? In what way might a precautionary principle limit the WTO requirement that environmental-protective measures must have a scientific justification?

3. If Professor Brunnée is correct about the reason for the US insistence on a precautionary "approach," then what does this tell you about the way in which customary international law is made? Despite any skepticism that you might have about the reality of international law, the US is treating international political processes as though they are capable of generating customary principles with real bite, and it is using its influence in those political processes to impact the shape and legal force of the norms that are generated. Isn't this exactly what you would expect to happen (and what is supposed to happen) if the international political process is, in fact, an arena in which real law is made?

4. What does it mean to say that "lack of full scientific certainty" should not be used as a reason for postponing action to address environmental problems "where there are threats of serious or irreversible damage"? Does this mean that even the most speculative and unsupported fear must be addressed if the alleged risk is great enough? Or must there be some scientific support for the alleged threat? And how much action must be taken in response to alleged risks when there is a "lack of full scientific certainty" about them? Would it be enough to continue studying the problem? Or does the precautionary principle mean that states must take action to eliminate the alleged threat? Suppose it is claimed that a chemical will cause cancer in 10% of people who are exposed to it, but the time between exposure and the development of cancer ranges from 10–20 years, so it is difficult to verify the accuracy of the fears about the chemical. Must states act immediately or at all to ban the chemical? If not, what must they do? If a state bans the chemical and another state challenges the ban as scientifically unjustified, what is the impact of the precautionary principle? Does it matter if the issue is one that potentially affects a few people or species versus hundreds of thousands of people or species?

5. Is the precautionary principle as much a procedural principle as a substantive norm? Carolyn Raffensperger and Katherine Barrett argue that the precautionary principle promotes democratic process by ensuring that neither the environment nor human health can be put at risk without a considered evaluation of likely harms. *See* Carolyn Raffensperger & Katherine Barrett, *In Defense of the Precautionary Principle*, 19 Nature Biotechnology 811 (Sept. 2011). Cass R. Sunstein replies that the principle "is too vague and abstract, and too incoherent, to provide a sensible basis for structuring democratic discussion." Moreover, a democratic public might choose to run risks and "decline to take precautions"? Cass R. Sunstein, Laws of Fear: Beyond the Precautionary Principle 55 (2005).

(f) The Polluter-Pays Principle

OECD COUNCIL RECOMMENDATION ON GUIDING PRINCIPLES CONCERNING THE INTERNATIONAL ECONOMIC ASPECTS OF ENVIRONMENTAL POLICIES, PRINCIPLES A(a)(1–5)

Adopted by the OECD Council, 26 May 1972. OECD Doc C(72)128 (Annex)

Cost Allocation: the Polluter-Pays Principle

2. Environmental resources are in general limited and their use in production and consumption activities may lead to their deterioration. When the cost of this deterioration is not adequately taken into account in the price system, the market fails to reflect the scarcity of such resources both at the national and international levels. Public measures are thus necessary to reduce pollution and to reach a better allocation of resources by ensuring that prices of goods depending on the quality and/or quantity of environmental resources reflect more closely their relative scarcity and that economic agents concerned react accordingly.

* * *

4. The principle to be used for allocating costs of pollution prevention and control measures to encourage rational use of scarce environmental resources and to avoid distortions in international trade and investment is the so-called "Polluter-Pays Principle." This Principle means that the polluter should bear the expenses of carrying out the above mentioned measures decided by public authorities to ensure that the environment is in an acceptable state. In other words, the cost of these measures should be reflected in the cost of goods and services which cause pollution in production and/or consumption. Such measures should not be accompanied by subsidies that would create significant distortions in international trade and investment.

5. This Principle should be an objective of Member countries, however, there may be exceptions or special arrangements, particularly for the transitional periods, provided that they do not lead to significant distortions in international trade and investment.

OECD COUNCIL RECOMMENDATION ON THE IMPLEMENTATION OF THE POLLUTER-PAYS PRINCIPLE

Adopted by the OECD Council, 14 November 1974. OECD Doc C(74)223

The Council, . . .

I. Reaffirms that:

1. The Polluter-Pays Principle constitutes for Member countries a fundamental principle for allocating costs of pollution prevention and control measures introduced by the public authorities in Member countries.

2. The Polluter-Pays Principle, as defined by the Guiding Principles concerning International Economic Aspects of Environmental Policies [C(72)128], which take account of particular problems possibly arising for developing countries, means that the polluter should bear the expenses of carrying out the measures, as specified in the previous paragraph, to ensure that the environment is in an acceptable state. In other words, the cost of these measures should be reflected in the cost of goods and services which cause pollution in production and/or consumption.

* * *

II. Notes that:

1. There is a close relationship between a country's environmental policy and its overall socio-economic policy;

2. In exceptional circumstances, such as the rapid implementation of a compelling and especially stringent pollution control regime, socio-economic problems may develop of such significance as to justify consideration of the granting of governmental assistance, if the environmental policy objectives of a Member country are to be realised within a prescribed and specific time;

3. Aid given for the purpose of stimulating experimentation with new pollution-control technologies and development of new pollution-abatement equipment is not necessarily incompatible with the Polluter-Pays Principle;

4. Where measures taken to promote a country's specific socio-economic objectives, such as the reduction of serious inter-regional imbalances, would have the incidental effect of constituting aid for pollution-control purposes, the granting of such aid would not be inconsistent with the Polluter-Pays Principle.

III. Recommends that:

1. Member countries continue to collaborate and work closely together in striving for uniform observance of the Polluter-Pays Principle, and therefore that as a general rule they should not assist the polluters in

bearing the costs of pollution control whether by means of subsidies, tax advantages or other measures;

2. The granting of any such assistance for pollution control be strictly limited, and in particular comply with every one of the following conditions:

a) it should be selective and restricted to those parts of the economy, such as industries areas or plants, where severe difficulties would otherwise occur;

b) it should be limited to well-defined transitional periods, laid down in advance and adapted to the specific socio-economic problems associated with the implementation of a country's environmental programme;

c) it should not create significant distortions in international trade and investment.

OECD COUNCIL RECOMMENDATION ON THE APPLICATION OF THE POLLUTER-PAYS PRINCIPLE TO ACCIDENTAL POLLUTION

Adopted by the OECD Council, 7 July 1989. OECD Doc C(89)88/Final

Application of the Polluter-Pays Principle

4. In matters of accidental pollution risks, the Polluter-Pays Principle implies that the operator of a hazardous installation should bear the cost of reasonable measures to prevent and control accidental pollution from that installation which are introduced by public authorities in Member countries in conformity with domestic law prior to the occurrence of an accident in order to protect human health or the environment.

* * *

8. Measures to prevent and control accidental pollution are those taken to prevent accidents in specific installations and to limit their consequences for human health or the environment.... *They do not include ... measures to compensate victims for the economic consequences of an accident.* [Emphasis added.]

* * *

11. A further specific application of the Polluter-Pays Principle consists in charging, in conformity with domestic law, the cost of reasonable pollution control measures decided by the authorities following an accident to the operator of the hazardous installation from which pollution is released. Such measures taken without undue delay by the operator or, in case of need, by the authorities would aim at promptly avoiding the spreading of environmental damage and would concern limiting the release of hazardous substances (e.g., by ceasing emissions at

the plant, by erecting floating barriers on a river), the pollution as such (e.g., by cleaning or decontamination), or its ecological effects (e.g., by rehabilitating the polluted environment).

RIO DECLARATION ON ENVIRONMENT AND DEVELOPMENT, PRINCIPLE 16

Adopted by consensus by the UN Conference on Environment and Development, 1 3 June 1992
U.N. Doc. A/CONF.151/26/Rev.1 (Vol. I), annex I (1992), *reprinted as* Basic Document 1.30

National authorities should endeavor to promote the internalization of environmental costs and the use of economic instruments, taking into account the approach that the polluter should, in principle, bear the cost of pollution, with due regard to the public interest and without distorting international trade and investment.

DISCUSSION NOTES/QUESTIONS

1. The polluter-pays principle is considered by some to be part of customary international law. For example, the preamble to the Convention on the Transboundary Effects of Industrial Accidents, 17 March 1992, describes it as a "general principle of international environmental law." But its precise meaning is not entirely clear.

2. Some of the earliest international expressions of the polluter-pays principle appeared in recommendations adopted by the Council of the Organization of Economic Cooperation and Development [OECD]. The OECD's version of the polluter-pays principle seems aimed primarily at discouraging states from assisting industries in paying for the costs of pollution control and prevention measures they take to reduce or control pollution. Under the OECD Recommendations, if a state mandates that industry take steps to reduce pollution, the polluter must pay for those measures, and the state should not assist in meeting the expenses. There is room for some exceptions, but the general policy is that states should not subsidize pollution prevention efforts.

Do you agree with this policy? Apart from avoiding alleged "distortions" of international trade, what are the advantages of requiring the polluter to pay the cost of pollution control? If Patria insists that its industries maintain high and costly environmental protection while its neighbor, Xandia, allows its industries to pollute, what is likely to be the effect of Patrian pollution-control regulation on the competitiveness of its industries? Why should it not subsidize those industries to help them maintain their competitiveness? Why should the polluter pay for the cost of pollution control when it benefits everyone in Patria?

3 The Rio Declaration says that polluters should "bear the cost of pollution," which implies that, in addition to paying for the expenses of pollution control, polluters should pay for any damage that their pollution

causes. Requiring polluters to pay for the costs of pollution damage as well as the costs of pollution control is sometimes described as a correction for the "market failure" that occurs when polluters are able to "externalize" pollution costs (that is, impose those costs on others). In a 1994 report, the OECD explained:

> Environmental problems ... are due to market and intervention failure.... Market failures can result from the failure of polluters to take into account the environmental costs of their activities ..... [T]he environmental costs are externalized rather than internalized in the prices of goods and services.

OECD, The Environmental Effects of Trade 8 (1994). Can you explain why "externalizing" the cost of pollution is described as a "market failure"? In what way does the market fail when pollution costs are externalized? The general explanation is that pollution should be considered a cost of production of a good. If the producer does not bear that cost, then the producer will produce the goods even when the total cost of production exceeds the price that consumers are willing to pay. To put the point another way, if all the costs are not reflected in the price, then the production of the goods will impose costs on society that are greater than the benefits that consumers derive from using the goods. In that case, the market has failed to generate a socially optimal level of production.

One way to deal with such a market failure is to impose liability on polluters for the costs they impose. But that is not the only way. If, the polluter and those injured by the pollution can easily bargain about the matter, and if the pollution damage that is caused exceeds the value of production of the goods, the injured persons may be able to pay the polluter to cease production or to take steps to minimize pollution damage. Or, if the value of production exceeds the pollution damage, the polluter may be willing to pay for the right to pollute. In short, it may be possible to negotiate an arrangement that maximizes social value. *See* Ronald Coase, *The Problem of Social Cost,* 3 J. Law & Econ. 1 (1960). Recall, for example, that the polluter in the Trail Smelter dispute (Chapter 3) initially sought to negotiate with landowners to compensate them in advance for the injury they suffered. Had Washington State law allowed it, the polluter would have sought to obtain a permanent smoke easement from the landowners most affected by its operation. Either result would have avoided the need for a post-hoc liability determination. Even if the polluter weren't liable, the affected landowners could, in principle, have paid the polluter to adopt pollution control measures if the damage suffered was sufficient to warrant such payments. The point is this—a polluter-pays liability rule is not the only way to deal with environmental externalities.

4. Examine paragraph 8 of the OECD's 1989 Recommendations on Accidental Pollution. That paragraph says explicitly that the polluter-pays principle does *not* mean that polluters must compensate the victims of accidental pollution. Why would the OECD have been unwilling to endorse a rule of liability for accidental pollution damage? Wouldn't that be one way to

force the internalization of environmental costs? In terms of correcting for "market failures," is accidental pollution different than intentional pollution? Could a rule of liability for accidental pollution result in too much pollution control?

Suppose that a chemical factory in Patria has an accident that results in serious harm to the Muddy River—the main source of water for Patria's irrigation-dependent fruit and vegetable farmers. Does the polluter-pays principle mean that the factory owners should bear the exclusive responsibility for compensating the fruit and vegetable farmers for any loss? That the factory owners should have exclusive responsibility for paying for any cleanup of the river? What if the factory owners cannot pay without bankrupting the company and putting hundreds of people out of work?

If a government wishes to adopt a liability rule for accidental pollution damage, what factors should it consider in structuring that rule? Should it cap potential damages? Limit the categories of damage that are recoverable? Require polluters to obtain insurance?

5. Only a handful of multilateral environmental agreements impose liability on private polluters for pollution damage. These agreements apply to certain particularly dangerous activities that carry a high risk of environmental harm in the event of an accident. These agreements include provisions limiting the scope of private-party liability and requiring that potential polluters have a substantial amount of insurance coverage. *See, e.g.*, Vienna Convention on Civil Liability for Nuclear Damage, 21 May 1963, 1063 UNTS 265 (extensively amended by 1997 Protocol); International Convention on Civil Liability for Oil Pollution Damage, 27 November 1992. For discussion of these treaties, *see* Problems 6-3 and 10-2, *infra*.

Apart from treaties concerning oil pollution and nuclear damage, states have been unable to agree on the establishment of rules imposing liability on private actors for accidental pollution damage. For example, although the Convention on the Transboundary Effects of Industrial Accidents endorses the polluter-pays principle in its preamble, and states are directed to "support appropriate international efforts to elaborate rules, criteria and procedures in the field of responsibility and liability," the operative provisions of the Convention do not impose liability on polluters. In 2003, a protocol to the convention was adopted that would impose liability on polluters in some cases, but that protocol has been adopted by only one state (as of June 2019) and is not in force. *See* Protocol on Civil Liability and Compensation for Damage Caused by the Transboundary Effects of Industrial Accidents on Transboundary Waters, 21 May 2003 **(Basic Document 3.17b)**.

Similarly, the Basel Convention on the Control of Transboundary Movements of Hazardous Wastes and their Disposal, 22 March 1989, 1673 UNTS 57 **(Basic Document 4.7)**, has no provisions imposing liability on the owners or transporters of hazardous waste, even in situations where the waste causes serious environmental harm. A protocol adopted in 1999 was designed to correct this situation, but it has received only a handful of signatures and insufficient ratifications to enter into force. *See* Basel Protocol on Liability and Compensation, 10 December 1999 **(Basic Document 4.7a)**.

6. If the international community is unable to reach agreement on the liability of polluters for transboundary harm from industrial accidents or for harm from the transboundary movement of hazardous wastes, then perhaps the polluter-pays principle is not yet a principle of customary international law or, perhaps, it does not mean that polluters should compensate for accidental damage they cause. If the polluter-pays principle does not require compensation for accidental damage, then what does it mean?

(g) The Principle of Common but Differentiated Responsibilities

BEIJING MINISTERIAL DECLARATION ON ENVIRONMENT AND DEVELOPMENT

Adopted on 19 June 1991 by ministers from 41 developing countries, at the Ministerial Conference on Environment and Development in Beijing
U.N. Doc. A/46/293 (Annex) (9 July 1991)

While the protection of the environment is in the common interests of the international community, the developed countries bear the main responsibility for the degradation of the global environment. Ever since the industrial revolution, the developed countries have over-exploited the world's natural resources through unsustainable patterns of production and consumption, causing damage to the global environment, to the detriment of the developing countries.

RIO DECLARATION ON ENVIRONMENT AND DEVELOPMENT, PRINCIPLE 7

Adopted by consensus by the UN Conference on Environment and Development, 14 June 1992
U.N. Doc. A/CONF.151/26/Rev.1 (Vol. I), annex I (1992) (Basic Document 1.30)

States shall cooperate in a spirit of global partnership to conserve, protect and restore the health and integrity of the Earth's ecosystem. In view of the different contributions to global environmental degradation, States have common but differentiated responsibilities. The developed countries acknowledge the responsibility that they bear in the international pursuit of sustainable development in view of the pressures their societies place on the global environment and of the technologies and financial resources they command.

US STATEMENT FOR THE RECORD PRIOR TO ADOPTION OF THE RIO DECLARATION

Written statement submitted for the record, 14 June 1992
Report of the UN Conference on the Environment and Development at Rio de Janeiro, 3–14 June 1992, U.N. Doc. A/Conf.151/26/Rev.1 (vol. II), p. 17–18 (1993)

The United States understands and accepts that Principle 7 highlights the special leadership role of the developed countries, based on our industrial development, our experience with environmental protection policies and actions, and our wealth, technical expertise, and capabilities.

The United States does not accept any interpretation of Principle 7 that would imply a recognition or acceptance by the United States of any international obligations or liabilities, or any diminution in the responsibilities of developing countries.

AGENDA 21, PARA. 39(1) & (3)

Approved by consensus by the UN Conference on Environment and Development, 14 June 1992
Report of the UN Conference on the Environment and Development at Rio de Janeiro, 3–14 June 1992, U.N. Doc. A/CONF.151/26 (Vols I–III) (1993) (Basic Document 1.31)

39.1. . . . The following vital aspects of the . . . treaty-making process should be taken into account:

* * *

At the global level, the essential importance of the participation in and the contribution of all countries, including the developing countries, to treaty making in the field of international law on sustainable development. Many of the existing international legal instruments and agreements in the field of the environment have been developed without adequate participation and contribution of developing countries, and thus may require review in order to reflect the concerns and interests of developing countries and to ensure a balanced governance of such instruments and agreements.

* * *

39.3 Specific objectives [in the review and development of international environmental law] are:

* * *

(c) To promote and support the effective participation of all countries concerned, in particular developing countries, in the negotiation, implementation, review and governance of international agreements or instruments, including appropriate provision of technical and financial assistance and other available mechanisms for this purpose, as well as the use of differential obligations where appropriate;

(d) To promote . . . international standards for the protection of the environment that take into account the different situations and capabilities of countries.

DISCUSSION NOTES/QUESTIONS

1. According to the principle of common but differentiated responsibility, all states have a "common responsibility for the protection of the environment," but each state's obligation in that regard is differentiated and dependent upon the state's "*contribution* to the creation of a particular environmental problem and its *ability* to prevent, reduce and control the threat." Philippe Sands, Principles of International Environmental Law 286 (2d ed. 2003). *See also* Yoshiro Matsui, *The Principle of "Common but Differentiated Responsibilities,"* in International Law and Sustainable Development: Principles and Practice 73–79 (Nico Schrijver & Friedl Weiss eds., 2004).

2. What is the source of the common responsibility for protection of the environment? Matsui traces it to "the reality of ecological interdependence, and the concomitant recognition of the global nature of environmental problems." Environmental protection, he says, has become the "common concern of humankind, and not solely a matter of domestic jurisdiction of each individual State." But in practice is it not likely that the "common responsibility" of developing nations will become subsumed into "differentiated responsibilities" so that, in fact, nothing will be expected of them? How does one avoid this outcome? Through obligations phased-in over time? Through obligations tied to a nation's per capita income?

3. Many international treaty regimes incorporate the principle of common but differentiated responsibility in one way or another. For example, the Montreal Protocol on Substances that Deplete the Ozone Layer **(Basic Document 2.8)** gives developing countries a longer time to phase out the use of ozone-depleting substances than it gives developed countries. The United Nations Framework Convention on Climate Change **(Basic Document 2.4)** explicitly endorses the principle of common but differentiated responsibility, and the Kyoto Protocol **(Basic Document 2.5)** imposed emission reduction obligations on developed countries but not on developing countries (which is one reason the United States refused to ratify the Kyoto Protocol). The Montreal Protocol and the UNFCCC both have provisions requiring developed countries to provide financial support to meet the costs incurred by developing countries in complying with their obligations under those treaties. *See* Montreal Protocol, article 10(1); UNFCCC, article 4(3). The Biodiversity Convention similarly provides for the transfer of financial resource to developing countries to assist them in fulfilling the goals of the Convention. *See* Convention on Biological Diversity, article 21 **(Basic Document 5.6)**.

4. Philippe Sands, *supra* discussion note/question 1, links the concept of common responsibility to the problem of dealing with shared natural resources on the global level. When a particular natural resource is not the property of a

particular state, then the problem emerges of how to ensure that no state over-exploits the resource. To deal with this problem, Sands observes, the international community developed the concept of unowned resources being "of common concern" to the exploiting nations and thus a subject for cooperative rather than unilateral behavior. The concept of "common concern" gave way to stronger claims for community authority, including the declaration of outer space as the "province of all mankind," the designation of deep seabed resources as "the common heritage of mankind," and the identification of plant genetic resources as "a heritage of mankind."

> While each of these formulations differs, and must be understood and applied in the context of the circumstances in which they were adopted, these attributions of 'commonality' do share common consequences. . . . [L]egal responsibilities [to prevent damage to these shared resources] are attributable to all states, [although] the extent and legal nature of that responsibility will differ for each resource . . . and each state. . . .

Do the concepts of "common concern" and "common heritage" suggest that the so-called "un-owned" areas and resources of the planet are, in fact more appropriately treated as a "commons" that is owned by all? Does the concept of a jointly-owned "commons" allow for forms or methods of governance that can do a better job than existing approaches to controlling the exploitation of unowned global resources? *See* Chapter 11, *infra* (Managing the Global Commons in Antarctica). *See generally* Burns H. Weston & David Bollier, Green Governance: Ecological Survival, Human Rights, and the Law of the Commons (2013).

5. Does the concept of "common responsibility" support the suggestion in Agenda 21 **(Basic Document 1.31)** that legal instruments and agreements in the environmental field "may require review in order to reflect the concerns and interests of developing countries" if they have been developed "without adequate participation and contribution of developing countries?" In other words, should principles and norms (e.g., the polluter-pays principle) that originally emerged in legal instruments created by industrial countries independent of developing countries be considered suspect insofar as such developing countries are concerned? Should those principles and norms be modified retroactively to reduce the obligations of developing countries, in keeping with the principle of "differentiated responsibility"?

6. The Beijing Declaration and the Rio Declaration justify the principle of "differentiated responsibility" partly in terms of the greater historical contribution of rich countries to "global environmental degradation" and the continuing "pressures [that developed country] societies place on the global environment." Matsui, *supra* discussion note/question 1, suggests that this concept of "differentiated responsibility" could lead to a concrete

> legal responsibility on the part of developed countries to take measures in order to tackle global environmental degradation. This responsibility of developed countries may be characterized as a kind

> of application of the polluter-pays principle. Though the context appears to be different, the underlying rationale of the polluter-pays principle "is reflected in those provisions referring to the historic responsibility of developed countries for the problem of climate change and the loss of biodiversity," as Philippe Sands argues.

Do you agree that application of the polluter-pays principle to global environmental problems would require developed countries to pay the bulk of the costs of addressing environmental degradation? Should we read this into the concept of "differentiated responsibility"?

7. What is the impact of the U.S. statement made at Rio? If the concept of "differentiated responsibility" were interpreted to give rise to a customary obligation on developed countries "to take measures . . . to take global environmental degradation," could the US resist application of the principle to it on the ground that it is a persistent objector?

8. Does equity support the concept of differentiated responsibility? In *Global Environment and International Inequality,* 75 Int'l Affairs 531 (1999), social philosopher Henry Shue contends that it does.

> When a party has in the past taken unfair advantage of others by imposing costs upon them without their consent, those who have been unilaterally put at a disadvantage are entitled to demand that in the future the offending party shoulder burdens that are unequal at least to the extent of the unfair advantage previously taken, in order to restore equality.

Do you agree? If so, how should developed countries go about "shouldering" these burdens? When do we know that "equality" has been restored? And how likely is it that developed country taxpayers will be willing to meet the demands of equity? If you think it is not very likely, then is "differentiated responsibility" just an empty concept? Or are there ways for developed countries to "shoulder the burden" that will meet the demands of equity without creating politically unacceptable consequences for rich country governments?

(h) Cooperation, Notification, Consultation, and Negotiation

UN GENERAL ASSEMBLY RESOLUTION 2995 CONCERNING COOPERATION BETWEEN STATES IN THE FIELD OF THE ENVIRONMENT

Adopted by the UN General Assembly, 5 Dec 1972
G.A. Res. 2995 (Dec. 5, 1972)

[I]n exercising their sovereignty over their natural resources, States must seek . . . to preserve and improve the environment;

[I]n the . . . development of their natural resources, States must not produce significant harmful effects in zones situated outside their national jurisdiction;

[C]ooperation between States in the field of the environment . . . will be effectively achieved if official and public knowledge is provided of the technical data relating to the work to be carried out by States within their national jurisdiction, with a view to avoiding significant harm that may occur in the environment of the adjacent area;

[T]he technical data referred to . . . will be given and received in the best spirit of co-operation and good-neighbourliness, without this being construed as enabling each State to delay or impede . . . [projects for the] development of the natural resources of the States in whose territories such . . . projects are carried out.

ILA RULES ON INTERNATIONAL LAW APPLICABLE TO TRANSFRONTIER POLLUTION, ARTS. 5 & 6

Adopted by the International Law Association, 4 September 1982
60 ILA 158 (Basic Document 1.26)

Article 5 (Prior Notice)

(1) States planning to carry out activities which might entail a significant risk of transfrontier pollution shall give early notice to States likely to be affected. . . .

* * *

Article 6 (Consultations)

(1) Upon request of a potentially affected States, the State furnishing the information should enter into consultations on transfrontier pollution problems connected with the planned activities and pursue such consultations in good faith and over a reasonable period of time. . . .

LEGAL PRINCIPLES FOR ENVIRONMENTAL PROTECTION AND SUSTAINABLE DEVELOPMENT, PRINCIPLES 16, 17 & 22

Adopted by the WCED Experts Group on Environmental Law, 18–20 June 1986
U.N. Doc. WCED/86/23/Add.1 (1986) (Basic Document 1.28)

Article 16
Prior notice of planned activities, environmental impact assessment

1. States planning to carry out or permit activities which may entail [a significant transboundary environmental interference or risk thereof] shall give timely notice to the States concerned. . . .

* * *

Article 17
Consultations

Consultations shall be held in good faith, upon request, [among States affected by a transboundary environmental interference]. . . .

* * *

Article 22

1. States . . . shall settle disputes [concerning an environmental interference] by peaceful means in such a manner that international peace and security, and justice, are not endangered.

2. States shall accordingly seek a settlement of such disputes by negotiation, good offices, enquiry, mediation, conciliation, arbitration, judicial settlement . . . or by any other peaceful means. . . .

RIO DECLARATION ON ENVIRONMENT AND DEVELOPMENT, PRINCIPLE 19

Adopted by consensus by the UN Conference on Environment and Development, 14 June 1992 U.N. Doc. A/CONF.151/26/Rev.1 (Vol. I), annex I (1992) (Basic Document 1.30)

States shall provide prior and timely notification and relevant information to potentially affected States on activities that may have a significant adverse transboundary environmental effect and shall consult with those States at an early stage and in good faith.

DRAFT PREAMBLE AND DRAFT ARTICLES ON PREVENTION OF TRANSBOUNDARY HARM FROM HAZARDOUS ACTIVITIES, ARTS. 4, 8 & 9

Adopted by the International Law Commission, 11 May 2001 Report of the International Law Commission on the Work of its Fifty-third Session, U.N. Doc. A/56/10, at 146–48 (2001) (Basic Document 1.16)

Article 4 Cooperation

States concerned shall cooperate in good faith and, as necessary, seek the assistance of one or more competent international organizations in preventing significant transboundary harm or at any event in minimizing the risk thereof.

Article 8 Notification and information

1. If the assessment referred to in article 7 indicates a risk of causing significant transboundary harm, the State of origin shall provide the State likely to be affected with timely notification of the risk and the assessment and shall transmit to it the available technical and all other relevant information on which the assessment is based.

2. The State of origin shall not take any decision on authorization of the activity pending the receipt, within a period not exceeding six months, of the response from the State likely to be affected.

Article 9 Consultations on preventive measures

1. The States concerned shall enter into consultations, at the request of any of them, with a view to achieving acceptable solutions regarding measures to be adopted in order to prevent significant transboundary harm or at any event to minimize the risk thereof. The States concerned shall agree, at the commencement of such consultations, on a reasonable time-frame for the consultations.

2. The States concerned shall seek solutions based on an equitable balance of interests in the light of article 10.

3. If the consultations referred to in paragraph 1 fail to produce an agreed solution, the State of origin shall nevertheless take into account the interests of the State likely to be affected in case it decides to authorize the activity to be pursued, without prejudice to the rights of any State likely to be affected.

DISCUSSION NOTES/QUESTIONS

1. The obligations of cooperation, notification, consultation, and negotiation are reflected in many international instruments on the environment. In addition to the instruments noted above, a particularly noteworthy expression of these obligations is contained in 1978 UNEP Council's Draft Principles of Conduct in the Field of the Environment **(Basic Document 1.24)**. These obligations seem to involve primarily an obligation to talk. What good does talking do? If failed negotiations will lead to formal adjudication of a dispute, the parties may have a strong incentive to negotiate to avoid that result. If one party has the ability to sanction the other, there may still be reason to negotiate. But do you think that there is any good to be achieved by notification and consultation when neither litigation nor the possibility of sanction looms?

2. To what extent should the obligation to notify and consult include an obligation to share information? How important is the information-sharing aspect of consultation?

(i) Environmental Impact Assessment

STOCKHOLM DECLARATION OF THE UNITED NATIONS CONFERENCE ON THE HUMAN ENVIRONMENT, PRINCIPLES 14 & 15

Adopted by the UN Conference on the Human Environment, 16 June 1972
U.N. Doc. A/CONF.48/14/Rev.1 at 5 (1972) (Basic Document 1.21)

Principle 14

Rational planning constitutes an essential tool for reconciling any conflict between the needs of development and the need to protect and improve the environment.

Principle 15

Planning must be applied to human settlements and urbanization with a view to avoiding adverse effects on the environment and obtaining maximum social, economic and environmental benefits for all. . . .

DRAFT PRINCIPLES OF CONDUCT IN THE FIELD OF THE ENVIRONMENT FOR GUIDANCE OF STATES IN THE CONSERVATION AND HARMONIOUS UTILIZATION OF NATURAL RESOURCES SHARED BY TWO OR MORE STATES, PRINCIPLES 5, 7, 8 & 13

Adopted by the UN Environment Programme Governing Council, 19 May 1978
U.N. Doc. UNEP/IG12/2 (1978) (Basic Document 1.24)

Principle 5

States sharing a natural resource should, to the extent practicable, exchange information and engage in consultations on a regular basis on its environmental aspects.

Principle 7

Exchange of information, notification, consultations and other forms of co-operation regarding shared natural resources are carried out on the basis of the principle of good faith and in the spirit of good neighbourliness and in such a way as to avoid any unreasonable delays either in the forms of co-operation or in carrying out development or conservation projects.

Principle 8

When it would be useful to clarify environmental problems relating to a shared natural resource, States should engage in joint scientific studies and assessments, with a view to facilitating the finding of appropriate and satisfactory solutions to such problems on the basis of agreed data.

Principle 13

It is necessary for States, when considering, under their domestic environmental policy, the permissibility of domestic activities, to take into account the potential adverse environmental effects arising out of the utilization of shared natural resources, without discrimination as to whether the effects would occur within their jurisdiction or outside it.

WORLD CHARTER FOR NATURE PRINCIPLES 11(b) & 11(c)

Adopted by the UN General Assembly, 28 October 1982
G.A. Res. 37/7 (Annex) (Oct. 28, 1982) (Basic Document 1.27)

Activities which are likely to pose a significant risk to nature shall be preceded by an exhaustive examination; their proponents shall demonstrate that expected benefits outweigh potential damage to nature, and where potential adverse effects are not fully understood, the activities should not proceed.

Activities which may disturb nature shall be preceded by assessment of their consequences, and environmental impact studies of development projects shall be conducted sufficiently in advance, and if they are to be undertaken, such activities shall be planned and carried out so as to minimize potential adverse effects; . . . .

UNITED NATIONS CONVENTION ON THE LAW OF THE SEA (UNCLOS), ART. 206

Concluded, 10 Dec. 1982. Entered into Force, 16 Nov. 1984
1833 UNTS 3 (Basic Document 3.4)

When States have reasonable grounds for believing that planned activities under their jurisdiction or control may cause substantial pollution of or significant and harmful changes to the marine environment, they shall, as far as practicable, assess the potential effects of such activities on the marine environment and shall communicate reports of the results of such assessment [to the competent international organizations, which should make them available to all States].

LEGAL PRINCIPLES FOR ENVIRONMENTAL PROTECTION AND SUSTAINABLE DEVELOPMENT, PRINCIPLE 16

Adopted by the WCED Experts Group on Environmental Law, 18–20 June 1986,
U.N. Doc. WCED/86/23/Add.1 (1986) (Basic Document 1.28)

When a State has reasonable grounds for believing that planned activities may have [significant adverse transboundary environmental] effects. . ., it shall make an assessment of those effects before carrying out or permitting the planned activities.

CONVENTION ON ENVIRONMENTAL IMPACT ASSESSMENT IN A TRANSBOUNDARY CONTEXT (ESPOO CONVENTION), ART. 2(2)

Concluded, 25 Feb. 1991. Entered into Force, 10 Sept. 1997
1989 UNTS 309 (Basic Document 1.38)

Each Party shall take the necessary legal, administrative or other measures to implement. . ., with respect to [activities] . . . that are likely to cause significant adverse transboundary impact, . . . an environmental impact assessment procedure that permits public participation and preparation of . . . environmental impact assessment documentation. . . .

RIO DECLARATION ON ENVIRONMENT AND DEVELOPMENT, PRINCIPLE 17

Adopted by consensus by the UN Conference on Environment and Development, 14 June 1992
U.N. Doc. A/CONF.151/26/Rev.1 (Vol. I), annex I (1992) (Basic Document 1.30)

Environmental impact assessment, as a national instrument, shall be undertaken for proposed activities that are likely to have a significant adverse impact on the environment and are subject to a decision of a competent national authority.

AGENDA 21, PARAS. 8.4 & 8.5

Approved by consensus by the UN Conference on Environment and Development, 14 June 1992
Report of the UN Conference on the Environment and Development at Rio de Janeiro, 3–14 June 1992, U.N. Doc. A/CONF.151/26 (Vols I–III) (1993) (Basic Document 1.31)

8.4. . . . Governments should . . . improve the processes of decision-making so as to achieve the progressive integration of economic, social and environmental issues in the pursuit of development that is economically efficient, socially equitable and responsible and environmentally sound. . . .

* * *

8.5. . . . Governments . . . should . . . strengthen procedures so as to facilitate the integrated consideration of social, economic and environmental issues. . . ., [including by] [a]dopting comprehensive analytical procedures for prior and simultaneous assessment of the impacts of decisions, including the impacts within and among the economic, social and environmental spheres; these procedures should extend beyond the project level to policies and programmes; analysis should also include assessment of costs, benefits and risks. . . .

DRAFT PREAMBLE AND DRAFT ARTICLES ON PREVENTION OF TRANSBOUNDARY HARM FROM HAZARDOUS ACTIVITIES, ART. 7

Adopted by the International Law Commission, 11 May 2001
Report of the International Law Commission on the Work of its Fifty-third Session, U.N. Doc. A/56/10, at 146–48 (2001) (Basic Document 1.16)

Any decision in respect of the authorization of an activity within the scope of the present articles shall, in particular, be based on an assessment of the possible transboundary harm caused by that activity, including any environmental impact assessment.

DISCUSSION NOTES/QUESTIONS

1. Most of the international pronouncements on environmental impact assessment are aimed at securing such assessments when there is likely to be a significant and adverse transboundary environmental effect. But the Rio Declaration **(Basic Document 1.30)** and Agenda 21 **(Basic Document 1.31)** appear to call upon states to conduct environmental impact assessment even when the anticipated environmental impact is purely local. Is that justified? Why? Why not?

2. In a 1996 book evaluating environmental assessment, its author described it as "a highly successful policy instrument, possibly . . . one of the major policy innovations of the 20th Century." Barry Sadler, Environmental Assessment in a Changing World 24 (1996). In support of that conclusion, Sadler observed that, as of 1996, more than 100 states had adopted national environmental assessment requirements and that environmental assessment policies were under consideration in many more states. In 1989, in fact, the World Bank began requiring environmental assessments in all investment projects financed by the Bank. Other development banks quickly followed suit. In addition, many donor countries make environmental assessment a condition of grants of foreign aid. Finally, the business community has embraced environmental assessment as an essential component of their risk management practices.

3. Environmental impact assessment has been adopted as an international legal obligation in several treaties. Most noteworthy is the 1991 Convention on Environmental Impact Assessment in a Transboundary Context (Espoo Convention) **(Basic Document 1.38)**, which was adopted under the auspices of the UN Economic Commission for Europe and has 45 Member States. The United Nations Convention on the Law of the Sea **(Basic Document 3.4)**, with a global membership, requires environmental impact assessment for any planned activities that "may cause substantial pollution of or significant and harmful changes to the marine environment" (art. 206). The Protocol on Environmental Protection to the Antarctic Treaty **(Basic Document 6.5)** requires environmental impact assessment of all activities in the Antarctic Treaty area. Some regional seas treaties also require environmental assessment in certain circumstances. *See, e.g.,* Protocol

Concerning Pollution from Land-Based Sources and Activities to the [Cartagena] Convention for the Protection and Development of the Marine Environment of the Wider Caribbean, art. VII **(Basic Document 3.5a)**.

4. Suppose that an environmental assessment reveals that an important economic development project in a developing country is likely to have a significant and adverse effect on a neighboring country. Then what? Does the project have to be altered to eliminate or reduce the effect? Can the state that wishes to undertake the project insist on assistance from the neighboring state relative to bearing the cost of making the project more environmentally friendly? If an anticipated adverse environmental effect cannot be eliminated or reduced, is it necessary to abandon the project? What do the principles addressed earlier in this chapter tell us should be the answer to these questions?

5. In the United States, agencies of the federal government have been required to conduct environmental impact assessments of their activities since the passage of the National Environmental Policy Act (NEPA) in 1969, P.L. 91–190, 83 Stat. 852 (1969). One early review of the process by Professor Joseph Sax was unrelentingly harsh in its assessment:

> . . . I know of no solid evidence to support the belief that requiring articulation, detailed findings or reasoned opinions enhances the integrity or propriety of . . . administrative decisions. I think the emphasis on the redemptive quality of procedural reform [such as the requirement of environmental impact assessment] is about nine parts myth and one part coconut oil.
>
> * * *
>
> [Without changes in the incentives facing decision-makers, they will not change their behavior], whether or not there is a NEPA and whether or not courts require them to file elaborate, multi-volume impact statements.
>
> * * *
>
> Unless we are ready to face these hard realities, we can expect laws like NEPA to produce little except fodder for law review writers and contracts for that newest of growth industries, environmental consulting.

Joseph L. Sax, *The (Unhappy) Truth about NEPA*, 26 Okla. L. Rev. 239, 240, 248 (1973).

But several years later, Professor Sax changed his mind:

> NEPA, and its requirement of an environmental impact statement open to public view and comment, ventilated the planning processes of federal agencies . . . [and made the citizen] a legitimate participant. . . . [L]egitimating public participation, and demanding openness in planning and decisionmaking, has been indispensable to

> a permanent and powerful increase in environmental protection, and [the] presence of citizen-initiated litigation is a major factor that keeps public agencies from slackening in their resolve to see that environmental laws are enforced.

Joseph L. Sax, *Environmental Law: More Than Just a Passing Fad*, 19 U. Mich. J.L. Rev. 797, 309–04 & n.28 (1986).

NEPA was the trigger for the global movement toward environmental assessment. But is the US experience in this regard transferable to other nations with different administrative processes and different expectations about public participation in government decisions?

6. How are environmental assessment, the duty to cooperate, and access to information related?

(j) Public Participation, Access to Information, Access to Justice

UNIVERSAL DECLARATION OF HUMAN RIGHTS, ARTS. 19 & 21(1)

Adopted by the UN General Assembly, 10 December 1948
G.A. Res. 217A (Dec. 10, 1948) (Basic Document 7.9)

Article 19

Everyone has the right to freedom of opinion and expression; this right includes freedom to hold opinions without interference and to seek, receive and impart information and ideas through any media and regardless of frontiers.

Article 21

1. Everyone has the right to take part in the government of his country, directly or through freely chosen representatives. . . .

STOCKHOLM DECLARATION OF THE UNITED NATIONS CONFERENCE ON THE HUMAN ENVIRONMENT, PRINCIPLE 22

Adopted by the UN Conference on the Human Environment, 16 June 1972
U.N. Doc A/CONF.48/14/Rev.1 at 5 (1972) (Basic Document 1.21)

States shall co-operate to develop further the international law regarding liability and compensation for the victims of pollution and other environmental damage caused by activities within the jurisdiction or control of such States to areas beyond their jurisdiction.

DRAFT PRINCIPLES OF CONDUCT IN THE FIELD OF THE ENVIRONMENT FOR GUIDANCE OF STATES IN THE CONSERVATION AND HARMONIOUS UTILIZATION OF NATURAL RESOURCES SHARED BY TWO OR MORE STATES, PRINCIPLE 14

Adopted by the UN Environment Programme Governing Council, 19 May 1978
U.N. Doc. UNEP/IG12/2 (Basic Document 1.24)

States should endeavour, in accordance with their legal systems and, where appropriate, on a basis agreed by them, to provide persons in other States who have been or may be adversely affected by environmental damage resulting from the utilization of shared natural resources with equivalent access to and treatment in the same administrative and judicial proceedings, and make available to them the same remedies as are available to persons within their own jurisdictions who have been or may be similarly affected.

WORLD CHARTER FOR NATURE, PRINCIPLE 23

Adopted by the UN General Assembly, 28 October 1982
G.A. Res. 37/7 (Annex) (Oct. 28, 1982) (Basic Document 1.27)

All persons, in accordance with their national legislation, shall have the opportunity to participate, individually or with others, in the formulation of decisions of direct concern to their environment, and shall have access to means of redress when their environment has suffered damage or degradation.

LEGAL PRINCIPLES FOR ENVIRONMENTAL PROTECTION AND SUSTAINABLE DEVELOPMENT, PRINCIPLE 6

Adopted by the WCED Experts Group on Environmental Law, 18–20 June 1986
U.N. Doc. WCED/86/23/Add.1 (1986) (Basic Document 1.28)

States shall inform all persons in a timely manner of activities which may significantly affect their use of a natural resource or their environment and shall grant the concerned persons access to and due process in administrative and judicial proceedings.

RIO DECLARATION ON ENVIRONMENT AND DEVELOPMENT, PRINCIPLE 10

Adopted by consensus by the UN Conference on Environment and Development, 14 June 1992
U.N. Doc. A/CONF.151/26/Rev.1 (Vol. I), annex I (1992) (Basic Document 1.30)

Environmental issues are best handled with the participation of all concerned citizens, at the relevant level. At the national level, each individual shall have appropriate access to information concerning the environment that is held by public authorities, including information on hazardous materials and activities in their communities, and the opportunity to participate in decision-making processes. States shall facilitate and encourage public awareness and participation by making information widely available. Effective access to judicial and administrative proceedings, including redress and remedy, shall be provided.

AGENDA 21, PARA. 23.2

Approved by consensus by the UN Conference on Environment and Development, 14 June 1992
Report of the UN Conference on the Environment and Development at Rio de Janeiro, 3–14 June 1992, U.N. Doc. A/CONF.151/26 (Vols I–III) (1993) (Basic Document 1.31)

One of the fundamental prerequisites for the achievement of sustainable development is broad public participation in decision-making. . . . This includes the need of individuals, groups and organizations to participate in environmental impact assessment procedures and to know about and participate in decisions, particularly those which potentially affect the communities in which they live and work. Individuals, groups and organizations should have access to information relevant to environment and development held by national authorities, including information on products and activities that have or are likely to have a significant impact on the environment, and information on environmental protection measures.

DISCUSSION NOTES/QUESTIONS

1. Based on the foregoing materials, would you say that people have a right to participate in decisions that affect their environment? If so, how would one articulate that right? If a governmental decision will affect the environment, is the right to participation limited to citizens of the government involved or does it extend also to people within the country who are not citizens? To people in neighboring countries who might be affected by the decision? Is there a right for civic participation when the environment-affecting decision is made by a private actor—e.g., a decision by a farmer to clear some of his forested land in order to plant more crops? How can other citizens participate in that decision? Affected non-citizens?

2. Is there a right to receive information related to environmental decision-making? What kind of information? Suppose a business applies for a permit to discharge industrial waste into a river. Do people (citizens and non-citizens alike) who are actually or potentially affected have a right to know what will be in the waste? Do they have a right to know all the chemicals used in the process that produces the waste? Do they have such a right even if the chemicals used in that process are a closely-guarded trade secret of the business involved?

3. Do people (citizens and non-citizens) have a right to be compensated for any harm they suffer as a result of pollution? If a nation gives its citizens such a right, must it extend that right to citizens of other nations?

4. A few treaties provide private individuals with the right to gain access to private information. *See, e.g.*, Convention for the Protection of the Marine Environment of the North-East Atlantic (1992 OSPAR Convention), 22 September 1992, art. 9. The most significant international effort to date aimed at protecting the right of private persons to participate in decisions affecting the environment is the 1998 Aarhus Convention on Access to Information, Public Participation in Decision-Making and Access to Justice in Environmental Matters **(Basic Document 1.39)**. This Convention was adopted under the auspices of the UN Economic Commission for Europe and has 47 parties, all European or Eurasian states. *See* Problem 5-1, *infra*.

3. INTERNATIONAL ENVIRONMENTAL TREATIES

Following the 1972 Stockholm Conference there was an explosion of treaty-making in the environmental arena. Some of the new treaties were continuations of efforts to deal with problems that had long been recognized as requiring international solutions (e.g., oceanic oil pollution). Other treaties dealt with newly recognized problems (e.g., depletion of the ozone layer).

Although each treaty or treaty regime is unique, there are some commonalities worth noting. Perhaps the most significant feature of modern environmental treaties is the extent to which they embrace the principle that developed and developing states have "common but differentiated responsibilities" with respect to global environmental problems. In some cases, the principle is reflected in treaty provisions that impose different obligations (or different timetables for fulfilling obligations) on developed and developing country Parties. In other cases, the principle is reflected in provisions that require developed countries to provide financial assistance to developing countries and that excuse the developing countries from their obligations if financial assistance is not forthcoming. Some treaties have both kinds of provisions.

A second important development is the rise of the "framework" treaty. A framework treaty is a treaty that lays down basic objectives, articulates guiding principles, and establishes an organizational and decision-making structure within which the participating states will cooperate to study and address a particular environmental problem. Framework treaties include few or no provisions mandating specific actions by states to "stop polluting" or otherwise "preserve the environment." Instead a framework treaty contemplates that the Parties will take future actions to address the relevant environmental problem, and the treaty includes provisions aimed at facilitating future action. The facilitative provisions include provisions promoting research and analysis of the problem along with provisions that allow the Parties to the treaty to adopt subsequent protocols imposing stronger regulations on themselves.

Many of the most important international environmental agreements—including the Convention on Long-range Transboundary Air Pollution **(Basic Document 2.1)**, the Vienna Convention on Substances that Deplete the Ozone Layer **(Basic Document 2.7)**, and the UN Framework Convention on Climate Change **(Basic Document 2.4)**—are of this type. So, too, are the various conventions negotiated under the auspices of UNEP's Regional Seas Programme,

A third important feature of modern environmental treaties, an outgrowth of the move toward framework treaties, is their creation of international organizations that "have changed both the process by which international law is made as well as its content."[8] Many environmental treaties call for periodic meetings of the Parties to the treaty and authorize those meetings (typically called a "Conference of the Parties" or a "Meeting of the Parties") to adopt decisions and rules on a wide variety of matters relating to the operation of the treaty. A COP may establish principles for the settlement of disputes involving the operation of the treaty, or it may be authorized to grant various kinds of exemptions from treaty rules. The situation is aptly described by Alvarez:

> A large portion of the rules that we have to govern nations, both those that are formally legally binding and those that are not, are now initiated, formulated, negotiated, interpreted, and often implemented through the efforts of IOs [international organizations]. * * * [A large] body of international rules, most of it generated by these organizations, is now subject to various forms of institutionalized dispute settlement, formal and informal, creating an ever increasing body of judicial and quasi-judicial opinions in discrete areas of the law.[9]

For a comprehensive discussion of this phenomenon, see Robin R. Churchill & Geir Ulfstein, *Autonomous Institutional Arrangements in Multilateral Environmental agreements: a Little-noticed Phenomenon in International Law*, 94 Am. J. Int'l L. 623 (2000).

A fourth development of importance is the rise of global agreements. Although, to be sure, regional agreements are still an important means of addressing regional problems, there has been an explosion of treaties with global membership. Even treaties that would appear to concern directly only a relatively small number of countries have seen their membership explode, although this is not always viewed as a good thing by the original participants. *See, e.g.,* the discussion of the International Whaling Convention in Chapter 1.

Here is a list of a few of the most important environmental treaties ratified in the 30 years from the Stockholm Conference in 1972 to the World

---

8 Jose E. Alvarez, International Organizations as Law-Markers xv (2005).

9 *Id.*

Summit on Sustainable Development, held in Johannesburg, South Africa in September 2002. Several of these treaties are discussed in greater detail in the problems in this book. The dates in parentheses are the dates of adoption and entry into force, respectively. We also include the number of parties as of January 2018.[10] A quick scan will give you a sense of the speed at which international environmental law developed after Stockholm and the breadth of issues it covers. Remember, though, that this is only a fraction of the treaty activity that occurred. In particular, most regional treaties are excluded as are most of the protocols to these treaties.

Convention Concerning the Protection of the World Cultural and Natural Heritage (16 Nov 1972/17 Dec 1975) (193 parties)

Convention on the Prevention of Marine Pollution by Dumping of Wastes and Other Matter (29 Dec 1972/30 Aug 1975) (87 parties)

Convention on International Trade in Endangered Species of Wild Fauna and Flora (CITES) (3 Mar 1973/1 Jul 1975) (183 parties)

International Convention for the Prevention of Pollution from Ships and 1978 Protocol (MARPOL 73/78) (2 Nov 1973/2 Oct 1983) (17 Feb 1978/2 Oct 1983) (156 parties)

Convention on the Conservation of Migratory Species of Wild Animals (23 Jun 1979/1 Nov 1983) (126 parties)

Convention on Long-Range Transboundary Air Pollution (LRTAP) (13 Nov 1979/16 Mar 1983) (51 parties) (multiple protocols to this Convention have been adopted but are not listed here)

Convention on the Conservation of Antarctic Marine Living Resources (20 May 1980/7 Apr 1982) (25 parties)

United Nations Convention on the Law of the Sea (10 Dec 1982/16 Nov 1994) (168 parties)

Vienna Convention for the Protection of the Ozone Layer (22 Mar 1985/22 Sep 1988) (197 parties)

IAEA Convention on Early Notification of a Nuclear Accident (26 Sep 1986/27 Oct 1986) (121 parties)

IAEA Convention on Assistance in the Case of a Nuclear Accident or Radiological Emergency (26 Sep 1986/26 Feb 1987) (115 parties)

Montreal Protocol on Substances that Deplete the Ozone Layer (16 Sep 1987/1 Jan 1989) (197 parties)

---

[10] For purposes of comparison, the United Nations has 193 Member States (as of July 28, 2019).

Basel Convention on the Control of Transboundary Movements of Hazardous Wastes and their Disposal (22 Mar 1989/5 May 1992) (186 parties)

International Convention on Oil Pollution Preparedness, Response and Cooperation (30 Nov 1990/13 May 1995) (112 parties)

Convention on Environmental Impact Assessment in a Transboundary Context (25 Feb 1991/10 Sep 1997) (45 parties)

Protocol on Environmental Protection to the Antarctic Treaty (4 Oct 1991/14 Jan 1998) (40 parties)

Convention on the Protection and Use of Transboundary Watercourses and International Lakes (17 Mar 1992/6 Oct 1996) (42 parties)

Convention on the Transboundary Effects of Industrial Accidents (17 Mar 1992/19 Apr 2000) (41 parties)

United Nations Framework Convention on Climate Change (9 May 1993/21 Mar 1994) (197 parties)

Convention on Biological Diversity (5 Jun 1992/29 Dec 1993) (196 parties)

International Convention on Civil Liability for Oil Pollution Damage, 1992 (27 Nov 1992/30 May 1996) (137 parties)

International Convention on the Establishment of an International Fund for Compensation for Oil Pollution Damage, 1992 (27 Nov 1992/30 May 1996) (115 parties)

United Nations Convention to Combat Desertification in those Countries Experiencing Serious Drought and/or Desertification, Particularly in Africa (17 Jun 1994/26 Dec 1996) (197 parties)

IAEA Convention on Nuclear Safety (20 Sep 1994/24 Oct 1996) (84 parties)

Agreement for the Implementation of the Provisions of the United Nations Convention on the Law of the Sea of 10 December 1982, relating to the Conservation and Management of Straddling Fish Stocks and Highly Migratory Fish Stocks (4 Aug 1995/11 Dec 2001) (88 parties)

Convention on the Law of Non-Navigational Uses of International Watercourses (21 May 1997/17 Aug 2014) (36 parties)

Kyoto Protocol to the United Nations Framework Convention on Climate Change (10 Dec 1997/16 Feb 2005) (192 parties)

Convention on Access to Information, Public Participation in Decision-Making and Access to Justice in Environmental Matters (25 Jun 1998/30 Oct 2001) (47 parties)

Convention on the Prior Informed Consent Procedure for Certain Hazardous Chemicals and Pesticides in International Trade (10 Sep 1998/24 Feb 2004) (160 parties)

Stockholm Convention on Persistent Organic Pollutants (22 May 2001/17 May 2004) (182 parties)

4. SUSTAINABLE DEVELOPMENT

The concept of "sustainable development" is today accepted as a central principle of international environmental law. Although hints of the idea of sustainability can be found in the Stockholm Declaration's discussion of the relationship between environmental protection and development, 'sustainable development' was first articulated as an organizing principle for international environmental law in the Brundtland Commission report (the first reading in this section). The "sustainable development" perspective of the Brundtland Commission report had a powerful impact on participants in the 1992 United Nations Conference on Environment and Development at Rio de Janeiro, and the Rio Declaration reflects that impact, as you will see in the second reading.

WORLD COMMISSION ON ENVIRONMENT AND DEVELOPMENT, OUR COMMON FUTURE[10]

UN Doc A/42/427 (Annex) at 54–60, 73–74 (1987)

Sustainable development is development that meets the needs of the present without compromising the ability of future generations to meet their own needs. It contains within it two key concepts:

- the concept of "needs," in particular the essential needs of the world's poor, to which overriding priority should be given; and
- the idea of limitations imposed by the state of technology and social organization on the environment's ability to meet present and future needs.

Thus the goals of economic and social development must be defined in terms of sustainability in all countries—developed or developing, market-oriented or centrally planned. Interpretations will vary, but must share certain general features and must flow from a consensus on the basic concept of sustainable development and on a broad strategic framework for achieving it.

Development involves a progressive transformation of economy and society. A development path that is sustainable in a physical sense could theoretically be pursued even in a rigid social and political setting. But

[10] Also known as the Brundtland Commission Report, after Norwegian Prime Minister Gro Brundtland, who chaired the Commission.

physical sustainability cannot be secured unless development policies pay attention to such considerations as changes in access to resources and in the distribution of costs and benefits. Even the narrow notion of physical sustainability implies a concern for social equity between generations, a concern that must logically be extended to equity within each generation.

I. The Concept of Sustainable Development

The satisfaction of human needs and aspirations is the major objective of development. The essential needs of vast numbers of people in developing countries—for food, clothing, shelter, jobs—are not being met, and beyond their basic needs these people have legitimate aspirations for an improved quality of life. A world in which poverty and inequity are endemic will always be prone to ecological and other crises. Sustainable development requires meeting the basic needs of all and extending to all the opportunity to satisfy their aspirations for a better life.

Living standards that go beyond the basic minimum are sustainable only if consumption standards everywhere have regard for long-term sustainability. Yet many of us live beyond the world's ecological means, for instance in our patterns of energy use. Perceived needs are socially and culturally determined, and sustainable development requires the promotion of values that encourage consumption standards that are within the bounds of the ecologically possible and to which all can reasonably aspire.

Meeting essential needs depends in part on achieving full growth potential, and sustainable development clearly requires economic growth in places where such needs are not being met. . . . But growth by itself is not enough. High levels of productive activity and widespread poverty can coexist, and can endanger the environment. Hence sustainable development requires that societies meet human needs both by increasing productive potential and by ensuring equitable opportunities for all.

* * *

A society may in many ways compromise its ability to meet the essential needs of its people in the future—by overexploiting resources, for example. The direction of technological developments may solve some immediate problems but lead to even greater ones. Large sections of the population may be marginalized by ill-considered development.

Settled agriculture, the diversion of watercourses, the extraction of minerals, the emission of heat and noxious gases into the atmosphere, commercial forests, and genetic manipulation are all examples of human intervention in natural systems during the course of development. Until recently, such interventions were small in scale and their impact limited. Today's interventions are more drastic in scale and impact, and more threatening to life-support systems both locally and globally. This need not happen. At a minimum, sustainable development must not endanger the natural systems that support life on Earth: the atmosphere, the waters, the soils, and the living beings.

Growth has no set limits in terms of population or resource use beyond which lies ecological disaster. . . . But ultimate limits there are, and sustainability requires that long before these are reached, the world must ensure equitable access to the constrained resource and reorient technological efforts to relieve the pressure.

Economic growth and development obviously involve changes in the physical ecosystem. Every ecosystem everywhere cannot be preserved intact. A forest may be depleted in one part of a watershed and extended elsewhere, which is not a bad thing if the exploitation has been planned and the effects on soil erosion rates, water regimes, and genetic losses have been taken into account. In general, renewable resources like forests and fish stocks need not be depleted provided the rate of use is within the limits of regeneration and natural growth. But most renewable resources are part of a complex and interlinked ecosystem, and maximum sustainable yield must be defined after taking into account system-wide effects of exploitation.

As for non-renewable resources, like fossil fuels and minerals, their use reduces the stock available for future generations. But this does not mean that such resources should not be used. In general the rate of depletion should take into account the criticality of that resource, the availability of technologies for minimizing depletion, and the likelihood of substitutes being available. Thus land should not be degraded beyond reasonable recovery. With minerals and fossil fuels, the rate of depletion and the emphasis on recycling and economy of use should be calibrated to ensure that the resource does not run out before acceptable substitutes are available. Sustainable development requires that the rate of depletion of non-renewable resources should foreclose as few future options as possible.

Development tends to simplify ecosystems and to reduce their diversity of species. And species, once extinct, are not renewable. The loss of plant and animal species can greatly limit the options of future generations; so sustainable development requires the conservation of plant and animal species.

So-called free goods like air and water are also resources. The raw materials and energy of production processes are only partly converted to useful products. The rest comes out as wastes. Sustainable development requires that the adverse impacts on the quality of air, water, and other natural elements are minimized so as to sustain the ecosystem's overall integrity.

In essence, sustainable development is a process of change in which the exploitation of resources, the direction of investments, the orientation of technological development, and institutional change are all in harmony and enhance both current and future potential to meet human needs and aspirations.

* * *

IV. Conclusion

In its broadest sense, the strategy for sustainable development aims to promote harmony among human beings and between humanity and nature. In the specific context of the development and environment crises of the 1980s, which current national and international political and economic institutions have not and perhaps cannot overcome, the pursuit of sustainable development requires:

- a political system that secures effective citizen participation in decision making,
- an economic system that is able to generate surpluses and technical knowledge on a self-reliant and sustained basis,
- a social system that provides for solutions for the tensions arising from disharmonious development,
- a production system that respects the obligation to preserve the ecological base for development,
- an international system that fosters sustainable patterns of trade and finance, and
- an administrative system that is flexible and has the capacity for self-correction.

These requirements are more in the nature of goals that should underlie national and international action on development. What matters is the sincerity with which these goals are pursued and the effectiveness with which departures from them are corrected.

RIO DECLARATION ON ENVIRONMENT AND DEVELOPMENT, PRINCIPLES 1–5

Adopted by consensus by the UN Conference on Environment and Development, 14 June 1992
U.N. Doc. A/CONF.151/26/Rev.1 (Vol. I), annex I (1992) (Basic Document 1.30)

Principle 1

Human beings are at the centre of concerns for sustainable development. They are entitled to a healthy and productive life in harmony with nature.

Principle 2

States have, in accordance with the Charter of the United Nations and the principles of international law, the sovereign right to exploit their own resources pursuant to their own environmental and developmental policies, and the responsibility to ensure that activities within their jurisdiction or control do not cause damage to the environment of other States or of areas beyond the limits of national jurisdiction.

Principle 3

The right to development must be fulfilled so as to equitably meet developmental and environmental needs of present and future generations.

Principle 4

In order to achieve sustainable development, environmental protection shall constitute an integral part of the development process and cannot be considered in isolation from it.

Principle 5

All States and all people shall cooperate in the essential task of eradicating poverty as an indispensable requirement for sustainable development, in order to decrease the disparities in standards of living and better meet the needs of the majority of the people of the world.

DISCUSSION NOTES/QUESTIONS

1. Do you think the first five principles of the Rio Declaration place greater importance on a) environmental protection or b) development? Or is there a fair balance between the two? Some commentators were highly critical, seeing in the Rio Declaration a near abandonment of Stockholm's focus on environmental protection. *See, e.g.,* Marc Pallemearts, *International Environmental Law from Stockholm to Rio: Back to the Future?* 1 Receil 256 (1992).

2. There is ongoing debate about what "sustainability" means. Consider, for example, the following remarks by a leading economist and former U.S. government official:

> The argument that a moral obligation to future generations demands special treatment of environmental investments is fatuous. We can help our descendants as much by improving infrastructure as by preserving rain forests, as much by educating children as by leaving oil in the ground, as much by enlarging our scientific knowledge as by reducing carbon dioxide in the air.

Lawrence Summers, *On Sustainable Growth,* The Economist, 30 May 1992, at 65. If Summers is right, then the choice between building a road and preserving a forest depends on the return on investment that either option would yield. Do you agree? Do we have the tools to appropriately value environmental investments? Do we know how to calculate, for example, the value of the services provided to humans by intact ecosystems, like forests or wetlands? *See* Problem 7-3, *infra.*

3. Nicholas Brunton describes the type of analysis offered by Summers as the "very weak sustainability" position. Under this view, "if the resources of the biosphere (natural capital) are depleted, then this depletion can be substituted by an increase in wealth (man-made capital) or other forms of capital." Nicholas Brunton, *Environmental Regulation: The Challenge Ahead: Governmental Policy Needs to Adopt the 'Strong Sustainability' Ecological Principle,* 1999 Alt. L. J. 24 (1999). A "weak sustainability" position takes the view that "sustained economic growth is possible without environmental damage if consideration of environmental impacts [is] systematically integrated into economic decisions." Appropriate government actions to protect "ecosystem stability and resilience" should be adopted, but that can be done without unduly retraining development. A "strong sustainability" approach, on the other hand, argues that "economic growth cannot continue with current patterns of resource use and waste production, and that fundamental changes to society, the economy and its institutions are required." Finally, the "very strong sustainability" position "emphasizes that economic and population growth ought to be close to zero" because the planet has reached the limit of its carrying capacity. *Id.* Are either the "strong sustainability" or the "very strong sustainability" approaches consistent with sustainable development? Don't those approaches take the view, in essence, that further economic development is unsustainable? Where on this spectrum of approaches to sustainability do you find yourself? What are the risks of your position to the environment? To the reasonable desire of developing nations to rise out of poverty?

5. ADJUDICATION OF ENVIRONMENTAL ISSUES

Since 1972, there have been quite a large number of disputes about environmental matters that have been the subject of international judicial opinions. Although these cases generally have been decided on the basis of treaty law, the environmental principles and rules discussed previously have often influenced the outcome. Even when adjudicators are unwilling to conclude that a particular principle is part of customary international law, they may find that the principle is implicit in the treaty provisions being interpreted. We here reproduce excerpts from three illustrative cases.

THE GABCÍKOVO-NAGYMAROS PROJECT (HUNGARY V. SLOVAKIA)

1997 ICJ 7 (Sept. 25)

[*Eds.*—The Danube River is the second longest river in Europe. It originates in the Black Forest Mountains of Germany and flows east to the Black Sea, passing through nine countries (Germany, Austria, Slovakia, Hungary, Croatia, Serbia, Bulgaria, Romania, and Ukraine) on the way. The river is navigable for most of its course, and three national capitals (Vienna, Budapest, and Belgrade) are built on its banks. The Danube has been used for commercial transportation for centuries. It is also used by several nations for hydroelectric power generation, for agricultural irrigation, and as a dump for industrial and other wastes. Both accidental and intentional pollution have caused grave harm to the Danube's ecosystem and sometimes rendered its waters unfit for drinking or irrigation.

In 1977, the Hungarian People's Republic and the Czechoslovak People's Republic signed a treaty "aimed at the production of hydroelectricity, the improvement of navigation on the relevant section of the Danube, and the protection of the areas along the banks against flooding." The treaty called for the construction of two hydroelectric power plants, one at Gabcíkovo, in Czechoslovakia, and one at Nagymaros, in Hungary. A system of locks and dams was to be constructed to support each power plant.

The dam that was to support the Gabcíkovo power plant (in Czechoslovakia) was to be built at Dunakiliti, in Hungary, with a resulting reservoir stretching upstream into Czechoslovakia. Water was to be diverted from the Danube (and the reservoir) via a bypass canal (in Czechoslovak territory). The Gabcíkovo power plant and the Gabcíkovo System of Locks (for navigation of boats and barges) were to be constructed on the bypass, and the water was to be returned to the old bed of the Danube downstream. The Nagymaros portion of the project (including locks and a hydroelectric power plant) was to be built downstream of the Gabcíkovo/Dunakiliti works, entirely in Hungarian territory.

The parties regarded the Gabcíkovo/Nagymaros Project as "a single and indivisible operational system of works." They agreed to participate equally in the cost of the works and in sharing the power created by the hydroelectric plants. They also "undertook to ensure that the quality of water in the Danube" would not be impaired by the Project, and "that compliance with the obligations for the protection of nature arising in connection with the construction and operation of the System of Locks would be observed."

Work on the Project started in 1978. In 1983, work was slowed by mutual agreement, and the date for putting the power plants into operation was postponed. In February 1989, however, the parties agreed to accelerate the project. But that plan was undermined by an emerging concern for the environment (and worries about the adverse environmental consequences of development projects) that swept Eastern Europe during this time.]

Excerpts from the Judgment of the Court

32. In the wake of the profound political and economic changes which occurred ... in central Europe [around 1989 and thereafter], the Gabcíkovo-Nagymaros Project was the object, in Czechoslovakia and more particularly in Hungary, of increasing apprehension, both within a section of public opinion and in some scientific circles. The uncertainties not only

about the economic viability of the Project, but also, and more so, as to the guarantees it offered for preservation of the environment, engendered a climate of growing concern and opposition with regard to the Project.

33. It was against this background that, on 13 May 1989, the Government of Hungary adopted a resolution to suspend works at Nagymaros. . . .

* * *

[*Eds.*—Hungary and Czechoslovakia negotiated over the fate of the project for the next four years, during which no agreement was reached and Hungary persisted in its refusal to complete the project. In early 1993, Hungary and Slovakia (then a newly independent state) agreed to submit their dispute to the ICJ for decision. There were multiple issues in the case, including whether Hungary's suspension of work on the project was a violation of the 1977 Treaty.]

40. Throughout the proceedings, Hungary contended that . . . it never suspended the application of the 1977 Treaty itself. To justify its conduct, it relied essentially on a "state of ecological necessity."

* * *

50. In the present case, the Parties are in agreement in considering that the existence of a state of necessity must be evaluated in the light of the criteria laid down by the International Law Commission in Article 33 of the Draft Articles on the International Responsibility of States that it adopted on first reading. That provision is worded as follows:

Article 33. State of necessity

1. A state of necessity may not be invoked by a State as a ground for precluding the wrongfulness of an act of that State not in conformity with an international obligation of the State unless:

(a) the act was the only means of safeguarding an essential interest of the State against a grave and imminent peril; and

(b) the act did not seriously impair an essential interest of the State towards which the obligation existed.

2. In any case, a state of necessity may not be invoked by a State as a ground for precluding wrongfulness:

(a) if the international obligation with which the act of the State is not in conformity arises out of a peremptory norm of general international law; or

(b) if the international obligation with which the act of the State is not in conformity is laid down by a treaty which, explicitly or implicitly, excludes the possibility of invoking the state of necessity with respect to that obligation; or

(c) if the State in question has contributed to the occurrence of the state of necessity."

In its Commentary, the Commission defined the "state of necessity" as being

> the situation of a State whose sole means of safeguarding an essential interest threatened by a grave and imminent peril is to adopt conduct not in conformity with what is required of it by an international obligation to another State (ibid., para. 1).

It concluded that "the notion of state of necessity is . . . deeply rooted in general legal thinking."

51. The Court considers, first of all, that the state of necessity is a ground recognized by customary international law for precluding the wrongfulness of an act not in conformity with an international obligation. It observes moreover that such ground for precluding wrongfulness can only be accepted on an exceptional basis. . . .

* * *

52. In the present case, the following basic conditions set forth in Draft Article 33 are relevant: it must have been occasioned by an "essential interest" of the State which is the author of the act conflicting with one of its international obligations; that interest must have been threatened by a "grave and imminent peril"; the act being challenged must have been the "only means" of safeguarding that interest; that act must not have "seriously impair[ed] an essential interest" of the State towards which the obligation existed; and the State which is the author of that act must not have "contributed to the occurrence of the state of necessity". Those conditions reflect customary international law. . . .

* * *

57. The Court [evaluated the environmental concerns raised by Hungary and concluded] that, with respect to both Nagymaros and Gabcíkovo, the perils invoked by Hungary, without prejudging their possible gravity, were not sufficiently established in 1989, nor were they "imminent"; and that Hungary had available to it at that time means of responding to these perceived perils other than the suspension and abandonment of works with which it had been entrusted. What is more, negotiations were under way which might have led to a review of the Project and the extension of some of its time-limits, without there being need to abandon it. . . .

Moreover, the Court notes that Hungary decided to conclude the 1977 Treaty . . . [and that] Hungary was . . . presumably aware of the situation as then known, [including the existence of environmental risks], when it assumed its obligations under the Treaty. Hungary contended before the

Court that [earlier environmental] studies had been inadequate and that the state of knowledge at that time was not such as to make possible a complete evaluation of the ecological implications of the Gabcíkovo-Nagymaros Project. It is nonetheless the case that although the principal object of the 1977 Treaty was the construction of a System of Locks for the production of electricity, improvement of navigation on the Danube and protection against flooding, the need to ensure the protection of the environment had not escaped the parties, as can be seen from Articles 15, 19 and 20 of the Treaty.

* * *

59. In the light of the conclusions reached above, the Court . . . finds that Hungary was not entitled to suspend and subsequently abandon, in 1989, the works on the Nagymaros Project and on the part of the Gabcíkovo Project for which the 1977 Treaty and related instruments attributed responsibility to it.

* * *

104. Hungary further argued that it was entitled to invoke a number of events which, cumulatively, would have constituted a fundamental change of circumstances [justifying its failure to perform the treaty]. In this respect it specified profound changes of a political nature, the Project's diminishing economic viability, the progress of environmental knowledge and the development of new norms and prescriptions of international environmental law. . . .

* * *

The prevailing political situation was certainly relevant for the conclusion of the 1977 Treaty. But the Court will recall that the Treaty provided for a joint investment programme for the production of energy, the control of floods and the improvement of navigation on the Danube. In the Court's view, the prevalent political conditions were thus not so closely linked to the object and purpose of the Treaty that they constituted an essential basis of the consent of the parties and, in changing, radically altered the extent of the obligations still to be performed. The same holds good for the economic system in force at the time of the conclusion of the 1977 Treaty. Besides, even though the estimated profitability of the Project might have appeared less in 1992 than in 1977, it does not appear from the record before the Court that it was bound to diminish to such an extent that the treaty obligations of the parties would have been radically transformed as a result.

The Court does not consider that new developments in the state of environmental knowledge and of environmental law can be said to have been completely unforeseen. What is more, the formulation of Articles 15, 19 and 20, designed to accommodate change, made it possible for the parties to take account of such developments and to apply them when implementing those treaty provisions.

[Thus, the] changed circumstances advanced by Hungary are, in the Court's view, not of such a nature, either individually or collectively, that their effect would radically transform the extent of the obligations still to be performed in order to accomplish the Project. A fundamental change of circumstances must have been unforeseen; the existence of the circumstances at the time of the Treaty's conclusion must have constituted an essential basis of the consent of the parties to be bound by the Treaty. The negative and conditional wording of Article 62 of the Vienna Convention on the Law of Treaties is a clear indication moreover that the stability of treaty relations requires that the plea of fundamental change of circumstances be applied only in exceptional cases.

* * *

111. Finally, the Court will address Hungary's claim that it was entitled to terminate the 1977 Treaty because new requirements of international law for the protection of the environment precluded performance of the Treaty.

112. Neither of the Parties contended that new peremptory norms of environmental law had emerged since the conclusion of the 1977 Treaty, and the Court will consequently not be required to examine the scope of Article 64 of the Vienna Convention on the Law of Treaties. On the other hand, the Court wishes to point out that newly developed norms of environmental law are relevant for the implementation of the Treaty and that the parties could, by agreement, incorporate them through the application of Articles 15, 19 and 20 of the Treaty. These articles do not contain specific obligations of performance but require the parties, in carrying out their obligations to ensure that the quality of water in the Danube is not impaired and that nature is protected, to take new environmental norms into consideration when agreeing upon the means to be specified in the Joint Contractual Plan.

By inserting these evolving provisions in the Treaty, the parties recognized the potential necessity to adapt the Project. Consequently, the Treaty is not static, and is open to adapt to emerging norms of international law. By means of Articles 15 and 19, new environmental norms can be incorporated in the Joint Contractual Plan.

* * *

139. The Court is of the opinion that the Parties are under a legal obligation [to conduct negotiations] to consider, within the context of the 1977 Treaty, in what way the multiple objectives of the Treaty can best be served, keeping in mind that all of them should be fulfilled.

140. It is clear that the Project's impact upon, and its implications for, the environment are of necessity a key issue. The numerous scientific reports which have been presented to the Court by the Parties—even if their conclusions are often contradictory—provide abundant evidence that this impact and these implications are considerable.

In order to evaluate the environmental risks, current standards must be taken into consideration. This is not only allowed by the wording of Articles 15 and 19, but even prescribed, to the extent that these articles impose a continuing—and thus necessarily evolving—obligation on the parties to maintain the quality of the water of the Danube and to protect nature.

The Court is mindful that, in the field of environmental protection, vigilance and prevention are required on account of the often irreversible character of damage to the environment and of the limitations inherent in the very mechanism of reparation of this type of damage.

Throughout the ages, mankind has, for economic and other reasons, constantly interfered with nature. In the past, this was often done without consideration of the effects upon the environment. Owing to new scientific insights and to a growing awareness of the risks for mankind—for present and future generations—of pursuit of such interventions at an unconsidered and unabated pace, new norms and standards have been developed, set forth in a great number of instruments during the last two decades. Such new norms have to be taken into consideration, and such new standards given proper weight, not only when States contemplate new activities but also when continuing with activities begun in the past. This need to reconcile economic development with protection of the environment is aptly expressed in the concept of sustainable development.

For the purposes of the present case, this means that the Parties together should look afresh at the effects on the environment of the operation of the Gabcíkovo power plant. In particular they must find a satisfactory solution for the volume of water to be released into the old bed of the Danube and into the side-arms on both sides of the river.

DISCUSSION NOTES/QUESTIONS

1. Hungary sought to justify its refusal to complete the Gabcíkovo/ Nagymaros project on the basis of the environmental harm the project would cause. Among other legal theories, it claimed that the potential environmental harm created a state of "ecological necessity" warranting suspension of the project. It also argued that the environmental harm, coupled with the dramatic change in the political situation following the fall of the Berlin Wall and the collapse of the communist system in Eastern Europe, constituted a "fundamental change of circumstances" warranting its withdrawal from the

treaty. *See* Vienna Convention on the Law of Treaties, art. 62 **(Basic Document 1.14)**. Why did the Court reject those arguments?

2. Toward the end of its opinion, the Court acknowledges that new international standards require that states "reconcile economic development with protection of the environment." Hungary's position was that suspension of the treaty is the only way to accomplish that goal. What is the Court's response? For a critique, *see* Stephen Stec & Gabriel Eckstein, *Of Solemn Oaths and Obligations: The Environmental Impact of the ICJ's Decision in the Case of the Gabcíkovo-Nagymaros Project,* 8 Yearbook Int'l Envtl. L. 41 (1998).

3. The Court directed Hungary and Slovakia to negotiate. As of this writing (June 2019), they still have not reached agreement and the Hungarian portions of the project remain uncompleted.

UNITED STATES—IMPORT PROHIBITION OF CERTAIN SHRIMP AND SHRIMP PRODUCTS

WTO Appellate Body Report, 12 October 1998
WTO Doc WT/DS58/AB/R

[*Eds.*—The United States required domestic shrimp trawlers to equip their nets with turtle excluder devices (TEDs) to prevent the nets from entrapping sea turtles and drowning them. The United States also banned importation of shrimp from other countries unless those countries had similar requirements in place for their shrimp trawlers. India, Malaysia, Pakistan and Thailand filed a complaint alleging that the shrimp import restrictions violated the rules of an international trade agreement known as the General Agreement on Tariffs and Trade, or GATT 1994.

The US claimed that its ban on shrimp imports from states that did not require shrimp trawlers to use TEDs was justified under GATT Article XX, which authorizes the imposition of trade restrictions "relating to the conservation of exhaustible natural resources." A central question in the case was whether "sea turtles" were an "exhaustible natural resource" within the meaning of that GATT provision.]

Excerpts from the Appellate Body Report

114. [The "customary rules of interpretation of public international law"] call for an examination of the ordinary meaning of the words of a treaty, read in their context, and in the light of the object and purpose of the treaty involved. A treaty interpreter must begin with, and focus upon, the text of the particular provision to be interpreted. . . . Where the meaning imparted by the text itself is equivocal or inconclusive, or where confirmation of the correctness of the reading of the text itself is desired, light from the object and purpose of the treaty as a whole may usefully be sought.

* * *

127. We begin with the threshold question of whether Section 609 is a measure concerned with the conservation of "exhaustible natural resources" within the meaning of Article XX(g). . . . India, Pakistan and Thailand contended that a "reasonable interpretation" of the term "exhaustible" is that the term refers to "finite resources such as minerals, rather than biological or renewable resources." In their view, such finite resources were exhaustible "because there was a limited supply which could and would be depleted unit for unit as the resources were consumed." Moreover, they argued, if "all" natural resources were considered to be exhaustible, the term "exhaustible" would become superfluous. They also referred to the drafting history of Article XX(g), and, in particular, to the mention of minerals, such as manganese, in the context of arguments made by some delegations that "export restrictions" should be permitted for the preservation of scarce natural resources. . . .

128. We are not convinced by these arguments. Textually, Article XX(g) is *not* limited to the conservation of "mineral" or "non-living" natural resources. The complainants' principal argument is rooted in the notion that "living" natural resources are "renewable" and therefore cannot be "exhaustible" natural resources. We do not believe that "exhaustible" natural resources and "renewable" natural resources are mutually exclusive. One lesson that modern biological sciences teach us is that living species, though in principle, capable of reproduction and, in that sense, "renewable' " are in certain circumstances indeed susceptible of depletion, exhaustion and extinction, frequently because of human activities. Living resources are just as "finite" as petroleum, iron ore and other non-living resources.

129. The words of Article XX(g), "exhaustible natural resources' " were actually crafted more than 50 years ago. They must be read by a treaty interpreter in the light of contemporary concerns of the community of nations about the protection and conservation of the environment. . . . The preamble of the WTO Agreement—which informs not only the GATT 1994, but also the other covered agreements—explicitly acknowledges "the objective of *sustainable development*":

* * *

130. From the perspective embodied in the preamble of the *WTO Agreement*, we note that the generic term "natural resources" in Article XX(g) is not "static" in its content or reference but is rather "by definition, evolutionary." It is, therefore, pertinent to note that modern international conventions and declarations make frequent references to natural resources as embracing both living and non-living resources. For instance, the 1982 United Nations Convention on the Law of the Sea ("UNCLOS") **[Basic Document 3.4]**, in [Article 56, 61 and 62] repeatedly refers . . . to "living resources" in specifying rights and duties of states in their exclusive

economic zones. The Convention on Biological Diversity uses the concept of "biological resources." Agenda 21 speaks most broadly of "natural resources" and goes into detailed statements about "marine living resources". . . .

131. Given the recent acknowledgement by the international community of the importance of concerted bilateral or multilateral action to protect living natural resources, and recalling the explicit recognition by WTO Members of the objective of sustainable development in the preamble of the *WTO Agreement*, we believe it is too late in the day to suppose that Article XX(g) of the GATT 1994 may be read as referring only to the conservation of exhaustible mineral or other non-living natural resources. Moreover, two adopted GATT 1947 panel reports previously found fish to be an "exhaustible natural resource" within the meaning of Article XX(g). We hold that, in line with the principle of effectiveness in treaty interpretation, measures to conserve exhaustible natural resources, whether *living* or *non-living*, may fall within Article XX(g).

132. We turn next to the issue of whether the living natural resources sought to be conserved by the measure are "exhaustible" under Article XX(g). That this element is present in respect of the five species of sea turtles here involved appears to be conceded by all the participants and third participants in this case. The exhaustibility of sea turtles would in fact have been very difficult to controvert since all of the seven recognized species of sea turtles are today listed in Appendix 1 of the Convention on International Trade in Endangered Species of Wild Fauna and Flora ("CITES"). The list in Appendix 1 includes "all species *threatened with extinction* which are or may be affected by trade" (emphasis added).

* * *

DISCUSSION NOTES/QUESTIONS

1. According to the WTO Appellate Body, the "customary rules of interpretation" of treaties are the rules codified in Articles 31 and 32 of the Vienna Convention on the Law of Treaties **(Basic Document 1.14)**. Vienna Convention article 31(3)(c) calls upon treaty interpreters to take into account "any relevant rules of international law applicable in the relations between the parties." In this case, the Appellate Body relied heavily on developments in international environmental law in reaching the conclusion that the phrase "exhaustible natural resources" included living species that are regarded as "threatened with extinction." What if one or more of the complaining countries is not a signatory or a party to the environmental instruments on which the Appellate Body relied? Could the Appellate Body still rely on international environmental law to support its treaty interpretation?

2. Here, the WTO Appellate Body relies on background legal principles relating to environmental protection to interpret key provisions of a trade

agreement. A somewhat similar interpretive approach was taken in the *North Atlantic Coast Fisheries Case* and the *Lake Lanoux Arbitration, supra.* In both those cases, the arbitrators invoked the international law principle of sovereignty to reject treaty interpretations that would have subjected Canadian and French decisions about the management of resources within their borders to a requirement that those decisions be made with the consent of other affected nations. In each case, the background principle of sovereignty guided the arbitrators away from an interpretation that would impinge on sovereignty in a fundamental way.

3. The language that the WTO Appellate Body was interpreting was written 50 years prior to its decision. Yet the Appellate Body turned to "contemporary concerns of the community of nations about the protection and conservation of the environment" for guidance in interpreting that old language. Is this justified? In the case of the GATT, perhaps, because the GATT was "readopted" in 1994 as part of the Agreement Creating the World Trade Organization, and that Agreement expressly mentioned concern for "sustainable development."

But suppose an agreement that was adopted 50 years or more in the past and was not "reenacted" or renewed in any way. Should such an agreement be interpreted as it would have been understood at the time of adoption? Or should it be interpreted in light of contemporary concerns?

This question arose in a dispute between Belgium and the Netherlands over Belgium's desire to reactivate a railroad that ran through a portion of the Netherlands. The treaty at issue was adopted in 1839. The issues in the dispute were whether a) the Netherland's treaty obligation to allow activation of the railroad limited its right to impose environmental protection measures on the railroad and b) whether Belgium's treaty obligation to bear the "cost and expense" of "agreed works" on the railroad line included an obligation to pay for environmental protection measures. *See Iron Rhine Railway Arbitration (Belg. V. Neth.),* 27 UNRIAA 127 (24 May 2005).

Applying the interpretive rule in Article 31(3)(c) of the Vienna Convention (see note 1, *supra*), the Tribunal concluded that contemporary international environmental law imposed on states "a duty to prevent, or at least mitigate" any "significant harm to the environment" that might be caused by development. Accordingly, Belgium's right to reactivate the railway line in question must be exercised in a way that took into account "the environmental protection measures necessitated by the intended use of the railway line" and that "fully integrated" those measures "into the project and its costs." *Id.* at paragraphs 58, 59 and 223.

But what about the fact that the treaty in question was adopted long before such environmental concerns existed? The Tribunal said the following:

> [The intertemporal rule with respect to treaty interpretation provides that] regard should be had in interpreting [the treaty provisions] to juridical facts as they stood in 1839. . . . [But it] has long been

> established that the understanding of conceptual or generic terms in a treaty may be seen as "an essentially relative question; it depends on the development of international relations." . . . Some terms are "not static," but were "by definition evolutionary. . . ." Where a term can be classified as generic "the presumption necessarily arises that its meaning was intended to follow the evolution of the law. . . ."
>
> In the present case it is not a conceptual or generic term that is in issue, but rather new technical developments relating to the operation and capacity of the railway. But here, too, it seems that an evolutive interpretation, which would ensure an application of the treaty that would be effective in terms of its object and purpose, will be preferred to a strict application of the intertemporal rule."

Id. at paragraphs 79–80. Do you agree? In applying the rule that treaties should take account of other rules of international law that are applicable between the parties, should a treaty interpreter focus only on the rules that existed when the treaty was adopted? Or is it permissible to consider new rules of international law that emerged decades after the treaty was adopted? Does it depend on the nature of the treaty provision in question?

PULP MILLS ON THE RIVER URUGUAY (ARGENTINA V. URUGUAY)

2010 I.C.J. 18 (Apr. 20)

[*Eds.* Argentina brought an action complaining that Uruguay's construction of two pulp mills on the River Uruguay, which forms the border between the two countries, had been authorized and conducted in violation of an agreement between the two countries concerning use of the River (the "1975 Statute") and would, or had, caused damage to the quality of the river's waters.

In Chapter 3, we reproduced excerpts from the case in which the Court concluded that Uruguay had not violated its treaty obligation to "protect and preserve the aquatic environment and, in particular, to prevent its pollution." The following excerpts consider whether Uruguay fulfilled its procedural obligations under the treaty and customary law.]

26. The boundary between Argentina and Uruguay in the River Uruguay is defined by the bilateral Treaty entered into for that purpose at Montevideo on 7 April 1961 . . . Article 7 [of the Treaty] provides for the establishment by the parties of a "régime for the use of the river" covering various subjects, including the conservation of living resources and the prevention of water pollution of the river. . . .

27. The "régime for the use of the river" contemplated in Article 7 of the 1961 Treaty was established through the 1975 Statute. . . . Article 1 of the 1975 Statute states that the parties adopted it "in order to establish the joint machinery necessary for the optimum and rational utilization of

the River Uruguay, in strict observance of the rights and obligations arising from treaties and other international agreements in force for each of the parties." . . . The 1975 Statute sets up the Administrative Commission of the River Uruguay (hereinafter "CARU",. . . .)

* * *

III. THE ALLEGED BREACH OF PROCEDURAL OBLIGATIONS

81. . . . [Articles 7–12 of the Statute impose] procedural obligations of informing, notifying and negotiating [under the auspices of CARU]. . . . These obligations are all the more vital when a shared resource is at issue, as in the case of the River Uruguay, which can only be protected through close and continuous co-operation between the riparian States.

* * *

101. The Court points out that the principle of prevention, as a customary rule, has its origins in the due diligence that is required of a State in its territory. It is "every State's obligation not to allow knowingly its territory to be used for acts contrary to the rights of other States" (Corfu Channel (United Kingdom v. Albania), Merits, Judgment, I.C.J. Reports 1949, p. 22). A State is thus obliged to use all the means at its disposal in order to avoid activities which take place in its territory, or in any area under its jurisdiction, causing significant damage to the environment of another State. . . .

102. In the view of the Court, the obligation to inform CARU allows for the initiation of co-operation between the Parties which is necessary in order to fulfil the obligation of prevention. . . .

* * *

106. The Court observes that, in the present case, Uruguay did not transmit to CARU the information required by Article 7, first paragraph, in respect of the CMB (ENCE) and Orion (Botnia) mills, despite the requests made to it by the Commission to that effect on several occasions[.] . . .

* * *

119. The Court notes that the environmental impact assessments which are necessary to reach a decision on any plan that is liable to cause significant transboundary harm to another State must be notified by the party concerned to the other party, through CARU, pursuant to Article 7, second and third paragraphs, of the 1975 Statute. This notification is intended to enable the notified party to participate in the process of ensuring that the assessment is complete, so that it can then consider the

plan and its effects with a full knowledge of the facts (Article 8 of the 1975 Statute).

* * *

121. In the present case, the Court observes that the notification to Argentina of the environmental impact assessments for the CMB (ENCE) and Orion (Botnia) mills did not take place through CARU, and that Uruguay only transmitted those assessments to Argentina after having issued the initial environmental authorizations for the two mills in question. . . . Uruguay ought not, prior to notification, to have issued the initial environmental authorizations and the authorizations for construction on the basis of the environmental impact assessments submitted to DINAMA. Indeed by doing so, Uruguay gave priority to its own legislation over its procedural obligations under the 1975 Statute and disregarded the well-established customary rule reflected in Article 27 of the Vienna Convention on the Law of Treaties, according to which "[a] party may not invoke the provisions of its internal law as justification for its failure to perform a treaty."

122. The Court concludes from the above that Uruguay failed to comply with its obligation to notify the plans to Argentina through CARU under Article 7, second and third paragraphs, of the 1975 Statute.

* * *

139. . . . [T]he negotiation provided for in Article 12 of the 1975 Statute forms part of the overall procedure laid down in Articles 7 to 12, which is structured in such a way that the parties, in association with CARU, are able, at the end of the process, to fulfil their obligation to prevent any significant transboundary harm which might be caused by potentially harmful activities planned by either one of them.

* * *

144. [A]s long as the procedural mechanism for co-operation between the parties to prevent significant damage to one of them is taking its course, the State initiating the planned activity is obliged not to authorize such work and, a fortiori, not to carry it out.

* * *

149. The Court concludes from the above . . . that by authorizing the construction of the mills and the port terminal at Fray Bentos before the expiration of the period of negotiation, Uruguay failed to comply with the obligation to negotiate laid down by Article 12 of the Statute. Consequently, Uruguay disregarded the whole of the co-operation mechanism provided for in Articles 7 to 12 of the 1975 Statute.

* * *

204. It is the opinion of the Court that in order for the Parties properly to comply with their obligations under Article 41 (a) and (b) of the 1975 Statute [to prevent pollution], they must, for the purposes of protecting and preserving the aquatic environment with respect to activities which may be liable to cause transboundary harm, carry out an environmental impact assessment. As the Court has observed in the case concerning the Dispute Regarding Navigational and Related Rights,

> there are situations in which the parties' intent upon conclusion of the treaty was, or may be presumed to have been, to give the terms used—or some of them—a meaning or content capable of evolving, not one fixed once and for all, so as to make allowance for, among other things, developments in international law (Dispute Regarding Navigational and Related Rights (Costa Rica v. Nicaragua), Judgment of 13 July 2009, para. 64).

In this sense, the obligation to protect and preserve, under Article 41 (a) of the Statute, has to be interpreted in accordance with a practice, which in recent years has gained so much acceptance among States that it may now be considered a requirement under general international law to undertake an environmental impact assessment where there is a risk that the proposed industrial activity may have a significant adverse impact in a transboundary context, in particular, on a shared resource. Moreover, due diligence, and the duty of vigilance and prevention which it implies, would not be considered to have been exercised, if a party planning works liable to affect the régime of the river or the quality of its waters did not undertake an environmental impact assessment on the potential effects of such works.

205. The Court observes that neither the 1975 Statute nor general international law specify the scope and content of an environmental impact assessment. . . . Consequently, it is the view of the Court that it is for each State to determine in its domestic legislation or in the authorization process for the project, the specific content of the environmental impact assessment required in each case, having regard to the nature and magnitude of the proposed development and its likely adverse impact on the environment as well as to the need to exercise due diligence in conducting such an assessment. The Court also considers that an environmental impact assessment must be conducted prior to the implementation of a project. Moreover, once operations have started and, where necessary, throughout the life of the project, continuous monitoring of its effects on the environment shall be undertaken.

DISCUSSION NOTES/QUESTIONS

1. Note that in this case, as in previous cases, the tribunal turns to modern international environmental law to give meaning to the provisions of

a treaty adopted several years before that law developed. How does it deal with the "intertemporal" issue discussed in the *Iron Rhine Railway Arbitration* (*see* note 3 following the previous case). Do you think the Court's rejection of the intertemporal rule and adoption of an evolutionary approach to treaty interpretation was appropriate? Was its use of background principles of international environmental law persuasive or useful? Was the result consistent with the "object and purpose" of the underlying treaty as it is described in paragraphs 26 and 27 of the opinion?

2. The Court says that "it may now be considered a requirement under general international law to undertake an environmental impact assessment where there is a risk that the proposed industrial activity may have a significant adverse impact in a transboundary context, in particular, on a shared resource." The Court's basis for this conclusion is its unsupported claim that environmental impact assessment is "a practice" that has "gained so much acceptance among States" that it may be considered part of customary international law. Do you think the Court is correct?

3. There are three additional post-Stockholm cases that are of interest because of their use or application of some of the principles discussed in section B.2, *supra*. Although space precludes us from reproducing them at length, a short summary of each case is provided here.

In the *Southern Bluefin Tuna Cases* (NZ v. Japan; Aust. v. Japan) (Provisional Measures), ITLOS Cases Nos. 3 & 4 (27 Aug. 1999) the International Tribunal for the Law of the Sea (ITLOS) concluded that the parties should, in the face of "scientific uncertainty" about the state of the southern Bluefin tuna fishery, "act with prudence and caution to ensure that effective conservation measures are taken." In an apparently deliberate attempt to avoid deciding whether precaution is a requirement of customary international law, the Tribunal's opinion did not mention the phrase "precautionary principle" or "precautionary approach." Two concurring judges expressed the view that the adoption of a "precautionary approach" was appropriate whether or not the precautionary principle was a part of customary international law. On 4 August 2000, an Arbitral Tribunal constituted under Annex VII of UNCLOS determined that it lacked jurisdiction over the dispute and terminated the provisional measures (which were based on the assumption that an UNCLOS tribunal would have jurisdiction). *See Southern Bluefin Tuna (New Zealand-Japan, Australia-Japan)*, 23 UNRIAA 1 (4 August 2000).

In *The MOX Plant Case (Ire v. UK) (Provisional Measures)*, ITLOS Case No. 10, (3 December 2001), ITLOS issued provisional measures in a case concerning a UK facility for reprocessing nuclear fuel (the "MOX Plant") that planned to make radioactive discharges into ocean waters. The provisional measures directed the disputing parties to cooperate by entering into consultations, exchanging information on the environmental risks of the activities in question, monitoring those risks, and devising measures to prevent pollution. In so doing, the Tribunal "identified the duty to cooperate as a fundamental principle [under UNCLOS] and general international law." (Joint Declaration of Judges Caminos, Yamamoto, Park, Akl, Marsit, Eiriksson and Jesus). The case was terminated on 6 June 2008, following Ireland's withdrawal of its claim.

In 2003, in another case involving the MOX Plant, an Arbitral Tribunal considered the scope of the "access to information" provisions of the 1992 Convention for the Protection of the Marine Environment of the North-East Atlantic (the Ospar Convention). Those provisions require Contracting Parties to make available information "on the state of the maritime area" and "on activities or measures adversely affecting or likely to affect" the maritime area covered by the Convention. Ireland had asked the UK to provide it with copies of a report prepared by British Nuclear Fuels, plc (BNFL), concerning the "economic justification for the MOX Plant." The report had been released, but with substantial redactions of material that BNFL felt would damage its "commercial operations" or the "economic case for the MOX plant" if released. Over a strong dissent, a majority of the Tribunal concluded that the redacted information (which concerned business and commercial aspects of the plant's operation) was not "information" that was subject to disclosure under the agreement because it was not "information . . . on the state of the maritime area." *Dispute Concerning Access to Information Under Article 9 of the OSPAR Convention (Ire. V. UK),* 23 UNRIAA 59 at paragraphs 163 & 168 (2 July 2003). The dissent pointed out that the economic information was necessary to an assessment of whether the anticipated environmental harm from the project was "legitimate" and whether the project "should be authorized." Thus, he concluded, the economic information was of "direct relevance to the state of the marine environment," as it would determine whether pollution of that environment would be allowed or not. *Id.*, dissenting opinion of Gavan Griffith, at paragraph 111.

C. THE FUTURE

The sheer number of treaties and other international instruments that address environmental problems is impressive. The documentary supplement to the third edition of this Coursebook was over 1500 pages long, and it did not include all that it could have.

But the pace of progress in solving global environmental problems has not matched the pace of lawmaking. While we have made real progress in some areas (e.g., repair of the ozone layer), other problems have worsened, despite the existence of laws and legal regimes aimed specifically at solving those problems. For example, we are nowhere close to a solution of the problem of climate change. Human emissions of greenhouse gases grow every year, despite our knowledge of the disaster that awaits if we do not stop that trend and despite the adoption of three important multilateral agreements on the subject. Similarly, the planet is losing its biodiversity at an unprecedented rate, again despite the existence of many global and regional treaties devoted to preserving biodiversity and reducing human threats to the survival of other species.

The question naturally presents itself: what is the international community doing wrong and what can it do better? Although we don't pretend to have any definitive answer to this question, we share here some thoughts by a number of scholars who have tried to understand why our progress on global environmental issues is so slow and what we might do to improve the situation.

In the first reading, Sir Geoffrey Palmer (one of the authors of this coursebook) recommends the creation of a new international organization, dedicated to addressing environmental problems, and given the authority to set international standards and take measures to secure compliance with those standards. The second reading discusses the problem of "treaty fatigue." The final reading argues that the problem is more fundamental—the author contends that environmental protection is no longer a priority on the global agenda. Following these readings, we offer a possible solution—a blueprint for the international environmental organization envisioned by Sir Geoffrey over 25 years ago.

NEW WAYS TO MAKE INTERNATIONAL ENVIRONMENTAL LAW

SIR GEOFFREY W.R. PALMER
87 AJIL 259, 259–60, 262, 264, 273–74, 278–81 (1992)

The purpose of this article is to suggest new ways to make international law for the environment. The existing methods are slow, cumbersome, expensive, uncoordinated and uncertain. Something better must be found if the environmental challenges the world faces are to be dealt with successfully. . . .

As matters stand today, we lack many of the necessary rules and the means for devising them; we lack institutions capable of ensuring that the rules we have are effective. I do not wish to sound apocalyptic. In fact, the proposals put forward here build on existing international law and institutions. But * * * unless we devise a better way to make international law for the environment, future progress is likely to be piecemeal, fitful, unsystematic and even random. If the appropriate steps are not taken now, the manifestly unsatisfactory situation we have will limp toward crisis. Assuredly, action will be necessary in the end; it will be easier if we start soon.

* * *

. . . [T]he United Nations lacks any coherent institutional mechanism for dealing effectively with environmental issues. . . . At present, environmental responsibilities are divided among a number of the specialized agencies. . . . UNEP itself is a creature of a mere General Assembly resolution. The Economic and Social Council has the task of coordinating all of these diffuse efforts and it is fair to say that the task has not been accomplished.

* * *

Many of these problems are widely recognized, but the logical inference from the facts seems politically unpalatable; the only way to cure the problem is to create a proper international environmental agency within the United Nations system that has real power and authority. . . . With determination the task could be achieved without spending more resources in total than are expended now. They should be regrouped and reorganized.

* * *

One of the biggest obstacles that must be overcome in international negotiations is the rule of unanimous consent. This rule impels each negotiating body to search for the lowest common denominator; it adds to the difficulty of negotiations because sometimes a single nation can resist the development of a common position and demand concessions as the price of securing unanimous consent. While it is doubtful that the rule of unanimous consent can be banished from international global negotiations, the introduction of new institutional mechanisms may provide ways around it, which would speed up the process and result in instruments of greater potency.

What is missing from the present institutional arrangements is the equivalent of a legislature: some structured and coherent mechanism for making the rules of international law. For such an institution to succeed, it must have access to high-quality streams of advice. An effective way of ensuring the availability of appropriate scientific information is essential. To maintain the authority of the rules that are made, international efforts must be devoted to effective monitoring, assessment and enforcement.

* * *

[In recent years] there have been developments in the way some international organizations create norms. . . . [I]t is now possible for nations that do not agree with a particular norm to be bound by it. Unanimous consent is not required. This development has been achieved by a process of prolepsis.

Procedures for the creation of norms are agreed upon. Those procedures include a provision that in respect of certain rules or in certain circumstances unanimous consent is not required. The norms created by using the procedures did not necessarily receive unanimous consent but are binding on any nation that did not consent because they were created by agreed procedures. Nations thus consent in advance to be bound by norms whose content is unknown at the time of the consent.

* * *

The proleptic method of avoiding the rule of unanimous consent has already been employed in the environmental sphere in the Montreal Protocol on Substances that Delete the Ozone Layer of 1987. . . .

* * *

Acceptance that nations can be bound without their consent opens the door to a quite different legal context from that in which international law has developed. . . . It offers the practical means of securing the higher standards that may be required by an objective assessment of the scientific evidence, however politically inconvenient a particular measure may be for an individual country. The search for the lowest common denominator in environmental matters, as in others, can be a grinding and laborious diplomatic search that hungrily consumes energies and time—both of which are too scarce. Nations that do not want to change can sit tight an avoid change. A recurring theme at international conferences is the last-minute effort to persuade one country or another to go along. Language is softened, material is removed, and much of substance is lost. Herein lies a fundamental difference between the legislative and the diplomatic process. With legislation everyone is bound by the outcome, including those who do not agree. With treaties those who do not agree simply do not become bound.

* * *

There are basically four policy options in the institutional area. First, things could be left as they are. Second, UNEP could be strengthened and given formal responsibilities. Third, the secretariat approach of the Vienna Convention could be embroidered upon and developed so that a series of secretariats operate for separate environmental issues. . . . The fourth broad option is to create a new international institution.

* * *

The International Labour Organisation is the most advanced supertreaty system in terms of providing legislative outcomes of any of the international agencies. Borrowing loosely from the ILO Constitution, a new International Environmental Organization could be established with the following features.

(1) A General Conference, comprising all members, to be called together annually and more often if the Governing Council so decides. The conference shall consist of four representatives from each member; two shall be government delegates and two others

shall represent business and environmental organizations, respectively.

(2) A Governing Council of forty people—twenty representing governments, ten representing business organizations and ten representing environmental organizations.

(3) The ability of the conference to set international environmental regulations by a two-thirds majority of the votes cast by delegates present. The regulations would become binding without further action. There would also be provision for recommendations to be made to members.

(4) A Director-general and staff of the International Environment Office, to have explicit international responsibilities for educating people about the global environmental problems and what they can do to help.

(5) The office to have defined functions for gathering information and monitoring compliance, including verification of compliance with the regulations. There should be regular reviews of the environmental policies of member states and their compliance with the regulations.

(6) A thorough preparatory process, in which there are ample notice, thorough scientific and technical preparation, and consultation before regulations are made.

(7) Formal provision for authoritative and widely representative scientific advice and papers to be available to the organization.

(8) Detailed requirements for nations to report annually on action taken to implement agreed regulations. The environment and business representatives would be required to report separately from governments.

(9) Provision for any member to be able to submit complaints regarding nonobservance in respect of any other member to the International Environment Office.

(10) Discretion of the council to refer such complaints to a commission of inquiry for a full report. The commission shall consist of three appropriate experts of recognized impartiality and be chaired by a lawyer. The commission is to make findings of fact and rule on the steps to be taken to deal with the complaint and the time by which the steps must be taken. Refusals by governments to accept these findings are to be referred to the full conference.

(11) Authority for the council to recommend measures to the conference to secure compliance when it is lacking.

A word needs to be said here about the last feature, on measures to secure compliance. For them to be effective, there must be some strong incentives to join the organization and stay in it. For many countries these will probably reside in technical assistance, information, advice, technology transfer and even financial assistance for dealing with environmental problems. From a practical point of view, the sanctions should include the withholding of benefits by the organization and of direct contacts with delinquent governments, and the mobilization of the politics of shame. Few nations like to be regarded as international pariahs and shame as a sanction ought not to be underestimated.

"TREATY CONGESTION" IN CONTEMPORARY INTERNATIONAL ENVIRONMENTAL LAW

DONALD K. ANTON

ANU College of Law Research Paper No. 12-05, at 1–2, 8 (January 2012)

Looking back now, the rapid growth of international environmental conventional norms that took place over roughly the last thirty years of the twentieth century is striking. Few fields have burst on the scene with as much unplanned fecundity. . . .

* * *

[This has generated a problem of] what came to be known as "treaty congestion". . . .

The essence of treaty congestion lies in the appearance of too much law, too fast. . . .

* * *

Treaty congestion in a particular field of international law, especially when proliferating treaties are widely ratified, will invariably be accompanied by treaty over-commitment for significant numbers of states. Over-commitment has been a feature of contemporary international environmental law. At a fundamental level, over-commitment seriously challenges the capacity of states to implement and comply with their international obligations. This is especially so for states without the requisite human, institutional, and technological resources to deal effectively, if at all, with expanding obligations. . . .

Over-commitment caused by treaty congestion poses a number of capacity challenges. Three in particular have been the source of concern for international environmental law. First, as noted, the basic ability to comply with substantive obligations is undermined by an unmanageable number of commitments. Second, as treaty bodies and institutions proliferate along with the growing corpus of conventions, the capacity of states to meaningfully participate in institutional activities to advance their interests is eroded. Third, the ability of states to adequately monitor and report on the implementation of their obligations, as international environmental treaties increasingly require, is hampered by treaty congestion.

FROM STOCKHOLM TO NEW YORK, VIA RIO AND JOHANNESBURG: HAS THE ENVIRONMENT LOST ITS WAY ON THE GLOBAL AGENDA?

PAOLO GALIZZI
29 Fordham Int'l L.J. 952 (2006)

Over thirty years ago, . . . delegates from 113 States (nearly all the members of the international community at the time) attended the United Nations Conference on the Human Environment [the Stockholm Conference]. . . . The lively and sometimes heated discussions at the UNCHE reflected different views on the environment among the members of the international community. . . . Finally, the UNCHE's participants achieved a consensus on the first truly universally shared environmental agenda.

* * *

[Twenty years later, in 1992,] the Earth Summit [in Rio de Janeiro] was attended by delegates from 176 States, including 103 Heads of State or Government. States came to Rio with different views and objectives. The developed world, in particular, wanted the Summit to re-energize the international community's environmental agenda, while the developing world wanted to put development and economic growth on the center stage. Following lengthy discussions, a new international "environmental agenda" emerged: an agenda for sustainable development. "Environment" and "development" were now on par on the global stage, reflecting a compromise and a new consensus between developed and developing countries.

* * *

[In 2002,] the international community gathered in Johannesburg for the World Summit on Sustainable Development ("WSSD") . . . to assess the state of the implementation of the Rio agenda, ten years after the Earth Summit.[11] This was to be the second review of the implementation of the Rio agreements.

[The] Johannesburg [Summit] was supposed to reenergize the international environmental agenda and improve the role of environmental

[11] The Summit was convened by a resolution of the U.N. General Assembly. *See* Ten-Year Review of Progress Achieved in the Implementation of the Outcome of the United Nations Conference on Environment and Development, G.A. Res. 55/199, U.N. GAOR, 55th Sess., 87th plen. mtg., U.N. Doc. A/RES/55/199 (Dec. 20, 2000).

issues within the context of the sustainable development agenda, but achieved neither.

Johannesburg arguably betrayed the spirit of Stockholm and Rio. Development appeared to have overtaken the environment on the international agenda. Sustainable development now seemed more like "development *tout court*" with insufficient consideration paid to its environmental dimensions.

An analysis of the Johannesburg Declaration on Sustainable Development ("Johannesburg Declaration") **[Basic Document 1.35]** and the Plan of Implementation of the World Summit on Sustainable Development ("Plan of Implementation") **[Basic Document 1.36]**, the two documents adopted at the Conference, provides ample support for the critical views on the summit's (lack of) environmental "achievements."

The Johannesburg Declaration contains very weak environmental language and hardly mentions specific environmental objectives. Recognizing that the "global environment continues to suffer," the Declaration reiterates the commitment to Agenda 21 and the Rio Declaration. The commitment is to the sustainable development agenda, however, rather than to an environmental one. The few references to the environment are, in fact, almost always to be understood in the context of sustainable development: "We the representatives of the people of the world . . . reaffirm our commitment to sustainable development" and "assume a collective responsibility to advance and strengthen the interdependent and mutually reinforcing pillars of sustainable development—economic development, social development and environmental protection—at the local, national, regional and global levels."[12]

[Although] the Johannesburg Declaration recognizes the contribution of the historical Stockholm and Rio Conferences and, particularly, UNCED's role in shaping the "new" agenda for sustainable development[,] . . . [the] Declaration mainly emphasizes developmental objectives and, generally, environmental goals are mentioned only when relevant to economic and social development.

The Plan of Implementation is hardly more encouraging from an environmental point of view. Again, the environment seems to be relevant only in the context of development. . . .

The World Summit on Sustainable Development failed to produce a strong and renewed environmental consensus in the international community. At Johannesburg, the environment was treated as a sideshow and focus was mostly placed on development and poverty eradication. As observed above, there are hardly any truly "ecological" or environmental

[12] Johannesburg Declaration, paragraphs 3, 5.

references in the documents adopted at the Summit. Most references are, in any event, purely related to the environment as a tool to promote economic and social development.

* * *

A chance to reaffirm the importance of the environment within the global agenda was not far away. World leaders would soon gather in New York for the 2005 World Summit to monitor the progress in the implementation of the Millennium Declaration. . . .

* * *

World leaders representing every Member State of the U.N. attended the 2005 World Summit. In the Summit's Outcome Document, Heads of State and Government renewed their commitment to the values and principles of the U.N. and its Charter and agreed to

> [C]reate a more peaceful, prosperous and democratic world and to undertake concrete measures to continue finding ways to implement the outcome of the Millennium Summit and the other major United Nations conferences and summits so as to provide multilateral solutions to problems in the four following areas:
>
> - Development
> - Peace and collective security
> - Human rights and the rule of law
> - Strengthening of the United Nations.[13]

. . . [T]he international community did not include environmental protection among the four areas for which new measures need to be identified to "create a more peaceful, prosperous and democratic world."

* * *

The 2005 World Summit rightly identified four priority areas where international cooperation and actions are needed to create a peaceful, secure, and more prosperous world: (1) development; (2) peace and collective security; (3) human rights and the rule of law; and (4) strengthening the U.N. It seems, however, that world leaders forgot the prerequisite for development to occur, peace and security to be guaranteed, human rights to be protected and enjoyed, the rule of law to be established, and the U.N. to be strengthened—the environment. The inclusion of the environment simply as an item within the development agenda reflects the lack of political support at the global stage for a strong and effective international environmental agenda. This has resulted in the absence of

[13] G.A. Res. 60/1, *2005 World Summit Outcome* (Oct. 24, 2005).

strong initiatives to aggressively and urgently address the environmental threats and challenges the world is facing.

DISCUSSION NOTES/QUESTIONS

1. There has been a proliferation of international environmental agreements, each with their own governance mechanisms, as Sir Geoffrey foresaw in 1992. As Professor Anton points out, this causes significant problems for developing countries, many of which simply lack the resources to participate in a significant way in so many different law-making and decision-making arenas. Would Sir Geoffrey's recommendation for the creation of an International Environmental Organization have helped deal with that capacity problem?

Although many environmental agreements have separate governance structures, there have been efforts to consolidate functions to achieve efficiency. For example, a single Secretariat serves the Parties to the Stockholm Convention on Persistent Organic Pollutants, the Rotterdam Convention on the Prior Informed Consent Procedure for Certain Hazardous Chemicals and Pesticides in International Trade, and the Basel Convention on the Control of Transboundary Movements of Hazardous Wastes and Their Disposal. In addition, the Global Environment Facility is the financial mechanism for 5 international environmental conventions: the UN Framework Convention on Climate Change, the Convention on Biological Diversity, the UN Convention to Combat Desertification, the Minamata Convention on Mercury, and the Stockholm Convention on Persistent Organic Pollutants.

2. Has sustainable development proved to be a Trojan Horse, undermining the international environmental movement from within? Does the Johannesburg Declaration resolve the tension between protecting the environment and promoting economic development by coming down squarely on the side of economic development? Or is Galizzi's assessment too pessimistic? The Rio +20 Declaration **(Basic Document 1.37)**, adopted by the United Nations Conference on Sustainable Development in 2012, strongly reaffirms the importance of international action to address environmental problems.

3. If you think development has been elevated to primacy in the "environment/development" balance in global discussions, is that a bad or a good thing? If poor countries were richer, they would have more resources to commit to environmental protection in general and to participation in environment treaties specifically. Doesn't that fact, by itself, warrant giving substantial attention to development as a means of furthering an environmentalist agenda? Or is it the case that development on the established Western model will simply worsen our environmental problems?

4. A new treaty, the "Global Pact for the Environment," has been proposed as a means for moving the environment and development agendas forward. A substantial portion of the proposed treaty is presented in the next reading.

PRELIMINARY DRAFT GLOBAL PACT FOR THE ENVIRONMENT

Adopted at La Sorbonne, Paris by Le Club des Jurists (24 June 2017)

Article 1
Right to an ecologically sound environment

Every person has the right to live in an ecologically sound environment adequate for their health, well-being, dignity, culture and fulfilment.

Article 2
Duty to take care of the environment

Every State or international institution, every person, natural or legal, public or private, has the duty to take care of the environment. To this end, everyone contributes at their own levels to the conservation, protection and restoration of the integrity of the Earth's ecosystem.

Article 3
Integration and sustainable development

Parties shall integrate the requirements of environmental protection into the planning and implementation of their policies and national and international activities, especially in order to promote the fight against climate change, the protection of oceans and the maintenance of biodiversity.

They shall pursue sustainable development. To this end, they shall ensure the promotion of public support policies, patterns of production and consumption both sustainable and respectful of the environment.

Article 4
Intergenerational Equity

Intergenerational equity shall guide decisions that may have an impact on the environment.

Present generations shall ensure that their decisions and actions do not compromise the ability of future generations to meet their own needs.

Article 5
Prevention

The necessary measures shall be taken to prevent environmental harm.

The Parties have the duty to ensure that activities under their jurisdiction or control do not cause damage to the environments of other Parties or in areas beyond the limits of their national jurisdiction.

They shall take the necessary measures to ensure that an environmental impact assessment is conducted prior to any decision made to authorise or engage in a project, an activity, a plan, or a program that is likely to have a significant adverse impact on the environment.

In particular, States shall keep under surveillance the effect of an above-mentioned project, activity, plan, or program which they authorise or engage in, in view of their obligation of due diligence.

Article 6
Precaution

Where there is a risk of serious or irreversible damage, lack of scientific certainty shall not be used as a reason for postponing the adoption of effective and proportionate measures to prevent environmental degradation.

Article 7
Environmental Damages

The necessary measures shall be taken to ensure an adequate remediation of environmental damages.

Parties shall immediately notify other States of any natural disasters or other emergencies that are likely to produce sudden harmful effects on the environment of those States. Parties shall promptly cooperate to help concerned States.

Article 8
Polluter-Pays

Parties shall ensure that prevention, mitigation and remediation costs for pollution, and other environmental disruptions and degradation are, to the greatest possible extent, borne by their originator.

Article 9
Access to information

Every person, without being required to state an interest, has a right of access to environmental information held by public authorities.

Public authorities shall, within the framework of their national legislations, collect and make available to the public relevant environmental information.

Article 10
Public participation

Every person has the right to participate, at an appropriate stage and while options are still open, to the preparation of decisions, measures, plans, programmes, activities, policies and normative instruments of public authorities that may have a significant effect on the environment.

Article 11
Access to environmental justice

Parties shall ensure the right of effective and affordable access to administrative and judicial procedures, including redress and remedies, to challenge acts or omissions of public authorities or private persons which contravene environmental law, taking into consideration the provisions of the present Pact.

Article 12
Education and training

The Parties shall ensure that environmental education, to the greatest possible extent, is taught to members of the younger generation as well as to adults, in order to inspire in everyone a responsible conduct in protecting and improving the environment.

The Parties shall ensure the protection of freedom of expression and information in environmental matters. They support the dissemination by mass media of information of an educational nature on ecosystems and on the need to protect and preserve the environment.

Article 13
Research and innovation

The Parties shall promote, to the best of their ability, the improvement of scientific knowledge of ecosystems and the impact of human activities. They shall cooperate through exchanges of scientific and technological knowledge and by enhancing the development, adaptation, dissemination and transfer of technologies respectful of the environment, including innovative technologies.

Article 14
Role of non-State actors and subnational entities

The Parties shall take the necessary measures to encourage the implementation of this Pact by non- State actors and subnational entities, including civil society, economic actors, cities and regions taking into account their vital role in the protection of the environment.

Article 15
Effectiveness of environmental norms

The Parties have the duty to adopt effective environmental laws, and to ensure their effective and fair implementation and enforcement.

Article 16
Resilience

The Parties shall take necessary measures to maintain and restore the diversity and capacity of ecosystems and human communities to withstand environmental disruptions and degradation and to recover and adapt.

Article 17
Non-regression

The Parties and their sub-national entities refrain from allowing activities or adopting norms that have the effect of reducing the global level of environmental protection guaranteed by current law.

Article 18
Cooperation

In order to conserve, protect and restore the integrity of the Earth's ecosystem and community of life, Parties shall cooperate in good faith and in a spirit of global partnership for the implementation of the provisions of the present Pact.

Article 19
Armed conflicts

States shall take pursuant to their obligations under international law all feasible measures to protect the environment in relation to armed conflicts.

Article 20
Diversity of national situations

The special situation and needs of developing countries, particularly the least developed and those most environmentally vulnerable, shall be given special attention.

Account shall be taken, where appropriate, of the Parties' common but differentiated responsibilities and respective capabilities, in light of different national circumstances.

Article 21
Monitoring of the implementation of the Pact

A compliance mechanism to facilitate implementation of, and to promote compliance with, the provisions of the present Pact is hereby established.

This mechanism consists of a Committee of independent experts and focuses on facilitation. It operates in a transparent, non-adversarial and non-punitive manner. The committee shall pay particular attention to the respective national circumstances and capabilities of the Parties.

One year after the entry into force of the present Pact, the Depositary shall convene a meeting of the Parties which will establish the modalities and procedures by which the Committee shall exercise its functions.

Two years after the Committee takes office, and at a frequency to be determined by the meeting of the Parties, not exceeding four years, each Party shall report to the Committee on its progress in implementing the provisions of the Pact.

Article 22
Secretariat

The Secretariat of the present Pact shall be provided by the Secretary-General of the United Nations [or the Executive Director of the United Nations Environment Program].

The Secretary-General [or the Executive Director of the United Nations Environment Program] convenes in as much as necessary meeting of Parties.

* * *

DISCUSSION NOTES/QUESTIONS

1. Of what significance is an umbrella agreement of this sort? It does not displace any existing agreements. It simply adds a new agreement on core principles. One claim is that such an agreement is useful because it takes steps toward unifying international environmental law by articulating core principles for the field. Another claim is that it would reorient international priorities toward environmental protection and, perhaps, lead to the "greening" of international policies other areas, such as trade and investment. In general, supporters of the Pact see it as having potential to reinvigorate international efforts to protect the environment. What do you think?

2. Perhaps the most obvious way in which the proposed Pact adds to international environmental law is its recognition (in Article 1) that humans have a "right" to live in an "ecologically sound environment adequate for their health, well-being, dignity, culture and fulfilment." Although some have advocated for such a right, or argued that it flows logically from other human rights, it has not been authoritatively recognized. Would you be supportive of global recognition of such a right? What obligations, if any, would the existence of such a right create and who has those obligations? Supporters of the Pact say that the recognition of such a right will help those suffering from environmental harms. But how? Through judicially imposed liability on those whose activities have led to the harm? The Pact also recognizes an individual right "to access to administrative and judicial procedures, including redress and remedies, to challenge acts or omissions of public authorities or private persons which contravene environmental law. . . ." (Article 11). Does that answer the question of how the Pact's authors anticipate that the right to a healthy environment will be enforced?

The Pact also recognizes a right to access to environmental information (Article 9) and a right to participate in decisions that may have a significant environmental effect (Article 10).

3. Apart from the provisions on environmental rights and the possibility of direct enforcement of those rights against governments or private actors, is there anything in the Pact that represents a significant departure from international environmental law as it is described in this chapter?

PART TWO

CHALLENGES IN ADDRESSING EARTH'S MOST PRESSING ENVIRONMENTAL THREATS

■ ■ ■

In Chapters 1–3 of this coursebook, we began our study of international environmental law by exploring the sources and application of international law, guided and instructed by litigation over whaling in the Southern Ocean, the environmentally provoked "case" of the *Rainbow Warrior,* and the dispute between the United States and Canada over transboundary air pollution. Chapter 4 addressed the development of some of the basic principles of international environmental law that are broadly relevant to all global environmental problems. As you move forward in your study, it is important that you have comprehended Chapter 4 *thoroughly.* The matters addressed therein are relevant in one way or another to all that follows.

In this Part II, we examine how international law is used to address particular environmental problems. Each of the remaining chapters of the book contains two or more hypothetical fact scenarios designed to raise issues related to the role of international law in dealing with the kind of environmental problem addressed in that chapter. There are 17 different problems in Chapters 5–12, which give your instructor plenty of coverage options.

We have chosen to start Part II with problems related to transboundary air pollution in Europe (Problem 5-1) and depletion of the stratospheric ozone layer (Problem 5-2). This is a deliberate choice: these are both areas in which international environmental law is quite mature and operating effectively even if not always sufficiently. We think it is useful for students to understand the potential for effective use of international law before they encounter, later in the book, its troubling failures and, especially, its failure effectively to address two of the most significant problems we face—loss of biodiversity (Problem 7-3) and climate change (Chapter 9).

Your instructor, of course, may choose a completely different starting point for your study of these problems. Indeed, in previous editions of this book we, the editors, chose to begin with the most difficult issues of all. But wherever your study of the problems begins, we encourage you to get into the spirit of the problem method—think hard and have fun!

CHAPTER FIVE

PROTECTING THE ATMOSPHERE

■ ■ ■

The Earth's atmosphere, a mixture of gases and water vapor essential to earthly life and good health, is today being threatened. Industrial and other human activities are altering its chemical balance and consequently endangering the life forms it supports, causing long-term contamination of the food chain, sickness, and related assaults upon the biosphere. Acid rain, ozone pollution, and ozone depletion, while less tangible than many other forms of pollution, are among the principal culprits.

Broadly speaking, "acid rain" refers to the deposit from the atmosphere—in the form of dew, fog, frost, hail, rain, sleet, snow, and dry deposits—of acidic "inputs" into the Earth's ecosystems derived from sulfur and nitrogen oxide emissions brought about by automotive, industrial, and other human activity. Those same activities lead also to chemical emissions that prompt the development of so-called "bad" ozone in the lower troposphere, where it is a threat to human health and the environment. So-called "good" ozone, the ozone layer in the upper atmosphere, operates as a thin shield that protects earthly life from the ultraviolet rays of the sun, but unfortunately this layer of "good" ozone is being destroyed by chlorofluorocarbons, halons, and other human-made substances that interfere with the way ozone is created and broken down, consequently reducing its concentration in the upper atmosphere.

Ironically, each of these threats to the atmosphere is a result largely of human progress. Sulfur, nitrogen oxides, and volatile organic compounds (important in the development of ozone pollution) derive from industrial innovations such as combustion. Ozone-depleting substances are used in refrigerators, air-conditioners, spray propellants, and other luxuries of modern—mainly "First World"—life.

Despite their similar human-based origins, however, these many threats raise different issues of law and policy. Addressing ozone depletion is a relatively simple proposition because only a few identifiable countries and industries are responsible for most of the production and use of ozone-depleting substances, and, what is more, alternatives to those substances exist. Not so acid rain and ozone pollution. While their sources clearly reside in industrial society, the causal links between emissions and pollution are complex, and transboundary atmospheric transfer of the key pollutants makes it hard to identify achievable strategies for controlling the problem.

On the other hand, all these atmosphere-threatening problems share in common the need to account in law and policy for disparate production and consumption patterns as between different countries and regions of the world. Disparate—particularly disproportionate—production and consumption patterns, one can argue, should create different degrees of legal accountability and responsibility; and in this connection the legal protection of the atmosphere must take additionally into account different commitments to prevention and redress. Moreover, one must recognize that political realities in particular countries may prevent achievement of the optimum level of pollution control. The question arises how to accommodate those realities in particular cases without inviting more widespread departures from policy goals.

A. AIR POLLUTION

According to the World Health Organization, air pollution is the largest environmental cause of human health problems.[1] Exposure to air pollution contributes to a variety of maladies, including asthma, heart disease, respiratory diseases and cancer. More than 91% of the world's population is exposed daily to levels of air pollution that exceed WHO's air quality guidelines, and WHO estimates that more than four million deaths per year can be attributed to air pollution.

In addition to threatening human health, air pollution has adverse environmental effects. For example, emissions of sulfur dioxide and nitrogen oxides "acidify lakes and streams; harm sensitive forests; harm sensitive coastal ecosystems; and accelerate the decay of building materials, paints, and cultural artifacts such as buildings, statues, and sculptures."[2] Reducing the damage caused by acid deposition (acid rain) was a major impetus for adoption of the Convention on Long-Range Transboundary Air Pollution.[3] In the United States, the cap-and-trade program for emissions of SO_2 from electric power plants was also adopted largely in response to this problem.

Another significant problem is low-level ozone produced when nitrogen oxides and volatile organic carbons (VOCs) react to sunlight. Ozone has toxic effects on plants, and it contributes to reduced crop yields and damage to forest ecosystems in affected areas. It can also reduce human lung

---

[1] World Health Organization, Ambient air pollution: A global assessment of exposure and burden of disease 15 (2016).

[2] Executive Office of the President of the United States, *National Acid Precipitation Assessment Program [NAPAP] Report to Congress: An Integrated Assessment* 1 (2003).

[3] *See* Chapter 3, *supra*.

function, irritate air passages, and cause unpleasant respiratory symptoms.

There are seven air pollutants of primary concern to scientists and public health experts. They are:

- Carbon monoxide (CO);
- Sulfur dioxide (SO_2);
- Nitrogen oxides (NO_X);
- Ozone (O_3);
- Heavy metals (cadmium, lead and mercury);
- Persistent organic pollutants (POPs)[4]; and
- Particulate matter (PM).

Volatile organic carbons (VOCs)[5] are also of concern primarily because of their role as precursors to ozone.[6]

Causes of air pollution

Most air pollution is caused by human activity.[7] In particular, the burning of fossil fuels for transportation, energy production, and industrial purposes is a primary cause of the pollutants that lead to acid rain. In 2002, for example, 66% of total sulfur dioxide emissions and 22% of total NO_X emissions in the United States were the result of burning fossil fuels for electricity generation. Another 56% of NO_X emissions and 5% of SO_2 emissions came from transportation sources. Other significant sources of emissions include industrial plants, stationary engines, and non-road vehicles. Modern agricultural practices also contribute to soil emissions of

[4] POPs are toxic chemicals with adverse impacts on human and animal health. They persist in the environment and can be transported across the globe by wind, water, or in the tissue of animals. Some POPs are intentionally produced and used for a variety of purposes. They are used in pest and disease control, in crop production, and in a variety of industrial applications. Others, such as dioxins, are an unintended byproduct of human activity.

[5] VOCs are chemical compounds containing carbon that are emitted in gaseous form from various solids or liquids, including paints, cleaners and disinfectants, office equipment such as copiers and printers, glues, adhesives and many other materials. There are also natural sources of VOCs (trees emit VOCs). In fact, natural sources are responsible for most of the VOCs in the Earth's atmosphere. However, the human sources are generally the main source of air pollution problems because they tend to be highly concentrated in particular areas.

[6] VOCs can also sometimes be found in high concentrations in indoor locations where they may be hazardous in their own right. Their health effects vary greatly, depending on the particular pollutant, the level of exposure and the length of time of exposure. According to the EPA, not much is presently known about the effects of VOC exposure in the home. EPA, Volatile Organic Compounds' Impact on Indoor Air Quality, https://www.epa.gov/indoor-air-quality-iaq/volatile-organic-compounds-impact-indoor-air-quality (last visited Sept. 8, 2018).

[7] In Southeast Asia, transboundary haze is one of the most serious air pollution problems. It might be seen as a natural phenomenon, as it is caused primarily by fires in forests and peatlands that occur in the area on a regular basis. While some of these fires might have a natural or accidental origin, many (perhaps most) are deliberately set to clear land for agricultural purposes.

nitrogen oxides, which are responsible for about 10% of total global NOx emissions.[8]

Ground-level ozone pollution is formed when pollutants such as NOx, VOCs, methane and carbon monoxide react in sunlight. These ozone precursor gases come from a variety of sources, both human and natural. In 2008, the World Health Organization reported the following:

> At present, the most important source of anthropogenic **NOx** emissions on the global scale is road transport (29% in 2000), followed by combustion in power plants and industry (27%). Some 17% of global emissions come from international maritime shipping, 10% from non-road vehicles and 2% from aircraft. Open burning of biomass due to forest fires, savannah burning and agricultural practices accounts for approximately 15% of global anthropogenic emissions. Natural sources include soils and lightning.
>
> There are a large number of **non-methane VOCs** in the atmosphere that contribute to ozone formation. Important anthropogenic sources include incomplete combustion of fossil fuels, evaporative losses of fuels, solvent use, various industrial production processes, agricultural activities and biomass burning. Globally, however, it is believed that natural sources of VOCs far outweigh anthropogenic sources.
>
> On a global scale, emissions of **carbon monoxide** from deforestation, savannah burning and the burning of agricultural waste account for about half of anthropogenic emissions. The rest come from fuel combustion, with a quarter from household solid fuels and about 20% from road transport. The primary natural sources of carbon monoxide are vegetation, oceans and wildfires (biomass burning).
>
> Globally, most **methane** emissions are anthropogenic, with an important fraction of biogenic emissions directly connected to human activities such as rice cultivation. The major anthropogenic sources include coal mining, the gas and oil industries, landfill, ruminant animals, rice cultivation and biomass burning. The single largest natural source of methane is wetlands.[9]

---

[8] US Environmental Protection Agency (EPA), *Integrated Science Assessment for Oxides of Nitrogen and Sulfur—Ecological Criteria* 2–2 to 2–17 (Dec. 2008) [hereinafter EPA Assessment]. World Health Organization-Europe, Health Risks of Ozone from Long-Range Transboundary Air Pollution 21–3) (2008).

[9] World Health Organization-Europe, Health Risks of Ozone from Long-Range Transboundary Air Pollution 21–3 (2008).

The wide variety of sources of air pollutants creates obvious challenges for regulatory policy.

Control of air pollution

While it is possible to reduce emissions from human activities, it is also costly to do so. Consequently, regulatory efforts meet resistance from the companies and individuals who are asked to bear the cost of emission reductions. Moreover, all these polluting activities (electricity generation, transportation, manufacturing, fertilizer-intensive agriculture) are central to life in a modern economy, and economic development and growth generally means concomitant growth in each of these activities. Thus, even when controls on the emission of pollutants are in place, economic expansion can lead to an increase in emissions, absent an offsetting strengthening of pollution controls.

Compounding the inherent political and economic difficulties of reducing air pollution is the fact that air pollutants are subject to transport through the atmosphere, sometimes traveling hundreds or thousands of miles from the place where they were emitted. This means that efforts to control emissions in one region or nation can be thwarted by atmospheric "importation" of sulfur and nitrogen oxides from a region where emission controls are not in place.

> Emitted NO_X, SO_X, NH_X and other pollutants can be transported vertically by convection into the upper part of the mixed layer on one day, then transported overnight in a layer of high concentrations. Once pollutants are lofted to the middle and upper troposphere, they typically have a much longer lifetime and, with the generally stronger winds at these altitudes, can be transported long distances from the source regions. The length scale of this transport is highly variable owing to differing chemical and meteorological conditions encountered along the transport path. . . . [While in the atmosphere, these pollutants interact and can transform into] secondary aerosols like ammonium nitrate and ammonium sulfate. . . .
>
> The emitted, transported, and transformed pollutants reach the surface where they can have ecological effects largely through deposition. Direct and indirect wet and dry deposition to specific locations like watersheds depend on air pollutant emissions and concentrations in the airshed above the watershed, but the shape and areal extent of the airshed is quite different from that of the watershed owing to the transport and transformation of emitted pollutants described above.[10]

[10] EPA Assessment, *supra* note 8, at 3–4.

As a result of these complexities, it can be difficult to attribute a problem like acid rain to a particular source. Even if attribution is possible, it may be difficult to hold a source accountable for a pollution problem if the source is in a different jurisdiction.

International law and air pollution

As illustrated in Chapter 3 (Transboundary Pollution), *supra,* there are at least three legal processes that might be invoked to address a problem of transboundary air pollution. First, it could be handled as a bilateral dispute between states and resolved through traditional dispute settlement methods and on the basis of customary international law. This was the approach taken by the United States and Canada in the original *Trail Smelter* arbitration. Second, the contending states could attempt to address the problem by creating new international conventional law aimed specifically at addressing the particular pollution problem they face. This, as you learned, was the approach taken to address the acid rain problem in Europe. A new framework treaty was negotiated on transboundary air pollution and a protocol aimed at reducing sulfur emissions quickly followed.[11] Finally, it is possible to address transboundary pollution problems by allowing affected parties access to judicial and administrative authorities in the polluting state (or in their own state) to seek action to address the problem or remedial measures to compensate for any harm caused. In the original *Trail Smelter* dispute, Canada had indicated that the American complainants could access Canadian courts to seek a remedy, but those complainants preferred to seek their government's assistance. In the later dispute involving water pollution in the United States attributable to the Trail smelter, the American plaintiffs sought their remedy in American administrative agencies and courts and through the application of local law.

Customary international law and the obligation not to cause transboundary harm

Although the *Trail Smelter* principle—that states have a duty to ensure that activities under their jurisdiction and control do not cause significant transboundary harm—is widely accepted, the *Trail Smelter* result (a payment of compensation and an agreement to place strict controls on a single source of pollution) has been less trend-setting. Despite repeated calls by the international community for the further development of "international law regarding liability and compensation,"[12] there is little evidence of progress on this front. There are no recent examples of remedies comparable to those in the *Trail Smelter* arbitration being imposed on

[11] Convention on Long-Range Transboundary Air Pollution, 13 Nov. 1979, 1302 UNTS 217; Protocol on the Reduction of Sulphur Emissions or their Transboundary Fluxes by at least 30 per cent, 8 July 1985, 1480 UNTS 215.

[12] *See* Stockholm Declaration, principle 22 **(Basic Document 1.21)** and Rio Declaration, principle 13 **(Basic Document 1.30)**.

account of transboundary pollution, even when the damages caused were extreme.[13] International treaties and treaty bodies often sidestep the issue of liability and compensation, and, when it has been addressed explicitly in a treaty, the treaty remains unratified.[14] When the International Law Commission decided to include "protection of the atmosphere" in its work program, it expressly excluded any discussion of the liability of states or their nationals.[15]

States have honored their obligation to prevent significant transboundary harm primarily by entering treaties and other cooperative arrangements aimed at controlling activities that might cause harm. The no-harm principle has rarely been used as a basis for imposing liability on polluting states or as the basis for an adjudicatory order to a state to control emissions of pollutants that are causing damage across borders.[16]

Air pollution treaties

The most important treaty regime aimed at the control of transboundary air pollution is the Convention on Long-Range Transboundary Air Pollution (CLRTAP) **(Basic Document 2.1)** and its protocols. Negotiated under the auspices of the UN Economic Commission for Europe (UNECE), the Convention has been ratified by 51 of the 56 UNECE States. This means the treaty covers much of the northern hemisphere, as UNECE's geographical scope includes North America, Western Europe, Eastern Europe and Western Asia.

---

[13] Devereaux F. McClatchey, *Chernobyl and Sandoz One Decade Later: The Evolution of State Responsibility for International Disasters, 1986–1996*, 25 Ga. J. Int'l & Comp. L. 659, 673–75, 676–78, 680 (1996).

[14] For example, the Convention on Transboundary Effects of Industrial Accidents **(Basic Document 2.2)**, adopted in the wake of the Sandoz chemical spill in Switzerland, says only that Parties "shall support appropriate international efforts to elaborate rules, criteria and procedures in the field of responsibility and liability." A 2003 protocol **(Basic Document 3.17b)** that addresses issues of civil liability and compensation has only one ratification and is not yet in force. The 1999 Basel Protocol on Liability and Compensation for Damage Resulting from Transboundary Movements of Hazardous Wastes and their Disposal **(Basic Document 4.7a)** likewise is not yet in force. The Nagoya-Kuala Lumpur Supplementary Protocol on Liability and Redress to the Cartagena Protocol on Biosafety **(Basic Document 5.6b)** is an apparent exception to this pattern, as it entered into force with 41 Parties on 5 Mar. 2018. But, in fact, this agreement neither creates nor articulates international standards of liability for transboundary harm. It primarily calls upon states to develop, as part of their domestic law, "rules and procedures that address damage" caused to "the conservation and sustainable use of biological diversity" by living modified organisms. It does not specify required standards of liability, levels of compensation, or types of compensable damage. It does, however, obligate states to require responsible persons to take "appropriate response measures," including measures to prevent or minimize damage and to "restore biological diversity." Id. arts. 5 & 12. The Protocol does not address "the rights and obligations of States under the rules of general international law." *Id.* art. 11.

[15] Int'l Law Comm'n, Report on the Work of its Sixty-Fifth Session, U.N. Doc. A/68/10, at 115, para. 168 (2013).

[16] For a discussion of customary international law developments related to protection of the atmosphere, *see* Shinya Murase, Int'l Law Comm'n, *First report of the Special Rapporteur on the protection of the atmosphere, Report on the Work of Its Sixty-Sixth Session*, U.N. Doc A/CN.4/667 at 35–42 (2014).

The CLRTAP establishes a framework for cooperation on air pollution matters. It is supplemented by eight protocols, seven of which establish national emission reduction targets for specific pollutants. There have been far fewer ratifications of the protocols than of the treaty itself. Hence, the geographic coverage of protocols establishing limits on emissions of particular pollutants varies and is generally smaller than the entire UNECE region. A list of the emissions-control protocols and the number of parties to each (as of June 28, 2019) follows:

- 1985 Protocol on the reduction of **sulphur** emissions or their transboundary fluxes by at least 30 per cent (25 parties);
- 1988 Protocol concerning the control of emissions of **nitrogen oxides** or their transboundary fluxes (35 parties);
- 1991 Protocol concerning the control of emissions of **volatile organic compounds** or their transboundary fluxes (24 parties);
- 1994 Protocol on further reduction of **sulphur** emissions (29 parties);
- 1998 Protocol on **heavy metals** (34 parties);
- 1998 Protocol on **persistent organic pollutants** (33 parties); and
- 1999 Protocol to abate acidification, eutrophication and ground-level ozone (Gothenburg Protocol) **(Basic Document 2.1a)** (27 parties) (establishing emissions limits for **sulphur, nitrogen oxides, ammonia, and volatile organic compounds**).

Amendments have been adopted to strengthen the emissions controls in the 1998 and 1999 protocols, but those amendments have so far not received sufficient ratifications to enter into force.

In other parts of the world, a number of regional agreements on air pollution have been adopted, but none of these efforts has had the regulatory impact of the CLRTAP system. Regional efforts to address air pollution in Africa,[17] southern Asia,[18] and South America[19] have resulted in the adoption of several framework agreements, but these are generally

[17] Regional arrangements in Africa include: the Air Pollution Information Network for Africa (APINA); the 2008 Southern Africa Policy Dialogue on Air Pollution; the 2008 Eastern Africa Regional Framework Agreement on Air Pollution; and the 2009 West and Central Africa Regional Framework agreement on Air Pollution.

[18] Malé Declaration on Control and Prevention of Air Pollution and its Likely Transboundary Effects for South Asia (Apr. 1998).

[19] Regional Plan of Action on Atmospheric Pollution, Decision 8 of the XIX Meeting of the Forum of Ministers of Environment for Latin America and the Caribbean (11–14 March 2014) (adopted as a "voluntary guide for the development of national action plans").

in the form of soft-law instruments that lack binding commitments.[20] The 2002 ASEAN Agreement on Transboundary Haze Pollution, though technically a binding agreement, has been described in reality as a "somewhat toothless instrument of limited enforceability."[21] Various regional seas treaties have provisions calling for the protection of the marine environment from various sources of pollution, including from air pollution. But actions taken under these conventions have focused primarily on dumping and water pollution. Little has been done to directly address air pollution.[22]

Finally, there has been international action to address particular sources of air pollution. Annex VI to MARPOL 73/78 establishes limits on emissions from ship diesel engines of nitrogen oxides, sulfur oxides, and volatile organic compounds.[23] Annex 16 of the International Convention on Civil Aviation establishes standards aimed at reducing emissions from aircraft engines of common pollutants such as sulfur oxides, nitrogen oxides and particulates.[24]

Remedies under local law and related procedural approaches to transboundary pollution (including air pollution)

One way to handle transboundary pollution problems is for injured persons in other states to seek relief from authorities in the polluter's state. The effectiveness of such a solution will depend on two things: a) the availability of adequate local remedies, and b) access to those remedies for persons from outside the state. The extent to which particular states provide remedies for pollution damage is beyond the scope of this book. But it is worth noting that international treaties on compensation for nuclear pollution damage and oil pollution damage address both aspects of remedial effectiveness—they require states to impose liability on certain polluters, and they ensure that injured persons (regardless of nationality) have access to judicial means of recovering compensation.[25]

---

20 Yulia Yamineva & Seita Romppanen, *Is Law Failing to Address Air Pollution? Reflections on International and EU Developments,* 26 Review of European, Comp. & Int'l Envtl. L. 189, 193 (2017).

21 Shawkat Alam & Laely Nurhidayah, *The International Law of Transboundary Haze Pollution: What Can We Learn from the Southeast Asia Region?,* 26 Review of European, Comp. & Int'l Envtl. L. 243, 250 (2017).

22 *See, e.g.,* Convention on the Protection and Development of the Marine Environment of the Wider Caribbean Region (Cartagena Convention), Mar. 24, 1983, art. 9, 1506 UNTS 157 **(Basic Document 3.5)**; Convention for the Protection of the Natural Resources and Environment of the South Pacific Region (Noumea Convention), Aug. 22, 1990, art. 9, 1990 ATS 31.

23 Regulations for the Prevention of Air Pollution from Ships, Protocol of 1997 to Amend the International Convention for the Prevention of Pollution from Ships, 1973, as modified by the Protocol of 1978 relating thereto (MARPOL 73/78), 1341 UNTS 3 (adding Annex VI).

24 International Civil Aviation Organization, Annex 16 [to the International Convention on Civil Aviation]—*Environmental Protection,* Volume II—*Aircraft Engine Emissions* (3rd ed., July 2008).

25 *See, e.g.,* Vienna Convention on Civil Liability for Nuclear Damage, May 21, 1963, as amended by the 1997 Protocol, Sept. 12, 1997, 2241 UNTS 270 **(Basic Document 2.12)**;

In addition to providing remedies for harm, states can address environmental issues by making good decisions about the public projects they undertake, the private projects they approve, and the environmental regulations they adopt. As the Stockholm Declaration **(Basic Document 1.21)** recognized, "rational planning" is "an essential tool" for reconciling conflicts between "the needs of development and the need to protect and improve the environment." One way to improve the quality of planning decisions is to ensure that they are made with full information and with input from persons who will be affected by them. Thus, Principle 10 of the Rio Declaration **(Basic Document 1.30)** provides:

> Environmental issues are best handled with participation of all concerned citizens, at the relevant level. At the national level, each individual shall have appropriate access to information concerning the environment that is held by public authorities, including information on hazardous materials and activities in their communities, and the opportunity to participate in decision-making processes. States shall facilitate and encourage public awareness and participation by making information widely available. Effective access to judicial and administrative proceedings, including redress and remedy, shall be provided.

UNEP has described the three rights mentioned in Principle 10—access to information, the opportunity to participate in decision-making processes, and access to judicial and administrative proceedings—as "key pillars of sound environmental governance." However, the careful reader will note that Principle 10 refers to the "participation of concerned *citizens*." When environment problems have a transboundary dimension (as with air pollution), "sound environmental governance" would require that these participatory rights also be provided to affected persons from outside the state.

Two treaties adopted under the auspices of the UNECE recognize the importance of giving a transboundary reach to procedural rights in the environmental context. Article 2 of the 1991 Convention on Environmental Impact Assessment in a Transboundary Context (Espoo Convention) **(Basic Document 1.38)** requires Parties to establish an environmental impact assessment procedure to be used with respect to certain activities when those activities are likely to cause "significant adverse transboundary impact." The environmental impact procedure must provide an opportunity for public participation in the EIA process, and that participatory right must be extended to "the public in the areas likely to be

International Convention on Civil Liability for Oil Pollution Damage, Nov. 27, 1992, 1956 UNTS 255 **(Basic Document 3.9)** (although oil pollution damage is not necessarily transboundary in nature, the oil tanker or ship causing the damage is often under the jurisdiction of a state other than the state where the incident occurs).

affected," i.e. it must include persons in other states where a significant transboundary impact is likely.

The second treaty providing for procedural rights is the 1998 Convention on Access to Information, Public Participation in Decision-Making and Access to Justice in Environmental Matters (Aarhus Convention) **(Basic Document 1.39)**. The Aarhus Convention establishes a broad right of access to environmental information on the part of members of the public. It also requires that the public be given an opportunity to participate in the making of various decisions and the formulation of various policies relating to the environment. It requires that judicial remedies be provided to persons who wish to contest certain administrative decisions or to challenge private or public acts that contravene national law. In this context, the "public" includes "the public affected or likely to be affected by, or having an interest in, the environmental decision-making." So the rights that states must provide under these treaties will be granted to non-citizens when there is a transboundary impact and possibly also in other situations where non-citizens might have an interest in the impact of a project (e.g., if the project impacted a local cultural site of importance to non-citizens).

In March 2018, representatives of 24 Latin American and Caribbean states adopted a Regional Agreement on Access to Information, Public Participation and Access to Justice in Environmental Matters. The agreement will open for signature in September 2018 at U.N. headquarters in New York. If it is ratified, it will be the first such regional agreement applicable outside the UNECE region.

Problem 5-1

Problem 5-1 is a multi-issue problem. Your instructor may ask you to study the entire problem or to focus on particular parts of it. Part A of the problem concerns the European Union and the laws it has adopted to address air pollution. Part B of the problem examines the operation of the Espoo and Aarhus Conventions. Part C of the problem deals with both customary law and the Convention on Long-Range Transboundary Air Pollution.

PROBLEM 5-1: ACID RAIN AND OZONE POLLUTION IN DONAUVIA

Section 1. Facts

The Emerald Forest is an ancient forest of pine, spruce, and other firs located in a mountainous region of Donauvia,[26] an Eastern European democracy bordering on the Azurian Sea near the AzMed straits, which

[26] Pronounced Dnowvia.

connect the Azurian Sea with the Mediterranean Sea. Renowned for the beauty of its evergreen-covered mountains, deep lakes, river gorges, and waterfalls, the Emerald Forest is also home to an endangered species of owl found nowhere else. Its natural beauty, ancient stone churches and unique castles attract tourists from across Donauvia, Europe, and the world. In 1990, the Emerald Forest was recognized on the World Heritage List as a natural area "of outstanding universal value from the point of view of science, conservation or natural beauty."[27]

In recent years, the Emerald Forest has come under serious stress. Large areas of pine are stunted and dying. The annual growth of young trees averages less than 70% of the average growth of prior years. Trees are losing their needles at unusual rates, and tree loss from insect damage, winter ice, and disease is much higher than in the past. The streams and lakes of the forest also are faring poorly. Twenty-five percent of the lakes are essentially "dead," lacking the trout and other fish that used to inhabit them, as well as plankton and other microscopic life. In addition, there are reports of unusual wear and deterioration of the castles and churches in the forest—large areas of stone work are turning black, the detail on intricate stone carvings is eroding, and cracks are developing in stone that has been stable for centuries.

Two years ago, the Donauvian Environmental Protection Agency published a report about the problems in the Emerald Forest, concluding that the damage to the trees in the forest was caused by acid rain and ozone pollution. The dead or dying lakes and streams were discovered to have pH levels less than 5.0, making the water too acidic for most plant and fish life. And the unusual damage to the forest's stone churches and castles appears to have been caused by the erosive and other effects of acid rain. Ambient ozone levels in the forest during the summer months were found to be excessively high—well above the limits set by EU Directive 2008/50/EC (the Ambient Air Quality Directive).

The Donauvian report concluded that a number of factors contributed to the problems in the Emerald Forest. The summertime ozone pollution was attributable primarily to heavy—mostly Donauvian—summertime road traffic in the forest and to emissions of ozone precursors from steady—oftentimes hourly—maritime traffic through the AzMed Straits.[28] The acid rain problem, the report further concluded, was the result of emissions of acidifying gases both from ships navigating the AzMed Straits and from coal-fired power plants in the Caucasian Republic of Haikastan and some

[27] UNESCO Convention for the Protection of the World Cultural and Natural Heritage, Nov. 16, 1972, art. 2, 1037 UNTS 151.

[28] For purposes of this problem, you should assume that any ships traveling through the AzMed Straits are exercising their right of innocent passage under the UN Convention on the Law of the Sea (**Basic Document 3.4**, art. 19) and that Donauvia has no right to impose any restrictions on those ships.

of its Caucasian neighbors, many kilometers east of Donauvia across the Azurian Sea.

In response to this report, a group of concerned Donauvians formed a non-governmental organization called Friends of the Emerald Forest [FOEF]. FOEF is organized under the laws of Donauvia, and its statutes call for it to engage in research and advocacy aimed at preserving the Emerald Forest. Although it is less than two years old, FOEF has already over 100,000 members, all Donauvian citizens. Also, its political pressure has been instrumental in causing the Donauvian government to address the problems in the Emerald Forest seriously.

A

Last year, Mate Boban, a wealthy Donauvian citizen who owns a large estate in the Emerald Forest, filed suit against the Donauvian Environmental Protection Agency in Donauvian courts. Boban's suit alleges that the Donauvian EPA has violated EU Directive 2008/50/EC (Ambient Air Quality) **(Basic Document 2.3)** by failing to adopt a plan sufficient to significantly reduce the ozone problem in the Emerald Forest. The Donauvian EPA's current plan (which has been implemented) seeks to discourage road traffic in the Emerald Forest by imposing a road access fee of 50 euros per vehicle per entry. Although the fee has somewhat reduced the number of vehicles traveling in the Forest, the reduction has not affected ozone levels.

Boban's suit alleges, and the Donauvian government concedes, that ambient ozone levels in the forest regularly exceed the applicable "target values," "long-term objectives," and "alert thresholds" for ozone pollution, as specified in Annexes VII and XII to the EU Ambient Air Quality Directive.

Boban has asked the court to require the Donauvian EPA to adopt a new plan that bans all tourism-related road traffic in the Emerald Forest during the summer months and severely restricts it during the winter. Alternatively, Boban has suggested that the Donauvian EPA could solve the problem by requiring all light-duty vehicles (automobiles and small trucks) licensed in Donauvia to be equipped with modern emissions-control devices (catalytic converters) to reduce their emissions of ozone-precursors.

The Donauvian EPA resists taking any of these actions. It claims that the elimination of tourist-related road travel in the Emerald Forest would do excessive harm to the local economy, that requiring all light-duty vehicles to be equipped with modern catalytic converters would be prohibitively expensive for Donauvian automobile owners, and that the ozone problem would continue due to emissions from ships in the AzMed Straits.

B

Carpathia is an independent state located on the Azurian Sea, about 150 kilometers north of Donauvia. It is not a member of the European Union, but it has recently indicated its desire to become a candidate for membership.

Three months ago, the Government of Carpathia issued a press release announcing plans to double the size of its port facilities at Balaknopt, its second largest city. The press release stated that the expansion was primarily intended to ensure that the port could accommodate the growing Carpathian navy and coast guard as well as visiting NATO ships. But the government also noted that the new construction would allow the port to accept the very largest ocean-going ships and tankers and was expected to increase international commercial ship traffic to and from the port.

Carpathia did not provide any prior public notice that it was planning this project, nor did it allow public comment on the likely environmental or economic impact of the port expansion. In response to a properly filed inquiry and request for documents submitted by FOEF, the Carpathian Information Agency stated that

> the environmental and economic impact of the project was analyzed in a report prepared by the Office of Environmental Compliance of the Ministry of Defense. That report concluded that the project would have no direct transboundary environmental effect. Because the report concerns expansion of an important military asset and related port facilities, national security considerations prevent us from releasing it.

FOEF is concerned that the port project will significantly worsen the problem in the Emerald Forest by contributing to growth in maritime traffic through the AzMed Straits (the only route by which ships engaged in international trade can reach Carpathia). FOEF filed a lawsuit in Carpathia, alleging that the Carpathian government had violated its own national law, as well as international treaties to which it is a party, by failing to permit public participation in the environmental impact analysis of the port expansion and by refusing to release the analysis of the environmental impact of the project. In particular, FOEF has complained that the Carpathian government refuses to provide detailed information about the expected increases in commercial ship traffic to the port and what percentage of the visiting vessels are expected to travel through the AzMed Straits.

The Carpathian court ruled that FOEF had properly exhausted all its administrative remedies. But it concluded that FOEF lacked standing, and it dismissed the lawsuit. Under Carpathian law, a nongovernmental environmental organization is automatically granted standing to contest governmental non-compliance with environmental laws, but only if the organization has been in existence for at least five years and has at least 500 members in Carpathia.

FOEF has complained to the Donauvian government that Carpathia's actions are in violation of the Espoo Convention on Environmental Impact Assessment in a Transboundary Context **(Basic Document 1.38)** and the Aarhus Convention on Access to Information, Public Participation in Decision-Making and Access to Justice in Environmental Matters **(Basic Document 1.39)**. Both countries are parties to those treaties. Neither accepts ICJ jurisdiction or arbitration as compulsory for the resolution of disputes under either treaty.

C

As noted earlier, the acid rain problem afflicting the Emerald Forest is due, in part, to pollution from coal-fired power plants in Haikastan. Donauvia has sought Haikastan's cooperation in addressing this problem. Both Donauvia and Haikastan are parties to the 1979 Convention on Long-Range Transboundary Air Pollution **(Basic Document 2.1)** and the related Gothenburg Protocol to Abate Acidification, Eutrophication and Ground-level Ozone **(Basic Document 2.1(a))**. Neither country accepts ICJ jurisdiction or arbitration as compulsory for the resolution of disputes under the Convention or Protocol.

EMEP data[29] show that emissions of acidifying compounds—primarily sulphur dioxide (SO_2), nitrous oxides, and ammonia (NH_3)—from sources in Haikastan contribute substantially to acid deposition in the Emerald Forest. But those same data show that current emissions in Haikastan are within the emission ceilings applicable to that country under the Gothenburg Protocol. However, Haikastan has recently announced plans to build five new coal-fired power plants in the next year. From reports and specifications released by Haikastan, it is clear that emissions of sulphur dioxides and nitrous oxides from these plants will greatly exceed the limit values for new stationary sources established by Article 3(2) of the Gothenburg Protocol and the relevant annexes.

Donauvia has demanded that Haikastan refrain from constructing the plants or provide assurances that they would be outfitted with appropriate pollution control technology. After a month of consultation and negotiation between the two countries, Haikastan withdrew from the discussions and issued the following statement:

> The Government of Haikastan is committed to a clean environment. It has long been our wish to meet the growing energy needs of our people through the construction of clean and green nuclear power plants. In fact, several new plants are under

[29] The European Monitoring and Evaluation Programme (EMEP) is a program under the Convention on Long-Range Transboundary Air Pollution that, among other things, compiles emissions data relevant to transboundary air pollution. *See* Reading 9, *infra*.

> construction and, if they were completed, we would have no need to build coal-fired plants. However, our civilian nuclear program has been halted as a result of unwarranted sanctions imposed upon us by the UN Security Council and the International Atomic Energy Agency in response to false reports that we are developing nuclear weapons. Those sanctions have prevented us from obtaining the equipment and technology we need to complete the nuclear plants in which we have already invested so heavily. Until the boycott is lifted, we have no choice but to build coal-fired plants, and we must build them as quickly and as cheaply as possible. Having invested so much in nuclear energy, we cannot afford the expensive pollution control now demanded by Donauvia. However, we will immediately cease construction of the coal-fired plants if Donauvia will meet its obligations under Article 4 of the Gothenburg Protocol by providing us with the technology and assistance we need to complete our nuclear power plants.

For its part, Donauvia indicated that it would honor the "lawful sanctions imposed on Haikastan by the international community," and that those sanctions "do not excuse Haikastan's announced decision to disregard its treaty commitments and its obligation, under customary international law, to avoid causing transboundary environmental harm."

You are a lawyer in the Donauvian Environmental Protection Agency's international affairs section. You have been asked to provide advice on whether Boban's suit has any merit. You have also been asked to advise on whether Carpathia or Haikastan or both have violated international law. In addition, you should identify actions that Donauvia might take to secure the cooperation of Carpathia and Haikastan in reducing the pollution that is damaging the Emerald Forest.

Section 2. Questions Presented

1. Has Donauvia violated EU law by failing to adopt an effective plan for reducing emissions of ozone-producing gases? Is Mate Boban entitled to the remedy he seeks?

2. Has Carpathia violated its obligations under the Espoo and Aarhus Conventions with respect to its assessment of the environmental impact of the port project and its response to FOEF's request for information and subsequent lawsuit?

3. If Haikastan builds the planned coal-fired plants and refuses to install pollution control technology, will it be in violation of its legal obligations under the Gothenburg Protocol or customary international law?

Does it have a valid defense based on Donauvia's refusal to provide it with technology and assistance to complete construction of its unfinished nuclear power plants?

Section 3. Assignments

A. *Reading Assignment*

Study the Readings presented in Section 4, *infra*, and the Discussion Notes/Questions that follow.

B. *Recommended Writing Assignment*

Prepare a comprehensive, logically sequenced, and *argumentative* brief in the form of an outline of the primary and subsidiary *legal* issues raised by the questions presented above. Also, from the perspective of the independent judge or arbitrator, indicate which side ought to prevail on each issue and why. Retain a copy of your issue-outline/brief for class discussion.

C. *Recommended Oral Assignment*

Assume you are legal counsel for Donauvia, Carpathia, or Haikastan (as designated by your instructor); then, relying upon the Readings (and your issue-outline if prepared), present a 15–20 minute oral argument of your party's likely position on each issue relevant to it.

D. *Recommended Reflective Assignment*

Consider (and recommend) alternative norms, institutions, and/or procedures that you believe might be more effective than existing world order arrangements in resolving situations of the kind posed by this problem. In so doing, but without insisting upon *immediate* feasibility, identify the particular transition steps that would be needed to make your alternatives a reality.

Section 4. Readings

(A) Readings Relevant to Problem 5-1(A)

1. Editors' Note on the European Union (EU)

Problem 5-1(A) requires some basic knowledge about the European Union. In this reading, we provide you with some background information about the EU. The two subsequent readings look at the nature of EU law and the ability of citizens to enforce it. Finally, we present excerpts from the EU's Ambient Air Quality Directive, which is at issue in this problem.

A Different Kind of International Organization

The European Union has been described as a "new legal order of international law."[30] Although the EU "remains a part of the old order of public international law from which it grew," its evolution has followed a path that

> has significantly moved the "goal post" of traditional international law. It extends the scope of possibilities available under international law. One important achievement is the wholesale change in our perceptions of how international law can work as a dynamic and effective force. The Community legal order has done so most notably by granting to nonstate actors rights that they can enforce before national courts and the European Court of Justice, by applying the doctrines of direct effect, supremacy, and implied powers, and by instituting a decisionmaking process based on qualified majority, rather than unanimous, voting.

Phillipe Sands, *European Community Environmental Law: The Evolution of a Regional Regime of International Environmental Protection*, 100 Yale L.J. 2511, 2518–19 (1991).

Today, the EU resembles an independent federation more than a treaty organization, and its past and continued development shows the transformative capacity of international law.

The Treaties

The European Union's origins trace to the efforts of far-sighted European politicians who, after living through the experience of World War II—the second continent-wide, all-out war in Europe in the span of 30 years—believed that the only hope for a peaceful and prosperous future Europe was through closer political and economic cooperation among the leading European powers. Spurred on by a fear of the Soviet Union's control of Eastern Europe and by US support and encouragement, these leaders began in the 1940s and 1950s to pursue a variety of actions aimed at building stronger international partnerships on the European continent.

Early steps toward European integration were cautious and relatively modest efforts aimed at building a framework that could be used to harmonize national policies in certain key areas—trade and economic relations, atomic energy policy, and policies affecting the coal and steel industry. In 1952, the European Coal and Steel Community (ECSC) was created by treaty.[31] Six years later, the six ECSC states—France, Germany, Italy, Belgium, Luxembourg, and the Netherlands—entered treaties establishing the European Economic Community and the

[30] Case 26/62, Van Gend en Loos v. Netherlands Inland Revenue Admin., 1963 E.C.R. 1, 2.

[31] Treaty Instituting the European Coal and Steel Community, Apr. 18, 1951, 261 UNTS 140.

European Atomic Energy Community.[32] In 1965, the institutional structures of these three "communities" were merged.

In the years since their adoption, the treaties establishing the European communities have been amended many times. Each amendment has aimed at strengthening the European institutions and deepening the economic or political integration of the member states. In 1987, for example, the Single European Act (SEA) gave the European Parliament an increased role in decision-making at the European level, thus improving the perceived democratic legitimacy of European Community actions. The SEA also expanded the circumstances in which European legislation could be passed by a qualified majority of states rather than requiring unanimous agreement. This reduced the ability of individual states to block the development of European law.

In 1993, the Treaty on European Union (also called the Maastricht Treaty),[33] changed the name of the European Economic Community to "the European Community," and broadened the scope of cooperation among member governments to include foreign policy, defense and "justice and home affairs." This broader cooperative structure, going beyond as well as encompassing economic affairs, was called the European Union (EU). Further changes aimed at improving the functioning of the EU and consolidating the key treaties into a single version were made by the Treaty of Amsterdam (entered into force in 1999) and the Treaty of Nice (entered into force in 2003).[34]

In 2009, the Treaty of Lisbon entered into force,[35] amending the key EU and EC treaties in ways that have brought the European Union even closer to resembling a nation-state rather than a traditional treaty organization. The European Parliament is given a stronger role than ever in EU legislation, with nearly as much authority in some areas as the Council of the European Union (which represents the member state governments). The ability of a qualified majority of states to pass legislation over the objection of other member states is expanded to new policy areas. The new treaty also includes provisions aimed at clarifying the respective legislative authority of the European Union and the Member states, including identifying areas in which the European Union's authority is exclusive.

But the European Union's roots in public international law remain evident. The Treaty of Lisbon for the first time affirms the right of member

[32] Treaty Establishing the European Economic Community, Mar. 25, 1957, 298 UNTS 3; Treaty Establishing the European Atomic Energy Community, Mar. 25, 1957, 298 UNTS 167.

[33] Treaty on European Union, Feb. 7, 1992, 1759 UNTS 3.

[34] Treaty of Amsterdam, Oct. 2, 1997, OJEC C340 (10 Nov 1997), *reprinted in* 37 ILM 56 (1998); Treaty of Nice, Feb. 26, 2001, OJEC C325 (24 Dec 2002).

[35] Treaty of Lisbon amending the Treaty on European Union and the Treaty Establishing the European Community, Dec. 13, 2007, OJEC C306 (Dec. 17, 2007).

states to withdraw from the Union, it provides that amendments to the treaty require unanimous agreement of all member states, and it requires that each member state must ratify amendments in accord with that state's own constitutional procedures for entering a treaty.

Legal Personality

A distinction that was often confusing in the past was the contrast between the European Community and the European Union. The distinction was based on the fact that the legal foundation of the European Union is not a single document but several treaties, including most prominently the Treaty Establishing the European Community and the Treaty on European Union.[36] When a European institution acted under the authority of the Treaty Establishing the European Community, it was acting as the legally separate "European Community" and not as the European Union. As noted earlier, the entry into force of the Treaty of Lisbon has eliminated this distinction, and the European institutions now have a single legal personality. Regardless of the treaty pursuant to which they are acting, they act as the European Union.

Members

As the structure and scope of integration in Europe has evolved, so has the membership of the European Union. The original six members of the European communities were joined in 1973 by Denmark, Ireland, and the United Kingdom. Greece joined in 1981, and Spain and Portugal followed in 1986. Austria, Finland and Sweden joined in 1995. During the expansion in Western Europe, Norway and Switzerland remained outside the EU and have not applied for membership as of this writing. Ten more states joined in 2004 (Cyprus, Czech Republic, Estonia, Hungary, Latvia, Lithuania, Malta, Poland, Slovak Republic, and Slovenia). Two joined in 2007 (Bulgaria and Romania), and the final member of the 28 (Croatia) joined in 2013.

These 28 states make today's European Union an economic and political powerhouse with a combined population of over 500 million and an economy about 25% larger than the United States. From the 1950s, when the earliest European Community treaties were adopted, to 2009, when the Treaty of Lisbon entered into force, the history of Europe has been a history of increasing economic and political integration through international law.

On 29 March 2017, the United Kingdom notified the Union of its intent to withdraw. Assuming that it completes the process of withdrawal, it will leave the EU sometime in the fall of 2019. The UK's decision to leave the EU has led some commentators to question whether the EU will survive.

---

[36] *Supra* notes 32–33.

But as of this writing, no other countries are proposing to leave the EU, and its future looks secure.

Key Institutions

The key institutions of the European Union are the Commission, the Council of the European Union (which becomes the European Council when it meets at the Heads of State or Government level), the European Parliament, and the Court of Justice. The governance responsibilities of these institutions can be described, in oversimplified fashion, as follows:

> The Commission is the executive arm of the EU. It has the power to initiate legislative proposals and the responsibility to enforce EU law.
>
> The Council, consisting of a representative of the government of each Member State, is the EU's legislature. It adopts EU laws and concludes international agreements on behalf of the Union.
>
> The European Parliament, for many years a primarily advisory body in Community affairs, has in recent years been granted expanded powers. Today it shares a significant amount of legislative power with the Council, it can ask the Commission to submit legislative proposals, and its assent is needed before the EU can enter certain kinds of international agreements.
>
> The European Court of Justice has jurisdiction to interpret and apply EU law, including the various treaties. It hears actions against Member States and against EU institutions. At the request of Member State courts, it can offer rulings on the meaning and validity of EU acts.

EU Legislation

In most cases, the European Commission has the sole power to propose EU legislation, whereas the Council and Parliament have the authority to pass the laws through the so-called ordinary legislative procedure, which requires both bodies to agree on proposed legislation before it can become law.

EU legislation takes two main forms: directives and regulations. An EU "regulation" is "binding in its entirety and directly applicable in all Member States." A "directive," on the other hand, is not ordinarily directly applicable and is binding on Member States only "as to the result to be achieved." *See* Article 288 of the Treaty on the Functioning of the European Union. Directives aim to align each Member State's national law with EU policy, and their effectiveness depends on how and when they are transformed into national law. The following European Parliament Fact Sheet provides more detail about these forms of EU legislation, along with other EU prescriptive acts.

2. European Parliament, Fact Sheets on the European Union: Sources of European Union Law, http://www.europarl.europa.eu (accessed on 2 March 2010)

a. Regulations

They have general application, are binding in their entirety and are directly applicable in all Member States. As 'Union law', regulations must be complied with fully by those to whom they apply (private persons, Member States, Union institutions). Regulations apply directly in all the Member States, without requiring a national act to transpose them. As soon as they enter into force (on the date stipulated or, failing this, on the twentieth day following their publication in the Official Journal of the European Union), they become part of national legal orders.

Regulations serve to ensure the uniform application of Union law in all the Member States. At the same time, they prevent the application of national legal rules which are incompatible with their substantive clauses.

b. Directives

Nature and scope

They are binding, as to the result to be achieved, upon the Member States to whom they are addressed. However, those Member States are left the choice of form and methods to achieve their objectives. Directives may be addressed to individual, several or all Member States. In order to ensure that the objectives laid down in directives become applicable to individual citizens, an act of transposition (or "national implementing measure") by national legislators is required, whereby national law is adapted to the objectives laid down in directives. Individual citizens are given rights and bound by the legal act only when the directive is transposed into national law. Since the Member States are only bound by the objectives laid down in directives, they have some discretion, in transposing them into national law, in taking account of specific national circumstances. Transposition must be effected within the period laid down in a directive. In transposing directives, the Member States must select the national forms which are best suited to ensure the effectiveness of Union law, based on the principle of sincere cooperation enshrined in Article 4(3) TEU. Directives must be transposed in the form of binding national legislation which fulfils the requirements of legal certainty and legal clarity and establishes a position whereby individuals can rely on the rights derived from the directive. Regulations which have been adopted as a result of directives may not subsequently be amended contrary to the objectives of those directives ("blocking" effect of directives).

Possible direct applicability

Directives are not directly applicable, in principle. The European Court of Justice, however, has nevertheless ruled that individual provisions of a directive may, exceptionally, have a direct effect in a Member State without requiring an act of transposition by that Member State beforehand (consistent case-law since 1970: ECR pp. 1213 et seq.) where the following conditions are satisfied:

- the period for transposition has expired and the directive has not been transposed or has been transposed incorrectly,
- the provisions of the directive are imperative and sufficiently clear and precise,
- the provisions of the directive confer rights on individuals.

If these requirements are fulfilled, individuals may cite the provisions of the directive against all agencies in which State power is vested. Such agencies are organisations and establishments which are subordinate to the State or on which the State confers rights that exceed those arising from the law on relations between private persons (Court judgment of 22 June 1989 in Case 103/88 Fratelli Costanzo). The case-law is mainly justified on the principles of "*effet utile*" and the uniform application of Community law. But even when the provision concerned does not seek to confer any rights on the individual, and only the first and second conditions are satisfied, the Court's consistent case-law says the Member State authorities have a legal duty to comply with the untransposed directive. This case-law is mainly justified on the grounds of "*effet utile,*" the penalisation of violations of the Treaty and legal protection. On the other hand, an individual may not directly invoke against another individual (the "horizontal effect") the direct effect of an untransposed directive. . . .

<u>Responsibility for failure to transpose a directive</u>

According to Court case-law (Francovich case, [1991] ECR p. 5357 et seq.), an individual citizen is entitled to claim compensation from a Member State which has not transposed a directive or has done so inadequately where:

- the directive is intended to confer rights on individuals,
- the substance of the rights can be ascertained on the basis of the directive,
- and where there is a causal connection between the breach of the duty to transpose the directive and the loss sustained by the individual.

Fault on the part of the Member State does not then have to be demonstrated in order to establish liability. If the Member State has powers of discretion in transposing the law, the violation must also, in addition to the three criteria above, qualify as defective or non-existent transposition: it must be substantial and evident (Court of Justice,

Brasserie du Pêcheur/Factortame 5 March 1996, Cases 46/93 and 48/93, ECR I–1029).

c. *Decisions*

They are binding in their entirety. Where those to whom they are addressed are stipulated, they are binding only on them. These may be Member States or natural or legal persons. Decisions serve to regulate actual circumstances vis-à-vis specific entities addressed thereby. Like directives, decisions may include an obligation on a Member State to grant individual citizens a more favourable legal position. In this case, as with directives, an act of transposition on the part of the Member State concerned is required as a basis for claims by individuals. Decisions may be directly applicable under the same preconditions as the provisions of directives.

d. *Recommendations and opinions*

They have no binding force, that is to say they do not establish any rights or obligations for those to whom they are addressed, but do provide guidance as to the interpretation and content of Community law.

3. Case C-237/07, Dieter Janecek v. Freistaat Bayern, 2008 E.C.R. I–06221

GROUNDS

1. This reference for a preliminary ruling concerns the interpretation of Article 7(3) of Council Directive 96/62/EC of 27 September 1996 on ambient air quality assessment and management [Directive 96/62]. . . .

* * *

Community legislation

3. According to the 12th recital in the preamble to Directive 96/62:

> ". . . in order to protect the environment as a whole and human health, it is necessary that Member States take action when limit values are exceeded in order to comply with these values within the time fixed."

5. Article 7 of Directive 96/62, headed "Improvement of ambient air quality—General requirements," provides:

> "1. Member States shall take the necessary measures to ensure compliance with the limit values. . . .
>
> 3. Member States shall draw up action plans indicating the measures to be taken in the short term where there is a risk of the limit values and/or alert thresholds being exceeded, in order to

reduce that risk and to limit the duration of such an occurrence. . . ."

* * *

National legislation

9. Directive 96/62 was transposed into German law by the . . . Federal Law on protection against the harmful effects of air pollution, noise, vibrations and other types of nuisance on the environment. . . .

* * *

The dispute in the main proceedings and the questions referred for a preliminary ruling

13. Mr. Janecek lives on the Landshuter Allee on Munich's central ring road, approximately 900 metres north of an air quality measuring station.

14. Measurements taken at that station have shown that, in 2005 and 2006, the limit value fixed for emissions of particulate matter (PM 10) was exceeded much more than 35 times, even though that is the maximum number of instances permitted under the Federal Law on combating pollution.

15. It is common ground that an air quality action plan exists in respect of the city of Munich, that action plan having been declared mandatory on 28 December 2004.

16. However, the applicant in the main proceedings brought an action before the Verwaltungsgericht (Administrative Court) Munich for an order requiring the Freistaat Bayern to draw up an air quality action plan in the Landshuter Allee district, so as to determine the measures to be taken in the short-term in order to ensure compliance with the maximum permitted number of instances—35 per year of the emission limit value for particulate matter PM 10 being exceeded. The Verwaltungsgericht Munich dismissed that action as unfounded.

17. On appeal, the Verwaltungsgerichtshof (Higher Administrative Court) took a different view, holding that the residents concerned may require the competent authorities to draw up an action plan, but that they are not entitled to insist that it must include the particular measures that would guarantee compliance in the short-term with the emission limit values for particulate matter PM 10. According to the Verwaltungsgerichtshof, the national authorities are required only to ensure that such a plan pursues that objective to the extent to which it is possible and proportionate for it to do so. Consequently, it ordered the Freistaat Bayern to draw up an action plan complying with those requirements.

18. [On appeal from this decision, the Bundesverwaltungsgericht (Federal Administrative Court) held that] the applicant in the main proceedings cannot rely on any entitlement to have an action plan drawn up pursuant to Paragraph 47(2) of the Federal Law on combating pollution. The Bundesverwaltungsgericht takes the view, moreover, that neither the spirit nor the letter of Article 7(3) of Directive 96/62 confers a personal right to have an action plan drawn up.

* * *

The Court's findings

The preparation of action plans

* * *

35. [Article 7(3) of Directive 96/62] places the Member States under a clear obligation to draw up action plans both where there is a risk of the limit values being exceeded and where there is a risk of the alert thresholds being exceeded. That interpretation, which follows from a straightforward reading of Article 7(3) of Directive 96/62, is, moreover, confirmed in the 12th recital in the preamble to the directive. What is laid down in relation to the limit values applies all the more with regard to the alert thresholds, in respect of which, moreover, Article 2—which defines the various terms used in the directive—provides that "immediate steps shall be taken by the Member States as laid down in this Directive."

36. In addition, the Court has consistently held that individuals are entitled, as against public bodies, to rely on the provisions of a directive which are unconditional and sufficiently precise (see, to that effect, Case 148/78 Ratti [1979] ECR 1629, paragraph 20). It is for the competent national authorities and courts to interpret national law, as far as possible, in a way that is compatible with the purpose of that directive (see, to that effect, Case C–106/89 Marleasing [1990] ECR I4135, paragraph 8). Where such an interpretation is not possible, they must disapply the rules of national law which are incompatible with the directive concerned.

37. As the Court of Justice has noted on numerous occasions, it is incompatible with the binding effect which Article 249 EC [now Article 288] ascribes to a directive to exclude, in principle, the possibility of the obligation imposed by that directive being relied on by persons concerned. That consideration applies particularly in respect of a directive which is intended to control and reduce atmospheric pollution and which is designed, therefore, to protect public health.

38. Thus, the Court has held that, whenever the failure to observe the measures required by the directives which relate to air quality and drinking water, and which are designed to protect public health, could endanger human health, the persons concerned must be in a position to rely on the mandatory rules included in those directives (see Case C–361/88

Commission v Germany; Case C–59/89 Commission v Germany; and Case C–58/89 Commission v Germany).

39. It follows from the foregoing that the natural or legal persons directly concerned by a risk that the limit values or alert thresholds may be exceeded must be in a position to require the competent authorities to draw up an action plan where such a risk exists, if necessary by bringing an action before the competent courts.

40. The fact that those persons may have other courses of action available to them—in particular, the power to require that the competent authorities lay down specific measures to reduce pollution, which, as indicated by the referring court, is provided for under German law—is irrelevant in that regard.

* * *

The content of action plans

43. By its second and third questions, the Bundesverwaltungsgericht is asking whether the competent national authorities are obliged to lay down measures which, in the short term, would ensure that the limit value is attained, or whether they can confine themselves to taking measures to ensure a reduction in instances of the limit value being exceeded or limits on their duration and which are, consequently, liable to make it possible for the situation to be improved gradually.

44. According to Article 7(3) of Directive 96/62, action plans must include the measures "to be taken in the short term where there is a risk of the limit values and/or alert thresholds being exceeded, in order to reduce that risk and to limit the duration of such an occurrence." It follows from that very wording that the Member States are not obliged to take measures to ensure that those limit values and/or alert thresholds are never exceeded.

45. On the contrary, it is apparent from the broad logic of the directive—which seeks an integrated reduction of pollution—that it is for the Member States to take measures capable of reducing to a minimum the risk of the limit values and/or alert thresholds being exceeded and the duration of such an occurrence, taking into account all the material circumstances and opposing interests.

46. It must be noted in this regard that, while the Member States thus have a discretion, Article 7(3) of Directive 96/62 includes limits on the exercise of that discretion which may be relied upon before the national courts (see, to that effect, Case C–72/95 Kraaijeveld and Others [1996] ECR I5403, paragraph 59), relating to the adequacy of the measures which must be included in the action plan with the aim of reducing the risk of the limit values and/or alert thresholds being exceeded and the duration of such an occurrence, taking into account the balance which must be maintained

between that objective and the various opposing public and private interests.

47. Therefore, the answer to the second and third questions must be that the Member States are obliged, subject to judicial review by the national courts, only to take such measures—in the context of an action plan and in the short term—as are capable of reducing to a minimum the risk that the limit values or alert thresholds may be exceeded and of ensuring a gradual return to a level below those values or thresholds, taking into account the factual circumstances and all opposing interests.

4. Council Directive 2008/50/EC on Ambient Air Quality, arts. 2, 17, 25, & 33, 2008 O.J. (L152/1) (EC)

Article 2. Definitions

* * *

3. 'level' shall mean the concentration of a pollutant in ambient air or the deposition thereof on surfaces in a given time; * * *

9. 'target value' shall mean a level fixed with the aim of avoiding, preventing or reducing harmful effects on human health and/or the environment as a whole, to be attained where possible over a given period;

10. 'alert threshold' shall mean a level beyond which there is a risk to human health from brief exposure for the population as a whole and at which immediate steps are to be taken by the Member States; * * *

14. 'long-term objective' shall mean a level to be attained in the long term, save where not achievable through proportionate measures, with the aim of providing effective protection of human health and the environment; * * *

Article 17. Requirements in zones and agglomerations where ozone concentrations exceed the target values and long-term objectives

1. Member States shall take all necessary measures not entailing disproportionate costs to ensure that the target values and long-term objectives are attained.

2. For zones and agglomerations in which a target value is exceeded, Member States shall ensure that * * *, if appropriate, an air quality plan is implemented in order to attain the target values, save where not achievable through measures not entailing disproportionate costs * * *.

Article 24. Short-term action plans

1. Where, in a given zone or agglomeration, there is a risk that the levels of pollutants will exceed one or more of the alert thresholds specified in Annex XII, Member States shall draw up action plans indicating the measures to be taken in the short term in order to reduce the risk or duration of such an exceedance. * * *

However, where there is a risk that the alert threshold for ozone specified in * * * Annex XII will be exceeded, Member States shall only draw up such short-term action plans when in their opinion there is a significant potential, taking into account national geographical, meteorological and economic conditions, to reduce the risk, duration or severity of such an exceedance. * * *

2. The short-term action plans referred to in paragraph 1 may, depending on the individual case, provide for effective measures to control and, where necessary, suspend activities which contribute to the risk of the respective limit values or target values or alert threshold being exceeded. Those action plans may include measures in relation to motor-vehicle traffic, construction works, ships at berth, and the use of industrial plants or products and domestic heating. * * *

Article 25. Transboundary air pollution

1. Where any alert threshold, limit value or target value plus any relevant margin of tolerance or long-term objective is exceeded due to significant transboundary transport of air pollutants or their precursors, the Member States concerned shall cooperate and, where appropriate, draw up joint activities, such as the preparation of joint or coordinated air quality plans * * * in order to remove such exceedances through the application of appropriate but proportionate measures.

2. The Commission shall be invited to be present and to assist in any cooperation referred to in paragraph 1. * * *

5. In drawing up plans as provided for in paragraphs 1 and 3 and in informing the public as referred to in paragraph 4, Member States shall, where appropriate, endeavour to pursue cooperation with third countries, and in particular with candidate countries.

(B) Readings Relevant to Problem 5-1(B)

5. Convention on Environmental Impact Assessment in a Transboundary Context (Espoo Convention), as amended, arts. 1–3, 5–6, 15 & appendix I, Feb. 25, 1991, 1989 UNTS 209 (Basic Document 1.38)

Article 1—Definitions

For the purposes of this Convention,

(i) "Parties" means, unless the text otherwise indicates, the Contracting Parties to this Convention;

(ii) "Party of origin" means the Contracting Party or Parties to this Convention under whose jurisdiction a proposed activity is envisaged to take place;

(iii) "Affected Party" means the Contracting Party or Parties to this Convention likely to be affected by the transboundary impact of a proposed activity;

(iv) "Concerned Parties" means the Party of origin and the affected Party of an environmental impact assessment pursuant to this Convention;

(v) "Proposed activity" means any activity or any major change to an activity subject to a decision of a competent authority in accordance with an applicable national procedure;

(vi) "Environmental impact assessment" means a national procedure for evaluating the likely impact of a proposed activity on the environment;

(vii) "Impact" means any effect caused by a proposed activity on the environment including human health and safety, flora, fauna, soil, air, water, climate, landscape and historical monuments or other physical structures or the interaction among these factors; it also includes effects on cultural heritage or socio-economic conditions resulting from alterations to those factors;

(viii) "Transboundary impact" means any impact, not exclusively of a global nature, within an area under the jurisdiction of a Party caused by a proposed activity the physical origin of which is situated wholly or in part within the area under the jurisdiction of another Party;

(ix) "Competent authority" means the national authority or authorities designated by a Party as responsible for performing the tasks covered by this Convention and/or the authority or authorities entrusted by a Party with decision-making powers regarding a proposed activity;

(x) "The Public" means one or more natural or legal persons and, in accordance with national legislation or practice, their associations, organizations or groups.

Article 2—General Provisions

1. The Parties shall, either individually or jointly, take all appropriate and effective measures to prevent, reduce and control significant adverse transboundary environmental impact from proposed activities.

2. Each Party shall take the necessary legal, administrative or other measures to implement the provisions of this Convention, including, with respect to proposed activities listed in Appendix I that are likely to cause significant adverse transboundary impact, the establishment of an environmental impact assessment procedure that permits public participation and preparation of the environmental impact assessment documentation described in appendix II.

3. The Party of origin shall ensure that in accordance with the provisions of this Convention an environmental impact assessment is

undertaken prior to a decision to authorize or undertake a proposed activity listed in Appendix I that is likely to cause a significant adverse transboundary impact.

4. The Party of origin shall, consistent with the provisions of this Convention, ensure that affected Parties are notified of a proposed activity listed in Appendix I that is likely to cause a significant adverse transboundary impact.

* * *

6. The Party of origin shall provide, in accordance with the provisions of this Convention, an opportunity to the public in the areas likely to be affected to participate in relevant environmental impact assessment procedures regarding proposed activities and shall ensure that the opportunity provided to the public of the affected Party is equivalent to that provided to the public of the Party of origin.

* * *

8. The provisions of this Convention shall not affect the right of Parties to implement national laws, regulations, administrative provisions or accepted legal practices protecting information the supply of which would be prejudicial to industrial and commercial secrecy or national security.

* * *

Article 3—Notification

1. For a proposed activity listed in Appendix I that is likely to cause a significant adverse transboundary impact, the Party of origin shall, for the purposes of ensuring adequate and effective consultations under Article 5, notify any Party which it considers may be an affected Party as early as possible and no later than when informing its own public about that proposed activity.

* * *

5. Upon receipt of a response from the affected Party indicating its desire to participate in the environmental impact assessment procedure, the Party of origin shall, if it has not already done so, provide to the affected Party:

(a) Relevant information regarding the environmental impact assessment procedure, including an indication of the time schedule for transmittal of comments; and

(b) Relevant information on the proposed activity and its possible significant adverse transboundary impact.

6. An affected Party shall, at the request of the Party of origin, provide the latter with reasonably obtainable information relating to the potentially affected environment under the jurisdiction of the affected Party, where such information is necessary for the preparation of the environmental impact assessment documentation. The information shall be furnished promptly and, as appropriate, through a joint body where one exists.

7. When a Party considers that it would be affected by a significant adverse transboundary impact of a proposed activity listed in Appendix I, and when no notification has taken place in accordance with paragraph 1 of this Article, the concerned Parties shall, at the request of the affected Party, exchange sufficient information for the purposes of holding discussions on whether there is likely to be a significant adverse transboundary impact. If those Parties agree that there is likely to be a significant adverse transboundary impact, the provisions of this Convention shall apply accordingly. If those Parties cannot agree whether there is likely to be a significant adverse transboundary impact, any such Party may submit that question to an inquiry commission in accordance with the provisions of Appendix IV to advise on the likelihood of significant adverse transboundary impact, unless they agree on another method of settling this question.

8. The concerned Parties shall ensure that the public of the affected Party in the areas likely to be affected be informed of, and be provided with possibilities for making comments or objections on the proposed activity, and for the transmittal of these comments or objections to the competent authority of the Party of origin, either directly to this authority or, where appropriate, through the Party of origin.

* * *

Article 5—Consultations on the Basis of the Environmental Impact Assessment Documentation

The Party of origin shall, after completion of the environmental impact assessment documentation, without undue delay enter into consultations with the affected Party concerning, *inter alia,* the potential transboundary impact of the proposed activity and measures to reduce or eliminate its impact. . . .

* * *

Article 6—Final Decision

1. The Parties shall ensure that, in the final decision on the proposed activity, due account is taken of the outcome of the environmental impact assessment, including the environmental impact assessment documentation, as well as the comments thereon received pursuant to

Article 3, paragraph 8 and Article 4, paragraph 2, and the outcome of the consultations as referred to in Article 5.

2. The Party of origin shall provide to the affected Party the final decision on the proposed activity along with the reasons and considerations on which it was based.

* * *

Article 15—Settlement of Disputes

1. If a dispute arises between two or more Parties about the interpretation or application of this Convention, they shall seek a solution by negotiation or by any other method of dispute settlement acceptable to the parties to the dispute.

* * *

Appendix I: List of Activities

1. Crude oil refineries. . . .

2. Thermal power stations [and] nuclear power stations. . . .

7. Construction of motorways, express roads and lines for long-distance railway traffic and of airports. . . .

8. Large-diameter pipelines. . . .

9. Trading ports . . . which permit the passage of vessels of over 1,350 metric tons. * * *

6. Convention on Access to Information, Public Participation in Decision-Making and Access to Justice in Environmental Matters (Aarhus Convention), arts. 1–4, 6, 9 & 16, June 25, 1998, 2161 UNTS 447 (Basic Document 1.39)

Article 1—Objective

In order to contribute to the protection of the right of every person of present and future generations to live in an environment adequate to his or her health and well-being, each Party shall guarantee the rights of access to information, public participation in decision-making, and access to justice in environmental matters in accordance with the provisions of this Convention.

Article 2—Definitions

For the purposes of this Convention,

1. "Party" means, unless the text otherwise indicates, a Contracting Party to this Convention;

2. "Public authority" means:

(a) Government at national, regional and other level;

* * *

This definition does not include bodies or institutions acting in a judicial or legislative capacity;

3. "Environmental information" means any information in written, visual, aural, electronic or any other material form on:

(a) The state of elements of the environment, such as air and atmosphere, water, soil, land, landscape and natural sites, biological diversity and its components, including genetically modified organisms, and the interaction among these elements;

(b) Factors, such as substances, energy, noise and radiation, and activities or measures, including administrative measures, environmental agreements, policies, legislation, plans and programmes, affecting or likely to affect the elements of the environment within the scope of subparagraph (a) above, and cost-benefit and other economic analyses and assumptions used in environmental decision-making;

(c) The state of human health and safety, conditions of human life, cultural sites and built structures, inasmuch as they are or may be affected by the state of the elements of the environment or, through these elements, by the factors, activities or measures referred to in subparagraph (b) above;

4. "The public" means one or more natural or legal persons, and, in accordance with national legislation or practice, their associations, organizations or groups;

5. "The public concerned" means the public affected or likely to be affected by, or having an interest in, the environmental decision-making; for the purposes of this definition, non-governmental organizations promoting environmental protection and meeting any requirements under national law shall be deemed to have an interest.

Article 3—General Provisions

1. Each Party shall take the necessary legislative, regulatory and other measures, including measures to achieve compatibility between the provisions implementing the information, public participation and access-to-justice provisions in this Convention, as well as proper enforcement measures, to establish and maintain a clear, transparent and consistent framework to implement the provisions of this Convention.

* * *

4. Each Party shall provide for appropriate recognition of and support to associations, organizations or groups promoting environmental protection and ensure that its national legal system is consistent with this obligation.

* * *

9. Within the scope of the relevant provisions of this Convention, the public shall have access to information, have the possibility to participate in decision-making and have access to justice in environmental matters without discrimination as to citizenship, nationality or domicile and, in the case of a legal person, without discrimination as to where it has its registered seat or an effective centre of its activities.

Article 4—Access to Environmental Information

1. Each Party shall ensure that, subject to the following paragraphs of this article, public authorities, in response to a request for environmental information, make such information available to the public * * *.

2. The environmental information referred to in paragraph 1 above shall be made available as soon as possible and at the latest within one month after the request has been submitted, unless the volume and the complexity of the information justify an extension of this period up to two months after the request. The applicant shall be informed of any extension and of the reasons justifying it.

3. A request for environmental information may be refused if:

(a) The public authority to which the request is addressed does not hold the environmental information requested;

(b) The request is manifestly unreasonable or formulated in too general a manner; or

(c) The request concerns material in the course of completion or concerns internal communications of public authorities where such an exemption is provided for in national law or customary practice, taking into account the public interest served by disclosure.

4. A request for environmental information may be refused if the disclosure would adversely affect:

(a) The confidentiality of the proceedings of public authorities, where such confidentiality is provided for under national law;

(b) International relations, national defence or public security;

(c) The course of justice, the ability of a person to receive a fair trial or the ability of a public authority to conduct an enquiry of a criminal or disciplinary nature;

(d) The confidentiality of commercial and industrial information, where such confidentiality is protected by law in order to protect a legitimate economic interest. Within this framework, information on emissions which is relevant for the protection of the environment shall be disclosed;

(e) Intellectual property rights;

* * *

The aforementioned grounds for refusal shall be interpreted in a restrictive way, taking into account the public interest served by disclosure and taking into account whether the information requested relates to emissions into the environment.

* * *

6. Each Party shall ensure that, if information exempted from disclosure under paragraphs 3 (c) and 4 above can be separated out without prejudice to the confidentiality of the information exempted, public authorities make available the remainder of the environmental information that has been requested.

* * *

Article 6—Public Participation in Decisions on Specific Activities

1. Each Party:

(a) Shall apply the provisions of this article with respect to decisions on whether to permit proposed activities listed in annex I[37];

(b) Shall, in accordance with its national law, also apply the provisions of this article to decisions on proposed activities not listed in annex I which may have a significant effect on the environment. To this end, Parties shall determine whether such a proposed activity is subject to these provisions; and

(c) May decide, on a case-by-case basis if so provided under national law, not to apply the provisions of this article to proposed activities serving national defence purposes, if that Party deems that such application would have an adverse effect on these purposes.

2. The public concerned shall be informed, either by public notice or individually as appropriate, early in an environmental decision-making procedure, and in an adequate, timely and effective manner, inter alia, of:

(a) The proposed activity and the application on which a decision will be taken;

(b) The nature of possible decisions or the draft decision;

(c) The public authority responsible for making the decision;

(d) The envisaged procedure . . . .

* * *

3. The public participation procedures shall include reasonable time-frames for the different phases, allowing sufficient time for informing the

[37] Annex I is substantially similar to Appendix I of the Espoo Convention and, for purposes of this problem, should be assumed to be identical.

public in accordance with paragraph 2 above and for the public to prepare and participate effectively during the environmental decision-making.

* * *

6. Each Party shall require the competent public authorities to give the public concerned access for examination, upon request where so required under national law, free of charge and as soon as it becomes available, to all information relevant to the decision-making referred to in this article that is available at the time of the public participation procedure, without prejudice to the right of Parties to refuse to disclose certain information in accordance with article 4, paragraphs 3 and 4. . . .

7. Procedures for public participation shall allow the public to submit, in writing or, as appropriate, at a public hearing or enquiry with the applicant, any comments, information, analyses or opinions that it considers relevant to the proposed activity.

* * *

Article 9—Access to Justice

1. Each Party shall, within the framework of its national legislation, ensure that any person who considers that his or her request for information under article 4 has been ignored, wrongfully refused, whether in part or in full, inadequately answered, or otherwise not dealt with in accordance with the provisions of that article, has access to a review procedure before a court of law or another independent and impartial body established by law.

In the circumstances where a Party provides for such a review by a court of law, it shall ensure that such a person also has access to an expeditious procedure established by law that is free of charge or inexpensive for reconsideration by a public authority or review by an independent and impartial body other than a court of law.

Final decisions under this paragraph 1 shall be binding on the public authority holding the information. Reasons shall be stated in writing, at least where access to information is refused under this paragraph.

2. Each Party shall, within the framework of its national legislation, ensure that members of the public concerned

(a) Having a sufficient interest or, alternatively,

(b) Maintaining impairment of a right, where the administrative procedural law of a Party requires this as a precondition, have access to a review procedure before a court of law and/or another independent and impartial body established by law, to challenge the substantive and procedural legality of any decision, act or omission subject to the provisions of article 6 and, where so provided for under national law and without prejudice to paragraph 3 below, of other relevant provisions of this Convention.

What constitutes a sufficient interest and impairment of a right shall be determined in accordance with the requirements of national law and consistently with the objective of giving the public concerned wide access to justice within the scope of this Convention. To this end, the interest of any non-governmental organization meeting the requirements referred to in article 2, paragraph 5, shall be deemed sufficient for the purpose of subparagraph (a) above. Such organizations shall also be deemed to have rights capable of being impaired for the purpose of subparagraph (b) above.

* * *

3. In addition and without prejudice to the review procedures referred to in paragraphs 1 and 2 above, each Party shall ensure that, where they meet the criteria, if any, laid down in its national law, members of the public have access to administrative or judicial procedures to challenge acts and omissions by private persons and public authorities which contravene provisions of its national law relating to the environment.

4. In addition and without prejudice to paragraph 1 above, the procedures referred to in paragraphs 1, 2 and 3 above shall provide adequate and effective remedies, including injunctive relief as appropriate, and be fair, equitable, timely and not prohibitively expensive. Decisions under this article shall be given or recorded in writing. Decisions of courts, and whenever possible of other bodies, shall be publicly accessible.

5. In order to further the effectiveness of the provisions of this article, each Party shall ensure that information is provided to the public on access to administrative and judicial review procedures and shall consider the establishment of appropriate assistance mechanisms to remove or reduce financial and other barriers to access to justice.

Article 16—Settlement of Disputes

1. If a dispute arises between two or more Parties about the interpretation or application of this Convention, they shall seek a solution by negotiation or by any other means of dispute settlement acceptable to the parties to the dispute. . . .

7. Third Meeting of the Parties to the Convention on Access to Information, Public Participation in Decision-Making and Access to Justice in Environmental Matters, Report of the Compliance Committee, U.N. Doc. ECE/MP.PP/2008/5 at 17–18 (22 May 2008).

Access to justice (article 9, paragraph 3)

62. Some of the communications referred to alleged failures by Parties to comply with article 9, paragraph 3, i.e. to ensure the communicants' opportunities to challenge acts and omissions by private persons and public authorities which contravene provisions of national law relating to the environment. One issue dealt with by the Committee was the scope of discretion given to the Parties in defining criteria for standing for member of the public. While article 9, paragraph 3, refers to "the criteria, if any, laid down in national law," the Convention neither defines these criteria nor sets out the criteria to be avoided. Rather, the Convention is intended to allow a great deal of flexibility in defining which members of the public have access to justice. On the one hand, the Parties are not obliged to establish a system of popular action (*actio popularis*) in their national laws with the effect that anyone can challenge any decision, act or omission relating to the environment. On the other hand, Parties should not take the clause "where they meet the criteria, if any, laid down in its national law" as an excuse for introducing or maintaining criteria that are so strict that they effectively bar all or almost all environmental organizations or other members of the public from challenging acts or omissions that contravene national law relating to the environment. The Convention does not prevent a Party from applying general criteria of a legal interest or requiring demonstration of an individual interest, provided the application of these criteria does not lead to effectively barring all or almost all members of the public from challenging acts and omissions and from availing of effective remedies. Accordingly, the phrase "the criteria, if any, laid down in national law" implies the exercise of self-restraint by the Parties.

63. When evaluating whether a Party complies with article 9, paragraph 3, the Committee pays attention to the general picture, i.e. to whether national law effectively has such blocking consequences for members of the public in general, including environmental organizations, or if there are remedies available for them to challenge the act or omission in question. In this evaluation, article 9, paragraph 3, should be read in conjunction with articles 1 to 3, and in the light of the purpose reflected in the preamble that "effective judicial mechanisms should be accessible to the public, including organizations, so that its legitimate interests are protected and the law is enforced." The Committee found support for this interpretation in paragraph 16 of decision II/2 of the Meeting of the Parties on promoting effective access to justice, which invites those Parties which

choose to apply criteria in the exercise of their discretion under article 9, paragraph 3, "to take fully into account the objective of the Convention to guarantee access to justice."

64. In some countries, a special category of NGOs operating in the public interest has been created and only those NGOs falling in this category have standing in administrative cases, including in matters related to the environment. However, even where such a special category of legal status has been in place for a long time, very few NGOs actually achieve it.

65. The Committee has also given consideration to what is to be understood by "national law" in article 9, paragraph 3, with regard to the European Union (EU) Member States. The Committee notes that, in different ways, European Community legislation constitutes a part of national law of the EU Member States. It also notes that article 9, paragraph 3, applies to the European Community as a Party, and that the reference to "national law" should therefore be understood as the domestic law of the Party concerned. While the impact of European Community law in the national laws of the EU Member States depends on the form and scope of the legislation in question, in some cases national courts and authorities are obliged to consider EC directives relating to the environment even when they have not been fully transposed by a Member State. For these reasons, in the context of article 9, paragraph 3, applicable European Community law relating to the environment should be considered to be part of the domestic, national law of a Member State.

8. Access to Information under Article 9 of the OSPAR Convention (Ire v. UK), 23 UNRIAA 59 (Decision of the Arbitral Tribunal, 2 July 2003)

1. This matter concerns a dispute between Ireland as claimant and the United Kingdom of Great Britain and Northern Ireland ("the United Kingdom") as respondent, determined by a Tribunal constituted pursuant to the 1992 Convention for the Protection of the Marine Environment of the North-East Atlantic ("the OSPAR Convention"). The issue concerns access to information as defined by the OSPAR Convention. Ireland has requested access to information redacted from reports prepared as part of the approval process for the commissioning of a Mixed Oxide Plant ("the MOX Plant") in the United Kingdom, based on Ireland's understanding of Article 9 of the OSPAR Convention.[38] The United Kingdom has declined to

---

[38] *Eds.* Article 9 of the OSPAR Convention reads in full, as follows:

ARTICLE 9

ACCESS TO INFORMATION

1. The Contracting Parties shall ensure that their competent authorities are required to make available the information described in paragraph 2 of this Article to any natural or legal person, in response to any reasonable request, without that person's

provide the information requested based on its understanding of the OSPAR Convention.

15. British Nuclear Fuels, plc ("BNFL"), a public limited company wholly owned by the United Kingdom, owns and operates a licensed nuclear enterprise at Sellafield in Cumbria. In 1993, BNFL applied to the local authority for permission to build a MOX Plant to process spent nuclear fuels by retrieving and blending separated plutonium oxide and uranium oxide into pellets to be reused as fuel in nuclear reactors. . . .

* * *

18. [Before the MOX Plant could be commissioned and put into operation, the United Kingdom had to fulfil a number of] international legal obligations with respect to the environmental consequences of commissioning [the Plant]. . . . [In particular], the domestic agency approving the Plant was required to ensure whatever environmental detriments it might cause were economically justified. . . .

* * *

25. [BNFL] selected the PA Consulting Group, London ("PA") to carry out a detailed assessment [of the business case for the project, including whether it was economically justified.]

26. . . . PA submitted the full version of its report ("the PA Report") to BNFL . . . . [A] public version of the PA Report [was] released in December 1997 . . . [with] redactions [justified] on "commercial confidentiality" grounds under section 4(2) of the United Kingdom's Environmental Information Regulations (1992) ("the 1992 Regulations"). . . .

---

having to prove an interest, without unreasonable charges, as soon as possible and at the latest within two months.

2. The information referred to in paragraph 1 of this Article is any available information in written, visual, aural or data-base form on the state of the maritime area, on activities or measures adversely affecting or likely to affect it and on activities or measures introduced in accordance with the Convention.

3. The provisions of this Article shall not affect the right of Contracting Parties, in accordance with their national legal systems and applicable international regulations, to provide for a request for such information to be refused where it affects:

(a) the confidentiality of the proceedings of public authorities, international relations and national defence;

(b) public security;

(c) matters which are, or have been, sub judice, or under enquiry (including disciplinary enquiries), or which are the subject of preliminary investigation proceedings;

(d) commercial and industrial confidentiality, including intellectual property;

(e) the confidentiality of personal data and/or files;

(f) material supplied by a third party without that party being under a legal obligation to do so;

(g) material, the disclosure of which would make it more likely that the environment to which such material related would be damaged.

4. The reasons for a refusal to provide the information requested must be given.

* * *

[*Eds.* BNFL prepared a new document "setting out the economic justification for the MOX Plant" and that document, as well as public comments on the plant, were evaluated by a consulting firm in the so-called ADL Report. The ADL Report was released to the public with redactions of "that information whose publication would cause unreasonable damage to BNFL's commercial operations or to the economic case for the MOX plant." Ireland demanded release of unredacted copies of both the PA Report and the ADL Report.]

* * *

43. The United Kingdom refused to disclose [either the full PA Report or the full ADL Report], contending . . . that:

First, Article 9 of the OSPAR Convention does not establish a direct right to receive information. Rather it requires Contracting Parties to establish a domestic framework for the disclosure of information. This the United Kingdom has done. . . .

Second, . . . the information [sought by Ireland] is insufficiently proximate to the state of the maritime area or to measures or activities affecting or likely to affect it. It is not information within the scope of Article 9(2) of the Convention. . . .

Third, in the event that the United Kingdom is wrong on this point, Article 9(3)(d) of the Convention affirms the right of the Contracting Parties, in accordance with their national legal systems and applicable international regulations, to provide for a request for information to be refused on grounds of commercial confidentiality. The United Kingdom has legislated to this effect. Its refusal to disclose the particular information requested by Ireland is consistent with both national law and applicable international regulations.

* * *

123. The [first] issue [is] whether . . . the obligation of a Contracting Party under Article 9(1) is completely discharged by putting in place an appropriate domestic regulatory framework so that disputes about specific applications of the obligations under Article 9 are to be exclusively determined within the municipal law of the Contracting Party. . . .

* * *

133. In the context of the language used within Article 9, it . . . appear[s] plain to the Tribunal that the obligation expressed in Article 9(1) by the requirement that a Contracting Party "shall ensure" the stipulated result is a reflection of a deliberate rather than a lax choice of vocabulary. It illustrates the application of a chosen (and strong) level of expression,

deftly applied by the drafters to the particular and, to them, important subject matter of disclosure of information to any persons, whether nationals or not, who request it. . . .

134. On that approach, the Tribunal finds that the obligation is to be construed as expressed at the mandatory end of the scale. The applied requirement of Article 9(1) is read by the Tribunal as imposing an obligation upon the United Kingdom, as a Contracting Party, to ensure something, namely that its competent authorities "are required to make available the information described in paragraph 2 . . . to any natural legal person, in response to any reasonable request."

* * *

137. For these reasons in this aspect it appears to the Tribunal that Article 9(1) is advisedly pitched at a level that imposes an obligation of result rather than merely to provide access to a domestic regime which is directed at obtaining the required result.

* * *

144. The proposed reading of Article 9(1) also is consistent with contemporary principles of state responsibility. A State is internationally responsible for the acts of its organs. On conventional principles, a State covenanting with other States to put in place a domestic framework and review mechanisms remains responsible to those other States for the adequacy of this framework and the conduct of its competent authorities who, in the exercise of their executive functions, engage the domestic system.

* * *

146. It follows as an ordinary matter of obligation between States, that even where international law assigns competence to a national system, there is no exclusion of responsibility of a State for the inadequacy of such a national system or the failure of its competent authorities to act in a way prescribed by an international obligation or implementing legislation. Adopting a contrary approach would lead to the deferral of responsibility by States and the frustration of the international legal system.

* * *

161. . . . In its Memorial, Ireland identified . . . 14 categories [of redacted information, including] information relating to: (A) Estimated annual production capacity of the MOX facility; (B) Time taken to reach this capacity; (C) Sales volumes; (D) Probability of achieving higher sales volumes; (E) Probability of being able to win contracts for recycling fuel in 'significant quantities'; (F) Estimated sales demand; (G) Percentage of plutonium already on site; (H) Maximum throughput figures; (I) Life span of the MOX facility; (J) Number of employees; (K) Price of MOX fuel; (L)

Whether, and to what extent, there are firm contracts to purchase MOX from Sellafield; (M) Arrangements for transport of plutonium to, and MOX from, Sellafield; (N) Likely number of such transports.

* * *

163. Article 9(2), whose chapeau is "Access to Information," establishes the scope of information to which, subject to specific enumerated rights of refusal in Article 9(3), the obligation in Article 9(1) relates. The scope of the information in the provision is not environmental, in general, but, in keeping with the focus of the OSPAR Convention, "the state of the maritime area." It is manifest to the Tribunal that none of the above 14 categories in Ireland's list can plausibly be characterized as "information * * * on the state of the maritime area." * * *

The Claims by Ireland are dismissed.

(C) Readings Relevant to Problem 5-1(C)

9. United Nations Economic Commission for Europe [UNECE], Strategies and Policies for Air Pollution Abatement: 2006 Review Prepared Under the Convention on Long-range Transboundary Air Pollution, U.N. Doc. ECE/Eb.AIR/93 at 5, 13–18 (2007)

The Convention on Long-range Transboundary Air Pollution **[Basic Document 2.1]**, signed in Geneva in 1979, is a landmark international agreement. For more than 25 years it has been instrumental in reducing emissions contributing to transboundary air pollution in the UNECE [United Nations Economic Commission for Europe] region through coordinated efforts on research, monitoring and the development of emission reduction strategies on regional air pollution and its effects.

* * *

B. The Convention's Executive Body and its main subsidiary bodies

The Executive Body (the meeting of the Parties) is the governing and decision-making body of the Convention. At its meetings, its three main subsidiary bodies and the Convention's Implementation Committee provide reports on their work. The Executive Body is responsible for adopting protocols, decisions, reports (such as this review) and agreeing its annual workplans as well as developing strategies for its future work.

Reflecting the Convention's science-based approach to emission control strategies, the Executive Body has two scientific subsidiary bodies, the Working Group on Effects and the EMEP Steering Body. The Working Group on Strategies and Review is the main negotiating body for the Convention and is responsible for reviewing protocols, identifying any need for amendment or revision and making recommendations for such changes.

The Implementation Committee consists of 9 elected members covering a cross-section of the geographical spread and expertise of the Convention. It draws the attention of the Executive Body to cases of non-compliance by Parties with their obligations under the protocols to the Convention and recommends action for encouraging compliance. The work of the three main subsidiary bodies is described below with reference to recent structural changes and achievements. . . .

Activities of EMEP

EMEP was established before the adoption of the Convention but its implementation and development, including reference to work on monitoring, modelling and emissions reporting, is described within the text of article 9 of the Convention. The programme is comprised of four main elements: (a) collection of emission data; (b) measurements of air and precipitation quality; (c) modelling of atmospheric transport and deposition of air pollution; and (d) integrated assessment modelling.

* * *

Emission data are used . . . to model the transport of pollutants between countries. Models . . . cover all the pollutants of the protocols and they form the basis for developing strategies for abatement measures to protect human populations and sensitive ecosystems. . . .

C. Capacity-building activities

The Executive Body is placing increased emphasis on the implementation of the Convention and its protocols and has stressed the importance of capacity-building for Parties with economies in transition.

* * *

D. Future work under the Convention

* * *

In addition to the scientific work, the policy focus of the Convention may also need to be extended. Ship and aircraft emissions contribute an increasing proportion of the pollution load in Europe and mechanisms for developing strategies for their control need to be developed. There are also problems when pollution is transported from non-UNECE countries.

10. Convention on Long Range Transboundary Air Pollution (LRTAP), arts. 2–5 & 13, Nov. 13, 1979, 1302 UNTS 217 (Basic Document 2.1)

FUNDAMENTAL PRINCIPLES

Article 2

The Contracting Parties, taking due account of the facts and problems involved, are determined to protect man and his environment against air pollution and shall endeavour to limit and, as far as possible, gradually reduce and prevent air pollution including long-range transboundary air pollution.

Article 3

The Contracting Parties, within the framework of the present Convention, shall by means of exchanges of information, consultation, research and monitoring, develop without undue delay policies and strategies which shall serve as a means of combating the discharge of air pollutants, taking into account efforts already made at national and international levels.

Article 4

The Contracting Parties shall exchange information on and review their policies, scientific activities and technical measures aimed at combating, as far as possible, the discharge of air pollutants which may have adverse effects, thereby contributing to the reduction of air pollution including long-range transboundary air pollution.

Article 5

Consultations shall be held, upon request, at an early stage between, on the one hand, Contracting Parties which are actually affected by or exposed to a significant risk of long-range transboundary air pollution and, on the other hand, Contracting Parties within which and subject to whose jurisdiction a significant contribution to long-range transboundary air pollution originates, or could originate, in connexion with activities carried on or contemplated therein.

SETTLEMENT OF DISPUTES

Article 13

If a dispute arises between two or more Contracting Parties to the present Convention as to the interpretation or application of the Convention, they shall seek a solution by negotiation or by any other method of dispute settlement acceptable to the parties to the dispute.

11. Gothenburg Protocol to the 1979 Convention on Long-range Transboundary Air Pollution to Abate Acidification, Eutrophication and Ground-level Ozone, arts. 3, 9 & 11, Nov. 30, 1999, 2319 UNTS 80 (Basic Document 2.1a)

Article 3—Basic Obligations

1. Each Party having an emission ceiling in any table in annex II shall reduce and maintain the reduction in its annual emissions in accordance with that ceiling and the timescales specified in that annex. Each Party shall, as a minimum, control its annual emissions of polluting compounds in accordance with the obligations in annex II.

2. Each Party shall apply the limit values specified in annexes IV, V and VI to each new stationary source within a stationary source category as identified in those annexes, no later than the timescales specified in annex VII . As an alternative, a Party may apply different emission reduction strategies that achieve equivalent overall emission levels for all source categories together.

Article 9—Compliance

Compliance by each Party with its obligations under the present Protocol shall be reviewed regularly. The Implementation Committee established by decision 1997/2 of the Executive Body at its fifteenth session shall carry out such reviews and report to the Parties at a session of the Executive Body in accordance with the terms of the annex to that decision, including any amendments thereto.

Article 11—Settlement of Disputes

1. In the event of a dispute between any two or more Parties concerning the interpretation or application of the present Protocol, the parties concerned shall seek a settlement of the dispute through negotiation or any other peaceful means of their own choice. The parties to the dispute shall inform the Executive Body of their dispute.

2. When ratifying, accepting, approving or acceding to the present Protocol, or at any time thereafter, a Party which is not a regional economic integration organization may declare in a written instrument submitted to the Depositary that, in respect of any dispute concerning the interpretation or application of the Protocol, it recognizes one or both of the following means of dispute settlement as compulsory ipso facto and without special agreement, in relation to any Party accepting the same obligation:

(a) Submission of the dispute to the International Court of Justice;

(b) Arbitration in accordance with procedures to be adopted by the Parties at a session of the Executive Body, as soon as practicable, in an annex on arbitration.

* * *

5. Except in a case where the parties to a dispute have accepted the same means of dispute settlement under paragraph 2, if after twelve months following notification by one party to another that a dispute exists between them, the parties concerned have not been able to settle their dispute through the means mentioned in paragraph 1, the dispute shall be submitted, at the request of any of the parties to the dispute, to conciliation.

6. For the purpose of paragraph 5, a conciliation commission shall be created. The commission shall be composed of an equal number of members appointed by each party concerned or, where parties in conciliation share the same interest, by the group sharing that interest,

and a chairperson chosen jointly by the members so appointed. The commission shall render a recommendatory award, which the parties to the dispute shall consider in good faith.

Section 5. Discussion Notes/Questions

1. European Union environmental law began with a 1972 decision by the Heads of Government of the EC Member states determining that an EC-wide environmental policy was necessary if certain environmental problems were to be addressed successfully. Subsequent treaties contained specific language addressing environmental policy. Today, environmental protection is one of the principal areas of EU activity and is mentioned as an important goal throughout the Treaty on the Functioning of the European Union. Article 191(1) of that Treaty establishes the goals for EU environmental policy: i) preserving, protecting and improving environmental quality, ii) protecting human health, iii) ensuring prudent use of natural resources, and iv) promoting international cooperation in environmental protection. Article 191(2) provides further that policy should "aim at a high level of protection" and be based on the principles of precaution, prevention, remedying pollution at its source, and polluter-pays. EU member states are expressly authorized to adopt environmental legislation that is more stringent than EU legislation. *See* Article 193.

2. The EU Commission has general responsibility to "ensure the application" of EU law. Article 17, Treaty on European Union. In particular, Article 258 of the Treaty on the Functioning of the European Union authorizes the Commission to take action against any Member States that fail to satisfy their treaty obligations, including the obligation to adhere to the requirements of binding directives. The Commission must first provide the Member State with a "reasoned opinion" setting out the Commission's view of the matter. If the Member State does not comply with the opinion, the Commission may bring the matter to the Court of Justice.

The Commission has made clear that it will not pursue Article 258 actions in every case of alleged violation of an environmental directive. Instead, its pursuit of infringement actions will focus on "directives that set the main framework for environmental protection" and cases where "defective or incomplete national legislation . . . significantly compromises the results to be achieved." Communication from the Commission on implementing European Community Environmental Law, COM (2008) 773 final (18 November 2008). It will also act where there are "breaches of core, strategic obligations on which fulfilment of other obligations depends," or where there are "systemic breaches of environmental quality or other environmental protection requirements presenting serious adverse consequences or risks for human health . . . or for aspects of nature that have high ecological value." *Id.*

Although such cases rarely reach the Court of Justice, Article 259 of the Treaty on the Functioning of the European Union authorizes the Court to hear actions brought by Member States against one another alleging a failure to fulfil a treaty obligation. Before bringing such an action, a Member State must bring its complaint to the Commission and allow the Commission to deliver a reasoned opinion on the matter.

3. The Court of Justice of the European Union has two types of jurisdiction that are of particular importance in the environmental protection context. First, as discussed in the previous note, it hears actions brought by the Commission alleging that a Member State has failed to fulfill its treaty obligations, including its obligation to comply with a directive. *See* Article 258. Second, the preliminary ruling procedure allows the Court to provide binding decisions on the validity and interpretation of EU law when EU law issues are before national courts. National courts may always request such rulings from the Court of Justice if they believe an EU law issue has been raised in a case. When an EU law issue is raised in a case pending before the highest national court, that court must bring the matter to the Court of Justice. Article 267, Treaty on the Functioning of the European Union.

4. The problem states that ambient levels of ozone in the Emerald Forest exceed target values, long-term objectives, and alert values set by EC Directive 2008/50/EC. What can be done about this? Does the Directive satisfy the conditions necessary for it to have "direct effect" under EU law? Can a Donauvian citizen bring an action in Donauvian courts to enforce the directive against the Donauvian government? If so, what would be an appropriate remedy? In 2016, the European Parliament's Directorate-General for Internal Policies reported that ambient air quality standards for particulate matter and nitrogen oxides were exceeded in 2014 in all but five Member States. In 2016, the European Commission had 29 open infringement actions against a total of 19 Member States. *See* Directorate-General for Internal Policies, *Implementation of the Ambient Air Quality Directive* at 9 (2016).

5. An important and complex issue in EU law concerns the competence of the European Union to enter into international agreements. The legal rules are relatively easy to describe, but difficult to apply. In some circumstances, the EU has exclusive competence to negotiate and conclude international agreements. In other circumstances, only Member States can do so. In still other circumstances, both the EU and the Member States are entitled to participate in negotiating and ratifying an agreement (mixed agreements). The determination whether a particular agreement is a mixed agreement or whether it falls within the exclusive competence of the EU or the Member States depends on the subject matter of the agreement and the extent to which, if at all, that subject matter falls within the EU's competence. Environmental agreements are generally mixed agreements, which means both Member States and the EU have authority to ratify. This does not mean, however, that the EU must await Member State ratification before exercising its authority.

Consider the Gothenburg Protocol. It is a mixed agreement and has been ratified by the EU as well as by most (but not all) of the EU Member States. It was amended in 2012, and those amendments have not yet received sufficient acceptances to enter into force. Indeed, fewer than half the Member States of the EU have accepted the amendments. But the European Union notified its acceptance of the amendments in August 2017, and, even before that, it incorporated the updated Gothenburg rules into EU law. *See* Council Directive 2016/2284, 2016 O.J. (L344/1) (EC).

6. Did Carpathia's actions in relation to its port expansion project violate the Espoo Convention or the Aarhus Convention? If either Convention was violated, what remedies are available? Do you believe those remedies will be effective? If not, what steps could be taken to make the Conventions more effective?

7. What does the decision in the OSPAR Convention case suggest about Carpathia's right to withhold information relating to the volume of commercial traffic expected in its port? Is this information purely commercial and economic? Or is it "environmental information" within the meaning of the relevant conventions? The dissenting judge in the OSPAR Convention arbitration observed that information required to be disclosed under Article 9(2) of that Convention is not limited to information on "the state of the maritime area," but includes any information on "activities" likely to affect the maritime area. Given that the MOX Plant was likely to affect the maritime area, information about it, including about its economic justification, was within Article 9(2). Indeed, such information was "necessary for [the] harmful activity to occur" given that, without such information, the harmful activity "would not be authorized to occur." Hence, the information should be disclosed. *See* Dissenting Opinion of Gavan Griffith QC, paragraphs 38, 93–96, 110, 23 UNRIAA 59 (2003).

8. Is Carpathia's law regarding the legal standing of nongovernmental environmental organizations consistent with the Aarhus Convention?

On its face, the Aarhus Convention appears to allow states to apply their own national laws to determine the legal standing of individuals or organizations seeking to challenge governmental action in court. National laws on legal standing vary widely. Generally, in order to challenge governmental action on the grounds that it violates environmental law, individuals must show an interest in the matter and an impairment of their rights. But national laws can differ significantly in their application of this standard, especially with respect to the concept of an "interest." In some countries, environmental organizations are given privileged access to the courts. But standing might be limited to organizations that meet certain criteria, such as time in existence, purposes, organization, or membership. *See generally* Esther Pozo Vera and Nathy-Rass Masson, *Summary Report by Milieu Limited on behalf of DG Environment: Inventory of EU Member States' Measures on Access to Justice in Environmental Matters* 6–10 (2007). What limits, if any, does the Aarhus Convention impose on a state's rules for legal standing in environmental matters? Would the Convention permit a state to limit standing to its own citizens? Would it permit a state to limit standing to organizations formed under its own laws? To individuals who suffer direct adverse effects as a result of the decision being challenged? Is the Report of the Compliance Committee quoted in Reading 7 helpful in resolving these issues?

9. Are Haikastan's plans to build new coal-burning power plants a violation of its obligations under the LRTAP Convention or its Gothenburg Protocol? If so, what remedies are available under the treaty or the Protocol? If the law of state responsibility were applied to this situation, and Carpathia were found to have violated its treaty or customary law obligations, would it have a necessity defense? Any other defense? *See* International Law Commission, Draft Articles on the Responsibility of States for Internationally Wrongful Acts, arts. 21–27 **(Basic Document 1.15)**.

10. One problem for Donauvia is that emissions from maritime shipping that contribute to pollution in the Emerald Forest are not subject to the Gothenburg Protocol or the relevant EU Directives. Moreover, such emissions are on the rise and will rise further when Carpathia's port expansion project is completed. Because of the principle of freedom of navigation on the high seas and the right of foreign ships to "innocent passage" through a state's territorial sea, it is unlikely that Donauvia could take any unilateral action to address this problem.[39] What might be done internationally? In 1997, regulations for the prevention of air pollution for ships were adopted as part of a protocol that amended MARPOL 73/78 (the International Convention for the Prevention of Pollution from Ships, 1973, as modified by the Protocol of 1978 relating thereto) **(Basic Document 3.3)**. The regulations, contained in Annex VI: Prevention of Air Pollution from Ships, went into force in May 2005. Annex VI imposes limits on both SOX and NOX emissions, as well as emissions of particulate matter. But those limits have not been sufficient to prevent a steady increase in pollutant emissions from maritime traffic in many parts of Europe. *See* European Environment Agency, Europe's Environment—The Fourth Assessment 78 (2007).

11. What about customary law? Have either Carpathia or Haikastan violated their customary legal obligations to cooperate in the solution of environmental problems? Their customary obligation to prevent transboundary environmental harm? *See* Chapter Three.

Regarding causation and proof in respect of state responsibility for transfrontier environmental harm, consider the following from Jutta Brunnée, Acid Rain and Ozone Depletion: International Law and Regulation 119 (1988):

> In transfrontier air pollution cases one of the most difficult aspects is to actually establish a chain of causation between the alleged polluter and the damage suffered. For a state attempting to hold another state responsible, an additional difficulty arises from

[39] However, passage is not innocent if the foreign ship engages in an act "of willful and serious pollution" in violation of the requirements of the UN Convention on the Law of the Sea (UNCLOS). States are entitled to adopt and apply laws regulating air pollution insofar as those laws "implement applicable international rules and standards established through competent international organizations or diplomatic conference." UNCLOS, art. 222. *See generally* Chapter Six, *infra*.

> the burden of proof. Generally, each side has to prove facts on which it banks its rights and claims. The victim country might thus have to prove the existence of the rule broken by the polluting state *and* the causation of the damage. Considering that most evidence with respect to the latter may well be beyond the reach of the victim country, such distribution of the burden of proof does not seem equitable. If we placed more emphasis on territorial integrity, we could more readily establish an assumption that transfrontier pollution is illegal. This would result in a shift of the burden of proof, at least with regard to the existence of rules prohibiting pollution. However, at this point it does not seem likely that major source countries would favor such a shift. Also, in some cases victim countries may at another occasion assume the role of the polluter. Thus they too may not be willing to press too hard for a general shift of the burden of proof in order to "protect" themselves from future claims.

Brunnée wrote in 1988. In the years since, the EMEP program's work on monitoring, modelling, and emissions reporting in Europe has greatly increased knowledge about the sources and transboundary movement of air pollution in Europe. Is the time now ripe for aggressive enforcement of the customary law regarding transboundary pollution? Or are there still problems with enforcement of the law? If they aren't "proof" problems, what are they?

B. OZONE DEPLETION

At ground level, ozone (O_3) is a pollutant. In the upper reaches of the atmosphere, ozone is a life saver. The stratospheric ozone layer absorbs most of the ultraviolet B (shortwave) light that reaches the Earth from the sun. In excessive amounts, ultraviolet B radiation is extremely deleterious to human and plant health. It causes sunburn and skin cancer and has been linked to cataracts, crop damage, and damage to marine life. It also suppresses the immune system and damages DNA. By preventing most of that radiation from reaching the Earth's surface, the ozone layer is one of the features of the Earth's environment that makes life on this planet possible.

Under natural conditions, ozone molecules are constantly formed and destroyed in the atmosphere. Atmospheric concentrations of ozone vary over time, depending on a variety of natural factors. Record-keeping over several decades has established that the natural concentration of ozone in the stratosphere is relatively stable, with periods of decline being followed quickly by periods of recovery.

In the 1970s and 1980s, researchers discovered that chlorofluorocarbons (CFCs)—man-made chemicals invented in the 1920s and used as refrigerants, propellants, and solvents—were a key link in a chain of chemical reactions that was destroying ozone molecules in the stratosphere at a rate faster than natural processes could replace them. When chlorofluorocarbon molecules are released into the atmosphere, they rise into the stratosphere where they are bombarded by ultraviolet radiation that causes them to break apart and release chlorine. The released chlorine atoms, in turn, interact with ozone molecules, triggering an ozone-destroying chain reaction:

$Cl + O_3 = ClO + O_2$

The chlorine monoxide released in this reaction will further react with stray oxygen molecules in a way that re-releases the original chlorine atom.

$ClO + O = Cl + O_2$

And thus the cycle begins again. It has been estimated that one chlorine atom released in the atmosphere will result in the destruction of 100,000 ozone molecules.[40]

Chlorofluorocarbons are not the only substances responsible for depletion of the ozone layer. Bromine atoms have a similar impact on ozone as chlorine atoms. So ozone depletion can be caused by any substance that rises in the atmosphere and releases either chlorine atoms or bromine atoms when exposed to intense stratospheric ultraviolet radiation. Ozone-depleting substances include many highly useful chemicals, including chlorofluorocarbons (CFCs), halon, carbon tetrachloride (CCl_4), methyl chloroform (CH_3CCl_3), hydrobromofluorocarbons (HBFCs), hydrochlorofluorocarbons (HCFCs), methyl bromide (CH_3Br), and bromochloromethane (CH_2BrCl).

How serious a problem?

Once the ozone-depleting effect of CFCs and similar substances was discovered, researchers began investigating the likely consequences of a significantly diminished ozone layer. A 1989 article, summarized the research on human and plant health:

> Theoretically, the complete destruction of the ozone layer would result in the extinction of life on earth. While there is still considerable academic debate over the extent to which a "decreasing" ozone layer would affect life on earth, that impact would definitely be adverse. Some of the predictions include:
>
> a. a 2 to 5 percent increase in squamous skin cancer for each 1.0 percent depletion in the ozone layer;
>
> b. a 1.0 to 3 percent increase in basal skin cancer for each 1.0 percent depletion of the ozone layer;

[40] F. Sherwood Rowland, *Stratospheric Sink for Chlorofluoromethanes: Chlorine Atom—Catalysed Destruction of Ozone*, 249 Nature 810 (1974).

c. a 1.0 to 2 percent increase in incidence and a 0.8 to 1.5 percent increase in mortality for melanoma skin cancer (which during 1986 killed 5,000 U.S. citizens) for each 1.0 percent depletion of the ozone layer;

d. a suppression of the immune system in humans, increasing the number and severity of some diseases (e.g., herpes, leishmaniasis, and other infectious cutaneous diseases);

e. a 0.3 to 0.6 percent increase in cataract cases for each 1.0 percent depletion in the ozone layer;

f. an alteration in competition between plant species and a reduction in crop yields (e.g., a twenty-five percent reduction in soybean yield given a twenty percent ozone depletion);

g. alterations in aquatic ecosystems and possible effects on aquatic food chains . . . .[41]

The figures in this list are for a 1% depletion in the ozone layer. A study published in 2009 estimated that, without effective international action to stop the production of chlorofluorocarbons, 17% of the world's stratospheric ozone would have been gone by 2020 and 67% by 2065.[42] The result, at a minimum, would have been many millions more cases of skin cancer and cataracts every year in the US alone.

Happily, effective international action was taken, as described below. Emissions of ozone-depleting substances have diminished as a result of this action, and the ozone layer is expected to return to 1980 levels by the middle of this century.[43]

Efforts to protect the ozone layer

In the late 1970s, in response to the growing scientific evidence that chloroflourocarbons were damaging the ozone layer, several countries, including the United States, banned CFC aerosols. However, as Carol Petsonk writes, in *The Role of the United Nations Environment Programme (UNEP) in the Development of International Environmental Law*, 5 Am. U. J. Int'l L. & Pol'y 351, 367–68 (1990), "[g]lobal CFC consumption continued

[41] John Warren Kindt & Samuel Pyeatt Menefee, *The Vexing Problem of Ozone Depletion in International Environmental Law and Policy*, 24 Tex. Int'l L.J. 261, 262–67 (1989).

[42] P.A. Newman, et al., *What would have happened to the ozone layer if chlorofluorocarbons (CFCs) had not been regulated?*, 9 Atmos. Chem. Phys. 2113 (2009).

[43] *See* National Oceanic and Atmospheric Administration (United States), National Aeronautics and Space Administration (United States), United Nations Environment Programme, World Meteorological Organization & European Commission, SCIENTIFIC ASSESSMENT OF OZONE DEPLETION: 2014, WMO Global Ozone Research and Monitoring Project, Report No. 56 (2014) [hereinafter Ozone Assessment]. At this writing, the 2018 assessment of ozone depletion is in progress and a new report is expected by the end of the year.

to climb . . . as the chemicals were put to other uses. In 1980, the Governing Council [GC] directed UNEP to undertake measures to protect the ozone layer from modifications due to human activities, and in 1981 the GC called for a convention."

UNEP hoped that global negotiations would lead to adoption of both a framework convention and a protocol to control ozone-depleting substances. But, Petsonk writes, "[t]here was no scientific consensus . . . on the extent of CFC-catalyzed ozone layer depletion[, and several] CFC-producing countries, most notably Japan, questioned the need for a CFC protocol."[44] As a result, by early 1985 consensus was reached only on the terms of the framework convention.

That convention, the Vienna Convention for the Protection of the Ozone Layer **(Basic Document 2.7)**, did not directly control the use or production of ozone depleting substances. Instead, it established a general goal of "protect[ing] human health and the environment against adverse effects resulting or likely to result from human activities which modify or are likely to modify the ozone layer," (art. 2(1)), and it created a procedure for the adoption of protocols (art. 8, 9, 13, and 17). However, the discovery of an "ozone hole" over Antarctica soon convinced world leaders that a framework convention was not enough. Within three years, controls on CFCs and halons had been negotiated as part of the Montreal Protocol.

In addition to establishing controls over CFCs and halons,[45] the 1987 Montreal Protocol created an innovative process for ratcheting up the level of those controls. Under the Protocol's procedures, once a chemical is listed as a "controlled substance" in the Annexes to the Protocol, then the level of controls imposed on the production and consumption of that substance can be adjusted by the parties to the Protocol, as the need arises. The Parties must make every effort to reach agreement by consensus on the adjustment of control measures; but if there is no consensus, decisions "shall, as a last resort, be adopted by two-third majority vote of the Parties present and voting representing a majority of the parties operating under paragraph 1 of Article 5 present and voting and a majority of the parties not so operating present and voting."[46] Such "adjustments" to the restrictions on production and use of controlled substances are binding on all Parties to the Protocol, even those that vote against them.

---

[44] CFCs were widely used at the time for a variety of purposes—as propellants in aerosol sprays, as coolants in refrigerators and air conditions, for the blowing of various foam products, and as a cleaning agent for various electrical processes and appliances, including computers. Thus, CFC consumers and consuming countries were also initially reluctant to agree to curbs on their production or use.

[45] Halons, also powerful ozone-depleting substances, are used to extinguish fires.

[46] The quoted language is from Article 2(9) of the Protocol as amended by the 1990 London Amendments. It effectively means that an adjustment must be supported by a majority of both the developing and developed country Parties to the Protocol who are present and voting at a meeting and by a super-majority (2/3) of those Parties taken altogether.

Adding new substances to the Protocol's list of controlled substances is more difficult. A 2/3 majority vote of the Parties may add substances, but the addition of new substances is treated as an amendment to the Protocol (rather than an "adjustment"), and is subject to the Ozone Convention's normal procedures for amending protocols. Under those procedures, amendments do not go into effect for parties that do not accept them; the rule of consent is fully operational. *See* Montreal Protocol article 2(10) **(Basic Document 2.8)** and Ozone Convention, article 9(5) **(Basic Document 2.7)**.

The Montreal Protocol has been amended five times since 1987, most recently in 2016. As a result of these amendments, controls are now in place on a wide variety of ozone-depleting substances (ODS). In addition to the controls originally imposed on CFCs and halons, the Montreal Protocol today limits the production and use of carbon tetrachloride, methyl chloroform, hydrochlorofluorocarbons, hydrobromofluorocarbons, methyl bromide, bromochloromethane, and hydrofluorocarbons. Every amendment has so far been ratified by nearly every party to the Protocol with the sole exception of the 2016 Kigali Amendment, which imposed controls on hydrofluorocarbons. In addition to these several amendments, the adjustment process has been used a total of 13 times, usually to strengthen limits on the production or use of particular ozone-depleting substances. As noted earlier, adjustments are binding on all parties to the Protocol (provided the party has ratified the amendment that brought the relevant ODS within the Protocol).

Keys to success?

The Vienna Convention/Montreal Protocol regime is probably the single most successful international effort to address and solve an environmental problem. It also provided a model that influenced the content of the United Nations Framework Convention on Climate Change. For these reasons, it is worth considering the challenges that faced negotiators and the steps they took to overcome those challenges.

One significant challenge to securing widespread adherence to the Montreal Protocol's regulatory scheme was to convince developing nations that they should join in the effort. Many developing countries insist that their right to develop trumps any obligation they might have to participate in global action to protect the environment. Current global environmental problems, they correctly observe, were caused primarily by actions in industrialized countries. Moreover, industrialized countries continue to be the leading contributors to those problems.

In response to these claims, developing countries with particularly low levels of per capita consumption of a controlled substance (called "Article 5 parties") were given an additional 10 years to comply fully with any international controls imposed on the production and consumption of a particular ozone-depleting substances.[47] They were also promised that a financial mechanism would be established to provide "financial transfers" to Article 5 parties sufficient to "meet all agreed incremental costs of such Parties in order to enable their compliance with the control measures of the Protocol."[48] Finally, they were promised access to "the best available safe substitutes and related technology," to be funded in part by the promised financial mechanism.[49] Some of these provisions appeared in the original Protocol, but others (including Article 10A on technology transfer) were added by an amendment adopted at the 1990 London meeting in response to "some tough arguing from the Indian Environment Minister, Maneka Gandhi."[50]

Developed nations, too, were concerned that the severe restrictions on ozone-depleting substances being negotiated might be too strict, especially if affordable substitutes for those substances could not be found. One provision aimed at assuaging this concern was Article 9, calling on the parties to cooperate in researching alternative products and technologies for the "containment, recovery, recycling or destruction of controlled substances,"[51] and to share information on those matters. Perhaps a more important protection, however, was the inclusion of a provision that qualified the ban imposed on certain ozone-depleting substances. That provision says that, despite a putative ban on consumption or production of a particular ODS, the Parties may "permit the level of production or consumption that is necessary to satisfy uses agreed by them to be critical uses."[52] In other words, an ozone-depleting substance may be "banned," but that doesn't necessarily mean that all production and use will cease. If the Parties agree, by decision at a Meeting of the Parties, production and consumption of the ODS may still continue for "critical uses." What counts as a critical use is for the Parties to decide.

Finally, the negotiators faced the threat of free riders. The effectiveness of the Montreal Protocol depends on widespread, if not universal, adherence to the agreement. If only a few countries continue to produce, consume, and release ozone-depleting substances, the problem of ozone depletion will continue. It is possible that some benefits could be achieved even in the presence of free-riding: the rate of depletion of the ozone layer might diminish. But the problem itself could not be solved if a significant number of countries stayed outside the Protocol.

---

47 *See, e.g.*, Montreal Protocol, article 2H.

48 *Id.*, art. 10.

49 *Id.*, art. 10(a).

50 Sylvia Maureen Williams, *The Protection of the Ozone Layer in Contemporary International Law*, 10 INT'L REL. 167, 176–77 (1990).

51 If an ODS could be contained and destroyed following use, then it would not reach the stratosphere and restrictions on its production or consumption could be kept relatively lenient.

52 *See, e.g.*, Montreal Protocol, art. 2A(4), 2B(2), 2C(3), 2D(2), 2E(3), 2G, 2H(5).

The provisions mentioned earlier provided some incentive to countries to join the Protocol. But, to bolster those incentives, the negotiators included trade measures designed to punish holdouts. Article 4 prohibits parties to the Protocol from importing or exporting any controlled substances to non-parties. Consider what this might mean for a country that stayed out of the Protocol. Generally, controls on ozone-depleting substances are imposed gradually, and it is usually many years before an outright ban is imposed. During the phase-in period, countries can continue to produce and consume substantial quantities of the substance. But a producing country that declined to join the Protocol would completely lose access to export markets in any participating country. A consuming country with no domestic production capability (and this would have been the situation of many developing countries) would completely lose access to the substance if it didn't join the Protocol, but would have access for many years (albeit at declining levels) if it did join.

Whether because of the seriousness of the threat of ozone depletion, or because of the many incentives to join that are built into the terms of the Montreal Protocol, membership in the regime is effectively universal. 197 states have ratified or accepted the Protocol. Almost all have also ratified or accepted each of the amendments to the Protocol (with the exception of the recent Kigali Amendment).

This global effort has led to a dramatic reduction in the emission of ozone-depleting substances, and the ozone layer appears to be on the mend. The 2014 WMO/UNEP assessment of ozone depletion noted that the abundance of chlorine- and bromine-containing substances in the stratosphere had declined by 10–15% from levels of ten to fifteen years previously.[53] And, in contrast to the 1980s and 1990s when stratospheric ozone was declining, recent measurements show stability in the overall amount of stratospheric ozone since year 2000 and a "clear increase" in ozone in the upper part of the stratosphere.[54] In short, the Vienna Convention/Montreal Protocol regime appears, for the most part, to be working.

This does not mean, however, that there is not work that remains to be done. The 2014 assessment noted that emissions of hydrochlorofluorocarbons (HCFCs) and halon-1301 have continued to increase. Moreover, NOAA recently reported that emissions of CFC-11 (an ozone-depleting chemical whose use should be near zero) have risen 25% since 2012, suggesting that it is being illegally produced somewhere in the world.[55]

---

[53] Ozone Assessment, *supra* note 42.

[54] *Id.*

[55] Chris Mooney, *Someone, somewhere, is making a banned chemical that destroys the ozone layer, scientists suspect*, Washington Post (May 17, 2018).

DISCUSSION NOTES/QUESTIONS

1. What does the history of the ozone regime teach us about the process of making effective international environmental law? The impact of CFCs on the ozone layer came to public attention in 1974. *See* Mario J. Molina & F. Sherwood Rowland, *Chlorofluorocarbons: Chlorine Atom-Catalyzed Destruction of Ozone*, 249 Nature 810 (1974). Yet, even after the problem was identified, skepticism about the existence and seriousness of the threat meant that effective efforts to address the problem were still several years away.

In *The Evolution of Policy Responses to Stratospheric Ozone Depletion,* 29 N.R.J. 793 (1989), Peter M. Morrisette, argues that the approach to ozone can best be understood as a two-stage process. The first stage involved the emergence of ozone depletion as a domestic issue in the United States and several other countries in the 1970s. The second stage was its transformation to an international issue in the 1980s. Morrisette maintains that factors critical to building international consensus on the need for strong measures controlling the production and use of CFCs were: the evolving scientific understanding of the problem, increasing public concern based on the threat of skin cancer, the perception of potential global catastrophe associated with the discovery of the Antarctic ozone hole (the "dread" factor), and the availability of acceptable substitutes.

How do the Ozone Convention **(Basic Document 2.7)** and the Montreal Protocol **(Basic Document 2.8)** seek to overcome the problems of scientific uncertainty and skepticism about environmental risk? *See* Ozone Convention, articles 2, 3, 6; Montreal Protocol, articles 6, 9. How do the agreements address the problem of finding substitute products? What does Morrisette's analysis mean for other environmental issues, like the loss of biodiversity, climate change, and deforestation?

2. The ozone layer as a global commons is a classic case of what Garrett Hardin calls, in his seminal article, the *Tragedy of the Commons. See* Garrett Hardin, *The Tragedy of the Commons*, 162 Science 1243 (1968). The ozone layer is a "pasture open to all," and is therefore likely to be "overgrazed" unless every nation limits its use of ozone-depleting substances. Hardin's suggestion that overuse can be solved by privatization of the commons obviously is not a feasible approach for the ozone layer. So how else can we protect against overuse of the commons? Obviously, by adopting some form of regulation of use. But, in a legal system built on consent, there is no guarantee that all the users of the commons will accept controls on their use.

Do global commons problems of this sort require a rethinking of the traditional concepts of state sovereignty? Is it now time to recognize that state sovereignty in certain matters (e.g., the use of hazardous chemicals) is subject to international restraint in the interests of environmental protection, regardless of whether the state consents to that restraint or not?

Consider how the Montreal Protocol **(Basic Document 2.8)** does (and does not) modify traditional views about the role of state consent in the creation of international treaty commitments. For example, adjustments to the Montreal Protocol go into effect even for those countries that voted against them. What does this mean for the rule of unanimous consent? Why was it necessary? Are there other environmental issues where a similar approach would be justified?

On the other hand, the Montreal Protocol provides that any party can withdraw from the Protocol at any time after four years of assuming the obligation of reducing the consumption of controlled substances. The withdrawal takes effect one year after giving notice. Should a nation be able to withdraw from a treaty as essential to planetary health as the Montreal Protocol? What is the purpose of allowing withdrawal only after five years of assuming treaty obligations (four years before notice can be given, then one additional year before the withdrawal takes effect)? Could this help deter withdrawal? How?

3. Given the universal adherence to the Montreal Protocol and its amendments, would it be fair to say that there is now a customary law obligation to reduce emissions of ozone-depleting substances?

4. Why does the ozone regime make designations of new controlled substances effective only against nations that accept the necessary amendment? Given the seriousness of the threat to the ozone layer, the universal acceptance of the Ozone Convention/Montreal Protocol regime as the proper means to address it, the regime's acknowledgment of the need to abandon the rule of unanimous consent to enable quick action to control ozone-depleting substances, and the regime's reliance on scientific evidence to support its control decisions, might one argue that *any* revisions in the regime necessary to address the threat of ozone depletion, including new designations of controlled substances, are binding on all nations, whether they consent or not? In short, is there now a general consensus that the international community has the right and power to control ozone-depleting substances? Is that consensus strong enough to warrant a conclusion that the traditional rule of *pacta tertiis* (treaties do not bind non-parties) has been modified in this context?

5. Like other global environmental issues, ozone depletion is closely linked to issues of industrial development and the international economy. Developing countries, embarking on large-scale expansion of their refrigeration, air conditioning, plastics, and electronics industries, are asked to substitute more expensive chemicals for the cheaper ozone-depleting substances previously used by developed countries. Developing countries must not go through the evolutionary process of previous industrialization, but, rather, must "leapfrog" directly from a state of underdevelopment to efficient, environmentally benign technologies.

6. At the 1990 meeting of the Parties to the Montreal Protocol, the developing nations successfully argued that they should not have to pay for the move from cheaper (ozone-depleting) to more expensive (non-ozone-depleting) technologies. India and China made creation of a fund to help pay for the move

a condition of their ratification of the Montreal Protocol. The London Amendments to the Protocol authorized the creation of a Multilateral Fund to facilitate compliance by developing countries, and India and China did, in fact, become Parties to the Protocol after the Fund was established.

7. The Multilateral Fund has been used to support the conversion of industry away from the use of ozone-depleting substances; to support necessary technology transfer, technical assistance and other projects designed to slow the use of ozone-depleting substances in developing countries; and to promote future reductions. The Chief Officer of the Fund reported to the UNEP Governing Council in 2007 that "technical assistance and capacity building" support had been provided to 141 developing countries and that "most of these countries are currently in compliance with the Protocol." She described the Fund as "a prime example of successful international environmental cooperation" that had "succeeded in stunting the growth in consumption of ODS in developing countries." Maria Nolan, Statement of the Chief Officer of the Multilateral Fund for the Implementation of the Montreal Protocol to the 24th Governing Council of UNEP (7 Feb. 2007).

8. Trade controls currently in force require Protocol parties to ban trade with non-parties in controlled substances and in certain products containing controlled substances. Two serious problems have emerged. First, a significant black market has developed for international trade in banned ozone-depleting substances. In part, this is because the Montreal Protocol allows developing countries to continue producing ozone-depleting substances after they are banned in developed countries. The United States has brought several successful criminal prosecutions against smugglers, but the problem continues. *See* Graham Donnelly Welch, Note, *HFC Smuffling: Preventing the Illicit (and Lucrative) Sale of Greenhouse Gases,* 44 B.C. Envtl. Aff. L. Rev. 525 (2017). What other solutions can you think of? *See generally Illicit trade in ozone-depleting substances (ODS) from East Asia to the world,* in Transnational Organized Crime in East Asia and the Pacific 113 (United Nations Office on Drugs and Crime, 2013).

A second problem concerns the transfer of outmoded technology from industrialized countries to developing countries. Some developing countries contend that their efforts to reduce the use of CFCs by their industries is hurt by Western companies which "dump" their outmoded CFC-using technology in developing countries at artificially low prices. As a result, developing country industries are attracted to technology which uses CFCs at the same time that developing country governments are undertaking long-term obligations to reduce CFC use. The developing countries contend, moreover, that international trade rules forbid them from banning such imports and that they lack the resources to do so in any event. *See Report of the Seventeenth Meeting of the Open-Ended Working Group of the Parties to the Montreal Protocol,* U.N. GAOR U.N. Doc. UNEP/OzL.Pro/WG.1/17/3, para. 77 (1998). Should the industrialized countries forbid the sale to developing countries of products that use ozone-depleting substances? Only if the country requests such a ban? What if the developing country allows its own industries to build new ODS-using equipment? Should imports of cheap equipment from industrialized countries still be banned?

9. One useful side-effect of the Montreal Protocol is that it appears to have contributed to the effort to mitigate climate change. Some of the ozone-depleting substances that are controlled by the Protocol are powerful greenhouse gases. Phasing out their production and use has been estimated to have had an impact on reducing greenhouse gas emissions from 1985–2010 equivalent to a reduction of 10–12 gigatons of CO_2. *See* Guus J. M. Velders, et al., *The importance of the Montreal Protocol in protecting climate,* 104 PNAS 4814 (2007). However, some ODS substitutes, especially fluorinated gases, are themselves super-powerful greenhouse gases, with a greenhouse effect up to 23,000 times more powerful that the same amount of carbon dioxide. As consumption of these substitutes grows, the contribution of the Montreal Protocol to mitigation of climate change may be reduced or completely eliminated.

10. Problem 5-2 takes a closer look at the operation of the Montreal Protocol and its effort to control the production and use of methyl bromide.

PROBLEM 5-2: NUEVA GRANADA VERSUS THE OZONE LAYER

Section 1. Facts

Nueva Granada is a developing nation of nearly thirty-five million people in southern South America. In recent years, Nueva Granada's economic situation has gradually improved, in part because of an increasingly prosperous agricultural sector. One reason for this success has been the growing use by local farmers of modern farming techniques, including the heavy use of fertilizer and pesticides.

One of Nueva Granada's most important trading partners is the Commonwealth of New Britannia (CNB), a developed country located about 2000 miles north of Nueva Granada. Like Nueva Granada, CNB has a large and important agricultural sector. But Nueva Granadan farmers have found that they can compete with CNB farmers, especially with respect to the sale of fruits and vegetables during November–February, CNB's winter season.

Methyl bromide is a colorless, odorless, toxic gas that is widely used as a pesticide in both Nueva Granada and the Commonwealth of New Britannia. The heaviest use of methyl bromide in both countries is by tomato and strawberry farmers, who use the gas to fumigate the soil before planting their crops. Methyl bromide is also used to eradicate a variety of pests, including insects and rodents, from warehouses, food-processing plants, and containers that are used to transport agricultural products. Finally, because of the widespread adoption of an international standard requiring pest-eradication treatment of certain wooden packing materials that are used in international trade, sterilization facilities in seaports in both countries have recently increased their use of methyl bromide to treat the affected kinds of wooden packing materials before they leave the port for a foreign destination.

Until recently, commercial production of methyl bromide occurred in only three countries in the world—Israel, the United States, and the Commonwealth of New Britannia. Two years ago, however, underground brine deposits containing high concentrations of bromide salts (used in the production of methyl bromide) were discovered in Nueva Granada. Shortly after that discovery, a Nueva Granadan firm began production of methyl bromide, and the country now produces five times as much methyl bromide as it needs, exporting the excess to tomato and strawberry producers in other developing countries.

Unfortunately, methyl bromide is an ozone-depleting substance with a relatively high ozone-depleting potential (ODP). In addition, methyl bromide's various uses all involve high rates of release of the gas into the atmosphere. As a result, international action to protect the ozone layer includes action designed to eliminate (or substantially reduce) the production and use of methyl bromide.

Nueva Granada and the Commonwealth of New Britannia are both parties to the 1985 Vienna Convention for the Protection of the Ozone Layer and the 1987 Montreal Protocol on Substances that Deplete the Ozone Layer. When ratifying the Vienna Convention, both countries indicated their acceptance of mandatory submission of disputes to the International Court of Justice pursuant to Article 11:3(b) of that Convention.

The Commonwealth of New Britannia has ratified all amendments to the Montreal Protocol. Nueva Granada, on the other hand, despite operating under the special rules applicable to developing countries under Article 5, paragraph 1 of the Protocol, has refused accept the 1992 Copenhagen Amendments, which added methyl bromide as a controlled substance under the Protocol.

In 2006, a dispute developed between Nueva Granada and the Commonwealth of New Britannia concerning the use and production of methyl bromide. The dispute was triggered when methyl bromide producers in CNB complained to their government that Nueva Granada was selling large quantities of methyl bromide in international markets. According to the CNB producers, the excess quantities of methyl bromide on the world market were depressing prices and thus discouraging the use and development of methyl-bromide alternatives.

When CNB complained to Nueva Granada, Nueva Granada denied that it was violating any of its obligations under international law, and it accused CNB of failing to live up to CNB's own commitments in relation to protection of the ozone layer. In particular, Nueva Granada accused CNB of using its critical use exemption[56] from the ban on methyl bromide in a manner that was inconsistent with the terms of relevant decisions of the Parties to the Montreal Protocol, and of unlawfully consuming and selling stockpiled methyl bromide.

Several weeks of negotiations did not resolve the dispute, and CNB threatened to impose trade sanctions against Nueva Granadan imports if Nueva Granada did not agree to reduce its exports of methyl bromide. In response to this threat, Nueva Granada brought a complaint against CNB before the International Court of Justice, alleging that CNB was in violation of both the Vienna Convention and the Montreal Protocol because of its "abuse of the critical use exemption" with respect to methyl bromide. In its response to the complaint, CNB asserted a) that it was acting in full compliance with its international legal obligations, b) that Nueva Granada had no standing to complain of any alleged violation involving methyl bromide given that Nueva Granada was not a party to the Copenhagen Amendments, and c) that any dispute about the operation of the Montreal Protocol should be resolved exclusively through the dispute resolution mechanism established by the Parties to the Protocol. CNB also filed a counterclaim against Nueva Granada, alleging that its uncontrolled production of methyl bromide was a violation of its Vienna Convention obligations and of customary international law.

Data collected by the Ozone Secretariat reveals the following about the stockpiling, production and use of methyl bromide in both the Commonwealth of New Britannia and Nueva Granada:

In 1991, the Commonwealth of New Britannia's "calculated level of consumption" of methyl bromide was 1000 metric tons. Pursuant to a 2017 Decision of the Parties to the Montreal Protocol, CNB was granted a critical use exemption totaling 500 tons of methyl bromide for pre-planting fumigation of tomato and strawberry fields in both 2018 and 2019.

In 2018, the Commonwealth of New Britannia had 4000 metric tons of stockpiled methyl bromide. Producers in CNB produced an additional 500 metric tons of methyl bromide. 600 tons of methyl bromide were used by tomato and strawberry producers in CNB, 40 tons of methyl bromide were used for pre-shipment treatment of wooden packaging, 300 tons of methyl bromide were exported to other countries, and 100 tons of methyl bromide were used in unspecified other uses (mostly involving pre-planting fumigation on CNB's many golf courses). At the end of 2018, CNB had 3,460 tons of methyl bromide remaining in its stockpile.

---

56 *See* Readings 2 through 5, *infra*.

Data for Nueva Granada is not as accurate, but it appears that Nueva Granada produced no methyl bromide during the years 1995–1998. At that time, however, its farmers were beginning to increase tomato and strawberry production, and its consumption of methyl bromide during those years rose from 30 metric tons in 1995 to 90 metric tons in 1998. The three-year average was 60 metric tons per year.

Nueva Granada's production and use of methyl bromide has risen steadily in the past several years. In 2018, Nueva Granada produced 700 tons of the substance. It exported 560 tons to other developing nations. 120 tons were used by its strawberry and tomato farmers, and 20 tons were used to treat wood packaging material prior to shipment of the material in international trade. Nueva Granada does not control the exportation of methyl bromide, so there is no way of determining how the exported methyl bromide was used.

Section 2. Questions Presented

1. Is the Commonwealth of New Britannia violating international law? Is so, should the International Court of Justice issue a ruling in Nueva Granada's favor?

2. Is Nueva Granada violating international law?

Section 3. Assignments

A. Reading Assignment

Study the Readings presented in Section 4, *infra*, and the Discussion Notes/Questions that follow.

B. Recommended Writing Assignment

Prepare a comprehensive, logically sequenced, and *argumentative* brief in the form of an outline of the primary and subsidiary *legal* issues you see requiring resolution by the International Court of Justice. Also, from the perspective of an independent objective observer, indicate which side ought to prevail on each issue and why. Retain a copy of your issue-outline/brief for class discussion.

C. Recommended Oral Assignment

Assume you are legal counsel for Nueva Granada or the Commonwealth of New Britannia (as designated by your instructor); then, relying upon the Readings (and your issue-outline if prepared), present a 15–20 minute oral argument of "your" government's likely positions before the Legal Adviser.

D. Recommended Reflective Assignment

Consider (and recommend) alternative norms, institutions, and/or procedures that you believe might do better than existing world order arrangements to contend with situations of the kind posed by this problem. In so doing, but without insisting upon *immediate* feasibility, identify the particular transition steps that would be needed to make your alternatives a reality.

Section 4. Readings

1. Vienna Convention for the Protection of the Ozone Layer, arts. 2 & 11, Mar. 22, 1985, 1513 UNTS 293 (Basic Document 2.7)

Article 2—General Obligations

1. The Parties shall take appropriate measures in accordance with the provisions of this Convention and of those protocols in force to which they are party to protect human health and the environment against adverse effects resulting or likely to result from human activities which modify or are likely to modify the ozone layer.

2. To this end the Parties shall, in accordance with the means at their disposal and their capabilities:

(a) Co-operate by means of systematic observations, research and information exchange in order to better understand and assess the effects of human activities on the ozone layer and the effects on human health and the environment from modification of the ozone layer;

(b) Adopt appropriate legislative or administrative measures and co-operate in harmonizing appropriate policies to control, limit, reduce or prevent human activities under their jurisdiction or control should it be found that these activities have or are likely to have adverse effects resulting from modification or likely modification of the ozone layer;

(c) Co-operate in the formulation of agreed measures, procedures and standards for the implementation of this Convention, with a view to the adoption of protocols and annexes;

(d) Co-operate with competent international bodies to implement effectively this Convention and protocols to which they are party.

3. The provisions of this Convention shall in no way affect the right of Parties to adopt, in accordance with international law, domestic measures additional to those referred to in paragraphs 1 and 2 above, nor shall they affect additional domestic measures already taken by a Party, provided that these measures are not incompatible with their obligations under this Convention.

4. The application of this article shall be based on relevant scientific and technical considerations.

Article 11—Settlement of Disputes

1. In the event of a dispute between Parties concerning the interpretation or application of this Convention, the parties concerned shall seek solution by negotiation.

2. If the parties concerned cannot reach agreement by negotiation, they may jointly seek the good offices of, or request mediation by, a third party.

3. When ratifying, accepting, approving or acceding to this Convention, or at any time thereafter, a state or regional economic integration organization may declare in writing to the Depositary that for a dispute not resolved in accordance with paragraph 1 or paragraph 2 above, it accepts one or both of the following means of dispute settlement as compulsory:

(a) Arbitration in accordance with procedures to be adopted by the Conference of the Parties at its first ordinary meeting;

(b) Submission of the dispute to the International Court of Justice.

4. If the parties have not, in accordance with paragraph 3 above, accepted the same or any procedure, the dispute shall be submitted to conciliation in accordance with paragraph 5 below unless the parties otherwise agree.

5. A conciliation commission shall be created upon the request of one of the parties to the dispute. The commission shall be composed of an equal number of members appointed by each party concerned and a chairman chosen jointly by the members appointed by each party. The commission shall render a final and recommendatory award, which the parties shall consider in good faith.

6. The provisions of this article shall apply with respect to any protocol except as otherwise provided in the protocol concerned.

2. Montreal Protocol on Substances That Deplete the Ozone Layer (as amended and adjusted), arts. 1, 2H(5–6), 3 & 8, Sept. 16, 1987, 1522 UNTS 3 (Basic Document 2.8)

Article 1—Definitions

For the purposes of this Protocol:

1. "Convention" means the Vienna Convention for the Protection of the Ozone Layer, adopted on 22 March 1985.

2. "Parties" means, unless the text otherwise indicates, Parties to this Protocol.

3. "Secretariat" means the Secretariat of the Convention.

4. "Controlled substance" means a substance in Annex A, Annex B, Annex C or Annex E to this Protocol, whether existing alone or in a mixture. It includes the isomers of any such substance, except as specified in the relevant Annex, but excludes any controlled substance or mixture which is in a manufactured product other than a container used for the transportation or storage of that substance.

5. "Production" means the amount of controlled substances produced, minus the amount destroyed by technologies to be approved by the Parties and minus the amount entirely used as feedstock in the manufacture of other chemicals. The amount recycled and reused is not to be considered as "production."

6. "Consumption" means production plus imports minus exports of controlled substances.

7. "Calculated levels" of production, imports, exports and consumption means levels determined in accordance with Article 3.

8. "Industrial rationalization" means the transfer of all or a portion of the calculated level of production of one Party to another, for the purpose of achieving economic efficiencies or responding to anticipated shortfalls in supply as a result of plant closures.

Article 2H—Methyl Bromide (paragraphs 5–6)

* * *

5. Each Party shall ensure that for the twelve-month period commencing on 1 January 2005, and in each twelve-month period thereafter, its calculated level of consumption of the controlled substance in Annex E[57] does not exceed zero. Each Party producing the substance shall, for the same periods, ensure that its calculated level of production of the substance does not exceed zero. However, in order to satisfy the basic domestic needs of the Parties operating under paragraph 1 of Article 5, its calculated level of production may, until 1 January 2002 exceed that limit by up to fifteen per cent of its calculated level of production in 1991; thereafter, it may exceed that limit by a quantity equal to the annual average of its production of the controlled substance in Annex E for basic domestic needs for the period 1995 to 1998 inclusive. This paragraph will apply save to the extent that the Parties decide to permit the level of production or consumption that is necessary to satisfy uses agreed by them to be critical uses.

5 *bis*. Each Party shall ensure that for the twelve-month period commencing on 1 January 2005 and in each twelve-month period thereafter, its calculated level of production of the controlled substance in

[57] *Eds.* The only substance listed in Annex E is methyl bromide, CH_3Br.

Annex E for the basic domestic needs of the Parties operating under paragraph 1 of Article 5 does not exceed eighty per cent of the annual average of its production of the substance for basic domestic needs for the period 1995 to 1998 inclusive.

5 *ter*. Each Party shall ensure that for the twelve-month period commencing on 1 January 2015 and in each twelve-month period thereafter, its calculated level of production of the controlled substance in Annex E for the basic domestic needs of the Parties operating under paragraph 1 of Article 5 does not exceed zero.

6. The calculated levels of consumption and production under this Article shall not include the amounts used by the Party for quarantine and pre-shipment applications.

Article 3—Calculation of Control Levels

[E]ach Party shall, for each group of substances in . . . Annex E determine its calculated levels of:

(a) Production by multiplying its annual production of each controlled substance by the ozone depleting potential specified [which is 0.6 for methyl bromide] * * *

(b) Imports and exports, respectively, by following, mutatis mutandis, the procedure set out in subparagraph (a); and

(c) Consumption by adding together its calculated levels of production and imports and subtracting its calculated level of exports as determined in accordance with subparagraphs (a) and (b). * * *

Article 8—Non-compliance

The Parties, at their first meeting, shall consider and approve procedures and institutional mechanisms for determining non-compliance with the provisions of this Protocol and for treatment of Parties found to be in non-compliance.

3. Decision of the Parties to the Montreal Protocol on a Non-compliance Procedure (1998), in UNEP, Handbook for the Montreal Protocol on Substances That Deplete the Ozone Layer, Sec. 3.5 (7th ed. 2006).

The following procedure has been formulated pursuant to Article 8 of the Montreal Protocol. It shall apply without prejudice to the operation of the settlement of disputes procedure laid down in Article 11 of the Vienna Convention.

1. If one or more Parties have reservations regarding another Party's implementation of its obligations under the Protocol, those concerns may be addressed in writing to the Secretariat. Such a submission shall be supported by corroborating information.

2. The Secretariat shall, within two weeks of its receiving a submission, send a copy of that submission to the Party whose implementation of a particular provision of the Protocol is at issue. Any reply and information in support thereof are to be submitted to the Secretariat and to the Parties involved within three months of the date of the dispatch or such longer period as the circumstances of any particular case may require. If the Secretariat has not received a reply from the Party three months after sending it the original submission, the Secretariat shall send a reminder to the Party that it has yet to provide its reply. The Secretariat shall, as soon as the reply and information from the Party are available, but not later than six months after receiving the submission, transmit the submission, the reply and the information, if any, provided by the Parties to the Implementation Committee referred to in paragraph 5, which shall consider the matter as soon as practicable.

* * *

5. An Implementation Committee is hereby established. . . .

* * *

7. The functions of the Implementation Committee shall be:

(a) To receive, consider and report on any submission in accordance with paragraphs 1, 2 and 4;

(b) To receive, consider and report on any information or observations forwarded by the Secretariat in connection with the preparation of the reports referred to in Article 12 (c) of the Protocol and on any other information received and forwarded by the Secretariat concerning compliance with the provisions of the Protocol;

(c) To request, where it considers necessary, through the Secretariat, further information on matters under its consideration;

(d) To identify the facts and possible causes relating to individual cases of non-compliance referred to the Committee, as best it can, and make appropriate recommendations to the Meeting of the Parties;

(e) To undertake, upon the invitation of the Party concerned, information-gathering in the territory of that Party for fulfilling the functions of the Committee;

(f) To maintain, in particular for the purposes of drawing up its recommendations, an exchange of information with the Executive Committee of the Multilateral Fund related to the provision of financial and technical cooperation, including the transfer of technologies to Parties operating under Article 5, paragraph 1, of the Protocol.

8. The Implementation Committee shall consider the submissions, information and observations referred to in paragraph 7 with a view to

securing an amicable solution of the matter on the basis of respect for the provisions of the Protocol.

9. The Implementation Committee shall report to the Meeting of the Parties, including any recommendations it considers appropriate. The report shall be made available to the Parties not later than six weeks before their meeting. After receiving a report by the Committee the Parties may, taking into consideration the circumstances of the matter, decide upon and call for steps to bring about full compliance with the Protocol, including measures to assist the Parties' compliance with the Protocol, and to further the Protocol's objectives.

* * *

Indicative list of measures that might be taken by a meeting of the Parties in respect of non-compliance with the Protocol

[Source: Annex V of the report of the Fourth Meeting of the Parties]

A. Appropriate assistance, including assistance for the collection and reporting of data, technical assistance, technology transfer and financial assistance, information transfer and training.

B. Issuing cautions.

C. Suspension, in accordance with the applicable rules of international law concerning the suspension of the operation of a treaty, of specific rights and privileges under the Protocol, whether or not subject to time limits, including those concerned with industrial rationalization, production, consumption, trade, transfer of technology, financial mechanism and institutional arrangements.

4. Decision IX/6 of the Parties to the Montreal Protocol: Critical-use Exemptions for Methyl Bromide

The *Ninth Meeting of the Parties* decided in *Dec. IX/6*:

1. To apply the following criteria and procedure in assessing a critical methyl bromide use for the purposes of control measures in Article 2 of the Protocol:

(a) That a use of methyl bromide should qualify as "critical" only if the nominating Party determines that:

(i) The specific use is critical because the lack of availability of methyl bromide for that use would result in a significant market disruption; and

(ii) There are no technically and economically feasible alternatives or substitutes available to the user that are acceptable from the standpoint of environment and health and are suitable to the crops and circumstances of the nomination;

(b) That production and consumption, if any, of methyl bromide for critical uses should be permitted only if:

(i) All technically and economically feasible steps have been taken to minimize the critical use and any associated emission of methyl bromide;

(ii) Methyl bromide is not available in sufficient quantity and quality from existing stocks of banked or recycled methyl bromide, also bearing in mind the developing countries' need for methyl bromide;

(iii) It is demonstrated that an appropriate effort is being made to evaluate, commercialize and secure national regulatory approval of alternatives and substitutes, taking into consideration the circumstances of the particular nomination and the special needs of Article 5 Parties, including lack of financial and expert resources, institutional capacity, and information. Non-Article 5 Parties must demonstrate that research programmes are in place to develop and deploy alternatives and substitutes. Article 5 Parties must demonstrate that feasible alternatives shall be adopted as soon as they are confirmed as suitable to the Party's specific conditions and/or that they have applied to the Multilateral Fund or other sources for assistance in identifying, evaluating, adapting and demonstrating such options. . . .

5. Hypothetical[58] Decision XXIX/6 of the Parties to the Montreal Protocol: Critical-use Exemptions for Methyl Bromide for 2019 and subsequent years

Recognizing that the production and consumption of methyl bromide for critical uses should be permitted only if methyl bromide is not available in sufficient quantity and quality from existing stocks of banked or recycled methyl bromide,

Recognizing also that parties operating under critical-use exemptions should take into account the extent to which methyl bromide is available in sufficient quantity and quality from existing stocks of banked or recycled methyl bromide in licensing, permitting or authorizing the production and consumption of methyl bromide for critical uses,

* * *

1. [Decides] To permit, for the agreed critical-use categories for 2019 and subsequent years set forth in table A of the annex to the present decision for each party, subject to the conditions set forth in decision Ex.

[58] The content of the tables to this decision has been altered for purposes of this problem and does not accurately reflect the actual decision.

I/4, to the extent that those conditions are applicable, the levels of production and consumption for 2019 and subsequent years set forth in table B of the annex to the present decision, which are necessary to satisfy critical uses, with the understanding that additional production and consumption and categories of uses may be approved by the Meeting of the Parties in accordance with decision IX/6;

* * *

3. That each party that has an agreed critical-use exemption shall renew its commitment to ensuring that the criteria in paragraph 1 of decision IX/6, in particular the criterion laid down in paragraph 1(b)(ii) of decision IX/6, are applied in licensing, permitting or authorizing critical uses of methyl bromide, with each party requested to report on the implementation of the present provision to the Secretariat. . . .

Hypothetical Table A—Agreed Critical Use Categories

Australia:	Strawberry runners
Argentina:	Strawberry fruit; tomatoes
Canada:	Strawberry runners
New Britannia:	Strawberry runners; tomatoes

Hypothetical Table B—Permitted Levels of Production and Consumption (level permitted each year for 2019 and subsequent years)

Australia:	30 metric tons
Argentina:	100 metric tons
Canada:	40 metric tons
New Britannia:	500 metric tons

6. Natural Resources Defense Council v. Environmental Protection Agency, 464 F.3d 1 (D.C. Cir. 2006)

I.

In the mid-1970s, scientists discovered that certain man-made chemicals can destroy the layer of ozone gas in the stratosphere approximately ten to twenty-five miles above the Earth's surface. Stratospheric ozone absorbs ultraviolet radiation; as the ozone layer thins, less radiation is absorbed. Increased human exposure to ultraviolet radiation is linked to a range of ailments, including skin cancer and cataracts.

Amidst growing international concern about ozone depletion, the United States and twenty-four other nations entered into the Montreal Protocol **[Basic Document 2.8]**. The Protocol requires signatory nations—which now number 189—to reduce and eliminate their production and use of ozone-depleting chemicals in accordance with agreed-upon timetables. Montreal Protocol arts. 2–2I. The Senate ratified the treaty in 1988, and Congress incorporated its terms into domestic law through the Clean Air Act Amendments of 1990. Since then, the United States has reduced its use of methyl bromide to less than 39% of its 1991 baseline.

In 1997, the Parties "adjusted" the Protocol to require developed-country Parties to cease "production" and "consumption"[59] of methyl bromide by 2005. *See* Montreal Protocol art. 2H(5).[60] In response, Congress amended the Clean Air Act to require EPA to "promulgate rules for reductions in, and terminate the production, importation, and consumption of, methyl bromide under a schedule that is in accordance with, but not more stringent than, the phaseout schedule of the Montreal Protocol Treaty as in effect on October 21, 1998." 42 U.S.C. § 7671c(h).

Methyl bromide is a naturally occurring gas produced by oceans, grass and forest fires, and volcanoes. It is also man-made and used as a broad-spectrum pesticide. Methyl bromide is typically injected into soil as a fumigant before several types of crops are planted. The United States regulates methyl bromide as a "class I" ozone-depleting substance. . . . It is not nearly as destructive as chlorofluorocarbons and most other class I substances, almost all of which were phased out in 2000. On the other hand, it is significantly more destructive than "class II" substances, which are to be phased out in 2030.

In light of methyl bromide's wide use and the lack of comparable substitute pesticides, the Protocol allows exemptions from the general ban "to the extent that the Parties decide to permit the level of production or consumption that is necessary to satisfy uses agreed by them to be critical uses." Montreal Protocol art. 2H(5); *see also* 42 U.S.C. § 7671c(d)(6) ("To the extent consistent with the Montreal Protocol, the [EPA] Administrator . . . . may exempt the production, importation, and consumption of methyl bromide for critical uses."). The Parties to the Protocol meet annually to "decide to permit the level of production or consumption that is necessary to satisfy uses agreed by them to be critical uses." Montreal Protocol art. 2H(5). At one of these meetings the Parties set general guidelines for implementing the critical-use exemptions, and at another the Parties approved exemptions for 2005. The United States formally began the

[59] "Production" is defined as "the amount of controlled substances produced, minus the amount destroyed [under the Protocol] and minus the amount entirely used [to produce other chemicals]." Montreal Protocol, art. 1(5). "Consumption" is "production plus imports minus exports of controlled substances." *Id.* art. 1(6).

[60] Current article 2H was added by "adjustment" at the Ninth Meeting of the Parties. *See* U.N. Env't Programme, *Report of the Ninth Meeting of the Parties to the Montreal Protocol on Substances that Deplete the Ozone Layer,* U.N. Doc. UNEP/OzL.Pro.9/12, Annex III (Sept. 25, 1997) ("*Ninth Report*"). The Protocol allows "adjustments" to be made without formal amendment and ratification. *See* Montreal Protocol art. 2(9). In incorporating the Protocol into domestic law, Congress defined the Protocol to include "adjustments adopted by the Parties thereto and amendments that have entered into force." 42 U.S.C. § 7671(9).

process of establishing its 2005 critical-use exemptions in May 2002, when EPA published a notice in the *Federal Register* seeking applications for 2005 and 2006 critical uses of methyl bromide and the amounts of new production and consumption needed to satisfy those uses. EPA teams composed of biologists and economists reviewed each application and decided which to include in the aggregate U.S. nomination to the Parties. The final U.S. nomination, submitted to the Montreal Protocol's administrative body (the "Ozone Secretariat") in February 2003, requested a total exemption of about ten-thousand metric tons of methyl bromide for sixteen different uses.

The process then moved to the international stage. Two working groups operating under the auspices of the Ozone Secretariat—the "Methyl Bromide Technical Options Committee" and the "Technology and Economic Assessment Panel"—evaluated each country's nomination and made a recommendation to the Parties at their November 2003 meeting. At that meeting, the Parties deadlocked over the proposed critical-use exemptions and called an "extraordinary meeting" to make the final decisions.

The Parties reached agreement at their First Extraordinary Meeting in March 2004. They granted the United States critical uses in sixteen categories, amounting to 8,942 metric tons of methyl bromide. To satisfy these critical uses, the Parties authorized 7,659 metric tons of new production and consumption, with the remainder (1,283 metric tons) to be made up from existing stocks of methyl bromide. *See* U.N. Env't Programme, *Report of the First Extraordinary Meeting of the Parties to the Montreal Protocol on Substances that Deplete the Ozone Layer,* U.N. Doc. UNEP/OzL.Pro.ExMP/1/3, at 14–15, 26 (Mar. 27, 2004) ("Decision Ex.I/3"). Decision Ex.I/3 noted that "each Party which has an agreed critical use should ensure that the criteria in paragraph 1 of decision IX/6[61] are applied when . . . authorizing the use of methyl bromide and that such procedures take into account available stocks." *Id.* ¶ 5.

With Decision Ex.I/3 in hand, EPA proposed rules to implement the critical-use exemption. Many parties, including NRDC, submitted comments. The Final Rule, issued in December 2004, authorized new production and consumption up to the limit established in Decision Ex.I/3. It also authorized the use of stocks as permitted by the decision, and permitted noncritical users to draw upon existing stocks.

NRDC believes the Final Rule violated Decision IX/6 and Decision Ex.I/3 because EPA failed to disclose the full amount of existing stocks, failed to offset new production and consumption by the full amount of these stocks, and failed to reserve the stocks for critical uses, and because the

[61] Decision IX/6 permits exemptions only when all technically and economically feasible steps have been taken to minimize the required use and when methyl bromide is not available from existing stocks. *Id.* ¶ 1(b)(i), (ii).

total amount of methyl bromide critical use the Final Rule authorized is not the technically and economically feasible minimum. These claims depend upon the legal status of Decisions IX/6 and Ex.I/3.

After oral argument, we ordered supplemental briefing to address the question whether consensus decisions of the Parties are "cognizable in federal court actions brought to enforce the Protocol and the relevant terms of the Clean Air Act." EPA and NRDC agree that the decisions are not "adjustments" to the Protocol. But they disagree on the legal consequences of the decisions.

* * *

III.

On the merits, NRDC argues that "EPA's 2005 critical-use rule violates the express terms of the Montreal Protocol Parties' unanimous Decisions," and therefore is "not in accordance with law."

Decision Ex.I/3, in which the Parties reached agreement on methyl bromide critical-use exemptions for 2005, stated that the United States had a critical need for 8,942 metric tons of methyl bromide. To meet this need, the Parties agreed to allow new production and consumption in the amount of 7,659 metric tons, with the remaining critical uses to be met by drawing down existing stocks. The decision also stated that each Party "which has an agreed critical use should ensure that the criteria in paragraph 1 of decision IX/6 are applied" when implementing the exemption, "and that such procedures *take into account available stocks*." *Id.* ¶ 5 (emphasis added). Paragraph 1 of Decision IX/6 directs the Parties to authorize new production and consumption of methyl bromide only if it "is not available in sufficient quantity and quality from existing stocks," Decision IX/6 ¶ 1(b)(ii), and only after "[a]ll technically and economically feasible steps have been taken to minimize the critical use," *id.* ¶ 1(b)(i).

NRDC believes EPA's rule departs from these post-treaty agreements in three respects. First, the rule authorizes 7,659 metric tons of new production and consumption—the maximum agreed upon in Decision Ex.I/3—without offsetting this amount by existing stocks. EPA declined to disclose the size of the total nationwide methyl bromide stockpile, an action NRDC claims is itself a violation of the Clean Air Act, 42 U.S.C. § 7607(d)(4)(B)(i). Still, the record suggests that the stockpile is at least as large as the United States' total critical-use allocation for 2005. Second, EPA's rule allows noncritical users to draw down existing stocks. NRDC claims that the "decisions" implicitly reserve the stocks for critical users only. Third, EPA approved 8,942 metric tons of critical uses—again the maximum agreed upon in Decision Ex.I/3—without considering anew whether this was the minimum amount feasible. EPA counters that it adhered to the agreed-upon critical-use and new production and consumption levels, and that the remainder of the decisions are "hortatory."

NRDC fashions the entirety of its argument around the proposition that the "decisions" under the Protocol are "law." This premise is flawed. The "decisions" of the Parties—post-ratification side agreements reached by consensus among 189 nations—are not "law" within the meaning of the Clean Air Act and are not enforceable in federal court.

The Clean Air Act authorizes EPA to "exempt the production, importation, and consumption of methyl bromide for critical uses" only "[t]o the extent consistent with the Montreal Protocol." 42 U.S.C. § 7671c(d)(6); *see also id.* § 7671m(b).[62] The Protocol bans the production or consumption of methyl bromide after December 31, 2004, except "to the extent that the Parties decide to permit the level of production or consumption that is necessary to satisfy uses agreed by them to be critical uses." Montreal Protocol art. 2H(5). NRDC argues that because the Clean Air Act requires EPA to abide by the Protocol, and because the Protocol authorizes future agreements concerning the scope of the critical-use exemption, those future agreements must "define the scope of EPA's Clean Air Act authority." Supp. Br. for Pet'r 4.

* * *

The legal status of "decisions" of this sort appears to be a question of first impression. There is significant debate over the constitutionality of assigning lawmaking functions to international bodies. A holding that the Parties' post-ratification side agreements were "law" would raise serious constitutional questions in light of the nondelegation doctrine, numerous constitutional procedural requirements for making law, and the separation of powers.

[But] we need not confront the "serious likelihood that the statute will be held unconstitutional." *Almendarez-Torres v. United States,* 523 U.S. 224, 238 (1998). It is far more plausible to interpret the Clean Air Act and Montreal Protocol as creating an ongoing international political commitment rather than a delegation of lawmaking authority to annual meetings of the Parties.

Nowhere does the Protocol suggest that the Parties' post-ratification consensus agreements about how to implement the critical-use exemption are binding in domestic courts. The only pertinent language in Article 2H(5) states that the Parties will "decide to permit" production and consumption necessary to satisfy those uses that they "agree[ ]" to be critical uses. The Protocol is silent on any specific conditions accompanying

---

[62] The Montreal Protocol includes the Protocol itself and any "adjustments adopted by Parties thereto and amendments that have entered into force." 42 U.S.C. § 7671(9). NRDC and EPA agree that the "decisions" are not "adjustments" to the Protocol. Supp. Br. for Pet'r 1; Supp Br. for the Resp. 2–5.

the critical-use exemption. Post-ratification agreements setting these conditions are not the Protocol.

To illustrate, suppose the President signed and the Senate ratified a treaty with Germany and France to conserve fossil fuel. How this is to be accomplished the treaty does not specify. In a later meeting of representatives of the signatory countries at the United Nations, a consensus is reached to lower the speed limits on all major highways of the signatory nations to a maximum of 45 miles per hour. No one would say that United States law has thus been made.

EPA characterizes the decisions as "subsequent consensus agreements of the Parties that address the interpretation and application of the critical use provision. . . . " Final Rule, 69 Fed.Reg. at 76,985. This may be so. Like any interpretive tool, however, the "decisions" are useful only to the extent they shed light on ambiguous terms in the Protocol. But the details of the critical-use exemption are not ambiguous. They are nonexistent. The "decisions" do not interpret treaty language. They fill in treaty gaps.

Article 2H(5) thus constitutes an "agreement to agree." The parties agree in the Protocol to reach an agreement concerning the types of uses for which new production and consumption will be permitted, and the amounts that will be permitted. "Agreements to agree" are usually not enforceable in contract. And the fruits of those agreements are enforceable only to the extent that they themselves are contracts. There is no doubt that the "decisions" are not treaties.

The Parties' post-ratification actions suggest their common understanding that the decisions are international political commitments rather than judicially enforceable domestic law. The Parties met to decide the 2006 critical-use exemptions well after EPA's rule went into effect. Yet they did not invoke the Protocol's internal noncompliance procedure against the United States, nor did they admonish the United States to change its interpretation of the previous decisions.[63] This course of dealing suggests that the Parties intended the side agreements to be enforceable as a political matter at the negotiating table.

Section 5. Discussion Notes/Questions

1. The Commonwealth of New Britannia has large stockpiles of methyl bromide, and it is apparently using those stockpiles as a source of methyl bromide for exportation, for non-critical uses (golf course pesticide), and for

---

[63] NRDC points to a change in the language from Decision Ex.I/3 (the 2005 decision) to Decision Ex.II/1 (the 2006 decision). *Compare* Decision Ex.I/3 ¶ 5 ("[Each Party] *should ensure* that the criteria in paragraph 1 of decision IX/6 are applied. . . ." (emphasis added)), *with Second Extraordinary Report, supra* note 4, at 5–6 ¶ 5 ("Decision Ex.II/1") ("[Each Party] *renews its commitment to ensure* that the criteria in paragraph 1 of decision IX/6 are applied. . . ." (emphasis added)). But this change in diplomatic language can hardly be said to change the United States' substantive commitments under the Protocol.

treatment of wood containers used in international trade. In using stockpiles in this way, is the Commonwealth of New Britannia violating its obligations under paragraphs 5 or 6 of Article 2H of the Montreal Protocol **(Basic Document 2.8)**? Is its "calculated level of consumption" of methyl bromide in excess of zero? To answer, you must read the treaty provisions with care, including the definitions.

2. By permitting new production of methyl bromide for critical uses, rather than requiring the use of existing stocks, is CNB violating its obligations under paragraph 3 of decision XXIX/6 to "ensure that the criteria in paragraph 1 of decision XI/6 are applied"?

In 2006, the decision on critical-use exemptions for methyl bromide provided that "a Party with a critical use exemption in excess of permitted levels of production and consumption for critical uses is to make up any such differences between those levels by using quantities of methyl bromide from stocks that the Party has recognized to be available." *See* Decision XVIII/13, paragraph 4. If such language were included in the decision in this case, would that change your analysis of CNB's legal obligations?

Are decisions of the Parties to the Montreal Protocol legally binding under international law? Nothing in the Protocol says so expressly. On what basis might they be binding? If they are not binding in and of themselves, can they be used as a basis for interpretation of the language of Article 2H, paragraph 5. *See* Vienna Convention on the Law of Treaties, art 31 (general rule of interpretation of treaties) **(Basic Document 1.14)**. In particular, do the decisions suggest that production or consumption of methyl bromide is not "necessary" so long as there are sufficient stocks in place to meet critical needs? Or do they suggest just the opposite?

3. As described by the court in the *National Resources Defense Council* decision, the United States ratified the Montreal Protocol and Congress "incorporated its terms into domestic law" in 1990. Presumably, this means that the incorporated terms of the Protocol could be enforced against the EPA in court if, for example, the EPA authorized production and consumption of an ozone-depleting substance in violation of the Protocol? Why, then, are the decisions of the Parties concerning critical-use exemptions unenforceable? Suppose the NRDC had not argued that the EPA violated a decision of the parties to the Protocol, but had argued instead that the EPA violated Article 2H(5) of the Protocol, which forbids methyl bromide production or consumption except as "necessary" for "uses agreed by [the Parties] to be critical uses." In the NRDC's view, production of additional methyl bromide is not "necessary" so long as stockpiles exist that are sufficiently large to satisfy agreed critical uses. Has the Protocol been violated under these circumstances? Are the decisions of the Parties relevant to answering that question? If you think the decisions are relevant, is your conclusion on that point consistent with the court's opinion? Note that the United States considers the rules of treaty interpretation referenced in the previous note to be part of customary international law.

4. Given that Nueva Granada has not accepted the amendments to the Montreal Protocol that restrict production of methyl bromide, does it have any right to complain to the ICJ about CNB's methyl bromide policy? *See* Vienna Convention on the Law of Treaties, art. 34 ("A treaty does not create either obligations or rights for a third State without its consent.") and art. 36(1) ("A right arises for a third State from a provision of a treaty if the parties to the treaty intend the provision to accord that right . . . to all States, and the third State assents thereto. . . .") In the preamble to the Montreal Protocol, the Parties state that they are "determined to protect the ozone layer by taking precautionary measures to control equitably total global emissions" of ozone-depleting substances, "bearing in mind the developmental needs of developing countries." Does this indicate that the Parties to the Protocol recognized a right in other states to be protected from ozone depletion, even if those other states needed to continue emitting ozone-depleting substances for developmental purposes? Would that satisfy the conditions of Vienna Convention art. 36(1) with respect to the creation of rights for non-party states?

5. Does the International Court of Justice have jurisdiction to hear this dispute? Review Article 11 of the 1985 Vienna Convention and Article 8 of the Montreal Protocol. If the ICJ does have jurisdiction, would its adjudication of the case be consistent with the approach to dispute settlement adopted by the parties to the Protocol? Which approach to dispute settlement do you prefer under circumstances like these?

6. As a non-party to the Copenhagen Amendments, is Nueva Granada subject to any restrictions on its production or use of methyl bromide. Does Article 3 of the Vienna Convention impose any obligations on it in this regard? What about customary international law? Sylvia Maureen Williams, in *A Historical Background on the Chlorofluorocarbon Ozone Depletion Theory and Its Legal Implications*, *in* Transboundary Air Pollution 267, 274–77 (Cees Flinterman et al. eds., 1986), writes:

> The well-known principle underlying the *Trail Smelter* arbitration and later, the *Corfu Channel* judgment, that no state has the right to allow its territory to be used for acts contrary to the rights of other states is, without doubt, applicable to the ozone depletion problem except that conditions are somewhat different. Whereas in the *Trail Smelter* and *Corfu Channel* cases the responsibility of the state causing the damage arises *vis-à-vis* another specific country and, therefore, indemnities are more easily determined, in the present instance, the damage affecting the ozone layer—perhaps irreversible and, certainly, retarded—would be reaching the whole international community. The state would, therefore, be responsible *erga omnes* for environmental damage. It necessarily follows that the assessment of the damage and the obligation to restore to the *status quo ante* become far more complex. However so, there exists today a rule of general international law prohibiting states to allow the use of their territory in a way that affects the rights of other states. This rule—which clearly covers the possibility of ozone depletion by the use of

> CFCs—is binding upon all states and its breach entails the international responsibility of the state causing the injury.

Do you agree with this assessment? Williams adds that international legal principles "relating to abuse of rights and good neighborliness" might also be implicated. Do you think that a developing country's refusal to join the regulatory regime for methyl bromide is a violation of these legal principles? Of any of the other principles discussed in Chapter 4?

7. Should the trade ban imposed by the Montreal Protocol be extended to products "produced" with controlled substances, as an incentive to induce nations to join the Copenhagen Amendments relating to methyl bromide? If such a ban were imposed, could it be determined whether methyl bromide had been used in the production, for example, of strawberries imported into the Commonwealth of New Britannia from Nueva Granada? Would it be fair to ban such imports when strawberry producers in CNB use methyl bromide for the same purposes as producers in Nueva Granada?

8. Three categories of uses of methyl bromide are exempt from the phase out: use as a chemical feedstock in the production of other chemicals (a relatively minor use in which most of the methyl bromide is consumed in chemical reaction); uses deemed "critical" by the Parties (as discussed in this problem); and use for eliminating pests from plants and plant products (including wooden shipping materials) in international trade during quarantine or preshipment treatment. The latter exemption is because methyl bromide fumigation of imported agricultural commodities is regarded as essential to preventing unwanted pests from entering into agricultural areas where they are not already present. In fact, methyl bromide fumigation is one of only two acceptable treatment options for wood packaging material in international trade under International Standard for Phytosanitary Measures (ISPM) No. 15, adopted pursuant to the International Plant Protection Convention. Importing countries will generally refuse to accept shipments packaged in wood unless the wood has been treated in compliance with ISPM 15. *See generally* Methyl Bromide: Quarantine and Preshipment Uses (2007) (Brochure jointly prepared by the Secretariates of the Montreal Protocol and the International Plant Protection Convention).

CHAPTER SIX

PROTECTING THE OCEANS

■ ■ ■

The immensity of our planet's oceans is almost impossible to grasp. Ocean waters cover more than 70% of the Earth's surface at an average depth of 12,100 feet. This amounts to 321 million cubic *miles* of water—97% of the planet's total. Over 250,000 species of plants and animals have been discovered in the oceans, and scientists predict that millions more remain to be discovered. Some 80% of life on Earth is ocean life, and it is amazingly diverse, surviving in habitats ranging from the icy waters of arctic regions to the tropical seas and from the sunlit waters of the surface to the lightless depths of the deepest ocean trenches.

Oceans regulate our atmosphere and our climate. One-half of the oxygen we breathe is produced by oceanic plant life. The oceans are also a major carbon dioxide sink, absorbing vast amounts of CO_2 and helping slow the rate of global warming. About 90% of the water that falls as life-giving rain on our farms and communities was originally evaporated from the oceans. By moving warm water from the tropics to arctic regions and vice versa, ocean currents determine weather patterns in many areas of the world, help moderate temperature extremes and keep human-settled regions habitable.

We rely on the oceans for other services as well, especially food, transport, and recreation. 17% of the animal protein consumed in the world is supplied by ocean fisheries, and more than a billion people rely on these fisheries as their main source of protein. 90% of the goods traded between countries (whether raw materials or finished products) are carried by sea. More than 23% of the planet's population lives within 100 kilometers of a coast. Migration to coastal regions is common, and population densities in those regions are far higher than elsewhere in both developed and developing countries.

Unfortunately, human threats to our oceans are significant and growing. Overfishing is depleting ocean fish stocks at an alarming rate. From 1974 to 2013, the percentage of fisheries being exploited at biologically unsustainable levels rose from 10% to 32%. Similarly, coral reefs and mangrove forests, both critical ocean ecosystems, face threats from a variety of sources, including land-based pollution and coastal development. An estimated 8 million tons of plastic litter enters the oceans each year, killing fish, seabirds, sea turtles, and seals at ever-increasing rates. Finally, oceans are not immune from the effects of anthropogenic changes to the atmosphere: human emissions of carbon dioxide are warming and acidifying the oceans with increasingly adverse effects on many ocean species, including ocean corals.

In this chapter, we first provide a brief overview of ocean law (the "law of the sea"). We then examine three threats to ocean ecosystems and the particular law that has been developed to address those threats. Problem 6-1 focuses on the problem of overfishing. Problem 6-2 examines land-based pollution of the ocean. Finally, Problem 6-3 illustrates how international law was used to address (and to a large extent solve) the problem of accidental pollution related to the oceanic transport of crude oil.

A. INTRODUCTION TO THE LAW OF THE SEA

In *Mare Liberum*, first published in 1609, Hugo Grotius, a Dutch jurist sometimes called "the father of international law," proposed that

> the sea is common to all, because it is so limitless that it cannot become a possession of any one, and because it is adapted for the use of all, whether we consider it from the point of view of navigation or of fisheries.[1]

It took two centuries, and much warfare, before the idea of freedom of the seas became widely accepted. But by the 19th century, it was a well-established concept in European international law. Thus, as you learned in Chapter One, the tribunal in the 1893 fur seals arbitration was unwilling to recognize any right in the United States to stop the unsustainable harvest of fur seals on the high seas. As the tribunal expressed it, "We have felt obliged to maintain intact the fundamental principles of that august law of nations, which extends itself like the vault of heaven above all countries." In particular, the tribunal affirmed the principle that no nation could subject the high seas to its jurisdiction or control, even when the exercise of jurisdiction was said to be necessary to prevent the extinction of a valuable species of animal. *See Bering Sea Fur Seals Arbitration,* in Chapter One, *supra.*

By the middle of the 20th century, however, the principle of freedom of the seas was under pressure on a number of fronts. The United States and other countries began to assert exclusive jurisdiction over their entire continental shelves (and the oil, minerals, and other resources contained therein), ignoring the traditional three-mile limit to national jurisdiction beyond the coast.[2] Similarly, Iceland claimed a special interest in fisheries near its coast but well beyond its three-mile limit, and seized a British

---

[1] Hugo Grotius, Mare Liberum 27–28 (J.B. Scott, ed., R. van D. Magoffin, trans. 1916).

[2] These claims to the continental shelf were preceded by a long history of nations claiming title to sedentary fisheries beyond the three-mile limit as well as claiming the right to extract resources from the seabed beyond the three-mile limit.

fishing vessel that violated its unilaterally imposed fishing rules. Latin American countries claimed the right to control fishing up to 200 miles beyond their coasts. Other states rejected the traditional three-mile limit and claimed territorial sovereignty up to 12 miles beyond their coasts. None of these developments directly challenged the principle of freedom of the seas; they did, however, seek to expand the authority of coastal states in a manner that would prevent the exercise of traditional high seas freedoms in some ocean areas.

In 1956, the first United Nations Conference on the Law of the Sea (UNCLOS I) began in Geneva, Switzerland. Two years later, four law-of-the-sea treaties were concluded.[3] Although those treaties mostly codified customary law-of-the-sea principles, they were unsatisfactory to many states. For one thing, the Territorial Sea Convention failed to define the breadth of the territorial sea (three miles or 12 miles), thus leaving a crucial issue up in the air. A second UN Conference on the Law of the Sea, convened in 1960 to deal with that issue, failed to resolve the matter. A second problem was fishing. The 1958 Fishing Convention recognized the special interest coastal states had in nearby fisheries. It did not, however, recognize any exclusive right of the coastal state to control such fisheries, despite the fact that several states were seeking such authority in response to increasing evidence of over-utilization of oceanic fish stocks.

In 1973, facing ever-increasing exploitation of oceanic resources and the constant risk that unresolved disputes would lead to open conflict, the United Nations convened a third conference on the law of the sea. Nine years later, the conference ended with the adoption of the Convention on the Law of the Sea,[4] perhaps the most consequential treaty yet concluded under the auspices of the United Nations.

1. THE UNITED NATIONS CONVENTION ON THE LAW OF THE SEA (UNCLOS)

The 1982 United Nations Convention on the Law of the Sea **(Basic Document 3.4)** contains both conservative and revolutionary provisions. On one hand, it strongly affirms traditional high seas freedoms. On the other hand, it extends the scope of coastal state jurisdiction in a variety of ways. It also breaks completely new ground in declaring the seabed and ocean floor beyond the limits of national jurisdiction to be "the common heritage of mankind"[5] and asserting that activities in that area are subject

---

3 Convention on the High Seas, 29 April 1958, 450 UNTS 82; Convention on the Continental Shelf, 29 April 1958, 499 UNTS 311; Convention on the Territorial Sea and Contiguous Zone, 29 April 1958, 516 UNTS 205; Convention on Fishing and Conservation of the Living Resources of the High Seas, 29 April 1958, 559 UNTS 285.

4 United Nations Convention on the Law of the Sea, 10 December 1982, 1833 UNTS 3.

5 *Id.* at art. 136.

to international control.[6] A general obligation to "protect and preserve the marine environment"[7] is complemented by specific obligations relating to dumping, land-based pollution, and pollution from vessels along with a general duty to ensure "prompt and adequate compensation" for pollution damage.[8] The freedom to fish is limited by conservation obligations.[9] A system of compulsory adjudication is established for the decision of disputes that aren't resolved by a negotiated settlement or voluntary conciliation.[10]

The Convention consists of 320 articles and five annexes. We cannot do justice to it here, but we can highlight some of the main provisions essential for understanding the problems in this chapter.

High seas freedoms

UNCLOS declares that "the high seas are open to all States," and it affirms the following high seas freedoms:

- Freedom of navigation;
- Freedom of fishing;
- Freedom of overflight;
- Freedom of scientific research;
- Freedom to lay submarine cables and pipelines; and
- Freedom to construct artificial islands and other installations.

Each of these freedoms is subject to "the conditions laid down by this Convention and by other rules of international law," including a general obligation to give "due regard for the interests of other States."[11]

Jurisdiction over vessels on the high seas

UNCLOS continues the traditional rule that "no State may validly purport to subject any part of the high seas to its sovereignty."[12] This means that coastal states cannot generally interfere with vessels of other states when those vessels are navigating or fishing on the high seas. Ships that are registered in a nation and are flying its flag are subject to its *exclusive* jurisdiction when on the high seas.[13]

---

6 *Id.* at art. 153.

7 *Id.* at art. 192–222.

8 *Id.* at art. 235.

9 *Id.* at arts. 116–120.

10 *Id.* at arts. 279–299.

11 *Id.* at art. 87.

12 *Id.* at art. 89. Twelve miles is a maximum. A state can declare a smaller territorial sea if it wishes.

13 *Id.* at art. 92 ("Ships shall sail under the flag of one State only and . . . shall be subject to its exclusive jurisdiction on the high seas.") Vessels without nationality (i.e. vessels that are not

Enforcement of international laws on the high seas is left primarily to flag states. Thus, the flag state has the responsibility to "effectively exercise its jurisdiction and control in administrative, technical and social matters over ships flying its flag."[14] The flag state must also police its flagged vessels' compliance with pollution-control rules[15] and ensure that its fishing vessels are subject to restrictions "necessary for the conservation of the living resources of the high seas."[16]

Coastal state authority

UNCLOS expanded coastal state authority in several ways. First, it specified that the territorial sea has a breadth of 12 miles, measured from the coastline.[17] The coastal state has sovereignty over the territorial sea, the airspace above it, and the underlying seabed. Foreign vessels have a right to navigate through a state's territorial sea so long as their passage is innocent—i.e. not prejudicial to the peace, good order, or security of the coastal state.[18] The coastal state may regulate the innocent passage of foreign vessels for a variety of reasons, including ensuring the safety of navigation and preventing pollution.[19] A coastal state can also exercise authority up to 24 miles beyond its coast when necessary to prevent or punish certain violations of its laws that have occurred or could occur within the territorial sea.[20]

The most important expansion of coastal state authority under UNCLOS was the recognition of coastal state sovereign rights in an "exclusive economic zone (EEZ)" beyond the territorial sea and extending up to 200 nautical miles from the coast. These sovereign rights include the rights to exploit the natural resources of the EEZ and to engage in any other kind of economic activity (e.g., the production of wind power).[21] Subject to various restrictions, the coastal state may adopt pollution-control measures applicable to foreign vessels in the EEZ[22] and may, in some serious situations, take direct enforcement action against a polluting vessel.[23] It also has the right to control fishing in the EEZ, subject to an obligation to allow other states access to surplus stocks,[24] and may take enforcement action, including "boarding, inspection, arrest and judicial

---

registered in any State) are subject to the jurisdiction of all states. Vessels that fly more than one flag are not entitled to the protection of any state and are treated as without nationality.

14 *Id.* at art. 94.

15 *Id.* at art. 217.

16 *Id.* at art. 117.

17 *Id.* at art. 3.

18 *Id.* at arts. 17–19.

19 *Id.* at art. 21.

20 *Id.* at art. 33. The area from 12–24 miles is called the "contiguous zone."

21 *Id.* at art. 56.

22 *Id.* at arts. 211 & 216.

23 *Id.* at art. 220(6).

24 *Id.* at art. 62.

proceedings" against foreign vessels violating its fishing conservation and management laws in the EEZ.[25]

Environmental protection

UNCLOS obligates Member States generally to "protect and preserve the marine environment."[26] This includes the obligations to take necessary measures to reduce or prevent pollution of the marine environment;[27] to ensure that activities under their jurisdiction or control do not damage the environments of other states;[28] to protect and preserve fragile ecosystems and critical ocean habitats;[29] to notify other states of imminent or actual pollution damage;[30] and to undertake impact assessments of activities that may adversely affect the marine environment.[31] In addition to these general rules, there are specific rules dealing with pollution from land-based sources; from sea-bed activities; from dumping; and from vessels.[32]

One important innovation of UNCLOS relates to the establishment and enforcement of laws designed to protect the marine environment from pollution from ships. Flag states are required to give effect to "generally accepted international rules and standards, established through the competent international organization" for the prevention of pollution from vessels.[33] This appears to require flag states to follow such rules, even if they are not a party to the instrument that adopts them. The phrase "international rules and standards established through the competent international organization" is generally understood to refer to anti-pollution rules adopted under the auspices of the International Maritime Organization (IMO). Coastal states have enhanced authority to enforce such rules against vessels navigating in their territorial sea and EEZ.[34]

UNCLOS also has a number of provisions mandating protection for the living resources of the oceans. Coastal states' authority over their EEZs is balanced by an express obligation to adopt conservation and management measures designed to prevent over-exploitation of the living resources in the EEZ.[35] States fishing on the high seas have a similar "duty to take, or to cooperate with other states in taking, such measures . . . as may be necessary for the conservation of the living resources of the high

---

[25] *Id.* at art. 73(1).

[26] *Id.* at art. 192.

[27] *Id.* at art. 194(1).

[28] *Id.* at art. 194(2).

[29] *Id.* at art. 194(5).

[30] *Id.* at art. 198.

[31] *Id.* at art. 206.

[32] *See, e.g., id.* at arts. 207 (land-based sources), 208–09 (sea-bed activities), 210 (dumping), 211 (vessels).

[33] *Id.* at art. 211(2).

[34] *See id.* at arts. 21(2), 211(4–5), & 220.

[35] *Id.* at art. 61(2).

seas."[36] And coastal states and high-seas-fishing states have a shared responsibility to cooperate in the protection of fish stocks that migrate between or straddle a high-seas area and an EEZ.[37]

2. THE INTERNATIONAL MARITIME ORGANIZATION

The International Maritime Organization (IMO) is a specialized agency of the United Nations. The treaty establishing the IMO (originally the Inter-Governmental Maritime Consultative Organization) was adopted in 1948.[38] However, many states were reluctant to approve a treaty providing for international involvement in the regulation of ocean shipping, and the treaty did not enter into force until 1958. The IMO held its first official meeting in January 1959.

The IMO's concern is with international ocean shipping. It focuses particularly on "maritime safety, efficiency of navigation and prevention and control of marine pollution from ships," and it is charged with encouraging the adoption of "the highest practicable standards" in relation to those matters. Its environmental authority extends beyond pollution control to "any matters concerning . . . the effect of shipping on the marine environment."[39]

More than 30 conventions have been adopted under IMO auspices. They establish rules governing such matters as the construction and design of ships, the equipping of ships, the training of crews, and the navigation of ships. Many of the most important IMO conventions relate to environmental protection. Some of those include:

- International Convention Relating to Intervention on the High Seas in Cases of Oil Pollution Casualties, 1969 **(Basic Document 3.1)**
- Convention on the Prevention of Marine Pollution by Dumping of Wastes and Other Matter, 1972 (London Convention) **(Basic Document 3.2)** and the 1996 London Protocol **(Basic Document 3.2a)**
- MARPOL 73/78: International Convention for the Prevention of Pollution from Ships, 1973, as modified by the Protocol of 1978 and the Protocol of 1997 **(Basic Document 3.3)**

---

[36] *Id.* at art. 117.

[37] *Id.* at arts. 63 & 64.

[38] Convention on the International Maritime Organization, 6 March 1948, 289 UNTS 48. The Convention has been amended many times. A current version is available from the IMO at its website, www.imo.org.

[39] *Id.* at art. 1.

- 1990 International Convention on Oil Pollution Preparedness, Response and Co-operation **(Basic Document 3.8)**
- 1992 International Convention on Civil Liability for Oil Pollution Damage **(Basic Document 3.9)**
- 2004 International Convention for the Control and Management of ships' Ballast Water and Sediments
- 2009 Hong Kong International Convention for the Safe and Environmentally Sound Recycling of Ships

Some of the rules and standards adopted in these agreements will be binding even on non-ratifying states. As noted earlier, some provisions of UNCLOS provide that all seafaring states are bound by rules and standards adopted by "the competent international organization" (i.e. the IMO) if those rules and standards become "generally accepted." Most IMO conventions will not enter into force unless and until they are accepted by states representing a majority of the world's merchant vessels. Hence, the entry into force of an IMO convention means that its rules are widely applicable to the world's shipping fleet and are well on their way to becoming "generally accepted."[40]

In Problem 6-3, we take a closer look at the IMO and at some of the conventions listed above.

3. REGIONAL SEAS AGREEMENTS

There are 14 multilateral agreements aimed at environmental protection of particular ocean regions around the world. These agreements are typically "framework" agreements. They set up a structure through which states in a region can cooperate to protect the marine environment of that region. While they may include specific commitments to "take all appropriate measures" to prevent land-based pollution, protect fragile ecosystems, stop ocean dumping, or control pollution from ships, they are generally complemented by the adoption of protocols or annexes addressing particular environmental issues in greater detail. One of these regional agreements, the Convention for the Protection and Development of the Marine Environment of the Wider Caribbean Region (Cartagena Convention) **(Basic Document 3.5)**, is the subject of Problem 6-2. Other regional seas agreements include:

---

[40] The "three conventions that include the most comprehensive sets of rules and standards on safety, pollution prevention and training and certification of seafarers, namely, SOLAS, MARPOL and STCW Conventions," have been ratified by states that flag more than 90% of the world's merchant fleet, "representing approximately 99% gross tonnage" of that fleet." IMO Secretariat, *Implications of the United Nations Convention on the Law of the Sea for the International Maritime Organization* 12, IMO Doc LEG/MISC.6 (Sept. 10, 2008).

- 1976 Convention for the Protection of the Mediterranean Sea Against Pollution (amended in 1995 and renamed the Convention for the Protection of the Marine Environment and the Coastal Region of the Mediterranean)
- 1978 Kuwait Regional Convention for Co-operation on the Protection of the Marine Environment from Pollution
- 1981 Convention for the Protection of the Marine Environment and Coastal Zones of the South-East Pacific (Lima Convention)
- 1982 Regional Convention for the Conservation of the Red Sea and the Gulf of Aden Environment (Jeddah Convention)
- 1986 Convention for the Protection of the Natural Resources and Environment of the South Pacific Area (Noumea Convention) **(Basic Document 3.7)**
- 1992 Convention on the Protection of the Marine Environment of the Baltic Sea Area (Helsinki Convention)
- 1992 Convention on the Protection of the Black Sea Against Pollution
- 1992 Convention for the Protection of the Marine Environment of the North-East Atlantic (OSPAR Convention)

In addition, the ocean areas surrounding the Antarctic are protected by the Protocol on Environmental Protection to the Antarctic Treaty **(Basic Document 6.5)**, the Convention for the Conservation of Antarctic Seals **(Basic Document 6.2)** and the Convention on the Conservation of Antarctic Marine Living Resources **(Basic Document 6.3)**. These treaties are discussed in Chapter 11, *infra*.

4. FISHERIES CONSERVATION

States have been entering into fisheries agreements for hundreds of years. The International Environmental Agreements (IEA) Database Project at the University of Oregon includes multiple bilateral agreements on marine fisheries dating back to 1351. The earliest listed multilateral agreement on ocean fisheries is an 1882 agreement to police over-fishing in the North Sea.[41] Today, there are many such agreements.

Modern fisheries agreements generally establish an organization that is authorized to develop regulations aimed at preventing over-fishing. The organization will have responsibility to police fishing in a particular ocean

---

[41] Ronald B. Mitchell, International Environmental Agreements (IEA) Database Project, https://iea.uoregon.edu (last visited July 25, 2018).

area.[42] Sometimes its authority will be limited to a particular species of fish.[43] These regional fisheries management organizations (RFMOs) are generally charged with using the best available scientific evidence to evaluate a fishery and take measures aimed at ensuring that exploitation of the fishery is sustainable.[44] To that end, the organization may limit the amount of fish that can be caught during a season, establish open and closed seasons, prohibit certain fishing methods and fishing gear, or prescribe a minimum size for fish that can be caught.[45]

Even if the members of an RFMO agree on appropriate conservation measures for a particular species of fish in a particular region, those measures may be utterly ineffective if vessels from other fishing states ignore the regulations. There are two principal legal issues that present themselves in such a scenario.

First, there is the question whether those non-party states (and their fishing vessels) are bound by the conservation measures adopted by the RFMO. Pursuant to basic treaty law, of course, a state is not bound by an agreement to which it has not consented. That would suggest that a state that is not a member of an RFMO would have no obligation to require its fishing vessels to respect an RFMO's fishing regulations.

On the other hand, whether a state has joined a particular RFMO or not, it has an obligation (either as a matter of customary law or pursuant to UNCLOS) to cooperate in the conservation of oceanic fish stocks in areas where its flagged vessels fish. So, arguably, that state's failure to join a relevant fisheries organization, or to conform to measures deemed necessary (according to the "best scientific evidence available") to conservation of the relevant fishery, could be viewed as a violation of its legal obligations. But such a conclusion only leads to the second legal problem: if the RFMO's rules are binding on fishing vessels from non-RFMO states, who can enforce those rules against those vessels?

The flag state's *exclusive* jurisdiction over its vessels on the high seas, and the inability of states to otherwise exercise sovereignty on the high seas, are both fundamental principles of customary international law and of UNCLOS. Application of those principles means, of course, that no state other than the flag state can (without the flag state's consent) take

[42] *See, e.g.*, International Convention for the Northwest Atlantic Fisheries, 8 February 1949, art. I, 157 UNTS 157.

[43] *See, e.g.*, Agreement for the Establishment of the Indian Ocean Tuna Commission, 25 November 1993, 1927 UNTS 329.

[44] RFOs are, in effect, the means by which their Member States cooperate to implement the fishery conservation obligations imposed by UNCLOS on states that utilize high seas fisheries. *See* UNCLOS art. 119 (states must use the "best scientific evidence available" to take measures designed "to maintain or restore populations of harvested species at levels which can produce the maximum sustainable yield."

[45] *See, e.g.*, Agreement for the Establishment of the Regional Commission for Fisheries (RECOFI), 11 November 1999, art. III(1), 2144 UNTS 105.

enforcement action against its fishing vessels on the high seas. If a flag state is unwilling to require its vessels to adhere to internationally established fisheries conservation measures, there is no action that other states can take against those vessels so long as they remain on the high seas.

Three international agreements address this enforcement problem. The 1993 FAO Compliance Agreement **(Basic Document 5.12)**[46] takes the modest step of stating clearly that a flag state has a duty to "ensure that fishing vessels entitled to fly its flag do not engage in any activity that undermines the effectiveness of international conservation and management measures." This duty applies whether or not the flag state is a party to the conservation and management measures at issue. In other words, flag states must ensure that their fishing vessels comply with RFMO-mandated conservation rules, even if the state has not joined the RFMO. Of course, this duty applies only if the flag state is a party to the Compliance Agreement. And the Compliance Agreement does not authorize any non-flag state to take enforcement action against vessels flying another state's flag.

The 1995 United Nations Fish Stocks Agreement **(Basic Document 5.14)**[47] made a more substantial effort to overcome the enforcement problem. It provides that fishing states *must* either join relevant RFMOs or adhere unilaterally to the conservation and management measures adopted by those RFMOs. It further provides that any member of an RFMO may authorize its fisheries inspectors to "board and inspect" the fishing vessels of nonmember states for the purpose of enforcing the RFMO's rules. If evidence of a violation is found, the flag state is informed and it must either investigate or authorize the inspecting state to do so. If a violation is found, the flag state must either take appropriate enforcement action or authorize the inspecting state to do so. Of course, a great weakness of this approach is, again, that these rules *only bind states that ratify or accept the Fish Stocks Agreement.* Fishing vessels flying the flag of a state that is not a party to the Agreement are not subject to the enforcement regime established by that Agreement.

A third agreement of importance to the enforcement of international fishing regulations is the 2009 Agreement on Port State Measures to Prevent, Deter and Eliminate Illegal, Unreported and Unregulated (IUU) Fishing. The Port State Measures Agreement provides that Member States will deny entry to their ports to the fishing vessels of other states if those

[46] Agreement to Promote Compliance with International Conservation and Management Measures by Fishing Vessels on the High Seas, 24 November 1993, 2221 UNTS 91 (FAO Compliance Agreement) **(Basic Document 5.12)**.

[47] Agreement for the Implementation of the Provisions of the United Nations Convention of the Law of the Sea of 10 December 1982 Relating to the Conservation and Management of Straddling Fish Stocks and Highly Migratory Fish Stocks, 4 August 1995, 2167 UNTS 3 (UN Fish Stocks Agreement) **(Basic Document 5.14)**.

fishing vessels are determined to have engaged in IUU fishing. This includes vessels that fish in another state's EEZ without permission or that fish in contravention of the conservation and management measures adopted by an RFMO. The denial of port access extends to vessels that have engaged in activities in support of IUU fishing (e.g., the processing of fish).

Problem 6-1 examines the challenges of managing high-seas fisheries.

DISCUSSION NOTES/QUESTIONS

1. As of July 2019, 168 states were parties to UNCLOS. Several important seafaring states were not, including Colombia, Iran, North Korea, Peru, Turkey and the United States. This does not mean, however, that UNCLOS rules are inapplicable to those non-party states. There is widespread agreement that many UNCLOS provisions—in particular, the provisions pertaining to navigation, coastal state jurisdiction, high seas freedoms, and the obligations to control pollution and cooperate in the protection of fisheries—either reflected customary law at the time UNCLOS was adopted or have since ripened into customary law as a result of the widespread adoption of the convention and adherence to the rules by non-Party as well as Party states. For a recent review of cases that treat various provisions of UNCLOS as part of customary international law, *see* J. Ashley Roach, *Today's Customary International Law of the Sea,* 45 Ocean Dev. & Int'l L. 239 (2014).

The United States government has long taken the position that many of UNCLOS's key rules are part of customary international law. For example, a few months after announcing that he would not sign UNCLOS, President Reagan issued a statement declaring (consistently with UNCLOS) a 200-mile EEZ and announcing that the United States would "act in accordance with the balance of interests relating to traditional uses of the oceans" reflected in the Convention, as those provisions "generally confirm existing maritime law and practice." *See* Ronald Reagan: "Statement on United States Oceans Policy," March 10, 1983. As early as 1987, the Third Restatement of U.S. Foreign Relations Law asserted that "many of the provisions of the Convention follow closely provisions in the 1958 conventions . . . which largely restated customary law as of that time. Other provisions in the LOS Convention set forth rules that, if not law in 1958, became customary law since that time, as they were accepted at the Conference by consensus and have influenced, and came to reflect, the practice of states." 2 Restatement (Third), Foreign Relations Law of the United States Part V, Introduction at p. 5 (1987).

2. As noted earlier, Article 287 of UNCLOS requires Member States to agree to some form of mandatory and binding adjudication to resolve disputes about the interpretation or application of the Convention. The parties to a dispute are free to resolve it by "any peaceful means of their own choice" (Art. 280). But if they fail to do so, either party may demand binding adjudication or arbitration of the dispute (Art. 286). It is unusual for a multilateral treaty to require its parties to submit to mandatory adjudication, although many treaties allow states to opt-in to such provisions at the time of ratification. *See,*

e.g., United Nations Framework Convention on Climate Change, 9 May 1992, art. 14(2), 1771 UNTS 107 (states may, at the time of ratification, opt in to adjudication or arbitration); Vienna Convention for the Protection of the Ozone Layer, 22 March 1985, art. 11(3), 1513 UNTS 293 (same).

What are the advantages and disadvantages of requiring UNCLOS Member States to accept binding adjudication or arbitration as a means of resolving their disputes? Do you think such a requirement is an incentive or disincentive for states to join the treaty? What factors would influence a state's views about that question?

3. Denial of port access can be a powerful enforcement tool against vessels that do not comply with internationally agreed rules. Consider the case of IUU fishing. A port state's decision to deny port access would, at the very least, force a fishing or fish-processing vessel to make a long and expensive journey to another port to dispose of its fish (thus eliminating or reducing the profits derived from IUU fishing). If many states all agreed to deny port access (at this writing, there are 54 State Parties to the 2009 Port State Measures Agreement), the denial of port access could effectively deny a fishing or processing vessel any market at all for its catch.

It has been said that "the ports of every state must be open to foreign merchant vessels and can only be closed when the vital interests of the state so require." *Saudi Arabia v. Aramco,* 27 ILR 117, 212 (Arb. Trib. 1958). But this dicta has been widely questioned and may never have been applicable to fishing vessels in any event. For example, the 1923 Statute on the International Regime of Maritime Ports, 9 December 1923, arts. 2 & 14, 58 LNTS 285, while establishing a conventional right of port access for foreign vessels, did so only on the basis of reciprocity and with the specific exclusion of "fishing vessels" and "their catches" from the rights created by the treaty.

If a state does allow foreign vessels to access its ports, there is a question as to how much authority it can exercise over those vessels while they are within its waters. There is no doubt that it can control and regulate the behavior of the vessel once in port, and it can also surely punish violations of its law that occur within its territorial sea or EEZ. But can it investigate and take action against a foreign vessel for events that occurred on the high seas (e.g., unlawful fishing or illegal dumping)? To allow the port state to do so would seem inconsistent with the notion that the flag state has exclusive jurisdiction over the vessel on the high seas.

Article 218 of UNCLOS addresses this issue with respect to pollution. It authorizes a port state to investigate and, "where the evidence so warrants, institute proceedings" against any foreign vessel with respect to discharges on the high seas when those discharges are "in violation of applicable international rules and standards established through the competent international organization or general diplomatic conference." Should a similar right to enforce internationally agreed fishing restrictions be recognized in port states? *See generally* Arron N. Honniball, *The Exclusive Jurisdiction of Flag States: A limitation on Pro-active Port States?,* 31 Intl J. Marine & Coastal L.

499 (2016); Sophia Kopela, *Port-State Jurisdiction, Extraterritoriality, and the Protection of Global Commons,* 47 Ocean Dev. & Int'l L., 89 (2016).

B. THREE THREATS TO OCEAN ECOSYSTEMS

1. DEPLETION OF LIVING RESOURCES

In pursuit of human needs and wants, the living resources of the seas are being plundered beyond sustainable limits. Excessive fishing of *target species* is part of the problem. But an equally serious problem is the use of fishing gear and fishing techniques that kill *non-target species* in large quantities and destroy critical ocean habitat.

In Problem 6-1 (Drift-Net Fishing in the Indian Ocean) we address the legal challenges of policing over-fishing and preventing the use of internationally disfavored fishing gear. First, however, review the following three readings on the problems facing high-seas fisheries.

OCEANS AND THE LAW OF THE SEA: REPORT OF THE SECRETARY GENERAL

UN GAOR., 60th Sess., Agenda Item 79, U.N. Doc. A/60/63/Add.1 (2005)

Impacts of fishing

132. By and large, the dominant human-caused direct effect on fisheries ecosystems is fishing itself, thus making the global impact of fishing activities on marine ecosystems a major concern for the international community. As an anthropogenic activity in the marine environment, fishing affects marine habitats worldwide and has the potential to alter the functioning and state of marine ecosystems, in particular vulnerable ecosystems as well as the biodiversity associated with them. Compounding the effects of fishing activities on the marine environment, unsustainable fishing practices, such as over-exploitation of fishery resources, illegal, unreported and unregulated fishing, the use of non-selective fishing gear, as well as destructive fishing practices and techniques in fishing operations, have aggravated the ecosystem effects of fishing activities and made such fishing practices the single greatest risk to vulnerable marine ecosystems and associated biodiversity.

* * *

134. Fishing pressure on stocks is generally high. While close to 25 per cent of stocks are moderately or under-exploited, 52 per cent of the stocks are fully exploited and 25 per cent of them are over-exploited, depleted or recovering. Considering stocks for which information is available, overfishing appears widespread and the majority of stocks are fully exploited. The percentage of stocks exploited at or beyond their maximum sustainable levels varies greatly by area. Assessments regularly conducted

on the 17 major tuna stocks indicate that close to 60 per cent requires stock rebuilding and/or reduction of fishing pressure.

* * *

Pelagic fisheries

136. In high-seas pelagic fisheries, catches of tuna and tuna-like species have been increasing throughout the years. The rate of increase has been much higher in comparison to other epipelagic species and tuna catches are still growing at a rapid pace, while those of other species have decreased in recent years. Trends in catch per unit effort over nine oceanic areas indicate that tuna and billfish biomass has declined by approximately 90 per cent, with a shift towards dominance by smaller pelagic species. Reduction of fish stocks below 30 per cent of their unfished biomass is generally not considered sustainable.

By-catch

137. Pelagic open-ocean fisheries seriously affect several groups of species, such as whales, sharks, seabirds, dolphins and turtles, whose biological characteristics render them vulnerable to depletion or even extinction. Oceanic sharks, primarily blue (*Prionace glauca*), oceanic whitetip (*Carcharhinus longimanus*), and silky shark (*Carcharhinus falciformis*), are taken in large numbers as by-catch of longline fisheries and their highly prized fins are removed. This catch is largely unreported and unregulated.

138. Seabirds are taken as incidental by-catch by pelagic longliners, most notably those targeting tuna and toothfish in the Southern Ocean. Albatrosses are particularly vulnerable, as they are long-lived and slow-breeding. Modifications to longline equipment and deployment techniques as well as other mitigation measures are being implemented to reduce seabird by-catch. FAO has adopted international plans of action for both seabirds and sharks that should assist in reducing the incidental catch of these two species in longline fisheries.

139. All seven species of sea turtle are endangered and some are on the verge of extinction. Among the major threats to sea turtles are incidental capture and drowning during commercial fishing with gill nets, shrimp nets, trawls, set nets, traps and longline equipment. Modifications to fishing equipment, such as the use of circle hooks and whole-fish bait, could substantially reduce sea turtle mortality.

140. The death of large numbers of dolphins caught as by-catch by purse-seiners targeting tuna [in the Eastern Tropical Pacific] in the late 1960s alarmed the public and led to government action to modify net design and fishing practices, which have reduced dolphin by-catch to a level of mortality considered to be sustainable. However, by-catch problems remain for juvenile tuna, endangered turtles and other non-target species

attracted to logs and other floating objects associated with some tuna schools.

Drift nets

141. Drift gill nets up to 60 kilometres in length were used to fish for dispersed species of salmon, squid, tuna and billfish on the high seas until the General Assembly, in its resolution 46/215 of 20 December 1991, called on the international community to ensure that a global moratorium on the use of large-scale pelagic drift-net fishing on the high seas was implemented. An estimated 40 per cent of the catch by this type of equipment was unwanted catch, including sea turtles, seabirds and marine mammals. Although the moratorium has been widely observed, recent reports indicate that some drift-net fishing may still occur, particularly in the Mediterranean Sea.[48]

Deep sea fisheries

142. Until 1975, catches of deep-water species were relatively small, ranging between 2 and 10 per cent of the total oceanic catches. Since the late 1970s, however, their contribution has consistently been greater than 20 per cent, reaching 30 per cent of the total oceanic catches in recent years. The life history attributes of deep-sea fish species (long lifespan, high age at maturity, low natural mortality, low fecundity, low levels of recruitment, high inter-annual variation in recruitment and aggregation over small areas) make them highly vulnerable to depletion by fishing. A reduction of adult biomass by fishing may have a stronger negative effect on deep-sea fish species than for species living on the shelf. This would mean that exploited populations of deep-sea fish species are likely to reduce quickly and take decades, or longer, to recover. For instance, some species, such as orange roughy, become more vulnerable by aggregating on isolated topographic features, such as seamounts.

143. Deep-trawl fisheries, which target bottom fish species on the high seas, are largely unregulated and unreported fishing activities. Often important biological information relevant to the conservation and management of target species has simply not been collected prior to commencement of the fisheries or following the exploitation of specific deep-sea areas. Deep-water fisheries tend to be more intermittent, less predictable and so less manageable than shallow-water fisheries. They are often characterized as being "serial" or "sequential depletion" fisheries, because fishing vessels find and deplete a stock then move on and repeat the practice. Altogether, it is believed that 62 deep-water species have been fished commercially. Owing to their biological characteristics, most target species are easily over-exploited. Stocks are typically depleted within 5 to

[48] The use of large driftnets by high-seas fishing vessels has not ended, despite the hopeful use of the past tense in this paragraph. *See* Problem 6-1, *infra*.

10 years. Some scientists believe that all deep-sea fisheries present in 2003 will be commercially extinct by 2025.

144. In addition, bottom fisheries are known to induce considerable damage to benthic habitats and other underwater features.

145. Deep-water fisheries often target features, such as seamounts and ridges, where food inputs advected by topographically enhanced currents support benthic communities dominated by hard and soft corals, sponges and other suspension feeders. Bottom trawls pick up these benthic communities as by-catch or otherwise reduce them to rubble. Given the slow growth of deep-water corals and uncertain rates of recruitment, the re-establishment of deep-water coral reefs will probably take centuries to millennia. Continued unrestricted fishing could destroy reefs in many areas, leading to extinction for the large proportion of seamount species with highly restricted distribution. Management of bottom trawling has been considered by the General Assembly (see resolution 59/25) and control measures have been taken by some States and regional fisheries management organizations.

LARGE SCALE PELAGIC DRIFTNET FISHING AND ITS IMPACT ON THE LIVING MARINE RESOURCES OF THE WORLD'S OCEANS AND SEAS: REPORT OF THE SECRETARY GENERAL

UN GAOR, 45th Sess., Agenda Item 79, 26–33, U.N. Doc. A/45/663 (1990)

26. A driftnet is a fishing gear made of a single or several rectangular panels of net webbing linked together and suspended vertically in the water by floats on the top of the panels and sinkers at the bottom. They drift with the winds and the currents, thus creating a webbing curtain in which the fish [and other not-target species] are enmeshed. By adjusting the size and the weight of the floats and sinkers it is possible to modify the buoyancy of the net and to suspend it at various depths in the water column. Driftnets belong to a broader category of nets called gillnets. The other types of gillnets include set-gillnets, encircling gillnets and fixed gillnets.

27. Until the 1950s the size of driftnets was necessarily limited by the weight of the natural fibres (hemp or cotton) of which they were made. The introduction of synthetic fibres and the growing utilization of hydraulic winches allowed fishermen to fish with longer sets of nets, thus increasing the fishing power of the gear, but also increasing the incidental catches of non-targeted species, in particular marine mammals.

28. The gear is now used both by modern industrial fleets operating on the high seas (with nets from 5 to 50 km in length) and by artisanal and semi-industrial fishermen of developing countries in coastal areas (with nets from a few hundred metres up to more than 10 km in length).

* * *

57. Two types of impact of large-scale pelagic driftnet fishing have caused the most widespread concern; first, commercially important species that are landed in poor condition or discarded, perhaps due to long soak time or damage by predators, and second, the incidental by-catch of non-targeted fish and other animals. . . . The by-catches and discards may consist of various categories:

(a) Other commercial fish (apart from the targeted species) retained as part of the catch;

(b) Fish of commercial value discarded and thus forming part of the waste from the fishery;

(c) Species without commercial importance that may be important to the ecosystem or valued for other reasons.

* * *

60. Category (c), by-catches of non-commercial but otherwise important to the ecosystems, represents a grave problem. Of greatest public concern is the prospect of high catch numbers of incidentally caught marine mammals (such as dolphins, small whales and fur seals), turtles and birds. Some of these species are listed among the world's threatened and endangered species of wildlife. Virtually all of them reproduce at a considerably lower rate than the targeted species.

TRANSNATIONAL ORGANIZED CRIME AND THE FISHING INDUSTRY

UNITED NATIONS OFFICE ON DRUGS AND ORGANIZED CRIME
16–20 (2011)

1.5.4 Decreasing fish stocks

At this point in history the future of global fish stocks is a pressing concern. The majority of the world's fish stocks are currently decreasing. Exploitation of these fish stocks cannot be expanded, [even with increasing effort], and in certain circumstances conservation efforts are urgently needed in order to avoid collapsing fish stocks and depletion.

In 2005 the FAO *Review of the World Marine Fishery Resources* revealed that of the fish stocks or species for which sufficient data was available to make an accurate assessment (approximately 76 per cent of the monitored species—or 80 per cent of the global catch), only 3 per cent were underexploited and 20 per cent moderately exploited; all of which were less profitable or low-value species. More than half of the fish stocks were fully exploited, meaning that there is no possibility of further expansion of the production. The remaining quarter was found over-exploited—with 7 per cent of the total fish stock depleted altogether.

The 2005 report indicated that there were some signs that the exploitation of fish stocks was decreasing. However, the revised figures in the 2010 FAO *State of the World's Fisheries and Aquaculture* report show that the category of under- and moderately exploited species now accounts for only 15 per cent in 2008, whereas overexploited and depleted species have increased to 32 per cent in the same time-period. 53 per cent of the world's fish-stocks are at present regarded as fully exploited.

According to the 2005 report the highest incidents of depleted fish stock are found around Europe (in particular the Mediterranean), the Black Sea, and Antarctica. Fish stocks in the northeast Atlantic are principally fully exploited, with a considerable percentage of over-exploited fish stock recovering. The least is known about the exploitation in southwest Atlantic, eastern Indian Ocean and the Caribbean, yet there are reasons to believe that due to lack of monitoring these areas will be susceptible to illegal fishing and thus a high degree of exploitation.

* * *

Depleted fish stocks are likely to significantly affect vulnerable coastal populations. For many of these communities fish is the main source of income and protein supply, and the lack of fish therefore undermines food security. Current prognoses suggest that depletion of fish stocks will intensify in the years to come.[49]

PROBLEM 6-1: DRIFT-NET FISHING IN THE INDIAN OCEAN

Section 1. Facts

Iberia is a European nation with a significant fishing industry that is financially supported by the Iberian government. Facing declining stocks in its own EEZ and in nearby high seas areas, the Iberian government authorized the Iberian fishing fleet to move their fishing operations to the Indian Ocean and to fish in that region. The Iberian fishing vessels are large and aim to target albacore, bigeye, southern Bluefin and yellowfin tuna in the Eastern Indian Ocean.

To support its fishing vessels in the Indian Ocean, Iberia entered into a government-to-government joint venture with Maniolae, an archipelagic nation in the Indian Ocean. Iberia agreed to provide financing for the construction of large fish-processing plants near the main Maniolaen port facilities. In exchange, Maniolae agreed to allow Iberian fishing vessels to fish in its EEZ, to call at its ports and to land their catches for processing. Maniolae anticipated that the arrangement with Iberia would help it build

49 And this is likely to be exacerbated by the impacts of climate change, especially on tropical shallow water coral reefs and their associated subsistence fisheries.

a new and profitable business exporting tuna to the United States and Europe.

The fish-processing plants were built, and the Iberian vessels began operating in Maniolae's EEZ in 2016. Although the Iberian vessels primarily fish in the Maniolaen EEZ, they are authorized by Iberia to fish in either the Maniolae EEZ or on the high seas. Iberia's authorization to its vessels generally requires them "to comply with all applicable Maniolaen and IOTC [Indian Ocean Tuna Commission] regulations."

The Iberian fishing vessels use the same fishing gear—large-scale driftnets—in both the Maniolaen EEZ and on the high seas. All the areas fished by the Iberian vessels are within the IOTC Area.

In 2017, the Indian Ocean Tuna Commission (IOTC) adopted Resolution 17/07 prohibiting the use of large-scale driftnets in the IOTC Area. (This resolution is reproduced in the readings, *infra.*)

Despite the adoption of Resolution 17/07, Maniolae has not forbidden the use of large-scale driftnets in its EEZ, and the Iberian vessels continue to fish with this equipment both within the EEZ and on those occasions that they venture beyond the EEZ. Their catches have been sizeable. Using information gleaned from signals intelligence intercepts (made available by certain IOTC members), as well as data on tuna exports from Maniolae, the Food and Agriculture Organization (FAO) has concluded that the Iberian fleet's catches have been so substantial as to endanger the future of several of the targeted stocks.

The FAO has notified the IOTC of its conclusions. Iberia and Maniolae, for their part, have informed the IOTC that they disagree with the FAO's conclusions and believe that the total annual catch of the Iberian vessels is no threat to stock sustainability and, in any event, should not be a matter of concern for the IOTC as 85% of the catch occurs within the Maniolaen EEZ.

New Holland, a member of the Indian Ocean Tuna Commission, has a significant long-line fleet that operates in the same high-seas tuna fishery where the Iberian vessels are active. It is outraged at the Iberian ships' defiance of the fishing-gear and quota restrictions imposed by IOTC and at Maniolae's facilitation of this situation. New Holland directed its navy to take all necessary steps to stop unlawful fishing on the high seas in the IOTC area. Shortly thereafter, a New Holland naval patrol observed three Iberian fishing vessels using large drift nets pass out of Maniolae's EEZ and onto the high sea. The New Holland patrol chased and arrested the Iberian fishing vessels. The ships were taken to New Holland's capital, Boorloo, and their catch was sold by the New Holland government, which retained the proceeds of the sale.

Iberia and Maniolae have protested this action. New Holland, in response, has demanded that Iberia and Maniolae cease their "illegal activities." New Holland has also reported its action to the IOTC Compliance Committee.

You are an attorney in private practice specializing in international law. The Secretariat of the Indian Ocean Tuna Commission has requested an opinion as to what breaches of international law may be present on these facts and what remedies are available. They wish to provide the opinion to the Compliance Committee of the Indian Ocean Tuna Commission at its upcoming meeting.

Iberia, Maniolae, and New Holland are all parties to the Agreement for the Establishment of the Indian Ocean Tuna Commission **(Basic Document 5.13)**. Each is an active member of the Commission, and none has objected to any conservation and management measure adopted by the Commission.

Iberia, New Holland, and Maniolae are also parties to the UN Convention on the Law of the Sea **(Basic Document 3.4)**, New Holland is a party to the UN Fish Stocks Agreement **(Basic Document 5.14)** and the FAO Compliance Agreement **(Basic Document 5.12)**, but neither Maniolae nor Iberia has ratified those agreements.

Section 2. Questions Presented

1. Is Maniolae in breach of international law for facilitating drift-net fishing for tuna in the Eastern Indian Ocean?

2. Are Iberia's fishing activities in the Eastern Indian Ocean in breach of international law?

3. Is New Holland in breach of international law for arresting and impounding the Iberian ships and selling their catch?

Section 3. Assignments

A. *Reading Assignment*

Study the Readings presented in Section 4, *infra*, and the Discussion Notes/Questions that follow.

B. *Recommended Writing Assignment*

Prepare a comprehensive, logically sequenced, and *argumentative* brief in the form of an outline of the primary and subsidiary *legal* issues you see requiring resolution in this dispute.

C. Recommended Oral Assignment

Assume you are legal counsel for Maniolae, Iberia, or New Holland (as designated by your instructor); then, relying upon the Readings (and your issue-outline if prepared), present a 15–20 minute oral argument of your government's likely positions before the Compliance Commission.

D. Suggested Reflective Assignment

Consider (and recommend) alternative norms, institutions, and/or procedures that you believe might do better than existing world order arrangements to contend with situations of the kind posed by this problem.

Section 4. Readings

1. Editors' Note: A Short History of International Action Against Driftnetting

Large-scale pelagic driftnets, which are suspended in the water like giant curtains and strung out as a wall for many miles, drift across the open ocean and indiscriminately catch everything in their path. In one sense, driftnetting of this type is very efficient. A single boat, suspending a number of nets in a long line simultaneously, can have up to 40 miles of such nets going down to a depth of about 48 feet below the surface of the ocean in a single positioning, and typically several vessels of a driftnet fleet will work together to fish in this manner. At its height in any given fishing season, driftnetting on the part of Japan, South Korea, and Taiwan, countries long and principally engaged in the practice because of the huge quantities of fish needed by their large populations for whom fish is a traditional and staple part of the diet, resulted in up to 22,500 miles of deep nets being drifted through the waters of the Pacific and Indian oceans each night—enough to stretch more than once around the Earth.

From an environmental or ecological perspective, however, large-scale pelagic driftnetting is very inefficient because of its unselective nature. Sometimes called a "wall of death," driftnets kill or maim most living things in their path. Marine creatures in search of food, and lured by fish already caught in the net, swim or dive into the webbing where they become entangled. If they do not drown or manage to escape, they may suffer for several months before dying from injury, starvation, or both. Tuna species (other than those allegedly targeted by the fishers), marlin, swordfish, and sharks are common victims. Also, the nets are dangerous for marine mammals and sea birds that must return to the surface to breathe because the nylon mesh often used in the nets is so sheer that it is invisible to mammals and birds and undetectable by dolphin sonar. People have been alerted to the dangers of driftnetting by graphic photographs of fur seals, sea lions, dolphins, and small whales all becoming entangled and dying as a result.

Because the marine life of the open sea is not inexhaustible, the real threat of driftnetting is to the marine ecosystems that are essential to life on Earth. Many of the victims of driftnetting are especially endangered because the reproductive rates of their species are very low and because we now are technologically capable of catching fish faster than they can breed. While not the only fishing technique that can result in overfishing, the indiscriminate impact of large-scale driftnetting on a variety of species and its incredible efficiency as a means of catching huge quantities of fish have brought it under special criticism and attack. The near collapse of the albacore tuna fishery in the South Pacific was blamed on the increase of large-scale driftnetting in the area. Driftnetting was also alleged to have contributed greatly to the serious decline of the North Pacific salmon fishery.

In addition to threatening stocks of individual fish species, driftnetting has repercussions throughout the marine ecosystem, endangering the diversity of marine life in our oceans. The survival of any one species in a marine ecosystem depends upon the existence of others—species rely upon each other as elements of the same food web, predator populations keep other populations in balance, and certain species rely on others as "hosts." In the North Pacific, driftnetters have taken heavily from albacore tuna and squid stocks, which are an essential part of the ocean food chain, and many people fear that widespread large scale driftnetting can cause irreversible damage to entire marine ecosystems.

In the late 1980s, driftnetters began to work the South Pacific albacore tuna fishing grounds, among the richest in the world. From the 1987–88 fishing season to that of 1988–89, the number of driftnet fishing vessels, each equipped with dozens of driftnets, grew from 20 Japanese and seven Taiwanese vessels to over 60 Japanese and up to 130 Taiwanese vessels, and all at a time when the South Pacific island countries with few resources were in various stages of developing longline fisheries for the albacore tuna (of great economic importance to these small countries notwithstanding its highly migratory nature). Prior to the 1988–89 fishing season, the South Pacific Albacore Research Group (SPAR), an informal organization of researchers from various countries, had estimated that continued fishing by driftnets at the levels then occurring would seriously deplete the entire stock of albacore tuna within two years, in large part because juvenile tuna, which swim near the surface and therefore are caught and killed by driftnets long before maturity, were being heavily depleted. Accordingly, a major economic resource—and with it the prospect of vigorous economic development—was seen by the otherwise resource-poor South Pacific countries to be slipping quickly from their grasp at the hands of distant water fishing nations plundering the available stocks.

At about the same time, several nongovernmental environmental organizations took up the issue. Earthtrust was able to film pictures of dolphins caught in driftnets and to produce a television documentary on the subject containing films that evoked a strong emotional response against driftnetting wherever shown. A big campaign was organized by several NGOs, particularly Earthtrust and Greenpeace. They provided information to public officials and otherwise lobbied governments, as well as making their case directly to the world's public.

The NGO campaign was run with a "piracy on the high seas" approach. The "wall of death," it was claimed, killed fish that never could be recovered; spelled death for marine mammals, seabirds, and fish other than those being pursued; posed hazards for navigation; and otherwise was a recipe for environmental degradation generally. People should not eat tuna caught by driftnets, it was argued.

The response of nations interested in defending driftnetting was no less adamant: no scientific evidence existed, they said, that the method was reducing stocks of fish to unsustainable levels or endangering the survival of particular species of fauna. But the intensive NGO campaign was highly successful. The issue had popular appeal. The alleged lack of scientific evidence was not persuasive.

The issue was closely studied by the Fisheries Agency of the South Pacific Forum, which was established by the Forum in 1979 with headquarters in Honiara in the Solomon Islands. The Forum Fisheries Agency (FFA) reported to the Heads of Government of the Forum after it had convened a meeting of interested countries in November 1988 at which it was concluded that the southern albacore fishery probably would collapse should the projected expansion of driftnet fishing in the South Pacific occur. Plans were put in place to collect data on landing, use of port facilities, and transhipment, and otherwise to secure as much information as possible using the resources of the governments involved. In March 1989, another meeting was convened by the FAA when it was clear that the situation was serious and that wider support was needed to pursue the issue. A review of the relevant law concluded that high sea driftnet operations were not being conducted in accordance with Part V of the 1982 United Nations Convention on the Law of the Sea, particularly Articles 87, 116–119, and 300 thereof.

In June 1989, a further consultation was held in Suva with members of the FFA, the distant water fishing nations engaged in the fishery, and scientists. While concern was clearly expressed about the sustainability of the present albacore tuna stocks, no agreement was reached. The South Pacific nations took the view that action was required while the distant water fishing nations contended that there was no proof that action was required. In any event, the distant water fishing nations certainly would not agree to stop.

In October 1989, the Prime Minister of New Zealand told the UN General Assembly that "[f]reedom of the high seas cannot be invoked to protect what is in effect a systematic assault on the regional marine ecosystem."[50] In the same month, the Commonwealth Heads of Government, meeting at Langkawi, Malaysia, stated in their Langkawi Declaration that they were committed to "seek to ban . . . pelagic drift-net fishing." With most of the South Pacific Forum countries being members of the Commonwealth and with a total of 42 countries in the Commonwealth, there now was something of an international bandwagon rolling against driftnet fishing.

Thereafter, a big diplomatic effort was made to inform governments of what a ban against driftnet fishing involved and to seek their support for a United Nations General Assembly resolution. The United States, New Zealand, and all the Forum countries co-operated in promoting General Assembly Resolution 44/225 **(Basic Document 5.10)** in 1989, which, in the end, was adopted without a vote although it was clear that Japan was unhappy with the course that developments had taken. Language was included sufficient to avoid Japanese objection, and Japan agreed to phase out driftnet fishing in the South Pacific.

But pressure for further action remained into late-1989 and 1990. The Forum countries worked fast to negotiate the Wellington Convention **(Basic Document 5.9)**, which entered into force on May 17, 1991, and prohibited driftnet fishing on the high seas and in the exclusive economic zones of countries lying within a large area of the Pacific defined by the Convention—a novel way of dealing with the problems of a particular fishery, by agreeing to an international convention to deal specially with it. However, the legal effects of the Convention were perhaps not as significant as its political and diplomatic consequences. It was a signal to the world that the South Pacific really cared about the practice of driftnet fishing and that it would go to considerable lengths to stop it. In the world of international diplomacy, this was equivalent to a regional full court press.

United Nations efforts hardened over the years as well, such that Japan, in July 1990, announced that it was ceasing driftnetting in the South Pacific a year earlier than it had undertaken to do. Taiwan, not being a member of the United Nations, was harder to reach, but finally it too announced its intention to stop. Additionally, the UN General Assembly, in Resolution 46/215 of 1991 **(Basic Document 5.11)**, called for "a global moratorium on all large-scale pelagic driftnet fishing . . . by 31 December 1992."

---

50 Provisional Verbatim Record of the Fifteenth Meeting, UN GAOR, 44th Sess., 15th mtg., at 75, U.N. Doc. A/44/PV.15 (prov. ed. 1989).

Today, driftnet fishing is not nearly as significant a problem as it was 20 years ago. It has been said that the 1991 UN General Assembly resolution was "as effective as any treaty in changing fishing behavior." David Balton & Dorothy C. Zbicz, *Managing Deep-Sea Fisheries: Some Threshold Questions*, 19 Intl J. Marine & Coastal L. 247, 253 (2004).

Nevertheless, large-scale driftnetting has not disappeared, and it remains a real concern in some parts of the world. Some nations continue to allow driftnetting within their EEZs, and vessels continue to fish on the high seas using large-scale driftnets in defiance of the alleged UN ban. And consider, is the "ban" even a ban? UN General Assembly Resolutions are not self-executing and theoretically not considered binding.

2. Resolution on Large-Scale Pelagic Driftnet Fishing and Its Impact on the Living Marine Resources of the World's Oceans and Seas, G.A. Res. 46/215, U.N. Doc. A/46/645/Add.6 (1991) (Basic Document 5.11)

The General Assembly,

* * *

Expressing deep concern about reports of expansion of large-scale pelagic drift-net fishing activities on the high seas in contravention of resolutions 44/225 and 45/197 . . .

* * *

Noting also the significant concerns expressed by members of the international community and competent regional fisheries bodies regarding the impact of large-scale pelagic drift-net fishing on the marine environment,

* * *

Recognizing that a moratorium on large-scale pelagic drift-net fishing is required, notwithstanding that it will have adverse socio-economic effects on the communities involved in high seas pelagic drift-net fishing operations,

* * *

3. *Calls upon* all members of the international community to implement resolutions 44/225 and 45/197 by, *inter alia*, . . . [taking action to] ensure that a global moratorium on all large-scale pelagic drift-net fishing is fully implemented on the high seas of the world's oceans and seas, . . . by 31 December 1992;

4. *Reaffirms* the importance it attaches to compliance with the present resolution and encourages all members of the international community to take measures, individually and collectively, to prevent

large-scale pelagic drift-net fishing operations on the high seas of the world's oceans and seas . . . ;

* * *

3. Editors' Note on the Indian Ocean Tuna Commission (IOTC)

The Indian Ocean Tuna Commission (IOTC) is an intergovernmental organisation responsible for the management of tuna and tuna-like species in the Indian Ocean.[51] It works to achieve this goal by promoting cooperation among its thirty-one Contracting Parties (Members) in order to ensure the conservation and appropriate utilisation of tuna stocks and encouraging the sustainable development of tuna fisheries. Three so-called Cooperating Non-Contracting Parties are able to participate in the Commission's activities based on their interest in the relevant Indian Ocean Fisheries. They need not make a financial contribution to the Commission, nor do they have voting rights, but they otherwise follow the same regulations as full Members.

The Commission has four key functions and responsibilities:

- to keep under review the conditions and trends of the stocks and to gather, analyse and disseminate scientific information, catch and effort statistics and other data relevant to the conservation and management of the stocks and to fisheries based on the stocks;
- to encourage, recommend, and coordinate research and development activities in respect of the stocks and fisheries covered by this Agreement, and such other activities as the Commission may decide appropriate, including activities connected with transfer of technology, training and enhancement, having due regard to the need to ensure the equitable participation of Members of the Commission in the fisheries and the special interests and needs of Members in the region that are developing countries;
- to adopt, in accordance with Article IX and on the basis of scientific evidence, conservation and management measures, to ensure the conservation of the stocks covered by this Agreement and to promote the objective of their optimum utilization throughout the Area;
- to keep under review the economic and social aspects of the fisheries based on the stocks covered by the Agreement

[51] *See* Agreement for the Establishment of the Indian Ocean Tuna Commission **(Basic Document 5.13)**.

bearing in mind, in particular, the interests of developing coastal States.[52]

The Compliance Committee of the Commission was created in 2002. Its terms of reference call upon it to review each IOTC Member's compliance with IOTC conservation and management resolutions and "make such recommendations" as the Committee thinks necessary to ensure the effectiveness of those resolutions. At the conclusion of its meetings, the Committee is charged with issuing an opinion "on the compliance status of each" IOTC Member and a formal "declaration of non compliance" with recommendations for "suitable actions" by the Commission with respect to non-compliant Members.

4. Agreement for the Establishment of the Indian Ocean Tuna Commission, arts. IX & X(1), 25 November 1993, 1927 UNTS 329 (Basic Document 5.13)

Article IX. Procedures Concerning Conservation and Management Measures

1. Subject to paragraph 2, the Commission may, by a two-thirds majority of its Members present and voting, adopt conservation and management measures binding on Members of the Commission in accordance with this Article.

2. Conservation and management measures for stocks for which a sub-commission has been established under paragraph 2 of Article XII, shall be adopted upon the proposal of the sub-commission concerned.

3. The Secretary shall, without undue delay, notify the Members of the Commission of any conservation and management measures adopted by the Commission.

4. Subject to paragraphs 5 and 6, conservation and management measures adopted by the Commission under paragraph 1, shall become binding on Members 120 days from the date specified in the Secretary's notification or on such other date as may be specified by the Commission.

5. Any Member of the Commission may, within 120 days from the date specified or within such other period as may be specified by the Commission under paragraph 4, object to a conservation and management measure adopted under paragraph 1. A Member of the Commission which has objected to a measure shall not be bound thereby. Any other Member of the Commission may similarly object within a further period of 60 days from the expiry of the 120-day period. A Member of the Commission may also withdraw its objection at any time and become bound by the measure immediately if the measure is already in effect or at such time as it may come into effect under this article.

[52] *Id.* at art. V(2)(a-d).

6. If objections to a measure adopted under paragraph 1 are made by more than one-third of the Members of the Commission, the other Members shall not be bound by that measure; but this shall not preclude any or all of them from giving effect thereto.

7. The Secretary shall notify each Member of the Commission immediately upon receipt of each objection or withdrawal of objection.

8. The Commission may, by a simple majority of its Members present and voting, adopt recommendations concerning conservation and management of the stocks for furthering the objectives of this Agreement.

Article X. Implementation

1. Each Member of the Commission shall ensure that such action is taken, under its national legislation, including the imposition of adequate penalties for violations, as may be necessary to make effective the provisions of this Agreement and to implement conservation and management measures which become binding on it under paragraph 1 of Article IX.

5. Resolution 17/07 on the Prohibition to Use Large-Scale Driftnets in the IOTC Area, Report of the 21st Session of the Indian Ocean Tuna Commission, 22–26 May 2017, FAO Doc. IOTC-2017-S21-R at 85

The Indian Ocean Tuna Commission (IOTC),

Recalling that the United Nations General Assembly (UNGA) Resolution 46/215 calls for a global moratorium on large-scale high seas driftnet fishing and that IOTC Resolution 12/12 prohibits the use of large-scale driftnets on the high seas in the IOTC; and also that both texts recognize the negative impact of such fishing gears;

Noting that a high number of vessels are engaged in large scale driftnet fishing in the Exclusive Economic Zones (EEZ) and offshore waters;

Mindful that large scale driftnet fisheries have a major impact in the ecosystems, the capacity to catch species of concern to the IOTC, and also that they are likely to undermine the effectiveness of IOTC Conservation and Management Measures;

* * *

Noting that large scale driftnets are regularly being used with lengths in excess of 4,000 m (and up to 7,000 m) within the EEZs and that those used within the EEZ may sometimes drift onto the high seas in contravention of Resolution 12/12;

Furthermore, *noting* that the Scientific Committee reiterated its previous recommendation that the Commission should consider whether a ban on large scale driftnets should also apply within the EEZs given the negative ecological impacts of large scale driftnets in areas frequented by marine mammals and turtles;

Adopts, in accordance with paragraph 1 of Article IX of the IOTC Agreement, that:

1. This Resolution applies to vessels registered on the IOTC Record of Authorised vessels that use driftnets for the purpose of targeting tuna and tuna-like species in the IOTC Area of competence.

2. The use of large-scale driftnets on the high seas within the IOTC area of competence shall be prohibited. The use of large-scale driftnets in the entire IOTC area of competence shall be prohibited by 1 January 2022.

3. Each Contracting Party and Cooperating Non-Contracting party (hereinafter referred to as CPCs) shall take all measures necessary to prohibit their fishing vessels from using large-scale driftnets while on the high seas in the IOTC area of competence. They shall take all measures necessary to prohibit their fishing vessels from using large-scale driftnets in the entire IOTC area of competence by 1 January 2022.

4. A CPC-flagged fishing vessel will be presumed to have used large-scale driftnets in the IOTC area of competence if it is found operating in the IOTC area of competence and is configured to use large-scale driftnets.

5. For the purposes of monitoring the implementation of this Resolution, CPCs must notify the Secretariat of any CPC-flagged vessel using large-scale driftnets in their EEZs before the 31st of December 2020.

6. CPCs shall include in their Annual Reports of implementation a summary of monitoring, control, and surveillance actions related to large-scale driftnet fishing in the IOTC area of competence.

7. The Commission shall periodically assess whether additional measures should be adopted and implemented to ensure that large-scale driftnets are not used in the IOTC area of competence and to take into account the latest advice of the Scientific Committee. The first such assessment shall take place in 2023.

8. Nothing in this measure shall prevent CPCs from applying more stringent measures to regulate the use of large- scale driftnets.

9. This Resolution supersedes Resolution 12/12 to prohibit the use of large-scale driftnets on the high seas in the IOTC area.

6. United Nations Convention on the Law of the Sea, arts. 62, 64(1), 65, 89, 92, 110–111, 116–117 & 119, 10 December 1982, 1833 UNTS 3 (Basic Document 3.4)

Article 62. Utilization of the living resources [of the EEZ]

1. The coastal State shall promote the objective of optimum utilization of the living resources in the exclusive economic zone. . . .

2. . . . Where the coastal State does not have the capacity to harvest the entire allowable catch [in the EEZ], it shall, through agreements or other arrangements . . . give other States access to the surplus of the allowable catch. . . .

* * *

4. Nationals of other States fishing in the exclusive economic zone shall comply with the conservation measures and with the other terms and conditions established in the laws and regulations of the coastal State. These laws and regulations shall be consistent with this Convention.

* * *

Article 64. Highly migratory species

1. The coastal State and other States whose nationals fish in the region for the highly migratory species listed in Annex I [including tuna] shall co-operate directly or through appropriate international organizations with a view to ensuring conservation and promoting the objective of optimum utilization of such species throughout the region, both within and beyond the exclusive economic zone. . . .

Article 65. Marine mammals

. . . States shall co-operate with a view to the conservation of marine mammals and in the case of cetaceans shall in particular work through the appropriate international organizations for their conservation, management and study.

Article 89. Invalidity of claims of sovereignty over the high seas

No State may validly purport to subject any part of the high seas to its sovereignty.

Article 92. Status of ships

1. Ships shall sail under the flag of one State only and, save in exceptional cases expressly provided for in international treaties or in this Convention, shall be subject to its exclusive jurisdiction on the high seas.

* * *

Article 110. Right of visit

1. Except where acts of interference derive from powers conferred by treaty, a warship which encounters on the high seas a foreign ship . . . is not justified in boarding it unless there is reasonable ground for suspecting that: (a) the ship is engaged in piracy; (b) the ship is engaged in the slave trade; (c) the ship is engaged in unauthorized broadcasting. . .; (d) the ship is without nationality; or (e) . . . the ship is, in reality, of the same nationality as the warship.

* * *

Article 111. Right of hot pursuit

1. The hot pursuit of a foreign ship may be undertaken when the competent authorities of the coastal State have good reason to believe that the ship has violated the laws and regulations of that State. Such pursuit must be commenced when the foreign ship or one of its boats is within the internal waters, the archipelagic waters, the territorial sea or the contiguous zone of the pursuing State, and may only be continued outside the territorial sea or the contiguous zone if the pursuit has not been interrupted.

* * *

8. Where a ship has been stopped or arrested outside the territorial sea in circumstances which do not justify the exercise of the right of hot pursuit, it shall be compensated for any loss or damage that may have been thereby sustained.

Article 116. Right to fish on the high seas

All States have the right for their nationals to engage in fishing on the high seas subject to:

(a) their treaty obligations;

(b) the rights and duties as well as the interests of coastal States provided for, *inter alia,* in article 63, paragraph 2, and articles 64 to 67; and

(c) the provisions of this section.

Article 117. Duty of States to adopt with respect to their nationals measures for the conservation of the living resources of the high seas

All States have the duty to take, or to cooperate with other States in taking, such measures for their respective nationals as may be necessary for the conservation of the living resources of the high seas.

Article 119. Conservation of the living resources of the high seas

1. In determining the allowable catch and establishing other conservation measures for the living resources in the high seas, States shall:

(a) take measures which are designed, on the best scientific evidence available to the States concerned, to maintain or restore populations of harvested species at levels which can produce the maximum sustainable yield, as qualified by relevant environmental and economic factors, including the special requirements of developing States, and taking into account fishing patterns, the interdependence of stocks and any generally recommended international minimum standards, whether subregional, regional or global;

(b) take into consideration the effects on species associated with or dependent upon harvested species with a view to maintaining or restoring populations of such associated or dependent species above levels at which their reproduction may become seriously threatened.

* * *

7. International Tribunal for the Law of the Sea, *The Sub-Regional Fisheries Commission (SRFC) Case,* Advisory Opinion of 2 April 2015, 2015 ITLOS Reports 4, paragraphs 85, 104–06, 115, 119–20, 124, 129, 131–32, 141, 146–48, 150

85. The first question submitted to the Tribunal is as follows:

What are the obligations of the flag State in cases where illegal, unreported and unregulated (IUU) fishing activities are conducted within the Exclusive Economic Zones of third party States?

104. Under the Convention, responsibility for the conservation and management of living resources in the exclusive economic zone rests with the coastal State, which, pursuant to article 56, paragraph 1, of the Convention, has in that zone sovereign rights for the purpose of exploring and exploiting, conserving and managing the natural resources, whether living or non-living. In this regard, in accordance with article 61, paragraphs 1 and 2, of the Convention, the coastal State is entrusted with the responsibility to determine the allowable catch of the living resources in its exclusive economic zone and to "ensure through proper conservation and management measures that the maintenance of the living resources in the exclusive economic zone is not endangered by over-exploitation." Pursuant to article 62, paragraph 2, of the Convention, the coastal State is required through agreements or other arrangements to give other States access to the surplus of the allowable catch if it does not have the capacity to harvest the entire allowable catch. To meet its responsibilities, in accordance with article 62, paragraph 4, of the Convention, the coastal

State is required to adopt the necessary laws and regulations, including enforcement procedures, which must be consistent with the Convention.

105. To ensure compliance with its laws and regulations concerning the conservation and management measures for living resources pursuant to article 73, paragraph 1, of the Convention, the coastal State may take such measures, including boarding, inspection, arrest and judicial proceedings, as may be necessary to ensure compliance with the laws and regulations adopted by it in conformity with the Convention.

106. Thus, in light of the special rights and responsibilities given to the coastal State in the exclusive economic zone under the Convention, the primary responsibility for taking the necessary measures to prevent, deter and eliminate IUU fishing rests with the coastal State.

115. Article 92 of the Convention stipulates that, save in exceptional cases expressly provided for in international treaties or in the Convention, ships are subject to the exclusive jurisdiction of the flag State on the high seas; by virtue of article 58, this also applies to the exclusive economic zone in so far as it is not incompatible with Part V of the Convention.

119. It follows from the provisions of article 94 of the Convention that as far as fishing activities are concerned, the flag State, in fulfilment of its responsibility to exercise effective jurisdiction and control in administrative matters, must adopt the necessary administrative measures to ensure that fishing vessels flying its flag are not involved in activities which will undermine the flag State's responsibilities under the Convention in respect of the conservation and management of marine living resources. If such violations nevertheless occur and are reported by other States, the flag State is obliged to investigate and, if appropriate, take any action necessary to remedy the situation.

120. Article 192 of the Convention imposes on all States Parties an obligation to protect and preserve the marine environment. Article 193 of the Convention provides that "States have the sovereign right to exploit their natural resources pursuant to their environmental policies and in accordance with their duty to protect and preserve the marine environment." In the *Southern Bluefin Tuna Cases*, the Tribunal observed that "the conservation of the living resources of the sea is an element in the protection and preservation of the marine environment." As article 192 applies to all maritime areas, including those encompassed by exclusive economic zones, the flag State is under an obligation to ensure compliance by vessels flying its flag with the relevant conservation measures concerning living resources enacted by the coastal State for its exclusive economic zone because, as concluded by the Tribunal, they constitute an integral element in the protection and preservation of the marine environment.

124. It follows from article 58, paragraph 3, and article 62, paragraph 4, as well as from article 192, of the Convention that flag States are obliged to take the necessary measures to ensure that their nationals and vessels flying their flag are not engaged in IUU fishing activities. . . . In other words, while under the Convention the primary responsibility for the conservation and management of living resources in the exclusive economic zone, including the adoption of such measures as may be necessary to ensure compliance with the laws and regulations enacted by the coastal State in this regard, rests with the coastal State, flag States also have the responsibility to ensure that vessels flying their flag do not conduct IUU fishing activities within the exclusive economic zones of [other States].

129. In the case of IUU fishing in the exclusive economic zones of the SRFC Member States, the obligation of a flag State . . . to ensure that vessels flying its flag are not involved in IUU fishing is also an obligation "of conduct." In other words, as stated in the Advisory Opinion of the Seabed Disputes Chamber, this is an obligation "to deploy adequate means, to exercise best possible efforts, to do the utmost" to prevent IUU fishing by ships flying its flag. However, as an obligation "of conduct" this is a "due diligence obligation," not an obligation "of result." This means that this is not an obligation of the flag State to achieve compliance by fishing vessels flying its flag in each case with the requirement not to engage in IUU fishing in the exclusive economic zones of the SRFC Member States. The flag State is under the "due diligence obligation" to take all necessary measures to ensure compliance and to prevent IUU fishing by fishing vessels flying its flag.

131. As to the meaning of "due diligence obligation," the Seabed Disputes Chamber referred to the following clarification provided by the ICJ in the *Pulp Mills on the River Uruguay* case:

> It is an obligation which entails not only the adoption of appropriate rules and measures, but also a certain level of vigilance in their enforcement and the exercise of administrative control applicable to public and private operators, such as the monitoring of activities undertaken by such operators, to safeguard the rights of the other party. The responsibility of a party to the 1975 Statute would therefore be engaged if it was shown that it had failed to act diligently and thus take all appropriate measures to enforce its relevant regulations on a public or private operator under its jurisdiction. (*Pulp Mills on the River Uruguay (Argentina v. Uruguay)*, Judgment, I.C.J. Reports 2010, p. 14, at p. 79, para. 197)

132. The Seabed Disputes Chamber in its Advisory Opinion pointed out that:

The content of "due diligence" obligations may not easily be described in precise terms. Among the factors that make such a description difficult is the fact that "due diligence" is a variable concept. It may change over time as measures considered sufficiently diligent at a certain moment may become not diligent enough in light, for instance, of new scientific or technological knowledge. It may also change in relation to the risks involved in the activity. . . . The standard of due diligence has to be more severe for the riskier activities. (*Responsibilities and obligations of States with respect to activities in the Area, Advisory Opinion,* 1 February 2011, ITLOS Reports 2011, p. 10, at p. 43, para. 117)

141. The second question submitted to the Tribunal is as follows:

To what extent shall the flag State be held liable for IUU fishing activities conducted by vessels sailing under its flag?

146. In the present case, the liability of the flag State does not arise from a failure of vessels flying its flag to comply with the laws and regulations of the SRFC Member States concerning IUU fishing activities in their exclusive economic zones, as the violation of such laws and regulations by vessels is not *per se* attributable to the flag State. The liability of the flag State arises from its failure to comply with its "due diligence" obligations concerning IUU fishing activities conducted by vessels flying its flag in the exclusive economic zones of the SRFC Member States.

147. The Tribunal is of the view that the SRFC Member States may hold liable the flag State of a vessel conducting IUU fishing activities in their exclusive economic zones for a breach, attributable to the flag State, of its international obligations referred to in the reply to the first question.

148. However, the flag State is not liable if it has taken all necessary and appropriate measures to meet its "due diligence" obligations to ensure that vessels flying its flag do not conduct IUU fishing activities in the exclusive economic zones of the SRFC Member States.

150. The Tribunal also wishes to address the issue as to whether isolated IUU fishing activities or only a repeated pattern of such activities would entail a breach of "due diligence" obligations of the flag State. As explained in paragraphs 146 to 148, the Tribunal finds that a breach of "due diligence" obligations of a flag State arises if it has not taken all necessary and appropriate measures to meet its obligations to ensure that vessels flying its flag do not conduct IUU fishing activities in the exclusive economic zones of the SRFC Member States. Therefore, the frequency of IUU fishing activities by vessels in the exclusive economic zones of the SRFC Member States is not relevant to the issue as to whether there is a breach of "due diligence" obligations by the flag State.

8. Agreement for the Implementation of the Provisions of the United Nations Convention of the Law of the Sea of 10 December 1982 Relating to the Conservation and Management of Straddling Fish Stocks and Highly Migratory Fish Stocks, arts. 2, 8, 18 & 21, 4 August 1995, 2167 UNTS 3 (Basic Document 5.14) ("U.N. Fish Stocks Agreement")

Article 2. Objective

The objective of this Agreement is to ensure the long-term conservation and sustainable use of straddling fish stocks and highly migratory fish stocks through effective implementation of the relevant provisions of the Convention.

Article 8. Cooperation for conservation and management

* * *

3. Where a subregional or regional fisheries management organization or arrangement has the competence to establish conservation and management measures for particular straddling fish stocks or highly migratory fish stocks, States fishing for the stocks on the high seas and relevant coastal States shall give effect to their duty to cooperate by becoming members of such organization or participants in such arrangement, or by agreeing to apply the conservation and management measures established by such organization or arrangement. . . .

4. Only those States which are members of such an organization or participants in such an arrangement, or which agree to apply the conservation and management measures established by such organization or arrangement, shall have access to the fishery resources to which those measures apply.

* * *

Article 18. Duties of the flag State

1. A State whose vessels fish on the high seas shall take such measures as may be necessary to ensure that vessels flying its flag comply with subregional and regional conservation and management measures and that such vessels do not engage in any activity which undermines the effectiveness of such measures.

2. A State shall authorize the use of vessels flying its flag for fishing on the high seas only where it is able to exercise effectively its responsibilities in respect of such vessels under the Convention and this Agreement.

* * *

Article 21. Subregional and regional cooperation in enforcement

1. In any high seas area covered by a subregional or regional fisheries management organization or arrangement, a State Party which is a member of such organization . . . may . . . board and inspect . . . fishing vessels flying the flag of another State Party to this Agreement, whether or not such State Party is also a member of the organization. . ., for the purpose of ensuring compliance with conservation and management measures . . . established by that organization. . . .

* * *

5. Where, following boarding and inspection, there are clear grounds for believing that a vessel has engaged in any activity contrary to the conservation and management measures referred to in paragraph 1, the inspecting State shall, where appropriate, secure evidence and shall promptly notify the flag State of the alleged violation.

6. The flag State shall respond [by either investigating and taking enforcement action or authorizing the inspecting State to investigate].

* * *

8. Where, following boarding and inspection, there are clear grounds for believing that a vessel has committed a serious violation, and the flag State has either failed to respond or failed to take action . . . the inspectors may remain on board [and take the vessel to port for further inspection].

* * *

11. For the purposes of this article, a serious violation means: . . . (e) using prohibited fishing gear. . . .

* * *

16. Action taken by States other than the flag State in respect of vessels having engaged in activities contrary to subregional or regional conservation and management measures shall be proportionate to the seriousness of the violation.

Section 5. Discussion Notes/Questions

1. Is it unlawful for Iberian fishing vessels to use large-scale driftnets in the Eastern Indian Ocean? Does it matter whether they are fishing on the high seas or in the Maniolaen exclusive economic zone? In this respect, notice that IOTC Resolution 12/12 (mentioned in the first preambulatory paragraph of Resolution 17/07) banned driftnetting on high seas areas in the IOTC Area. If high-seas driftnetting was already banned by an IOTC conservation measure, what was the point of Resolution 17/07? Are either Iberia or Maniolae or both bound by these resolutions?

2. What is the legal effect of United Nations General Assembly Resolution 46/215 (Reading 2)? Should important fisheries policy issues be decided in this way (i.e. by a massive public relations campaign followed by a vote in the General Assembly)? Some commentators were highly critical of this approach, arguing that the action taken "was based primarily on emotion and hyperbole rather than scientific data and interpretations." Thus, they argued, "the General Assembly disregarded the most basic canons of sound fisheries management: the use of the best available scientific data and the conscious assessment of alternative means to achieve the conservation objective." *See* William Burke, Mark Freeberg & Edward Miles, *The United Nations Resolutions on Driftnet Fishing: An Unsustainable Precedent for High Seas and Coastal Fisheries,* 25 Ocean Dev. & Int'l L. 127, 128 (1994).

3. Assuming that the Iberian vessels were fishing in an unlawful manner, did New Holland act lawfully in seizing them? If not, how could the IOTC rules be enforced against them? Would New Holland's actions have been lawful if the Fish Stocks Agreement were in force with respect to Iberia?

4. Did Maniolae have the right to authorize Iberia to fish in its exclusive economic zone? Is Maniolae required to ban the use of driftnets in its exclusive economic zone? In answering that question, be sure to consider Maniolae's obligations under the provisions of UNCLOS. Are large-scale driftnets so inherently destructive that allowing their use violates general duties of conservation with respect to the living resources of the oceans?

5. Although UNCLOS requires states to accept binding adjudication or binding arbitration for the resolution of disputes under the Convention, this obligation does not apply to certain categories of disputes listed in Article 297 and 298. In particular, a coastal state is not obliged to submit to binding adjudication or arbitration if the dispute concerns its sovereign rights in the management of fisheries in its exclusive economic zone, including its decisions regarding harvesting capacity, allowable catch, the allocation of surpluses to other states, and the terms of its conservation and management laws. Does this mean that Maniolae is, in essence, free to do what it wants in its EEZ, even if its actions profoundly affect migratory species or straddling stocks of importance to other states?

6. According to the United Nations, fish provide 1.5 billion people with 20% of their animal protein intake and 3 billion people with 15% of it. While the populations of some poor countries are heavily dependent on fish protein, developing countries are also the world's largest producers and exporters of fish. In fact, fish is the largest single agricultural commodity exported by the developing world, and countries defined by the FAO as "low-income food-deficit countries" actually exported $19.8 billion worth of fish to the developed world in 2008. Japan, the United States, and the European Union are the largest importers of fish, and exports to those countries doubled from 1998–2008.

What responsibility, if any, do major importing nations have to ensure that the fish they import were caught in a sustainable manner and in compliance with internationally agreed fishing restrictions? How could an importing state enforce rules about how fish are caught?

7. One possible approach to enforcing internationally agreed fishing restrictions might be to restrict imports of fish that are caught in unlawful ways or produced by states that have not joined relevant fisheries organizations. The U.S. Marine Mammal Protection Act, 16 U.S.C.A. § 1371 (1988) requires a ban on the importation of fish or products from fish that have been caught with commercial fishing technology that results in the incidental kill or serious injury of ocean mammals in excess of U.S. standards. *See also* Driftnet Act Amendments of 1990, Pub. L. 101–627, Title I, § 107(a), 28 Nov. 1990, 104 Stat. 4441, 16 USCA § 1826 (1988). These measures were further strengthened by the High Seas Driftnet Fisheries Enforcement Act of 1992, Pub. L. 102–582, Nov. 1992, 106 Stat. 4900, 16 U.S.C.A. §§ 1362, 1371, 1826(a) (1993). But the way in which ocean fish are caught and processed (described below) can obscure the origin of processed fish and make it difficult to enforce this type of law. In addition, some import restrictions could violate international trade rules. *See* Problem 12-1, *infra*.

Fish are highly perishable and must be quickly processed and frozen after being caught. Some large fishing vessels have processing and freezing capacity on board. Smaller vessels will quickly off-load their catch to so-called "reefer vessels," which have facilities for preparing and freezing the fish. Generally, ownership of the fish transfers to a buyer as soon as the fish is transshipped to the reefer vessel. The reefer vessel will gather fish from a number of vessels, freeze them, and eventually take the fish to a port and transfer them to a fish processing plant where they will be filleted and made ready for sale, often in an international market.

So, are fish that enter the international market a product of the flag state of the fishing vessel, the flag state of the reefer vessel, the nation where the fish was finally processed, or the nation in whose exclusive economic zone the fish were caught (if they weren't caught on the high seas)? If the goal is to ensure that fishing vessels comply with fishing rules, presumably we would want to link the fish to the catching vessel. But how could that be done? Reefer vessels might gather fish from a number of fishing vessels, and processing plants certainly take fish from many fishers.

The port state could, presumably, exercise some effective control by denying port access to either fishing vessels or reefer vessels that are suspected of IUU fishing. Techniques for monitoring fishing vessels are becoming increasingly sophisticated, so substantial information is available in this regard. But if the port state is a developing state, like Maniolae, that is establishing a fish processing industry, does it have any incentive to restrict purchases from vessels based on fishing techniques?

8. Is it realistic to expect flag states to police their fishing vessels around the world? Especially if a flag state is a poorer developing nation, it is unlikely to have a navy or the resources to monitor the activities of its fisherman in oceans on the other side of the globe. What is the solution other than to

authorize states other than the flag state to undertake investigation and enforcement actions?

This is the approach taken by the UN Fish Stocks Agreement **(Reading 8 and Basic Document 5.14)**. To date, there are 90 parties to this agreement, including the United States. But many fishing states are not parties, including China. Why would states not join an agreement that aims a) at ensuring the long-term sustainability of fish stocks and b) at easing the difficulty and expense flag states face in policing their fishing vessels?

9. Although global concern about world fisheries tends to focus on declining stocks of particular species and the economic and social impact of those declines, there is also the question of the impact of steep declines in fish populations on the entire marine ecosystem. A recent study indicates that the loss of species and diversity in an ocean ecosystem can accelerate the collapse of other species in the ecosystem and delay species recovery. Thus, argued the authors, protection of global fishery resources required a focus on "restoring marine biodiversity through sustainable fisheries management, pollution control, maintenance of essential habitats, and the creation of marine reserves. . . ." Absent serious action to restore marine ecosystems, we face "serious threats to global food security, coastal water quality, and ecosystem stability, affecting current and future generations." Boris Worm, et al., *Impacts of Biodiversity Loss on Ocean Ecosystem Services*, 314 Science 787, 790 (2006).

With that in mind, consider the comments of Sir Geoffrey Palmer at the 1992 Rio Conference on Environment and Development. Sir Geoffrey argued that real sustainability in the oceans required a rejection of traditional approaches to fisheries management (which often focus on a single species of fish) in favor of "a multi-species approach, conserving whole eco-systems." Expressing doubt that the framework established by UNCLOS was adequate to the task, he said: "I am of the opinion myself that these issues cannot easily be dealt with in piecemeal fashion. A new convention altogether appears to be needed to deal with conservation and use of living marine resources on the high seas. Such a convention ought to be firmly based on the ecosystem approach to assessing the impact of high seas fisheries on the marine environment." Geoffrey Palmer, Towards a New Ocean World Order, Address to Oceans Day at the Global Forum, Rio de Janeiro, 8 June 1992.

In 2015, the United Nations General Assembly decided to develop a legally binding instrument "on the conservation and sustainable use of marine biological diversity of areas beyond national jurisdiction." The instrument is intended to broadly address the conservation of marine biological diversity in areas beyond national jurisdiction (e.g., the high seas), including matters relating to "marine genetic resources," "the sharing of benefits," and "area-based management tools" such as "marine protected areas." G.A. Res. 69/292, para. 1 & 2 (15 June 2015). Is this a move toward the approach for which Sir Geoffrey advocated?

10. Even though fish stocks are in decline, consumption of fish is increasing. This is largely due to the rapid growth of aquaculture (fish farming)

around the world. But aquaculture has its own problems. Farm-raised fish must be fed, and much of the feed comes from capture production. Low-value species of fish captured in ocean fisheries are fed to high-value species being raised in aquaculture. An estimated 19 percent of the global catch is now used for this purpose.

It is not known precisely what impact this practice is having on ocean ecosystems. But the removal of low-value species from the oceans in large quantities will inevitably reduce the food available to wild fish, turtles, and marine mammals.

11. An increasingly serious threat to marine life is the accumulation of plastic waste in the oceans. *See* Food and Agriculture Organization of the United Nations, *Microplastics in fisheries and aquaculture* (2017). The main source of plastic waste affecting fisheries is discarded fishing gear, including lost or abandoned driftnets. But plastic waste enters the ocean in many other ways; the FAO reports that from 4.8 to 12.7 million tons of plastic waste entered the oceans in 2010 alone. Because plastic waste is durable and persists in the environment for long periods, there are today billions of pounds of plastic in the ocean.

Plastic pollution is a significant hazard to ocean creatures. Estimates are that thousands of sea turtles, sea birds, seals, and other marine mammals are killed each year as a result of ingesting plastic or becoming entangled in it. Microplastics (plastic waste less than 5 mm in any dimension) pose a particular hazard because they can be ingested by many aquatic organisms and they often contain toxic contaminants which accumulate in the bodies of the organisms that ingest them and are passed along through the marine food chain.

2. LAND-BASED POLLUTION

The infamous "dead zones" in the Gulf of Mexico and the Chesapeake Bay are probably the examples of land-based ocean pollution that are best known to residents of the United States. The dead zones (or hypoxic zones) in these areas are caused by nitrogen and phosphorus pollution. When nutrients like nitrogen and phosphorus are present in water in excessive amounts (eutrophication), they trigger excessive plant growth (e.g., algal blooms). When the algae decomposes, it uses up the oxygen in the water. The low-oxygen (hypoxic) conditions make it difficult for other marine life to survive.

What is happening in the Gulf of Mexico and the Chesapeake Bay is also happening elsewhere in the world, and the problem is getting worse, not better. In 1995, one report identified 195 coastal hypoxic zones worldwide. The same researchers, updating their work in 2008, identified over 400 hypoxic zones. 115 more sites were added in 2011, all from the

Baltic Sea. Most of the sites are downstream from major population centers or agricultural land.[53]

The next reading provides a quick overview of the causes and consequences of land-based pollution of the oceans. Following the reading, we examine some legal aspects of this issue through Problem 6-2 (Land-based Pollution in the Caribbean Sea).

A SEA OF TROUBLES

REPORT OF GESAMP (THE JOINT GROUP OF EXPERTS ON THE SCIENTIFIC ASPECTS OF MARINE ENVIRONMENTAL PROTECTION) 1–3, 5–9, 14–15, 21 (2001)

[POLLUTION]

Sewage pollution of the sea is, of course, as old as civilisation. It provides nutrients which, in moderation, can benefit sea life. The problem arises when there is too much of it in too small an area. . . .

This is more than just an aesthetic nuisance. Sewage pollution ruins large areas for fisheries, recreation and tourism, causing major economic loss. Eutrophication and blooms of algae, stimulated by too much nutrition from sewage and agricultural chemicals and wastes, does widespread and serious damage to the life of coastal waters. And there are frequent outbreaks of gastrointestinal disease such as cholera, typhoid and infectious hepatitis caused by contaminated seafood and bathing water—particularly in areas where there are many carriers of the pathogens, and sewage treatment and disposal is inadequate. A major outbreak of cholera in Naples in 1973, for example, came from eating shellfish. An even greater epidemic of the disease which affected many millions of people in Latin America from 1991 to 1995—and took 10,000 lives—started in the coastal cities of Peru.

Yet such dramatic outbreaks are responsible for only a small part of the toll of disease caused by sewage pollution. A new study sponsored by GESAMP and the World Health Organisation (WHO), now shows that—far from just causing isolated, local problems—microbiological contamination of the sea has precipitated a health crisis with massive global implications.

* * *

Many studies show that respiratory and intestinal diseases and infections among bathers rise steadily in step with the amount of sewage pollution in the water. They demonstrate, too, that bathers are at risk even in lightly contaminated waters that meet the pollution standards laid down by the European Union and the US Environmental Protection Agency. A

---

[53] S.S. Rabotyagov, et al., *The Economics of Dead Zones: Causes, impacts, Policy Challenges, and a Model of the Gulf of Mexico Hypoxic Zone*, 8 Rev. Envtl. Econ. & Pol'y 58, 59 (2014).

recent WHO report has estimated that one in every 20 bathers in "acceptable waters," will become ill after venturing just once into the sea.

* * *

This new evidence of the dangers of sewage pollution is just one example of a general reappraisal of the relative importance of different pollutants of the sea. Some of those once thought to be the most damaging worldwide are now believed to be much less important, either because more is known about them or because they have been brought under control.

The supposed effects of man-made radionuclides discharged into the sea still loom large in the minds of the general public and politicians. Although threats from accidental releases cannot be ruled out, radionuclides now probably worry scientists less than any other category of marine pollutants. Similarly, highly publicised and exaggerated concerns about the extent of contamination of the seas and their life by heavy metals cannot be justified; it is probably far less serious than pollution by nutrients and some persistent organic chemicals. The effects of even the most dramatic oil spills are generally localised; gross pollution from them disappears relatively rapidly, though some subtle effects may last for decades, with enormous economic costs.

Until recently, most attention concentrated on pollutants which directly or indirectly poisoned sea life and those consuming it—or were suspected of doing so. Less attention was paid to the potential effects of the persistent organic chemicals, some of which may have much more subtle, but possibly even more damaging effects. These include changes in the structure and function of communities of marine life, through disrupting reproduction and altering behaviour, and effects at the molecular level, such as causing cancer or mutations or disrupting endocrine systems. Evidence that concentrations of these substances now in the marine environment are causing such effects is mostly inconclusive. Risks to human health usually only occur where concentrations are high, or where people are exposed to them in unusual ways, such as in the Arctic where fish and seafood form an extremely high percentage of the diet.

* * *

EUTROPHICATION

Excessive growth of marine plant life—eutrophication—is potentially one of the most damaging of the many harmful effects that humans have on the oceans, both in its scale and its consequences. It can turn parts of the sea into wastelands.

Plants in the oceans, as on land, need adequate nourishment from minerals and organic substances if they are to grow well. Life is far more profuse in coastal waters, which are rich in these nutrients, than in the open oceans. Areas with poor supplies of nutrients support little life; their transparent and apparently 'clean' blue waters may be aesthetically attractive, but biologically they resemble deserts on land.

Waters, however, can have too much nutrient. When this happens, usually because of pollution from the land, plant life—phytoplankton or algae—proliferates. Longterm increases in phytoplankton, and their decay near the seabed, can deplete oxygen over large areas, either periodically or permanently—and dramatically alter ecosystems. Coastal areas with relatively little circulation of their waters are particularly vulnerable. A "dead zone" with far too little oxygen, for example, appears off Louisiana in the Gulf of Mexico each summer; excessive nitrogen from agricultural fertiliser used upstream, and flushed down the Mississippi River, has been blamed.

Increases in the abundance of phytoplankton also make water less transparent, and thus reduce the penetration of sunlight into the sea. Coral reefs, seagrass beds, and other ecosystems that depend on light, can suffer. And the reefs can be threatened in another way too. Eutrophication can cause seaweeds on the ocean floor to grow so fast that they outstrip the corals and smother them; the reefs stop growing and start to erode, and much of the diversity of the ecosystem is lost.

Eutrophication can also cause explosive blooms of algae—such as 'red tides'—which cover the surface of the sea. And changes in the relative amounts of different nutrients can stimulate the growth of toxic or otherwise harmful algae. The toxins can accumulate in shellfish and poison people who eat them. One explosion of algae in Chesapeake Bay, for example, killed thousands of fish, made dozens of people ill, and sent sales of crabs, oysters and fish plummeting. The poisons can also be blown to land, at times causing eye irritation, respiratory problems, and other complaints.

Toxic algae can also harm other marine life—including whales, dolphins and other marine mammals—and cause hundreds of millions of dollars worth of damage to commercial fisheries. They devastate tourism in areas like the Adriatic, and damage aquaculture, with massive economic and social costs. There are indications that the blooms, toxic or otherwise, are increasing.

Humanity mainly adds nutrients to the sea through agriculture (for example from fertilisers and animal wastes), in sewage, and by nitrogen oxides from burning fossil fuels, which fall out onto the waters. Naturally, municipal sewage tends to be the main source near cities, while agriculture predominates in rural areas. Worldwide most nutrients reach the seas down rivers (the main route for inshore areas) and by being blown in the winds (the main one for the open ocean).

* * *

[SOURCES OF MARINE POLLUTION]

[Industry is a major source of ocean pollution.] Pulp mills, also often sited on the coast, discharge a wide range of particulates and chemical compounds, sometimes including chlorinated dioxins and furans. Textile and food processing plants, and those refining metal ores are also among the most common industrial polluters of the sea, discharging organic and particulate matter, and chemicals including nutrients, oils and other compounds.

* * *

Globally, air pollution is as important as rivers in contaminating the open ocean with dissolved copper and nickel—and more important for cadmium, mercury, lead, zinc and, particularly, for synthetic organic compounds. Once emitted, many of these compounds stay in the air for weeks or more, and this is the major route by which they reach the open oceans. Once in the sea they may be taken up by the air again and dispatched to the polar regions by a process of global distillation, which boils the chemicals off the ocean in hotter areas, and allows them to condense out of the air again in colder ones.

* * *

Agriculture has an even greater effect on the sea than industry. Fertilisers and animal wastes—escaping from farms, and working their way into rivers and the sea—are major causes of eutrophication. Pesticides reach the ocean in a similar way. Soil eroded from fields adds greatly to the particulate load of rivers and coastal waters, increasing sedimentation—a problem that gets worse as forests are cut down to make way for farming.

* * *

[HABITAT DESTRUCTION]

The greatest of all threats to biodiversity, and the most widespread human impact on coastal zones, comes from the destruction and alteration of habitats. This can happen through a wide variety of means; physical, such as draining or 'reclaiming' land, extracting sand or gravel, or the deposition of sediments from soil erosion or deforestation; chemical, such as pollution; and biological, such as invasions of alien species. Habitats, of course, have changed naturally since long before the appearance of humanity, but the sheer scale of the present onslaught is unprecedented.

Half of the world's wetlands were lost during the course of the twentieth century, mostly in the last decades. Up to two thirds of those in Europe and North America have been destroyed, and 85 per cent of those remaining in Asia are threatened. These figures include inland wetlands as well as coastal ones, but these are usually important for watersheds, rivers and thus, ultimately, for coasts and seas.

Over half of the world's mangrove forests have been lost, too. Sixty per cent of them in Guinea and the Ivory Coast have been cut down, mainly for firewood and housebuilding: about seventy per cent of them have been destroyed in Liberia. Seventy per cent of coral reefs worldwide are threatened, while only about five per cent of Europe's coastline still remains undisturbed.

Destroying habitats often has dramatic knock-on effects. Take the widespread destruction of mangrove forests to provide wood and wood chips or to make way for such developments as aquaculture, road building and the spread of towns and cities. This hits fisheries, as mangroves are vital breeding areas and nurseries for many fish, crustaceans and mollusks. It increases the flow of sediments, normally trapped by mangrove roots. And it makes coasts and their peoples more vulnerable to storms—turning natural events into human disasters—as intact forests provide effective buffers against them. The loss of wetlands leads to a similar cascade of effects.

* * *

Coral reefs, arguably the richest of all the ecosystems in the sea, have been damaged in 93 of the 110 countries in whose waters they are to be found. Some 27 per cent of the world's reefs are at high risk of degradation: this figure rises to 80 per cent in populous areas. . . .

Mass bleaching of corals was discovered on reefs all over the world between 1996 and 1998. In 1998, it was found on two thirds of all the world's reefs; in some places, such as around the Maldive Islands, the proportion rose to 90 per cent. It is caused by the water at the sea surface getting warmer. These outbreaks took place at the same time as a strong El Niño event, but there is evidence that global warming over the longer term may also be having an effect.

PROBLEM 6-2: LAND-BASED POLLUTION IN THE CARIBBEAN SEA

Section 1. Facts

Puerto Cristo is a large island country in the Caribbean Sea, with an area of 95,682 square-kilometers and a population of 9.3 million. The interior is mountainous and supports a small zinc mining industry. Along the mountain slopes are numerous sugar and banana plantations owned by companies incorporated in the United States. The entire island is drained by a single river, the Malaguas, and its various tributaries. The capital of Puerto Cristo is the port city of Santo Paulo, which is located on the Northeast side of the island at the mouth of the Malaguas River.

In 2015, the Government of Puerto Cristo undertook three public works projects aimed at improving the local economy. First, an irrigation system was built to improve the productivity of the plantations located along the banks of the Malaguas. The irrigation system uses water from the Malaguas, sends it through the fields, and then returns it to the river.

Second, to deal with its growing sewage problem, which had been discharged directly into the Santo Paulo harbor, Puerto Cristo built a pipe to carry untreated household sewage to a deep-water outfall emptying four kilometers offshore on the northeast side of the island. When discharged at that point, the untreated sewage has a typical biochemical oxygen demand (BOD)[54] of 270 mg/l. However, the waters where it is discharged are seldom used by people and have no important or unique environmental or ecological characteristics.

Finally, the Puerto Cristo government upgraded its port area and began regular dredging of the mouth and estuary of the Malaguas River. The spoils from the dredging are dumped out to sea near the outlet of the sewer system.

From an economic standpoint, the projects have been very successful. The irrigation system has tripled agricultural output, leading to an increase in employment on the plantations and in processing facilities located in Santo Paulo. The dredging has revitalized the port at Santo Paulo, allowing larger cruise ships and cargo vessels to visit the port. Finally, the transport of sewage to a deep-water outfall has reduced sewage pollution of the Malaguas River and Santo Paulo's harbor, with the result that the incidence of pathogenic diseases in Santo Paulo has fallen by 50%.

On the other hand, many environmental problems remain. The Malaguas River is polluted with heavy metals from zinc mining. Agricultural runoff, already a problem, has increased as a result of the new irrigation system. And the river has very high levels of pesticides and fertilizers in it at all times of the year. In addition, sedimentation has increased in the river, which, in turn, has increased the need for regular dredging of the Santo Paulo harbor.

Forty miles northeast of Puerto Cristo lies a small island called St. Columba. St. Columba's economy is based on the fishing and tourism industries, both of which depend on St. Columba's extensive coral reef system. The tourism industry is especially important. Most of the world's major hotel companies have built large resorts and other attractions on the island, and more than 1.5 million tourists visited the island in 2017. Unfortunately, the infrastructure surrounding the hotels has not kept pace

[54] Biochemical oxygen demand (BOD) is a measure of the amount of organic pollution in water. A BOD test determines the amount of dissolved oxygen needed for aerobic biological organisms to break down the organic material present in a body of water. The more oxygen needed, the higher the level of BOD and the more polluted the water. Water with a BOD of 270 mg/l is highly polluted.

with the hotel development. Sewage and runoff from the hotels and the hotel grounds drain into canals that themselves drain directly into the waters off St. Columba. Scientists estimate the BOD of the polluted canal water averages about 35 mg/l.

In 2016, fish catches in St. Columba's waters declined significantly. In 2017, the decline was severe, with total fish catch falling by 60%. Divers along the reefs reported significant falls in fish population and apparent problems with the corals themselves. A large bloom of toxic algae occurred in mid-winter 2016 near St. Columba's largest city, and an outbreak of gastro-intestinal disorders among the tourist population was linked to a bacterial infection caused by eating contaminated shellfish. The first algae bloom was followed by a second in the same place a year later. At the same time, slicks of grey matter and dead fish began washing up on St. Columba's beaches.

An investigation by the St. Columba Ministry of Health found several areas around St. Columba that were completely de-oxygenated and the reefs severely damaged, with the corals in nearly 50% of the total reef area either dead or dying. The damage to the reefs was attributed to a variety of causes, including sedimentation, unusual turbidity of the water, an excess of nutrients (leading to growth of algae), and environmental stress from heavy metals found in the water, which the Department believe has rendered the reefs more susceptible to disease.

As a result of these findings, the St. Columba government commissioned an interdisciplinary group of scientists to discover the causes of the pollution. These scientists took samples of the waters around St. Columba, and also of the waters reaching St. Columba via the flow of the Gulf Stream. As the team moved up current from St. Columba to Puerto Cristo, the levels of pesticides and heavy metal pollutants in the water steadily increased, as did the BOD of the water and the volume of suspended sediments in the water. The scientists concluded that the high pollution levels in the waters around St. Columba were due to the Puerto Cristo's depositing of its sewage discharge and dredge spoils in waters that were located too close to the Gulf Stream, the strong current of which prevented the pollutants from settling until they reached St. Columba.

As the environment around St. Columba deteriorated, its government lodged several complaints with the government of Puerto Cristo. Puerto Cristo's government denied causing the pollution and cited its own scientific studies which concluded that the dredge spoils would remain as sediment without traveling a great distance. Puerto Cristo also stated that the BOD level of its discharged sewage was low enough that it would have been diluted to harmless levels long before it reached St. Columba. Puerto Cristo claimed that the pollution and damage to the reefs in St. Columba was obviously attributable to St. Columba's failure to update its own sewer system, and to its discharge of untreated sewage directly into waters near its reef system.

Both St. Columba and Puerto Cristo are parties to the 1982 United Nations Convention on the Law of the Sea **(Basic Document 3.4)**, the 1983 Convention for the Protection and Development of the Marine Environment of the Wider Caribbean (Cartagena Convention) **(Basic Document 3.5)** and its 1999 Protocol Concerning Pollution from Land-Based Sources (including all annexes to the Protocol) **(Basic Document 3.5a)**.

St. Columba and Puerto Cristo were unable to settle their dispute by negotiation, and Puerto Cristo refused conciliation. St. Columba therefore submitted the dispute to the International Tribunal for the Law of the Sea [ITLOS]. Both St. Columba and Puerto Cristo have accepted the jurisdiction of that tribunal, pursuant to Article 287(1)(a) of the UN Convention on the Law of the Sea. St. Columba has asked the tribunal to declare that Puerto Cristo violated its customary and conventional international law obligations regarding pollution of the marine environment, that St. Columba was damaged as a result, and that Puerto Cristo should pay reparations to St. Columba for lost fishing and tourism income and for research and action to restore its fisheries and the ecosystem of its harbor. Santo Cristo denies responsibility for the harms experienced by St. Columba and insists that, in any event, the tribunal lacks authority to grant the remedy requested by St. Columba.

Section 2. Questions Presented

1. Has Santo Cristo violated international law and, if so, how?
2. If so, what remedies should ITLOS grant to St. Columba, if any?

Section 3. Assignments

A. Reading Assignment

Study the Readings presented in Section 4, *infra*, and the Discussion Notes/Questions that follow.

B. Recommended Writing Assignment

Prepare a comprehensive, logically sequenced, and *argumentative* brief in the form of an outline of the primary and subsidiary *legal* issues you see requiring resolution by the International Tribunal for the Law of the Sea (ITLOS). Also, from the perspective of an independent objective judge, indicate which side ought to prevail on each issue and why. Retain a copy of your issue-outline/brief for class discussion.

C. *Recommended Oral Assignment*

Assume you are legal counsel for St. Columba or Puerto Cristo (as designated by your instructor); then, relying upon the Readings (and your issue-outline if prepared), present a 15–20 minute oral argument of your government's likely positions before the Tribunal.

D. *Suggested Reflective Assignment*

Consider (and recommend) alternative norms, institutions, and/or procedures that you believe might do better than existing world order arrangements to contend with situations of the kind posed by this problem. In so doing, but without insisting upon *immediate* feasibility, identify the particular transition steps that would be needed to make your alternatives a reality.

Section 4. Readings

1. Sherry Heileman, The Caribbean SIDS Region, in the State of the Marine Environment: Regional Assessments 214, 217–19, 221–24 (UNEP/GPA 2006)

The Caribbean Sea covers a surface area of about 1,943,000 km^2, and possesses many productive and biologically complex and diverse ecosystems including coral reefs, seagrass beds, mangroves, coastal lagoons, and beaches. With the majority of corals and coral reef-associated species being endemic, the Caribbean Sea is a biogeographically distinct area of coral reef development particularly important in terms of global biodiversity. . . .

. . . Areas of high [biological] productivity [in the region] include the plumes of continental rivers, localized upwelling areas, and nearshore habitats such as coral reefs, mangrove forests, and seagrass beds. Relatively high productivity also occurs off the northern coast of South America where nutrient input from rivers, estuaries, and wind-induced upwelling is greatest. . . . The remaining area of the Caribbean Sea is mostly comprised of clear, nutrient-poor waters.

* * *

Sewage

. . . Sewage is regarded as one of the most important and widespread causes of degradation of the coastal environment in the Caribbean. . . . As a result of rapidly expanding populations, poorly planned development, and inadequate or poorly designed and malfunctioning sewage treatment facilities in most Caribbean SIDS [Small Island Developing States], untreated sewage is often discharged into the environment. . . .

. . . Less than 2% of urban sewage is treated before disposal; this is even lower in rural communities. On some islands (e.g., Antigua and Barbuda, Dominica, Haiti) there is no sewerage system and sewage is disposed of mainly through septic tanks and pit latrines. . . .

The discharge of untreated sewage is likely to have an adverse effect on the quality of coastal waters and on the ecology of critical coastal ecosystems. One of the possible effects of sewage pollution is eutrophication near treatment facilities and sewage outfalls, with increased algal and bacterial growth, degradation of seagrass and coral reef ecosystems, and decreased fisheries production. . . .

Microbiological pollution from the discharge of untreated sewage is severe in the Caribbean SIDS and poses a serious threat to human health from direct contact with polluted waters or from the consumption of contaminated fish and shellfish. . . .

* * *

Heavy metals

The sources of heavy metals in the marine environment include industrial point sources. . . . Antifouling paints used on vessels are of particular concern, considering the growing recreational boating sector and servicing facilities in the region.

In 1995 only 39% of the investigated small industries in the Caribbean had undertaken treatment of residual waters. . . . Heavy metals are very persistent in the aquatic environment, bio-accumulate in marine organisms, and are highly toxic to humans when consumed.

* * *

Nutrients

. . . Organic and nutrient pollution is most widespread and is possibly the most serious marine pollution problem in the Caribbean. . . . The total estimated nutrient load from land-based sources in the Caribbean Sea is 13,000 tonnes/yr of nitrogen and 5,800 tonnes/yr of phosphorus. . . . The predominant source of nutrients is the discharge of untreated sewage, as well as non-point agricultural run-off as a result of the large quantities of agricultural fertilizers applied annually. . . .

* * *

The discharge of nutrients into coastal waters is a major cause of eutrophication. . . . Elevated nutrient inputs into coastal areas are associated with a range of conditions, including HABs [Harmful Algal Blooms], changes in the aquatic community structure, decreased biological diversity, fish kills, and oxygen depletion in the water column. HABs are frequently the cause of very serious human illness when the biomass produced are ingested in contaminated seafood. The illnesses most frequently associated with marine biotoxins include paralytic shellfish poisoning and ciguatera poisoning. . . .

Sediment mobilization

* * *

Discharges of suspended and dissolved solids have intensified due to inappropriate agricultural and land-use practices, including deforestation and poorly planned urbanization. . . . Dredging of shipping lanes in shallow coastal waters causes serious re-suspension of sediments. . . . [D]evelopment . . . has increased erosion and the input of sediments to coastal areas. . . . The region's rivers supply about 300 million tonnes/yr of suspended solids to the Caribbean Sea. . . .

Bauxite mining . . . releases large quantities of particulate matter that can be deposited in marine areas. . . .

Suspended solids have severe environmental impacts. . . . Damage to coastal habitats such as coral reefs . . . is a major concern. Increased water turbidity reduces the productivity of coral reefs and seagrass beds, as a consequence of reduced light penetration. . . . [P]hysical smothering of coral reefs, seagrasses, and associated filter feeders and other benthic organisms is also possible. . . .

* * *

Physical alteration and destruction of habitats [PADH]

Mangrove wetlands, seagrass meadows, and coral reefs play an important ecological role in the Caribbean SIDS. This includes harbouring high biological diversity, providing nursery grounds for the juveniles of many commercially important fish species, as well as providing coastal protection and stabilization against storm surges and erosion. . . . Mangroves and seagrass beds also purify freshwater before it reaches marine areas, including coral reefs. Along with their living resources, these habitats also underpin important economic activities such as fisheries and tourism, providing food and livelihoods for thousands of people as well as substantial national incomes.

PADH was identified as the principal environmental problem for the smaller islands. . . . The ultimate causes of PADH are exponential population growth and anthropogenically-driven changes in the coastal zone and in the adjacent watersheds. . . .

2. David A. Ring, Sustainability Dynamics: Land-Based Marine Pollution and Development Priorities in the Island States of the Commonwealth Caribbean, 22 Colum. J. Envtl. L. 65, 73, 78–79, 81–98, 112–13 (1997)

The Role of International Law in LBMP Control

1. Obstacles to International LBMP Control

Pollution from LBS [land-based sources] has been considered a major problem in the ocean environment for over twenty years. . . . However, the complexity of LBMP [Land-Based Marine Pollution] renders identification and attribution of cause and effect extremely problematic; virtually every human activity on land, especially those connected with economic development, poses some threat to the marine environment. LBMP is often overlooked because it is largely invisible and accumulative. Apportioning responsibility thus presents a dizzying task, particularly to the extent that LBS may interact in the marine environment.

While technical obstacles to LBMP control are substantial, political considerations will present the most serious hurdle in achieving local or international solutions. The nature of LBS is such that they are usually located within one state's sovereign territory. A sovereign state generally has full jurisdiction to deal with its own nationals, within its own territory, so long as its actions do not interfere with its international legal obligations. If sources and impacts occur within the same jurisdiction, marine pollution under traditional international law constitutes a purely domestic matter.

Sovereignty questions thus pervade international LBMP negotiations. Any state commitment in a relevant instrument will generally affect its national economic policies and development priorities. Sovereignty is of particular concern to developing countries, where priorities driven by poverty and debt servicing may favor development at the expense of environmental management. Moreover, the equity concerns that inform the North-South debate broadly implicate LBMP controls. International agreements limit the traditional right to pollute at self-determined levels, but in practice, "states that were able to industrialize first, or those that have vast territories, have been able to establish pollution levels quite independently of other countries."[55] Developing states might be expected to resist legal obligations on this basis, but international environmental law has to some degree overcome perceived inequities by virtue of the concept of differentiated responsibility.

[55] Edith Brown Weiss, *International Environmental Law: Contemporary Issues and the Emergence of a New World Order*, 81 Geo. L.J. 675, 704 (1993).

2. Legal Bases for International LBMP Control

The primacy of state actors in international law limits the conceptual bases for global or regional LBMP control. Of those bases, the prevention and control of transboundary pollution is most cognizable given its state sovereignty orientation and arguable customary law development. A second basis, the protection and preservation of shared resources and common interests, suggests some normative ingress on State sovereignty. In all, however, international LBMP law is in a state of infancy. . . . However, because LBMP is recognized as an international problem, recent multilateral agreements, based in part on evolving customary international law, have directly addressed LBMP.

a. Customary International Law and LBMP

The normative basis for transboundary LBMP control derives from the Roman maxim *sic utere tuo ut alienum non laedas*, or "use your property not to injure that of another." In 1972, the Stockholm Declaration crystallized this norm with respect to the global environment, thus suggesting tension between sovereign rights and international responsibility. This "good neighborliness" principle may comprise the sole substantive norm of customary international law applicable to LBMP. Moreover, the seminal Trail Smelter arbitration restricted this duty to cases where the damage was of serious consequence, established by clear and convincing evidence. The nature of LBMP renders this standard nearly impossible to meet with respect to state liability for transboundary effects.

The 1982 Convention on the Law of the Sea ("CLOS") goes some distance in codifying the *sic utere tuo* principle and reduces the Trail Smelter standard to mere "damage," which would seem to include chronic, low-level degradation characteristic of LBMP. The CLOS also suggests a much broader "obligation to protect and preserve the marine environment," defining states' responsibilities toward their own environment and the global marine environment. Such a norm would reach the commons aspect of LBMP. . . .

b. The Stockholm Conference

In response to a general rise in global environmental awareness . . ., the 1972 United Nations Conference on the Human Environment ("Stockholm Conference") became the "first international forum to consider the protection of the environment on a comprehensive basis." The twenty-six principles of its declaration constitute "soft law" that, without creating binding obligations, provide a basis for more precise, legally compelling obligations.

Principle 21 of the Stockholm Declaration articulates the *sic utere tuo norm*, but also, by referring to "areas beyond the limits of national jurisdiction," contributes to the legitimacy of the more general norm regarding protection and preservation of the marine environment. Moreover, under Principle 7, "[s]tates shall take all possible steps to prevent pollution of the seas by substances that are liable to create hazards to human health, to harm living resources and marine life, to damage amenities or to interfere with other legitimate uses of the sea." This indicates an intention to extend the basic norm regarding state responsibility for environmental protection to common spaces such as the high seas. . . .

c. *Early Regional Seas Agreements*

Regional agreements for the protection of the marine environment began to develop in the wake of the Stockholm Conference. States have preferred to adopt specific obligations with respect to prevention, monitoring, and assessment of marine pollution at the regional level. Various rationales support this general preference, including (1) the encouragement of "maximum participation by the regional nations, especially less developed countries which might otherwise stay away from a globally organized and technologically advanced system," and (2) generally, cost-effectiveness.

* * *

e. *The Montreal Guidelines*

The 1985 Montreal Guidelines for the Prevention of Pollution from Land-Based Sources ("Montreal Guidelines"), **[Basic Document 3.6]** . . ., represent the international community's first attempt to address LBMP at the global level. Purely recommendatory in nature, the guidelines provide a checklist of provisions suitable for inclusion in future bilateral and multilateral agreements and national programs. The guidelines also "provide guidance to Governments in areas not covered by any regional agreements, and potentially for the preparation of a global convention."

* * *

f. *The 1982 Convention on the Law of the Sea*

The most significant development to date in building a global regime to protect and preserve the marine environment was the entry into force of the Convention on the Law of the Sea ("CLOS") in November 1994. This comprehensive instrument attempts to develop global standards for LBMP control, but political volatility has reduced pertinent provisions to general duties, with clear priority for municipal law. . . .

3. United Nations Convention on the Law of the Sea (UNCLOS), arts. 192, 194, 207, 210, 213, 288 & 293, Dec. 10, 1982, 1833 UNTS 3 (Basic Document 3.4)

Article 192. General obligation

States have the obligation to protect and preserve the marine environment.

Article 194. Measures to prevent, reduce and control pollution of the marine environment

1. States shall take, individually or jointly as appropriate, all measures consistent with this Convention that are necessary to prevent, reduce and control pollution of the marine environment from any source, using for this purpose the best practicable means at their disposal and in accordance with their capabilities, and they shall endeavour to harmonize their policies in this connection.

2. States shall take all measures necessary to ensure that activities under their jurisdiction or control are so conducted as not to cause damage by pollution to other States and their environment, and that pollution arising from incidents or activities under their jurisdiction or control does not spread beyond the areas where they exercise sovereign rights in accordance with this Convention.

3. The measures taken pursuant to this Part shall deal with all sources of pollution of the marine environment. These measures shall include, inter alia, those designed to minimize to the fullest possible extent:

(a) the release of toxic, harmful or noxious substances, especially those which are persistent, from land-based sources, from or through the atmosphere or by dumping;

* * *

5. The measures taken in accordance with this Part shall include those necessary to protect and preserve rare or fragile ecosystems as well as the habitat of depleted, threatened or endangered species and other forms of marine life.

Article 207. Pollution from land-based sources

1. States shall adopt laws and regulations to prevent, reduce and control pollution of the marine environment from land-based sources, including rivers, estuaries, pipelines and outfall structures, taking into account internationally agreed rules, standards and recommended practices and procedures.

2. States shall take other measures as may be necessary to prevent, reduce and control such pollution.

3. States shall endeavour to harmonize their policies in this connection at the appropriate regional level.

4. States, acting especially through competent international organizations or diplomatic conference, shall endeavour to establish global and regional rules, standards and recommended practices and procedures to prevent, reduce and control pollution of the marine environment from land-based sources, taking into account characteristic regional features, the economic capacity of developing States and their need for economic development. Such rules, standards and recommended practices and procedures shall be re-examined from time to time as necessary.

5. Laws, regulations, measures, rules, standards and recommended practices and procedures referred to in paragraphs 1, 2 and 4 shall include those designed to minimize, to the fullest extent possible, the release of toxic, harmful or noxious substances, especially those which are persistent, into the marine environment.

Article 210. Pollution by dumping

1. States shall adopt laws and regulations to prevent, reduce and control pollution of the marine environment by dumping.

2. States shall take other measures as may be necessary to prevent, reduce and control such pollution.

* * *

5. Dumping within the territorial sea and the exclusive economic zone or onto the continental shelf shall not be carried out without the express prior approval of the coastal State, which has the right to permit, regulate and control such dumping after due consideration of the matter with other States which by reason of their geographical situation may be adversely affected thereby.

6. National laws, regulations and measures shall be no less effective in preventing, reducing and controlling such pollution than the global rules and standards.

Article 213. Enforcement with respect to pollution from land-based sources

States shall enforce their laws and regulations adopted in accordance with article 207 and shall adopt laws and regulations and take other measures necessary to implement applicable international rules and standards established through competent international organizations or diplomatic conference to prevent, reduce and control pollution of the marine environment from land-based sources.

Article 235. Responsibility and liability

1. States are responsible for the fulfilment of their international obligations concerning the protection and preservation of the marine environment. They shall be liable in accordance with international law.

* * *

3. With the objective of assuring prompt and adequate compensation in respect of all damage caused by pollution of the marine environment, States shall co-operate in the implementation of existing international law . . . .

Article 288. Jurisdiction

1. A court or tribunal referred to in article 287 [including the International Tribunal for the Law of the Sea] shall have jurisdiction over any dispute concerning the interpretation or application of this Convention which is submitted to it in accordance with this Part.

2. A court or tribunal referred to in article 287 shall also have jurisdiction over any dispute concerning the interpretation or application of an international agreement related to the purposes of this Convention, which is submitted to it in accordance with the agreement.

* * *

Article 293. Applicable law

1. A court or tribunal having jurisdiction under this section shall apply this Convention and other rules of international law not incompatible with this Convention.

2. Paragraph 1 does not prejudice the power of the court or tribunal having jurisdiction under this section to decide a case *ex aequo et bono,* if the parties so agree.

4. Cartagena Convention for the Protection and Development of the Marine Environment of the Wider Caribbean Region, arts. 4, 6–7, 10 & 12, Mar. 24, 1983, 1506 UNTS 157 (Basic Document 3.5)

Article 4. General Obligations

1. The Contracting Parties shall, individually or jointly, take all appropriate measures in conformity with international law and in accordance with this Convention and those of its protocols in force to which they are parties to prevent, reduce and control pollution of the Convention area and to ensure sound environmental management, using for this purpose the best practicable means at their disposal and in accordance with their capabilities.

* * *

Article 6. Pollution Caused By Dumping

The Contracting Parties shall take all appropriate measures to prevent, reduce and control pollution of the Convention area caused by dumping of wastes and other matter at sea from ships, aircraft or manmade structures at sea, and to ensure the effective implementation of the applicable international rules and standards.

Article 7. Pollution From Land-Based Sources

The Contracting Parties shall take all appropriate measures to prevent, reduce and control pollution of the Convention area caused by coastal disposal or by discharges emanating from rivers, estuaries, coastal establishments, outfall structures, or any other sources on their territories.

Article 10. Specially Protected Areas

The Contracting Parties shall, individually or jointly, take all appropriate measures to protect and preserve rare or fragile ecosystems, as well as the habitat of depleted, threatened or endangered species, in the Convention area. To this end, the Contracting Parties shall endeavour to establish protected areas. The establishment of such areas shall not affect the rights of other Contracting Parties and third States. In addition, the Contracting Parties shall exchange information concerning the administration and management of such areas.

Article 12. Environmental Impact Assessment

1. As part of their environmental management policies the Contracting Parties undertake to develop technical and other guidelines to assist the planning of their major development projects in such a way as to prevent or minimize harmful impacts on the Convention area.

2. Each Contracting Party shall assess within its capabilities, or ensure the assessment of, the potential effects of such projects on the marine environment, particularly in coastal areas, so that appropriate measures may be taken to prevent any substantial pollution of, or significant and harmful changes to, the Convention area.

3. With respect to the assessments referred to in paragraph 2, each Contracting Party shall, with the assistance of the Organization when requested, develop procedures for the dissemination of information and may, where appropriate, invite other Contracting Parties which may be affected to consult with it and to submit comments.

5. Protocol Concerning Pollution from Land-Based Sources and Activities to the Convention for the Protection and Development of the Marine Environment of the Wider Caribbean, arts. III(1), IV(2), IX & Annexes III & IV, Oct. 6, 1999, S. Treaty Doc 110–1 (Basic Document 3.5a)

Article III. General Obligations

1. Each Contracting Party shall, in accordance with its laws, the provisions of this Protocol, and international law, take appropriate measures to prevent, reduce and control pollution of the Convention area from land-based sources and activities, using for this purpose the best practicable means at its disposal and in accordance with its capabilities.

* * *

Article IV. Annexes

1. The Contracting Parties shall address the source categories, activities and associated pollutants of concern listed in Annex I to this Protocol through the progressive development and implementation of additional annexes for those source categories, activities, and associated pollutants of concern that are determined by the Contracting Parties as appropriate for regional or sub-regional action. Such annexes shall, as appropriate, include *inter alia*:

(a) effluent and emission limitations and/or management practices based on the factors identified in Annex II to this Protocol; and

(b) timetables for achieving the limits, management practices and measures agreed by the Contracting Parties.

2. In accordance with the provisions of the annexes to which it is party, each Contracting Party shall take measures to prevent, reduce and control pollution of the Convention area from the source categories, activities and pollutants addressed in annexes other than Annexes I and II to this Protocol.

3. The Contracting Parties may also develop such additional annexes as they may deem appropriate, including an annex to address water quality criteria for selected priority pollutants identified in Annex I to this Protocol.

Article IX. Transboundary Pollution

Where pollution from land-based sources and activities originating from any Contracting Party is likely to affect adversely the coastal or marine environment of one or more of the other Contracting Parties, the Contracting Parties concerned shall use their best efforts to consult at the request of any affected Contracting Party, with a view to resolving the issue.

Annex III. Domestic Wastewater

* * *

Each Contracting Party shall ensure that domestic wastewater that discharges into, or adversely affects, the Convention area, is treated by a new or existing domestic wastewater system whose effluent achieves the effluent limitations specified below:

[For discharges into Class II waters ("waters that . . . are less sensitive to the impacts of domestic wastewater and where humans or living resources that are likely to be adversely affected by the discharges are not exposed to such discharges") the BOD limit, based on a monthly average, is 150 mg/l.]

[For discharges into, or that adversely affect, Class I waters ("waters that, due to inherent or unique environmental characteristics or fragile biological or ecological characteristics or human use, are particularly sensitive to the impacts of domestic wastewater.") Class I waters include "waters containing coral reefs, seagrass beds, or mangroves." The BOD limit, based on a monthly average, is 30 mg/l.]

Annex IV. Agricultural Non-Point Sources of Pollution

Each Contracting Party shall . . . formulate policies, plans and legal mechanisms for the prevention, reduction and control of pollution of the Convention area from agricultural non-point sources of pollution that may adversely affect the Convention area. Programmes shall be identified . . . to mitigate pollution of the Convention area from agricultural non-point sources of pollution, in particular, if these sources contain nutrients (nitrogen and phosphorus), pesticides, sediments, pathogens, solid waste or other such pollutants that may adversely affect the Convention area.

* * *

6. Articles on the Responsibility of States for Internationally Wrongful Acts, arts. 31, 34 & 39, U.N. Doc. A/56/10 and Corr. 1 (2001) (Basic Document 1.15)

Article 31. Reparation

1. The responsible State is under an obligation to make full reparation for the injury caused by the internationally wrongful act.

2. Injury includes any damage, whether material or moral, caused by the internationally wrongful act of a State.

Article 34. Forms of reparation

Full reparation for the injury caused by the internationally wrongful act shall take the form of restitution, compensation and satisfaction, either singly or in combination, in accordance with the provisions of this chapter.

Article 39. Contribution to the injury

In the determination of reparation, account shall be taken of the contribution to the injury by willful or negligent action or omission of the injured State or any person or entity in relation to whom reparation is sought.

Section 5. Discussion Notes/Questions

1. Has Puerto Cristo violated any of its customary-law or treaty-based obligations with respect to land-based pollution? In answering this question, you should separately assess each of Puerto Cristo's actions (its sewage discharge, the dumping of dredge spoils, and its agricultural development activities).

2. If Puerto Cristo has violated international law, what remedies are appropriate? Is it relevant that activities in St. Columba may be contributing to the problems it is having? Even though St. Columba does not appear to be causing any transboundary harm, is it nonetheless violating some of its international obligations?

3. There are other international legal materials of potential relevance to this problem. In 1995, 110 conferees (including several Caribbean nations) adopted the so-called Washington Declaration on Protection of the Marine Environment from Land-Based Activities **(Basic Document 3.12)** and the Global Programme of Action for the Protection of the Marine Environment from Land-Based Activities **(Basic Document 3.11)**. Are these documents relevant to determining Puerto Cristo's international legal obligations?

In addition to the soft-law instruments mentioned above, there is widespread adherence among Caribbean nations to the London Convention on the Prevention of Marine Pollution by Dumping of Wastes and Other Matter, Dec. 29, 1972, 1046 UNTS 120 **(Basic Document 3.2)** & its 1996 Protocol on Dumping and Incineration of Wastes and Other Matter at Sea, **(Basic Document 3.2a)**. If Puerto Cristo were a party to these agreements, would they impose any obligations beyond those imposed by the Caribbean Sea Protocol on Pollution from Land-Based Sources?

Might the London Convention and its Protocol apply to Puerto Cristo even if it has not joined those agreements? Consider Article 210(6) of UNCLOS, quoted in Reading 3, *supra*.

4. A fundamental problem in resolving the dispute between Puerto Cristo and St. Columba is determining whose behavior is primarily responsible for the damage to St. Columba's coral reefs. Given the difficulty of determining causation in cases like this, the importance of monitoring becomes self-evident. It is not merely a question of determining liability in the (unlikely) event that legal action is taken. It is also a matter of having the knowledge necessary to develop strategies that can solve problems like this. In its 1990 report *The State of the Marine Environment*, GESAMP stated that:

> The difficulty of monitoring biological change, given its long-term and extensive geographic variation, and the problem of interpreting these observations in the light of the results of experimental exposures of a few species to a few known contaminants, are not easily resolved. Where changes are expected, for example, in areas receiving discharges, monitoring programmes may be initiated, but they may involve an expensive and long-term commitment of resources. . . . In addition, it is often charged that irreversible damage will ensue before the results of long-term programmes are accumulated and analyzed.
>
> It follows that long-term field observations seldom provide early warning of significant effects at population level, nor do they by themselves identify the principal or even important causative agents. Aside from catastrophic events, it is usually difficult to distinguish between natural and man-made causes of biological change. . . .

In the instant case of *St. Columba v. Santo Cristo*, what kind of monitoring might have helped solve the problem of causation? How can we deal with the fact that a significant portion of marine pollution is transported into the marine environment by air, often from places thousands of miles away? What kind of legal arrangements are required to address this problem?

5. In *An Oceans Manifesto: The Present Global Crisis,* 32 Fletcher Forum of World Affairs 39, 44, 49 (2008), Alan B. Sielen observes that our failure adequately to protect the marine environment is due, in part, to our failure to properly account for the true economic value of healthy oceans.

> As nations and citizens consider their interests in the oceans, it is important to cultivate a better understanding of the large-scale economic effects of coastal and marine ecosystems on regional, national, and local economies. The economic stakes in the oceans are especially high in much of the developing world, where fish and other marine resources play a large part in meeting basic human needs, including food and income. On a global scale, the world's terrestrial and marine ecosystems provide at least $33 trillion annually in services. The benefits from ecosystems include food, water, timber, livelihoods, recreation, and cultural values, among many others—almost two thirds of which is contributed by marine systems. The idea that a healthy and sustainable marine environment is an essential ingredient in the large economic engine of the world must be better understood and conveyed.
>
> * * *
>
> Better ocean economics . . . will help to establish the value of the oceans as "capital"—that is, their ability to produce income in the future through a sustainable flow of economic value derived from the many activities associated with them. Linking the economy's health to the oceans' health will not only underscore the serious

> consequences of ineffective environmental policies but also give environmental advocates a powerful tool for arguing their case before the public and their elected representatives.

As Sielen observes, the economic value of ocean resources means that there is also a national security dimension to marine environmental protection.

> Competition and the destruction of scarce resources can ignite hostilities and trigger large-scale migration, as seen in Haiti in the 1970s and 1980s. It can also incite armed conflict, as in Nigeria's oil-rich southern delta region. Competing claims to offshore oil and gas, such as the present dispute between China and Japan in the East China Sea, strain relations between neighboring states. Disagreements about fishing rights—a longstanding source of conflict—are exacerbated by the scarcity of living resources that results from overexploitation and pollution. Parts of the Middle East and the Horn of Africa continue to experience serious political tension over access to scarce supplies of fresh water.

Id. at 44. *See also* Ranee Khooshie Lal Panjabi, *The Pirates of Somalia: Opportunistic Predators or Environmental Prey?*, 34 Wm. & Mary Envtl. L. & Pol'y Rev. 377, 382 (2010) (attributing the growth and extent of piracy in the waters near Somalia to the "environmental devastation" and consequent loss of livelihoods that Somali citizens and fishermen have suffered at the hands of "predators from many nations" who have "polluted their waters . . . and looted their oceans of fish.")

6. To what extent is poverty an excuse for Puerto Cristo's failure to control its pollution of the marine environment? Does the relevant international law recognize a lack of financial and regulatory capacity as a mitigating factor? Do poor countries have a lesser obligation with respect to pollution control? What obligations do higher income countries have to assist poorer countries in dealing with their pollution problems?

7. In its 2001 report on the state of the oceans, GESAMP suggested that pollution of the ocean by radioactive waste is a less serious problem than it appears "in the minds of the general public and politicians." Not everyone would agree. In particular, there has long been significant concern about Russian dumping of radioactive wastes in the Arctic. This issue was addressed extensively in the second edition of this coursebook. *See* Lakshman D. Guruswamy, Sir Geoffrey W.R. Palmer, Burns H. Weston & Jonathan C. Carlson, International Environmental Law and World Order 1–14, 171–81 (2nd ed. 1999).

8. Is an instrument like the 1995 Global Programme of Action for the Protection of the Marine Environment from Land-Based Activities (Global Programme) **(Basic Document 3.11)** sufficiently "binding" to have any impact on state behavior? By its own terms, it offers non-binding "conceptual and practical guidance" on managing land-based pollution, rather than clear rules. Would a treaty be more effective?

Professor Suh-Yong Chung has suggested that treaties may, in fact, be less successful than soft-law solutions like the 1995 Programme of Action. Professor Chung argues that failures to control land-based pollution in the Mediterranean region may be due to the decision to use a "hard-law" based approach, which deters countries from pursuing aggressive environmental protection goals because of fear of legal consequences. Drawing a contrast to the successful use of soft-law approaches to secure international cooperation in cleaning up the Baltic and North Seas, he writes:

> The Barcelona Convention System is a set of legally binding rules. As demonstrated in the case of the Land-Based Sources Protocol, the main stakeholders' uncertainties about the level of their commitments to the legally binding standards delayed the adoption of the protocol that was presumed to be the most important and urgent. The standards of the Land-Based Sources protocol were also too low to control the pollutants due to a general reluctance by the states and the existence of conflicts of interests between the states. It may have been more effective if the Med Plan introduced a soft-law based institution which could have provided more flexibility to reluctant states and created like-minded enthusiasm among the states.

Suh-Yong Chung, *Is the Convention-Protocol Approach Appropriate for Addressing Regional Marine Pollution?: The Barcelona Convention System Revisited*, 13 Penn St. Envtl. L. Rev. 85, 101–02 (2004).

3. POLLUTION FROM SHIPS

Although most ocean pollution comes from land-based sources, pollution from ships is a significant threat, especially in enclosed seas and other areas of heavy maritime traffic. The carriage of people and goods on the world's oceans comes with some built-in hazards for the marine environment, including oil pollution (resulting from either operational or accidental discharges from ships); chemical pollution (generally from accidental discharges); intentional disposal by ships of raw sewage and garbage into the marine environment; and the spread of invasive species through ballast water discharges or by carriage on ships' hulls. Maritime traffic is also a significant source of air pollution, and concern is growing about the impact on marine life of noise pollution from ships. Putting aside ordinary maritime traffic, ships contribute to pollution problems when they engage in the deliberate disposal at sea of wastes or hazardous material including material gathered on shore (i.e. dumping) or when they reach the end of their useful life and must be scrapped.

The International Maritime Organization (IMO) and its Marine Environment Protection Committee (MEPC) have played a dominant role in international efforts to control and prevent ship-based pollution. The most relevant international agreements are listed in chronological order below. All of them are administered by IMO (to the extent administration is needed), and most were adopted under IMO auspices.

- 1969 International Convention Relating to Intervention on the High Seas in Cases of Oil Pollution Casualties
- 1973 Protocol Relating to Intervention on the High Seas in Cases of Marine Pollution by Substances other than Oil
- 1973 London Convention on the Prevention of Marine Pollution by Dumping of Wastes and other Matter and the 1996 London Protocol (London Dumping Convention)
- 1973 International Convention for the Prevention of Pollution from Ships, as amended by the Protocols of 1978 and 1997 (MARPOL or MARPOL 73/78)
- 1990 International Convention on Oil Pollution Preparedness, Response and Co-operation
- 2000 Protocol on Preparedness, Response and Co-operation to Pollution Incidents by Hazardous and Noxious Substances (other than oil)
- 2001 International Convention on the Control of Harmful Anti-Fouling Systems on Ships
- 2004 International Convention for the Control and Management of Ships' Ballast Water and Sediments
- 2009 Hong Kong International Convention for the Safe and Environmentally Sound Recycling of Ships

In addition to these environmentally focused agreements, other IMO agreements are of importance because of their role in promoting safe ships and safe navigation (both of which are critical to avoiding accidents and the pollution that stems from them). These safety-oriented agreements impose requirements related to ship design and construction, necessary onboard equipment, crew training, and navigational practices. Widespread adherence to the requirements imposed by these agreements has dramatically improved maritime safety. Three of the most important such agreements are the following.

- 1972 Convention on the International Regulations for Preventing Collisions at Sea
- 1974 International Convention for the Safety of Life at Sea (SOLAS)
- 1978 International Convention on Standards of Training, Certification and Watchkeeping for Seafarers

All of the international agreements mentioned above are subject to frequent updating and amendment. In many cases, amendments are by special processes under which an amendment that receives sufficient support to enter into force will bind all parties to the main agreement who do not expressly opt out of the amendment within a certain time period. This substantially eases the process of ensuring worldwide applicability of the amendments. In addition, the IMO Assembly and the Marine Environment Protection Committee issue resolutions and codes that contain important safety and environmental performance standards for the guidance of states and private ship operators.

Finally, beginning in 1969, the IMO has tackled the problem of liability and compensation for oil pollution damage through a series of conventions and protocols. The current versions of these agreements are:

- 1992 International Convention on Civil Liability for Oil Pollution Damage (1992 Civil Liability Convention)
- 1992 International Convention on the Establishment of an International Fund for Compensation for Oil Pollution Damage (1992 Fund Convention)
- 2003 Supplementary Fund Protocol to the 1992 Fund Convention

Problem 6-3 examines the operation of these liability and compensation conventions. It also presents issues related to the role of the International Maritime Organization in the context of the United Nations Convention on the Law of the Sea and of customary international law.

PROBLEM 6-3: AN OIL TANKER SPILL IN THE SOUTH CHINA SEA

Section 1. Facts

The Great Coral Reef is one of the ecological wonders of the world. Located in the South China Sea, the structure is actually a complex of reefs and islands that stretches for a length of 200 miles, just 10 miles off the western coast of the nation of Annam. The area is renowned for its beauty and for the diversity of the sea life that can be found there. The endangered Green and Hawksbill turtles nest on islands in the reef system, and other sea turtle species are regularly spotted in the surrounding waters. One hundred fifty different species of birds visit the reefs and islands each year, including 10 species that make their homes only there. Twenty-five species of cetaceans, 1200 species of fish, and a wide variety of mollusks live on the reef or in surrounding waters.

The Great Coral Reef has long been under Annamese control, and it is of tremendous social, cultural, and economic significance to the Annamese people. Its waters and resources were once central to the traditional way of life of the indigenous peoples of Annam, and 10,000 Annamese still fish the reef either commercially or for basic subsistence. Thousands of Annamese vacationers and foreign tourists visit the reef each year, and Annam's coastal hospitality and recreation industry is thriving as a result. Yet, despite all this activity, the area has remained relatively pristine, and most visitors value it for that characteristic. Ten years ago, Annam declared the entire area a national maritime park.

One constant threat to the Great Coral Reef is merchant shipping in the South China Sea. The central section of the South China Sea, where the reef is located, is only about 350 miles wide, and the western half of the sea is too shallow and too dotted with islands to serve as a major shipping route. Hence, vessels traveling north or south must travel in the eastern part of the Sea, where they pass by the reef.

There are two main routes past the reef. The shortest and fastest route is through the Tokin Passage, a 60-mile wide stretch of extremely deep open water bordered on the east by the Great Coral Reef and on the west by the Berkey Islands, a chain of uninhabited islands, many of them submerged, which, over the centuries, have been the site of frequent shipwrecks and ship groundings. The second shipping route is a slightly longer route through the Annamese Channel, a ten-mile wide stretch of water that separates the Great Coral Reef from Annam's coast.[56]

Most ship captains prefer to travel through the Tokin Passage. However, in bad weather, or if their ship has any mechanical problems, captains avoid the Tokin Passage because of the inherent dangers posed by the Berkey Islands and because the depth of the water in the Tokin Passage prevents ships from anchoring when in distress. Because its waters are shallower (permitting anchoring) and generally calmer in bad weather, the Annamese Channel is a safer route. Moreover, ships in the channel can easily reach Annam's main port in the event of an emergency.

Because of a number of minor accidents involving ship groundings on parts of the reef, Annam became concerned about the danger posed to the reef by the large number of oil tankers traveling through the South China Sea. Accordingly, in November of last year, Annam notified the IMO and maritime authorities around the world that, commencing January 1 of this year, that its territorial sea near the Great Coral Reed would be completely closed to oil tankers above 5000 DWT (deadweight tonnage). The area of closure extends from a point five miles south of the reef to a point five miles north of the reef and for the full width of the territorial sea between those points. That area includes two miles of territorial sea to the west of the

[56] Neither the Tokin Passage nor the Annamese Channel is an "international strait" as that term is used in the United Nations Convention on the Law of the Sea **(Basic Document 3.4)** and in customary international law.

reef, plus the entire Annamese Channel. The closure of the territorial sea also prevents tanker access to the port of Annam City, which is located on the Annamese Channel. Tankers traveling in the South China Sea near the Great Coral Reef would be required to use the Tokin Passage and remain at least two miles west of the reef at all times.

In July of this year, the *Eastern Star,* a 27-year-old oil tanker weighing 98,000 tonnes (deadweight), set sail from a port in the Persian Gulf loaded with a cargo of 84,000 tonnes of unrefined medium crude oil owned by Fortune Oil Company, a South Korean company. The ship's planned route would take it across the Indian Ocean, through the South China Sea, then on to South Korea where it would off-load the oil at a refinery owned by Fortune Oil.

The *Eastern Star* is a double-hulled oil tanker of the Suezmax class. It is registered in Grand Isle, a small Caribbean island state, and it sails under that nation's flag. It is owned by Eastern Tankers, Inc., a Grand Isle corporation. Late last year, the *Eastern Star* was inspected by Tanker Survey, Inc., a ship classification organization incorporated in Grand Isle and authorized by Grand Isle to conduct surveys on behalf of Grand Isle of ships flying the Grand Isle flag. Tanker Survey reported to Grand Isle that it had completed a so-called ESP survey of the ship (a survey following the protocols established by the IMO's Enhanced Survey Program) and that the ship satisfied all parameters for safe operation of a ship of its age. Tanker Survey also renewed the *Eastern Star's* required international certificates (signifying that the vessel was in compliance with various IMO Conventions, including MARPOL 73/73 and SOLAS).

The *Eastern Star*'s voyage was uneventful until the seventh day when it encountered high seas and gale force winds shortly after entering the South China Sea. The ship seemed to be holding its own in the stormy weather until, about 70 miles south of the Great Coral Reef, the crew discovered that a ballast tank was leaking and that a small crack had developed in the ship's outer hull.

Concerned about the safety of the ship, especially in light of a forecasted worsening of the storm, the *Eastern Star's* captain contacted the port authorities at Annam City, explained the situation, and asked for permission to enter port to effect repairs. The Annamese authorities refused, citing their ban on port calls by oil tankers and their concern about the possibility of pollution, especially given the damage to the *Eastern Star*. They suggested that the captain proceed to the port of Daungan on the island nation of Marganda, located 40 miles north of the Great Coral Reef.

The captain radioed again, pointing out that the storm was forecast to worsen and requesting permission to proceed north through the Annamese Channel, where he could anchor and make repairs if necessary. The Annamese authorities informed the captain that oil tankers were banned completely from the Annamese territorial sea in the area of the Great Coral Reef and directed him to proceed north via the Tokin Passage.

With no nearer harbor available, the *Eastern Star* steamed into the Tokin Passage, heading for Daungan. Unfortunately, the storm intensified. After several hours of battering by 20-foot waves and high winds, the ship began to break apart. The crew abandoned ship and were able to safely make their way to an island in the Great Coral Reef, but the ship's entire cargo of oil was spilled into the sea.

The oil was carried northeast by prevailing currents where it eventually polluted the reefs and islands at the northern end of the Great Coral Reef, as well as the surrounding sea. The environmental damage was enormous. Hundreds of sea birds were killed or injured, and their breeding grounds saturated in an "oily mousse." Oil residue washed into coves and inlets and on to reefs, damaging the reefs, killing local land vegetation, polluting sea turtle nesting sites, and defacing the pristine scenery. Commercial fishing in the area was completely banned for six months while Annam attempted to clean up the spill. After pictures of the damage done by the oil spill were shown throughout the world, thousands of tourists cancelled their trips to Annam, with dire consequences for local hotels, restaurants, shops, and service businesses.

A subsequent investigation by the Annamese maritime authority concluded that the survey of the *Eastern Star* had failed to detect severe corrosion in both the outer and inner hulls of the vessel, that the surveyor employed by Tanker Survey had failed to personally supervise the taking of critical thickness measurements that would have revealed the corrosion, and that the *Eastern Star* would have failed its survey, and been denied the Certificates it needed to sail, if the corrosion had been detected.

The Annamese authorities also discovered that five other ships surveyed by Tanker Survey in the last year had been detained by ship inspectors in ports where the ships had stopped when it was determined that the ships were structurally unsound. The appropriate authorities of Grand Isle were informed of these detentions, but they did not investigate or discuss the matter with Tanker Survey.

Within two months of the *Eastern Star's* accident, multiple actions were filed in the courts of Annam against Eastern Tankers, Inc. and Tanker Survey, Inc. The actions were consolidated into a single action, and Eastern Tankers deposited a sum of money with the court equal to the full amount of its potential liability under the 1992 International Convention on Civil Liability for Oil Pollution Damage.

The total claims filed in the actions are more than double the amount of recovery available under the Civil Liability Convention. The largest claim is by the government of Annam seeking recovery for past and future clean-up costs. Other large claimants are the Fortune Oil Company (seeking to recover the value of the lost oil, plus damage to its reputation stemming from the spill), Annamese commercial fishing interests (lost profits), Annamese tourist industries (lost profits), several international airlines (lost revenue due to a decline in air travel to Annam), and Annamese indigenous peoples organizations and environmental groups (damages for loss of spiritual and recreational enjoyment of the reef).

Eastern Tankers has moved to dismiss all claims against it. The accident, it argues, was caused by an irresistible natural force. Alternatively, it alleges that the Annamese government's claim is inadmissible because the accident was caused by Annam's "illegal, wrongful, and negligent refusal to allow the *Eastern Star* to enter its port or territorial waters." In addition, Eastern Tankers asserts that damages cannot be recovered for the "pure economic loss" suffered by the fishermen, the tourist industry and the airlines, or for the alleged loss of "spiritual and recreational enjoyment of the reef" or for the lost cargo.

Tanker Survey, Inc. has moved to dismiss all claims against it on the basis that nothing in international law makes a ship survey company liable under these circumstances. It also alleges that it is immune from liability pursuant to the Civil Liability Convention and Grand Isle law.

Annam and Grand Isle are members of the International Maritime Organization and parties to the 1982 United Nations Convention on the Law of the Sea, the 1992 International Convention on Civil Liability for Oil Pollution Damage ("the Liability Convention"), and the 1992 International Convention on the Establishment of an International Fund for Compensation for Oil Pollution Damage ("the Fund Convention"). Grand Isle and Annam are also parties to the 1973 International Convention for the Prevention of Pollution from Ships, 1973, as modified by the Protocol of 1978 (MARPOL 73/78). Under the Annamese constitution, "ratified treaties and established customary international law" are the "law of the land" and may be applied by the courts in judicial proceedings.

Section 2. Questions Presented

1. Should the Annamese court hold Eastern Tankers liable for the damage caused by the accident? If so, which of the claimants are entitled to recover from Eastern Tankers? From the International Oil Pollution Compensation Fund?

2. Assuming its survey of the *Eastern Star* was negligent, should the Annamese court hold Tanker Survey liable for the oil pollution damage? What law should the court apply to answer this question?

Section 3. Assignments

A. Reading Assignment

Study the Readings presented in Section 4, *infra*, and the Discussion Notes/Questions that follow.

B. Recommended Writing Assignment

Prepare a comprehensive, logically sequenced, and *argumentative* brief in the form of an outline of the primary and subsidiary *legal* issues you see requiring resolution by the Annamese court? Also, from the perspective of an independent objective judge, indicate which side ought to prevail on each issue and why. Retain a copy of your issue-outline/brief for class discussion.

C. Recommended Oral Assignment

Assume you are legal counsel for Annam, for Eastern Tankers, or for Tanker Survey (as designated by your instructor); then, relying upon the Readings (and your issue-outline if prepared), present a 15–20 minute oral argument of your client's likely positions before the court.

D. Recommended Reflective Assignment

Consider (and recommend) alternative norms, institutions, and/or procedures that you believe might do better than existing world order arrangements to contend with situations of the kind posed by this problem. In so doing, but without insisting upon *immediate* feasibility, identify the particular transition steps that would be needed to make your alternatives a reality.

Section 4. Readings

1. U.S. Fish & Wildlife Service (Alaska Region), Effects of Oil Spills on Wildlife and Habitat (Dec. 2004), available at http://alaska.fws.gov (last accessed Mar.1, 2011).

Oil spills affect wildlife and their habitats in many ways. The severity of the injury depends on the type and quantity of oil spilled, the season and weather, the type of shoreline, and the type of waves and tidal energy in the area of the spill.

Oil can be categorized into five groups, ranging from very light to very heavy oils. Most oil has a density less than water, so it floats. Oil tends to spread into a thin layer on the water surface as a sheen. Once in the water, oil undergoes weathering, a process that describes the physical, chemical, and biological changes that occur when oil interacts with the environment.

Weathering reduces the more toxic elements in oil products over time, as exposure to air, sunlight, wave and tidal action, and certain microscopic organisms degrades and/or disperses oil. Weathering rates depend on factors such as type of oil, weather, temperature, and the type of shoreline and bottom that occur in the spill area.

Types of Oil

Very light oils (jet fuel, gasoline) are highly volatile and evaporate quickly. Very light oils are one of the most acutely toxic oils and generally affect aquatic life (fish, invertebrates, and plants) that live in the upper water column.

Light oils (diesel, light crude, heating oils) are moderately volatile and can leave a residue of up to one third of the amount spilled after several days. Light oils leave a film on intertidal resources and have the potential to cause long-term contamination.

Medium oils (most crude oils) are less likely to mix with water and can cause severe and long-term contamination to intertidal areas. Medium oils can also severely impact waterfowl and fur-bearing marine mammals.

Heavy oils (heavy crude, No. 6 fuel oil and Bunker C) do not readily mix with water and have far less evaporation and dilution potential. These oils tend to weather slowly. Heavy oil can cause severe long-term contamination of intertidal areas and sediments. Heavy oils have severe impacts on waterfowl and fur-bearing marine mammals. Cleanup of heavy oil is difficult and usually long-term.

Very heavy oils can float, mix, sink, or hang in the water. These oils can become oil drops and mix in the water, or accumulate on the bottom, or mix with sediment and then sink.

Wildlife and Habitat

Oil causes harm to wildlife through physical contact, ingestion, inhalation and absorption. Floating oil can contaminate plankton, which includes algae, fish eggs, and the larvae of various invertebrates. Fish that feed on these organisms can subsequently become contaminated. Larger animals in the food chain, including bigger fish, birds, terrestrial mammals, and even humans may then consume contaminated organisms.

Initially, oil has the greatest impacts on species that utilize the water surface, such as waterfowl and sea otters, and species that inhabit the nearshore environment. Although oil causes immediate effects throughout the entire spill site, it is the external effects of oil on larger wildlife species that are often immediately apparent.

Plants

Marine algae and seaweed respond variably to oil, and oil spills may result in die-offs for some species. Algae may die or become more abundant in response to oil spills. Although oil can prevent the germination and growth of marine plants, most vegetation, including kelp, appears to recover after cleanup.

Invertebrates

Oil can be directly toxic to marine invertebrates or impact them through physical smothering, altering metabolic and feeding rates, and altering shell formation. These toxic effects can be both acute (lethal) and chronic (sub-lethal). Intertidal benthic (bottom dwelling) invertebrates may be especially vulnerable when oil becomes highly concentrated along the shoreline. Additionally, sediments can become reservoirs for the spilled petroleum. Some benthic invertebrates can survive exposure, but may accumulate high levels of contaminants in their bodies that can be passed on to predators.

Fish

Fish can be impacted directly through uptake by the gills, ingestion of oil or oiled prey, effects on eggs and larval survival, or changes in the ecosystem that support the fish. Adult fish may experience reduced growth, enlarged livers, changes in heart and respiration rates, fin erosion, and reproductive impairment when exposed to oil. Oil has the potential to impact spawning success, as eggs and larvae of many fish species, including salmon, are highly sensitive to oil toxins.

Birds and Mammals

Physical contact with oil destroys the insulation value of fur and feathers, causing birds and fur-bearing mammals to die of hypothermia. In cold climates, an inch diameter oil drop can be enough to kill a bird. Heavily oiled birds can lose their ability to fly and their buoyancy, causing drowning.

In efforts to clean themselves, birds and sea otters ingest and inhale oil. Ingestion can kill animals immediately, but more often results in lung, liver, and kidney damage and subsequent death. Seals and sea lions may be exposed to oil while breathing or resting at the water's surface or through feeding on contaminated species.

Long-term or chronic effects on birds and marine mammals are less understood, but oil ingestion has been shown to cause suppression to the immune system, organ damage, skin irritation and ulceration, damage to the adrenal system, and behavioral changes. Damage to the immune system can lead to secondary infections that cause death, and behavioral changes may affect an individual's ability to find food or avoid predators. Oil also affects animals in non-lethal ways such as impairing reproduction.

Avian and mammalian scavengers such as ravens, bald eagles, and arctic foxes are also exposed to oil by feeding on carcasses of contaminated fish and wildlife. Direct mortality and reduced reproduction in bald eagles were attributed to the Exxon Valdez oil spill.

Habitat

Oil has the potential to persist in the environment long after a spill event and has been detected in sediment 30 years after a spill. Oil spills may cause shifts in population structure, species abundance and diversity, and distribution. Habitat loss and the loss of prey items also have the potential to affect fish and wildlife populations.

Oil remains in the environment long after a spill event, especially in areas sheltered from weathering processes, such as the subsurface sediments under gravel shorelines, and in some soft substrates. However, pelagic and offshore communities are fairly resilient and rebound more quickly than inshore habitats. Although oil is still present in the sediment and coastal areas 15 years after the Exxon Valdez oil spill in Prince William Sound, Alaska, some wildlife populations have recovered. It is believed that continued effects will most likely be restricted to populations that reside or feed in isolated areas that contain oil.

2. Editors' Note

The international regime governing compensation for oil pollution damage is based upon three widely adopted treaties:

- The 1992 International Convention on Civil Liability for Oil Pollution Damage (1992 CLC) **(Basic Document 3.9)**,[57]
- The 1992 International Convention on the Establishment of an International Fund for Compensation for Oil Pollution Damage (1992 Fund Convention) **(Basic Document 3.10)**,[58] and
- The 2003 Supplementary Fund Protocol **(Basic Document 3.13)**.[59]

These treaties establish a three-tier structure for providing compensation to persons and businesses injured as a result of pollution from an oil tanker accident. (Relevant excerpts from the 1992 Civil Liability Convention and the 1992 Fund Convention appear immediately after this reading.)

---

[57] Protocol of 1992 to amend the International Convention on Civil Liability for Oil Pollution Damage, Nov. 27, 1992, 1956 UNTS. 1992. The 1992 Civil Liability Convention had 138 Contracting States as of 10 April 2019.

[58] Protocol of 1992 to amend the International Convention on the Establishment of an International Fund for Compensation for Oil Pollution Damage, Nov. 27, 1992, 1953 UNTS. 330. The 1992 Fund Convention had 116 Contracting State as of 10 April 2019.

[59] Protocol of 2003 to the International Convention on the Establishment of an International Fund for Compensation for Oil Pollution Damage, 1992, May 16, 2003, 2012 UKTS 48. The Supplementary Fund Protocol had 32 Contracting States as of 10 April 2019.

A. *The three-tier compensation structure*

Compensation from the shipowner (1992 Civil Liability Convention). In the first instance, compensation for oil pollution damage can be sought from the shipowner. A shipowner is strictly liable for damage caused by an oil-carrying vessel as a result of an oil-pollution incident involving that vessel. No fault need be shown, and the shipowner can escape liability only in three limited circumstances specified in article III(2) of the Convention.

The shipowner's total potential liability for any one incident is capped at an amount determined by the tonnage of the ship, and the shipowner is obliged to "maintain insurance or other financial security" in that amount. This liability cap protects the shipowner in all cases unless it is proved that the pollution damage resulted from the shipowner's "personal act or omission, committed with the intent to cause such damage, or recklessly and with knowledge that such damage would probably result."

Compensation from the 1992 International Oil Pollution Compensation Fund (the 1992 Fund). The 1992 Fund is an intergovernmental organization established pursuant to the 1992 Fund Convention. The 1992 Fund provides additional compensation for oil pollution damage to persons who are unable to obtain full and adequate compensation under the terms of the 1992 CLC. Compensation from the Fund is available when the shipowner is not liable under the 1992 CLC, when the shipowner is liable but is unable to meet its obligations, or when the recoverable damages caused by the oil pollution incident exceed the shipowner's liability limits under the 1992 CLC. The amount of compensation paid by the Fund for pollution damage from any one incident is capped at 203 million SDRs (Special Drawing Rights),[60] less whatever amounts are actually paid for that damage pursuant to the 1992 Civil Liability Convention.

Financial support for the Fund is provided by mandatory "contributions" from persons (nature or legal, including states and state organizations) who receive oil that has been carried by sea. If a person (alone or in conjunction with associated persons) has received more than 150,000 tons of oil in the territory of a Contracting State during any one calendar year, it is required to make a contribution toward the expenses of the Fund. The amount of these contributions is not fixed, but fluctuates. Each person's contribution is determined by a complex formula that depends on the Fund's total expenses and the amount of oil received by each entity in the calendar year when the expenses were incurred.

Compensation from the Supplementary Fund. The Supplementary Fund, like the 1992 Fund, is an intergovernmental organization financed by contributions paid by persons who receive oil by sea transport. The

[60] The unit of account in each of these Conventions is the "Special Drawing Right" or SDR. The SDR is an international reserve asset developed by the International Monetary Fund. Its value is based on the market exchange rates of a basket of major currencies.

Supplementary Fund was established by the Protocol of 2003 to the 1992 International Fund Convention (Supplementary Fund Protocol). To receive compensation from the Supplementary Fund, a person must have a claim that would have been fully compensated by the 1992 Fund but for the limit on compensation established by the 1992 Fund Convention.

B. Compensable damage

Compensation under any of the three Conventions is only available for "pollution damage" that occurs in the territory, territorial sea, or exclusive economic zone of a Contracting State. Pollution damage is defined in an open-ended way by Article I, paragraph 6 of the 1992 Civil Liability Convention, leaving room for dispute over what types of damage are covered. The 2019 Claims Manual published by the International Oil Pollution Compensation Funds identifies five categories of compensable damage under the Civil Liability and Fund Conventions.

1. The costs of *clean-up and preventive measures.*

2. Compensation for *property damage*, i.e. the cost of cleaning, repair or replacement necessary to restore property that has been damaged due to contamination by oil.

3. Compensation for *consequential losses* incurred by persons whose property has been damaged by oil, such as the loss of earnings that a fisherman might suffer if contamination of his nets prevents him from fishing.

4. Compensation for some so-called *pure economic losses.* These are losses of earnings suffered by people as a result of pollution *but not* as a result of direct harm to their property. For example, fishermen may be unable to fish in a polluted area even if their fishing gear is unaffected by the pollution. Similarly, industries catering to the tourist trade may lose earnings due to pollution of a nearby public beach even if their property is untouched by the pollution.

5. Compensation for *environmental damage*, but limited to "loss of profit" caused by environmental impairment and the "costs of reasonable measures of reinstatement actually undertaken or to be undertaken."

Compensation for pure economic losses has been somewhat controversial. When a major oil spill occurs, its effects are not limited to persons whose property is directly damaged by the spill. Others may lose earnings and profits because of other impacts of the oil spill. For example, fishermen may discover that damage to fish stocks in the area adversely impacts the size of their catch. A hotel may lose clientele because the public beaches that attract tourists are contaminated. A real estate agent in a coastal community may see a decline in commissions because home sales in the area have slowed following a local oil spill. Local taxi drivers may lose business because of a decline in tourism.

National laws differ in their treatment of pure economic losses. Courts in common law countries "have been very reluctant to accept claims for pure economic loss."[61] In other countries, such losses may be compensable so long as the connection of the losses to the oil pollution incident is close enough and the amount of the loss attributable to the incident can be determined with a fair degree of certainty.[62]

The IOPC Funds Claims Manual allows for the compensation of pure economic losses so long as there is a "sufficiently close link of causation between the contamination and the loss or damage." Relevant factors for making this determination include:

i) the geographic proximity of the claimant's business to the oil contamination;

ii) whether the claimant's business is economically dependent on an affected resource (e.g., by contaminated fishing grounds);

iii) whether the claimant protect its business by utilizing resources other than those affected by oil contamination (e.g., nearby non-contaminated fishing grounds); and

iv) how closely integrated the claimant's business is with other economic activity in the area affected by the oil spill ("for example whether a claimant's business is located or has assets in the affected area, or provides employment for people living there").

Persons seeking compensation from the Funds for particular types of pure economic losses (e.g., loss of wages) must satisfy additional specific criteria established by the Funds.

C. *Process of obtaining compensation*

Following an oil pollution incident, an action for compensation for damage may be brought against the shipowner or its insurer in the courts of the Contracting State within which the damage occurred.[63] Similarly, an action may be brought against the 1992 Fund[64] before the same court. Such actions must be brought within three years from the date when the damage

---

[61] Mäns Jacobsson, *Liability and Compensation for Ship-Source Pollution,* in The IMLI Manual on International Maritime Law: Volume III: Marine Environmental Law and International Maritime Security Law, at § 9.2.5.4 (2016).

[62] *See id.*

[63] 1992 Civil Liability Convention, art. IX, *supra* note 56.

[64] 1992 Fund Convention, art. 7, *supra* note 57. When the Supplementary Fund also has an obligation to pay compensation, a claim against the 1992 Fund is automatically considered a claim against the Supplementary Fund as well. *See* 2003 Supplementary Fund Protocol, art. 6.2, *supra* note 58.

occurred but no later than six years from the date of the incident that caused the damage.[65]

In practice, most claims under the Conventions are settled out of court without the need for litigation. Following an oil pollution incident, the shipowner or its insurer will establish a fund for the payments of claims and a process for receiving and evaluating claims. If it appears that the claims may exceed the owner's liability limits, the 1992 Fund may also establish a process for receiving claims. In some case, the 1992 Fund and the insurer will jointly establish an office in the country where the damage occurred for easier processing of claims. However, where that occurs, decisions on whether to pay any particular claim will still be made by the shipowner/insurer and the Fund, respectively, and not by the processing office. In the vast majority of cases, claims for compensation are submitted to the shipowner/insurer or to the 1992 Fund and are resolved without the need for litigation.

D. Compensation from other entities

National law may permit persons damaged by oil pollution to seek compensation from persons or entities other than the shipowner/insurer. But the so-called "channeling provision" of the Civil Liability Convention limits such claims. Article III(4) of the Convention provides as follows:

> 4. . . . [N]o claim for compensation for pollution damage under this Convention or otherwise may be made against:
>
> (a) the servants or agents of the owner or the members of the crew;
>
> (b) the pilot or any other person who, without being a member of the crew, performs services for the ship;
>
> (c) any charterer (how so ever described, including a bareboat charterer), manager or operator of the ship;
>
> (d) any person performing salvage operations with the consent of the owner or on the instructions of a competent public authority;
>
> (e) any person taking preventive measures;
>
> (f) all servants or agents of persons mentioned in subparagraphs (c), (d) and (e);
>
> unless the damage resulted from their personal act or omission, committed with the intent to cause such damage, or recklessly and with knowledge that such damage would probably result.

Thus, for states that have ratified the Conventions, most claims against entities other than the shipowner will be prohibited unless the claim

---

[65] 1992 Civil Liability Convention, art. VIII, *supra* note 56; 1992 Fund Convention, art. 6, *supra* note 57.

alleges that the damage was caused by the "personal act or omission" of the person being sued and that the act was committed "with the intent to cause" pollution damage or "recklessly and with knowledge" that such damage would probably result.

In a state, like the United States, that has not joined any of these Conventions, national law will determine all issues of liability for oil pollution damage occurring within the jurisdiction of that state. For example, the Oil Pollution Act of 1990, 33 U.S.C. 2701–2761, establishes a liability and compensation regime for oil pollution damage that occurs in U.S. navigable waters. That regime has features similar to the international liability and compensation regime but, of course, is governed entirely by U.S. law and regulations.

3. International Convention on Civil Liability for Oil Pollution Damage, 1992, arts. I, II, III, V, IX & X, Nov. 27, 1992, 1956 UNTS 255 (Basic Document 3.9)

Article I

For the purposes of this Convention:

* * *

2. "Person" means any individual or partnership or any public or private body, whether corporate or not, including a State or any of its constituent subdivisions.

3. "Owner" means the person or persons registered as the owner of the ship or, in the absence of registration, the person or persons owning the ship. . . .

* * *

6. "Pollution damage" means:

(a) loss or damage caused outside the ship by contamination resulting from the escape or discharge of oil from the ship, wherever such escape or discharge may occur, provided that compensation for impairment of the environment other than loss of profit from such impairment shall be limited to costs of reasonable measures of reinstatement actually undertaken or to be undertaken;

(b) the costs of preventive measures and further loss or damage caused by preventive measures.

7. "Preventive measures" means any reasonable measures taken by any person after an incident has occurred to prevent or minimize pollution damage.

8. "Incident" means any occurrence, or series of occurrences having the same origin, which causes pollution damage or creates a grave and imminent threat of causing such damage.

* * *

Article II

This Convention shall apply exclusively:

(a) to pollution damage caused:

(i) in the territory, including the territorial sea, of a Contracting State, and

(ii) in the exclusive economic zone of a Contracting State. . . .

(b) to preventive measures, wherever taken, to prevent or minimize such damage.

Article III

1. Except as provided in paragraphs 2 and 3 of this Article, the owner of a ship at the time of an incident, or, where the incident consists of a series of occurrences, at the time of the first such occurrence, shall be liable for any pollution damage caused by the ship as a result of the incident.

2. No liability for pollution damage shall attach to the owner if he proves that the damage:

(a) resulted from an act of war, hostilities, civil war, insurrection or a natural phenomenon of an exceptional, inevitable and irresistible character, or

(b) was wholly caused by an act or omission done with intent to cause damage by a third party, or

(c) was wholly caused by the negligence or other wrongful act of any Government or other authority responsible for the maintenance of lights or other navigational aids in the exercise of that function.

3. If the owner proves that the pollution damage resulted wholly or partially either from an act or omission done with intent to cause damage by the person who suffered the damage or from the negligence of that person, the owner may be exonerated wholly or partially from his liability to such person.

4. No claim for compensation for pollution damage may be made against the owner otherwise than in accordance with this Convention. Subject to paragraph 5 of this Article, no claim for compensation for pollution damage under this Convention or otherwise may be made against:

(a) the servants or agents of the owner or the members of the crew;

(b) the pilot or any other person who, without being a member of the crew, performs services for the ship;

(c) any charterer (howsoever described, including a bareboat charterer), manager or operator of the ship;

(d) any person performing salvage operations with the consent of the owner or on the instructions of a competent public authority;

(e) any person taking preventive measures;

(f) all servants or agents of persons mentioned in subparagraphs (c), (d) and (e); unless the damage resulted from their personal act or omission, committed with the intent to cause such damage, or recklessly and with knowledge that such damage would probably result.

5. Nothing in this Convention shall prejudice any right of recourse of the owner against third parties.

Article V

1. The owner of a ship shall be entitled to limit his liability under this Convention in respect of any one incident to an aggregate amount calculated as follows:

[As of July 2018, the liability limit applicable to a tanker of the size of the *Eastern Star* (98,000 tonnes) was 4.51 million SDR (Special Drawing Rights)[66] plus 631 SDR for each gross tonne over 5000.]

2. The owner shall not be entitled to limit his liability under this Convention if it is proved that the pollution damage resulted from his personal act or omission, committed with the intent to cause such damage, or recklessly and with knowledge that such damage would probably result.

Article IX

1. Where an incident has caused pollution damage in the territory, including the territorial sea or an area referred to in Article II, of one or more Contracting States or preventive measures have been taken to prevent or minimize pollution damage in such territory including the territorial sea or area, actions for compensation may only be brought in the Courts of any such Contracting State or States. Reasonable notice of any such action shall be given to the defendant.

2. Each Contracting State shall ensure that its Courts possess the necessary jurisdiction to entertain such actions for compensation.

3. After the fund has been constituted in accordance with Article V the Courts of the State in which the fund is constituted shall be exclusively competent to determine all matters relating to the apportionment and distribution of the fund.

---

[66] The unit of account in the Convention is the "Special Drawing Right" or SDR. The SDR is an international reserve asset developed by the International Monetary Fund. Its value is based on the market exchange rates of a basket of major currencies.

Article X

1. Any judgment given by a Court with jurisdiction in accordance with Article IX which is enforceable in the State of origin where it is no longer subject to ordinary forms of review, shall be recognized in any Contracting State, except:

(a) where the judgment was obtained by fraud; or

(b) where the defendant was not given reasonable notice and a fair opportunity to present his case.

2. A judgment recognized under paragraph 1 of this Article shall be enforceable in each Contracting State as soon as the formalities required in that State have been complied with. The formalities shall not permit the merits of the case to be re-opened.

4. International Convention on the Establishment of an International Fund for Compensation for Oil Pollution Damage, 1992, arts. 1–4, Nov. 27, 1992, 1953 UNTS 330 (Basic Document 3.10)

Article 2

1. An International Fund for compensation for pollution damage, to be named "The International Oil Pollution Compensation Fund 1992" and hereinafter referred to as "the Fund," is hereby established with the following aims:

(a) to provide compensation for pollution damage to the extent that the protection afforded by the 1992 Liability Convention is inadequate;

(b) to give effect to the related purposes set out in this Convention.

* * *

Article 4

1. For the purpose of fulfilling its function under Article 2, paragraph 1(a), the Fund shall pay compensation to any person suffering pollution damage if such person has been unable to obtain full and adequate compensation for the damage under the terms of the 1992 Liability Convention,

(a) Because no liability for the damage arises under the 1992 Liability Convention;

(b) Because the owner liable for the damage under the 1992 Liability Convention is financially incapable of meeting his obligations in full and any financial security that may be provided under Article VII of that Convention does not cover or is insufficient to satisfy the claims for compensation for the damage; . . .

(c) Because the damage exceeds the owner's liability under the 1992 Liability Convention. . . .

Expenses reasonably incurred or sacrifices reasonably made by the owner voluntarily to prevent or minimize pollution damage shall be treated as pollution damage for the purposes of this Article.

2. The Fund shall incur no obligation under the preceding paragraph if:

(a) It proves that the pollution damage resulted from an act of war, hostilities, civil war or insurrection or was caused by oil which has escaped or been discharged from a warship or other ship owned or operated by a State and used, at the time of the incident, only on Government non-commercial service; or

(b) The claimant cannot prove that the damage resulted from an incident involving one or more ships.

3. If the Fund proves that the pollution damage resulted wholly or partially either from an act or omission done with the intent to cause damage by the person who suffered the damage or from the negligence of that person, the Fund may be exonerated wholly or partially from its obligation to pay compensation to such person. The Fund shall in any event be exonerated to the extent that the shipowner may have been exonerated under Article III, paragraph 3, of the 1992 Liability Convention. However, there shall be no such exoneration of the Fund with regard to preventive measures.

* * *

5. United Nations Convention on the Law of the Sea (UNCLOS), arts. 17–19, 21–22, 24, 94, 194, 197 & 211, Dec. 10, 1982, 1833 UNTS 3 (Basic Document 3.4)

Article 17. Right of innocent passage

Subject to this Convention, ships of all States, whether coastal or land-locked, enjoy the right of innocent passage through the territorial sea.

Article 18. Meaning of passage

1. Passage means navigation through the territorial sea for the purpose of: (a) traversing that sea without entering internal waters or calling at a roadstead or port facility outside internal waters; or (b) proceeding to or from internal waters or a call at such roadstead or port facility.

2. Passage shall be continuous and expeditious. However, passage includes stopping and anchoring, but only in so far as the same are incidental to ordinary navigation or are rendered necessary by force majeure or distress or for the purpose of rendering assistance to persons, ships or aircraft in danger or distress.

Article 19. Meaning of innocent passage

1. Passage is innocent so long as it is not prejudicial to the peace, good order or security of the coastal State. Such passage shall take place in conformity with this Convention and with other rules of international law.

2. Passage of a foreign ship shall be considered to be prejudicial to the peace, good order or security of the coastal State if in the territorial sea it engages in any of the following activities:

(a) any threat or use of force against the sovereignty, territorial integrity or political independence of the coastal State, or in any other manner in violation of the principles of international law embodied in the Charter of the United Nations;

* * *

(h) any act of wilful and serious pollution contrary to this Convention;

* * *

Article 21. Laws and regulations of the coastal State relating to innocent passage

1. The coastal State may adopt laws and regulations, in conformity with the provisions of this Convention and other rules of international law, relating to innocent passage through the territorial sea, in respect of all or any of the following:

(a) the safety of navigation and the regulation of maritime traffic;

(b) the protection of navigational aids and facilities and other facilities or installations;

(c) the protection of cables and pipelines;

(d) the conservation of the living resources of the sea;

(e) the prevention of infringement of the fisheries laws and regulations of the coastal State;

(f) the preservation of the environment of the coastal State and the prevention, reduction and control of pollution thereof;

(g) marine scientific research and hydrographic surveys;

(h) the prevention of infringement of the customs, fiscal, immigration or sanitary laws and regulations of the coastal State.

2. Such laws and regulations shall not apply to the design, construction, manning or equipment of foreign ships unless they are giving effect to generally accepted international rules or standards.

3. The coastal State shall give due publicity to all such laws and regulations.

Article 22. Sea lanes and traffic separation schemes in the territorial sea

1. The coastal State may, where necessary having regard to the safety of navigation, require foreign ships exercising the right of innocent passage through its territorial sea to use such sea lanes and traffic separation schemes as it may designate or prescribe for the regulation of the passage of ships.

2. In particular, tankers, nuclear-powered ships and ships carrying nuclear or other inherently dangerous or noxious substances or materials may be required to confine their passage to such sea lanes.

3. In the designation of sea lanes and the prescription of traffic separation schemes under this article, the coastal State shall take into account:

(a) the recommendations of the competent international organization;

(b) any channels customarily used for international navigation;

(c) the special characteristics of particular ships and channels; and

(d) the density of traffic.

4. The coastal State shall clearly indicate such sea lanes and traffic separation schemes on charts to which due publicity shall be given.

Article 24. Duties of the coastal State

1. The coastal State shall not hamper the innocent passage of foreign ships through the territorial sea except in accordance with this Convention. In particular, in the application of this Convention or of any laws or regulations adopted in conformity with this Convention, the coastal State shall not:

(a) impose requirements on foreign ships which have the practical effect of denying or impairing the right of innocent passage; or

(b) discriminate in form or in fact against the ships of any State or against ships carrying cargoes to, from or on behalf of any State.

2. The coastal State shall give appropriate publicity to any danger to navigation, of which it has knowledge, within its territorial sea.

Article 94. Duties of the flag State

1. Every State shall effectively exercise its jurisdiction and control in administrative, technical and social matters over ships flying its flag.

2. In particular every State shall:

(a) maintain a register of ships containing the names and particulars of ships flying its flag, except those which are excluded from generally accepted international regulations on account of their small size; and

(b) assume jurisdiction under its internal law over each ship flying its flag and its master, officers and crew in respect of administrative, technical and social matters concerning the ship.

3. Every State shall take such measures for ships flying its flag as are necessary to ensure safety at sea with regard, inter alia, to:

(a) the construction, equipment and seaworthiness of ships;

(b) the manning of ships, labour conditions and the training of crews, taking into account the applicable international instruments;

(c) the use of signals, the maintenance of communications and the prevention of collisions.

4. Such measures shall include those necessary to ensure:

(a) that each ship, before registration and thereafter at appropriate intervals, is surveyed by a qualified surveyor of ships, and has on board such charts, nautical publications and navigational equipment and instruments as are appropriate for the safe navigation of the ship;

(b) that each ship is in the charge of a master and officers who possess appropriate qualifications, in particular in seamanship, navigation, communications and marine engineering, and that the crew is appropriate in qualification and numbers for the type, size, machinery and equipment of the ship;

(c) that the master, officers and, to the extent appropriate, the crew are fully conversant with and required to observe the applicable international regulations concerning the safety of life at sea, the prevention of collisions, the prevention, reduction and control of marine pollution, and the maintenance of communications by radio.

5. In taking the measures called for in paragraphs 3 and 4 each State is required to conform to generally accepted international regulations, procedures and practices and to take any steps which may be necessary to secure their observance.

6. A State which has clear grounds to believe that proper jurisdiction and control with respect to a ship have not been exercised may report the facts to the flag State. Upon receiving such a report, the flag State shall investigate the matter and, if appropriate, take any action necessary to remedy the situation.

7. Each State shall cause an inquiry to be held by or before a suitably qualified person or persons into every marine casualty or incident of navigation on the high seas involving a ship flying its flag and causing loss of life or serious injury to nationals of another State or serious damage to ships or installations of another State or to the marine environment. The flag State and the other State shall cooperate in the conduct of any inquiry

held by that other State into any such marine casualty or incident of navigation.

Article 194. Measures to prevent, reduce and control pollution of the marine environment

1. States shall take, individually or jointly as appropriate, all measures consistent with this Convention that are necessary to prevent, reduce and control pollution of the marine environment from any source, using for this purpose the best practicable means at their disposal and in accordance with their capabilities, and they shall endeavour to harmonize their policies in this connection.

2. States shall take all measures necessary to ensure that activities under their jurisdiction or control are so conducted as not to cause damage by pollution to other States and their environment, and that pollution arising from incidents or activities under their jurisdiction or control does not spread beyond the areas where they exercise sovereign rights in accordance with this Convention.

3. The measures taken pursuant to this Part shall deal with all sources of pollution of the marine environment. These measures shall include, inter alia, those designed to minimize to the fullest possible extent:

* * *

(b) pollution from vessels, in particular measures for preventing accidents and dealing with emergencies, ensuring the safety of operations at sea, preventing intentional and unintentional discharges, and regulating the design, construction, equipment, operation and manning of vessels.

* * *

4. In taking measures to prevent, reduce or control pollution of the marine environment, States shall refrain from unjustifiable interference with activities carried out by other States in the exercise of their rights and in pursuance of their duties in conformity with this Convention.

5. The measures taken in accordance with this Part shall include those necessary to protect and preserve rare or fragile ecosystems as well as the habitat of depleted, threatened or endangered species and other forms of marine life.

Article 197. Cooperation on a global or regional basis

States shall cooperate on a global basis and, as appropriate, on a regional basis, directly or through competent international organizations, in formulating and elaborating international rules, standards and recommended practices and procedures consistent with this Convention, for the protection and preservation of the marine environment, taking into account characteristic regional features.

Article 211. Pollution from vessels

1. States, acting through the competent international organization or general diplomatic conference, shall establish international rules and standards to prevent, reduce and control pollution of the marine environment from vessels and promote the adoption, in the same manner, wherever appropriate, of routeing systems designed to minimize the threat of accidents which might cause pollution of the marine environment, including the coastline, and pollution damage to the related interests of coastal States. Such rules and standards shall, in the same manner, be re-examined from time to time as necessary.

2. States shall adopt laws and regulations for the prevention, reduction and control of pollution of the marine environment from vessels flying their flag or of their registry. Such laws and regulations shall at least have the same effect as that of generally accepted international rules and standards established through the competent international organization or general diplomatic conference.

* * *

4. Coastal States may, in the exercise of their sovereignty within their territorial sea, adopt laws and regulations for the prevention, reduction and control of marine pollution from foreign vessels, including vessels exercising the right of innocent passage. Such laws and regulations shall, in accordance with Part II, section 3, not hamper innocent passage of foreign vessels.

* * *

6. (a) Where the international rules and standards referred to in paragraph 1 are inadequate to meet special circumstances and coastal States have reasonable grounds for believing that a particular, clearly defined area of their respective exclusive economic zones is an area where the adoption of special mandatory measures for the prevention of pollution from vessels is required for recognized technical reasons in relation to its oceanographical and ecological conditions, as well as its utilization or the protection of its resources and the particular character of its traffic, the coastal States, after appropriate consultations through the competent international organization with any other States concerned, may, for that area, direct a communication to that organization, submitting scientific and technical evidence in support and information on necessary reception facilities. Within 12 months after receiving such a communication, the organization shall determine whether the conditions in that area correspond to the requirements set out above. If the organization so determines, the coastal States may, for that area, adopt laws and

regulations for the prevention, reduction and control of pollution from vessels implementing such international rules and standards or navigational practices as are made applicable, through the organization, for special areas. These laws and regulations shall not become applicable to foreign vessels until 15 months after the submission of the communication to the organization.

(b) The coastal States shall publish the limits of any such particular, clearly defined area.

(c) If the coastal States intend to adopt additional laws and regulations for the same area for the prevention, reduction and control of pollution from vessels, they shall, when submitting the aforesaid communication, at the same time notify the organization thereof. Such additional laws and regulations may relate to discharges or navigational practices but shall not require foreign vessels to observe design, construction, manning or equipment standards other than generally accepted international rules and standards; they shall become applicable to foreign vessels 15 months after the submission of the communication to the organization, provided that the organization agrees within 12 months after the submission of the communication.

7. The international rules and standards referred to in this article should include inter alia those relating to prompt notification to coastal States, whose coastline or related interests may be affected by incidents, including maritime casualties, which involve discharges or probability of discharges.

6. IMO Secretariat, Implications of the United Nations Convention on the Law of the Sea for the International Maritime Organization 60–64, IMO Doc LEG/MISC.6 (10 September 2008)

Routeing measures

Article 211(1) of UNCLOS **[Basic Document 3.4]** provides that States, acting through the competent international organization or general diplomatic conference, shall promote the adoption of routeing systems designed to minimize the threat of accidents which might cause pollution of the marine environment, including the coastline and related interests of coastal States. . . .

The General Provisions on Ships' Routeing (resolution A.572(14) adopted by the IMO Assembly in 1985) were amended in 1995 by the insertion of new paragraphs 3.6 and 3.7, which deal with routeing systems for the protection of environmentally sensitive areas. Paragraph 3.6 establishes the criteria to be taken into account when considering the adoption of a routeing system for the protection of the marine environment. Paragraph 3.7 sets limits for the adoption of routeing systems. In accordance with this paragraph IMO should not adopt a system that would impose unnecessary constraints on shipping, or establish an area to be avoided that would impede the passage of ships through an international strait. . . .

Territorial sea

In accordance with article 21(1) of UNCLOS the coastal State may adopt rules and regulations "in conformity with the provisions of this Convention and other rules of international law, relating to innocent passage through the territorial sea in respect of . . . (f) the preservation of the environment of the coastal State and the prevention, reduction and control of pollution thereof." In this connection, article 211(4) establishes that coastal States may "in the exercise of their sovereignty within their territorial sea, adopt laws and regulations for the prevention, reduction, and control of marine pollution from foreign vessels, including vessels exercising the right of innocent passage." This provision is complemented by a reference to the need not to hamper innocent passage of foreign vessels.

* * *

7. International Convention for the Safety of Life at Sea, annex, chapter V, Nov. 1, 1974, 1184 UNTS 277 (as amended)

Chapter V (Safety of Navigation), Regulation 10

1. Ships' routeing systems contribute to safety of life at sea, safety and efficiency of navigation and/or protection of the marine environment. Ships' routeing systems are recommended for use by, and may be made mandatory for, all ships, certain categories of ships or ships carrying certain cargoes, when adopted and implemented in accordance with the guidelines and criteria developed by the Organization.

2. The Organization is recognized as the only international body for developing guidelines, criteria and regulations on an international level for ships' routeing systems. Contracting Governments shall refer proposals for the adoption of ships' routeing systems to the Organization. The Organization will collate and disseminate to Contracting Governments all relevant information with regard to any adopted ships' routeing systems.

* * *

4. Ships' routeing systems should be submitted to the Organization for adoption. However, a Government or Governments implementing ships' routeing systems not intended to be submitted to the Organization for adoption or which have not been adopted by the Organization are encouraged to take into account, wherever possible, the guidelines and criteria developed by the Organization.

* * *

9. All adopted ships' routeing systems and actions taken to enforce compliance with those systems shall be consistent with international law, including the relevant provisions of the 1982 United Nations Convention on the Law of the Sea.

10. Nothing in this regulation nor its associated guidelines and criteria shall prejudice the rights and duties of Governments under international law or the legal regimes of straits used for international navigation and archipelagic sea lanes.

8. Aldo Chircop, Olof Linden, & Detlef Nielsen, Characterising the Problem of Places of Refuge for Ships, in Places of Refuge for Ships: Emerging Environmental Concerns of a Maritime Custom 3–6 (Aldo Chircop & Olof Linden eds., 2006)

Traditionally and over a long period of time, the international maritime community strongly supported an unwritten norm concerning the provision of assistance to ships in distress. For ease of reference, this norm will be referred to as the refuge custom. The expectations consist of a complementary right of the ship and crew to self-preservation and a responsibility on the part of coastal authorities to assist them. The two expectations form the core of a customary norm, i.e., an unwritten law, but law nonetheless because many states over a long period of time have considered the right and duty as having juridical value. The refuge custom is very old; historical evidence shows that the custom has persisted over a long period of time, through peaceful and belligerent times. Whether the decision-maker is a national maritime administration or a port authority, the duty boils down to a legal obligation of the state. Historically, not only was the ship in distress entitled to enter safe waters: it also enjoyed certain privileges based on the fact that the ship was not within the jurisdiction of the place of refuge voluntarily. . . .

In short, at least until very recently, if not to date, there has been a well-developed and widely practised custom to assist ships in distress, including by providing a place of refuge. Incidents since the 1970s, and most especially between 1999 and 2002, have called into question the extent of the right of a ship in distress to seek a refuge. . . .

9. John E. Noyes, Book Review: Places of Refuge for Ships, 37 Denv. J. Int'l L. & Pol'y 135, 135–36, 137–38 (2008)

The damaged tankers Erika and Prestige, denied access to ports or other places of refuge, sank in 1999 and 2002, respectively. They spilled their cargoes of oil, wreaking much environmental damage on French and Spanish coastlines and damaging the fishing and tourist industries. Another ship in distress, the Castor, was towed around the Mediterranean for over a month in 2001, having been denied entry by numerous states, before its cargo of gasoline was safely offloaded at sea. Denying refuge to a damaged tanker may alleviate understandable anxieties of local authorities, but this course of action may also render salvage operations impossible and contribute to an environmental catastrophe that could have been avoided.

When foreign flag vessels in distress seek access to places of refuge, complex problems arise. The issue of access to places of refuge illustrates how difficult it is to arrive at a new legal consensus when changes in technology and social attitudes challenge traditional legal understandings—in this case, the customary international law right of refuge in internal waters. Competing legal perspectives, reflecting the concerns of various affected constituencies, vie for prominence.

* * *

Value conflicts related to places of refuge have intensified in recent decades. The predominant humanitarian rationale for a right of access of vessels in distress to a place of refuge—a right often asserted as existing in customary international law—has been undermined. This is so because of changes in technology. These changes have helped to minimize the danger to humans, but have increased the risk of damage from ships. Traditionally, access to places of refuge was often necessary in order to save the lives of people on board a ship in distress. Refuge thus linked to a broader duty of assistance that also found expression in the international law rule that vessels have a duty to render assistance to those in danger of being lost at sea. Today, however, technology permits precise location of ships in distress, and passengers and crew members on board such ships often can be offloaded by helicopter or ship. Yet the need to insure the safety of the crew and passengers on board a vessel in distress never completely explained the customary international law rule allowing access to ports or places of refuge in situations of distress, for the rule also supported the interests of ship and cargo owners and the value of open commerce. These latter rationales remain, but they have come into increasing tension with environmental values.

Modern ships pose dangers that older vessels did not. Spills of oil or hazardous cargoes from tankers may devastate the marine environment or threaten the health and safety of coastal communities. These risks have been addressed through a variety of initiatives directed at vessel safety and restricting access of vessels to Particularly Sensitive Sea Areas. Yet these preventive measures are not the only ways to respond to increased environmental risks. The Law of the Sea Convention and other treaties also incorporate protective jurisdictional principles, allowing coastal states to counteract environmental threats from marine casualties. These protective principles provide a conceptual basis for qualifying the traditional customary right of access to places of refuge. State practice has moved toward requiring notice and consent for entry into a place of refuge, something that historically was not necessary except with respect to warships in distress. Recent authorities maintain that a ship in distress does not have an absolute right of access to a place of refuge. For example, the Irish High Court of Admiralty concluded that "[i]f safety of life is not a factor, then there is a widely recognised practice among maritime states to have proper regard to their own interests and those of their citizens in deciding whether or not to accede" to the request by a vessel in distress for access to a place of refuge. According to Aldo Chircop, "the right, according to customary international law, for a vessel in distress to be granted a place of refuge no longer appears to be recognised by many States as an absolute right."

10. Guidelines on Places of Refuge for Ships in Need of Assistance, adopted on Dec. 5, 2003 by the Assembly of the International Maritime Organization, Resolution A.949, 23d Sess., IMO Doc A 23/Res.949: paras 1.1–1.20, & 3.1–3.12, App. 1, n. 3, App. 2 (Basic Document 3.14)

1 General

Introduction

Objectives of providing a place of refuge

* * *

1.3 When a ship has suffered an incident, the best way of preventing damage or pollution from its progressive deterioration would be to lighten its cargo and bunkers; and to repair the damage. Such an operation is best carried out in a place of refuge.

1.4 However, to bring such a ship into a place of refuge near a coast may endanger the coastal State, both economically and from the environmental point of view, and local authorities and populations may strongly object to the operation.

1.5 While coastal States may be reluctant to accept damaged or disabled ships into their area of responsibility due primarily to the potential for environmental damage, in fact it is rarely possible to deal satisfactorily and effectively with a marine casualty in open sea conditions.

1.6 In some circumstances, the longer a damaged ship is forced to remain at the mercy of the elements in the open sea, the greater the risk of the vessel's condition deteriorating or the sea, weather or environmental situation changing and thereby becoming a greater potential hazard.

1.7 Therefore, granting access to a place of refuge could involve a political decision which can only be taken on a case-by-case basis with due consideration given to the balance between the advantage for the affected ship and the environment resulting from bringing the ship into a place of refuge and the risk to the environment resulting from that ship being near the coast.

* * *

3 Guidelines for Actions Expected of Coastal States

* * *

Event-specific assessment

Analysis factors

3.9 [When an event occurs, an analysis of the advantages and disadvantages of allowing a place of refuge should be performed.] This analysis should include the following points:

- seaworthiness of the ship concerned, in particular buoyancy, stability, availability of means of propulsion and power generation, docking ability, etc.;
- nature and condition of cargo, stores, bunkers, in particular hazardous goods;
- distance and estimated transit time to a place of refuge;
- whether the master is still on board;
- the number of other crew and/or salvors and other persons on board and an assessment of human factors, including fatigue;
- the legal authority of the country concerned to require action of the ship in need of assistance;
- whether the ship concerned is insured or not insured;
- if the ship is insured, identification of the insurer, and the limits of liability available;
- agreement by the master and company of the ship to the proposals of the coastal State/salvor to proceed or be brought to a place of refuge;
- provisions of the financial security required;
- commercial salvage contracts already concluded by the master or company of the ship;
- information on the intention of the master and/or salvor;
- designation of a representative of the company at the coastal State concerned;
- risk evaluation factors identified in Appendix 2 [including the risk of pollution and harm to areas of "high ecological value"]; and
- any measures already taken.

* * *

3.11 The analysis should include a comparison between the risks involved if the ship remains at sea and the risks that it would pose to the place of refuge and its environment. Such comparison should cover each of the following points:

- safeguarding of human life at sea;
- safety of persons at the place of refuge and its industrial and urban environment (risk of fire or explosion, toxic risk, etc.);
- risk of pollution;
- if the place of refuge is a port, risk of disruption to the port's operation (channels, docks, equipment, other installations);
- evaluation of the consequences if a request for place of refuge is refused, including the possible effect on neighbouring States; and
- due regard should be given, when drawing the analysis, to the preservation of the hull, machinery and cargo of the ship in need of assistance.

After the final analysis has been completed, the maritime authority should ensure that the other authorities concerned are appropriately informed.

Decision-making process for the use of a place of refuge

3.12 When permission to access a place of refuge is requested, there is no obligation for the coastal State to grant it, but the coastal State should weigh all the factors and risks in a balanced manner and give shelter whenever reasonably possible.

11. Editors' Note

If a flag state doesn't do its job and, as a result, a substandard ship causes oil pollution damage, the flag state is likely immune from suit by private parties who are harmed by the spill, although another state could make a claim against the flag state for breach of its international legal obligations.

What other parties are subject to suit? Certainly the shipowner, but the shipowner may be a shell corporation with few or no assets available to pay damages claims. Should the cargo owner be liable? How about the company that chartered the ship for the voyage? What about the ship's crew? The International Convention on Civil Liability for Oil Pollution Damage (Reading 2, *supra*) provides a partial answer to these questions. But not all issues of liability are resolved by the relevant treaties. Where the treaties are silent, states are free to impose liability on whichever parties they believe should bear it.

One of the emerging questions is whether classification societies (known as "Recognized Organizations" when they perform ship inspection services on behalf of flag states) should be held responsible for losses caused by a ship's unseaworthiness. Classification societies play a vital role in ensuring the success of the international system for ship safety. As stated in *Carbotrade S.p.A. v. Bureau Veritas*, 99 F.3d 86, 88, 1997 AMC 98, 99–100 (2d Cir. 1996):

> A classification society sets standards for the quality and integrity of vessels and performs surveys to determine whether vessels are in compliance with the classification society's rules and regulations, national laws, and international conventions. If a vessel passes inspection, the classification society either issues a certificate attesting to the vessel's conformity with the applicable rules, regulations, laws, and conventions or endorses an existing certificate with a visa reflecting the survey. If the vessel fails to pass the inspection, the classification society either does not issue the certificate or withdraws the existing certificate.

In a formal legal sense, classification societies generally act on behalf of flag states and shipowners. But aren't they also acting on behalf of the international community as a whole? *See* Machale A. Miller, *Liability of Classification Societies from the Perspective of United States Law*, 22 Tul. Mar. L. J. 75, 75 (1997) ("Classification societies serve as the unofficial policemen of the maritime world, using independent verification processes to ensure that seaworthy vessels are in service."). Traditionally, classification societies have not been held responsible for loss caused by a ship's unseaworthiness, even if the society certified that the ship was up to required standards. Should that rule change? Whose law should determine the liability of a classification society? The law of the coastal state? The flag state? The state where the society is organized? The final few readings in this chapter address these questions.

12. MARPOL 73/78: Protocol of 1978 Relating to the International Convention for the Prevention of Pollution From Ships 1973, Annex I, Regulations 6–7, Feb. 17, 1978, 1341 UNTS 3 (as amended) (Basic Document 3.3)

Regulation 6. Surveys

1. Every oil tanker of 150 gross tonnage and above, and every other ship of 400 gross tonnage and above shall be subject to the surveys specified below:

> .1 an initial survey before the ship is put in service. . . .
>
> .2 a renewal survey at intervals specified by the Administration, but not exceeding 5 years. . . . The renewal survey shall be such as to ensure that the structure, equipment,

systems, fittings, arrangements and material fully comply with applicable requirements of this Annex;

* * *

.4 an annual survey within 3 months before or after each anniversary date of the Certificate, including a general inspection of the structure, equipment, systems, fittings, arrangements and material referred to in paragraph 1.1 of this regulation to ensure that they have been maintained in accordance with paragraphs 4.1 and 4.2 of this regulation and that they remain satisfactory for the service for which the ship is intended. Such annual surveys shall be endorsed on the Certificate issued under regulation 7 or 8 of this Annex; and

* * *

3.1 Surveys of ships as regards the enforcement of the provisions of this Annex shall be carried out by officers of the Administration. The Administration may, however, entrust the surveys either to surveyors nominated for the purpose or to organizations recognized by it. Such organizations, including classification societies, shall be authorized by the Administration in accordance with the provisions of the present Convention [and with the Code for Recognized Organizations (RO Code)].

* * *

3.3 When a nominated surveyor or recognized organization determines that the condition of the ship or its equipment does not correspond substantially with the particulars of the Certificate or is such that the ship is not fit to proceed to sea without presenting an unreasonable threat of harm to the marine environment, such surveyor or organization shall immediately ensure that corrective action is taken and shall in due course notify the Administration. If such corrective action is not taken the Certificate shall be withdrawn and the Administration shall be notified immediately. . . .

3.4 In every case, the Administration concerned shall fully guarantee the completeness and efficiency of the survey and shall undertake to ensure the necessary arrangements to satisfy this obligation.

4.1 The condition of the ship and its equipment shall be maintained to conform with the provisions of the present Convention to ensure that the ship in all respects will remain fit to proceed to sea without presenting an unreasonable threat of harm to the marine environment.

* * *

Regulation 7. Issue or endorsement of certificate

1. An International Oil Pollution Prevention Certificate shall be issued, after an initial or renewal survey in accordance with the provisions of regulation 6 of this Annex, to any oil tanker of 150 gross tonnage and above and any other ships of 400 gross tonnage and above which are engaged in voyages to ports or offshore terminals under the jurisdiction of other Parties to the present Convention.

2. Such certificate shall be issued or endorsed as appropriate either by the Administration or by any persons or organization duly authorized by it. In every case the Administration assumes full responsibility for the certificate.

13. Vincent J. Foley & Christopher R. Nolan, The Erika Judgment—Environmental Liability and Places of Refuge: A Sea Change in Civil and Criminal Responsibility That the Maritime Community Must Heed, 33 Tul. Mar. L. J. 41, 42–46, 65–72 (2008)

The ERIKA was "a nearly twenty-five year old tanker, flying a Maltese flag" and controlled by two Liberian companies. The technical manager of the ship was an Italian company, and the vessel had been issued a class certificate which was renewed on November 24, 1999. The vessel was time chartered by a Bahamian company to an intermediary company and voyage chartered by the intermediary to a subsidiary of a large French-based oil company. The ERIKA was loaded with a cargo of 30,884.471 metric tons of fuel oil at the port of Dunkirk and was fixed for destination as "per order, in an Italian port."

The ERIKA departed the port of Dunkirk on her final voyage on December 8, 1999. The tanker experienced unfavorable weather conditions almost immediately upon leaving the port and by December 11 issued her first distress message while in the Bay of Biscay heading towards the port of Donges. A little before 6:00 a.m. on December 12, 1999, the ERIKA issued a new distress message that the ship was breaking apart. The crew was safely evacuated. At that time, the product spilled was estimated to be seven to ten thousand tons. Due to the weather conditions, the oil was directed towards the south of the Bay of Biscay and polluted over 400 kilometers of coast.

After eight years of litigation and a four-month trial involving scores of witnesses, voluminous documentary evidence, and testimony from individual experts as well as detailed submissions from judge-appointed boards of inquiry, the Erika judgment was rendered on January 16, 2008. In an extraordinary 278-page opinion, the court meticulously reviewed the history of ownership, operation, management, inspections, and trading patterns of the ERIKA and extended criminal and civil liability for oil pollution beyond the traditionally liable shipowner to include the vessel's classification society and her oil company charterer. The court found culpable conduct by each of these maritime safety-chain entities and found that this conduct caused or contributed to the oil pollution. . . .

The court held the shipowner and classification society were criminally and civilly liable, finding they had deliberately acted together to reduce the amount of steel used for structural repairs in order to save costs at the expense of jeopardizing the safety of the ship, her crew, and the marine environment. The oil company was also liable for its negligence in chartering a vessel far beyond her intended life expectancy to transport the most dangerous and persistent oil products.[67]

* * *

The authors consider this case to be a groundbreaking departure from well-entrenched principles of liability that have limited exposure for pollution liabilities to the shipowner and its insurers. Courts have shown a determined reluctance to hold classification societies responsible for approving deficient repairs to ship structures that allow a ship to continue carrying oil cargos despite a dangerously weakened structural condition. But make no mistake, this narrow view of classification liability has been shattered by the Erika court's ruling. This is also the first significant extension of liability to a charterer, an entity that is not involved with any maintenance or repair of the vessel. Charterers are "on notice" that by simply hiring a problem ship, they could be exposed to liability for the wrongful and criminal conduct of others. In particular, the Erika court's holding should be considered a stern warning to shipowners, managers, classification societies, and oil companies alike: adhere to safe shipping practices or face criminal charges and potentially limitless civil liability for endangering seafarers and causing harm to the environment.

* * *

In the light of the Erika court's analysis of the ship repair process, the traditional defenses to liability raised by classification societies would seem to be abrogated by the active role of the classification society in hiding the vessel's deficiencies. Classification societies have typically relied upon the following rationales to avoid liability for their negligence in surveys and classification of vessels: (1) they have immunity under the law of the vessel's flag state; (2) contractual limitations in their agreement with the shipowner preclude liability because the amount of fees charged do not justify imposition of liability for the loss of the vessel; (3) the shipowner has exclusive responsibility and control over the vessel and cannot delegate this responsibility to the classification society; and (4) the purpose of classification certificates is limited to allowing the shipowner to take

[67] Tribunal de grande instance [Criminal Court of First Instance] Paris, 11ème ch., Jan. 16, 2008, No. 9934895010, slip op. at 141 (Erika), *translated in* The LanguageWorks, Inc., Erika Judgment 141 (Apr. 22, 2008). . . .

advantage of favorable insurance rates and should not form the basis of more extensive liability.

The Erika court's analysis squarely rejected flag state immunity as grounds for protection of the classification society. The court also denied the classification society any protection under article III(4)(b) of 1992 CLC because it did not participate in the navigational or nautical operation of the ERIKA on the incident voyage. . . .

The Erika court's finding that the classification society, through its surveyor, acted in concert with the shipowner's representative to jeopardize deliberately the safety of the ship, and thereby endanger third parties, is a sound basis on which to hold classification societies liable for creating unreasonably dangerous conditions. As a result of the Erika court's analysis, for the first time, classification society negligence has been declared to be the legal and proximate cause of the environmental harm caused by a structural failure on a vessel at sea. In our view, it will not be the last.

14. Editors' Note

In March 2010, the Court of Appeal in Paris confirmed the lower court's judgment (described in the prior reading) that the classification society RINA, was liable for damage caused by its negligent inspection of the Erika. But the Court of Appeal ruled that Total SA (the cargo owner) was de facto the charterer of the Erika and did not have civil liability because of the channeling provision of Article III.4(c) of the 1992 CLC. The Court of Appeal also determined that the classification society would have been entitled to assert the flag state's immunity, but that it failed to raise the issue at the appropriate time and therefore waived the defense. *See* International Oil Pollution Compensation Funds, *Incidents Involving the IOPC Funds—1992 Fund, ERIKA, Note by the Director*, para. 4.2.3, IMO Doc IOPC/JUN10/3/1 (May 17, 2010).

The Court of Appeal decision was itself appealed to the Cour de Cassation. In September 2012, that court (essentially, the French equivalent of the Supreme Court of the United States) determined that classification societies were also protected by the channeling provision in the 1992 CLC. But, the Court of Cassation concluded, the classification society's lack of care amounted to "recklessness," which removed its protection under the CLC. Moreover, while agreeing that Total SA was also protected by the channeling rule in the CLC, the Court concluded that Total's lack of care also amounted to recklessness and denied it any CLC protection.

Compare the French courts' conclusions concerning the liability of the classification society to the conclusions reach by two district courts in the United States in the next two readings.

15. Reino de España v. The American Bureau of Shipping, Inc., 729 F. Supp. 2d 635, 636–38, 642–44, 645–46 (S.D.N.Y. 2010)

This action arises from the sinking of the *M.T. Prestige*, an oil tanker (the "Prestige"), off the coast of Plaintiff Reino de España ("Plaintiff" or "Spain") on November 19, 2002. The Prestige discharged millions of gallons of oil into Plaintiff's territorial waters before sinking 140 miles from the Spanish coast, causing devastating environmental and economic effects. Plaintiff seeks compensatory damages in excess of $1,000,000,000 and punitive damages from Defendants American Bureau of Shipping, ABS Group of Companies, Inc., and ABSG Consulting, Inc. f/k/a ABS Marine Services, Inc. (collectively, "Defendants" or "ABS"), alleging principally that ABS was reckless in classifying the Prestige as fit to carry fuel cargoes. . . .

* * *

ABS is a not-for-profit classification society that maintains its headquarters in Houston, Texas. . . . ABS performs classification surveys to determine whether a ship's structure and condition satisfy ABS's rules. . . . ABS also conducts statutory surveys for the benefit of states that are parties to various international treaties that oblige them to regulate ships sailing under their flags. Statutory certificates certify that vessels comply with specific international treaties.

* * *

The Commonwealth of the Bahamas (the "Bahamas"), under whose flag the Prestige sailed at all relevant times, is a party to various international maritime conventions that require it to regulate ships sailing under its flag and permit it to delegate the inspection and survey of ships to a Recognized Organization ("RO"). ABS is an RO that, pursuant to a contract with the Bahamas, is authorized to carry out statutory classification surveys of Bahamian flag ships. The Prestige was registered in the Bahamas in 1994 and sailed under the flag of the Bahamas from that time until the casualty on November 19, 2002. The Prestige was class certified by ABS upon its construction in 1976 and was surveyed and classed by ABS throughout its operational life.

ABS conducted a special survey and statutory surveys of the Prestige in Guangzhou, China, commencing on April 2, 2001, and concluding on May 19, 2001. . . .

ABS conducted annual class and statutory surveys of the Prestige in the United Arab Emirates from May 15–22, 2002, which were led by a surveyor from ABS's Dubai office. Following the survey, ABS's assigned surveyor endorsed the Prestige's classification certificates on May 27, 2002. . . .

* * *

Both the issuance of the five-year classification certificate in Houston in 2001 and the endorsement in the UAE in 2002 were necessary predicates for the Prestige's ability to sail at the time of the casualty. There is no evidence that Spain communicated with ABS or reviewed any of the certifications prior to the casualty. Plaintiff alleges that, approximately three months before the casualty, an individual who had captained the Prestige sent ABS's Houston headquarters a facsimile alerting ABS to dangerous conditions aboard the ship.

* * *

ABS argues that it is entitled under U.S. maritime law to judgment dismissing Spain's claim because U.S. law imposed no duty on it with respect to the Prestige that is enforceable by Spain. Spain, contending that it would be entitled to recover from ABS if it could prove that ABS acted recklessly in setting its classification standards and/or certifying the Prestige as meeting such standards, argues that ABS's motion must be denied.

* * *

Spain has identified no precedent for the duty it posits to avoid recklessness, and this Court is not persuaded that any such duty to coastal states attended ABS's vessel certification activities under federal maritime law. Spain's proposed rule—that a classification society owes a duty to refrain from reckless behavior to all coastal states that could foreseeably be harmed by failures of classified ships—would constitute an unwarranted expansion of the existing scope of tort liability. More importantly, by relieving shipowners of their ultimate responsibility for certified ships, such a rule would be inconsistent with the shipowner's nondelegable duty to ensure the seaworthiness of the ship, a duty that is grounded in the practical reality that the shipowner is ultimately . . . in control of the activities aboard ship. Spain's proposal would also run afoul of the intentions of the shipowners and classification societies contracting for classification services, as demonstrated by the instant certification's explicit disclaimer of any representation to a third party, and the disproportionality between the relatively small fee paid to the classification society and the potentially limitless scope of third party liability.

Spain, without citing any legal authority, argues that the "significant public consequences" of the Prestige catastrophe nonetheless warrant a different result. The Court accepts Spain's characterization of the ramifications of the Prestige casualty for the purposes of adjudicating the instant motions, and recognizes the general imperative to hold appropriate parties accountable for oil spills that cause major economic and environmental damage. However, the only question before the Court in this action is whether a classification society that performed services on behalf of a shipowner can properly be held liable to an injured coastal state on the basis of reckless certification-related conduct. The legal authorities discussed above demonstrate that it cannot; they do not distinguish between damages that are limited to private parties and damages suffered widely by the public. Accordingly, ABS is entitled to summary judgment and its motion is granted.

16. Sundance Cruises Corporation v. American Bureau of Shipping, 7 F.3d 1077 (2d Cir. 1993)

[*Eds.*—Suit by a shipowner against a classification society for breach of contract and negligence, alleging that the classification society had failed to detect serious problems with the watertight integrity of the vessel that caused the loss of the vessel.]

The district court ultimately held that law of the flag, Bahamian law, governs this dispute. Judge Knapp determined "this factor to be the most compelling because of the flag state's clear and powerful interest in the actions that are at the heart of this case." We agree. The SOLAS and Load Line certificates [issued by the classification society] were necessary for Sundance to register the ship in the Bahamas, and Sundance had freely chosen the Bahamian flag for the *Sundancer* for its own reasons of convenience.

* * *

Bahamian law confers immunity upon its agents:

> Every officer appointed under this Act, and every person appointed or authorized under this Act for any purpose of this Act, shall have immunity from suit in respect of anything done by him in good faith or admitted to be done in good faith in the exercise or performance, or in the purported exercise or performance, of any power, authority or duty conferred or imposed on him under this Act.

Bahamian Merchant Shipping Act of 1976 § 279 (the "Act").

ABS was nominated under Bahamian regulations pursuant to the Act as one of six classification societies authorized to perform surveys on behalf of the Bahamian government.

* * *

The Bahamian immunity statute does not immunize everything that a classification society may do in the course of its business. Section 279 provides immunity for "anything done * * * in good faith * * * in the exercise or performance * * * of any power, authority or duty conferred or imposed on him under [the Merchant Shipping Act]."

In the present context that immunity extends to the statutorily required SOLAS and Load Line certificates. . . .

Section 5. Discussion Notes/Questions

1. Article III of the 1992 Civil Liability Convention (CLC) **(Basic Document 3.9)** imposes liability for pollution damage caused by a ship on the owner of the ship. To determine the extent of Eastern Tankers's liability for damage caused by the *Eastern Star*, consider the following questions:

   a. Can Eastern Tankers successfully assert any of the defenses to liability stated in CLC Article III:2?

   b. Did Annam violate the provisions of UNCLOS by requiring oil tankers to traverse its coast via the Tokin Passage and to avoid the Annamese Channel?

   c. Did Annam violate international law by refusing to allow the *Eastern Star* to seek refuge in its port or in the Annamese Channel?

   d. If Annam violated international law, can Eastern Tankers avoid liability to the Annamese government pursuant to CLC Article III:3?

   e. Which of the claimants mentioned in the problem is entitled to recovery from Eastern Tankers pursuant to the CLC, and for what types of injuries can they recover? If a claimant cannot recover from Eastern Tankers, is that claimant entitled to compensation pursuant to the 1992 Fund Convention?

2. State practice is one of the law-making components of international law. But states sometimes take unilateral action in defiance of established international norms, sometimes even to change the law, either by prompting a new treaty or other international prescriptive action, or by contributing to the development of a shift in customary law. An example is found in the increasing tendency of coastal states, sometimes with catastrophic consequences, to deny refuge to damaged ships notwithstanding, first, the longstanding rule of customary international law requiring coastal states to provide places of refuge to ships in distress and, second, UNCLOS Article 18(2) which acknowledges this rule to the extent of affirming that ships engaged in innocent passage can stop and anchor insofar as that is made "necessary by *force majeure*." Are these denials of refuge a violation of international law? Or has a new custom been created? *See generally* Places of Refuge for Ships: Emerging Environmental Concerns of a Maritime Custom 3–6 (Aldo Chircop & Olof Linden eds., 2006).

What do you make of IMO Assembly Resolution A.949(23) **(Basic Document 3.14)**. Does it abrogate the customary rule of refuge? If so, does this mean that the IMO Assembly has become, in effect, an international legislature capable of modifying international law directly, without waiting for the development of new customs or the ratification of new treaties? If not, then what is the impact of this resolution?

3. The interest of coastal states in controlling the movement of oil tankers and other ships near their shores is evident from the readings. But

what of the interests of maritime nations in free navigation? Avoiding international straits and other areas within other states' EEZs or territorial waters can add significantly to the length, expense, and risks of a voyage. Examine any atlas. Do maritime states or states that receive goods from overseas have an interest in maintaining international navigational freedoms? Does the United States, for example, have an interest in the free navigation through international straits of oil tankers carrying Mideastern oil to U.S. oil refineries? Of its warships? Even if those ships are carrying potentially dangerous nuclear materials on board? Is the US likely to accede to unilateral claims of right to control navigation where that control hinders the right of innocent passage? Is any maritime nation? If unilateral claims are asserted only against maritime commerce from states too weak to protest, can the claims nevertheless create a new international rule as a result of the lack of protest? Are the US and other maritime nations more likely to view restraints on free navigation as tolerable if they have been approved by an international body like the IMO? *See generally* Stephen J. Darmody, *The Law of the Sea: A Delicate Balance for Environmental Lawyers*, 9 Nat. Resources & Env't 24 (1995).

4. The IMO Regulations on ship routeing systems and on surveys (Readings 7 and 12) were adopted pursuant to the tacit amendment/opt out procedures in the International Convention for the Safety of Life at Sea and MARPOL, respectively. Under this procedure, amendments to the conventions adopted by the appropriate IMO Committee enter into force automatically unless a stated number of states representing a high proportion of world merchant fleet tonnage explicitly rejects them. The amendments, moreover, are binding on all Convention parties which do not expressly reject them. What are the benefits of this procedure? Could a similar tacit amendment/opt out procedure be adopted for amendments to UNCLOS? Might the procedure be less acceptable in that context? Why? Why not?

5. Should Tanker Survey be deemed liable for damage caused by its negligent survey of the *Eastern Star*? If Grand Isle law extends state immunity to Tanker Survey because it is performing acts on behalf of Grand Isle, should the Annamese court respect that immunity? Is Tanker Survey protected from immunity by the 1992 Civil Liability Convention?

6. The 1992 CLC and 1992 Fund Conventions split the cost of compensating victims of oil spills between the shipping industry (i.e., tanker owners) and the oil industry (which contributes the monies that support payment of compensation under the Fund Convention). The 2003 Supplementary Fund was perceived as upsetting the balance by creating an additional compensation fund entirely supported by the oil industry. In response, the International Group of P & I Clubs created two agreements providing for shipowner reimbursement of the 1992 Fund and the 2003 Supplementary Fund for some portion of any payments made by those funds in connection with an oil spill involving a covered ship. Participation in the two agreements—the Small Tanker Oil Pollution Indemnification Agreement 2006 (STOPIA 2006) and the Tanker Oil Pollution Indemnification Agreement 2006

(TOPIA 2006) is voluntary. For a discussion, *see* Mans Jacobsson, *The International Liability and Compensation Regime for Oil Pollution from Ships—International Solutions for a Global Problem*, 32 Tul. Mar. L. J. 1, 17–19 (2007). What are the justifications for imposing the cost of oil pollution damage on shipowners? On the oil industry (cargo owners)?

7. Most international legal developments relating to oil spills have occurred in response to specific disasters. The *Torrey Canyon* disaster off the coast of Cornwall led to the adoption of the 1969 Civil Liability Convention, the 1969 International Convention Relating to Intervention on the High Seas in Cases of Oil Pollution Casualties, and the 1971 Fund Convention. The massive damage that occurred in the wake of the grounding of the supertanker *Amoco Cadiz* off the coast of France in March 1978 prompted finalization of a new oil pollution control regime, MARPOL 73/78, and led to negotiation of the International Convention on Salvage, Apr. 28, 1989, 1953 UNTS 165. In addition, it contributed to efforts to increase the amount of compensation available under the 1969 CLC and 1971 Fund Conventions. Those efforts culminated with the adoption of amendments that created the 1992 Civil Liability Convention and the 1992 Fund Convention.

In 1989, the *Exxon Valdez* oil spill in Alaska led directly to the establishment of national and international rules aimed at forcing a worldwide requirement that all large oil tankers have double hulls or their equivalent. It also prompted domestic and international efforts to improve oil pollution response capabilities, and negotiation of the 1990 International Convention on Oil Pollution Preparedness, Response, and Cooperation (OPRC) **(Basic Document 3.8)**. The *Erika* and *Prestige* disasters in Europe similarly led to an accelerated implementation of the double-hull requirement for oil tankers as well as adoption of the IMO guidelines on places of refuge and to the adoption of the 2003 Protocol establishing an International Oil Pollution Compensation Supplementary Fund, which increased the compensation available to victims of oil spills beyond the levels allowed by the 1992 Civil Liability and Fund Conventions.

8. Under UNCLOS, flag states have exclusive jurisdiction over vessels flying their flag and the responsibility to ensure that the vessels are in good condition and operated in a safe manner. But, according to the UN Secretary General, "a minority of flag states show little interest in these responsibilities." As a result, "their ships are substandard, and "through their physical condition, their operation or the activities of their crew, they fail to meet basic standards of seaworthiness, violate international rules and standards, and pose a threat to life and/or the environment." U.N. Secretary-General, *Oceans and the Law of the Sea,* para. 85, U.N. Doc. A/58/65 (March 3, 2003).

Assume that the *Eastern Star* was a substandard and unseaworthy vessel, and that a proper survey of the ship would have disclosed that fact. Does Grand Isle have an obligation to survey ships and ensure their seaworthiness? Is this an obligation of conduct (due diligence) or of result? Was Grand Isle entitled to delegate this responsibility to Tanker Survey? If so, is Grand Isle responsible to ensure that Tanker Survey performs its duties properly? Is this an obligation of conduct or of result? If Grand Isle violated any of its duties as a flag state, is it liable to Annam for the environmental damage caused by the *Eastern Star*?

Flag states usually delegate their responsibility to inspect ships to private companies. International rules adopted under the auspices of the International Maritime Organization require flag states to follow guidelines aimed at ensuring that the companies they select are reputable and operate in an effective manner. *See, e.g.*, Reading 12, Regulation 6, paragraph 3.1, *supra*. *See generally* The Code for Recognized Organizations (RO Code), IMO Resolutions MSC.349(2) & MEPCD.237(65).

9. In response to the perceived failure of flag states to ensure the seaworthiness of ships, the international community has made increasing use of inspections by port states to verify that the condition of a ship complies with international requirements. Several IMO Conventions (including SOLAS and MARPOL) authorize inspection of ships when they visit foreign ports. The effectiveness of such inspections, and the success of the Paris MOU on Port State Control, led the IMO Assembly to encourage the widespread adoption of such regional agreements. *See* IMO Assembly Resolution A.682(17) on Regional Co-operation in the Control of Ships and Discharges. To date, nine regional agreements on port state control have been adopted for the following regions: Asia and the Pacific (Tokyo MOU); Black Sea region (Black Sea MOU); Caribbean (Caribbean MOU); Europe and the north Atlantic (Paris MOU); Gulf Region (Persian Gulf and Gulf of Oman) (Riyadh MOU); Indian Ocean (Indian Ocean MOU); Latin America (Acuerdo de Viña del Mar); Mediterranean (Mediterranean MOU); West and Central Africa (Abuja MOU). The United States has established its own port state control regime.

10. Article 211(6) of UNCLOS authorizes coastal states to adopt special mandatory measures for the prevention of pollution from ships, including special navigational rules, for areas of its EEZ which, because of the "oceanographical and ecological conditions" in the area, require such measures for adequate protection of the environment and resources in those areas. Before imposing such measures, the coastal state must consult through the IMO with other concerned states, and may impose the measures following an IMO decision. Some coastal states, however, have proceeded without IMO approval and in ways that do not necessarily comply with international law. *See* Robert C. Beckman, PSSAs and Transit Passage—Australia's Pilotage System in the Torres Strait Challenges the IMO and UNCLOS, 38 Ocean Dvlpmt & Int'l L. 325, 326–27 (2007). *See generally* Glen Plant, The Relationship between International Navigation Rights and Environmental Protection: A Legal Analysis of Mandatory Ship Traffic Systems, in Competing Norms in the Law of Marine Environmental Protection (Henrik Ringbom ed., 1997).

To support such actions, the IMO Assembly has adopted Guidelines for the Identification and Designation of Particularly Sensitive Sea Areas

(PSSAs). IMO Assembly Resolution 982(24). 17 PSSAs have been designated to date, including two in the United States: the sea around the Florida Keys and the Papahānaumokuākea Marine National Monument.

11. Great progress has been made in limiting pollution damage from accidents involving oil tankers. In part, this is due to the IMO's successful phase out of single-hull oil tankers in favor of double-hull, or equivalently protected, tankers, a requirement that entered fully into force in 2015. Double-hulled tankers are far less likely to spill oil in minor accidents than are single-hulled tankers. *See, e.g., Single Hull Oil Tankers Barred from U.S. Waters,* Environment News Service (January 2, 2015). Improved inspection of ships, better training of seafarers, and enhanced navigational practices also likely play a role. As a result of these factors, ship accidents in general seem to be less frequent (at least relative to the amount of ship traffic). *See generally* B. Buzancic Primorac & J. Parunov, *Review of statistical data on ship accidents,* Maritime Technology and Engineering (Guedes, Soares & Santos, eds. 2016). In recent years, there have been relatively few significant oil spills. *See* ITOPF (International Tanker Owners Pollution Federation), Oil Tanker Spill Statistics 2017, available at www.itopf.org. This does not mean, however, that major pollution events from tanker accidents are entirely a thing of the past. *See* Gerry Mullany, *Wildlife at Risk after Fiery Tanker Disaster,* New York Times A5 (January 15, 2018).

CHAPTER SEVEN

PROTECTING NATURAL RESOURCES

■ ■ ■

In pursuit of human needs and wants, the living resources of the seas are being plundered, the grandest species are being endangered, freshwater resources are being depleted, and life-supporting ecosystems are being destroyed. Each of these developments, reflecting humanity's mounting demands upon the natural environment, represents a threat to biodiversity, to the intricately differing varieties of genes, species, and ecosystems that inhabit planet Earth. The pressures of contemporary economic and social reality, combined with increased technological ability, press the boundaries of environmental exploitation to their limits and beyond.

To some degree, the loss of biodiversity is a natural process; species extinction has always existed. But, according to the 2019 Report of the Intergovernmental Science-Policy Platform on Biodiversity and Ecosystem Service (IPBES), biodiversity is today declining at rates unprecedented in human history. The incredibly increased and accelerating rate at which humanity is decimating ecosystems and other species suggests that controls are needed—tough ones. This is especially the case with respect to the world's tropical forests, the so-called "lungs of the world"—jungles, rain forests, cloud forests, and swamp and mangrove forests. Together these forests, covering about twenty percent of the Earth's land surface, contain nearly half the world's species of plants and animals, including many from which modern crops and medicines are derived. They are, however, fast disappearing and, with them, the large percentage of biotic wealth that is stored in them.

Historically, international policies and programs designed to conserve and otherwise protect the biosphere, most of them of relatively recent origin, have foundered on the shoals of state sovereignty or, in the case of sea life, on derivations of the time-honored principle of freedom of the high seas. Invoking the Lotus doctrine of plenary state sovereignty,[1] states rely on their claimed right to pursue independent action within their jurisdictional boundaries so that the consensus needed to establish binding legal restraints becomes difficult to achieve. Under the state-centric principle of *res nullius*,[2] conflicts of interest in the global commons between

1 *See* S.S. "Lotus" (Fr. v. Turk.), 1927 PCIJ (ser. A.) No. 10, at 4.

2 Property owned by no one, but capable of being acquired through certain unilateral acts.

protective regimes and economic needs become oftentimes impossible to reconcile. Moreover, differing cultural values, as well as economic and political realities, militate against widespread compliance with agreed-upon protective measures. In addition, policing assaults upon the biosphere—as in driftnet fishing, elephant poaching, or tropical rainforest destruction—requires substantial enforcement resources, which many states do not have readily at hand. Thus, it should come as no surprise, international law and policy have so far responded to threats to biodiversity with only limited success.

Where success has been achieved, of course, the contributing factors demand to be analyzed, as they may be instructive for other settings. But given the interconnectedness and interdependence of the Earth's biosphere, fully comprehending that one state's behavior may ultimately affect the world community at large is, on final analysis, the most crucial lesson to be learned. Precisely because of its interpenetrating character, biodiversity is a source of global security; the adaptability it provides cannot be replaced by the most ingenious of synthetic alternatives. And so it seems wrong that its intrinsic values should be allowed to be overridden by the artificial boundaries of state territory or the short-term reference frames of the decision-makers within them. If we are serious about protecting and enhancing the biosphere, we must entertain at least the possibility that a vision or philosophy of sovereignty for our time must have a larger frame of reference than the state and human society alone, and that the old ideas built around the primacy of space must give way, at least in part, to perspectives that emphasize time and community. Time is a crucial factor with biodiversity; each day that goes by there is a significant loss of the Earth's biotic riches.

PROBLEM 7-1: WATER RESOURCE CONFLICTS IN THE FERTILE CRESCENT

Section 1. Facts

The Purattu River originates in the Torus Mountains of Korduene and flows southward for 1900 miles through the Middle East's Fertile Crescent before terminating in the Sabah Delta on the Persian Gulf. The Purattu is the most important source of fresh water for the three Middle Eastern countries in this historic region: Korduene, Palmyrene, and Sumer.

The Purattu emerges from a lake high in the Torus Mountains, growing in size and volume as it descends through the mountains and travels across the high plateau of southwestern Korduene. By the time the Purattu reaches Palmyrene, it is a very large river. Records kept during the 20th Century show that the river's natural flow at the Korduene/Palmyrene border averaged about 30 cubic kilometers of water per year.

The Purattu travels through Palmyrene for about 400 miles before entering Sumer. Several significant tributaries join the river in Palmyrene, so its historical flow by the time it reached the Sumer city of Hadar, just south of the Palmyrene border, was nearly 37 cubic kilometers per year. Because of Sumer's arid climate, the river picks up virtually no water on its gentle 600-mile meander through that country toward the Persian Gulf. The Purattu discharges into the Sabah Delta in southern Sumer, a vast marshland that was once larger than the Florida everglades.

People have farmed the fertile alluvial plains of the Purattu throughout recorded history and the area has been called the "cradle of civilization" because of the ancient cultures that developed on the river's banks. Palmyrene receives sufficient rainfall to support significant agricultural activities, but it depends on the river to supply irrigation water during dry periods. The Purattu supplies 20% of the water used in Palmyrene for household and industrial purposes, with 80% coming from other rivers or groundwater sources. There is little rainfall anywhere in Sumer, and its agricultural sector is completely dependent on the river. The Purattu also provides for 70% of the water Sumer consumes for industrial and household use; the rest of its water comes from aquifers.

Since 1990, the Purattu's natural flow has been altered considerably. Both Palmyrene and Sumer have built dams along the river to control seasonal flows of the river, to store water for dry periods, and to support new and expanded irrigation. These efforts have been quite successful. The use of Purattu river water for irrigation allowed Palmyrene to increase agricultural production significantly. Today, the agriculture sector accounts for 30% of Palmyrene's GNP and employs 20% of the population. Agricultural exports are Palmyrene's main source of foreign exchange. Average *per capita* income in Palmyrene has tripled over the past 20 years, due largely to the success of agricultural development efforts. In Sumer, increased irrigation has allowed agricultural production to keep pace with population growth, and reservoirs along the river have provided a stable water source for growing cities near the river.

Palmyrene's activities have reduced the amount of water that reaches Sumer by 50% from historical levels, and Sumer itself withdraws much more water than previously from the river. By the time the Purratu discharges into the Sabah Delta, the flow rate is a mere 20% of what it was as recently as 1990. As a result, the Delta's marshes have shrunk to less than a third of their former size, several species of birds are endangered, and the Sumer river otter is all but extinct. Additionally, the water entering the marsh is increasingly polluted from agricultural runoff in Palmyrene and Sumer, and the marsh is no longer sufficiently large to filter the water before it enters the Persian Gulf. Consequently, productivity in the fisheries in the Gulf is falling. Furthermore, several species of migratory birds that stop at the marsh on their journey between

Africa and Asia are dying in large numbers due to the lack of water and food, and the size of the migrating flocks is noticeably diminished.

Last year, a new threat to the river emerged when Korduene announced plans to build a series of 10 dams and reservoirs on the Purattu River and its tributaries in southern Korduene. The dams will provide hydroelectric power to towns and villages in the region. Some of the water stored in the reservoirs will be used locally, but much of it will be delivered via a planned system of canals, tunnels, and pipelines (the "Korduene Aqueduct") to farms and communities in impoverished arid regions of southeastern Korduene where the government plans to expand agricultural production to support economic development.

Korduene has informed Palmyrene and Sumer of its plans. It has told them that after the project is completed there will be a 90% decline in the flow of the Purattu while the reservoirs are being filled. However, Korduene has guaranteed Palymrene an average annual flow of 10 cubic kilometers on the Purattu, about 1/3 of the historical average, once the reservoirs are filled. It has made no promises to Sumer, indicating that the Purattu's flow into Sumer is a matter for Sumer and Palmyrene to determine.

Korduene, Palmyrene, and Sumer also share the Assyrian Aquifer, an extensive, relatively shallow water table aquifer located beneath the dry plains of southeastern Korduene, northeastern Palmyrene, and northwestern Sumer. It provides drinking and irrigation water for most of the communities in the dry regions of Korduene, Palmyrene, and Sumer that are not located near the Purattu River or its tributaries. As these regions have developed and grown in population, utilization of the aquifer has increased in all three countries, but especially in Sumer. As withdrawals from the aquifer have increased, there have been reports of wells running dry in Korduene and Palmyrene. In addition, some springs and streams that run from the highlands of east Palmyrene to the Purattu river system have dried up, suggesting a previously unsuspected link between the Assyrian Aquifer and the Purattu. The Assyrian is recharged exclusively from rainfall and snowmelt in the mountains of eastern Korduene. Scientists estimate that the annual recharge of the aquifer is only about 80% of current annual withdrawals.

Palmyrene has expressed outrage over Korduene's dam-building plans, contending that the proposed reduction in the volume of water reaching Palmyrene will disrupt Palmyrene's established uses of the Purattu and devastate Palmyrene's agricultural sector. A letter from Palmyrene's president to Korduene's president stated that "completion of the planned project would be a *causus belli*."

Sumer, for its part, has also protested Korduene's plans, and has asked Palmyrene to guarantee that the volume of water in the Purattu where it crosses into Sumer will be maintained at least at current levels. Sumer points out that increasing demands on the river in Sumer, combined with the diminished annual flow, mean that the Sabah Delta, one of the world's great wetlands, is slowly drying out and dying as it receives less and less water each year. Moreover, it says, a diminution in river flows would seriously imperil the health and well-being of its citizens, 90% of whom depend on river water for daily needs and lack access to any other water source.

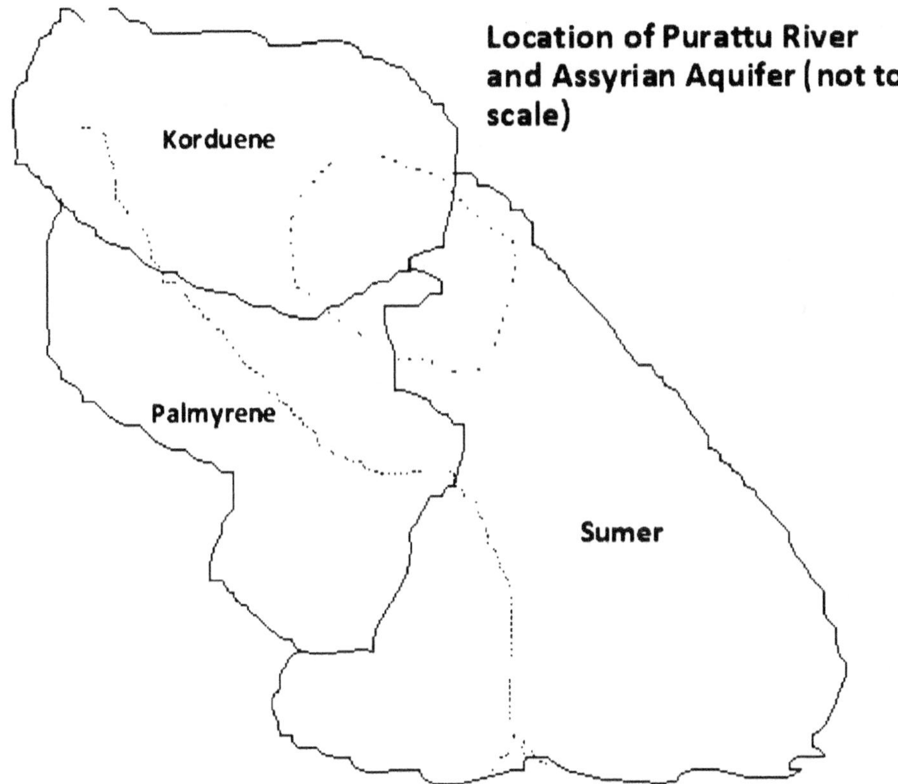

A dispute is also brewing over the Assyrian Aquifer. Sumer has announced plans to turn the oasis town of Kish into an upscale resort city. Kish was built at the site of a natural spring of the Assyrian Aquifer. The town is picturesque, and the desert landscapes around it are spectacular and filled with ancient archaeological sites. Sumer is convinced that Kish can become a major tourist destination, and it has lined up several major international resort companies to build hotels and golf courses around Kish. It anticipates that it will need to double the amount of water it withdraws from the Assyrian Aquifer to support this development. Palmyrene and Korduene have expressed "grave concern" over the impact of this plan on the aquifer.

These two disputes have been escalating among the three countries for several months, and the international community is concerned about the possibility of military conflict in the region. The World Bank recently announced that it would not provide any financing for Korduene's project on the Purattu until Korduene reaches an agreement with Palmyrene and Sumer on the use of the river. Similarly, the Multilateral Investment Guarantee Agency (MIGA), a member of the World Bank Group, has informed Sumer that it will not insure any private investments in Kish unless the three countries reach an agreement on extractions from the Assyrian Aquifer. Without support from the World Bank and MIGA, neither project can move forward.

Korduene, Palmyrene, and Sumer have agreed to convene a summit to discuss their differences with the aim of reaching some sort of formal arrangement concerning the use of the waters of the Purattu River and the Assyrian Aquifer. In pre-summit communiques, each country has stated its position as follows: Palmyrene insists that its existing uses of the river and aquifer are, and must be, absolutely protected against any development plans in the other countries that might disrupt those uses. Sumer believes that it has a sovereign right to utilize aquifers on its territory without interference from other states. It also claims that it is entitled to a resumption of the full natural flow of the Purattu River in order to ensure adequate water resources to meet its growing national needs and to restore the Sabah Delta. Korduene contends that it has an absolute right to control its water resources, which include all waters originating in Korduene, including the waters of the Purattu River and Assyrian Aquifer. However, Korduene is prepared to guarantee Sumer and Palmyrene a fixed allocation of water each year, albeit at a significantly lower level than the amount they use or receive at present.

All three countries are members of the United Nations. They all are signatories to the UN Convention on the Law of Non-Navigational Uses of International Watercourses **(Basic Document 3.18)**, although none of them has ratified that treaty.

Section 2. Questions Presented

1. What are the legal rights of Korduene, Palmyrene, and Sumer with respect to the Purattu River and the Assyrian Aquifer?

2. What elements should be included in any international agreement(s) reached concerning the utilization and exploitation of these water resources?

Section 3. Assignments

A. Reading Assignment

Study the Readings presented in Section 4, *infra*, and the Discussion Notes/Questions that follow.

B. Recommended Writing Assignments

Prepare (1) a comprehensive, logically sequenced, and *argumentative* brief in the form of an outline of the primary and subsidiary *legal* issues that are relevant to the Korduene-Palmyrene-Sumer dispute; and (2) a comprehensive and logically sequenced outline of the key elements you would include in a treaty aimed at resolving the Korduene-Palmyrene-Sumer water dispute. Retain copies of both the issue and elements outlines for class discussion.

C. Recommended Oral Assignment

Assume you are a negotiator for Korduene, Palmyrene, or Sumer (as designated by your instructor); then, relying upon the Readings (and your issue-outline if prepared), present a 15–20 minute oral argument of your government's likely positions at the negotiations, including its position on the legal situation as well as on the nature and content of any agreement(s) that might be reached concerning the Purattu Riveror the Assyrian Aquifer.

D. Recommended Reflective Assignment

Consider (and recommend) alternative norms, institutions, and/or procedures that you believe might do better than existing world order arrangements to contend with situations of the kind posed by this problem. In so doing, but without insisting upon *immediate* feasibility, identify the particular transition steps that would be needed to make your alternatives a reality.

Section 4. Readings

1. Malin Falkenmark, Foreword, The World's Water 2008–2009: The Biennial Report on Freshwater Resources (Peter H. Gleick ed., 2009)

When it comes to freshwater—the bloodstream of both the biosphere and the social sphere—the world is on the threshold to a new era. Humanity's profound dependence on freshwater makes basic water security a necessary condition for improving living conditions, securing food production to eradicate hunger, and providing employment and income to eliminate poverty.

Looking at countries from the perspective of water security reveals some important differences. Industrial countries have already tackled their hydroclimatic vulnerability, and have come far in expanding economic development and improving the quality of life for their populations. Emerging economies, on the other hand, remain hampered by water-related challenges such as flooding, drought, and severe water pollution. And the poorest economies in semi-arid climates still remain hostage to water problems and suffer large-scale poverty, disease, and uncurbed population growth.

To make matters worse, we now see evidence signaling the end of the era of easy access to freshwater. In many places, the perception of water security is starting to dissolve: overpumped aquifers under breadbasket regions of the world constitute economic "bubbles" ready to burst; excessive water consumption by irrigation is depleting rivers and deltas; neglect of pollutants in return flows from water use is contaminating potential raw water sources; and some city water-supply systems have started to crumble because of neglect of critical maintenance.

2. Stephen C. McCaffrey, Introduction: Politics and Sovereignty Over Transboundary Groundwater, Panel Discussion Entitled If Water Respects No Political Boundary, Does Politics Respect Transboundary Waters?, 102 Am. Soc'y Int'l L. Proc. 353, 353 (2008)

While much has been made of the prospect of global water shortages, what is perhaps not so well known is that most of the world's fresh water is shared by two or more states. There are more than 260 international drainage basins, which account for about 60 percent of global river flows. This figure does not include an increasingly important form of this resource, groundwater, much of which also straddles international boundaries. Perhaps this is in part what motivated UN Secretary-General Ban Ki-moon to say, at the World Economic Forum in Davos, Switzerland, in January of this year: "As the global economy grows, so will its thirst . . . many more conflicts lie over the horizon," and "too often, where we need water, we find guns."

3. Joseph W. Dellapenna, International Water Law in a Climate of Disruption, 17 Mich. St. J. Int'l L. 43, 68–71, 72–75 (2008)

A rich body of customary law regarding internationally shared fresh water has emerged, largely in the last century or so. Historically, the process of claim and counterclaim relating to internationally shared fresh waters focused on surface waters. The application of the resulting norms to international aquifers is a more recent development. . . .

There is one point on which all states agree: Only riparian states—states across which, or along which, a river flows—have any legal right, absent agreement, to use the water of a river, lake, or other surface source. Beyond that point, however, the patterns of international claim and counterclaim initially diverged sharply according to the riparian status of the state making the claim. The uppermost riparian state always initially claims "absolute territorial sovereignty"—often called the Harmon Doctrine—claiming the right to do whatever it chooses with the water regardless of its effect on other riparian states. Downstream states generally open by claiming a right to the "absolute integrity of the watercourse"—a claim that upper riparian states can do nothing that affects the quantity or quality of water that flows down the watercourse. The utter incompatibility of such claims guarantees that neither claim will prevail in the end, although the process of negotiating or otherwise resolving the dispute embodied in these claims might require decades. The usual solution is found in a concept of restricted sovereignty that goes by the name "equitable utilization." That rule assures each state a "fair" share of the available water, a right that is sometimes expressed as an obligation not to inflict unreasonable injury on water users in another state.

Documenting the process of claim and counterclaim that converts a convenient practice into a customary rule of law is easy for internationally shared waters. There are today literally hundreds of treaties specifying the terms of such sharing and no treaties embracing claims of either absolute sovereignty or absolute integrity. . . . [N]early all commentators conclude that the customary rule of equitable utilization rests on the now nearly innumerable treaties regarding internationally shared waters.

The International Law Association endorsed the principle of equitable utilization in the Helsinki Rules on the Uses of the Waters of International Rivers in 1966 and in the Berlin Rules on Water Resources in 2004 **[Basic Document 3.19]**, while the U.N. General Assembly endorsed the same principle by a vote of 103 to 3 (with twenty-seven declared abstentions) when it approved the U.N. Convention on the Law of Non-Navigational Uses of International Watercourses in 1997 **[Basic Document 3.18]**. No wonder the International Court of Justice felt able to endorse equitable utilization as the rule of customary international law in 1997.[3] . . .

4. Convention on the Law of the Non-Navigational Uses of International Watercourses, arts. 5–7, May 21, 1997, 2015 UKTS 5 (Basic Document 3.18)

Article 5

Equitable and reasonable utilization and participation

1. Watercourse States shall in their respective territories utilize an international watercourse in an equitable and reasonable manner. In particular, an international watercourse shall be used and developed by watercourse States with a view to attaining optimal and sustainable utilization thereof and benefits therefrom, taking into account the interests

[3] *See* The Gabcikovo-Nagymaros Project (Hungary v. Slovakia), 1997 I.C.J. No. 92, ¶¶ 78, 85. . . .

of the watercourse States concerned, consistent with adequate protection of the watercourse.

2. Watercourse States shall participate in the use, development and protection of an international watercourse in an equitable and reasonable manner. Such participation includes both the right to utilize the watercourse and the duty to cooperate in the protection and development thereof, as provided in the present Convention.

Article 6

Factors relevant to equitable and reasonable utilization

1. Utilization of an international watercourse in an equitable and reasonable manner within the meaning of article 5 requires taking into account all relevant factors and circumstances, including:

(a) Geographic, hydrographic, hydrological, climatic, ecological and other factors of a natural character;

(b) The social and economic needs of the watercourse States concerned;

(c) The population dependent on the watercourse in each watercourse State;

(d) The effects of the use or uses of the watercourses in one watercourse State on other watercourse States;

(e) Existing and potential uses of the watercourse;

(f) Conservation, protection, development and economy of use of the water resources of the watercourse and the costs of measures taken to that effect;

(g) The availability of alternatives, of comparable value, to a particular planned or existing use.

2. In the application of article 5 or paragraph 1 of this article, watercourse States concerned shall, when the need arises, enter into consultations in a spirit of cooperation.

3. The weight to be given to each factor is to be determined by its importance in comparison with that of other relevant factors. In determining what is a reasonable and equitable use, all relevant factors are to be considered together and a conclusion reached on the basis of the whole.

Article 7

Obligation not to cause significant harm

1. Watercourse States shall, in utilizing an international watercourse in their territories, take all appropriate measures to prevent the causing of significant harm to other watercourse States.

2. Where significant harm nevertheless is caused to another watercourse State, the States whose use causes such harm shall, in the absence of agreement to such use, take all appropriate measures, having due regard for the provisions of articles 5 and 6, in consultation with the affected State, to eliminate or mitigate such harm and, where appropriate, to discuss the question of compensation.

5. Joseph W. Dellapenna, International Water Law in a Climate of Disruption, 17 Mich. St. J. Int'l L. 43, 68–71, 72–75 (2008)

[*Eds.* The U.N. Convention on the Law of Non-Navigational Uses of International Watercourses was based upon a set of Draft Articles prepared by the International Law Commission. One of the difficult issues encountered by the International Law Commission and the United Nations General Assembly was reconciling a rule of reasonable and equitable use with the 'no harm' principle.]

Article 5 of the Commission's Draft Articles on the Law of Non-Navigational Uses of International Watercourses requires watercourse states to utilize an international watercourse in an equitable and reasonable manner with a view to attaining optimal utilization and benefits consistent with adequate protection in the watercourse. Article 5 also provides that watercourse states shall participate in the use, development, and protection of an international watercourse in an equitable and reasonable manner. The right to participate includes both the right to utilize the watercourse and the duty to cooperate in its protection and development.

The Commission's first reading of the Draft Articles also embraced a strong version of a "no harm rule": "Watercourse States shall utilize an international watercourse in such a way as not to cause appreciable harm to other watercourse States." This proposition flatly contradicted the rule of equitable utilization and therefore generated considerable controversy. The Commission therefore adopted a completely rewritten Article 7 in 1994 that required watercourse states to exercise due diligence in utilizing an international watercourse so as not to cause significant harm to other watercourse states. The meaning of the new Article 7 was not altogether clear. The problem became moot once the U.N. General Assembly converted the Draft Articles into a U.N. Convention. The Assembly, while making no material change to Article 5, approved a new Article 7 that made clear the subordination of the "no harm" rule to the rule of equitable utilization. Thus, while Article 7 requires watercourse states, in utilizing an international watercourse, to "take all appropriate measures to prevent the causing of significant harm to other watercourse States," if significant harm nevertheless is caused to another watercourse state, "the States whose use causes such harm shall, in the absence of agreement to such use, take all appropriate measures, having due regard for the provisions of

Articles 5 and 6, in consultation with the affected State, to eliminate or mitigate such harm and, where appropriate, to discuss the question of compensation." The duty to take "all appropriate measures" incorporates the relative standard of "due diligence," and the duty not to cause harm is also expressly limited in subsection (2) by "due regard for the provisions of Articles 5 and 6"—the articles on equitable utilization. The rule of equitable utilization seems unquestionably to be the primary rule with any obligation to prevent harm being subordinated to that primary rule.

* * *

"Equitable utilization" does not require "equality of use"—a confusion that arises in some non-common law countries that lack the notion of "equity" in its common law sense. "Equity" means fairness considering the water needs of the several riparian states and their ability to use the water efficiently. The merest perusal of the standards for equitable utilization demonstrates that while equal access is guaranteed, equal shares are not. Thus when each interested state agrees to the rule of equitable utilization, they still dispute the shares. The rule of equitable utilization is too general and too vague to be applied without the interested states negotiating the details in what is only an obligation of fairness. . . .

6. Hilal Elver, Palestinian/Israeli Water Conflict and Implementation of International Water Law Principles, 28 Hastings Int'l & Comp. L. Rev. 421, 435–37, 441–43 (2005)

The principle of equitable utilization . . . does not imply that each state should receive equal rights, but rather that all states share sovereignty over the water resource, and their interest must be reasonably balanced and upheld according to a range of factors. . . .

. . . The relative weight of the factors depends on the circumstances and the judgments of an interpreter. The content of the list, as a definition of the reasonableness of shared water use, has been criticized widely by various scholars and states. One criticism is, for instance, that the principle of equitable use does not a priori preclude states from sacrificing satisfaction of vital human needs for the sake of ill-fated plans to make deserts bloom.

Moreover, an emphasis on the social and economic needs of states can operate as a very unjust factor if the riparian countries are not at equal levels of development, such as is the case with respect to Israel and Palestine. Does Israel deserve more per capita and overall water use rights than the Palestinians, because they are economically wealthier than Palestinians?

Finally, equitable utilization principle was not developed with any broader consideration of the importance of the environmental protection of water resources. It affords an insufficient basis for measurement of more comprehensive environmental protection.

* * *

Due to the difficulty of agreeing upon the application of "equitable utilization," criteria that are generally vague and often contradictory, some have suggested allocation principles based on human needs rather than on legal rights. Based on an influential study of treaties relating to international water resources, the conclusion is reached that in practice, states almost never rely on broad conceptual ideas, and do not invoke extreme views of absolute sovereignty. Many of the treaties simply divide water equally between riparians. In arid regions, the assessors often shift quietly to a needs-based criterion for water allocations, as measured by some mutually agreeable parameter such as irrigable land or population, or the requirements of specific projects. . . .

Advocates of the need-based equity approach propose the consideration of new sources such as recycled waste-water or out-of-basin water allocations, made with the help of technological tools. The need-based approach also suggests efficiency measures to decrease demand or reduce population growth. However, given the nationalistic dimension of water projects, the domination of agricultural policy, asymmetrical power between the parties, and regional competition over already scarce water resources, the calculation of acceptable and reasonable "needs" of aspiring users is often highly problematic.

7. The Indus Waters Kishenganga Arbitration (Pakistan v. India), Partial Award (Perm. Ct. Arb., 18 Feb. 2013)

[*Eds.* The dispute concerned India's plans to build a hydroelectric power plant on a transboundary river (known as the Kishenganga in India and the Neelum in Pakistan). The dispute was governed primarily by the Indus Waters Treaty of 1960, and the Court concluded that the Treaty authorized India to build a hydroelectric power facility on the river. But the Court also concluded that India was required to guarantee a minimal flow of water to Pakistan. To support that conclusion, it relied in part on customary international law.]

447. India's duty to ensure that a minimum flow reaches Pakistan also stems from the Treaty's interpretation in light of customary international law. . . .

448. Well before the Treaty was negotiated, a foundational principle of customary international environmental law had already been enunciated in the Trail Smelter arbitration. There, the Tribunal held that

> no State has the right to use or permit the use of its territory in such a manner as to cause injury by fumes in or to the territory of another or the properties or persons therein, when the case is of

serious consequence and the injury is established by clear and convincing evidence.

A broader restatement of the duty to avoid transboundary harm is embodied in Principle 21 of the 1972 Stockholm Declaration, pursuant to which States, when exploiting natural resources, must "ensure that activities within their jurisdiction or control do not cause damage to the environment of other States or of areas beyond the limits of national jurisdiction."

449. There is no doubt that States are required under contemporary customary international law to take environmental protection into consideration when planning and developing projects that may cause injury to a bordering State. Since the time of Trail Smelter, a series of international conventions, declarations and judicial and arbitral decisions have addressed the need to manage natural resources in a sustainable manner. In particular, the International Court of Justice expounded upon the principle of "sustainable development" in Gabčíkovo-Nagymaros, referring to the "need to reconcile economic development with protection of the environment."

450. Applied to large-scale construction projects, the principle of sustainable development translates, as the International Court of Justice recently put it in Pulp Mills, into "a requirement under general international law to undertake an environmental impact assessment where there is a risk that the proposed industrial activity may have a significant adverse impact in a transboundary context, in particular, on a shared resource." The International Court of Justice affirmed that "due diligence, and the duty of vigilance and prevention which it implies, would not be considered to have been exercised, if a party planning works liable to affect the regime of the river or the quality of its waters did not undertake an environmental impact assessment on the potential effects of such works." Finally, the International Court of Justice emphasized that such duties of due diligence, vigilance and prevention continue "once operations have started and, where necessary, throughout the life of the project."

451. Similarly, this Court recalls the acknowledgement by the Tribunal in the Iron Rhine arbitration of the "principle of general international law" that States have "a duty to prevent, or at least mitigate" significant harm to the environment when pursuing large-scale construction activities. As the Iron Rhine Tribunal determined, this principle "applies not only in autonomous activities but also in activities undertaken in implementation of specific treaties, such as, it may be said, the present Treaty.

452. It is established that principles of international environmental law must be taken into account even when (unlike the present case)

interpreting treaties concluded before the development of that body of law. The Iron Rhine Tribunal applied concepts of customary international environmental law to treaties dating back to the mid-nineteenth century, when principles of environmental protection were rarely if ever considered in international agreements and did not form any part of customary international law. Similarly, the International Court of Justice in Gabčíkovo-Nagymaros ruled that, whenever necessary for the application of a treaty, "new norms have to be taken into consideration, and . . . new standards given proper weight." It is therefore incumbent upon this Court to interpret and apply this 1960 Treaty in light of the customary international principles for the protection of the environment in force today.

[The Court ordered the parties to provide further evidence on what the required minimal flow should be.]

8. The Indus Waters Kishenganga Arbitration (Pakistan v. India), Final Award (Perm. Ct. Arb., 20 Dec. 2013)

105. . . . [T]he effects of the [proposed hydropower project] on the environment and on power generation by Pakistan . . . both suggest the need for a higher minimum flow than India proposes . . . . . Taking environmental considerations alone, in the appreciation of the Court, would appear to suggest releasing a flow of some 12 cumecs[4] downstream of the [project] at all times. . . . [And, as determined in the Partial Award, the treaty must be interpreted in light of the customary law obligation to take environmental considerations into account.]

110. [However,] [a]s India has recalled to the Court, recourse to customary international law is conditioned by Paragraph 29 of Annexure G to the Indus Waters Treaty, which provides as follows:

> Except as the Parties may otherwise agree, the law to be applied by the Court shall be this Treaty and, whenever necessary for its interpretation or application, but only to the extent necessary for that purpose, the following in the order in which they are listed:
>
> (a) International conventions establishing rules which are expressly recognized by the Parties.
>
> (b) Customary international law.

111. [Through Paragraph 29, the Indus Waters Treaty] expressly limits the extent to which the Court may have recourse to, and apply, sources of law beyond the Treaty itself.

112. As the Court held in its *Partial Award*, "States have 'a duty to prevent, or at least mitigate' significant harm to the environment when pursuing large-scale construction activities.' In light of this duty, the Court

4 *Eds.* A "cumec" is a unit of flow equal to one cubic meter of water per second.

has no difficulty concluding that the requirement of an environmental flow (without prejudice to the level of such flow) is necessary in the application of the Treaty. At the same time, the Court does not consider it appropriate, and certainly not "necessary," for it to adopt a precautionary approach and assume the role of policymaker in determining the balance between acceptable environmental change and other priorities, or to permit environmental considerations to override the balance of other rights and obligations expressly identified in the Treaty—in particular the entitlement of India to divert the waters of a tributary of the Jhelum. The Court's authority is more limited and extends only to mitigating significant harm. Beyond that point, prescription by the Court is not only unnecessary, it is prohibited by the Treaty. If customary international law were applied not to circumscribe, but to negate rights expressly granted in the Treaty, this would no longer be *"interpretation or application" of* the Treaty but the substitution of customary law *in place of* the Treaty. . . .

113. [Noting that "a flow of 12 cumecs would be appropriate" if "environmental considerations were the sole consideration," the Court emphasized that environmental concerns are not the only factor to be considered. India's right to develop a power plant and operate it effectively were also significant considerations.]

115. The Court therefore concludes that a minimum flow criterion of 9 cumecs is consistent with Pakistan's analysis of environmental flows, given the need to balance power generation with environmental and other downstream uses, and, based on India's data, would maintain the natural flow regime in the most severe winter conditions.

9. Gabriel E. Eckstein, Commentary on the U.N. International Law Commission's Draft Articles on the Law of Transboundary Aquifers, 18 Colo. J. Int'l Envtl. L. & Pol'y 537, 537–38, 553–56, 560–68, 570–73 (2007)

Ground water is the most extracted natural resource in the world. It provides more than half of humanity's freshwater for everyday uses such as drinking, cooking, and hygiene, as well as twenty percent of irrigated agriculture. Despite our increasing reliance, ground water resources have long been the neglected stepchild of international water law; regulation and management of and information about ground water resources are sorely lacking, especially in the international context. Presently, there is no international agreement squarely addressing ground water resources that traverse an international boundary. Moreover, there is only one treaty in the entire world pertaining to the management of a transboundary aquifer, and few nations possess the relevant technical information necessary to enter into such agreements. The result is overexploitation and degradation of many of the world's transboundary aquifers, and considerable harmful impacts on border communities, economies, and ecosystems dependent on transboundary ground water resources.

Recently, the United Nations International Law Commission embarked on an effort to address this shortcoming and to consider the international law applicable to transboundary aquifers. This undertaking follows and builds on the Commission's prior work on international watercourses, which culminated in the 1997 U.N. Convention on the Non-Navigational Uses of International Watercourses **[Basic Document 3.18]**. It also builds on the work of other organizations, including that of the International Law Association and its Helsinki, Seoul, and Berlin Rules. . . .

* * *

Use of the term "transboundary" in the [Draft Articles on the Law of Transboundary Aquifers **(Basic Document 3.20)**] is intentional and of considerable consequence. Subparagraph (c) of Article 2 provides that " 'transboundary aquifer' or 'transboundary aquifer system' means, respectively, an aquifer or aquifer system, parts of which are situated in different States." Under the original mandate from the UNILC, the Special Rapporteur was tasked with addressing ground water resources within the rubric of "shared natural resources." Following the submission of his First Report, various Members of the UNILC and its parent body, the Sixth Committee of the United Nations expressed considerable doubt about the use of the term "shared." The term "shared" intimates collective ownership and suggests that the resource at issue may be subject to common or equal ownership and potentially to the common heritage of humankind. Referring to the UN General Assembly Resolution 1803 (XVII) on "Permanent Sovereignty over Natural Resources" **[Basic Document 1.20]** some UNILC and Sixth Committee Members voiced their opposition to the possibility that a transboundary aquifer could be collectively owned. Given such sensitivities, and with the support of the UNILC, the Special Rapporteur amended the focus of his work to "transboundary" ground water resources.

* * *

. . . [An] aquifer is international [for purposes of the Watercourse Convention] where it is "part of a system where groundwater interacts with surface water that is at some point intersected by a boundary." Thus, a purely domestic aquifer hydraulically linked to a river traversing an international political boundary would constitute an international aquifer, or an aquifer that is a part of an international watercourse. . . . However, such an aquifer would not fulfill the characteristics of a transboundary aquifer for the purposes of the present Draft Articles. The Special Rapporteur defines a "transboundary" aquifer as a "groundwater body that is intersected by a boundary itself." The defining criterion for this category is that the aquifer must traverse an international political boundary to fall under the scope of the Draft Articles. . . .

Some aquifers, however, could fall under both the Watercourse Convention and the present Draft Articles. This duality would occur where a transboundary aquifer or aquifer system has a hydraulic relationship with a transboundary river. In such a case, the transboundary nature of the river, coupled with the river's hydraulic relationship with the aquifer, would make it subject to the Watercourse Convention. However, the aquifer's transboundary character would also subject it to the present Draft Articles. The dual application of the two, conceivably, could create conflicting rights and obligations. . . . If the Draft Articles develop into a binding international instrument, the new treaty and the Watercourse Convention would have to be harmonized or a process would have to be developed to determine which instrument applies.

* * *

[Thus,] not all transboundary aquifers can be classified as international aquifers, and not all international aquifers constitute transboundary aquifers. The key is determining whether or not the aquifer at issue traverses an international political boundary. From a practical perspective, making such a determination presents a much more difficult task than making a similar determination for a river. The very fact that aquifers are hidden from sight requires more sophisticated approaches that rely on various technologies and methodologies including well drilling, core sampling, isotope tracing, conceptual modeling, and other science-based tactics. Such assessments are essential for determining which set of international norms govern the resource. Accordingly, as noted above, the present set of definitions has a strong foundation in the science of water. The consequence, though, is that scientific research and understanding becomes critical for the proper application of the Draft Articles.

* * *

Throughout much of the debate leading to the Draft Articles, numerous Members of the UNILC and of the Sixth Committee opined that permanent sovereignty over natural resources was central to the subject matter and must be recognized in the Draft Articles. . . . Still, others doubted whether there was any role for the principle of sovereignty given that if transboundary aquifers were recognized as shared natural resources, no aquifer State could rightly claim permanent sovereignty over such resources. Moreover, they contended that it was highly unlikely that the principle of sovereignty would be undermined or diminished even if excluded from the Draft Articles.

In the end, those arguing for an explicit recognition of sovereignty in a separate article succeeded in their objective, at least in form. Draft Article

3 provides that: "Each aquifer State has sovereignty over the portion of a transboundary aquifer or aquifer system located within its territory. It shall exercise its sovereignty in accordance with the present draft articles." Careful scrutiny, though, suggests that some measure of compromise also was achieved. The first sentence of Draft Article 3 certainly comports with traditional notions of sovereignty over natural resources. The second sentence, however, tempers that position in that it explicitly recognizes that sovereignty is not absolute and that aquifer States "shall" moderate their rights to ensure that their actions adhere to the requirements of the Draft Articles. In essence, States that agree to the terms of the Draft Articles relinquish some measure of sovereignty to the extent that they give up their sovereign right to act contrary to the Draft Articles.

Although innocuous in appearance, this latter language ultimately may strengthen the position of those who argued for a limited role for sovereignty in the Draft Articles. . . . [T]he principles contained in the Draft Articles, such as equitable and reasonable utilization, no significant harm, exchange of data, monitoring, and others clearly place considerable restrictions and obligations on what aquifer States can do with regard to the utilization of a transboundary aquifer. These obligations implicitly, if not explicitly, prevent aquifer States from sustaining claims of absolute sovereignty.

* * *

. . . Article 4 of the Draft Articles provides that "Aquifer States shall utilize a transboundary aquifer or aquifer system according to the principle of equitable and reasonable utilization." It further provides in subparagraph (a) that aquifer States "shall utilize the transboundary aquifer or aquifer system in a manner that is consistent with the equitable and reasonable accrual of benefits therefrom to the aquifer States concerned."

In substance, the principle of equitable and reasonable utilization is a utilitarian concept employing a cost-benefit analysis that attempts to maximize the beneficial uses of limited water resources while minimizing the burdens. . . .

* * *

. . . [T]he principle of equitable and reasonable utilization is also grounded in the notion that transboundary resources are shared, meaning that the two—or more—countries in whose territories the aquifer lays [*sic*] agree that they must allocate the use of the waters of the aquifer. This notion is derived from the objective of equity, which requires aquifer States to fairly distribute the waters of an aquifer or its benefits. Conceivably, fairness and equity might compel a more developed aquifer State to allot a greater percentage of the waters of a transboundary aquifer to a lesser developed aquifer State, even where the majority of the aquifer lies underneath the more developed State. Such possibilities, however, were at the core of objections to the notion of "shared natural resources," as discussed above. When considering ground water resources, many states are reluctant to accept the notion that natural resources could be divided in relation to equity rather than geography, or worse, subject to common ownership. Of particular note, this concern was observed during the development of the Watercourse Convention. Accordingly, given the degree to which many states asserted claims to sovereignty over underground natural resources, it is remarkable that the principle of equitable and reasonable utilization of Draft Article 4 found consensus among the Members of the UNILC.

Sub-paragraph (b) is noteworthy in that equitable and reasonable utilization is defined, in part, through the maximization of "the long-term benefits derived from the use of water" of an aquifer. This provision recognizes two important facts about aquifers: that by definition, a non-recharging aquifer is a non-renewable resource; and that a recharging aquifer could become non-renewable if overexploited. In so recognizing, the provision acknowledges the principle of sustainable utilization as tailored to the characteristics and potential benefits of the resource. . . .

The final two sub-paragraphs of Draft Article 4 are particularly significant to the extent that they are novel enhancements of the principle of equitable and reasonable utilization. The first one—sub-paragraph (c)—requires that aquifer States "establish individually or jointly an overall utilization plan, taking into account present and future needs of, and alternative water sources for, the aquifer States," and is unique in that it mandates the development of a long-term strategy for the equitable and reasonable utilization of transboundary aquifers. . . . [I]t is a rather progressive obligation in that many countries, including those in the developed world, have rarely undertaken such planning. Nevertheless, if aquifer States truly adopt such a commitment, it could result in considerable benefits in terms of managing the resource for present and future needs.

Sub-paragraph (d) of the Draft Article, however, is possibly more novel than Sub-paragraph (c) by mandating that aquifer States "shall not utilize a recharging transboundary aquifer or aquifer system at a level that would prevent continuance of its effective functioning." In effect, this provision recognizes the unique characteristic of aquifers generally, and recharging aquifers specifically, as dynamic but fragile mechanisms for transporting, storing, and processing water. The modification or removal of any segment of the mechanism—such as a reduction in recharge or overexploitation of the aquifer, both of which could reduce water flow and possibly drain the aquifer, as well as pollution of the aquifer or removal of the aquifer matrix (e.g., for its mineral content)—could have considerable consequences to the effective functioning of the aquifer.

10. Int'l Law Comm'n, Draft Articles on the Law of Transboundary Aquifers, art. 4, Report on the Work of its Sixty-Sixth Session, U.N. Doc. A/63/10, at 4 (2008) (Basic Document 3.20)

Article 4. Equitable and reasonable utilization

Aquifer States shall utilize transboundary aquifers or aquifer systems according to the principle of equitable and reasonable utilization, as follows:

(a) they shall utilize transboundary aquifers or aquifer systems in a manner that is consistent with the equitable and reasonable accrual of benefits therefrom to the aquifer States concerned;

(b) they shall aim at maximizing the long-term benefits derived from the use of water contained therein;

(c) they shall establish individually or jointly a comprehensive utilization plan, taking into account present and future needs of, and alternative water sources for, the aquifer States; and

(d) they shall not utilize a recharging transboundary aquifer or aquifer system at a level that would prevent continuance of its effective functioning.

11. Jonathan Lautze & Mark Giordano, Equity in Transboundary Water Law: Valuable Paradigm or Merely Semantics?, 17 Colo. J. Int'l Envtl. L & Pol'y 89, 90–1, 94–5, 98, 110–11 (2006)

Enshrined in the 1966 Helsinki Rules on the Uses of the Waters of International Rivers (1966 Helsinki Rules) and the United Nation's 1997 Convention on the Non-Navigational Uses of International Watercourses (IWC) **[Basic Document 3.18]**, equity is now one of the most frequently applied concepts in transboundary water agreements, particularly as related to water allocation. Despite its importance in academic debates and treaty texts, the actual impact of equity on transboundary water treaties remains a subject of dispute. While all sides admit that equitable language in international water agreements contains high levels of ambiguity, some observers nevertheless assert that application of the IWC provides a basis for negotiation and facilitates interstate cooperation and communication. For example, Stephen McCaffrey[5] contends that the IWC's application contributes to equitable and sustainable use of international waterways and works to preserve ecosystems. Others, however, are not so optimistic.

[5] Stephen McCaffrey, Water Scarcity: Institutional and Legal Responses, in The Scarcity of Water Emerging Legal and Policy Responses 43, 55–56 (Edward H.P. Brans et al. eds., 1997).

Ellen Hey[6] and Asit Biswas[7] point out that the language of the IWC is far from clear or explicit, thereby accomplishing nothing in the way of regulating states' discretionary powers to reach agreement on water related issues. Similarly, Aaron Wolf[8] and Peter Beaumont[9] note that the IWC's language of equity provides no practical guidelines for water allocation, which is arguably one of the most important components of international water treaties.

* * *

The ambiguity associated with use of equitable language in international water law leads to two key questions. First, has inclusion of equitable language really made a difference in transboundary water law at the basin level? And if so, what substantive difference has it made? To answer these questions, the authors compiled a collection of . . . agreements, treaties, protocols, and significant amendments concerning transboundary waters in Africa. The collection is the result of a systematic search of available literature, published general treaty collections, online collections of international water and environmental law, as well as interviews with experts in this field. It includes only agreements that consider water as a scarce or consumable resource, a quantity to be managed, or an ecosystem to be improved or maintained, and excludes those dealing "only with boundaries, navigation, or fishing rights."[10]

* * *

[A review of the treaties clearly shows] growing incorporation of equitable language into African transboundary water law in recent decades. . . . This shift in emphasis in transboundary water agreements raises questions as to whether increased use of equitable language in Africa is indicative of an actual change in treaty content, the hollow byproduct of global changes in international water management thought, or something in between.

* * *

[Our analysis shows that] in terms of treaty content, equity agreements are much more likely to include the provisions generally

6 Ellen Hey, *The Watercourses Convention: To What Extent Does it Provide a Basis for Regulating Uses of International Watercourses?*, 7 Rev. Eur. Community & Int'l Envtl. L. 291, 294 (1998).

7 Asit Biswas, *Management of International Waters: Opportunities & Constraints*, 15 Int'l J. Water Res. Dev. 429, 439 (1998).

8 Aaron T. Wolf, *Conflict and Cooperation Along International Waterways*, 1 Water Pol'y 251, 252 (1998).

9 Peter Beaumont, *The 1997 UN Convention on the Law of Non-Navigational Uses of International Watercourses: Its Strengths and Weaknesses from a Water Management Perspective and the Need for New Workable Guidelines*, 16 Water Res. Dev. 475, 487 (2000). . . .

10 Aaron Wolf, *The Transboundary Freshwater Dispute Database Project*, 24 Water Int'l 160, 160 (1999).

considered important to a treaty's resilience—conflict resolution mechanisms, amendment mechanisms, provisions for exchange of hydrologic data, and consideration of water quality. In terms of actual water allocations, arguably the true measure by which equity should be judged, those equity agreements in fact appear to be more equitable in their allocations. Equity agreements allocate water more proportionately to runoff, land area, and population contribution than nonequity agreements. In response to the title question of whether equity in transboundary water law is a valuable paradigm or merely semantics, the results here indicate that use of equitable language is more than window-dressing. The incorporation of equitable language has contributed, at least within Africa, to a body of basin level transboundary water law that is more equitable.

These findings have a few clear implications. First, they work to support the assertion that generalized legal principles are significant in that they help to influence practical policymaking. Second, they indicate that nations that are parties to transboundary water agreements do in fact have considerable understanding of how to interpret and apply equity in water utilization, despite marked ambiguities in the term. In conclusion, they indicate that more widespread inclusion of equity in treaties is a positive development, and more common use of such language should be supported.

12. Stephen C. McCaffrey & Kate J. Neville, Small Capacity and Big Responsibilities: Financial and Legal Implications of a Human Right to Water for Developing Countries, 21 Geo. Int'l Envtl. L. Rev. 679, 681–85, 693, 696, 700–02 (2009)

Given that humans must have water to live—we cannot go without it for more than a few days—it is remarkable that none of the principal human rights instruments mentions a right to water. The pattern was set by the 1948 Universal Declaration of Human Rights **[Basic Document 7.10]** and was carried through into the two agreements that grew out of the Universal Declaration: the International Covenant on Civil and Political Rights (CP Covenant) **[Basic Document 7.12]** and the International Covenant on Economic, Social and Cultural Rights (ESC Covenant) **[Basic Document 7.11]**. Whether this omission was due to a reluctance to state the obvious—that water, like air, is a precondition for enjoying all other human rights—whether water simply had not yet become a pressing issue even by the mid-1960s or whether nations were cognizant even in the mid-20th century of the enormity of the challenge of implementing a right to water, the failure of these instruments to enshrine such a right seems today to be a rather serious oversight.

GENERAL COMMENT 15

Perhaps in recognition of this omission, in 2002 the United Nations Committee on Economic, Social and Cultural Rights, which monitors implementation of the corresponding Covenant, adopted a General Comment (General Comment No. 15, "The right to water . . .") finding that a right to water exists as an independent right, by necessary implication from Articles 11 (right to an adequate standard of living) and 12 (right to health) of the Covenant. Specifically, this document provides that:

> The human right to water entitles everyone to sufficient, safe, acceptable, physically accessible and affordable water for personal and domestic uses. An adequate amount of safe water is necessary to prevent death from dehydration, reduce the risk of water-related disease and provide for consumption, cooking, personal and domestic hygienic requirements.[11]

This is the first recognition by a United Nations human rights body of an independent and generally applicable human right to water. While it is no doubt an authoritative interpretation of the ESC Covenant, this finding is not binding per se on parties to the Covenant, nor does it "create" a previously nonexistent human right to water (indeed, as indicated above, the Committee found that the right already exists by necessary implication from other rights set forth in the Covenant). However, the General Comment does serve notice that the ESC Committee will expect the 160 parties to the Covenant to indicate the status of their implementation of the right to water in the course of their general reports on implementation of the rights under the ESC Covenant.

* * *

In General Comment No. 15, the Committee finds that there are "a number of core obligations in relation to the right to water," and, crucially, that they "are of immediate effect . . ." The Committee states this despite the fact that the governments that ratified the ESC Covenant only accepted an obligation to "achiev[e] progressively the full realization of the rights" it recognizes.

The Committee identifies the following nine core obligations in relation to the right to water:

> (a) To ensure access to the minimum essential amount of water . . .;
>
> (b) To ensure the right of access to water and water facilities and services on a non-discriminatory basis . . .;
>
> (c) To ensure physical access to water facilities or services that provide sufficient, safe and regular water; that have a sufficient number of water outlets to avoid prohibitive

[11] United Nations Economic and Social Council, Committee on Economic, Social and Cultural Rights, *General Comment No. 15 (2002), The Right to Water (Articles 11 and 12 of the International Covenant on Economic, Social and Cultural Rights)*, UN ESCOR Doc. E/C. 12/2002/11 (Nov. 26, 2002) [hereinafter General Comment 15] at ¶ 2.

waiting times; and that are at a reasonable distance from the household;

(d) To ensure personal security is not threatened when having to physically access to [sic] water;

(e) To ensure equitable distribution of all available water facilities and services;

(f) To adopt and implement, [on the basis of a participatory and transparent process,] a national water strategy and plan of action addressing the whole population;

(g) To monitor the extent of the realization, or the non-realization, of the right to water;

(h) To adopt relatively low-cost targeted water programs to protect vulnerable and marginalized groups;

(i) To take measures to prevent, treat and control diseases linked to water, in particular ensuring access to adequate sanitation.

It bears emphasis that according to the ESC Committee, this rather long list of obligations is of immediate applicability. It would not be surprising if some parties to the Covenant objected on the grounds that: 1) they did not accept obligations of this magnitude that would be immediately applicable, and 2) they simply do not have the financial and capacity-related resources to implement the items identified as core obligations in relation to the right to water. The obligations identified in paragraphs (a) and (c) alone would be extremely difficult for many developing countries to meet in the near future, let alone immediately. The United Nations Millennium Development Goals **[Basic Document 1.34]**, adopted in 2000 by all U.N. member states, call for "reduc[ing] by half the proportion of people without sustainable access to safe drinking water" by 2015, not for ensuring immediate access to "the minimum essential amount of water" for all. Having imposed these heavy obligations on state parties, the ESC Committee places at minimum a moral responsibility on wealthy nations and international financial institutions for seeing that they are fulfilled: "For the avoidance of any doubt, the Committee wishes to emphasize that it is particularly incumbent on States parties, and other actors in a position to assist, to provide international assistance and cooperation, especially economic and technical which enables developing countries to fulfill their core obligations. . . ." Although the international donor community will doubtless continue to provide assistance to developing countries in the water sector to the best of its ability, in today's economic and financial climate it seems uncertain whether the Committee's lofty expectations can be met. This places additional pressure on States parties.

* * *

. . . High standards for improving basic living conditions and human rights should be encouraged and promoted. However, our view is that such standards should be set in the form of goals, which can be achieved through flexible means depending on the circumstances and needs of the affected polity, as revealed in a participatory process. Indeed, the formula contained in Article 2(1) of the ESC Covenant . . . would seem the most appropriate approach, especially if implemented through broad citizen participation. As we have seen, this formula calls for progressive realization of the rights in question, bringing to bear the maximum of a state's available resources with the economic and technical assistance of the international community in the case of the Covenant.

* * *

Asit Biswas, the founder and president of the Third World Centre for Water Management in Mexico, and a former senior scientific advisor to the Executive Director of the United Nations Environment Programme, articulates this concern of insufficient capacity, suggesting that some countries are hesitant to recognize water as a right because they:

> are worried that human rights to water may mean free provision of clean water and proper wastewater management for everyone, which they simply cannot afford. Since this simply cannot be achieved within the foreseeable future, these countries prefer not to recognize this concept until their responsibilities and accountabilities are clarified, as well as those of the consumers.[12]

13. Joseph W. Dellapenna, International Water Law in a Climate of Disruption, 17 Mich. St. J. Int'l L. 43, 76–83, 84, 86–90, 92 (2008)

The International Law Association's Berlin Rules on Water Resources **[Basic Document 3.19]** provide a clear, cogent, and coherent summary of the customary international law applicable to water resources, incorporating the experience of the four decades since the Association approved the Helsinki Rules. The Berlin Rules take into account the innovations in . . . several important fields of customary international law that developed after the Helsinki Rules were approved, primarily international environmental law and international human rights law. . . .

* * *

Most of the chapters pertaining to all waters (national and international) either are new or are significantly different from the content of the Helsinki Rules and the U.N. Convention, both of which restricted

[12] Asit K. Biswas, *Water as a Human Right in the MENA Region: Challenges and Opportunities*, 23 Int'l J. Water Resources Dev. 209, 215 (2007).

their coverage solely to international waters. Chapter IV addresses the rights of persons, including the right of access to water, the right to participate in decisions and to access information, and the rights of identifiable communities. Chapter V deals in considerable detail with the protection of the aquatic environment, including the obligations to protect its ecological integrity, apply the precautionary approach, and to prevent, eliminate, reduce, or control pollution as appropriate (including a special rule on hazardous substances). Chapter VI addresses the assessment of the environmental impacts of programs, projects, or activities relating to all waters-national and international. Chapter VII sets forth obligations for cooperative and separate responses to extreme situations, including highly polluting accidents, floods, and droughts.

* * *

The Berlin Rules represent a bold departure when compared to the Helsinki Rules or the U.N. Convention, yet when compared to international environmental law and the international law of human rights, the Berlin Rules are not bold at all. The nature of customary international law always leaves room for debate about whether a particular practice of states has become binding as international law and also about the precise content of the customary rules. Still, the new articles in the Berlin Rules are firmly grounded in international human rights law or are supported strongly by international environmental agreements that have entered into force and are widely followed, even in nations that have not ratified them. As the International Law Association unanimously concluded, the Berlin Rules correctly summarize the current state of customary international law as it pertains to water resources. . . .

14. International Law Association, Berlin Rules on Water Resources, arts. 10–16, 22, & 36–42, Aug. 21, 2004, 71 ILA 337 (Basic Document 3.19)

15. A. Dan Tarlock, Four Challenges for International Water Law, 23 Tul. Envtl. L. J. 369, 371, 375, 377–78, 383–84, 385–88, 396–98, 402–03, 404–08 (2010)

[I]nternational water law use[s] the concept of equitable apportionment to provide the legal basis to constrain unilateral action, positing that all states are entitled to make equitable and reasonable utilization of international rivers. . . .

Unfortunately, on the ground the project of constraining unilateral action can at best be described as a very limited success. States such as China, India, and Turkey continue to engage in large multipurpose water projects unilaterally. Asia is now rife with conflicts between proposed dams in headwaters states and downstream states. . . .

These conflicts reflect the fact that geopolitics, not law, drives unilateral action, but international water law shares some of the blame because the equitable apportionment factors are vague. All uses of international rivers are correlative and thus can only be determined in relationship to the uses of other riparians. The geography, hydrology and climate of the basin, past utilization, the population and economic and social needs of the basin, and the availability of alternative sources of supply are among the relevant factors to be considered in determining what is a reasonable and equitable use of the water. The vagueness of the factors combined with inadequate enforcement institutions create incentives for nations to continue to dam and divert first and respond to objections second. . . .

* * *

Two models, shared benefits and cooperative management, have been offered to supplement customary law's restraints on unilateral action, to address [global climate change], to encourage more sustainable dam projects, and to promote aquatic ecosystem conservation and restoration. The two models can overlap and be complementary in any given situation. However, there are important distinctions among them that can affect stresses such as large dam construction and ecosystem conservation differently. Both models rely on integrated water resources management planning to promote sufficient cooperation, and to address environmental protection and climate change adaptation.

A. Shared Benefits

In recent years, there have been increasing calls to address the inefficiencies and injustices of the race to dam by shifting the focus of international disputes from the allocation of rivers to benefit sharing throughout the basin. The shared benefits model accepts the need for large dams but substitutes money for the use and control of wet water. Nations can forgo the construction of a dam or even the actual use of wet water in return for monetary or in kind compensation that satisfies other domestic needs, thus making it possible for other states to put the water to its most efficient use.

* * *

The idea of shared benefits arose from the 1961 Columbia River Treaty between Canada and the United States, and has developed into a basic principle of international water and environmental law. The signatories entered the treaty in hopes of damming the Columbia for power plants and flood control. . . . Canada's basic problem was that it wanted to develop its hydro potential but had little internal demand for electricity or flood control storage. In protesting a planned U.S. dam, Canada asked for the sharing of benefits from Canadian storage throughout the river downstream. The United States initially rejected Canada's expansive view of shared benefits, but eventually came around to the idea as Canada threatened out-of-basin diversion, which would decrease the river's flow into the Libby Dam. . . .

Pursuant to the treaty, Canada has developed 15.5 million acre feet of storage among three different projects. Most of the storage provides flood-control benefits, 50% of which the United States shares. The United States has paid Canada US$64.4 million for flood control benefits through 2024, and a consortium of U.S. power companies paid her US$254 million for a hydropower entitlement that ended in 2003.

* * *

B. Shared Management

To correct the defects of a static equitable apportionment doctrine, commentators have proposed an expansion of the core principle of equitable apportionment—that each riparian state is entitled to a fair "wet" share of an international river—to include continuing shared management of international rivers. . . . The immediate legal foundation is article 8 of the Watercourses Convention **[Basic Document 3.18]**, which imposes a duty on states to "cooperate on the basis of sovereign equality, territorial integrity, mutual benefit and good faith in order to attain optimal utilization and adequate protection of an international watercourse." The Berlin Rules **[Basic Document 3.19]** posit a much stronger cooperative management duty, derived from Hungary v. Slovakia, compared to the Watercourses Convention. Article 11 posits that "Basin States shall cooperate in good faith in the management of waters of an international drainage basin for the mutual benefit of the participating States.". . .

Shared management is an aspirational principle, but if it is implemented, it can better help nations address all four stresses provided that any regime satisfies four conditions. First, the regime must impose procedural duties that go beyond the customary duty of prior notice and consultation to include a wide range of voices and perspectives in major development and use decisions. Second, it must have stringent and continuing environmental assessment and monitoring duties that meet the standards set out by the World Commission on Dams in Dams and Development and the evolving international standard. Third, it must have substantive rules that constrain unilateral state behavior. Fourth, the management regimes must have the flexibility to adjust quickly to changing hydrologic conditions. No single existing or proposed allocation regime currently exhibits all four characteristics. Therefore, the model must be assembled from a variety of sources.

* * *

C. Integrated Water Resource Management and Adaptive Management

Integrated Water Resource Management (IWRM) has been progressively adopted as the international water management standard. . . .

* * *

IWRM has widespread support because it has been adopted by European donor nations as the price for water development aid. It was endorsed in Agenda 21 [**Basic Document 1.31**], the environmental action plan for the twenty-first century agreed to at the 1992 United Nations Rio de Janeiro Conference on Environment and Development (UNCED). It was incorporated into the four principles adopted at the 1992 Dublin Conference on Water and the Environment. Between UNCED in 1992 and the follow-up 2002 World Summit on Sustainable Development (WSSD), or Rio Plus 10, in Johannesburg, South Africa, IWRM was endorsed by the Commission on Sustainable Development, the General Assembly of the United Nations, the Ministerial Declaration of the International Conference on Freshwater, and was reaffirmed by the WSSD. The 2000 European Union Water Framework Directive adopts IWRM to improve the water quality of the Union's heavily used rivers. It requires a river basin management plan that prioritizes risks and establishes cost-effective measures to reduce pollution loads and flood damage.

IWRM's substantive message is that new demands for water must be recognized as potential constraints on existing, especially inefficient uses to accommodate new environmental and social equity uses. IWRM posits that freshwater is a finite and vulnerable resource, and calls for holistic management that integrates sectoral water plans and programs within a broader framework of economic and social policy. The specific objectives of IWRM, as articulated in Agenda 21, are:

1. [To] promot[e] . . . a dynamic, interactive, iterative and multisectoral approach to water resources management, including the identification and protection of potential sources of freshwater supply, that integrates technological, socioeconomic, environmental and human health considerations;
2. [To] plan[ ] . . . strategies for the sustainable and rational utilization, protection, conservation and management of water resources based on community needs and priorities within the framework of national economic development policy;
3. To design, implement and evaluate projects and programmes that are both economically efficient and socially appropriate

within clearly defined strategies, based on an approach of full public participation, including that of women, youth, indigenous people and local communities in water management policy-making and decision-making;

4. [To] identify[ ] [and] strengthen[ ] or develop[ ], as required, in particular in developing countries, the appropriate institutional, legal and financial mechanisms to ensure that water policy and its implementation are [a] catalyst [ ] for sustainable social progress and economic growth.

Ideally, IWRM would function as a series of nested plans and management strategies starting at the subbasin level and be progressively integrated into a multinational planning and management regime for the entire river basin. However, [experience shows that it is not always easy to apply IWRM in concrete situations.]

Section 5. Discussion Notes/Questions

1. As you think through the legal issues in this problem, consider the following questions:

a. What procedural obligations does international law impose on Korduene with respect to its proposed dam-building project. Has it satisfied all those obligations by notifying Palmyrene and Sumer and agreeing to meet with them? What else, if anything, must it do? Must it conduct an environmental impact assessment? Should it be required to do so?

b. Is Korduene's proposed project an "equitable and reasonable" use of the river? Does the law give any special protection to the prior uses of Palmyrene and Sumer? If Korduene's project substantially diminished the water available for irrigation, household, and industrial uses in Palmyrene and Sumer, would that be "significant harm" to those countries? Is it appropriate to privilege prior uses, given that they represent investments already made and settled expectations? What are the countervailing considerations?

c. Does international law require some portion of the flow of the Purattu to be maintained to preserve the Sabah Delta? If it does not, should it?

d. Does international law privilege some uses over others? For example, suppose it can be demonstrated that Sumer's proposed use of the Assyrian Aquifer to provide water to luxury resorts in Kish will result in a diminution of the water available to poor villages and farms in southeastern Korduene. Does international law privilege the use of water to meet basic needs over its use to fill swimming pools and water golf courses at a playground for the rich? Should it privilege basic needs? Or is the use of water to promote economic development—even development of tourism—an equally valuable use? Or is the relative importance of different uses a question that international law should leave to individual nations to decide?

2. Is there is a human right to water? If so, is that a factor in resolving international water disputes? Suppose that many Sumeran citizens have substantial difficulty securing access to adequate, safe water supplies to the extent that Sumeran courts have concluded that they are denied their "human right to water." Sumer seems to have an international obligation to do something about that situation. Does Korduene have any such obligation? Could Korduene's increased utilization of the Parattu River be considered a violation of the human rights of Sumeran citizens if it diminished the availability of water in Sumer to the point where it was impossible for basic needs to be met?

3. As Professor Dellapenna points out in Reading 13, the Berlin Rules incorporate principles derived from international environmental law and from international human rights law into their "restatement" of international water law. Is that appropriate? Absent supportive State practice, is it appropriate to assume that States would incorporate principles from environmental law into their decisions about water allocation? How about principles of human rights law?

If the Berlin Rules are expressive of customary law, do they mandate a different result in this case than the provisions of the International Watercourses Convention?

4. Assuming they both express customary international law, should the International Watercourses Convention or the Draft Articles on Transboundary Aquifers be applied to resolve the dispute over use of the Assyrian Aquifer? Do they differ in any significant way? Is Sumer's proposed use "equitable and reasonable" under the formulations in either document. Are there more facts that we need to know to evaluate its use of the aquifer or the law that governs? Will it be easy to learn those facts?

5. What elements do you think should be included in any agreement that Korduene, Palmyrene and Sumer might reach concerning the Puratttu River?

a. Would you favor an agreement that provided a guaranteed allocation to Palmyrene and Sumer? What would be the advantages of such an approach? What would be the disadvantages? What would happen if, for example, a prolonged drought caused Palmyrene's other water sources to diminish significantly? Or suppose that climate change further dries out the region on a long-term basis? What is the alternative to a fixed allocation of water?

b. What kind of governance mechanisms should be included in a water agreement between the three countries? Should there be a scientific body? What would it do? Should there be a standing body that is always available for discussion of river-related issues? What decision-making authority, if any, should it have?

c. Should an agreement on the use of the Purattu consider environmental or ecological issues? How would you address those issues in the agreement?

d. Should the Assyrian Aquifer be covered by the same agreement that covers the Purattu or by a separate agreement? What reasons can you give to support your answer?

e. How do the concepts of "shared benefits" and "shared management" apply to this problem? Are there benefits from Korduene's proposed project that could be shared with Sumer or Palmyrene in a way that would make either country more open to the project? What might be the benefits to the three countries, if any, of "shared management" of either the Purattu or the Assyrian Aquifer? What provisions would you put in the treaty to facilitate shared management and future shared benefits? Is this something that can be institutionalized in the treaty, or do such arrangements have to be done on a project-by-project basis?

6. There are many examples throughout world history of disputes over water being settled by violence. *See* Pacific Institute, *Water Conflict Chronology,* at http://www.worldwater.org/conflict/index.html (last visited Apr. 20, 2011). Conflict over water supplies is seen by many people as a dangerous flash point for conflict in many of the water scarce regions of the world, and a threat to global security. A recent report by the staff of the U.S. Senate's Committee on Foreign Relations began:

> Water scarcity is often overlooked, underfunded, and undervalued within foreign policy. Yet a government's ability to provide and manage access to water is critical for ensuring political, economic, and social stability.
>
> In Central and South Asia, particularly in Afghanistan and Pakistan, the impacts of water scarcity are fueling dangerous tensions that will have repercussions for regional stability and U.S. foreign policy objectives. The national security implications of this looming water shortage—directly caused or aggravated by agriculture demands, hydroelectric power generation, and climate instability—will be felt all over the world.

Majority Staff Report, *Avoiding Water Wars: Water Scarcity and Central Asia's Growing Importance for Stability in Afghanistan and Pakistan,* United States Senate Committee on Foreign Relations, 112th Cong., 1st Sess. 1 (Feb. 22, 2011). There are frequent predictions of a "coming water war" in the Middle East and, more recently, in the Far East. *See, e.g.,* John Bulloch, Adil Darwish, & Adel Darwish, Water Wars: Coming Conflicts in the Middle East (1993); Denis D. Gray, *Water wars? Thirsty, energy-short China stirs fear,* San Francisco Chronicle, Apr. 16, 2011, http://www.sfgate.com.

Not everyone, however, is so pessimistic. Jerome Delli Priscoli and Aaron T. Wolf suggest that many past conflicts commonly attributed to disputes over water were not about water at all or did not actually involve armed conflict. While the potential for water disputes to end violently is always present, they report that "the record of acute conflict over international water resources is historically overwhelmed by the record of cooperation." They identified 37 violent disputes over international water resources since the 1950s, as against 157 signed treaties. Over the full historical record, "the total number of water-related events among nations . . . is likewise weighted toward cooperation . . . implying that violence over water is not strategically rational, hydrographically effective, or economically viable." Jerome Delli Priscoli & Aaron T. Wolf, Managing and Transforming Water Conflicts 12 (2009).

7. Recent analysis posits that the Syrian civil war and the rise of ISIS were both the result, ultimately, of water shortage in Syria. Extreme drought and the government's poor water management policies caused historic crop failures in Syria, leading to massive rural-to-urban migration, consequent social and civil unrest, and, ultimately, civil war. *See, e.g.,* Peter H. Gleick, *War, Drought, Climate Change, and Conflict in Syria,* 6 Weather, Climate & Soc'y 331 (2014).

To add insult to injury, there have been allegations that Turkey has taken advantage of the weakness of Syria and Iraq to withdraw more water from the Euphrates River than it is allowed under the agreement governing its utilization of that resource. *See* Zaid Saba, et al., *Water Shortages Uniting Iraqi Government, Islamic State Militants Against Turkey,* Bloomberg BNA Water L. & Pol'y Monitor (Jul. 2, 2015).

8. Since 2011, Ethiopia has been at work on a massive dam on the Nile River known as the Grand Ethiopian Renaissance Dam (GERD). The project has been controversial from the start, particularly in Egypt, which fears the impact of the dam on the flow of the Nile that country. On several occasions, Egypt has threatened military action if the dam project alters flows guaranteed to Egypt by colonial-era water agreements. Ethiopia, for its part, claims that the dam will have minimal downstream impact, while providing substantial electrical power for Ethiopia and improving local agriculture. Ethiopia also insists that it is not bound by the prior agreements involve the flow of the Nile, as it was not a party to those agreements, which were made by Great Britain (in its capacity as a colonial power with control over much of the Nile River basin) and Egypt. As of this writing (December 2018) talks among Ethiopia, Egypt and Sudan were ongoing. *See generally* Adam Allington, *Is a Water War About to Break Out Along the Nile?,* Bloomberg BNA Water L. & Pol'y Monitor (Jan. 26, 2018).

9. Southeast Asia is another area of the world where an upstream State's water projects have led to international conflict. For several years, China has been constructing hydropower facilities in its section of the Mekong River basin (known as the Lancang River in China). The transboundary impacts of this construction are substantial and have caused regional friction,

but the countries involved appeared to be resolving their differences amicably. During a 2016 drought, China increased flow rates from its dams to ease water shortages in Vietnam. In addition, in early 2016, China joined the Lancang-Mekong Cooperation Mechanism, an arrangement aimed at facilitating cooperation among basin States in the management of the Mekong River Basin. (In China, the river is known as the Lancang). *See Lancang-Mekong Cooperation,* http://www.lmcchina.org (last accessed December 8, 2018). China, Laos, Thailand, Cambodia, Myanmar and Vietnam are all participants in the Lancang-Mekong Mechanism. *See generally* Michael Standaert, *China Hydropower Having Major Impact Along Mekong River: Study*, Bloomberg BNA Water L. & Pol'y Monitor (Jan. 19, 2017).

10. The Ramsar Convention on Wetlands of International Importance **(Basic Document 5.2)** was adopted in February 1971 and entered into force in December 1975. It aims to "stem the progressive encroachment on and loss of wetlands now and in the future." (Preamble, paragraph 4.) If the Sabah Delta were included on the Ramsar List of Wetlands of International Importance, how would that affect the problem (assuming Sumer, Korduene, and Palmyrene are parties to the Convention)? Does the Convention impose any obligation(s) on Korduene and Palmyrene with respect to the health of wetlands in Sumer? If so, what is the nature of the obligation? *See* Ramsar Convention, Articles 3, 5 & 6. Does the Convention provide an additional forum where discussions among the countries could take place?

PROBLEM 7-2: POACHING ELEPHANTS IN USAMBARA

Section 1. Facts

Located in central East Africa, the small nation of Bawanda was once a haven for wildlife, its wide savannahs home to immense herds of elephant, gazelle, and numerous other species. However, twelve years of violent civil war and a long period of drought devastated the countryside. The once abundant herds slowly vanished and were displaced by tens of thousands of homeless human refugees, expanding deserts, and guerrilla warfare. Hardest hit were the elephants—most of the elephant population in Bawanda was decimated by hunting, both for food, which the refugees desperately needed, and for ivory, which could be sold on the black market for a small fortune by soldiers and refugees alike. Indeed the proceeds of the ivory trade were an important factor in the purchase of arms by the combatants.

The recent arrival of peace has brought a new coalition government to Bawanda. This government has ratified a number of international environmental agreements, and it has passed strict laws banning the killing of elephants for any reason. But it is devoting most of its energy and resources to feeding and relocating Bawanda's suffering population. Because little funding is available for law enforcement, wildlife crime is widespread and there is a thriving black market in ivory. This has put Bawanda's few remaining elephants in increasing danger, and it has also driven poachers in Bawanda into neighboring Usambara in search of elephant tusks that they can then sell in Bawanda, generally for export abroad.

Unlike its less fortunate neighbor to the north, the government of Usambara long ago set aside a 60,000 square kilometers park to protect its indigenous wildlife, including elephants. There, the once endangered elephant population has risen from 10,000 to 40,000 over the past fifteen years. This turn of events has resulted in a booming tourism industry that provides substantial revenue to the Usambara government and supports a generally stable economy. Indeed, Usambara's elephants have increased in numbers to such a degree that Usambara recently has begun to allow hunters, for a very high fee and on government-sponsored safaris, actually to kill selected animals so as to maintain an appropriate ecological balance in the elephant population. In addition, in 1997 and again in 2008, Usambara sought and received permission from the CITES Standing Committee to make single sales of raw ivory from existing stocks of ivory gathered from elephants that have died as a result of natural causes or from culling. Proceeds from the sales are used to help fund Usambara's elephant conservation programs.

The poachers coming from Bawanda, it now appears, have begun to have a serious negative impact on Usambara's ecologically driven tourism industry. Despite many appropriately addressed formal complaints by Usambara to Bawanda, however, no steps have been taken to remedy the poaching problem, either through enforcement action or legislation. The Government of Bawanda has explained politely that it simply does not have the resources necessary to provide the protection Usambara requests. Additionally, it claims that Usambara is partially to blame for the problem, as its official hunting safaris and its participation in the ivory trade have the effect of providing an incentive to poach in its park.

In January 2008, 600 contraband ivory tusks were seized by Hong Kong customs officials, acting in concert with the Interpol Working Group on Wildlife Crime,[13] the Lusaka Agreement Task Force,[14] and TRAFFIC,[15] an international wildlife trade monitoring network. The tusks were seized

---

[13] Interpol is an international police organization with 188 member countries. Originally formed in 1923, Interpol facilitates police cooperation across a broad range of law enforcement activities. *See About Interpol* at http://www.interpol.int (accessed July 21, 2011).

[14] The Lusaka Agreement Task Force is a law enforcement organization and the Secretariat of the Lusaka Agreement on Co-operative Enforcement Operations Directed at Illegal Trade in Wild Flora and Fauna, Sept. 8, 1994, 1950 UNTS 35. *See* http://www.lusakaagreement.org (accessed July 21, 2011).

[15] TRAFFIC is a wildlife trade monitoring network, formed by a partnership between the World Wildlife Federation (WWF) and the International Union for Conservation of Nature (IUCN). For more information, *see About TRAFFIC* at http://www.traffic.org.

after they were offloaded from a vessel that had arrived in Hong Kong from Bawanda. Genetic analysis of the tusks revealed that they had come from a specific population of elephants located in a portion of Usambara's wildlife park.

Alerted by Interpol and TRAFFIC, Usambaran authorities stepped up their patrols in the identified area of the park and, in May of last year, Usambaran troops surprised a band of poachers who had been in the midst of butchering elephants three and one half kilometers into Usambaran territory. The poachers shot at the troops, wounding two Usambaran soldiers. They then took off in their vehicles and made for the Bawandaan border. The troops pursued the poachers and, with the help of helicopters, were eventually able to apprehend them at their base camp, which was located about two kilometers inside Bawandaan territory. Before entering Bawandaan territory to arrest the poachers, the Usambaran troops had sought and obtained permission to do so from the highest levels of the Usambaran government.

Following the poachers' surrender, the Usambaran forces discovered forty-eight elephant tusks hidden in a pit at the poachers' camp. The troops seized the tusks (thought to be worth nearly $2 million), took the poachers into custody, transported them back to detention in Usambara, and eventually tried, convicted, and imprisoned each of them for breach of Usambara's laws protecting elephants. No effort was made to determine whether the tusks came from elephant populations in Usambara or in Bawanda or elsewhere.

All the poachers in question, as it turned out, were Bawandaan nationals, and they had launched their raid from Bawandaan territory. Indeed, there is evidence to suggest that such was their usual mode of operation. Nevertheless, Bawanda demanded their immediate return and the return of the tusks to its custody. Bawanda pledged to prosecute the poachers and to destroy the tusks. Usambara refused this offer, noting that the poachers were already in prison and stating that it would stockpile the seized ivory for future sale in support of its conservation efforts.

A war of increasingly hostile words ensued. Usambara claims that Bawanda's failure to stop elephant poaching and eliminate the black market for ivory within its borders is an on-going violation of international law for which Bawanda is responsible. Usambara wants a promise from Bawanda that it will act effectively to stop cross-border poaching and compensation for the harm the poachers have inflicted on Usambara's elephant population. Bawanda, for its part, denies any legal responsibility to act, and claims that Usambara's safari policy is itself a violation of international law. It also claims that Usambara's support for, and participation in, a 'legal' ivory trade encourages poaching. Each government has indicated that it will cease cooperating with the other in environmental matters until this dispute is resolved.

Distressed by these developments, the Director-General of the United Nations Environment Programme (UNEP) intervened, and has persuaded both governments that the appropriate way to deal with the dispute is to submit it to her mediation since UNEP is headquartered in Africa and since both disputants are African nations. Both countries agreed and accepted that her mediation should be guided by the relevant doctrines, principles, and rules of international law.

Both countries have signed and ratified the 1973 Convention on International Trade in Endangered Species of Wild Fauna and Flora (CITES) and the 2003 Revised African Convention on the Conservation of Nature and Natural Resources. Additionally, both have ratified the 1992 Convention on Biological Diversity. Usambara is a party to the Lusaka Agreement on Co-operative Enforcement Operations Directed at Illegal Trade in Wild Fauna and Flora; Bawanda is not. Usambara's elephant population is listed in Appendix II of CITES, subject to the same rules as are applicable to elephant populations in Botswana, Namibia, South Africa and Zimbabwe.

You are head of UNEP's Legal Division and you are asked by UNEP's Director-General to prepare a comprehensive outline of the legal issues present in this dispute. She specifically asks for an evaluation of each side's arguments in respect of each issue and the likely result were the dispute to be submitted to the Permanent Court of Arbitration at The Hague as set out in Article XVIII of the 1973 CITES Convention.

Section 2. Questions Presented

1. To what extent, if any, is Bawanda in breach of its obligations under international law and, assuming such breach, to what extent, if any, can Usambara claim reparation therefor?

2. Should the ivory seized by Usambara be returned to Bawanda?

Section 3. Assignments

A. *Reading Assignment*

Study the Readings presented in Section 4, *infra*, and the Discussion Notes/Questions that follow.

B. *Recommended Writing Assignment*

Prepare a comprehensive, logically sequenced, and *argumentative* brief in the form of an outline of the primary and subsidiary *legal* issues you see requiring clarification for the Director-General of the United Nations Environment Programme. Also, from the perspective of an independent objective judge, indicate which side ought to prevail on each issue and why. Retain a copy of your issue-outline/brief for class discussion.

C. Recommended Oral Assignment

Assume you are legal counsel for Bawanda or Usambara (as designated by your instructor); then, relying upon the Readings (and your issue-outline if prepared), present a 15–20 minute oral argument of your government's likely positions before the Director-General of UNEP.

D. Recommended Reflective Assignment

Consider (and recommend) alternative norms, institutions, and/or procedures that you believe might do better than existing world order arrangements to contend with situations of the kind posed by this problem. In so doing, but without insisting upon *immediate* feasibility, identify the particular transition steps that would be needed to make your alternatives a reality.

Section 4. Readings

1. John B. Heppes & Eric J. McFadden, The Convention on International Trade In Endangered Species of Wild Fauna and Flora: Improving the Prospects for Preserving Our Biological Heritage, 5 Boston U. Int'l L.J. 229, 229–32 (1987)

Illegal trafficking in wildlife species and products has been one of the primary contributing factors to the precipitous decline of wildlife species in recent years. The US Department of Interior has estimated that as many as 300 species now face extinction each decade. An even less sanguine assessment estimates that the current rate of extinction may be as high as several species per day. Hundreds of mammal, reptile, and bird species are in imminent danger of extinction, as well as 20,000–25,000 species of plants. Many experts calculate that species extinction is now occurring at a greater rate than at any time since the last great extinction cycle at the end of the Pleistocene era more than 65 million years ago, when dinosaurs gradually disappeared.

Species diminution has several adverse consequences. First, utilitarian benefits that can be derived from flora and fauna species, both currently known and potentially discoverable, are lost irretrievably when a species is rendered extinct by over-exploitation. If preserved, rare species of animals and plants ultimately may help to alleviate the world's food crisis. For example, scientists in recent years discovered that *Zea diploperennis*, a rare Mexican tall grass, may be crossed with corn through techniques of genetic engineering to create a perennial, virus resistant hybrid which could substantially increase the world's food supply in the future. In recent years, water shortages have proven to be the primary constraint against expansion of food productivity. The crossing of commercial tomatoes with a rare wild tomato from the Galapagos Islands has yielded a hybrid that can be irrigated with 70% sea water, helping to alleviate pressures on irrigation systems in developing countries.

Wildlife species also yield important pharmacological benefits. Extracts from certain marine species show promise as anti-cancer agents. Marine sponges have yielded a large number of important antibiotics in recent years. Additionally, pharmacologically active ingredients in other species of fauna and flora are utilized in a wide range of heart drugs, analgesics, anticoagulants, and hormones.

Wildlife species also perform obscure yet critical functions in the regulation of the ecosystem. For example, certain species of wild birds eat water plants and other green water contaminants, ensuring clean reservoirs essential for the survival of other species. Certain species of flora also help to regulate rainfall, recycle matter, and resist soil erosion. Wild species of flora and fauna also protect watersheds and coastal areas from floods and droughts by acting as a buffer. Impoverishment of biodiversity threatens to upset the delicate balance of nature that supports life on earth as we know it. Several members of the National Academy of Sciences view the ramifications of a loss of biodiversity "as second only in severity to the consequences of large scale nuclear warfare."

Wildlife is also a significant source of economic benefits for many nations. For example, a survey conducted by Statistics Canada in 1982 estimated that Canadians spent an estimated $4.2 billion on wildlife-related activities in 1981 alone. This figure does not include the additional foreign exchange that is earned from tourist expenditures on wildlife-related activities.

The diminution of wildlife species also threatens to deny society the aesthetic and spiritual benefits of nature. Throughout history, mankind has celebrated its bond with animal and plant life in art, music, and literature. In recent years, society has begun to accept its role as protector of nature for its own sake:

> [T]his non-humanistic value of communities and species is the simplest of all to state: they should be conserved because they exist and because this existence itself is but the present expression of a continuing historical process of immense antiquity and majesty.[16]

2. Michael Glennon, Has International Law Failed the Elephant?, 84 AJIL 1, 1–3 (1990)

If, as Lao-tse said, nature is not anthropomorphic, some fellow creatures nonetheless seem to share the better angels of our character;

[16] David W. Ehrenfeld, The Arrogance of Humanism 207–08 (1978).

among these animals, none is grander than the African elephant.[17] Elephants live in close-knit "families" of about ten members that seem to do just about everything synchronously—feeding, walking, resting, drinking or mud wallowing.[18] Each unit has a matriarchal structure: it is headed by the oldest female and consists of younger females and their calves, as male calves tend to leave the family and strike out on their own when they reach sexual maturity between the ages of 10 and 15. Fighting is rare.

Elephants are the largest land animals on earth. They grow for their entire life, weighing up to 6 tons and eating up to 300 pounds of food a day, consisting primarily of grasses and bark. Left alone, they can live past 60. They seem able to communicate with low-frequency calls that carry for 6 miles, which may explain the coordinated movement and behavior of separate groups. On the same day that the culling of elephants began in Hwange National Park in Zimbabwe, elephants 90 miles away fled to the opposite corner of the reserve.

Elephants are quite tactile. They often touch each other with their trunks, and tend to stand and even walk bunched together, leaning on or rubbing each other. After being apart for a while, they greet each other by intertwining trunks, clashing tusks and flapping ears, exhibiting great excitement even if the separation has lasted for only a few days. They aid other members of the group that are threatened or disabled.

Elephants have a haunting sense of death. When a member of the family dies, they touch the carcass gently with their trunks and feet, and cover it with loose earth and branches. They do not react to the remains of other species but are fascinated by those of their own:

> When they come upon an elephant carcass they stop and become quiet and yet tense. . . . First they reach their trunks toward the body to smell it, and then they approach slowly and cautiously and begin to touch the bones, sometimes lifting them and turning them with their feet and tusks. They run their trunk tips along the tusks and lower jaw and feel in all the crevices and hollows in the skull [probably] trying to recognize the individual.[19]

Observers noticed one 7-year old male lingering at such a site long after the others had gone, "repeatedly feeling and stroking the jaw and turning it with his foot and trunk." It was the remains of his mother. Females whose calves have died have seemed lethargic and depressed for many days afterwards. When the matriarch dies, the entire family can

[17] This article deals with the African elephant, *Laxodonta africana.* The Asian elephant, *Elephas maximus,* is somewhat smaller and more often tuskless. *A Program to Save the African Elephant,* World Wildlife Fund Letter, No. 2, 1989, at 1–2 [hereinafter *To Save the Elephant*].

[18] The following text draws heavily on Cynthia Moss, Elephant Memories: Thirteen Years in the Life of an Elephant Family (1988).

[19] *Id.* at 270.

disintegrate, its former members seemingly becoming asocial and aggressive.

Elephants have no natural enemies; threats come entirely from man. Licensed hunting continues to account for several hundred deaths per year. The Governments of South Africa and Zimbabwe conduct culling programs aimed at maintaining their elephant populations at a level the available habitat can support. As with many other species, loss of habitat to human encroachment is a major problem. Elephants and cattle compete for some of the same food, and as Africa has become increasingly agricultural, the natural range of the elephant has diminished. Certain native groups have engaged in random killing of elephants: the Masai, for example, spear elephants as proof of their bravery and even as a form of political protest. As the Masai began to grow crops, their harassment of elephants increased.

Tourism, too, has had its effect. Tourist lodges in the parks have garbage pits that attract various animals, including elephants. Plastic bags and gloves, medicine bottles, broken glass, metal, wrappings and containers have all turned up in elephant dung. A psychiatrist has concluded that these environmental pressures may drive the elephant to increased feeding on fermenting food: "environmental stress can be an important variable in the self-administration of alcohol [from fermented fruits and grains] in these natural habitats. Elephants drink, perhaps, to forget . . . the anxiety produced by shrinking rangeland and the competition for food. And I think that we can see a little bit of ourselves in this kind of behavior."[20]

By far the greatest threat to the elephant's survival is poaching. The elephant is killed for its ivory tusks, which are carved and used for dice, jewelry, trinkets, ornaments, billiard balls, piano keys and knife handles. A principal use is for *hanko*, personalized signature seals considered status symbols in Japan. International conservation groups estimate that the illegal killing of elephants for their ivory has reduced Africa's elephant population from 1.5 million to fewer than 500,000 in the last decade. By some estimates, the poachers kill two to three hundred a day; at this rate, the African elephant could be extinct by the end of the century. . . .

[20] Rodger Yaeger & Norman Miller, Wildlife, Wild Death: Land Use and Survival in Eastern Africa 115 (1986).

3. Mario Del Baglivo, CITES at the Crossroad: New Ivory Sales and Sleeping Giants, 14 Fordham Envtl. L. J. 279, 285–301 (2003)

III. The Convention on International Trade in Endangered Species of Flora and Fauna

A. History

In response to the alarming global decline in both the population and varieties of endangered species of wild animals and plants, the World Conservation Union ("IUCN") drafted the Convention on International Trade in Endangered Species of Flora and Fauna **[Basic Document 5.3]** during the late 1960's and early 1970's.

* * *

CITES was initially signed by twenty-one nations in 1973 and ratified by ten nations. The Convention entered into force on July 1, 1975. Currently, there are 158 Parties to CITES.[21]

Unlike the Convention on Biodiversity **[Basic Document 5.6]**, CITES does not regulate the efforts of Parties to avoid habitat destruction or modification. Nor does CITES directly or indirectly control the takings of any species of plant or animal. CITES was drafted to provide a regulatory framework to limit world-wide trade in endangered and threatened species and to control trade in other species on a sustainable basis. Regulation of trade in endangered species under CITES is accomplished through a system of permits for the importation and exportation of living specimens of these species and any products derived from them. Currently, some 34,000 species of plants and animals are protected to some extent by the Convention.

Parties join CITES voluntarily. However, Parties to the Convention are legally bound to implement the treaty; each member nation must adopt domestic legislation that implements the rules of CITES.

B. Regulatory Structure

The trade permit system which serves as the regulatory backbone of CITES is tied to the placement of a particular species on one of three Appendices that list all plants and animals protected by CITES. Placement of a species on a CITES Appendix is, in turn, dependent on the overall viability of the species in its native range.

CITES requires Parties to the Convention to meet every two years.[22] At each biennial meeting, the Parties review the three Appendices to

[21] *Eds.*—As of December 2018, there were 183 Parties to CITES.

[22] *Eds.*—Article XI of the treaty allows the Conference of the Parties to alter the frequency of its meetings. In recent years its practice has been to meet every 2–3 years, rather than on a strict biennial schedule.

determine whether to add, delete, or move a species from one listing to another. Any amendments to Appendix I or II must be approved by a two-thirds majority of Parties in attendance and voting at the meeting. Changes to the Appendices enter into force ninety days after the meeting closes.

Appendix I contains those species of flora and fauna for which the limitations on trade are the strictest. Trade in Appendix I species requires an import permit from the recipient nation, as well as an export permit from the country of origin (trade in Appendix II or III species requires only a permit from the exporting nation.) Under CITES, a species can only be placed on Appendix I if it is "threatened with extinction." Trade between nations in these species may only take place under circumstances deemed exceptional and only for noncommercial purposes. Any potential threat to the viability of an Appendix I species of plant or animal from trade activity requires Parties to CITES to halt such trade. It is widely accepted that an Appendix I listing serves as a de facto ban on all international trade in living specimens or products of a species.

Plant and animal species listed in Appendix II of CITES are those deemed to be less in danger of extinction than Appendix I species. Commercial trade in Appendix II species is allowed by CITES and regulated under the permit system. Parties must closely monitor the effect of trade on these plants and animal species to assess the impact on their viability within the exporting country. Any trade in species listed in Appendix II requires accompanying permits stating that the scientific authority of the exporting nation has determined that trade will not be detrimental to the survival of the species.

Appendix III contains species that are protected by at least one member nation. It is the country of origin that primarily controls export of an Appendix III species, i.e. the member nation itself decides what level of trade of an Appendix III species or its products is appropriate, if any. The CITES permit system operates to regulate international trade in Appendix III species by mandating that, upon request by a fellow Party to the Convention, other Parties must monitor importation of the species to assist the requesting exporting nation in controlling illegal trade exports of the species.

CITES does not provide a direct mechanism for global enforcement of Convention rules. Instead, CITES primarily relies on each Party to implement the Convention by adopting national legislation regulating trade in endangered species with other nations. Within their own borders, Parties are required to penalize illegal traffickers and confiscate live specimens and/or products of a species protected under CITES. The Convention, therefore, relies on the internal police powers of each member nation to impose criminal and/or monetary sanctions on persons convicted of illegally exporting or importing living specimens of a protected endangered species or products of the species.

To implement CITES outside their borders, Parties must refrain from trade in endangered species or their products with non-member nations unless the latter uses trade permits comparable to those used by member nations. However, there is no provision in the Convention requiring Parties to sanction offending nations. Rather, CITES merely recommends that Parties penalize countries that engage in trade that violates the Convention.

Critics who charge that CITES is ineffective in stopping illegal trade in endangered and threatened species (and their products) often point out that "regulation" of the trade too often falls far short of "prohibiting" the trade.

One controversial feature of CITES makes total prohibition of trade in an endangered or threatened species virtually impossible. Any member State may make a unilateral statement, or reservation, that it will not be bound by the provisions of the Convention regulating trade in a particular species or product of a species. Once a Party "takes" a reservation on a particular species, it is not considered a Party to the Convention for that species and may engage in exports and imports of the species.

IV. The Ivory Ban Under CITES

[T]he Parties to CITES kept the elephant listed on Appendix II from 1977 to 1990. During that time, CITES' protection of the elephant was limited to a complex registration system that is now recognized as a failure. About half of the African Parties to the Convention ignored the CITES rules governing ivory trading and, in those nations that observed the restrictions, ivory traders used various methods to escape prosecution for illegally exporting ivory.

As the toll of African elephants killed each day for their ivory rose into the hundreds in the mid-1980s, some nations acted on their own to ban the importation of any ivory past their borders. Japan, the nation that imported more ivory than any other, banned ivory imports in 1985. Recognizing that CITES was failing to protect the African elephant from impending extinction within the decade, the United States Congress passed the African Elephant Conservation Act in 1988. The Act halted importation of all raw and worked ivory into the U.S. The European Union passed similar legislation in 1989. These unilateral actions by the United States and European nations were credited with significantly decreasing the worldwide demand for ivory.

At the same time that nations were unilaterally acting to halt the ivory trade to slow the massive slaughter of African elephants, some Parties to CITES, including several African nations, were agitating to have the elephant designated an endangered species by moving it from Appendix II to Appendix I. Kenya and Tanzania, which sought a complete ban on ivory trade, were the most vocal of the African nations supporting this amendment. Southern African nations, including South Africa, Zimbabwe, and Botswana, argued against changing the status of the elephant to endangered by moving it to Appendix I. However, at the 1990 Seventh Conference of the Parties (COP 7), the voting members moved the African elephant to Appendix I, thereby banning all elephant products (including ivory) from international trade.

Most observers credit the CITES Ivory Ban with virtually ending the poaching crisis throughout Africa. Moving the African elephant from Appendix II to Appendix I had a dramatic effect on worldwide ivory prices and, in turn, the intensity of poaching of elephants in Africa. For example, in Kenya, where as many as 3,500 elephants were killed by poachers each year during the crisis, the numbers of elephants poached per year dropped to 50 by 1993.

Widely accepted as the only means to saving the African elephant from extinction, the 1989 Ivory Ban worked well at achieving this end at two important levels. As already stated, the Ban dramatically reduced the poaching of elephants for their tusks because the profit motive at the critical supplier (poacher) end of the ivory market was greatly diminished. But the Ban, and the global publicity surrounding it, also succeeded in raising the consciousness of buyers of ivory. Some ten years after imposition of the Ivory Ban, jewelers reported that the international demand for ivory was "dead." A Johannesburg, South Africa, jewelry wholesaler described the dramatic effect of the Ban on the perception of ivory as a commodity among the public—even in Africa—when he stated "People are too embarrassed or ashamed to ask about ivory." The 1989 Ivory Ban, therefore, was highly successful both in halting the mass slaughter of elephants for their tusks and in publicizing the issue to the point that many found it unconscionable to purchase any ivory, even that stockpiled from elephants that died from natural causes.

With pressure from intense poaching eliminated, the elephant population of Africa stabilized and underwent a recovery throughout the continent unmatched by any species in the history of CITES. In Kenya alone, the elephant population grew by 13,300 in the decade following the imposition of the ivory ban in 1989.

V. The 1999 Ivory Sale

A. CITES Approval and Conditions to the Sale

As a result of moving the African elephant to Appendix I and the de facto Ivory Ban implemented by this action, the population of African elephants rose dramatically, particularly in southern Africa. The increasing size of the elephant herds put pressure on humans who shared the same range with the elephant and who competed with the species for habitat, i.e. food, water, and shelter. With African elephants protected from slaughter by poachers solely for their tusks, elephant range states spent increasingly large sums to manage elephant herds. At the same time, ivory from "legal" sources, including the natural death and culling of elephants, was being added to the supply of stockpiled ivory that African nations already had on hand from the interdiction of poachers. With the Ivory Ban in place, these nations now had to pay to protect the stockpiled ivory from theft and to keep it stored in humidified conditions. As one commentator noted, the stockpiles of "legal" ivory went from "financial assets to liabilities overnight."

As the elephant population grew throughout its range, southern African nations managing elephants became increasingly resentful of the CITES ban on the ivory trade. Several sought some relief to the absolute ban on the sale of ivory from elephants. In particular, Zimbabwe, Namibia, and Botswana (countries in which the elephant population staged a significant population growth) mounted a campaign to move the African elephant back to Appendix II so that they could once again use the species as a source of much needed foreign currency. These southern African nations were aided in this effort by a handful of non-African Parties to CITES who also sought a resumption of the ivory trade at some level under the close supervision of the Convention. The southern African nations gained additional support for their proposal to move the elephant back to Appendix II when the CITES Panel of Experts, appointed at the last Conference of the Parties, reported that the African elephant population in Zimbabwe, Namibia, and Botswana no longer met the biological criteria for an Appendix I listing.

Although the proposal to move the elephant from Appendix I to Appendix II in Zimbabwe, Namibia, and Botswana met with strong opposition from many nations outside the continent, as well as several eastern and central African Parties, the measure passed by the required two-thirds vote at the 1997 COP 10 in Harare, Zimbabwe. Additionally, the Parties voted to allow these three nations to conduct a one-time sale of stockpiled ivory to Japan to be concluded eighteen months after COP 10 ended. One important requirement for the sale to occur was that all proceeds were to be earmarked for elephant conservation in Zimbabwe, Namibia, and Botswana. Once the sale to Japan was completed in 1999, no further sales were allowed without the approval of a two-thirds majority of the Parties to the Convention.

After the eighteen-month waiting period had elapsed, the CITES Standing Committee announced in February 1999 that Zimbabwe, Namibia, Botswana, and Japan had met the preconditions imposed on the sale and authorized that it proceed. The sale to Japan took place in April 1999 and raised $5,000,000.

B. The Post-Sale Period

At the April 2000 Convention of the Parties (COP 10) in Nairobi, the CITES Standing Committee reported that Zimbabwe, Namibia, and Botswana had not manipulated "legal" sources of ivory to increase government stockpiles prior to the sale and that the sale had not served as an opportunity for the laundering of poached ivory. The Committee also stated there was no significant increase in the poaching of elephants in the three nations attributed to the one-time sale to Japan and that the sale was a complete success in that it had not prompted any significant increase in illegal elephant deaths on the African continent.

However, critics of the 1999 sale paint a very different picture of the effects of the sale on poaching and, ultimately, the threat it posed to the survival of the African elephant as a species. The International Fund for Animal Welfare (IFAW) reported that elephant poaching in Zimbabwe, Zambia, the Democratic Republic of Congo, the Central African Republic, Ghana and other African countries began to escalate as early as 1997, when the decision to allow the sale was announced. IFAW reported a 50% increase in elephant poaching in Zimbabwe alone in 1997 and 1998. Numerous studies conducted by other international nongovernmental (environmental) organizations documented increased elephant poaching and ivory smuggling across the African continent after the 1999 sale.

According to the International Fund for Animal Welfare, poachers believed the ban had been lifted throughout Africa and were building up stockpiles of poached ivory in anticipation of renewed trade. These reports were attacked as unreliable by organizations representing the sustainable-use position of several African nations. Vendors and craftsmen in West and Central Africa, upon hearing of the ivory sales in southern Africa, prepared for what they believed would be the beginning of the end for the Ivory Ban throughout Africa.

After the approval of the sale of stockpiled ivory, a significant increase in poaching was reported in Kenya's Tsavo and Damburu wildlife reserves; recorded ivory seizures also increased 400% in Kenya during 1999. Poachers in Kenya's Tsavo National Park killed 29 elephants in 1999, five times the average annual total during the CITES Ivory Ban. It is estimated that the price for ivory rose from $22 before the 1999 sale to approximately $300 in the year following the sale. International NGO's reported the results of studies showing that the demand for ivory stimulated by the "one-time" sale to Japan also led to increased poaching of elephants in Southeast Asia. One report credited the sale for the illegal killing of over 6,000 elephants in Africa and Asia during 1998 and 1999.

C. Reinstitution of the Ivory Ban

At the Convention of the Parties to CITES in Nairobi in 2000 (COP 11), Zimbabwe, Namibia, and Botswana proposed maintaining the elephant on Appendix II in their nations and requested further CITES approved sales of stockpiled "legal" ivory. South Africa joined the three nations in proposing future sales of stockpiled ivory, with the proceeds of the sales to be used for elephant conservation programs in southern Africa. At the same time, Kenya and India, fearful that further sales would lead to increased elephant poaching (as occurred after the 1999 sale), proposed returning the African elephant to Appendix I in all Party nations, thereby resuming a total global ban on ivory sales.

A compromise was reached whereby the four southern African nations requesting further sales withdrew the proposal for two years and Kenya and India in turn withdrew their proposal to return the African elephant to Appendix I in all range states. As part of the compromise, Parties agreed to delay any ivory sales until an effective system was in place to prevent the widespread poaching of elephants. Pending scientific study of elephant population statistics and the potential impacts of future limited ivory trade, the compromise agreement stayed any further discussion of additional ivory sales until the next Convention of the Parties (COP 12) in November 2002.

4. Editors' Note

Conservationists and the international legal community have largely embraced the notion that protection of species is most effective when local human communities derive benefits from that protection.[23] Thus, there is little objection to policies like eco-tourism, which seeks to generate revenue to local communities from conservation efforts, but which does not involve any trade in the endangered species or its parts. When "sustainable use" policies go further, however, and propose that human exploitation of an endangered species should include taking, trade or, indeed, any use of the animal, so long as species existence is not threatened, then serious disagreements emerge.[24] As the preceding reading explained, one of the most intense conflicts has been over the question whether to permit commercial trade in elephant parts, especially ivory. The next two readings examine the issues and make the case for allowing some legal sales of elephant ivory.

5. Sam B. Edwards III, Legal Trade in African Elephant Ivory: Buy Ivory to Save the Elephant?, 7 Animal Law 119, 128–131 (2001)

Wildlife represents a common, shared resource. In 1968, biology professor Garrett Hardin systematically analyzed this idea of a commons

---

[23] For a discussion of efforts to involve local communities in wildlife management programs, including efforts by African countries which explicitly affect elephant conservation, *see* Gregory F. Maggio, *Recognizing the Vital Role of Local Communities in International Legal Instruments for Conserving Biodiversity*, 16 UCLA J. Envtl. L & Pol'y 179, 196–200 (1998).

[24] *See* Chapter 1 ("Whaling"), *supra*, for further discussion of this point.

from which all citizens are allowed to benefit. Hardin's thesis is that a common pasture open to all will result in the ultimate destruction of the shared resource, the public pasture. Each citizen will seek to maximize his or her individual utility by grazing more and more cattle in the common pasture, even though the collective result is overgrazing and destruction of the pasture. Hardin succinctly summarizes the problem: "[f]reedom in a commons brings ruin to all."

There are two primary solutions to the problem of the commons: 1) fence the commons while controlling access; and 2) privatize the commons and give each citizen his own share of the commons to manage. Under the fencing scheme, the government controls access and manages the commons for the benefit of all. The privatization scheme, by contrast, divides the commons and allocates a section to each citizen under the assumption that each individual will maximize his own utility, thereby effectively managing his section of the commons. In the context of wildlife management, these two solutions are manifest in strategies of pure protectionism and sustained use.

1. Pure Protectionism

African nations have taken varying approaches to preserving their elephant populations. On one side are the 'fencing in' countries like Kenya, which has opted for a command-and-control system. Such command-and-control systems involve a complete ban on all hunting and cultivation of wildlife resources, and instead focuses on nonconsumptive activities such as tourism. In Kenya, where the country enjoys a robust tourism industry heavily reliant on safaris in public parks, a command-and-control system is appropriate. If the commons were divided, such safaris would not be possible because safari guides would have to obtain permission from multiple landowners over a large area.

Under the Kenyan program, the government has destroyed large numbers of stockpiled tusks to send the message that no use of ivory is permissible. Rather than focus on the sale of ivory for income, Kenya has developed a very robust tourism industry. Kenya's tourism industry is closely linked with the survival of species, such as the elephant, since most tourism revenue comes from safaris. Wildlife tourism in Africa provides more than $4 billion annually to urban and rural communities, reflecting tourists' desire to see elephants and other African wildlife in their natural habitats. However, the fencing solution is costly and difficult to enforce. One of Kenya's primary arguments against delisting the elephant in southern Africa is that it will lead to additional poaching in Kenya. To combat such enforcement problems, officials have had to rely on armed patrols and other coercive measures to protect wildlife.

2. Sustainable Use

In contrast to the pure protection approach of Kenya, some countries have followed a completely different path and employed a version of the privatization scheme, often referred to as 'sustainable use' or 'sustained use.' This scheme is similar to the privatization solution, in that each country or region is permitted to manage its own elephant stocks.

At the opening of the Tenth Meeting of the Parties [to CITES **(Basic Document 5.3)**] in 1997, Zimbabwe's President Robert Mugabe said that '[w]e believe a species must pay [its] own way to survive.' Mugabe's opinion clearly expresses the idea of sustained use: treating species as resources to be used, rather than merely preserved. Under this 'active management' approach, local residents manage wildlife within their region and keep some of the resulting profits. Sustained use is based on the concept of sustainable development.

The idea of sustainable development is not new. It emerged as early as 1972 at the United Nations Conference on the Human Environment. Former Director of the United Nations Environment Program, Mostafa Tolba, provided a good definition of the concept:

> At its core is the requirement that current practices not undermine future living standards: present economic systems must maintain or improve the resource and environmental base, so that future generations will be able to live as well as or better than the present one. Sustainable development does not require the preservation of the current stock of natural resources or any particular mix of human, physical, or natural assets, nor does it place artificial limits on economic growth, provided that such growth is both economically and environmentally sustainable.[25]

The idea is that current generations may use natural resources so long as they leave future generations as well off as or better than the current generation. While this concept of sustainable development appears straightforward, it is actually very difficult to define which actions are truly sustainable. Moreover, scientific uncertainty in assessing the environmental impacts of human activities contributes to the difficulty in defining sustainable development.

'Sustainable wildlife resource management' or 'sustained use' is sustainable development as it applies to wildlife management. Sustained use encompasses three primary concepts:

1) ensuring the sustainable utilization of species and ecosystems;

2) promoting genetic diversity; and

[25] Mostafa K. Tolba & Iwona Rummel-Bulska, Global Environmental Diplomacy: Negotiating Environmental Agreements for the World, 1973–1992 3 (MIT Press 1998).

3) maintaining the essential ecological processes and the life-support systems on which human survival and development depend.

For example, culling is considered an essential part of many wildlife management schemes. The sale of pelts, tusks, and other parts of the culled animals is allowed. Sustained use permits countries to cull enough animals to maintain healthy populations, thereby ensuring the existence of the resource for future generations. Moreover, through the sale of the culled animal products, countries are able to take economic advantage of their wildlife resources.

The concept of sustained use was first discussed at the 1992 CITES Conference. By the 1994 Meeting of the Parties, the shift away from pure protectionism to sustainable use was evident. The primary supporters of the sustained use strategy are several southern African nations, China, and Japan. The split of nations favoring and opposing sustained use roughly mirrors the north-south split of developed and developing nations. Developing nations of the south have often complained that they have borne an unequal burden in preserving and protecting the species listed in CITES. These nations seek to use their natural resources, including wildlife, to earn much needed revenue. Thus, the idea of a species having to 'pay its own way' exemplifies this idea of sustained use.

A much-heralded example of this sustained use strategy is the Communal Areas Management Programme for Indigenous Resources (CAMPFIRE) program in Zimbabwe. Under the CAMPFIRE program, local people manage 1% of their area's elephant population as they see fit. This generally results in the community allowing the culling or trophy hunting of some elephants in exchange for hard currency. The program has proven successful, and in 1989 one community was able to support above-average conservation efforts and purchase otherwise unaffordable social services from the sale of wildlife products, including ivory and elephant hides.

Under this type of program, citizens have a vested interest in preserving elephant populations, since such preservation yields economic benefits to their communities. In some instances, citizens have turned farming areas back into elephant habitat since the revenue from the elephants far exceeds the value of the crops. If the local people have a financial incentive, they will seek to protect the elephant populations so they can continue to reap benefits from the legal taking of individual animals.

Critics of this approach highlight moral and practical problems inherent in any sustainable use program. Some critics argue that humans cannot morally kill other species. Practical problems include the difficulty in counting the numbers of elephants, calculating what constitutes 'sustainable use,' and monitoring the taking of elephants and sales of elephant parts. Additionally, if countries allow the use of some elephants, albeit sustainably, they also open the door to illegal hunting. Since it is difficult to determine the origin of ivory, it follows that it is quite difficult to distinguish legally culled ivory from poached ivory.

Which strategy offers the best use of the elephant as a resource without jeopardizing the future of the elephant? The 'correct' management scheme depends on many changing factors such as the state of the elephant's habitat, the health of the populations, the effectiveness of worldwide controls on illegal sales, as well as policy preferences of the decision makers. Given these variables, it is doubtful that a single 'correct' management strategy exists. However, under the recent decision to permit the limited sale from Botswana, Zimbabwe, and Namibia, at least three countries will be able to implement an active management scheme.

6. Frances Cairncross, Costing the Earth—The Challenge for Governments, the Opportunities for Business 134–38, 141 (1992)

Can the concept of sustainable use, rather than conservation, save two of the world's most endangered and precious natural resources, the large mammals and the tropical rain forests? Perhaps, though old-fashioned conservationists are skeptical. Take the example of the African elephant, whose numbers have been halved by poaching, falling from about 1.2m in 1981 to just over 600,000 by 1989. In some countries the decline has been even more appalling: Kenya's elephant population fell by two-thirds between 1981 and 1989, Zambia's and Tanzania's by almost three-quarters. The beasts have been killed primarily for their ivory. In the hope of stemming the slaughter, a decision was taken in October 1989 to ban trade in ivory. The richest of the final consumers of ivory—the United States, the EC and Japan—all banned its import. Splendid, said conservationists. In the wake of the ban, the price of ivory plummeted and poaching fell sharply. The elephant, it seemed, might possibly have been saved. Since trade in the skins of wild cats, including leopards, was banned, their numbers have greatly revived. On the other hand, the black rhino was given the same protection in 1975, yet its numbers dropped from 500,000 to fewer than 40,000 by 1991.

Which fate awaits the elephant? The most convincing answer comes from a group of economists at the London Environmental Economics Centre (LEEC) in a study[26] they carried out in 1988–89 as part of the groundwork for the conference that eventually banned the ivory trade. They argue powerfully that a ban may eventually speed up the disappearance of the elephant from the wild, because it destroys one of the main ways in which governments could—if they chose—earn back the costs they incur in conserving the species. They suggest that the ivory trade did not cause the elephant's decline. The key factor was the failure of African governments to use the world ivory market to their best advantage. A ban

[26] Edward B. Barbier et al., Elephants, Economics and Ivory (1990).

on the trade will not help, for two reasons. First, the initial effect will be to cause a sharp drop in ivory prices. That will encourage a new demand for ivory among potential importers previously priced out of the market, such as South Korea, Taiwan and African countries themselves. This trade will be unmonitored, because new importers have not subscribed to the international convention that governs trade in endangered species.

* * *

Second, a ban destroys a possible incentive to preserve elephants. If elephants are to survive, they must be seen in Africa as an immensely valuable source of foreign exchange. The problem for the elephant is not that it lacks value, but that it is too valuable, and that it is, in effect, available to anybody who wants to risk killing it.

But conserving elephants is expensive. Even if the ivory trade were indeed to be stopped effectively by the ban, elephants might still continue to vanish. "If they are not killed for their ivory, they will be killed for the land they occupy," argue the LEEC economists. Conserving elephants not only means forgoing the use of the land on which they forage, but also spending hugely to prevent poachers. Zimbabwe reckons that it costs $200 per square km to protect wild elephants from illegal hunting. For Africa as a whole an effective war against poachers might well cost $80 million–100 million a year.

With a ban in place, only a few countries have an incentive to conserve, and they are the ones whose tourist trade has been built on showing wildlife to visitors. Elephants are one of the mainstays of the Kenyan tourist trade. Properly exploited, they might bring in even more than they do. A back of an envelope survey of tourists in Kenya, by Gardner Brown of the University of Washington in Seattle, found that the average tourist was happy to pay a $100 surcharge to protect the elephant. Even allowing for exaggeration, that suggests Kenya's 1 million game park tourists could bring in an extra $20 million a year in revenues, one-third as much as all Africa gets from killing the beasts.

The elephant's best hope of survival in other countries still lies mainly in its tusks. The aim should be to cull elephants at a sustainable rate and use the revenue to help to pay for conservation. One intriguing study in Botswana compared the value of managing elephant herds with the value if tourism is combined with elephant cropping. The cropping reduces yields from tourism by about 10%, but leads to other gains, such as tanning elephant hides, ivory carving and producing meat for crocodile farming. The extra benefits almost double the total economic value of a herd.

* * *

With the ban [on the ivory trade], however, the elephant's future is uncertain. Temporarily, the collapse of demand in the rich industrial countries will discourage poaching. The price of ivory within Africa has fallen dramatically. Large new dollops of aid from the West are helping to improve the pay and equipment of park guards. The danger is that poaching will revive. New markets will be developed. Some people who in the past bought ivory legally will now buy it illegally. That will drive up the black market price, raising the profitability of poaching and increasing the risks that poachers are willing to take.

7. Editors' Note: Legal Developments

In 2008, after years of discussion and debate, a second legal sale of ivory was authorized by CITES. This time, the sellers were the three African nations involved in the 1997 sale (Botswana, Namibia and Zimbabwe) plus South Africa. China joined Japan as a purchaser. The auctioned ivory was from stockpiles gleaned from animals that died of natural causes or were killed during controlled culls of elephant herds. Following authorization of the sale, the CITES Secretariat commented that "linking legal supplies of raw ivory from southern African countries with the legal demand in countries in Asia should help reduce the motivation for the poaching of elephants and illegal trade in ivory." At the same time, it indicated that it would monitor the internal markets in China and Japan to ensure that there was no laundering of ivory from illegal sources. *See* Fifty-seventh meeting of the Standing Committee, *Control of Trade in Elephant Ivory*, CITES Doc. SC57 Doc. 33.2 (2008). Proceeds of the sale were earmarked for elephant conservation.

The issue of how to deal with the ivory trade remains contentious, both internationally and within individual countries. At the 17th meeting of the Conference of the Parties to CITES in 2016, Namibia and Zimbabwe proposed to remove the annotation that restricts ivory sales from populations of elephants listed in CITES Appendix II. The countries indicated a desire to sell stockpiled ivory from natural elephant deaths and poaching seizures in order to fund conservation efforts. The move was rejected by the CITES Parties. A competing proposal was made by several other African countries to move elephant populations in Botswana, Namibia, South Africa and Zimbabwe from Appendix II back to Appendix I. That proposal was also rejected by the CITES Parties. The next CITES Conference of the Parties is scheduled for August 2019 in Geneva, Switzerland.

In a move widely hailed by wildlife campaigners, China announced in 2017 that it would shut down its domestic ivory market. The ban came into effect on the last day of 2017, although China had been shutting down shops and factories throughout 2017. The immediate reported effects were a significant decline in the price of raw ivory (because of the huge loss of demand attributable to the Chinese ban) and a decline in seizures of ivory entering China illegally.

On the other hand, Botswana, which has banned trophy hunting of elephants since 2014 was considering (as of 2018) lifting the ban and allowing the export of elephant trophies. Botswana is home to the world's largest elephant population, and parliamentarians advocating a return to trophy hunting cited growing conflict between humans and elephants as a reason. Crop losses caused by elephants in northwestern Botswana are significant, and income generated by trophy hunting is seen as one way to generate revenue for local communities adversely affected by large elephant populations.

The United States, which banned the import of elephant trophies during the Obama Administration, lifted the ban in March 2018 and now allows the import of elephant trophies from several African countries, so long as it can be shown that the hunting is sustainable and benefits the elephant population overall (e.g., by reinvestment of the proceeds into support for conservation efforts).

8. Editors' Note: What the Numbers Say About Sustainable Use Versus Pure Protection

The population of African elephants fell from an estimated 1.3 million in 1979 to about 600,000 in 1989. Poaching declined considerably after the imposition of the ban on commercial trade in ivory, but it by no means disappeared, and by the mid-1990s it was on the rise again. Despite the differing views over whether allowing ivory sales would promote or reduce poaching, no adequate method for monitoring the situation was in place at the time of the 1997 one-off ivory sale, so evaluations of its impact on the poaching situation are highly speculative.

However, better methods for estimating poaching rates and overall elephant numbers have been put in place since 2000. Following the 2008 ivory sale, two scholars used the new data to try to determine whether the sale had led to an increase or decrease in poaching. Their conclusion: "legal sale of ivory triggered an increase in black market ivory production [poaching] by increasing consumer demand and/or reducing the cost of supplying black market ivory, and these effects dominated any competitive displacement that occurred."[27] The lawful sale of ivory appeared, in fact, to have led directly to increased elephant poaching, as many feared.

Before one concludes, however, that the sales of ivory by Botswana, Namibia, South Africa, and Zimbabwe were failures from an elephant conservation point of view, it is worth considering what happened in the countries that made the sales. The IUCN's 2016 estimate of African elephant populations reported an overall decline in population numbers of approximately 104,000—114,000 from 2007–2016, and concluded that the

[27] Solomon Hsiang & Nitin Sekar, *Does Legalization Reduce Black Market Activity? Evidence from a Global Ivory Experiment and Elephant Poaching Data*, NBER Working Paper 22314 (National Bureau of Economic Research, June 2016).

decline was "largely caused by the surge in poaching that began around 2006." The same report concluded that populations in some of the countries (Namibia, South Africa, and Zimbabwe) were "stable or increasing." In Botswana, the elephant population appears to be in decline, but the reliability of the estimate is considered quite low. *See generally* International Union for Conservation of Nature and Natural Resources, *African Elephant Status Report 2016: An Update from the African Elephant Database,* Occasional Paper Series of the IUCN Species Survival Commission, no. 60 (2016). Furthermore, the Hsiang & Sekar report showed no statistically significant increase in poaching in any of the countries from which ivory sales were made.

Thus, perhaps we must reach a mixed conclusion. Legalizing ivory sales does appear to create an incentive for increased elephant poaching, both by increasing consumer demand for ivory (by legalizing it) and by making it difficult to distinguish legal from illegal ivory sales. On the other hand, the revenue that range states gain from such sales may assist them in their conservation efforts and, in those states at least, help support effective conservation efforts.

The following readings from material in the Documents Supplement are important for analysis of this problem. Pay particular attention to Reading 9 (CITES) and Reading 10 (Revised African Convention on the Conservation of Nature).

9. Convention on International Trade in Endangered Species of Wild Fauna and Flora (CITES), arts. I–III, VII–IX, XIV, XXIII, XXIV & Appendix II, March 3, 1973, 993 UNTS 243 (Basic Document 5.3)

10. Revised African Convention on the Conservation of Nature and Natural Resources, arts. VII–IX, July 11, 2003 (Basic Document 5.8)

11. Stockholm Declaration on the Human Environment, Principles 2–4, 11, 13, 21, 24, & 25, U.N. Doc. A/CONF.48/14 at 2–65 (June 16, 1972) (Basic Document 1.21)

12. Draft Principles of Conduct in the Field of the Environment for Guidance of States in the Conservation and Harmonious Utilization of Natural Resources Shared by Two or More States, Principles 1–5, 7–8, 10, 12.1, & 13, May 19, 1978, UNEP/IG.12/2, at 11–14 (Basic Document 1.24)

13. World Charter for Nature, Principles 1–4, 6, 7, 9–11, 14, 19, & 24 (Oct. 28, 1982), G.A. Res. 37/7, U.N. GAOR, 37th Sess., Supp. No. 51, at 17, UN Doc A/37/51 (Basic Document 1.27)

14. Rio Declaration on Environment and Development, Principles 4, 12, & 14, June 14, 1992, Report of the UN Conference on the Environment and Development at Rio de Janeiro, U.N. Doc. A/CONF.151/26 (1992) (Basic Document 1.30)

15. Michael Glennon, Has International Law Failed the Elephant?, 84 AJIL 1, 30–33 (1990)

It is now possible to conclude that customary international law requires states to take appropriate steps to protect endangered species. Customary norms are created by state practice "followed by them from a sense of legal obligation."[28] Like highly codified humanitarian law norms that have come to bind even states that are not parties to the instruments promulgating them, wildlife protection norms also have become binding on nonparties as customary law. Closely related to this process of norm creation by practice is that of norm creation by convention: customary norms are created by international agreements "when such agreements are intended for adherence by states generally and are in fact widely accepted."[29] Several such agreements are directed at wildlife protection, and CITES is one of them. It is intended for adherence by states generally and is accepted by the 103 states that have become parties. In addition, some nonparties comply with certain CITES documentary requirements so as to trade with parties. CITES is not "rejected by a significant number of states";[30] only the United Arab Emirates has withdrawn from the agreement. In such circumstances, the International Court of Justice has observed, international agreements constitute state practice and represent law for nonparties.

Moreover, customary norms are created by the "general principles of law recognized by civilized nations."[31] Because CITES requires domestic implementation by parties to it, and because the overall level of compliance seems quite high, the general principles embodied in states' domestic endangered species laws may be relied upon as another source of customary law. Even apart from the CITES requirements, states that lack laws protecting endangered species seem now to be the clear exception rather than the rule. That there exists *opinio juris* as to the binding character of this obligation is suggested by the firm support given endangered species protection by the UN General Assembly and various international conferences.

While the existence of a norm requiring the protection of endangered species thus seems likely, its scope remains uncertain. To the extent that the norm derives from CITES and laws implementing CITES, that scope

---

[28] Restatement (Third) of the Foreign Relations Law of the United States, pt. VI (1987).

[29] *Id.* § 102(3).

[30] *Id.* § 102 comment i.

[31] I.C.J. Statute **[Basic Document 1.2]**, Art. 38(1)(c).

would be fairly narrow, for the norm would cover only species in international trade, not those taken for domestic consumption or those endangered by threats to their habitat. Even if it could be shown that major legal systems generally comprise endangered species legislation, more work needs to be done to determine exactly what elements those laws have in common. What constitutes an "endangered species," for example, is debatable. Is it one that is endangered in every state, or only in the state making the assessment? And to what lengths must a state go in protecting a species it finds "endangered"? Must it do everything necessary to protect that species, notwithstanding the cost or the ecological significance of the species?

As to the elephant in particular, it is hard to argue under customary international law that states such as South Africa and Zimbabwe are prohibited from selling ivory by a new customary norm, corresponding generally to the CITES restrictions. In the *North Sea Continental Shelf* case, the International Court of Justice said:

> Although the passage of only a short period of time is not necessarily, or of itself, a bar to the formation of a new rule of customary international law on the basis of what was originally a purely conventional rule, an indispensable requirement would be that within the period in question, short though it might be, State practice, including that of States whose interests are specially affected, should have been both extensive and *virtually uniform* in the sense of the provision invoked. . . .[32]

The nonparticipation of southern African states suggests that any such custom is not "virtually uniform." In fact, the southern African elephant "excess" states might be seen as partaking in a regional custom of the sort considered in the *Asylum* case.[33] Or they might be seen as "persistent objectors" to an emerging norm during the inchoate stages of its development.

It thus appears doubtful that a customary norm concerning the elephant or any other endangered species can yet play any significant role in its protection. But the trend cannot be doubted; and once its contours are more clear, the customary norm requiring states to protect endangered species ought to take on the character of an obligation *erga omnes.* Ordinarily, claims for the violation of an international obligation may be made only by the state to which the obligation is owed. Obligations *erga omnes*, however, run to the international community as a whole; thus, their breach is actionable by any state since such matters are "[b]y their very

---

[32] 1969 ICJ 3, 43 (emphasis added).

[33] Asylum (Colum./Peru), 1950 ICJ 266 (Judgment of Nov. 20).

nature . . . the concern of all States. . . . [T]hey are obligations *erga omnes*."[34]

Section 5. Discussion Notes/Questions

1. Was Bawanda's failure to stop poachers from entering Usambara, and presumably transporting illegally-obtained ivory back to Usambara, a violation of its legal obligations under CITES, other treaty law, or customary international law?

2. Did the Usambaran troops violate international law when they transported ivory from Bawanda to Usambara?

3. Do either government's conservation policies violate international law. In particular, is Bawanda's failure to protect its own elephant populations a violation of international law?

4. As the readings indicate, there is great disagreement about the impact that a strictly limited legal ivory trade will have on conservation of elephant populations. At COP 10, the CITES Contracting Parties established two programs aimed at ascertaining whether a resumption of legal international trade in ivory would have on illegal hunting of elephants and the illegal ivory trade. One program, known as MIKE (Monitoring the Illegal Killing of Elephants) gathers information within elephant range states to measure levels and trends in the illegal hunting of elephants. A second program, known as ETIS (Elephant Trade Information System) seeks to track illegal trade in ivory and other elephant products. ETIS is managed by Traffic on behalf of the CITES parties. At COP12, reports generated from ETIS data led Traffic to conclude that the illegal trade in ivory is driven by large, unregulated *domestic* ivory markets in Africa and Asia. If this is true, then what measures are likely to be most effective in reducing the illegal trade? How does this impact the decision to allow occasional legal *international* sales of ivory from countries with well-managed elephant populations? Although knowing where ivory is traded is certainly useful, one problem in assessing the effectiveness of a ban on trade, or the impact of limited legal trade, is that either policy approach could be beneficial or harmful to elephant populations, depending on a variety of circumstances, including how income from trade (or protection) is used. *See* Andrew M. Lemieux & Ronald V. Clarke, *The International Ban on Ivory Sales and its Effects on Elephant Poaching in Africa,* 49 Brit. J. Criminology 451 (2009); Daniel Stiles, *CITES-approved Ivory Sales and Elephant Poaching*, 45 Pachyderm 150 (2008–09). The data generated by MIKE and the ETIS were important to the conclusion of Hsiang & Sekar (*see* Reading 8) that the 2008 ivory sale led to an increase in poaching.

5. China's internal ivory market was the largest in the world, and its ban on the internal sale of ivory will go a long way toward reducing international demand for ivory. But ivory markets remain open and active in

[34] Barcelona Traction, Light & Power Co., Ltd. (Belg. v. Spain), Second Phase, 1970 ICJ 3, 32 (Judgment of Feb. 5).

other Asian countries and in some African countries. Tourists (including Chinese tourists) are often the main buyers.

6. In *Summarizing the Evidence on the International Trade in Illegal Wildlife,* 7 EcoHealth 24 (2010), Gail Emilia Rosen & Katherine F. Smith concluded that illegal wildlife trade may be one of the world's largest illegitimate businesses. They summarize, at p. 27:

> The illegal wildlife trade is vast in species diversity and geographic scope, evidence that large numbers of illegal wildlife are traded successfully on a regular basis. Efforts to control illegal wildlife trade vary nationally. Many governments face challenges in enforcement due to the remoteness of areas where poaching occurs, lack of infrastructure, corrupt officials, the involvement of transnational crime networks, and a shortage of wildlife law enforcement officers.

Similarly, Samuel K. Wasser, et al., writes:

> The illegal wildlife trade is booming around the world. Illegal trade in wildlife products has reached over $20 billion a year. China is the largest market, with the United States and Japan running close seconds. The illegal trade has become a high-profit enterprise with exceptionally low risks. Prosecutions of illegal wildlife traffickers are relatively rare, largely because law enforcement officers, prosecutors, and judicial systems typically consider such crime a low priority. Not surprisingly, evidence now indicates that organized crime has become heavily involved in illegal wildlife trafficking. There has been a conspicuous increase in frequency of seizures of large consignments of contraband, including coral, snake skins, conch shells, ivory, the Tibetan antelope chiru or shahtoosh, abalone, and other wildlife products, each recently characterized by authorities as the largest of this type in history. Wildlife traffickers are exploiting the globalization and liberalization of legal international trade and taking advantage of the most modern commercial and technological developments, both of which make illegal trade in wildlife products nearly impossible to track once the product has left the source country.

Samuel K. Wasser, et al., *Combating the Illegal Trade in African Elephant Ivory With DNA Forensics*, 22 Conservation Biology 1065, 1066–67 (2008).

Elephants are by no means the only large mammals on the list of endangered species as a result of consumer demand and international trade. For example, tigers are being hunted to a point which they are now reaching extinction. There is a flourishing market in tiger bones in some Asian countries, and it seems that the "few remaining wild tiger populations may not survive beyond the end of this decade." *See Tiger Bone Survey—Undercover Survey of Markets Reveals Tons of Tiger Bone For Sale*, Earth Trust Chronicles 14 (Summer, 1993). Similarly, the rhinoceros is in trouble, as well as some species of dolphin and whales.

7. International cooperation to address this illegal international trade is increasing and includes the joint efforts of NGOs like TRAFFIC; international organizations, including CITES and Interpol; regional enforcement bodies, such as the ASEAN Wildlife Enforcement Network; and national governments. But efforts to foster international cooperation are not always successful. The Lusaka Agreement on Co-operative Enforcement Operations Directed at Illegal Trade in Wild Fauna and Flora, September 8, 1994, 1950 UNTS 35, was a promising effort to address the problem of illegal trade in endangered species within Africa. Unfortunately, only a handful of African countries signed or ratified the Agreement. At this writing, there are only six parties to the agreement: Congo (Brazzaville), Kenya, Tanzania, Uganda, Zambia and Lesotho.

DNA testing may become an important tool in combating illegal wildlife trade. Through DNA testing, a "geographic origin" can be assigned "to seized wildlife products." Once that is done, law enforcement can be directed to those areas. "Focusing law enforcement on areas where poaching is most concentrated potentially thwarts the trade before it enters into an increasingly complex web of international criminal activity that is extraordinarily expensive and difficult to track. This approach can also prevent countries from denying their poaching problems at home and may ultimately stop the trade before the wildlife is actually killed." Samuel K. Wasser, et al., *Combating the Illegal Trade in African Elephant Ivory With DNA Forensics*, 22 Conservation Biology 1065, 1066–67 (2008).

8. Why save the elephant? Is there an obligation on States to preserve global environmental resources? Is the elephant a "global resource," part of the "common heritage"? If so, do non-elephant countries have an obligation to help elephant countries meet their custodial obligations to elephant populations? What would these support obligations involve? Should they apply to the opportunity cost of forgoing the sale of ivory as well as the cost of conservation programs? Should all who benefit from elephant protection share the cost? How might this be done? *See* Michael Glennon, *Has International Law Failed the Elephant?*, 84 AJIL 1, 34–43 (1990). What about debt for nature swaps? How about debt for ivory? *See generally* Amanda Spitler, *Exchanging Debt for Conservation*, 37 Bioscience 781 (1987); *A Debt to Nature*, ECONOMIST, Aug. 19, 1989, at 35.

9. A frequent complaint about international policy concerning the elephant is that it is unduly influenced by the sentimental and unrealistic views of the elephant held by animal protectionists in developed nations. There is a tendency to overlook or underestimate the hazards of large elephant populations to the people of the developing countries in which the elephant resides. Elephants are difficult to support and can do tremendous destruction to the natural environment and human settlements. The average elephant eats 18 hours a day, consuming up to 300 pounds of vegetation. It takes a minimum of 4 square kilometers per elephant to support a healthy population. During a drought elephants compete with other species, including humans, for limited food. As they roam, they can strip entire areas clear of vegetation, leading to

the demise of other species. In the past, this has led governments to undertake efforts to exterminate elephants as pests. *See* Paul Ehrlich & Anne Ehrlich, Extinction—The Causes and Consequences of the Disappearance of Species 128 (1981).

Although government extermination programs aimed at elephants are probably a thing of the past, concern over human-elephant conflict is not. Elephants often raid and destroy crops of poor African farmers, and no effective mechanisms to confine them to particular areas (or to fence them out of cropland) have been developed. Elephants are also dangerous to humans whose paths they cross (and vice versa, of course). Reports of elephants killing people are common and regular in Africa, and human-elephant conflict can only escalate as populations of both species grow. See generally Joseph R. Berger, The African Elephant, Human Economies, and International Law: Bridging a Great Rift for East and Southern Africa, 13 Geo. Int'l Envtl. L. Rev. 417 (2001).

In short, preservation of the elephant imposes significant costs on the peoples and countries in which elephants live. Consideration of this reality has prompted efforts to develop sustainable-use approaches to conservation that make it pay, not only for the world at large, but also for the directly-affected human populations.

10. Is the desire to protect the elephant simply cultural imperialism, reflecting the affluent West's sentimental attachment to large mammals? The Japanese have argued, with respect to whaling, that preservation concerns are motivated by culturally specific values; the imposition of these values on countries and cultures that do not share them, is a form of imperialism. *See* Kazuo Sumi, *The "Whale War" Between Japan and the US: Problems and Prospects*, 17 Den. J. Int'l L. & Pol'y 317 (1989); Sidney Holt, *Whale Mining, Whale Saving,* 9 Marine Pol'y 192 (1985). For an in-depth examination of the whaling issue, see Chapter 1. *See also* Eugene Hargrove, *An Overview of Conservation and Human Values: Are Conservation Goals Merely Cultural Attitudes?*, *in* Conservation for the Twenty-First Century 227 (David Western & Mary Pearl eds. 1989); Bryan Norton, *The Cultural Approach to Conservation Biology*, *in id.*, at 241.

11. Illegal international trade in animal parts is not the main cause of animal extinctions globally. Other threats include resource conflicts with humans (e.g., habitat destruction), competition from other non-human species (including invasive species), and local consumption of endangered animals. Yet these other problems are not addressed adequately, or at all, by international law. CITES, for example, "does not address the issue of local community harvesting and consumption . . . for domestic subsistence or commercial purposes, despite the extensive documentation that local consumption of species [including the elephant] otherwise protected under CITES is a significant conservation issue." *See* Gregory Maggio, *Recognizing the Vital Role of Local Communities in International Legal Instruments for Conserving*

Biodiversity, 16 UCLA J. Envtl. L. & Pol'y 179, 206–07 (1998). How does the Convention on Biological Diversity address these other problems?

12. In the case of the elephant, human encroachment on elephant habitat (and the killing of elephants in the resulting human-elephant conflicts) may be as significant a problem as illegal ivory poaching. Setting aside game preserves does not necessarily solve the problems. Elephants can, and do, leave reserves and deprecate bordering cropland, which may lead to killings of elephants by local communities. Moreover, the land set aside for game land is often good land as it must support vegetation. This means that there will be pressure to open the land for farming or to otherwise support impoverished local populations.

Should elephants or other wildlife be required to justify economically the allocation of land and resources that are necessary for their protection? Is it worth the cost to the human population to save elephants? For a detailed discussion of the different approaches taken by different African nations to the issues of human-elephant conflicts, *see* Joseph R. Berger, *The African Elephant, Human Economies, and International Law: Bridging a Great Rift for East and Southern Africa,* 13 Geo. Int'l Envtl. L. Rev. 417 (2001).

13. A related consideration is that excessively large elephant populations can threaten the natural biodiversity of an area, as they choke out other species and, then, the species that fed on them. What is to be done about this? Should international law allow the thinning of elephant populations by governments that have effective elephant conservation programs? Should they be allowed to sell the ivory on the legal market? To give the food to local persons (elephant meat dries to a sturdy jerky which will preserve for up to one year)? What about a hunting season, much like the United States has with deer or elk? Shouldn't countries with a strong elephant conservation program be allowed to profit from their successful management by "selling" the right to take a controlled number of surplus animals, as Usambara has done? *See* Berger, *supra*.

14. Is there anything that the international community can (or should) do about threats to endangered species that are completely local in origin? If so, what? Or are local threats of local concern only? If the elephant is destroyed in a country because of local consumption of the animal for food, is that a matter of importance to the international community? If game preserves are destroyed to make room for farms, is that a matter of international concern? If so, should the international community ease up on trade restrictions and allow the profits from international trade in ivory, and other uses of elephants, to be used to address local concerns and discourage excessive local consumption of elephants (by raising standards of living)? Or is that an apologist's pipedream? *See* Max Abesperg-Traun, *CITES, Sustainable Use of Wild Species and Incentive-Driven Conservation in Developing Countries, With an Emphasis on Southern Africa*, 142 Biol. Cons. 948 (2009).

15. What if Bawanda wanted to raise elephants on farms and trade in ivory. Would this be permitted by CITES? *See* Hubertus Welsch, *Trade in Appendix I Species*, 13 Envtl. Pol'y & L. 100 (1984). At COP–10 in Harare in

June 1997, significant decisions were taken with the aim of encouraging ranching activities aimed at threatened species (albeit aimed at species other than the elephant). *See generally* Richard Damania & Erwin H. Bulte, *The Economics of Wildlife Farming and Endangered Species Conservation,* 62 Ecol. Econ. 461 (2007).

16. One might argue that protecting elephants is an essential element of protecting biodiversity. But some preservationist strategies may go well beyond what is necessary in that regard. When elephants are protected, they place disproportionate demands on the available ecosystem. Some in Botswana believe, for example, that its current elephant population is at least double what the land area can reasonably support. Some conservationists also question the focus on a single species like the elephant:

> Biotic diversity is not linked to the distribution of elephants, rhinos, and other so-called charismatic megaherbivores. The massive investment in conservation campaigns directed at these species does more for the souls of the donors and the egos of the elephant experts than it does for biotic diversity, which is centered on less exciting communities of montane, forests, Mediterranean heathlands, wetlands, lakes and rivers.

Brian Huntley, *Conserving and Monitoring Biotic Diversity: Some African Examples, in* BIODIVERSITY 248, 259 (E. Wilson ed. 1988). Is an ecosystem approach preferable? What would it mean to adopt such an approach? *See* Anne Batchelor, *The Preservation of Wildlife Habitat in Ecosystems: Towards a New Direction Under International Law to Prevent Species' Extinction,* 3 Fla. Int'l L.J. 307 (1988). *See also* Sarah Fitzgerald, International Wildlife Trade: Whose Business Is It? (1989).

PROBLEM 7-3: SAVING THE SEMINOLE SWAMP

Section 1. Facts

The Seminole Swamp covers more than 1 million acres of a subtropical peninsula located in the southeast corner of the Federation of Columbia (FC). The swamp is actually a series of diverse interconnected wetlands, including shallow rivers, sawgrass marshes, cypress swamps, wet prairies, and mangrove forests. It is a Ramsar Convention "wetland of global importance" and a World Heritage site, and it hosts a diverse variety of plant and animal life, much of which is found nowhere else in the Federation. Three hundred fifty bird species make their home in the swamp, including 10 endangered species. Twenty-nine varieties of snake live there, as well as alligators living in the freshwater swamps and crocodiles in the coastal mangroves. More than 120 different species of marsh plants have been identified in the swamp; in addition to the ubiquitous sawgrass, floating aquatic plants like water lily and maidencane are abundant.

Amidst the marshes and wet prairies of the swamp are numerous tree islands—small groupings of trees and shrubs that have adapted to the wet environment of the Seminole Swamp. Tree islands increase the habitat options for animals living in the swamp and thus contribute to the diversity of its flora and fauna. Bay, willow, and cypress trees flourish on the islands. Shrubs and flowing plants that could not survive in the swamp itself grow abundantly on the islands, including many species of fern and several varieties of orchid.

The tree islands are vital to the Seminole Swamp ecosystem. They are home to many mammals that live in the Swamp, including whitetail deer. Alligators nest on tree islands. They are also the site of the rookeries of many of the wading and migratory bird species in the Swamp. Recent scientific studies have revealed that the tree islands are an important sink for excess phosphorus and nitrogen that enters the Swamp as a result of agricultural activity in surrounding areas. They play a disproportionate role in carbon cycling as well.

Estimates of the value to the local economy of the Seminole Swamp exceed $2 billion annually. The swamp is an important tourist attraction, it supports a significant commercial fishing industry, and it provides recreational opportunities (including fishing, hunting, birdwatching, boating, and camping) for the 7 million people living in the area. The swamp's most important ecosystem service, however, is purification of water and recharging of aquifers. The ability of the swamp to absorb and recycle nutrients and chemicals significantly reduces pollution in surface waters. Water from the swamp also recharges and helps maintain the quality of water in the heavily utilized aquifers in the region.

The tree islands in the swamp are currently under grave threat from an invasive species known as Amazonian marsh grass. Amazonian marsh grass is a perennial grass that grows rapidly (as much as 12 feet in one season) and densely. When it takes root on a tree island, it quickly crowds out native surface plants and shrubs. It grows so thickly that small mammals accustomed to seeking shelter on the tree island can no longer do so. Worse, while small surface fires are frequent on tree islands in the swamp and are an important means for the ecosystem to regenerate and make room new growth, a fire on a tree island infested with Amazonian marsh grass can be devastating. Because of the height of the marsh grass, fire travels along it into the canopy of the trees, which kills the trees and destroys the rookeries of the birds nesting there. Some scientists believe that if the grass continues to spread at current rates, two-thirds of the tree islands in the Seminole Swamp will be destroyed within 20 years, with disastrous consequences for the entire swamp ecosystem.

Amazonian marsh grass was imported into the Federation of Columbia five years ago from South America. The importer, Seminole BioFuels LLC

(SB), believed that the plant would prove to be a valuable source of cellulosic biomass for biofuel production. Amazonian marsh grass grows rapidly, can be harvested multiple times a year, thrives in a wet environment, and has high yields of biomass. Unfortunately, the plant escaped from cultivated fields and spread rapidly across the swamp. With no natural insect predators in the swamp, it has thrived and is threatening to overwhelm local vegetation.

Under FC law, SB is responsible for controlling the spread of the marsh grass that escaped from its facilities. SB staff scientists have been working to develop a plan for eliminating Amazonian marsh grass from the Seminole Swamp. Because of the grave threat to the swamp, the FC Environmental Protection Agency has assigned several of its scientists to work with SB in addressing the problem. So far, however, these efforts have been unsuccessful. Traditional herbicides cannot be used to control the Amazonian marsh grass because of their impact on other plant species on the infected tree islands. No other realistic control options have yet been identified.

The Government of Amazonia, a large, middle-income developing nation in South America, recently created a database to serve as a repository of traditional knowledge about the uses of plants and animals found within the country—the Amazonian Traditional Knowledge Database (ATKD). Amazonian scientists, working with indigenous peoples, prepare information recording traditional uses of different components of biodiversity in the country. Access to the database is available to bioprospectors for a fee. If a biosprospector finds information that has promise, the bioprospector can apply for limited access to the resource itself. Access is granted on terms set by the Amazonian Office for the Protection of Genetic Resources (AOGPR). Before removing genetic resources from Amazonia, a prospector must also sign a contract with AOGPR on terms negotiated with AOGPR on a case-by-case basis.

While searching the Amazonia Traditional Knowledge Database, a scientist working for Seminole BioFuels discovered that the Anámo people of the Amazon rainforest use the ground root of small local plant—the canamatar—as a means to eradicate infestations of Amazonian marsh grass from their garden plots. The entry in the database indicates that the root of canamatar appears to produce a selective herbicide that kills the marsh grass, but does not affect surrounding vegetation.

Seminole BioFuels immediately hired an anthropologist who previously had worked with the Anámo to arrange for a team of scientists to visit a traditional Anámo village located in the Northern Amazonia National Park, an area that Amazonia has set aside for preservation and protection from development. The anthropologist contacted elders of the village, who were eager to help. The Anámo revere the natural environment and believe strongly in sharing their knowledge and resources to assist in its preservation. The village elders agreed to host a team of FC scientists to help them identify canamatar, and to demonstrate canamatar's properties, for a payment of $50,000 to the village.

When SB contacted the Amazonian Office for Protection of Genetic Resources (AOPGR), they were told that visas would not be issued for their proposed scientific expedition, nor would they be allowed to acquire samples of canamatar, unless SB and the FC signed an "access to biodiversity resources" agreement with AOPGR. The proposed access agreement includes the following terms and requirements:

1. SB must to pay a $250,000 "bioprospecting fee" to the Amazonian Biodiversity Trust Fund (ABTF) prior to the commencement of the expedition. The ABTF is a fund established to help cover the expenses of maintaining national parks and other protected areas in Amazonia.
2. Researchers from the Universidade Católica de Amazonia must be included on the scientific team established by SB to acquire and evaluate samples of canamatar.
3. No samples of canamatar can be taken out of the country for research purposes. All research to determine canamatar's effectiveness as an herbicide must be conducted at the Universidade Católica de Amazonia, with the participation of Amazonian scientists paid by Seminole BioFuels or the Federation of Columbia. SB scientists will be permitted to lead and participate in the research effort.
4. If research on canamatar leads to development of an effective herbicide against Amazonian marsh grass, SB must agree that the herbicide can be freely used and produced in Amazonia.
5. SB must pay 20% of earned profits from annual sales of any canamater-derived herbicide to the Amazonian Biodiversity Trust Fund.
6. In the event that a herbicide derived from canamatar is used to control the spread of Amazonian marsh grass in the Seminole Swamp, Amazonia will be compensated for its contribution to saving the swamp by annual payments of $1 billion (50% of the estimated annual economic value of the Seminole Swamp) for a period of five years. Payments are to be made by the Federation of Columbia government to the Amazonian Biodiversity Trust Fund.
7. No access to canamatar of any sort will be allowed until the Federation of Columbia government ratifies the 2010 Nagoya

> Protocol on Access to Genetic Resources and the Fair and Equitable Sharing of Benefits Arising from their Utilization.

The Federation of Columbia and Seminole BioFuels objected to the terms of the proposed access agreement. They proposed alternative terms aimed primarily at reducing the financial obligations of the agreement and permitting them to perform research on canamatar at SB's research facilities in the FC. They also asked AOPGR to remove the obligation concerning ratification of Nagoya Protocol because, they said, such a coercive condition was an inappropriate interference with FC's sovereignty and that securing legislative approval of the Protocol (a precondition to FC's ratification) will take too long given the immediacy of the threat posed by the spread of swamp grass. The AOPGR, however, refused to modify any of its access conditions.

In a letter sent to the head of AOPGR and subsequently released to the press, the Federation of Columbia's Minister for Environmental Protection said the following:

> The conditions imposed by the AOPGR are harsh, unfair, and entirely inconsistent with Amazonia's obligations under the 1992 Convention on Biological Diversity. The canamatar could provide the only means available to save the Seminole Swamp, one of the world's great biodiversity preserves. While the Federation is willing to accept reasonable terms, Amazonia's conditions, imposed with knowledge of the ecological catastrophe we are facing, amount to environmental blackmail. Export of the canamatar plant to the Federation will cause no harm to Amazonia or to the Anámo people. Our scientists are more experienced than Amazonian scientists and can quickly investigate the plant's potential and develop a useful herbicide if that is possible. Moreover, Amazonia's conditions violate the rights of the Anámo people who have invited SB to visit their village and who stand to gain tremendously from this relationship.

Amazonia's Minister for Sustainable Development replied:

> Private companies and scientists from the Federation of Columbia have been engaged in widespread theft of our genetic resources for decades. Billions of dollars have been made from pharmaceuticals and other products derived from Amazonian plants and animals, with little or no compensation to Amazonia or to the indigenous people whose knowledge led to the so-called "discovery" by exploitative and unethical Northern scientists. We have the right under international law to demand a share of the value our resources will provide to the Federation of Columbia as the price of allowing access to those resources. We are also entitled to

adequate compensation for the development opportunities we lose by choosing to preserve our wetlands, forests, and waterways where these immense stores of biodiversity are found.

Following receipt of this reply, the Federation of Columbia requested conciliation pursuant to Article 27(4) and Annex II, Part 2 of the 1992 Convention on Biological Diversity (CBD) **(Basic Document 5.6)**. A five-member conciliation commission has been appointed and has scheduled a hearing in the matter.

Both Amazonia and the Federation of Columbia are parties to the CBD. Amazonia, but not the Federation of Columbia, has also ratified all the protocols[35] adopted by the parties to the CBD. Both countries are parties to the 1971 Ramsar Convention on Wetlands of International Importance Especially as Waterfowl Habitat **(Basic Document 5.2)** and the 1972 Convention Concerning the Protection of the World Cultural and Natural Heritage. Amazonia voted in favor of the 2007 United Nations Declaration on the Rights of Indigenous Peoples **(Basic Document 7.17)**. The Federation of Columbia voted against that resolution.

Section 2. Questions Presented

1. Are Amazonia's access conditions consistent with its rights and obligations under the 1992 Convention on Biological Diversity?

2. Does Amazonia's refusal to provide access to canamatar (except on the specified conditions) violate any other conventional or customary rule of international law?

Section 3. Assignments

A. Reading Assignment

Study the Readings presented in Section 4, *infra*, and the Discussion Notes/Questions that follow.

B. Recommended Writing Assignments

Prepare a comprehensive, logically sequenced, and *argumentative* brief in the form of an outline of the primary and subsidiary *legal* issues that are relevant to the Amazonia-Federation of Columbia dispute. Also, from the perspective of an independent objective conciliator, indicate which side ought to prevail on each issue and why. Retain a copy of your issue-outline/brief for class discussion.

---

[35] The 2000 Cartagena Protocol on Biosafety **(Basic Document 5.6a)**, the 2010 Nagoya Protocol on Access to Genetic Resources and the Fair and Equitable Sharing of Benefits Arising from their Utilization **(Basic Document 5.6c)**, and the 2010 Nagoya-Kuala Lumpur Supplementary Protocol on Liability and Redress to the Cartagena Protocol on Biosafety **(Basic Document 5.6b)**.

C. Recommended Oral Assignment

Assume you are counsel for Amazonia or the Federation of Columbia (as designated by your instructor); then, relying upon the Readings (and your issue-outline if prepared), present a 15–20 minute oral argument of your government's likely positions before the conciliation commission.

D. Recommended Reflective Assignment

Consider (and recommend) alternative norms, institutions, and/or procedures that you believe might do better than existing world order arrangements to contend with situations of the kind posed by this problem. In so doing, but without insisting upon *immediate* feasibility, identify the particular transition steps that would be needed to make your alternatives a reality.

Section 4. Readings

1. Vicki Breazeale, Introduction: A Perspective on Sustainable Pathways Toward Preservation of Biodiversity, 10 Sustainable Dev. L. & Pol'y 2 (2010)

Biodiversity describes the vast variety of all species of life on Earth. Ecosystems are where species live, and the health, size, and nature of intact ecosystems directly affect their biodiversity. The structure, complexity, inhabitant species, organism interactions, and fragility of ecosystems vary. Tropical rainforests, for example, are the most complex and diverse ecosystems on earth, and more than half of all species live in tropical forests.

Biodiversity has steadily increased on Earth since life began some 3.2 billion years ago, but now it is on a precipitous decline due to human activity. The biologically diverse ecosystems on earth constitute our life support system—they are responsible for our atmosphere, our clean water, our medicines, and the food we eat. If ecosystems collapse and biodiversity continues to decline at the current rate, humans will be at great risk.

There are many ways to describe the accelerating loss of biodiversity on earth and the difficulty humans have in grasping the depth of the problem. The most rapid changes in biodiversity in history have occurred in only the last 50 years. The major human created threats to ecosystem health and biodiversity are:

1. invasive species that out-compete and cause extinction of native species,
2. climate change due to increased carbon dioxide in the atmosphere,
3. habitat change or destruction,

4. over exploitation of ecosystems such as removing top carnivores or over-fishing of oceans, and
5. nutrient loading and pollution from nitrogen and phosphorous fertilizer.

According to the International Union for the Conservation of Nature ("IUCN"):

> Loss of biodiversity—the variety of animals, plants, their habitats and their genes on which so much of human life depends, is one of the world's most pressing crises. It is estimated that the current species extinction rate is between 1,000 and 10,000 times higher than it would naturally be. The main drivers of this loss are converting natural areas to farming and urban development, introducing invasive alien species, polluting or over-exploiting resources including water and soils and harvesting wild plants and animals at unsustainable levels.[36]

The Ecological Footprint has been calculated globally on the basis of United Nations statistics and other well-established data. It shows the ratio between humanity's demand and the Earth's productive capacity, or biocapacity (the ability of the flora, fauna, water and atmosphere to sustain the balance of life on Earth), in each year, and how this ratio has changed over time. Humanity has moved from using, in net terms, about half the planet's biocapacity in 1961 to 1.2 times the biocapacity of the Earth in 2001. The global demand for resources thus exceeds the biological capacity of the Earth to renew these resources by some 20%—in other words, it takes the biosphere one year and nearly three months to renew what humanity uses in one year. This "ecological deficit" or "overshoot" means ecosystem assets are being liquidated and wastes are accumulating in the biosphere, and the potential for future biocapacity is reduced. Overshoot is possible because, for example, forests can be cut faster than they grow, fish can be harvested faster than their natural replacement rate, water can be withdrawn faster than aquifers are replenished, and carbon dioxide ("CO2") emitted faster than it is sequestered. We must stop cutting down our forest and earnestly support global reforestation efforts.

2. Secretariat of the Convention on Biological Diversity, Executive Summary, Global Biodiversity Outlook (GBO) 3 (2010)

The word biodiversity, a contraction of the synonymous phrase "biological diversity," is defined by the Convention on Biological Diversity (CBD) **[Basic Document 5.6]** as "the variability among living organisms from all sources including, inter alia, terrestrial, marine and other aquatic ecosystems and the ecological complexes of which they are part; this

[36] Int'l Union for Conservation of Nature, Biodiversity, http://www.iucn.org/what/tpas/biodiversity/ (last visited May 3, 2010).

includes diversity within species, between species and of ecosystems." This is the definition used throughout this document.

* * *

There are multiple indications of continuing decline in biodiversity in all three of its main components—genes, species and ecosystems . . .:

- Species which have been assessed for extinction risk are on average moving closer to extinction. Amphibians face the greatest risk and coral species are deteriorating most rapidly in status. Nearly a quarter of plant species are estimated to be threatened with extinction.
- The abundance of vertebrate species, based on assessed populations, fell by nearly a third on average between 1970 and 2006, and continues to fall globally, with especially severe declines in the tropics and among freshwater species.
- Natural habitats in most parts of the world continue to decline in extent and integrity, although there has been significant progress in slowing the rate of loss for tropical forests and mangroves, in some regions. Freshwater wetlands, sea ice habitats, salt marshes, coral reefs, seagrass beds and shellfish reefs are all showing serious declines.
- Extensive fragmentation and degradation of forests, rivers and other ecosystems have also led to loss of biodiversity and ecosystem services.
- Crop and livestock genetic diversity continues to decline in agricultural systems.
- The five principal pressures directly driving biodiversity loss (habitat change, overexploitation, pollution, invasive alien species and climate change) are either constant or increasing in intensity.
- The ecological footprint of humanity exceeds the biological capacity of the Earth by a wider margin than at the time the 2010 target was agreed.

The loss of biodiversity is an issue of profound concern for its own sake. Biodiversity also underpins the functioning of ecosystems which provide a wide range of services to human societies. Its continued loss, therefore, has major implications for current and future human well-being. The provision of food, fibre, medicines and fresh water, pollination of crops, filtration of pollutants, and protection from natural disasters are among those ecosystem services potentially threatened by declines and changes in biodiversity. Cultural services such as spiritual and religious values, opportunities for knowledge and education, as well as recreational and aesthetic values, are also declining.

* * *

Many actions in support of biodiversity have had significant and measurable results in particular areas and amongst targeted species and ecosystems. This suggests that with adequate resources and political will, the tools exist for loss of biodiversity to be reduced at wider scales. For example, recent government policies to curb deforestation have been followed by declining rates of forest loss in some tropical countries. Measures to control alien invasive species have helped a number of species to move to a lower extinction risk category. It has been estimated that at least 31 bird species (out of 9,800) would have become extinct in the past century, in the absence of conservation measures.

However, action to implement the Convention on Biological Diversity has not been taken on a sufficient scale to address the pressures on biodiversity in most places. There has been insufficient integration of biodiversity issues into broader policies, strategies and programmes, and the underlying drivers of biodiversity loss have not been addressed significantly. Actions to promote the conservation and sustainable use of biodiversity receive a tiny fraction of funding compared to activities aimed at promoting infrastructure and industrial developments. Moreover, biodiversity considerations are often ignored when such developments are designed, and opportunities to plan in ways that minimize unnecessary negative impacts on biodiversity are missed. Actions to address the underlying drivers of biodiversity loss, including demographic, economic, technological, socio-political and cultural pressures, in meaningful ways, have also been limited.

Most future scenarios project continuing high levels of extinctions and loss of habitats throughout this century, with associated decline of some ecosystem services important to human well-being.

For example:

- Tropical forests would continue to be cleared in favour of crops and pastures, and potentially for biofuel production.
- Climate change, the introduction of invasive alien species, pollution and dam construction would put further pressure on freshwater biodiversity and the services it underpins.
- Overfishing would continue to damage marine ecosystems and cause the collapse of fish populations, leading to the failure of fisheries.

Changes in the abundance and distribution of species may have serious consequences for human societies. The geographical distribution of species and vegetation types is projected to shift radically due to climate change, with ranges moving from hundreds to thousands of kilometres towards the poles by the end of the 21st century. Migration of marine species to cooler waters could make tropical oceans less diverse, while both boreal and temperate forests face widespread dieback at the southern end of their existing ranges, with impacts on fisheries, wood harvests, recreation opportunities and other services.

There is a high risk of dramatic biodiversity loss and accompanying degradation of a broad range of ecosystem services if ecosystems are pushed beyond certain thresholds or tipping points. The poor would face the earliest and most severe impacts of such changes, but ultimately all societies and communities would suffer.

Examples include:

- The Amazon forest, due to the interaction of deforestation, fire and climate change, could undergo a widespread dieback, with parts of the forest moving into a self-perpetuating cycle of more frequent fires and intense droughts leading to a shift to savanna-like vegetation. While there are large uncertainties associated with these scenarios, it is known that such dieback becomes much more likely to occur if deforestation exceeds 20–30% (it is currently above 17% in the Brazilian Amazon). It would lead to regional rainfall reductions, compromising agricultural production. There would also be global impacts through increased carbon emissions, and massive loss of biodiversity.
- The build-up of phosphates and nitrates from agricultural fertilizers and sewage effluent can shift freshwater lakes and other inland water ecosystems into a long-term, algae-dominated (eutrophic) state. This could lead to declining fish availability with implications for food security in many developing countries. There will also be loss of recreation opportunities and tourism income, and in some cases health risks for people and livestock from toxic algal blooms. Similar, nitrogen-induced eutrophication phenomena in coastal environments lead to more oxygen-starved dead zones, with major economic losses resulting from reduced productivity of fisheries and decreased tourism revenues.
- The combined impacts of ocean acidification, warmer sea temperatures and other human induced stresses make tropical coral reef ecosystems vulnerable to collapse. More acidic water—brought about by higher carbon dioxide concentrations in the atmosphere—decreases the availability of the carbonate ions required to build coral skeletons.

> Together with the bleaching impact of warmer water, elevated nutrient levels from pollution, overfishing, sediment deposition arising from inland deforestation, and other pressures, reefs worldwide increasingly become algae-dominated with catastrophic loss of biodiversity and ecosystem functioning, threatening the livelihoods and food security of hundreds of millions of people.

3. Dale D. Goble, What Are Slugs Good For? Ecosystem Services and the Conservation of Biodiversity, 22 J. Land Use & Envtl. L. 411, 412, 422–24 (2007)

What are slugs good for? They aren't tasty like cows or corn. They can't be bottled in garlic oil and sold as faux escargot. Slugs are neither charismatic nor megafauna. Slugs are just icky.

Slugs do, however, serve a role in the ecosystems they inhabit. They are decomposers, chewing up leaves, feces, and other detritus and helping to recycle the nutrients back into the soil. Slugs thus contribute to what has become known as "ecosystem services." In Gretchen Daily's frequently cited definition, ecosystem services are "the conditions and processes through which natural ecosystems . . . sustain and fulfill human life."[37] The service to which slugs contribute is replenishing soil fertility.

* * *

Ecosystem goods are familiar. They are the tangible bits of ecosystem composition that are commodities—the bauxite, timber, fish, Taxol, and all the other "natural resources." Although banana slugs are structural components of the Pacific rainforest ecosystem, they are not goods—at least until someone can re-conceive and package them as marketable commodities. In other words, goods are compositional elements of ecosystems, but not all compositional components are goods.

Ecosystem services, on the other hand, are less familiar—in part—because Daily and her colleagues have only recently crafted the concept. Ecosystem services are also less familiar because the physical, biological, and chemical processes at work in ecosystems (the ecosystem functions) are seldom experienced directly (or even seen) by those who benefit from those functions. As processes, they are simply part of the background that is the taken-for-granted world. The decomposition services provided by slugs, for example, is invisible to most people—and when it isn't, it's because slugs are decomposing something of value to humans. Although some services are provided by structural components of ecosystems, such as the pollination by animals, the tsunami protection afforded by coral reefs, and the flood risk reduction by wetlands, most ecosystem services are provided

---

[37] Gretchen C. Daily, *Introduction: What are Ecosystem Services?*, *in* Nature's Services 1, 3 (Gretchen C. Daily ed., 1997).

by ecosystem functions rather than structure. This array of "services" include:

- purification of air and water
- mitigation of droughts and floods
- generation and preservation of soils and renewal of their fertility
- detoxification and decomposition of wastes
- pollination of crops and natural vegetation
- dispersal of seeds
- cycling and movement of nutrients
- control of the vast majority of potential agricultural pests
- protection of coastal shores from erosion by waves
- protection from the sun's harmful ultraviolet rays
- stabilization of the climate
- moderation of weather extremes and their impacts
- provision of aesthetic beauty and intellectual stimulation that lift the human spirit

4. Yuhong Zhao, The War Against Biotic Invasion—A New Challenge of Biodiversity Conservation for China, 24 UCLA J. Envtl. L. & Pol'y 459, 460, 462–63 (2005–06)

The international community is aware of the serious threat posed by alien invasive species to the ecosystem, biodiversity, human health and socio-economic wellbeing. Studies show that, among the causes of biodiversity loss, the introduction of non-indigenous species is only second to direct habitat destruction. The Convention on Biological Diversity ("CBD") reflects the international consensus in response to the potential irreversible harm created by biological invasion. Under article 8(h), Contracting Parties should, as far as possible and as appropriate, "prevent the introduction of, control or eradicate those alien species which threaten ecosystem, habitats and species." . . .

* * *

An introduced alien species that spreads beyond human control may die out after a certain period of time, or remain in the area without disrupting local biota or ecosystem. However, invasion occurs when an alien species not only persists, but proliferates and becomes a threat to native species, local habitats and the ecosystem. This happens because an alien species living within a new ecosystem may not have the same natural restraints, such as predation, competition for food, and disease, which exist in their original habitat. Absent nature's checks on an alien species' growth and reproduction, its population can grow exponentially in the new ecosystem. Prolific alien species typically transform unprotected ecosystems by predation, competition, altering landscapes, or a combination of these effects.

5. Editors' Note

In 2011, the Conference of the Parties to the Convention on Biological Diversity adopted a "Strategic Plan for Biodiversity (2011–2020)" along with a set of 20 target indicators (the Aichi Biodiversity Targets). At its 14th meeting, in November 2018, the COP assessed global progress toward meeting the targets. The conclusion was not encouraging: "despite many positive actions by Parties and others," the COP reported, "most of the Aichi Biodiversity Targets are not on track to be achieved by 2020." *See* Conference of the Parties to the Convention on Biological Diversity, *Updated Assessment of Progress Towards Selected Aichi Biodiversity Targets and Options to Accelerate Progress,* UN Doc. CBD/COP/14/L.2 (21 November 2018). This conclusion was consistent with the assessment in Global Biodiversity Outlook 4 (2014), which found continuing declines in biodiversity worldwide, including: resource consumption that continued to outpace the Earth's biocapacity; continued fragmentation and degradation of forests, grasslands, wetlands and river systems; increasing problems with invasive species; continuing declines in coral reefs and other ecosystems; and no reductions in the risk of extinction for endangered species.

International law addresses threats to biodiversity in a variety of ways. There are international agreements in place to protect particular species[38] or particular categories of species[39] from over-exploitation and other threats. There are also treaties designed to address specific human threats to biodiversity, such as trade in endangered species[40] or pollution[41] or the transport of invasive species from one part of the planet to another.[42]

---

[38] *See, e.g.,* Agreement for the Establishment of the Indian Ocean Tuna Commission (25 Nov 1973) **(Basic Document 5.13)**; Convention for the Conservation of Antarctic Seals (11 Feb 1972) **(Basic Document 6.2)**.

[39] *See, e.g.,* Convention on the Conservation of Antarctic Marine Living Resources (20 Ma7 1980) **(Basic Document 6.3)**; Convention on the Conservation of Migratory Species of Wild Animals (23 Jun 1979) **(Basic Document 5.5)**.

[40] *See, e.g.,* Convention on International Trade in Endangered Species of Wild Fauna and Flora (3 Mar 1973) **(Basic Document 5.3)**.

[41] *See, e.g.,* Kuwait Regional Convention for Co-Operation on the Protection of the Marine Environment from Pollution (24 Apr 1978), 1140 UNTS 155.

[42] *See, e.g.,* International Convention for the Control and Management of Ships' Ballast Water and Sediments (13 Feb 2004), IMO Doc BWM/CONF/36 (Annex).

Several regional conventions aim to encourage nations to protect biodiversity by protecting habitats and species under national law.[43]

The focus of this problem is on three global treaties. The most important of these treaties for this problem is the Convention on Biological Diversity **(Basic Document 5.6)**, which was opened for signature at the Rio Conference in 1992, entered into force in 1993, and currently has 196 Parties, including every member of the United Nations except the United States. The Ramsar Convention on Wetlands of International Importance **(Basic Document 5.2)** creates a global system for the protection of wetland habitat and is in force in 170 countries. Finally, the Convention Concerning the Protection of the World Cultural and Natural Heritage, which is in force for 193 countries, aims at protecting "parts of the cultural or natural heritage" that are "of outstanding interest and therefore need to be preserved as part of the world heritage of mankind as a whole."

Each of these agreements shares in common a focus on encouraging States to protect biodiversity by designating and protecting special conservation areas within the nation. The Convention on Biological Diversity, however, goes much further than this. It requires its members to develop national strategies for biodiversity protection, to promote both in-situ and ex-situ conservation of the components of biodiversity, and to work toward the sustainable use of biodiversity in support of local development. As is the case with other Rio Conventions, the Biodiversity Convention contemplates that developed countries will assist developing countries in biodiversity protection through the transfer of technology, financial assistance, and other forms of cooperation. A key principle of the Convention is that States have the sovereign right to control their natural resources and the right to control access to their genetic resources and biodiversity.

6. Convention on Wetlands of International Importance Especially as Waterfowl Habitat (Ramsar Convention), preamble & arts. 1–5, Feb. 2, 1971, 996 UNTS 245 (Basic Document 5.2)

The Contracting Parties * * *

Considering the fundamental ecological functions of wetlands as regulators of water regimes and as habitats supporting a characteristic flora and fauna, especially waterfowl;

Being Convinced that wetlands constitute a resource of great economic, cultural, scientific, and recreational value, the loss of which would be irreparable;

* * *

---

[43] *See, e.g.,* Revised African Convention on the Conservation of Nature and Natural Resources (11 July 2003) **(Basic Document 5.8)**; Convention on Nature Protection and Wildlife Preservation in the Western Hemisphere (12 Oct 1940) **(Basic Document 5.1)**.

Being Confident that the conservation of wetlands and their flora and fauna can be ensured by combining far-sighted national policies with co-ordinated international action;

Have agreed as follows:

Article 2

1. Each Contracting Party shall designate suitable wetlands within its territory for inclusion in a List of Wetlands of International Importance, hereinafter referred to as "the List" which is maintained by the bureau established under Article 8. . . .

* * *

Article 3

1. The Contracting Parties shall formulate and implement their planning so as to promote the conservation of the wetlands included in the List, and as far as possible the wise use of wetlands in their territory.

* * *

Article 5

1. The Contracting Parties shall consult with each other about implementing obligations arising from the Convention especially in the case of a wetland extending over the territories of more than one Contracting Party or where a water system is shared by Contracting Parties. They shall at the same time endeavour to coordinate and support present and future policies and regulations concerning the conservation of wetlands and their flora and fauna. . . .

7. Royal C. Gardner, Kim Diana Connolly & Abou Bamba, African Wetlands of International Importance: Assessment of Benefits Associated With Designations Under the RAMSAR Convention, 21 Geo. Int'l Envtl. L. Rev. 257, 258–64, 285–90 (2009)

The Ramsar Convention was concluded in Ramsar, Iran in February 1971. The Convention was the culmination of more than eight years of efforts by nongovernmental organizations and concerned countries. The negotiations included representatives from western Europe and the former Soviet Union, a notable development during the Cold War. Indeed, the Soviet invasion of Czechoslovakia in 1968 almost derailed the process. With seven ratifications (South Africa, under the apartheid regime, was the sole African country), the Ramsar Convention entered into force in 1975. . . .

As one of the oldest multilateral environmental agreements (and the first to focus on a specific ecosystem), the Ramsar Convention is a relatively short framework convention. Not surprisingly, although the Ramsar Convention opens with the sweeping language of its noble purposes, the duties imposed on Ramsar Parties are general and permit a large degree of flexibility in their implementation. The "three pillars of implementation," or overarching obligations, are: (1) to designate sites as Wetlands of International Importance; (2) to apply a wise-use concept to all wetlands within a Party's territory; and (3) to engage in international cooperation.

To accomplish the first obligation, Article 2 of the Ramsar Convention calls on each Party to "designate suitable wetlands within its territory for inclusion in a List of Wetlands of International Importance." The Ramsar Convention states that a wetland may be listed based on its "international significance in terms of ecology, botany, zoology, limnology or hydrology." As currently interpreted, a wetland may meet this significance threshold if it satisfies at least one of nine criteria; for example, a site could qualify if it contains a representative, rare or unique wetland type, or if its biological diversity meets certain requirements. While the focus of the Convention initially was on wetlands as waterfowl habitat, current listing criteria include provisions related to fish and other nonavian, wetland-dependent species.

* * *

Beyond an obligation to designate at least one site as a Wetland of International Importance, the second pillar obligates each Party to "formulate and implement . . . planning so as to promote . . . as far as possible the wise use of wetlands in their territory." The wise-use concept has been viewed as a forerunner of, and compatible with, the notion of sustainable use or development. A Party can satisfy the obligation of wise use by adopting national wetland legislation or policies, by implementing programs on wetland inventories, monitoring, research, and education, and by developing plans to "take action" at individual wetland sites. The wise-use concept applies to all wetlands in a Party's territory, not just Ramsar sites.

The third pillar of the Ramsar Convention is international cooperation. Article 5 requires Parties to consult with each other over transboundary wetlands or shared water basins, codifying a principle that is now typically viewed as part of customary international law. International cooperation in the Ramsar context also contemplates the sharing of experiences and data, providing financial assistance (by some countries) to aid with wetland conservation efforts, and promoting the sustainable harvest of wetland-related products in international trade.

* * *

BENEFITS OF RAMSAR DESIGNATION

All the [African] sites [that were the subject of the survey] have a conservation status in addition to their Ramsar designations (e.g.,

Important Bird Area, National Park, National Wildlife Refuge or Reserve, World Heritage Site). The survey asked whether Ramsar designation had contributed additional benefits in several specific areas. While it can be difficult to quantify some benefits, the survey data demonstrate that Ramsar designation can and does provide value to the sites and local communities. In particular, Ramsar designation has been instrumental in providing increased support for protection and management of the sites, scientific studies, funding opportunities, tourism, and poverty alleviation.

8. Convention for the Protection of the World Cultural and Natural Heritage, arts. 2, 4 & 6, Nov. 23, 1972, 1037 UNTS 15

Article 2

For the purposes of this Convention, the following shall be considered as "natural heritage":

> natural features consisting of physical and biological formations or groups of such formations, which are of outstanding universal value from the aesthetic or scientific point of view;
>
> geological and physiographical formations and precisely delineated areas which constitute the habitat of threatened species of animals and plants of outstanding universal value from the point of view of science or conservation;
>
> natural sites or precisely delineated natural areas of outstanding universal value from the point of view of science, conservation or natural beauty.

Article 4

Each State Party to this Convention recognizes that the duty of ensuring the identification, protection, conservation, presentation and transmission to future generations of the cultural and natural heritage referred to in Articles 1 and 2 and situated on its territory, belongs primarily to that State. It will do all it can to this end, to the utmost of its own resources and, where appropriate, with any international assistance and co-operation, in particular, financial, artistic, scientific and technical, which it may be able to obtain.

Article 6

1. Whilst fully respecting the sovereignty of the States on whose territory the cultural and natural heritage mentioned in Articles 1 and 2 is situated, and without prejudice to property right provided by national legislation, the States Parties to this Convention recognize that such heritage constitutes a world heritage for whose protection it is the duty of the international community as a whole to co-operate.

2. The States Parties undertake, in accordance with the provisions of this Convention, to give their help in the identification, protection,

conservation and presentation of the cultural and natural heritage referred to in paragraphs 2 and 4 of Article 11 if the States on whose territory it is situated so request.

3. Each State Party to this Convention undertakes not to take any deliberate measures which might damage directly or indirectly the cultural and natural heritage referred to in Articles 1 and 2 situated on the territory of other States Parties to this Convention.

9. John Charles Kunich, Losing Nemo: The Mass Extinction Now Threatening the World's Ocean Hotspots, 30 Colum. J. Envt'l L. 1, 66–69 (2005)

The Convention Concerning the Protection of the World Cultural and Natural Heritage (the World Heritage Convention or WHC) **[Basic Document 7.14]** was adopted by the General Conference of UNESCO in 1972. The WHC provides an international framework for the protection of natural and cultural areas of "outstanding universal value." To date, some 177 countries have adhered to the WHC[44] (the overwhelming majority of the Member States of the United Nations), including key nations with both terrestrial and marine hotspots.

The Preamble states with clarity the core principles relevant to the preservation of all resources that are locally situated yet have global significance. Although neither the term "biodiversity hotspot," nor any of the alternative means for establishing biodiversity conservation priorities (e.g., Global 200 Eco-regions, Endemic Bird Areas, Centres of Plant Diversity, WORLDMAP), specifically appear anywhere in the WHC, the vexing challenges that assail such natural treasures are nonetheless recognized in the Preamble: "deterioration or disappearance of any item of the cultural or natural heritage constitutes a harmful impoverishment of the heritage of all the nations of the world . . . parts of the cultural or natural heritage are of outstanding interest and therefore need to be preserved as part of the world heritage of mankind as a whole. . . ."

Building on this philosophical and factual predicate, the WHC establishes, as its centerpiece, a list of specific places in the world that meet its overarching criterion of "outstanding universal value." The World Heritage List is the compendium of sites, in either the natural heritage or "cultural heritage" category, that have been recognized formally according to the terms of the WHC.

The WHC defines the type of natural or cultural sites which can be considered for inclusion in the World Heritage List, and sets forth the duties of States Parties in identifying potential sites and their roles in protecting them. Specifically with regard to "natural heritage" sites, the WHC supplies the following criteria:

---

[44] At the time this coursebook went to press, there were 193 parties to the Convention.

> [N]atural features consisting of physical and biological formations or groups of such formations, which are of outstanding universal value from the aesthetic or scientific point of view; geological and physiographical formations and precisely delineated areas which constitute the habitat of threatened species of animals and plants of outstanding universal value from the point of view of science or conservation; natural sites or precisely delineated natural areas of outstanding universal value from the point of view of science, conservation, or natural beauty.

The Convention, in Article 4, places the primary "duty of ensuring the identification, protection, conservation, presentation and transmission to future generations of the cultural and natural heritage" sites on the World Heritage List with the nation that is host to each site. Each host nation is to "do all it can to this end, to the utmost of its own resources." Additionally, where appropriate, each host nation may also draw upon "any international assistance and co-operation, in particular, financial, artistic, scientific and technical, which it may be able to obtain." More detailed requirements are delineated in Article 5, which unfortunately prefaces its worthy mandates with the multi-layered qualifier that each State Party "shall endeavor, in so far as possible, and as appropriate for each country" . . . .

. . . Nations that are predisposed to take effective action to preserve their natural and cultural heritage will do so, and perhaps would do so even absent Article 5 of the WHC. Those that lack this predisposition will find ample room for discretion and exception in the introductory clause to justify a very comfortable inaction. As a result, the efficacy of these provisions in questionable even within the confines of Article 5 itself. . . .

Article 6 is at the core of the WHC, insofar as it is a potential source of succor for at least some of the hotspots of the world, because it declares that the World Heritage List sites are indeed a world heritage, which the entire international community has a duty to protect, in a cooperative effort. . . .

10. Convention on Biological Diversity, arts. 1, 4–5, 10 & 14–15, June 5, 1992, 1760 UNTS 79 (Basic Document 5.6)

Article 1. Objectives

The objectives of this Convention, to be pursued in accordance with its relevant provisions, are the conservation of biological diversity, the sustainable use of its components and the fair and equitable sharing of the benefits arising out of the utilization of genetic resources, including by appropriate access to genetic resources and by appropriate transfer of relevant technologies, taking into account all rights over those resources and to technologies, and by appropriate funding.

Article 4. Jurisdictional Scope

Subject to the rights of other States, and except as otherwise expressly provided in this Convention, the provisions of this Convention apply, in relation to each Contracting Party:

(a) In the case of components of biological diversity, in areas within the limits of its national jurisdiction; and

(b) In the case of processes and activities, regardless of where their effects occur, carried out under its jurisdiction or control, within the area of its national jurisdiction or beyond the limits of national jurisdiction.

Article 5. Cooperation

Each Contracting Party shall, as far as possible and as appropriate, cooperate with other Contracting Parties, directly or, where appropriate, through competent international organizations, in respect of areas beyond national jurisdiction and on other matters of mutual interest, for the conservation and sustainable use of biological diversity.

Article 8. In-situ Conservation

Each Contracting Party shall, as far as possible and as appropriate:

(a) Establish a system of protected areas or areas where special measures need to be taken to conserve biological diversity;

* * *

(j) Subject to its national legislation, respect, preserve and maintain knowledge, innovations and practices of indigenous and local communities embodying traditional lifestyles relevant for the conservation and sustainable use of biological diversity and promote their wider application with the approval and involvement of the holders of such knowledge, innovations and practices and encourage the equitable sharing of the benefits arising from the utilization of such knowledge, innovations and practices;

* * *

Article 10. Sustainable Use of Components of Biological Diversity

Each Contracting Party shall, as far as possible and as appropriate:

(a) Integrate consideration of the conservation and sustainable use of biological resources into national decision-making;

(b) Adopt measures relating to the use of biological resources to avoid or minimize adverse impacts on biological diversity;

(c) Protect and encourage customary use of biological resources in accordance with traditional cultural practices that are compatible with conservation or sustainable use requirements;

(d) Support local populations to develop and implement remedial action in degraded areas where biological diversity has been reduced; and

(e) Encourage cooperation between its governmental authorities and its private sector in developing methods for sustainable use of biological resources.

Article 14. Impact Assessment and Minimizing Adverse Impacts

1. Each Contracting Party, as far as possible and as appropriate, shall:

* * *

(b) Introduce appropriate arrangements to ensure that the environmental consequences of its programmes and policies that are likely to have significant adverse impacts on biological diversity are duly taken into account;

* * *

(d) In the case of imminent or grave danger or damage, originating under its jurisdiction or control, to biological diversity within the area under jurisdiction of other States or in areas beyond the limits of national jurisdiction, notify immediately the potentially affected States of such danger or damage, as well as initiate action to prevent or minimize such danger or damage; and

(e) Promote national arrangements for emergency responses to activities or events, whether caused naturally or otherwise, which present a grave and imminent danger to biological diversity and encourage international cooperation to supplement such national efforts and, where appropriate and agreed by the States or regional economic integration organizations concerned, to establish joint contingency plans.

* * *

Article 15. Access to Genetic Resources

1. Recognizing the sovereign rights of States over their natural resources, the authority to determine access to genetic resources rests with the national governments and is subject to national legislation.

2. Each Contracting Party shall endeavour to create conditions to facilitate access to genetic resources for environmentally sound uses by other Contracting Parties and not to impose restrictions that run counter to the objectives of this Convention.

3. For the purpose of this Convention, the genetic resources being provided by a Contracting Party, as referred to in this Article and Articles 16 and 19, are only those that are provided by Contracting Parties that are

countries of origin of such resources or by the Parties that have acquired the genetic resources in accordance with this Convention.

4. Access, where granted, shall be on mutually agreed terms and subject to the provisions of this Article.

5. Access to genetic resources shall be subject to prior informed consent of the Contracting Party providing such resources, unless otherwise determined by that Party.

6. Each Contracting Party shall endeavour to develop and carry out scientific research based on genetic resources provided by other Contracting Parties with the full participation of, and where possible in, such Contracting Parties.

7. Each Contracting Party shall take legislative, administrative or policy measures, as appropriate, and in accordance with Articles 16 and 19 and, where necessary, through the financial mechanism established by Articles 20 and 21 with the aim of sharing in a fair and equitable way the results of research and development and the benefits arising from the commercial and other utilization of genetic resources with the Contracting Party providing such resources. Such sharing shall be upon mutually agreed terms.

11. Stuart R. Harrop & Diana J. Pritchard, A Hard instrument Goes Soft: The Implications of the Convention on Biological Diversity's Current Trajectory, 21 Global Environ. Change 474 (2011)

Negotiations for the [Convention on Biological Diversity] were fraught with conflicts concerning its core objectives and its priorities. The debate was particularly marked by the divide between North and South perspectives, primarily regarding environment and development imperatives. For industrialised states the aim was to promote conservation, although this key concept is not defined in the convention. Developing countries, which are the 'collective repository' of four-fifths of the world's biodiversity, stressed that the goal was for the sustainable use of biological resources . . . coupled with mechanisms to secure equitable financial and technological transfers. . . .

12. Rachelle Adam, Missing the 2010 Biodiversity Target: A Wake-Up Call For the Convention on Biodiversity?, 21 Colo. J. Int'l Envtl. L. & Pol'y 123, 133–38, 140–41, 145 (2010)

The CBD **[Basic Document 5.6]** was adopted at the United Nations Conference on Environment and Development ("UNCED") in 1992, together with the United Nations Framework Convention on Climate Change ("UNFCCC"). Along with the United Nations Convention to Combat Desertification ("UNCCD"), these agreements are known as the three "Rio Agreements." The conservation of biological diversity is one of the CBD's three objectives; the other objectives are the sustainable use of biological diversity's components and the "fair and equitable sharing of the benefits arising out of the utilization of genetic resources." . . .

* * *

Notwithstanding the importance that the preamble attaches to the protection and conservation of biodiversity, the agreement makes clear that committing developing states to addressing biodiversity loss has its price: increased financial and technological assistance from developed states. Thus, the CBD emphasizes not only ending biodiversity loss, but also recognizes "that economic and social development and poverty eradication are the first and overriding priorities of developing countries." The significance of the preamble's declarations for protecting biodiversity is further weakened by the insistence of governments on entrenching recognition of their sovereignty over biodiversity by "Reaffirming that States have sovereign rights over their own biological resources," thus contradicting the conceptualization of biodiversity as a global common resource. The above declaration has been qualified to a certain extent by Article 3, which, after confirming the principle of state sovereignty, attaches the no-harm principle that charges states "to ensure that activities within their jurisdiction of control do not cause damage to the environment of other States or of areas beyond the limits of national jurisdiction." However, the bottom line remains that states are entitled to exploit—or protect—biodiversity found within their territorial borders as they see fit, and the agreement imposes no effective safeguards to prevent its degradation.

* * *

The CBD does little to turn its preamble's declarations on the importance of biodiversity into operative provisions. Attempts to impose binding substantive obligations to reduce biodiversity loss on the Contracting Parties culminated in ambiguous, weak, and qualified commitments. For example, Article 5, entitled "Cooperation," obligates each Contracting Party to cooperate with others "for the conservation and sustainable use of biological diversity," but only in "areas beyond national jurisdiction" (emphasis added) and "as far as possible and as appropriate." This qualifying phrase weaves throughout the convention text like a red skein, leaving enfeebled commitments in its wake. It has transformed both Article 6(b), which obligates parties to integrate the conservation and sustainable use of biodiversity into national plans and policies, and Article 7, which obligates parties to identify and monitor both components of biodiversity and activities which impact it, into non-compliable obligations since verification of compliance with them is virtually impossible. Moreover, the phrase "in accordance with its particular conditions and capabilities" further qualifies the responsibility of "each Contracting Party" in performing its obligations.

Article 8 could have constituted the core of a binding biodiversity conservation strategy. It obligates parties to undertake specific measures to protect biodiversity in situ, including the establishment of protected areas, the sustainable management of biological resources, the protection of ecosystems and natural habitats, the "maintenance of viable populations of species," the rehabilitation and restoration of degraded ecosystems and threatened species, the control and eradication of alien species, the implementation of legislation for the protection of species, the regulation or management of activities that have adverse effects on biodiversity and cooperation in providing financial aid to support in situ conservation in developing countries. However, the same escape clause text "as far as possible and as appropriate" was added to its chapeau. Thus Article 8, instead of being the nucleus of the agreement to protect, manage, and restore biodiversity, has been rendered amorphous by these words.

* * *

In contrast to the qualified and conditional nature of the CBD's substantive provisions for protecting biodiversity, provisions of a technical or financial nature are more focused and specific. The Contracting Parties have an unqualified obligation to establish educational programs for biodiversity education, promote research in the conservation and sustainable use of biological diversity, promote public education and awareness of biodiversity issues, exchange information, engage in technical and scientific cooperation to strengthen national capabilities, train personnel, and exchange experts. Article 20, "Financial Resources," obligates developed country Parties to "provide new and additional financial resources to enable developing country Parties to meet the agreed full incremental costs to them of implementing measures which fulfil the obligations of this Convention." Significantly, the CBD notes [in Article 20(4)] that:

> The extent to which developing country Parties will effectively implement their commitments under this Convention will depend on the effective implementation by developed country Parties of their commitments under this Convention related to financial resources and transfer of technology and will take fully into account the fact that economic and social development and eradication of poverty are the first and overriding priorities of the developing country Parties.

Thus, implementation by developing countries is conditional to implementation by developed countries of their commitments for increased financial resources and technology transfer. Moreover, the recognition granted in the preamble that "economic and social development and poverty eradication are the first and overriding priorities of developing countries" removes any doubt as to their intentions in negotiating the agreement. And even assuming that the developing countries implement their commitments, in light of the ambiguous nature of the CBD's substantive provisions dealing with biodiversity protection, defining their effective implementation would be an elusive task.

* * *

Lakshman Guruswamy critiques the CBD: "[t]he Convention on Biological Diversity fails to address the problems it was meant to remedy. It declined to institutionalize the common responsibility of humanity to protect biodiversity, rejected the extension of state responsibility for damage to the global commons, and effectively spurned the concept of sustainable development."[45] Guruswamy enumerates three points to support his argument that the CBD cannot reverse biodiversity loss: 1) it contradicts the principle of sustainable development by prioritizing the economic development of developing countries; 2) it does not impose binding "substantive protection obligation[s]" on its state parties; and 3) it rejects the notion of protecting biodiversity as a common global responsibility, instead favoring the entrenchment of national sovereignty over biological resources.

By adopting the CBD, governments created a myth that action is underway to stem biodiversity loss by means of an international agreement, while in reality the agreement cannot "deliver the goods." As demonstrated by the above review, the amorphous nature of the CBD's obligations for biodiversity conservation makes compliance verification an almost impossible feat. More significantly, the CBD does not address the underlying causes of biodiversity loss. Thus, strengthening compliance with the CBD [will not] reverse ongoing biodiversity loss. . . .

13. George Frisvold & Kelly Day-Rubenstein, Biosprospecting and Biodiversity Conservation: What Happens When Discoveries Are Made?, 50 Ariz. L. Rev. 545, 546–54 (2008)

I. Bioprospecting, Property Rights, and Biodiversity Conservation

Bioprospecting is the search among living organisms for compounds that have commercial value as active ingredients in pharmaceuticals, pesticides, and other products. Natural products, derived from plants and animals, remain a basic source of many pharmaceuticals. . . . [R]oughly a quarter of prescription drugs contain some natural products. This percentage increases when one considers traditional medicines used in developing countries. Despite advances in chemistry and biotechnology,

[45] Lakshman D. Guruswamy, *The Convention on Biological Diversity: A Polemic*, in Protection of Global Biodiversity 351 (Lakshman Guruswamy & Jeffery A. McNeely eds., 1998).

production of these drugs via synthesis, tissue culture, or genetic manipulation often remains uneconomical. The anti-malaria drugs quinine and quinidine, for example, are still produced from chinchona bark. Madagascar's rosy periwinkle, *Catharansus roseus*, remains the basic ingredient in the anti-cancer drugs vincristine and vinblastine, as well as the anti-hypertension drug ajmalicine. Artimisinin, used to treat drug-resistant malaria, is produced through semisynthesis using material isolated from the shrub *Artemisia annua,* long used in traditional Chinese medicine. Semisynthesis uses large, complex molecules isolated from plants, animals or bacteria as building blocks to produce a wide range of drugs and other chemicals.

In addition to providing raw materials for medicines, natural products also provide information for pharmaceutical development: the molecular structures of natural products serve as blueprints or as leads in developing compounds. Millions of years of evolution have led to molecules organic chemists would not dream of producing. These molecules often have novel mechanisms of action against diseases. With advances in biotechnology, the scope for using this genetic information to develop new medicines has increased. Wildlands, where species reside, have an option value as a potential source of genetic materials and information.

. . . . Based on sheer numbers, areas rich in biodiversity, such as tropical rainforests, appear promising for exploration of new drugs. Biologists estimate that the tropics are home to most of the world's plant and animal species, with the tropical forests especially rich in species. Mendelsohn and Balick identified forty-seven major pharmaceuticals derived from compounds from tropical flowering plants.[46] Extrapolating from past discoveries and estimates of species numbers, they estimated that over 300 undiscovered drugs remain in tropical forests and that these drugs are worth $147 billion to society.

Yet, 42 million acres of tropical forests are cleared annually, primarily for subsistence agriculture and cattle ranching, and the resulting habitat conversion is considered the primary cause of biodiversity loss. These circumstances beg the question: if genetic resources have such value (actual or potential) for pharmaceutical development, why are they being depleted so quickly? While conserving genetic resources that are potential sources of new medicines may make sense from a social perspective, private decision-makers may often lack incentives to do so.

While natural products have been important sources of pharmaceutical materials and information, historically the pharmaceutical industry has hesitated to engage in much collecting and testing of genetic materials. This reluctance may stem from public-good aspects of

[46] Robert Mendelsohn & Michael J. Balick, *The Value of Undiscovered Pharmaceuticals in Tropical Forests,* 49 Econ. Botany 223, 224 (1995).

information about the value of genetic materials. A firm collecting and screening biological samples would have difficulty excluding others from the information that a sample showed promising medical activity. This would be particularly true as a compound's origins, mechanism of action, and efficacy were revealed through required disclosures during the drug-development application process and through clinical trials. Although the knowledge of a compound's medical activity may be valuable, firms have an incentive to free-ride off the search and discovery activities of others. Thus, expected private economic gains to bioprospecting by individual companies are considerably less than social gains.

Another disincentive for natural product collection and screening can be traced to historically weaker intellectual property protection for biological innovations, compared with mechanical or chemical innovations. The mere discovery of a new plant, animal, or other organism found in the wild cannot be patented. This legal rule limits firms' abilities to exclude others from access to raw genetic materials once discovery becomes known. Because of these disincentives for private sector collection, large-scale, sustained search and screening of plant and animal materials for medical or agricultural applications historically has been carried out by the public sector.

Tropical countries have also been unable to exercise intellectual property rights and capture gains from products developed from their raw genetic materials. For example, while Eli Lilly, maker of vinblastine and vincristine, derived from Madagascar's rosy periwinkle, earned $100 million per year from these drugs. Madagascar, the source of the raw materials, received no royalties from sale of the drug.

Yet another disincentive for conservation is competing demands for lands that serve as wildlife habitats. Returns to these other uses (such as timber harvesting, farming, or ranching) represent opportunity costs of habitat preservation. In principle, forests could be used as extractive reserves where medicinal plants (and other products) are harvested renewably. . . .

In the 1980s and 1990s, technological and institutional changes led to increased incentives for and renewed interest in natural product development. Advances in biotechnology have increased the ability of scientists to genetically engineer new organisms. In *Diamond v. Chakrabarty*, the Supreme Court ruled that organisms bred or genetically modified for novel traits could be patented. The U.S. Patent and Trademark Office extended the Supreme Court's decision, ruling that utility patents could be awarded for human-developed traits in plants and animals.

Not only did United States law redefine property rights in natural products; international agreements took part in this shift as well.

Historically, it was common practice for botanists or plant scientists to send materials back to their home countries for screening without the knowledge or consent of the country of origin. The United Nations Convention on Biological Diversity **[Basic Document 5.6]**, which entered into force on December 29, 1993, seeks to change that practice. Article 15 of the Convention asserts that (a) countries have sovereign rights to their genetic resources (section 1), (b) access to genetic resources shall be subject to prior informed consent of the source country (section 5), and (c) access shall be on mutually agreed terms (section 4).

In addition, Article 15 (7) of the Convention states:

> Each Contracting Party shall take legislative, administrative or policy measures . . . with the aim of sharing in a fair and equitable way the results of research and development and the benefits arising from the commercial and other utilization of genetic resources with the Contracting Party providing such resources. Such sharing shall be upon mutually agreed terms.

This provision formalizes the right of a country to use its property rights over genetic resources to gain a greater share of the benefits from technologies using those resources.

. . . In the wake of these redefinitions of property rights over both naturally occurring and human-modified genetic resources, a number of biologists and conservationists have touted bioprospecting arrangements as ways to simultaneously develop medicines and improve conservation incentives by allowing developing countries to capture gains from new product development.

Indeed, a number of bioprospecting arrangements reflecting these trends have arisen. The most studied was one between the pharmaceutical multinational Merck, the Instituto Nacional de Bioversidad ("INBio"), a Costa Rican non-profit private organization, and the government of Costa Rica. The agreement originally was a two-year collection contract, in which INBio received a $1 million payment plus more than $100,000 in equipment. INBio scientists received technical training locally and at Merck facilities. INBio was also to receive an undisclosed percentage of royalty payments for any discoveries Merck made, to be shared with Costa Rica's Ministry of Natural Resources. Merck retained first rights to patent discoveries, however. In February of 1997, the agreement was renewed, with Merck expected to provide an additional $1 million in research funds during 1997 and 1998. In addition, INBio was paid for sample collection and processing. The Costa Rican government and INBio also cooperated with Cornell University and Bristol-Myers Squibb to collect and screen insects as a source of drugs.

Federal government agencies in the United States have also attempted to encourage bioprospecting agreements. In 1992, the U.S.

Agency for International Development implemented a program encouraging joint biodiversity research and development between developing countries and private industry. The U.S. National Cancer Institute ("NCI") has entered into contracts with organizations in Madagascar, Tanzania, Zimbabwe, and the Philippines, while the British firm Biotics has signed agreements with organizations in Ghana and Malaysia.

The International Cooperative Biodiversity Group ("ICBG") was initiated by the U.S. National Institute of Health ("NIH"), the U.S. National Science Foundation, and the U.S. Agency for International Development in 1993 to promote drug discovery, biodiversity research, and conservation by funding research consortia and encouraging royalty payments to developing countries in the event of discoveries. Since then, they have financed several consortia of government agencies in developing countries, U.S. universities, and private firms.

As these examples illustrate, the terms of these bioprospecting agreements often vary greatly. A source country may simply provide access to natural resources, or it can provide complete prospecting services, such as screening and evaluating the samples. Agreement terms also depend on search strategy. Drug prospecting entails collecting samples that are screened for activity against a certain disease (e.g., cancer or AIDS). Prospecting can focus on random collections of plants or other living things. Drug companies often prefer random collection because it yields more diverse samples. Prospecting can also be targeted, with collectors using ethno-botanical or ethno-medical information to narrow the search. Targeted samples are usually collected and screened on a slower, smaller scale. In this type of prospecting, the source country often supplies traditional knowledge.

The methods of compensating source countries vary and can be complex. In the simplest model, the source country is paid a fee for samples. Often, agreements provide the source country with royalties from the sale of a successful product, should one be developed. Here, the source country faces the possibility that such a compound may not be found, and thus, no royalty payments may be received. Royalty provisions often have an inverse relationship with up-front payments: the larger the up-front payments, usually the smaller the royalty rate.

A more complex model involves the use of ethno-botanical or ethno-medical data, which can raise complicated intellectual property rights issues over how suppliers of traditional knowledge are compensated. A royalty scheme may become further complicated if indigenous knowledge was used to select the sample and the sale of the product takes place some time in the future. For example, identifying which group or groups initially developed the knowledge may be difficult to identify. Determining who has

a right to compensation for "traditional" knowledge could also be difficult. Other forms of compensation may include technology transfer, training, job opportunities, and the right of first refusal as supplier of the resource.

To summarize thus far, biologists and conservationists suggest bioprospecting contracts can simultaneously find new medical breakthroughs and provide developing countries with economic incentives to conserve genetic resources. Advances in biotechnology and changing definitions of intellectual property rights over biological innovations have spurred a number of bioprospecting arrangements. . . .

II. Economic Assessments of Bioprospecting Contracts

While many biologists and environmentalists have seen bioprospecting agreements as avenues to improve incentives for habitat conservation, economists, by and large, have taken a more skeptical view. Simpson et al. noted that while biodiversity as a whole is extremely valuable, for bioprospecting, it is the value of a marginal species that matters.[47] They argued that this marginal value of habitat will be low (e.g., $21/hectare). When several species produce the same chemical compound, the probability of discovering the compound's value is high, but discovery in one species will render other species redundant as a source of that compound. In cases where a compound is rarely found (for example, in one and only one species), the probability of finding a useful lead will be quite small.

Rausser and Small, in contrast, found that marginal values of species from bioprospecting could be large (over $9,000/hectare).[48] In such cases, private bioprospecting contracts could indeed create incentives to conserve biological diversity. Rausser and Small attribute this difference to the role of information search process. While Simpson et al. assume a random search process, Rausser and Small assume that prospectors can use information to carry out more efficient searches. By using scientific information, one could search for bioprospecting leads in a more efficient order instead of carrying out random searches. This targeting—so their argument goes—raises the value of new searches at the margin. An important policy implication of this argument is that investment in scientific information can stimulate biodiversity-conserving contracting agreements.

[47] The word "marginal," here, refers to the incremental contribution of one species to making a commercial discovery. R David Simpson, Roger A. Sedjo & John W. Reid, *Valuing Biodiversity for Use in Pharmaceutical Research*, 104 J. Pol. Econ. 163, 163 (1996).

[48] Gordon C. Rausser & Arthur A. Small, *Valuing Research Leads: Bioprospecting and the Conservation of Genetic Resources*, 108 J. Pol. Econ. 173, 193 (2000).

14. Gurdial Singh Nijar, Incorporating Traditional Knowledge in an International Regime on Access to Genetic Resources and Benefit Sharing: Problems and Prospects, 21 Eur. J. Int'l L. 457, 458–59 (2010)

Traditional knowledge of indigenous and local communities (ILCs) associated with genetic resources is at the centre of the current negotiations[49] for an international regime on access and benefit-sharing (ABS) of these resources. . . .

It is widely acknowledged that it is the TK associated with genetic resources that is of value to industry. TK's contribution to modern medicine illustrates this rather vividly. It is estimated that three quarters of the plants that provided active ingredients for prescription drugs came to the attention of researchers because of their use in traditional medicine. Of the 120 active compounds currently isolated from the higher plants and widely used in medicine today, 74 per cent show a positive correlation between their modern therapeutic use and the traditional use of the plant from which they were derived. TK's role in increasing the efficiency of screening plants for medicinal properties is often highlighted, with various calculations—that it increases the efficiency by more than 400 per cent or that it enhances the probability of drug development at the lead discovery stage by as much as 0.5 or a 50 per cent chance of success. Shaman Pharmaceuticals of the US calculates its rate of scoring a marketable hit as one in every two plants studied with the use of TK. The comparable success rate for random bioprospecting in plants, animals, and microorganisms is one in 10,000 compounds. The current value of the world market for medicinal plants derived from such leads is estimated at US $43 billion.

15. Atul Kaushik, Protecting Traditional Knowledge, Innovations and Practices: The Indian Experience in Protecting and Promoting Traditional Knowledge: Systems, National Experiences and International Dimensions 85, 85–89, (Sophia Twarog & Promila Kapoor, eds., 2004), U.N. Doc. UNCTAD/DITC/TED/10 (2004)

[Traditional knowledge (TK)] associated with biological resources is an intangible component of the resource itself. It has the potential of being translated into commercial benefits by providing leads for development of useful products and processes. The valuable leads provided by TK save time and money that industry would otherwise invest in research and

[49] These negotiations concluded on October 29, 2010 with the adoption of the Nagoya Protocol on Access to Genetic Resources and the Fair and Equitable Sharing of Benefits Arising from their Utilization by the Conference of the Parties to the Convention on Biological Diversity **(Basic Document 5.6c)**.

product development. Hence, a share of these benefits must be returned to the creators and holders of TK.

India is a party to the Convention on Biological Diversity (CBD) **[Basic Document 5.6]**. The CBD envisages that the benefits accruing from commercial use of TK have to be shared with the people responsible for creating, refining and using this knowledge. . . .

. . . India has, therefore, proposed to enact legislation to realize the benefits provided for by the Convention. The bill, which was introduced in the Parliament in the 2000 budget session, addresses the basic concerns of access to and collection and utilization of biological resources and knowledge by foreigners, and sharing of benefits arising therefrom. The legislation provides for a National Authority that will grant approvals for access, subject to conditions designed to ensure equitable sharing of benefits.

Recently, there have been several cases of biopiracy of TK from India. First a patent was issued for the wound-healing properties of haldi (turmeric); now patents have been obtained in other countries for the hypoglycaemic properties of karela (bitter gourd), brinjal, and other plants. An important criticism in this context relates to foreigners' obtaining patents based on Indian biological materials. . . . A patent granted on neem as a fungicide was contested and subsequently revoked in the European Patent Office in May 2000. However, since the time and money involved in getting individual patents examined and revoked in foreign patent offices are prohibitive, an internationally accepted solution to such biopiracy is necessary.

The problem of biopiracy may not be resolved by such revocation actions and domestic biodiversity legislation alone. There is a need to provide appropriate legal and institutional means at the international level for recognizing the rights of tribal communities to their TK based on biological resources. There is also a need to institute mechanisms for sharing benefits arising out of the commercial exploitation of biological resources using such TK. . . .

* * *

Documentation of traditional knowledge

Some believe that proper documentation of associated TK could help check biopiracy. Some also assume that if knowledge or materials are documented, they can be made available to patent examiners the world over, so that prior knowledge in the case of inventions based on such knowledge or materials is readily available. It is also hoped that such documentation will facilitate the tracing of indigenous communities with whom the benefits of commercialization of such materials or knowledge have to be shared.

Others, however, believe that documentation may facilitate biopiracy. They argue that the trade secrets of an indigenous community can be maintained only as long as they are closely held by the community: as soon as they are put on paper, they will become accessible to pirates and be purloined. This dilemma is the subject of discussions in national and international debates on benefit sharing. Some suggest empowering the indigenous communities themselves so that they are able to get legal protection for closely held knowledge without the involvement of outside agencies. Nevertheless, documentation has one clear benefit: It would prevent the issuing of patents based on public-domain TK that today are difficult to prevent because patent examiners lack some necessary information.

In India, the preparation of village-specific Community Biodiversity Registers for documenting all knowledge, innovations and practices has been undertaken in a few states.

Traditional Knowledge Digital Library

Recently, there have been several cases of biopiracy of TK from India. To prevent such instances in the future, there is a need to develop digital databases of prior knowledge related to herbs that is already in the public domain. Following problems experienced with patents for brinjal and other plants, an exercise has been initiated in India to prepare an easily navigable database of documented TK relating to the use of medicinal and other plants that is already in the public domain. This database, to be known as the Traditional Knowledge Digital Library, would enable patent offices all over the world to search for and examine existing uses or prior knowledge of the enabling knowledge from which an "invention" may have been derived.

While documentation of TK is one means of recognizing knowledge holders, mere documentation may not lead to the sharing of benefits arising from the use of such knowledge, unless the documentation is accompanied by some mechanism for protecting the knowledge. In other words, documentation of TK may serve the defensive purpose of preventing the patenting of this knowledge in the form in which it exists, but documentation alone will not facilitate benefit sharing with the holders of TK.

* * *

. . . For ensuring equitable sharing of benefits arising from the use of biological resources and associated knowledge, Sections 19 and 21 [of India's Biodiversity Bill, 2000] stipulate that the approval of the National Biodiversity Authority (NBA) must be secured before the resources can be accessed. While granting approval, the NBA will also impose terms and conditions that secure equitable sharing of benefits. Section 6 provides that anybody seeking any kind of IPR to research based on biological resources or knowledge obtained from India needs to first obtain their approval of the NBA, which will impose benefit-sharing conditions. Section 18(iv) stipulates that one of the functions of NBA is to take measures to oppose the grant of IPR in any country outside India to any biological resource obtained from India or on knowledge associated with such a biological resource.

* * *

Even though provisions of Article 8(j) of the CBD are subject to national legislation, India believes that securing benefits arising out of the use of TK related to biodiversity cannot be limited to national action, and that a basic understanding of and respect for an internationally recognized regime to protect the rights of these communities is an absolute must. These two requirements, therefore, have to go hand in hand. To secure this, India's representatives in international forums under the aegis of the CBD as well as the WTO have suggested that applications for patents be required to disclose the following:

- The source of knowledge and biological material; and
- State that the prevalent laws and practices of the country of origin have been fully respected.

16. Paul J. Heald, The Rhetoric of Biopiracy, 11 Cardozo J. Int'l & Comp. L. 519, 519–20, 531–34, 538–39 (2003)

. . . [A]dvocates for long-term occupant communities ("LTOC Advocates") . . . argue for the creation of sui generis intellectual property rights in plant genetic resources. LTOC Advocates share common goals: they want to nurture and maintain long-term occupant communities (particularly in the developing countries of the southern hemisphere); they want to preserve habitat and maintain bio-diversity (particularly in the rain forest); and they want to ensure the survival of valuable traditional knowledge (particularly about plant genetic resources). Using a vocabulary grounded primarily in terms of moral obligation, unjust enrichment, and free-riding, they advocate granting new intellectual property rights to long-term occupant communities in order to achieve these ends. . . .

* * *

I offer two normative arguments below to demonstrate why even policymakers with a natural sympathy for long-term occupant communities will be unlikely to heed the call for new intellectual property rights.

A. Don't We Want a Cure for Cancer?

Corporate interests and anthropologists agree on the vast potential of the world's rapidly disappearing plant genetic resources. Hundreds of important and efficacious drugs have already been developed from plants found in developing countries. In fact, four-fifths of all drugs have their basis in natural plant resources. The world's biodiversity is also an important source of new agricultural products, for instance, crops that produce more per acre and are more resistant to disease than previous strains. . . . A cure for cancer may well be found in the rain forest, and we certainly hope someone will find it.

New property rights for long-term occupant communities would raise the cost of bio-prospecting and therefore the cost of developing new drugs and crops from existing plant genetic resources. Pharmaceutical companies, agribusiness and bio-tech firms would be forced to buy information and germplasm from rights holders and might well encounter refusals to deal. Although principles of unjust enrichment suggest that the biopirates should pay, and principles of group autonomy militate in favor of respecting the cultural and religious practices of disempowered groups, policymakers will weigh the cost to the sick and hungry against privileging these principles. A strong normative argument will be offered that the interest of the world community is not well served by the creation of new property rights, especially when the practice of biopiracy does not entail depriving long-term occupant communities of their traditional medicines or food. With biopirates providing medicine and food to much of the world, policymakers may well demand an especially compelling argument as to why they should be economically sanctioned.

B. Preserving Biodiversity

The loggers are winning. Despite efforts by environmentalists and LTOC Advocates, the world's biodiversity is disappearing at an alarming rate. This environmental disaster implicates not only forest dwellers, but those who wish to be cured and fed by products made with plant genetic resources. It also threatens the future profits of the pharmaceutical, agribusiness, and bio-tech firms who would like to make and sell new medicines and food. Biopirates, in other words, are the natural enemies of those who would log the existing primeval forests to extinction. While this essay is not the place to settle the debate over whether market forces alone can save the rain forests, it is clear that biopirates lose potential income as rain forest disappears. This insight has implications for the creation of new intellectual property rights for long-term occupant communities. Do environmentalists and anthropologists (not to mention those who consume new medicines and food products) really want to make the rain forest a less attractive source of profits for the natural enemies of logging interests?

A recent article in the Journal of Political Economy concluded that "[n]umerical simulation results suggest that, under plausible conditions, the bioprospecting value of certain genetic resources could be large enough to support market-based conservation of biodiversity."[50] The key to Rausser and Small's finding, that pharmaceutical companies may have a financial incentive to engage in conservation efforts, is the notion that "research leads" significantly diminish the cost of bio-prospecting. If firms were to test plants randomly in the hope of identifying valuable germ plasm, the cost of bio-prospecting would be so significant that expending resources on conservation would not be feasible. In practice, Rausser and Small note, bio-prospecting is not random, but rather driven by "research leads" that significantly reduce the cost of searching. If research leads provided by long-term occupant communities are key to bio-prospecting success and the success of bio-prospectors is directly related to preserving habitats, do we really want to establish new property rights in that information? Policymakers must consider the argument that bio-prospecting in threatened areas should be made cheaper, rather than more expensive.

* * *

The rhetoric of justice and the insistence on moral principles has not stopped the ongoing destruction of the world's remaining biologically rich ecosystems and the communities who live there. It is time to reexamine the rhetorical strategy of those who argue that justice and fairness require the creation of new intellectual property rights for long-term occupant communities. Given that one sure solution to the preservation problem would be to set aside vast tracts of wilderness (a real property answer, not an intellectual property answer), it may be time to set sail with the biopirates and attempt to co-opt their wealth and political clout. Preservation is in the direct financial interest of some of the most powerful private institutions on the earth—international pharmaceutical, agribusiness and bio-tech firms—and it is worth convincing them to support the effort. . . .

17. Nagoya Protocol on Access to Genetic Resources and the Fair and Equitable Sharing of Benefits Arising From Their Utilization, arts. 1, 6–9, 11 & 12, Oct. 29, 2010, Report of the Tenth Meeting of the Conference of the Parties to the Convention on Biological Diversity at 87, UNEP/CBD/COP/10/27, Decision X/1 (Annex) (2011) (Basic Document 5.6c)

18. United Nations Declaration on the Rights of Indigenous Peoples, arts. 29, 31–32, & 36, Sep. 13, 2007, GA Res 61/295, UN Doc A/RES/61/295 (Basic Document 7.17)

[50] Gordon Rausser & Arthur Small, *Valuing Research Leads: Bioprospecting and the Conservation of Genetic Resources*, 108 J. Pol. Econ. 173 (2000).

Section 5. Discussion Notes/Questions

1. Does the Convention on Biological Diversity **(Basic Document 5.6)** give Amazonia the right to restrict access to the canamatar plant? Why? Should nations have the right to control genetic resources located in their borders, or should such resources be made available freely to all (assume that can be done without depleting them) on the grounds that the Earth's natural biological diversity is part of the common heritage of humankind and not the property of any individual nation?

2. If Amazonia can restrict access to canamatar, does the Convention on Biological Diversity impose any limits on its right to control access? Are the limits imposed by Amazonia reasonable?

3. Apart from the Convention on Biological Diversity, does Amazonia have any other legal obligations that might require it to provide the Federation of Columbia with access to canamatar? Does the Ramsar Convention **(Basic Document 5.2)** impose any obligations on Amazonia to cooperate in protecting the Seminole Swamp? What about the World Heritage Convention? What about customary law?

4. Does the Convention on Biological Diversity require Amazonia to consult the Anámo before making a decision about allowing access to canamatar? Does it require Amazonia to share any benefits of an access agreement with the Anámo? Consider Articles 3, 8(j), 15 and 19.

Is the United Nations Declaration on the Rights of Indigenous Peoples **(Basic Document 7.17)** relevant here? Do the Anámo have the right to share their traditional knowledge and invite foreign nationals to their territory regardless of the wishes of the Amazonian government? Does the Amazonian government have the right to restrict dealings between the Anámo and the outside world? To demand compensation for use of Anámo traditional knowledge that is greater than the Anámo themselves would demand? Should the Anámo have been consulted by Amazonia before it crafted its laws and regulations on this subject? If they were consulted, does that affect your analysis of Amazonia's rights? *See generally* Jason Gray, *Indigenous Communities and Biodiversity Conservation: Protected Areas and the Right to Consultation,* 12 Gonz. J. Int'l L. 3 (2008–09); Humberto Márquez, *Biopiracy Leaves Native Groups Out in the Cold* (Inter Press Service, Feb. 9, 2011) (reporting researchers extracted plant samples that might become new source of anti-cancer drug Taxol without notifying local communities or providing any benefits.)

5. The Conference of the Parties to the Convention on Biological Diversity has recently addressed the implementation of Article 8(j) by adopting voluntary guidelines on the treatment of indigenous knowledge. The Mo'otz Kuxtal Voluntary Guidelines, adopted in 2016, include the following key substantive elements: i) access should be on the basis of indigenous peoples' "prior and informed consent," "free, prior and informed consent," or "approval and involvement," depending on national circumstances; ii) there should be

"fair and equitable sharing of benefits"; and iii) unlawful appropriation should be reported and prevented. Conference of the Parties to the Convention on Biological Diversity, 13th meeting, Decision XIII/18, CBD/COP/DEC/XIII/18 (17 December 2016). At the 14th COP, in November 2018, the Contracting Parties adopted the Rutzolijirisaxik Voluntary Guidelines for the Repatriation of Traditional Knowledge Relevant for the Conservation and Sustainable Use of Biological Diversity. *See* U.N. Doc. CBD/COP/14/L.14 (25 November 2018).

6. If the Federation of Columbia ratifies the Nagoya Protocol to gain access to the canamatar plant, is its consent to the Protocol valid? Under what circumstances should coercion invalidate consent to a treaty? Would consent be valid if it was coerced by a threat of military force in violation of the United Nations Charter? Is environmental coercion any different? If consent is invalidated by coercion, is it invalidated as to all other parties to the Protocol, or only as to Amazonia, which engaged in the coercive behavior? *See* Article 52 of the Vienna Convention on the Law of Treaties **(Basic Document 1.14)**. The Vienna Convention speaks of coercion by the "threat or use of force in violation of the principles of international law." During negotiation of the Vienna Convention, there was no general agreement on the meaning of force. A group of 19 states requested an amendment to make clear that "force" included economic and political coercion. That effort failed, but a declaration was adopted on the prohibition of various kind of coercion in the entry of treaties. *See* Mark E. Villiger, Commentary on the 1969 Vienna Convention on the Law of Treaties (2009). *See also* Stuart S. Malawer, *A New Concept of Consent and World Public Order: "Coerced Treaties" and the Convention on the Law of Treaties*, 4 Vanderbilt Int'l L. J. 1 (1970).

7. Much of Earth's remaining terrestrial biodiversity is located in forests in developing countries. Those forests are also carbon sinks, and their preservation will help in the effort to control atmospheric greenhouse gas concentrations. *See infra* Ch. 9. At one time it was thought that the economic potential of bioprospecting might generate sufficient funds to support forest preservation worldwide, but that hope has so far not been realized. The United Nations Collaborative Programme on Reducing Emissions from Deforestation and Forest Degradation in Developing Countries (UN-REDD), launched in 2008, addresses the problem of preserving forests by promoting their value as carbon sinks. The basic idea is that donor countries will make funds available to assist tropical forest countries in sustainable development in forest regions if those countries commit to slowing the rate of forest destruction in their borders. The hope is that the economic value associated with forests as carbon sinks will be enough to secure their preservation. Do you think this will work? Or is this scheme likely to encounter the same economic reality as preservation for bioprospecting—that alternative uses of tropical forests will offer higher returns to the people of developing countries than western governments or businesses are willing to pay to secure the forests as carbon sinks? *See generally* Oscar Venter, William F. Laurance, Takuya Iwamura, Kerrie A. Wilson, Richard A. Fuller & Hugh P. Possingham, *Harnessing Carbon Payments to Protect Biodiversity,* 326 Science 1368 (2009).

8. Are political systems capable of choosing biodiversity preservation over short term economic gains, especially when economic conditions are as difficult as they are in many tropical forest countries? Consider the following evaluation of the Convention on Biological Diversity:

> The particular case of international agreements for global biodiversity protection requires a curtailment of a state's sovereignty over its natural resources and in so doing cuts across a wide range of political, social and economic interests. Protection of biological resources imposes costs on member states for advantages that give no payback for the investing states within the normal political event horizon. . . . The collective manifestation is an unwillingness of the international political community to build an environmentally sound foundation for a politically distant—but biologically imminent—future since governments typically respond "only to short-term and parochial considerations." . . . As a consequence [the CBD's] provisions are "expressed as overall goals and policies" . . . in a text that is beleaguered by vague commitments, ambiguous phrases and escape clauses that permit avoidance of obligations. . . .

Stuart R. Harrop & Diana J. Pritchard, *A hard instrument goes soft: The implications of the Convention on Biological Diversity's current trajectory*, 21 Global Environ. Change 474 (2011). How can this problem be overcome?

9. There is a widespread assumption that the value of natural products as inputs into pharmaceuticals or biotechnologies will contribute to forest preservation. But, as George Frisvold and Kelly Day-Rubenstein have observed, the value of the natural resource can trigger devastating over-harvesting. Their study of taxol (an important cancer drug derived from the Pacific and Asian yew trees) demonstrated "that bioprospecting, by creating a valuable product with open access sources of supply, can have unintended negative implications for biodiversity conservation." George Frisvold & Kelly Day-Rubenstein, *Bioprospecting and Biodiversity Conservation: What Happens When Discoveries are Made*, 50 Ariz. L. Rev. 545, 556 (2008). In part because of overharvesting for taxol production, Asian yew species are now threatened or endangered in Pakistan, India, Nepal and China. *Id.* at 571–575.

10. One of the most significant impacts of the Convention on Biological Diversity **(Basic Document 5.6)** and other treaties aimed at the preservation of ecosystems may be the inducement they provide for nations to pay attention to biodiversity issues and to establish protected areas within national borders. Although it is easy to lament the fact that the Earth's biodiversity is rapidly disappearing, one should not forget that strides are being made in improving protection of biodiverse 'hotspots.' *See* Colin Crawford & Guilherme Pignataro, *The Insistent (and Unrelenting) Challenges of Protecting Biodiversity in Brazil: Finding 'The Law That Sticks,'* 39 U. Miami Inter-Am. L. Rev. 1 (2007). The national reports filed by parties to the Convention on Biological Diversity are a good source of information about the progress that is being made, as is the IUCN World Database on Protected Areas. Today, protected areas "cover 12%

of the Earth's land area" and studies show that they are effective in "slowing deforestation," and "decreas[ing] habitat loss and other threats" to biodiversity. Thomas M. Brooks, S. Joseph Wright, & Douglas Sheil, *Evaluating the Success of Conservation Actions in Safeguarding Tropical Forest Biodiversity*, 23 Conservation Biology 1448 (2009).

11. Climate change poses new threats to biodiversity. "Changes in temperature, humidity and weather patterns have consequences for species and ecosystems," including the possibility that species may have to migrate to new areas to survive. Given the fragmentation of protected areas and wide separation between undeveloped natural areas, species survival may depend on human actions "facilitating [species] movement between (current and future) habitats," such as "wildlife-friendly corridors" or "translocation through direct human intervention." Arie Trouwborst, *International Nature Conservation Law and the Adaptation of Biodiversity to Climate Change: a Mismatch?*, 21 J. Envtl. L. 419, 426 (2009).

12. Biodiversity in marine ecosystems is also under threat from many of the same forces threatening terrestrial ecosystems, including habitat destruction, pollution, climate change, and invasive species. *See* John Charles Kunich, *Losing Nemo: the Mass Extinction Now Threatening the World's Ocean Hotspots,* 30 Colum. J. Envt'l L. 1 (2005). The key treaties discussed in this problem—the Convention on Biological Diversity, the Ramsar Convention, and the World Heritage Convention—all apply to marine areas.

PROBLEM 7-4: EXPANDING DRYLANDS IN MITUMBA

Section 1. Facts

Mitumba, a land-locked developing nation located in east central Africa, is one of the world's poorest countries with an annual gross domestic product of less than $800 per capita. The poorest area is in northern Mitumba, where the semi-arid climate and periodic droughts make life very difficult for the people living in the small farming villages that dot the region.

Over 80% of Mitumba's population lives in rural areas, and most depend for their survival on subsistence agriculture. As population has increased, farmers in northern Mitumba have cut down or burned most of its woodlands and large parts of its grasslands to clear land for crops. The cleared land is farmed intensively, and the soil quickly becomes nutrient-poor, causing fields to be abandoned. Few plants will grow in the eroded and nutrient-poor fields, and they retain very little water as a result. In many areas of northern Mitumba, the land is so degraded that the region has been identified globally as a prime example of desertification. During periodic droughts, large portions of the arable land are unusable because of lack of water.

Except during the short rainy season in November and December, rainfall in northern Mitumba is too minimal to support crops, so water for crops must be carried to the fields from village wells or from the main water source in the region—the Upper Oboti River. The task of keeping crops watered and weed-free is nearly all-consuming for the women and girls who are responsible for maintaining village crops as well as their homes. Few girls go to school, and women have little time for any activity other than transporting water, tending crops, and cooking meals. Agricultural production has not kept up with population growth, and hunger is widespread.

In addition to farming, Mitumban villagers raise cattle. Men have primary responsibility for the herds, which are mostly grazed on land within a day's walk of the owner's village. Over-grazing is common, and much of the rangeland near Mitumban villages is seriously degraded due to soil compaction, erosion, and the emergence of low-value grass and shrubs in place of the more nutritious species eaten by the cattle.

After extensive nationwide consultations, including public discussions with citizens and NGOs in every region of the country, Mitumba's government recently adopted a national Poverty Reduction Action Plan (PRAP) based on four main principles—promotion of economic growth, good governance, supporting the ability of the poor to increase their incomes, and improving the quality of life for the poor. In addition, the government adopted a National Action Plan to Combat Drought and Desertification (NAPCDD). That plan is focused on improving farming methods and cattle-raising techniques to protect against land degradation; increasing the availability of water to rural villages; enhancing the income-earning potential of rural villagers; and raising the education level in rural areas.

Both these plans were adopted with the support of the largest NGO in Mitumba, the Poverty Reduction Network (PRN), a group devoted to promoting sustainable development by building the capacity of women and youth to improve their lives. To this end, the plans involve building small dams along the Upper Oboti River to store water, and supplying pumps and pipes to transport water from the river reservoirs to nearby villages for household use and to irrigate crop land and cattle paddocks when rainfall is inadequate. Villagers would be encouraged to produce cash crops (e.g., cotton and sugar cane) as well as subsistence crops, and to practice more effective farming techniques. Also, Mitumba would grant farmers (for the first time) exclusive rights to their farmland and authorize them to fence the range lands surrounding their villages. The responsibility to make land allocations to specific families would be delegated to village elders.

The Global Mechanism (GM) of the 1994 United Nations Convention to Combat Desertification[51] is a team of individuals with the responsibility of assisting nations suffering from land degradation and desertification to mobilize the resources needed to implement their plans to prevent or reverse such degradation. Officials from the GM have identified three potential funding sources for the Mitumban plan: the World Bank, the Federation of Columbia's International Development Agency (FCIDA), and Hanguo's Agricultural Assistance Department (HAAD). Both Hanguo and the Federation of Columbia regularly finance development projects in Africa; the two countries use development aid to compete for influence in Africa and votes in international organizations.

GM officials organized an international workshop in Mitumba's capital city, Kahuzi, to discuss the Mitumban plan. A general invitation was issued to potential donor organizations. Two potential donors agreed to attend: the World Bank and FCIDA. HAAD indicated interest but stated that it preferred to deal with the Mitumban government directly.

A general invitation also was issued to all interested governments, intergovernmental organizations, and transnational NGOs, as well as to Mitumban political leaders, national NGOs, and citizens.

At the workshop, officials from the World Bank and FCIDA heard from the Mitumban government as well as Mitumban political leaders, national NGOs, and citizens. All expressed strong support for the plan, which was explained in a lengthy report prepared by experts hired by the Mitumban government. The report evaluated the environmental and developmental benefits and costs of the plan. It concluded that the planned dams and irrigation system would provide significant benefits to several Mitumban villages and would not cause any significant harm to the Upper Obiti River ecosystem. Village leaders and Mitumban NGOs, including the PRN, argued that implementation of the plan would reduce land degradation, increase incomes of village families, and ease burdens on women and children, allowing the children to pursue education and the women to pursue other projects aimed at improving their lives and the lives of their families.

However, the potential donors also heard from a representative of the Government of Equatoria (a country that borders Mitumba to the north) who expressed serious reservations about the plan. She argued that Mitumba's plan was inconsistent with the rights and interests of the Ngi Turkana people living in northern Mitumba and southern Equatoria.

The Ngi Turkana (or Turkana) are a nomadic pastoral people who have grazed cattle in the drylands of east central Africa for generations. They

[51] *I.e.*, United Nations Convention to Combat Desertification in those Countries Experiencing Serious Drought and/or Desertification, Particularly in Africa **(Basic Document 4.11)**.

spend most of each year moving their cattle herds from location to location in search of the best grazing land. Their ancestral lands covered wide swathes of what are, today, several separate African nations. They have gradually been forced from much of their traditional grazing territory and now graze cattle primarily within the borders of Equatoria and Mitumba.

In any given year, the Turkana spend the bulk of their time in Equatoria, they maintain semi-permanent settlements there, and they are considered citizens of that state. However, Turkana herdsmen drive their cattle into Mitumba and graze there for long periods each year, particularly along stretches of the Upper Oboti River, where grasses can be found during even the driest times of year.

Equatoria's representative told the GM donors' workshop that the Mitumban development plan could negatively affect the sustainability of Turkana culture. First, she said, the proposed dams in the Upper Okoti River would reduce water flow in lower stretches of the river sufficiently to cause a loss of the fertile riverside grasslands where the Turkana typically graze their cattle for several weeks during the east African dry season. Second, she contended, irrigated paddock-based cattle ranching and the fencing of open rangeland would deprive the Turkana of access to grazing areas that traditionally they have used during their annual migrations through northern Mitumba.

The Mitumban government alleged that the Turkana themselves are largely responsible for the regular exhaustion of their pasturelands in Equatoria because they are grazing that land beyond its carrying capacity. The government explained that it had allowed the Turkana to graze in northern Mitumba because their activities had so far not interfered with Mitumba's development plans. But the Turkana have no legal right to any Turkana land or to its water resources, according to the government. The appropriate solution to any problems they may experience from rural development in Mitumba is for them to trim the size of their herds and graze within Equatoria's borders.

Following the workshop in Mitumba, officials of the World Bank and the Federation of Columbia scheduled a joint meeting to discuss whether they should support the Mitumban plan.

Equatoria, the Federation of Columbia, and Mitumba are each members of the United Nations and parties to the 1994 United Nations Convention to Combat Desertification.

The Federation of Columbia's International Development Agency is charged by statute to use its development funding "to support sustainable development in countries with per capita incomes under $1200 per annum," "to leverage funding whenever possible through partnerships with the World Bank and other multilateral lenders," and "by so doing, to further Federation foreign policy and promote good relations with developing nations."

Section 2. Questions Presented

1. Would support for the development project proposed by Mitumba be consistent with the goals and provisions of the 1994 Desertification Convention and Operational Policies 4.01 and 4.10 of the World Bank?

2. Would support for the development project be consistent with the policy goals of the Federation of Columbia's International Development Agency?

Section 3. Assignments

A. Reading Assignment

Study the Readings presented in Section 4, *infra,* and the Discussion Notes/Questions that follow.

B. Recommended Writing Assignment

Assume you are an adviser to the head of the Federation of Columbia's International Development Agency. Prepare a comprehensive, logically sequenced, and *argumentative* memorandum in the form of an outline of the primary and subsidiary *legal and policy* issues you see requiring resolution as part of the decision to provide funding in support of the Mitumban project. Also, from the perspective of an independent observer interested in promoting sustainable development, indicate whether you would support funding for the project. Retain a copy of your issue-outline/memorandum for class discussion.

C. Recommended Oral Assignment

Assume you are counsel for Mitumba, on the one hand, or Equatoria, on the other (as designated by your instructor); then, relying upon the Readings (and your issue-outline if prepared), present a 15–20 minute oral argument of your government's likely position on the consistency of Mitumba's plan with international law and policy.

D. Recommended Reflective Assignment

Consider (and recommend) alternative norms, institutions, and/or procedures that you believe might be more effective than existing world order arrangements in resolving situations of the kind posed by this problem. In so doing, but without insisting upon *immediate* feasibility, identify the particular transition steps that would be needed to make your alternatives a reality.

Section 4. Readings

1. William C. Burns, The International Convention to Combat Desertification: Drawing a Line in the Sand?, 16 MICH. J. INT'L L. 831, 832–48 (1995)

The process known as desertification, which can be broadly characterized as degradation of land, resulting in decreased productivity, is not a new phenomenon. 4200 years ago, the world's first empire, the Akkadian in Mesopotamia, collapsed after only a century of prosperity as a result of severe drought that induced desert-like conditions throughout what is now Iraq, Syria, and parts of Southern Turkey.

In the sixth century B.C., the capital of the Kingdom of Kush, Napata, was abandoned because of overgrazing by herds, resulting in erosion and advancement of the desert. More recently, in the latter part of the 19th Century and early part of the 20th, desertification seriously denuded the productivity of large portions of rangelands in the United States and Australia.

However, in the past three decades the rate of desertification has increased dramatically in the forty percent of land surface classified as arid or semi-arid, dealing particularly harsh blows to the besieged inhabitants of developing nations. During the present decade, the amount of land degraded by desertification will be double that of the past two decades. This translates into the staggering loss of about 58 thousand square kilometers of once productive land annually, an aggregate area about the size of the state of West Virginia. By 1993, more than 3.6 billion hectares of the total area of the drylands was [sic] subject to some degree of desertification, representing nearly one quarter of the global land mass. On the African continent, eighty percent of sub-Saharan drylands and rangelands, or about 1.5 billion hectares show significant signs of desertification, as well as seventy-two percent of the drylands in South America and seventy percent in Asia.

Several nations in the developing world are suffering disproportionately. In China, desertification is advancing by 2100 square kilometers per year, with over one-sixth of the nation's total land mass subject to some degree of degradation. In India, forty percent of the land is desertified, encompassing about 120 million hectares. An astounding eighty-five percent of the landmass of Kenya is experiencing some degree of desertification, with almost twenty percent currently severely degraded.

The United Nations has estimated that "desertification threatens the future of more than 785 million people, or 17.7 percent of the world's population who live in . . . drylands. . . . Of this number between sixty and one hundred million people are affected directly by decreases in productivity associated with the current desertification process." Moreover, the United Nations Environment Program [UNEP] has estimated that if trends continue unabated, about eight billion acres of grazing land, irrigated zones, and croplands will be in jeopardy by the end of the century, threatening the livelihoods of 1.2 billion of the world's 5.5 billion people.

* * *

The term "desertification" is defined in the Convention [to Combat Desertification **[Basic Document 4.11]** as "land degradation in arid, semi-arid and dry sub-humid areas resulting from various factors, including climatic variations and human activities." As this definition implies, desertification is attributable to both human and natural factors.

* * *

A. Causes of Desertification

1. Human Factors

Human-induced desertification is caused primarily by four activities: overcultivation, overgrazing, deforestation, and poor irrigation practices.

a. Overcultivation

Overcultivation occurs when farmers crop lands more intensively than is sustainable by the land's natural fertility. Drylands are particularly susceptible to overcultivation. Soils in arid and semi-arid regions are formed by processes where water is extremely limited. As a consequence, the soils are not leached and the evaporative process produces an accumulation of soluble salts near the land surface. This results in a severe shortage of important nutrients, especially nitrogen and phosphorous. The paucity of these nutrients in turn results in low soil organic matter (humus) content, rendering the soil highly susceptible to erosion.

Soil and wind erosion are primary causes of desertification in the world's drylands. Erosion results in exposed topsoil becoming crusted, which reduces its ability to absorb water or causes it to be blown away by wind or washed away by water. The subsoil that remains after the valuable nutrient layer of topsoil is removed is largely infertile and is characterized by reduced water absorption properties.

Erosion also wreaks havoc with vegetation; wind carrying soil particles can "sand-blast" plants, shredding leaves through abrasion, killing them outright, or burying them under sand and dust. The loss of surface vegetation results in an acceleration of the desertification process, exposing topsoil to further erosion and destabilizing its composition. Vegetation that does subsequently grow under such conditions will usually respond less well to rain, produce less biomass, and die at increasingly earlier stages of drought. The impoverishment of the soil also leads desperate farmers to expand into more marginal rangelands, which quickly become degraded, exacerbating the desertification cycle.

Overcultivation in dryland areas can be primarily attributed to two factors: population pressures necessitating increased crop production and the expansion of cash cropping.

In areas where desertification is of particular concern, such as sub-Saharan Africa and the Middle East, population growth rates of more than three percent are severely taxing food resources.

* * *

Reduction in fallow periods is particularly harmful to the viability of agricultural lands. Fallow periods permit a land's fertility to regenerate naturally. Additionally, farmers often plant trees on land lying fallow, which provide nitrogen fixing nutrients for the soil and help prevent erosion. Fallow lands also often provide grazing resources for livestock, which, in turn, provide fertilizer for the fields.

At one time, dryland farmers could shift cereal cultivation from field to field, with fallow periods ranging from a few years up to a few decades. Increased population densities now preclude this in many dryland regions, and fallow periods have been severely reduced or eliminated. In some nations, fallowing is actively discouraged by law. For example, in Senegal, a farmer who does not plough her land within a three-year period can be stripped of ownership.

As commodity prices have plummeted in recent years, many developing nations have turned to the cultivation of monocultural cash crops, such as cotton and groundnuts, to obtain revenue for development and to service foreign debt. Many developed nations have actively encouraged this strategy by tying aid to cash crop production.

* * *

Cash crops are particularly stressful on drylands. Groundnut cropping in the Sahelian region of Africa, for example, has substantially reduced the productivity of dryland soils and has reduced the area used for food crops and fallow time, which further exacerbates soil deterioration. Similarly, the decision of farmers in Thailand to switch from cultivation of rice to tapioca has resulted in deforestation and overcultivation of soil, important precursors of desertification.

b. Overgrazing

Overgrazing occurs when livestock density becomes excessive and too many animals are grazed on the same area of rangeland. It is a major cause of desertification in the drylands, the site of one-half of the world's cattle, one-third of its sheep, and two-thirds of its goats.

In recent years, population pressures have substantially increased the size of livestock herds in dryland areas while the area available for grazing has declined as pastoralists are displaced by farmers. This has resulted in

the concentration of high volumes of livestock in extremely limited areas, contributing to desertification in several ways. First, livestock overgrazing results in the loss of vegetation, which is consumed or trampled, contributing to soil erosion. . . . Overgrazing also may result in the displacement of desirable species of plants, such as palatable grass species, which help to hold soil together, by drought-resistant shrubs, which do little to maintain soil viability or prevent erosion.

Second, the trampling of soil, particularly at places where livestock congregate, such as watering holes, results in the pulverization of the soil, contributing to erosion. In addition, pounding by livestock hooves can result in the compaction of soil. This results in surface crusting, which reduces infiltration of water into the soil and accelerates the process of water erosion.

c. Deforestation

Deforestation is proceeding at a tragic rate in many parts of the developing world, including dryland regions in Africa, Asia, and the Middle East. According to the Food & Agriculture Organization, four million hectares [i.e., circa 10 million acres] of land are deforested every year in arid lands. On the African continent, ten times more wood is harvested annually than is produced in the continent's forests. Two particularly disheartening examples in Africa are in Ethiopia, where ninety percent of the vegetation has been stripped away since the beginning of the century, and in Uganda where forest cover has declined from thirty-one thousand square kilometers to less than six thousand square kilometers in the last ninety years.

* * *

The pressure on forests in drylands comes from two directions. First, the desperate need to expand food production has resulted in the clearing of large areas of forestland for crop cultivation. For example, in the Senegalese Mbegue forest, over seven hundred kilometers of forest was [sic] cleared for cultivation in less than one month. . . . Overall, it has been estimated that seventy to eighty percent of ongoing deforestation can be attributed to clearance of land for crop production.

A second primary cause of deforestation is demand for fuel wood. About one-third of the world's population, and ninety percent in the developing world, rely exclusively on wood and woody materials as a source of heat for cooking and warmth. As supplies of farmland trees and the scrubby woodlands of unfarmed areas have been depleted, poaching has increased in ecologically critical national forests. This has resulted in the diminution or elimination of natural growths of forest and steppes in many dryland regions.

* * *

The loss of tree cover is often the first step in the process of desertification. "[T]rees play a vital role in protecting and retaining soils." Tree and plant roots help to anchor soil down, preventing wind and water erosion. . . . In Ethiopia, where national forest cover has fallen from sixteen percent a few decades ago to just three percent currently, soil is washed away in some areas by rains at the rate of twenty tons per hectare per year.

Diminution of tree cover also diminishes the water retention capacity of soil, contributing to the buildup of silt deposits and impairing the effectiveness of irrigation schemes and water reservoirs. Finally, trees provide a hospitable microclimate for grasses and supply important nutrients through stem flow to soil.

d. Irrigation/Salinization

One of the primary constraints to increasing food production in dryland regions is a shortage of water. Controlled application of water can help expand production in the short-term in the drylands. However, the construction of irrigation schemes that direct the flow of water to root zones in optimum quantities is critical for long-term gains.

Unfortunately, poor-planned irrigation projects can lead to desertification. When irrigated land is not properly drained, the soluble salts contained in irrigation water accumulate in the system and contiguous soil because the outflow of saline water is prevented or hindered. Additionally, expansion of irrigation schemes may cause the ground water table to rise, bringing salts up to the soil profile. The accumulation of salts in soils creates desert-like conditions because its constituent elements, including sodium chlorides and sodium sulfates, reduce soil fertility, stunt plant growth, and impair the metabolism between the compounds of soil, atmosphere, and hydrosphere that supply the biosphere with nutrients.

* * *

Overall, the environmental organization Earth Action reports that 1.25 million acres are desertified each year because of improper irrigation practices. Recent research pegs the annual loss of farmland from salinization at almost one percent. If current trends continue, nearly thirty percent of the world's presently irrigated acreage will be lost by 2025, rising to nearly fifty percent by 2050.

2. Climatic Factors

The role of climatic factors in contributing to the desertification process has been a constant source of controversy.

* * *

Climate clearly plays a role in the desertification process, though its precise contribution is hard to calculate. Rainfall variations are a primary cause of variations in forage production and decisions as to how to utilize rangelands. Moreover, a substantial amount of the year-to-year variation in vegetation cover in arid and hyper-arid areas can be attributed to changes in rainfall. As indicated earlier, sparse vegetation cover leads to erosion, which accelerates the process of desertification.

B. Impact of Desertification

1. Productivity Losses: Agricultural

In contradistinction to the popular image of dryland regions as barren, hostile expanses of land, arid regions are a critical source of food production, accounting for at least one-fifth of the world's supply. Unfortunately, desertification has substantially denuded food production in the drylands in the past two decades, and this process threatens to accelerate cataclysmically as this decade closes.

Approximately eighty percent of the agricultural land in arid regions suffers from moderate to severe degrees of desertification. Over sixty million acres of agricultural land are directly affected by decreases in productivity associated with desertification, and an additional fifty to seventy thousand square kilometers of useful land go out of production annually.

The degradation of agricultural lands translates directly into a decline in crop production. For example, in Africa, soil fertility losses linked to desertification has reduced dryland crop yields by twenty-five to fifty percent in severely desertified areas. Per capita grain production on the continent has plummeted twelve percent since 1981 and twenty-two percent since 1967.

Burgeoning population rates make future declines in food production potentially catastrophic. The world population, currently at 5.8 billion, is increasing by ninety-three to ninety-five million annually, the fastest rate in history.

* * *

The United Nations recently averred: "If the process of desertification is not arrested in the near future, the world shortage of food will increase dramatically within a few decades." Perhaps the most chilling portent of this conclusion is on the African continent where desertification is contributing to stagnating or even declining levels of agricultural production.

2. Stefanie M. Herrmann & Charles F. Hutchinson, The Scientific Basis: Links between Land Degradation, Drought, and Desertification, in Governing Global Desertification 18–19 (Pierre Marc Johnson, Karel Mayrand, & Marc Paquin eds. 2006)

Generally, the alleged human causes of land degradation and desertification are subsumed under the headings of overgrazing, overcultivation, and deforestation, often portrayed as almost inevitable consequences of population growth and poverty.

* * *

Labelling these land uses as causes of land degradation, however, stems from subjective judgements [sic] and is often based on misunderstanding of indigenous land use systems on the part of western scientists. As a result of their long and intimate contact with their environment, most indigenous people have developed strategies to cope with uncertainties that make economic and ecological sense. Unless droughts hit with unusual severity, these strategies generally help to sustain rather than destroy their resource base. However, socioeconomic factors such as poverty, marginality to local power structures, and uncertain or unfavorable land tenure relationships often undermine these strategies.

3. Uriel Safriel & Azfar Adeel (coordinating lead authors), Chapter 22: Dryland Systems, in Ecosystems and Human Well-being: Current State and Trends 623, 626, 636–37, 645–50 (by the Millennium Ecosystem Assessment)[52]

22.4.1.3.3 Responses to keep ahead of degradation

The desertification paradigm is grounded in simplistic, mechanistic thinking about human responses to the dryland environment and the processes of desertification. This section presents the crux of the counter-paradigm. An understanding of the dynamism of human responses helps explain why degradation estimates based on carrying capacity concepts of the desertification paradigm can be somewhat misleading.

. . . The premise of the desertification paradigm is that land users, in response to their needs, increase pressure on the land in unsustainable ways, leading to decreasing productivity and a downward spiral of poverty and further degradation. However, there is increasing evidence that these negative feedback loops need not occur. Rather, dryland populations, building on long-term experience with their dynamic environments as well as active innovation, can stay ahead of degradation by intensifying their agricultural practices and enhancing pastoral mobility in a sustainable way. In these scenarios, population growth does not lead to degradation

---

[52] Copyright 2005 Millenium Ecosystem Assessment. Reproduced by permission of Island Press, Washington, D.C.

and poverty but to a Boserupian-style[53] intensification and improved environmental management. . . .

There is, for example, a mounting body of evidence that in the African Sahel region, once considered the centerpiece of the desertification paradigm, land users are achieving higher productivity by both intensifying and improving their land management practices—capitalizing on improved organization of labor, more extensive soil and water conservation, increased use of mineral fertilizer and manure, and new market opportunities.

These studies have shown that yields per hectare and food output per capita and livestock sales are largely determined by policies and market opportunities within the constraints posed by the natural environment. It is also argued that population growth is not the overriding driver of either desertification or sustainable land management, but that the impact of population growth is largely determined by the rate of change and the way in which people adjust to their increasing numbers, mediating the effect on the environment and their own well-being through adaptations of local informal institutions, technological innovations, income diversification, and livelihood options and strategies.

The message of the counter-paradigm is that the interacting direct and indirect drivers combined with the local situation can create a range of different outcomes and that raising a general alarm based on questionable scientific evidence in the end is much less effective than identifying individual problem areas where large influxes of refugees or other complicating factors have led to an unsustainable local response. It is also crucial to distinguish between problems originating from the natural harsh and unpredictable conditions of dryland ecosystems and problems caused by unsustainable management of the environment, since the remedies will often be different.

* * *

22.4.2.1 Policy Drivers—Successes and Failures

Top-down policies with minimal participation of local communities often lead to land degradation, whereas policies encouraging participation and local institutions can induce a sustainable intensification of primary production. For example, a study of eight countries in West Asia and North Africa (Hazell et al. 2002) revealed that past agricultural policies favoring only rich farmers promoted agricultural growth that led to environmental degradation. On the other hand, policies that emphasize risk-reducing strategies, that secure property rights, and that take into account both technical and socioeconomic constraints do ensure adequate incentives for

[53] *Eds.* Ester Boserup, a Danish economist, argued that rising population density causes land use patterns to change in favor of practices that make the land more productive.

participation in resource management and can thus avoid degradation. Community-based land use decision-making and social networks also contribute to the success of non-degrading agriculture in drylands.

* * *

22.4.2.2 Demographic Drivers

* * *

Migrating populations can be a source of additional pressure on dryland environments and on resource management when livestock temporarily concentrate at key resources such as water points. Under these circumstances, conflicts over water often arise between nomads and farmers (as in the dry subhumid part of Tanzania). A transition between migration as a temporary livelihood strategy to permanent migration creates additional pressure on drylands, as described later.

Nomadism can be described as a rangeland management practice that over the centuries has proved to be sustainable and within the carrying capacity of drylands. Sedentarisation of nomads and other policies and infrastructure that promote farming in rangelands at the lower limit of cropping viability can act as drivers of land degradation. The concentration of human and livestock populations in particular areas can reduce the ability of nomads to adjust their socioeconomic activities in the face of stresses such as droughts, and a Convention on Nomadic Pastoralism to protect pastoralists' rights and empower them economically, socially, and politically has been suggested (CENESTA 2002). . . .

22.4.2.3 Land Tenure Policies

Land tenure practices and policies in drylands can also act as indirect drivers of land degradation. When farmers and herders lose control or long-term security over the land they use, the incentives for maintaining environmentally sustainable practices are lost. Problems of water scarcity, groundwater depletion, sedimentation, and salinity can all be symptoms of deeper policy and institutional failures, including a lack of well-defined, secure, tradable property rights. According to this argument, it is essential that people perceive that they have secure ownership over local natural resources for management to be effective. However, security of tenure need not imply systems of private property rights. For instance, long-established collective and community-based management of village tank systems has been more effective than the current proliferation of privately owned boreholes.

22.4.2.4 Water Policies

Water policies are relevant to many provisioning and supporting services in dryland areas. These policies include allocation systems, pricing, government investments in water resource development, and priorities in conservation measures. Water allocation for irrigation has caused degradation in some dryland areas where flows in semiarid rivers used for irrigation, such as the River Ord in Western Australia, are highly variable and unpredictable. Therefore the proportionate water release strategies have been found to be unsuitable and to cause detrimental effects to the riverine ecosystem. Irrigation policy decisions also depend on other factors, such as water availability and pricing and anticipated crop prices. Increasing water scarcity and degradation of quality are also linked to water sharing between upstream-downstream riparian users. A frequent policy focus on the aggregate availability of water—more specifically, the ratio between the number of people in a country or region and the amount of water that is naturally available—hides how much of that water can and is withdrawn and used by different people. Therefore, a shift from the mindset of resource development to one of resource management and conflict resolution is more useful.

* * *

22.4.3.1 Water Use

Freshwater resources like lakes, rivers, and aquifers are essential to the transition of rangelands to croplands by providing fresh water for irrigation. The intensity of this driver decreases with distance of the dryland from the source. The proximity of fresh water generates interventions in water transportation infrastructure, which accelerate the use of the provisioning services. These interventions can cause a degradation of several dryland services.

4. Convention to Combat Desertification in Those Countries Experiencing Serious Drought and/or Desertification, Particularly in Africa, arts. 1–5, 7–11, 19, & 28, & Annex I, arts. 1–4, & 7–8, June 17, 1994, 1954 UNTS 3 (Basic Document 4.11)

5. Kyle W. Danish, International Environmental Law and the Bottom-Up Approach: A Review of the Desertification Convention, 3 Ind. J. Global Legal Stud. 133 (1995)

The hallmark of the Desertification Convention is its elaboration of a bottom-up approach for combating desertification.

* * *

1. The "Bottom-Up" Approach: Participation in Desertification Action Programmes and in Sustainable Development Programmes

The Convention says that the national action programmes—the "central element of the strategy" to combat desertification—should consist of local development programmes that are based on participatory mechanisms. The national action programmes therefore shall:

> [P]rovide for effective participation at the local, national and regional levels of non-government organizations and local populations, both women and men, particularly resource users, including farmers and pastoralists and their representative organizations, in policy planning, decision-making, and implementation and review of national action programmes.

Notably, the Parties are obligated to provide for "effective participation" of local stakeholders and NGOs. A duty to provide merely for their "participation" arguably could be discharged by making only modest attempts to keep local stakeholders and NGOs informed and involved. The Parties must provide participation not only in implementing the programmes but also in deciding on the content of the programmes. Participation is required during continuing elaboration and revision; the plans "shall be updated through a continuing participatory process. . . ." This paragraph also gives identity to the land users and land user groups of central importance—women as well as men, pastoralists as well as farmers, and NGOs.

* * *

The African Parties agreed to obligations not only to enhance participation of land users in desertification action programmes, but also to develop a process which can maximize their participation in planning national sustainable development programmes generally. In Article 6, concerning the "[s]trategic planning framework for sustainable development," these Parties agree to undertake a "consultative and participatory process" involving local populations and NGOs to "provide guidance on a strategy . . . to allow maximum participation from local populations and communities." This language seems to create a binding obligation of decentralized development planning within the African country Parties. Such obligations should help to alleviate the political marginalization of rural land users. As noted earlier, this marginalization is one of the socio-economic conditions at the root of desertification.

2. The "Bottom-Up" Approach: Capacity-Building

Additional evidence of the bottom-up process's centrality in the Desertification Convention is its extensive section on "Capacity building, education, and public awareness." Though the language in this section more closely approximates policy recommendations than strictly binding obligations, one should not conclude that the parties are placing little emphasis on this aspect of the response to desertification.

* * *

The article defines capacity-building as "institution building, training and development of relevant local and national capacities." In addition to some measures aimed at institutions, the Parties agree to promote capacity-building through a range of activities involving the key local actors identified in earlier articles.

* * *

The section on educational awareness programs contains strictly binding obligations for the Parties. They are obligated to create and support programs to educate the public in affected countries about the causes and effects of desertification. To meet these objectives the Parties "shall" among other things, organize awareness campaigns and "promote" permanent public access to "relevant information."

* * *

4. The "Bottom-Up" Approach: Special Roles for NGOs

NGOs were an important element of the negotiations and the text reflects their central role in the bottom-up process created by the Convention.

* * *

In the last few decades, the role of non-governmental organizations in developing, implementing, and enforcing international environmental initiatives has increased substantially. Non-governmental organizations are participating in the drafting of international agreements, sometime as members of the delegation of state parties. They monitor the performance of state parties. They shame and expose those parties that do not comply with their obligations. NGOs also are playing a major role in carrying out environmental initiatives both in tandem with state agencies and independently.

Nonetheless, according to the majority view, NGOs do not have legal personality in international law. Arguably, some legal personality attaches to those NGOs with which intergovernmental organizations and convention secretariats have established formal relationships.

* * *

Given this current state of international law, the Desertification Convention represents a significant leap forward. In the text of the Convention itself, there are twenty-two separate references to NGOs. These references do not merely establish that a future desertification secretariat or intergovernmental organization should create a formal relationship with an NGO. The text obligates the state parties themselves to work with NGOs. According to the international law established under the Convention, non-governmental organizations shall be an integral element of the international and national-level policy responses to desertification.

The Convention acknowledges two important roles of NGOs in the bottom-up process. Because of their special links to the grass-roots, NGOs are recognized as effective conduits through which the international community can channel resources, information, and power to local populations. Thus, within the text, they are consistently grouped among the key local actors—women, farmers, pastoralists, local communities, local populations, etc.

The other role of NGOs recognized by the Convention is that of expert bodies. Implicitly, NGOs are placed on equal footing with intergovernmental organizations as organizations with whom Parties should consult and coordinate. In fact, the Convention consistently refers to intergovernmental organizations and non-governmental organizations in tandem. The Parties agree to develop national and field-level operational mechanisms to coordinate the efforts of developed country Parties, developing country Parties, and "relevant intergovernmental and non-governmental organizations." . . . In undertaking educational and awareness-building programs, the Parties "shall" cooperate with "competent intergovernmental organizations, as well as non-governmental organizations." Any financial mechanisms developed by the Conference of the Parties shall provide information on available sources of funds "to interested Parties and relevant intergovernmental and non-governmental organizations" in order to promote cooperation among them.

6. William C. Burns, The International Convention to Combat Desertification: Drawing a Line in the Sand?, 16 Mich. J. Int'l L. 831, 876–80 (1995)

As the drafters of both Agenda 21 and the Convention recognized, women play a critical role in land management in developing nations. Women play a predominant role in the production of food crops, producing ninety to ninety-five percent of the crops in Africa, are responsible for a large proportion of animal husbandry, and collect the vast majority of fuelwood. Thus, any effort to address the root causes of desertification must actively engage women in the process. As one commentator noted, "the energy and skills of women as natural resource managers may be a decisive factor in the battle against land degradation."

Unfortunately, many developed nations actively degrade the role of women in the context of land, denying them security of tenure, access to credit, and educational services. Affected Parties to the Convention should strive to improve the lot of women in several ways. First, the laws in many developing nations need to be reformed to permit women to inherit land, and to provide for daughters and single women to hold title to land. Second, credit policies which often deny women access to capital, or exact exorbitant interest payments, need to be eliminated. The [Food and Agricultural Organization] FAO has estimated that women receive ten percent or less of all agricultural credit, even when they are the sole breadwinners. As a consequence, women are unable to invest in sounder agricultural practices, purchase technologies to reduce demand for fuelwood, or gain access to timesaving equipment, which would make it easier to them to concentrate on sound land management. Third, efforts should be made by dryland governments to target land management training programs to women. This will require the reorientation of extension agencies in many nations which almost exclusively direct their services at men.

* * *

Unfortunately, women's educational levels are abject in many developing nations. Of the 960 million illiterate individuals in the world (most of whom are in the developing world) two-thirds are women. In many developing nations, religious customs and patriarchal institutions deny women educational opportunities and ensure unchecked population growth. Thus, the prospects for enhancing the status of women is contingent on a meaningful commitment by affected Party governments to achieve gender equity.

Finally, increasing security of land tenure, discussed earlier in this article, might yield the ancillary benefit of reducing population growth rates. A recent study indicates that in nations where private land rights are weak there is an incentive to have more children because they can be sent out to "capture" open-access resources such as firewood, animal fodder, grazing, and fish.

* * *

E. Emphasis on Local Decisionmaking and Empowerment

A final significant aspect of the Convention is its recognition of the importance of participation by groups and individuals at the local level in affected nations. Implicit in the Convention's approach is a commitment to decentralization, defined as:

> [T]he transfer of responsibility for planning, management, and the raising and allocation of resources from the central government and its agencies to field units of central government ministries or agencies, subordinate units or levels of government, semi-autonomous public authorities or corporations, area-wide, regional or functional authorities, or nongovernmental private or voluntary organizations.[54]

[54] Harlan Hobgood, Sahel Decentralization Policy Rpt. (Vol. 11): Facilitating Transitions from Centralized to Decentralized Politics I–2 (Apr. 1992) (on file with the *Michigan Journal of International Law*).

[P]rograms reflecting the "top down" concept, whereby programs are formulated at an aggregate decisionmaking level (such as a government ministry or donor organization), often fail "because local circumstances vary greatly over time and space. The informed, key decision-makers are the farmers and pastoralists themselves."[55]

7. Editors' Note

Not everyone is convinced that the Convention's emphasis on local decisionmaking and local empowerment is wise. Alon Tal and Jessica A. Cohen suggest that some amount of "top-down" pressure for reform of land use practices is necessary for two reasons. First, local empowerment is insufficient to ensure the adoption of necessary and beneficial reforms. "The problem is," they write, that

> there are many critical and cost-effective land management practices that will not be adopted for a variety of cultural, political, economic and practical reasons. Human history clearly teaches that the tragedy of the commons will often not be solved by consultation or by galvanizing the collective wisdom and goodwill of affected communities. If sustainable practices are not imposed or strongly encouraged, ecological collapse is often inevitable.[56]

On the other hand, "command-and-control" regulations can change behavioral patterns and enable the adoption of beneficial soil conservation policies. Moreover, policies imposed from above can "shape public opinion" in positive ways that local empowerment can't match. "Anti-desertification laws, especially when supplemented with educational campaigns, may forge a new public awareness and commitment to protecting land resources."

A second problem with local empowerment is that local communities often lack access to resources to implement anti-desertification policies. Because most of those resources will be provided by international donors, it is essential to be able to persuade donors that their funds will be used in a beneficial fashion. A "top-down" approach to combating desertification gives poor countries the opportunity "to show donors that they are indeed serious about land stewardship and that they will make the necessary societal and legislative commitment to address the problem of desertification." Such a "demonstration of seriousness," through the adoption of meaningful national laws and policies, can help convince

[55] Johannes Kotschi et al., Towards Control of Desertification in African Drylands: Problems, Experiences, Guidelines 28 (1986); *see also* Michael Carley & Ian Christie, Managing Sustainable Development 26 (1993).

[56] Alon Tal & Jessica A. Cohen, Bringing "Top-down" to "Bottom-up": A New Role for Environmental Legislation in Combating Desertification, 31 Harv. Envtl. L. Rev. 163, 215–217 (2007).

donors that money spent funding initiatives to combat land degradation will not be wasted.

Thus, Tal and Cohen urge countries not to adhere too slavishly to bottom-up governance, but to follow the lead of those countries that have successfully used "centralized policies" and "a myriad of laws" to combat desertification and promote land restoration.

Before concluding, however, that top-down approaches can help local communities overcome their destructive land-use practices, one must be sure that those top-down policies will be wise. As the next reading suggests, sometimes the received wisdom about wise land management can be incorrect.

8. Ced Hesse & Sue Cavanna, Modern and Mobile: The Future of Livestock Production in Africa's Drylands 15, 19, 37, 40, 47, 84 (International Institute for Environment & Development 2010)

Understanding mobile livestock production systems can be a challenge, with most of the confusion being about why pastoralists always seem to be on the move. Essentially pastoralists move to take their animals to places where they can find the best quality grazing. This is not as simple as it sounds, and requires a great deal of preparation and years of experience in an environment where errors can be unforgiving.

It is commonly believed that pastoralists move in response to pasture shortage. While this happens sometimes it is not the main reason why they move. As a general rule pastoralists are much more concerned with the quality of the diet (grasses, shrubs, tree leaves and water), as measured by their animals' health and productivity. They usually move towards higher quality rather than away from low quantity. The better the diet of the livestock, the more milk there is of a better taste and a higher fat content. Livestock on a good diet will put on weight quicker, be healthier and reproduce faster. Animals must be fed particularly well during the rainy season, when the fresh grass is high in nutrients, so as to optimize their weight gain so they can survive the inevitable weight loss during the dry season.

In the dry rangelands the timing and distribution of the nutrients is highly variable and unpredictable. This variability is due not only to the erratic rainfall, but also different soil types, different plant species and even the different stages of a plant's growth cycle.

To an outsider the grasses, shrubs and trees of the drylands may look much the same, but in fact pasture quality varies on a daily, seasonal and annual basis, and most importantly is not evenly spread across the landscape. It is this scattering of different pastures over different places, at different times, which makes mobile livestock keeping so productive in what is otherwise a difficult environment. Because fresh green pasture does not sprout in the same place at the same time, it means it is available over a longer time period than would be the case if it rained everywhere at the same time. To sedentary livestock keepers who rely on uniformity and economies of scale, randomly variable concentrations of nutrients on the range would be a serious constraint to productivity, but to pastoralists, who are mobile and maintain populations of selectively feeding animals, it represents a resource.

By being mobile with their livestock, pastoralists can take advantage of the ever-changing diversity of dryland ecology. They track the random concentrations of nutrients in space and time. The result of this strategy, when unhindered, is that their livestock are able to feed on a diet that is substantially richer than the average nutritional value of the range they live on. They can thus attain a much better level of nutrition than livestock feeding off natural pastures that remain in one place. And this means their livestock are more productive—producing more milk and meat than sedentary animals reared in the same environmental conditions.

* * *

Modern ranching is often believed to be an improvement over traditional livestock management. Many governments in Africa believe ranches will produce more and better quality beef and milk than pastoralism. Ranches, which control stocking densities and invest in high-yielding cattle breeds, water development and veterinary inputs, are able to meet the international health standards required for the export trade. But research in Ethiopia, Kenya, Botswana and Zimbabwe comparing the productivity of ranching against pastoralism all came to the same conclusion: pastoralism consistently outperforms ranching, and to a quite significant degree. Whether measured in terms of meat production, generating energy (calories) or providing cash, pastoralism gives a higher return per hectare of land than ranching. Whereas commercial cattle ranching tends to specialise in only one product—meat—pastoralism provides a diverse range of outputs including meat, milk, blood, manure, traction, which when added up is of greater value than meat alone.

* * *

The obstacles to mobility

Pastoralists are regularly in the news. However, a careful look at these incidents shows the problem is often more complex than initially appears and that in many cases it is obstacles to the safe and free movement of livestock that is the starting point.

Incidents of crop damage by pastoral animals are escalating into violent conflicts between herders and farmers. Confrontations over access to water are becoming more frequent and turning bloody. Pastoralists are clashing with private owners or government officers over access to conservation areas. Border skirmishes are intensifying in frequency and ferocity.

Instead of being mobile and productive, pastoralists are increasingly constrained. Farms frequently block access to their grazing areas; national border controls hinder their trade patterns; and the areas they traditionally preserve for times of drought are now national parks or agricultural schemes. In other areas national government policies actively encourage pastoralists to settle and be "modern." These policies are often driven by unfounded perceptions that pastoralism is economically inefficient and environmentally destructive. Alternative land uses, including large-scale agriculture and national parks, are believed to bring in more national revenues and to have less environmental impact. But this is not evidence based.

* * *

And it is not just the sheer extent of the lost land that is so important; it is the nature of that lost land that is so critical. Much of the alienation concerns strategic areas such as wetlands or riverine forests. Here, because of higher and more stable moisture, pastures of higher nutritional content can be found, particularly in the dry season when the surrounding range is dry and poor.

These areas represent "islands" of high quality pasture where livestock feed until the arrival of new fresh grass with the next rainy season. The loss of these areas undermines the profitability and resilience of the whole pastoral system.

Little research has been carried out to calculate the economic and environmental impacts the loss of these areas have had on national economies, and whether the expected benefits from the new land use systems are greater than the benefits lost as a result of displacing pastoralism.

* * *

Obstacles to mobility reduce productivity

When livestock are unable to access grazing or cross borders, the whole pastoral system becomes less efficient and the economy suffers. When livestock are forced to remain in one place, pressure on natural resources increases, particularly around water points. Faced with the threat of destitution, pastoralists make every effort to remain mobile, and this can result in conflict if their way is blocked.

Across the drylands inappropriate policies are blocking livestock mobility. Enduring perceptions of pastoralism as an outdated, economically inefficient and environmentally destructive land use system continue to drive rangeland and livestock policy in much of Africa. Yet, none of these perceptions are evidence-based, informed by past failure or reflect current scientific knowledge of the dynamics in dry land environments and livelihood systems. Nor are they designed with the participation of pastoral communities. These persistent beliefs must be left behind in the 20th century.

* * *

[Recommendation 3.] Mobile livestock production is a complex system that requires a holistic response. Securing access to relatively small but highly productive areas—along rivers, on hills, or in alluvial plains—during the critical dry season/drought allows pastoralists to access much larger areas at other times. Protecting these ecologically valuable areas from appropriation or exploitation by other users, and facilitating livestock's access to them, particularly during periods of drought stress, is essential to maintaining the health of the system as a whole.

9 International Bank for Reconstruction and Development (World Bank), World Bank Safeguard Policies, at http://go.worldbank.org/QL7ZYN48M0 (accessed on December 8, 2018)

The World Bank has developed a series of safeguard policies to help staff promote socially and environmentally sustainable approaches to development as well as to ensure that Bank operations do not harm people and the environment. These safeguard policies include the Bank's policy on Environmental Assessment (EA) and those policies that fall within the scope of EA: Cultural Property; Disputed Areas; Forestry; Indigenous Peoples; International Waterways; Involuntary Resettlement; Natural Habitats; Pest Management; and Safety of Dams.

The World Bank conducts Environmental Assessments (EA) of each proposed investment loan to determine the appropriate extent and type of environmental impact analysis to be undertaken, and whether or not the project may trigger other safeguard policies. The Bank classifies the proposed project into one of four categories (A, B, C, and FI) depending on the type, location, sensitivity, and scale of the project and the nature and magnitude of its potential environmental impacts.

The government is responsible for the assessments required by the Safeguard Policies while the World Bank is responsible for overall compliance with these policies. The Bank's Legal Vice Presidency monitors compliance with the policies addressing international waterways and disputed areas. The Sustainable Development (SD) Network monitors all other safeguard policies through the multi-disciplinary Quality Assurance and Compliance Unit (QACU).

During the appraisal process, the International Finance Corporation (IFC) identifies which of these policies are applicable to a project. If IFC invests, the project's performance is monitored against these policies.

Compliance is the expected standard, in addition to compliance with applicable local, national, and international laws.

10. International Bank for Reconstruction and Development (World Bank), Operational Policies (OP) 4.00, 4.01, and 4.10, The World Bank Operations Manual (March 2005) (Basic Document 1.42)

Section 5. Discussion Notes/Questions

1. The Desertification Convention **(Basic Document 4.11)** envisions progress in combating land degradation through partnerships between affected countries and donor organizations and governments from the developed world. To date, this cooperation has not resulted in a great deal of financial support for developing nation anti-desertification programs, despite the fact that a Convention body, the Global Mechanism, is specifically designed to foster the needed financial support. To what would you attribute this failure?

2. A report by the UN's Joint Inspection Unit (JIU) on the performance of the Global Mechanism offered a number of technical criticisms of the process by which the Global Mechanism had gone about its work and questioned whether it had been hindered by attempting to engage in activities outside its mandate. But the JIU also noted some fundamental problems with the Desertification Convention itself, including a relative absence of "a sound scientific basis and evidence-based approaches to support policy strategies," and a lack of agreement among the parties to the Convention on whether desertification should be treated "as an environmental or a developmental challenge." *See* Even Fontaine Ortiz & Tadanori Inomata, UN Joint Inspections Unit, *Assessment of the Global Mechanism of the United Nations Convention to Combat Desertification* 3–5 (2009). Is there an even more fundamental issue of state interests? What interest do donor countries have in contributing to a resolution of an environmental problem that does not affect them and is primarily local or regional in scope?

3. One argument that was made during negotiation of the Desertification Convention was that desertification affects everyone because it contributes to the problem of environmental refugees—people fleeing their homelands because of catastrophic environmental destruction. So-called environmental refugees can be found worldwide, including in the United States where much illegal immigration from Mexico and Central America is said to stem from environmental degradation in that region. But whether there is a significant problem of environmental migration (as opposed to economic migration) and, if so, how it should be addressed, is subject to much dispute. Some migratory movements may be appropriate local or regional adaptation to the realities of living in drylands. For discussion, *see* Norman Myers and Jennifer Kent, Environmental Exodus: An Emergent Crisis in the Global Arena (1995); William C. Burns, *The International Convention to Combat Desertification: Drawing a Line in the Sand?*, 16 Mich. J. Int'l L. 831, 847–48

(1995); Arthur C. Helton, *The Legal Dimensions of Preventing Forced Migration,* 90 Am. Soc'y Int'l L. Proc. 545, 548 (1996); Stephen Castles, *Environmental Change and Forced Migration: Making Sense of the Debate,* New Issues in Refugee Research: Working Paper No. 70 (October 2002).

4. As Readings 1–3 illustrate, there is disagreement among scientists about the nature of the desertification problem, not to mention its solution. Hermann and Hutchinson argue that "the scientific basis for recognition of desertification as an irreversible process remains rather weak," but the "term 'desertification' is still widely used in scientific or popular circles to refer to a multitude of land-cover change phenomena, despite its acknowledged limitations and lack of clarity about the fundamental nature of the problem and the lack of measurable criteria." Stefanie M. Herrmann & Charles F. Hutchinson, *The Scientific Basis: Links between Land Degradation, Drought, and Desertification,* in Governing Global Desertification 12 (2006). On the other hand, there is no doubt that the drylands of the world are home to many of the very poorest people, and that their efforts to earn a living on marginally productive land very frequently leads to degradation and lower productivity of that land.

5. In addressing the problem of land degradation, how should policy be formulated? Should the views of local people always be given preference? What if local elites dominate local governance processes to the detriment of everyone else? Do you agree that top-down policy frameworks, imposed by central governments, may be necessary to put a stop to harmful local practices, as suggested by Reading 7? What reforms would you suggest? For example, should traditional land use practices such as communal ownership and customary shared rights be replaced by some sort of exclusive private ownership? Can local communities successfully manage a shared resource, or is their failure to do so part of the problem?

6. In determining whether to fund Mitumba's proposal or not, what factors should the World Bank and the Federation of Columbia consider? Should they seek to determine whether Mitumba's plan is the best solution to land degradation in northern Mitumba and, if not, should they refuse funding? Or should they rely on Mitumba's judgment about the viability of its plan?

7. Is the likelihood of an adverse impact on the Turkana herdsmen a consideration against Mitumba's plan? Is Mitumba obliged to consider the desire of the Turkana to use its land and water resources when they are citizens of another state? Should it be obliged to consider their interests? Despite the artificial borders drawn by colonial powers, isn't it likely that parts of Mitumba and Equatoria are a single ecosystem, which the Turkana have learned to utilize productively and sustainably? Should their successful example of sustainable development, operating across generations, be impaired in the interests of conducting an experiment in sustainable development using modern irrigation technology (which has had disastrous consequences in some parts of the world, *see* Problem 12-1, *infra*)?

8. If the World Bank and the Federation of Columbia refuse to provide funding for Mitumba's project, Hanguo might. Ethiopia's attempt to secure funding for a large dam on the Omo River was refused by the World Bank and other western donors. Two Chinese banks offered significant funding to help the project move forward, and the dam was completed in 2016. Ethiopia is now considering two additional dams on the river. *See* Kevin Mwanza, *Ethiopia's dams threaten thousands of Kenyans: environmentalists,* Big Story 10, Reuters (July 3, 2018), https://www.reuters.com/article/us-kenya-water-ethiopia/ethiopias-dams-threaten-thousands-of-kenyans-environmentalists-idUSKBN1JT1QU (accessed Dec. 8, 2018). Is it significant to the World Bank that Hanguo might provide funding for the Mitumba project if the Bank does not? Is it significant to the Federation of Columbia?

9. Is it a consideration in Mitumba's favor that the irrigation project will improve the lives of women and girl children in the affected villages? Desertification and other environmental problems are, arguably, a result of women's subordination and lack of power. Rapid population growth in developing countries can be attributed, at least in part, to a lack of birth control means available to women. Moreover, women are often less educated than their male counterparts, lacking knowledge that could help them improve their economic and living circumstances, even though they often have primary responsibility for ensuring the family's livelihood. The Desertification Convention **(Basic Document 4.11)** requires education and local action as part of the fight against desertification. If women are targeted in this effort—and educated about health issues, farming techniques, and the economic, political and social issues that impact their lives—there is potential for exponential impacts. On the other hand, if women are excluded from the picture, can the battle against desertification be won?

Do you agree or disagree with this suggested link between desertification problems and the lack of input by, and education for, women? Why or why not? What are some specific ways in which the voices of women would make a difference in combating desertification? Other environmental problems?

10. If the World Bank decides to fund Mitumbo's project, despite the impact on the Ngi Turkana, they might have a remedy through the World Bank's Inspection Panel. The Inspection Panel was established by the Executive Directors of the World Bank in response to complaints about the adverse impact of World Bank-supported projects on some local communities. The Inspection Panel investigates whether the Bank is following its own policies (including those identified in Reading 10).

a. The Panel process is triggered by a Request for Inspection from at least two Requesters alleging that the Bank has violated its own policies or procedures. The Panel determines the eligibility of the request, but only the Bank's Board of Executive Directors can authorize the Panel to engage in an inspection and evaluation of the merits of the request. At the conclusion of an investigation, the Panel submits its report to the Bank's Management, and Bank

Management then submits a response and recommendations to the Board of Executive Directors. Management's recommendations are intended to bring the Bank into compliance with its policies (if non-compliance is found) and may include remedial measures. The Board makes the final determination whether to approve Management's recommendations.

b. A Request for Inspection must come from adversely affected peoples in the country where the Bank-financed project is located. The request must establish that the people live in the project area and will suffer harm because of the Bank's failure to follow its own policy. If the Bank financed Mitumbo's project, would the Ngi Turkana qualify to make a request for an Inspection Panel Investigation? *See generally* Dana Clark, Jonathan Fox & Kay Treakle, Demanding Accountability: Civil-Society Claims and the World Bank Inspection Panel (2003); Ibrahim F. I. Shihata, The World Bank Inspection Panel In Practice (2000); Enrique R. Carrasco & Alison Guernsey, *The World Bank's Inspection Panel: Promoting True Accountability through Arbitration,* 41 Cornell Int'l L. J. 577 (2008); E. Tammy Kim, Note, *Unlikely Formation: Contesting and Advancing Asian/African "Indigenousness" at the World Bank Inspection Panel*, 41 N.Y.U. J. Int'l L. & Pol. 131 (2008).

CHAPTER EIGHT

PREVENTING CHEMICAL POLLUTION

■ ■ ■

The two problems in this chapter identify two fundamental truisms. First, human activities, ranging from those that cater to the prodigal life styles of the rich industrial countries to those that are necessary for the development of poor nations, almost inexorably end up fouling our nest, i.e., the environment we inhabit. Second, although we sometimes conceptualize the global environment in terms of its component parts—the atmosphere, the hydrosphere, the lithosphere, and the biosphere—this division does not faithfully mirror nature or the ways in which environmental problems emerge in the real world. Rather, each part of the environment is connected to every other. Pollution of the air or groundwater will find its way into the lakes, rivers, and oceans. Pollution in water will affect plants and animals that use the water or live in it. Pollutants that accumulate in plant and animal life become part of a food chain that eventually includes human consumers.

In rich countries, pollution results from a staggering array of household, commercial, and industrial uses that maintain abundant and wasteful life-styles. The natural resources required to satisfy modern living standards—extravagant by any historical criterion—include, but are not limited to, the energy we consume to heat and cool and to move ourselves and our goods in speedy fashion by air, land, and water; the pesticides, fungicides, insecticides and other chemicals upon which we have become dependent to produce our food; and, of course, the luxurious materials we assemble to build and furnish our homes, cars, and boats, and to attire ourselves from head to foot. All of which puts enormous pressure on our natural resources, particularly the nonrenewable kind, and on the fragile ecosystems that support them.

This massive exploitation of renewable and nonrenewable resources gives rise to another problem. The matter and energy that is necessary to satisfy our life styles are neither created nor destroyed; they are merely transformed, so that massive quantities of wastes or residuals become the unavoidable and punishing by-products of today's living. In short, in addition to depleting non-renewable resources, we today appear to be—in advanced industrial societies certainly, but also in some developing countries—locked into a profligate cycle of waste production, as Problem 8-1 suggests.

And what about the dangers of the many hazardous chemicals that play an important role in improving the quality of human life but are subject to misuse and overuse that threatens the environment and human health? How might international law pragmatically assist in arresting the damage caused by such chemicals without denying developing nations access to their benefits? Problem 8-2 addresses that issue.

PROBLEM 8-1: E-RE SENDS USED ELECTRONICS TO LUZONAN

Section 1. Facts

Luzonan is an island country located in Southeast Asia with Luzona City as its capital. Its population of 40,000,000 is multi-ethnic, the country having been originally settled by Malayo Polynesian peoples, but including sizable numbers people of Chinese, Spanish, British, American, Indian, Arab, Japanese, and Indonesian descent. Luzonan is a democracy governed by a president and a bicameral legislature. While autocratic administrations governed the nation in the 1960s, 70s, and 80s, Luzonan has had regular elections and peaceful exchanges of power for nearly 20 years.

Luzonan is a middle-income developing country. Important economic activities include agriculture, mining, manufacturing, and tourism. There is a significant and growing middle class, but the majority of its people still live below the government-identified poverty level, more than a third of them living on less than $2 a day. Also, while the country has a strong educational system, its large workforce of highly skilled workers earn very low wages in comparison to similarly skilled workers in more developed nations.

Prior to World War II, Luzonan was a colony of Iberia, an industrialized country in southwestern Europe and a member to the European Union. Luzonan and Iberia continue to have strong business and political ties, and Iberian business people frequently vacation in Luzonan.

A few years ago, Juan Barril, a frequent visitor to Luzonan and a senior executive in a multinational European electronic waste management company, E-Re Corporation, realized that Luzonan presented a huge potential market for the refurbishing and sale of electronic equipment that had become obsolete by European standards. As Barril explained to his company's board of directors, "One man's waste is another man's treasure. Equipment that Europeans regard as hopelessly outdated would be accepted with delight by Luzonanians who cannot afford better. What's more, Luzonan has a skilled labor force which will work for a fraction of European wages. That makes it practical to repair and re-use equipment in Luzonan that would be discarded in Europe." Convinced by

Barril's arguments, E-Re decided to explore the export of used electronic equipment to Luzonan—primarily computers, cell phones, and televisions.

E-Re found a willing partner in Used Tech, a Luzonan corporation that repairs and refurbishes electronic equipment and then sells it to retailers across Luzonan. They agreed that E-Re would supply Used Tech with monthly shipments of used electronic equipment "for the purpose of repair and reuse" at prices calculated on a "per ton" basis and adjusted once each year.

For five years, E-Re has been shipping used electronic equipment to Used Tech in Luzonan. The invoices for every shipment indicate that the shipment includes "used electronic equipment for repair and re-use." The electronic equipment that E-Re sends is donated to E-Re by people and organizations from all over Europe—by businesses that no longer want it, from charities which themselves collect the equipment from consumers, and from product manufacturers who have re-acquired outmoded consumer electronic devices under "take-back" plans for products whose useful life has ended. E-Re's policy is to accept only equipment that is "in working order," but it admits that it does not test the equipment. Instead it informs donors that donated equipment must be in good working order, and it relies on them to comply.

In fact, only about 60% of the electronic equipment shipped to Luzonan by E-Re is in working order and only about 80% is even repairable. Upon inspection, at least 20% is unusable junk. That junk is discarded by Used Tech at a dump site that it owns on the outskirts of Luzona City. Moreover, when Used Tech must repair equipment, it generally ends up replacing major components of the equipment, such as circuit boards and old laptop computer batteries. The parts that are replaced also end up at the dump site. Yet, despite the fact that 20% of E-Re's supply product is unusable, Used Tech has been willing to deal with E-Re because E-Re's prices are much lower than the prices charged by firms that pre-inspect products or guarantee 100% usable products. This, in turn, affords Used Tech a competitive advantage in Luzonan. There is a large market for Used Tech products because they have a good reputation for quality—despite being technologically outmoded by European standards—and because they are inexpensive.

GreenWorld is an environmental NGO headquartered in Iberia. Twelve months ago, it began to investigate E-Re's business practices and discovered that E-Re had been shipping as many as 40,000 used computers to Luzonan every month. When its investigators traced the shipments, they discovered Used Tech's operation, including its dump site on the edge of Luzona City which quickly became the focus of a GreenWorld video documentary.

GreenWorld's video documentary was shown across Europe to a horrified audience. The Used Tech dump site, it turns out, was located about 200 meters from a shantytown near a river approximately 10 kilometers from Luzona City. Barefoot children and elderly people from the shantytown would each day visit the dump site to "recycle" the used electronic equipment, dismantling it to get at the valuable metals inside. The recycling processes on display were primitive and dangerous. The recyclers would break open cathode ray tubes with hammers, burn wires to destroy the insulation covering the copper inside, and melt circuit boards in pans over open fires.

Dumped electronic equipment contains many toxic substances, including lead, cadmium, barium, beryllium, mercury, and brominated flame retardants. The destruction of the equipment at the Used Tech dump site released these substances into the environment in the area, and the burning of plastic-covered wire created smoke filled with dioxins and furans, highly poisonous substances in their own right.

When GreenWorld released its video, the Government of Luzonan immediately sent a team of scientists and doctors to the dump site. They determined that the groundwater in the area was so contaminated with hazardous chemicals that it was not fit to drink. They also learned that almost 90% of the children living in the area had high levels of toxic lead in their blood. The adults working in the dump site reported nausea, headaches, and chest and respiratory problems, which the investigators attribute to exposure to the hazardous materials in the electronic equipment and the toxic fumes generated when the equipment burned.

The Luzonan authorities immediately fined Used Tech $100,000 for maintenance of an illegal dump site. They also condemned the shantytown and moved the residents a few kilometers away. The dump site has not been cleaned up, however, because no Luzonan law requires Used Tech to do so and because Luzonan authorities are unwilling to pursue further action against Used Tech. Its owners are closely connected to top Luzonan politicians.

Under Iberian law, any person who commits a "willful violation of any rule or principle of domestic or international law protecting the environment" is liable for any injuries caused thereby, including for the costs of environmental cleanup. The Iberian courts have taken the position that individuals and businesses are in violation of international environmental law if they engage in conduct that is contrary to any treaty-based norm that is binding on Iberia, even if private conduct was not under the auspices of government authority. The Iberian courts have also held that damages can be sought for injuries that occur in other nations if the allegedly unlawful conduct occurred in Iberia or was committed by an Iberian citizen.

Luzonan has filed suit against E-Re in Iberia seeking $10 million in damages, which it estimates is the cost of relocating the shantytown and providing medical care to persons who were injured by exposure to hazardous wastes from the dump site. Luzonan has also approached the Iberian government through diplomatic channels and demanded that it take back all the dumped electronic equipment that remains at the Used Tech dump site. Iberia contends that any dumping that occurred in Luzonan was by Used Tech, and that it was Luzonan's responsibility to ensure that Used Tech and all other Luzonanian companies handled their waste appropriately.

Luzonan and Iberia are parties to the Basel Convention on the Control of the Transboundary Movement of Hazardous Wastes and Their Disposal **(Basic Document 4.7)**. Both have adopted domestic legislation that seeks to control the import and export of hazardous waste consistently with that Convention. In addition, Iberia, as a member of the OECD, has agreed to be bound by OECD Council decisions, including the 1986 OECD *Decision/ Recommendation on Exports of Hazardous Wastes from the OECD Area* **(Basic Document 4.6)**.

Section 2. Questions Presented

1. Did E-Re's conduct constitute a "willful violation of any rule or principle of . . . international law protecting the environment"?

2. Is Iberia obligated to take back the dumped electronic equipment that E-Re shipped to Luzonan?

Section 3. Assignments

A. Reading Assignment

Study the Readings presented in Section 4, *infra*, and the Discussion Notes/Questions that follow.

B. Recommended Writing Assignment

Prepare a comprehensive, logically sequenced, and *argumentative* brief in the form of an outline of the primary and subsidiary *legal* issues you see requiring resolution by the Iberian court in the suit by Luzonan or by the two countries in their diplomatic negotiations. Also, from the perspective of an independent objective judge, indicate which side ought to prevail on each issue and why. Retain a copy of your issue-outline/brief for class discussion.

C. Recommended Oral Assignment

Assume you are legal counsel for Luzonan, on the one hand, or E-Re/Iberia on the other (as designated by your instructor); then, relying upon the Readings (and your issue-outline if prepared), present a 15–20 minute oral argument of your client's position.

D. Recommended Reflective Assignment

Consider (and recommend) alternative norms, institutions, and/or procedures that you believe might do better than existing world order arrangements to contend with situations of the kind posed by this problem. In so doing, but without insisting upon *immediate* feasibility, identify the particular transition steps that would be needed to make your alternatives a reality.

Section 4. Readings

1. Editors' Note

Industrialized countries export a significant amount of their hazardous waste. The wastes involved cover a wide spectrum and include municipal solid wastes, incinerator ash, asbestos wastes, sewage sludge, old tires, and radioactive wastes. Exported waste may be processed and disposed of properly in the importing country, or it may be simply dumped, buried, or burned. The extent of the hazardous waste trade is not known accurately, however, and the facts are controversial. In Reading 2, *infra*, *Transboundary Toxic Waste Disposal: Understanding the Gravity of the Problem and Addressing the Issue through the Human Rights Commission*, 1-Fall Int'l Dimensions (1997), Andrea Marcus provides some specific accounts.

The international trade in waste has grown in response to strong legal and economic incentives. Businesses face strict and costly regulations for waste disposal at home. Moreover, there often is a shortage of disposal sites within industrialized nations, and the "not in my backyard" (NIMBY) philosophy of nearby residents exacerbates this problem. For some countries, there are geological, topographical, and other factors that make the building of adequate disposal facilities difficult or impossible. Finally, in many cases, the cost of transporting and disposing of waste abroad is less than disposing of hazardous wastes at home. *See, e.g.*, Hao-Nhien Q. Vu, *The Law of Treaties And The Export of Hazardous Waste*, 12 UCLA J. Envtl. L. & Pol'y 389 (1994) (discussing the numerous reasons for the transfrontier movements of hazardous wastes from industrialized nations to developing nations).

Although it is economically attractive for industrial countries to ship their waste abroad, poorer countries often have minimal or no hazardous waste disposal facilities, and even when they do, they have minimal regulations and often no mechanisms to enforce them. But developing countries face a dilemma: hazardous waste disposal can provide major and much needed revenue. For example, "in 1992, Italian and Swiss companies took advantage of the confused political situation in war-torn, famine-stricken Somalia to secure an $80 million, twenty-year contract for dumping toxic wastes there. The contract was supposedly signed by the Somali Minister of Health, but at the time none of the warring factions in Somalia truly held power." *Id.* This dilemma is not limited to the Horn of Africa.

International Regulation of the Waste Trade—Early Action at the OECD

Significant international action to address the trade in wastes began under the auspices of the Organization for Economic Cooperation and Development (OECD), a group of industrialized countries. In 1974, OECD formed a Waste Management Policy Group (WMPG). In 1976, following a report from WMPG, the OECD Council recommended that its Members adopt "comprehensive waste management policies" and work with other countries to ensure that their waste management practices "do not have a detrimental effect on other countries."[1] The 1976 OECD Recommendation articulated a set of principles for waste management that have shaped international policy to this day. Those principles included:

- Ensuring that "the necessity to protect human and natural environment is duly taken into account at every stage of the production-consumption-disposal chain";
- Encouraging the adoption of measures "aiming at avoiding or reducing the generation of waste, when beneficial on a social cost basis";
- "[P]romoting recycling in all cases where waste reclamation and upgrading is beneficial";
- Applying the "Polluter-Pays Principle" to "encourage waste prevention and recycling by allowing market forces to work on a more rational basis."
- Adopting measures to ensure "that competent authorities" are provided with "all necessary information to ensure that waste disposal or reclamation is realized in the most economic and judicious way with regard to environmental protection."

In 1984, the OECD Council adopted a Decision-Recommendation on Transfrontier Movements of Hazardous Waste **(Basic Document 4.5)**. That Decision-Recommendation, which is still in effect, directed OECD Members to "control the transfrontier movements of hazardous waste" and "ensure that the competent authorities of the countries concerned are provided with adequate and timely information concerning such

[1] Recommendation of the Council on a Comprehensive Waste Management Policy, OECD Doc. OECD/LEGAL/0147 (adopted Sept. 28, 1976).

movement."[2] A set of recommended "Principles Concerning Transfrontier Movements of Hazardous Waste" were attached to the decision. They included the following:

- Internal activities related to "generation, transport and disposal or recovery of hazardous waste" should be regulated to ensure that such waste "is managed in such a way as to protect man and the environment."
- Waste generators and persons acting on their behalf should be required to ensure that any transfrontier movement of waste occurs only in compliance with "the laws and regulations applicable in the countries concerned."
- Waste generators and persons acting on their behalf should provide the exporting, transit, and importing countries with "adequate and timely information" about any proposed movement of hazardous wastes, including the type of waste involved, the environment risks of the movement, and the identity of all entities involved with the movement or disposal of the waste. Exporting countries should assist in ensuring that importing and transit countries receive relevant information about proposed transboundary movements.
- A decision of a transit or importing country to oppose (under its own laws) a particular transfrontier movement of hazardous waste should be respected, and the exporting country should prohibit movements that would violate another country's laws or accept the reimport of the waste in question if the movement has already begun.

In 1986, the OECD Council adopted an additional decision-recommendation specifically aimed at the problem of exports of hazardous waste to countries outside the OECD area.[3] Member countries were directed to prohibit movements of hazardous waste to a final destination outside the OECD unless a) all transit countries had been notified of the waste movement; b) the destination country had been notified and had consented to receive the waste; and c) the wastes were being sent to "an adequate disposal or recovery facility" in the destination country. Recommended measures for implementation of the prior notification/ consent system were set out at the end of the decision. In addition, the Council recommended that Member countries "conclude bilateral or multilateral agreements with nonmember countries to which frequent exports of hazardous wastes are taking place or are foreseen to take place."

---

[2] Decision-Recommendation of the Council on Transfrontier Movements of Hazardous Waste, OECD Doc. OECD/LEGAL/0209 (adopted February 1, 1984).

[3] Decision-Recommendation of the Council on Exports of Hazardous Wastes from the OECD Area, OECD Doc. OECD/LEGAL/0224 (adopted June 5, 1986) **(Basic Document 4.6)**.

The OECD's Environmental Policy Committee had been asked in 1985 to develop a draft international agreement on the hazardous waste trade, and it was instructed to "take account of the elements of this Decision-Recommendation" when completing that task.

Actions outside the OECD

A 1982 decision of the UNEP Governing Council had identified the development of global "guidelines, principles or conventions" on hazardous waste management as a top priority.[4] An Ad Hoc Working Group of Experts was formed and, after two years of study and discussion, the Working Group adopted the 1985 Cairo Guidelines and Principles for the Environmentally Sound Management of Hazardous Wastes.[5] Among other things, the Cairo Guidelines endorsed the principle that transboundary movements of hazardous waste should be subject to a regime of notification and prior consent by transit and importing states. In 1987, the UNEP Governing Council adopted the Cairo Guidelines and directed UNEP's Executive Director to convene a group of experts to "prepare a global convention on the control of transboundary movements of hazardous wastes, drawing on the Cairo Guidelines and Principles and the relevant work of national, regional and international bodies."[6] The Working Group was formed and held its first organizational meeting in October 1987.

In mid-1988, the world was shocked by news that two Italian firms had paid a farmer in Koko, Nigeria $100 per month to allow them to dump over 18,000 containers of hazardous waste. When the dumping was discovered, some of the containers were already leaking and hazardous chemicals were leaching into the local river, causing chemical burns and deaths among the local population. Italy at first denied that the wastes were harmful, but when an independent analysis proved the contrary, it ordered the firms to repackage and remove the waste. Nigeria responded by banning all hazardous waste imports.

This incident, and reports of similar activities in other developing countries, created a sense of urgency around the international negotiations. In late 1988, the United Nations General Assembly adopted a resolution urging the negotiators to consider certain key principles as they worked toward consensus. Those principles, mirroring the principles adopted by the OECD and UNEP, were that:

- "All transboundary movement of toxic and dangerous wastes" should be prohibited unless the prior consent of importing

---

4 UNEP, Montevideo Programme for the Development and Periodic Review of Environmental Law, Decision 10/21 of the Governing Council (31 May 1982).

5 *See* UNEP, Report of the Executive Director to the UNEP Governing Council at its Fourteenth Session, U.N. Doc. UNEP/GC.14/17 at para. 2 (2 April 1987).

6 *See* Final Report of the Ad Hoc Working Group of Legal and Technical Experts with a Mandate to Prepare a Global Convention on the Control of Transboundary Movements of Hazardous Wastes, para. 1, U.N. Doc. UNEP/IG.80/4 (22 Mar 1989).

countries was secured and the "sovereign rights of transit countries" recognized.

- Prior notification should be given to both importing and transit countries, including "full disclosure of the nature of the substances" involved in the movement and "all information required to ensure proper management of the wastes."
- Wastes should be disposed of "in the country of origin to the maximum extent possible consistent with environmentally sound disposal."[7]

Thus, by the end 1988, a strong consensus had emerged that trade in hazardous wastes was a serious problem requiring prompt international action to address it. Moreover, there appeared to be broad agreement on the basic principles that should govern transboundary movements of hazardous wastes. Within a few months, negotiations had concluded. The Basel Convention on the Control of Transboundary Movements of Hazardous Wastes and their Disposal **(Basic Document 4.7)** was adopted on 22 March 1989.[8]

The Basel Convention

The Basel Convention reflected the work previously done within the OECD and under the auspices of UNEP. It adopted four key principles in the form of binding obligations. First, transboundary movements of hazardous waste should not occur without the prior notification and prior consent of transit and importing countries.[9] Second, wastes should be exported only to destinations where they will be managed in an environmentally sound manner.[10] Third, exporting countries have an obligation to police their exporter's compliance with the prior notification and consent rules and to take back wastes that are exported in violation of those rules.[11] Fourth, the main responsibility for the disposal of hazardous wastes lies with the state of generation.[12] Wastes should be exported only for recovery or recycling or when the exporting state lacks the capacity to dispose of the waste in an "environmentally sound and efficient manner."[13] Where a proposed contract for recovery, recycling or disposal of waste in another country cannot be completed, the exporting country has an

[7] G.A. Res. 43/212 (on the Responsibility of States for the protection of the environment) (Dec. 20,1988).

[8] Convention on the Control of Transboundary Movements of Hazardous Wastes and their Disposal, March 22, 1992, 1673 U.N.T.S. 57 [hereinafter Basel Convention]. The Basel Convention entered into force in May 1992. There were 186 parties to the convention as of September 2018.

[9] Id. at art. 6(1), 6(4), & 6(7).

[10] Id. at art. 4(2)(e, g), & 4(8).

[11] Id. at arts. 6(1), 6(3), 9(2), & 9(5).

[12] Id. at art. 4(2)(a-d).

[13] Id. at art. 4(9).

obligation to accept the return of the waste and to deal with the problem itself.[14]

To carry out their Basel obligations, ratifying states must designate a "competent authority" that is responsible for providing notice of a transboundary movement of hazardous wastes, for receiving and responding to such notifications, and for verifying completion of the movement as specified in the notification.[15] The information that must be included in a notification is spelled out in detail in Annex VA of the Convention, and some of this information must also accompany the shipment in a movement document.[16] The movement document must be signed by each person "who takes charge of a transboundary movement of hazardous wastes," and the exporting state must be notified when disposal is completed as specified in the original notification. If the exporting state is not informed that the movement has been completed as planned, it must inform the importing state of the apparent problem.

The regulatory regime established by Basel applies to wastes defined as hazardous pursuant to Annexes I, III, VIII and IX of the Convention or identified as "other wastes" under Annex II. It also applies, in relevant part, to wastes defined as hazardous by the domestic legislation of any exporting, importing, or transit state that is a party to the Convention. Basel Parties are not permitted to engage in hazardous-waste transactions with non-Parties[17] except pursuant to an agreement that ensures the "environmentally sound management" of the wastes.[18]

The Basel Convention established a Conference of the Parties that has worked actively to supplement the Convention with additional rules. In 1995, the COP adopted the so-called "Ban Amendment" which aimed to prohibit all exports of hazardous waste from developed countries to developing countries.[19] As of this writing, the amendment is not in force. Similarly, a Protocol on Liability and Compensation **(Basic Document 4.7a)**, adopted by the COP in 1999, has not yet received sufficient ratifications for entry into force. By contrast, Annexes VIII and IX, which clarify the definition of hazardous waste in Annexes I and III, were added by amendment in 1998 and have entered into force pursuant to a tacit consent procedure.[20]

---

14 Id. at art. 4(8).

15 Id. at arts. 2(6), 5(1), 6(1) & 6(9).

16 Id. at art. 4(7)(c) & Annex V B.

17 Id. at art. 4(5).

18 Id. at art. 11.

19 Id. at art. 4A.

20 Article 18(2) of the Convention provides that new annexes will automatically enter into force six months after notice of their adoption. A Party may avoid having a new annex apply to it by giving written notification to the Depositary within those six months of its non-acceptance of the annex. Otherwise, all Parties are deemed to have accepted any adopted annex and are bound by it. The same procedure applies to amendments to an annex.

The Conference of the Parties has also adopted over two dozen documents containing technical guidelines. These guidelines are aimed at assisting countries in ensuring that their standards for the management of hazardous wastes are at a level sufficient to satisfy the Basel requirement of "environmentally sound management." The documents include technical guidelines to assist in the determination whether a particular waste stream exhibits characteristics that make it hazardous within the meaning of the Convention,[21] as well as guidelines on the environmentally sound management of specific types of wastes.[22]

The Bamako Convention

In January 1991, twelve African nations adopted the Bamako Convention on transboundary hazardous waste movements in Africa. The Convention bans the importation into Africa of hazardous wastes from outside the region. It also seeks to control transboundary movements within Africa in a way that parallels the regulatory regime established by the Basel Convention.[23] To date, the Bamako Convention has not been particularly effective. Although it entered into force in 1998, the first Conference of the Parties under the Convention was not held until 2013. A second COP was held in 2018. The meeting focused on discussions of the challenges of implementing the Convention.

Post-Basel OECD Actions

In the years following entry into force of the Basel Convention, the OECD adopted two additional decisions on hazardous wastes, both of which (with amendments) remain in force. The first decision, adopted in 1991 and significantly amended in 2001, requires OECD Members to develop the capacity to dispose of wastes in their own territory insofar as that is "consistent with environmentally sound and efficient management practices," and "to reduce their transfrontier movements to the minimum justified by environmentally sound and efficient management."[24] These requirements mirror the obligation of parties to the Basel Convention to "ensure that the transboundary movement" of wastes "is reduced to the minimum consistent with the environmentally sound and efficient management of such wastes."[25] The decision recognizes also, however, that

---

[21] *See, e.g.*, Guidance paper on hazard characteristic H6.2 (infectious substances), UN Doc UNEP/CHW.7/11/Add.1/Rev.1 (27 October 2004).

[22] *See, e.g.*, Technical guidelines on the environmentally sound management of wastes consisting of, containing or contaminated with mercury or mercury compounds, UN Doc UNEP/CHW.12/5/Add.8/Rev.1 (20 July 2015).

[23] Convention on the Ban of Import into Africa and the Control of Transboundary Movement and Management of Hazardous Wastes within Africa, Jan. 30, 1991, 2101 U.N.T.S. 177 **(Basic Document 4.8)**. The Convention entered into force on April 22, 1998. It currently has 27 parties. 28 African countries have not yet ratified the Convention.

[24] Decision-Recommendation of the Council on the Reduction of Transfrontier Movements of Wastes, OECD Doc. OECD/LEGAL/0260 (adopted January 31, 1991).

[25] Basel Convention, art. 4(2)(d).

transboundary movements might be necessary when domestic waste infrastructure does not exist and cannot be developed. In such circumstances, disposal and recovery facilities in other states may be utilized, but the countries concerned should cooperate to ensure the "environmentally sound management of the wastes" at the receiving facilities.

In 1992, the OECD Council adopted a Decision on the Control of Transboundary Movements of Wastes Destined for Recovery Operations.[26] The decision applies only to movements within the OECD area. It sets up an elaborate control system, with notification and movement documents as set out in the agreement. The decision has been modified several times, most notably in 2001, to ensure that its elements are consistent with the Basel Convention, especially in terms of the wastes that it regulates strictly and those that flow more easily across frontiers.

Illegal trade in hazardous waste

The Basel Convention defines hazardous waste trade that does not comply with its terms as "illegal traffic," and it requires Parties to the Convention to adopt appropriate legislation to "prevent and punish illegal traffic."[27] Illegal traffic most commonly involves shipments of hazardous waste under documents containing false declarations of the contents of a shipment and shipments in a form that conceals their true nature (e.g., mislabeled containers). When illegal traffic is detected, the state of export has responsibility for ensuring the proper management of the wastes if the illegality was the result of the conduct of the exporter or generator of the waste. If the illegal conduct was attributable to the importer or disposer, the state of import bears the obligation to ensure environmentally sound management of the waste.

As the next three readings illustrate, these various international agreements have not solved the problem of dumping of hazardous wastes in countries that lack capacity to handle the wastes. One of the ongoing challenges is illegal traffic. Another challenge is deciding whether a certain substance or object is "waste" that is (or should be) subject to the regulatory system set up by the Basel Convention.

---

[26] Decision of the Council on the Control of Transboundary Movements of Wastes Destined for Recovery Operations, OECD Doc. OECD/LEGAL/0266 (March 30, 1992).

[27] Basel Convention, art. 9.

2. Andrea Marcus, Transboundary Toxic Waste Disposal: Understanding the Gravity of the Problem and Addressing the Issue Through the Human Rights Commission, 1 Int'l Dimensions 11–13 (1997)

The following are just a few of the thousands of examples of illegal toxic waste dumping, import, and export, that result in the continuing degradation of the environment, and often fatal violations of human rights:

1. In November of 1994, in South Africa, African National Congress President Nelson Mandela visited victims of the international toxics trade. At Thor Chemicals, the world's largest recycler of mercury wastes, one worker at the Natal plant died, and almost a third of the workforce reportedly suffered some form of mercury poisoning, including one man who had been in a coma for years. Certain types of mercury wastes cannot be legally disposed of in the United States, and Thor's suppliers include at least three U.S. corporations and the U.S. Department of Energy. On February 21, 1994 an ANC inspection team found more than 10,000 barrels of mercury wastes from three U.S. companies stockpiled at the plant.

2. In early 1994, Thor Chemicals returned a shipment of waste mercury to its source, Borden Chemicals and Plastics, in the United States. The documentation for the shipment indicated that it was activated carbon, which is no more hazardous than charcoal. Thor Chemicals spokesman John MacDonald confirmed that the shipment contained mercuric chloride, but said that Thor had the means to dispose of it safely.

3. In 1992, Italian and Swiss companies, who claimed to have agreements with a Somalian government official, planned to dump half a million tons of hazardous waste each year for the next 20 years in Somalia. This prompted the Swiss government to request U.N. help to track down any of its companies involved. During these alleged agreements, Somalia was suffering political turmoil and severe famine, making it particularly vulnerable to corrupt bargaining between impostors claiming to hold authority in Somalia, and opportunistic companies exporting toxic waste. On October 6, 1992, the Executive Director of the United Nations Environment Programme (UNEP), Mostafa K. Tolba, stated that the deal had been aborted, and that UNEP was "pleased to have played a role in heading off an environmental tragedy in Somalia."

4. In 1990, U.S. Customs Officials discovered lead waste in an empty truck returning to the United States. The officials tracked the waste to an American-owned battery "recycling" plant in Mexico, where batteries shipped from the United States were simply opened and their acid dumped on the ground. The extracted lead was then shipped back to the U.S. for resale. In response to felony charges in California for unlawfully transporting hazardous waste across the border, the facility owner pleaded no contest and paid a $25 million fine.

5. In 1991, instead of paying the $300 per ton price for disposal in the U.S., an American corporation sold 1000 tons of dust containing lead and calcium to a waste broker for $45 per ton. The broker sold the dust to another American company which later sold it to Bangladesh as fertilizer. The poisonous quality was discovered only after one third of the "fertilizer" had already been spread on fields, and fifty-pound bags of the fertilizer were on shelves in local markets. In July of 1993, after months of pressure from environmentalists, the financier of the scheme, the Asian Development Bank, sent a team of epidemiologists and toxicologists to investigate. It also tentatively agreed to fund the return to the U.S. of the toxic that is still warehoused. No date had been set for the return of the waste because the U.S. government had not yet agreed to accept it. Late in 1992, the company that generated the waste, Gaston Copper, pleaded guilty to violating U.S.—waste export reporting procedures and accepted a $1 million fine.

6. In 1992, a U.S. firm shipped 8,000 tons of contaminated soil from California to be used as landfill for a causeway project in the Marshall Islands. Local protests led by Greenpeace and other green groups prompted the U.S. environmental protection authorities to impound the ship in Guam, and later send it back to the United States.

7. In October 1992, the S.S. United States, after being purchased by a consortium that planned to refurbish it for luxury cruising, was sent to Turkey to have its more than 500,000 square feet of asbestos removed. In Turkey, the asbestos removal was estimated at about $2 million, instead of the $100 million it would have cost in the United States. However, the Turkish government, citing the dangers, refused to allow the asbestos to be removed there. In October of 1993, the ship was hauled to the Black Sea port of Sevastopol in Ukraine, where the government did not object to the hazards of the asbestos removal.

8. In March 1994, Philippine customs officials impounded two 12-meter long containers of computer waste from Australia after a Greenpeace ship intercepted the shipment at sea at night. When this sort of waste lands in China, workers strip the cables for copper wire and the remaining material is either burned or stockpiled. Computer waste contains chlorinated compounds and rare metals which produce dioxins and other toxic substances when burned. For example, computer keyboards emit brominated dioxins, a substance linked to cancer and immune system disorders.

9. Australian laws do not control the export of waste if it is being sent for "recycling and recovery purposes." As a result, Australian exports to Asia include plastic scrap, lead car batteries, metal scrap, and other hazardous wastes, and more recently, computer junk. Between 1992 and 1993, Australia sent hundreds of tons of plastic waste to the following

Asian countries: China Hong Kong, India, Kiribati, Malaysia, the Philippines, Singapore, South Korea, Papua New Guinea, Taiwan and Vauatu.

10. In October 1993, Chinese customs officials discovered that a shipment declared and documented as fuel oil instead contained chemical wastes produced in Korea by the Macao International Limited Corporation.

11. In November 1993, a train from Germany carrying 239 tons of hazardous pesticides stored in leaking drums, stood unwanted at the northern Albanian border. The pesticides, stored in 17 railroad cars, were ordered from Germany but not admitted to Albania because the new democratic government did not want the cargo and asked the German government to take it back. Environment Minister Klaus Toepfer said he would immediately send 1.4 million marks ($817,000) to ensure the pesticides caused no danger. In the meantime, the leaking toxic pesticides were left waiting at the border. The German train endangered Lake Shkoder, and the water supply of large parts of the Southern Balkans.

12. In January of 1993, the German waste trading company Rimex, sent 230 tons of various kinds of toxic wastes and chemicals to the Ukrainian town of Rovno. The waste included three barrels (about 180 kg) of extremely toxic mercury wastes; chemical reagents (expired in 1976 and 1978); waste paints containing heavy metals; outdated pesticides; wood preservatives; pure DDT; prussic acid (hydro cyanic acid); laboratory chemicals and pharmaceuticals in glass containers and cardboard boxes; and red and white phosphorus which can ignite at any time without outside influence. Except for the mercury, which was not declared at all, Rimex declared the wastes it exported to Ukraine as "building materials" and "consumer goods." In June of 1993, German Chancellor Helmut Kohl, visited the Ukraine, and agreed to send a team of experts to the eastern region city of Rovno to examine and package safely the wastes.

13. February 6, 1996, Alexandr Nikitin was arrested and charged with espionage and acts of high treason because of his involvement in the production of a Bellona Foundation report on atomic safety in Russian Northern Fleet installations and submarines based on the Kola peninsula. The charge carried a penalty from ten years of imprisonment up to and including the death sentence. The Norwegian Minister of Foreign Affairs stated, in response to the arrest of Nikitin, that openness regarding environmental and nuclear safety questions and the possibility of citizens and organizations to freely engage in environmental work are among the most important changes the new times have brought to Russia. Regrettably, many countries still do not permit their citizens to engage freely in environmental work. Nikitin's arrest and imprisonment is only one of many examples of people being imprisoned or executed for their attempts to bring their countries environmental hazards to light.

These incidents illustrate that industrialized countries can easily unload their toxic waste in lesser developed countries due both to economic incentives and the lack of sufficient regulatory mechanisms in lesser developed countries. Not only does this harm the receiving countries, but it greatly reduces incentives for countries to regulate and reduce the amount of toxic waste they produce.

3. Editors' Note, Continued Hazardous Waste Dumping and Its Consequences

Abuses like those described in the previous reading continue today. In August 2006, the *Probo Koala*, a ship chartered by a Netherlands company, off-loaded 500 tons of toxic waste in Côte d'Ivoire (the Ivory Coast). The waste was trucked around the country and dumped in multiple locations. By November, 10 people were dead and more than 100,000 had sought medical care. Similar incidents occur regularly, though not usually as dramatically. The fact is that the trade in hazardous waste, both legal and illegal, is dangerous and continues apace.

There are numerous risks posed by the hazardous wastes trade. Many developing countries have totally uncontrolled hazardous waste disposal practices. Others do not have the technical expertise or means of enforcement to handle these dangerous substances properly. Sometimes nations do not know what they are receiving due to mislabeling (or labeling in foreign languages unknown to them) and the deliberate mixing of hazardous material with harmless material. Often waste brokers handle the transaction, which increases the risks of mishandling and subterfuge.

The risks for the receiving country are not only contaminated air, soil, water, and foodstuffs. Rates of cancer, birth defects, and other health problems can be alarmingly high in areas contaminated by hazardous wastes. Many hazardous wastes have a long-life span in the environment. The effects of poorly managed wastes may take generations to show up. There can be direct, physically harmful effects on neighboring states. Of major concern is the possible effect on the biosphere.

The transboundary shipment of waste is also not in the interests of the waste-exporting industrialized nations as there is no guarantee that the wastes will then be properly managed. Food-importing industrialized nations may experience a "boomerang effect," with poisons ending up on their dining room tables because of contaminated food imports from largely agrarian developing countries. And there are reports that lead recovered from electronic waste has been shipped back to the United States as a key ingredient in children's jewelry.[28]

---

[28] Jeffrey D. Weidenhamer & Michael L. Clement, *Evidence of Recycling of Lead Battery Waste into Highly Leaded Jewelry,* 69 Chemosphere 1670 (2007).

4. Electronic Waste: EPA Needs to Better Control Harmful U.S. Exports Through Stronger Enforcement and More Comprehensive Regulation, United States General Accounting Office, GAO–08–1044 (Aug. 2008)

According to EPA, a vast majority of used electronics (including their component parts and commodities) donated for reuse or recycling are exported, both responsibly and irresponsibly. Responsible recyclers often test used electronics to determine which components can be reused, then separate the remaining materials into their component parts and commodities before exporting. Recyclers like these have told us that they operate at a competitive disadvantage against companies that export whole, untested units.

Exporting used electronics from the United States brings important benefits. For example, export leads to viable and productive secondhand use of electronic devices in developing countries—a practice known as "bridging the digital divide"—where they can be purchased for 1/10th the price of a new unit and contribute significantly to the operations of schools, small businesses, and government agencies. Moreover, extending the life cycle of electronic products prevents substantial environmental damage. A United Nations University study found that the manufacturing phase takes up 80 percent of the natural resources used during the life cycle of computers, so extending the lifetime of computers provides an important environmental service.

In addition, strong demand exists overseas to recycle the raw materials contained within electronic devices. State-of-the-art recycling facilities in developed countries, such as Belgium, can extract precious metals and salable commodities. Recycling in this fashion also provides an important environmental benefit: metals can often be extracted from used electronics with less environmental impact than from mining. The U.S. Geological Survey, for instance, reports that 1 metric ton of computer scrap contains more gold than 17 metric tons of ore and much lower levels of harmful elements common to ores, such as arsenic, mercury, and sulfur.

In recent years, concerns have been raised because toxic substances such as lead, which have well-documented adverse health effects, can potentially leach from discarded electronic products, especially if disposed of improperly. Nearly all the substances of concern in an electronic appliance are in solid, nondispersible form, so there is no cause for concern with respect to human exposure or release into the environment through normal contact. Instead, human health and environmental concerns related to the presence of these substances arise if the equipment is improperly disassembled or incinerated. EPA has identified lead, mercury, and cadmium (which are typically found in computers or monitors) as priority toxic chemicals for reduction. According to EPA, these toxic substances do not break down when released into the environment and can be dangerous, even in small quantities. . . .

Used Electronics Are Exported Worldwide and Often Handled and Disposed of Unsafely

Some exported used electronics can be handled responsibly in countries with effective regulatory regimes and by companies with advanced technologies. A substantial quantity, however, ends up in countries where the items are handled and disposed of in a manner that threatens human health and the environment.

Some Exported Used Electronics Appear to Be Handled Responsibly

Certain developed countries have regulatory regimes that require safe handling and disposal of used electronics. Member states of the European Union, for example, must comply with the Waste Electrical and Electronic Equipment Directive of 2002, which established comprehensive take-back and recycling requirements involving retailers, manufacturers, and importers of electrical and electronic products. The directive requires member countries to ensure that producers and importers finance the separate collection, treatment, recovery, and environmentally sound disposal of "waste electronics," either on their own or through collective systems financed by themselves and other members of the industry.

European Union countries are also parties to the Basel Convention **[Basic Document 4.7]**. The aim of the convention is to protect human health and the environment from the adverse effects caused by the export of hazardous wastes, especially to developing countries, where the risk of unsafe hazardous waste management is often higher. As part of European Union countries' implementation of the Basel Convention, hazardous wastes intended for disposal cannot be shipped to non-OECD countries. Exports of waste occur only under the following circumstances: (1) if the exporting country does not have sufficient disposal capacity, (2) if the exporting country does not have disposal sites that can dispose of the waste in an environmentally sound manner, and (3) if the wastes are required as a raw material for recycling or recovery industries in the importing country.

In addition to being governed by comprehensive regulatory controls, some companies in European Union countries use advanced technologies to recycle used electronics. For example, the recycler Umicore, according to its own documents, operates a state-of-the-art facility in Belgium, where it uses advanced technologies and processes to extract precious metals from circuit boards and responsibly handles waste by-products. Umicore samples electronic scrap to determine the presence of hazardous materials. The company then captures hazardous materials, such as cadmium and mercury, in the extraction process and disposes of them in an environmentally sound manner, state company documents. Over 95 percent of the electronic items that Umicore recycles become new electronic products, and many of the remnants are recycled into construction materials.

Some companies located in developing countries also appear to safely recycle and dispose of used electronics using advanced technologies. Samsung Corning, for example, operates a plant in Malaysia that not only recycles CRT glass but also manufactures new CRT televisions containing as much as 50 percent recycled-glass content. . . . Malaysia's regulatory regime helps ensure safe recycling and disposal practices for CRTs; these products may be exported to Malaysia only if they meet certain conditions, according to Malaysian environmental protection officials. If local facilities lack the capacity or ability to safely carry out recycling activities, the government of Malaysia will not allow companies to import CRTs from the United States, according to a Malaysian government document. In addition, officials with the country's Department of Environment and Department of Customs have said CRTs cannot be legally imported from other countries if destined for final disposal.

Many Countries Receiving Used Electronics Lack the Capacity to Safely Handle and Dispose of Them

While the United States has the landfill and institutional capacity to provide safe handling and disposal of used electronics domestically, many foreign countries, particularly those in the developing world, do not. According to surveys made on behalf of the United Nations Environment Programme [UNEP], many developing countries lack the infrastructure to safely manage waste, including hazardous waste. These surveys found that large quantities of used electronic items are imported by developing countries, particularly in Southeast Asia, where they are improperly handled and, in some cases, informally recycled in "backyard" operations involving open-air burning of copper wire and acid baths to recover valuable metals.

Upon importation, brokers, recyclers, and refurbishment companies in some developing countries examine items to determine how they can be used most profitably. According to individuals familiar with the international electronics industry, to maximize profit, working units are resold, repairable products are refurbished, and broken units are disassembled into component parts for further reclamation. Reusable electronics—those that can be directly resold or easily refurbished—generally have the highest value and are sold in retail shops in some developing countries. For nonworking or otherwise broken units, workers disassemble those that cannot be resold into their component parts, generally by hand. After disassembly, metals and plastics are recovered from the component parts, using methods that may lead to pollution and contamination. For instance, in some cases, workers burn the plastic coating off wires to recover copper and submerge circuit boards in open acid baths to extract gold and other metals. Unsalvageable computer parts are often burned in the open air.

* * *

Used Electronics are Exported to Western Africa Primarily for Reuse

In contrast to the situation in many Asian countries, used electronics exported to West African countries are intended for reuse. Businesses importing used computers, for example, can sell functional units for as little as $100, well below the cost of a new computer, bringing technology within the reach of more people, according to one African computer importer. Recycling is not as prevalent in West Africa as it is in Southeast Asia, in part because West Africa is farther from markets where recycled commodities are sought. In addition, shipping costs to Africa are considerably higher than to Hong Kong and Southeast Asian countries. One recycler told us that rates from the United States to West Africa range from $4,000 to $7,000 per 20-foot container—considerably more expensive than the $750 it costs to ship 40-foot containers from the United States to Hong Kong.

Some U.S. recyclers mix broken units with working units in shipments to Africa, and the nonworking units are often dumped and left for scavengers. Accepting "junk" equipment is often part of the "arrangement" U.S. recyclers make with African importers, according to a used computer importer in Senegal. Negotiating the amount of working versus broken equipment is routinely part of the agreement, and this importer told us that even if he receives a shipment of up to 40 percent "junk," he can still make a profit. Often, the "junk" computers are dumped in the countryside and burned, he explained. In addition, in 2007, an official with the Basel Convention Regional Centre for Africa for Training and Technology Transfer noted, on the basis of his experience that a high proportion of the units that arrive in Nigeria are unusable, that used electronics are rarely tested for functionality before export to developing countries like those in Africa.

5. Waste Crime—Waste Risks: Gaps in Meeting the Global Waste Challenge, A UNEP Rapid Response Assessment 7–8, 13–17 (Ieva Racevska, et al., contributors) (UNEP and GRID-Arendal 2015)

The exact size of the global illegal waste trade is unknown. The latest research on e-waste, a product of one of the world's largest and fastest growing manufacturing industries, estimates that about 41.8 million metric tonnes (Mt) of e-waste was generated in 2014 and that this number will increase to 50 Mt already by 2018. According to various estimates, the amount of e-waste properly recycled and disposed of ranges between 10 to 40 per cent. The presence of the informal economy makes solid estimates of the value for the sector difficult. However, using an estimate previously used by INTERPOL of an average value of e-waste at USD 500 per tonne, the range of e-waste handled informally or unregistered, including illegally, amounts to USD 12.5–18.8 billion annually. It is not known how much of this e-waste that is subject to the illegal trade or simply dumped.

* * *

Serious crimes may take place in any part of the waste chain, including exposing populations to toxic material through improper handling and disposal. They are not necessarily associated with breach of soft, unclear or waste environmental regulations. Rather, serious crimes such as tax fraud or money laundering, take place as the large-scale economic and transport sector of waste receives very little attention. Furthermore, larger business interests may deliberately bypass environmental legislation and tax laws for profit. In some cases some recyclable waste such as plastics, paper or metals may be used directly to cover or hide hazardous waste, although the scale of this remains unknown. Companies can be paid significant sums for appropriate treatment, but instead dump large quantities mixed with regular waste for substantial profit. Thus, these companies may commit environmental crimes (with important health implications), such as fraud through falsification of customs forms, or tax fraud through over- or under invoicing costs and incomes.

Waste is also deliberately classified as other items to deceive law enforcement authorities. This is often done by using non-hazardous waste codes for hazardous wastes or using product codes for hazardous wastes. As e-waste is largely categorized as hazardous due to the presence of toxic materials such as mercury, lead and brominated flame retardants, it requires proper management. E-waste may also contain precious metals such as gold, copper and nickel, and rare materials of value such as indium and palladium making it an attractive trade. However, in practice, many shipments of e-waste are disguised as second hand goods.

Inadequate resources for monitoring, enforcement and low penalties provide an environment of major opportunity for transnational organized criminal actors to commit large-scale breaches of environmental laws. As volumes are unknown, this situation in effect generates a permissive environment for tax fraud.

Key destinations for large-scale shipments of hazardous wastes, such as electrical and electronic equipment, include Africa and Asia. In West Africa, a significant recipient is Ghana and Nigeria, but high volumes also go to, but not limited to, Cote D'Ivoire, and the Republic of the Congo. South Asia and Southeast Asia also appear to be major regional destinations, including, but not limited to, China, Hong Kong, Pakistan, India, Bangladesh, and Vietnam.

The key driver for illegal waste shipments to destination countries is the profit generated from payments for safe disposal of waste that in reality is either dumped or unsafely recycled. It may, however, also include an additional profit from recycling certain components. While the latter appears to be positive, in practice it develops environments that are hazardous to health, and typically leads to subsequent dumping of majority of the waste. Profit is the fundamental objective of the different players in illegal waste shipments. These may include exporters, middlemen and informal recyclers. Their activities are usually structured along a legal chain of operations, albeit where the players take advantage of loopholes in control regimes and actual control capacities.

Both small- and large-scale smuggling techniques can be observed all over the world, from organized truck transport across Europe and North America to the use of major smuggling hubs in South Asia, including widespread container transport by sea. Large numbers of abandoned waste containers with unknown contents are stored in different ports in Asia and in other parts of the world. Dumping at sea or even more so in ports is logistically easy. The use of such methods warrants much further investigation given the possible scale of tax fraud and larger organized breaches of environmental regulations.

Stringent enforcement in one country commonly leads to changes in illegal shipment routes through neighbouring countries. Strong enforcement practices, such as China's Green Fence campaign, have been changing the traditional routes for illegal waste shipments.

The shipment of toxic material and electronic waste poses a particular [*sic*] acute threat for involvement and growth of organized crime. It entails money laundering, increased criminal proceeds revenues and an opportunity for further diversification of criminal proceeds. There is likely no other area of organized crime that provides such a significant opportunity for money laundering and tax fraud as waste disposal, with its near complete lack of monitoring, statistics or reporting.

Without any significant enforcement efforts dedicated to the mapping, investigation and possible prosecution of criminals involved in illegal waste collection, illegal dumping and transport activities are likely to grow, as will the associated threats to human health and environmental security.

* * *

Legal framework: What is waste

The first and probably most complex question is whether a certain substance or object is waste. Modern recycling involves innovative technologies to move waste back into the production or consumption chain.

Waste with positive value, such as paper, plastic, and metal, can rejoin the value chain and serve as a resource for new products. When investigating waste crimes, it is necessary first to prove the status of the substance or object as waste before applying the laws and regulations that cover waste management and its transboundary movement.

Even though the Basel Convention contains a definition of waste, there are various interpretations of the term and what exactly it covers. Unclear definitions or obligations may lead to both unintentional and intentional breaches of the legal framework dealing with waste management and transboundary movement. The problem is further compounded by a lack of harmonization between the codes of different countries, or by different requirements between countries with respect to the conditions under which a substance or object must be disposed of and thus considered a waste. To remedy this situation, the Indonesian-Swiss Country-Led Initiative was launched in 2011 to provide additional legal clarity with respect to certain terms used in the Convention, such as clarifying the distinction between wastes and non-wastes. Another initiative developed within the framework of the Basel Convention and aimed at providing greater legal certainty is the development of technical guidelines on transboundary movements of electronic and electrical waste and used electrical and electronic equipment.

Not only do lack of clarity or differing understandings create challenges for the law enforcement community, but they might also be taken advantage of intentionally by organized criminal groups and individuals to export wastes in contravention of the applicable legal framework.

In addition to defining waste, the Basel Convention defines two types of waste falling within its scope: "hazardous" wastes, based on their origin and/or composition and their characteristics; and "other wastes," such as household waste and incinerator ash as listed in Annex II to the Convention. Hazardous wastes are defined in Annexes I, III, VIII, and IX of the Convention, bearing in mind that a Party has also the possibility to define additional wastes as "hazardous" under its national legislation. Throughout the years, some Parties to the Convention have developed further criteria to support the process of distinguishing waste from non-waste. In the European Union, end-of-waste criteria have been developed to specify when certain waste ceases to be waste and achieves the status of a product or a secondary raw material—for example, if the substance or object is commonly used for specific purposes; if there is an existing market or demand for the substance or object and the use is lawful (substance or object fulfils the technical requirements for the specific purposes and meets the existing legislation and standards applicable to products); and the use will not lead to overall adverse environmental or human health impacts.

It is estimated that thousands of tonnes of e-waste declared as second-hand goods are regularly exported from developed countries to developing countries (Secretariat of the Basel Convention 2011). The Basel Convention technical guidelines referred to above have the potential to draw a clear line between used electronic and electrical equipment and waste electronic and electrical equipment falling within the scope of the Basel Convention and its export and import control regime.

What is hazardous waste

Once the waste status has been established or assumed (in some cases, in court as a result of legal proceedings), the question is whether the waste is "hazardous" or "other," given that this determines whether the Basel Convention's regulatory regime applies to its export, transit, and import.

Basel Convention	Examples
Annex I Hazardous wastes requiring prior informed consent (Y codes)	Clinical wastes, waste mineral oils, or residues arising from industrial waste operations
Annex II Other wastes requiring prior informed consent (Y codes)	Wastes collected from households
Annex III List of hazardous characteristics	Explosive, corrosive, or toxic
Annex VIII (List A) List of hazardous wastes covered by the Convention (A codes) unless the use of Annex III demonstrates that a waste is not hazardous	Waste lead-acid batteries, glass from cathode ray tubes, or fluff-light fraction from shredding
Annex IX (List B) List of wastes not covered by the Convention (B codes), unless they contain Annex I material to an extent causing them to exhibit an Annex III characteristic	Waste end-of-life motor vehicles containing neither liquids nor other hazardous components, paper wastes, or textile wastes.

* * *

In Asia, many countries have adopted regulations prohibiting or restricting the import of hazardous and other wastes that are, in some cases, even more stringent than the requirements of the Basel Convention. However, due to the need for resources and raw materials for their development, many of them allow the import of second-hand materials and used electrical and electronic equipment (EEE). For example, China and Vietnam regulate the import and export of scraps and second-hand EEE through permits. Yet most of the countries that allow the import of scraps or second-hand EEE do not have more specific requirements for distinguishing scraps and second-hand EEE, rubber/ tires, plastic, and metal scraps from wastes. This leads to an enormous "grey area" for distinguishing legal from illegal waste shipments and makes enforcement very difficult.

To address the grey area, some countries have set certain criteria for the percentage of waste contents (allowable percentage of contamination) in shipments. For example, China's allowable percentage of contaminated wastes in a shipment is the following: 0.5% (scrap plastics, PET beverage bottles); 1.0% (refining residue, waste textiles, compressed auto); 1.5% (waste wood, waste paper); 2.0% (waste steel, non-ferrous metals, motors, cables, and assorted metals).

However, inconsistency in the regulations between the exporting and the importing countries pose challenges for effectively controlling illegal waste trafficking. For example, EU countries may allow a certain percentage of contaminated waste to be exported to other countries, while the importing countries may have different criteria. Indonesia has adopted a "zero tolerance" policy for contaminated waste. If any contamination is found, a shipment has to turn back to the country of export. This can lead to a dispute between the exporting country and the importing country, since a shipment that is legal in one country might be illegal in the other country.

6. Basel Convention on the Control of Transboundary Movements of Hazardous Waste, preamble, arts. 1, 2, 4, 8, 9 & Annexes I, III, VIII & IX, Mar. 22, 1989, 1673 UNTS 57, (Basic Document 4.7)

Article 1. Scope of the Convention

1. The following wastes that are subject to transboundary movement shall be "hazardous wastes" for the purposes of this Convention:

(a) Wastes that belong to any category contained in Annex I, unless they do not possess any of the characteristics contained in Annex III; and

(b) Wastes that are not covered under paragraph (a) but are defined as, or are considered to be, hazardous wastes by the domestic legislation of the Party of export, import or transit.

2. Wastes that belong to any category contained in Annex II that are subject to transboundary movement shall be "other wastes" for the purposes of this Convention.

* * *

Article 2. Definitions

1. "Wastes" are substances or objects which are disposed of or are intended to be disposed of or are required to be disposed of by the provisions of national law;

* * *

4. "Disposal" means any operation specified in Annex IV to this Convention;

* * *

8. "Environmentally sound management of hazardous wastes or other wastes" means taking all practicable steps to ensure that hazardous wastes or other wastes are managed in a manner which will protect human health and the environment against the adverse effects which may result from such wastes[.]

* * *

Article 4. General Obligations

1. . . . (c) Parties shall prohibit or shall not permit the export of hazardous wastes and other wastes if the State of import does not consent in writing to the specific import . . . .

2. Each Party shall take the appropriate measures to: . . .

(f) Require that information about a proposed transboundary movement of hazardous wastes and other wastes be provided to the States concerned, according to Annex V A, to state clearly the effects of the proposed movement on human health and the environment;

(g) Prevent the import of hazardous wastes and other wastes if it has reason to believe that the wastes in question will not be managed in an environmentally sound manner; . . . .

3. The Parties consider that illegal traffic in hazardous wastes or other wastes is criminal.

4. Each Party shall take appropriate legal, administrative and other measures to implement and enforce the provisions of this Convention, including measures to prevent and punish conduct in contravention of the Convention. . . .

7. Furthermore, each Party shall:

(a) Prohibit all persons under its national jurisdiction from transporting or disposing of hazardous wastes or other wastes unless such persons are authorized or allowed to perform such types of operations;

(b) Require that hazardous wastes and other wastes . . . be packaged, labelled, and transported in conformity with generally accepted and recognized international rules and standards . . . .

(c) Require that hazardous wastes and other wastes be accompanied by a movement document from the point at which a transboundary movement commences to the point of disposal.

8. Each Party shall require that hazardous wastes or other wastes, to be exported, are managed in an environmentally sound manner in the State of import or elsewhere. Technical guidelines for the environmentally sound management of wastes subject to this Convention shall be decided by the Parties at their first meeting.

9. Parties shall take the appropriate measures to ensure that the transboundary movement of hazardous wastes and other wastes only be allowed if:

(a) The State of export does not have the technical capacity and the necessary facilities, capacity or suitable disposal sites in order to dispose of the wastes in question in an environmentally sound and efficient manner; or

(b) The wastes in question are required as a raw material for recycling or recovery industries in the State of import; or

(c) The transboundary movement in question is in accordance with other criteria to be decided by the Parties, provided those criteria do not differ from the objectives of this Convention.

10. The obligation under this Convention of States in which hazardous wastes and other wastes are generated to require that those wastes are managed in an environmentally sound manner may not under any circumstances be transferred to the States of import or transit.

* * *

Article 8. Duty to Re-Import

When a transboundary movement of hazardous wastes or other wastes to which the consent of the States concerned has been given . . . cannot be completed in accordance with the terms of the contract, the State of export shall ensure that the wastes in question are taken back into the State of export, by the exporter, if alternative arrangements cannot be made for their disposal in an environmentally sound manner . . . .

Article 9. Illegal Traffic

1. For the purpose of this Convention, any transboundary movement of hazardous wastes or other wastes:

(a) without notification pursuant to the provisions of this Convention to all States concerned; or

(b) without the consent pursuant to the provisions of this Convention of a State concerned; or

(c) with consent obtained from States concerned through falsification, misrepresentation or fraud; or

(d) that does not conform in a material way with the documents; or

(e) that results in deliberate disposal (e.g. dumping) of hazardous wastes or other wastes in contravention of this Convention and of general principles of international law,

shall be deemed to be illegal traffic.

2. In case of a transboundary movement of hazardous wastes or other wastes deemed to be illegal traffic as the result of conduct on the part of the exporter or generator, the State of export shall ensure that the wastes in question are:

(a) taken back by the exporter or the generator or, if necessary, by itself into the State of export, or, if impracticable,

(b) are otherwise disposed of in accordance with the provisions of this Convention . . . .

3. In the case of a transboundary movement of hazardous wastes or other wastes deemed to be illegal traffic as the result of conduct on the part of the importer or disposer, the State of import shall ensure that the wastes in question are disposed of in an environmentally sound manner by the importer or disposer . . . .

* * *

Annex I. Categories of Wastes to be Controlled

Waste Streams . . .

Y10—Waste substances and articles containing or contaminated with polychlorinated biphenyls (PCBs) and/or polychlorinated terphenyls (PCTs) and/or poliybrominated biphyenyls (PBBs). . . .

Wastes Having as Constituents . . .

Y22—Copper compounds

Y23—Zinc compounds

Y24—Arsenic; arsenic compounds . . .

Y26—Cadmium; cadmium compounds . . .

Y29—Mercury; mercury compounds . . .

Annex II. Categories of Wastes Requiring Special Consideration

Y46—Wastes collected from households . . . .

Annex III. List of Hazardous Characteristics

* * *

H6.1 Poisonous (Acute): Substances or wastes liable either to cause death or serious injury or to harm human health if swallowed or inhaled or by skin contact. . . .

H11 Toxic (Delayed or chronic): Substances or wastes which, if they are inhaled or ingested or if they penetrate the skin, may involve delayed or chronic effects, including carcinogenicity.

H12 Ecotoxic: Substances or wastes which if released present or may present immediate or delayed adverse impacts to the environment by means of bioaccumulation and/or toxic effects upon biotic systems.

H13 Capable, by any means after disposal, of yielding another material, e.g. leachate, which possesses any of the characteristics listed above. . . .

Annex VIII. List A

Wastes contained in this Annex are characterized as hazardous under Article 1, paragraph 1(a) of this Convention, and their designation on this Annex does not preclude the use of Annex II to demonstrate that a waste is not hazardous. . . .

A1180—Waste electrical and electronic assemblies or scrap containing components such as accumulators and other batteries . . . , mercury-switches, glass from cathode-ray tubes and other activated glas and PCB-capacitors, or contaminated with Annex I constituents (e.g. cadmium, mercury, lead, polychlorinated biphenyl) to an extent that they possess any of the characteristics contained in Annex III . . . .

Annex IX. List B

Wastes contained in the Annex will not be wastes covered by Article 1, paragraph 1(a) of this Convention unless they contain Annex I material to an extent causing them to exhibit an Annex III characteristic. . . .

B1090—Waste batteries conforming to a specification, excluding those made with lead, cadmium or mercury . . .

B1110—Electrical and electronic assemblies:

- Electronic assemblies consisting only of metals or alloys; . . .
- Electrical and electronic assemblies (including printed circuit boards, electronic components and wires) destined for direct reuse, and not for recycling or final disposal.

  Note: Reuse can include repair, refurbishment or upgrading, but not major reassembly. . . .

7. Technical guidelines on transboundary movements of electrical and electronic waste and used electrical and electronic equipment, in particular regarding the distinction between waste and non-waste under the Basel Convention, adopted by the Conference of the Parties to the Basel Convention at its 12th Meeting, 23 June 2015, U.N. Doc. UNEP/CHW.12/5/Add.1/Rev.

2. The present guidelines focus on clarifying aspects related to transboundary movements of e-waste and used equipment that may or may not be waste. Countries define and evaluate the distinction between waste and non-waste in different manners when considering used equipment destined, e.g., for direct reuse or extended use by the original owner for the purpose for which it was conceived, or for failure analysis, repair and refurbishment. Certain parties may consider used equipment destined for failure analysis, repair or refurbishment to be waste, while others may not. Further, the present guidelines consider which e-waste is hazardous waste or "other waste" and therefore would fall under the provisions of the Convention. Such distinctions will be helpful for enforcement agencies to assess if the provisions of the Basel Convention on transboundary movements apply, as the Convention only applies to hazardous wastes and other wastes.

* * *

8. The volume of e-waste being generated is growing rapidly due to the widespread use of electrical and electronic equipment in both developed and developing countries. The total amount of global e-waste generated in 2005 was estimated to be 40 million tonnes (StEP, 2009). The latest estimates indicate that in 2012 48.9 million tonnes of e-waste were generated globally (Huisman, 2012). The amount of e-waste in the European Union was estimated at between 8.3 million and 9.1 million tonnes in 2005 and was expected to reach some 12.3 million tonnes in 2020 (United Nations University, 2007). Currently e-waste is exported to countries that are not likely to possess the infrastructure and societal safety nets to prevent harm to human health and the environment, due to factors such as exports being less expensive than managing the waste domestically, the availability of markets for raw materials or recycling facilities, and the location of manufacturers of electrical and electronic equipment. However, there are also examples of formal recycling facilities in developing countries and economies in transition that are repairing, refurbishing and recycling used equipment and e-waste in an environmentally sound manner. However, in some cases the practices outside such facilities, e.g., downstream waste management, may not constitute environmentally sound management.

* * *

22. The Convention defines wastes as "substances or objects which are disposed of or are intended to be disposed of or are required to be disposed of by the provisions of national law" (Article 2, paragraph 1). It defines disposal in Article 2, paragraph 4, as "any operation specified in Annex IV to this Convention." It is important to note that national provisions concerning the definition of waste may differ and, therefore, the same material may be regarded as waste in one country but as non-waste in another country.

23. Hazardous wastes are defined in Article 1, paragraphs 1(a) and 1(b), of the Convention as "(a) wastes that belong to any category contained in Annex I, unless they do not possess any of the characteristics contained in Annex III ["List of hazardous characteristics"]; and (b) wastes that are not covered under paragraph 1(a) but are defined as, or considered to be, hazardous wastes by the domestic legislation of the Party of export, import or transit." The definition of hazardous waste therefore incorporates domestic law such that material regarded as a hazardous waste in one country but not another is defined as hazardous waste under the Convention. The Convention also requires that parties inform the other parties, through the Secretariat of the Convention, of their national definitions (Article 3). Providing detailed and specific information on the national definitions of hazardous waste can promote compliance and avoid ambiguity concerning the applicability of national definitions.

24. To help parties to distinguish hazardous wastes from non-hazardous wastes for the purpose of Article 1, paragraph 1 (a), two annexes have been added to the Convention. Annex VIII lists wastes considered to be hazardous according to Article 1, paragraph 1 (a), of the Convention unless they do not possess any of the characteristics of Annex III ("List of hazardous characteristics"). Annex IX lists wastes that are not covered by Article 1, paragraph 1 (a), unless they contain Annex I material to an extent that causes them to exhibit an Annex III characteristic. Both Annex VIII and Annex IX list various types of e-waste. More information on the distinction between hazardous and non-hazardous e-waste is included in section IV.B of the present guidelines.

25. To determine if used equipment is waste it may be necessary to examine all circumstances, including the history of an item and its proposed fate, on a case-by-case basis. However, there are characteristics of used equipment that are likely to indicate whether or not the equipment is waste.

* * *

30. Used equipment is waste in a country if it is defined as or considered to be waste under the provisions of that country's national legislation. Without prejudice to paragraph 31, used equipment should normally be considered waste if:

(a) The equipment is destined for disposal or recycling, instead of failure analysis or reuse, or its fate is uncertain;

(b) The equipment is not complete—essential parts are missing and the equipment cannot perform its key functions;

(c) The equipment shows a defect that materially affects its functionality and fails relevant functionality tests;

(d) The equipment shows physical damage that impairs its functionality or safety, as defined in relevant standards, and cannot be repaired at a reasonable cost;

(e) The protection against damage during transport, loading and unloading operations is inappropriate, e.g., the packaging or stacking of the load is insufficient;

(f) The equipment is particularly worn or damaged in appearance and its appearance reduces its marketability;

(g) The equipment has among its constituent part(s) hazardous components that are required to be disposed of under national legislation or are prohibited to be exported or are prohibited for use in such equipment under national legislation;

(h) There is no regular market for the equipment;

(i) The equipment is destined for disassembly and cannibalization (to gain spare parts); or

(j) The price paid for the equipment is significantly lower than would be expected for fully functional equipment intended for reuse.

31. Used equipment should normally not be considered waste:

(a) When it is not destined for any of the operations listed in Annex IV of the Convention (recovery or disposal operations) and it is destined for direct reuse, or extended use by the original owner for the purpose for which it was originally intended and the following is provided or is in place both prior to and during transport:

(i) [Documentation that includes] a signed declaration that indicates that the equipment has been tested and is destined for direct reuse and fully functional . . .;

(ii) Evidence of evaluation or testing . . . (certificate of testing—proof of functionality) on every item within the shipment . . .;

(iii) A declaration made by the person who arranges the transport of the equipment that none of the equipment within the shipment is defined as or is considered to be waste in any of the countries involved in the transport (countries of export and import and, if applicable, countries of transit);

(iv) Each piece of equipment is individually protected against damage . . . .

(b) When the person who arranges the transport of the used equipment claims that the equipment is destined for failure analysis, or for repair and refurbishment with the intention of reuse, or extended use by the original owner, for its originally intended purpose, provided that the criteria set out in sub-paragraphs (a) (iii) and (a) (iv) of paragraph 31 above and all of the following conditions are met:

(i) . . .;

(ii) A valid contract exists between the person who arranges the transport and the legal representative of the facility where the equipment is to be repaired or refurbished or undergo failure analysis. The contract should contain a minimum set of provisions, including the following:

a. The intention of the transboundary transport (failure analysis, repair or refurbishment);

b. Provisions on adherence to the principles of ESM for the treatment of any residual hazardous waste generated through the failure analysis, repair or refurbishment activities;

c. A provision stating the responsibility of the person who arranges the transport to comply with applicable national legislation and international rules, standards and Basel Convention guidelines. . . .;

d. A provision allocating responsibility to specific persons throughout the whole process, from export until the equipment is either analysed or repaired or refurbished to be fully functional, including cases where the equipment is not accepted by a facility and has to be taken back;

e. A provision requiring the facility to provide the person who arranged the transport with a feedback report on the failure analysis, repair or refurbishment activities that were performed on the equipment and on the management of any residual hazardous waste that may have been generated from such activities. . . .

Section 5. Discussion Notes/Questions

1. Is used electronic equipment "waste" within the meaning of the Basel Convention? If so, is it also "hazardous waste"? In 2015, the Basel COP adopted technical guidelines on the transboundary movement of electronic waste (Reading 7). Those guidelines appear to set out rules for distinguishing electronic "waste" from other shipments of used electronics. Are the guidelines consistent with the Convention? Are the guidelines binding? Does the treaty authorize the COP to adopt such rules? *See* Basel Convention, art. 4(8), 10(2)(e), & 15(5) **(Basic Document 4.7)**.

2. Was E-Re's conduct inconsistent with any international legal norms? Does the Basel Convention forbid the exportation of used electronic products when they are intended to be refurbished and reused? If E-Re knows that refurbishing will include replacing defective circuit boards, is E-Re exporting circuit boards for "disposal"? Should E-Re be obliged to ascertain that the electronics are in working order before exporting them? Do OECD or EU rules impose any different obligations on E-Re than are imposed by the Basel Convention? If E-Re did not violate international law, did Iberia? If E-Re did violate international law, is Iberia obliged to take back the dumped electronic equipment?

3. What about Luzonan? Isn't the real problem here that Luzonan failed to monitor the activities of a Luzonanian business? As between Luzonan and Iberia, which government has responsibility to monitor and prevent dumping by a company like Used Tech?

4. Following the adoption of the Basel Convention, many people argued that it did not go far enough. They contended that the exportation of wastes from developed countries for disposal in developing countries should be completely prohibited (not just regulated on a prior consent basis). Greenpeace, for example, pointed to the reaction of a prominent waste trader who said that obtaining the signature of one government official required by the Convention would not be a significant problem compared to the other hurdles faced in shipping wastes to developing countries. There was, accordingly, great concern that the shipment of wastes to developing countries would continue, and that those wastes would continue to be disposed of improperly. The incidents described in Reading 2, all of which post-dated the Basel Convention, suggested that such concerns were warranted.

In 1995, the Basel COP responded to these concerns by adopting the so-called Ban Amendment. The amendment added a new Article 4A, which bans shipment of hazardous wastes from developed to developing countries when those wastes are destined for disposal operations. As of July 2019, 95 countries had ratified the amendment, which is far short of the 140 ratifications needed for it to enter into force.

5. Another concern of developing countries is how to deal with the cost of cleanup and other damages caused when wastes are improperly dumped in their countries or when the inevitable accident occurs. In 1999, the COP adopted a Protocol on Liability and Compensation for Damage Resulting from Transboundary Movements of Hazardous Wastes and their Disposal **(Basic Document 4.7a)**. The Protocol provides for strict liability on exporters and disposers of hazardous waste for accidents occurring when the waste is in their possession or control. That liability is limited if the exporter and disposer acted in compliance with the Convention. The Protocol also imposes liability on any person whose "lack of compliance" with the Convention or other "wrongful intentional, reckless or negligent acts or omissions" contribute to damage. Such fault-based liability is not limited.

Like the Ban Amendment, the Liability Protocol has not yet received sufficient ratifications to enter into force.

6. Transboundary shipments of hazardous waste present a different legal and philosophical situation from the typical transboundary pollution problem which involves one state's involuntary invasion of another. Here, in theory, willing sellers and willing buyers of risk are involved. Should the law interfere with such voluntary agreements? Does the lack of informed consent invalidate a voluntary agreement? Indeed, is the consent of a developing country really voluntary? Do developing countries actually have a choice? Often the choice is between accepting hazardous waste imports and starvation. Who is informed about the risks? Generally not the local community that ends up with the waste. Should informed consent require a process whereby the people affected have the opportunity to make a decision on the risks? How can they be represented in the decision-making? *See generally, e.g.*, Panel Discussion (Robert E. Lutz, Ved P. Nanda, David A. Wirth, Daniel Magraw, & Günter Handl), *International Transfer of Hazardous Technology and Substances: Caveat Emptor or State Responsibility? The Case of Bhopal, India*, 79 Proceed. Am' Soc'y Int'l L. 303 (1985).

7. Does the international hazardous waste trade work against environmentally sound and long-term solutions to the problem? Does the export of wastes mean there is less incentive to develop or use technologies that minimize waste at its source? Is there an ethical issue here, too? When wastes are exported, the populations and environments of the receiving countries suffer from the unsustainable production processes of the industrialized world. Should international law permit this?

On the other hand, high-tech facilities for recovering or destroying hazardous waste exist, but they are expensive to build and operate. For that reason, certain kinds of recovery operations may be conducted in only a few places, and those places may include developing countries. Does it not make sense to allow countries to export waste when the best facilities for handling it are in other countries?

8. Industrialized nations have found that the best way to control waste is to control what goes into the "waste stream." The first place to start in dealing with hazardous waste problems is to stop the production of the waste at its source. Changes to in-plant processes and raw materials can mean clean production. Where hazardous waste exists, it can sometimes be recycled. It can also be treated before disposal to render it less hazardous. UNEP's Technology Facilitation Mechanism aims to help developing countries access clean technologies for a variety of purposes, including waste management.

9. The EU has adopted two path-breaking directives aimed at improving the handling of electronic waste. The RoHS 2 directive[29] mandates more clean production, and cleaner products, by restricting the use of

[29] Directive 2011/65/EU of the European Parliament and the Council of 8 June 2011 on the restriction of the use of certain hazardous substances in electrical and electronic equipment, OJ L 174 (July 1, 2011).

particular substances in electrical and electronic equipment. Is this an approach that can or should be adopted internationally?

In 2003, the EU adopted the so-called WEEE Directive, which aimed at encouraging the recycling of electrical and electronic waste by creating collection mechanisms that permitted consumers to recycle electronic waste free of charge. The directive was significantly amended in 2012. Among other things, the amended directive continues the obligation to maintain free-of-charge electronic waste collection mechanisms (separate from unsorted waste disposal), encourages the adoption of "eco-design requirements" that facilitate re-use and recovery of electronic waste, and requires treatment of electronic waste prior to disposal to limit the threat posed to human health and the environment.[30] Would it be a good international solution to the electronic waste problem?

PROBLEM 8-2: RAJAPUR EXPORTS HAZARDOUS, BUT USEFUL, PRODUCTS TO AFRICA

Section 1. Facts

Rajapur is a densely populated, developing nation. It has been an independent nation and a functioning democracy since 1947. Its constitution establishes Rajapur as a federated republic, with legislative authority divided between 29 highly autonomous state governments and a national government with limited, but significant, powers. Chemical manufacturing and building-product manufacturing are two of Rajapur's most important industries.

Rajapur is the developing world's leading producer of asbestos cement products—construction materials made with cement reinforced with chrysotile asbestos fibers. The production and use of asbestos cement products is forbidden or heavily restricted in most developed countries, but they are still popular building materials in many developing countries. Manufacturers from Rajapur sell their asbestos cement products (primarily roofing materials, building siding, and cement pipes) throughout Rajapur and in many African nations.

Although Rajapur's national government does not restrict the production or sale of asbestos cement products, it does regulate workplaces where such products are produced. Its workplace regulations list chrysotile asbestos as a hazardous substance and establish strict limits on worker exposure to chrysotile asbestos fibers. The five largest states in Rajapur, comprising 56% of the nation's population, ban the use of asbestos cement products in public construction projects (e.g., schools, government buildings and public infrastructure). The Rajapuran national railway bans

[30] Directive 2012/19/EU of the European Parliament and of the Council of 4 July 2012 on waste electrical and electronic equipment (WEEE) (recast), OJ L 197/38 (July 24, 2012).

the use of asbestos cement roofing and siding in terminals and other publicly accessible structures owned by the railway.

On the other hand, Rajapur's government regularly speaks out against efforts to ban or restrict international trade in chrysotile asbestos. It has frequently joined Russia, China and a handful of other countries in blocking attempts to have chrysotile asbestos listed in Annex III of the 1998 Rotterdam Convention on the Prior Informed Consent Procedure for Certain Hazardous Chemicals and Pesticides **(Basic Document 4.1)**. Rajapur contends that building materials containing chrysotile asbestos are perfectly safe if properly used.

Yoribo is an African nation that recently emerged from a long period of civil war. In the first free elections held in Yoribo in over 30 years, Elijah Udam, a western-educated economist and former finance minister, was elected President. Udam was a close college friend of Arjun Khatri, Prime Minister of Rajapur, and he contacted Khatri seeking assistance for Yoribo's reconstruction efforts.

Udam's plan for Yoribo's reconstruction focused on an ambitious program to promote economic development by raising educational standards and improving public health. As part of this plan, Udam proposed to build new schools throughout Yoribo, to construct new water treatment facilities, and to embark on a major program to combat malaria, a disease that kills nearly 150,000 Yoribons every year. Khatri pledged to support Udam's plan by providing extensive financial assistance to Yoribo. One month after the two leaders reached this agreement, the Rajapur parliament authorized $200 million in foreign assistance to support Yoribo's reconstruction. The legislation required Yoribo to spend the money for the purchase of Rajapur-origin products.

Shortly after passage of the legislation, the Yoribon government entered into a contract with Chrysotile Construction Products, Ltd., a Rajapuran company, to supply fibreboard and piping for use in the construction of new schools and water treatment facilities in Yoribo. The government also entered a contract with Rajapur Chemicals, Ltd. for the provision of DDT.[31] Yoribo provided Rajapur's trade ministry with a certification that the DDT was intended for the use of individual homeowners in northern Yoribo for indoor spraying to control malaria-carrying mosquitoes and that any other use would violate Yoribon law.

Over the next two years, Elijah Udam's development plan for Yoribo seemed to be working very well. Fifty new schools were completed in the poorest villages in the country, ten new water treatment plants were completed, and a malaria-control program, focused on the indoor

[31] The abbreviation DDT is from the common name of the chemical: dichlorodiphenyltrichlorethane. The scientific name of DDT is *1,1,1-trichloro-2,2-bis-(p-chlorophenyl) ethane.*

application of DDT to control mosquitoes, cut the number of new cases of malaria by 90%.

Late last year, on the eve of presidential elections, things began to unravel for Udam. First, European Union (EU) food inspectors discovered DDT residue on fruit and vegetable imports from Yoribo. The EU immediately banned all food imports from Yoribo, thus cutting off one of Yoribo's main sources of export earnings. An investigation by the Yoribon Department of Agriculture revealed that Yoribon farmers had been ordering more DDT from the government than they needed for indoor application and applying the excess DDT to their crops and fields, both to kill breeding mosquitoes and to eliminate other pests that damaged their crops.

Second, the *Yoribo Times*, a muckraking newspaper associated with Udam's political opponents, published well-documented stories reporting that the fiberboard and pipe imported from Rajapur contained chrysotile asbestos. The products were not labeled in any fashion indicating that they contained a hazardous material, nor were they accompanied by any information regarding their proper or safe use. As a result, workers in the construction industry had been using power tools to cut the pipe and fiberboard, releasing large quantities of asbestos-laden dust into their work environment without taking any precautions to control the dust or protect themselves from asbestos inhalation. Even more troubling were reports that village children frequently congregated at the construction sites and were also exposed to asbestos.

Udam's reelection bid failed, and he was replaced by Jeremiah Udah, a well-respected lawyer who won the presidency in a landslide. Immediately upon taking office, Udah banned the use of DDT and chrysotile asbestos products in Yoribo. Also, at Udah's direction, the foreign minister of Yoribo instituted proceedings against Rajapur in the International Court of Justice (ICJ) at The Hague.

In the ICJ proceedings, Yoribo alleges that its citizens are so frightened by what they have heard about chrysotile asbestos that they refuse to enter any school or drink water treated in any facility that was constructed using asbestos-cement building materials. In addition, it says, the EU has refused to resume food imports from Yoribo unless Yoribo implements a mandatory program of testing for pesticide residue on all exported food crops.

Yoribo asserts that Rajapur's sales of DDT and chrysotile-asbestos products to Yoribo were carried out in a manner that was inconsistent with Rajapur's obligations under both the aforementioned Rotterdam Convention and the 2001 Stockholm Convention on Persistent Organic Pollutants **(Basic Document 4.2)**, as well as its obligations under customary international law. Yoribo has requested reparations in the form of payment for Yoribo's mandatory pesticide-residue testing program, environmentally-sound removal and replacement of the schools and water-treatment facilities built with chrysotile-asbestos products, and establishment of a trust fund to pay the medical expenses of people who might be afflicted by abestos-related illnesses in the future.

Rajapur and Yoribo are members of the United Nations and parties to the Statute of the International Court of Justice. Both have consented to the Court's compulsory jurisdiction. Both countries also are parties to the Rotterdam Convention, but only Rajapur is a party to the Stockholm Convention. Rajapur is listed as a producer and user of DDT on the Stockholm Convention's DDT Register.

Section 2. Questions Presented

1. Did Rajapur violate international law in allowing the export of DDT to Yoribo? If so, is the ICJ likely to grant Yoribo's request for reparations?

2. Did Rajapur violate international law with respect to its exports of chrysotile-asbestos products? If so, is the ICJ likely to grant Yoribo's request for reparations?

Section 3. Assignments

A. *Reading Assignment*

Study the Readings presented in Section 4, *infra*, and the Discussion Notes/Questions that follow.

B. *Recommended Writing Assignments*

Prepare a comprehensive, logically sequenced, and *argumentative* brief in the form of an outline of the primary and subsidiary *legal* issues you see requiring resolution by the International Court of Justice. Also, from the perspective of an independent objective judge, indicate which side ought to prevail on each issue and why. Retain a copy of your issue-outline/brief for class discussion.

C. *Recommended Oral Assignment*

Assume you are legal counsel for Rajapur or Yoribo (as designated by your instructor); then, relying upon the Readings (and your issue-outline if prepared), present a 15–20 minute oral argument of your government's likely positions before the International Court of Justice.

D. *Recommended Reflective Assignment*

Consider (and recommend) alternative norms, institutions, and/or procedures that you believe might do better than existing world order arrangements to contend with situations of the kind posed by this problem.

In so doing, but without insisting upon *immediate* feasibility, identify the particular transition steps that would be needed to make your alternatives a reality.

Section 4. Readings

1. Editors' Note

There is a common pattern in the global regulation of hazardous chemicals. This pattern is most often seen in connection with products used as pesticides (like DDT), but it has also occurred with products, like asbestos and PCBs, used in other applications. First, a chemical product is discovered to have useful applications and, as a result, becomes widely used, sometimes with significant positive impacts. Then, after the product has been in the marketplace for many years, scientific researchers discover that it also has significant adverse impacts on human health, the environment or both. As these adverse impacts are revealed and public concern about the product grows, legislators and regulators in developed countries kick into gear and ban the product or severely restrict its use. However, manufacturers of the product may be allowed to continue exporting it to countries where it is regulated weakly or not at all.

There may be good reasons for a country that has banned a product to allow its exportation to other countries. Respect for sovereignty dictates that each country be allowed to make its own decisions about what environmental or health risks are tolerable and what are not. As Principle 11 of the Rio Declaration states, environmental "standards applied by some countries may be inappropriate and of unwarranted economic and social cost to other countries." The fact that a product is banned in a wealthy country because of its potential adverse health impacts does not mean it should be banned in a poorer country, where the judgment of local policymakers may be that the advantages gained from using the product outweigh concerns about adverse health impacts. In principle, at least, decisions to ban or tolerate dangerous products are decisions to be made by sovereign states in their own interests.

At least three considerations, however, may justify the imposition of some controls on the exportation of dangerous products from countries in which they are banned. First, the importing countries may be willing to accept the dangerous product, and consumers in that country may be willing to use it, only because they are unaware of its dangers. Many developing countries lack the regulatory capacity to evaluate the thousands of chemicals and chemical products in use in the world today. They also often lack the resources needed to develop labeling rules, guidelines for product use, and other standards necessary to ensure that a hazardous product is handled safely. In such circumstances, the international community has reached the conclusion that an exporting country that has banned or restricted a product has a responsibility to ensure that importing countries are fully informed of the hazards posed by the product.

A second reason that restrictions have been imposed on the exportation of hazardous products is the so-called "circle of poison." The phrase usually denotes a situation in which pesticides that have been banned in a country show up as residues on agricultural products imported from countries where the products are not banned. Sometimes, in fact, the banned products have been locally produced and exported to a developing country before being reimported and consumed by local citizens in the developed country. Because it is virtually impossible (economically, at least) to test all imported food, concern about the "circle of poison" has led to efforts to turn certain chemical restrictions in developed countries into worldwide bans.

A final motivation for creating global rules on the use of dangerous chemicals is that some toxic chemicals persist in the environment over long time periods. These chemicals, particularly the Persistent Organic Pollutants, have characteristics that can make them a global threat, even if they are used only in limited parts of the world. They:

- remain intact for exceptionally long periods of time (many years);
- become widely distributed throughout the environment as a result of natural processes involving soil, water and, most notably, air;
- accumulate in the fatty tissue of living organisms including humans, and are found at higher concentrations at higher levels in the food chain; and
- are toxic to both humans and wildlife.[32]

Many POPs are carcinogenic. Others are believed to be "endocrine disrupters," which "undermine the reproductive capacities of mammals, including humans."[33] Because of their persistence and ability to spread through the environment, "POPs can be found throughout the planet, including places where they have never been used."[34] States that have banned such chemicals will naturally wish to see them banned everywhere, particularly when the local ban is attributable to the adverse long-term

---

[32] Secretariat of the Stockholm Convention, What are POPs?, http://chm.pops.int/Convention/ThePOPs/tabid/673/language/en-US/Default.aspx (last accessed May 27, 2011).

[33] Don Mayer, *The Precautionary Principle and International Efforts to Ban DDT,* 9 S.C. Envtl L. J. 135, 142–151 (2002).

[34] Pep Fuller & Thomas O. McGarity, *Beyond the Dirty Dozen: The Bush Administration's Cautious Approach to Listing New Persistent Organic Pollutants and the Future of the Stockholm Convention,* 28 Wm. & Mary Envtl L. & Pol. Rev. 1, 1–9 (2003).

health effects caused by the presence of the chemicals in the environment. A local ban by itself cannot eliminate the risk that the chemical poses.

International Cooperation—Early Efforts

The Stockholm Declaration **(Basic Document 1.21)** called upon states to halt "the discharge of toxic substances" in "quantities or concentrations" that exceeded "the capacity of the environment to render them harmless." For the first decade following the Stockholm Conference, the developed countries led the way in the study and regulation of toxic chemicals. In the United States, for example, less than two weeks after the Stockholm Conference ended, EPA Administrator William Ruckelshaus announced a widespread ban on "all uses of DDT for crop production and nonhealth purposes."[35] In 1976, Congress passed the Toxic Substances Control Act, providing the EPA with enhanced authority to study chemical substances and to regulate those determined to "present an unreasonable risk of injury to health or the environment."[36] This law controlled the domestic distribution and use of dangerous chemicals, but did not affect international trade in the chemicals and did not restrict the export activities of domestic chemical producers.[37]

In 1973, an OECD Council Decision called upon Member countries to restrict the use of PCBs (polychlorinated biphenyls) in their own territories and also to control the "export of bulk PCBs." While the OECD thus recognized that international action on PCBs was needed "to minimize their escape into the environment," it imposed no specific restrictions on the export of PCBs, or of products containing PCBs, to developing countries for uses prohibited in the OECD countries.[38]

One of the recommendations made by the Stockholm Conference was for the development of an international registry that would contain information about chemicals and their impact on health and the environment. In 1974, UNEP began studying the feasibility of establishing such a registry, and in 1976 UNEP established the International Register of Potentially Toxic Chemicals (IRPTC) in Geneva at the headquarters of the World Health Organization.

The first significant action aimed at controlling international trade in hazardous or toxic substances came in 1982, in the form of a United Nations General Assembly resolution. The resolution, which articulated the principle of prior informed consent in embryonic form, is worth quoting at length.

---

[35] Environmental Protection Agency, Consolidated DDT Hearings, Opinion ad Order of the Administrator, June 30, 1972, 37 Fed. Reg. 13369.

[36] Toxic Substances Control Act, '2, P.L. 94–469, 90 Stat. 2003 (Oct. 11, 1976).

[37] *Id.* at § 12 (provisions of law do not apply to chemical substances intended for export).

[38] OECD Council Decision on Protection of the Environment by Control of Polychlorinated Biphenyls, February 12, 1973, C(73)1 (Final) (abrogated November 9, 1992).

> *The General Assembly,*
>
> *Aware* of the damage to health and the environment that the continued production and export of products that have been banned and/or permanently withdrawn on grounds of human health and safety from domestic markets is causing in the importing countries,
>
> *Aware* that some products, although they present a certain usefulness in specific cases and/or under certain conditions, have been severely restricted in the consumption and/or sale owing to their toxic effects on health and the environment, . . .
>
> *Considering* that many developing countries lack the necessary information and expertise to keep up with developments in this field,
>
> *Considering* the need for countries that have been exporting the above-mentioned products to make available the necessary information and assistance to enable the importing countries to protect themselves adequately, . . .
>
> 1. *Agrees* that products that have been banned from domestic consumption and/or sale because they have been judged to endanger health and the environment should be sold abroad by companies, corporations or individuals only when a request for such products is received from an importing country or when the consumption of such products is officially permitted in the importing country;
>
> 2. *Agrees* that all countries that have severely restricted or have not approved the domestic consumption and/or sale of specific products, in particular pharmaceuticals and pesticides, should make available full information on the products with a view to safeguarding the health and environment of the importing country, including clear labelling in a language acceptable to the importing country; . . . .

The Resolution concluded by calling upon the Secretary-General to work with other organizations to prepare for use of all countries a consolidated list of products that had been banned or restricted in any country, along with a summary of the reasons for the restrictions.[39]

In 1985, the United Nations Food and Agricultural Organization (FAO) responded to the General Assembly's call for action by adopting an *International Code of Conduct on the Distribution and Use of Pesticides.*[40]

---

[39] G.A. Res. 37/137, Protection against products harmful to health and the environment (Dec. 12,1982).

[40] FAO International Code of Conduct on the Distribution and Use of Pesticides, 23 FAO Conf. Res. 10/85 (November 28, 1985).

This nonbinding document set forth "voluntary standards of conduct for all public and private entities engaged in or affecting the distribution and use of pesticides, particularly where there is no or an inadequate national law to regulate pesticides." It called upon manufacturers and distributors of pesticides a) to test their products for safety (with respect to human health and the environment) and efficacy, including under conditions prevailing in the particular countries or regions of intended use; b) to label products with information about risks and safe use, in a language understandable to users in the place where it is to be used; and c) to ensure that pesticides entering international trade conform to international standards of quality and are at least of the same quality as the same goods sold domestically.

The FAO Code of Conduct also called upon the governments of exporting countries to play an active role in policing the international sale of hazardous substances. Any country that banned or severely restricted a pesticide was asked to notify other countries of its action and the reasons for it. Before permitting the export of a banned or restricted product, the exporting country should inform the importing country of its control action and should not permit export without the prior informed consent of the importing country. Finally, exporting country governments were expected to police the actions of their exporters and ensure their compliance with the Code of Conduct (e.g., with respect to product labelling and quality) and to provide assistance to developing countries in assessing the wisdom of allowing the importation and use of particular pesticides.

Two years later, in 1987, the UNEP Governing Council adopted a similar document, but one that was not restricted in its scope to pesticides. UNEP's *London Guidelines for the Exchange of Information on Chemicals in International Trade*[41] were aimed broadly at promoting information exchange on all internationally traded chemicals. Special provisions addressed trade in chemicals that were "banned or severely restricted" by a government for "health or environmental reasons." The *London Guidelines* directed states that had banned or restricted a chemical product to provide notice of the restriction and the reasons for it to the IRPTC. The IRPTC then would make that available to all other states. The *London Guidelines* established a prior-informed-consent procedure (PIC procedure) aimed at ensuring that banned or restricted chemicals would not be exported to developing countries without their consent. Under the PIC procedure, the IRPTC would provide information about banned or severely restricted products to potential importing countries. Those countries would then decide whether "to permit use and importation, to prohibit use and importation or to permit importation only under specified stated conditions." Exporting country governments were responsible for taking

[41] UNEP Governing Council Decision on London Guidelines for the Exchange of Information on Chemicals in International Trade, U.N. Doc. UNEP/GC/DEC/15/30 (June 19, 1987).

action "to ensure that exports do not occur contrary to the PIC decisions of participating importing countries."

Global Treaties on Chemical Regulation

The international efforts to regulate trade in chemicals through voluntary arrangements described above have long since been supplanted by treaties that establish binding obligations in this regard. But the prior-informed- consent approach adopted by the UN General Assembly in 1982 and developed in the FAO Code of Conduct and the London Guidelines remains a cornerstone of international regulation in this area. However, it is no longer the only approach to international regulation. Some modern treaties aim to ban completely, on a global basis, the production and use of certain chemicals. The remainder of this introductory note gives a brief overview, in chronological order, of the major treaties seeking to restrict international use or trade of dangerous chemicals.

The *Montreal Protocol on Substances that Deplete the Ozone Layer* **(Basic Document 2.8)** was adopted in 1987 and entered into force on January 1, 1989. It aims at protecting the stratospheric ozone layer by ending the production and consumption of ozone-depleting chemicals. It includes restrictions on international trade in ozone-depleting chemicals and in products containing such chemicals. *See* Problem 5-2, *supra*.

The *Basel Convention on the Control of Transboundary Movements of Hazardous Waste and their Disposal* **(Basic Document 4.7)** was adopted in 1989 and entered into force on May 5, 1992. Its goal is to restrict the transboundary movement of hazardous chemical wastes. It imposes a prior-informed-consent rule, along with requirements aimed at ensuring that hazardous waste will be handled and disposed of in an environmentally sound manner. *See* Problem 8-1, *supra*.

The *Rotterdam Convention on the Prior Informed Consent Procedure for Certain Hazardous Chemicals and Pesticides in International Trade* **(Basic Document 4.1)** was adopted in 1998 and entered into force on February 24, 2004. It is designed to ensure that countries that import hazardous chemicals are fully informed of the risks of the product. Countries proposing to export a product that is included in the Convention's list of hazardous chemicals must first determine that the importing country has agreed to receive the chemical before allowing the export to proceed. Other requirements, including labelling requirements, are aimed at ensuring that end-users are informed about the chemicals properties and use it safely. The requirements apply to chemicals listed in Annex III of the Convention. This problem is focused, in part, on the *Rotterdam Convention*.

The *Stockholm Convention on Persistent Organic Pollutants* **(Basic Document 4.2)** was adopted in 2001 and entered into force on May 17, 2004. The Stockholm Convention seeks to ban or severely restrict the production and use of certain persistent organic pollutants on a global basis. Annex A of the Convention includes a list of POPs that are banned: production and use of the listed chemicals is forbidden, as is the exportation or importation of those chemicals. There are certain limited exceptions to the ban. Chemicals listed in Annex B are not banned, but are subject to severe restrictions on their production, use or trade. Finally, the Convention encourages countries to use the best available techniques for reducing or eliminating releases of unintentionally produced POPs listed in Annex C. The Convention is addressed in the current problem.

The *Minimata Convention on Mercury* **(Basic Document 4.4)** was adopted in 2013 and entered into force on August 16, 2017. It aims to reduce the emission of mercury into the environment. To that end, the Convention bans the opening of new mercury mines, provides for the phasing out of existing mines, and regulates small-scale gold mining (which often results in releases of mercury). The Convention calls on Member States to phase out mercury use in certain products and processes and to impose controls on emissions of mercury into the air or releases of mercury on land or into water. The Convention also seeks to regulate storage and disposal of mercury waste.

2. Paula Barrios, The Rotterdam Convention on Hazardous Chemicals: A Meaningful Step Toward Environmental Protection, 16 Geo. Int'l Envtl. L. Rev. 679–82, 725–33 (2004)

During the last three decades, the production of chemicals increased spectacularly. Realizing that some of these substances pose serious threats to the environment and to human health, governments in most industrialized countries promulgated strict regulations dealing with their registration, testing, production, distribution and sale, and several hazardous chemicals were banned or severely restricted for domestic use. At the same time, regulations were silent or lenient with regard to exports, allowing these substances to be sent abroad.

Developing countries have been and continue to be a favored destination of hazardous chemicals, since they are less aware of the risks involved and they often depend on them to earn foreign currencies or to control vector-borne diseases. These countries usually lack appropriate environmental regulations to deal with hazardous chemicals, and when these regulations exist there is very limited capacity to enforce them. Developing countries also generally lack the ability and the infrastructure to handle these materials in an environmentally sound manner (i.e., in a way that protects the environment and human health from their negative effects). The consequences of these exports should thus come as no surprise. The most alarming figures involve the use of hazardous pesticides by farmers in the South. Reviews of hospital data from the World Health Organization (WHO) indicate that there are about one million accidental poisonings and twenty thousand deaths due to pesticides every year, primarily in developing countries, and agricultural surveys suggest that there could be as many as twenty-five million agricultural workers in the developing world suffering from an episode of pesticide poisoning every year. In addition, there is evidence that pesticides banned in developed countries sometimes return to them in the form of residues in food imported from the developing world. This phenomenon is known as the "circle of poison."

These and other problems prompted a global response to deal with trade in hazardous chemicals between developed and developing countries in the late 1980s. The initial reaction of states was to adopt two voluntary instruments that created a system of information exchange on hazardous chemicals and pesticides. They are the International Code of Conduct on the Distribution and Use of Pesticides, adopted in 1985 and the London Guidelines for the Exchange of Information on Chemicals in International Trade, adopted in 1987. In 1989, the prior informed consent (PIC) procedure was introduced into both instruments in order to give importing countries the opportunity to refuse future imports of a number of certain hazardous chemicals banned or severely restricted (i.e., banned for virtually all uses) in other countries. In 1998, the PIC system was transformed into a legally binding procedure, with the adoption of the Rotterdam Convention on the Prior Informed Consent Procedure for Certain Hazardous Chemicals and Pesticides in International Trade **[Basic Document 4.1]**. . . .

* * *

i. Information Exchange, Export Notification and PIC Procedure

Like the London Guidelines and the [FAO] Code of Conduct, the Rotterdam Convention covers three types of procedures: (1) information exchange; (2) export notification of domestically banned or severely restricted chemicals not subject to PIC; and (3) prior informed consent for the chemicals listed in Annex III.

Information exchange requires each party to notify the Secretariat in writing of each ban or severe restriction on a chemical it adopts. The chemical could potentially be included in Annex III and thus be subject to the PIC procedure, providing some requirements—moderately stricter than those of the voluntary system—are met. Export notification, in turn, requires a party that plans to export a banned or severely restricted chemical for use within its territory to inform the importing party of such export before the first shipment and annually thereafter. This obligation ceases if the chemical is listed in Annex III, since it is then covered by the PIC procedure. As in the voluntary system, the exporting party must also provide an updated export notification if it has adopted a final regulatory action that has resulted in a major change of the ban or severe restriction of the chemical being exported.

Lastly, the PIC procedure applies to Annex III chemicals. Once a decision has been made to include a chemical in Annex III, a decision guidance document (DGD) with all the relevant information must be sent by the Secretariat to all parties so that they can decide whether to import the chemical in the future. . . . [I]f a party decides to refuse an import or consents to an import under certain conditions, the same restrictions must apply to imports of that chemical from any source and to domestic production. Exporting parties must take appropriate legislative or administrative measures to ensure that exporters within their jurisdiction comply with the decisions of importing parties in relation to PIC decisions. According to Article 11(2), exporting parties must also ensure that, in the absence of a response by an importing party, no export takes place. . . .

Article 11(2) seems to establish the rule that no export should take place unless expressly agreed upon by the importing country, and a narrow exemption that an export without such consent can occur under three exceptional circumstances. In practice, however, Article 11(2), referred to as the "status quo" clause, guarantees that trade in hazardous chemicals will continue unless the importing country impedes it through effective participation in the PIC procedure. This is because the three exceptional circumstances contemplated by the rule are very broad, placing the burden of preventing an export on the importing country. To prevent an export, the importing country must give a negative response on the import of the substance through the PIC system. This requirement presumes that the importing country has, among other things, the technical capacity, sufficient qualified staff, and adequate laboratories to establish a basis for its negative response. In order to give that response, the country must be able to analyze the data received to study the possible effects of the substance under its own environmental conditions, and to consider viable and affordable alternatives. Perhaps more importantly, the country must make sure that its response, whether provisional or final, is consistent with the rules of international trade. Thus, in order to ensure that its decision will not be challenged in international trade tribunals because it contradicts, for instance, the principle of non-discrimination, the importing country must disclose whether it is currently importing the chemical, the history of imports from different sources, and whether there is local production of the chemical. Since many countries lack the capacity to fulfill these requirements, they might prefer to give an interim response which allows the import of the chemical, or to register no decision at all, as evidenced by the high occurrences of failures to respond.

One could argue that by ensuring that trade of hazardous chemicals will continue unless there is an explicit prohibition by the importing state, the Rotterdam Convention is inconsistent with the Rio Declaration's principle of state responsibility for transboundary harm. According to the Rio Declaration's rule, states have the duty to take all appropriate measures to prevent significant transboundary harm when carrying out lawful activities. Thus, as a preventive measure, a state that has banned, restricted or failed to register a substance because it poses unacceptable risks to the environment or human health should not export it to other states. This is true particularly if the importing country has relatively less capacity to guarantee its safe use. The application of the state responsibility principle would entail, therefore, a presumption that substances that are harmful in the North will cause harm in the South unless there is enough evidence contradicting that assumption. Therefore, the rule would be that the prohibition on the export of PIC chemicals exists unless the import was expressly agreed to by the importing state, and the exceptions would apply only if the exporter provided sufficient evidence that the substance to be exported would cause no significant harm in the importing country.

ii. Chemicals Covered by PIC and Export Notification Under Rotterdam

a. Severely Hazardous Pesticide Formulations

Besides the categories of banned and severely restricted chemicals that qualify as candidates of the PIC procedure, the Rotterdam Convention introduces the notion of "severely hazardous pesticide formulation." The Convention also allows a developing country or country with an economy in transition that is experiencing problems with the use of a "severely hazardous" substance within its territory, to propose the chemical's inclusion in Annex III. . . . This may be problematic because . . . developing countries generally lack the infrastructure needed to document and report incidents as contemplated by the Convention. . . .

b. Banned and Severely Restricted Chemicals

. . . The Rotterdam Convention [provides] that the definition of banned chemical includes a chemical that has been denied approval or been withdrawn by industry either from the domestic market or from further consideration in the domestic approval process when there is "clear evidence" that such action was taken to protect human health or the environment. The same applies to the notion of "severely restricted" . . . . [T]he Rotterdam Convention . . . makes clear that the definition includes a chemical that has, for "virtually all uses," been refused approval or been withdrawn by industry either from the domestic market or from further consideration in the domestic approval process, to protect the environment or human health.

The definitions in Rotterdam incorporate those situations in which a chemical is voluntarily withdrawn by industry, without requiring formal regulatory action. This clarification was necessary to fill a gap in the voluntary system, which did not expressly cover those chemicals subject to voluntary action even when motivated by reasons of the environment or health. . . .

* * *

Regrettably, . . . the Rotterdam Convention requires "clear evidence" that the action by the government to refuse approval of a chemical, or the decision by industry to withdraw its product from the market or from further consideration in the domestic approval process, has been taken in order to protect human health or the environment. This can be difficult in the case of a voluntary action, even for a developed country. In the United States, for instance, if companies voluntarily pull their product out of the market once it is subject to investigation but before a risk assessment has been completed and published, government officials will not invest resources to develop a full risk/benefit analysis of that substance. As a result, the "clear evidence" required by the Convention might not be available. Again, the obligation upon states to prevent significant transboundary harm would dictate that, as a preventive measure, states should not allow the export of substances that were refused for approval or withdrawn by industry if there were sufficient reasons to believe that they were withdrawn or refused to protect health or the environment. Given the preventive nature of the customary obligation of states to prevent significant transboundary harm, the "clear evidence" seems to constitute an unacceptably high standard.

c. Never Registered Chemicals

As in the voluntary system, chemicals for which no registration has been sought remain completely outside the scope of the Rotterdam Convention. This could be an important loophole because many exporting countries allow the export of chemicals never registered for domestic use, and no specific testing requirements apply to these chemicals. The lack of interest on the part of a manufacturer to register its product in the domestic market might simply reflect, to give an example, that the pest is not a problem in the exporting country. Yet this lack of interest could also be a conscious decision to prevent a substance from being rejected for environmental or health reasons in its own country. This possibility underlines the need to eliminate double standards in relation to testing requirements so that producers are obliged to use similar testing procedures for their products, regardless of whether those products will be used domestically or abroad. . . .

iii. Labeling Requirements

In relation to labeling, the Convention requires that the export of chemicals included in the PIC procedure, and other chemicals that are banned or severely restricted domestically, when exported, be subject to labeling requirements that ensure adequate disclosure of the risks and/or hazards to human health or the environment, taking into account relevant international standards. If the chemicals exported are to be used for occupational purposes, e.g., by farmers, the exporting party must ensure that a safety data sheet, that follows an internationally recognized format and sets out the most up-to-date information available, is sent to the importer. However, the exporter "should, as far as practicable," provide the information on the label and on the data sheet in one or more of the official languages of the importing party. Logic dictates that the minimum precondition for the importing party to ensure the appropriate use of a chemical would be that its citizens understand the label. The Rotterdam Convention, however, does not demand that the label be in at least one of the official languages of the importing country.

In addition, the Rotterdam Convention does not require the exportation of a chemical that is subject to handling restrictions, but which is not covered by PIC or banned or severely restricted in the exporting country, to comply with labeling requirements that ensure adequate availability of information with regard to risks and/or hazards to human health or the environment. . . .

3. Rotterdam Convention on the Prior Informed Consent Procedure for Certain Hazardous Chemicals and Pesticides in International Trade, arts. 1, 2, 5, 10, 11, 12, 13, & 15, & Annex V, September 10, 1998, 2244 UNTS 337 (Basic Document 4.1)

Article 1. Objective

The objective of this Convention is to promote shared responsibility and cooperative efforts among Parties in the international trade of certain hazardous chemicals in order to protect human health and the environment from potential harm and to contribute to their environmentally sound use, by facilitating information exchange about their characteristics, by providing for a national decision-making process on their import and export and by disseminating these decisions to Parties.

Article 2. Definitions

For the purposes of this Convention: . . .

(b) "Banned chemical" means a chemical all uses of which within one or more categories have been prohibited by final regulatory action, in order to protect human health or the environment. It includes a chemical that has been refused approval for first-time use or has been withdrawn by industry either from the domestic market or from further consideration in the domestic approval process and where there is clear evidence that such action has been taken in order to protect human health or the environment;

(c) "Severely restricted chemical" means a chemical virtually all use of which within one or more categories has been prohibited by final

regulatory action in order to protect human health or the environment, but for which certain specific uses remain allowed. It includes a chemical that has, for virtually all use, been refused for approval or been withdrawn by industry either from the domestic market or from further consideration in the domestic approval process, and where there is clear evidence that such action has been taken in order to protect human health or the environment;

. . .

(e) "Final regulatory action" means an action taken by a Party, that does not require subsequent regulatory action by that Party, the purpose of which is to ban or severely restrict a chemical; . . .

(g) "Party" means a State or regional economic integration organization that has consented to be bound by this Convention and for which the Convention is in force; . . . .

Article 5. Procedures for banned or severely restricted chemicals

1. Each Party that has adopted a final regulatory action shall notify the Secretariat in writing of such action. Such notification shall be made as soon as possible, and in any event no later than ninety days after the date on which the final regulatory action has taken effect, and shall contain the information required by Annex I, where available.

* * *

Article 7. Listing of chemicals in Annex III

1. For each chemical that the Chemical Review Committee has decided to recommend for listing in Annex III, it shall prepare a draft decision guidance document. The decision guidance document should, at a minimum, be based on the information specified in Annex I, or, as the case may be, Annex IV, and include information on uses of the chemical in a category other than the category for which the final regulatory action applies.

2. . . . The Conference of the Parties shall decide whether the chemical should be made subject to the Prior Informed Consent procedure and, accordingly, list the chemical in Annex III and approve the draft decision guidance document.

3. When a decision to list a chemical in Annex III has been taken and the related decision guidance document has been approved by the Conference of the Parties, the Secretariat shall forthwith communicate this information to all Parties.

* * *

Article 10. Obligations in relations to imports of chemicals listed in Annex III

1. Each Party shall implement appropriate legislative or administrative measures to ensure timely decisions with respect to the import of chemicals listed in Annex III.

2. Each Party shall transmit to the Secretariat, as soon as possible, and in any event no later than nine months after the date of dispatch of the decision guidance document referred to in paragraph 3 of Article 7, a response concerning the future import of the chemical concerned. . . .

* * *

4. A response under paragraph 2 shall consist of either:

(a) A final decision, pursuant to legislative or administrative measures:

(i) To consent to import;

(ii) Not to consent to import; or

(iii) To consent to import only subject to specified conditions;

or

(b) An interim response, which may include [a decision to consent to import, to consent with conditions or not to consent during the interim periods. A Party may also request information or assistance from the Secretariat in evaluating a chemical.]

* * *

6. A final decision should be accompanied by a description of any legislative or administrative measures upon which it is based.

* * *

9. A Party that, pursuant to paragraphs 2 and 4 above and paragraph 2 of Article 11, takes a decision not to consent to import of a chemical or to consent to its import only under specified conditions shall, if it has not already done so, simultaneously prohibit or make subject to the same conditions:

(a) Import of the chemical from any source; and

(b) Domestic production of the chemical for domestic use.

10. Every six months the Secretariat shall inform all Parties of the responses it has received. . . .

Article 11. Obligations in relation to exports of chemicals listed in Annex III

1. Each exporting Party shall: . . .

(b) Take appropriate legislative or administrative measures to ensure that exporters within its jurisdiction comply with decisions in each response [from an importing country] no later than six months after the date on which the Secretariat first informs the Parties of such response in accordance with paragraph 10 of Article 10;

* * *

2. Each Party shall ensure that a chemical listed in Annex III is not exported from its territory to any importing Party that, in exceptional circumstances, has failed to transmit a response or has transmitted an interim response that does not contain an interim decision, unless:

(a) It is a chemical that, at the time of import, is registered as a chemical in the importing Party; or

(b) It is a chemical for which evidence exists that it has previously been used in, or imported into, the importing Party and in relation to which no regulatory action to prohibit its use has been taken; or

(c) Explicit consent to the import has been sought and received by the exporter through a designated national authority of the importing Party. The importing Party shall respond to such a request within sixty days and shall promptly notify the Secretariat of its decision.

The obligations of exporting Parties under this paragraph shall apply with effect from the expiration of a period of six months from the date on which the Secretariat first informs the Parties, in accordance with paragraph 10 of Article 10, that a Party has failed to transmit a response or has transmitted an interim response that does not contain an interim decision, and shall apply for one year.

Article 12. Export notification

1. Where a chemical that is banned or severely restricted by a Party is exported from its territory, that Party shall provide an export notification to the importing Party. The export notification shall include the information set out in Annex V.

2. The export notification shall be provided for that chemical prior to the first export following adoption of the corresponding final regulatory action. Thereafter, the export notification shall be provided before the first export in any calendar year. The requirement to notify before export may be waived by the designated national authority of the importing Party.

* * *

Article 13. Information to accompany exported chemicals

* * *

2. Without prejudice to any requirements of the importing Party, each Party shall require that both chemicals listed in Annex III and chemicals banned or severely restricted in its territory are, when exported, subject to labelling requirements that ensure adequate availability of information with regard to risks and/or hazards to human health or the environment, taking into account relevant international standards.

* * *

4. With respect to the chemicals referred to in paragraph 2 that are to be used for occupational purposes, each exporting Party shall require that a safety data sheet that follows an internationally recognized format, setting out the most up-to-date information available, is sent to each importer.

5. The information on the label and on the safety data sheet should, as far as practicable, be given in one or more of the official languages of the importing Party.

Article 22. Adoption and amendment of annexes

* * *

5 (b). The Conference of the Parties shall take its decision on adoption [of amendments to Annex III] by consensus; . . . .

4. Joseph LaDou, et al., The Case for a Global Ban on Asbestos, 118 Environ. Health Perspect. 897 [doi:10.1289/ehp.1002285] (2010)

All forms of asbestos are now banned in 52 countries, and safer products have replaced many materials that once were made with it. Nonetheless, a large number of countries still use, import, and export asbestos and asbestos-containing products. In many countries that have banned other forms of asbestos, the so-called controlled use of chrysotile asbestos is exempted from the ban, an exemption that reflects the political and economic influence of the asbestos mining and manufacturing industry lobbies.

All forms of asbestos cause asbestosis, a progressive, debilitating fibrotic disease of the lungs. All forms of asbestos also cause malignant mesothelioma and lung and laryngeal cancers, and may cause ovarian, gastrointestinal, and other cancers. . . . The scientific community is in overwhelming agreement that there is no safe level of exposure to asbestos. . . . Moreover, there is no evidence of a threshold level below which there is no risk of mesothelioma. . . .

The Asbestos Cancer Pandemic

Occupational exposures to asbestos

About 125 million people around the world are exposed to asbestos in their work environments (WHO 2006), and many millions more workers have been exposed to asbestos in years past.

* * *

Environmental exposures to asbestos

Nonoccupational, environmental exposure to asbestos from the use of construction materials that contain asbestos is also a serious and often neglected problem throughout the world. In developed countries, large quantities of asbestos remain as a legacy of past construction practices in many thousands of schools, homes, and commercial buildings. In developing countries, where asbestos is used today in large quantities in construction, asbestos-contaminated dust is now accumulating in thousands of communities, with virtually all people burdened with asbestos fibers in their lungs and bodies. . . .

* * *

Chrysotile Asbestos

Chrysotile represents nearly 100% of the asbestos produced and used worldwide today . . . and 95% of all the asbestos used worldwide since 1900. . . . There is general agreement among scientists and physicians, and widespread support from agencies in countries around the world, that chrysotile causes various cancers, including mesothelioma and lung cancer.

* * *

The Chrysotile Institute (Montreal, Quebec, Canada),[42] a registered lobby group for the Quebec asbestos mining industry, takes the position that chrysotile can be handled safely. Numerous epidemiologic studies, case reports, controlled animal experiments, and toxicological studies refute the assertion that chrysotile is safe. . . . These studies demonstrate that the so-called controlled use of asbestos is a fallacy. . . . Workers exposed to chrysotile fiber alone have excessive risks of lung cancer and mesothelioma. . . .

* * *

[42] *Eds.* The Chrysotile Institute closed in 2012. Today, the International Chrysotile Association is the primary advocate for continued production and use of chrysotile asbestos and chrysotile-asbestos products. It argues that a ban on chrysotile is unnecessary, as a "safe and responsible use" approach to regulation can ensure that permissible exposure levels are kept below the limits at which health risks are detected. *See* www.chrysotileassociation.com/sfuse/default.php (Safe Use of Chrysotile) (last visited July 2, 2019).

Current Production and Use of Asbestos

Despite all that is known about the dangerous and adverse health effects of asbestos, annual world production remains at >2 million tons. Russia is now the leading producer of asbestos worldwide, followed by China, Kazakhstan, Brazil, Canada, Zimbabwe, and Colombia. These six countries accounted for 96% of the world production of asbestos in 2007. Russia has mines rich enough in asbestos deposits to last for >100 years at current levels of production. Most of the 925,000 tons of asbestos extracted annually in Russia is exported.

All forms of asbestos are now banned in 52 countries (International Ban Asbestos Secretariat 2010), including all European Union member countries. Nonetheless, these 52 countries make up less than one-third of WHO member countries. A much larger number of WHO member countries still use, import, and export asbestos and asbestos-containing products. These are almost all countries in Asia, Eastern Europe, Latin America, and Africa. Most of the world's people still live in countries where asbestos use continues, usually with few safeguards. More than 85% of the world production of asbestos is used today to manufacture products in Asia and Eastern Europe. . . . In developing countries, where too often there exists little or no protection of workers and communities, the asbestos cancer pandemic may be the most devastating. China is by far the largest consumer of asbestos in the world today, followed by Russia, India, Kazakhstan, Brazil, Indonesia, Thailand, Vietnam, and Ukraine.

* * *

Repeated efforts to include chrysotile asbestos under the Rotterdam Convention have failed, not because its Chemical Review Committee has not recommended the listing of chrysotile, but because of the Convention's requirement for unanimity and as a result of the determined opposition of asbestos mining and manufacturing countries. At the 2008 conference of parties on the Convention, Kazakhstan, Kyrgyzstan, Vietnam, Russia, and Zimbabwe opposed listing chrysotile asbestos in Annex III. A few asbestos-importing countries thwarted the will of >100 other countries.

The Need for a Universal Ban on Asbestos

The profound tragedy of the asbestos pandemic is that all illnesses and deaths related to asbestos are preventable. Safer substitutes for asbestos exist, and they have been introduced successfully in many nations. Currently, asbestos cement products account for >85% of world consumption . . ., and in about 100 countries, asbestos-containing pipes and sheets are manufactured to be used as low-cost building materials. . . . However, these asbestos cement water-pipe products could be replaced with ductile iron pipe, high-density polyethylene pipe, and metal-wire—reinforced concrete pipe. Many substitutes exist for roofing as well as interior building walls and ceilings, including fiber-cement flat and corrugated sheet products that are made with polyvinyl alcohol fibers and cellulose fibers. . . . For roofing, lightweight concrete tiles can be made and used in the most remote locations using locally available plant fibers, such as jute, hemp, sisal, palm nut, coconut coir, and wood pulp. Galvanized iron roofing and clay tiles are among the other alternative materials.

5. Pep Fuller & Thomas O. McGarity, Beyond the Dirty Dozen: The Bush Administration's Cautious Approach to Listing New Persistent Organic Pollutants and the Future of the Stockholm Convention, 28 Wm. & Mary Envtl L. & Pol. Rev. 1, 1–9 (2003)

. . . POPs are toxic, manmade chemicals that resist photolytic, chemical, and biological degradation and therefore accumulate and persist in the environment. Because they are hydrophobic and lipid soluble, they tend to accumulate in human and animal fat and biomagnify as they move up the food chain. Because they can travel great distances in both air and water, POPs can be found throughout the planet, including places where they have never been used. Although the chronic toxicity of most POPs has been a controversial subject through the years, many are probably carcinogenic in humans and cause adverse reproductive and endocrine effects. For all of these reasons, POPs warrant special attention by environmental regulators.

* * *

The Stockholm Convention **[Basic Document 4.2]** . . . requires nations that become parties to eliminate or restrict the production, use, and/or release of the twelve listed [POPs]. The implementing countries must eliminate production and use of all of the ten intentionally produced POPs except DDT, which may continue to be produced and used for disease vector control, primarily to fight malaria, while development of effective and economically viable alternatives continue. The parties must develop national action plans to address the two byproduct POPs, dioxins and furans, and use best available technologies to reduce emissions from certain new sources of these POPs. Parties must also control handling of POPs wastes and trade in POPs chemicals. The Convention contains a well-articulated process for adding new chemicals when a panel employing a science-based process determines that a chemical possesses the characteristics of a POP and the Conference of the Parties concurs.

6. Stockholm Convention on Persistent Organic Pollutants, arts. 1, 3, 6 & Annex B, May 22, 2001, 2256 UNTS 119 (Basic Document 4.2)

Article 1. Objective

Mindful of the precautionary approach as set forth in Principle 15 of the Rio Declaration on Environment and Development, the objective of this Convention is to protect human health and the environment from persistent organic pollutants.

* * *

Article 3. Measures to reduce or eliminate releases from intentional production and use

1. Each Party shall: . . .

(a) Prohibit and/or take the legal and administrative measures necessary to eliminate:

(i) Its production and use of the chemicals listed in Annex A subject to the provisions of that Annex; and

(ii) Its import and export of the chemicals listed in Annex A in accordance with the provisions of paragraph 2; and

(b) Restrict its production and use of the chemicals listed in Annex B in accordance with the provisions of that Annex.

2. Each Party shall take measures to ensure: . . .

(b) That . . . a chemical listed in Annex B for which any production or use specific exemption or acceptable purpose is in effect, taking into account any relevant provisions in existing international prior informed consent instruments, is exported only:

(i) For the purpose of environmentally sound disposal as set forth in paragraph 1 (d) of Article 6;

(ii) To a Party which is permitted to use that chemical under Annex A or Annex B; or

(iii) To a State not Party to this Convention which has pro-vided an annual certification to the exporting Party. Such certification shall specify the intended use of the chemical and include a statement that, with respect to that chemical, the importing State is committed to:

a. Protect human health and the environment by taking the necessary measures to minimize or prevent re-leases;

b. Comply with the provisions of paragraph 1 of Article 6; and

c. Comply, where appropriate, with the provisions of paragraph 2 of Part II of Annex B.

The certification shall also include any appropriate supporting documentation, such as legislation, regulatory instruments, or administrative or policy guidelines. The exporting Party shall transmit the certification to the Secretariat within sixty days of receipt.

* * *

Article 6. Measures to reduce or eliminate releases from stockpiles and wastes

1. In order to ensure that stockpiles consisting of or containing chemicals listed either in Annex A or Annex B and wastes, including products and articles upon becoming wastes, consisting of, containing or contaminated with a chemical listed in Annex A, B or C, are managed in a manner protective of human health and the environment, each Party shall:

(a) Develop appropriate strategies for identifying:

(i) Stockpiles consisting of or containing chemicals listed either in Annex A or Annex B; and

(ii) Products and articles in use and wastes consisting of, containing or contaminated with a chemical listed in Annex A, B or C;

(b) Identify, to the extent practicable, stockpiles consisting of or containing chemicals listed either in Annex A or Annex B on the basis of the strategies referred to in subparagraph (a);

(c) Manage stockpiles, as appropriate, in a safe, efficient and environmentally sound manner. . . .

* * *

Annex B

PART I

DDT Production: *Acceptable purpose:* Disease vector control use in accordance with Part II of this Annex. . . .

DDT Use: *Acceptable purpose:* Disease vector control in accordance with Part II of this Annex. . . .

* * *

PART II—DDT (1,1,1-trichloro-2,2-bis(4-chlorophenyl)ethane)

1. The production and use of DDT shall be eliminated except for Parties that have notified the Secretariat of their intention to produce

and/or use it. A DDT Register is hereby established and shall be available to the public. The Secretariat shall maintain the DDT Register.

2. Each Party that produces and/or uses DDT shall restrict such production and/or use for disease vector control in accordance with the World Health Organization recommendations and guidelines on the use of DDT and when locally safe, effective and affordable alternatives are not available to the Party in question.

* * *

5. With the goal of reducing and ultimately eliminating the use of DDT, the Conference of the Parties shall encourage:

(a) Each Party using DDT to develop and implement an action plan as part of the implementation plan specified in Article 7. That action plan shall include:

(i) Development of regulatory and other mechanisms to ensure that DDT use is restricted to disease vector control;

(ii) Implementation of suitable alternative products, methods and strategies, including resistance management strategies to ensure the continuing effectiveness of these alternatives;

(iii) Measures to strengthen health care and to reduce the incidence of the disease.

7. Don Mayer, The Precautionary Principle and International Efforts to Ban DDT, 9 S.C. Envtl L. J. 135, 142–151 (2002)

While the benefits of chlorine-based chemicals were immediately appreciated, the understanding of their risks to animal and human health developed far more gradually. One by one, the organochlorines have come under scientific scrutiny, and numerous studies have suggested strong risk factors in their use and accumulation in the environment. DDT, PCBs, CFCs and kepone are some of the better known organochlorines that have been banned or restricted after well-demonstrated risks to human and animal health. Many other organochlorines such as dioxin, furans, aldrin, trichloroethylene, perchloroethylene, methylene chloride, chloroform, pentachlorophenol (PCP), dieldrin, dicofol, dienochlor, endosulfan, lindane, hexaclorobenzene and methoxychlor show signs of being "endocrine disrupters" that may undermine the reproductive capacities of mammals, including humans. Among other attributes, these chemicals are toxic, persistent, and bioaccumulative.

. . . Contrary to general public perceptions, the toxicity of [organochlorines] is not necessarily their carcinogenic properties, but their potential as "endocrine disrupters" that trick reproductive systems in fish, amphibians, and mammals. They have the potential to be, if not carcinogenic, then either mutagenic[43] and teratogenic.[44] Moreover, there are over fifty chemicals suspected of having endocrine disrupting effects, and humans may be exposed to them through products, food, water, and air. They are not only persistent but also widely used for a number of purposes and thoroughly ingrained into our economic activities.

There is a wealth of literature on endocrine disrupters. The work of Theo Colborn is perhaps the best known. Her studies and the book that summarized them—*Our Stolen Future*[45]—has been compared to the work of Rachel Carson in *Silent Spring*.[46] In essence, endocrine disrupters may interfere with normal human endocrine disruption in a number of ways: they can "disrupt the synthesis, storage, release, transport, and clearance of hormones, and they can disturb receptor recognition, receptor binding, or post-receptor responses within cells." Some EDCs [endocrine-disrupting chemicals] mimic hormones that bind to protein receptors in place of the natural hormones. Some enhance (an agonistic effect) or inhibit (an antagonistic effect) the action of hormones. Other EDCs may directly affect the overall production of certain hormones in the body. . . .

* * *

. . . The EPA Risks Assessment Forum summarized the scientific literature by recognizing that endocrine-disrupting chemicals have been associated with reduced fertility, birth defects, cancer, endometriosis, malformed reproductive organs, glandular dysfunction, and neurological disorders. Both breast and prostate cancer have been linked to hormone exposure, particularly to DDT exposure. In general, the body mistakes chemicals that mimic hormones and reacts to them "in ways that cause deep and permanent trouble, especially when exposure occurs during the critical period of development, before, and immediately after birth."

* * *

The more sobering studies relate to the potential effects of EDCs on embryos. Some studies show serious deficits in children of mothers who consumed large amounts of Great Lakes fish. One similarity between human and animal studies indicates small amounts of endocrine-

---

43 Chemicals that cause chemical changes in DNA are called mutagens. Many mutagens are carcinogens, but DNA can be changed in other ways. . . .

44 In the process of an embryo's development, the single cell ovum begins to proliferate by making a series of divisions. In human beings, a remarkable process of cell differentiation begins around the ninth day; the specific kinds of cells (neurons, liver cells, etc.) that make up the human body begin to form and to migrate to their specific positions within the body. The embryonic period where organs form—organogenesis—lasts until the fourteenth week of gestation, when the "fetal" period begins, ending at birth. Teratogenic chemicals alter the normal development during organogenesis. . . .

45 *Eds.* Theo Colborn, Dianne Dumanoski, & John Peterson Myers, Our Stolen Future: Are We Threatening Our Fertility, Intelligence and Survival?—A Scientific Detective Story 26, 157 (1996).

46 *Eds.* Rachel Carson, Silent Spring (1962).

mimicking chemicals can negatively affect a developing fetus far more than a mature adult. Moreover, since humans and large mammals are at the top of the food chain, the bioaccumulation of persistent toxic substances greatly magnifies the amount of toxins a mammalian mother may ingest.

* * *

Thus, while there is no conclusive proof that EDCs cause reproductive or non-reproductive harm, there are reasons to be cautious. . . .

8. David L. Mulliken, Jennifer D. Zambone, & Christine G. Rolph, DDT: A Persistent Lifesaver, 19 Nat. Res. & Envt. 3 (Spring 2005)

After [World War II], DDT became the main method of insect control throughout the world. The use of DDT was found to be able to control, partially or completely, nearly thirty diseases (including malaria, dengue, urban yellow fever, plague, dysentery, and cholera). DDT's success lay in its persistence. . . . DDT continued to kill lice, mosquitoes, and insects long after its application. The characteristic that [was] initially considered DDT's great flaw—persistence—actually was its great virtue. It prevented epidemics from starting, much less spreading through the population or being carried to other areas. Thus, DDT's lethality and persistence made it an ideal pesticide for many uses.

U.S. public health officials soon deployed DDT widely to fight malaria, which had become an endemic disease pervasive in southern states from the Carolinas to Texas. As a result of this effort, mosquito transmission of malaria was brought to an end in the United States. The use of DDT helped to drop the number of American malaria cases from at least 1 million in 1940 to zero in 1952.

The success of the U.S. eradication program emboldened world health organizers to undertake a campaign to eliminate malaria worldwide. The World Health Organization and activist Fred Soper initiated the Global Malaria Eradiation Programme, using DDT as the chosen medicine and with substantial financial backing from the United States. By using DDT, malaria was eliminated in Taiwan, much of the Caribbean, the Balkans, parts of northern Africa, the northern region of Australia, and a large swath of the South Pacific. In 1943, Venezuela had 8,171,115 cases of malaria; by 1958, after the use of DDT, the number was down to 800. In Italy, the number of malaria cases dropped from 411,602 in 1945 to only 37 in 1968 after a DDT program. Sri Lanka (then Ceylon) used DDT to cut the incidence of malaria from 3 million cases to just 29 cases within twenty years. In India, 75 million people a year suffered from malaria. Through the use of DDT, India managed to reduce the number of cases to 75,000 in 1961. Ultimately, as the *New Yorker* recently explained, Soper and his Eradication Programme succeeded in eliminating malaria from the developed world, and from many parts of the developing world, thanks to DDT.

* * *

From Savior to Pariah

In 1962, marine biologist Rachel Carson published Silent Spring—a book that blamed pesticides such as DDT for harming the environment and killing wildlife. She also argued that DDT was dangerous to humans because of its bioaccumulative properties. While others previously had claimed that DDT caused various ailments or diseases, Carson's book was evocative and compellingly written and touched a chord with the public.

Emboldened by the book and with increasing public support, environmentalists began pushing for the banning of DDT on state and federal levels. However, many of the most notable scientific organizations in the United States refused to support any ban on DDT . . . .

* * *

[In 1972, over the opposition of many scientific groups, the EPA announced a ban on DDT.] While EPA reserved the possibility of using DDT in emergencies, the ban effectively ended use of DDT in the United States. . . . The ban also served to compromise DDT's use internationally. Because of political pressures, financial funding, and societal changes, countries began to use less and less DDT even for public health purposes.

The Malaria Epidemic

Almost twenty-five years after the ban, in the late 1990s, an active debate about DDT surfaced again. The United Nations Environment Programme (UNEP) began to develop an international treaty phasing out the use of certain chemicals. A coalition consisting of the World Wildlife Fund, Greenpeace, Physicians for Social Responsibility, and the International Pesticides Elimination Network, demanded that DDT be among the chemicals phased out by 2007. Labeling DDT as a persistent organic pollutant (POP), this coalition launched a vigorous campaign to include DDT in the Stockholm Convention on Persistent Organic Pollutants, arguing that DDT needed to be banned to protect the environment. The campaign seemed certain of success until public health officials raised the issue of DDT's efficacy in fighting malaria.

A parasitic disease caused by the *Plasmodium* protozoan and transmitted by the *Anopheles* mosquito, malaria remains epidemic in the developing world. Malaria infects 650 million to 750 million a year and kills 1 million to 2 million, mainly pregnant women and children under the age of 5. Every thirty seconds a child dies from malaria. Dr. Wenceslaus Kilama, chair of Malaria Foundation International, puts it in even more graphic terms: "The malaria epidemic is like loading up seven Boeing 747 airliners each day, then deliberately crashing them into Mt. Kilimanjaro."

Malaria takes its toll upon the living as well. Malaria thrives in Central and South America, and Southeast and South Asia, but 90 percent of all malaria cases occur in sub-Saharan Africa, where it contributes to the poverty of Africa. Even when controlling for determinants such as human capital, life expectancy, and geography, countries with a high rate of *P. falciparum* malaria infection have annual economic growth rates 1.3 percent lower than those of nonmalarious countries. Over the long term, the effect of malaria is that the per capita gross national product (GNP) of highly malarious countries is reduced by more than half compared to the GNP in nonmalarious countries. In dollars, Africa loses about $12 billion a year due to the drop in economic productivity due to malaria. Malaria causes this reduction in a variety of ways: It impacts the cognitive development of children, which can decrease their ability to function as productive members of society; the fear of infection and a compromised workforce drive away economic investment; and the treatment of the disease cuts into what little money families have been able to save.

As a parasitic vector-borne disease, malaria is extremely complex. It can be controlled successfully, but public health authorities have to use a variety of measures: drugs to kill the *Plasmodium* parasite, insecticide-treated bed nets to protect sleepers and to kill mosquitoes, and pesticides applied to a house in what is known as Indoor Residual Spraying (IRS). Malaria cannot be controlled for any significant amount of time if a control program uses only one or two of these methods. An effective malarial control program must use all methods available, including IRS.

The *Anopheles* mosquito is a night biter. It will fly into a house, rest on the walls, and wait to take blood until it is dark. IRS takes advantage of this behavior. In an IRS program, "spraymen" spray a small amount of pesticide on the interior walls of houses and under the eaves. The idea is that the mosquitoes will land on the treated walls, be exposed to the pesticide, and die.

Four classes of pesticides are effective in IRS: carbamates, synthetic pyrethroids, organophosphates, and organochlorines, of which DDT is the only remaining member. Four classes may sound like plenty of pesticide alternatives, but it is not. For malaria-control programs to effectively use pesticides, they must rotate them so that mosquitoes do not develop resistance. Banning DDT would effectively drop the number of classes to three and mosquito-control experts have flatly stated that running effective control programs with so few classes of pesticides would be nearly impossible.

South Africa, for example, switched to using pyrethroids in its malarious areas in 1996. Within five years the mosquitoes developed resistance to these pesticides, probably because agriculture also extensively uses synthetic pyrethroids. Malaria rates rocketed in South Africa from 5,991 in 1995 to 61,934 in 2000. In 2000, South Africa decided it could no longer endure the havoc that malaria was wreaking on the population and switched back to using DDT. By 2002, the number of malaria cases decreased to 14,474. South Africa was not alone in having rising malaria rates after ending the use of DDT. Madagascar, Venezuela, and Belize all had similar experiences.

Nor is South Africa alone in having falling malaria rates after reintroducing DDT. In the early 1980s Zambia, one of the poorest countries in Africa, discontinued its insecticide spraying program, due largely to financial constraints. As a result, the incidence of malaria increased from approximately 120 cases per one thousand people in the late 1970s to more than 330 cases per one thousand in the late 1990s.

In 2000, a privately funded malaria-control program in the Zambian Copperbelt began using DDT in an IRS program that protected a population of approximately 360,000 at a cost of $6 per household with an average of eleven people per household. After just one spraying season, malaria cases declined by 50 percent, and since the start of the program, malaria cases have declined by 80 percent. Impressed by the success of this program, Zambia implemented DDT use in IRS programs in other parts of the country with equally good results. As a result of the successes seen there, the Global Fund to Fight AIDS, Tuberculosis, and Malaria has agreed to fund nationwide IRS programs, including ones that use DDT, in Zambia.

DDT's success as an indoor residual pesticide lies in its triplicate effect and its persistence. In addition to its lethality, DDT possesses repellant and irritant properties. When applicators spray a small amount of DDT on the walls and under the eaves of a house, DDT's repellant property keeps mosquitoes, even mosquitoes that might be resistant to DDT, from entering the treated house. If mosquitoes enter the house and land on the walls, the irritant property causes more mosquitoes to leave. If the remaining mosquitoes are not resistant to it, DDT kills them.

DDT's persistence causes it to be effective for a much longer time than other pesticides, an important consideration when treating houses in remote areas. Spraymen may have to make only one application of DDT per year rather than the three or four required by other pesticides. Additionally, DDT is usually the cheapest pesticide available, an important consideration as malaria-plagued countries are usually cash-strapped as well. Finally, the amounts of DDT used in these programs are so small that they offer no discernable threat to the environment. The amount of DDT that was used on one thousand acres of cotton during a growing season in the United States back in the 1950s could today protect the entire nation of Guyana from malaria for a year.

The malaria-control and public health communities were outraged by the effort to permanently ban DDT. They launched a vigorous and ultimately partially successful campaign to support the public heath use of DDT. Instead of being banned outright, the delegates to the POPs Convention placed DDT in Annex B of the Stockholm Convention **[Basic Document 4.2]**. According to the terms of Annex B, countries that declare their intent to produce and/or use DDT for public health purposes may do so as long as they comply with the strictures laid out in the Annex and elsewhere in the Convention.

While the option to continue using DDT according to Annex B is desirable and welcome, it comes with a number of onerous obligations on those DDT—exempted countries. The conditions might not be onerous for western countries, but they could be very burdensome for poor countries, such as Eritrea and Mozambique, that are struggling to rebuild after civil wars and may have other far more urgent national priorities than complying with the standards of the international bureaucracy.

The Convention also stipulates that DDT may only be used in accordance with WHO recommendations and guidelines and only when "safe, effective and affordable alternatives are not available to the Party in question." If, for example, the price of carbamates were to drop dramatically, malaria-control programs in poor countries would have a safe and affordable alternative to DDT, but they would also have one less reliable insecticide upon which to base malaria control. Given the problem of insecticide resistance, this would be highly risky. Good pest-management practice requires the rotation of insecticides. Thus, until the invention of more effective techniques or pesticides, malaria-control programs will still need to use DDT to manage insecticide resistance.

Every three years in consultation with WHO, the Conference of Parties (COP) will review the DDT exemption. There are concerns that COP, where malarial countries have been historically underrepresented and developed countries overrepresented, might ban DDT even while it is still needed in malaria control. In all, while the Stockholm Convention recognizes the ongoing need for DDT in public health programs, the COP could severely undermine public health efforts, removing decision-making from health experts and scientists in developing countries and burdening governments of poor countries with excessive reporting and bureaucratic requirements.

Meanwhile more and more malaria-plagued countries are turning to DDT for help in combating malaria. The Uganda government recently announced its intention to launch IRS programs that use DDT, an intention that its parliament supports. Debate continues in Kenya and Tanzania about incorporating DDT in their programs as well. Given the success in South Africa and Zambia, it seems likely that more African countries will seriously consider adopting the use of DDT to quell a disease that kills so many of its citizens and stultifies the countries' economic development.

DDT was discovered but ignored in the nineteenth century, lauded then vilified in the twentieth. As it enters the twenty-first century, DDT reflects its most famous characteristic: it persists. It persists because its usefulness has not yet ended. Until science finds other methods for malaria control, the responsible use of persistent and effective DDT may remain the best hope for saving and improving millions of lives.

9. Hindrick Bouwman, Henk van den Berg, & Henrik Kylin, DDT and Malaria Prevention: Addressing the Paradox, 119(6) Envtl. Health Perspect doi: 10.1289/ehp.1002127 (Jun 2011)

Should DDT be used? Overall, community health is significantly improved through all the many malaria control measures, which include IRS with DDT. The pro-DDT lobby has advocated for the continued use of DDT. . . .

The evidence of adverse health effects due to DDT (as for many other chemicals) is mounting as more research is published . . ., clearly indicating that it is time now, at the very least, to invoke precaution on DDT used in malaria control. Clearly, protecting lives is the priority, but who will take care of those protected but harmed, and what can be done to reduce exposure? Developing safe and effective alternatives to DDT would be a major step forward.

The mounting evidence of a DDT-associated health burden should not be ignored, even if such a health burden does not nearly equate with malaria morbidity and mortality. Advancing an argument that DDT should be continued as DDT's negative effects are so much less than malaria's effects on mortality or morbidity . . . and then ending the discussion there, ignores the rights of people to a safe environment, or at least to live safely in a compromised environment. . . . Much more attention should therefore be focused on informing the public about the advantages of malaria control even if this still requires DDT, and ways and means to reduce exposures. . . .

10. World Health Organization, Conclusion of the 2011 Position Statement on DDT in Indoor Residual Spraying: Human Health Aspects, WHO/HTM/GMP/2011 (2011)

DDT is still needed and used for disease vector control simply because there is no alternative of both equivalent efficacy and operational feasibility, especially for high-transmission areas. The reduction and ultimate elimination of the use of DDT for public health must be supported technically and financially. It is essential that adequate resources and technical support are rapidly allocated to countries so that they can adopt appropriate measures for sound management of pesticides in general and of DDT in particular. There is also an urgent need to develop alternative products and methods, not only to reduce reliance on DDT and to achieve its ultimate elimination, but also to sustain effective malaria vector control.

11. Conference of the Parties to the Stockholm Convention at its Sixth Meeting, Decision SC-6/1: DDT, UNEP/POPS/COP.6/33 (25 June 2013)

The Conference of the Parties . . .

2. *Concludes* that countries that are relying on DDT for disease vector control may need to continue such use until locally safe, effective, affordable and environmentally sound alternatives are available for a sustainable transition away from DDT;

3. *Notes* the necessity to provide technical, financial and other assistance to developing countries, least developed countries, small island developing States and countries with economies in transition for a transition away from reliance on DDT for disease vector control, with due priority accorded to ensuring that adequate systems and institutional capacity are in place to enable evidence-based decision-making. . . .

Section 5. Discussion Notes/Questions

1. Chrysotile asbestos is not listed in Annex III of the Rotterdam Convention **(Basic Document 4.1)**. But its use is banned in many countries. Is it "banned" in Rajapur? Is it "severely restricted" there? If it is banned or severely restricted in Rajapur, what obligations does Rajapur have relative to the exportation of chrysotile asbestos?

2. The Rotterdam Convention's Chemical Review Committee has recommended that chrysotile asbestos should be listed in Annex III of the Convention. *See Consideration of the draft decision guidance document for chrysotile asbestos,* UNEP/FAO/RC/CRC.2/19 (Nov. 8, 2005). Exporting countries have continually blocked any such listing, pursuant to the Convention's unanimity requirement for new Annex III listings. If chrysotile were listed in Annex III, how would that change Rajapur's obligations? Would production or use of chrysotile products be forbidden? Would exports to Yoribo be forbidden? If not, why have producing countries resisted amending Annex III to add chrysotile? *See generally* Christopher P.H. Bitonti, *Exporting Ignorance: Canada's Opposition to the Regulation of the International Chrysotile Asbestos Trade Under the Rotterdam Convention,* 9 ASPER REV. INT'L BUS. & TRADE L. 171 (2009).

3. As a party to the Stockholm Convention **(Basic Document 4.2)**, is Rajapur allowed to export DDT to a non-party? What conditions must it satisfy before doing so? *See* Article 3(2)(b).

4. If Rajapur has violated the Stockholm Convention, does Yoribo, a non-party to the Convention, have standing to complain of the violation? The Vienna Convention on the Law of Treaties **(Basic Document 1.14)** provides that "a treaty does not create either obligations or rights for a third State without its consent," but also that "a right arises for a third State from a provision of a treaty if the parties to the treaty intend the provision to accord that right either to the third State, or to a group of States to which it belongs, or to all States, and the third State assents thereto. Its assent shall be presumed so long as the contrary is not indicated . . . ." *See* Vienna Convention, arts. 34 & 36. *See also* Articles on State Responsibility, art. 42 **(Basic Document 1.15)**. Given that the Stockholm Convention's rules are designed to protect against world-wide transmission of POPS, are those rules *erga omnes* norms that even non-Party States can use as the basis of a claim against a Party State?

5. Does Rajapur have a customary law obligation to ensure that importing countries are warned of the hazards of products exported from Rajapur? To ensure that importing countries are capable of managing the products in a safe way? Does it matter whether the threatened harm from the products is global or local in nature?

6. Article 20 of the Articles on State Responsibility provides that "valid consent by a State to the commission of a given act by another state precludes the wrongfulness of that act . . . to the extent that the act remains within the limits of that consent." If Yoribo consented to Rajapur's exportation of DDT and asbestos cement products, is it therefore precluded from complaining about that action? If Yoribo could establish that it lacks the resources to police effectively the use of dangerous products or even to assess the extent of that danger, does that make its consent "invalid"? Does Rajapur have any obligation to assure itself of Yoribo's capacity and, in the absence of capacity, to protect Yoribo (and the rest of the world) from itself by not exporting a dangerous product? Or is Yoribo's consent a defense even to that obligation (assuming no evidence of harm to any other country)?

7. International regulation of hazardous chemicals raises difficult and important policy questions. How does one compare the benefits associated with use of a particular chemical (e.g., DDT) with the harm or potential harm from that chemical? DDT is not acutely toxic to humans, although it might have long-term toxic effects and it is persistent and bio-accumulative, so the long term must be considered. On the other hand, DDT is tremendously effective in the fight against malaria and other insect-borne diseases. How should the long-term risks be balanced against the significant short-term benefits?

A related question is how the cost-benefit determination should be made and at what governmental level? Some asbestos producers have argued that ensuring "workplace health and safety is a sovereign responsibility of importing countries," and that those countries, not exporters, have the duty to ensure that chrysotile asbestos is not a health hazard. With respect to dangerous pesticides, many argue that a ban on domestic use in a country should not lead to an export ban because exporting countries cannot appropriately weigh the costs and benefits of such chemicals for other countries where conditions may differ. Usually these arguments are used to justify exports of dangerous products from developed countries (where they are banned or restricted) to developing countries (where there are not).

Are you persuaded by these arguments? Or do developed nations have a duty to protect developing nations which, in general, have significantly less capacity to evaluate or regulate hazardous chemicals? What is your view on the proper regulatory level? Assuming no risk of global effects, should regulation of pesticides be exclusively the responsibility of the country in which those pesticides are used?

8. When France banned the sale of chrysotile and chrysotile-asbestos products, Canada challenged the ban before the World Trade Organization. Canada argued that chrysotile asbestos was safe when handled and used properly. France argued that safe use could not be guaranteed and, in fact, that many users were unlikely to follow proper precautions, thus putting themselves at unacceptable risk for serious asbestos-induced illnesses. The WTO Appellate Body ruled in France's favor and upheld the ban. *European Communities-Measures Affecting Asbestos and Asbestos-Containing Products*, WTO Doc WT/DS135/AB/R (12 Mar 2001). Although it did not say so, the Appellate Body may have had in mind the comments it made in an earlier case:

> the risk that is to be evaluated . . . is not only risk ascertainable in a science laboratory operating under strictly controlled conditions, but also risk in human societies as they actually exist, in other words, the actual potential for adverse effects on human health <u>in the real world where people live and work and die.</u>

EC Measures Concerning Meat and Meat Products (Hormones), WTO Doc. WT/DS26/AB/R (Jan. 16, 1998) (emphasis added).

For more on the intersection of international trade law and international environmental law, *see infra* Problem 12-1.

9. Is the PIC procedure sufficient to protect people in the developing world from the risks of dangerous chemicals? Is it adequate for "the real world where people live and work and die"?

10. The case against the production and use of chrysotile-asbestos products seems much stronger than the case against DDT, at least in terms of the evidence of its harm to human health. At the same time, the need for DDT seems much clearer and more pressing than the need for chrysotile asbestos products. So cost-benefit analysis would seem to favor more stringent restrictions on chrysotile-asbestos products and less-stringent restrictions on DDT. Yet international law takes exactly the opposite approach. Why? Does it have something to do with the sovereignty considerations discussed in Discussion Note/Question 7, *supra*?

11. Is it possible that the real explanation for the different treatment of chrysotile-asbestos products and DDT is that international law simply

privileges the interests of the powerful industrialized countries and their citizens over the interests of developing nations? In *Note, The Regulation of DDT: A Choice Between Evils*, 41 Vand. J. Transnat'l L. 677, 693 (2008), Ashley K. Martin observes that the heavy restrictions imposed on the use of DDT by the Stockholm Convention ignore the fact that

> the actual secondary effects of DDT are far more uncertain and far less harmful than its reputation throughout the world would suggest. Many independent studies of DDT have produced no sound evidence to support its ban because the harmful consequences of DDT on the environment and humans have not been shown to be of a magnitude great enough to outweigh its safe, effective, and inexpensive nature.

Martin goes on to suggest that the structure of the Convention allows "the interest of developed countries in protecting the environment [to] trump the interest of the developing countries in using DDT," despite the weight of evidence favoring DDT's use. Moreover, she says, *id.* at 703, critical decisions about how to structure malarial control programs and the role that DDT should play in those programs are made at the international level, and subject to undue influence of the rich Northern countries:

> Experts in developing countries need the majority of the discretion in the use of DDT because they are better able to understand and evaluate their need for DDT as they confront the realities and consequences of the malaria epidemic on a daily basis. The absence of the malaria epidemic in developed countries contributes to their reluctance to advocate DDT's continued use; because the problem is not visible in those developed countries, the countries' representatives cannot fully comprehend the pervasiveness and gravity of the disease, and thus do not fully comprehend the need for DDT. Easing the requirements for exemption and returning more control to experts in developing countries will increase the likelihood that DDT is available where needed, and will therefore address developing countries' interests in the regulation of DDT.

On the other hand, Paula Barrios describes the Rotterdam Convention's focus on informed consent as reflecting a "double standard" in which Northern countries protect their own citizens from hazardous chemicals while allowing their companies to poison impoverished people in the developing world. She says the Rotterdam Convention "does not address the needs of developing countries in any meaningful way."

Do you agree? Does the Stockholm Convention over-regulate DDT and other persistent pesticides and the Rotterdam Convention under-regulate non-persistent pesticides and other hazardous chemicals? Is this because the rich countries of the North have chosen to protect themselves against small risks and expose poor countries to grave risks? Or is there some principled explanation for the structure of these treaties? One could argue that the scope of the two conventions can be explained by the fact that DDT and other POPs pose global threats and require global determinations about their use, whereas other hazardous chemicals pose local threats and require local determinations about their use. Do you accept that explanation?

12. One of UNEP's priority focus areas is harmful substances and hazardous wastes. In this connection, it promotes "international activities related to the sound management of chemicals," with a goal of "promot[ing] chemical safety and provid[ing] countries with access to information on toxic chemicals." UNEP, *Harmful Substances and Hazardous Waste,* http://www.unep.org (last visited June 3, 2011). UNEP played an instrumental role in the adoption of the Minimata Convention on Mercury **(Basic Document 4.4)**, and it has promoted international efforts to address the health and environmental effects of lead and cadmium. *See* UNEP, *Governing Council Decision Relating to Lead and Cadmium,* adopted at the 26th session of the Governing Council/Global Ministerial Environment Forum, Nairobi, 21–24 February 2011.

UNEP additionally supported the development of the Strategic Approach to International Chemicals Management (SAICM), a "policy framework to foster the sound management of chemicals" adopted by the International Conference on Chemicals Management (ICCM) in early 2006. The relevant instruments comprising SAICM are the Dubai Declaration on International Chemicals Management **(Basic Document 4.3)**, and an accompanying Overarching Policy Strategy and Global Plan of Action. SAICM emphasizes voluntary business support for sound chemical management and international efforts to build regulatory capacity in developing countries. *See* UNEP, *Strategic Approach to International Chemicals Management: SAICM texts and resolutions of the International Conference on Chemicals Management* (2006), available at http://www.saicm.org (last visited June 3, 2011).

13. Writing about SAICM two years before its adoption, a representative of business interests commented that the global chemical industry supported the goal of safe use and handling of chemicals, but was resistant to the adoption of new binding international instruments. Rainer Koch, *Global strategy on chemicals management: opportunities and risks,* UNEP Industry and Environment 7–8 (Apr.–Sept. 2004).

Mr. Koch, endorsed the idea of a global strategy for chemicals management (SAICM) in principle, provided that the final SAICM package was

> a balanced outcome, levering the need for command and control systems with a sound, flexible and practical strategic approach that will promote and support industry's stewardship of chemicals, and one that is aimed at more regulatory efficiency, integration, coherence and consistency, less bureaucracy, and strengthening of industry voluntary activities and cooperation among all stakeholders in a new partnership.

If, on the other hand, the strategy was "the basis for additional, even more stringent, legally binding regulatory approaches at the national, regional or international levels" that "would not always contribute to more effective chemical safety" and might harm overall efforts to achieve sound management of chemicals.

Do you agree? Are voluntary efforts aimed at partnerships with business better than regulatory efforts? If your answer is, "it depends," then what factors are relevant to determining the appropriate approach to promoting chemical safety on a global level?

14. The SAICM approach is broadly consistent with a move at the 2002 Johannesburg World Summit on Sustainable Development away from "new treaties, . . . new international institutions, and . . . major new financial commitments" toward a focus on implementation with "development 'partnerships' " at the heart of the effort. The Summit "brought a new formal recognition" to "voluntary, cooperative ventures, involving self-selected groups of governments, international agencies, nongovernmental organizations, and corporations." S. Jacob Scherr & R. Juge Gregg, *Johannesburg and Beyond: the 2002 World Summit on Sustainable Development and the Rise of Partnerships,* ALI-ABA Course of Study, SM083 ALI-ABA 679 (April 12–13, 2007). What are the advantages of such partnerships? What are the weaknesses?

15. On June 1, 2007, a new European Union regulation on chemicals and their safe use entered into effect. Regulation (EC) No. 1907/2006, commonly called REACH (an acronym for Registration, Evaluation, and Authorization of Chemicals), requires manufacturers and importers of chemicals to register chemicals and to provide basic data about the registered substance, including information on the properties of the substance, its intended use, and labeling. For substances produced in quantities above a certain level, information on health and environmental effects and risks of the product must also be provided. Manufacturers have responsibility to ensure that the chemicals they produce are safe or that risks are adequately controlled. Chemicals with certain hazardous properties can be subject to further regulation, including a ban on production or use or appropriate restrictions on production, sale, or use. There are obligations to phase out particularly dangerous chemicals as quickly as suitable substitutes can be found. *See generally* Isabelle Laborde, *REACH: The New European Union Chemicals Regulations,* 23 NAT. RESOURCES & ENV'T 63 (Winter 2009); Diana Bowman & Geert van Calster, *Reflecting on Reach: Global Implications of the European Union's Chemicals Regulation,* 4 NANOTECHNOLOGY L. & BUS. 375 (2007); Michael P. Walls, *REACH 101: Understanding and Preparing for the New EU Chemicals Legislation,* ALI-ABA Course of Study, SN044 ALI-ABA 635 (Feb. 6–8, 2008). Professor Applegate suggests that REACH provides some lessons for reform of US legislation on toxic chemicals. *See* John S. Applegate, *Synthesizing TSCA and REACH: Practical Principles for Chemical Regulation Reform,* 35 ECOLOGY L.Q. 721 (2008).

Might REACH provide a model for a global treaty? Why should every state have duplicative registration and regulation of chemicals? If a chemical is unsafe for use in the EU, isn't it unsafe everywhere? If certain safety precautions are required in the EU, shouldn't they be required everywhere? What arguments, if any, would you make against a unified international regulatory approach? Wouldn't it be administratively cheaper and more efficient than having 190 separate national regulatory systems?

CHAPTER NINE

CONFRONTING CLIMATE CHANGE

■ ■ ■

In this chapter we consider the problem of climate change, the most profound environmental threat ever to face human society and the most difficult to solve. Human civilization developed during a period of relative climate stability, the current geological epoch known as the Holocene, which began some 12,000 years ago.[1] Much of human culture—our agricultural practices, the locations of our major cities, our heavy use of the "free" resources of our oceans and forests—assumes that relative climate stability will continue into the foreseeable future. Today, however, human actions are causing fundamental shifts in the Earth's climate system that differ in kind and impact from anything that has occurred since the dawn of civilization. Unless we confront climate change seriously and soon, we can expect to see massive disruptions of global agricultural systems, the displacement of tens of millions of people from their homes and even their countries, disruption and change in local flora and fauna ecosystems as pests and disease shift locations in response to the changing climate, and changes in ocean chemistry (as the ocean absorbs CO_2). These ecosystem disruptions are certain to reduce the already dwindling oceanic resources upon which many people depend for livelihood and sustenance. There is little doubt in our minds that these changes will undermine fundamental human rights and breed new political conflict as well as contribute to the worsening of existing conflicts in many areas of the world.

Addressing the challenge of climate change will not be easy. The fundamental difficulty can be stated simply: the human activity that makes the most significant contribution to climate change is the production of energy via the burning of fossil fuels, and the production of energy is absolutely essential to the maintenance of modern industrial life. While there are many cost-effective ways to reduce energy consumption, pursuing greater efficiency in the use of energy will not alone solve the problem. The overall demand for energy will continue to grow as population increases and as people in poorer countries seek to improve their lives and their economic circumstances. So we must either scale back our *per capita* energy consumption, or we must find ways of producing massive amounts of energy without emitting greenhouse gases (GHGs).

1 *See* Brian Fagan, The Long Summer (2004).

To date, however, there is no method of producing energy on a large scale that is as inexpensive as burning fossil fuels;[2] and to date the burning of fossil fuels inevitably leads to the emission of greenhouse gases. Even if non-GHG-emitting methods of producing energy become more cost effective and are promoted diligently, it will take many years before enough of this alternative energy can be produced to satisfy a substantial portion of energy demand at an affordable price. Until then, people and nations will opt to produce fossil-fuel energy.

Well-designed policies can facilitate and promote a shift away from fossil-fuel energy. However, the countries, the industries, and the people that profit from the production and use of fossil fuels resist the adoption of any such policies. In many parts of the world, including our own, small steps have been taken, but everyone acknowledges that the steps are tiny relative to the length of the journey before us.

Acknowledging the difficulty of the challenge that faces us does not lessen our obligation to respond to that challenge. As the late Professor Burns H. Weston wrote:[3]

> This much we know with certainty: climate change exists, global warming included; it is today caused largely by human activity; and, with each passing day, it looms ever larger as a major threat to the worldwide human and natural environment. We also know with certainty that its worst effects will be severe if left unabated and that these will be felt primarily by today's children and the generations that follow them, especially if they are poor or otherwise without capacity to protect themselves.
>
> Ask almost anyone about this perilous state of affairs and they will agree: each of us living today has a responsibility to prevent the looming catastrophe. At a minimum, each of us has a moral responsibility to ensure that today's children and future generations inherit a global environment at least no worse than the one we received from our predecessors.

The three problems in this chapter introduce you to some of the legal, political, and economic challenges involved in confronting climate change. The first problem, a negotiation exercise, explores the difficulty of convincing nation-states to commit to the actions needed to combat the causes and effects of climate change. The second problem asks how international law could respond if a nation decided to attempt to solve climate change by embarking on a policy of unilateral "geoengineering."

---

[2] We recognize, of course, that burning fossil fuels is relatively inexpensive only because the adverse environmental impacts of fossil-fuel use are generally not factored into the cost of the energy produced.

[3] Burns H. Weston, *Climate Change and Intergenerational Justice: Foundational Reflections*, 9 Vt. J. Envtl. L. 375, 375–76 (2008).

The third and final problem considers what to do when climate change seriously disrupts an existing human culture, and whether international law has any contribution to make in the effort to protect and assist people who are adversely impacted by climate change.

We begin with some essential background.[4]

A. CLIMATE CHANGE: A BRIEF OVERVIEW

1. EVIDENCE AND SCIENCE

Greenhouse gases (GHGs)—so named for their heat-trapping properties—are an essential component of life on Earth. Through a process popularly referenced as the "greenhouse effect," GHGs capture a substantial amount of infrared energy from the sun that enters Earth's atmosphere. Without GHGs, surface temperatures on the Earth would be too low to sustain life—negative 80°F on average. In contrast, excess concentrations of GHGs, such as in Venus's atmosphere, maintain surface temperatures at around 870°F, too hot for life to subsist. In classic Goldilocks fashion, concentrations of GHGs in Earth's atmosphere are just right for sustaining life by maintaining temperatures that average roughly 60°F. The increasing concentration of GHGs in Earth's atmosphere as a result of human activity, however, is now altering climatic patterns and ecosystems around the planet in unpredictable and alarming ways.

The greenhouse gases are carbon dioxide (CO_2), methane (CH_4), nitrous oxide (N_2O), ozone (O_3), halocarbons (human-made compounds that contain chlorine or bromine and carbon atoms), and water vapor.[5] Each gas is a by-product of several processes. The main source of nitrous oxide, for example, is the application of nitrogen fertilizer in agricultural operations. The major sources of methane are geologic deposits, livestock, and landfills. Carbon dioxide, on the other hand, is emitted from the incomplete combustion of fossil fuels including coal, oil, and natural gas. Therefore, the primary sources of CO_2 emissions are the electricity generation, industrial, and transportation sectors. GHG concentrations are also affected by "sinks." Forests and oceans, for example, are sinks for carbon dioxide because they absorb carbon dioxide out of the atmosphere.

Climate "forcings" are externally imposed factors that affect the climate. Positive forcings, such as industrial emission of GHGs or increases in solar radiation, have warming effects; and negative forcings, such as volcanic eruptions or human emissions of aerosols, have cooling effects. In addition to directly affecting the climate, forcings also contribute to positive

---

[4] The editors thank Adam Abelkop, research assistant to Professor Carlson at The University of Iowa College of Law during 2008–2010, for his substantial contributions to this chapter and, in particular, for his assistance in preparing the Editors' Notes and problem facts.

[5] Intergovernmental Panel on Climate Change 2007 [hereinafter "IPCC 2007"], Changes in Atmospheric Constituents and in Radiative Forcing 131–33 (2007).

and negative "feedbacks." A feedback occurs when an external forcing causes an energy change within the climatic system itself, which in turn either augments or dampens the effects of the original forcing. For example, CO_2 emissions could cause temperatures' to rise at certain locations across the globe, causing permafrost to melt and release methane. The release of methane into the atmosphere would accelerate the warming process. The methane release, then, would constitute a positive feedback to the climate change process.

To understand and predict how the climate will react to forcings and feedbacks—e.g., to certain levels of GHG concentration and temperature increases—scientists input enormous amounts of data into climate models that are run on advanced supercomputers. Over the past three decades or so, the accuracy of these climate models has increased considerably as computing power and our knowledge about the global climate have improved.[6]

Climate change data is gathered in a variety of ways, which taken together reflect temperature changes and climatic trends on an aggregate or system-wide level. Surface temperature measurements are taken at fixed locations on land and buoys and ships at sea. Atmospheric temperature measurements are obtained via weather balloons and, since 1979, from satellites as well. Scientists then compile the measurements from these individual monitors and analyze them together to discern trends in temperature levels. Scientists gather information on atmospheric GHG concentrations in much the same way. In addition to direct measurements though, researchers can analyze hydrogen and oxygen isotopes in ice cores drilled out of polar or mountain ice caps to determine temperatures far into the past. Air trapped in the ice can also be used to determine past GHG concentrations. Researchers have also examined tree rings, corals, and sediments to infer past temperatures. Finally, climate scientists compare these data with observational data gathered from around the world. Observational data includes melting of ice in the Arctic sea, melting of glaciers across the planet, decreases in snow cover, earlier blooming of plants, changes in animal ranges and migratory patterns, rises in sea level, and the frequency of droughts, floods, and hurricanes.

Taken together, these data have led the Intergovernmental Panel on Climate Change (IPCC)—a Nobel Prize winning consortium of top scientists from across the globe—to conclude that "[w]arming of the climate system is unequivocal" and that human activity, particularly the burning of fossil fuels, is the primary cause.[7] The IPCC's Fifth Assessment, released

[6] The National Academies, Understanding and Responding to Climate Change 14–15 (2008).

[7] IPCC, *Summary for Policymakers*, in Climate Change 2013: The Physical Science Basis. Contribution of Working Group I to the Fifth Assessment Report of the Intergovernmental Panel on Climate Change 4, 17 (2013) [hereinafter "IPCC 2013, *Summary for Policymakers*"].

in 2013, indicates, with medium confidence, that the years 1983 through 2012 were "*likely* the warmest 30-year period of the last 1400 years."[8] The changes to global climate patterns that have been observed are too great to be explained by natural events, and rising temperatures and climatic changes correspond very closely with increases in atmospheric GHG concentrations.

Of the GHGs that have contributed to planetary warming, carbon dioxide is the most important. The preindustrial CO_2 concentration was around 280 parts per million molecules (ppm). The CO_2 concentration in 2011 was roughly 391 ppm, which, as the IPCC notes, "now substantially exceed[s] the highest concentrations recorded in ice cores during the past 800,000 years."[9] The increase in GHG emissions has corresponded with a temperature increase of roughly 1.5°F (0.85°C) from 1880–2012. Global CO_2 emissions continue to rise. Annual emissions hit an all-time high in 2014, and are nearly twice as high as they were as recently as the 1970s.[10] The average atmospheric concentration of CO_2 reached 411 ppm in May 2018.[11]

If these trends are not reversed, we can expect continued temperature rises throughout this century and beyond. Models based on a worst-case scenario (ever-rising emissions due to population increases and economic development) forecast temperature increases by the end of the century of 5.8–9.7°F (3.2–5.4°C) above the average that prevailed during the period 1850–1900. Moreover, the effects of emissions today will persist into the future, even if emissions are eventually reduced. CO_2 has a long atmospheric lifetime: nearly one-half of CO_2 emissions will remain in the atmosphere after 100 years, and roughly one-fifth of it will remain after 1,000 years.[12] Unless we take rapid action to reduce emissions, we are creating the conditions for dramatic climate changes that will be irreversible on human time scales.

---

[8] *Id.* at 5.

[9] *Id.* at 11.

[10] T.A. Boden, et al., *Global, Regional, and National Fossil-Fuel CO2 Emissions*, Carbon Dioxide Information Analysis Center, Oak Ridge National Laboratory, U.S. Department of Energy, Oak Ridge, Tenn. U.S.A. doi 10.3334/CDIAC/00001_V2017 (2017).

[11] As measured by the United States National Oceanic & Atmosphere Administration at its Mauna Loa Observatory in Hawaii. National Oceanic & Atmospheric Administration, *Trends in Atmospheric Carbon Dioxide,* https://www.esrl.noaa.gov/gmd/ccgg/trends/ (last updated June 5, 2018) (last visited June 12, 2018).

[12] United States Global Change Research Program, Global Climate Change Impacts in the United States 40 (Thomas R. Karl, Jerry M. Melillo & Thomas C. Peterson eds., 2009).

GLOBAL CLIMATE CHANGE

GLOBAL CLIMATE CHANGE IMPACTS IN THE UNITED STATES 14–15
Thomas R. Karl, Jerry M. Melillo, & Thomas C. Peterson eds., 2009

Climate is influenced by a variety of factors, both human-induced and natural. The increase in the carbon dioxide concentration has been the principal factor causing warming over the past 50 years. Its concentration has been building up in the Earth's atmosphere since the beginning of the industrial era in the mid-1700s, primarily due to the burning of fossil fuels (coal, oil, and natural gas) and the clearing of forests. Human activities have also increased the emissions of other greenhouse gases, such as methane, nitrous oxide, and halocarbons. These emissions are thickening the blanket of heat-trapping gases in Earth's atmosphere, causing surface temperatures to rise.

Heat-trapping gases

Carbon dioxide concentration has increased due to the use of fossil fuels in electricity generation, transportation, and industrial and household uses. It is also produced as a by-product during the manufacturing of cement. Deforestation provides a source of carbon dioxide and reduces its uptake by trees and other plants. Globally, over the past several decades, about 80 percent of human-induced carbon dioxide emissions came from the burning of fossil fuels, while about 20 percent resulted from deforestation and associated agricultural practices. The concentration of carbon dioxide in the atmosphere has increased by roughly 35 percent since the start of the industrial revolution.

Methane concentration has increased mainly as a result of agriculture; raising livestock (which produce methane in their digestive tracts); mining, transportation, and use of certain fossil fuels; sewage; and decomposing garbage in landfills. About 70 percent of the emissions of atmospheric methane are now related to human activities.

Nitrous oxide concentration is increasing as a result of fertilizer use and fossil fuel burning.

Halocarbon emissions come from the release of certain manufactured chemicals to the atmosphere. Examples include chlorofluorocarbons (CFCs), which were used extensively in refrigeration and for other industrial processes before their presence in the atmosphere was found to cause stratospheric ozone depletion. The abundance of these gases in the atmosphere is now decreasing as a result of international regulations designed to protect the ozone layer. Continued decreases in ozone-depleting halocarbon emissions are expected to reduce their relative influence on climate change in the future. Many halocarbon replacements, however, are potent greenhouse gases, and their concentrations are increasing.

Ozone is a greenhouse gas, and is continually produced and destroyed in the atmosphere by chemical reactions. In the troposphere, the lowest 5 to 10 miles of the atmosphere near the surface, human activities have increased the ozone concentration. . . .

In the stratosphere, the layer above the troposphere, ozone exists naturally and protects life on Earth from exposure to excessive ultraviolet radiation from the Sun. As mentioned previously, halocarbons released by human activities destroy ozone in the stratosphere and have caused the ozone hole over Antarctica. Changes in the stratospheric ozone layer have contributed to changes in wind patterns and regional climates in Antarctica.

Water vapor is the most important and abundant greenhouse gas in the atmosphere. Human activities produce only a very small increase in water vapor through irrigation and combustion processes. However, the surface warming caused by human-produced increases in other greenhouse gases leads to an increase in atmospheric water vapor, since a warmer climate increases evaporation and allows the atmosphere to hold more moisture. This creates an amplifying "feedback loop," leading to more warming.

Other human influences

In addition to the global-scale climate effects of heat-trapping gases, human activities also produce additional local and regional effects. Some of these activities partially offset the warming caused by greenhouse gases, while others increase the warming. One such influence on climate is caused by tiny particles called "aerosols" (not to be confused with aerosol spray cans). For example, the burning of coal produces emissions of sulfur-containing compounds. These compounds form "sulfate aerosol" particles, which reflect some of the incoming sunlight away from the Earth, causing a cooling influence at the surface. Sulfate aerosols also tend to make clouds more efficient at reflecting sunlight, causing an additional indirect cooling effect.

Another type of aerosol, often referred to as soot or black carbon, absorbs incoming sunlight and traps heat in the atmosphere. Thus, depending on their type, aerosols can either mask or increase the warming caused by increased levels of greenhouse gases. On a globally averaged basis, the sum of these aerosol effects offsets some of the warming caused by heat-trapping gases.

The effects of various greenhouse gases and aerosol particles on Earth's climate depend in part on how long these gases and particles remain in the atmosphere. After emission, the atmospheric concentration of carbon dioxide remains elevated for thousands of years, and that of methane for decades, while the elevated concentrations of aerosols only persist for days to weeks. The climate effects of reductions in emissions of carbon dioxide and other long-lived gases do not become apparent for at least several decades. In contrast, reductions in emissions of short-lived compounds can have a rapid, but complex effect since the geographic patterns of their climatic influence and the resulting surface temperature responses are quite different. One modeling study found that while the greatest emissions of short-lived pollutants in summertime by late this century are projected to come from Asia, the strongest climate response is projected to be over the central United States.

Human activities have also changed the land surface in ways that alter how much heat is reflected or absorbed by the surface. Such changes include the cutting and burning of forests, the replacement of other areas of natural vegetation with agriculture and cities, and large-scale irrigation. These transformations of the land surface can cause local (and even regional) warming or cooling. Globally, the net effect of these changes has probably been a slight cooling of the Earth's surface over the past 100 years.

Natural influences

Two important natural factors also influence climate: the Sun and volcanic eruptions. Over the past three decades, human influences on climate have become increasingly obvious, and global temperatures have risen sharply. During the same period, the Sun's energy output (as measured by satellites since 1979) has followed its historical 11-year cycle of small ups and downs, but with no net increase. The two major volcanic eruptions of the past 30 years have had short-term cooling effects on climate, lasting 2 to 3 years. Thus, these natural factors cannot explain the warming of recent decades; in fact, their net effect on climate has probably been a slight cooling influence over this period. Slow changes in Earth's orbit around the Sun and its tilt toward or away from the Sun are also a purely natural influence on climate, but are only important on timescales from thousands to many tens of thousands of years.

The climate changes that have occurred over the last century are not solely caused by the human and natural factors described above. In addition to these influences, there are also fluctuations in climate that occur even in the absence of changes in human activities, the Sun, or volcanoes. One example is the El Niño phenomenon, which has important influences on many aspects of regional and global climate. Many other modes of variability have been identified by climate scientists and their effects on climate occur at the same time as the effects of human activities, the Sun, and volcanoes.

OBSERVED CHANGES IN THE CLIMATE SYSTEM[13]

INTERGOVERNMENTAL PANEL ON CLIMATE CHANGE, 2014
Climate Change 2014: Synthesis Report. Contribution of Working Groups I, II and III to the Fifth Assessment Report of the IPCC 40–42
(Core Writing Team, R.K. Pachauri & L.A. Meyer, eds.)

Warming of the climate system is unequivocal, and since the 1950s, many of the observed changes are unprecedented over decades to millennia. The atmosphere and ocean have warmed, the amounts of snow and ice have diminished, and sea level has risen.

1.1.1 Atmosphere

Each of the last three decades has been successively warmer at the Earth's surface than any preceding decade since 1850. The period from 1983 to 2012 was very likely the warmest 30-year period of the last 800 years in the Northern Hemisphere, where such assessment is possible (high confidence) and likely the warmest 30-year period of the last 1400 years (medium confidence).

The globally averaged combined land and ocean surface temperature data as calculated by a linear trend show a warming of 0.85 [0.65 to 1.06] °C over the period 1880 to 2012 .... For the longest period when calculation of regional trends is sufficiently complete (1901 to 2012), almost the entire globe has experienced surface warming.

* * *

1.1.2 Ocean

Ocean warming dominates the increase in energy stored in the climate system, accounting for more than 90% of the energy accumulated between 1971 and 2010 (high confidence) with only about 1% stored in the atmosphere. On a global scale, the ocean warming is largest near the surface, and the upper 75 m warmed by 0.11 [0.09 to 0.13] °C per decade over the period 1971 to 2010. It is virtually certain that the upper ocean (0–700 m) warmed from 1971 to 2010, and it likely warmed between the 1870s and 1971. It is likely that the ocean warmed from 700 to 2000 m from 1957 to 2009 and from 3000 m to the bottom for the period 1992 to 2005. . . .

Since the beginning of the industrial era, oceanic uptake of CO2 has resulted in acidification of the ocean; the pH of ocean surface water has decreased by 0.1 (high confidence), corresponding to a 26% increase in acidity, measured as hydrogen ion concentration. There is medium confidence that, in parallel to warming, oxygen concentrations have decreased in coastal waters and in the open ocean thermocline in many

---

[13] *Eds.* The IPCC report italicizes words such as *likely, very likely, high confidence,* and *medium confidence* to signal that those are terms of art with a technical meaning. The italicization is omitted here. The technical definitions of the terms can be found in the full report, available on the IPCC's webpage. Internal citations have also been deleted.

ocean regions since the 1960s, with a likely expansion of tropical oxygen minimum zones in recent decades.

* * *

1.1.3 Cryosphere

Over the last two decades, the Greenland and Antarctic ice sheets have been losing mass (high confidence). Glaciers have continued to shrink almost worldwide (high confidence). Northern Hemisphere spring snow cover has continued to decrease in extent (high confidence). There is high confidence that there are strong regional differences in the trend in Antarctic sea ice extent, with a very likely increase in total extent.

* * *

1.1.4 Sea level

Over the period 1901–2010, global mean sea level rose by 0.19 [0.17 to 0.21] m. The rate of sea level rise since the mid-19th century has been larger than the mean rate during the previous two millennia (high confidence).

2. IMPACTS

There are a number of ways in which climate change will adversely affect the quality of human life.

It is likely that global warming will cause (and probably already is causing) severe weather events such as heat waves, droughts, floods, and even hurricanes to occur more regularly. The number of days during which temperatures reach above 90°F is likely to increase throughout warmer regions of the planet.[14] Along with an increase in temperature, residents in traditionally warmer regions can expect drought conditions that are more frequent and severe. As the temperature increases, so too will the rate of water evaporation. More water vapor in the air means longer periods of heavy precipitation in certain areas. Therefore, while certain regions are experiencing extended drought conditions, other regions will undergo more frequent flooding. In addition, an increase in the atmospheric concentration of water vapor will create another positive feedback, accelerating the warming process. Models project that warmer oceans and greater atmospheric instability contribute to more frequent and powerful hurricanes.

Warmer temperatures are also causing the sea level to rise. Before the Twentieth Century, the sea level had remained relatively constant for at least 2,000 years. Over the last century, however, the global sea level has risen by roughly 8 inches. As it warms, ocean water expands. In addition,

[14] United States Global Change Research Program, Global Climate Change Impact in the United States 33–34 (Thomas R. Karl, Jerry M. Melillo & Thomas C. Peterson eds., 2009).

rising temperatures are causing ice sheets and glaciers across the planet to melt at accelerated rates. The surge of melting water into the oceans could raise the sea level by 2 to 4 feet by 2100. Furthermore, melting ice sheets and glaciers are introducing vast amounts of fresh water into the ocean, particularly in the North Atlantic. The influx of freshwater into Northern Atlantic could dilute the Atlantic Meriodonal Overturning Circulation (Atlantic MOC, or the Gulf Stream), which is responsible for carrying warm water to northern Europe. The Atlantic MOC could reach a tipping point after which the Gulf Stream would simply shut down. Cut off from the flow of warm ocean currents, the result would be a mini-ice age throughout Western Europe.

In more temperate regions of the world, rising ocean surface temperatures are already having substantial negative impacts on ocean ecosystems. Rising temperatures, for example, cause coral to lose algae and turn white in a process known as coral bleaching. This stress can kill coral or make coral more susceptible to disease. Warming has already killed or severely damaged one-third of the ocean's corals.[15] Because oceans absorb carbon dioxide, increased CO_2 concentrations also cause ocean acidification, which diminishes the ability of corals and other sea creatures to form shells and skeletons.

Climate change will also impact ecosystems on the land. Many habitats and species are already stressed due to overharvesting, deforestation, or other forms of pollution. Climate change will exacerbate these stresses by changing certain ecosystem functions and also the natural ranges of a vast number of species. The IPCC estimates that between 20% and 30% of all known species would be far removed from their natural temperature ranges and placed at risk of extinction if the planet warms by 3.5 to 5.5°F.[16] Thus, climate change will drastically alter migration and hibernation patterns and will influence species to move towards areas with temperatures that match their natural temperature ranges. In warmer climates, invasive species will likely outcompete native species, providing a further stress on fragile ecosystems. Insects also thrive in warmer climates. The result will be more frequent and severe insect outbreaks in forests and possible disease outbreaks as insects carry pathogens to new areas.

Changes to the natural environment will also carry economic, social, and political costs. Droughts, floods, insects, and invasive plant species will significantly affect agricultural production, limiting the availability of food and driving up its price. Drier conditions and melting glaciers will place substantial limits on freshwater resources. Disease outbreaks could kill a substantial amount of people, hinder economic growth, and could cause

---

[15] *Id.* at 84–85.

[16] *Id.* at 81–82.

nations to place restrictions on international travel. Severe weather and the rising sea level may decimate entire cities, creating large populations of refugees. In response to climate change, nations could come into conflict over access to natural resources. The changing climate will test the limits of international cooperation. If society is unprepared and slow to adapt, then climate change could stress the global economy to its breaking point and incite conflicts across the globe.

In its 2014 Assessment, the IPCC summarized these impacts by identifying four key areas of risk "that span sectors and regions":

1. Risk of severe ill-health and disrupted livelihoods resulting from storm surges, sea level rise and coastal flooding; inland flooding in some urban regions; and periods of extreme heat.

2. Systemic risks due to extreme weather events leading to breakdown of infrastructure networks and critical services.

3. Risk of food and water insecurity and loss of rural livelihoods and income, particularly for poorer populations.

4. Risk of loss of ecosystems, biodiversity and ecosystem goods, functions, and services.[17]

The next three readings briefly discuss these risks. The first reading examines climate-change impacts in the United States. The second reading offers an estimate of the economic costs associated with the physical impacts of climate change. The final reading examines the possibility that the climate system could reach various "tipping points" that would precipitate extremely rapid, dramatic, or irreversible changes globally or in particular regions of the world.

CLIMATE SCIENCE SPECIAL REPORT

Highlights of the Findings of the U.S. Global Change Research Program, Fourth National Climate Assessment, Volume I (D.J. Wuebbles, et al., eds. 2017)

New observations and new research have increased our understanding of past, current, and future climate change since the Third U.S. National Climate Assessment (NCA3) was published in May 2014. This Climate Science Special Report (CSSR) is designed to capture that new information and build on the existing body of science in order to summarize the current state of knowledge and provide the scientific foundation for the Fourth National Climate Assessment (NCA4).

Since NCA3, stronger evidence has emerged for continuing, rapid, human-caused warming of the global atmosphere and ocean. This report

[17] IPCC, Climate Change 2014: Synthesis Report 65 (2014).

concludes that "it is *extremely likely*[18] that human influence has been the dominant cause of the observed warming since the mid-20th century. For the warming over the last century, there is no convincing alternative explanation supported by the extent of the observational evidence."

The last few years have also seen record-breaking, climate-related weather extremes, the three warmest years on record for the globe, and continued decline in arctic sea ice. These trends are expected to continue in the future over climate (multidecadal) timescales. Significant advances have also been made in our understanding of extreme weather events and how they relate to increasing global temperatures and associated climate changes. Since 1980, the cost of extreme events for the United States has exceeded $1.1 trillion; therefore, better understanding of the frequency and severity of these events in the context of a changing climate is warranted.

* * *

Recent droughts and associated heat waves have reached record intensity in some regions of the United States; however, by geographical scale and duration, the Dust Bowl era of the 1930s remains the benchmark drought and extreme heat event in the historical record. (*Very high confidence*).

* * *

Extreme temperatures in the contiguous United States are projected to increase even more than average temperatures (*very high confidence*). Both extremely cold days and extremely warm days are expected to become warmer. Cold waves are predicted to become less intense while heat waves will become more intense. The number of days below freezing is projected to decline while the number above 90°F will rise. *(Very high confidence).*

The frequency and intensity of heavy precipitation events in the United States are projected to continue to increase over the 21st century (*high confidence*). . . .

* * *

Substantial reductions in western U.S. winter and spring snowpack are projected as the climate warms. Earlier spring melt and reduced snow water equivalent have been formally attributed to human-induced warming (*high confidence*) and will *very likely* be exacerbated as the climate continues to warm (*very high confidence*). Under higher scenarios, and assuming no change to current water resources management, chronic, long-duration hydrological drought is increasingly possible by the end of this century (*very high confidence*). . . .

---

[18] *Eds.* The italicized terms in this reading are terms of art intended to indicate the level of scientific certainty attached to particular factual statements. For definitions of these terms, the reader should consult the original report.

* * *

The incidence of large forest fires in the western United States and Alaska has increased since the early 1980s (*high confidence*) and is projected to further increase in those regions as the climate warms, with profound changes to certain ecosystems (*medium confidence*).

* * *

Global mean sea level (GMSL) has risen by about 7–8 inches (about 16–21 cm) since 1900, with about 3 of those inches (about 7 cm) occurring since 1993 (*very high confidence*). . . .

* * *

Relative to the year 2000, GMSL is *very likely* to rise by 0.3–0.6 feet (9–18 cm) by 2030, 0.5–1.2 feet (15–38 cm) by 2050, and 1.0–4.3 feet (30–130 cm) by 2100 (*very high confidence* in lower bounds; *medium confidence* in upper bounds for 2030 and 2050; *low* confidence in upper bounds for 2100). Future emissions pathways have little effect on projected GMSL rise in the first half of the century, but significantly affect projections for the second half of the century (*high confidence*).

Emerging science regarding Antarctic ice sheet stability suggests that, for higher scenarios, a GMSL rise exceeding 8 feet (2.4 m) by 2100 is physically possible, although the probability of such an extreme outcome cannot currently be assessed. Regardless of emission pathway, it is *extremely likely* that GMSL rise will continue beyond 2100 (*high confidence*). . . .

* * *

As sea levels have risen, the number of tidal floods each year that cause minor impacts (also called "nuisance floods") have increased 5- to 10-fold since the 1960s in several U.S. coastal cities (*very high confidence*). Rates of increase are accelerating in over 25 Atlantic and Gulf Coast cities (*very high confidence*). Tidal flooding will continue increasing in depth, frequency, and extent this century (*very high confidence*).

Assuming storm characteristics do not change, sea level rise will increase the frequency and extent of extreme flooding associated with coastal storms, such as hurricanes and nor'easters (*very high confidence*). A projected increase in the intensity of hurricanes in the North Atlantic (*medium confidence*) could increase the probability of extreme flooding along most of the U.S. Atlantic and Gulf Coast states beyond what would be projected based solely on relative sea level rise. However, there is *low confidence* in the projected increase in frequency of intense Atlantic hurricanes, and the associated flood risk amplification, and flood effects could be offset or amplified by such factors, such as changes in overall storm frequency or tracks.

* * *

Residents of Alaska are on the front lines of climate change. Crumbling buildings, roads, and bridges and eroding shorelines are commonplace. Accelerated melting of multiyear sea ice cover, mass loss from the Greenland Ice Sheet, reduced snow cover, and permafrost thawing are stark examples of the rapid changes occurring in the Arctic. Furthermore, because elements of the climate system are interconnected, changes in the Arctic influence climate conditions outside the Arctic. . . .

* * *

Atmospheric circulation patterns connect the climates of the Arctic and the contiguous United States. Evidenced by recent record warm temperatures in the Arctic and emerging science, the midlatitude circulation has influenced observed arctic temperatures and sea ice (*high confidence*). However, confidence is low regarding whether or by what mechanisms observed arctic warming may have influenced the midlatitude circulation and weather patterns over the continental United States. The influence of arctic changes on U.S. weather over the coming decades remains an open question with the potential for significant impact.

* * *

There is significant potential for humanity's effect on the planet to result in unanticipated surprises and a broad consensus that the further and faster the Earth system is pushed towards warming, the greater the risk of such surprises.

There are at least two types of potential surprises: *compound events*, where multiple extreme climate events occur simultaneously or sequentially (creating greater overall impact), and *critical threshold* or *tipping point events*, where some threshold is crossed in the climate system (that leads to large impacts). The probability of such surprises—some of which may be abrupt and/or irreversible—as well as other more predictable but difficult-to-manage impacts, increases as the influence of human activities on the climate system increases.

STERN REVIEW: THE ECONOMICS OF CLIMATE CHANGE

SIR NICHOLAS STERN
Executive Summary i–x (2006)

Climate change presents a unique challenge for economics: it is the greatest and widest-ranging market failure ever seen. The economic analysis must therefore be global, deal with long time horizons, have the economics of risk and uncertainty at centre stage, and examine the possibility of major, non-marginal change. . . .

The benefits of strong, early action on climate change outweigh the costs.

* * *

The evidence shows that ignoring climate change will eventually damage economic growth. Our actions over the coming few decades could create risks of major disruption to economic and social activity, later in this century and in the next, on a scale similar to those associated with the great wars and the economic depression of the first half of the 20th century.

And it will be difficult or impossible to reverse these changes. Tackling climate change is the pro-growth strategy for the longer term, and it can be done in a way that does not cap the aspirations for growth of rich or poor countries. The earlier effective action is taken, the less costly it will be.

At the same time, given that climate change is happening, measures to help people adapt to it are essential. And the less mitigation we do now, the greater the difficulty of continuing to adapt in future.

* * *

Under a BAU [Business As Usual] scenario, the stock of greenhouse gases could more than treble by the end of the century, giving at least a 50% risk of exceeding 5°C global average temperature change during the following decades. This would take humans into unknown territory. An illustration of the scale of such an increase is that we are now only around 5°C warmer than in the last ice age.

Such changes would transform the physical geography of the world. A radical change in the physical geography of the world must have powerful implications for the human geography—where people live, and how they live their lives. . . . The risks of serious, irreversible impacts of climate change increase strongly as concentrations of greenhouse gases in the atmosphere rise.

* * *

Warming will have many severe impacts, often mediated through water:

- Melting glaciers will initially increase flood risk and then strongly reduce water supplies, eventually threatening one-sixth of the world's population, predominantly in the Indian sub-continent, parts of China, and the Andes in South America.
- Declining crop yields, especially in Africa, could leave hundreds of millions without the ability to produce or purchase sufficient food. At mid to high latitudes, crop yields may increase for moderate temperature rises (2–3°C), but

then decline with greater amounts of warming. At 4°C and above, global food production is likely to be seriously affected.

- In higher latitudes, cold-related deaths will decrease. But climate change will increase worldwide deaths from malnutrition and heat stress. Vector-borne diseases such as malaria and dengue fever could become more widespread if effective control measures are not in place.
- Rising sea levels will result in tens to hundreds of millions more people flooded each year with warming of 3 or 4°C. There will be serious risks and increasing pressures for coastal protection in South East Asia (Bangladesh and Vietnam), small islands in the Caribbean and the Pacific, and large coastal cities, such as Tokyo, New York, Cairo and London. According to one estimate, by the middle of the century, 200 million people may become permanently displaced due to rising sea levels, heavier floods, and more intense droughts.
- Ecosystems will be particularly vulnerable to climate change, with around 15–40% of species potentially facing extinction after only 2°C of warming. And ocean acidification, a direct result of rising carbon dioxide levels, will have major effects on marine ecosystems, with possible adverse consequences on fish stocks.

The damages from climate change will accelerate as the world gets warmer.

Higher temperatures will increase the chance of triggering abrupt and large-scale changes.

- Warming may induce sudden shifts in regional weather patterns such as the monsoon rains in South Asia or the El Niño phenomenon—changes that would have severe consequences for water availability and flooding in tropical regions and threaten the livelihoods of millions of people.
- A number of studies suggest that the Amazon rainforest could be vulnerable to climate change, with models projecting significant drying in this region. One model, for example, finds that the Amazon rainforest could be significantly, and possibly irrevocably, damaged by a warming of 2–3°C.
- The melting or collapse of ice sheets would eventually threaten land which today is home to 1 in every 20 people.

While there is much to learn about these risks, the temperatures that may result from unabated climate change will take the world outside the range of human experience. This points to the possibility of very damaging consequences.

The impacts of climate change are not evenly distributed—the poorest countries and people will suffer earliest and most. And if and when the damages appear it will be too late to reverse the process. Thus we are forced to look a long way ahead.

Climate change is a grave threat to the developing world and a major obstacle to continued poverty reduction across its many dimensions. First, developing regions are at a geographic disadvantage: they are already warmer, on average, than developed regions, and they also suffer from high rainfall variability. As a result, further warming will bring poor countries high costs and few benefits. Second, developing countries—in particular the poorest—are heavily dependent on agriculture, the most climate-sensitive of all economic sectors, and suffer from inadequate health provision and low-quality public services. Third, their low incomes and vulnerabilities make adaptation to climate change particularly difficult.

Because of these vulnerabilities, climate change is likely to reduce further already low incomes and increase illness and death rates in developing countries. Falling farm incomes will increase poverty and reduce the ability of households to invest in a better future, forcing them to use up meagre savings just to survive. At a national level, climate change will cut revenues and raise spending needs, worsening public finances.

[W]e estimate the total cost over the next two centuries of climate change . . . [is] equivalent to an average reduction in global per-capita consumption of at least 5%, now and forever. While this cost estimate is already strikingly high, it also leaves out much that is important.

The cost of BAU would increase still further, were [we] systematically to take account of three important factors:

- First, including direct impacts on the environment and human health (sometimes called 'non-market' impacts) increases our estimate of the total cost of climate change on this path from 5% to 11% of global per-capita consumption. There are difficult analytical and ethical issues of measurement here. The methods used in this model are fairly conservative in the value they assign to these impacts.
- Second, some recent scientific evidence indicates that the climate system may be more responsive to greenhouse-gas emissions than previously thought, for example because of the existence of amplifying feedbacks such as the release of methane and weakening of carbon sinks. Our estimates, based on modelling a limited increase in this responsiveness,

indicate that the potential scale of the climate response could increase the cost of climate change on the BAU path from 5% to 7% of global consumption, or from 11% to 14% if the non-market impacts described above are included.

- Third, a disproportionate share of the climate-change burden falls on poor regions of the world. If we weight this unequal burden appropriately, the estimated global cost of climate change at 5–6°C warming could be more than one-quarter higher than without such weights.

Putting these additional factors together would increase the total cost of BAU climate change to the equivalent of around a 20% reduction in consumption per head, now and into the future.

In summary, analyses that take into account the full ranges of both impacts and possible outcomes—that is, that employ the basic economics of risk—suggest that BAU climate change will reduce welfare by an amount equivalent to a reduction in consumption per head of between 5 and 20%. Taking account of the increasing scientific evidence of greater risks, of aversion to the possibilities of catastrophe, and of a broader approach to the consequences than implied by narrow output measures, the appropriate estimate is likely to be in the upper part of this range.

COMPOUND EXTREMES AND TIPPING POINTS

Climate Science Special Report: Fourth National Climate Assessment, Volume I, Chapter 15 (D.J. Wuebbles, et al., eds. 2017)

Some areas are susceptible to multiple types of extreme events that can occur simultaneously. For example, certain regions are susceptible to both flooding from coastal storms and riverine flooding from snow melt, and a compound event would be the occurrence of both simultaneously. Compound events can also result from shared forcing factors, including natural cycles like the El Niño-Southern Oscillation (ENSO); large-scale circulation patterns, such as the ridge observed during the 2011–2017 California drought; or relatively greater regional sensitivity to global change, as may occur in "hot spots" such as the western United States. Finally, compound events can result from mutually reinforcing cycles between individual events, such as the relationship between drought and heat, linked through soil moisture and evaporation, in water-limited areas. . . .

* * *

Compound events may surprise in two ways. The first is if known types of compound events recur, but are stronger, longer-lasting, and/or more widespread than those experienced in the observational record or projected by model simulations for the future. . . . [An] example would be the concurrent and more severe heavy precipitation events that have occurred in the U.S. Midwest in recent years. After record insurance payouts following the events, in 2014 several insurance companies, led by Farmers Insurance, sued the city of Chicago and surrounding counties for failing to adequately prepare for the impacts of a changing climate. Although the suit was dropped later that same year, their point was made: in some regions of the United States, the insurance industry is not able to cope with the increasing frequency and/or concurrence of certain types of extreme events.

The second way in which compound events could surprise would be the emergence of new types of compound events not observed in the historical record. . . . An example is Hurricane Sandy, where sea level rise, anomalously high ocean temperatures, and high tides combined to strengthen both the storm and the magnitude of the associated storm surge. At the same time, a blocking ridge over Greenland—a feature whose strength and frequency may be related to both Greenland surface melt and reduced summer sea ice in the Arctic—redirected the storm inland to what was, coincidentally, an exceptionally high-exposure location.

* * *

Different parts of the Earth system exhibit critical thresholds, sometimes called "tipping points." These parts, known as tipping elements, have the potential to enter into self-amplifying cycles that commit them to shifting from their current state into a new state: for example, from one in which the summer Arctic Ocean is covered by ice, to one in which it is ice-free. . . .

One important tipping element is the Atlantic meridional overturning circulation (AMOC), a major component of global ocean circulation. Driven by the sinking of cold, dense water in the North Atlantic near Greenland, its strength is projected to decrease with warming due to freshwater input from increased precipitation, glacial melt, and melt of the Greenland Ice Sheet. A decrease in AMOC strength is probable and may already be culpable for the "warming hole" observed in the North Atlantic . . . .

A slowing or collapse of the AMOC would have several consequences for the United States. A decrease in AMOC strength would accelerate sea level rise off the northeastern United States, while a full collapse could result in as much as approximately 1.6 feet (0.5 m) of regional sea level rise, as well as a cooling of approximately 0°–4°F (0°–2°C) over the country. . . .

Another tipping element is the atmospheric-oceanic circulation of the equatorial Pacific that, through a set of feedbacks, drives the state shifts of the El Niño-Southern Oscillation. . . . Climate model experiments suggest that warming will reduce the threshold needed to trigger extremely strong

El Niño and La Niña events. As evident from recent El Niño and La Niña events, such a shift would negatively impact many regions and sectors across the United States . . . .

* * *

The Antarctic and Greenland Ice Sheets are clear tipping elements. . . . At least one study suggests that warming of 2.9°F (1.6°C) above a preindustrial baseline could commit Greenland to an 85% reduction in ice volume and a 20 foot (6 m) contribution to global mean sea level over millennia. . . . In Antarctica, the amount of ice that sits on bedrock below sea level is enough to raise global mean sea level by 75.5 feet (23 m). This ice is vulnerable to collapse over centuries to millennia due to a range of feedbacks involving ocean-ice sheet-bedrock interactions. . . .[19]

Finally, tipping elements also exist in large-scale ecosystems. . . . As [an] example, coral reef ecosystems, such as those in Florida, are maintained by stabilizing ecological feedbacks among corals, coralline red algae, and grazing fish and invertebrates. However, these stabilizing feedbacks can be undermined by warming, increased risk of bleaching events, spread of disease, and ocean acidification, leading to abrupt reef collapse.

3. MITIGATION AND ADAPTATION OPTIONS

What can we do about climate change? Adaptation is one option. Farmers can change their agricultural practices in response to shifts in rainfall patterns. People and businesses in low-lying coastal areas can relocate to higher ground. Indeed, given that some significant amount of climate change is inevitable (because of existing atmospheric levels of greenhouse gases and the future warming to which we are already committed), adaptation is not really an option; it's a necessity.

But if we wish to avoid the risk of truly catastrophic climate change, we must take steps toward mitigation as well. We must find ways to reduce our emissions of greenhouse gases dramatically in order to ensure that atmospheric concentrations of such gases peak at a safe level. Unfortunately, no one really knows exactly what level will be safe. Some scientists believe it is necessary for planetary safety to limit atmospheric concentrations of greenhouse gases to a highly ambitious 450 ppm CO2e; others endorse a more plausible goal of 550 ppm CO2e (approximately double pre-industrial levels).

---

[19] *Eds.* There is recent evidence that both the West and East Antarctic ice sheets are melting at a much faster rate than previously believed. This has profound implications for the future rate and amount of sea level rise. *See* Qian Shen, et al., *Recent high-resolution Antarctic ice velocity maps reveal increased mass loss in Wilkes Land, East Antarctica,* 8 Nature: Scientific Reports No. 4477 (2018); P. Milillo, et al., *Heterogeneous retreat and ice melt of Thwaites Glacier, West Antarctica,* 5 Science Advances No. 1, eaau3433 (30 Jan. 2019).

In the Paris Agreement **(Basic Document 2.6)**, the international community endorsed a goal of stabilizing global warming below two degrees Celsius (relative to the pre-industrial period). The IPCC's Fifth Assessment Report estimated that the temperature increase at 550 ppm CO2e would fall within a range of 1.5–4.5° C, with it being *"more unlikely than likely"* that the increase would be below two degrees Celsius. On the other hand, the IPCC calculated that it was *"likely"* that the temperature change could be kept to less than two degrees Celsius if atmospheric GHG concentrations were stabilized at 450–500 ppm by 2100 (although temporarily overshooting the 500 ppm target could undermine that goal).[20] Meeting any of those targets requires prompt action. One recent study concluded that "peaking global emissions before 2020, cutting them at least 50 per cent below 1990 levels by 2050 and continuing reductions thereafter gives us a reasonable chance of staying within a budget [of total cumulative emissions] consistent with limiting warming to 2°C."[21] Clearly, meeting such a goal poses an enormous challenge: global GHG emissions are currently well above 1990 levels and rising every day.

Fortunately, we have currently the technological means to reduce GHG emissions to safe levels,[22] and we know how to design policies to ensure that this is done as cheaply as possible.[23] Moreover, if we begin aggressively to move toward a low-emission world, technological breakthroughs will almost certainly further reduce the cost of making the transition to a low-carbon economy. But good technology and policy sophistication will not be enough to solve the problem. Society must also muster the political will to act. So far at least, the necessary political will has been lacking, in the United States especially.

The remaining readings in this overview consider mitigation and adaptation options from both a policy and a technological perspective.

STABILIZATION WEDGES: SOLVING THE CLIMATE PROBLEM FOR THE NEXT 50 YEARS WITH CURRENT TECHNOLOGIES

STEPHEN PACALA & ROBERT H. SOCOLOW

305 Sci. 968, 968 (2004)

Humanity already possesses the fundamental scientific, technical, and industrial know-how to solve the carbon and climate problem for the next half-century. A portfolio of technologies now exists to meet the world's

[20] *See* IPCC, *Summary for Policymakers* in Mitigation of Climate Change, Contribution of Working Group III to the Fifth Assessment Report of the Intergovernmental Panel on Climate Change (2014).

[21] Myles Allen, et al., *The Exit Strategy* (Apr. 30, 2009), http://www.nature.com (last accessed June 10, 2010).

[22] Stephen Pacala & Robert Socolow, *Stabilization Wedges: Solving the Climate Problem for the Next 50 Years with Current Technologies,* 305 SCIENCE 968 (2004).

[23] Organization for Economic Cooperation and Development [OECD], Climate Change Mitigation: What Do We Do 18–21 (2008).

energy needs over the next 50 years and limit atmospheric CO2 to a trajectory that avoids a doubling of the preindustrial concentration. Every element in this portfolio has passed beyond the laboratory bench and demonstration project; many are already implemented somewhere at full industrial scale. Although no element is a credible candidate for doing the entire job (or even half the job) by itself, the portfolio as a whole is large enough that not every element has to be used.

* * *

[*Eds.*—The authors then discuss several examples of "options that are already deployed at an industrial scale and that could be scaled up further": improved vehicle fuel economy, reduced reliance on cars, more efficient buildings, more efficient power plants, use of natural gas rather than coal, carbon capture and storage, greater use of renewable energies (wind, solar, hydrogen, biofuels), enhancement of natural sinks (forests and agricultural lands).]

STERN REVIEW: THE ECONOMICS OF CLIMATE CHANGE

SIR NICHOLAS STERN
Executive Summary x–xxi (2006)

This Review has focused on the feasibility and costs of stabilisation of greenhouse gas concentrations in the atmosphere in the range of 450–550ppm CO2e.

Stabilising at or below 550ppm CO2e would require global emissions to peak in the next 10–20 years, and then fall at a rate of at least 1–3% per year. . . . By 2050, global emissions would need to be around 25% below current levels. These cuts will have to be made in the context of a world economy in 2050 that may be 3–4 times larger than today—so emissions per unit of GDP would need to be just one quarter of current levels by 2050.

To stabilise at 450ppm CO2e, without overshooting, global emissions would need to peak in the next 10 years and then fall at more than 5% per year, reaching 70% below current levels by 2050.

Theoretically it might be possible to "overshoot" by allowing the atmospheric GHG concentration to peak above the stabilisation level and then fall, but this would be both practically very difficult and very unwise. Overshooting paths involve greater risks, as temperatures will also rise rapidly and peak at a higher level for many decades before falling back down. Also, overshooting requires that emissions subsequently be reduced to extremely low levels, below the level of natural carbon absorption, which may not be feasible. Furthermore, if the high temperatures were to weaken the capacity of the Earth to absorb carbon—as becomes more likely with overshooting—future emissions would need to be cut even more rapidly to hit any given stabilisation target for atmospheric concentration.

* * *

Reversing the historical trend in emissions growth, and achieving cuts of 25% or more against today's levels is a major challenge. Costs will be incurred as the world shifts from a high-carbon to a low-carbon trajectory. But there will also be business opportunities as the markets for low-carbon, high-efficiency goods and services expand.

Greenhouse-gas emissions can be cut in four ways. Costs will differ considerably depending on which combination of these methods is used, and in which sector:

- Reducing demand for emissions-intensive goods and services
- Increased efficiency, which can save both money and emissions
- Action on non-energy emissions, such as avoiding deforestation
- Switching to lower-carbon technologies for power, heat and transport

* * *

[This report's] central estimate [of the costs of these changes] is that stabilisation of greenhouse gases at levels of 500–550ppm CO2e will cost, on average, around 1% of annual global GDP by 2050. This is significant, but is fully consistent with continued growth and development, in contrast with unabated climate change, which will eventually pose significant threats to growth.

* * *

Costs of mitigation of around 1% of GDP are small relative to the costs and risks of climate change that will be avoided. However, for some countries and some sectors, the costs will be higher. There may be some impacts on the competitiveness of a small number of internationally traded products and processes. These should not be overestimated, and can be reduced or eliminated if countries or sectors act together; nevertheless, there will be a transition to be managed. For the economy as a whole, there will be benefits from innovation that will offset some of these costs. All economies undergo continuous structural change; the most successful economies are those that have the flexibility and dynamism to embrace the change.

There are also significant new opportunities across a wide range of industries and services. Markets for low-carbon energy products are likely to be worth at least $500bn per year by 2050, and perhaps much more. Individual companies and countries should position themselves to take advantage of these opportunities.

Climate-change policy can help to root out existing inefficiencies. At the company level, implementing climate policies may draw attention to money-saving opportunities. At the economy-wide level, climate-change policy may be a lever for reforming inefficient energy systems and removing distorting energy subsidies, on which governments around the world currently spend around $250bn a year.

Policies on climate change can also help to achieve other objectives. These co-benefits can significantly reduce the overall cost to the economy of reducing greenhouse-gas emissions. If climate policy is designed well, it can, for example, contribute to reducing ill-health and mortality from air pollution, and to preserving forests that contain a significant proportion of the world's biodiversity.

National objectives for energy security can also be pursued alongside climate change objectives. Energy efficiency and diversification of energy sources and supplies support energy security, as do clear long-term policy frameworks for investors in power generation. Carbon capture and storage is essential to maintain the role of coal in providing secure and reliable energy for many economies.

* * *

Comparing the social costs of carbon on a BAU [Business as Usual] trajectory and on a path towards stabilisation at 550ppm CO2e, we estimate the excess of benefits over costs, in net present value terms, from implementing strong mitigation policies this year, shifting the world onto the better path: the net benefits would be of the order of $2.5 trillion. This figure will increase over time. This is not an estimate of net benefits occurring in this year, but a measure of the benefits that could flow from actions taken this year; many of the costs and benefits would be in the medium to long term.

* * *

[T]he analysis of the costs of climate change used in the Review all point to the desirability of strong action, given estimates of the costs of action on mitigation. But how much action? . . .

The current evidence suggests aiming for stabilisation somewhere within the range 450–550ppm CO2e. Anything higher would substantially increase the risks of very harmful impacts while reducing the expected costs of mitigation by comparatively little. Aiming for the lower end of this range would mean that the costs of mitigation would be likely to rise rapidly. Anything lower would certainly impose very high adjustment costs in the near term for small gains and might not even be feasible, not least because of past delays in taking strong action.

Uncertainty is an argument for a more, not less, demanding goal, because of the size of the adverse climate-change impacts in the worst-case scenarios.

* * *

Three elements of policy for mitigation are essential: a carbon price, technology policy, and the removal of barriers to behavioural change. Leaving out any one of these elements will significantly increase the costs of action.

* * *

The first element of policy is carbon pricing. Greenhouse gases are, in economic terms, an externality: those who produce greenhouse-gas emissions are bringing about climate change, thereby imposing costs on the world and on future generations, but they do not face the full consequences of their actions themselves.

Putting an appropriate price on carbon—explicitly through tax or trading, or implicitly through regulation—means that people are faced with the full social cost of their actions. This will lead individuals and businesses to switch away from high-carbon goods and services, and to invest in low-carbon alternatives. Economic efficiency points to the advantages of a common global carbon price: emissions reductions will then take place wherever they are cheapest.

* * *

The second element of climate-change policy is technology policy, covering the full spectrum from research and development, to demonstration and early stage deployment. The development and deployment of a wide range of low-carbon technologies is essential in achieving the deep cuts in emissions that are needed. The private sector plays the major role in R & D and technology diffusion, but closer collaboration between government and industry will further stimulate the development of a broad portfolio of low carbon technologies and reduce costs.

Many low-carbon technologies are currently more expensive than the fossil-fuel alternatives. But experience shows that the costs of technologies fall with scale and experience. . . .

Carbon pricing gives an incentive to invest in new technologies to reduce carbon; indeed, without it, there is little reason to make such investments. But investing in new lower-carbon technologies carries risks. Companies may worry that they will not have a market for their new product if carbon-pricing policy is not maintained into the future. And the knowledge gained from research and development is a public good; companies may under-invest in projects with a big social payoff if they fear they will be unable to capture the full benefits. Thus there are good economic reasons to promote new technology directly.

* * *

The third element is the removal of barriers to behavioural change. Even where measures to reduce emissions are cost-effective, there may be barriers preventing action. These include a lack of reliable information, transaction costs, and behavioural and organisational inertia. The impact of these barriers can be most clearly seen in the frequent failure to realise the potential for cost-effective energy efficiency measures.

Regulatory measures can play a powerful role in cutting through these complexities, and providing clarity and certainty. Minimum standards for buildings and appliances have proved a cost-effective way to improve performance, where price signals alone may be too muted to have a significant impact.

Information policies, including labelling and the sharing of best practice, can help consumers and businesses make sound decisions, and stimulate competitive markets for low-carbon and high-efficiency goods and services. Financing measures can also help, through overcoming possible constraints to paying the upfront cost of efficiency improvements.

Fostering a shared understanding of the nature of climate change, and its consequences, is critical in shaping behaviour, as well as in underpinning national and international action. Governments can be a catalyst for dialogue through evidence, education, persuasion and discussion. Educating those currently at school about climate change will help to shape and sustain future policy-making, and a broad public and international debate will support today's policy-makers in taking strong action now.

BRIDGING THE GAP—SECTORAL GREENHOUSE GAS EMISSION REDUCTION POTENTIALS IN 2030

KORNELIS BLOK, ANGÉLICA AFANADOR, DETLEF VAN VUUREN, ET AL.
The Emissions Gap Report 2017, Chapter 4 (UNEP 2017)

[*Eds.* In this UNEP Report, an international team of scientists evaluated various options for reducing global greenhouse gas emissions by 2030 to a level sufficient to meet the Paris Agreement goal of holding global warming to well below 2 degrees Celsius. The analysis focused on identifying emission reductions that would be "economically attractive from a social cost perspective." An economically attractive reduction was defined as one that could be achieved "at a marginal cost of no more than US$100/t$CO_2$e, at current prices." The analysis focused on six economic sectors—agriculture, buildings, energy, forestry, industry, and transport. The following excerpts present the authors' conclusions.]

[B]ased on proven technologies and relatively precautionary assumptions regarding potentials in 2030, [we conclude there is] a total emission reduction potential in 2030 of 33 GtCO2 e/year (uncertainty 30—36 GtCO2 e). . . .[This] estimated total potential . . . is sufficient to bridge the emissions gap in 2030 for 2°C (>66 percent chance) and 1.5°C (50 to 66 percent chance). It exceeds the estimated difference in 2030 between emissions under the current policy scenario and the emission levels consistent with a likely chance of staying below 2°C and a medium chance of staying below 1.5°C of about 17 and 22.5 GtCO2 e respectively, as indicated in the introduction to this chapter.

An important question is what the efforts and costs of realizing these emission reductions are. Although it is beyond the scope of the current chapter to answer this question in full, a number of observations can be made. It is remarkable that a large part of the potential consists of just six categories, that is, solar and wind energy, efficient appliances, efficient passenger cars, afforestation and stopping deforestation. These six categories sum up a potential of 18.5 GtCO2 e in 2030 (range: 15–22 GtCO2 e), making up more than half of the basic potential. Equally important, all these measures can be realized at modest cost, and are predominantly achievable through proven policies:

- *Solar photovoltaics and wind energy.* Many countries around the world have targets for renewable energy and have policies in place to stimulate its adoption. The most dominant policy instruments are feed-in tariffs or feed-in premiums, which have been implemented in 75 countries and 29 states or provinces in the world, providing long-term power purchase agreements with a specified price or premium price per kWh for a renewable energy technology. An instrument with increasing popularity is competitive bidding or auctioning, especially for large scale developments, where the renewable energy market is mature and governments have already achieved a degree of success with renewable installation through feed-in-tariffs. Costs of electricity from solar and wind electricity have already declined to levels comparable with fossil-fuel based electricity, and auctions have accelerated this trend. Continuation of feed-in policies and/ or a shift to auctions are a straightforward and cheap approach to rapid decarbonization of the power sector.

- *Energy efficient appliances and cars.* A combination of labelling and minimum energy performance standards are the dominant policies to stimulate the uptake of efficient appliances. Over 60 countries have adopted or pledged to adopt policies to shift to more energy-efficient lighting. Under the United for Efficiency (U4E) public-private-partnership,

UN Environment is supporting developing countries and emerging economies to move their markets to energy-efficient appliances and equipment. In terms of performance standards for cars, several countries have opted to implement fuel economy standards in miles per gallon or CO2 emission standards in gCO2 per km; these standards exist in Brazil, the EU, India, Japan, Mexico and the USA. Typically, energy efficiency standards are implemented in such a way that life-cycle costs are minimized, hence leading to net negative costs for the consumer. Similar policies are in place in many countries for new building construction. Further continuation of these policies, scaling them up to more countries while raising ambitions is a way forward to limit the growth of energy use and hence reducing emissions.

- *Stopping deforestation and restoration of degraded forests.* There are several examples of policies successfully stopping deforestation, the most largescale being the Brazilian 'Action Plan for Prevention and Control of Deforestation in the Amazon', consisting of (1) territorial and land-use planning, (2) environmental control and monitoring, and (3) fostering sustainable production activities. The programme led to a reduction of the rate of deforestation by more than 80 percent. Costs are found to be US$13/tCO2 e on average. For reforestation of degraded forests, the scale of operations is not of that size, but promising examples are available for China, Costa Rica, and the Republic of Korea. Costs are comparable with the costs of stopping deforestation.

These are examples of a few of the options that can be implemented at relatively low cost and based on significant existing experience. Together they represent more than half of the basic potential identified. Previous Emissions Gap Reports provide many more examples of scaling up of existing policies and programmes, as do other studies, including the study Green to Scale.

Although the available studies prevent an explicit, economic assessment of all emission reduction options, there is a relatively high degree of confidence that all options included [in this estimate] have costs below US$100/tCO2 e avoided. In many cases, this is explicit in the source documents. For some, however, it is not clear whether the costs will be below US$100/tCO2 e. For example, some electricity sources may show costs above US$100/tCO2 e, as there are large variations in costs (Lazard, 2016). However, given that there are abundant options in the electricity sector, leaving out these options will not affect the total potential.

ADAPTATION

U.S. ENVIRONMENTAL PROTECTION AGENCY
Climate Change—Health and Environmental Effects
http://www.epa.gov./climatechange/effects/adaptation.html (accessed Nov. 11, 2010)

The Intergovernmental Panel on Climate Change (IPCC) defines adaptation as the "adjustment in natural or human systems in response to actual or expected climatic stimuli or their effects, which moderates harm or exploits beneficial opportunities."

The extent of climate change impacts upon different ecosystems, regions and sectors of the economy will depend not only on the sensitivity of those systems to climate change, but also on the systems' ability to adapt to climate change.

* * *

All climate-sensitive systems of society and the natural environment, including agriculture, forestry, water resources, human health, coastal settlements, and natural ecosystems, will need to adapt to a changing climate or possibly face diminished productivity, functioning and health.

In unmanaged natural systems, adaptation is not planned but occurs when forced to do so. For example, as the climate warms, tree and animal species may migrate northward to remain in suitable climatic conditions and habitat (to the extent that human barriers, such as roads and cities, allow such migration).

In human society, much of adaptation may be planned and undertaken by private decision makers and by public agencies or governments. For humans, adaptation is a risk-management strategy that has costs and is not foolproof. The effectiveness of any specific adaptation requires consideration of the expected value of the avoided damages against the costs of implementing the adaptation strategy.

* * *

Furthermore, adaptive capacity is uneven across and within societies. There are individuals and groups within all societies that have insufficient capacity to adapt to climate change, and high adaptive capacity does not necessarily translate into actions that reduce vulnerability. For example, despite a high capacity to adapt to heat stress through relatively inexpensive adaptations, residents in urban areas in some parts of the world continue to experience high levels of mortality.

Regarding ecosystems, and on species diversity in particular, effects are expected to be negative at all but perhaps the lowest magnitudes of climate change because of the limited ability of natural systems to adapt. Although biological systems have an inherent capacity to adapt to changes in environmental conditions, given the rapid rate of projected climate change, adaptive capacity is likely to be exceeded for many species.

Furthermore, the ability of ecosystems to adapt to climate change is severely limited by the effects of urbanization, barriers to migration paths, and fragmentation of ecosystems, all of which have already critically stressed ecosystems independent of climate change itself.

Illustrative examples of potential adaptation measures in different sectors include the following:

Human Health

- Many diseases and health problems that may be exacerbated by climate change can be effectively prevented with adequate financial and human public health resources, including training, surveillance and emergency response, and prevention and control programs.
- Urban tree planting to moderate temperature increases
- Weather advisories to alert the public about dangerous heat conditions
- Grain storage, emergency feeding stations
- Adjusting clothing and activity levels, increasing fluid intake

Coastal Areas and Sea Level Rise

- Developing county-scale maps depicting which areas will require shore protection (e.g. dikes, bulkheads, beach nourishment) and which areas will be allowed to adapt naturally
- Analyzing the environmental consequences of shore protection
- Promoting shore protection techniques that do not destroy all habitat
- Identifying land use measures to ensure that wetlands migrate as sea level rises in some areas
- Engaging state and local governments in defining responses to sea level rise
- Improving early warning systems and flood hazard mapping for storms
- Protecting water supplies from contamination by saltwater

Agriculture and Forestry

- Altering the timing of planting dates to adapt to changing growing conditions

- Altering cropping mix and forest species that are better suited to the changing climatic conditions
- Breeding new plant species and crops that are more tolerant to changed climate condition
- Promoting fire suppression practices in the event of increased fire risk due to temperature increases
- Controlling insect outbreaks

Ecosystems and Wildlife

- Protecting and enhancing migration corridors to allow species to migrate as the climate changes
- Identifying management practices that will ensure the successful attainment of conservation and management goals
- Promoting management practices that confer resilience to the ecosystem

Water Resources

- Altering infrastructure or institutional arrangements
- Changing demand or reducing risk
- Improving water use efficiency, planning for alternative water sources (such as treated wastewater or desalinated seawater), and making changes to water allocation
- Conserving soil moisture through mulching and other means
- Protecting coastal freshwater resources from saltwater intrusion

Energy

- Increasing energy efficiency to offset increases in energy consumption due to warming
- Protecting facilities against extreme weather events
- Diversifying power supply in the event of power plant failures due to excess demand created by extreme heat, or by extreme weather events

DISCUSSION NOTES/QUESTIONS

1. The widespread consensus in the peer-reviewed and published scientific literature is that human activity is changing the concentration of greenhouse gases in the atmosphere, that this change is warming the planet, and that the resulting warming is causing significant changes in Earth's climate. This consensus view is reflected in IPCC Reports and in reports and statements by major scientific bodies in the United States, including the

National Academy of Sciences, the American Meteorological Society, the American Geophysical Union, and the American Association for the Advancement of Science. *See* Naomi Oreskes, *Beyond the Ivory Tower: The Scientific Consensus on Climate Change*, Science, Dec. 2004, at 1686.

Nonetheless, there continues to be a small, but vocal, group of skeptics who oppose taking action to mitigate climate change. Some of these skeptics question or deny the scientific evidence of global warming. Other skeptics accept the reality of climate change, but do not believe we know enough to forecast future consequences with any certainty. *See, e.g.*, Richard S. Lindzen, *The Climate Science Isn't Settled: Confident Predictions of Catastrophe Are Unwarranted*, Wall Street Journal Online Opinion Journal, Nov. 30, 2009. There also are some who acknowledge climate change, but who doubt that we should take steps to reduce greenhouse gas emissions, arguing that mitigation will be far too costly and that the money would be better spent on other pressing social needs (such as bringing clean water to impoverished villages in developing nations). *See, e.g.*, Bjorn Lomborg, Cool It (2007).

As a policy matter, how should the international community respond to uncertainty related to global climate change? Suppose the consensus view is that average mean temperatures will increase by 2–4.5 degrees Celsius if atmospheric greenhouse gas concentrations exceed 550 ppm CO2e, but that there is a 5% chance of catastrophic warming of ten degrees Celsius at that level, and also a 10% probability that warming will be no greater than 1 degree Celsius. Assuming we cannot know which of these possibilities will actually occur until we reach the future, what should our policy be for now? Should we take mitigation steps to ensure against the possibility of the worst outcomes, or should we hope for the best outcomes and spend our resources on other things? *See generally* Richard A. Posner, Catastrophe: Risk and Response (2004).

2. What about the argument that we have better things to spend our money on than stopping climate change? If you had a choice between spending a billion dollars to mitigate climate change for the benefit of future generations and spending a billion dollars to bring clean water to millions of people in Africa (thus saving hundreds of thousands of lives now), which would you choose? Is that a fair way to express the choice we face? If we do not act to mitigate climate change, will we necessarily use the money we save to fund clean water projects in developing countries?

If we do act to mitigate climate change, does that mean we can't fund clean water projects as well? As Richard Posner observes, it is a "fallacy . . . to think that we have a choice between only two policies": funding clean water projects or combatting climate change. "We can do both. We would just have to give up something else. If the something else . . . is a less valuable use of our resources, then giving it up" to achieve both clean water and climate-change mitigation "would be a good trade." *Id.* at 115.

3. UNEP's Emissions Gap Report 2017 calculated that we could reduce emissions by 33 GtCO2 e/year by 2030 using techniques that cost no more than

US$100/tCO2 e avoided. A back-of-the-envelope calculation yields a total yearly cost of meeting this target of $3.3 trillion, although this undoubtedly overstates the cost because much mitigation can be accomplished at a cost of much less than US$100/tCO2 e avoided. But even if you cut this figure in half—$1.65 trillion—it is still a very large figure. According to World Bank estimates, total global production in 2016 was $76 trillion. So meeting the target in the UNEP Report would cost the equivalent of 2% of the world's GDP at a price of US$50/tCO2 e avoided and more than 4% of world GDP at a price of US$100/tCO2 e avoided.

Is it worth it? That depends, obviously, on the amount of damage that will be caused if we fail to mitigate, the amount we will need to spend on adaptation to a changed climate, and the value one places on avoiding the very real risk that climate change will be more rapid and severe than we currently anticipate. Calculating the costs of NOT taking action is obviously important. In the Stern Report, Dr. Nicholas Stern argued that those costs would be equal to about 20% of world GDP by 2050. Others have calculated the costs of inaction at much lower levels. *See generally* John Carey, *Calculating the True Cost of Global Climate Change*, YaleEnvironment360 (January 6, 2011), https://e360.yale.edu/features/calculating_the_true_cost_of_global_climate_change (last accessed June 14, 2018); Dante Disparte, *If You Think Fighting Climate Change Will Be Expensive, Calculate the Cost of Letting It Happen,* Harv. Bus. Rev. (June 12, 2017); Solomon Hsiang, et al., *Estimating economic damage from climate change in the United States,* 356 Sci. 1362 (2017).

4. A related issue is how to compare the value of *future* benefits (from reduced climate change damage) against the cost of *present* action to mitigate climate change. If we spend a billion dollars today to avoid a billion dollars of damage in 50 years, is that a sensible expenditure? Most economists would say it is not—the future damages must be discounted to present value. But the choice of a discount rate matters greatly. Cass R. Sunstein & David A. Weisbach explain in *Climate Change and Discounting the Future: A Guide for the Perplexed,* Harvard Law School Program on Risk Regulation, Research Paper No. 08–12, p. 13 (2008):

> Suppose that we were going to invest $100 billion to reduce carbon emissions, producing a benefit in 100 years of $400 billion. This represents a rate of return of 1.4%, the discount rate used in the Stern Review. The positivists reason that if the market rate of return over that time period is 5.5% (the Nordhaus rate), the same $100 billion could be invested to produce over $21 *trillion* in 100 years, almost 53 times as much. Equivalently, we could give the future $400 billion dollars by investing about $2 billion at the market rate, keeping the remaining $98 million to spend on riotous living now. It does not make any sense, argue the positivists, to invest the $100 billion to reduce the effects of climate change under this hypothetical set of facts. To do so would be to throw away vast resources: either $98 billion today or more than $20 trillion in 100 years.

Thus, critics of the Stern Review argue that the discount rate he used to determine relative costs and benefits across time was artificially low and that the market rate should have been chosen.

However, not everyone finds this reasoning persuasive. Consider the comments of Julie Rehmeyer, in *'Discounting' the future cost of climate change: Economists develop new methods to quantify the trade-off between spending now and spending later,* ScienceNews Web edition (Friday, May 21st, 2010):

> Play this [i.e. discounting] out over many years, though, and the consequences are peculiar. For example, at a 5 percent annual interest rate, a penny that belonged to Julius Caesar would have expanded to the bogglingly huge sum of 3×10^{41} dollars today—more than the entire world economic output over the last 2,000 years multiplied by the number of stars in the sky. So the brutal arithmetic of discounting (at a 5 percent social discount rate) would shrink any imaginable catastrophe today to far less than a penny in Caesar's time, and an economist would have therefore recommended that Caesar not spend even so tiny an amount to avoid it.

There is a vast literature on this topic. *See, e.g.,* Frank Ackerman & Lisa Heinzerling, Priceless: On Knowing the Price of Everything and the Value of Nothing (2004); William D. Nordhaus, A Question of Balance (2008); Richard L. Revesz & Michael A. Livermore, Retaking Rationality: How Cost-Benefit Analysis Can Better Protect the Environment and Our Health (2008); Nicholas Stern, *The Economics of Climate Change,* 98 Am. Econ. Rev. 1 (2008); Partha Dasgupta, *Discounting Climate Change,* 36 J. Risk & Uncertainty (2008); Martin Weitzman, Why the Far-Distant Future Should be Discounted at its Lowest Possible Rate, 36 J. Envtl. Econ. & Mgmt. (2008).

5. Some countries will likely benefit from climate change. Russia and Canada, for example, might experience increased agricultural productivity and other benefits from a warmer climate. For other countries, such as the United States, the costs of adaptation to climate change might be much less than the costs of mitigation. Do those countries have any ethical or legal obligation to participate in mitigation efforts? How can they be induced to do so? For discussions of these and related questions, *see* Jonathan C. Carlson, *Reflections on a Problem of Climate Justice: Climate Change and the Rights of States in a Minimalist International Legal Order,* 18 Transnat'l L. & Contemp. Probs. 101 (2009); Eric A. Posner & Cass R. Sunstein, *Climate Change Justice,* 96 Geo. L. J. 1565 (2008); Daniel A. Farber, *The Case for Climate Compensation: Justice for Climate Change Victims in a Complex World,* 2008 Utah L. Rev. 377.

6. In an insightful paper, Francesco Bosello, Carlo Carraro, & Enrica De Cian examine several key differences between adaptation and mitigation as strategies to respond to climate change. *See* Challenge Paper: Climate Change, Adaptation (Copenhagen Consensus 2012). One significant difference is that the benefits of expenditures on adaptation to climate change will be realized by the local community where the expenditures are made. The benefits from expenditures on mitigation, on the other hand, will be realized globally.

A second difference is that adaptation measures are "immediately effective in reducing the damage" from climate change, whereas mitigation has an impact (if at all) only in the far future. A third difference is that mitigation, if it works, is a permanent solution. Adaptation is temporary and further adaptive steps may need to occur as climate change continues. Do these differences make adaptation or mitigation a better choice from a politician's point of view? What other factors should influence the decision about how much effort is devoted to adaptation and how much effort is devoted to mitigation?

7. Most scientists believe we are already committed to a level of climate change that will produce profound, harmful, and irreversible damage to Earth ecosystems, including ocean acidification (damaging coral reef ecosystems), mountain glacier loss (disrupting rivers and irrigation systems), shifts in precipitation patterns (extending drylands and deserts), and sea level rise (interfering with coastal human settlements). *See* UNEP, Climate Change Science Compendium 2009. What assistance should be provided to countries and peoples who cannot afford to take the steps necessary to adapt to these ecosystem changes? Is it relevant that the richer countries are, in general, responsible for the rise in atmospheric greenhouse gas concentrations that is warming the planet? Putting ethics aside, are there any prudential reasons for richer countries to assist poorer countries in adapting to climate change?

8. In a 2007 study, a dozen retired admirals and generals concluded that "[p]rojected climate change poses a serious threat to America's national security." Unlike most conventional security threats that involve a single entity acting in specific ways and points in time, climate change has the potential to result in multiple chronic conditions, occurring globally within the same time frame. Economic and environmental conditions in already fragile areas will further erode as food production declines, diseases increase, clean water becomes increasingly scarce, and large populations move in search of resources. Weakened and failing governments, with an already thin margin for survival, foster the conditions for internal conflicts, extremism, and movement toward increased authoritarianism and radical ideologies. *See* CNA Corporation, National Security and the Threat of Climate Change 6 (2007). A study that focused on abrupt climate change also warned of a heightened risk of external conflict and its implications for US geopolitical strategy:

> Nations with the resources to do so may build virtual fortresses around their countries, preserving resources for themselves. Less fortunate nations especially those with ancient enmities with their neighbors, may initiate in struggles for access to food, clean water, or energy. Unlikely alliances could be formed as defense priorities shift and the goal is resources for survival rather than religion, ideology, or national honor.

Peter Schwartz and Doug Randall, *An Abrupt Climate Change Scenario and Its Implications for United States National Security* 2, GBN Global Business Network (Oct. 2003), *available from the Defense Technical Information Center, Accession Number ADA469325.*

Do you agree with the recommendations of the CNA Corporation report: That national security and national defense strategies should consider the national security consequences of climate change? That "the U.S. should commit to a stronger national and international role to help stabilize climate change"? That "the U.S. should commit to global partnerships that help less developed nations build the capacity and resiliency to better manage climate impacts"?

There are an increasing number of studies linking climate change to conflict around the world. *See, e.g.,* Colin P. Kelley, et al., *Climate Change in the Fertile Crescent and implications of the recent Syrian drought,* 112 Proc. Nat'l Acad. Sci. 3241 (Mar 2015) (attributing Syrian civil war to displacement of people by unprecedented drought); U.S. Department of Defense, Report to the Senate Committee on Appropriations, *National Security Implications of Climate-Related Risks and a Changing Climate* 3 (23 July 2015) (concluding that "climate change is an urgent and growing threat to our national security, contributing to increased natural disasters, refugee flows, and conflicts over basic resources such as food and water.")

9. The Stern Review suggests that mitigating climate change will require putting a price on the carbon that is emitted into the atmosphere. There are a number of different ways to "put a price on carbon." One possibility is to impose a tax on carbon emissions. Such a tax could be imposed on the producers of fossil fuels (based, for example, on the carbon content of the products they sell). Or the consumers of the fuels could be taxed based, again, on the carbon content of the fuel they purchase.

An alternative way of pricing carbon is to create a "cap-and-trade system." Under a cap-and-trade system, an overall cap would be set on the amount of carbon that could be emitted by a certain group of emitters (e.g., utility companies that burn fossil fuels to produce electricity). Emitters would then be given (or purchase) licenses to emit a certain quantity of carbon. They could then trade those licenses. If the cap were set below current emission levels, emitters would need either to find a way to reduce emissions or to purchase the right to emit from other emitters. In that way a price would be set on carbon. A cap and trade system could be applied economy-wide or to a particular economic sector.

There are some key differences between carbon taxes and cap-and-trade systems. A carbon tax "provides price certainty." A carbon emitter "can calculate how much their emissions will cost them in taxes and take the appropriate abatement actions to reduce those costs." However, one cannot be certain about the impact of the tax on the level of emissions, as some polluters will choose to pay the tax rather than reduce emissions. A cap-and-trade system, on the other hand, guarantees a limit on emissions (the cap), but polluters can't be sure about the price they will have to pay to purchase the right to emit and that price may fluctuate in ways that make it difficult to plan.

Another difference is that a carbon tax would generate a considerable amount of revenue. That revenue could be used to lower taxes in countries where the tax is paid, to fund emissions-reduction efforts or research on emissions-reduction technologies, or to support abatement efforts. Even a cap-and-trade system that allocated emission permits by auction would be unlikely to generate the substantial revenue stream that a carbon tax would create.

But cap-and-trade systems are more common way to address the problem of GHG emissions. Although some nations have experimented with carbon taxes, they have not been seriously considered at the international level. The OECD suggests politics might be a reason for this. Not only are "taxes" generally unpopular in many places, but any system that is put in place will face challenges to its legitimacy from time to time. It may be easier for governments to maintain cap-and-trade systems because, once such systems are established, "a constituency progressively develops that has a clear interest in seeing the scheme continue—namely market holders and other market actors" who have invested in permits. The advantage of a tax system, on the other hand, is that it "generates government revenue and thus in principle provides scope to lower other taxes." *See generally* Organization for Economic Cooperation and Development, Climate Change Mitigation: What Do We Do? 18–21, Box 7.2 (2008).

10. There are other policies the international community could adopt that might help reduce emissions. For example, automobiles that are traded internationally are already subject to certain technical safety and design requirements established by international agreement. Should there also be international fuel efficiency standards for automobiles? For airplanes? International standards for power-plant emissions? Efficiency standards for home appliances?

11. The US has sponsored or participated in several multilateral initiatives aimed at promoting technological solutions to the GHG emissions problem. Those efforts include the International Partnership for a Hydrogen Economy; the Carbon Sequestration Leadership Forum; the Methane to Markets Partnership; the Generation IV Nuclear Forum; the International Thermonuclear Experimental Reactor; and the Asia-Pacific Partnership on Clean Development and Climate. Do you think that technology will permit us to achieve the necessary reductions in greenhouse gas emissions without reducing energy consumption, altering consumption patterns, or changing economic growth trajectories? If so, is there any reason to commit to reductions now, or should we wait until the needed technology is commercially available?

While new technological breakthroughs would certainly be welcome, many people believe that governments must do more than simply support and promote the development of new energy technologies. Unless there are incentives to use the new technology, private firms and individuals will continue to rely primarily on proven, and cheaper, fossil-fuel-based energy technologies. One way to create such incentives is to set a price on carbon emissions, as discussed in Note 9.

12. Altering global patterns of land use is also an important mitigation technique. Currently, carbon emissions from deforestation and the draining of

peaty wetlands are estimated to account for nearly 20% of global greenhouse gas emissions. Most, but not all, of this activity occurs in developing countries. Reducing deforestation is a relatively low-cost way to reduce global emissions, and it comes with other benefits such as protecting biodiversity.

13. Considering the various options discussed above, what kinds of cooperative international actions to address climate change would you support? Putting a price on carbon? If so, through taxes or cap-and-trade? Research into low-emissions technologies? Restrictions on land-use changes that lead to increased emissions or the creation of incentives for changes that reduce emissions and sequester carbon?

What are the chances that the U.S. and other nations would support your preferred approach to this problem?

B. THE CURRENT LEGAL FRAMEWORK OF CLIMATE GOVERNANCE

Transnational cooperation among scientists and scientific organizations is one of the earliest and best examples of civil society organizing itself across national borders to promote shared interests and advance human wellbeing. Citizen-scientists, cooperating privately but on an international basis, have been the catalyst for significant advances in inter-governmental cooperation on many important issues. The story of how climate change became a matter of international concern is illustrative.

For our purposes, this story begins in 1952, when the International Council of Scientific Unions (ICSU), a non-governmental organization, called upon the nations of the world to join in a coordinated, worldwide study of Earth's geophysical systems. The proposed period of scientific research and data-gathering, dubbed the International Geophysical Year (IGY), was planned for July 1, 1957 through December 31, 1958. A central theme of the IGY was international cooperation. The IGY organizing committee emphasized that "all observational data shall be available to scientists and scientific institutions in all countries," and scientists organized the creation of World Data Centers to serve as repositories of the data gathered during the event.

The United States participated enthusiastically in the IGY. Among the activities funded and promoted by the U.S. government were two that proved to be of particular importance to the study of climate and climate change. One project was the launch of a series of satellites (Explorers 1–5), the first satellites ever put into orbit by the United States. Although two launches failed, three succeeded, and the scientific value of orbiting satellites was convincingly demonstrated when the information gathered by the satellites led to the discovery of the radiation belts which circle the Earth. The second project of importance to the history of climate change was the U.S. Weather Bureau's sponsorship of the measurement of atmospheric carbon dioxide at the Mauna Loa observatory in Hawaii, which began in March 1958, right in the middle of the International Geophysical Year.

The success of the Explorer satellite program led the United States to launch the world's first weather satellite, TIROS-1, in April 1960. TIROS-1 was operational for only three months, but those were a "historic" three months for meteorology and climate science. The data gathered demonstrated the power of the satellite as a "global means of observing a global phenomenon" and "an ideal tool for the meteorological exploration of the earth."[24] The project changed weather forecasting forever. It also led directly to the first concerted international action on climate.

In late 1961, the United Nations General Assembly, noting that "advances in outer space" had opened an opportunity for significant progress "in meteorological science and technology," called upon the international community to cooperate in "weather research and analysis" with the hope that cooperative scientific study would "provide greater knowledge of basic physical forces affecting climate and the possibility of large-scale weather modification."[25] In response to the General Assembly's call to action, the World Meteorological Organization (WMO), a specialized agency of the UN, initiated two new programs. First, it launched World Weather Watch program in 1963. Then, in 1967, WMO partnered with the International Council of Scientific Unions to establish the Global Atmospheric Research Program (GARP).

At this time, of course, neither the General Assembly nor the WMO was concerned with climate change or its causes. Their interest reflected only the age-old human desire to better understand, predict and, if possible, control the weather. But the scientists engaged in climate research quickly found their focus shifting to the problem of human-induced climate change.

GARP addressed two major objectives: advancing the range of deterministic weather prediction and understanding the physical basis of climate. Although much GARP activity was highly relevant to climate research, the primary challenge of weather prediction absorbed most of the energies of GARP's participants. However, as the program neared its culmination with the Global Weather Experiment in 1979, the second objective acquired additional urgency. Deepening droughts and famines in Africa, unfavorable years in major world food producing regions, and collapse of the exceptionally productive South American fisheries revealed

[24] National Aeronautics and Space Administration, Technical Report R-131, Final Report on the TIROS I Meteorological Satellite System 6 (1962), available at https://ntrs.nasa.gov/archive/nasa/casi.ntrs.nasa.gov/19640007992.pdf (accessed on June 21, 2018).

[25] G.A. Res. 1721C (XVI), on international co-operation in the peaceful uses of outer space (20 Dec 1961).

global societal vulnerability to climate variability. At the same time, long-held concerns about the impact of human activities on global climate were heightened by measurements of increasing carbon dioxide concentrations and model predictions of significant climatic consequences. Discussions within the parent organizations of GARP, notably by a panel of experts of the WMO Executive Committee, led to the decision to hold the 1979 World Climate Conference.[26]

The 1979 Climate Conference was convened by the World Meteorological Organization in collaboration with several other UN specialized agencies as well as various nongovernmental scientific organizations. The meeting reviewed the emerging science on climate change and culminated with a resolution urging the "nations of the world" to continue to promote increased knowledge about Earth's climate and "to foresee and prevent potential man-made changes in climate that might be adverse to the well-being of humanity." Shortly after this First Climate Conference closed, WMO held its 8th World Meteorological Congress in Geneva. Responding to the findings of the Climate Conference, WMO established a World Climate Programme aimed at promoting the acquisition of climate data, facilitating climate research, and furthering the study of the impact of climate variation. At the same time, the ICSU Scientific Committee on Problems of the Environment was undertaking its own assessments of emerging climate science.[27]

Some years previously, in 1969, Charles Keeling had reported to the American Philosophical Society that his ongoing measurements of atmospheric carbon dioxide at Mauna Loa (originally begun during the International Geophysical Year) had established clearly that CO2 concentrations were on the rise and that fossil fuel combustion was the likely cause. He warned that this trend, if unchecked, created the potential for significant climate change in the 21st Century.[28] His analysis did not immediately attract widespread attention. But, as scientific understanding of the atmosphere and the climate improved, other scientists began to share Keeling's worries. The participants in a 1985 conference on atmospheric science in Villach, Austria forecast the likelihood of significant global temperature increases in the 21st century. They called for periodic assessments of climate science and urged the organizations that sponsored the conference (UNEP, WMO and ICSU) to be prepared to recommend international action to address climate change if the science showed it was necessary.[29] In *Our Common Future,* the 1987 Report of the World

---

26 Eric J. Barron, et al., A Decade of International Climate Research: The First Ten Years of the World Climate Research Program 1–2 (1992).

27 *See generally* John W. Zillman, *A History of Climate Activities,* 58(3) WMO Bulletin (2009).

28 *Id.*

29 Lester de Souza, *Villach Conference,* in *Encyclopedia of Global Warming and Climate Change* (S. George Philander, ed.), http://dx.doi.org/10.4135/9781412963893.n696 (last viewed June 21, 2018).

Commission on Environment and Development (the Brundtland Commission), the findings of the Villach Conference were cited in support of the recommendations with respect to climate change. Specifically, the Commission called for:

- Improved monitoring and assessment of the evolving phenomena;
- Increased research to improve knowledge about the origins, mechanisms, and effects of the phenomena;
- The development of internationally agreed policies for the reduction of the causative gases; and
- Adoption of strategies needed to minimize damage and cope with the climate changes, and rising sea level.[30]

In 1988, responding to the growing international concern, the WMO and UNEP jointly established an Intergovernmental Panel on Climate Change (IPCC).[31] The mandate given to the IPCC was to (i) assess the scientific information on climate change and its "environmental and socio-economic consequences" and (ii) formulate "realistic response strategies." Although IPCC was established expressly as an *intergovernmental* organization, most of its work is done by scientists, many of whom participate "in their own right" and not as national representatives or political appointees.[32]

In August, 1990, IPCC completed its first assessment and issued a lengthy report which concluded, among other things, that "emissions from human activities are substantially increasing the atmospheric concentrations of the greenhouse gases," and that those increases would result "in an additional warming of the Earth's surface." The assessment also predicted, although with a high degree of uncertainty, significant adverse impacts on agriculture, natural ecosystems (both terrestrial and oceanic), freshwater availability, and human settlements (especially those vulnerable to flooding or sea level rise).[33]

---

[30] Report of the World Commission on Environment and Development: Our Common Future, chapter 7, ¶ 24 (1987).

[31] *Resolution on the Intergovernmental Panel on Climate Change,* Resolution 4 (EC-XL) of the Fortieth Session of the Executive Council of the World Meteorological Organization (June 7–16, 1988). Membership in the IPCC is open to all WMO and UN Member countries.

[32] National representatives to the IPCC are the appointed representatives of sovereign governments. They may be scientists with expertise in some area of IPCC work, but they need not be. The IPCC's assessments and reports, however, are prepared by scientists and subject to peer review by expert scientists as well as review by governments. Although governments may nominate experts to serve in the assessment process, most scientists serving the IPCC are invited "in their own right" (i.e. not as national representatives) to contribute to the IPCC's work. *See* Principles Governing IPCC Work, adopted by the IPCC at its Fourteenth Session (Vienna 1–3 October 1998) and amended in 2003, 2006, 2012, and 2013.

[33] IPCC First Assessment Report, Overview (1990).

The IPCC's assessment was met with a quick response. Two months after the IPCC released its assessment, scientists meeting at the Second World Climate Conference in Geneva called upon governments to take strong action to reduce greenhouse gas emissions and enhance greenhouse gas sinks. However, the heads of government and governmental ministers participating in the conference were not prepared to commit immediately to serious action. They did, however, call for the negotiation of a treaty on climate change. On December 21, 1990, the United Nations General Assembly established an Intergovernmental Negotiating Committee (INC), open to all UN Members, and charged it with responsibility to prepare "an effective framework convention on climate change."[34] Less than two years later, in May 1992, the INC reached agreement on the text of the United Nations Framework Convention on Climate Change (UNFCCC). One month later, the UNFCCC was signed by 144 countries at the Rio Conference on Environment and Development.

We tell this story for two reasons. First, it illustrates the central role played by science and scientists in the development of international law in the environmental arena. Scientists were first to understand that climate change posed a threat to human wellbeing, and scientists were first to call for cooperative international action to address it. Scientific knowledge has been, and will be, vital to the identification of solutions to the problem.

Second, the story of how climate change became an international issue illustrates the significant role that transnational civil society plays in the modern international system. The International Geophysical Year, a milestone in global scientific cooperation, was initiated by the International Council of Scientific Unions (ICSU), a nongovernmental organization.[35] Some of the most important subsequent initiatives and events related to climate change were the product of partnerships between ICSU and various specialized agencies of the United Nations. The modes by which civil society operates—for example, through meetings at scientific conferences—lack the formality and regularity that characterize many governmental interactions on the international stage. But such informal cooperation among civil society actors has proven to be a valuable means to transmit information and build consensus on the international level, thus helping pave the way toward the adoption of formal and binding instruments of international environmental policy.

We turn now to those formal and binding instruments. There are three. The first to be adopted was the just-mentioned 1992 United Nations Framework Convention on Climate Change [UNFCCC] **(Basic Document 2.4)**, which entered into force in 1994 and, at this writing, boasts over 190 State Parties. The UNFCCC was quickly followed by the 1997 Kyoto

[34] G.A. Res. 45/212, Protection of global climate for present and future generations of mankind (Dec. 21, 1990).

[35] ICSU is today known as the International Council for Science.

Protocol. The Kyoto Protocol entered into force in 2005 and imposed emissions-reduction obligations that were in effect from 2008–2012.[36] In 2015, the Parties to the UNFCCC adopted the Paris Agreement, which takes a radically new "choose your own adventure" approach to reducing GHG emissions. The Paris Agreement entered into force in November 2016, and has 186 Parties at this writing (July 2019).

1. UNITED NATIONS FRAMEWORK CONVENTION ON CLIMATE CHANGE (UNFCCC)

The UNFCCC was modelled on previous framework treaties aimed at pollution control, including the 1979 Convention on Long-range Transboundary Air Pollution (discussed in Chapter 3, *supra*) and the 1985 Vienna Convention for the Protection of the Ozone Layer (1985) (discussed in Chapter 5, *infra*). As a framework treaty, the UNFCCC did not impose specific GHG-emissions-reduction obligations on any of its parties. However, it did include a means for the adoption of subsequent agreements if stronger action were deemed necessary "to prevent dangerous anthropogenic interference with the climate system." The objective of the treaty and agreed principles of action were expressed in Articles 2 and 3.

> Article 2: Objective
>
> The ultimate objective of this Convention and any related legal instruments . . . is to achieve . . . stabilization of greenhouse gas concentrations in the atmosphere at a level that would prevent dangerous anthropogenic interference with the climate system. Such a level should be achieved within a time-frame sufficient to allow ecosystems to adapt naturally to climate change, to ensure that food production is not threatened and to enable economic development to proceed in a sustainable way.
>
> Article 3: Principles
>
> In their actions to achieve the objective of the Convention and to implement its provisions, the Parties shall be guided, *inter alia,* by the following:
>
> 1. The Parties should protect the climate system for the benefit of present and future generations of humankind, on the basis of equity and in accordance with their common but differentiated responsibilities and respective capabilities. Accordingly the developed country Parties should take the lead in combating climate change and the adverse effects thereof.

[36] The so-called Doha Amendment to the Kyoto Protocol was adopted in 2012. It seeks to extend and strengthen the emissions-reduction commitments of the Protocol. As of this writing, the Doha Amendment has not entered into force, and it seems unlikely that it will ever do so.

2. The specific needs and special circumstances of developing country Parties, especially those that are particularly vulnerable to the adverse effects of climate change, and of those Parties, especially developing country Parties, that would have to bear a disproportionate or abnormal burden under the Convention, should be given full consideration.

3. The Parties should take precautionary measures to anticipate, prevent or minimize the causes of climate change and mitigate its adverse effects. Where there are threats of serious or irreversible damage, lack of full scientific certainty should not be used as a reason for postponing such measures, taking into account that policies and measures to deal with climate change should be cost-effective so as to ensure global benefits at the lowest possible cost. To achieve this, such policies and measures should take into account different socio-economic contexts, be comprehensive, cover all relevant sources, sinks and reservoirs of greenhouse gases and adaptation, and comprise all economic sectors. Efforts to address climate change may be carried out cooperatively by interested Parties.

4. The Parties have a right to, and should, promote sustainable development. Policies and measures to protect the climate system against human-induced change should be appropriate for the specific conditions of each Party and should be integrated with national development programmes, taking into account that economic development is essential for adopting measures to address climate change.

5. The Parties should cooperate to promote a supportive and open international economic system that would lead to sustainable economic growth and development in all Parties, particularly developing country Parties, thus enabling them better to address the problems of climate change. Measures taken to combat climate change, including unilateral ones, should not constitute a means of arbitrary or unjustifiable discrimination or a disguised restriction on international trade.

Obligations under the Framework Convention

The Framework Convention divides countries into three different groups: "Annex I Parties," "Annex II Parties," and "non-Annex I Parties." The Annex I Parties (i.e. the Parties listed in Annex I of the Convention) are drawn from two groups of industrialized nations. Annex I includes countries that were members of the Organization for Economic Cooperation and Development (OECD) at the time the UNFCCC was adopted. It also includes several European states, including Russia, that were formerly part of the Soviet bloc.[37] These states are sometimes referred to as the EIT or economies-in-transition group. The "non-Annex I Parties." Roughly speaking, then, one might say that Annex I Parties are the industrialized nations, non-Annex I Parties are developing nations, and Annex II Parties are a relatively rich subset of industrialized nations.

All Parties (Annex I and non-Annex I) have several basic obligations under the Convention. Those basic obligations, as summarized by the Convention's secretariat, are as follows:

> They agree to compile an inventory of their greenhouse gas emissions, and submit reports—known as national communications—on actions they are taking to implement the Convention. To focus such actions, they must prepare national programmes containing:
>
> - Climate change mitigation measures, i.e. measures to control GHG emissions
> - Provisions for developing and transferring environmentally friendly technologies
> - Provisions for sustainably managing carbon "sinks" (a term applied to forests and other ecosystems that can remove more greenhouse gases from the atmosphere than they emit)
> - Preparations to adapt to climate change
> - Plans for climate research, observation of the global climate system and data exchange
> - Plans to promote education, training and public awareness relating to climate change.[38]

In addition to these basic obligations, each Annex I Party committed specifically to adopt national measures "limiting its anthropogenic emissions of greenhouse gases and protecting and enhancing its greenhouse gas sinks and reservoirs." Though no particular emissions limitations were identified, the Convention says that Annex I Parties actions should "demonstrate that developed countries are taking the lead in modifying longer-term trends in anthropogenic emissions." Their "aim"

---

[37] This description of the countries included in Annex I and Annex II is somewhat overgeneralized, and the Annexes must be read to determine their exact composition. For example, Monaco is an Annex I country, although it is neither a former Soviet bloc country nor a member of the OECD. Turkey is an OECD member, but it was deleted from Annex II by an amendment to the Convention that entered into force in 2002. Several countries that joined the OECD after 1992 are included in Annex I but not in Annex II.

[38] Secretariat of the United Nations Framework Convention on Climate Change, Uniting on Climate: A Guide to the Climate Change Convention and the Kyoto Protocol 17 (2007).

should be to return "individually or jointly" to 1990 levels of emissions.[39] Annex I Parties also have enhanced reporting obligations.[40]

The Annex II Parties (the richer developing nations) have several financial commitments. They are obligated to "provide new and additional financial resources" to meet the "agreed full incremental costs" incurred by developing country Parties" in fulfilling their obligations under the Convention. They also are obligated to "assist the developing countries that are particularly vulnerable to the adverse effects of climate change" in adapting to those effects. Finally, they "shall take all practicable steps to promote, facilitate and finance" access by developing countries to "environmentally sound technologies."[41]

The flip side of this financial commitment by the richer developed countries is a qualification on the commitments of developing countries if the rich countries don't fulfil their financial obligations. Article 4, paragraph 7 of the Convention specifies that "the extent to which developing country Parties will effectively implement their commitments" depends on whether developed country Parties meet their financial and technology-transfer obligations. The Parties also agree that special solicitude is required to meet the needs of Parties that are especially vulnerable to climate change as well as the needs of the least developed countries.[42]

Institutional Structure

Article 7 of the Convention establishes a "Conference of the Parties" (COP) as the "supreme body of this Convention." The Conference of the Parties is nothing more than the yearly meeting of all the Parties to the Convention.[43] When acting as the COP, the Parties "may adopt, and shall make, within [the COP's] mandate, the decisions necessary to promote the effective implementation of the Convention." Article 7 contains a lengthy list of items that are within the COP's mandate, including assessing the effect of measures taken under the Convention, reporting on the implementation of the Convention and making related recommendations, establishing subsidiary bodies in addition to those established by the Convention itself, and "seek[ing] to mobilize financial resources." But the COP cannot, by its own action, alter or add to any of the substantive obligations under the Convention.

The Convention establishes two subsidiary bodies. The Subsidiary Body for Scientific and Technological Advice (SBSTA) is charged with

---

39 Framework Convention **(Basic Document 2.4)**, article 4(2).

40 *Id.*, article 12(2), (5).

41 *Id.*, article 4(3).

42 *Id.*, article 4(8)–(10).

43 Extraordinary sessions of the COP may be held at other times, and the COP itself may change the schedule of its regular meetings. Framework Convention, article 7(4)–(5).

providing the COP with "timely information and advice on scientific and technological matters relating to the Convention."[44] The Subsidiary Body for Implementation (SBI) "assists" the COP in "the assessment and review of the effective implementation of the Convention." The subsidiary bodies generally meet twice a year.

In addition to the Convention-established subsidiary bodies, the COP itself has constituted a number of committees and other groups to work on such matters as adaptation, financing, capacity-building, and compliance. The Convention also establishes a Secretariat (a group of international civil servants) which provides technical and administrative assistance to the COP and the other bodies established under the Convention. The Secretariat is headquartered in Bonn, Germany.

The Kyoto Protocol and the Paris Agreement each have organizational structures that, in effect, piggyback on the structure already created by the Convention. Thus, the Kyoto Protocol's supreme body is the CMP—the "Conference of the Parties serving as the meeting of the Parties to the Kyoto Protocol." The Paris Agreement's supreme body is the CMA—the "Conference of the Parties serving as the meeting of the Parties to the Paris Agreement." The subsidiary bodies of the Convention also serve as subsidiary bodies for the CMP and the CMA. The Convention Secretariat likewise provides secretariat services to the CMP and the CMA.

Finally, the COP, the CMA and the CMP have established a Bureau to make decisions regarding management of the process of intergovernmental engagement under all three agreements. The members of the Bureau are representatives of Parties and are elected from each of the five United Nations regional groups as well as the group of Small Island Developing States. Among other things, the Bureau examines the credentials of representatives of Parties prior to meetings and reports to the Conference on intergovernmental organizations and nongovernmental organizations that wish to attend Convention meetings.

Protocols and amendments

The Parties to the Framework Convention contemplated that its general obligations would be supplemented by more specific obligations if analysis of the climate change problem indicated that further action was required. Article 17 of the Convention thus authorizes the Conference of the Parties to adopt protocols to the Convention. As a legal matter, such a protocol is separate treaty from the Convention. Adoption of a protocol by the COP does not make the protocol binding on any particular State. Rather, to be bound to a protocol, individual States must accept the protocol as binding. In addition, each adopted protocol must establish the terms

[44] Framework Convention, article 9.

under which it will enter into force (e.g., the number of ratifications required before it will be given legal effect).

The Convention can be amended. Amendments to the Convention text should be adopted by consensus but can, if a consensus cannot be achieved, be adopted by a three-quarters majority vote of the Parties "present and voting" at the meeting. Three-quarters of the Parties must ratify the amendment for it to enter into force. An amendment does not bind any party that does not ratify it.

Annexes may also be amended. The process for adoption of annex amendments is similar to the process for adoption of amendments to the Convention. But amendments to the annexes enter into force automatically except for Parties that communicate their non-acceptance of the amendment within six months of receiving notice of its adoption.

DISCUSSION NOTES/QUESTIONS

1. Why did the World Meteorological Organization and UNEP decide to create the Intergovernmental Panel on Climate Change? What are the advantages to having an intergovernmental body review and report on the science (as opposed to, for example, simply relying on the unmediated reports of scientists and scientific organizations)? What are the disadvantages?

2. Do you agree with the principles set out in Article 3 of the Framework Convention? What is your reaction to the way in which the Convention implements the principle of common-but-differentiated responsibilities? Do you agree with the special obligations placed on developed countries? With the various efforts made to limit the obligations of developing countries?

3. The emissions-reduction obligation imposed on developed countries by Article 4(2) of the Convention is arguably quite a "soft" obligation. No specific emissions-reduction requirements are imposed. Instead, developed nations are to take the lead in "modifying longer-term trends" in emissions. That doesn't necessarily mean reducing emissions; it could mean reducing the rate of increase in emissions. And, moreover, the obligation is qualified by the statement that actions should be "consistent with the objective of the Convention." That objective is to "prevent dangerous anthropogenic interference with the climate system" in a "time-frame sufficient" to allow adaptation. This raises the questions (to which different countries will have different answers) of what level of climate change might be "dangerous," whether adaptation is a realistic response to even very significant climate change, and in what time frame significant emissions reduction is needed to allow effective adaptation to changes. If a country concluded that accomplishment of the objective of the Convention did not require dramatic reductions in emissions of greenhouse gases, that country would presumably conclude that not much would be required of it to satisfy its Article 4 obligation.

However, consider the precautionary principle expressed in Article 2(3). Does that obligate countries to assume that the worst will happen if emissions continue to rise?

4. With the Kyoto Protocol (discussed in the next session), the Parties to the Convention sought to achieve the goal (expressed in Article 4 of the Convention) of returning the GHG emissions of the developed countries to their 1990 levels. The United States refused to ratify the Kyoto Protocol or to participate in any other binding emissions-reduction effort. The official reasons given by the U.S. for not ratifying the Kyoto Protocol were (a) that it would be ineffective because it did not require developing countries to cap their greenhouse gas emissions, (b) that adherence to the emission restrictions in the Protocol would cause too much economic harm to the United States, and (c) that climate science was too uncertain to warrant taking economically harmful mitigation measures. How do you evaluate these arguments in light of the Framework Convention, which the US has ratified? Do you think the United States violated its obligations under Article 4(2) of the Convention by refusing to ratify the Kyoto Protocol? What if the United States was taking other actions to reduce emissions—such as encouraging energy efficiency and a wider use of renewable energy resources?

5. Why is it easier to amend an annex than to amend the Convention or to adopt an enforceable protocol? Should the opt-out process used for amendments of the annexes be extended to include the amendment of the Convention or the adoption of enforceable protocols? That is to say, should the COP be empowered to adopt protocols that bind all members by a three-quarters vote, subject to the right of each country to opt out of the new obligation within six months after its adoption? Or do you favor continuing to require ratification by members as a prerequisite to entry into force of protocols and amendments to the Convention text?

2. THE KYOTO PROTOCOL

The second international treaty on this subject, the 1997 Kyoto Protocol **(Basic Document 2.5)** to the UNFCCC, was the answer to the UNFCCC's lack of regulatory mechanisms. Entered into force in 2005, it is, expressly, a regulatory agreement. Its goal is to reduce greenhouse gas emissions by industrialized nations (the so-called "Annex I" parties), and at this writing over 160 countries are party to it. The United States and Canada (which withdrew from the Protocol in 2011) are the only industrialized nations not among them.

UNITING ON CLIMATE: A GUIDE TO THE CLIMATE CHANGE CONVENTION AND THE KYOTO PROTOCOL

SECRETARIAT OF THE UNITED NATIONS FRAMEWORK CONVENTION ON CLIMATE CHANGE 12, 27–29, 31–32, 35 (2007)

Even as they adopted the [Framework] Convention . . ., governments were aware that its provisions would not be sufficient by themselves to tackle climate change in all its aspects. At the first Conference of the Parties (COP 1), held in Berlin, Germany in early 1995, a new round of talks was launched to discuss firmer, more detailed commitments for industrialized countries, a decision known as the Berlin Mandate.

THE KYOTO PROTOCOL EVOLVES

In December 1997, after two and a half years of intensive negotiations, a substantial extension to the Convention that outlined legally binding commitments to emissions cuts was adopted at COP 3 in Kyoto, Japan. This Kyoto Protocol sketched out basic rules, but did not specify in detail how they were to be applied. It also required a separate, formal process of signature and ratification by governments before it could enter into force.

A fresh round of negotiations launched in Buenos Aires, Argentina at COP 4 in November 1998 linked negotiations on the Protocol's rules to implementation issues—such as finance and technology transfer—under the umbrella of the Convention. In July 2001. Governments struck a political deal—the Bonn Agreements—signing off the controversial aspects of the Buenos Aires Plan of Action. A third report from the IPCC, meanwhile, improved the climate for negotiations by offering the most compelling scientific evidence so far presented, of a warming world.

At COP 7, held a few months later in Marrakesh, Morocco, negotiators built on the Bonn Agreements and brought a major negotiating cycle to a close by adopting a broad package of decisions. The Marrakesh Accords spelt out more detailed rules for the Protocol as well as advanced prescriptions for implementing the Convention and its rules. These rules were further elaborated by subsequent decisions at COP 8, 9 and 10.

The Protocol could only enter into force after at least 55 Parties to the Convention had ratified it, including enough industrialized countries listed in the Convention's Annex I to encompass 55 per cent of that group's carbon dioxide emissions in 1990. The first Parties ratified the Protocol in 1998. With the ratification by the Russian Federation on 18 November 2004, the prescribed 90-day countdown was set in motion: The Kyoto Protocol entered into force on 16 February 2005.

* * *

EMISSION TARGETS AND ASSIGNED AMOUNTS

At the heart of the Protocol lie its legally binding emissions targets for Annex I Parties. These targets are listed in Annex B to the Protocol, which lists GHG reduction or limitation targets for 38 developed countries and for the European Community as a whole. The 15 member States of the European Community (prior to the EU expansion to 25 states in May 2004) agreed to redistribute their reduction targets among themselves, forming the so-called "EU bubble."

Annex B emission targets are set relative to each Party's GHG emissions in a specific reference year, called the base year. For most Parties, the base year is 1990. However, some EIT Parties, have another base year. In addition, any Party may choose a base year of either 1990 or 1995 for its emissions of HFCs, PFCs and SF6. . . . The emission target covers the six GHGs from sources and sectors listed in Annex A of the Protocol. Annex A excludes emissions and removals from the LULUCF sector,[45] which are treated differently than emissions from the other sectors.

The Protocol establishes a specific time frame, called the commitment period, for achieving emission targets. A five-year period was preferred to a single target year as a way to smooth out annual fluctuations in emissions arising from unforeseen factors such as economic cycles or weather patterns. During the commitment period, each Annex I Party must ensure that its total GHG emissions from Annex A sources do not exceed its allowable level of emissions. The allowable level of emissions is called the Party's assigned amount. For the first commitment period (2008–2012), the assigned amount of each Party is calculated by multiplying the Party's base year GHG emissions from Annex A, by its emission target, by five (for the five years of the commitment period.) The resulting quantity is denominated in individual units called assigned amount units or AAUs. Each AAU represents an allowance to emit one metric tonne of carbon dioxide equivalent over the commitment period.

Unlike other multilateral environmental agreements, the Kyoto Protocol allows Annex I Parties to change the level of their allowed emissions over the commitment period through participation in the Kyoto Protocol mechanisms and enhancement of carbon sinks. Through these activities, Parties may generate or acquire additional emission allowances, which are then added to the Party's assigned amount. Each of the mechanisms, and sink activities have a specific emission allowance associated with it, which are collectively referred to as Kyoto Protocol units and are subject to explicit rules for how they can be used.

---

[45] LULUCF means "land use, land-use change, and forestry."

THE KYOTO MECHANISMS

The Kyoto Protocol broke new ground with three innovative mechanisms (joint implementation, the clean development mechanism and emissions trading) designed to boost the cost-effectiveness of climate change mitigation by opening ways for Parties to cut emissions, or enhance carbon "sinks," more cheaply abroad than at home. Although the cost of limiting emissions or expanding removals varies greatly from region to region, the effect for the atmosphere is the same regardless where the action is taken. Even so, concerns have been voiced that the mechanisms could allow Parties to avoid taking climate change mitigation action at home, or could confer a "right to emit" on Annex I Parties or lead to exchanges of fictitious credits, undermining the Protocol's environmental goals. The Marrakesh Accords sought to dispel such fears, asserting that the Protocol creates no "right, title or entitlement" to emit. They call on Annex I Parties to implement domestic action to reduce emissions in ways that could help to narrow per capita differences between developed and developing countries, while pursuing the Convention's ultimate objective.

The Marrakesh Accords imposed no quantitative limits on the extent to which the mechanisms could be used to meet emissions targets. Annex I Parties were obliged, however, to provide information in their national communication showing that their use of the mechanisms is "supplemental to domestic action" and that domestic policies and measures constitute "a significant element" of efforts to meet commitments.

To be eligible to participate in the mechanisms, Annex I Parties must have ratified the Kyoto Protocol and must meet specific eligibility criteria, based on the methodological and reporting requirements related to GHG inventories and tracking of assigned amounts. These eligibility criteria help to ensure that an Annex I Party is accounting accurately for its emissions and assigned amount, so that use of the Kyoto mechanisms will not jeopardize the Party's ability to meet its emission commitment. Each Party's eligibility to participate in each of the Kyoto mechanisms will be determined as a normal outcome of reporting, review and compliance procedures under the Protocol.

Kyoto Protocol units acquired from another Party under the Kyoto mechanisms are added to an Annex I Party's assigned amount, whereas units transferred to another Annex I Party are subtracted from the Annex I Party's assigned amount.

THE CLEAN DEVELOPMENT MECHANISM (CDM)

The CDM is a mechanism by which Annex I Parties can invest in emission reduction projects or afforestation or reforestation projects in developing countries and receive credit for the emission reductions or removals achieved. These projects contribute to sustainable development of the host country and generate emission allowances, called certified emission reductions (CERs) that can be used by the Annex I Party in meeting its emission target.

Investments in CDM projects are to be additional to the finance and technology transfer commitments of Annex II Parties under the Convention and the Kyoto Protocol and must not result in a diversion of official development assistance. The CDM is generating significant investment in developing countries, especially from the private sector, to enhance the transfer of environmentally friendly technologies and thus promote their sustainable development. Already, the CDM has resulted in a significant flow of resources to developing countries. The World Bank estimates that as of the third quarter of 2006, almost US$5.2 billion has been invested through the CDM.

CDM projects must have the approval of all Parties involved. This must be gained from designated national authorities set up by Annex I and non-Annex I Parties. Projects must lead to real, measurable and long-term climate benefits in the form of emission reductions or removals that are additional to any that would have occurred without the project. To demonstrate this, CDM projects must meet detailed requirements and procedures for registration, validation, verification, and certification to demonstrate that reductions or removals associated with the project are additional to what would otherwise occur in the absence of the project. The emission reductions or removals resulting from a CDM project must be calculated and monitored according to specific methodologies, including for project baselines (the starting point for measuring emissions and removals), and verified by designated operational entities.

Additional rules apply to afforestation and reforestation projects, which generate two special types of CERs called temporary certified emission reductions (tCERs) and long-term certified emission reductions (lCERs). Annex I Parties are limited in how much they may use CERs from such "sink" activities towards their targets—up to 1 per cent of the Party's emissions in its base year, for each of the five years of the commitment period.

* * *

JOINT IMPLEMENTATION

Joint implementation is also a project-based mechanism. It allows Annex I Parties to implement projects that reduce emissions, or increase removals using sinks, in other Annex I countries. Emission reduction units (ERUs) generated by such projects can then be used by investor Annex I Parties to help meet their emissions targets. To avoid double counting, a corresponding subtraction is made from the host Party's assigned amount.

The term "joint implementation" is convenient shorthand for this mechanism, although it does not appear in the Kyoto Protocol. In practice, joint implementation projects are most likely to take place in EIT countries, where there is generally more scope for cutting emissions at lower costs. Joint implementation projects must have the approval of all Parties involved and must lead to emission reductions or removals that are additional to any that would have occurred without the project. Projects such as reforestation schemes involving activities in the LULUCF sector must conform to the Protocol's wider rules on this sector and Annex I Parties are to refrain from using ERUs generated from nuclear facilities to meet their targets. Only projects starting from the year 2000 that meet these rules may be listed.

There are two approaches for verification of emission reductions under JI, commonly called "track one" and "track two." Under track one, a host Party that meets all eligibility requirements may verify its own JI projects and issue ERUs for the resulting emission reductions or removals. Annex I Parties operating under track one are required to inform the secretariat of their national guidelines and procedures for approving these projects and to make information about each project publicly available.

The eligibility requirements for track two are less strict than those for track one, and are thus applicable for host Parties that do not meet the eligibility requirements for track one. Under track two, each JI project is subject to verification procedures established under the supervision of the Joint Implementation Supervisory Committee (JISC). . . .

Track two procedures are similar to that of the CDM, in that each project must be reviewed by an accredited independent entity to determine whether the project meets the requirements. The emission reductions or removals resulting from the project must also be verified by an independent entity, accredited by the JISC, in order for the Party concerned to issue ERUs. Each project must adhere to strict monitoring requirements, and use approved methodologies for calculation the project baseline and the associated emission reductions or removals.

* * *

EMISSIONS TRADING

Emissions trading enables Annex I Parties to acquire AAUs from other Annex I Parties that are able to more easily reduce emissions. It enables Parties to pursue cheaper opportunities to curb emissions or increase removals wherever those opportunities exist, in order to reduce the overall cost of mitigating climate change.

Annex I Parties may also acquire, from other Annex I Parties, CERs from CDM projects, ERUs from joint implementation projects, or RMUs from sink activities. To answer concerns that some Parties could "oversell" and then be unable to meet their own targets, each Annex I Party is required to hold a minimum level of credits at all times. . . .

Annex I Parties may choose to implement domestic or regional systems under which legal entities, such as industrial or power plants that are subject to GHG controls, can trade emission allowances and credits. Although the Kyoto Protocol does not address domestic or regional emissions trading, it provides an umbrella under which national and regional trading systems operate, in that the entity-level trading uses Kyoto Protocol units and needs to be reflected in the Kyoto Protocol accounting. Any transfer of units between entities in different Parties under domestic or regional trading systems is also subject to Kyoto Protocol rules. The emissions trading scheme (ETS) of the European Union is one example of a regional trading system, operating under the Kyoto Protocol umbrella.

THE INTERNATIONAL CARBON MARKET

The implementation of the Kyoto Protocol has stimulated the development of national and regional ghg emission trading systems, as well as the emergence of multiple organizations and tools to facilitate the trading of emission allowances and credits. Even countries that are not Party to the Kyoto Protocol are seeing the emergence of emission crediting services and voluntary trading systems. Collectively, these trading systems, and the organization and tools that support it, are referred to as "carbon markets," in that the standard unit for measuring GHG emission allowances under the Kyoto Protocol is one tonne of carbon dioxide equivalent.

At the center of the international carbon market are the companies that are subject to GHG controls imposed by Parties to meet their Kyoto Protocol targets, or that anticipate future GHG controls. These companies are the end-users of emission allowances and credits, and as such, drive the overall volume and price of trades. But there are many other players in the carbon market: companies that verify and certify emission credits under the CDM, JI and the various voluntary offset programmes; trading exchanges, such as the European Climate Exchange and the Chicago Climate Exchange, which provide platforms for trading of emissions allowances and credits; and a whole host of brokerages, advisors and analysts to help companies find and manage their emission allowances and credits.

The carbon market is important for the international efforts to address climate change because it helps reduce the overall cost of reducing greenhouse gas emissions. It does this in three ways: by enabling companies that can not reduce emissions cheaply to buy lower cost emission reductions elsewhere; by providing opportunities for companies that are cleaner, and more efficient to profit from their technologies and practices by selling excess allowances, and by making it easier for buyers and sellers to find each other, thereby lowering the transaction costs.

SINKS AND SAFEGUARDS

Climate change can be partially counteracted at relatively low cost by removing greenhouse gases from the atmosphere—for example through planting trees or improving forest management. But it is often difficult to estimate emissions and removals from the land use, land-use change and forestry (LULUCF) sector. For this reason, LULUCF activities under the Kyoto Protocol are subject to special rules.

Unlike the Convention, which includes all emissions and removals from LULUCF in a Party's total emissions, the Protocol restricts the accounting of for emissions and removals to specific LULUCF activities, as long as they were begun in or after 1990. First, each Party must account for emissions and removals from all afforestation, reforestation and deforestation activities. Second, Parties may choose to account for forest management, cropland management, grazing land management and re-vegetation. Parties must make this choice before the commitment period and it may not be changed subsequently. To help ensure consistency and comparability among Parties, common definitions are established for the term "forest" and for each of the seven classes of activity. Some variation is permitted, to allow for national conditions, but must be applied consistently.

In contrast to emissions from Annex A sources, emissions and removals from LULUCF activities are accounted by adding to or subtracting from Parties' assigned amount. Net removals from LULUCF activities result in the issuance of additional emission allowances, called removal units (RMUs,) which a Party may add to its assigned amount; while Parties must account for any net emissions from LULUCF activities by cancelling Kyoto Protocol units. Calculation of the quantity of emission allowances to be issued or cancelled is subject to specific rules and limits, which differ for each LULUCF activity.

* * *

THE COMPLIANCE COMMITTEE

The Kyoto Protocol establishes a Compliance Committee to facilitate, promote and enforce Parties' compliance with its commitments. It considers "questions of implementation" concerning a Party's compliance with the Kyoto Protocol requirements. . . .

EDITORS' NOTE

At the conclusion of the first commitment period (2008–2012), the 36 industrialized countries that had remained in the Kyoto Protocol had met their target. Cumulative emissions for these countries were well below the levels (on an annual basis) of their emissions in 1990. Several of the countries met their targets by making liberal use of the flexibility mechanisms (i.e. by purchasing the right to emit from others, rather than by actually reducing their own emissions). But even taking into account purchases of CERs under the Clean Development Mechanism (which do not represent reductions from 1990 levels), the overall emissions reductions were enough to meet the Kyoto targets. What's more, if the emissions of Canada and the United States were added to the pool, the Kyoto targets would still have been met.[46]

Whether this success is attributable to the Kyoto Protocol itself is debatable. Even before the Kyoto Protocol was adopted, total annual emissions of the Annex B Parties as a group were below 1990 levels because of the severe economic decline in the former Soviet bloc countries that followed the breakup of the Soviet Union. In addition, there was a global recession at the start of the commitment period. That naturally kept emissions levels down, and recovery from the recession was slow. So there were economic factors that contributed to the decline in emissions, and it is hard to make definitive statements about how much of the decline is attributable to policy and how much to the impact of unintended economic declines.

It is possible, however, to say that the Kyoto Protocol demonstrated that countries could adopt policies that promote emissions reductions without significant economic harm. The Protocol also "has been identified as an important driver of the diffusion of emissions trading around the globe."[47]

When the Kyoto Protocol was negotiated, the United States insisted that it include an emissions trading component (the flexibility mechanisms). Several countries resisted that approach, although the U.S. view ultimately prevailed (ironically, given that the United States never ratified the agreement). Despite the initial resistance to emissions trading, it was eventually embraced in Europe. Several developing nations, moreover, became involved as hosts to Clean Development Mechanism projects (which can sell CERs—certified emission reduction units—to private parties or to national government agencies). The CDM gave rise "to an entire industry of consultancies, carbon brokers and verification/validation firms,"[48] which, in a way, made emissions trading respectable. As a result:

> The policy instrument of greenhouse gas (GHG) emissions trading has gained prominence since the early 2000s. At the end of 2016, twenty-one distinct GHG emissions trading systems (ETSs) covering thirty-five countries were operating worldwide (ICAP 2017). China has announced the launch of a national ETS for the second half of 2017, which is expected to become the world's largest carbon market. A number of other countries and subnational jurisdictions, including

---

[46] *See* Igor Shishlov, Romain Morel & Valentin Bellassen, *Compliance of the Parties to the Kyoto Protocol in the first commitment period*, 16 Climate Policy 768 (2016).

[47] Katja Biedenkopf, Patrick Müller, Peter Slominski & Jørgen Wettestad, *A Global Turn to Greenhouse Gas Emissions Trading? Experiments, Actors, and Diffusion*, 17 GLOBAL ENVIRONMENTAL POLITICS 1 (2017). *See also* David Bellis & Bart Kerremans, *The socialization potential of the CDM in EU-China climate relations*, 16 International Environmental Agreements: Politics Law & Economics 543 (2016).

[48] *Id.* at 548.

Thailand, Mexico, and Oregon, are considering the adoption of a GHG ETS.[49]

Many of these multilateral, national, and subnational emissions trading systems are indirectly linked by the fact that they allow CERs issued under the Kyoto Clean Development Mechanism to be traded within their systems. This trading in CDM CERs continues, despite the expiration of the Kyoto Protocol's commitment period.

A second Kyoto commitment period (2013–2020) with new emissions-reduction targets was established in 2012 by the Doha Amendment to the Kyoto Protocol. However, the Doha Amendment has so far not received sufficient ratifications to enter into force, and it is unlikely to do so.

DISCUSSION NOTES/QUESTIONS

1. You can test your understanding of the cap-and-trade aspects of the Kyoto Protocol by analyzing the following hypothetical:

> Country A is an Annex I party to the Framework Convention. Country A has ratified the Kyoto Protocol. Its "quantified emission limitation and reduction commitment" in Annex B is 95%. In 1990, Country A emitted 1000 metric tons CO_2e of the greenhouse gases listed in Annex A. In 2008, Country A's greenhouse gas emissions (CO_2e) amounted to 1300 metric tons. In 2009 and 2010, during the economic downturn, its emissions were 900 metric tons each year. Its emissions in 2011 rose to 1050 metric tons, but fell to 1000 metric tons in 2012. In 2009, Country A sponsored a project in a developing country to burn waste rice hulls in place of coal in a power plant. The project is certified as reducing the developing country's greenhouse gas emissions by 10 metric tons per year, beginning in 2010. Country A has also sponsored several projects in Country B (also an Annex I party to the Framework Convention and a party to the Kyoto Protocol) to convert coal-burning power plants to natural gas. These projects, in total, will reduce Country B's emissions of greenhouse gases by 25 metric tons a year beginning in 2010. Country B has agreed that Country A can receive credit for these reductions. Country A has also purchased 150 AAUs from Country C. Finally, Country A's efforts at reforestation have been calculated to have increased removal of CO_2 from the atmosphere by 5 metric tons per year for every year of the commitment period, and Country A has been issued the appropriate number of RMUs for these efforts.

Is Country A in compliance with its Kyoto commitments? Explain. How does the arrangement between Country A and Country B affect Country B's Kyoto commitments? Explain. How about the arrangement with Country C? How do Country A's reforestation efforts affect its Kyoto commitment?

[49] Biedenkopf, et al., *supra* note 31.

2. If the Kyoto Protocol was a success, why have most industrialized countries not signed on to a second commitment period? One reason may be that reduction of emissions by the industrialized nations alone will do little to mitigate climate change in the long run. GHG emissions have continued to grow dramatically in countries not covered by Annex B of Kyoto. Indeed, some analysts believe that there was a large "leakage" problem under Kyoto: private businesses would reduce their local emissions in Kyoto-bound countries, but they would move production (and emissions) to other countries not bound by Kyoto requirements.

Thus, a problem with the Kyoto Protocol is simply this: even if it is fully implemented for a second commitment period, it will not prevent climate change. In fact, it will barely have an impact. Growth in emissions from China and other developing countries will swamp emission reductions elsewhere. Under those circumstances, many states fail to see the point of continuing with the Kyoto Protocol approach.

3. THE PARIS AGREEMENT

The Paris Agreement **(Basic Document 2.6)** was adopted by the 21st session of the UNFCCC Conference of the Parties on December 12, 2015. It entered into force on November 4, 2016. As of this writing, it has 186 Parties. The principal goals and key methodology of the Agreement are stated in Articles 2 and 3.

> Article 2
>
> 1. This Agreement, in enhancing the implementation of the Convention, including its objective, aims to strengthen the global response to the threat of climate change, in the context of sustainable development and efforts to eradicate poverty, including by:
>
> (a) Holding the increase in the global average temperature to well below 2°C above pre-industrial levels and pursuing efforts to limit the temperature increase to 1.5°C above pre-industrial levels, recognizing that this would significantly reduce the risks and impacts of climate change;
>
> (b) Increasing the ability to adapt to the adverse impacts of climate change and foster climate resilience and low greenhouse gas emissions development, in a manner that does not threaten food production; and
>
> (c) Making finance flows consistent with a pathway towards low greenhouse gas emissions and climate-resilient development.
>
> 2. This Agreement will be implemented to reflect equity and the principle of common but differentiated responsibilities

and respective capabilities, in the light of different national circumstances.

Article 3

As nationally determined contributions to the global response to climate change, all Parties are to undertake and communicate ambitious efforts as defined in Articles 4, 7, 9, 10, 11 and 13 with the view to achieving the purpose of this Agreement as set out in Article 2. The efforts of all Parties will represent a progression over time, while recognizing the need to support developing country Parties for the effective implementation of this Agreement.

Emissions reduction obligations under the Paris Agreement

The goal of limiting global temperature rise to "well below 2°C above pre-industrial levels" is ambitious and will likely require rapid and significant reductions in global greenhouse gas emissions. Unlike the Kyoto Protocol, however, the Paris Agreement does not seek to achieve this goal by imposing specific emission-reduction targets on any particular country or group of countries. Rather, it requires all parties (developed and developing countries alike) to determine, on their own, what actions they will take to reduce GHG emissions. A combination of required reporting of these "nationally determined contributions" and peer assessments of each country's actions is intended to promote a high degree of ambition in each nation's plans, ensure that countries will be held accountable for meeting their commitments, and thus secure meaningful reductions in GHG emissions.

Toward this end, Article 4 requires Parties to "prepare, communicate and maintain successive nationally determined contributions that it intends to achieve" with respect to emissions reductions. For developed countries, these contributions should consist of "economy-wide absolute emission reduction targets." Developing countries are encouraged to move "over time" toward targets for emissions reduction or limitation "in the light of different national circumstances." Emissions reductions can be achieved either by reducing anthropogenic emissions or enhancing removals by sinks.

Parties are expected to "account for their nationally determined contributions" in a fashion that shows that they are meeting their commitments. Parties communicate a new nationally determined contribution every five years. The agreement seems to contemplate a one-way ratchet: parties may "adjust" their nationally determined contributions, but only "with a view to enhancing [the Party's] level of ambition."

Article 2 states explicitly that the Agreement will be implemented in a way that reflects "the principle of common but differentiated responsibilities and respective capabilities." The emissions-reduction obligations of Article 4, in turn, draw a clear differentiation between developed and developing country parties. As noted earlier, developed country parties are expected to "continue taking the lead" by adopting more demanding emission-reduction targets than developing countries. The "least developed countries and small island developing States" are authorized to communicate plans for "low greenhouse gas emissions development reflecting their special circumstances." This seems to contemplate that for these countries, at least, emissions can continue to rise.

For those countries that restrict their emissions, the Agreement authorizes a continuation of the Kyoto Protocol's emissions trading system, albeit with new terminology. Article 6 allows Parties to use "internationally transferred mitigation outcomes" in order to achieve their nationally determined contributions. It also establishes "a mechanism to contribute to the mitigation of greenhouse gas and support sustainable development." This mechanism, similar to Kyoto's Clean Development Mechanism, is intended to incentivize public and private investment in projects that mitigate greenhouse gas emissions in a host country and to allow the transfer of credits for the emissions reduction to another country to assist it in fulfilling its nationally determined contribution.

Other nationally determined contributions

The Paris Agreement's provisions on emissions reduction are undoubtedly the most important provisions with respect to its climate mitigation goal. But Parties to the Agreement are expected to make and communicate "nationally determined contributions" in a number of other areas.

- Each Party must communicate a nationally determined contribution to adaptation, "which may include its priorities, implementation and support needs, plans and actions." Article 7(10).

- Developed countries are expected to "provide financial resources to assist developing country Parties with respect to both mitigation and adaptation." They are required to report biennially on their "projected levels of public financial resources to be provided to developing country Parties." Article 9, paragraphs 1 and 5.

- Article 3 also requires countries to "undertake and communicate ambitious efforts" with respect to technology transfer (Article 10) and capacity-building in developing countries (Article 11).

Article 13 further spells out many of these reporting obligations and authorizes the "Conference of the Parties serving as the meeting of the Parties to this Agreement" (CMA) to adopt "common modalities, procedures and guidelines" to ensure "the transparency of action and support" across the full range of nationally determined contributions. Article 15 establishes a "compliance mechanism" consisting of a committee that "shall be expert-based and facilitative in nature and function in a manner that is transparent, non-adversarial and non-punitive."

DISCUSSION NOTES/QUESTIONS

1. The Paris Agreement is an obvious attempt to answer the critics of the Kyoto Protocol who argued that significant climate mitigation could never be achieved if developing countries were not required to limit (and in some cases reduce) their GHG emissions. The Paris Agreement requires commitments from all nations, but each nation will determine for itself what its climate-mitigation commitments should be.

This approach was first adopted in the Copenhagen Accord, a deal reached by some of the UNFCCC Parties at the 15th meeting of the COP in 2009. A number of countries signed on, but the COP merely "took note of" the Accord and did not adopt or endorse it. Nevertheless, the Paris Agreement is in many ways a continuation of the approach taken in 2009.

Do you think this approach can move the mitigation effort forward? What are the advantages and disadvantages of letting countries set their own emissions-reduction targets?

2. The Paris Agreement continues to draw a distinction between what is expected of developed countries with respect to mitigation and what is expected of developing countries. Is it "unfair" to developed countries, as some political leaders in the United States have argued? If the distinction between developed and developing countries leads the United States to withdraw from the Agreement, then what is left of the principle of common but differentiated obligations?

3. In the 2009 Copenhagen Accord, the developed nations committed "to a goal of mobilizing jointly USD 100 billion dollars a year by 2020 to address the needs of developing countries." The Paris Agreement's financial provisions are premised on the assumption that that financial commitment remains in place. The COP's decision adopting the Paris Agreement provides that the "existing collective [financial] mobilization goal" will be carried out through the mechanism of Article 9, paragraph 3, of the Paris Agreement and that, prior to 2025, a new financial mobilization goal will be established with "from a floor of USD 100 billion per year." *See* Report of the Conference of the Parties on its twenty-first session, Addendum, Decision 1/CP.21, paragraph 53, UN Doc FCCC/CP/2015/10/Add.1 (29 Jan. 2016).

4. FINANCIAL MECHANISMS

Each of the climate change agreements has one or more provisions aimed at securing financial assistance for developing countries. For example, Article 11 of the UNFCCC provides, in part, as follows:

> Article 11: Financial Mechanism
>
> 1. A mechanism for the provision of financial resources on a grant or concessional basis, including for the transfer of technology, is hereby defined. It shall function under the guidance of and be accountable to the Conference of the Parties, which shall decide on its policies, programme priorities and eligibility criteria related to this Convention. Its operation shall be entrusted to one or more existing international entities.

The Kyoto Protocol provided that a portion of the proceeds from the sale of CERs generated by Clean Development Mechanism projects should be allocated "to assist developing country Parties that are particularly vulnerable to the adverse effects of climate change." (Kyoto Protocol, article 12(8)) And, of course, as noted earlier, the Paris Agreement requires developed countries to "provide financial resources to assist developing country Parties with respect to both mitigation and adaptation in continuation of their existing obligations under the Convention," including the USD 100 billion collective commitment made in the Copenhagen Accord. (Paris Agreement, article 9(1))

Over the years, the UNFCCC Parties have developed several different means for providing financial assistance to help developing countries with climate-change mitigation and adaptation. The operation of the Financial Mechanism of the Convention was originally entrusted entirely to the Global Environment Facility (GEF), which channels funds to developing countries on a grant or loan basis. The GEF, established in 1991, describes itself as "an international partnership of 183 countries, international institutions, civil society organization and the private sector." It is governed by a Council of 32 Members appointed by various constituencies (14 from developed countries, 16 from developing countries, and 2 from economies in transition). The World Bank is the GEF Trustee.

The GEF administers the financial mechanisms for several international environmental treaties. The GEF reports to the COP annually on its funding for climate-change-related projects, and the COP provides policy guidance to the GEF on such matters as program priorities and appropriate eligibility criteria.

The COP has established two special funds to support climate-change-related projects: the Special Climate Change Fund (SCCF) and the Least Developed Countries Fund (LDCF). These special funds were created in part as an effort to increase contributions from developed countries by providing identifiable "climate funds" to which contributions could be made. Both are managed by the GEF, under guidance from the COP.

In 2001, an Adaptation Fund was created to receive a share of the proceeds from Clean Development Mechanism project activities under the Kyoto Protocol. Management of this Fund was delegated to an Adaption Fund Board established by the CMP in 2007.

Finally, in 2010, the UNFCCC Parties set up a Green Climate Fund, to be operated as part of the Convention's financial mechanism. Thus, operation of the financial mechanism is now split between the GEF and the Green Climate Fund. Unlike the GEF, the Green Climate Fund's exclusive focus is to finance climate-change mitigation and adaptation activities. It is governed by its own Board, although its governing document provides that it will be "accountable to" and function "under the guidance of the COP."

Developed country parties thus have a number of avenues for making financial contributions to assist developing countries in responding to climate change. Presumably, developed countries will determine which of these various funds makes a use of their money that is most in line with their preferences and contribute there. Alternatively, a developed country could provide funding directly, bypassing entirely the international financial mechanisms.

DISCUSSION NOTES/QUESTIONS

1. At its 19th session in Warsaw, Poland, in 2013, the COP established the Warsaw international mechanism for loss and damage. The Warsaw international mechanism (WIM) is an institutional arrangement for organizing efforts "to address loss and damage associated with impacts of climate change, including extreme events and slow onset events, in developing countries that are particularly vulnerable to the adverse effect of climate change." It is run by an Executive Committee that is "under the guidance of, and accountable to, the Conference of the Parties." The WIM's focus is not exclusively, or even heavily, on providing financial support for adaptation efforts. Rather, it seeks to organize a variety of resources to help vulnerable nations deal with the damage that climate change is likely to cause. *See* Decision 2/CP.19 (23 Nov. 2013), UN Doc FCCC/CP/2013/10/Add.1 at 6 (2014).

As instructed by the COP, the WIM's primary functions are to "promote the implementation of approaches" that will:

- Enhance "knowledge and understanding of comprehensive risk management approaches" to climate-change-induced loss and damage;
- Strengthen "dialogue, coordination, coherence, and synergies among relevant stakeholders";

- Enhance "action and support, including finance, technology and capacity-building" related to addressing climate-change-induced loss and damage.

It carries out these functions by "facilitat[ing] support of actions to address loss and damage"; "coordinat[ing]" the work of existing Convention bodies relevant to loss and damage; convening meetings of experts and stakeholders; compiling and reviewing information on loss and damage; "provid[ing] technical guidance and support"; and making recommendations on how to enhance efforts to deal with loss and damage.

2. Beginning in 2007, the Conference of the Parties has adopted a series of decisions aimed at "encourag[ing] developing country Parties to contribute to mitigation" of climate change by a) reducing deforestation and forest degradation and b) enhancing forest carbon sinks through sustainable management. *See, e.g.,* Decision 1/CP.16, paragraph 70, UN Doc FCCC/CP/2010/7/Add.1. This program, called REDD+ (Reducing Emissions from Deforestation and Forest Degradation in Developing Countries), is currently governed by the so-called Warsaw Framework for REDD+, seven decisions adopted in Warsaw at COP 19.

To date, the COP has not created any special institution structure to manage the REDD+ program. However, shortly after the first COP decision addressing deforestation and forest degradation, three UN agencies created their own institutional structure to support REDD activities. This program, the United Nations Collaborative Programme on Reducing Emissions from Deforestation and Forest Degradation in Developing Countries (UN-REDD) was started in 2008. It is operated jointly by the UN Food and Agricultural Organization (FAO), the UN Development Programme (UNDP), and UNEP. It is governed by a small Executive Board with members who represent donor countries, countries conducting REDD programs, and the three UN agencies. Permanent "observers" also have a seat on the Board to represent the interests of indigenous peoples and civil society organizations, respectively. A much larger UN-REDD Programme Assembly has representation from the same groups, as well as from the private sector and from other international programs and funds.

3. In Chapter 4, we quoted from Professor Donald Anton's comments on the problem of "treaty congestion" as it impacts international environmental law. Professor Anton observed that one aspect of the treaty-congestion problem is the proliferation of treaty bodies and institutions. This phenomenon, he argued, erodes "the capacity of states to meaningfully participate in institutional activities to advance their interests," as they have an "unmanageable number of commitments."

Does the climate change regime provide an example of this problem? Are there good reasons for having multiple financing arrangements, often with separate governing bodies, priorities, and eligibility criteria? Does it make sense to create another institution to promote and coordinate adaptation efforts related to climate loss and damage? Does it make sense to have a

REDD+ program within the UNFCCC framework and a separate UN-REDD programme, organized by different UN agencies, but addressing the same problems and issues? Is the climate-change regime simply pulling resources into bureaucratic management activities when those resources are desperately needed elsewhere? Or can you think of sound reasons for having a variety of institutional arrangements to support climate mitigation and adaptation activities in developing countries?

C. THREE PROBLEMS IN CONFRONTING CLIMATE CHANGE

The remainder of this chapter consists of three problems on climate change. Problem 9–1 poses some of the formidable issues that confront international negotiators and challenges you to see whether you, in the role of such a negotiator, can simultaneously defend your nation's interest and build cooperation among members of the global community who, despite their differing economic and social priorities, confront a common threat to their security. Problem 9-2 considers the possibility that some states might seek to limit global warming via geo-engineering. Problem 9-3 examines the human rights dimensions of climate change, a normative approach.

PROBLEM 9-1: STABILIZING GREENHOUSE GASES AND NEGOTIATING CLIMATE FINANCE WITHIN THE FRAMEWORK OF THE PARIS AGREEMENT

Section 1. Facts

Brazil, China, the European Union, Grenada, India, Saudi Arabia, the United States, and Zimbabwe have come together, along with the other Parties to the Paris Agreement, to negotiate their commitments in three areas: emissions reductions (Article 4); conservation and enhancement of forest sinks (Article 4(1)(d) and Article 5); and provision of (Article 9), or need for (Article 13(1)), financial support. Each negotiating party is expected to make national commitments ("nationally determined contributions") in each of these three areas. Hence, each negotiating party will decide: *First,* how deeply and how rapidly it will reduce its emissions of greenhouse gases. *Second,* what commitments it will make to reduce deforestation or to increase reforestation or afforestation. *Third,* how much financing it will contribute to, or request from, the Green Climate Fund. The collective goals for the negotiation were established by the COP when it adopted the Paris Agreement. On the first and second issues, the objective is a combination of activities that hold the "global average temperature to well below 2 degrees Celsius above pre-industrial levels" and that aim to "limit the temperature increase to 1.5 degrees Celsius above pre-industrial levels." (Paris Agreement, article 2)

With respect to financing, all the participants at the 2015 COP agreed that the developed nations should provide significant financial support to assist developing countries in addressing climate change, and the Paris Agreement so provides in Article 9. The developed countries have previously accepted a collective obligation, as a group, to commit a minimum of $100 billion per year to support adaptation, mitigation, and REDD (reducing emissions from deforestation and forest degradation). At the time the Paris Agreement was adopted, the developed countries accepted the proposition that the $100 billion/year commitment was a floor, and that more funding might be necessary.

Section 2. Questions Presented

1. At what level and within what time frame should the Parties to the Paris Agreement stabilize or reduce their greenhouse gas emissions?

2. How vigorously should the Parties to the Paris Agreement pursue efforts to stop forest destruction and degradation and promote afforestation and reforestation?

3. At what levels should developed nations make significant funds available to assist developing nations in taking actions to mitigate and adapt to climate change? What amount of funding should be demanded by developing countries as a condition of taking climate action?

Section 3. Assignments

The purpose of this exercise is to simulate an international negotiation on climate change. This can be structured in a number of ways, and the precise approach will be in the hands of your instructor. However, in lieu of differing instructions from your instructor, you should assume the following:

a) Each member of the class will be assigned to serve as a member of a delegation from one of the countries participating in the negotiation. (The countries we have named as participants may be changed by your instructor.)

b) Each country's delegation will be expected, at various points in the negotiation (to be determined by your instructor, acting as chair of the proceedings), to make "offers" of nationally determined contributions as follows:

i) *on GHG emissions:* the year the country's emissions will peak; the year it will begin reducing emissions; and the annual rate at which it will reduce emissions;

ii) *on deforestation and afforestation:* a statement of the effort it will make to stop deforestation or promote afforestation in terms of a percentage. For example, a decision to make no effort (to continue with "business as usual") would be a zero percent effort. A 100% effort would mean that the country is committing to do the maximum possible to stop deforestation and to support afforestation within its territory.

iii) *on financial matters:* each country will state (on an annual basis) either the amount it will contribute to global funds for adaptation and mitigation or the amount it will request from those funds to assist its mitigation and adaptation efforts.

The members of each delegation will be expected to do sufficient research to make offers in each of the above areas that bear some relationship to the real-world circumstances of their country. This does not mean that one must slavishly follow the most recent pronouncements of the current political leadership of a particular country. It does mean that one should take into account what is realistically possible for a country (or what its real needs are) when making commitments or making requests for funding. Of course, negotiating strategy will also influence your decisions in this regard.

c) The negotiation will begin with a five-minute opening statement from each delegation as to the stance their country takes and the proposals it intends to make. Often the most productive negotiations will occur in informal groups outside the plenary negotiating meeting. The negotiation will continue for as many class periods as your instructor determines. Your instructor will determine how much negotiating time will be spent in formal discussion and debate in plenary session and how much time will be devoted to informal negotiations outside the plenary.

d) Prior to the start of negotiations, you will be expected to prepare the following materials and provide them to your instructor:

i) *A full powers document, granting you the authority to negotiate and take decisions on behalf of your country with respect to these negotiations. See* Vienna Convention on the Law of Treaties, art. 1(c); United Nations Treaty Collection, *Model Instruments in the Six Official UN Languages,* https://treaties.un.org.

ii) *A description of your assigned country's negotiating position on each of the three points that are the subject of negotiation.*

Your negotiating position should be based on background research that includes such matters as: i) your country's economic situation and development needs; ii) the likely impact of climate change on your country; iii) past positions your country has taken in climate negotiations; iv) the range of actions available to your country to contribute to climate-mitigation efforts (e.g., countries with no forests are in a different position than countries with forests); and v) relevant actions your country has already taken or is planning to take in the near future.

Relevant research can be conducted easily on the internet.

c) *A negotiating plan.* Your plan will depend largely on your negotiating positions. The plan should:

- Identify and prioritize specific and concrete negotiating goals. You should set high expectations, but you should also pick goals that you believe are justifiable and achievable.
- Write out justifications for each goal (i.e. reasons why you're entitled to make this particular demand and why others should accept it.) You should be prepared to use these justifications during the negotiation as explanations and/or arguments for your position.
- Identify both an aspirational and a fallback position for each goal. (You may wish to ask for more than your goal, and you ought to be prepared to settle for less.)
- Identify key points that the other side is likely to raise, and identify the arguments you will make in response to those points. Also identify possible compromise offers you could make.
- Law should be part of your plan. If there are legal principles that support your position in the negotiations, you should be prepared to raise those legal points during the negotiation. Note those points in your plan.
- Decide on your tactics: cooperative or obstructionist? A mix of both? What, if anything, will you do to facilitate the negotiation (e.g., have alternative positions available to propose to the group to move the negotiation forward?)

In many negotiations, the object is to reach some kind of an agreement. This negotiation is a little different because it is not necessary to reach a consensus position for which countries will vote. Each country determines its own contribution to meeting the shared objectives.

Finally, you are welcome—indeed, encouraged—to communicate with representatives of other delegations between sessions, and particularly in advance of the first session. For example, you may wish to circulate a written version of your opening statement either before or after you deliver it. The Secretariat (your instructor) will make every effort to distribute documents to all delegations within twenty-four (24) hours of receipt, but only those documents that are intended for general distribution. Bilateral or other confidential communications should be undertaken directly with the other participating delegations. However, whatever the distributional character of the document, be sure to mark it with your name, the date, and a heading "Proposal of the Delegation of X" or similar description identifying your role.

A. *Reading Assignment*

Study the Readings presented in Parts A and B of this Chapter, *supra*, and in Section 4, *infra*.

B. *Negotiating Assignment*

Assume you are a member of one of the delegations to the negotiation (as designated by your instructor); then, relying upon your research and negotiating plan, negotiate the nationally determined commitments that you and the other negotiating countries will make toward accomplishment of the goals of the Paris Agreement.

C. *Post-Negotiation Writing Assignment*

Prepare a memorandum from your delegation to your Foreign Office justifying and explaining the final nationally determined contributions negotiated by you and your associate negotiating diplomats.

D. *Suggested Reflective Assignment*

Consider (and recommend) alternative norms, institutions, and/or procedures that you believe might work better than existing world order arrangements to contend with situations of the kind posed by this problem. In so doing, but without insisting upon immediate feasibility, identify the particular transition steps that would be needed to make your alternatives a reality.

Section 4. Readings

1. Paris Agreement, arts. 2, 3, 4.1–4.2, 5, 7.10, 9.1, 9.5, 13.8, & 13.9, Dec. 12, 2015, UN Reg. No. 54113, available at https://treaties.un.org (Basic Document 2.6)

2. United Nations Environment Programme (UNEP), The Emissions Gap Report 2014, *Executive Summary* xiii—xviii (2014).

As noted by the IPCC, scientists have determined that an increase in global temperature is proportional to the build-up of long-lasting greenhouse gases in the atmosphere, especially carbon dioxide. Based on this finding, they have estimated the maximum amount of carbon dioxide that could be emitted over time to the atmosphere and still stay within the 2 °C limit. This is called the carbon dioxide emissions budget because, if the world stays within this budget, it should be possible to stay within the 2 °C global warming limit. In the hypothetical case that carbon dioxide was the only human-made greenhouse gas, the IPCC estimated a total carbon dioxide budget of about 3,670 gigatonnes of carbon dioxide (Gt CO2) for a likely chance of staying within the 2 °C limit. Since emissions began rapidly growing in the late 19th century, the world has already emitted around 1,900 Gt CO2 and so has used up a large part of this budget. Moreover, human activities also result in emissions of a variety of other substances that have an impact on global warming and these substances also reduce the total available budget to about 2,900 Gt CO2. This leaves less than about 1,000 Gt CO2 to "spend" in the future. The key questions are: how can these emissions best be spread out over time; at what point in time should net carbon dioxide emissions fall to zero—that is, when should we become budget neutral in the sense that we sequester as much as we emit; and how much can we spend of the budget at different points in the future and still stay within the temperature limit?

What does the budget approach say about emission levels and their timing to meet the 2 °C limit?

To stay within the 2 °C limit, global carbon neutrality will need to be achieved sometime between 2055 and 2070.

Using the carbon budget approach and information from integrated assessment models it is possible to estimate when or if global carbon neutrality will need to be reached during the 21st century in order to have a likely chance of staying within the 2 °C limit.

Here global carbon neutrality means that annual anthropogenic carbon dioxide emissions are net zero on the global scale. Net zero implies that some remaining carbon dioxide emissions could be compensated by the same amount of carbon dioxide uptake (negative emissions) so long as the net input of carbon dioxide to the atmosphere due to human activities is zero.

The fact that global emissions will continue to be larger than zero in the immediate future means that at some point we will exhaust the carbon dioxide emissions budget and annual net emissions will have to drop to zero to avoid exceeding the budget. If we do exceed the budget, then negative emissions will be required to stay within the 2 °C limit.

Based on a subset of scenarios from the IPCC Fifth Assessment Report (AR5) scenario database, the best estimate is that global carbon neutrality is reached between 2055 and 2070 in order to have a likely chance of staying within the 2 °C limit. This same subset of scenarios is used throughout this Summary for calculating emissions consistent with the 2 °C limit, with the exception of the calculation of the 2020 gap, as explained in Section 5 of the Summary.

To stay within the 2 °C limit, total global greenhouse gas emissions need to shrink to net zero sometime between 2080 and 2100.

An important point about carbon neutrality is that it only refers to carbon dioxide emissions. Nonetheless, it is well known that other greenhouse gases also cause global temperature increases. Among these are methane, nitrous oxide and hydrofluorocarbons. Current and likely future emissions of these and other non-carbon dioxide greenhouse gases have been taken into account in the above estimation of when carbon neutrality should be reached. The next question is, when must total greenhouse gas emissions (carbon dioxide plus non-carbon dioxide) reach net zero in order to stay within the emissions budget?

Based on additional assumptions about non-carbon dioxide emissions, it has been estimated that global total greenhouse gas emissions will need to reach net zero sometime between 2080 and 2100. Although this is somewhat later than the timing for carbon neutrality it does not assume slower reductions of non-carbon dioxide emissions. On the contrary, non-carbon dioxide and carbon dioxide emissions are assumed to be reduced with about the same level of effort.

The estimates here are again based on a subset of scenarios that have a likely chance of staying within the 2 °C limit. As in the case of carbon neutrality, the net part of net zero emissions means that any global residual emissions from society could be compensated by enough uptake of carbon dioxide and other greenhouse gases from the atmosphere (negative emissions) to make sure that the net input of total greenhouse gases to the atmosphere is zero.

Bringing global emissions down to below the pledge range in 2020 allows us to postpone the timing of carbon neutrality and net zero total emissions.

An important consequence of the carbon budget is that the lower the annual emissions in the immediate future, including in the years up to 2020, the relatively higher they can be later, and the longer the time we have before exhausting the emissions budget. This would allow us to push back the timing of carbon neutrality and net-zero total emissions. Hence taking more action now reduces the need for taking more extreme action later to stay within the 2 °C limit.

Following the budget approach, the levels of annual global emissions consistent with the 2 °C limit have been estimated. Under these circumstances, global emissions in 2050 are around 55 per cent below 2010 levels. By 2030 global emissions have already turned the corner and are more than 10 per cent below 2010 levels after earlier peaking.

Countries took the important decision at the Durban Climate Conference to pursue a new climate agreement, expected to enter into effect in 2020. This raises the crucial question about which global emission levels after 2020 are consistent with staying within the 2 °C limit. The estimates in the following table were made with this question in mind.

[The table is omitted here. It estimates that global greenhouse gas emissions will need to be 4% below 2010 levels by 2015, 14% below 2010 levels by 2030, and 55% below 2010 levels by 2050 for a 66% chance of staying within the 2 degrees Celsius target.]

What are the consequences of delayed action?

The consequences of postponing stringent emission reductions will be additional costs and higher risks to society.

The current pathway of global emissions is consistent with scenarios that assume only modest emission reductions up to 2020 and then stringent mitigation thereafter. By postponing rigorous action until 2020, this pathway will save on costs of mitigation in the near term. But it will bring much higher costs and risks later on, such as:

i: much higher rates of global emission reductions in the medium term;

ii: greater lock-in of carbon-intensive infrastructure;

iii: greater dependence on using all available mitigation technologies in the medium-term;

iv: greater costs of mitigation in the medium and long-term, and greater risks of economic disruption;

v: greater reliance on negative emissions; and

vi: greater risks of failing to meet the 2 °C target, which would lead to substantially higher adaptation challenges and costs.

Delaying stringent action till 2030 will further aggravate these risks and reduce the likelihood of meeting the 2 °C target to 50 per cent or less. Conversely, putting greater effort into reducing emissions over the next few years would reduce all of these risks and would bring many co-benefits along with climate mitigation (see Section 7 of the Summary).

The higher the emissions level in the near term, the higher the level of negative emissions needed later in the century as compensation. Although scenarios routinely assume a substantial amount of global negative emissions, the feasibility of these assumptions still needs to be explored.

* * *

Where are we headed under business-as-usual conditions?

Although it is clear from the science that emissions soon need to peak to stay within the 2 °C target, global greenhouse gas emissions continue to rise. Without additional climate policies global emissions will increase hugely up to at least 2050.

Since 1990, global emissions have grown by more than 45 per cent and were approximately 54 Gt CO2e in 2012. Looking to the future, scientists have produced business-as-usual scenarios as benchmarks to see what emission levels would be like in the absence of additional climate policies, also assuming country pledges would not be implemented. Under these scenarios, global greenhouse gas emissions would rise to about 59 Gt CO2e in 2020, 68 Gt CO2e in 2030 and 87 Gt CO2e in 2050. It is clear that global emissions are not expected to peak unless additional emission reduction policies are introduced.

3. Organization for Economic Cooperation and Development, Climate Change Mitigation: What Do We Do 12 (2008)

Ambitious GHG abatement is economically rational, but it will not be cheap. The costs would be lower if a less stringent emissions pathway were chosen, or if greater overshooting were allowed. For instance, allowing more interim overshooting [of a 550 ppm CO2e target] (to over 600 ppm instead of about 560 ppm) could lower the GDP loss in 2050 to around 2% [rather than the 4.8% GDP loss predicted with a 550 ppm target with moderate overshooting]. But such overshooting would come at the price of greater risks of irreversible damage from climate change and would merely postpone some of the costs farther in the future.

4. Editors' note on atmospheric concentrations of greenhouse gases and the 2-degrees-Celsius goal

According to the IPCC's 5th Assessment Report, if atmospheric greenhouse gas concentrations at the end of the century reach 550 ppm CO2 equivalent, there is less than a 50% chance that we will meet the Paris Agreement goal of keeping the temperature increase below 2 degrees Celsius. To have a better than 50% chance of meeting the goal, end-of-the-century concentrations must be below 530 ppm CO2e. If concentrations can be maintained below 480 ppm, chances of meeting the goal are around 80%.

According to the National Oceanic & Atmospheric Administration (NOAA), atmospheric greenhouse gas concentrations in 2017 reached 493 ppm CO2e. Of that total, 405 ppm were provided by CO2 alone. The rest comes from other greenhouse gases, primarily nitrous oxide, methane, CFC-12 and CFC-11. *See* The NOAA Annual Greenhouse Gas Index (AGGI), https://www.esrl.noaa.gov/gmd/aggi/aggi.html (last visited June 29, 2018).

As was pointed out in Reading 3, we could allow atmospheric concentrations to rise temporarily above target levels if emissions were reduced sufficiently thereafter to bring the concentration levels back down. That might make mitigation less expensive. It might also result in overshooting the 2 degree target, although some projections suggest that the temperature increase could return to less than 2 degrees if concentration levels were rapidly brought back to 480 ppm or below. For a full discussion, *see* Leon Clarke, Kejun Jiang, et al., *Assessing Transformation Pathways* in CONTRIBUTION OF WORKING GROUP III TO THE

FIFTH ASSESSMENT REPORT OF THE INTERGOVERNMENTAL PANEL ON CLIMATE CHANGE (2014).

5. Jane A. Leggett & Richard K. Lattanzio, Status of the Copenhagen Climate Change Negotiations (Congressional Research Service, November 5, 2009)

[*Eds. This reading describes the thinking and negotiating positions at the Copenhagen COP in 2009. The so-called "Copenhagen Accord," though not adopted by the COP, established an approach that eventually became the Paris Agreement. This analysis of the Copenhagen negotiations (although it is a decade old) remains a useful guide to the issues that will be of importance to various countries during negotiations within the framework established by the Paris Agreement. A comparison of the Paris Agreement to the negotiating positions described here usefully reveals the compromises that are reflected in the Paris Agreement and the issues that were tacitly set aside for discussion at another time.*]

The negotiations toward a "Copenhagen agreement" are intended to be the next steps toward meeting the objective of the UNFCCC, to stabilize greenhouse gas concentrations in the atmosphere at a level that would prevent dangerous anthropogenic interference with the climate system. Most parties conclude the objective requires avoiding a 2° Celsius increase in global mean temperature and reducing global greenhouse gas (GHG) emissions by 80%–95% by 2050. The UNFCCC principle of "common but differentiated responsibilities" among parties permeates debate about obligations of different forms, levels of effort, and verifiability. Key disagreements remain among parties:

1. **GHG mitigation**: Some countries, including the United States, seek GHG actions by all parties; many developing countries argue that differentiation should exclude them from quantified and verifiable GHG limitations. Many vulnerable countries are alarmed that GHG targets proposed by wealthy countries are inadequate to avoid 2°C of temperature increase and associated serious risks.

2. **Adaptation to climate change**: Many countries, including the United States, wish to use bilateral and existing international institutions, with incremental financial assistance, targeted at the most vulnerable populations; many developing countries seek a fully financed, systemic, and country-determined effort to avoid damages of climate change, to which they have made minor historical contribution.

3. **Financial assistance to developing countries**: Many wealthy countries, including the United States, propose private sector mechanisms such as GHG trading, along with

investment-friendly economies, as the main sources of financing, with a minor share from public funds; many developing countries argue for predictable flows of unconditioned public monies, with direct access to an international fund under the authority of the Conference of the Parties.

4. **Technology**: Many countries, including the United States, maintain that private sector mechanisms are most effective at developing and deploying the needed advanced technologies, enabled by balanced trade and intellectual property protection; some countries seek new institutional arrangements and creative mechanisms to share technologies to facilitate more effective technology transfer.

* * *

Annex I Parties' Views [on GHG Mitigation]

The United States, the EU, and many other Annex I countries insist that a Copenhagen outcome be a comprehensive framework for action by all parties. They propose alternate versions of differentiated, quantified emission limits for Annex I parties, with key issues including the form, nature and depth ("comparability") of GHG mitigation commitments. Furthermore, Annex I parties propose differentiated commitments for non-Annex I parties to establish strategies that would reduce their current GHG growth trajectories, as well as Nationally Appropriate Mitigation Actions (NAMAs), to delineate specific actions that they would submit to be inscribed into an internationally measured schedule or registry. Eligibility for countries to receive financial or technological assistance would be incumbent upon taking and reporting such GHG mitigation programs.

U.S. GHG Mitigation Proposals

The United States has described its positions as follows:

– that Annex I countries make robust and absolute emission reductions in the mid-term (i.e., around 2020) from a base year (1990 or 2005);

– that major developing countries take actions in the mid-term that will significantly reduce their emissions compared to business-as-usual paths;

– that least developed countries need not make any commitments to reduce emissions, only to prepare low carbon growth plans for which they will be supported; and

– that other developing countries, likewise, need not make commitments. Rather, they should focus on developing and implementing low carbon growth plans and implementing nationally appropriate mitigation actions (NAMAs) to help guide them on a long-term development path.

Further, the United States outlined a proposal on measuring, reporting and verification (MRV) for all parties, which builds on the existing frameworks, and would introduce enhanced reporting, independent review by experts, and public peer review. The U.S. promised financial support for countries not capable of meeting MRV costs, and said that the "sub-elements" of the broad framework would be different, for instance, for the LDCs and for non-Annex I countries that have more capacity and responsibility. . . .

Non-Annex I Parties' Views [on GHG Mitigation]

The Bali Action Plan included ambiguous language regarding mitigation commitments by developing countries. Its key phrase was:

> consideration of mitigation actions that would include: . . . (ii) Nationally appropriate mitigation actions by developing country Parties in the context of sustainable development, supported and enabled by technology, financing and capacity building, in a measurable, reportable and verifiable manner;

China and many large developing countries continue to resist the idea that any non-Annex I countries might take on quantitative and enforceable commitments. However, by mid-2009 some non-Annex I countries favored beginning to differentiate among the non-Annex I country parties. Uganda, speaking for the Least Developed Countries (LDCs), expressed the position that all countries will need to take actions, including the LDCs.

Such proposals, and those of the United States and EU, are strongly opposed by many non-Annex I countries, especially Brazil, India and China—among the non-Annex I parties most pressured to take on quantified GHG commitments. They contend that these proposals seek to erase the differentiation between Annex I and developing countries embodied in the UNFCCC. These countries also oppose "Measuring, Reporting, and Verification" (MRV) proposals that would make all countries more accountable for their mitigation commitments.

Adapting to Impacts of Climate Change

For low-income countries, many of which have the populations most vulnerable to climate and climate change, near-term assistance to adapt is as high a priority as mitigating long-term climate change. Key issues include how much financial assistance might be provided; how to measure, report and verify (MRV) whether wealthier countries meet their commitments; and through what mechanisms financial aid would flow.

The G–77/China and Africa Groups wish to establish quantified commitments for financial transfers by the wealthier countries. Some argue for payments as "compensation" for unavoidable climate change impacts, though the UNFCCC mentions only "consideration" of actions (not compensation). Non-Annex I countries voice concern over access to financing, conditions imposed on receiving assistance, criteria to judge "vulnerability," and the burdens of processes and mechanisms, among additional issues.

* * *

Financial Assistance to Low-income Countries

The United States and all other parties to the UNFCCC committed to promoting adaptation, cooperation to develop and deploy new technologies, and a host of additional but unquantified obligations. The wealthier countries (including the United States) also committed to provide financial and technical assistance to underpin developing countries' efforts to meet their obligations. In the current negotiations, developing countries are calling for financial resources that will be "new, additional, adequate, predictable and sustained," for mitigation, adaptation, and development and transfer of technologies, to flow through UNFCCC specialized funds. They call for the resources to be publicly financed (not private) and to be provided on a grant or concessional basis.

Financial assistance—its amount, predictability, and "conditionality"—ties into all other aspects of the Copenhagen negotiations. Deep divisions exist among parties over four proposals now in the negotiating text:

- one or more funds established under the UNFCCC Conference of the Parties (COP), managed by one or more Trustees, with funds generated through levies on international maritime transport and aviation; a share of proceeds from accessing international emissions trading; assessed contributions from parties; and voluntary contributions from parties and other donors; OR assessed contributions from Annex I parties as a percent of Gross National Product;
- a World Climate Change Fund or Green Fund under the authority and guidance of the UNFCCC COP, administered by an existing financial institution, with funding from assessed contributions from all parties except the Least Developed Countries (LDCs);
- a Global Fund for Climate (U.S. proposal) as an operating entity of the (existing) financial mechanism (the World

Bank's Global Environment Facility), funded by multiyear, voluntary contributions of all parties except LDCs; and

- use of existing financial institutions, such as the Global Environment Facility (GEF), multilateral development banks, etc., with a Facilitative Platform under the authority and Guidance of the COP to register and link needs to support, and to monitor and evaluate the information in the registry.

Amounts of Financing

A variety of international institutions and non-governmental organizations have tried to estimate the costs of adaptation to developing countries and the associated needs for public funding. . . . [F]igures range from $4 billion to several hundreds of billions of dollars annually by the year 2030. . . . For GHG mitigation, the International Energy Agency's World Energy Outlook 200915 concludes that, in a scenario to stabilize atmospheric GHG concentrations at 450 ppm, "the energy sector in non-OECD16 countries would need around $200 billion of additional investment in clean energy and efficiency in 2020—including $70 billion for nationally appropriate mitigation actions (NAMAs) and a similar amount to achieve sectoral standards in transport and industry." . . .

Heads of State in the European Union (the European Council) propose that 5 to 7 billion euros of public financing, particularly for least developed countries, should be provided in each year of 2010 to 2012, as a "fast-start" in the context of a Copenhagen agreement. The European Council has concluded that 100 billion euros annually by 2020 will be necessary to help developing countries to mitigate and adapt to climate change.

Some non-Annex I countries (e.g., China) call for amounts of public financing that many view as unrealistic—up to 1% of GDP on top of other Overseas Development Assistance.

Public versus Private Financing

Countries differ on the appropriate sources of funds. The G–77 and China argue that developed nations' governments should provide public funds as the main source of climate change financing for mitigation, adaptation, technology cooperation, and capacity building. Annex I nations, however, underscore the importance of private sector finance through GHG trading mechanisms and other investments, with public funds as smaller and more targeted shares. . . .

European Union heads of state concluded that the net incremental costs of up to 100 billion euros by 2020 in developing countries18 should be met through a combination of non-Annex I countries' own efforts, the international carbon market and international public finance. They propose that the international public finance portion may be in the range of 22 to 50 billion euros per year, but subject to a "fair burden sharing" among parties to the UNFCCC, agreement on how to manage the funds, and application of the funds to "specific mitigation actions and ambitious Low Carbon Development Strategies/Low Carbon Growth Plans." . . . They conclude that all parties except the least developed should contribute to the public financing, with assessments based heavily on emission levels, as well as on Gross Domestic Product. EU leaders have stated they will provide their "fair share" of this amount, though they have not specified a precise amount. Their contribution will be conditioned on other countries' offers.

Public finances have been proposed to come from a variety of levies, including charges on maritime and aviation fuels, a percentage of GHG offsets internationally (such as exists now under the Kyoto Protocol's Clean Development Mechanism), contribution of a share of national allowances to auction, etc.

* * *

Mechanisms for Financing

Besides the magnitude and terms of financing available, substantial disagreement continues over appropriate mechanisms that would manage publicly provided financing under a new agreement. Much assistance passes through bilateral arrangements, although some countries complain that these are difficult to verify and may represent a shift in funding, not additional funding. Multilaterally, an array of mechanisms is available to help finance capacity building, technology cooperation, GHG mitigation policy development and measures, and adaptation analysis, planning, and actions. Such mechanisms include the Global Environment Facility (GEF) as the financial mechanism of the UNFCCC; the Special Climate Change Fund; and funds for specialized activities (e.g., the Adaptation Fund of the Kyoto Protocol) or groups of countries (e.g., the Least Developed Countries Fund of the Kyoto Protocol). In 2008, multilateral development banks with several governments and stakeholders established the Climate Investment Funds (CIF) under management of the World Bank. Many additional sources of funding, such as through other MDBs, are active. Their processes, terms, and responsiveness vary.

Some countries are concerned about the plethora of funds, administrative and management costs, and strategic provision of funds to maximize the effectiveness of the monies. Many non-Annex I countries complain that much financing is managed bilaterally or through the Multilateral Development Banks, particularly the World Bank, which some believe are not as responsive to the priorities of the recipient countries. These critics prefer financing to be managed by institutions created under the UNFCCC, in which they have "one-country, one-vote," or at least equal regional representation as the industrialized nations. Also, while Annex I parties generally prefer and promote means for the private sector to finance mitigation and adaptation investment, many non-Annex I countries prefer more "predictable" public sector flows.

* * *

The United States participates in the financing deliberations with impaired credibility, being almost $170 million in arrears for its assessed contribution to the Global Environment Facility (the financial mechanism of the UNFCCC and other treaties).

6. Aaron Cosbey, Developing Country Interests in Climate Change Action and the Implications for a Post-2012 Climate Change Regime, U.N. Doc. UNCTAD/DITC/BCC/2009/2 at 6, 9–15 (United Nations Conference on Trade and Development, 2009)

2.4. There are a number of potential conflicts between economic growth and action on climate change

This is a fairly straightforward proposition: as the economy grows, so too will GHG emissions. The equation appears simplest for carbon emissions associated with increased use of energy in industrial, residential/ commercial (lighting, heating and appliances) and transportation sectors. All of these tend to increase with income, other things being equal. . . .

* * *

[Growth in the size of a developing country's economy will result in negative environmental effects, but that negative effect can sometimes be offset by improvements in technology or shifts in consumer preferences or in production to cleaner goods.] Thus, the final impact of any economic growth is, ex ante, indeterminate. It will often boil down to a contest between the scale and technique effects—a contest, however, that is almost always won by the power of scale. That is, the rate of development and dissemination of new technology does not normally keep pace with the rate of growth in scale. For example, the Chinese Government's current five-year plan involves a 20 per cent reduction in the energy intensity of its economy—a level of ambition with few international precedents. But over those five years at current rates of growth, China's GDP will be almost 55 per cent larger. . . .

The same dynamic can be seen repeatedly over time: for example, the improving efficiency of automobiles is routinely swamped by increased miles driven. . . .

* * *

2.5. But there are synergies between climate change goals and development

While it may be true that economic growth often conflicts with climate change objectives, this is not necessarily the case for development (which is, in the end, the object of growth). In fact there are important synergies between development and climate change objectives. There are, for example, a number of ways in which development efforts can lead to mitigation:

(a) Efforts to restore forest cover or avoid deforestation/land degradation, for example, can have significant development payoffs, including reduced time spent collecting fuelwood, reduced indoor air pollution from inefficient biomass use and flood control in watersheds. In the process, such efforts also address a source of some 20 per cent of total anthropogenic emissions, reducing GHGs emitted and increasing carbon sink capacity;

(b) Efforts to provide energy to the poor constitute development in their own right. If that energy is in the form of renewables (e.g., biogas digesters, micro hydro, solar cookers, photovoltaic panels), then those efforts will count toward mitigating emissions, compared to a baseline of conventional new energy provision;

(c) Fuel-switching efforts may be aimed at reducing the burden of import costs, improving balance of payments and generating domestic employment. At the firm level they may simply be about increasing efficiency and/or saving on fuel costs, but they can also yield significant emissions reductions;

* * *

There are also a number of ways in which efforts to mitigate GHG emissions can contribute to development:

(a) Efforts to achieve energy efficiency have enormous potential to reduce GHG emissions. Household energy efficiency programmes can also reduce expenditures on heating and lighting (yielding particularly strong development benefits when targeted at the poor). And overall energy efficiency, other things being equal, leads to a stronger, more competitive economy, with significant economic benefits for all;

(b) Efforts to avoid the emissions associated with deforestation, as in the provision of improved cookstoves or solar cookers to fuelwood users, can yield significant development benefits as well, including reduced indoor air pollution. As noted above, avoided deforestation itself yields a number of development benefits;

(c) Efforts to capture methane emissions from landfills and livestock operations contribute powerfully to GHG emission

> reductions. Such efforts also reduced odours and often the containment technologies used significantly lower the risk of leaching and containment spills—a benefit to local populations.

As well as the links to mitigation efforts, development objectives have strong links to adaptation. This stands to reason: the key objective of adaptation measures is to reduce vulnerability to the immiserating impacts of climate change, so any successful adaptation efforts will, by definition, constitute development.

* * *

2.7. The international community should focus on advancing development goals sustainably in developing and least developed countries

The line of argument laid out in the previous sections holds true for developed countries as well as developing. Economic growth and development are key priorities for policymakers the world over, and climate change impacts will likewise be felt everywhere. In all countries there needs to be a focus on the types of win-win solutions that advance development goals and simultaneously achieve climate change objectives.

That said, as the international community addresses climate change there are a number of reasons why it should focus in particular on advancing development goals in developing and least developed countries.

First, while it is true that economic growth and development are priorities in all countries, the needs in developing and least developed countries are on a different scale altogether than that in the developed world. . . .

Second, current development paths indicate the greatest need for investment to alter energy paths is in developing countries. IEA's baseline projections predict that between 2007 and 2030 non-OECD countries will account for 87 per cent of the world's increase in primary energy demand and practically all (97 per cent) of the global increase in energy-related CO2 emissions.

Third, developing and least developed countries are particularly vulnerable to climate change impacts. Many are more exposed to climate change impacts because of their tropical geography. Further, developing countries, and particularly their poorest populations, are generally more sensitive to any climate change impacts, given a high dependence on agriculture, strong reliance on ecosystem services, rapid growth and concentration of population and relatively poor health. And developing countries generally have less capacity to adapt to climate change impacts, having inadequate infrastructure (particularly in water supply and management), meager household income and savings and limited supporting public services.

Fourth, there is a strong argument to be made on equity grounds. The very countries that are most vulnerable are, for the most part, those that have contributed least to the current atmospheric concentrations of GHGs. It can be argued that there is therefore a responsibility among the largest historic contributors to assist them in achieving development goals in ways that contribute to adaptation and mitigation goals.

Finally, if developing and least developed countries are to contribute meaningfully to efforts toward mitigation of climate change impacts, they will need the strengthened capacity that comes with development. The UNFCCC rightly holds, among its principles, that "economic development is essential for adopting measures to address climate change". That is, states that experience development are more likely to be able to play a meaningful role addressing the international challenge that is climate change.

7. John C. Dernbach, Achieving Early and Substantial Greenhouse Gas Reductions Under a Post-Kyoto Agreement, 20 Geo. Int'l Envtl. L. Rev. 573, 573–574, 582, 594–597, 599–603 (2008)

It has been more than 15 years since the United Nations Framework Convention on Climate Change was opened for signature in 1992, and more than a decade since the Kyoto Protocol was agreed to in 1997. We are now at the beginning of the 2008–2012 compliance period for the Kyoto Protocol, the first and only agreement under the Framework Convention that imposes binding greenhouse gas emission limitations. Yet little evidence exists to indicate that either agreement has had any significant effect on overall greenhouse gas emissions, and substantial doubt that the Kyoto Protocol can achieve significant reductions by 2012 even among the parties that are subject to Kyoto's emissions reduction targets.

* * *

Achieving substantial short-term emissions reductions should be a key objective for a post-Kyoto agreement for several reasons. These reasons include the climate science itself, the precautionary approach, the current availability of cost-effective policies and measures, the need to reduce the costs of climate change, the availability of considerable non-climate benefits from climate change mitigation, the need for governments to establish credibility in addressing climate change, the difficulty of achieving long-term reductions without short-term reductions, the ethical and equitable consequences of delay, and the need to build international confidence that mitigation is possible. . . .

* * *

Some analysts appear to oppose short-term reductions. Many analysts argue that the temporal distribution of greenhouse gas reductions should be guided by cost-benefit analysis. Such analyses tend to indicate that the great bulk of the necessary emissions reductions are most appropriately achieved after 2030. Many factors counsel for this result—the high costs of greenhouse gas mitigation, the fact that future costs are subject to a discount rate, the fact that needed technologies will take time to develop, and the long-term nature of the climate change problem. The economic argument has added force when we consider that countries will decide whether to participate in a post-Kyoto agreement based on their understanding of the costs they will bear as a result. Finally, the specific Kyoto targets have been criticized as unrealistic, especially for the United States, which experienced a 37 percent growth in GDP during the 1990s. The Kyoto Protocol, which would have required the United States to reduce its greenhouse gas emissions 5 percent from 1990 levels by 2008–2012, would have forced the United States to reduce its greenhouse gas emissions by 25–30 percent from business-as-usual levels. . . .

To a significant degree, this line of analysis has merit. Some reductions appear to be possible only in the long run, and the high costs of mitigating some sources of greenhouse gases will be reduced only through the development and deployment of technologies that do not now exist. But this is not true of all mitigation options, particularly those that are now available and cost-effective, as well as those that provide significant co-benefits and reduce the potential impacts of climate change. Developed countries have an ethical and even legal duty under the Framework Convention to implement such policies and measures. Significantly, these issues—co-benefits, benefits from reducing climate change impacts, and ethical responsibilities—are not addressed in macro-economic analyses that tend to indicate a preference for an approach that relies almost entirely on long-term action.

The argument for primarily long-term reductions also appears to rest on a more benevolent understanding of the potential effect of climate change than is warranted by the evidence. It is not prudent to postpone implementation of these options in the face of mounting scientific information about the impact of climate change, the desirability of the lowest possible stabilization level, and the sensitivity of the climate to human greenhouse gas emissions. This is particularly true when the implementation and achievement of long-term reductions will depend on actions taken in the immediate future. Nor does postponing short-term measures create the kind of political momentum and confidence building in the mitigation effort that is needed to provide a sound foundation for future actions. *Some* significant fraction of the world's greenhouse gas emissions can be reduced now or in the near future, and ample reasons exist to accomplish those reductions in a post-Kyoto agreement.

* * *

A. SHORT-TERM EMISSIONS STABILIZATION GOAL

The parties should consider a goal for stabilizing global greenhouse gas emissions by no later than 2020. . . .

This short-term emissions stabilization goal would be consistent with scientific evidence indicating that early action is needed and that lower stabilization levels involve lower costs and risks than higher stabilization levels. . . . This goal would also be consistent with the warning of scientist James Hansen, who said in 2006 that we have at most ten years—not ten years to decide upon action, but ten years to alter fundamentally the trajectory of global greenhouse emissions. . . .

B. DEVELOPED AND DEVELOPING COUNTRIES

A post-Kyoto agreement is more likely to achieve early and substantial reductions if it requires reductions by both developed and developing countries. Broadening participation to include developing countries is, of course, an important goal for any post-Kyoto agreement; otherwise the United States is not likely to ratify it. Participation by developing countries also enhances the likelihood of early and substantial results. To begin with, developing countries account for a significant and growing share of overall greenhouse gas emissions. At least two-thirds of the projected global increase in carbon dioxide emissions between now and 2030 will be from developing countries. China's emissions, in fact, are growing more than have previously been projected; the size of the projected increase by 2010 is several times larger than the reductions sought in the Kyoto Protocol.

Another reason to engage developing countries is to ensure that developed countries fully account for their greenhouse gas impact. There is evidence, for example, that global carbon dioxide emissions from European Union consumption are 12 percent higher than European Union production. This results from the fact that Europe imports are more energy-intensive and pollution-intensive than the products that it exports.

Finally, engaging developing countries to implement policies and measures that save energy, produce other benefits, and reduce the impacts of climate change would further sustainable development and alleviate poverty in those countries. Such early actions, in other words, have economic, social, environmental, and security benefits that exceed their mitigating effect on climate change. Indeed, focusing early action on such measures could help overcome the perception existing throughout the developing world that environmental controls are a luxury.

Section 5. Discussion Notes/Questions

1. As you prepare to negotiate with your classmates, you may find it helpful to consider past positions taken by states on the critical negotiation issues. You can find such information by a simple search of material on the

web. If you are more ambitious, climate change has been debated many times in the UN General Assembly, and its verbatim records may yield useful information. In addition, the UNFCCC website provides information on the nationally determined contributions (NDCs) your country has already pledged to make. You might want to check those out. But beware: as of this writing there is no agreed methodology for the format or content of such pledges, so you cannot assume that the existing pledges of various countries will be easily compared or that they are in a form that allows them to be used in this negotiation.

There are also many studies of climate negotiations that may provide useful background information and can be easily accessed on line. *See, e.g.*, POLIMP Project, *Role of Countries in Climate Negotiations,* CLIMATE POLICY INFO HUB, https://climatepolicyinfohub.eu/role-countries-climate-negotiations (last visited June 28, 2018); Swiss Network for International Studies (SNIS), *Negotiating Climate Change* (includes links to a number of relevant working papers), https://snis.ch/project/negotiating-climate-change/ (last visited June 28, 2018). Apart from these sources, an internet search will reveal a substantial amount of information about climate negotiations, including information about the negotiating positions taken by your assigned country.

2. In UNEP's 2017 Emissions Gap Report, it was estimated that on the world's "current policy trajectory," annual emissions of greenhouse gases would be 55.4 gigatons CO2e by 2025 and 58.9 gigatons by 2030. By contrast, the least-cost pathway to 2 degrees Celsius would require emissions of no more than 47.7 gigatons CO2e by 2025 and 41.8 gigatons by 2030.

To put this in context, the World Resources Institute has reported total greenhouse gas emissions (excluding land-use change and forestry) in 2014 for the countries in this problem as follows: Brazil, 1.05 gigaton CO2e; China, 11.91 gigatons; the European Union, 4.05 gigatons; Grenada, 0.002 gigatons; India, 3.08 gigatons; Saudi Arabia, 0.58 gigatons; the United States, 6.37 gigatons; and Zimbabwe, 0.028 gigatons. Figures from other sources vary slightly, but not inordinately so. According to the US EPA, US greenhouse gas emissions totaled 6.76 gigatons CO2e in 2014, 6.64 gigatons in 2015, and 6.5 gigatons in 2016.

3. Should developed countries be required to make reductions in their emissions of greenhouse gases that are sufficiently large to allow growth in emissions by developing countries while still ensuring that total atmospheric concentrations are at a safe level? Is it fair to aim at an equal *per capita* emissions level for all countries, or are there reasons to allow variations among countries?

4. Granted that emissions must be limited in the future, how does one equitably determine the allowable emissions for different countries? One suggested idea is that nations agree on a "global emission budget" for the period 1900 to 2050 that reflects the total greenhouse gas emissions that could be allowed during that period consistent with an acceptable level of planetary warming. That emissions budget could then be divided among all countries on

a *per capita* basis. Each country would be allowed to emit their part of the budget, taking into account the emissions they've already made since 1900. If a country has already met or exceeded its budget, it can buy emissions rights from other countries for future periods. What do you think?

Does equity have any role to play in the choose-your-own-adventure approach to emissions reduction under the Paris Agreement?

5. In a provocative paper released in May 2010, Professor Gwyn Prins and 13 other analysts declared the UNFCCC/Kyoto model "structurally flawed and doomed to fail." They argued that, instead of focusing on reducing greenhouse gas emissions, government policies should focus on doing things that carry other significant benefits and that therefore are "politically attractive and relentlessly pragmatic" as well as happening to have some climate-related benefits. For example, the eradication of black carbon (soot), a significant climate forcing agent, could be justified, it just so happens, entirely on public health grounds. So, one could seek to control black carbon pollution for good reasons that would be politically attractive, while indirectly making a positive contribution to reducing climate change. Similarly, policies focused on the promotion of energy efficiency are pro-development policies with economic benefits for individuals, businesses, and entire economies, but they also serve the goal of combating global warming. Finally, investment in research and innovation aimed at decarbonizing the energy supply will serve long-term climate change goals while being "harmonious with economic growth" and far more likely to secure "political traction" than an emissions reduction policy that stunts growth. *See* Gwyn Prins et al., *The Hartwell Paper: A New Direction for Climate Policy after the Crash of 2009* (2010).

What advantages and/or disadvantages do you see to this approach? Is it enough? To answer the question, you must first try to identify the various policies that are desirable and politically attractive on their own merits and simultaneously helpful in combating climate change. Try it, and see how many you can think of.

6. What are the issues in the negotiations over funding (other than the total amount)? One issue is how to split the funding between mitigation and adaptation. If you were a developed nation, would you prefer to finance mitigation or adaptation? Any particular kind of mitigation you would prefer to fund? How about reductions in deforestation? If you were a developing nation, would you prefer funding for mitigation or adaptation? Article 9.4 of the Paris Agreement provides that "the provision of scaled-up financial resources should aim to achieve a balance between adaptation and mitigation." But developed nations could satisfy their own preferences in this regard by their decisions about where to direct funding. Do developing nations have any leverage that will allow them to insist on consideration of their preferences (e.g., for adaptation support) when funding is allocated?

Some developed nations argue that a significant amount of climate-change-related financing should come from the private sector. Do you understand how private investment is supposed to work? What would induce private firms to invest in climate change mitigation or adaptation projects in developing countries? Perhaps the prospect of earning tradeable emission reduction credits? Anything else? Article 9.3 of the Paris Agreement tosses a bone to the developed-nation position by stating that climate finance should be mobilized "from a wide variety of sources, instruments and channels." But it also notes the "significant role of public funds."

7. There are many important issues under discussion at the international level that have not been addressed in this problem. One of the most important negotiation topics is technology transfer. For a general discussion, *see* Cynthia Cannady, *Access to Climate Change Technology by Developing Countries: A Practical Strategy*, ICTSD Issue Paper No. 25 (2009). *See also* Article 10 of the Paris Agreement.

PROBLEM 9-2: HANGUO GEOENGINEERS THE CLIMATE

Section 1. Facts

The People's Republic of Hanguo ("Hanguo") is a large developing nation in Eastern Asia. It has grown rapidly in recent years, and this economic growth has led to a dramatic increase in its domestic industrial production and energy consumption. Although it is experimenting with alternative forms of electricity generation such as solar and wind power, Hanguo has huge reserves of coal, and most of its factories are powered by coal. Hanguo has kept up with steadily rising demand for electricity by building several new coal-fired power plants every year. Furthermore, as the Hanguoan middle class has grown, the automobile has become ubiquitous in Hanguoan cities, and Hanguo has become the world's largest importer of oil. As a result of these developments, Hanguo is now one of the top five greenhouse-gas-emitting nations in the world. It also is one of the most powerful states in its region due to its large economy, its large and well-equipped military, and an arsenal of nuclear weapons.

As Hanguo's middle class has grown, its citizens and government have become more attentive to environmental issues, and concern has been increasing about the potential adverse consequences of climate change for the future well-being of the state. Particularly worrisome are current models projecting significant sea level rise by the end of the 21st Century. Approximately 400 million citizens of Hanguo live in low-lying cities and rural communities along Hanguo's lengthy Pacific coastline, and sea level rises of even half of a meter would displace a significant portion of that coastal population.

Last year, Hanguo's president determined that the country should take steps to reduce and mitigate the effects of climate change as quickly as possible. However, convinced that reductions in domestic emissions of carbon dioxide and other greenhouse gases would seriously retard Hanguo's economic development, the president decided that Hanguo's climate change policy should focus on two so-called "geoengineering" solutions to the problem. First, the president ordered Hanguo's navy to begin iron fertilization in Hanguo's exclusive economic zone to augment phytoplankton growth in the ocean. Marine biologists in Hanguo believe that larger phytoplankton populations will remove large amounts of carbon dioxide from the atmosphere, thereby reducing total greenhouse gas concentrations. Second, the president directed Hanguo's air force to use dirigibles to emit sulfur dioxide directly into the stratosphere. Hanguoan climatologists posit that the injection of sulfate aerosols into the stratosphere will directly reduce global average temperatures by blocking sunlight from entering the upper atmosphere and providing an additional barrier to solar energy by increasing cloud cover.

Although Hanguo did not publicly announce these efforts, they were immediately detected and denounced by a coalition of developed states, led by the Federation of Columbia. The FC President claimed that "unilateral geoengineering creates grave risks of harm to the environment of other states and is contrary to established principles of international law, including the duty to cooperate on environmental matters."

Ignoring these protests, Hanguo continued its efforts. A year later, climate scientists across the world have detected a decline in average global temperatures due, they believe, to Hanguo's injection of sulfate aerosols into the stratosphere. There are also well-verified reports of exceptionally large plankton blooms in the Pacific Ocean, east of Hanguo.

In response to evidence of the impact of Hanguo's actions, some developing states (especially several small island states) have expressed appreciation to Hanguo for its "leadership in responding to the climate change crisis." However, not all states approve of what is happening. The Federation of Columbia has denounced Hanguo for conducting an "irresponsible experiment" with the planet, and other countries have expressed similar concerns. Two of Hanguo's neighbors, Bihar and Greater LiuQui, have raised more immediate objections to Hanguo's actions, and have brought their complaints to the UN Security Council.

Bihar, located to the southwest of Hanguo, is a large developing nation with a modern military and nuclear weapons capability. The border between Hanguo and Bihar has been in dispute for many years, with Hanguo claiming ownership of Arun, a prosperous agricultural region in the north of Bihar. The two countries fought a brief shooting war more than 40 years ago that ended without a settlement of the border issue. Recent relations between the two states, though tense, have remained peaceful. The international community generally recognizes Arun as part of Bihar.

Bihar alleges that Hanguo's injection of sulfate aerosols into the upper atmosphere has substantially altered rainfall patterns throughout Asia and has effectively shut down the annual monsoon rains that are vital to agriculture in Bihar, especially in the Arun region. According to Bihar, the current year's rainfall totals are only 10% of normal and crop failures in Arun and elsewhere are widespread. Hanguo has responded that the rainfall declines in Bihar are likely due to climate change, and that Hanguo's actions will help reverse the process in the long run. However, Hanguo has offered to provide Arun farmers with access to water from nearby Hanguoan mountain reservoirs, provided that Bihar "cease its illegal occupation of Arun and turn the region over to the proper Hanguoan government authorities."

On the other side of Hanguo, located about 1000 kilometers to the east in the Pacific Ocean, is the island state of Greater LiuQui, another neighbor with which Hanguo's relations are tense. Greater LiuQui claims and administers the Siyu Islands, located approximately 150 kilometers off its western coast. Hanguo has long claimed that the Siyu Islands belong to it and that Greater LiuQui is illegally occupying them. Although Hanguo has sometimes threatened military action to recover the islands, it has in fact never made any attempt to take them by force.

Greater LiuQui is now complaining that the large plankton blooms stimulated by Hanguo's iron fertilization program have been carried by prevailing winds into the waters surrounding the Siyu Islands, and that they are adversely affecting the ecology of those areas, resulting in significantly declining stocks of key fish species. Hanguo has replied that the fish stocks in question have been declining for years and the current decline cannot be attributed to its actions. However, it has offered to provide all assistance necessary to secure the livelihoods of the Siyu Islanders, including access to fishing grounds in Hanguoan waters provided Greater LiuQui surrenders administrative control of the Siyu Islands to Hanguo.

Following unsuccessful negotiations with Hanguo, Bihar and Greater LiuQui jointly submitted a complaint against Hanguo to the United Nations Security Council, alleging that Hanguo's actions were illegal and a threat to international peace and security in the region. Moreover, they say, Hanguo's actions were not taken primarily to address the problem of climate change, but in fact to gain advantage in its territorial disputes with Bihar and Greater LiuQui. For its part, Hanguo contends that its geoengineering program is completely peaceful in intent, and is aimed at combating climate change and its consequences, specifically sea-level rise, which pose a clear and present danger to Hanguo's coastal population, as well as those of Bihar and Great LiuQui.

Bihar and Greater LiuQui have asked the Security Council to condemn Hanguo's actions as a violation of international law and to direct Hanguo to provide assistance to both countries in remedying the harm caused by Hanguo's geoengineering program. All three states are members of the United Nations, but not of the Security Council. Each state has ratified the 1972 Convention on the Prevention of Marine Pollution by Dumping of Wastes and Other Matter; the 1977 Convention on the Prohibition of Military or Any Other Hostile Use of Environmental Modification Techniques ("Environmental Modification Convention"); the 1982 United Nations Convention on the Law of the Sea; the 1985 Vienna Convention for the Protection of the Ozone Layer; the 1992 UN Framework Convention on Climate Change; and the 1992 Convention on Biological Diversity.

You are legal counsel to the Foreign Minister of Savoy, a permanent member of the Security Council. The Foreign Minister has asked you to advise Savoy's U.N. ambassador concerning the legal issues raised in this matter.

Section 2. Questions Presented

1. Does Hanguo's policy of injecting sulfate aerosols into the stratosphere violate international law? If so, is there any basis for Security Council action?

2. Does Hanguo's policy of ocean fertilization violate international law? If so, is there any basis for Security Council action?

Section 3. Assignments

A. *Reading Assignment*

Study the Readings presented in Parts A and B of this Chapter, *supra*, and in Section 4, *infra*.

B. *Recommended Writing Assignment*

Prepare a memorandum for the Foreign Minister of Savoy in the form of an outline of the primary and subsidiary *legal* issues you see as relevant to any decision that might be made by the Security Council in this matter. Indicate how you think the issues should be resolved under international law and why. Retain a copy of your issue-outline for class discussion.

C. *Recommended Oral Assignment*

Assume you are legal counsel for one of the states involved in this dispute (as designated by your instructor). Relying upon the Readings (and your issue-outline if prepared), present a 15–20 minute oral argument of your government's position in the matter.

D. Recommended Reflective Assignment

Consider (and recommend) alternative norms, institutions, and/or procedures that you believe might do better than existing world order arrangements to contend with situations of the kind posed by this problem. In so doing, but without insisting upon *immediate* feasibility, identify the particular transition steps that would be needed to make your alternatives a reality.

Section 4. Readings

1. Adam D.K. Abelkop & Jonathan C. Carlson, Reining in Phaëthon's Chariot: Principles for the Governance of Geoengineering, 21 Trans. L. & Contemp. Prob. 101 (2012) (as updated and revised by the authors)

The myth of the mortal Phaëthon is a cautionary tale. According to Greek lore, the young Phaëthon convinced his father, the sun god Helios, to allow the boy any single wish he desired. More than anything, Phaëthon yearned to drive the god's "chariot," the sun, from east to west across the sky and through the heavens as the sun god himself did each day. Helios cautioned Phaëthon, however, that no other being—not even the almighty Zeus himself—could maintain control of the sun. Disregarding this warning from his father, Phaëthon took charge of the fiery chariot. Just as Helios had feared, Phaëthon lost control of the unyielding sun, melting glaciers and scorching the earth as he careened about the planet. Intervening to save Earth from climatic ruin, Zeus destroyed Phaëthon and returned the sun to Helios's control.

The tale of Phaëthon is an apt metaphor for the position in which humanity finds itself today. Indeed, the earth has entered a new epoch in its geological history that many are coming to call the "Anthropocene" to mark the increasing human influence on global natural systems. It is an era in which humankind increasingly bears "responsibility for the welfare and future evolution of life on the planet"[50] because of the profound impacts human activities are having on the planet. As a result of anthropogenic greenhouse gas emissions in particular, the climate of the planet will, for millennia, significantly deviate from its natural trajectory.

* * *

As data begins to confirm some of the worst-case projections from climate scientists around the world, policymakers seem to be at an impasse on enacting a solution. Despite initial hope for the 2015 Paris Agreement, the United States has announced its intention to withdraw from the agreement at the earliest possibility, and the emissions-reduction

---

[50] Robert L. Olson, Woodrow Wilson Int'l Ctr. for Scholars, Geoengineering for Decision Makers 2 (2011).

commitments made by the parties to the agreement are far short of what is needed to avoid dangerous temperature increases. According to the 2018 UN Environment Emissions Gap Report, the level of ambition reflected in the initial set of Nationally Determined Contributions filed by the parties to the Paris Agreement "needs to be roughly tripled" to keep warming below 2 degrees Celsius and needs to be "increased around fivefold" to meet the 1.5 degree target.[51]

The lack of progress reflects the fact that climate change has all the makings of a "wicked problem"—a problem that "defies resolution because of the enormous interdependencies, uncertainties, circularities, and conflicting stakeholders implicated."[52] Climate change is wrought with "temporal and spatial complexities,"[53] a deficiency in governance, powerful economic incentives for the polluters to resist mitigation, and no single solution.[54] Moreover, climate change creates spin-off problems that are themselves wicked problems with deficiencies in governance.

Geoengineering represents one such problem. Geoengineering is "intentional large-scale manipulation of the environment."[55] Whereas mitigation efforts seek to reduce humanity's influence on the natural world, geoengineering "seeks to ameliorate the effects of existing anthropogenic interferences with natural processes by introducing additional anthropogenic interferences."[56] Indeed, a group of notable scientists has emerged to tell us that they have discovered the secret to manipulating earth's radiative balance and that they can restore climate stability if given the money and power to do so.[57] These modern-day Phaëthons would grab the reins of Helios's chariot and, like the sun god himself, select a path for the global environment that will restore climatic equilibrium to the planet. Yet, like climate change, geoengineering

---

[51] UNEP, *Executive Summary,* The Emissions Gap Report 2018 at 4.

[52] Cinnamon P. Carlarne, *Arctic Dreams and Geoengineering Wishes: The Collateral Damage of Climate Change,* 49 Colum. J. Transnat'l L. 602, 606 (2011) (quoting Richard J. Lazarus, *Super Wicked Problems and Climate Change: Restraining the Present To Liberate the Future,* 94 Cornell L. Rev. 1153, 1159 (2009)).

[53] Alan Carlin, *Why a Different Approach Is Required if Global Climate Change Is to Be Controlled Efficiently or Even at All,* 32 Wm. & Mary Envtl. L. & Pol'y Rev. 685, 685 (2008).

[54] Carlarne, *supra* note 3, at 606–09; William F. Ruddiman, Plows, Plagues, and Petroleum 183 (2005).

[55] David Keith, *Geoengineering the Climate: History and Prospect,* 25 Ann. Rev. Energy Env't 245, 245 (2000).

[56] Albert C. Lin, *Geoengineering Governance,* 8 Issues Legal Scholarship 3, 14 (2009) (internal citation omitted).

[57] The Royal Soc'y, Geoengineering the Climate: Science, Governance And Uncertainty 57 (2009) [hereinafter Royal Soc'y 2009], available at http://royalsociety.org/uploadedFiles/Royal_Society_Content/policy/publications/2009/8693.pdf; *see* Symposium, *Geoengineering the Climate? A Southern Hemisphere Perspective,* Nat'l Comm. for Earth Sys. Sci. (Sept. 26, 2011), http://science.org.au/natcoms/nc-ess/documents/GEsymposium.pdf; Div. of Ecological & Earth Sciences, U.N. Educ., Scientific, & Cultural Org., Engineering the Climate: Research Questions and Policy Implications (Nov. 1, 2011), *available at* http://unesdoc.unesco.org/images/0021/002144/214496e.pdf.

solutions are themselves wicked problems that challenge our understanding of the climatic system and raise questions of risk, equity, and justice. Even if climate engineering reduces the global mean temperature, it is virtually inevitable that some group of people will be harmed in the process. . . .

Geoengineering raises fundamental philosophical, political, scientific, and legal questions. What type of relationship should humankind maintain with the natural environment? Is geoengineering an answer to collective action problems in the governance of the global climate commons? Which methods warrant a closer examination? What parameters should govern the choice of one geoengineering technique over another? How should the public be involved in decision making on climate engineering? Should those communities harmed by geoengineering be compensated and, if so, how? The legal and policy questions themselves are numerous and dense, and are increasingly the subject of international discussion and concern.

* * *

A. *Geoengineering: History and Rationale*

The concept of engineering the climate predates the climate crisis. In fact, the notion that humans could (and should) attempt to deliberately alter weather patterns dates to at least the 1830s. By the late 1930s, the Soviet Union and the United States were both actively exploring techniques of climate modification to, for example, open shipping routes through the Arctic or gain tactical military advantages. One of the earliest mentions of geoengineering as a technology to reduce the human impact on the climate came in a 1965 report issued to Lyndon B. Johnson by the President's Science Advisory Council—notably, one of the first high-level acknowledgements of the human hand in climate change. By 2008, China was employing 50,000 laborers and spending more than $100 million annually using artillery to seed clouds with silver iodide in an attempt to control the weather for the 2008 Summer Olympic Games. Today, the possibility of geoengineering the climate is receiving attention not only from the policy and natural science communities, but also from non-governmental organizations ("NGOs"), the media, legal and social scholars, philosophers, research corporations, and wealthy philanthropists. The IPCC's 5th Assessment Report on the Mitigation of Climate Change included an extensive discussion of geoengineering options.

Geoengineering options are receiving a great deal of attention for a variety of reasons. First, there is a growing recognition that the governance mechanisms in place—at both domestic and international levels—are inadequate to overcome collective action problems in time to stave off harmful global warming. Even if humanity were to stop emitting CO_2 today, the planet would continue to warm an additional 0.5 degrees Celsius over the next two centuries due to the hundred-year residence time of CO_2

in the atmosphere. Furthermore, the improving knowledge of the global climatic system suggests that the positive feedbacks mentioned above could trigger climate tipping points, which would require response mechanisms that have quicker effects on the climate than mitigation techniques have. In fact, some technologies could begin to have a measurable effect on the global climate within a matter of months after deployment. Climate engineering advocates, therefore, promote geoengineering as an "insurance mechanism," "Plan B," or "last resort" in the face of climate emergencies and as an interim measure to buy time for a mitigation strategy to be selected and take effect.

Second, many advocates support geoengineering—regardless of its usefulness as an emergency option—as a cost savings mechanism vis-à-vis economically disruptive mitigation measures, the most effective of which would require substantial reductions in GHG emissions. They suggest that certain techniques could act as a complement to mitigation while others have the potential to displace the need for mitigation altogether. The exact capital investments and operating costs involved vary with the engineering technique and deployment method, but for many of the methods being widely discussed, the costs are low enough for single nations or even corporations to carry out geoengineering unilaterally. David Victor notes that "the discounted present cost of a geoengineering programme extended into perpetuity is of the order of $100 billion"—an amount he finds to be "shockingly small."[58] On the other hand, Nicholas Stern estimates that the cost of conventional mitigation would be approximately one trillion dollars—between 1 and 2 percent of global GDP—per year.[59] To William Nordhaus, this difference in cost between mitigation and geoengineering is so great that he treats the act of developing and deploying geoengineering as essentially "costless."[60]

The combination of low cost and quick benefits allows geoengineering to escape most collective action problems. Every stage of research, development, and deployment of geoengineering can be done unilaterally—by wealthy individuals and corporations as well as nations. At least a dozen nations already possess the technological and economic capacity to conduct a planetary geoengineering effort by themselves.[61] It is not inconceivable that one of these nations would decide that the harm it faces from climate change is so grave that it should resort to manipulating the climate, especially if it concludes that the harmful effects of climate modification

[58] David G. Victor, *On the Regulation of Geoengineering*, 24 Oxford Rev. Econ. Pol'y 322, 326 (2008).

[59] Nicholas Stern, The Economics of Climate Change: The Stern Review 232, 238–39 (2007).

[60] William D. Nordhaus, *An Optimal Transition Path for Controlling Greenhouse Gases*, 258 Science 1315, 1317 (1992).

[61] *See* Bipartisan Policy Ctr., Task Force on Climate Remediation Research, Geoengineering: A National Strategic Plan for Research on the Potential Effectiveness, Feasibility, and Consequences of Climate Remediation Technologies 6–7 (2011).

would fall outside its borders. The fear of unilateral action with planetary effects, therefore, provides a third reason why geoengineering proposals are drawing attention—particularly from stakeholders who take an interest in designing potential governance mechanisms.

Geoengineering represents a novel challenge, as no regulatory structure exists to govern implementation or research and development efforts. Nonetheless, experiments on several geoengineering techniques are already underway. Scientists and corporations are seeking funding while governments are eagerly reviewing findings to determine what role geoengineering should play in their mix of technological responses to climate change. That no governing mechanism exists to constrain geoengineering activity only increases the likelihood that some nation or group will actually attempt climate modification in the coming decades. The uncertain risks inherent in all geoengineering techniques, combined with the threat of unilateral climate manipulation by undisciplined and unaccountable public or private actors, create a pressing need for the development of governance mechanisms to inform the public and stakeholders, guide research and development, and allow governments to responsibly consider deployment options.

B. Methods

Geoengineering includes any large-scale technique designed to manipulate the environment. In the context of climate change, there are two primary classes of proposed geoengineering options: carbon dioxide removal ("CDR") technologies are being designed to draw CO_2 from the atmosphere to increase the amount of outgoing longwave, thermal infrared radiation, whereas solar radiation management ("SRM") technologies are being designed to lower the amount of incoming shortwave solar radiation. Geoengineering methods are not "one size fits all." The costs and timeframes for implementation and climate response differ with each method. Thus, the choice of method will turn on the nature of the climate emergency at hand. For example, a predictable future climate impact (e.g., sea-level rise) may call for a slower CDR method, while a sudden and unexpected climate emergency (e.g., the rapid onset of severe droughts) may call for an SRM method with a quick climate response.

1. Carbon Dioxide Removal

Methods that remove CO_2 from the atmosphere have an advantage over SRM measures because CDR technologies address the underlying cause of climate change. Though other greenhouse gases—methane (CH_4), nitrous oxide (N_2O), ground-level ozone (O_3), halocarbons, and water vapor—contribute to global warming, carbon dioxide is by far the primary greenhouse gas responsible for climate change. Thus, CDR methods seek to remove CO_2 from the atmosphere by employing chemical, biological, or physical mechanisms to enhance existing carbon sinks in the land and ocean or to create new carbon sinks altogether.

Certain CDR technologies will undoubtedly play an indispensable role in the solution to climate change: "In the long-term, the only way to return atmospheric CO_2 to pre-industrial levels is to permanently store (in some combination of the crust, sediments, soils, oceans, and terrestrial biosphere) an equivalent amount of CO_2 to the total emitted to the atmosphere."[62]

Methods that enhance land carbon sinks are the least invasive CDR approaches. For example, afforestation and reforestation measures involve growing forests on non-forested land, thereby creating new carbon sinks in terrestrial vegetation. Other methods that have been discussed include chemically altering soil minerals to uptake additional carbon, increasing the use of biomass energy sources, and carbon capture from emissions streams or even the ambient air, paired with geologic sequestration.

Attempts to enhance ocean carbon sinks are more demanding than land-based measures. The ocean stores CO_2 through two natural mechanisms: a solubility pump and a biological pump. The solubility pump functions through an inorganic physio-chemical process whereby the surface ocean absorbs carbon dioxide from the atmosphere and the CO_2-rich water sinks to great depths.[63] Through this process, the ocean absorbs roughly one quarter of the anthropogenic CO_2 that we emit into the atmosphere each year. On a millennial timescale, nearly all anthropogenic CO_2 emissions will end up in the deep ocean. The biological pump, on the other hand, functions through planktonic algae, which absorbs CO_2 through photosynthesis.[64] Though much of the CO_2 taken into the ocean through this process is degassed back into the atmosphere, some CO_2 sinks into deep waters within the remains of planktonic algae and in other debris from the food chain.

Scientists could enhance the solubility pump by increasing the rate at which CO_2-rich waters sink and by altering the chemistry of the surface water to increase the amount of CO_2 absorbed into the ocean. For example, some scientists have suggested that it would be possible to increase downwelling (sinking) of CO_2-rich waters by mechanically cooling the ocean's surface. On the other hand, increasing the alkalinity of surface water by adding carbonate minerals would increase the surface water's physio-chemical absorption of CO_2.

Though enhancing the solubility pump may be a more effective long-term solution, advocates of geoengineering have given more attention to

---

[62] Naomi E. Vaughan & Timothy M. Lenton, *A Review of Climate Geoengineering Proposals*, 109 Climatic Change 745, 750 (2011).

[63] *Id.*; Royal Soc'y 2009, *supra* note 8, at 19.

[64] *Id.*

methods that enhance the biological pump. Advocates have given iron fertilization particular attention.[65] In the Equatorial Pacific and Southern Ocean, a deficiency in iron limits the growth of phytoplankton. Dispersing iron particles into the ocean, therefore, will stimulate the growth of phytoplankton, which, through photosynthesis, will draw in CO_2. More than a dozen small-scale experiments conducted in the open ocean have demonstrated the potential of iron fertilization; however, a great deal of uncertainty still surrounds iron fertilization as an effective geoengineering technique. Although additional phytoplankton takes in a great deal of CO_2, much of this CO_2 is released back into the atmosphere through physio-chemical respiration. Feeding by zooplankton and crustaceans on the phytoplankton also keeps a notable amount of the CO_2 near the surface. Therefore, "only a small fraction [of absorbed CO_2] is finally transported and sequestered deep in the water column or in the sediments."[66] Finally, iron fertilization in one area could draw down concentrations of other essential nutrients—e.g., nitrogen and phosphorous—in other, downstream areas in a process called "nutrient robbing." Thus, iron fertilization's effectiveness will turn on an assessment of the entire ocean carbon system.

2. Solar Radiation Management

Whereas CDR methods would slowly draw down levels of atmospheric CO_2, SRM methods have the potential to stimulate rapid changes in the climate and are relatively cheaper to deploy. Full implementation of several SRM techniques could take as little as one year, and the climate would respond quickly with surface temperatures potentially decreasing to pre-industrial levels within a matter of years thereafter.

SRM methods are designed to lower the amount of incoming shortwave solar radiation. They aim to accomplish this by deflecting incoming solar radiation from space or by increasing the reflectivity, or albedo, of the earth itself. Reducing the amount of incoming solar radiation will, in turn, lower the global mean temperature. Yet, although SRM methods block solar radiation from reaching the earth, a fundamental shortcoming of these methods is that they do not decrease the atmospheric concentration of CO_2. As a result, SRM methods do not address the problem of ocean acidification. Moreover, absent controls on atmospheric concentrations of GHGs, their cessation would result in rapid warming. Nonetheless, many climate scientists support the use of SRM insofar as it appears necessary to avoid the radiative forcing that would accompany a doubling of atmospheric CO_2 from pre-industrial levels.

---

[65] Less promising proposals involve increasing the concentrations of nitrogen and/or phosphorous to areas of ocean that are deficient in those macronutrients by either adding the nutrients to the water or by mechanically enhancing upwelling, which would transport nutrient rich deep water to the surface to stimulate algal growth.

[66] Royal Soc'y 2009, *supra* note 8, at 17.

A variety of space-based deflection techniques have been discussed in the literature, including reflective mirrors, or "solar shields," which would extend for 4.7 million square kilometers to achieve the desired amount of deflection. To keep pace with increasing GHG emissions, additional space shades would need to be added each year. For the most part, space-based solar deflection methods are unrealistic at this point in time given the large capital investments required to develop and deploy the technology. In addition, there are no nations with both the capacity and political will to deploy space-based SRM.

In contrast, the simplest SRM methods involve enhancing the surface albedo of the earth. These measures involve increasing the reflectivity of human settlements—for example, painting roofs and paved areas white. Efforts like this are not likely to have a global effect, but could reduce the temperature in cities from the urban-heat-island effect. In addition to altering human settlements, scientists have suggested that selecting more reflective plant varieties, or even genetically modifying plants to be more reflective, could enhance surface albedo. Finally, others have suggested covering deserts and oceans with reflective surfaces. Each of these methods would likely reduce the global mean temperature, but they would also each present countervailing ecological risks.

On the other hand, some scientists have suggested that enhancing the albedo of clouds is an "ecologically benign" SRM method. Indeed, vessels could seed clouds with sea-salt by spraying ocean water into the atmosphere with the effect of increasing the ocean clouds' droplet concentrations—in other words, "whitening" the clouds—and thereby making them more reflective. Despite the initial appeal of this approach as ecologically friendly, little is known about the effects of enhancing cloud albedo, and therefore, some experts have grown skeptical.

The most frequently discussed method of all of the SRM geoengineering proposals, however, is aerosol injection. This method involves the dispersal of aerosols—e.g., hydrogen sulfide (H_2S) or sulfur dioxide (SO_2)—into the stratosphere to reflect solar radiation back towards space, thus limiting the amount of shortwave radiation that can heat the earth. Aerosol injection has drawn a great deal of attention because observational data indicates that this method is theoretically sound. Indeed, aerosol injection proposals are attempts to mimic the effects of volcanic eruptions, which expel massive amounts of dust and debris into the atmosphere. "The cooling impact of these large volcanic eruptions is well documented—[SO_2] ejected into the stratosphere reacts to form sulphate aerosols, which scatter shortwave and absorb and emit longwave radiation."[67] Moreover, dispersing aerosols can be accomplished in a relatively straightforward manner: potential delivery mechanisms for the

[67] Vaughan & Lenton, *supra* note 13, at 764 (noting that smaller particles are ideal because they do not absorb outgoing longwave radiation).

gaseous particles include aircraft, artillery shells, and stratospheric balloons. In addition, developing and deploying this technology would be relatively inexpensive. In fact, deploying a fleet of airplanes to disperse aerosols into the stratosphere would only cost several billion dollars per year—less than the operating costs of major airlines.

It is perhaps ironic that aerosol injection has received the most enthusiasm from geoengineering advocates, because analyses conducted thus far hint that it also presents the most ecological danger of any climate engineering technique.[68]

C. *Ecological Hazards of Geoengineering*

Though climate engineering is advocated as a technique to protect the planet from major environmental harm, nearly all of the geoengineering techniques mentioned above involve some non-zero risk of causing environmental harm of their own. Researchers and decisionmakers will need to evaluate and balance these risks against the risks of climate change before attempting large-scale climate engineering. In this section, we briefly consider some of the known ecological hazards associated with the two most widely discussed geoengineering techniques: ocean iron fertilization and aerosol injection.

All else being equal, decisionmakers should prefer CDR over SRM techniques because CDR addresses the root cause of the climate problem—carbon dioxide emissions. However, CDR methods, including ocean iron fertilization, also raise the potential for harm to ecosystems and those communities who depend on them for their wellbeing. Fertilization-induced algal blooms could contribute to eutrophication and hypoxia, causing a loss of biodiversity. Moreover, fertilization could incite changes in the macronutrient balance that would undermine productivity in some parts of the ocean, and it may also worsen the growing problem of ocean acidity. Finally, iron fertilization could result in a positive climate feedback through the release of methane and nitrous oxide emissions from chemical interactions associated with algae blooms—limiting the overall effectiveness of iron fertilization as a climate change solution in the first place.

The suite of hazards associated with aerosol injection is broader. One potential problem with SRM, whether through aerosol injection or otherwise, is that it works by reducing the amount of sunlight reaching the surface of the planet. This is likely to have a negative effect on plant photosynthesis, and it may have other adverse impacts that are not yet fully understood. In addition, because scientists do not know exactly how much sunlight to deflect in order to stabilize atmospheric temperatures at

---

[68] *See, e.g.*, Vaughan & Lenton, *supra* note 18, at 765 ("The uncertainties surrounding the effects of sulphate aerosol addition to the stratosphere are much greater and more meteorologically complicated than those related to mitigating CO_2 emissions.").

any particular level, all forms of SRM carry an inherent risk of overshooting or undershooting target temperature ranges. Because aerosol injection can be stopped relatively quickly, this risk is not as significant as it might otherwise be for this type of SRM. On the other hand, the ease with which aerosol injection can be reversed is also a problem: if a successful program of aerosol injection were used to cool the earth, the abrupt termination of that program would lead to a more rapid and sustained temperature increase than if the program had not been started in the first place.

A more troubling set of hazards relates to the possible impacts of aerosol injection on planetary systems, including the hydrological cycle and the ozone layer. Significant changes in rainfall patterns (e.g., modification of the Asian or African summer monsoons) would disrupt agriculture and could potentially impact the food supply for billions of people, leading to widespread famine in some areas of the world. Even if there are not extreme consequences, reduced evaporation (and hence precipitation) is a likely consequence with possible negative effects on freshwater availability. Scientists also expect that aerosol injection would contribute to ozone depletion—setting back current efforts to repair the hole in the ozone layer over Antarctica.

Whether large-scale ocean fertilization or aerosol injection efforts would actually result in any of these harms is unknown. Moreover, the timeframes associated with those impacts are unknown as well. Harm to the environment from fertilization and aerosol injection—or any geoengineering technique for that matter—is likely to be unpredictable and non-linear. Therefore, the size of the at-risk population is also indeterminate. Careful environmental monitoring following any geoengineering effort will be absolutely critical. Even a simple account of the hazards of geoengineering, though, makes it plain that any undesirable impact will almost certainly be transboundary in nature. This raises the likelihood that any geoengineering effort will have an unbalanced distributional impact: some communities will suffer more than others as a direct result of geoengineering.

2. Editors' Note

The remaining readings in this section consist of primary legal materials that you may find relevant when assessing the legality of Hanguo's behavior as described in the facts of the problem. In addition to these readings, your analysis of this problem should take account of the following:

a) Articles 2 & 3 of the UNFCCC, in part B of this chapter;

b) The materials on state responsibility and the duty to prevent transboundary harm, in Chapter 3;

c) The principles of international environmental law discussed in Chapter 4.

Your instructor may identify additional material you should consider.

The setting for this problem is in the United Nations Security Council, which is considering whether to take any action with respect to Hanguo's climate engineering activities. To familiarize you with the principles of the United Nations and the role of the Security Council, we begin with some excerpts from the United Nations Charter.

3. Charter of the United Nations, art. 1–2, & 33–38, June 26, 1945, 1976 YBUN 1043, 59 Stat 1031, TS 993 (Basic Document 1.1)

Article 1

The Purposes of the United Nations are:

1. To maintain international peace and security, and to that end: to take effective collective measures for the prevention and removal of threats to the peace, and for the suppression of acts of aggression or other breaches of the peace, and to bring about by peaceful means, and in conformity with the principles of justice and international law, adjustment or settlement of international disputes or situations which might lead to a breach of the peace;

2. To develop friendly relations among nations based on respect for the principle of equal rights and self-determination of peoples, and to take other appropriate measures to strengthen universal peace;

3. To achieve international co-operation in solving international problems of an economic, social, cultural, or humanitarian character, and in promoting and encouraging respect for human rights and for fundamental freedoms for all without distinction as to race, sex, language, or religion; and

4. To be a centre for harmonizing the actions of nations in the attainment of these common ends.

Article 2

The Organization and its Members, in pursuit of the Purposes stated in Article 1, shall act in accordance with the following Principles.

1. The Organization is based on the principle of the sovereign equality of all its Members.

2. All Members, in order to ensure to all of them the rights and benefits resulting from membership, shall fulfill in good faith the obligations assumed by them in accordance with the present Charter.

3. All Members shall settle their international disputes by peaceful means in such a manner that international peace and security, and justice, are not endangered.

4. All Members shall refrain in their international relations from the threat or use of force against the territorial integrity or political independence of any state, or in any other manner inconsistent with the Purposes of the United Nations.

5. All Members shall give the United Nations every assistance in any action it takes in accordance with the present Charter, and shall refrain from giving assistance to any state against which the United Nations is taking preventive or enforcement action.

6. The Organization shall ensure that states which are not Members of the United Nations act in accordance with these Principles so far as may be necessary for the maintenance of international peace and security.

7. Nothing contained in the present Charter shall authorize the United Nations to intervene in matters which are essentially within the domestic jurisdiction of any state or shall require the Members to submit such matters to settlement under the present Charter; but this principle shall not prejudice the application of enforcement measures under Chapter VII.

Article 33

1. The parties to any dispute, the continuance of which is likely to endanger the maintenance of international peace and security, shall, first of all, seek a solution by negotiation, enquiry, mediation, conciliation, arbitration, judicial settlement, resort to regional agencies or arrangements, or other peaceful means of their own choice.

2. The Security Council shall, when it deems necessary, call upon the parties to settle their dispute by such means.

Article 34

The Security Council may investigate any dispute, or any situation which might lead to international friction or give rise to a dispute, in order to determine whether the continuance of the dispute or situation is likely to endanger the maintenance of international peace and security.

Article 36

1. The Security Council may, at any stage of a dispute of the nature referred to in Article 33 or of a situation of like nature, recommend appropriate procedures or methods of adjustment.

* * *

Article 39

The Security Council shall determine the existence of any threat to the peace, breach of the peace, or act of aggression and shall make recommendations, or decide what measures shall be taken in accordance with Articles 41 and 42, to maintain or restore international peace and security.

Article 41

The Security Council may decide what measures not involving the use of armed force are to be employed to give effect to its decisions, and it may call upon the Members of the United Nations to apply such measures. These may include complete or partial interruption of economic relations and of rail, sea, air, postal, telegraphic, radio, and other means of communication, and the severance of diplomatic relations.

Article 42

Should the Security Council consider that measures provided for in Article 41 would be inadequate or have proved to be inadequate, it may take such action by air, sea, or land forces as may be necessary to maintain or restore international peace and security. Such action may include demonstrations, blockade, and other operations by air, sea, or land forces of Members of the United Nations.

Legal materials potentially relevant to Hanguo's SRM program

4. Vienna Convention for the Protection of the Ozone Layer, art. 2.1, Mar. 22, 1985, 1513 UNTS 293 (Basic Document 2.7)

Article 2

1. The Parties shall take appropriate measures in accordance with the provisions of this Convention and of those protocols in force to which they are party to protect human health and the environment against adverse effects resulting or likely to result from human activities which modify or are likely to modify the ozone layer.

5. Convention on Long Range Transboundary Air Pollution (LRTAP), arts. 1 & 2, Nov. 13, 1979, 1302 UNTS 217 (Basic Document 2.1)

Article 1: Definitions

For the purposes of the present Convention:

(a) "Air Pollution" means the introduction by man, directly or indirectly, of substances or energy into the air resulting in deleterious effects of such a nature as to endanger human health, harm living resources and ecosystems and material property and impair or interfere with amenities and other legitimate uses of the environment, and "air pollutants" shall be construed accordingly;

(b) "Long-range transboundary air pollution" means air pollution whose physical origin is situated wholly or in part within the area under the national jurisdiction of one State and which has adverse effects in the area under the jurisdiction of another State at such a distance that it is not generally possible to distinguish the contribution of individual emission sources or groups of sources.

Article 2: Fundamental Principles

The Contracting Parties, taking due account of the facts and problems involved, are determined to protect man and his environment against air pollution and shall endeavour to limit and, as far as possible, gradually reduce and prevent air pollution including long-range transboundary air pollution.

Legal materials potentially relevant to Hanguo's ocean fertilization program

6. United Nations Convention on the Law of the Sea (UNCLOS), arts. 1, 192—194 & 235, Dec. 10, 1982, 1833 UNTS 3 (Basic Document 3.4)

Article 1: Use of terms and scope

1(4): "pollution of the marine environment" means the introduction by man, directly or indirectly, of substances or energy into the marine environment, including estuaries, which results or is likely to result in such deleterious effects as harm to living resources and marine life, hazards to human health, hindrance to marine activities, including fishing and other legitimate uses of the sea, impairment of quality for use of sea water and reduction of amenities.

Article 192: General obligation

States have the obligation to protect and preserve the marine environment.

Article 193: Sovereign right of States to exploit their natural resources

States have the sovereign right to exploit their natural resources pursuant to their environmental policies and in accordance with their duty to protect and preserve the marine environment.

Article 194: Measures to prevent, reduce and control pollution of the marine environment

1. States shall take, individually or jointly as appropriate, all measures consistent with this Convention that are necessary to prevent,

reduce and control pollution of the marine environment from any source . . . .

2. States shall take all measures necessary to ensure that activities under their jurisdiction or control are so conducted as not to cause damage by pollution to other States and their environment, and that pollution arising from incidents or activities under their jurisdiction or control does not spread beyond the areas where they exercise sovereign rights in accordance with this Convention.

* * *

Article 235: Responsibility and Liability

1. States are responsible for the fulfilment of their international obligations concerning the protection and preservation of the marine environment. They shall be liable in accordance with international law.

7. Convention on the Prevention of Marine Pollution by Dumping of Wastes and Other Matter, 1972 (London Convention), arts. I, III & IV(1), 1046 UNTS 120 (Basic Document 3.2)

Article I

Contracting Parties shall individually and collectively promote the effective control of all sources of pollution of the marine environment, and pledge themselves especially to take all practicable steps to prevent the pollution of the sea by the dumping of waste and other matter that is liable to create hazards to human health, to harm living resources and marine life, to damage amenities or to interfere with other legitimate uses of the sea.

Article III

1. (a) "Dumping" means: (i) any deliberate disposal at sea of wastes or other matter from vessels, aircraft, platforms or other man-made structures at sea; (ii) any deliberate disposal at sea of vessels, aircraft, platforms or other manmade structures at sea.

(b) "Dumping" does not include: . . . (ii) placement of matter for a purpose other than the mere disposal thereof, provided that such placement is not contrary to the aims of this Convention.

* * *

Article IV

1. In accordance with the provisions of this Convention Contracting Parties shall prohibit the dumping of any wastes or other matter in whatever form or condition except as otherwise specified below:

(a) the dumping of wastes or other matter listed in Annex I is prohibited;

(b) the dumping of wastes or other matter listed in Annex II requires a prior special permit;

(c) the dumping of all other wastes or matter requires a prior general permit.

[*Eds.* neither of the annexes covers the materials used by Hanguo in its ocean fertilization program.]

8. Resolution LC-LP.1 on the Regulation of Ocean Fertilization, adopted by the 30th Meeting of the Contracting Parties to the London Convention and the Third Meeting of the Contracting Parties to the London Protocol, Oct. 31, 2008.

[The Contracting Parties to the London Convention and the London Protocol]

1. *Agree* that the scope of the London Convention and Protocol includes ocean fertilization activities;

2. *Agree* that for the purposes of this resolution, ocean fertilization is any activity undertaken by humans with the principle intention of stimulating primary productivity in the oceans;

3. *Agree* that in order to provide for legitimate scientific research, such research should be regarded as placement of matter for a purpose other than the mere disposal thereof under Article III.1(b)(ii) of the London Convention and Article 1.4.2.2 of the London Protocol;

4. *Agree* that scientific research proposals should be assessed on a case-by-case basis using an assessment framework to be developed by the Scientific Groups under the London Convention and Protocol;

5. *Agree* that the aforementioned assessment framework should include, inter alia, tools for determining whether the proposed activity is contrary to the aims of the Convention and Protocol;

6. *Agree* that until specific guidance is available, Contracting Parties should be urged to use utmost caution and the best available guidance to evaluate the scientific research proposals to ensure protection of the marine environment consistent with the Convention and Protocol;

7. *Agree* that for the purposes of this resolution, legitimate scientific research should be defined as those proposals that have been assessed and found acceptable under the assessment framework;

8. *Agree* that, given the present state of knowledge, ocean fertilization activities other than legitimate scientific research should not be allowed. To this end, such other activities should be considered as contrary to the aims of the Convention and Protocol and not currently qualify for any exemption from the definition of dumping in Article III.1(b) of the Convention and Article 1.4.2 of the Protocol;

9. *Agree* that this resolution should be reviewed at appropriate intervals in light of new and relevant scientific information and knowledge.

9. Convention on Biological Diversity, arts. 10 & 14, June 5, 1992, 1760 UNTS 79 (Basic Document 5.6)

Article 10. Sustainable Use of Components of Biological Diversity

Each Contracting Party shall, as far as possible and as appropriate:

(a) Integrate consideration of the conservation and sustainable use of biological resources into national decision-making;

(b) Adopt measures relating to the use of biological resources to avoid or minimize adverse impacts on biological diversity;

(c) Protect and encourage customary use of biological resources in accordance with traditional cultural practices that are compatible with conservation or sustainable use requirements;

(d) Support local populations to develop and implement remedial action in degraded areas where biological diversity has been reduced; and

(e) Encourage cooperation between its governmental authorities and its private sector in developing methods for sustainable use of biological resources.

Article 14. Impact Assessment and Minimizing Adverse Impacts

1. Each Contracting Party, as far as possible and as appropriate, shall:

(a) Introduce appropriate procedures requiring environmental impact assessment of its proposed projects that are likely to have significant adverse effects on biological diversity with a view to avoiding or minimizing such effects and, where appropriate, allow for public participation in such procedures;

(b) Introduce appropriate arrangements to ensure that the environmental consequences of its programmes and policies that are likely to have significant adverse impacts on biological diversity are duly taken into account;

(c) Promote, on the basis of reciprocity, notification, exchange of information and consultation on activities under their jurisdiction or control which are likely to significantly affect adversely the biological diversity of other States or areas beyond the limits of national jurisdiction, by encouraging the conclusion of bilateral, regional or multilateral arrangements, as appropriate;

(d) In the case of imminent or grave danger or damage, originating under its jurisdiction or control, to biological diversity within the area under jurisdiction of other States or in areas beyond the limits of national jurisdiction, notify immediately the potentially affected States of such danger or damage, as well as initiate action to prevent or minimize such danger or damage; and

(e) Promote national arrangements for emergency responses to activities or events, whether caused naturally or otherwise, which present a grave and imminent danger to biological diversity and encourage international cooperation to supplement such national efforts and, where appropriate and agreed by the States or regional economic integration organizations concerned, to establish joint contingency plans. * * *

10. Decision IX/16C on biodiversity and climate change, adopted by the Conference of the Parties to the Convention on Biological Diversity at its Ninth Meeting, 30 May 2008, U.N. Doc UNEP/CBD/COP/DEC/IX/16 (2008)[69]

The Conference of the Parties, * * *

4. *Bearing in mind* the ongoing scientific and legal analysis occurring under the auspices of the London Convention (1972) and the 1996 London Protocol, *requests* Parties and *urges* other Governments, in accordance with the precautionary approach, to ensure that ocean fertilization activities do not take place until there is an adequate scientific basis on which to justify such activities, including assessing associated risks, and a global, transparent and effective control and regulatory mechanism is in place for these activities; with the exception of small scale scientific research studies within coastal waters. Such studies should only be authorized if justified by the need to gather specific scientific data, and should also be subject to a thorough prior assessment of the potential impacts of the research studies on the marine environment, and be strictly controlled, and not be used for generating and selling carbon offsets or any other commercial purposes . . . .

11. U.N. Conference on Sustainable Development, *Rio+20 Declaration, The Future We Want*, U.N. Doc. A/CONF.216/16 at 1, 32 (June 22, 2012) (Basic Document 1.37)

167. We stress our concern about the potential environmental impacts of ocean fertilization. In this regard, we recall the decisions related to ocean fertilization adopted by the relevant intergovernmental bodies, and resolve

[69] The Conference of the Parties to the Convention on Biological Diversity has adopted three subsequent decision on climate engineering. Paragraph 8(w) of Decision X/33 briefly reaffirms the proposition that "no climate-related geo-engineering activities that may affect biodiversity" should take place "until there is an adequate scientific basis on which to justify such activities and appropriate consideration of the associated risks." Decision X/33 on biodiversity and climate change, 29 Oct. 2010, U.N. Doc UNEP/CBD/COP/DEC/X/33. At its 11th Meeting, the Conference adopted a decision that also addressed solar radiation management. That decision is reproduced below (reading 12), in relevant part. At its 13th Meeting, the Conference reaffirmed its earlier positions on climate engineering. *See* Decision XIII/14 on climate-related geoengineering, 9 Dec. 2016, U.N. Doc CBD/COP/DEC/XIII/14.

to continue addressing with utmost caution ocean fertilization, consistent with the precautionary approach.

Legal materials potentially relevant to all of Hanguo's climate engineering activities

12. Decision XI/20 on climate-related geoengineering, adopted by the Conference of the Parties to the Convention on Biological Diversity at its 11th Meeting, 19 Oct. 2012, U.N. Doc. UNEP/CBD/COP/DEC/XI/20 (2012)

The Conference of the Parties, * * *

4. *Emphasizes* that climate change should primarily be addressed by reducing anthropogenic emissions by sources and by increasing removals by sinks of greenhouse gases under the United Nations Framework Convention on Climate Change, noting also the relevance of the Convention on Biological Diversity and other instruments;

5. *Aware* of existing definitions and understandings, . . . and ongoing work in other forums, including the Intergovernmental Panel on Climate Change, *notes*, without prejudice to future deliberations on the definition of geoengineering activities, that climate-related geoengineering may include:

(a) Any technologies that deliberately reduce solar insolation or increase carbon sequestration from the atmosphere on a large scale and that may affect biodiversity (excluding carbon capture and storage from fossil fuels when it captures carbon dioxide before it is released into the atmosphere);

(b) Deliberate intervention in the planetary environment of a nature and scale intended to counteract anthropogenic climate change and/or its impacts;

(c) Deliberate large-scale manipulation of the planetary environment;

(d) Technological efforts to stabilize the climate system by direct intervention in the energy balance of the Earth for reducing global warming;

6. *Notes* . . . that there is no single geoengineering approach that currently meets basic criteria for effectiveness, safety and affordability, and that approaches may prove difficult to deploy or govern;

7. *Also notes* that there remain significant gaps in the understanding of the impacts of climate-related geoengineering on biodiversity, including:

(a) How biodiversity and ecosystem services are likely to be affected by and respond to geoengineering activities at different geographic scales;

(b) The intended and unintended effects of different possible geoengineering techniques on biodiversity;

(c) The socio-economic, cultural and ethical issues associated with possible geoengineering techniques, including the unequal spatial and temporal distribution of impacts;

8. *Notes* the lack of science-based, global, transparent and effective control and regulatory mechanisms for climate-related geoengineering, the need for a precautionary approach, and that such mechanisms may be most necessary for those geoengineering activities that have a potential to cause significant adverse transboundary effects, and those deployed in areas beyond national jurisdiction and the atmosphere, noting that there is no common understanding on where such mechanisms would be best placed;

* * *

11. *Notes* that the application of the precautionary approach as well as customary international law, including the general obligations of States with regard to activities within their jurisdiction or control and with regard to possible consequences of those activities, and requirements with regard to environmental impact assessment, may be relevant for geoengineering activities but would still form an incomplete basis for global regulation[.]

* * *

13. Convention on the Prohibition of Military or Any Other Hostile Use of Environmental Modification Techniques (ENMOD), arts. I–III, Dec. 10, 1976, 1108 UNTS 151 (Basic Document 7.19)

Article I

1. Each State Party to this Convention undertakes not to engage in military or any other hostile use of environmental modification techniques having widespread, long-lasting or severe effects as the means of destruction, damage or injury to any other State Party.

2. Each State Party to this Convention undertakes not to assist, encourage or induce any State, group of States or international organization to engage in activities contrary to the provisions of paragraph 1 of this article.

Article II

As used in article 1, the term "environmental modification techniques" refers to any technique for changing—through the deliberate manipulation of natural processes—the dynamics, composition or structure of the Earth, including its biota, lithosphere, hydrosphere and atmosphere, or of outer space.

Article III

1. The provisions of this Convention shall not hinder the use of environmental modification techniques for peaceful purposes and shall be without prejudice to the generally recognized principles and applicable rules of international law concerning such use.

2. The States Parties to this Convention undertake to facilitate, and have the right to participate in, the fullest possible exchange of scientific and technological information on the use of environmental modification techniques for peaceful purposes. States Parties in a position to do so shall contribute, alone or together with other States or international organizations, to international economic and scientific co-operation in the preservation, improvement and peaceful utilization of the environment, with due consideration for the needs of the developing areas of the world.

Section 5. Discussion Notes/Questions

1. Do Hanguo's actions violate international law? What problems of proof would you confront in establishing that Hanguo was liable for causing transboundary environmental harm? Do you think the ENMOD Convention is applicable to this scenario? What other international norms might Hanguo have violated?

It is possible that the injection of sulfate aerosols into the stratosphere would worsen the problem of ozone depletion. Would this be a violation of the Vienna Convention for the Protection of the Ozone Layer? Would ocean fertilization violate the UN Convention on the Law of the Sea if it had adverse ecological effects? What if ocean fertilization also proved to be an effective tool to combat global climate change? Would it still violate UNCLOS?

2. Is the United Nations Security Council an appropriate forum in which to resolve the legal issues raised in this problem? Does unilateral geoengineering raise issues of international peace and security? "If the losers from climate change use geoengineering to cool temperatures, might the winners use geoengineering to *absorb*, rather than to scatter, radiation[, thus raising temperatures]? (Might there be geoengineering wars?)" Scott Barrett, *The Incredible Economics of Geoengineering*, 39 Envtl. Resource Econ. 45, 51 (2008).

3. If geoengineering is as cheap and effective as some people believe, it seems likely that the temptation to experiment with it will be irresistible, especially if evidence of serious climate change continues to accumulate and efforts to reduce global greenhouse gas emissions continue to disappoint. How should the international community seek to govern geoengineering? Abelkop & Carlson argue that "international environmental law has developed a suite of norms . . . that provide a workable set of guideposts for the negotiation of an international agreement aimed at the regulation of geoengineering." Among the norms they mention are the obligations of notification, consultation, and

information-sharing; the requirement of environmental impact assessment of activity likely to have an adverse transboundary impact; and the principle that those who cause environmental harm should provide compensation to injured parties. Adam D.K. Abelkop & Jonathan C. Carlson, *Reining in Phaëton's Chariot: Principles for the Governance of Geoengineering,* 21 Transnat'l L. & Contemp. Prob. 101, 129, 135–139 (2012). Do you agree that the norms you've studied in this course provide a sound basis for regulating climate engineering activities?

Gareth Davies cautions against attempting to rely on existing law to govern climate engineering activities:

> [C]urrent law should not be allowed to constrain decision-making on geoengineering. The legal framework for liability and of environmental law was designed without this particular issue in mind. This is of course true of other environmental issues, but geoengineering is qualitatively very distinct. While, for example, pollution or conservation principles may be transferable from one pollutant or species to another, man-made cooling raises unique issues that demand a specific analysis and probably a specific regime. Even insofar as environmental law deals with climate change, it is concerned with warming, but the political dynamics of warming, which is generally a side-effect of other actions, are importantly different from geoengineering, which would entail the deliberate pursuit of cooling as an end in itself. Moreover, the consequences and gains that might result from climate manipulation are of a vast and global scale, meaning that failing to have an appropriate legal regime could be disastrous for both planet and population. The conclusion is that geoengineering is simply too important to become the victim of legacy law—of accidentally relevant rules not suited to this new context. Any approach to geoengineering needs to begin with the policy issues, and then change the law to fit.

Gareth T. Davies, *Law and Policy Issues of Unilateral Geoengineering: Moving to a Managed World, in* 2 Select Proc. Eur. Soc'y Int'l L. 627 (2008). Are you persuaded?

The question of governance includes basic issues concerning the applicable norms that should be applied: Is geoengineering, in and of itself, a "dangerous anthropogenic interference" with the climate that should be avoided absent a clear international consensus that it is necessary? Should individual nations be free at least to experiment with it, as their capabilities allow and interests demand? Should nations be permitted to use it, if they believe they can do so without serious harm to others?

4. The question of governance also raises the question of how, and by whom, these basic norms should be developed. The Royal Society report on geoengineering argues that

> There are at present no international treaties or institutions with a sufficiently broad mandate to regulate the broad range of possible geoengineering activities and there is a risk that methods could be applied by individual nation states, corporations or one or more wealthy individuals without concern for their transboundary implications. Mechanisms by which deployment (and where necessary, research) and be controlled and regulated are therefore necessary.

The Society's report recommends starting with a review, by a broad-based body such as the UN Commission for Sustainable Development, of existing mechanisms that could govern geoengineering. The review would be aimed at identifying regulatory gaps and establishing a "process for the development of mechanisms to address these gaps." The Royal Society, *Geoengineering the Climate* 60 (Sept. 2009).

In contrast to the Royal Society's inclusive, global governance approach, Alan Carlin has suggested that control and governance of geoengineering should be turned over to a relatively small number of like-minded developed countries. He writes:

> Less developed countries . . . generally express the view that climate change has been mainly caused by developed countries; thus in their view it is the developed world's responsibility to solve it. As a result, the choice of an organization [to govern geoengineering] representing developed countries [such as NATO or the OECD] would seem appropriate. Presumably only those countries willing to make a financial contribution would be involved so as to minimize the number of players and improve the speed with which decisions could be made. It would also be reasonable for the organization to retain control over all policy issues, but to contract out the actual implementation, presumably on the basis of competitive bidding.

Alan Carlin, *Implementation & Utilization of Geoengineering for Global Climate Change Control,* 7 Sustainable Dev. L. & Pol'y 56 (2007).

Other commentators favor governance approaches that make use of existing governance frameworks. Albert Lin, for example, believes that geoengineering can be addressed within the existing UNFCCC structure. Despite the UNFCCC's "general orientation toward emission reductions," he says, its basic principles, governance structure, and established technical bodies provide the framework necessary to "facilitate research, peer review, discussion, and development of consensus in this area." While the development of new rules, norms, and governance processes for geoengineering is essential, Lin believes this can occur within the framework provided by the UNFCCC. Albert C. Lin, *Geoengineering Governance,* 8:3 Issues in Legal Scholarship article 2, 18–19 (2009).

Scott Barrett, on the other hand, agrees that existing mechanisms should be employed in this area, but also thinks that revision of the UN Framework

Convention on Climate Change is necessary because of its current emphasis on emissions reduction as the solution to climate change. Thus, he suggests that the IPCC prepare a report on the pros and cons of geoengineering, to be followed by the adoption of an amendment to the UNFCCC that would emphasize "the need to reduce climate change risk," including through geoengineering. The revised convention would then be supplemented by a geoengineering protocol specifying "whether and under what conditions geoengineering should be allowed (even if only for research purposes), or possible even required, and how the costs of any efforts should be shared." Scott Barrett, *The Incredible Economics of Geoengineering, supra* Reading 5, at 53.

Abelkop & Carlson, *supra* at 106, argue for a new treaty with its own governance structure:

> 1. An international structure should be established for the governance of geoengineering and geoengineering research on a multilateral, global level. There should be a ban on geoengineering activities outside that governance framework.
>
> 2. The following principles should be applied to the governance of geoengineering within that international framework:
>
> a. Relative climate stability is a common heritage of humankind and a shared natural resource. For that reason, any geoengineering activities aimed at stabilizing climate should be undertaken in the interests of all states and peoples. Principles of precaution and equity should guide decision making. Decisions should be made on the basis of sound science.
>
> b. Geoengineering activities should be approved only after notification and consultation with all states.
>
> c. Information concerning geoengineering activities should be publicly disclosed at the planning stage (i.e., before an activity is approved or undertaken), once an activity is initiated, and after the activity has been completed.
>
> d. An environmental impact assessment should be required for all geoengineering activity, and the results of that assessment should be included in the information disclosed prior to approval of the activity.
>
> e. Compensation should be provided to persons harmed by geoengineering activities, whether directly or indirectly as a result of its effects on weather or the environment.
>
> 3. An *effective* governance mechanism must be established. This means abandoning the one-nation/one-vote, conference-oriented governance structure of most international environmental agreements in favor of weighted voting and governance by a relatively small executive body charged with responsibility to evaluate and make decisions concerning geoengineering proposals.

Among the various suggested approaches to developing norms and procedures for geoengineering governance, which make most sense to you? Do you have any alternative suggestions? For a recent and comprehensive review of legal and governance issues, *see* Climate Engineering and the Law: Regulation and Liability for Solar Radiation Management and Carbon Dioxide Removal (Michael B. Gerrard & Tracy Hester, eds. 2018).

5. Geoengineering appears to have great potential as a tool in the effort to "prevent dangerous anthropogenic interference with the climate system." On the other hand, the risks and uncertainties are large. As climate change skeptics are fond of pointing out, scientists lack full understanding of how the climate system operates, and, as Ronald Prinn, a professor of atmospheric sciences at MIT put it, "how can you engineer a system you don't fully understand"? Kevin Bullis, *The Geoengineering Gambit,* MIT Technology Review (January/February 2010). *See also* Patrick Huyghe, *Geoengineering our way out of trouble,* 21stC, issue 2.1 (2009).

However, although many scientists believe it is not wise to rely on geoengineering as a first defense against climate change, there are some who argue that we must begin studying it now so that it is available as a tool to protect the planet if warming and climate change trends begin to reach critical tipping points. Moreover, the failure of the international community to take geoengineering seriously may simply mean that no rules will be in place to govern the activity when someone—whether a state or an eccentric billionaire—decides to undertake unilateral efforts to prevent catastrophic climate change.

6. Assuming that the international community does adopt policies on geoengineering, what rules should be included to protect states, like Bihar and Greater Liuqui, that may be hurt by particular geoengineering strategies? Should they be provided with compensation? And what about those states that view a warming climate as a benefit? Should they be compensated for the harm they might suffer if global warming is stopped or reversed? Would you rely upon an international 'tort' system that allows the states that lose from a geoengineering scheme to seek compensation from the geoengineers? Or would you prefer an international fund arrangement of some sort, in which states seek compensation from an international body administering monies that are set aside for that basis? Or would you prefer no compensation at all? For discussion of these and related issues, *see, e.g.,* Scott Barrett, The Incredible Economics of Geoengineering, 39 Envtl. Resource Econ. 45, (2007); Gareth T. Davies, *Law and Policy Issues of Unilateral Geoengineering: Moving to a Managed World* (29 Jan. 2009); The Royal Society, *Geoengineering the climate: science, governance and uncertainty* 40 (Sept. 2009); Albert Lin, *Geoengineering Governance,* 8:3 Issues in Legal Scholarship Article 2, 13–15 (2009); Adam D.K. Abelkop & Jonathan C. Carlson, *Reining in Phaëton's Chariot: Principles for the Governance of Geoengineering,* 21 Transnat'l L. & Contemp. Prob. 101, 131–135, 137–139 (2012).

PROBLEM 9-3: CLIMATE CHANGE AND THE CHUKSUK OF THE ARCTIC

Section 1. Facts

The Chuksuk are an indigenous people native to the northernmost parts of Europe and Asia, with settlements spanning from Scandinavia to Western Volhynia. They have existed for over a millennium in these areas and have adapted to the harsh life on the outskirts of the Arctic Circle.

Chuksuk culture is distinguished by dependence on subsistence harvesting. Their diet consists mainly of seal, fish, reindeer, berries, and occasionally whale and polar bear, and they rely on snow and ice for travel, building materials for igloos, and food preservation. The Chuksuk also share a common base of traditional knowledge. This knowledge base, passed down generationally, includes familiarity with the terrain such that hunters and travelers know where they may travel safely over sea-ice and where certain animal populations may be found in abundance for hunting.

Some Chuksuk settlements have adopted certain western practices such as partially cash-based economies, yet much of Chuksuk culture remains substantially constant via the continuous use of centuries old practices. Chuksuk leaders believe that maintenance of traditional Chuksuk lifestyle practices provides their people with necessary spiritual and cultural affirmation.

Global warming and consequent climate change present a serious threat to the continued existence of the Chuksuk people. Rising Arctic temperatures are causing deterioration of the extent and thickness of sea-ice, a decline in snowfall and in the quality of snow, fluctuations in weather patterns, and unpredictable permafrost melts, which themselves cause slumping, landslides, and coastal erosion.

All of these changes threaten the Chuksuk way of life. Deterioration and loss of sea-ice is particularly harmful, isolating communities by making travel and hunting more difficult. It has similar effects on certain animal species, including ice-living seals, walrus, marine birds, and polar bears. Arctic populations of these species, upon which the Chuksuk depend, are in decline, and over the next century, climate change threatens several of the Arctic species that the Chuksuk people rely on for food and shelter with extinction. Thin sea-ice also poses a safety risk to travelers and hunters. Communal knowledge of the safety of sea-ice in traditional hunting and traveling routes has become unreliable, and several Chuksuk have perished by falling through thin ice in historically safe areas. Sea-ice also acts as a natural buffer to storms, so a decline in sea-ice makes coastal Chuksuk communities more vulnerable to severe weather.

Warmer temperatures also make permafrost susceptible to unpredictable and earlier seasonal thaws. Sudden spring permafrost thaws have caused severe flooding, which has damaged Chuksuk homes and property and forced many to relocate away from their traditional settlement areas. Flooding also contributes to erosion on the coast and into freshwater habitats. Climate oscillation and higher temperatures in general contribute to more rapid evaporation in post-flood areas, leaving less freshwater resources available to the Chuksuk and to local species. Lower freshwater levels and erosion also harm fish populations in several ways, including making reproduction more difficult because the fish are unable to reach their spawning grounds. In the winter, the altered freeze-thaw cycle creates layers of ice underneath the snow, making foraging difficult for game animals.

Rising temperatures contribute to a host of other problems as well. Less snow and lower quality snow make igloo construction, an important part of Chuksuk culture for centuries, extremely difficult. Warming temperatures require Chuksuk hunters and travelers to use tents which are both more cumbersome when traveling and generally not as effective as igloos for protection from harsh weather conditions. They also make food preservation more difficult and contribute to unprecedented heat-related public health problems for the Chuksuk, including severe sunburn, skin cancer, cataracts, and immune system disorders. Finally, shifts in temperature, weather patterns, and Arctic terrain are causing many species to alter their migration patterns. As a result, the Chuksuk are finding that many of their traditional hunting techniques, which have been passed down for generations, are obsolete.

Volhynia, a northern European country with a significant Chuksuk population, has worked with local Chuksuk communities to address some of these climate change challenges. In most cases, the only viable solution has been to relocate Chuksuk communities away from coastal regions and to provide them with financial assistance to compensate the Chuksuk for the loss of their traditional means of subsistence. But Chuksuk leaders are adamant that this is not enough and thus have demanded that Volhynia do more to prevent climate change so as to ensure the survival of their Chuksuk culture.

Volhynia is a party to the 1992 United Nations Framework Convention on Climate Change, the Kyoto Protocol and the Paris Agreement. Its emissions of greenhouse gases (GHGs) constitute about 1.5% of the global total. It has been an active and aggressive participant in climate change negotiations, and has proposed radical cuts in GHGs by all countries in the world. These efforts have been to no avail, however.

Determined to demonstrate its good faith to the Chuksuk people, and to fulfill what it sees as its obligation to them under international law, the

Volhynian government decided to take legal action against some of the nations that have been most resistant to combatting climate change. Volhynia's leaders believe that such legal action will call attention to the plight of the Chuksuk in ways that will create global political pressure for action on climate change. The government's legal advisors have said, furthermore, that Volhynia might actually have a valid legal claim against the world's largest greenhouse gas emitters under international human rights law.

Consequently, acting on behalf of the Chuksuk population located within its borders, Volhynia filed a complaint against the governments of Hanguo and the Federation of Columbia (FC), respectively, in the International Court of Justice. Both Hanguo and the FC are among the top ten GHG emitting nations in the world. Both refused to ratify the Kyoto Protocol. Each is a party to the Paris Agreement, and each has submitted NDCs (nationally determined contributions) on greenhouse gas emissions. But neither country's NDCs involve making substantial near-term reductions in that country's greenhouse gas emissions. Together, the two countries account for anywhere from 44% to 53% of global GHGs, depending on the year.

Hanguo, a densely-populated rapidly developing nation that has only recently become a major GHG emitter, has said that it will not agree to any caps on GHG emissions until developing nations reduce their emissions to the per capita levels of Hanguo. The FC, a sparsely-populated large developed nation, has been a leading emitter of GHGs for many decades. It has said that it will work to increase the use of renewable energy in its economy, but that it cannot agree to strict limits on its greenhouse gas emissions because such limits would harm its economy and do little to slow climate change given the continued growth in emissions in Hanguo and other developing nations.

Volhynia's complaint against Hanguo and the FC alleges, among other things, that climate change violates the international human rights of the Chuksuk people, and that Hanguo and the FC are responsible for that violation on account of the volume and significance of their GHG emissions and their failure to take any meaningful steps to reduce those emissions. No Chuksuk people live in either the FC or Hanguo.

Volhynia's complaint requests four remedies. First, it prays for the ICJ to initiate a mandatory cap on each nation's emissions of each greenhouse gas. Second, it requests that the ICJ order the FC and Hanguo to negotiate with the Government of Volhynia and designated leaders of the Chuksuk community to establish a plan to protect Chuksuk culture and resources. Third, the complaint requests that the ICJ order the FC and Hanguo to establish a $4 billion fund, to be administered by the Volhynian government in cooperation with designated leaders of the Chuksuk community, to facilitate the adaptation of the Chuksuk to any inevitable harmful effects from climate change. Fourth, it requests any other relief that the ICJ considers appropriate and just.

All three countries have accepted the compulsory jurisdiction of the ICJ pursuant to Article 36(2) of the Court's Statute.

Section 2. Questions Presented

1. Have the FC and Hanguo violated international human rights law as a result of their inaction on climate change and, if so, how?

2. If so, what remedial orders should the International Court of Justice make in this case?

Section 3. Assignments

A. *Reading Assignment*

Study the Readings presented in Parts A and B of this Chapter, *supra*, and in Section 4, *infra*.

B. *Recommended Writing Assignment*

Prepare an issue-outline: a comprehensive, logically sequenced, and argumentative brief in the form of an outline of the primary and subsidiary legal issues raised by the questions presented above. Also, from the perspective of the independent judge or arbitrator, indicate which side ought to prevail on each issue and why. Retain a copy of your issue-outline/brief for class discussion.

C. *Recommended Oral Assignment*

Assume you are legal counsel for Volhynia, Hanguo, or the Federation of Columbia (as designated by your instructor); then, relying upon the Readings (and your issue-outline if prepared), present a 15–20 minute oral argument of your party's likely position on each issue relevant to it.

D. *Recommended Reflective Assignment*

Consider (and recommend) alternative norms, institutions, and/or procedures that you believe might do better than existing world order arrangements to contend with situations of the kind posed by this problem. In so doing, but without insisting upon *immediate* feasibility, identify the particular transition steps that would be needed to make your alternatives a reality.

Section 4. Readings

1. Editors' Note

On December 7, 2005, the Inuit people filed a petition with the Inter-American Commission on Human Rights seeking "relief from human rights violations resulting from the impacts of global warming and climate change caused by acts and omissions of the United States." The Commission declined to hear the case, but that was hardly the end of the matter. Since 2005, the question of the connection between climate change and human rights has been prominent on the international agenda.

In 2007, the Alliance of Small Island States, meeting in the Maldives, adopted the Malé Declaration on the Human Dimension of Global Climate Change, which recognized "that climate change has clear and immediate implications for the full enjoyment of human rights" and which called for "detailed study" of the effects of climate change in that regard. In response to that call, the Office of the United Nations High Commissioner for Human Rights undertook a number of studies on the links between climate change and human rights.[70] At the same time, the United Nations Human Rights Council issued a series of resolutions emphasizing the adverse impacts of climate change on the "effective enjoyment of human rights" and noting that those adverse impacts would "be felt most acutely by those segments of the populations who are already in a vulnerable situation."[71]

Prior to the 21st Conference of the Parties to the UNFCCC (held in Paris in 2015), the Office of the High Commission for Human Rights made a submission arguing that "failure to take affirmative measures to prevent human rights harms caused by climate change, including foreseeable long-term harms" would be a breach of the legal obligation of States to "respect, protect, fulfil and promote all human rights for all persons without discrimination." The lengthy submission called upon the Conference of the Parties to adopt a "rights-based approach to climate change." It urged that "global efforts to mitigate and adapt to climate change should be guided by relevant human rights norms and principles including the rights to participation and information, transparency, accountability, equity, and

---

[70] *See, e.g.*, the following reports of the Office of the United Nations High Commissioner for Human Rights: *Report on the relationship between climate change and human rights*, U.N. Doc. A/HRC/10/61 (15 January 2009); *Analytical study on the relationship between climate change and the human right of everyone to the enjoyment of the highest standard of physical and mental health*, U.N. Doc. A/HRC/32/23 (6 May 2016); *Analytical study on the relationship between climate change and the full and effective enjoyment of the rights of the child*, U.N. Doc. A/HRC/35/13 (4 May 2017).

[71] Human Rights Council Resolution 10/4 on human rights and climate change, adopted at its 41st meeting (25 March 2009). *See also* HRC Resolution 7/23 (March 2008), HRC Resolution 18/22 (September 2011); HRC Resolution 26/27 (July 2014), HRC Resolution 29/15 (July 2015), and HRC Resolution 32/33 (July 2016).

non-discrimination. Simply put, climate change is a human rights problem and the human rights framework must be part of the solution."[72]

Why a human-rights approach to climate change?

From an advocacy perspective, one reason to adopt a human-rights approach to climate change, is that it "offers a number of advantages over the inter-governmental negotiating process."[73] Professor Bodansky explains:

> if the activities that contribute to climate change violate human rights law, then we do not need to wait for governments to agree to cut their emissions; our current practices are illegal already. Under existing law we can make legal arguments about what countries must do, as opposed simply to policy arguments about what they should do.
>
> Human rights law promises not only legal arguments but also forums in which to make those arguments. In contrast to international environmental law, where dispute resolution mechanisms are in short supply, human rights law is full of tribunals to hear complaints and rapporteurs to investigate more general situations. These procedures give victims of climate change, who generally have little influence in inter-governmental negotiations, a forum in which they possess greater power.

A second, related reason for emphasizing the human-rights dimension of climate change is that putting the issues forward in a human-rights forum can "put a human face on climate change and make the impacts more concrete."[74] Professor Amy Sinden elaborates the point:

> Thinking of climate change as a human-rights issue can help us see that it is not just a matter of aggregate costs and benefits but of winners and losers—of the powerful few preventing the political system from acting to protect the powerless many. But perhaps even more importantly, treating climate change as a human-rights issue simply begins to imbue it with a sense of gravity and moral urgency that communicates to all of us: this is something different; this is an issue that must be understood to stand apart

---

[72] Submission of the Office of the High Commissioner for Human Rights to the 21st Conference of the Parties to the United Nations Framework Convention on Climate Change at 2, 6 (27 November 2015), available at www.ohchr.org/Documents/Issues/CLIMATECHANGE/COP 21.pdf (accessed 4 July 2018).

[73] Daniel Bodansky, *Introduction: Climate Change and Human Rights: Unpacking the Issues,* 38 Georgia J. Int'l & Comp. L. 511, 516–519 (2010).

[74] *Id.*

from the normal clatter and noise of day to day politics and to demand attention from our best selves.[75]

Finally, there is the argument that human-rights principles should guide our actions in responding to climate change for the simple reason that our actions are likely to be better if they are so guided. Thus, decisions about mitigation and adaptation are likely to be sounder decisions if basic procedural human-rights principles (e.g., rights to participation and information) are honored and people have an opportunity to be heard concerning the impact of climate change and climate-change response measures on their lives. More substantively, to the extent that concern for human well-being is at the center of our concern for the environment,[76] a human-rights approach can help policymakers focus on developing responses to climate change that will best further the goal of promoting human welfare.

Thus, human-rights issues can be raised in the context of climate change as purely legal issues—as part of an argument before a tribunal alleging a rights violation and seeking an appropriate remedy. Or, those same issues can be raised purely as policy issues and negotiation points—as part of an effort to ensure that international action to address climate change includes action aimed explicitly at addressing its impacts on the well-being of human beings and that proposed solutions to climate change are similarly formulated with attention to the well-being of the persons affected by them. Put simply, "human rights obligations, standards and principles have the potential to inform and strengthen international and national policymaking in the area of climate change."[77]

In this problem, we ask you to approach this issue from a primarily legal perspective. We do this because we think that setting these issues in an adjudicatory context will help you focus on certain key issues. There are "three crucial questions pertaining to the human rights climate change interface":

1. Is there a relationship between climate change and human rights, and if so, what is the nature of that relationship?

---

[75] Amy Sinden, *Climate Change & Human Rights,* 27 J. Land, Resources & Env't L. 255, 271 (2007).

[76] While some environmentalists reject a human-centered approach to environmental protection, a concern for human well-being is prominent in the international community's articulations of environmental principles and policies. *See, e.g.,* Rio Declaration **(Basic Document 1.30)**, principle 1 ("Human beings are at the centre of concerns for sustainable development. They are entitled to a healthy and productive life in harmony with nature."); Stockholm Declaration **(Basic Document 1.21)**, paragraph 2 ("The protection and improvement of the human environment is a major issue which affects the well-being of peoples and economic development throughout the world.").

[77] Human Rights Council Res. 18/22, perambulatory paragraph 6, U.N. Doc. A/HRC/RES/18/22 (30 September 2011).

2. Does climate change constitute a violation of human rights, especially the rights of vulnerable people?

3. Irrespective of whether climate change represents a human rights violation, what are states' national-level and international-level human rights obligations pertaining to climate change?[78]

Keep these questions in mind as you analyze the Chukuk's case in light of the following readings. In the next two readings, excerpts from the primary globally applicable human rights treaties, consider not only the content of the declared rights but also the stated scope of state obligations to fulfill those rights.

2. International Covenant on Civil and Political Rights, arts. 1(1–2), 2, 6(1), & 12, Dec. 16, 1966, 999 UNTS 171 (Basic Document 7.12)

Article 1 (paragraphs 1 & 2 only))

1. All peoples have the right of self-determination. By virtue of that right they freely determine their political status and freely pursue their economic, social and cultural development.

2. All peoples may, for their own ends, freely dispose of their natural wealth and resources without prejudice to any obligations arising out of international economic co-operation, based upon the principle of mutual benefit, and international law. In no case may a people be deprived of its own means of subsistence.

Article 2

1. Each State Party to the present Covenant undertakes to respect and to ensure to all individuals within its territory and subject to its jurisdiction the rights recognized in the present Covenant, without distinction of any kind, such as race, colour, sex, language, religion, political or other opinion, national or social origin, property, birth or other status.

2. Where not already provided for by existing legislative or other measures, each State Party to the present Covenant undertakes to take the necessary steps, in accordance with its constitutional processes and with the provisions of the present Covenant, to adopt such legislative or other measures as may be necessary to give effect to the rights recognized in the present Covenant.

---

[78] Marc Limon, *Human Rights Obligations and Accountability in the Face of Climate Change*, 38 Ga. J. Int'l & Comp. L 543, 545 (2010).

3. Each State Party to the present Covenant undertakes:

(a) To ensure that any person whose rights or freedoms as herein recognized are violated shall have an effective remedy, notwithstanding that the violation has been committed by persons acting in an official capacity;

(b) To ensure that any person claiming such a remedy shall have his right thereto determined by competent judicial, administrative or legislative authorities, or by any other competent authority provided for by the legal system of the State, and to develop the possibilities of judicial remedy;

(c) To ensure that the competent authorities shall enforce such remedies when granted.

Article 6 (paragraph 1 only)

1. Every human being has the inherent right to life. This right shall be protected by law. No one shall be arbitrarily deprived of his life.

Article 12

1. Everyone lawfully within the territory of a State shall, within that territory, have the right to liberty of movement and freedom to choose his residence.

2. Everyone shall be free to leave any country, including his own.

3. The above-mentioned rights shall not be subject to any restrictions except those which are provided by law, are necessary to protect national security, public order (ordre public), public health or morals or the rights and freedoms of others, and are consistent with the other rights recognized in the present Covenant.

4. No one shall be arbitrarily deprived of the right to enter his own country.

3. International Covenant on Economic Social and Cultural Rights, arts. 2, 11, 12, & 15, Dec. 16, 1966, 993 UNTS 3 (Basic Document 7.11)

Article 2

1. Each State Party to the present Covenant undertakes to take steps, individually and through international assistance and co-operation, especially economic and technical, to the maximum of its available resources, with a view to achieving progressively the full realization of the rights recognized in the present Covenant by all appropriate means, including particularly the adoption of legislative measures.

2. The States Parties to the present Covenant undertake to guarantee that the rights enunciated in the present Covenant will be

exercised without discrimination of any kind as to race, colour, sex, language, religion, political or other opinion, national or social origin, property, birth or other status.

3. Developing countries, with due regard to human rights and their national economy, may determine to what extent they would guarantee the economic rights recognized in the present Covenant to nonnationals.

Article 11

1. The States Parties to the present Covenant recognize the right of everyone to an adequate standard of living for himself and his family, including adequate food, clothing and housing, and to the continuous improvement of living conditions. The States Parties will take appropriate steps to ensure the realization of this right, recognizing to this effect the essential importance of international cooperation based on free consent.

2. The States Parties to the present Covenant, recognizing the fundamental right of everyone to be free from hunger, shall take, individually and through international co-operation, the measures, including specific programmes, which are needed:

(a) To improve methods of production, conservation and distribution of food by making full use of technical and scientific knowledge, by disseminating knowledge of the principles of nutrition and by developing or reforming agrarian systems in such a way as to achieve the most efficient development and utilization of natural resources;

(b) Taking into account the problems of both food-importing and food-exporting countries, to ensure an equitable distribution of world food supplies in relation to need.

Article 12

1. The States Parties to the present Covenant recognize the right of everyone to the enjoyment of the highest attainable standard of physical and mental health.

2. The steps to be taken by the States Parties to the present Covenant to achieve the full realization of this right shall include those necessary for: (a) The provision for the reduction of the stillbirth-rate and of infant mortality and for the healthy development of the child; (b) The improvement of all aspects of environmental and industrial hygiene; (c) The prevention, treatment and control of epidemic, endemic, occupational and other diseases; (d) The creation of conditions which would assure to all medical service and medical attention in the event of sickness.

Article 15 (paragraphs 1 & 2 only)

1. The States Parties to the present Covenant recognize the right of everyone: (a) To take part in cultural life; (b) To enjoy the benefits of scientific progress and its applications; (c) To benefit from the protection of

the moral and material interests resulting from any scientific, literary or artistic production of which he is the author.

2. The steps to be taken by the States Parties to the present Covenant to achieve the full realization of this right shall include those necessary for the conservation, the development and the diffusion of science and culture.

4. United Nations Declaration on the Rights of Indigenous Peoples, arts. 1, 8, 10, 18 25, 26(1), 28, 29(1) & 32, 13 Sept. 2007, GA Res 61/295, UN GAOR, 61st Sess., 106/107th mtg, U.N. Doc. A/61/L.67 (2007) (Basic Document 7.17)

Article 1

Indigenous peoples have the right to the full enjoyment, as a collective or as individuals, of all human rights and fundamental freedoms as recognized in the Charter of the United Nations, the Universal Declaration of Human Rights and international human rights law.

Article 8

1. Indigenous peoples and individuals have the right not to be subjected to forced assimilation or destruction of their culture.

2. States shall provide effective mechanisms for prevention of, and redress for:

(a) Any action which has the aim or effect of depriving them of their integrity as distinct peoples, or of their cultural values or ethnic identities;

(b) Any action which has the aim or effect of dispossessing them of their lands, territories or resources;

(c) Any form of forced population transfer which has the aim or effect of violating or undermining any of their rights;

(d) Any form of forced assimilation or integration;

(e) Any form of propaganda designed to promote or incite racial or ethnic discrimination directed against them.

Article 10

Indigenous peoples shall not be forcibly removed from their lands or territories. No relocation shall take place without the free, prior and informed consent of the indigenous peoples concerned and after agreement on just and fair compensation and, where possible, with the option of return.

Article 18

Indigenous peoples have the right to participate in decision-making in matters which would affect their rights, through representatives chosen by themselves in accordance with their own procedures, as well as to maintain and develop their own indigenous decision-making institutions.

Article 25

Indigenous peoples have the right to maintain and strengthen their distinctive spiritual relationship with their traditionally owned or otherwise occupied and used lands, territories, waters and coastal seas and other resources and to uphold their responsibilities to future generations in this regard.

Article 26 (paragraph 1 only)

1. Indigenous peoples have the right to the lands, territories and resources which they have traditionally owned, occupied or otherwise used or acquired.

Article 28

1. Indigenous peoples have the right to redress, by means that can include restitution or, when this is not possible, just, fair and equitable compensation, for the lands, territories and resources which they have traditionally owned or otherwise occupied or used, and which have been confiscated, taken, occupied, used or damaged without their free, prior and informed consent.

2. Unless otherwise freely agreed upon by the peoples concerned, compensation shall take the form of lands, territories and resources equal in quality, size and legal status or of monetary compensation or other appropriate redress.

Article 29 (paragraph 1 only)

1. Indigenous peoples have the right to the conservation and protection of the environment and the productive capacity of their lands or territories and resources. States shall establish and implement assistance programmes for indigenous peoples for such conservation and protection, without discrimination.

Article 32

1. Indigenous peoples have the right to determine and develop priorities and strategies for the development or use of their lands or territories and other resources.

2. States shall consult and cooperate in good faith with the indigenous peoples concerned through their own representative institutions in order to obtain their free and informed consent prior to the approval of any project affecting their lands or territories and other resources, particularly in connection with the development, utilization or exploitation of mineral, water or other resources.

3. States shall provide effective mechanisms for just and fair redress for any such activities, and appropriate measures shall be taken to mitigate adverse environmental, economic, social, cultural or spiritual impact.

5. Charter of the United Nations, arts. 55–56, 26 June 1945, 1976 YBUN 1043, 59 Stat 1031, TS 993 (Basic Document 1.1)

Article 55

With a view to the creation of conditions of stability and well-being which are necessary for peaceful and friendly relations among nations based on respect for the principle of equal rights and self-determination of peoples, the United Nations shall promote:

a. higher standards of living, full employment, and conditions of economic and social progress and development;

b. solutions of international economic, social, health, and related problems; and international cultural and educational cooperation; and

c. universal respect for, and observance of, human rights and fundamental freedoms for all without distinction as to race, sex, language, or religion.

Article 56

All Members pledge themselves to take joint and separate action in co-operation with the Organization for the achievement of the purposes set forth in Article 55.

6. United Nations High Commissioner for Human Rights, Report on the Relationship Between Climate Change and Human Rights, U.N. Doc. A/HRC/10/61 (2009)

16. An increase in global average temperatures of approximately 2° C will have major, and predominantly negative, effects on ecosystems across the globe, on the goods and services they provide. Already today, climate change is among the most important drivers of ecosystem changes, along with overexploitation of resources and pollution. Moreover, global warming will exacerbate the harmful effects of environmental pollution, including higher levels of ground-level ozone in urban areas. In view of such effects, which have implications for a wide range of human rights, it is relevant to discuss the relationship between human rights and the environment.

17. Principle 1 of the 1972 Declaration of the United Nations Conference on the Human Environment (the Stockholm Declaration) **[Basic Document 1.21]** states that there is "a fundamental right to freedom, equality and adequate conditions of life, in an environment of a quality that permits a life of dignity and well-being". The Stockholm Declaration reflects a general recognition of the interdependence and interrelatedness of human rights and the environment.

18. While the universal human rights treaties do not refer to a specific right to a safe and healthy environment, the United Nations human rights treaty bodies all recognize the intrinsic link between the environment and the realization of a range of human rights, such as the right to life, to health, to food, to water, and to housing. . . .

* * *

1. The right to life

21. The right to life is explicitly protected under the International Covenant on Civil and Political Rights and the Convention on the Rights of the Child. The Human Rights Committee has described the right to life as the "supreme right," "basic to all human rights," and it is a right from which no derogation is permitted even in time of public emergency. . . .

22. A number of observed and projected effects of climate change will pose direct and indirect threats to human lives. IPCC AR4 projects with high confidence an increase in people suffering from death, disease and injury from heatwaves, floods, storms, fires and droughts. Equally, climate change will affect the right to life through an increase in hunger and malnutrition and related disorders impacting on child growth and development; cardiorespiratory morbidity and mortality related to ground-level ozone.

23. Climate change will exacerbate weather-related disasters which already have devastating effects on people and their enjoyment of the right to life, particularly in the developing world. For example, an estimated 262 million people were affected by climate disasters annually from 2000 to 2004, of whom over 98 per cent live in developing countries. Tropical cyclone hazards, affecting approximately 120 million people annually, killed an estimated 250,000 people from 1980 to 2000.

* * *

2. The right to adequate food

25. The right to food is explicitly mentioned under the International Covenant on Economic, Social and Cultural Rights, the Convention on the Rights of the Child and the Convention on the Rights of Persons with Disabilities and implied in general provisions on an adequate standard of living of the Convention on the Elimination of All Forms of Discrimination against Women and the International Convention on the Elimination of All Forms of Racial Discrimination. In addition to a right to adequate food, the International Covenant on Economic, Social and Cultural Rights also enshrines the fundamental right of everyone to be free from hunger. Elements of the right to food include the availability of adequate food (including through the possibility of feeding oneself from natural resources) and accessible to all individuals under the jurisdiction of a State. Equally,

States must ensure freedom from hunger and take necessary action to alleviate hunger, even in times of natural or other disasters.

26. As a consequence of climate change, the potential for food production is projected initially to increase at mid to high latitudes with an increase in global average temperature in the range of 1–3° C. However, at lower latitude s crop productivity is projected to decrease, increasing the risk of hunger and food insecurity in the poorer regions of the word. According to one estimate, an additional 600 million people will face malnutrition due to climate change, with a particularly negative effect on sub-Saharan Africa. Poor people living in developing countries are particularly vulnerable given their disproportionate dependency on climate-sensitive resources for their food and livelihoods.

* * *

3. The right to water

28. CESCR [Committee on Economic, Social and Cultural Rights[79]] has defined the right to water as the right of everyone to sufficient, safe, acceptable, physically accessible and affordable water for personal and domestic uses, such as drinking, food preparation and personal and household hygiene. . . .

29. Loss of glaciers and reductions in snow cover are projected to increase and to negatively affect water availability for more than one-sixth of the world's population supplied by meltwater from mountain ranges. Weather extremes, such as drought and flooding, will also impact on water supplies. Climate change will thus exacerbate existing stresses on water resources and compound the problem of access to safe drinking water, currently denied to an estimated 1.1 billion people globally and a major cause of morbidity and disease. In this regard, climate change interacts with a range of other causes of water stress, such as population growth, environmental degradation, poor water management, poverty and inequality.

* * *

4. The right to health

31. The right to the highest attainable standard of physical and mental health (the right to health) is most comprehensively addressed in article 12 of the International Covenant on Economic, Social and Cultural Rights and referred to in five other core international human rights treaties. This right implies the enjoyment of, and equal access to, appropriate health care and, more broadly, to goods, services and

[79] The CESCR is a body of independent experts elected by the UN Economic and Social Council to monitor implementation of the International Covenant on Economic, Social and Cultural Rights. *See* ECOSOC Resolution 1985/17 (28 May 1985).

conditions which enable a person to live a healthy life. Underlying determinants of health include adequate food and nutrition, housing, safe drinking water and adequate sanitation, and a healthy environment. Other key elements are the availability, accessibility (both physically and economically), and quality of health and health-care facilities, goods and services.

32. Climate change is projected to affect the health status of millions of people, including through increases in malnutrition, increased diseases and injury due to extreme weather events, and an increased burden of diarrhoeal, cardiorespiratory and infectious diseases. Global warming may also affect the spread of malaria and other vector borne diseases in some parts of the world. Overall, the negative health effects will disproportionately be felt in sub-Saharan Africa, South Asia and the Middle East. Poor health and malnutrition increases vulnerability and reduces the capacity of individuals and groups to adapt to climate change.

* * *

5. The right to adequate housing

35. The right to adequate housing is enshrined in several core international human rights instruments and most comprehensively under the International Covenant on Economic, Social and Cultural Rights as an element of the right to an adequate standard of living. The right to adequate housing has been defined as "the right to live somewhere in security, peace and dignity." Core elements of this right include security of tenure, protection against forced evictions, availability of services, materials, facilities and infrastructure, affordability, habitability, accessibility, location and cultural adequacy.

36. Observed and projected climate change will affect the right to adequate housing in several ways. Sea level rise and storm surges will have a direct impact on many coastal settlements. In the Arctic region and in low-lying island States such impacts have already led to the relocation of peoples and communities. Settlements in low-lying mega-deltas are also particularly at risk, as evidenced by the millions of people and homes affected by flooding in recent years.

37. The erosion of livelihoods, partly caused by climate change, is a main "push" factor for increasing rural to urban migration. Many will move to urban slums and informal settlements where they are often forced to build shelters in hazardous areas. Already today, an estimated 1 billion people live in urban slums on fragile hillsides or flood-prone riverbanks and face acute vulnerability to extreme climate events.

38. Human rights guarantees in the context of climate change include: (a) adequate protection of housing from weather hazards (habitability of housing); (b) access to housing away from hazardous zones;

(c) access to shelter and disaster preparedness in cases of displacement caused by extreme weather events; (d) protection of communities that are relocated away from hazardous zones, including protection against forced evictions without appropriate forms of legal or other protection, including adequate consultation with affected persons.

* * *

C. Effects on specific groups

* * *

51. Climate change, together with pollution and environmental degradation, poses a serious threat to indigenous peoples, who often live in marginal lands and fragile ecosystems which are particularly sensitive to alterations in the physical environment. Climate change-related impacts have already led to the relocation of Inuit communities in polar regions and affected their traditional livelihoods. Indigenous peoples inhabiting low-lying island States face similar pressures, threatening their cultural identity which is closely linked to their traditional lands and livelihoods.

* * *

53. The United Nations Declaration on the Rights of Indigenous Peoples sets out several rights and principles of relevance to threats posed by climate change.[80] Core international human rights treaties also provide for protection of indigenous peoples, in particular with regard to the right to self-determination and rights related to culture.[81] The rights of indigenous peoples are also enshrined in ILO Convention No. 169 (1989) concerning Indigenous and Tribal Peoples in Independent Countries.

7. John H. Knox, Climate Change and Human Rights Law, 50 Va. J. Int'l L. 163, 191–193 (2009)

Two particularly vulnerable communities, the Inuit and the Maldivians, have shown in detail how climate change interferes with their human rights. In December 2005, the Inuit filed a petition with the Inter-American Commission on Human Rights alleging that the United States failed to comply with its obligations under human rights law, by failing to take effective measures to abate the effects of climate change on the rights of the Inuit. . . .

---

[80] Key provisions include the right to effective mechanisms for prevention of, and redress for, actions which have the aim or effect of dispossessing them of their lands, territories or resources (art. 8); the principle of free, prior and informed consent (art. 19), the right to the conservation and protection of the environment and indigenous lands and territories (art. 29), the right to maintain, control, protect and develop their cultural heritage and traditional knowledge and cultural expressions (art. 31).

[81] *See* the provisions on cultural rights in ICCPR, art. 27 **[Basic Document 7.17]**, and ICESCR, art. 15 **[Basic Document 7.16]**.

The Inuit petition describes how climate change is affecting the Arctic environment on which the Inuit depend. The petition explains how those effects interfere with many Inuit human rights, including rights to life, health, property, cultural identity, and self-determination. The Inuit's right to life, for example, is infringed because "[c]hanges in ice and snow jeopardize individual Inuit lives, critical food sources are threatened, and unpredictable weather makes travel more dangerous at all times of the year."[82] Individual lives are at risk because the sea ice on which the Inuit travel and hunt freezes later, thaws earlier, and is thinner; critical food sources are threatened because harvested species are becoming scarcer and more difficult for the Inuit to reach; the increase in sudden, unpredictable storms and the decrease of snow from which to construct emergency shelters have contributed to death and injuries among hunters; and the decrease in summer ice has caused rougher seas and more dangerous storms, increasing danger to boaters.

The Inuit community also argued that climate change affects the Inuit right to health: as sea ice disappears and local weather conditions change, the fish and game on which the Inuit rely for nutrition disappear; new diseases move northward; quality and quantity of drinking water diminishes; and the dramatic changes in the circumstances of their lives damage the Inuit's mental health. Furthermore, climate change also interferes with the Inuit's ability to enjoy their right to property in their traditional lands. "Sea ice, a large and critical part of coastal Inuit's property, is literally melting away."[83] Coastal erosion and melting permafrost are forcing the Inuit to relocate homes and, sometimes, entire communities further inland. By undermining the ability of the Inuit to sustain themselves, climate change also threatens their rights to enjoy their cultural identity, and deprives them of their means of subsistence in violation of their right to self-determination.

* * *

The September 2008 submission by the Maldives to the OHCHR describes the threats climate change poses to the human rights of its people. Climate change threatens harm to small island states like the Maldives by intensifying tropical storms and cyclones, changing patterns of precipitation, increasing temperatures, and, most importantly, causing sea levels to rise

Composed of small islands in the Indian Ocean, the Maldives has an average height above sea level of less than two meters. As its submission describes, sea levels have been rising at an accelerating pace. In 2007, the

---

[82] Petition to the Inter-American Commission on Human Rights Seeking Relief from Violations Resulting from Global Warming Caused by Acts and Omissions of the United States (Dec. 7, 2005), at 90.

[83] *Id.* at 82.

IPCC projected that the average rise in sea level will be between 0.19 and 0.58 meters by the end of the century, but recent studies indicate that the Greenland and Antarctic ice sheets are melting more rapidly than previously realized, and project that sea levels will actually rise between 0.5 and 1 meter by 2100. Rising sea levels exacerbate inundation, storm surges, and erosion. An increase of 0.5 meters would inundate 15% of Malé, the most populous island in the Maldives, by 2025, and flood half of it by 2100. A sea surge 0.7 meters higher than the average sea level, which would flood most of the islands in the Maldives, has been expected to occur only once per century, but by 2050 may occur at least annually.

Rising sea levels threaten many of the Maldivians' human rights. Because 42% of the population and 47% of the housing structures in the Maldives are located within 100 meters of the shoreline, "even partial flooding of the islands is likely to result in drowning, injury, and loss of life."[84] Flooding and the resulting loss of land interferes not only with the right to life, but also the rights to health, property, housing, and water, among others, by "eliminat[ing] the physical area necessary for the establishment of homes, services infrastructure, economic activities, and the sites of all political, social, and cultural activities. Land is, in this sense, a fundamental pre-cursor to the enjoyment of all other rights."[85] If sea level rise is not halted, it will eventually inundate so much of the Maldives that continued human existence there will no longer be possible. "The extinction of their State would violate the fundamental right of Maldivians to possess nationality and the right of the Maldives people to self-determination."[86]

8. Daniel Bodansky, Introduction: Climate Change and Human Rights: Unpacking the Issues, 38 Ga. J. of Int'l & Comp. L. 511, 516–19 (2010)

It is sometimes said that climate change violates human rights. If this is simply a shorthand way of saying that climate change will affect the realization and enjoyment of a variety of widely recognized human rights, then it is very likely true. Although the extent and nature of these harms are still unclear and will vary from region to region, climate change is likely to affect the right to life, the right to adequate food and water, the right to health, and the right to self-determination, among others. . . .

To the extent that conceptualizing climate change as a human rights problem serves a symbolic or political function, then identifying these human harms may be enough. In essence, the argument is that climate change will severely impact the enjoyment of important human rights-the

[84] Submission of the Maldives to the Office of the High Commissioner for Human Rights 21 (2008), *available at* https://www.ohchr.org/Documents/Issues/ClimateChange/Submissions/Maldives_Submission.pdf.

[85] *Id.*

[86] *Id.* [Eds. In the Pacific Ocean, Turalu and Kiribati will be affected in almost exactly the same way as the Maldives in the Indian Ocean.]

right to life, the right to food, the right to health, the right to self-determination, and so forth. Therefore we need to prevent it.

But although this reasoning may be compelling as a policy argument, it is insufficient as a legal argument. Legally, climate change no more violates human rights than does a hurricane, earthquake, volcanic eruption, or meteor impact. Human rights are "human" by virtue of not only their victims but also their perpetrators. And they represent human rights "violations" only if there is some identifiable duty that some identifiable duty-holder has breached. . . . Thus, in considering the connections of human rights and climate change, we need to focus as much, if not more, on the nature of the duties involved as the nature of the rights.

9. United Nations High Commissioner for Human Rights, Report on the Relationship Between Climate Change and Human Rights, U.N. Doc. A/HRC/10/61 (2009)

69. There exists broad agreement that climate change has generally negative effects on the realization of human rights. This section seeks to outline how the empirical reality and projections of the adverse effects of climate change on the effective enjoyment of human rights relate to obligations assumed by States under the international human rights treaties.

70. While climate change has obvious implications for the enjoyment of human rights, it is less obvious whether, and to what extent, such effects can be qualified as human rights violations in a strict legal sense. Qualifying the effects of climate change as human rights violations poses a series of difficulties. First, it is virtually impossible to disentangle the complex causal relationships linking historical greenhouse gas emissions of a particular country with a specific climate change-related effect, let alone with the range of direct and indirect implications for human rights. Second, global warming is often one of several contributing factors to climate change-related effects, such as hurricanes, environmental degradation and water stress. Accordingly, it is often impossible to establish the extent to which a concrete climate change-related event with implications for human rights is attributable to global warming. Third, adverse effects of global warming are often projections about future impacts, whereas human rights violations are normally established after the harm has occurred.

* * *

72. Under international human rights law, individuals rely first and foremost on their own States for the protection of their human rights. In the face of climate change, however, it is doubtful, for the reasons mentioned above, that an individual would be able to hold a particular State responsible for harm caused by climate change. Human rights law

provides more effective protection with regard to measures taken by States to address climate change and their impact on human rights.

73. For example, if individuals have to move away from a high-risk zone, the State must ensure adequate safeguards and take measures to avoid forced evictions. Equally, several claims about environmental harm have been considered by national, regional and international judicial and quasi-judicial bodies, including the Human Rights Committee, regarding the impact on human rights, such as the right to life, to heath, to privacy and family life and to information. Similar cases in which an environmental harm is linked to climate change could also be considered by courts and quasi-judicial human rights treaty bodies. In such cases, it would appear that the matter of the case would rest on whether the State through its acts or omissions had failed to protect an individual against a harm affecting the enjoyment of human rights.

74. In some cases, States may have an obligation to protect individuals against foreseeable threats to human rights related to climate change, such as an increased risk of flooding in certain areas. In that regard, the jurisprudence of the European Court of Human Rights gives some indication of how a failure to take measures against foreseeable risks could possibly amount to a violation of human rights. The Court found a violation of the right to life in a case where State authorities had failed to implement land-planning and emergency relief policies while they were aware of an increasing risk of a large-scale mudslide. The Court also noted that the population had not been adequately informed about the risk.

* * *

76. While international human rights treaties recognize that some aspects of economic, social and cultural rights may only be realized progressively over time, they also impose obligations which require immediate implementation. First, States parties must take deliberate, concrete and targeted measures, making the most efficient use of available resources, to move as expeditiously and effectively as possible towards the full realization of rights.108 Second, irrespective of resource limitations, States must guarantee non-discrimination in access to economic, social and cultural rights. Third, States have a core obligation to ensure, at the very least, minimum essential levels of each right enshrined in the Covenant. For example, a State party in which "any significant number of individuals is deprived of essential foodstuffs, of essential primary health care, of basic shelter and housing, or of the most basic forms of education" would be failing to meet its minimum core obligations and, prima facie, be in violation of the Covenant.

77. In sum, irrespective of the additional strain climate change-related events may place on available resources, States remain under an obligation to ensure the widest possible enjoyment of economic, social and

cultural rights under any given circumstances. Importantly, States must, as a matter of priority, seek to satisfy core obligations and protect groups in society who are in a particularly vulnerable situation.

10. John H. Knox, 2016 Report of the Special Rapporteur on the issue of human rights obligations relating to the enjoyment of a safe, clean, healthy and sustainable environment, U.N. Doc. A/HRC/31/52 (1 February 2016)

34. In some respects, the application of [human rights] obligations [to environmental problems] is relatively straightforward. However, the scale of climate change introduces complicating factors. Unlike most environmental harms to human rights that have been considered by human rights bodies, climate change is truly a global challenge. Greenhouse gases emitted anywhere contribute to global warming everywhere. Billions of people contribute to climate change and will experience its effects, and the causal chains linking individual contributions with specific effects may be impossible to discern with certainty.

35. These complications led OHCHR to warn in 2009 that "while climate change has obvious implications for the enjoyment of human rights, it is less obvious whether, and to what extent, such effects can be qualified as human rights violations in a strict legal sense". Specifically, OHCHR stated that it would be "virtually impossible to disentangle the complex causal relationships" linking emissions from a particular country to a specific effect, and noted that "global warming is often one of several contributing factors to climate change-related effects such as hurricanes". In addition, it stated that the "adverse effects of global warming are often projections about future impacts, whereas human rights violations are normally established after the harm has occurred" [see Reading 9, para. 70].

36. These conclusions can be challenged. As scientific knowledge improves and the effects of climate change become larger and more immediate, tracing causal connections between particular contributions and resulting harms becomes less difficult. But whether or not climate change legally violates human rights norms is not the dispositive question. As OHCHR emphasized, even in the absence of such a finding, "human rights obligations provide important protection to the individuals whose rights are affected by climate change" [see Reading 9, para. 71].

37. Specifically, States have obligations to protect against the infringement of human rights by climate change. This conclusion follows from the nature of their obligations to protect against environmental harm generally. Human rights bodies have made clear that States should protect against foreseeable environmental impairment of human rights whether or not the environmental harm itself violates human rights law, and even

whether or not the States directly cause the harm. An illustrative example is a case of the European Court of Human Rights arising from mudslides in the Caucasus that killed several inhabitants of the town of Tyrnauz. The Government did not cause the mudslide, but the Court held that it still had a responsibility to take appropriate steps to safeguard the lives of those within its jurisdiction.

38. Above all, the Court stated, Governments must adopt legal frameworks designed to effectively deter threats to the right to life from natural disasters as well as dangerous human activities. While each State has discretion to choose particular preventive measures and "an impossible or disproportionate burden must not be imposed on the authorities," the discretion of the State is not unlimited. In reviewing whether a State has met its obligations, the Court indicated that relevant factors include the foreseeability of the threat, whether the State undertook appropriate investigations and studies, and whether it followed its own law. The authorities must respect the right to information, including by providing for a system of advance warnings. Finally, the Court stated that where lives have been lost in circumstances that may engage the responsibility of the State, the State must provide an adequate response to the disaster, to ensure that the legal framework designed to protect the right to life is properly implemented.

39. The reasoning of the European Court in this respect is typical of the approach taken by other regional tribunals and human rights mechanisms. The duty to protect against harmful interference with the enjoyment of human rights is accepted as a pillar of human rights law, and many human rights bodies have applied that duty to such interference occurring as a result of environmental degradation.

40. Apart from questions of causation and responsibility, the nature of climate change also requires us to consider how human rights norms apply to a global environmental threat. Most human rights bodies that have examined the application of human rights norms to environmental issues have examined harm whose causes and effects are felt within one country. Climate change obviously does not fit within this pattern.

41. A possible response is to treat climate change as a matter of extraterritoriality—that is, to conclude that it implicates the obligation of each State to protect the human rights of those outside, as well as those within, its own jurisdiction. The Special Rapporteur is aware that the question of extraterritorial human rights obligations has been controversial in other contexts. However, he believes that attempting to describe the extraterritorial human rights obligations of every State in relation to climate change would be of limited usefulness even apart from its potential for controversy. In the human rights context, climate change is probably not best understood as a set of simultaneously occurring

transboundary harms that should be addressed by each State trying to take into account its individual contribution to the effects of climate change in every other State in the world. The practical obstacles to such an undertaking are daunting, and it is instructive that the international community has not attempted to address climate change in this way.

42. Instead, from the creation of the Intergovernmental Panel on Climate Change in 1988, through the adoption of the United Nations Framework Convention on Climate Change in 1992, to the negotiation of the Paris Agreement in 2015, States have consistently treated climate change as a global problem that requires a global response. This approach not only makes the most practical sense. It is also in accord with, and can be seen as an application of, the duty of international cooperation.

43. The duty of international cooperation has support in the general practice of States and, more specifically, in the Charter of the United Nations. Article 55 of the Charter requires the United Nations to promote "universal respect for, and observance of, human rights and fundamental freedoms for all," and in Article 56, "all Members pledge themselves to take joint and separate action in co-operation with the Organization for the achievement of the purposes set forth in Article 55". Similarly, article 2 (1) of the International Covenant on Economic, Social and Cultural Rights requires each of its parties to take steps not only individually, but also "through international assistance and cooperation," towards the progressive realization of the rights recognized in the Covenant.

44. With respect to many threats to human rights, international cooperation needs to play only a supporting role. Environmental harms whose causes and effects are within the jurisdiction of one State can and should be addressed primarily by that State. However, some challenges require international cooperation. Outside the environmental context, the International Court of Justice has recognized "the universal character both of the condemnation of genocide and of the co-operation required 'in order to liberate mankind from such an odious scourge'." Climate change is a paradigmatic example of a global threat that is impossible to address effectively without coordinated international action. As States have acknowledged in the text of the United Nations Framework Convention on Climate Change itself, as well as in Human Rights Council resolutions 26/27 and 29/15, "the global nature of climate change calls for the widest possible cooperation by all countries and their participation in an effective and appropriate international response".

Section 5. Discussion Notes/Questions

1. Climate change will adversely impact millions of people worldwide, undermining their health, livelihoods, communities, and food security. For some people, their survival will be at risk, and many will not survive. However,

the adversities will not be felt evenly around the world. Some people are much more vulnerable than others; geographic location, poverty, and lack of political power place them at special risk of experiencing severe harms as the climate changes. Should they be given special attention and treatment? If so, what, how, and according to what legal theory or logic?

Consider people whose coastal homes, cities, and even countries are lost to rising seas, or communities that suffer extreme hunger because drought destroys their food supplies. Will their human rights have been violated? By whom? If there is not a legally cognizable violation of human rights that can be attributed to any human entity, is there a legally cognizable obligation under human rights law for states to assist the victims of climate change?

What in particular should be done about the alarming yet likely prospect that some island nations will be entirely submerged by rising sea levels? Where will the people go? Is any nation bound to accept them? Certain nations? Will they have rights to citizenship in nations that accept them? Will they have rights to self-determination, self-governance?

2. In the instant problem, Volhynia has provided assistance to the Chuksuk people. Was it legally obligated to do so? Volhynia also was careful to consult and engage with the Chuksuk people. Was it legally obligated to do so, or could it simply and unilaterally have moved threatened Chuksuk communities to safer areas?

What about Hanguo and the Federation of Columbia? If there were Chuksuk communities within their borders, would they have any obligation, based in human rights law, to assist such communities in adapting to climate change? Does either country have any similar obligation to Chuksuk communities outside their borders?

Do Hanguo and the Federation of Columbia have any obligation, based in human rights law, to reduce their greenhouse gas emissions or to cooperate in international efforts to reduce greenhouse gas emissions? Reducing emissions now will not stop current climate change or mitigate the adverse impacts currently being experienced by the Chuksuk people. The impact of today's reduced emissions will be felt decades from now. Do Hanguo and the Federation of Columbia owe any obligation to future generations of Chuksuk? What if, as seems likely, it can be shown that the Arctic homelands of the Chuksuk will have been long destroyed before current emission reductions will have any impact, is there any obligation under those circumstances?

3. One challenge in developing an argument based on human rights norms is that human rights norms are sometimes grounded in nonbinding texts. For example, the United Nations Declaration on the Rights of Indigenous Peoples was adopted by the United Nations General Assembly. Under the terms of the U.N. Charter, General Assembly actions are recommendatory only. *See* Charter of the United Nations, arts. 10, 11, and 13 **[Basic Document 1.1]**. The extent to which the norms articulated in such documents have become part of customary international law is frequently contested. John H.

Knox addressed this problem in a 2013 report to the Human Commission on the issue of human rights obligations relating to the enjoyment of a safe, clean, healthy and sustainable environment. In preparing his report, he relied on "a large and growing number of legal statements that together create a body of human rights norms relating to the environment." However, he acknowledged that many of the "legal statements" on which he relied were not actually binding on States. He explained:

> The Independent Expert understands that not all States have formally accepted all of these norms. While some of the statements cited are from treaties, or from tribunals that have the authority to issue decisions that bind the States subject to their jurisdiction, other statements are interpretations by experts that do not in themselves have binding effect. Despite the diversity of the sources from which they arise, however, the statements are remarkably coherent. Taken together, they provide strong evidence of converging trends towards greater uniformity and certainty in the human rights obligations relating to the environment. These trends are further supported by State practice reflected in the universal periodic review process and international environmental instruments. . . . In this light, the Independent Expert encourages States to accept these statements as evidence of actual or emerging international law. At a minimum, they should be seen as best practices that States should move to adopt as expeditiously as possible.

For purposes of this problem, does it matter whether we consider a purported "legal statement" concerning human rights and the environment to be "actual" international law, "emerging" international law, or "best practices"? What authority should the International Court of Justice have to apply "emerging" international law or a consideration of "best practices" in the decision of an international dispute? What authority does it have?

4. If there is no obligation owed to the Chuksuk people, what about other people (as yet unidentified and unborn) who will be adversely impacted by future climate change? Is it possible for rights to exist in generations of people yet unborn, in future human beings who are indeterminate, contingent, and lacking identity? Given that legal duties do not exist absent corresponding legal rights, on what legal theory, if any, can it be said that such persons have rights and that current generations have legal obligations to them? For pertinent discussion, *see, e.g.*, Burns H. Weston, *Climate Change, Human Rights, and Intergenerational Justice*, 9 Vt. J. Envtl. L. 375 (2008) and Burns H. Weston, *The Theoretical Foundations of Intergenerational Ecological Justice,* 34 Hum. Rts. Q. 251 (2012). *See also* Robert Nozick, Anarchy, State, and Utopia (1974); Joerg Chet Tremmel, A Theory of Intergenerational Justice (2009); Edith Brown Weiss, In Fairness to Future Generations: International Law, Common Patrimony, and Intergenerational Equity (1988–89); Wilfred Beckerman, *The Impossibility of a Theory of Intergenerational Justice, in* Handbook of Intergenerational Justice 53 (Joerg Chet Tremmel ed., 2006).

5. Some experts estimate that by 2050 there will be between 200–250 million refugees who have been displaced by environmental changes caused by climate change (including sea level rise, extreme weather events such as hurricanes, or extended droughts), vastly more than currently existing political refugees. Most environmental refugees will not cross international borders, but will continue an internal migration trend in developing countries from rural to urban areas. The 1951 Geneva Convention Relating to the Status of Refugees and its 1967 Protocol Relating to the Status of Refugees currently provide protection to political refugees, but that framework will not be sufficient for this new class of refugees. Some, such as the Government of the Maldives, have suggested expanding the Geneva Convention's definitions. Others have suggested an entirely new regime. Which position do you support? How would you define "environmental refugee" and what protections would you give such individuals? *See* Frank Biermann & Ingrid Boas, *Preparing for a warmer world: towards a global governance system to protect climate refugees*, 10 Global Envtl. Pol. 60–88 (2010). What about circumstances where the refugees do seek to move across international borders? In the case of internal or cross-border movements, there is a real risk of violent clashes between refugees and existing populations over resources and land. For general discussion, *see* Jon Barnett & W. Neil Adger, *Climate Change, Human Security and Violent Conflict*, 26 Pol. Geography 639–55 (2007). *See also* Office of the High Commissioner on Human Rights, OHCHR's Key Messages on Human Rights, Climate Change and Migration, available at https://www.ohchr.org/Documents/Issues/ClimateChange/Key_Messages_HR_CC_Migration.pdf (accessed 4 July 2018).

6. Although the current problem is set in the International Court of Justice, it is much more likely that attempts to litigate human rights claims related to climate change will be made in one or more of the several specialized tribunals that have been established specifically to hear human rights claims. Those tribunals have often responded favorably to claims of violations of human rights resulting from environmental degradation. The European Court of Human Rights, for example, has issued several rulings affirming that environmental harm can amount to a violation of human rights (e.g., the right to life, to health, to respect for private and family life). In 2001, the African Commission on Human and Peoples' Rights ruled that pollution and other environmental degradation caused by corporate oil and gas development violated multiple provisions of the African Charter on Human Rights and Peoples' Rights. *See* African Commission on Human and Peoples' Rights, *Decision in 155/96 The Social and Economic Rights Action Center and the Center for Social and Economic Rights/Nigeria,* 30th Sess., Oct 13–27, 2001. And in 2010, the Inter-American Commission on Human Rights, in the spirit of three earlier Commission decisions and one decision of the Inter-American Court of Human Rights, each defending the ecological rights of indigenous peoples in Latin America, determined that the "noxious effects of pollution" can be the basis for a "colorable claim" of a human rights violation under the 1948 American Declaration of the Rights and Duties of Man when the pollution was the result of the issuance of environmental permits allowing the

installation of toxic and hazardous industrial facilities near residential areas and its impact was felt disproportionately by minority groups. *See* Inter-American Commission on Human Rights, *Report No. 43/10, Petition 242–05, Admissibility, Mossville Environmental Action Now v. United States* (17 Mar. 2010). On the other hand, a 2005 petition to the Inter-American Commission on Human Rights on behalf of Inuit living in the Arctic regions of the United States and Canada has been, so far, completely unsuccessful. The petition alleged that "through its failure to take effective action to reduce greenhouse gas emissions, the United States is violating the Inuit's right to the benefits of culture," along with several other human rights. *See* Sheila Watt-Coutier, *Petition to the Inter-American Commission on Human Rights Seeking Relief from Violations Resulting from Global Warming Caused by Acts and Omissions of the United States* (7 Dec. 2005), *available at* http://www.ciel.org/Publications/ICC_Petition_7Dec05.pdf (last visited Feb 12, 2011). The Inter-American Commission declined to consider the petition, but did allow testimony on the general subject of "global warming and human rights" at a hearing on March 1, 2007, although without resolving the issue definitively.

7. Courts in the United States have also considered claims alleging that environmental degradation violates international human rights. Those claims are generally brought pursuant to the Alien Tort Statute (ATS), which gives federal courts jurisdiction over actions seeking to recover for torts committed "in violation of the law of nations or a treaty of the United States." 28 U.S.C. § 1350. *See supra* Chapter 2. One major obstacle to such actions is the Supreme Court's conclusion that ATS claims must rest on international norms that are as definite and as widely accepted as the "historical paradigms" that were recognized when the statute was adopted in the 18th century. *Sosa v. Alvarez-Machain,* 542 U.S. 692, 732 (2004). *See* Kathleen Jaeger, *Environmental Claims Under the Alien Tort Statute,* 28 Berkeley J. Int'l L. 519 (2010) (concluding that environmental norms are not yet sufficiently established in customary international law to support an ATS claim, but that it might be possible to bring claims where "human rights abuses and environmental wrongs overlap.") In addition, the Court has held that the ATS does not apply extraterritorially. It is not entirely clear what this means for cases alleging environmental harm attributable to U.S.-based actors, but it may mean that no case could ever be premised on environmental harm occurring outside the United States. *See Kiobel v. Royal Dutch Petroleum Co.* 569 U.S. 108 (2013). A further blow to ATS litigation over environmental harm was dealt by the Court's decision in *Jesner v. Arab Bank, PLC,* 136 S.Ct. 1386, 1394 (2018), which held that foreign corporations could not be held liable in ATS suits for international law violations absent a "specific direction from Congress" to impose liability on corporations.

8. Is litigation a good strategy for addressing climate change problems? As a member of the law community, and in light of the dismal results of the UN Framework Convention on Climate Change **(Basic Document 2.4)**, you might be supportive of efforts to seek judicial assistance in securing help for the victims of climate change or in forcing government action to address the

problem. But some commentators criticize those who turn to the courts for help on the grounds that litigation strategies are unlikely to be effective, that they may complicate efforts to find an international solution, and that the legislative and executive branches of government, not the courts, should decide whether to take action to combat climate change and what action to take. *See, e.g.,* Eric A. Posner, *Climate Change and International Human Rights Litigation: A Critical Appraisal,* 155 U. Pa. L. Rev. 1925 (2006). How do you respond to these concerns?

9. Is it relevant to combating climate change that people who are hurt by it may not have access to the executive and legislative branches of government in the states where the greatest volume of greenhouse gas emissions is occurring? What incentive do governments of emitting states have to reduce emissions if the people who are hurt by them do not have any vote in local elections or any voice in the local political process? Is not litigation before local courts an appropriate response for persons who lack power to influence local politicians? In what other ways can vulnerable groups from other countries influence the actions of a state with significant greenhouse gas emissions? Do international political processes provide adequate means for addressing transboundary environmental harms? Does it help in any of these settings to base claims on human rights doctrines, principles, or rules?

10. Should human rights norms limit action taken to mitigate climate change? Suppose a proposed hydroelectric dam will allow a State to reduce its emissions by shutting down a coal-fired power plant? Can it build the dam even if it means displacing local people? What about adaptation actions? If a state wishes to remove people from threatened coastal areas, can it do so over their protests? And what about the impact of geoengineering solutions? If geoengineering causes severe harm to particular groups or individuals, is that a human rights violation for which the geoengineers bear responsibility? *See* Naomi Roht-Arriaza, *"First Do No Harm": Human Rights and Efforts to Combat Climate Change,* 38 Ga. J. Int'l & Comp. L. 593 (2010).

11. Traditionally, human rights have served to redress state or public power. Today it is asserted that human rights may serve as well to redress corporate or private power, including multinational corporations with assets that clearly rival that of states. *See, e.g.,* Steven R. Ratner, *Corporations and Human Rights: A Theory of Legal Responsibility,* 111 Yale L. J. 443 (2001). It allows weaker parties to stand up to stronger forces and thus is increasingly held up as the best answer, rhetorically and legally, to the problem of climate change. Do you agree? What advantages do you see? Disadvantages? Do human rights allow those with little power to take on corporations? *See* Amy Sinden, *Climate Change and Human Rights,* 27 J. Land Resources & Envtl. L. 255–453 (2007). Do power imbalances make any other approaches more or less appealing to you? If not, what solutions would you recommend? Would you reform human rights law? Any other legal regimes? *See generally* Office of the High Commissioner on Human Rights, Guiding Principles on Business and Human Rights, U.N. Doc. A/HRC/17/31, annex (2011).

CHAPTER TEN

NUCLEAR THREATS TO THE ENVIRONMENT

■ ■ ■

Two "wicked problems" confront humanity: the nuclear weapons issue and climate change. It is hard to say which is worse. Big nuclear explosions, if they occur, will produce a nuclear winter that will make human life impossible to sustain. Anthropogenic climate change is heating up the atmosphere, raising sea levels, increasing ocean acidification and increasing the frequency and intensity of storms and other extreme weather events that will make life seriously endangered.

Both prohibiting nuclear weapons and combatting climate change raise issues for the future of people on this planet. The authors are hopeful we can meet both these challenges, but it ought not to be assumed in either instance. How to achieve the aim in both cases will require political and global leadership of a high order. Both topics raise issues of enormous complexity. In Chapter 9, we addressed issues related to climate change. In this chapter, we address the international laws pertaining to nuclear weapons and nuclear energy.

The nuclear weapons issue involves complicated geopolitical issues that reach far beyond the environment. It is 73 years since an atomic bomb was dropped on Hiroshima. A 14-kiloton weapon dropped on 6 August 1945 killed 140,000 people and caused horrific human suffering. Surrounded by mountains of thick green bush and magnificent seascapes, Hiroshima does not now look like a place visited by a nuclear disaster. It presents as a modern, attractive city of more than 1.2 million people. At its center, however, there is a museum that never fails to touch the humanity of any who visit it, demonstrating the appalling suffering that nuclear explosions can cause.

Nuclear energy also poses problems for people as demonstrated by the well-known disaster that occurred in the former Soviet Union at Chernobyl on 26 April 1986. The state-run nuclear power plant was near Kiev, in what is now Ukraine. A chemical explosion occurred in one of its four reactors. A fire in the damaged reactor caused release into the atmosphere of radioactive elements. Adjoining countries became seriously concerned. People died in Ukraine from radiation sickness or radiation-induced health impairments. Four thousand children were estimated to have developed thyroid cancer as a result of radiation exposure. More than 300,000 people were relocated. The clean-up in the region was massive.

More recently, catastrophic events in Japan arose from an earthquake and resultant tsunami that swamped the Fukushima 1 Nuclear Power Plant in 2011. It was not able to be shut down and the entire complex was flooded. Cooling systems failed, the reactors and spent fuel overheated causing a series of explosions that led to significant releases of radiological contamination into the environment. Three reactors experienced meltdown.

Serious safety issues exist about nuclear power and the variety of approaches by different countries around the world are evident. The issue here is what is the optimal regulatory system, and to what degree should it be, or must it be, international?

Part A of this Chapter addresses the law and policy pertaining to nuclear weapons. It begins with some general background material on law and policy in this arena. Then, in Problem 10-1, we concentrate specifically on the difficult law relating to the legality of the use of nuclear weapons.

In Part B, the Chapter examines the international law related to nuclear power. Problem 10-2 focuses attention on a multitude of issues that could arise in the event of a nuclear accident causing significant transboundary harm.

A. INTERNATIONAL REGULATION OF NUCLEAR WEAPONS

To understand international legal regulation of nuclear weapons, one must begin with the 1968 Treaty on the Non-Proliferation of Nuclear Weapons **(Basic Document 7.18)**, commonly known as the "Non-Proliferation Treaty" or the "NPT." At the core of the NPT is a deal struck between the five states that then possessed nuclear weapons (China, Great Britain, France, the United States, and the Union of Soviet Socialist Republics) and the non-nuclear-weapon states that ratified the treaty. The essential deal was this: in exchange for assistance in developing nuclear energy for peaceful purposes, the non-nuclear-weapon states (frequently abbreviated as NNWS) agreed not to develop nuclear weapons.

As part of the deal, the nuclear-weapon states (NWS) agreed to take steps to make nuclear technology, especially nuclear energy, available to non-nuclear-weapon states for peaceful purposes, so long as steps were taken to ensure the technology was not diverted to the production of nuclear weapons. The non-nuclear-weapon states agreed to accept oversight by the International Atomic Energy Agency (IAEA) **(Basic Document 1.3)** for the purpose of verifying that the non-nuclear-weapon states complied with their treaty obligations.

The NPT aimed at preventing the spread of nuclear weapons. But it did not aim at complete denuclearization of the world's military forces: the nuclear-weapon states did not agree to abandon their nuclear weapons. They did agree, however, to take steps to reduce the risks of nuclear war. Thus, the preamble to the treaty recites that the Parties to the treaty "declar[e] their intention to achieve at the earliest possible date the cessation of the nuclear arms race and to undertake effective measures in the direction of nuclear disarmament." And in Article VI of the Treaty, the Parties agreed to "pursue negotiations in good faith on effective measures relating to cessation of the nuclear arms race at an early date and to nuclear disarmament . . . ."

The NPT was adopted in 1968. It entered into force in 1970. It has 190 parties, including the five original nuclear-weapon states. Four current nuclear-weapon states—India, Israel, North Korea[1] and Pakistan—are not parties to the NPT, which means, of course, that they are not bound by its Article VI commitment to negotiate about nuclear disarmament.

In addition to the NPT, there are two treaties dealing with nuclear-weapons testing. The 1963 Limited Nuclear Test Ban Treaty prohibits the testing of nuclear weapons in outer space, underwater or in the atmosphere. It has entered into force and has 125 parties. The 1996 Comprehensive Nuclear Test Ban Treaty has 144 parties, but has not entered into force. That's because its entry-into-force conditions require ratifications of 44 named countries, including all the nuclear-weapon states. At this time, several nuclear-weapon states have not ratified, including China, India, Israel, North Korea, Pakistan, and the United States.

In several regions of the world, states have adopted treaties aimed at establishing that region as a "Nuclear-Weapons-Free Zone." Currently, there are five such treaties: i) the 1967 Treaty of Tlatelolco (Prohibition of Nuclear Weapons in Latin America and the Caribbean); ii) the 1985 Treaty of Rarotonga **(Basic Document 7.21)** (South Pacific Nuclear Free Zone); iii) the 1995 Treaty of Bangkok (Southeast Asia Nuclear Weapon-Free Zone); iv) the 1996 Treaty of Pelindaba (African Nuclear Weapon Free Zone); and v) the 2006 Treaty on a Nuclear-Weapon-Free Zone in Central Asia. Each of these treaties has entered into force. Several other treaties forbid the presence of nuclear weapons in particular locations. They are the Antarctic Treaty **(Basic Document 6.1)**, the Treaty on Principles Governing the Activities of States in the Exploration and Use of Outer Space, the Agreement Governing the Activities of States on the Moon and Other Celestial Bodies, and the Treaty on the Prohibition of the Emplacement of Nuclear Weapons on the Sea-Bed Floor. Each of these treaties has also entered into force.

---

[1] North Korea was a party to the NPT but withdrew in 2003. The effectiveness of its withdrawal is disputed.

The United States and Russia have entered into a number of arms control agreements aimed at limiting the threat from nuclear weapons. Those agreements include the 1987 Intermediate-range Nuclear Forces (INF) Treaty (aimed at the elimination of intermediate-range nuclear missiles),[2] the New Start Treaty (NST) (aimed at reductions in strategic nuclear weapons), and the Plutonium Management and Disposition Agreement (PMDA) (aimed at the disposal of weapon-grade plutonium).

On September 20, 2017, 49 states signed the Treaty on the Prohibition of Nuclear Weapons **(Basic Document 7.24)**. As its name implies, this treaty aims at the complete elimination of nuclear weapons. At this writing, a total of 57 states had signed the treaty and eight had ratified it, although it is not yet in force. None of the five NPT nuclear-weapon states, and none of the four non-NPT nuclear-weapon states has yet signed or ratified the treaty.

With this background in mind, consider the following assessments of the current nuclear-weapons threat.

GARETH EVANS, INCORRIGIBLE OPTIMIST: A POLITICAL MEMOIR

(Melbourne University Press, 2017) 257–261

[Gareth Evans was Australia's Foreign Minister from 1988 to 1996. After he left politics he was engaged in many different and important diplomatic assignments. He convened the APLN group from 2011 until 2015 and is now Convenor Emeritus. He has written extensively on the issue of nuclear weapons.]

The problem posed by nuclear weapons can be very simply stated. There are only two threats to life on this planet as we know it which international policy failure can make real. One is global warming, and the other is nuclear annihilation—and nuclear weapons can kill us a lot faster than CO2. The scale of the casualties that would follow any kind of significant nuclear exchange is almost incalculably horrific—not only from the immediate blast and longer-term irradiation effects, but also the nuclear-winter effect on global agriculture. Although, with the Cold War now long over, the threats posed by the arsenals of the existing nuclear-armed states are constantly downplayed by those states and their allies the real-world risk of this occurring is still immediate and real.

Despite big reductions which occurred immediately after the end of the Cold War, and the continuing retirement or scheduling for dismantlement

---

2 On February 2, 2019, the United States indicated that it would withdraw from the INF treaty within six months, pursuant to Article XV of the Treaty. It also announced that it would immediately suspend its obligations under the treaty. Both actions were said to be taken in response to Russia's noncompliance with the treaty. Russia, for its part, denied any violation of the treaty.

since by Russia and the United States of many more, there are still, at the time of writing in April 2017, some 15 400 warheads still in existence, with a combined destructive capability of close to 100 000 Hiroshima- or Nagasaki-sized bombs. Russia and the United Sates are embarking on a massive new modernisation program, and in our own Asian region the number of weapons is not diminishing but increasing, with China, India and Pakistan all having active programs. Around 7300 nuclear weapons remain in the hands of Russia, 7000 with the United Sates, and around 1100 with the other nuclear-armed states combined (China, France, United Kingdom, India, Pakistan, Israel and—at the margin—North Korea). A large proportion of them—over 4000—remain operationally available. And, most extraordinarily of all, some 2000 of the US and Russian weapons remain on dangerously high alert, ready to be launched on warning in the event of a perceived attack, within a decision window for each president of four to eight minutes.

Having launch decision times measured in minutes creates an extraordinarily stressful situation for decision-makers. Some people might be at their ice-calm best in crisis situations, but all human experience teaches us that these are not circumstances in which, cool, objective, balanced judgment is guaranteed. Zbigniew Brzezinski has given a wonderful account of the pressures involved, describing a situation which arose when he was US national security adviser in 1979:

> I got a message from my military assistant, a general, who woke me up at 3:00 a.m. at night on the red phone and said, 'Sorry to wake you up. We're under nuclear attack'. That kind of wakes you up. And he adds 30 seconds ago, 200 Soviet missiles have been fired at the United States . . . I had three minutes in which to notify the President. During those three minutes, I had to confirm it in a variety of ways. And then he would have four minutes to decide how to respond. And then 28 minutes later, if we decided to respond with everything—just let it roll—then 85 million would be dead and we'd be living in a different age . . . Then the confirmations did not come in . . . within two minutes, prior to me calling him on the third minute, it was clear that this was a false alarm. So I did nothing. I went back to sleep.

Brzezinski's interviewer then asked: 'And if the confirmation had been a little late, could we have had a problem?' His masterfully understated reply: 'We might have had'. Those decision times, and presidential response times, continue to this day. About the only consolation I have ever derived from all of this was the news that emerged a few years ago that Bill Clinton, for several months of his presidency, completely mislaid the nuclear codes he was supposed to carry on a card in his pocket (the 'biscuit') at all times—perhaps not altogether surprisingly, given his reported tendency to mislay his trousers—which means that during that period, a US retaliatory nuclear strike could not in fact have been authorised even had anyone wanted to.

The key point is that we have been much closer to catastrophe in the past, and are now, than most people begin to appreciate. Over the years, communications satellite launches have been mistaken for nuclear missile launches; demonstration tapes of incoming missiles have been confused for the real thing; military exercises have been mistaken for real mobilisations; technical glitches have triggered real-time alerts; live nuclear weapons have been flown by mistake around the US without anyone noticing until the plane returned to base; and one hydrogen bomb-carrying plane actually crashed in the United States, with every defensive mechanism preventing an explosion failing, except one cockpit switch. One of the most chilling near-misses occurred during the Cuban missile crisis when, losing communication with Moscow after coming too close to a depth charge from a US ship blockading Cuban waters, and not knowing whether war had broken out or not, the commander of a Soviet submarine had to decide whether to launch his nuclear torpedo. Overwhelmed by the responsibility, he put it to a vote of the three senior officers aboard—and it was by a two-to-one majority of those officers, on that boat, that we escaped World War III.

As bad as the risks were during most of the Cold War years, when there were just two opposing major nuclear powers, they have become dramatically compounded since the proliferation developments that produced India, Pakistan and Israel as new nuclear-armed states in the 1970s, and more recently North Korea—in areas of great regional volatility, a history of violent conflict, and less sophisticated command and control systems. These risks would worsen even more dramatically were there to be further breakouts, particularly in the Middle East in response to Iran's perceived program, or in North-East Asia in response either to North Korea or a dramatic increase in Chinese military capability. Given what we know about how many times the supposedly very sophisticated command and control systems of the Cold War years were strained by mistakes and false alarms, human error and human idiocy; given what we also know about how much less sophisticated are the command and control systems of some of the newer nuclear-armed states; and given also what we both know and can guess about how much more sophisticated and capable cyber offence will be of overcoming cyber defence in the years ahead, that we have survived for over seven decades without a nuclear weapons catastrophe is not a matter of inherent system stability or great statesmanship—rather sheer dumb luck. And it is utterly wishful thinking to believe that this luck can continue in perpetuity.

The other kind of risk with nuclear weapons is that non-state terrorist actors will acquire, by theft of conspiracy, ill-secured nuclear weapons or dangerous nuclear material, or sabotage nuclear power reactors. These possibilities have, understandably, captured much more attention in the aftermath of 9/11 with the series of deeply troubling developments in the Middle East, and jihadist-driven terrorist attacks on a number of capitals. Of course, no-one can be complacent about the risks posed by these extremists. Should they ever get their hands on the necessary nuclear material, we have to assume they would have no moral compunction whatever about using it. But this debate needs to be conducted a little less emotionally, and a little more calmly and rationally, than has sometimes tended to be the case. While it cannot be assumed that intelligence and law enforcement institutions will become aware of, and be able to intercept, every conceivable kind of terrorist conspiracy, there is a big difference in sophistication and time lines between the kind of coordination necessary to unleash simultaneous Kalashnikov attacks and that needed to manufacture and explode a nuclear weapon. While the engineering know-how required to build a basic fission device like the Hiroshima or Nagasaki bomb is readily available, highly enriched uranium and weapons-grade plutonium are not at all easily accessible. To assemble and maintain—for a long period, out of sight of the huge intelligence and law enforcement resources that are now being devoted to this threat worldwide—the team of criminal operatives, scientists and engineers necessary to acquire the components of, build and deliver such a weapon, would be a formidably difficult undertaking.

To complete the nuclear weapons risk story, it has to be acknowledged that a manifestly less difficult undertaking—and one rather more likely to occur although, somewhat surprisingly, it hasn't yet—would be to assemble quantities of non-fissile radioactive material like caesium 137, much more readily available in multiple industrial and medical uses, and detonate it with a conventional explosive like TNT as a 'dirty bomb' in the middle of a city. The physical damage would be relatively small, certainly by comparison with a fission bomb, but the psychological damage unquestionably would be very great—made so largely by the way this threat continues to be talked-up by policymakers. Talk the risks down and it may be that much less likely to be perpetrated.

Addressing all these risks is about as tough as public policy gets. Despite the incalculable harm that would be done to our planet by any kind of a significant nuclear weapons exchange, the very real risk of that occurring, and the urgency, accordingly, of a robust international policy response, there seems to be no major public policy issue on which it has been harder to make serious and sustained progress than nuclear non-proliferation and disarmament. The issues are complex, the technical detail is often impenetrable to the uninitiated, and by and large both policymakers and publics are—despite an occasional frisson about Iran or North Korea—complacent and indifferent.

BARACK OBAMA, PRESIDENT OF THE UNITED STATES OF AMERICA, REMARKS

delivered in Hradčany Square in Prague, 5 April 2009

Now, one of those issues that I'll focus on today is fundamental to the security of our nations and to the peace of the world—that's the future of nuclear weapons in the 21st century.

The existence of thousands of nuclear weapons is the most dangerous legacy of the Cold War. No nuclear war was fought between the United States and the Soviet Union, but generations lived with the knowledge that their world could be erased in a single flash of light. Cities like Prague that existed for centuries, that embodied the beauty and the talent of so much of humanity, would have ceased to exist.

Today, the Cold War has disappeared but thousands of those weapons have not. In a strange turn of history, the threat of global nuclear war has gone down, but the risk of a nuclear attack has gone up. More nations have acquired these weapons. Testing has continued. Black market trade in nuclear secrets and nuclear materials abound. The technology to build a bomb has spread. Terrorists are determined to buy, build or steal one. Our efforts to contain these dangers are centered on a global non-proliferation regime, but as more people and nations break the rules, we could reach the point where the center cannot hold.

Now, understand, this matters to people everywhere. One nuclear weapon exploded in one city—be it New York or Moscow, Islamabad or Mumbai, Tokyo or Tel Aviv, Paris or Prague—could kill hundreds of thousands of people. And no matter where it happens, there is no end to what the consequences might be—for our global safety, our security, our society, our economy, to our ultimate survival.

Some argue that the spread of these weapons cannot be stopped, cannot be checked—that we are destined to live in a world where more nations and more people possess the ultimate tools of destruction. Such fatalism is a deadly adversary, for if we believe that the spread of nuclear weapons is inevitable, then in some way we are admitting to ourselves that the use of nuclear weapons is inevitable.

Just as we stood for freedom in the 20th century, we must stand together for the right of people everywhere to live free from fear in the 21st century. And as nuclear power—as a nuclear power, as the only nuclear power to have used a nuclear weapon, the United States has a moral responsibility to act. We cannot succeed in this endeavor alone, but we can lead it, we can start it.

So today, I state clearly and with conviction America's commitment to seek the peace and security of a world without nuclear weapons. (Applause.) I'm not naive. This goal will not be reached quickly—perhaps not in my lifetime. It will take patience and persistence. But now we, too, must ignore the voices who tell us that the world cannot change. We have to insist, "Yes, we can."

Now, let me describe to you the trajectory we need to be on. First, the United States will take concrete steps towards a world without nuclear weapons. To put an end to Cold War thinking, we will reduce the role of nuclear weapons in our national security strategy, and urge others to do the same. Make no mistake: As long as these weapons exist, the United States will maintain a safe, secure and effective arsenal to deter any adversary, and guarantee that defense to our allies—including the Czech Republic. But we will begin the work of reducing our arsenal.

To reduce our warheads and stockpiles, we will negotiate a new Strategic Arms Reduction Treaty with the Russians this year. President Medvedev and I began this process in London, and will seek a new agreement by the end of this year that is legally binding and sufficiently bold. And this will set the stage for further cuts, and we will seek to include all nuclear weapons states in this endeavor.

To achieve a global ban on nuclear testing, my administration will immediately and aggressively pursue U.S. ratification of the Comprehensive Test Ban Treaty. After more than five decades of talks, it is time for the testing of nuclear weapons to finally be banned.

And to cut off the building blocks needed for a bomb, the United States will seek a new treaty that verifiably ends the production of fissile materials intended for use in state nuclear weapons. If we are serious about stopping the spread of these weapons, then we should put an end to the dedicated production of weapons-grade materials that create them. That's the first step.

Second, together we will strengthen the Nuclear Non-Proliferation Treaty as a basis for cooperation.

The basic bargain is sound: Countries with nuclear weapons will move towards disarmament, countries without nuclear weapons will not acquire them, and all countries can access peaceful nuclear energy. To strengthen the treaty, we should embrace several principles. We need more resources and authority to strengthen international inspections. We need real and immediate consequences for countries caught breaking the rules or trying to leave the treaty without cause.

And we should build a new framework for civil nuclear cooperation, including an international fuel bank, so that countries can access peaceful power without increasing the risks of proliferation. That must be the right of every nation that renounces nuclear weapons, especially developing countries embarking on peaceful programs. And no approach will succeed if it's based on the denial of rights to nations that play by the rules. We must harness the power of nuclear energy on behalf of our efforts to combat climate change, and to advance peace opportunity for all people.

But we go forward with no illusions. Some countries will break the rules. That's why we need a structure in place that ensures when any nation does, they will face consequences.

Just this morning, we were reminded again of why we need a new and more rigorous approach to address this threat. North Korea broke the rules once again by testing a rocket that could be used for long range missiles. This provocation underscores the need for action—not just this afternoon at the U.N. Security Council, but in our determination to prevent the spread of these weapons.

Rules must be binding. Violations must be punished. Words must mean something. The world must stand together to prevent the spread of these weapons. Now is the time for a strong international response now is the time for a strong international response, and North Korea must know that the path to security and respect will never come through threats and illegal weapons. All nations must come together to build a stronger, global regime. And that's why we must stand shoulder to shoulder to pressure the North Koreans to change course.

Iran has yet to build a nuclear weapon. My administration will seek engagement with Iran based on mutual interests and mutual respect. We believe in dialogue. But in that dialogue we will present a clear choice. We want Iran to take its rightful place in the community of nations, politically and economically. We will support Iran's right to peaceful nuclear energy with rigorous inspections. That's a path that the Islamic Republic can take. Or the government can choose increased isolation, international pressure, and a potential nuclear arms race in the region that will increase insecurity for all.

So let me be clear: Iran's nuclear and ballistic missile activity poses a real threat, not just to the United States, but to Iran's neighbors and our allies. The Czech Republic and Poland have been courageous in agreeing to host a defense against these missiles. As long as the threat from Iran persists, we will go forward with a missile defense system that is cost-effective and proven. If the Iranian threat is eliminated, we will have a stronger basis for security, and the driving force for missile defense construction in Europe will be removed.

So, finally, we must ensure that terrorists never acquire a nuclear weapon. This is the most immediate and extreme threat to global security. One terrorist with one nuclear weapon could unleash massive destruction. Al Qaeda has said it seeks a bomb and that it would have no problem with using it. And we know that there is unsecured nuclear material across the globe. To protect our people, we must act with a sense of purpose without delay.

So today I am announcing a new international effort to secure all vulnerable nuclear material around the world within four years. We will set new standards, expand our cooperation with Russia, pursue new partnerships to lock down these sensitive materials.

We must also build on our efforts to break up black markets, detect and intercept materials in transit, and use financial tools to disrupt this dangerous trade. Because this threat will be lasting, we should come together to turn efforts such as the Proliferation Security Initiative and the Global Initiative to Combat Nuclear Terrorism into durable international institutions. And we should start by having a Global Summit on Nuclear Security that the United States will host within the next year.

Now, I know that there are some who will question whether we can act on such a broad agenda. There are those who doubt whether true international cooperation is possible, given inevitable differences among nations. And there are those who hear talk of a world without nuclear weapons and doubt whether it's worth setting a goal that seems impossible to achieve.

But make no mistake: We know where that road leads. When nations and peoples allow themselves to be defined by their differences, the gulf between them widens. When we fail to pursue peace, then it stays forever beyond our grasp. We know the path when we choose fear over hope. To denounce or shrug off a call for cooperation is an easy but also a cowardly thing to do. That's how wars begin. That's where human progress ends.

There is violence and injustice in our world that must be confronted. We must confront it not by splitting apart but by standing together as free nations, as free people. I know that a call to arms can stir the souls of men and women more than a call to lay them down. But that is why the voices for peace and progress must be raised together.

Those are the voices that still echo through the streets of Prague. Those are the ghosts of 1968. Those were the joyful sounds of the Velvet Revolution. Those were the Czechs who helped bring down a nuclear-armed empire without firing a shot.

Human destiny will be what we make of it. And here in Prague, let us honor our past by reaching for a better future. Let us bridge our divisions, build upon our hopes, accept our responsibility to leave this world more prosperous and more peaceful than we found it. Together we can do it.

ASIA-PACIFIC AND GLOBAL NUCLEAR ORDERS IN THE SECOND NUCLEAR AGE

RAMESH THAKUR

(APLN-CNND, PB 21, July 2016)

Summary

All global nuclear risks and threats are present in the Asia-Pacific and in some cases are even more acute in this region. Security complexes and the main drivers of nuclear weapons policy tend to be primarily regional rather than global. Asia is the principal site of strategic rivalry in the second nuclear age and the theatre of the least unlikely nuclear war. The nuclear disarmament norm continues to be breached most egregiously in Asia as the only continent where warhead numbers are growing. The most serious violations of the non-proliferation norm have occurred here in the last two decades and it is the sole site of nuclear testing today. There is no architecture in place to promulgate and police regional regulatory norms and standards for the safe operation of nuclear reactors. And Asia also has some of the most acute nuclear security vulnerabilities.

1. Of the world's nine nuclear weapons possessor countries—China, India, North Korea, Pakistan, France, Israel, Russia, the United Kingdom and the United States—four are in Asia. Not surprisingly, therefore, nuclear risks and threats that exist globally are also present in Asia, and in some cases are even more acute in this region.[3] It is also worth remembering that security complexes and the main drivers of nuclear weapons policy tend to be primarily regional—and indeed, in Asia-Pacific, sub-regional[4]—rather than global, although obviously there are cross-linkages between these two and the national levels of analyses.

The Asia-Centric Second Nuclear Age

2. The first nuclear age was shaped by the overarching ideological rivalry of the bipolar Cold War protagonists, the competitive nuclear arms build-up and doctrines of the two superpowers and the development of robust mechanisms for maintaining strategic stability. Effectively there were the five 1968 Nuclear Non-Proliferation Treaty (NPT)-licit nuclear weapons states (NWS) and the non-NWS, albeit with the ambiguous

[3] This Policy Brief is based on a paper prepared for the Berlin Conference on Asian Security, 19–21 June 2016.

[4] Moreover, the subregional nuclear insecurity complex across Asia does not always coincide with the geographical subregion. For example in the subcontinent, there is a triangular nuclear relationship between China, India and Pakistan. The other South Asian states are largely irrelevant to the core dynamics of the nuclear equation, although they would be severely impacted with any use of nuclear weapons and with a nuclear accident. By contrast, in Northeast Asia every country is part of the nuclear equations complex. In Southeast Asia and Oceania, no country has or is likely to seek nuclear weapons in the foreseeable future, although Australia is a nuclear umbrella country; some Southeast Asian countries are interested in nuclear power but Oceania is entirely free of nuclear power reactors; and both subregions are covered by nuclear-weapon-free zones.

exception of Israel. Today there are also the non-NPT nuclear-armed states,[5] with two of the three (India, Israel, and Pakistan) being in Asia. In addition, the world's only NPT non-NWS country to have announced its withdrawal from the treaty in order to pursue nuclear weapons, namely North Korea, is also in Asia. Three US allies depend for their national security on the extended (nuclear) deterrence provided by US nuclear weapons. And of course Asia is the only continent where nuclear weapons have ever been used.

3. The site of great power rivalry has shifted from Europe to Asia in the second nuclear age[6] characterized by a multiplicity of nuclear powers with criss-crossing ties of cooperation and conflict, the fragility of command and control systems, the critical importance of cybersecurity, threat perceptions between three or more nuclear-armed states simultaneously,, asymmetric perceptions of the military and political utility of nuclear weapons,[7] and the resulting greater complexity of deterrence relations between the nine nuclear-armed states. Changes in the nuclear posture of one can generate a cascading effect on several others. The nuclear relationship between India and Pakistan, for example, is conceptually, politically and strategically deeply intertwined with China as a nuclear power. The strategic boundary between nuclear warheads and conventional precision munitions is being steadily eroded.

4. The NPT is the normative anchor of the global nuclear orders on disarmament, nonproliferation, safety and security. Asia—and only Asia—contains states with the full spectrum of nuclear weapons status in relation to the NPT: a NWS, two non-NPT nuclear-armed states, an NPT defector state, three umbrella states, and a vast majority of non-NWS States Parties to the NPT.

5. China is Asia's only NPT-recognized NWS, and also the sole Asian permanent member of the United Nations Security Council which functions as the global enforcement authority in the maintenance of international peace and security, including nuclear peace. Pakistan is the only one of the nine nuclear-armed states where nuclear weapons were developed by the military, are essentially under military control and the decision to use them will be made by the military rather than civilian

---

[5] The NPT's arbitrary chronological definition of a NWS restricts that status to countries that conducted nuclear tests before 1 January 1967 (the five NWS). It is possible to work around the legal restriction by describing any country that possesses nuclear weapons as a nuclear-armed state.

[6] Paul Bracken, *The Second Nuclear Age: Strategy, Danger, and the New Power Politics* (New York: Henry Holt, 2012); Toshi Yoshihara and James R. Holmes, eds., *Strategy in the Second Nuclear Age: Power, Ambition, and the Ultimate Weapon* (Washington DC: Georgetown University Press, 2012); Gregory D. Koblentz, *Strategic Stability in the Second Nuclear Age* (New York: Council on Foreign Relations, Special Report No. 71, November 2014).

[7] Toby Dalton and George Perkovich, *India's Nuclear Options and Escalation Dominance* (Washington DC: Carnegie Endowment for International Peace, May 2016), pp. 5, 11; http://carnegieendowment.org/files/CP_273_India_Nuclear_Final.pdf.

leadership. India is the only nuclear-armed state to have territorial conflicts with two nuclear-armed states, China and Pakistan, over long and contested borders.

6. North Korea is unique in the family of nations: a communist dynastic dictatorship (the third generation is currently in control) that has committed acts of aggression and serial provocations against its more populous, prosperous and democratic southern kin state; acts of state criminality in kidnapping Japanese citizens in Japan and smuggling them into North Korea; and acts of terrorism. It is similarly unique in relation to the non-proliferation regime as the world's sole NPT defector state.

7. The other three Asian nuclear-armed states also have their own sets of troubling issues and problems. These include inventing the legal fiction of a 'peaceful nuclear explosion' while violating the terms of international civilian nuclear assistance; acting as the enabler for another nuclear-armed state; and pursuing a policy of managed nuclear instability vis-à-vis a major irredentist claim on a neighbour.[8]

8. There are far fewer nuclear weapons today than during the Cold War and they play a lesser role in shaping relations between Moscow and Washington, so that the risk of a nuclear war between them is very low.[9] Yet the overall risks of nuclear war have grown with more countries with weaker command and control systems in more unstable regions possessing these deadly weapons, terrorists wanting them and vulnerability to human error, system malfunction and cyber attack.

9. The geostrategic environment of the subcontinent had no parallel in the Cold War, with shared borders, major territorial disputes, history of many wars since 1945, compressed timeframes for using or losing nuclear weapons, and political volatility and instability.[10] Even a "limited" regional nuclear war, in which India and Pakistan used 50 Hiroshima-size (15kt) bombs each, could, in addition to direct casualties, lead to a famine that kills up to two billion people.[11]

10. The toxic cocktail of growing nuclear stockpiles, expanding nuclear platforms, irredentist territorial claims and out of control jihadist

---

[8] Shaun Gregory, "Pak toxic chaos plan changes nuke debate," *Times of India*, 6 March 2011, http://timesofindia.indiatimes.com/home/sundaytimes/all-that-matters/Pak-toxic-chaos-plan-changesnuke-debate/articleshow/7637964.cms.

[9] However, the flare-up of geopolitical tensions over Ukraine in 2014 heightened the danger of an unintended nuclear war: Robert E. Berls and Leon Ratz, "Rising Nuclear Dangers: Assessing the Risk of Nuclear Use in the Euro-Atlantic Region," *NTI Paper* (Washington: Nuclear Threat Initiative, October 2015), http://www.nti.org/media/pdfs/NTI_Rising_Nuclear_Dangers_Paper_FINAL.pdf?_=1443443566.

[10] Ramesh Thakur, "The Inconsequential Gains and Lasting Insecurities of India's Nuclear Weaponization," *International Affairs* 90:5 (2014), pp. 1101–24.

[11] Ira Helfand, *Nuclear Famine: Two Billion People at Risk? Global Impacts of Limited Nuclear War on Agriculture, Food Supplies, and Human Nutrition* (Somerville, MA: International Physicians for the Prevention of Nuclear War, 2013), *available at* https://www.ippnw.org/nuclear-famine.html.

groups makes the Indian subcontinent a high risk region of concern.[12] Premeditated large-scale conventional attacks and preemptive nuclear strikes seem unlikely pathways to a nuclear exchange between India and Pakistan or China and India. But the subcontinental rivalry is not free of the risk of a nuclear exchange triggered by acts of terror committed on Indian territory by individuals and groups linked to networks across the border in Pakistan. No one can be confident that another Mumbai style terrorist attack (November 2008) on a major Indian city will not take place, with links back to jihadists based in Pakistan;[13] that India will not retaliate militarily; and that this will not escalate to another war which then crosses the nuclear threshold. That is, the brittleness of deterrence stability is a function of fragile crisis stability mechanisms. Moreover, each party will feel more insecure with every increase in the other's nuclear weapons stockpiles and capabilities.

11. Northeast Asia is the world's most dangerous cockpit for a possible nuclear war that could directly involve three NWS (China, Russia, the US) plus North Korea as a non-NPT nuclear-armed state and South Korea, Japan and Taiwan as major US allies. North Korea's nuclear threat and the risk of war in Korea involving US troops, potential direct conflict with China, risk to the Taiwan Straits, risk to South Korea and Japan, and risk of DPRK direct use against the US homeland are critical and demand immediate, urgent attention.

Evading the Duty to Disarm

12. All the nine nuclear-armed states pay only lip-service to the ultimate elimination of nuclear weapons while their actions with respect to weapons arsenals, fissile material stocks, force modernization plans, declared doctrines and observable deployment practices demonstrate the intent to retain nuclear weapons indefinitely.[14] Even though their combined stockpiles total only three per cent of global nuclear arsenals, warhead numbers are growing in all four Asian nuclear-armed states (and in none of the other five).

13. Of the four, only China is legally bound by Article 6 of the NPT to nuclear disarmament. Instead, heavily dependent on land-based missiles, China is actively modernizing them to increase the survivability and strengthen the retaliatory capabilities of its nuclear forces.[15] With relatively small nuclear forces, China is concerned that its nuclear

[12] *See* Pervez Hoodbhoy and Zia Mian, "Nuclear battles in South Asia," *Bulletin of the Atomic Scientists*, 4 May 2016, http://thebulletin.org/nuclear-battles-south-asia9415.

[13] Ramesh Thakur, "Delinking Destiny from Geography: The Changing Balance of India-Pakistan Relations," *India Quarterly* 67:3 (September 2011), pp. 197–212.

[14] Gareth Evans, Tanya Ogilvie-White and Ramesh Thakur, *Nuclear Weapons: The State of Play 2015* (Canberra: Centre for Nuclear Non-Proliferation and Disarmament, 2015), https://cnnd.crawford.anu.edu.au/publication/cnnd/5328/nuclear-weapons-state-play-2015.

[15] 3 Li Bin, "Tracking Chinese Strategic Mobile Missiles," *Science & Global Security* 15:1 (2007), pp. 4–5.

deterrent is vulnerable to planned US conventional precision munitions that pose a potential a threat to Beijing's conventional and nuclear weapons systems, as well as its command-and-control centres.[16] A credible, near-continuous sea-based deterrent capability would significantly increase the survivability of its nuclear forces.

14. The growing accuracy and lethality of US conventional precision munitions, the continuing interest in ballistic missile defence (BMD) systems and the US refusal to adopt a no-first-use policy makes many Chinese nervous that Washington harbours doubts about China's survivable second-strike retaliatory capability. Chinese anxieties are strengthened by the US refusal to acknowledge mutual vulnerability vis-à-vis China. According to Gregory Kulacki, in "a significant—and dangerous—change in Chinese policy," China's military planners have for the first time begun to discuss putting the country's nuclear missiles on high alert, believing that this "would be a step toward assured retaliation."[17] If China follows the Russian and US lead, how long before the posture proliferates to India and Pakistan? Like nuclear terrorism, the launch of nuclear weapons on high alert by mistake, rogue launch, miscalculation of incoming information, or through system malfunction is low probability but high impact.

15. North Korea withdrew from the NPT in January 2003[18] and has conducted four nuclear weapon tests (2006, 2009, 2013, 2016) and several rocket and missile launches, although its capacity to target and hit other countries is still very limited. In May 2015 Pyongyang boasted it had successfully tested a submarine launched ballistic missile (SLBM). On 6 January 2016 it claimed to have successfully tested a hydrogen bomb followed by a rocket launch. As its restarted plutonium separation and uranium enrichment programs ramp up to full production, it will soon have the capability to produce several nuclear bombs every year. We will return to Korea in the next section on nonproliferation.

16. Neither India nor Pakistan has signed the NPT and therefore neither is bound by the Article 6 obligation to disarm. That said, it is difficult to challenge the claim—based on the NPT, the repeated demands

---

[16] Douglas Barrie, "China's Hypersonic Test—Behind the Headlines," *Military Balance Blog* (IISS), 30 January 2014, http://www.iiss.org/en/militarybalanceblog/blogsections/2014-3bea/january-1138/barrie-china-d0a8.

[17] Gregory Kulacki, *China's Military Calls for Putting Its Nuclear Forces on Alert* (Cambridge MA: Union of Concerned Scientists, January 2016), p. 1. http://www.ucsusa.org/sites/default/files/attach/2016/02/China-Hair-Trigger-full-report.pdf.

[18] A State Party has the right to withdraw from the NPT if it decides that "extraordinary events, related to the subject matter of [the] Treaty, have jeopardized the supreme interests of its country" (Article 10). North Korea announced its withdrawal from the NPT on 12 March 1993 but then suspended it on 11 June 1993, the day before the decision would have taken effect. In January 2003, North Korea ended the suspension, which for all practical purposes meant withdrawal with immediate effect. Christer Ahlstrom, "Withdrawal from arms control treaties," *SIPRI Yearbook 2004: Armaments, Disarmament and International Security* (Oxford: Oxford University Press, 2004), pp. 763–77.

from successive NPT Review Conferences, a multitude of UN General Assembly resolutions over the decades, and the humanitarian impacts initiative that has attracted over 150 states and a broad cross-section of civil society actors in the global arms control community—that there is a global norm to eliminate nuclear weapons.

17. India is estimated to possess around 110 warheads, is producing more bombs annually, and is working to create survivable nuclear forces based on a mix of different land, sea and air-based launch platforms. It is also developing and testing a mix of short, medium and long range missiles, plus nuclear-powered ballistic missile submarines. It has ambitions to design and build multistage ballistic rockets, remote sensing and communications satellites, and monitoring and guidance systems for putting different types of vehicles into space orbit. India's declared nuclear doctrine is "credible minimum nuclear deterrence." India says it will not be the first to use nuclear weapons but would "respond with punitive retaliation should deterrence fail"[19] and India is attacked by a weapon of mass destruction (WMD).

18. Pakistan has had a nuclear weapons program since the early 1970s and is currently estimated to have about 120 warheads for delivery by missiles and aircraft. Its nuclear arsenal is growing the fastest of any country in the world. Like India, its nuclear doctrine is based on the principle of "credible minimum deterrence," with resort to nuclear weapons envisaged only in response to an existential conventional or WMD threat.[20] Pakistan's nuclear doctrine is India-specific, although, particularly after the US raid on Abbotabad in May 2011 that killed Osama bin Laden and in light of continuing strong differences of opinion on regional security issues, the expansion and modernization of Pakistan's nuclear arsenal may also be driven partly by fears of a US raid to capture or secure its nuclear forces.[21]

19. The development of tactical nuclear weapons as a counter to India's superiority in conventional arms, and to compensate for its lack of strategic depth, would seem to leave open the possibility of first use of nuclear weapons against India, particularly in the case of invasion. Deployment of battlefield nuclear weapons requires the delegation of command and control to military units in the field. This increases the risks of miscalculation, accident, theft, and infiltration by militant groups.

20. In addition to four of the world's nine nuclear-armed states, Asia also accounts for several states that rely on the US for their security, including some who are explicitly umbrella states: that is, countries that

---

[19] Draft *Report of the National Security Advisory Board on Indian Nuclear Doctrine*, 17 August 1999; http://www.fas.org/nuke/guide/india/doctrine/990817- indnucld.htm.

[20] Ayaz Gul, "Pakistan rejects US call for curbing tactical nuke weapons," *Global Security Newswire*, 26 March 2016.

[21] Shyam Saran, "Dealing with Pakistan's brinkmanship," *Hindu*, 7 December 2012.

rely on the US extended nuclear deterrence. The argument has been expressed very sharply in the recent Australian Defence White Paper: "Only the nuclear and conventional military capabilities of the United States can offer effective deterrence against the possibility of nuclear threats against Australia."[22] The reliance of Japan and South Korea on the US nuclear umbrella is, if anything, even greater, given their propinquity to North Korea and China (as well as Russia as the third Northeast Asian nuclear-armed state). The particular significance of the US commitment here is seen as lying in its very strong incentive for Japan and South Korea not to acquire a deterrent nuclear capability of their own. If the various efforts at bilateral BMD cooperation involving the US, Australia, Japan and South Korea develop into a US-led Asia Pacific missile defence shield, China is likely to accelerate the expansion of its own nuclear and ballistic missile programs and possibly adopt a somewhat more robust nuclear deterrence doctrine.

Breaching the Non-Proliferation Norm

21. The first substantial breach of the NPT-centred non-proliferation norm occurred by Israel in the 1970s. On 18 May 1974, India conducted its first test, describing it disingenuously as a "peaceful nuclear explosion." India thus bears the primary responsibility for introducing the nuclear element into the subcontinental rivalry by heightening Pakistan's sense of insecurity and vulnerability to its more powerful neighbour. In 1998, India conducted another five nuclear tests and this time proclaimed itself to be a nuclear weapons possessor state.[23] Pakistan followed with six tests (to match India's six in 1974 and 1998 combined) of its own on 28 and 30 May 1998. Since then both countries have been more or less accepted as de facto nuclear-armed states.

22. India has also been granted a country-specific waiver by the Nuclear Suppliers Group for international trade in sensitive nuclear materials and signed bilateral civil nuclear supply agreements with several countries, despite its status as an NPT non-signatory. However justified these might be on grounds of India's self-proclaimed impeccable record of nonproliferation to third countries and as a means of drawing the country with growing geopolitical heft and diplomatic weight into global regimes, they have caused undoubted damage to the existing non-proliferation normative instruments.[24]

---

[22] Department of Defence, *2016 Defence White Paper* (Canberra: Government of Australia, 2016), paragraph 5.20.

[23] George Perkovich, *India's Nuclear Bomb: The Impact on Global Proliferation* (Berkeley CA: University of California Press, 1999).

[24] Ramesh Thakur, "Follow the Yellowcake Road: Balancing Australia's Security, Commercial and Bilateral National Interests against International Anti-Nuclear Interests," *International Affairs* 89:4 (2013), pp. 943–61.

23. For its part, China was the enabler for Pakistan's nuclear weapons. In 1983 a US State Department report concluded that there was "unambiguous evidence" that Pakistan was actively pursuing a nuclear weapons program. Thomas Reed, Secretary of the Air Force under presidents Gerald Ford and Jimmy Carter, has claimed that Pakistan's first nuclear weapon test was carried out for it by China on 26 May 1990.[25] The "deliberate act of proliferation" by China began in earnest in 1982 with the transfer of weapons-grade uranium and a blueprint for making a bomb that China had already tested.[26] Pakistan built 7–12 nuclear warheads "based on the Chinese design, assisted by Chinese scientists and Chinese technology."[27]

24. The Comprehensive Test Ban Treaty (CTBT), signed by 183 countries and ratified by 164, is a key barrier to both vertical and horizontal proliferation. This still leaves eight countries, out of 44 with nuclear reactors listed in Annex 2 of the treaty, whose ratifications are needed to bring it into force: China, Egypt, India, Iran, Israel, North Korea, Pakistan, and the US.[28] The other Asia-Pacific non-signatories are Bhutan, Mauritius, Tonga and Tuvalu. Myanmar, Nepal, Papua New Guinea, Solomon Islands, Sri Lanka, Thailand and Timor-Leste have signed but not yet ratified. Since the treaty's adoption in 1996, the handful of nuclear-weapon test explosions have all been in Asia in India, Pakistan and North Korea.

25. China, India and Pakistan maintain voluntary moratoria on testing. China also supports the treaty's early entry into force in principle, participates in the work of the Preparatory Commission for the CTBT Organization (CTBTO) and is preparing for national implementation of the treaty.[29] China's formal ratification would likely quickly follow US ratification, although Beijing neither acknowledges nor implies any link to ratification by another state. Similarly, it is not clear why India has not yet ratified, as there are no technical requirements for more tests within its

[25] Interview with Thomas C. Reed in Alex Kingsbury, "Why China helped countries like Pakistan, North Korea build nuclear bombs," *U.S. News & World Report*, 2 January 2009, http://www.usnews.com/articles/news/world/2009/01/02/why-china-helped-countries-like-pakistan-northkorea-build-nuclear-bombs.html. Reed also claims that China intentionally proliferated to North Korea too. See also William J. Broad, "Hidden travels of the atomic bomb," *New York Times*, 8 December 2008; Dan Vergano, "Scientists ponder how to get nuclear genie back in the bottle," *USA Today*, 14 December 2008, http://www.usatoday.com/tech/science/2008-12-14-nuclear-weapons_N.htm; and Thomas C. Reed and Danny B. Stillman (former director of the technical intelligence division at Los Alamos National Laboratory), *The Nuclear Express: A Political History of the Bomb and Its Proliferation* (Zenith Press, 2009).

[26] R. Jeffrey Smith and Joby Warrick "A nuclear power's act of proliferation," *Washington Post*, 13 November 2009.

[27] Tim Weiner, "U.S. and Chinese aid was essential as Pakistan built bomb," *International Herald Tribune*, 2 June 1998.

[28] http://www.ctbto.org/the-treaty/.

[29] Viyyanna Sastry, "The Poor Prospects of the CTBT Entering Into Force," 9 January 2012, Institute for Defence Studies and Analyses, http://www.idsa.in/idsacomments/ThePoorProspectsoftheCTBTEnteringIntoForce_cvsastry_090112.

professed doctrine of credible nuclear deterrence. Nor is there any reason why, as an earnest of its good faith in engaging with the global physical infrastructure, India could not actively participate in the CTBTO global system even without signing or ratifying the CTBT.[30]

26. A related treaty-based regime that does not yet exist but many deeply desire would prohibit additional production of fissile material for nuclear weapons. Pakistan has consistently blocked the adoption of any program of work in the CD in Geneva because it will not agree to negotiations on a fissile materials cut-off treaty (FMCT) in the absence of prior agreement to include existing stocks of weapons-grade fissile material, where it believes itself to be at a disadvantage vis-à-vis India.

27. The Additional Protocol (AP) is a formal document that grants the International Atomic Energy Agency (IAEA) complementary legal authority to verify a state's comprehensive, item-specific or voluntary offer safeguards obligations. Although voluntary, once an AP enters into force it becomes legally binding for the state. In March 2016, 127 states had an AP in force; another 19 had signed but were yet to bring it into force. Countries of the Asia-Pacific that signed or approved the AP, but for whom it is not yet in force, are Kiribati, Laos, Malaysia, Myanmar, Thailand and Timor Leste, of whom Malaysia and Thailand have significant nuclear activities.

28. The final plank of the non-proliferation structure relevant to Asia-Pacific is nuclear-weapon-free zones (NWFZ) that deepen and extend the scope of the NPT and embed the non-nuclear weapon status of NPT States Parties in additional treaty-based arrangements.[31] Asia-Pacific has two NWFZ covering the South Pacific and Southeast Asia. Mongolia and New Zealand have also declared themselves national NWFZ in law.

How to Solve a Problem Like North Korea

29. North Korea's pursuit of nuclear weapons began in the 1960s, accelerated in the 1980s and led to overt weaponization with four tests in the last decade. Its nuclear program has been enshrined in the constitution and embedded in party ideology, making reversal procedurally more challenging and politically more costly. To keep the scale and gravity of the North Korean threat in perspective, nevertheless, let us note that its nuclear tests have been on the small side, its claims are often exaggerated, and many of its attempted missile tests are known flops. Thus Pyongyang is still some distance from acquiring a reliable and deliverable nuclear weapon capability. But it does have a rudimentary capability and a few small bombs, and both are set to expand. Empirically, therefore, North Korea now belongs in the disarmament basket but its unique NPT-defector

---

[30] Ramesh Thakur and John Carlson, "How India can support the CTBT before signing," *Japan Times*, 9 April 2015.

[31] Ramesh Thakur, ed., *Nuclear Weapons-Free Zones* (New York: St. Martin's Press, 1998).

status imposes the straitjacket of having to deal with it still through the non-proliferation lens.

30. Can the Iranian model for getting to a denuclearization agreement be applied to the Northeast Asian pariah regime? Some key differences between the two situations are worth noting. Iran did not possess a single nuclear weapon. The challenge was to cap its capability in order to prevent a potential breakout.[32] By contrast, North Korea already has several and its delivery capability is also growing. In other words the train of non-proliferation left the Pyongyang station a decade ago and is now out of sight; it was stopped from ever arriving at a platform at Tehran station.

31. Second, North Korea is already deeply isolated and it is hard to see the incremental pain of still more sanctions tipping it into a search for compliance. Clearly the pain of sanctions is within the tolerance threshold for the regime. Nor is a comparable middle class youth cohort exerting pressure on the regime to re-engage with the international community, nor anything resembling the genuine political contestation in Iran with competing policy platforms.

32. Third, the West has very limited leverage with respect to North Korea. The only external actor with any meaningful—but not necessarily decisive—leverage is China. The key to any progress on the agenda lies in Beijing and China's ability and willingness to ratchet up the pressure on the North Korean regime. While preserving North Korea as a territorial buffer remains a critical Chinese security goal, with over 200,000 Chinese soldiers having been killed during the 1950s Korean War to this end and their ultimate sacrifice not forgotten, Pyongyang's unpredictable, erratic and provocative behaviour heightens regional instability, strengthens US alliances with Japan and South Korea, builds sentiment in the latter two countries for nuclear weaponization, and increases the risk of an unwanted conflict that would undermine China's own development goals. Instead of a P5 (China, France, Russia, UK, USA) +1 (Germany) formula, therefore, it might have to be a case of 1 (China) + P4 (France, Russia, UK, USA) + EA2 (Japan, South Korea).[33]

33. That said, the lessons that are relevant from the Iran example are (1) the importance of an international coalition that brings together mutually reinforcing UN, US, European and East Asian sanctions regimes; (2) a new diplomatic framework that discards the dated Six Party Talks that have long since passed their use-by date; (3) an abandonment of

---

[32] Ramesh Thakur, *To Stop Iran Getting the Bomb, Must We Learn to Live with Its Nuclear Capability?* Strategic Analysis 36:2 (2012), pp. 328–34.

[33] Bringing the two cases together like this in one sentence highlights another striking difference. The P5+1 Iran negotiations framework did not include a single regional actor beyond the country of concern. In Northeast Asia, any negotiating framework that excluded South Korea and Japan would be such a non-starter that it is hard to see it being seriously proposed.

complete denuclearization as a precondition for talks with Pyongyang; (4) a credible prospect of a lifting of sanctions as an inducement to Pyongyang to engage with external interlocutors; and (5) an agreed goal among East Asian and international partners on the final product.

34. For a mixed strategy of rewards and penalties to have any success, Pyongyang's insecurity complex will have to be addressed, including fears of vulnerability to forcible regime change by Washington. Senior North Korean officials have said to a former (1986–97) director of the Los Alamos National Laboratory that "if Slobodan Milosevic in Serbia, Saddam Hussein in Iraq and Muammar Gaddafi in Libya had had nuclear weapons, their countries would not have been at the mercy of the Americans and their regime-change tactics."[34] To this list we might now well add the Russian intervention in Ukraine and the annexation of Crimea in 2014 in clear violation of the 1994 Budapest Memorandum wherein Russia, the UK and the US had guaranteed Ukraine's territorial integrity in return for Kiev's agreement to remove 1,900 strategic and 2,500 tactical Russian nuclear weapons stationed in Ukraine.

35. Amid rising nationalism in the region, territorial disputes in the East and South China Seas, continued North Korean nuclear defiance, and concerns about the Obama administration's disarmament agenda, doubts about the reliability of US deterrence have been catalysts for pro-nuclear arguments in Japan and South Korea.[35] A leading conservative daily published an article pointing to how Seoul could get the bomb in 18 months.[36] In a written answer in parliament on 1 April (sic), the Abe government announced that while it remains firmly committed to Japan's three non-nuclear principles (no manufacture, possession or basing of nuclear weapons), in its view the war-renouncing Article 9 of the Constitution does not prohibit Japan from possessing and using nuclear weapons.[37] Japan has stockpiled about 11 tonnes of plutonium, enough to make more than 2,000 bombs.[38]

36. While the threshold for the nuclear weaponization debate has been lowered with serial North Korean provocations and Chinese belligerence, this remains most unlikely in the foreseeable future. Internationally, the NPT constrains the weapon option, the US nuclear

---

[34] Siegfried S. Hecker, "For Iran, a nuclear option more trouble than it was worth," *Bulletin of the Atomic Scientists*, 18 January 2016, http://thebulletin.org/iran-nuclearoption-more-trouble-it-was-worth9064.

[35] Peter Hayes and Chung-in Moon, *Should South Korea Go Nuclear*? EAF Policy Debates No. 7, 28 July 2014; Henry Sokolski, *Japan and South Korea may soon go nuclear*, Wall Street Journal, 8 May 2016.

[36] Lee Young-Wan, *6 Months to Produce Fissile Materials, 6–9 Months to Develop a Detonation Device. . .South Korea Could Arm Itself With a Nuclear Weapon in 1.5 Years*, Chosun Ilbo, 19 February 2016, trans. Raymond Ha; http://npolicy.org/article.php?aid=1313&rid=2.

[37] *Abe Cabinet says Article 9 does not ban possessing, using N-weapons*, Asahi Shimbun, 2 April 2016; http://www.asahi.com/ajw/articles/AJ201604020026.html.

[38] This is not counting over 35 tonnes that Japan has in the UK and France.

extended deterrence bolsters Japan's security confidence and weaponization could rupture relations with Washington. Tokyo is also acutely conscious of the extreme regional sensitivities to any nuclearization. Domestically, the three non-nuclear principles, the very strong nuclear allergy in public opinion, and the atomic energy basic law that limits nuclear activity to peaceful purposes are additional powerful constraints on the weapons option.

* * *

An Agenda for Action in the Second Nuclear Age

42. Based on this brief overview of the nuclear state of play in Asia against the global strategic backdrop, the overall objectives and strategy that the international community should be pursuing in relation to nuclear disarmament might realistically be described as a rapid movement towards further major overall reductions in the nuclear warhead numbers of Russia and the US which hold 93 per cent of global stockpiles. This should be accompanied by an immediate freeze in the stockpiles of the Asian nuclear-armed states. Once the two major nuclear powers have reduced their arsenals down to the hundreds, China could be drawn into the negotiations followed by the other nuclear-armed states.[39] With each new entrant into the multilateral arms control negotiations, it would become progressively more difficult for the remainder to stay outside the process.

43. North Korea demonstrates the weakness of the NPT withdrawal clause. It should not be possible for a country to gain the technology and materials benefits as an NPT non-NWS, decide on an entirely unilateral calculation that withdrawal from the treaty is justified, defect and yet keep all the benefits gained during membership. In addition, the cases of India and Pakistan (and Israel in the Middle East) show the strategic folly of the NPT's chronological rather than empirical or analytical definition of a NWS. The integrity and credibility of the NPT as the overarching regime for managing the world's nuclear orders is dented by the fact that four of the nine states that possess nuclear weapons fall outside the regime.

44. The non-proliferation leg can be strengthened with the entry into force of the CTBT, although it is an open question as to whether this is better pursued by demanding signature and ratification by the Annex 2 holdout states, or amending the entry-into-force formula to bring the CTBT into line with all other arms control regimes. A treaty-based freeze on fissile materials production is equally urgent. So too is the universalization of the Additional Protocol and the NWS adherence to relevant regional NWFZ protocols. Vertical proliferation by the nuclear armed states can be checked and reversed by Russia and the US taking their warheads off high

[39] James Cartwright, et al., *Modernizing U.S. Nuclear Strategy, Force Structure and Posture*, Global Zero U.S. Nuclear Policy Commission Report (Washington DC: Global Zero, May 2012), p. 4, http://www.globalzero.org/files/gz_us_nuclear_policy_commission_report.pdf.

alert and Pakistan and India aborting the pursuit of tactical nuclear weapons.

45. It may be worth testing Pyongyang on a freeze[40] in return for replacing the 1953 armistice by a peace treaty, as the prelude to difficult negotiations that culminate in a comprehensive peace settlement for the peninsula.[41] Part of the challenge in the latter goal would be to reconcile the West's call for denuclearization of the Korean Peninsula aimed at terminating the North's nuclear weapons program, with Pyongyang's insistence that denuclearization must include removal of the US nuclear umbrella. Moreover, because of the deep trust deficit in the region, any agreement will have to be underpinned by a robust and credible verification and monitoring system. A verifiable and irreversible denuclearization of North Korea would also be the most effective bulwark against the growth of pro-nuclear weapons sentiments in South Korea and Japan.

46. Finally, the negotiation of additional regional nuclear energy regulatory arrangements and regional and global nuclear fuel banks; the adoption of international standards and benchmarks on nuclear security; the extension of the nuclear security agenda to cover sensitive nuclear materials under military control that account for over 80 per cent of all such materials; and the universal take-up by all Asia-Pacific states with significant nuclear activities of regional and global safety and security conventions, would boost confidence in the safety and security practices of the peaceful uses of nuclear energy across the continent.

DISCUSSION NOTES/QUESTIONS

1. We have deliberately included readings that portray the political background to the legal issues presented. In international law, politics looms large and carries greater weight than it does in the domestic law of most countries. For example, it will not have escaped your notice that the five permanent members of the Security Council are all nuclear-weapon states and all have seats on the International Court of Justice.

Why would that be?

2. Smaller nations tend to put more weight upon international law than larger and more powerful and influential nations. What, if anything, can be done about that?

---

[40] Interestingly, in a recent set of articles on North Korea, the three Chinese, South Korean and Russian analysts agreed that the goal of "complete, verifiable and irreversible denuclearization" is fanciful and a freeze is the more realistic objective worth pursuing. Shen Dingli, "Acknowledging reality: A pragmatic approach to Pyongyang"; Chung-in Moon, "North Korea: A negotiated settlement remains the best hope"; and Andrei Lankov, "North Korea: Don't dream the impossible," *Bulletin of the Atomic Scientists*, 1 and 2 June 2016; http://thebulletin.org/northkoreas-nuclear-weapons-what-now.

[41] John Carlson, "Dealing with the North Korean Nuclear Threat," *The Interpreter*, 9 May 2016; http://www.lowyinterpreter.org/post/2016/05/09/Dealing-with-the-North-Korean-nuclear-threat.aspx.

3. Why do you suppose the Japanese Government, the only nation to have been subject to a nuclear attack, is now abandoning its low key defense policies in favor of a more assertive international security and diplomatic stance? The NTI website contains this paragraph:[42]

> In one of the largest shifts in Japan's security policy since the end of World War II, on 19 September 2015, Japan's parliament enacted a legislative package that would permit Japan's Self Defense Forces to engage in collective self-defense, the goal that has been pursued by Prime Minister Abe. While the degree of the engagement in collective self-defense is significantly limited mainly because of LDP's junior coalition partner, the New Komei Party's efforts to maintain the exclusively defensive nature of Japan's security policy, this deliberation process generated heated debates both inside and outside of the National Diet with concerns that Japan might abandon its pacifist security policy.

Japan took no part in the negotiations concerning the United Nations Treaty and there was domestic criticism in Japan that the country was abandoning its long held anti-nuclear stance. *The Japan Times* editorialized on 1 April 2017 as follows:[43]

> As talks began last week at the United Nations on a treaty that would outlaw nuclear weapons, Japan announced that it will not take part in the negotiations—which is most regrettable. The move could be taken as an indication that Japan is giving up its moral responsibility as the world's sole victim of nuclear attacks to play a proactive role in global efforts to eliminate nuclear weapons, and it will come as a great disappointment to people, including survivors of the 1945 atomic bombings of Hiroshima and Nagasaki, and non-nuclear states. At the very least the government needs to explain in concrete terms how it otherwise intends to work toward its stated goal of making the world free of nuclear arms.

4. Perhaps concerns about threats and risks of the use of nuclear weapons are exaggerated. After all, there has been no use of nuclear weapons on Planet Earth since Hiroshima and Nagasaki in 1945. Perhaps the doctrine of deterrence works? Consider the following comments by Dr. John J. Hamre, president of the Center for Strategic and International Studies:

> Last week I participated in a high-level discussion with a senior representative from the Administration. The topic was North Korea. And at one point, the individual said that the Administration believes "we are running out of time on North Korea." "What the hell are you talking about," I said. Let us go through this systematically.

---

[42] *See* http://www.nti.org/learn/countries/japan/nuclear/.

[43] *See* Japan Times, *A treaty to ban nuclear weapons, available at* https://www.japantimes.co.jp/opinion/2017/04/01/editorials/treaty-ban-nuclear-weapons/#.XUHw5vJKhEY (last accessed 31 July 2019).

We should survey the real facts—not what people want to believe, but what is true.

First, North Korea is not going to give up nuclear weapons just because we want them to. They are a failed economy with only one thing going for them—their nuclear weapons program. They will not give it up ever.

Second, China will put pressure on North Korea to express their displeasure, but not to break North Korea. China wants a divided Korean peninsula. The last thing they want is for North Korea to collapse and have South Korea take over. China is willing to put pressure on North Korea to get North Korea to stop doing things that are awkward for China. North Korea's provocative military gestures are awkward for China, which is why China is putting pressure on them now. But China will not break North Korea because they need North Korea. And North Korea knows this. China's real strategy is to drive a wedge between the United States and South Korea.

Third, we are never going to reward North Korea for becoming a weapon state. Somehow the North Koreans think that once they can threaten the United States, we will give up and give them something in exchange for being nice to us. That will never happen. We will support North Korea financially only when they abandon nuclear weapons. That won't happen, so there are no rewards on the horizon for North Korea.

Fourth, we anticipated North Korea's actions 20 years ago. We started then to deploy a missile defense system in Alaska designed to knock down North Korean missiles. It is in place, and we can expand it. The purpose of a missile defense system is not to keep blocking wave after wave of attacking missiles. The purpose of a missile defense system is to buy time—to block the initial attack long enough for us to retaliate with overwhelming nuclear destruction. That will happen. North Korea knows that will happen. North Korea is not suicidal.

Fifth, we are not going to invade North Korea to find their nuclear weapons and destroy them. The North Koreans know this. They also know that we are not going to pre-emptively attack them because they now have a nuclear retaliatory capability and the destruction of our South Korean (and maybe Japanese) ally would be horrendous and unacceptable.

Taking all this together, it is clear that we are not running out of time. Indeed, time has stopped for the path we have been on for 15 years. But deterrence has worked for 50 years with Russia, it will work for North Korea.

I am dismayed by our rhetoric in Washington. We are talking like frightened little rabbits, afraid of a wolf in the forest. We have

> nothing to be afraid of, and the more we act like frightened little critters, the more we reward North Korea for pursuing a dead-end strategy. We tried a policy of dissuasion for the past 15 years, and it has failed. But a strategy of deterrence has worked and will continue to work.
>
> This past weekend I heard a very prominent and influential senator say that we should not send families with American military personnel who are deployed to Korea. This only feeds the fear and paranoia about North Korea that goes nowhere. The five facts outlined above dictate a logical and calm policy—deterrence. It is time for everyone in the U.S. to stop running around with frightened cries of "we are running out of time." We are not running out of time. We have all the time we need. North Korea has no options for improving their situation, and we shouldn't give them the satisfaction of us being afraid of them. North Korea is trying to stampede us into a negotiation, and we have nothing to gain from that.
>
> Everyone in Washington should just calm down. Stop working ourselves up to a fevered pitch with breathless rhetoric that has no policy direction. We have lived with this before and we will live with it now. Thankfully, over a twenty-year period, we built the insurance policy we now need. The Brits had it right in World War II—"Keep calm, carry on."[44]

Is deterrence an adequate safeguard against all the risks posed by nuclear proliferation? Before you answer, review the comments of former Australian Foreign Minister Evans in the first reading in this chapter. What would he say in response to the argument made above?

5. The most useful book that contains a discussion of the practicalities of the issues concerning nuclear weapons is that by Gareth Evans, Tanya Ogilvie-White and Ramesh Thakur, *Nuclear Weapons: The State of Play 2015* (Australian National University, Centre for Nuclear Non-Proliferation and Disarmament, Crawford School of Public Policy, 2015).

PROBLEM 10-1: THE ASIA-PACIFIC AND NUCLEAR WEAPONS

Section 1. Facts

Substantial problems have arisen in recent years in the Asia-Pacific region as a result of the Democratic Republic of Korea (North Korea) developing a capacity to make and deliver nuclear weapons. Concern in the region has become acute and the Asia Pacific Leadership Network for Nuclear Non-proliferation and Disarmament (APLN) was formed some

[44] John J Hamre, "Running out of time," Bulletin of the Atomic Scientists, 19 December 2017.

years ago to try to make progress on the issue of a reduction in the number of nuclear weapons. The organization conducts regional meetings comprising former political leaders, academics, former senior public servants and experts to try to reduce tensions and reduce the risks posed by the existence of nuclear weapons. The countries from which the members are drawn are Australia, Japan, Malaysia India, New Zealand, Republic of Korea, China, Sri Lanka, Pakistan, Singapore, Vietnam, Mongolia, and Indonesia.

The APLN is paid for and affiliated to the Nuclear Security Project, within the Nuclear Threat Initiative (NPI), set up by US public officials George P. Shultz, William J. Perry, Henry A. Kissinger, and Sam Nunn to make progress on addressing the tough technical issues involved in taking concerted steps towards building a world without nuclear weapons. They aim to generate global momentum to build broad international support to reduce the risks posed by nuclear weapons among governments, political leaders, and the public.[45] Schultz, Perry, Kissinger, and Nunn have all occupied the posts of Secretary of State or Secretary of Defense and have close knowledge of the United States nuclear weaponry and the dangers nuclear weapons pose for the world.

Recent discussions at an APLN plenary revolved around the degree to which the use of nuclear weapons was prohibited by international law and whether there were means available to use international law to help curb the threat of nuclear weapons. The debate was influenced in part by the negotiation in 2017 of a new Treaty on the Prohibition of Nuclear Weapons. The successful negotiation on this Treaty is the most significant achievement on nuclear disarmament for many years. Its effectiveness is doubtful, however. The nuclear-weapons states did not attend the negotiations and will not be bound by the Treaty unless they ratify it, which seems unlikely. Nuclear-weapons states appear to be intending to retain their nuclear weapons indefinitely.

Nonetheless, the adoption of the treaty, combined with the entry into force of nuclear-weapons-free zones across the globe, suggests a growing international consensus that nuclear weapons should be eradicated. The question that has arisen at the APLN meeting is whether the outright prohibition on nuclear weapons contained in the Treaty, when understood in the context of existing features of international law, could mean that upon widespread ratification and entry into force of this Treaty, the use of nuclear weapons in all circumstances will become illegal, even for non-Party states.

---

[45] The Nuclear Security Project, A New Visions for a Changing World. The website is www. nuclearsecurityproject.org. The Project operates within the wider framework of the NTI (Nuclear Threat Initiative): www.nti.org/about/global-nuclear-policy/.

Section 2. Questions Presented

You are an attorney in New York with a practice in international law. You are a member of the American Association of International Law. You have been asked for an opinion for the APLN on the following questions:

1. In what circumstances is the use of nuclear weapons by States unlawful at international law?

2. What difference, if any, to the legal position will the Treaty on the Prohibition of Nuclear Weapons make, if it is ratified and enters into force according to its terms?

Section 3. Assignments

A. *Reading Assignment*

Study the Readings presented in Section 4, *infra*, and the Discussion Notes/Questions that follow.

B. *Recommended Writing Assignment*

Prepare a comprehensive, logically sequenced, and *argumentative* brief in the form of an outline of the primary and subsidiary *legal* issues raised by the questions presented above? Also, from the perspective of an independent objective judge, indicate which side ought to prevail on each issue and why. Retain a copy of your issue-outline/brief for class discussion.

C. *Recommended Oral Assignment*

As assigned by your instructor and relying upon the Readings (and your issue-outline if prepared), present a 15–20 minute oral argument of your position on the questions presented above.

D. *Recommended Reflective Assignment*

Consider (and recommend) alternative norms, institutions, and/or procedures that you believe might do better than existing world order arrangements to contend with situations of the kind posed by this problem. In so doing, but without insisting upon *immediate* feasibility, identify the particular transition steps that would be needed to make your alternatives a reality.

Section 4. Readings

1. *Legality of the Threat or Use of Nuclear Weapons, Advisory Opinion* [1996] ICJ Rep 226, footnotes omitted

ADVISORY OPINION

Present: President BEDJAOUI; *Vice-President* SCHWEBEL; *Judges* ODA, GUILLAUME, SHAHABUDDEEN, WEERAMANTRY, RANJEVA,

HERCZEGH, SHI, FLEISCHHAUER, KOROMA, VERESHCHETIN, FERRARI BRAVO, HIGGINS; *Registrar* VALENCIA-OSPINA.

On the legality of the threat or use of nuclear weapons,

THE COURT,

composed as above,

gives the following Advisory Opinion:

1. The question upon which the advisory opinion of the Court has been requested is set forth in resolution 49/75 K adopted by the General Assembly of the United Nations (hereinafter called the "General Assembly") on 15 December 1994. By a letter dated 19 December 1994, received in the Registry by facsimile on 20 December 1994 and filed in the original on 6 January 1995, the Secretary-General of the United Nations officially communicated to the Registrar the decision taken by the General Assembly to submit the question to the Court for an advisory opinion. Resolution 49/75 K, the English text of which was enclosed with the letter, reads as follows:

> "*The General Assembly,*
>
> *Conscious* that the continuing existence and development of nuclear weapons pose serious risks to humanity,
>
> *Mindful* that States have an obligation under the Charter of the United Nations to refrain from the threat or use of force against the territorial integrity or political independence of any State,
>
> *Recalling* its resolutions 1653 (XVI) of 24 November 1961, 33/71 B of 14 December 1978, 34/83 G of 11 December 1979, 35/152D of 12 December 1980, 36/92 I of 9 December 1981, 45/59 B of 4 December 1990 and 46/37D of 6 December 1991, in which it declared that the use of nuclear weapons would be a violation of the Charter and a crime against humanity,
>
> *Welcoming* the progress made on the prohibition and elimination of weapons of mass destruction, including the Convention on the Prohibition of the Development, Production and Stockpiling of Bacteriological (Biological) and Toxin Weapons and on Their Destruction and the Convention on the Prohibition of the Development, Production, Stockpiling and Use of Chemical Weapons and on Their Destruction,
>
> *Convinced* that the complete elimination of nuclear weapons is the only guarantee against the threat of nuclear war,
>
> *Noting* the concerns expressed in the Fourth Review Conference of the Parties to the Treaty on the Non-Proliferation

of Nuclear Weapons that insufficient progress had been made towards the complete elimination of nuclear weapons at the earliest possible time,

Recalling that, convinced of the need to strengthen the rule of law in international relations, it has declared the period 1990–1999 the United Nations Decade of International Law,

Noting that Article 96, paragraph 1, of the Charter empowers the General Assembly to request the International Court of Justice to give an advisory opinion on any legal question,

Recalling the recommendation of the Secretary-General, made in his report entitled 'An Agenda for Peace', that United Nations organs that are authorized to take advantage of the advisory competence of the International Court of Justice turn to the Court more frequently for such opinions,

Welcoming resolution 46/40 of 14 May 1993 of the Assembly of the World Health Organization, in which the organization requested the International Court of Justice to give an advisory opinion on whether the use of nuclear weapons by a State in war or other armed conflict would be a breach of its obligations under international law, including the Constitution of the World Health Organization,

Decides, pursuant to Article 96, paragraph 1, of the Charter of the United Nations, to request the International Court of Justice urgently to render its advisory opinion on the following question: 'Is the threat or use of nuclear weapons in any circumstance permitted under international law?' "

2. Pursuant to Article 65, paragraph 2, of the Statute, the Secretary-General of the United Nations communicated to the Court a dossier of documents likely to throw light upon the question.

3. By letters dated 21 December 1994, the Registrar, pursuant to Article 66, paragraph 1, of the Statute, gave notice of the request for an advisory opinion to all States entitled to appear before the Court.

4. By an Order dated 1 February 1995 the Court decided that the States entitled to appear before it and the United Nations were likely to be able to furnish information on the question, in accordance with Article 66, paragraph 2, of the Statute. By the same Order, the Court fixed, respectively, 20 June 1995 as the time-limit within which written statements might be submitted to it on the question, and 20 September 1995 as the time-limit within which States and organizations having presented written statements might submit written comments on the other written statements in accordance with Article 66, paragraph 4, of the Statute. In the aforesaid Order, it was stated in particular that the General

Assembly had requested that the advisory opinion of the Court be rendered "urgently"; reference was also made to the procedural time-limits already fixed for the request for an advisory opinion previously submitted to the Court by the World Health Organization on the question of the *Legality of the Use by a State of Nuclear Weapons in Armed Conflict*.

* * *

13. The question put to the Court by the General Assembly is indeed a legal one, since the Court is asked to rule on the compatibility of the threat or use of nuclear weapons with the relevant principles and rules of international law. To do this, the Court must identify the existing principles and rules, interpret them and apply them to the threat or use of nuclear weapons, thus offering a reply to the question posed based on law.

The fact that this question also has political aspects, as, in the nature of things, is the case with so many questions which arise in international life, does not suffice to deprive it of its character as a "legal question" and to "deprive the Court of a competence expressly conferred on it by its Statute" (*Application for Review of Judgement No. 158 of the United Nations Administrative Tribunal, Advisory Opinion, I.C.J. Reports 1973*, p. 172, para. 14). Whatever its political aspects, the Court cannot refuse to admit the legal character of a question which invites it to discharge an essentially judicial task, namely, an assessment of the legality of the possible conduct of States with regard to the obligations imposed upon them by international law (cf. *Conditions of Admission of a State to Membership in the United Nations (Article 4 of Charter), Advisory Opinion, 1948, I.C.J. Reports 1947–1948*, pp. 61–62; *Competence of the General Assembly for the Admission of a State to the United Nations, Advisory Opinion, I.C.J. Reports 1950*, pp. 6–7; *Certain Expenses of the United Nations (Article 17, paragraph 2, of the Charter), Advisory Opinion, I.C.J. Reports 1962*, p. 155).

Furthermore, as the Court said in the Opinion it gave in 1980 concerning the Interpretation of the Agreement of 25 March 1951 between the WHO and Egypt:

> "Indeed, in situations in which political considerations are prominent it may be particularly necessary for an international organization to obtain an advisory opinion from the Court as to the legal principles applicable with respect to the matter under debate . . ." (*I.C.J. Reports 1980*, p. 87, para. 33.)

The Court moreover considers that the political nature of the motives which may be said to have inspired the request and the political implications that the opinion given might have are of no relevance in the establishment of its jurisdiction to give such an opinion.

* * *

23. In seeking to answer the question put to it by the General Assembly, the Court must decide, after consideration of the great corpus of international law norms available to it, what might be the relevant applicable law.

* * *

24. Some of the proponents of the illegality of the use of nuclear weapons have argued that such use would violate the right to life as guaranteed in Article 6 of the International Covenant on Civil and Political Rights, as well as in certain regional instruments for the protection of human rights. Article 6, paragraph 1, of the International Covenant provides as follows: "Every human being has the inherent right to life. This right shall be protected by law. No one shall be arbitrarily deprived of his life."

In reply, others contended that the International Covenant on Civil and Political Rights made no mention of war or weapons, and it had never been envisaged that the legality of nuclear weapons was regulated by that instrument. It was suggested that the Covenant was directed to the protection of human rights in peacetime, but that questions relating to unlawful loss of life in hostilities were governed by the law applicable in armed conflict.

25. The Court observes that the protection of the International Covenant of Civil and Political Rights does not cease in times of war, except by operation of Article 4 of the Covenant whereby certain provisions may be derogated from in a time of national emergency. Respect for the right to life is not, however, such a provision. In principle, the right not arbitrarily to be deprived of one's life applies also in hostilities. The test of what is an arbitrary deprivation of life, however, then falls to be determined by the applicable *lex specialis*, namely, the law applicable in armed conflict which is designed to regulate the conduct of hostilities. Thus whether a particular loss of life, through the use of a certain weapon in warfare, is to be considered an arbitrary deprivation of life contrary to Article 6 of the Covenant, can only be decided by reference to the law applicable in armed conflict and not deduced from the terms of the Covenant itself.

26. Some States also contended that the prohibition against genocide, contained in the Convention of 9 December 1948 on the Prevention and Punishment of the Crime of Genocide, is a relevant rule of customary international law which the Court must apply. The Court recalls that in Article II of the Convention genocide is defined as

> "any of the following acts committed with intent to destroy, in whole or in part, a national, ethnical, racial or religious group, as such:
>
> (*a*) Killing members of the group;

(*b*) Causing serious bodily or mental harm to members of the group;

(*c*) Deliberately inflicting on the group conditions of life calculated to bring about its physical destruction in whole or in part;

(*d*) Imposing measures intended to prevent births within the group;

(*e*) Forcibly transferring children of the group to another group."

It was maintained before the Court that the number of deaths occasioned by the use of nuclear weapons would be enormous; that the victims could, in certain cases, include persons of a particular national, ethnic, racial or religious group; and that the intention to destroy such groups could be inferred from the fact that the user of the nuclear weapon would have omitted to take account of the well-known effects of the use of such weapons.

The Court would point out in that regard that the prohibition of genocide would be pertinent in this case if the recourse to nuclear weapons did indeed entail the element of intent, towards a group as such, required by the provision quoted above. In the view of the Court, it would only be possible to arrive at such a conclusion after having taken due account of the circumstances specific to each case.

* * *

27. In both their written and oral statements, some States furthermore argued that any use of nuclear weapons would be unlawful by reference to existing norms relating to the safeguarding and protection of the environment, in view of their essential importance.

Specific references were made to various existing international treaties and instruments. These included Additional Protocol 1 of 1977 to the Geneva Conventions of 1949, Article 35, paragraph 3, of which prohibits the employment of "methods or means of warfare which are intended, or may be expected, to cause widespread, long-term and severe damage to the natural environment"; and the Convention of 18 May 1977 on the Prohibition of Military or Any Other Hostile Use of Environmental Modification Techniques **[Basic Document 7.19]**, which prohibits the use of weapons which have "widespread, long-lasting or severe effects" on the environment (Art. 1). Also cited were Principle 21 of the Stockholm Declaration of 1972 **[Basic Document 1.21]** and Principle 2 of the Rio Declaration of 1992 **[Basic Document 1.30]** which express the common conviction of the States concerned that they have a duty

> "to ensure that activities within their jurisdiction or control do not cause damage to the environment of other States or of areas beyond the limits of national jurisdiction."

These instruments and other provisions relating to the protection and safeguarding of the environment were said to apply at all times, in war as well as in peace, and it was contended that they would be violated by the use of nuclear weapons whose consequences would be widespread and would have transboundary effects.

28. Other States questioned the binding legal quality of these precepts of environmental law; or, in the context of the Convention on the Prohibition of Military or Any Other Hostile Use of Environmental Modification Techniques, denied that it was concerned at all with the use of nuclear weapons in hostilities; or, in the case of Additional Protocol 1, denied that they were generally bound by its terms, or recalled that they had reserved their position in respect of Article 35, paragraph 3, thereof.

It was also argued by some States that the principal purpose of environmental treaties and norms was the protection of the environment in time of peace. It was said that those treaties made no mention of nuclear weapons. It was also pointed out that warfare in general, and nuclear warfare in particular, were not mentioned in their texts and that it would be destabilizing to the rule of law and to confidence in international negotiations if those treaties were now interpreted in such a way as to prohibit the use of nuclear weapons.

29. The Court recognizes that the environment is under daily threat and that the use of nuclear weapons could constitute a catastrophe for the environment. The Court also recognizes that the environment is not an abstraction but represents the living space, the quality of life and the very health of human beings, including generations unborn. The existence of the general obligation of States to ensure that activities within their jurisdiction and control respect the environment of other States or of areas beyond national control is now part of the corpus of international law relating to the environment.

30. However, the Court is of the view that the issue is not whether the treaties relating to the protection of the environment are or are not applicable during an armed conflict, but rather whether the obligations stemming from these treaties were intended to be obligations of total restraint during military conflict.

The Court does not consider that the treaties in question could have intended to deprive a State of the exercise of its right of self-defence under international law because of its obligations to protect the environment. Nonetheless, States must take environmental considerations into account when assessing what is necessary and proportionate in the pursuit of legitimate military objectives. Respect for the environment is one of the elements that go to assessing whether an action is in conformity with the principles of necessity and proportionality.

This approach is supported, indeed, by the terms of Principle 24 of the Rio Declaration, which provides that:

> "Warfare is inherently destructive of sustainable development. States shall therefore respect international law providing protection for the environment in times of armed conflict and cooperate in its further development, as necessary."

31. The Court notes furthermore that Articles 35, paragraph 3, and 55 of Additional Protocol 1 provide additional protection for the environment. Taken together, these provisions embody a general obligation to protect the natural environment against widespread, long-term and severe environmental damage; the prohibition of methods and means of warfare which are intended, or may be expected, to cause such damage; and the prohibition of attacks against the natural environment by way of reprisals.

These are powerful constraints for all the States having subscribed to these provisions.

32. General Assembly resolution 47/37 of 25 November 1992 on the "Protection of the Environment in Times of Armed Conflict" is also of interest in this context. It affirms the general view according to which environmental considerations constitute one of the elements to be taken into account in the implementation of the principles of the law applicable in armed conflict: it states that "destruction of the environment, not justified by military necessity and carried out wantonly, is clearly contrary to existing international law." Addressing the reality that certain instruments are not yet binding on all States, the General Assembly in this resolution "*[a]ppeals* to all States that have not yet done so to consider becoming parties to the relevant international conventions."

In its recent Order in the *Request for an Examination of the Situation in Accordance with Paragraph 63 of the Court's Judgment of 20 December 1974 in the* Nuclear Tests (New Zealand v. France) *Case*, the Court stated that its conclusion was "without prejudice to the obligations of States to respect and protect the natural environment" (*Order of 22 September 1995, I. C. J. Reports 1995*, p. 306, para. 64). Although that statement was made in the context of nuclear testing, it naturally also applies to the actual use of nuclear weapons in armed conflict.

33. The Court thus finds that while the existing international law relating to the protection and safeguarding of the environment does not specifically prohibit the use of nuclear weapons, it indicates important environmental factors that are properly to be taken into account in the

context of the implementation of the principles and rules of the law applicable in armed conflict.

* * *

34. In the light of the foregoing the Court concludes that the most directly relevant applicable law governing the question of which it was seised, is that relating to the use of force enshrined in the United Nations Charter and the law applicable in armed conflict which regulates the conduct of hostilities, together with any specific treaties on nuclear weapons that the Court might determine to be relevant.

* * *

35. In applying this law to the present case, the Court cannot however fail to take into account certain unique characteristics of nuclear weapons.

The Court has noted the definitions of nuclear weapons contained in various treaties and accords. It also notes that nuclear weapons are explosive devices whose energy results from the fusion or fission of the atom. By its very nature, that process, in nuclear weapons as they exist today, releases not only immense quantities of heat and energy, but also powerful and prolonged radiation. According to the material before the Court, the first two causes of damage are vastly more powerful than the damage caused by other weapons, while the phenomenon of radiation is said to be peculiar to nuclear weapons. These characteristics render the nuclear weapon potentially catastrophic. The destructive power of nuclear weapons cannot be contained in either space or time. They have the potential to destroy all civilization and the entire ecosystem of the planet.

The radiation released by a nuclear explosion would affect health, agriculture, natural resources and demography over a very wide area. Further, the use of nuclear weapons would be a serious danger to future generations. Ionizing radiation has the potential to damage the future environment, food and marine ecosystem, and to cause genetic defects and illness in future generations.

36. In consequence, in order correctly to apply to the present case the Charter law on the use of force and the law applicable in armed conflict, in particular humanitarian law, it is imperative for the Court to take account of the unique characteristics of nuclear weapons, and in particular their destructive capacity, their capacity to cause untold human suffering, and their ability to cause damage to generations to come.

* * *

37. The Court will now address the question of the legality or illegality of recourse to nuclear weapons in the light of the provisions of the Charter relating to the threat or use of force.

38. The Charter contains several provisions relating to the threat and use of force.

In Article 2, paragraph 4, the threat or use of force against the territorial integrity or political independence of another State or in any other manner inconsistent with the purposes of the United Nations is prohibited. That paragraph provides:

> "All Members shall refrain in their international relations from the threat or use of force against the territorial integrity or political independence of any State, or in any other manner inconsistent with the Purposes of the United Nations."

This prohibition of the use of force is to be considered in the light of other relevant provisions of the Charter. In Article 51, the Charter recognizes the inherent right of individual or collective self-defence if an armed attack occurs. A further lawful use of force is envisaged in Article 42, whereby the Security Council may take military enforcement measures in conformity with Chapter VII of the Charter.

39. These provisions do not refer to specific weapons. They apply to any use of force, regardless of the weapons employed. The Charter neither expressly prohibits, nor permits, the use of any specific weapon, including nuclear weapons. A weapon that is already unlawful per se, whether by treaty or custom, does not become lawful by reason of its being used for a legitimate purpose under the Charter.

40. The entitlement to resort to self-defence under Article 51 is subject to certain constraints. Some of these constraints are inherent in the very concept of self-defence. Other requirements are specified in Article 51.

41. The submission of the exercise of the right of self-defence to the conditions of necessity and proportionality is a rule of customary international law. As the Court stated in the case concerning *Military and Paramilitary Activities in and against Nicaragua (Nicaragua v. United States of America)*: there is a "specific rule whereby self-defence would warrant only measures which are proportional to the armed attack and necessary to respond to it, a rule well established in customary international law" (*I.C.J. Reports 1986*, p. 94, para. 176). This dual condition applies equally to Article 51 of the Charter, whatever the means of force employed.

42. The proportionality principle may thus not in itself exclude the use of nuclear weapons in self-defence in all circumstances. But at the same time, a use of force that is proportionate under the law of self-defence, must, in order to be lawful, also meet the requirements of the law applicable in armed conflict which comprise in particular the principles and rules of humanitarian law.

43. Certain States have in their written and oral pleadings suggested that in the case of nuclear weapons, the condition of proportionality must be evaluated in the light of still further factors. They contend that the very nature of nuclear weapons, and the high probability of an escalation of nuclear exchanges, mean that there is an extremely strong risk of devastation. The risk factor is said to negate the possibility of the condition of proportionality being complied with. The Court does not find it necessary to embark upon the quantification of such risks; nor does it need to enquire into the question whether tactical nuclear weapons exist which are sufficiently precise to limit those risks: it suffices for the Court to note that the very nature of all nuclear weapons and the profound risks associated therewith are further considerations to be borne in mind by States believing they can exercise a nuclear response in self-defence in accordance with the requirements of proportionality.

44. Beyond the conditions of necessity and proportionality, Article 51 specifically requires that measures taken by States in the exercise of the right of self-defence shall be immediately reported to the Security Council; this article further provides that these measures shall not in any way affect the authority and responsibility of the Security Council under the Charter to take at any time such action as it deems necessary in order to maintain or restore international peace and security. These requirements of Article 51 apply whatever the means of force used in self-defence.

45. The Court notes that the Security Council adopted on 11 April 1995, in the context of the extension of the Treaty on the Non-Proliferation of Nuclear Weapons, resolution 984 (1995) by the terms of which, on the one hand, it

> "*[t]akes note* with appreciation of the statements made by each of the nuclear-weapon States (S/1995/261, S/1995/262, S/1995/263, S/1995/264, S/1995/265), in which they give security assurances against the use of nuclear weapons to non-nuclear-weapon States that are Parties to the Treaty on the Non-Proliferation of Nuclear Weapons,"

and, on the other hand, it

> "*[w]elcomes* the intention expressed by certain States that they will provide or support immediate assistance, in accordance with the Charter, to any non-nuclear-weapon State Party to the Treaty on the Non-Proliferation of Nuclear Weapons that is a victim of an act of, or an object of a threat of, aggression in which nuclear weapons are used."

46. Certain States asserted that the use of nuclear weapons in the conduct of reprisals would be lawful. The Court does not have to examine, in this context, the question of armed reprisals in time of peace, which are considered to be unlawful. Nor does it have to pronounce on the question of

belligerent reprisals save to observe that in any case any right of recourse to such reprisals would, like self-defence, be governed *inter alia* by the principle of proportionality.

47. In order to lessen or eliminate the risk of unlawful attack, States sometimes signal that they possess certain weapons to use in self-defence against any State violating their territorial integrity or political independence. Whether a signalled intention to use force if certain events occur is or is not a "threat" within Article 2, paragraph 4, of the Charter depends upon various factors. If the envisaged use of force is itself unlawful, the stated readiness to use it would be a threat prohibited under Article 2, paragraph 4. Thus it would be illegal for a State to threaten force to secure territory from another State, or to cause it to follow or not follow certain political or economic paths. The notions of "threat" and "use" of force under Article 2, paragraph 4, of the Charter stand together in the sense that if the use of force itself in a given case is illegal—for whatever reason—the threat to use such force will likewise be illegal. In short, if it is to be lawful, the declared readiness of a State to use force must be a use of force that is in conformity with the Charter. For the rest, no State—whether or not it defended the policy of deterrence—suggested to the Court that it would be lawful to threaten to use force if the use of force contemplated would be illegal.

48. Some States put forward the argument that possession of nuclear weapons is itself an unlawful threat to use force. Possession of nuclear weapons may indeed justify an inference of preparedness to use them. In order to be effective, the policy of deterrence, by which those States possessing or under the umbrella of nuclear weapons seek to discourage military aggression by demonstrating that it will serve no purpose, necessitates that the intention to use nuclear weapons be credible. Whether this is a "threat" contrary to Article 2, paragraph 4, depends upon whether the particular use of force envisaged would be directed against the territorial integrity or political independence of a State, or against the Purposes of the United Nations or whether, in the event that it were intended as a means of defence, it would necessarily violate the principles of necessity and proportionality. In any of these circumstances the use of force, and the threat to use it, would be unlawful under the law of the Charter.

49. Moreover, the Security Council may take enforcement measures under Chapter VII of the Charter. From the statements presented to it the Court does not consider it necessary to address questions which might, in a given case, arise from the application of Chapter VII.

50. The terms of the question put to the Court by the General Assembly in resolution 49/75 K could in principle also cover a threat or use of nuclear weapons by a State within its own boundaries. However, this

particular aspect has not been dealt with by any of the States which addressed the Court orally or in writing in these proceedings. The Court finds that it is not called upon to deal with an internal use of nuclear weapons.

* * *

51. Having dealt with the Charter provisions relating to the threat or use of force, the Court will now turn to the law applicable in situations of armed conflict. It will first address the question whether there are specific rules in international law regulating the legality or illegality of recourse to nuclear weapons *per se*; it will then examine the question put to it in the light of the law applicable in armed conflict proper, i.e. the principles and rules of humanitarian law applicable in armed conflict, and the law of neutrality.

* * *

52. The Court notes by way of introduction that international customary and treaty law does not contain any specific prescription authorizing the threat or use of nuclear weapons or any other weapon in general or in certain circumstances, in particular those of the exercise of legitimate selfdefence. Nor, however, is there any principle or rule of international law which would make the legality of the threat or use of nuclear weapons or of any other weapons dependent on a specific authorization. State practice shows that the illegality of the use of certain weapons as such does not result from an absence of authorization but, on the contrary, is formulated in terms of prohibition.

* * *

53. The Court must therefore now examine whether there is any prohibition of recourse to nuclear weapons as such; it will first ascertain whether there is a conventional prescription to this effect.

54. In this regard, the argument has been advanced that nuclear weapons should be treated in the same way as poisoned weapons. In that case, they would be prohibited under:

(*a*) the Second Hague Declaration of 29 July 1899, which prohibits "the use of projectiles the object of which is the diffusion of asphyxiating or deleterious gases";

(*b*) Article 23 *(a)* of the Regulations respecting the laws and customs of war on land annexed to the Hague Convention IV of 18 October 1907, whereby "it is especially forbidden: . . . to employ poison or poisoned weapons"; and

(*c*) the Geneva Protocol of 17 June 1925 which prohibits "the use in war of asphyxiating, poisonous or other gases, and of all analogous liquids, materials or devices."

55. The Court will observe that the Regulations annexed to the Hague Convention IV do not define what is to be understood by "poison or poisoned weapons" and that different interpretations exist on the issue. Nor does the 1925 Protocol specify the meaning to be given to the term "analogous materials or devices." The terms have been understood, in the practice of States, in their ordinary sense as covering weapons whose prime, or even exclusive, effect is to poison or asphyxiate. This practice is clear, and the parties to those instruments have not treated them as referring to nuclear weapons.

56. In view of this. it does not seem to the Court that the use of nuclear weapons can be regarded as specifically prohibited on the basis of the above-mentioned provisions of the Second Hague Declaration of 1899, the Regulations annexed to the Hague Convention IV of 1907 or the 1925 Protocol (see paragraph 54 above).

57. The pattern until now has been for weapons of mass destruction to be declared illegal by specific instruments. The most recent such instruments are the Convention of 10 April 1972 on the Prohibition of the Development, Production and Stockpiling of Bacteriological (Biological) and Toxin Weapons and on Their Destruction—which prohibits the possession of bacteriological and toxic weapons and reinforces the prohibition of their use—and the Convention of 13 January 1993 on the Prohibition of the Development, Production, Stockpiling and Use of Chemical Weapons and on Their Destruction—which prohibits all use of chemical weapons and requires the destruction of existing stocks. Each of these instruments has been negotiated and adopted in its own context and for its own reasons. The Court does not find any specific prohibition of recourse to nuclear weapons in treaties expressly prohibiting the use of certain weapons of mass destruction.

58. In the last two decades, a great many negotiations have been conducted regarding nuclear weapons; they have not resulted in a treaty of general prohibition of the same kind as for bacteriological and chemical weapons. However, a number of specific treaties have been concluded in order to limit:

- the acquisition, manufacture and possession of nuclear weapons (Peace Treaties of 10 February 1947; State Treaty for the Re-establishment of an Independent and Democratic Austria of 15 May 1955; Treaty of Tlatelolco of 14 February 1967 for the Prohibition of Nuclear Weapons in Latin America, and its Additional Protocols; Treaty of 1 July 1968 on the Non-Proliferation of Nuclear Weapons; Treaty of Rarotonga of 6 August 1985 on the Nuclear Weapon-Free Zone of the South Pacific, and its Protocols; Treaty of 12

September 1990 on the Final Settlement with respect to Germany);

- the deployment of nuclear weapons (Antarctic Treaty of 1 December 1959; Treaty of 27 January 1967 on Principles Governing the Activities of States in the Exploration and Use of Outer Space, including the Moon and Other Celestial Bodies; Treaty of Tlatelolco of 14 February 1967 for the Prohibition of Nuclear Weapons in Latin America, and its Additional Protocols; Treaty of 11 February 1971 on the Prohibition of the Emplacement of Nuclear Weapons and Other Weapons of Mass Destruction on the Sea-Bed and the Ocean Floor and in the Subsoil Thereof; Treaty of Rarotonga of 6 August 1985 on the Nuclear-Weapon-Free Zone of the South Pacific, and its Protocols); and
- the testing of nuclear weapons (Antarctic Treaty of 1 December 1959; Treaty of 5 August 1963 Banning Nuclear Weapon Tests in the Atmosphere, in Outer Space and under Water; Treaty of 27 January 1967 on Principles Governing the Activities of States in the Exploration and Use of Outer Space, including the Moon and Other Celestial Bodies; Treaty of Tlatelolco of 14 February 1967 for the Prohibition of Nuclear Weapons in Latin America, and its Additional Protocols; Treaty of Rarotonga of 6 August 1985 on the Nuclear-Weapon-Free Zone of the South Pacific, and its Protocols).

59. Recourse to nuclear weapons is directly addressed by two of these Conventions and also in connection with the indefinite extension of the Treaty on the Non-Proliferation of Nuclear Weapons of 1968:

(a) the Treaty of Tlatelolco of 14 February 1967 for the Prohibition of Nuclear Weapons in Latin America prohibits, in Article 1, the use of nuclear weapons by the Contracting Parties. It further includes an Additional Protocol II open to nuclear-weapon States outside the region, Article 3 of which provides:

> "The Governments represented by the undersigned Plenipotentiaries also undertake not to use or threaten to use nuclear weapons against the Contracting Parties of the Treaty for the Prohibition of Nuclear Weapons in Latin America."

The Protocol was signed and ratified by the five nuclear-weapon States. Its ratification was accompanied by a variety of declarations. The United Kingdom Government, for example, stated that "in the event of any act of aggression by a Contracting Party to the Treaty in which that Party was supported by a nuclear-weapon State," the United Kingdom Government would "be free to reconsider the extent to which they could be regarded as committed by the provisions of Additional Protocol II." The United States made a similar statement. The French Government, for its part, stated that it "interprets the undertaking made in article 3 of the Protocol as being without prejudice to the full exercise of the right of self-defence confirmed by Article 51 of the Charter." China reaffirmed its commitment not to be the first to make use of nuclear weapons. The Soviet Union reserved "the right to review" the obligations imposed upon it by Additional Protocol II, particularly in the event of an attack by a State party either "in support of a nuclear-weapon State or jointly with that State." None of these statements drew comment or objection from the parties to the Treaty of Tlatelolco.

(b) the Treaty of Rarotonga of 6 August 1985 establishes a South Pacific Nuclear Free Zone in which the Parties undertake not to manufacture, acquire or possess any nuclear explosive device (Art. 3). Unlike the Treaty of Tlatelolco, the Treaty of Rarotonga does not expressly prohibit the use of such weapons. But such a prohibition is for the States parties the necessary consequence of the prohibitions stipulated by the Treaty. The Treaty has a number of protocols. Protocol 2, open to the five nuclear-weapon States, specifies in its Article 1 that:

> "Each Party undertakes not to use or threaten to use any nuclear explosive device against:
>
> *(a)* Parties to the Treaty; or
>
> *(b)* any territory within the South Pacific Nuclear Free Zone for which a State that has become a Party to Protocol 1 is internationally responsible."

China and Russia are parties to that Protocol. In signing it, China and the Soviet Union each made a declaration by which they reserved the "right to reconsider" their obligations under the said Protocol; the Soviet Union also referred to certain circumstances in which it would consider itself released from those obligations. France, the United Kingdom and the United States, for their part, signed Protocol 2 on 25 March 1996, but have not yet ratified it. On that occasion, France declared, on the one hand, that no provision in that Protocol "shall impair the full exercise of the inherent right of self-defence provided for in Article 51 of the . . . Charter" and, on the other hand, that "the commitment set out in Article 1 of [that] Protocol amounts to the negative security assurances given by France to non-nuclear-weapon States which are parties to the Treaty on . . . Non-Proliferation," and that "these assurances shall not apply to States which are not parties" to that Treaty. For its part, the United Kingdom made a declaration setting out the precise circumstances in which it "will not be bound by [its] undertaking under Article 1" of the Protocol.

(c) as to the Treaty on the Non-Proliferation of Nuclear Weapons, at the time of its signing in 1968 the United States, the United Kingdom and the USSR gave various security assurances to the non-nuclear-weapon States that were parties to the Treaty. In resolution 255 (1968) the Security Council took note with satisfaction of the intention expressed by those three States to

> "provide or support immediate assistance, in accordance with the Charter, to any non-nuclear-weapon State Party to the Treaty on the Non-Proliferation . . . that is a victim of an act of, or an object of a threat of, aggression in which nuclear weapons are used."

On the occasion of the extension of the Treaty in 1995, the five nuclear-weapon States gave their non-nuclear-weapon partners, by means of separate unilateral statements on 5 and 6 April 1995, positive and negative security assurances against the use of such weapons. All the five nuclear-weapon States first undertook not to use nuclear weapons against non-nuclear-weapon States that were parties to the Treaty on the Non-Proliferation of Nuclear Weapons. However, these States, apart from China, made an exception in the case of an invasion or any other attack against them, their territories, armed forces or allies, or on a State towards which they had a security commitment, carried out or sustained by a nonnuclear-weapon State party to the Non-Proliferation Treaty in association or alliance with a nuclear-weapon State. Each of the nuclear-weapon States further undertook, as a permanent member of the Security Council, in the event of an attack with the use of nuclear weapons, or threat of such attack, against a non-nuclear-weapon State, to refer the matter to the Security Council without delay and to act within it in order that it might take immediate measures with a view to supplying, pursuant to the Charter, the necessary assistance to the victim State (the commitments assumed comprising minor variations in wording). The Security Council, in unanimously adopting resolution 984 (1995) of 11 April 1995, cited above, took note of those statements with appreciation. It also recognized

> "that the nuclear-weapon State permanent members of the Security Council will bring the matter immediately to the attention of the Council and seek Council action to provide, in accordance with the Charter, the necessary assistance to the State victim";

and welcomed the fact that

> "the intention expressed by certain States that they will provide or support immediate assistance, in accordance with the Charter, to any non-nuclear-weapon State Party to the Treaty on the Non-Proliferation of Nuclear Weapons that is a victim of an act of, or an object of a threat of, aggression in which nuclear weapons are used."

60. Those States that believe that recourse to nuclear weapons is illegal stress that the conventions that include various rules providing for the limitation or elimination of nuclear weapons in certain areas (such as the Antarctic Treaty of 1959 which prohibits the deployment of nuclear weapons in the Antarctic, or the Treaty of Tlatelolco of 1967 which creates a nuclear-weapon-free zone in Latin America) or the conventions that apply certain measures of control and limitation to the existence of nuclear weapons (such as the 1963 Partial Test-Ban Treaty or the Treaty on the Non-Proliferation of Nuclear Weapons) all set limits to the use of nuclear weapons. In their view, these treaties bear witness, in their own way, to the emergence of a rule of complete legal prohibition of all uses of nuclear weapons.

61. Those States who defend the position that recourse to nuclear weapons is legal in certain circumstances see a logical contradiction in reaching such a conclusion. According to them, those Treaties, such as the Treaty on the Non-Proliferation of Nuclear Weapons, as well as Security Council resolutions 255 (1968) and 984 (1995) which take note of the security assurances given by the nuclear-weapon States to the non-nuclear-weapon States in relation to any nuclear aggression against the latter, cannot be understood as prohibiting the use of nuclear weapons, and such a claim is contrary to the very text of those instruments. For those who support the legality in certain circumstances of recourse to nuclear weapons, there is no absolute prohibition against the use of such weapons. The very logic and construction of the Treaty on the Non-Proliferation of Nuclear Weapons, they assert, confirm this. This Treaty, whereby, they contend, the possession of nuclear weapons by the five nuclear-weapon States has been accepted, cannot be seen as a treaty banning their use by those States; to accept the fact that those States possess nuclear weapons is tantamount to recognizing that such weapons may be used in certain circumstances. Nor, they contend, could the security assurances given by the nuclear-weapon States in 1968, and more recently in connection with the Review and Extension Conference of the Parties to the Treaty on the Non-Proliferation of Nuclear Weapons in 1995, have been conceived without its being supposed that there were circumstances in which nuclear weapons could be used in a lawful manner. For those who defend the legality of the use, in certain circumstances, of nuclear weapons, the acceptance of those instruments by the different non-nuclear-weapon States confirms and reinforces the evident logic upon which those instruments are based.

62. The Court notes that the treaties dealing exclusively with acquisition, manufacture, possession, deployment and testing of nuclear weapons, without specifically addressing their threat or use, certainly point to an increasing concern in the international community with these weapons; the Court concludes from this that these treaties could therefore

be seen as foreshadowing a future general prohibition of the use of such weapons, but they do not constitute such a prohibition by themselves. As to the treaties of Tlatelolco and Rarotonga and their Protocols, and also the declarations made in connection with the indefinite extension of the Treaty on the Non-Proliferation of Nuclear Weapons, it emerges from these instruments that:

(a) a number of States have undertaken not to use nuclear weapons in specific zones (Latin America; the South Pacific) or against certain other States (non-nuclear-weapon States which are parties to the Treaty on the Non-Proliferation of Nuclear Weapons);

(b) nevertheless, even within this framework, the nuclear-weapon States have reserved the right to use nuclear weapons in certain circumstances; and

(c) these reservations met with no objection from the parties to the Tlatelolco or Rarotonga Treaties or from the Security Council.

63. These two treaties, the security assurances given in 1995 by the nuclear-weapon States and the fact that the Security Council took note of them with satisfaction, testify to a growing awareness of the need to liberate the community of States and the international public from the dangers resulting from the existence of nuclear weapons. The Court moreover notes the signing, even more recently, on 15 December 1995, at Bangkok, of a Treaty on the Southeast Asia Nuclear-Weapon-Free Zone, and on 11 April 1996, at Cairo, of a treaty on the creation of a nuclear-weapons-free zone in Africa. It does not, however, view these elements as amounting to a comprehensive and universal conventional prohibition on the use, or the threat of use, of those weapons as such.

* * *

64. The Court will now turn to an examination of customary international law to determine whether a prohibition of the threat or use of nuclear weapons as such flows from that source of law. As the Court has stated, the substance of that law must be "looked for primarily in the actual practice and *opinio juris* of States" (*Continental Shelf (Libyan Arab Jarnahiriya/Malta), Judgment, I.C.J. Reports 1985*, p. 29, para. 27).

65. States which hold the view that the use of nuclear weapons is illegal have endeavoured to demonstrate the existence of a customary rule prohibiting this use. They refer to a consistent practice of non-utilization of nuclear weapons by States since 1945 and they would see in that practice the expression of an *opinio juris* on the part of those who possess such weapons.

66. Some other States, which assert the legality of the threat and use of nuclear weapons in certain circumstances, invoked the doctrine and practice of deterrence in support of their argument. They recall that they have always, in concert with certain other States, reserved the right to use those weapons in the exercise of the right to self-defence against an armed attack threatening their vital security interests. In their view, if nuclear weapons have not been used since 1945, it is not on account of an existing or nascent custom but merely because circumstances that might justify their use have fortunately not arisen.

67. The Court does not intend to pronounce here upon the practice known as the "policy of deterrence." It notes that it is a fact that a number of States adhered to that practice during the greater part of the Cold War and continue to adhere to it. Furthermore, the members of the international community are profoundly divided on the matter of whether non-recourse to nuclear weapons over the past 50 years constitutes the expression of an *opinio juris.* Under these circumstances the Court does not consider itself able to find that there is such an *opinio juris.*

68. According to certain States, the important series of General Assembly resolutions, beginning with resolution 1653 (XVI) of 24 November 1961, that deal with nuclear weapons and that affirm, with consistent regularity, the illegality of nuclear weapons, signify the existence of a rule of international customary law which prohibits recourse to those weapons. According to other States, however, the resolutions in question have no binding character on their own account and are not declaratory of any customary rule of prohibition of nuclear weapons; some of these States have also pointed out that this series of resolutions not only did not meet with the approval of all of the nuclear-weapon States but of many other States as well.

69. States which consider that the use of nuclear weapons is illegal indicated that those resolutions did not claim to create any new rules, but were confined to a confirmation of customary law relating to the prohibition of means or methods of warfare which, by their use, overstepped the bounds of what is permissible in the conduct of hostilities. In their view, the resolutions in question did no more than apply to nuclear weapons the existing rules of international law applicable in armed conflict; they were no more than the "envelope" or *instrumentum* containing certain pre-existing customary rules of international law. For those States it is accordingly of little importance that the *instrumentum* should have occasioned negative votes, which cannot have the effect of obliterating those customary rules which have been confirmed by treaty law.

70. The Court notes that General Assembly resolutions, even if they are not binding, may sometimes have normative value. They can, in certain circumstances, provide evidence important for establishing the existence of

a rule or the emergence of an *opinio juris*. To establish whether this is true of a given General Assembly resolution, it is necessary to look at its content and the conditions of its adoption; it is also necessary to see whether an *opinio juris* exists as to its normative character. Or a series of resolutions may show the gradual evolution of the *opinio juris* required for the establishment of a new rule.

71. Examined in their totality, the General Assembly resolutions put before the Court declare that the use of nuclear weapons would be "a direct violation of the Charter of the United Nations"; and in certain formulations that such use "should be prohibited." The focus of these resolutions has sometimes shifted to diverse related matters; however, several of the resolutions under consideration in the present case have been adopted with substantial numbers of negative votes and abstentions; thus, although those resolutions are a clear sign of deep concern regarding the problem of nuclear weapons, they still fall short of establishing the existence of an *opinio juris* on the illegality of the use of such weapons.

72. The Court further notes that the first of the resolutions of the General Assembly expressly proclaiming the illegality of the use of nuclear weapons, resolution 1653 (XVI) of 24 November 1961 (mentioned in subsequent resolutions), after referring to certain international declarations and binding agreements, from the Declaration of St. Petersburg of 1868 to the Geneva Protocol of 1925, proceeded to qualify the legal nature of nuclear weapons, determine their effects, and apply general rules of customary international law to nuclear weapons in particular. That application by the General Assembly of general rules of customary law to the particular case of nuclear weapons indicates that, in its view, there was no specific rule of customary law which prohibited the use of nuclear weapons; if such a rule had existed, the General Assembly could simply have referred to it and would not have needed to undertake such an exercise of legal qualification.

73. Having said this, the Court points out that the adoption each year by the General Assembly, by a large majority, of resolutions recalling the content of resolution 1653 (XVI), and requesting the member States to conclude a convention prohibiting the use of nuclear weapons in any circumstance, reveals the desire of a very large section of the international community to take, by a specific and express prohibition of the use of nuclear weapons, a significant step forward along the road to complete nuclear disarmament. The emergence, as *lex lata*, of a customary rule specifically prohibiting the use of nuclear weapons as such is hampered by the continuing tensions between the nascent *opinio juris* on the one hand, and the still strong adherence to the practice of deterrence on the other.

* * *

74. The Court not having found a conventional rule of general scope, nor a customary rule specifically proscribing the threat or use of nuclear weapons *per se*, it will now deal with the question whether recourse to nuclear weapons must be considered as illegal in the light of the principles and rules of international humanitarian law applicable in armed conflict and of the law of neutrality.

75. A large number of customary rules have been developed by the practice of States and are an integral part of the international law relevant to the question posed. The "laws and customs of war"—as they were traditionally called—were the subject of efforts at codification undertaken in The Hague (including the Conventions of 1899 and 1907), and were based partly upon the St. Petersburg Declaration of 1868 as well as the results of the Brussels Conference of 1874. This "Hague Law" and, more particularly, the Regulations Respecting the Laws and Customs of War on Land, fixed the rights and duties of belligerents in their conduct of operations and limited the choice of methods and means of injuring the enemy in an international armed conflict. One should add to this the "Geneva Law" (the Conventions of 1864, 1906, 1929 and 1949), which protects the victims of war and aims to provide safeguards for disabled armed forces personnel and persons not taking part in the hostilities. These two branches of the law applicable in armed conflict have become so closely interrelated that they are considered to have gradually formed one single complex system, known today as international humanitarian law. The provisions of the Additional Protocols of 1977 give expression and attest to the unity and complexity of that law.

76. Since the turn of the century, the appearance of new means of combat has—without calling into question the longstanding principles and rules of international law—rendered necessary some specific prohibitions of the use of certain weapons, such as explosive projectiles under 400 grammes, dum-dum bullets and asphyxiating gases. Chemical and bacteriological weapons were then prohibited by the 1925 Geneva Protocol. More recently, the use of weapons producing "non-detectable fragments," of other types of "mines, booby traps and other devices," and of "incendiary weapons," was either prohibited or limited, depending on the case, by the Convention of 10 October 1980 on Prohibitions or Restrictions on the Use of Certain Conventional Weapons Which May Be Deemed to Be Excessively Injurious or to Have Indiscriminate Effects. The provisions of the Convention on "mines, booby traps and other devices" have just been amended, on 3 May 1996, and now regulate in greater detail, for example, the use of anti-personnel land mines.

77. All this shows that the conduct of military operations is governed by a body of legal prescriptions. This is so because "the right of belligerents to adopt means of injuring the enemy is not unlimited" as stated in Article 22 of the 1907 Hague Regulations relating to the laws and customs of war

on land. The St. Petersburg Declaration had already condemned the use of weapons "which uselessly aggravate the suffering of disabled men or make their death inevitable." The aforementioned Regulations relating to the laws and customs of war on land, annexed to the Hague Convention IV of 1907, prohibit the use of "arms, projectiles, or material calculated to cause unnecessary suffering" (Art. 23).

78. The cardinal principles contained in the texts constituting the fabric of humanitarian law are the following. The first is aimed at the protection of the civilian population and civilian objects and establishes the distinction between combatants and non-combatants; States must never make civilians the object of attack and must consequently never use weapons that are incapable of distinguishing between civilian and military targets. According to the second principle, it is prohibited to cause unnecessary suffering to combatants: it is accordingly prohibited to use weapons causing them such harm or uselessly aggravating their suffering. In application of that second principle, States do not have unlimited freedom of choice of means in the weapons they use.

The Court would likewise refer, in relation to these principles, to the Martens Clause, which was first included in the Hague Convention II with Respect to the Laws and Customs of War on Land of 1899 and which has proved to be an effective means of addressing the rapid evolution of military technology. A modern version of that clause is to be found in Article 1, paragraph 2, of Additional Protocol 1 of 1977, which reads as follows:

> "In cases not covered by this Protocol or by other international agreements, civilians and combatants remain under the protection and authority of the principles of international law derived from established custom, from the principles of humanity and from the dictates of public conscience."

In conformity with the aforementioned principles, humanitarian law, at a very early stage, prohibited certain types of weapons either because of their indiscriminate effect on combatants and civilians or because of the unnecessary suffering caused to combatants, that is to say, a harm greater than that unavoidable to achieve legitimate military objectives. If an envisaged use of weapons would not meet the requirements of humanitarian law, a threat to engage in such use would also be contrary to that law.

79. It is undoubtedly because a great many rules of humanitarian law applicable in armed conflict are so fundamental to the respect of the human person and "elementary considerations of humanity" as the Court put it in its Judgment of 9 April 1949 in the *Corfu Channel case (I.C.J. Reports 1949*, p. 22), that the Hague and Geneva Conventions have enjoyed a broad accession. Further these fundamental rules are to be observed by all States

whether or not they have ratified the conventions that contain them, because they constitute intransgressible principles of international customary law.

80. The Nuremberg International Military Tribunal had already found in 1945 that the humanitarian rules included in the Regulations annexed to the Hague Convention IV of 1907 "were recognized by all civilized nations and were regarded as being declaratory of the laws and customs of war" (*Trial of the Major War Criminals, 14 November 1945-1 October 1946, Nuremberg, 1947*, Vol. 1, p. 254).

81. The Report of the Secretary-General pursuant to paragraph 2 of Security Council resolution 808 (1993), with which he introduced the Statute of the International Tribunal for the Prosecution of Persons Responsible for Serious Violations of International Humanitarian Law Committed in the Territory of the Former Yugoslavia since 1991, and which was unanimously approved by the Security Council (resolution 827 (1993)), stated:

> "In the view of the Secretary-General, the application of the principle *nullum crimen sine lege* requires that the international tribunal should apply rules of international humanitarian law which are beyond any doubt part of customary law . . .
>
> The part of conventional international humanitarian law which has beyond doubt become part of international customary law is the law applicable in armed conflict as embodied in: the Geneva Conventions of 12 August 1949 for the Protection of War Victims; the Hague Convention (IV) Respecting the Laws and Customs of War on Land and the Regulations annexed thereto of 18 October 1907; the Convention on the Prevention and Punishment of the Crime of Genocide of 9 December 1948; and the Charter of the International Military Tribunal of 8 August 1945."

82. The extensive codification of humanitarian law and the extent of the accession to the resultant treaties, as well as the fact that the denunciation clauses that existed in the codification instruments have never been used, have provided the international community with a corpus of treaty rules the great majority of which had already become customary and which reflected the most universally recognized humanitarian principles. These rules indicate the normal conduct and behaviour expected of States.

83. It has been maintained in these proceedings that these principles and rules of humanitarian law are part of *jus cogens* as defined in Article 53 of the Vienna Convention on the Law of Treaties of 23 May 1969. The question whether a norm is part of the *jus cogens* relates to the legal character of the norm. The request addressed to the Court by the General Assembly raises the question of the applicability of the principles and rules

of humanitarian law in cases of recourse to nuclear weapons and the consequences of that applicability for the legality of recourse to these weapons. But it does not raise the question of the character of the humanitarian law which would apply to the use of nuclear weapons. There is, therefore, no need for the Court to pronounce on this matter.

84. Nor is there any need for the Court to elaborate on the question of the applicability of Additional Protocol 1 of 1977 to nuclear weapons. It need only observe that while, at the Diplomatic Conference of 1974–1977, there was no substantive debate on the nuclear issue and no specific solution concerning this question was put forward, Additional Protocol 1 in no way replaced the general customary rules applicable to all means and methods of combat including nuclear weapons. In particular, the Court recalls that all States are bound by those rules in Additional Protocol 1 which, when adopted, were merely the expression of the pre-existing customary law, such as the Martens Clause, reaffirmed in the first article of Additional Protocol 1. The fact that certain types of weapons were not specifically dealt with by the 1974–1977 Conference does not permit the drawing of any legal conclusions relating to the substantive issues which the use of such weapons would raise.

85. Turning now to the applicability of the principles and rules of humanitarian law to a possible threat or use of nuclear weapons, the Court notes that doubts in this respect have sometimes been voiced on the ground that these principles and rules had evolved prior to the invention of nuclear weapons and that the Conferences of Geneva of 1949 and 1974–1977 which respectively adopted the four Geneva Conventions of 1949 and the two Additional Protocols thereto did not deal with nuclear weapons specifically. Such views, however, are only held by a small minority. In the view of the vast majority of States as well as writers there can be no doubt as to the applicability of humanitarian law to nuclear weapons.

86. The Court shares that view. Indeed, nuclear weapons were invented after most of the principles and rules of humanitarian law applicable in armed conflict had already come into existence; the Conferences of 1949 and 1974–1977 left these weapons aside, and there is a qualitative as well as quantitative difference between nuclear weapons and all conventional arms. However. it cannot be concluded from this that the established principles and rules of humanitarian law applicable in armed conflict did not apply to nuclear weapons. Such a conclusion would be incompatible with the intrinsically humanitarian character of the legal principles in question which permeates the entire law of armed conflict and applies to all forms of warfare and to all kinds of weapons, those of the past, those of the present and those of the future. In this respect it seems significant that the thesis that the rules of humanitarian law do not apply to the new weaponry, because of the newness of the latter, has not been advocated in the present proceedings. On the contrary, the newness of

nuclear weapons has been expressly rejected as an argument against the application to them of international humanitarian law:

> "In general, international humanitarian law bears on the threat or use of nuclear weapons as it does of other weapons.
>
> International humanitarian law has evolved to meet contemporary circumstances, and is not limited in its application to weaponry of an earlier time. The fundamental principles of this law endure: to mitigate and circumscribe the cruelty of war for humanitarian reasons." (New Zealand, Written Statement, p. 15, paras. 63–64.)

None of the statements made before the Court in any way advocated a freedom to use nuclear weapons without regard to humanitarian constraints. Quite the reverse; it has been explicitly stated,

> "Restrictions set by the rules applicable to armed conflicts in respect of means and methods of warfare definitely also extend to nuclear weapons" (Russian Federation, CR 95/29, p. 52);
>
> "So far as the customary law of war is concerned, the United Kingdom has always accepted that the use of nuclear weapons is subject to the general principles of the *jus in bello*" (United Kingdom, CR 95/34, p. 45);

and

> "The United States has long shared the view that the law of armed conflict governs the use of nuclear weapons—just as it governs the use of conventional weapons" (United States of America, CR 95/34, p. 85).

87. Finally, the Court points to the Martens Clause, whose continuing existence and applicability is not to be doubted, as an affirmation that the principles and rules of humanitarian law apply to nuclear weapons.

* * *

88. The Court will now turn to the principle of neutrality which was raised by several States. In the context of the advisory proceedings brought before the Court by the WHO concerning the *Legality of the Use by a State of Nuclear Weapons in Armed Conflict*, the position was put as follows by one State:

> "The principle of neutrality, in its classic sense, was aimed at preventing the incursion of belligerent forces into neutral territory, or attacks on the persons or ships of neutrals. Thus: 'the territory of neutral powers is inviolable' (Article 1 of the Hague Convention (V) Respecting the Rights and Duties of Neutral Powers and Persons in Case of War on Land, concluded on 18 October 1907); 'belligerents are bound to respect the sovereign

> rights of neutral powers . . .' (Article 1 to the Hague Convention (XIII) Respecting the Rights and Duties of Neutral Powers in Naval War. concluded on 18 October 1907), 'neutral states have equal interests in having their rights respected by belligerents . . .' (Preamble to Convention on Maritime Neutrality, concluded on 20 February 1928). It is clear, however, that the principle of neutrality applies with equal force to transborder incursions of armed forces and to the transborder damage caused to a neutral State by the use of a weapon in a belligerent State." (Nauru, Written Statement (1), p. 35, IV E.)

The principle so circumscribed is presented as an established part of the customary international law.

89. The Court finds that as in the case of the principles of humanitarian law applicable in armed conflict, international law leaves no doubt that the principle of neutrality, whatever its content, which is of a fundamental character similar to that of the humanitarian principles and rules, is applicable (subject to the relevant provisions of the United Nations Charter), to all international armed conflict, whatever type of weapons might be used.

* * *

90. Although the applicability of the principles and rules of humanitarian law and of the principle of neutrality to nuclear weapons is hardly disputed, the conclusions to be drawn from this applicability are, on the other hand, controversial.

91. According to one point of view, the fact that recourse to nuclear weapons is subject to and regulated by the law of armed conflict does not necessarily mean that such recourse is as such prohibited. As one State put it to the Court:

> "Assuming that a State's use of nuclear weapons meets the requirements of self-defence, it must then be considered whether it conforms to the fundamental principles of the law of armed conflict regulating the conduct of hostilities" (United Kingdom, Written Statement, p. 40, para. 3.44);

> "the legality of the use of nuclear weapons must therefore be assessed in the light of the applicable principles of international law regarding the use of force and the conduct of hostilities, as is the case with other methods and means of warfare" (*ibid.*, p. 75, para. 4.2 (3));

and

> "The reality . . . is that nuclear weapons might be used in a wide variety of circumstances with very different results in terms of

likely civilian casualties. In some cases, such as the use of a low yield nuclear weapon against warships on the High Seas or troops in sparsely populated areas, it is possible to envisage a nuclear attack which caused comparatively few civilian casualties. It is by no means the case that every use of nuclear weapons against a military objective would inevitably cause very great collateral civilian casualties." (*Ibid.*, p. 53, para. 3.70; see also United States of America, CR951 34, pp. 89–90.)

92. Another view holds that recourse to nuclear weapons could never be compatible with the principles and rules of humanitarian law and is therefore prohibited. In the event of their use, nuclear weapons would in all circumstances be unable to draw any distinction between the civilian population and combatants, or between civilian objects and military objectives, and their effects, largely uncontrollable, could not be restricted, either in time or in space, to lawful military targets. Such weapons would kill and destroy in a necessarily indiscriminate manner, on account of the blast, heat and radiation occasioned by the nuclear explosion and the effects induced; and the number of casualties which would ensue would be enormous. The use of nuclear weapons would therefore be prohibited in any circumstance, notwithstanding the absence of any explicit conventional prohibition. That view lay at the basis of the assertions by certain States before the Court that nuclear weapons are by their nature illegal under customary international law, by virtue of the fundamental principle of humanity.

93. A similar view has been expressed with respect to the effects of the principle of neutrality. Like the principles and rules of humanitarian law, that principle has therefore been considered by some to rule out the use of a weapon the effects of which simply cannot be contained within the territories of the contending States.

94. The Court would observe that none of the States advocating the legality of the use of nuclear weapons under certain circumstances, including the "clean" use of smaller, low yield, tactical nuclear weapons, has indicated what, supposing such limited use were feasible, would be the precise circumstances justifying such use; nor whether such limited use would not tend to escalate into the all-out use of high yield nuclear weapons. This being so, the Court does not consider that it has a sufficient basis for a determination on the validity of this view.

95. Nor can the Court make a determination on the validity of the view that the recourse to nuclear weapons would be illegal in any circumstance owing to their inherent and total incompatibility with the law applicable in armed conflict. Certainly, as the Court has already indicated, the principles and rules of law applicable in armed conflict—at the heart of which is the overriding consideration of humanity—make the conduct of

armed hostilities subject to a number of strict requirements. Thus, methods and means of warfare, which would preclude any distinction between civilian and military targets, or which would result in unnecessary suffering to combatants, are prohibited. In view of the unique characteristics of nuclear weapons, to which the Court has referred above, the use of such weapons in fact seems scarcely reconcilable with respect for such requirements. Nevertheless, the Court considers that it does not have sufficient elements to enable it to conclude with certainty that the use of nuclear weapons would necessarily be at variance with the principles and rules of law applicable in armed conflict in any circumstance.

96. Furthermore, the Court cannot lose sight of the fundamental right of every State to survival, and thus its right to resort to self-defence, in accordance with Article 51 of the Charter when its survival is at stake. Nor can it ignore the practice referred to as "policy of deterrence," to which an appreciable section of the international community adhered for many years. The Court also notes the reservations which certain nuclear-weapon States have appended to the undertakings they have given, notably under the Protocols to the Treaties of Tlatelolco and Rarotonga, and also under the declarations made by them in connection with the extension of the Treaty on the Non-Proliferation of Nuclear Weapons, not to resort to such weapons.

97. Accordingly, in view of the present state of international law viewed as a whole, as examined above by the Court, and of the elements of fact at its disposal, the Court is led to observe that it cannot reach a definitive conclusion as to the legality or illegality of the use of nuclear weapons by a State in an extreme circumstance of self-defence, in which its very survival would be at stake.

* * *

98. Given the eminently difficult issues that arise in applying the law on the use of force and above all the law applicable in armed conflict to nuclear weapons, the Court considers that it now needs to examine one further aspect of the question before it, seen in a broader context.

In the long run, international law, and with it the stability of the international order which it is intended to govern, are bound to suffer from the continuing difference of views with regard to the legal status of weapons as deadly as nuclear weapons. It is consequently important to put an end to this state of affairs: the long-promised complete nuclear disarmament appears to be the most appropriate means of achieving that result.

99. In these circumstances, the Court appreciates the full importance of the recognition by Article VI of the Treaty on the Non-Proliferation of Nuclear Weapons of an obligation to negotiate in good faith a nuclear disarmament. This provision is worded as follows:

"Each of the Parties to the Treaty undertakes to pursue negotiations in good faith on effective measures relating to cessation of the nuclear arms race at an early date and to nuclear disarmament, and on a treaty on general and complete disarmament under strict and effective international control."

The legal import of that obligation goes beyond that of a mere obligation of conduct; the obligation involved here is an obligation to achieve a precise result—nuclear disarmament in all its aspects—by adopting a particular course of conduct, namely, the pursuit of negotiations on the matter in good faith.

100. This twofold obligation to pursue and to conclude negotiations formally concerns the 182 States parties to the Treaty on the Non-Proliferation of Nuclear Weapons, or, in other words, the vast majority of the international community.

Virtually the whole of this community appears moreover to have been involved when resolutions of the United Nations General Assembly concerning nuclear disarmament have repeatedly been unanimously adopted. Indeed, any realistic search for general and complete disarmament, especially nuclear disarmament, necessitates the co-operation of all States.

101. Even the very first General Assembly resolution, unanimously adopted on 24 January 1946 at the London session, set up a commission whose terms of reference included making specific proposals for, among other things, "the elimination from national armaments of atomic weapons and of all other major weapons adaptable to mass destruction." In a large number of subsequent resolutions, the General Assembly has reaffirmed the need for nuclear disarmament. Thus, in resolution 808 A (IX) of 4 November 1954, which was likewise unanimously adopted, it concluded

"that a further effort should be made to reach agreement on comprehensive and co-ordinated proposals to be embodied in a draft international disarmament convention providing for: . . . *(b)* The total prohibition of the use and manufacture of nuclear weapons and weapons of mass destruction of every type, together with the conversion of existing stocks of nuclear weapons for peaceful purposes."

The same conviction has been expressed outside the United Nations context in various instruments.

102. The obligation expressed in Article VI of the Treaty on the Non-Proliferation of Nuclear Weapons includes its fulfilment in accordance with the basic principle of good faith. This basic principle is set forth in Article 2, paragraph 2, of the Charter. It was reflected in the Declaration on Friendly Relations between States (resolution 2625 (XXV) of 24 October

1970) and in the Final Act of the Helsinki Conference of 1 August 1975. It is also embodied in Article 26 of the Vienna Convention on the Law of Treaties of 23 May 1969, according to which "[e]very treaty in force is binding upon the parties to it and must be performed by them in good faith."

Nor has the Court omitted to draw attention to it, as follows:

> "One of the basic principles governing the creation and performance of legal obligations, whatever their source, is the principle of good faith. Trust and confidence are inherent in international co-operation, in particular in an age when this co-operation in many fields is becoming increasingly essential." (*Nuclear Tests (Australia v. France), Judgment, I.C.J. Reports 1974*, p. 268, para. 46.)

103. In its resolution 984 (1995) dated 11 April 1995, the Security Council took care to reaffirm "the need for all States Parties to the Treaty on the Non-Proliferation of Nuclear Weapons to comply fully with all their obligations" and urged

> "all States, as provided for in Article VI of the Treaty on the Non-Proliferation of Nuclear Weapons, to pursue negotiations in good faith on effective measures relating to nuclear disarmament and on a treaty on general and complete disarmament under strict and effective international control which remains a universal goal."

The importance of fulfilling the obligation expressed in Article VI of the Treaty on the Non-Proliferation of Nuclear Weapons was also reaffirmed in the final document of the Review and Extension Conference of the parties to the Treaty on the Non-Proliferation of Nuclear Weapons, held from 17 April to 12 May 1995.

In the view of the Court, it remains without any doubt an objective of vital importance to the whole of the international community today.

* * *

104. At the end of the present Opinion, the Court emphasizes that its reply to the question put to it by the General Assembly rests on the totality of the legal grounds set forth by the Court above (paragraphs 20 to 103), each of which is to be read in the light of the others. Some of these grounds are not such as to form the object of formal conclusions in the final paragraph of the Opinion; they nevertheless retain, in the view of the Court, all their importance.

* * *

105. For these reasons,

THE COURT,

(1) By thirteen votes to one,

Decides to comply with the request for an advisory opinion;

IN FAVOUR: *President* Bedjaoui; *Vice-President* Schwebel; *Judges* Guillaume, Shahabuddeen, Weeramantry, Ranjeva, Herczegh, Shi, Fleischhauer, Koroma, Vereshchetin, Ferrari Bravo, Higgins;

AGAINST: *Judge* Oda;

(2) *Replies* in the following manner to the question put by the General Assembly:

A. Unanimously,

There is in neither customary nor conventional international law any specific authorization of the threat or use of nuclear weapons;

B. By eleven votes to three,

There is in neither customary nor conventional international law any comprehensive and universal prohibition of the threat or use of nuclear weapons as such;

IN FAVOUR: *President* Bedjaoui; *Vice-President* Schwebel; *Judges* Oda, Guillaume, Ranjeva, Herczegh, Shi, Fleischhauer, Vereshchetin, Ferrari Bravo, Higgins;

AGAINST: *Judges* Shahabuddeen, Weeramantry, Koroma;

C. Unanimously,

A threat or use of force by means of nuclear weapons that is contrary to Article 2, paragraph 4, of the United Nations Charter and that fails to meet all the requirements of Article 51, is unlawful;

D. Unanimously,

A threat or use of nuclear weapons should also be compatible with the requirements of the international law applicable in armed conflict, particularly those of the principles and rules of international humanitarian law, as well as with specific obligations under treaties and other undertakings which expressly deal with nuclear weapons;

E. By seven votes to seven, by the President's casting vote,

It follows from the above-mentioned requirements that the threat or use of nuclear weapons would generally be contrary to the rules of international law applicable in armed conflict, and in particular the principles and rules of humanitarian law;

However, in view of the current state of international law, and of the elements of fact at its disposal, the Court cannot conclude definitively whether the threat or use of nuclear weapons would be lawful or unlawful in an extreme circumstance of self-defence, in which the very survival of a State would be at stake;

IN FAVOUR: *President* Bedjaoui; *Judges* Ranjeva, Herczegh, Shi, Fleischhauer, Vereshchetin, Ferrari Bravo;

AGAINST: *Vice-President* Schwebel; *Judges* Oda, Guillaume, Shahabuddeen, Weeramantry, Koroma, Higgins;

F. Unanimously,

There exists an obligation to pursue in good faith and bring to a conclusion negotiations leading to nuclear disarmament in all its aspects under strict and effective international control.

Done in English and in French, the English text being authoritative, at the Peace Palace, The Hague, this eighth day of July, one thousand nine hundred and ninety-six, in two copies, one of which will be placed in the archives of the Court and the other transmitted to the Secretary-General of the United Nations.

2. Editors' Note: Nuclear Explosions and Climate Change

The reference in the opinion above to the *Nuclear Test Cases* raises the issue about nuclear explosions causing air pollution as well as other environmental damage.

Australia and New Zealand argued at the International Court of Justice in 1974 that the French nuclear testing program was contrary to international law. New Zealand argued that the French government tests at French Polynesia in the South Pacific region that gave rise to radioactive fallout constituted a violation of New Zealand's rights. The Court gave interim relief.[46] It indicated that pending further stays of the case, France should cease testing. In December 1974 the Court held, following the issuance of a media release by the French government, that since France had promised not to test nuclear weapons in the atmosphere and was bound by its own promise to that effect, the proceedings could be terminated as they no longer had any purpose and the Court did not need to decide them.[47] France also moved to terminate its acceptance of the compulsory jurisdiction of the International Court of Justice under the optional clause as it was entitled to do. It resumed underground nuclear testing at the same location.

In 1995 the same case was resumed by New Zealand at the International Court of Justice. New Zealand filed with the Court a Request for an Examination of the Situation in light of the 1974 judgment because France announced it would conduct a series of eight tests of nuclear

---

46 *Nuclear Test Cases (New Zealand v France) (Provisional Measures)* [1973] ICJ Rep 135 at 138.

47 *Nuclear Test Cases (New Zealand v France) (Jurisdiction)* [1974] ICJ Rep 457.

weapons in the South Pacific, starting in September 1995.[48] The resumed case concerned underground testing, not the atmospheric testing that the French had ceased with the effect of rendering the original case moot. The argument was that underground testing and atmospheric testing had similar effects when it came to the marine environment. While request for an examination of the case by the court lost by 12 votes to 3, New Zealand was of the view that it had brought pressure to bear upon France. The Prime Minister Rt Hon Jim Bolger said:[49]

> It was New Zealand's view that any resumption of nuclear testing in the South Pacific was totally unacceptable, and contrary to the legal, environmental, and political developments of the last two decades. The Government looked, therefore, to every possible avenue to challenge the testing, including legal means.

Here is an example of a small state using international law to attempt to secure leverage against a larger and more powerful state. By taking a case that will produce publicity, there is the prospect of gaining support on the issue from international opinion. In such situations winning is not the only thing to aim for. Sir Geoffrey Palmer was New Zealand's Judge *ad hoc* in the case.

If nuclear testing causes atmospheric and other environmental damage of sufficient concern to raise questions about the legality of the tests, consider the much greater damage that could result from nuclear war. Even a small-scale nuclear conflict could have significant impacts on the global climate. *See* O.B. Toon, et al., *Atmospheric effects and societal consequences of regional scal nuclear conflicts and acts of individual nuclear terrorism,* 7 Atmos. Chem. Phys. 1973 (2007). Widespread nuclear war could produce a nuclear winter that would make it impossible to sustain human life on the planet. Alan Robock, et al., *Nuclear winter revisited with a modern climate model and current nuclear arsenals: Still catastrophic consequences,* 112 J. Geophys. Res. D13107 (2007).

3. Hiroshima Declaration on Nuclear Weapons, Hiroshima, Japan, 8 August 2015

We the undersigned members of the Asia Pacific Leadership Network for Nuclear Non-Proliferation and Disarmament (APLN),

Meeting in Hiroshima on the 70th anniversary of the indescribable horror of the world's first use of atomic weapons, deeply moved by our experience here, believing that all the world's political leaders and nuclear policymakers should share it, reinforced by that experience in our determination to ensure the elimination once and for all of the most

[48] *Request for an Examination of the Situation* [1995] ICJ Rep 288.

[49] New Zealand Ministry of Foreign Affairs & Trade *New Zealand at the International Court of Justice: French Nuclear Testing in the Pacific—Nuclear Tests Case New Zealand v France (1995)* (Wellington, 1996). Foreword by Rt Hon Jim Bolger at 7.

indiscriminately inhumane weapons ever devised, and supporting the continuing initiatives of Hiroshima toward nuclear non-proliferation and disarmament,

Recalling the words of a former mayor of Hiroshima that "It is important to look at the stark reality of war in terms of both aggrieved and aggriever so as to develop a common understanding of history,"

Profoundly disappointed at the failure of the Ninth NPT Review Conference held in April–May this year in New York, despite the pledge by more than 100 Member States in the UN General Assembly last year to take effective action to "stigmatize, prohibit and eliminate" nuclear weapons,

Conscious that the world's 16,000 remaining nuclear weapons are strongly concentrated in Asia Pacific powers, with the United States and Russia having over 90 per cent of the world's stockpile; China, India, and Pakistan all having significant and growing arsenals; and the breakout state of North Korea continuing to build its weapons and delivery capability,

Gravely concerned that the number of nuclear weapons in the Asia Pacific is increasing, substantial modernization programs are occurring, and reliance on nuclear weapons in national security policies is nowhere diminishing and in some cases growing, raising the risk of further proliferation,

Noting that most of the projected world growth in civil nuclear energy—with all the attendant proliferation, safety and security risks requiring close and effective regulation—will be in the Asia Pacific,

Believing that the risks associated with the possession of nuclear weapons in today's world far outweigh any deterrent utility they may have had in the past or continue to have,

Recalling and reaffirming our strong continuing commitment to a world and Asia Pacific region free of nuclear weapons, and expressing our strong continuing support for national, regional and global efforts to prevent the further proliferation of nuclear weapons and improve nuclear security and safety,

Reiterating our strong belief that a world free of nuclear weapons is achievable through a phased process of risk reduction, minimization and final elimination, pursued in tandem with efforts to improve regional and global security,

Emphasizing that regional organizations and mechanisms, including regional security dialogues aimed at building confidence and promoting cooperation, have a vital role to play in addressing both regional security generally and nuclear risks in particular,

Declare it unacceptable that the world should continue to live under the threat of complete nuclear destruction, and to that end, *call upon* policymakers in the Asia Pacific region to re-energize the nuclear disarmament, non-proliferation and security agendas, and to act accordingly as follows:

ON NUCLEAR DISARMAMENT

Modifying Nuclear Doctrine

1. As a first major step towards nuclear disarmament all states, including nuclear-armed states and allies and partners relying on their protection, should support changes to nuclear doctrine and posture which dramatically reduce the role of nuclear weapons in security policy, in order to promote confidence-building, strengthen the norm of non-use of nuclear weapons, reduce the risks of accidental and unauthorized use, and counteract crisis instability.

2. All nuclear-armed states should, pending the elimination of nuclear weapons and accepting the principle of undiminished security for all, adopt the principle that their sole purpose is to deter nuclear war, embrace the principle of 'No First Use' in their respective nuclear doctrines, and reinforce this by:

- taking nuclear weapons off high operational alert status,
- avoiding forward deployment of nuclear weapons, and
- separating warheads from land and air-based delivery vehicles and storing them physically apart in disassembled state.

3. All states should support the negotiation of a global Convention enshrining the principles of sole purpose and No First Use.

4. All states that have nuclear weapons should provide unconditional negative security assurances that they will not threaten to use, or use, such weapons against states that do not have them.

Minimizing Nuclear Weapons Numbers

5. Russia and the US should continue to abide by and implement all existing bilateral and multilateral agreements, and negotiate a new agreement to reduce dramatically the number of all nuclear weapons in their stockpiles.

6. Pending the elimination of nuclear weapons, all nuclear-armed states should commit not to increase their nuclear weapon stockpiles, *and* to reducing them to the lowest levels consistent with maintaining minimum effective retaliatory capability.

7. To help create the conditions for reducing nuclear weapons numbers, those states pursuing advanced conventional capabilities,

including missile defence and long-range precision strike, should make special efforts not to let these capabilities impede progress on nuclear non-proliferation and disarmament.

Eliminating Nuclear Weapons

8. All states should endorse the humanitarian impact initiative that draws sustenance from the 1996 Advisory Opinion of the ICJ and declare that it is in the interests of the very survival of humanity that nuclear weapons are never again used, under any circumstances.

9. Recognizing that the NPT has failed to make progress toward nuclear disarmament, like-minded states should negotiate a simple, normatively powerful Use Ban Convention that prohibits any use of nuclear weapons by any state or non-state actor under any circumstances.

10. Such a Convention, irrespective of whether it is joined by the nuclear-armed states, would be an important educational and advocacy vehicle for governments and civil society organizations, reinforcing understanding of the catastrophic humanitarian impact of any weapons use, and of the reality that the risks and costs associated with nuclear weapons far outweigh any possible benefit.

11. The final objective should be negotiation and adoption of a comprehensive and universal Nuclear Weapons Convention, backed by effective verification and enforcement mechanisms, absolutely prohibiting not only the use of nuclear weapons but their possession, manufacture or acquisition by any other means by state or non-state actors.

ON NUCLEAR NON-PROLIFERATION

12. The relevant authorities in Tehran and Washington should fully support the historic Joint Comprehensive Plan of Action negotiated between the P5+1 and Iran, which is to be warmly welcomed as a crucial step forward in minimizing the risk of nuclear proliferation in the Middle East and promoting the prospect of eventual denuclearization and elimination of all weapons of mass destruction of the region.

13. All relevant states should accede to the protocols of the relevant regional nuclear-weapon-free zones (NWFZ) and, where outstanding issues prevent this, work with NWFZ parties to find solutions. Initiatives for the negotiation of a new Nuclear Weapon Free Zone in North East Asia—comprising Japan, North and South Korea and Mongolia—should be warmly encouraged.

14. Recognizing that North Korea's nuclear program poses a serious threat to regional and global non-proliferation efforts and to the peace and stability of this region, all countries concerned should explore all ways and means, to advance the denuclearization of the Korean peninsula, including North Korea abandoning all its nuclear weapons and programs under the

terms and conditions stipulated by the Joint Statement of September 2005, and complying with all relevant Security Council resolutions.

15. States whose signature and/or ratification is necessary to bring the Comprehensive Nuclear Test Ban Treaty (CTBT) into force should so act as soon as possible, without awaiting such action by any other State Party, and in the meantime maintain a moratorium on all nuclear tests.

16. All states should support the urgent commencement of negotiations on a Fissile Material Cut-off Treaty (FMCT), preferably within the framework of the Conference on Disarmament. Pending negotiation of an FMCT, all relevant states should announce and apply a moratorium on the production of fissile material for nuclear weapons and declare their past production of fissile material, including current stockpiles.

17. All states should implement fully the requirements of UN Security Council Resolution 1540, to prohibit non-state actors developing, acquiring, or transferring weapons of mass destruction, including enacting and enforcing the required legislation and reporting to the UNSC 1540 Committee.

18. All states should ensure that peaceful nuclear energy programs do not contribute to the proliferation of nuclear weapons and do not endanger human and environmental health and safety.

ON NUCLEAR SECURITY AND SAFETY

19. All states should build and sustain strong nuclear security and safety cultures in relation to all fissile material, nuclear weapons and military and civil nuclear facilities, share best practices, and take steps to strengthen the international nuclear security architecture.

20. All states should minimize stocks of highly enriched uranium (HEU) and separated plutonium, convert reactor fuel from HEU to low enriched uranium, and support efforts to use non-HEU technologies.

21. All states should promote intensive dialogue among and between nuclear industry and government bodies, including national regulators, with a view to improving nuclear security and safety regulations, and regulatory effectiveness and transparency.

22. To strengthen nuclear energy governance in the region across all three crucial areas of safeguards, security and safety, the East Asia Summit should explore the concept of an Asia Pacific Nuclear Energy Community.

23. All states should promote knowledge and awareness of nuclear issues through appropriate advocacy, educational and training activities.

Hiroshima resonates powerfully around the world as a symbol of the need for nuclear weapons never again to be used under any circumstances, and ultimately eliminated from the face of the earth. We as members of the APLN will not rest until we realize that goal.

4. Editors' Note: Events Preceding the 2017 UN Treaty

Sixteen thousand remaining nuclear weapons are strongly concentrated in the Asia Pacific region with the United States and Russia having 90% of the stockpile. (There were nearly 18,000 in 2012.) China, India and Pakistan all have significant and growing arsenals. The situation promoted by North Korea's policy is producing real concern in that region. The out-dated doctrine of deterrence seems to be still dominating the policies of the nuclear powers, and efforts at nuclear disarmament are essentially at a halt. The Nuclear Security Summit held in Washington at the beginning of April 2016 may have improved the methods for controlling and safeguarding highly enriched uranium and plutonium somewhat. The agreement with Iran was a positive sign, although the Trump administration has retreated from that.

There is worrying evidence that significant funds are currently being expended in updating nuclear weapons. China, India, and Pakistan all have significant and growing arsenals. And very big money indeed is earmarked for updating nuclear weaponry. The growing numbers of tactical nuclear weapons pose real problems.

However, there was another hopeful sign. The Nuclear Weapons Open-ended Working Group had its first meeting in Geneva in February 2016. Although the nuclear-armed states did not participate, a large number of countries relying on nuclear weapons did. These included Japan, South Korea and Australia.

A different approach to the issue has somewhat revived hopes for successfully dealing with the nuclear problem. The humanitarian initiative on the nuclear issue was backed by 155 United Nations members of the General Assembly in October 2014. And in December 2014, the Vienna conference on Humanitarian Impact of Nuclear Weapons swelled further the support for that approach. Ultimately after long negotiations, the 2017 United Nations Treaty was successfully negotiated.

5. United Nations General Assembly Resolution 69/52 on united action towards the elimination of nuclear weapons, U.N. Doc. A/Res/69/52 (2 December 2014)

The General Assembly,

Recalling the need for all States to take further practical steps and effective measures towards the total elimination of nuclear weapons, with a view to achieving a peaceful and secure world free of nuclear weapons, and in this regard confirming the determination of Member States to take united action,

Noting that the ultimate objective of the efforts of States in the disarmament process is general and complete disarmament under strict and effective international control, . . .

Expressing deep concern at the catastrophic humanitarian consequences of any use of nuclear weapons, and reaffirming the need for all States at all times to comply with applicable international law, including international humanitarian law, while convinced that every effort should be made to avoid the use of nuclear weapons,

* * *

Reaffirming that the enhancement of international peace and security and the promotion of nuclear disarmament are mutually reinforcing,

Reaffirming also that further advancement in nuclear disarmament will contribute to consolidating the international regime for nuclear non-proliferation, which is, inter alia, essential to international peace and security,

Reaffirming further the crucial importance of the Treaty on the Non-Proliferation of Nuclear Weapons as the cornerstone of the international nuclear non-proliferation regime and an essential foundation for the pursuit of the three pillars of the Treaty, namely, nuclear disarmament, nuclear non-proliferation and the peaceful uses of nuclear energy,

* * *

Welcoming the entry into force on 5 February 2011 of the Treaty between the Russian Federation and the United States of America on Measures for the Further Reduction and Limitation of Strategic Offensive Arms and its continuing successful implementation,

Welcoming also the announcements and recent updates on overall stockpiles of nuclear warheads by France, the United Kingdom of Great Britain and Northern Ireland and the United States of America, as well as the update of the Russian Federation on its nuclear arsenal, which further enhance transparency and increase mutual confidence,

Expressing deep concern regarding the growing dangers posed by the proliferation of weapons of mass destruction, inter alia, nuclear weapons, including that caused by proliferation networks, . . .

Condemning in the strongest terms the nuclear tests conducted by the Democratic People's Republic of Korea, its launches using ballistic missile technology and its continued development of its nuclear and ballistic missile programmes, recognizing the importance of . . . full compliance with Security Council resolutions ... requirements ... that the Democratic People's Republic of Korea abandon all nuclear weapons and existing nuclear programmes, immediately cease all related activities and not conduct any further nuclear tests, ...

1. *Reaffirms* the importance of all States parties to the Treaty on the Non-Proliferation of Nuclear Weapons complying with their obligations under all the articles of the Treaty;

* * *

3. *Reaffirms* the vital importance of the universality of the Treaty on the Non-Proliferation of Nuclear Weapons, and calls upon all States not parties to the Treaty to accede as non-nuclear-weapon States to the Treaty promptly and without any conditions and, pending their accession to the Treaty, to adhere to its terms and take practical steps in support of the Treaty;

4. *Also reaffirms* the unequivocal undertaking of the nuclear-weapon States to accomplish the total elimination of their nuclear arsenals, leading to nuclear disarmament, to which all States parties to the Treaty on the Non-Proliferation of Nuclear Weapons are committed under article VI thereof;

5. *Calls upon* nuclear-weapon States to undertake further efforts to reduce and ultimately eliminate all types of nuclear weapons, deployed and non-deployed, including through unilateral, bilateral, regional and multilateral measures;

6. *Emphasizes* the importance of applying the principles of irreversibility, verifiability and transparency in relation to the process of nuclear disarmament and non-proliferation;

7. *Recognizes* that nuclear disarmament and achieving the peace and security of a world without nuclear weapons require openness and cooperation, affirms the importance of enhanced confidence through increased transparency and effective verification, and emphasizes the importance of the commitment made by the nuclear-weapon States at the 2010 Review Conference to accelerate concrete progress on the steps leading to nuclear disarmament contained in the Final Document of the 2000 Review Conference in a way that promotes international stability, peace and undiminished and increased security;

* * *

13. *Also calls upon* the nuclear-weapon States to promptly engage with a view to further diminishing the role and significance of nuclear weapons in all military and security concepts, doctrines and policies;

14. *Recognizes* the legitimate interest of non-nuclear-weapon States in receiving unequivocal and legally binding security assurances from nuclear-weapon States which could strengthen the nuclear non-proliferation regime;

* * *

16. *Encourages* the establishment of further nuclear-weapon-free zones, where appropriate, on the basis of arrangements freely arrived at among States of the region concerned and in accordance with the 1999 guidelines of the Disarmament Commission, recognizes that, by signing and ratifying relevant protocols that contain negative security assurances, nuclear-weapon States would undertake individual legally binding commitments with respect to the status of such zones and not to use or threaten to use nuclear weapons against States parties to such treaties, and welcomes in this regard the signature of the Protocol to the Treaty on a Nuclear-Weapon-Free Zone in Central Asia by the five nuclear-weapon States on 6 May 2014; * * *

22. *Encourages* every effort to secure all vulnerable nuclear and radiological material in order to, inter alia, prevent nuclear terrorism, and calls upon all States to work cooperatively as an international community to advance nuclear security, while requesting and providing assistance, including in the field of capacity building, as necessary;

23. *Encourages* all States to implement the recommendations contained in the report of the Secretary-General on the United Nations study on disarmament and non-proliferation education, in support of achieving a world without nuclear weapons, and to voluntarily share information on efforts they have been undertaking to that end;

24. *Commends and further encourages* the constructive role played by civil society in promoting nuclear non-proliferation and nuclear disarmament, and encourages all States to promote, in cooperation with civil society, disarmament and non-proliferation education which, inter alia, contributes to raising public awareness of the tragic consequences of the use of nuclear weapons and strengthens the momentum of international efforts to promote nuclear disarmament and non-proliferation . . . .

6. United Nations Treaty on the Prohibition of Nuclear Weapons, arts. 1 & 4 (opened for signature 20 September 2017)

Article 1 Prohibitions

1. Each State Party undertakes never under any circumstances to:

(a) Develop, test, produce, manufacture, otherwise acquire, possess or stockpile nuclear weapons or other nuclear explosive devices;

(b) Transfer to any recipient whatsoever nuclear weapons or other nuclear explosive devices or control over such weapons or explosive devices directly or indirectly;

(c) Receive the transfer of or control over nuclear weapons or other nuclear explosive devices directly or indirectly;

(d) Use or threaten to use nuclear weapons or other nuclear explosive devices;

(e) Assist, encourage or induce, in any way, anyone to engage in any activity prohibited to a State Party under this Treaty;

(f) Seek or receive any assistance, in any way, from anyone to engage in any activity prohibited to a State Party under this Treaty;

(g) Allow any stationing, installation or deployment of any nuclear weapons or other nuclear explosive devices in its territory or at any place under its jurisdiction or control.

Article 4 Towards the total elimination of nuclear weapons

1. Each State Party that after 7 July 2017 owned, possessed or controlled nuclear weapons or other nuclear explosive devices and eliminated its nuclear-weapon programme, including the elimination or irreversible conversion of all nuclear- weapons-related facilities, prior to the entry into force of this Treaty for it, shall cooperate with the competent international authority designated pursuant to paragraph 6 of this Article for the purpose of verifying the irreversible elimination of its nuclear-weapon programme. . . .

2. Notwithstanding Article 1 (a), each State Party that owns, possesses or controls nuclear weapons or other nuclear explosive devices shall immediately remove them from operational status, and destroy them as soon as possible but not later than a deadline to be determined by the first meeting of States Parties, in accordance with a legally binding, time-bound plan for the verified and irreversible elimination of that State Party's nuclear-weapon programme, including the elimination or irreversible conversion of all nuclear-weapons-related facilities. . . .

Section 5. Discussion Notes/Questions

1. What did the International Court of Justice conclude in 1995 concerning the legality of the use of nuclear weapons?

2. Do you think it may be argued that since this case was adjudicated upon in 1996 that the state of customary international law has moved on and it may now be possible to argue that the use of nuclear weapons would be unlawful at international law in all circumstances?

Consider, in particular, the following developments:

a. Nuclear-weapon-free zones are now in place in Latin America, Africa, southeast Asia, and central Asia. In each case, all or most of the NPT nuclear-weapon states have ratified a protocol to the applicable treaty that promises that the nuclear-weapon states will not use or threaten to use nuclear weapons against the states participating in the nuclear-weapon-free zone. *See, e.g.,* Article 4 of

Additional Protocol II to the Treaty for the Prohibition of Nuclear Weapons in Latin America and the Caribbean (Protocol to the Treaty of Tlatelolco).

b. The views expressed in United Nations General Assembly Resolution 69/52 (Reading 5), which passed by a vote of 170–1, with 14 absentions. Three nuclear-weapon states voted for the resolution (France, the United Kingdom and the United States). North Korea voted against it. Five nuclear-weapon states abstained (China, India, Israel, Pakistan and Russia).

c. Prior to their acquisition of nuclear weapons, the United Nations Security Council condemned efforts by India, Pakistan and North Korea to develop nuclear-weapons capability.

d. The adoption of the 2017 Treaty on the Prohibition of Nuclear Weapons.

3. In connection with the questions in paragraph 2, you will recall from Chapter 2 that the formation of new rules of customary international law requires both state practice and *opinio juris*. Is there evidence of state practice supporting the proposition that the use of nuclear weapons is illegal? *Opinio juris?* Consider also the following comments by the by the International Court of Justice in the *North Sea Continental Shelf Cases,* 1969 ICJ 3, 41–45 (paragraphs 72 & 74):

> [The process by which a rule,] while only conventional or contractual in its origin, has since passed into the general corpus of international law, and is now accepted as such by the *opinio juris*, so as to have become binding even for countries which have never, and do not, become parties to the [conventional rules] is a perfectly possible one and does from time to time occur: it constitutes indeed one of the recognized methods by which new rules of customary international law may be formed. At the same time this result is not lightly to be regarded as having been attained.
>
> * * *
>
> Although the passage of only a short period of time is not necessarily, or of itself, a bar to the formation of a new rule of customary international law on the basis of what was originally a purely conventional rule, an indispensable requirement would be that within the period in question, short though it might be, State practice, including that of States whose interests are specially affected, should have been both extensive and virtually uniform in the sense of the provision involved; and should moreover have occurred in such a way as to show a general recognition that a rule of law or legal obligation is involved.

You may wish also to consider the Court's comments in the case concerning *Military and Paramilitary Activities in and Against Nicaragua,* 1986 ICJ 14 (paragraphs 186 & 188):

> The Court does not consider that, for a rule to be established as customary, the corresponding practice must be in absolutely rigorous conformity with the rule. In order to deduce the existence of customary rules, the Court deems it sufficient that the conduct of States should, in general, be consistent with such rules and that instances of State conduct inconsistent with a given rule should generally have been treated as breaches of that rule, not as indications of the recognition of a new rule.
>
> * * *
>
> *[O]pinio juris* may, though with all due caution, be deuced from, *inter alia*, . . . the attitude of States towards . . . General Assembly resolutions * * *. The effect of consent to the text of such resolutions * * * may be understood as an acceptance of the validity of the rule or set of rules declared by the resolution * * *.

4. As to the United Nations Prohibition Treaty, once it is in force, how does it help the legal argument? How can nuclear-weapon states be bound by a Treaty they will not sign up to or ratify? Are there any circumstances in which the United States may be persuaded to ratify the Treaty? Or Russia? Or North Korea? Or India and Pakistan? What about France and the United Kingdom?

5. Can it be argued that the use of nuclear weapons is in the final analysis an issue akin to the political question doctrine in United States International Law, and therefore is not readily susceptible to being justiciable?

6. There is a significant body of international humanitarian law referred to in the ICJ opinion. Can the use of nuclear weapons ever be regarded as being humane?

Is the best argument in favour of the ICJ view that of self-defense by a sovereign nation when its very existence is threatened? But is it a sound argument?

7. Lawyers can make arguments about the legality of the use of nuclear weapons. But what judicial or other forums exist where those arguments can germinate into an enforceable decision that they are illegal?

B. INTERNATIONAL REGULATION OF NUCLEAR POWER

In December 1953, President Dwight D. Eisenhower delivered an address to the United Nations General Assembly known as the "Atoms for Peace" speech. In his remarks, Eisenhower noted the grave threat that nuclear weapons posed for the world and expressed the willingness of the United States to participate in efforts to end the "atomic armaments race which overshadows not only the peace, but the very life, of the world." But, he added,

> The United States would seek more than the mere reduction or elimination of atomic materials for military purposes. It is not enough to take this weapon out of the hands of the soldiers. It must be put into the hands of those who will know how to strip its military casing and adapt it to the arts of peace. . . . Who can doubt, if the entire body of the world's scientists and engineers had adequate amounts of fissionable material with which to test and develop their ideas, that this capability would rapidly be transformed into universal, efficient, and economic usage.

With those hopeful words as preamble, Eisenhower proposed the creation of an International Atomic Energy Agency to be formed with a dual purpose—to help prevent the proliferation of atomic weapons and, more importantly in Eisenhower's vision, to facilitate the application of atomic energy "to the needs of agriculture, medicine, and other peaceful activities. A special purpose would be to provide abundant electrical energy in the power-starved areas of the world."[50]

Early developments in the international regulation of nuclear power

Four years later, the Statute of the International Atomic Energy Agency (IAEA) **(Basic Document 1.3)** was adopted in New York. It was quickly ratified, including by the United States and the Soviet Union, and it entered into force on 29 July 1957. The functions assigned to the IAEA by its Statute closely paralleled the proposal made by President Eisenhower. The IAEA would

- "encourage and assist research on, and development and practical application of atomic energy for peaceful uses throughout the world,"
- provide "materials, services, equipment, and facilities" to that end and, in particular, to promote "the production of electric power, with due consideration" for the needs of developing countries,
- foster the exchange of information on peaceful uses of nuclear power,
- "establish and administer safeguards designed to ensure" that the support it provided was "not used in such a way as to further any military purpose," and
- "establish . . . standards of safety for protection of health and minimization of danger to life and property," and ensure those standards were applied to its own operations or to any

[50] Dwight D. Eisenhower, *Atoms for Peace,* Address before the General Assembly of the United Nations on Peaceful Uses of Atomic Energy, New York City, 8 December 1953, *available at* https://www.eisenhowerlibrary.gov/media/3378 (last accessed July 3, 2019).

> operations using materials, services, equipment, facilities or information made available by the IAEA.[51]

Today, the IAEA remains at the heart of international efforts to regulate the "peaceful uses of nuclear power," including for the production of nuclear energy, although its efforts now occur in the context of a broader network of treaties dealing with various aspects of this subject.

The negotiation and ratification of the IAEA Statute was quickly followed by the adoption of two separate treaties on the liability of operators of nuclear power plants for damage caused by nuclear accidents. One treaty, the 1960 Paris Convention on Third Party Liability in the Field of Nuclear Energy, was adopted under the auspices of the OECD. A non-OECD nation could join the Convention only with the unanimous consent of the parties to the Convention. A second treaty, the 1963 Vienna Convention on Civil Liability for Nuclear Damage was open to any member of the United Nations, the IAEA, or a UN specialized agency.

Both liability conventions were grounded on four basic principles. First, the operator of a nuclear installation would be strictly liable, without regard to fault (although subject to certain exceptions), for damage resulting from a nuclear accident associated with the facility. Second, the operator's liability would be exclusive—damages could be recovered from the operator (or an insurer or guarantor of the operator), and only from the operator, regardless of who was at fault in causing the accident. Third, the total amount of compensation an operator would be required to pay for any single nuclear incident was limited to an aggregate amount stated in each treaty. Fourth, nuclear operators were required to maintain insurance or other financial security sufficient to cover the total amount for which they might be liable.

Commercial nuclear power plants began to come online in the late 1950s and early 1960s. Several companies in various OECD countries developed competing power plant designs, and similar work was underway in the Soviet Union. By the mid-1980s, nuclear power plants had been installed in North America, in Western Europe, in the USSR and Eastern Europe, in Latin America, in Japan, and in South Africa. In 1974, the IAEA issued its first guidelines on safety, which reflected then-current understandings about how best to ensure safe plant operation and avoid damage in the event of an accident. But adherence to those safety recommendations made the construction and operation of nuclear power plants more expensive, and not every government was willing to impose those additional costs on its nuclear operators. The risks of such decisions eventually became clear.

---

51 IAEA Statute, art. III **(Basic Document 1.3)**.

The Chernobyl accident

On April 26, 1986, a chemical explosion occurred in one of the four reactors of the state-run Chernobyl nuclear power plant near Kiev, Ukraine, in the former Soviet Union. Over the following days, a fire in the damaged reactor caused the release into the atmosphere of radioactive elements. The radiation fall-out caused considerable concern and damage in many continental European countries. Scandinavia also experienced increased radiation levels. Reactions by nations to radiation levels varied. Some nations took preventive actions, such as banning the pasturing of cows and forbidding children in some regions to drink milk. A number of countries intervened in the import and sale of food. Some iodine 131 was detected in rainwater samples in the United States and the State of Oregon advised people not to drink rainwater.

The effects in the then-Federal Republic of Germany were described in *Legislative and Regulatory Activities, Federal Republic of Germany*, 38 Nuclear L. Bull. 7, 21 (Dec. 1986) as follows:

> The widespread radioactive contamination of the air, water and soil entailed direct damage to spring vegetables; milk-producing cattle had to be kept from grazing; the consumption of milk and other foodstuffs had to be supervised; import restrictions became necessary; the fixing of state intervention levels led to a change in consumers' eating and buying habits; travel agencies and transport undertakings specializing in Eastern European business lost their clientele; and finally, seasonal workers in agriculture lost their jobs.

In Ukraine itself, 39 people died within a few months of the accident, and more than 100 more suffered radiation sickness or radiation-induced health impairment. Four thousand children are estimated to have developed thyroid cancer as a result of radiation exposure from the Chernobyl accident, with at least 15 deaths so far. More than 300,000 people were relocated in the aftermath of the accident, and the clean-up in the region involved the decontamination of 60,000 buildings, 500 villages, and the building of a special subterranean concrete wall to prevent groundwater from penetrating into nearby rivers. Radioactive topsoil from several square miles was carted away; agricultural activities were forbidden on thousands of square kilometers of land.

For three days after the accident, the USSR remained silent, a fact that caused additional damage to its own people and to its European neighbors that could have been avoided had Moscow disclosed the mishap without delay. It was only later, after radioactivity spread throughout much of Europe and beyond, that the Soviet authorities, in a report to a "Post Accident Review Meeting" called by the IAEA in Vienna, described in detail the causes and circumstances of the accident, its evolution, the emergency actions taken by the Soviet authorities, and their efforts at site decontamination and rehabilitation during August 25–29, 1986. *See* IAEA, Summary Report on the Post Accident Review Meeting on the Chernobyl Accident (1986).

Despite the scale of the damage done, the Soviet Union rejected all demands for compensation, and no state made a formal claim against it. There was, moreover, no legislation in place in the Soviet Union that would have permitted individual victims to make a claim for compensation.

The response to Chernobyl

The Chernobyl accident revealed significant weaknesses in the international legal framework governing the use of nuclear energy. As noted above, prior to the Chernobyl accident, international law in this area was oriented largely toward the prevention of nuclear weapons proliferation and regulation of liability and compensation in the event of a nuclear accident. Although the IAEA had promulgated safety recommendations, safety and accident response were considered matters primarily of national concern.

The significant transboundary impacts of the Chernobyl accident caused states to reconsider this regulatory pattern. In the months and years following Chernobyl, at least 10 new international agreements were negotiated, in most cases under the auspices of the IAEA. Several of these agreements were aimed at securing better international cooperation and oversight in matters of safety and emergency response. Among the most important agreements are:

- the 1986 Convention on Early Notification of a Nuclear Accident **(Basic Document 2.9)**;
- the 1986 Convention on Assistance in the Case of a Nuclear Accident or Radiological Emergency **(Basic Document 2.10)**;
- the 1994 Convention on Nuclear Safety **(Basic Document 2.11)**;
- the 1997 Joint Convention on the Safety of Spent Fuel Management and on the Safety of Radioactive Waste Management; and
- the 1997 Convention on Supplementary Compensation for Nuclear Damage **(Basic Document 2.13)**

In addition, a number of protocols were adopted with the goal of improving the operation of the liability conventions, including a protocol amending and updating the Vienna Convention on Civil Liability for Nuclear Damage **(Basic Document 2.12)**. In 2005, concerns about terrorist threats to nuclear facilities led to the adoption of the International

Convention for the Suppression of Acts of Nuclear Terrorism **(Basic Document 7.23)**.

Despite these efforts, international regulation of nuclear energy remains relatively weak. Part of the problem is that many of the key international agreements have not received sufficiently widespread ratification. A different problem is that the agreements are, in some cases, substantively weak. For example, while the IAEA has some authority to establish health and safety standards to protect health and minimize danger to life and property, there are no mandatory international safety standards applicable to all nuclear installations, and a large number of member states oppose any effort to create binding standards. The 1994 Nuclear Safety Convention only goes a small way toward addressing that problem.

Another major problem for the IAEA is monitoring compliance with safety standards. On-site inspections are essential. However, on-site inspections frequently meet resistance from states inasmuch as an erosion of their territorial sovereignty is involved, particularly where there is nuclear power in military installations. On the positive side, the IAEA currently offers voluntary nuclear and radiological safety assessment services, and, as the number of countries using these services grows, political pressure is likely to increase on holdout states to make use of those services. States may find that there is political advantage in allowing such services, both domestically and in their relations with neighboring states.

In its 2017 Nuclear Safety Review, the IAEA reported increasing Member State requests for IAEA assistance in improving safety in existing nuclear power plants. It also organized multiple safety-oriented training events and capacity-building activities for Member States that have existing nuclear power facilities or that are developing new nuclear power programs.

Current trends in the nuclear power industry

In the years immediately following the Chernobyl accident, enthusiasm for nuclear power declined in the world. More recently, however, concerns about global warming have led to a resurgence of interest in nuclear power. Nuclear power plants do not emit greenhouse gases or other pollutants associated with the burning of fossil fuels and are therefore often characterized as a "clean" energy alternative. Moreover, as the Chernobyl catastrophe receded into the past, and nuclear plants worldwide were operated without any equivalent accidents, public concern about the safety of nuclear power began to diminish.

The 2011 nuclear disaster at the Fukushima Dai-ichi facility in Japan (*see* Discussion Note 5, *infra*) slowed the resurgence of the industry, and the current picture is mixed. In 2017, there were 405 nuclear reactors operating worldwide, which was one less than in the previous year. There were also 52 new reactors under construction. But there was evidence of difficulties within the industry, with fewer reactor startups than planned and some abandoned construction.[52]

Nonetheless, interest in nuclear power remains strong in some parts of the world. The following readings address both the continuing expansion of nuclear power and the challenges of operationalizing the safety regime established by the 1994 Convention on Nuclear Safety. After a few discussion notes and questions, this chapter concludes with a multi-issue problem designed to illustrate the variety and complexity of the legal issues that can arise in this area.

ASIA-PACIFIC AND GLOBAL NUCLEAR ORDERS IN THE SECOND NUCLEAR AGE

RAMESH THAKUR

(APLN-CNND, PB 21, July 2016)

37. Despite the 2011 Fukushima accident, interest in expanding nuclear power remains especially strong in Asia, led by China and India. The continent accounts for 28 and 25 per cent respectively of the number of reactors in operation and amount of electricity generated by nuclear power in the world at present. When looking at reactors under construction and planned, Asia's global share climbs dramatically to 58 and 51 per cent of reactors, and to 57 and 65 per cent of the share of electricity to be generated by nuclear power.

38. The Fukushima accident highlighted the need for stronger international governance and closer international cooperation on nuclear safety and security. There is also a continuing need to avoid proliferation risk from the growth in nuclear energy programs, particularly the spread of proliferation-sensitive technologies. Pending agreement on global solutions, practical steps can be taken at a regional level. An intergovernmental Asia-Pacific nuclear energy community could facilitate high-level consultation on nuclear plans and programs; regional cooperation and promotion of best practice in safeguards, security and safety; and collaborative arrangements for energy security and fuel cycle management.[53]

39. The 1994 Convention on Nuclear Safety aims to bind states operating land-based nuclear power plants to a high level of safety to international benchmarks set by the IAEA. The obligations cover siting, design, construction, operation, the availability of adequate financial and human resources, the assessment and verification of safety, quality

[52] *See* Mycle Schneider, *World Nuclear Industry Status as of 1 January 2018,* at https://www.worldnuclearreport.org (last visited July 11, 2018).

[53] John Carlson, "An Asia-Pacific Nuclear Energy Community," APLN/CNND *Policy Brief* No. 4 (June 2013). http://www.apln.org/?m=briefings&sm=briefings_view&seq=37.

assurance and emergency preparedness. Not all of the 70 states with significant nuclear activities have joined the Convention.[54] Asia-Pacific non-parties are Malaysia, North Korea, the Philippines (which signed on 14 October 1994 but is yet to ratify) and Thailand. There is also a lack of international standards, transparency and accountability. Many states with power reactors remain outside the liability regimes as well.

40. Nuclear security refers to measures designed to address the risks associated with theft and trafficking in nuclear and radiological materials, sabotage of nuclear facilities and the danger of terrorists acquiring and using a nuclear or radiological weapon. Because a major nuclear security incident anywhere would have far-reaching consequences, effective nuclear security is a global concern. Several worrying incidents are known to have taken place in recent years,[55] pointing to gaps in the existing national and multilateral machinery: lack of universality, binding standards, transparency and accountability mechanisms, and compulsory IAEA oversight; and insufficient attention to nuclear weapons. The terrorists who struck Brussels in March 2016 were apparently considering an attack on a nuclear power facility. The very notion of deterrence is irrelevant to groups that hold no territory or fixed assets that can be attacked in retaliation and whose members court martyrdom by suicide.

41. In the third biennial Nuclear Security Index,[56] in the theft rankings among the world's 24 states with weapons-useable nuclear materials, four or five of the six Asia Pacific countries are in the bottom half on all measures. On the risk of sabotage for 45 countries with nuclear power plants or research reactors, six or seven of the Asian countries plus Taiwan are in the bottom half of the table on all measures.

NOTE, THE PRACTICE OF PEER REVIEW IN THE INTERNATIONAL NUCLEAR SAFETY REGIME

MONICA J. WASHINGTON

72 N.Y.U. L. Rev. 430, 432–36 (1997)

The [International Atomic Energy Agency] is an autonomous intergovernmental organization within the United Nations system. Its mandate is embodied in the IAEA Statute, which defines the Agency's dual objectives as seeking to "accelerate and enlarge the contribution of atomic energy to peace, health and prosperity throughout the world [and to] ensure . . . that assistance provided by it . . . is not used in such a way as to further any military purpose." The Agency has definite statutory authority to require and recommend the observance of health and safety measures

[54] Evans, Ogilive-White and Thakur, *Nuclear Weapons: The State of Play* 2015, pp. 238–39.

[55] Ibid., Box 3.1, pp. 163–64.

[56] *NTI Nuclear Security Index: Building a Framework for Assurance, Accountability, and Action* (Washington DC: Nuclear Threat Initiative, January 2016).

and to promulgate safety standards in conjunction with some promotional activities and with safeguards. For both the Agency's own operations and for other operations making use of materials, services, equipment, facilities, and information made available through the Agency or at its request, compliance with Agency standards is mandatory. The Agency applies its standards pursuant to agreements with countries that receive assistance. With the exception of these two situations, the Agency has no power to impose its standards on any operation. States, however, are free to decide whether to adopt any or all of the Agency's standards by incorporating them into national regulatory legislation or through other means.

Although the IAEA Statute delineates a number of situations in which the Agency can legally exercise safety controls (through Agency-assisted projects or pursuant to bilateral or multilateral agreements), it has largely refrained from doing so. Instead, by establishing and encouraging the development of basic safety criteria, the Agency safety program focuses primarily on norm making and the harmonization of safety-related policies. During the early years of the Agency, the promulgation of safety standards was the principal safety-related activity it performed. The Health and Safety Document, first approved in March 1960, outlined the circumstances under which the Agency could impose health and safety controls in its projects. According to this document, the Agency could conclude agreements with states that required certain safety control features, such as periodic and special reports to the Agency, and could also dispatch safety inspectors to nuclear facilities under certain circumstances. Though a few agreements of this type were concluded, no uninvited safety inspections ever took place.

* * *

Underlying all of the Agency's hesitations [about regulating nuclear safety was] a concern about whether it [could] properly serve two masters, that is, whether it [could] simultaneously promote the peaceful use of nuclear energy worldwide and still promote safety in nuclear power plants. In this regard it is important to note that the potentially high monetary costs of implementing safety controls is often at odds with the promotion of nuclear power. Safety measures such as remote location, containment buildings, and lock-up features can multiply the capital requirements for a nuclear facility. Thus, states considering whether to embark on a nuclear power program may be dissuaded from doing so by additional expenses that may affect their competitiveness.

A second obstacle to the international regulation of nuclear power, which is conceptually related to the above discussion, is nuclear power states' misgivings regarding the application of any international standards of safety to them. Some opponents to the application of international health and safety standards maintain that the responsibility for weighing the risks and benefits of different operating procedures should be left to national governments. Some critics have argued that the safe use of nuclear energy depends upon economic, scientific, industrial, institutional, and legal factors that can vary widely among states. These critics therefore maintain that only national governments can determine the level of safety standards for domestic nuclear power operations. Another critic argues that because agreement on internationally enforced standards will only be possible at the level of the "lowest common denominator," these standards may be lower than those currently in force in some countries and thus could undermine the efforts of national regulatory regimes.

A third obstacle to the international regulation of nuclear power is the divergence of nuclear power plant designs. Nuclear power has become a major energy source, generating approximately seventeen percent of the world's total electricity. With the development of nuclear safety technology over the years, significant changes have been made in design standards and safety criteria. Today there exist considerable variations in the extent to which nuclear power plants have been upgraded in line with these advances. Older nuclear power plants, therefore, may not conform with current safety standards, and upgrading them may not be practicable. Defects in design, however, can often be compensated for by adjustments in operational procedures. Furthermore, an operator within an older plant may judge that the danger of a particular instance of noncompliance with later standards is acceptably small. The perception that any particular noncompliance with safety standards should be judged on its merits thus tends to inhibit the acceptance of uniform international standards of safety.

Differences in national priorities with respect to nuclear risk, economic allocation, and economic growth present a fourth impediment to international regulation of safety standards. The objective of safety regulation is to approach total freedom from risk or danger. For many countries, however, this may be too high a price to pay. As noted above, the Chernobyl reactor was of a type that would never have passed the stricter licensing requirements of Western states. The former USSR, however, was far more concerned with solving its energy problems than with the possibility of a nuclear accident. Many of the former Soviet republics now face the same predicament and are opting for the same alternative. Even within the West, safety standards differ in the extent to which they require overlap or redundancy to mitigate the effects of a major accident. Moreover, it is hard to prove that one regulatory approach is safer than another, and the fact that United States and European nuclear reactors differ in construction, operation, and regulation makes the drafting and monitoring of uniform standards even more difficult.

. . . [However, in the wake of Chernobyl] nuclear power facilities and nuclear power states reluctantly have recognized that safety is an international concern. Transboundary fears, public aversion to nuclear power, and the expanding activities of the Agency have helped to shape this consensus. On the other hand, states continue to resist significant intrusion on their decisionmaking power in this realm. Concerns of sovereignty, respected by the traditional role of the Agency and accentuated by design differences and diverging national priorities, all make a "frontal assault" on state-based regulation highly unlikely. . . .

* * *

[It was in this environment that the] Convention on Nuclear Safety was adopted by a Diplomatic Conference convened in Vienna from June 14–17, 1994, under the auspices of the Agency. The "first legal instrument to address directly the issue of safety of nuclear installations worldwide" entered into force on October 24, 1996, with the ratification of twenty-seven states.

THE CONVENTION ON NUCLEAR SAFETY

ODETTE JANKOWITSCH-PREVOR
Reprinted in International Nuclear Law in the Post-Chernobyl Period (OECD 2006) (originally published in 1994)

[*Eds.*—Prior to the negotiation of the Nuclear Safety Convention, a group of experts convened by the IAEA had produced a "Safety Fundaments" document that served as a kind of "template" for the Convention. Those "Safety Fundamentals," and their impact on the convention, are described here.]

The "elements for inclusion in a convention" were . . . to be drawn essentially from the principles and basic requirements contained [in the Safety Fundamentals document]: a legislative and regulatory framework, the "management" of safety, the technical aspects of safety, and verification of safety. The objectives to be achieved by the convention would also be based on the same source:

i) *a general nuclear safety objective*: "To protect individuals, society and the environment from harm by establishing and maintaining in nuclear installations effective defences against radiological hazards";

ii) *a radiation protection objective*: "To ensure that in all operational states radiation exposure within the installation or due to any planned release of radioactive material from the installation is kept below prescribed limits and as low as reasonably achievable, and to ensure mitigation of the radiological consequences of any accidents"; and as a main goal;

iii) *the technical safety objective*: "To take all reasonable practicable measures to prevent accidents in nuclear installations and to mitigate their consequences should they occur; to ensure with a high level of confidence that, for all possible accidents taken into account in the design of the installation, including those of very low probability, any radiological consequences would be minor and below prescribed limits; and to ensure that the likelihood of accidents with serious radiological consequences is extremely low."

The obligations of Parties to the convention would be derived from these "fundamental" principles: i.e. to establish a legislative and regulatory framework, which should define the discrete responsibilities of the government, the regulatory body and the operators; to take necessary measures for the education and training of the workforce; and for the safety of the nuclear facilities (including matters of siting, design, construction, commissioning, decommissioning), to require the continued surveillance of the safety of the facilities; to secure the safe operation and maintenance of the facilities; and to take necessary measures for the safe management and disposal of radioactive waste should such wastes be included in the scope of the convention.

It was clear however that a listing of general obligations defined only in terms of principles for the safe operation of nuclear installations would not suffice. If the convention was to contribute to promoting "the highest level of nuclear safety worldwide," it required a mechanism commensurate with the objectives set out.

The difficulty encountered in devising for the convention a mode of verifying compliance with the convention's obligations without introducing at the same time exceptions to the principle that the safety of nuclear power plants was primarily a question of national responsibility was resolved with the help of the convincing argument that enlightened self-interest of states in matters of nuclear safety would be stronger than any form of outside control devised under international law: this self-interest would be developed and promoted among the Contracting Parties with nuclear installations, that is the "peer group"; peer group "pressure" or "persuasion" would be effective in compelling the Parties to meet their obligations under the convention, and as a result, improve nuclear safety in all power plants. A "meeting" of all Contracting Parties would be the appropriate method of focusing these "peer group" effects.

CONVENTION ON NUCLEAR SAFETY

ARTS. 4, 5, 7, 8, 10, 14, 17, 18, & 19
June 17, 1994, 1963 UNTS 293 (Basic Document 2.11)

Article 4. Implementing Measures

Each Contracting Party shall take, within the framework of its national law, the legislative, regulatory and administrative measures and other steps necessary for implementing its obligations under this Convention.

Article 5. Reporting

Each Contracting Party shall submit for review, prior to each meeting referred to in Article 20, a report on the measures it has taken to implement each of the obligations of this Convention.

Article 7. Legislative and Regulatory Framework

1. Each Contracting Party shall establish and maintain a legislative and regulatory framework to govern the safety of nuclear installations.

2. The legislative and regulatory framework shall provide for: (i) the establishment of applicable national safety requirements and regulations; (ii) a system of licensing with regard to nuclear installations and the prohibition of the operation of a nuclear installation without a licence; (iii) a system of regulatory inspection and assessment of nuclear installations to ascertain compliance with applicable regulations and the terms of licences; (iv) the enforcement of applicable regulations and of the terms of licences, including suspension, modification or revocation.

Article 8. Regulatory Body

1. Each Contracting Party shall establish or designate a regulatory body entrusted with the implementation of the legislative and regulatory framework referred to in Article 7, and provided with adequate authority, competence and financial and human resources to fulfil its assigned responsibilities.

2. Each Contracting Party shall take the appropriate steps to ensure an effective separation between the functions of the regulatory body and those of any other body or organization concerned with the promotion or utilization of nuclear energy.

Article 10. Priority to Safety

Each Contracting Party shall take the appropriate steps to ensure that all organizations engaged in activities directly related to nuclear installations shall establish policies that give due priority to nuclear safety.

Article 14. Assessment and Verification of Safety

Each Contracting Party shall take the appropriate steps to ensure that:

(i) comprehensive and systematic safety assessments are carried out before the construction and commissioning of a nuclear installation and throughout its life. Such assessments shall be well documented, subsequently updated in the light of operating experience and significant new safety information, and reviewed under the authority of the regulatory body;

(ii) verification by analysis, surveillance, testing and inspection is carried out to ensure that the physical state and the operation of a nuclear installation continue to be in accordance with its design, applicable national safety requirements, and operational limits and conditions.

Article 17. Siting

Each Contracting Party shall take the appropriate steps to ensure that appropriate procedures are established and implemented:

(i) for evaluating all relevant site-related factors likely to affect the safety of a nuclear installation for its projected lifetime;

(ii) for evaluating the likely safety impact of a proposed nuclear installation on individuals, society and the environment;

(iii) for re-evaluating as necessary all relevant factors referred to in sub-paragraphs (i) and (ii) so as to ensure the continued safety acceptability of the nuclear installation;

(iv) for consulting Contracting Parties in the vicinity of a proposed nuclear installation, insofar as they are likely to be affected by that installation and, upon request providing the necessary information to such Contracting Parties, in order to enable them to evaluate and make their own assessment of the likely safety impact on their own territory of the nuclear installation.

Article 18. Design and Construction

Each Contracting Party shall take the appropriate steps to ensure that:

(i) the design and construction of a nuclear installation provides for several reliable levels and methods of protection (defense in depth) against the release of radioactive materials, with a view to preventing the occurrence of accidents and to mitigating their radiological consequences should they occur;

(ii) the technologies incorporated in the design and construction of a nuclear installation are proven by experience or qualified by testing or analysis;

(iii) the design of a nuclear installation allows for reliable, stable and easily manageable operation, with specific consideration of human factors and the manmachine interface.

Article 19. Operation

Each Contracting Party shall take the appropriate steps to ensure that:

(i) the initial authorization to operate a nuclear installation is based upon an appropriate safety analysis and a commissioning programme demonstrating that the installation, as constructed, is consistent with design and safety requirements;

(ii) operational limits and conditions derived from the safety analysis, tests and operational experience are defined and revised as necessary for identifying safe boundaries for operation;

(iii) operation, maintenance, inspection and testing of a nuclear installation are conducted in accordance with approved procedures;

(iv) procedures are established for responding to anticipated operational occurrences and to accidents; * * *

DISCUSSION NOTES/QUESTIONS

1. The Nuclear Safety Convention requires Contracting Parties to establish "applicable national safety requirements and regulations" (article 7) and a regulatory body (article 8) to implement those regulations. Why? The IAEA has expertise and experience. It would be more than capable of developing appropriate safety regulations and conducting inspections to verify compliance. Why not turn the job of regulation over to it? That would be a simpler and more efficient approach, would it not? Given the incompetence and corruption in some national bureaucracies, that would also be a safer approach, wouldn't it?

2. How much does the Nuclear Safety Convention say about the actual content of national safety regulations? Does it establish *any* safety minimums? Or are Contracting Parties free to do whatever they wish with respect to safety?

3. If the Nuclear Safety Convention had been in force in 1986, and if the Soviet Union had been a party, would compliance with the Convention's requirements have helped mitigate damage from the Chernobyl accident?

4. The safety of nuclear power is a much-debated question, and we will not try to answer it here. But some basic facts bear consideration.

The best modern reactor designs include many levels of safety systems that significantly reduce the risk of a nuclear accident. These safety systems are first designed to moderate the "chain reaction" of neutrons that split the fissionable uranium (or other nuclear fuel) and release heat. The moderating devices, "control rods" made of neutron-absorbing materials, can be quickly lowered into place between rods of fissionable uranium so that the production of energy in the reactor can be slowed, reducing the amount of heat that the reactor produces. A backup electric generator is used to supply power to the plant in the case of an emergency where electric power to the plant is interrupted, or plant operators would otherwise be unable to control the plant. In addition to the control rods and the backup power supply, more than one cooling system is installed, ensuring that the reactor core is kept from melting, losing its structural integrity and then fissioning uncontrollably—"melting down." They are designed to provide enough coolant to bring the core under control, to stop the plant from generating electricity, and thereby allow repairs to be undertaken. Finally, the reactor cores of most western style nuclear power plants are surrounded by a steel and concrete containment enclosure designed to withstand the force of any explosions that might accompany a "melt down." This last level of containment is aimed at lessening the environmental effects of an accident.

With the implementation of these technologies, the U.S. Nuclear Regulatory Commission (NRC) issued its 1977 Rassmussen Report, which found there was only a remote possibility of a nuclear reactor accident in a U.S. commercial power plant that could have serious environmental effects. Less than two years later, Three Mile Island (TMI) Unit 2 experienced a serious accident with some release of radioactive material beyond the containment structure, although most studies have concluded that the release was not significant enough to cause serious harm. Had the accident occurred in a reactor without a containment dome, like the reactors at the Chernobyl plant, the impact of the accident might have been much worse.

Thus, while good plant design can obviously enhance nuclear safety, a major contributing factor to the TMI accident and the Chernobyl catastrophe was human error and poor judgment. No amount of legal regulation can eliminate such factors, although legally mandated operator training can significantly reduce the risk.

And, of course, as the next note illustrates, it would be foolish to underestimate the power of nature and the possibility that a natural disaster could trigger a corresponding nuclear disaster.

5. On March 11, 2011, following a 9.0 magnitude earthquake, a huge tsunami swamped the Fukushima I Nuclear Power Plant on the eastern coast of Japan. Several nuclear power facilities around Japan were affected by tsunami waves but managed to shut down successfully. The situation at Fukushima Dai-ichi was different. The tsunami was more than 20 feet higher than the sea wall built to protect the six reactors at the plant, and the entire complex was flooded. All power sources were lost except for one emergency

diesel generator which provided emergency power to two of the six reactors; all control systems went down at reactors 1–4.

Only three reactors were operational at the time of the earthquake, but without cooling systems operating, the reactors and spent fuel overheated, causing a series of explosions that led to significant releases of radiological contamination into the environment. Three reactors experienced meltdown. Japan evacuated areas within 30 kilometers of the plant and restricted the distribution or consumption of certain foods in specific regions. Nonetheless, because the Fukushima reactors were inside containment structures, the radiation release was far less significant than the release in Chernobyl. *See* IAEA International Fact Finding Expert Mission of the Fukushima Dai-ichi NPP Accident Following the Great East Japan Earthquake and Tsunami, 24 May—2 June 2011, *Report to the IAEA Member States* (16 June 2011).

An IAEA Fact Finding Mission examined the causes of the Fukushima disaster and concluded that "there were insufficient defence-in-depth provisions for tsunami hazards" at the plant, even though the risk had been considered during the site evaluation and design of the plant. They recommended "an updating of [Japan's] regulatory requirements and guidelines" in line with "the relevant IAEA Safety Standards for comprehensively coping with earthquakes and tsunamis and external flooding and, in general, all correlated external events." They also stated expressly the somewhat obvious (in retrospect) conclusion: "There is a need to ensure that in considering external natural hazards: the siting and design of nuclear plants should include sufficient protection against infrequent and complex combinations of external events . . .—specifically those that can cause site flooding and which may have longer term impacts. . . ." *Id.* at 13–16.

As of this writing, the problems at Fukushima Dai-ichi are ongoing, but the situation is improving. As radiation levels fall, people are returning to their homes in towns and hamlets within the original 12-mile exclusion zone around the plant. In June 2018, Japan reported that radiation levels in seawater and groundwater were within safety margins established by government regulations. *See* IAEA, *Fukushima Daiichi Status Updates*, available at https://www.iaea.org (last visited July 11, 2018).

6. Quite apart from natural disasters, modern technology poses its own challenges. Instrumentation and control (I & C) systems are vital to nuclear safety, providing protection, control, supervision, and monitoring for nuclear power plants. The nuclear industry is beginning to face issues related to the updating of its analog I & C systems to digital I & C systems. Globally, 30 countries worldwide are operating 449 nuclear reactors for electricity generation and dozens of new nuclear plants are under construction. *See* Nuclear Energy Institute, World Statistics: Nuclear Energy Around the World (April 2017). And every one of those plants for which construction commenced post-1990 incorporates digital instrumentation and control. Issues for concern include not only common mishaps associated with digital information systems (such as the system error that forced the Hatch nuclear power plant in Georgia

into an emergency shutdown on March 7, 2008), but also the possibility of cyber-terrorism. For further discussion, *see* IAEA, *Instrumentation and Control (I & C) Systems in Nuclear Power Plants: A Time of Transition,* in Nuclear Technology Review 2008, Annex V, at 84 (2008).

7. Finally, in the world we live in today, we must worry about deliberate sabotage of nuclear facilities, including the theft of nuclear material for use in terrorist activities. The IAEA has led extensive international efforts to address these threats. Applicable treaties include the Convention on the Physical Protection of Nuclear Material and the International Convention for the Suppression of Acts of Nuclear Terrorism **(Basic Document 7.23)**.

8. In addition to the IAEA, there are two other multinational organizations that actively address nuclear issues: the Nuclear Energy Agency (NEA) of the Organization of Economic Cooperation and Development (OECD) and the European Atomic Energy Community (EURATOM). The NEA represents the industrialized market economy countries with the most advanced nuclear programs. EURATOM represents certain European countries only.

PROBLEM 10-2: A NUCLEAR ACCIDENT IN AZYKHSTAN

Section 1. Facts

Azykhstan's nuclear power program. Azykhstan, once part of the former Soviet Union, is an independent republic of some 17 million people located in Central Asia. Mountainous, with very harsh winters and relatively mild summers, it is quite highly developed, with a thriving agricultural sector, an abundance of natural resources, a per capita income in excess of $9,000 a year, and a near 100% adult literacy rate.

Three years ago, Azykhstan announced plans to develop a nuclear energy industry. To this end, it built a gas centrifuge uranium enrichment plant and authorized Elektrikon, its leading private energy company, to build a large nuclear power plant at the city of Yadersk.

Osteuria's objections. Azykhstan's plans were loudly protested by the Government of Osteuria, Azykhstan's economically and technologically advanced Eastern European neighbor to the west. Relations between Azykhstan and Osteuria have been strained for many years, primarily because Azykhstan claims that Scissuria, a resource rich province in eastern Osteuria, rightfully belongs to Azykhstan. In the past, Azykhstan has threatened to "recover" Scissuria by force, but has been deterred by its belief—neither confirmed nor denied by Osteuria—that Osteuria has a stockpile of nuclear weapons left over from the days when it was a Soviet Republic.

In opposing Azykhstan's nuclear energy plans, Osteurian leaders have expressed their belief that Azykhstan intends to develop nuclear weapons, that the already completed uranium enrichment facility would be used to produce weapons-grade uranium, and that the proposed power plant would be operated also to produce weapons-grade plutonium. Further, Osteuria has expressed concern about the risk of a nuclear accident in Azykhstan, pointing out that Azykhstan is one of the most seismologically active regions on Earth and that the prevailing winds in Azykhstan blow from east to west, i.e., toward Osteuria.

The IAEA gets involved. In response to Osteuria's concerns, Azykhstan agreed to inspections by the Vienna-based International Atomic Energy Agency (IAEA). The IAEA inspectors found no evidence that Azykhstan was enriching uranium to the levels required to produce nuclear weapons. Furthermore, they reported that Azykhstan had sited its proposed nuclear power plant at a location where the risk of significant seismic activity was relatively low.

Osteuria's warning. Despite the favorable IAEA inspection report, the Osteurian government continued to condemn Azykhstan's nuclear program, calling it an "unacceptable security risk to Osteuria" and warning Azykhstan to end the program or "face the consequences."

Azykhstan constructs the Yadersk facility. Ignoring Osteuria's warnings, Azykhstan authorized continued operation of the uranium enrichment facility and completion of the nuclear power plant at Yadersk. Elektrikon engaged Kernkraft, Ltd., an experienced nuclear plant construction company headquartered in Friesland, a technologically advanced western European country, to provide equipment design and construction services for the nuclear power plant project. Previously, Kernkraft had constructed the uranium enrichment facility.

Kernkraft provided a pressurized water reactor (PWR) for the Yadersk plant—i.e., a light water reactor in which the water is kept from boiling by maintaining high pressure inside the reactor. For safety, the Kernkraft design included a steel and concrete containment structure commonly used in nuclear plants throughout western Europe. In addition, Kernkraft installed sophisticated computer software of its own design that was programmed to monitor continuously the technical aspects of the plant's operation so as to reduce human error.

The project was completed expeditiously, and passed Azykhstani safety and licensing tests early last year. Before beginning operation of the plant, however, Azykhstan invited the IAEA to inspect the plant, and thereafter a team of senior regulators and technical experts from seven IAEA member states spent several days at the plant before issuing a report deeming it safe to operate. Azykhstan also created a new government office, the Office of Nuclear Safety (ONS), a division of the Ministry of Energy, to provide ongoing regulatory oversight of the Yadersk plant and any other plants that might be built in the future.

The Yadersk plant is damaged by an earthquake. The plant began operating on July 1 of last year. Later, in November, a minor earthquake cracked the foundation on which the Yadersk plant was built. Elektrikon reported to the Azykhstani Office of Nuclear Safety that the weakening of support structures in the foundation could compromise the outer containment shell of the power station in the event of an explosion or major seismic activity. Elektrikon also stated that the power station would need to be shut down for six to eight weeks to allow for repairs to the foundation, resulting in a 30% overall decline in electricity availability in Azykhstan.

The head of ONS met with the Azykhstani Minister of Energy to discuss the matter. Fearing that such a significant loss of electricity would lead to political unrest, particularly at the beginning of winter, and given the successful operation of the safety systems to date, the Energy Minister directed the head of ONS to authorize Elektrikon to forego the repairs until the following summer.

A nuclear disaster at Yadersk. On February 15 of this year, at 1:00 p.m. Azykhstani time, disaster struck at the Yadersk plant. The computer control systems at both the uranium enrichment facility and the nuclear power plant unexpectedly froze, locking facility employees out of the operating system. As power plant technicians attempted to regain control of the operating systems, a pressure spike at 9:00 p.m. produced an explosion in the cooling system which, in turn, ruptured the containment structure and caused the reactor to overheat resulting in a "melt down" and the release of a steady stream of smoke, gas, and radiation.

The Yadersk plant's operators informed the Azykhstan Ministry of Energy of the disaster at 4:00 a.m. on February 16, Azykhstan time. After confirming the report, and fearing widespread radioactive contamination, the Government of Azykhstan quickly moved to evacuate all inhabitants from the area and to destroy all local milk supplies and fresh produce. At 3:00 p.m., on February 16, the Azykhstan's Ministry of Energy informed the IAEA and neighboring countries of the possibility of radioactive contamination.

Upon learning officially of the accident, the Government of Osteuria mobilized its health care and military services to check its population and livestock for contamination. Additionally, it issued large quantities of iodide tablets to its people to combat possible health effects and ordered the destruction of all unsheltered agricultural produce and fresh milk supplies. It also destroyed large numbers of animals and crops over a wide area and paid compensation to the farmers who owned them. Finally, expensive measures were instituted to monitor the health of the population, so far as its exposure to radiation was concerned.

Azykhstani hospitals quickly became overwhelmed by the number of people seeking medical treatment. Azykhstan contacted Osteuria and

requested that it send health care workers to assist in treating injured workers and radiation-exposed citizens. Azykhstan also requested that its citizens be allowed to cross the border into Osteuria to receive treatment at Osteurian hospitals. Osteuria declined both requests, however, explaining that its emergency personnel and hospitals were fully occupied dealing with Osteurian casualties. In the end, 500 Azykhstani citizens died of radiation poisoning; in Osteuria, 30 people suffered symptoms of radiation sickness, but all recovered.

A joint investigation of the accident by the IAEA and Azykhstani authorities concluded that the computer shutdown was caused by a computer worm that infected the computer systems of the nuclear facilities from laptop computers of Kernkraft engineers used during initial tests of both systems. There was no evidence that any Kernkraft or Elektrikon employee was aware of the worm, and it lay dormant until it attacked and disabled the computer systems in the middle of the night on February 15. By itself, this disabling of the computer system would have damaged the facilities severely and prevented their operation for weeks; but it would not have caused any release of radioactivity, even coupled with the explosion at the power plant, if the containment structure had not been weakened by the earthquake-caused damage to the plant's foundation.

Lawsuits are filed and dismissed. Legal actions were filed in an Azykhstani court against Elektrikon and the Azykhstani Ministry of Energy. The court dismissed the actions on the ground that neither Elektrikon nor the Government of Azykhstan could be held liable for the accident, which was due either to a defect in software supplied by Kernkraft or to a terrorist act by a person or persons unknown. Asykhstan's highest court affirmed this dismissal.

Nuclear sabatoge is revealed. Shortly after the case was dismissed, top secret Osteurian government documents were leaked and posted on Wikileaks. Those documents revealed that the worm that attacked the Azykhstani facilities was created by a computer espionage team within Osteurian military intelligence headed by Igor Dahi, an Osteurian military officer. An Azykhstani court has issued an arrest warrant for Dahi on suspicion of nuclear sabotage, but Osteuria has refused to turn him over. Azykhstan also has claimed $1 billion in compensation from Osteuria for damage to its nuclear facilities.

For its part, Osteuria has disavowed any responsibility for the actions of Dahi, who it says was a "rogue agent" acting without authority. It has also protested the Azykhstani court's denial of its citizen's suits for damages, and is seeking $10 billion in compensation from Azykhstan to recover for injuries to its citizens as well as the costs of preventive and decontamination measures it took in the wake of the accident at the Yadersk plant.

A Commission of Inquiry is established. After several months of fruitless diplomatic exchanges, and on the verge of armed conflict, Azyhkstan and Osteuria agreed to bring their dispute before a Commission of Inquiry appointed by the UN Secretary General. The Commission of Inquiry is charged with making "formal recommendations to the parties aimed at resolving the matter consistently with international law." Both countries are members of the United Nations and the IAEA. Also, both are party to the Vienna Convention on Civil Liability for Nuclear Damage **(Basic Document 2.12)**; the Nuclear Non-Proliferation Treaty (NPT) **(Basic Document 7.18)**; the IAEA Convention on Early Notification of a Nuclear Accident **(Basic Document 2.9)**; the IAEA Convention on Assistance in the Case of Nuclear Accident or Radiological Emergency **(Basic Document 2.10)**; the 1994 Convention on Nuclear Safety **(Basic Document 2.11)**; and the 2005 International Convention for the Suppression of Acts of Nuclear Terrorism **(Basic Document 7.23)**.

Section 2. Questions Presented

1. Did Azykhstan violate any of its international legal obligations relating to the safety of the Yadersk nuclear power plant? If so, to what damages or other relief is Osteuria entitled?

2. Did Azykhstan violate the IAEA Notification Convention? If so, to what damages or other relief is Osteuria entitled?

3. Did Osteuria violate the IAEA Assistance Convention? If so, to what damages or other relief is Azykhstan entitled?

4. Does Osteuria bear state responsibility for the actions of Igor Dahi? If so, to what damages or other relief is Azykhstan entitled?

5. Does Osteuria have a legal obligation to extradite Dahi to Azykhstan?

Section 3. Assignments

A. Reading Assignment

Study the Readings presented in Section 4, *infra,* and the Discussion Notes/Questions that follow.

B. Recommended Writing Assignment

Prepare a comprehensive, logically sequenced and *argumentative* brief in the form of an outline of the primary and subsidiary *legal* issues you see requiring resolution by the Commission of Inquiry. Also, from the perspective of an independent objective judge, indicate which side ought to prevail on each issue and why. Retain a copy of your issue-outline/brief for class discussion.

C. Recommended Oral Assignment

Assume you are legal counsel for Azykhstan or Osteuria (as designated by your instructor); then, relying upon the Readings (and your issue-outline if prepared), present a 15–20 minute oral argument of your government's case to the members of the Commission of Inquiry.

D. Recommended Reflective Assignment

Consider (and recommend) alternative norms, institutions, and/or procedures that you believe might do better than existing world order arrangements to contend with situations of the kind posed by this problem. In so doing, but without insisting upon *immediate* feasibility, identify the particular transition steps that would be needed to make your alternatives a reality.

Section 4. Readings

(a) Nuclear Safety

1. Review the excerpts from the Convention on Nuclear Safety, arts. 4, 5, 7, 8, 10, 14, 17, 18, & 19, supra.

2. IAEA Action Plan on Nuclear Safety, approved by the IAEA Board of Governors on 13 September 2011 and endorsed by the IAEA General Conference during its 55th regular session, 22 September 2011.

Strengthening nuclear safety in light of the [Fukushima] accident is addressed through a number of measures proposed in this Action Plan including {the following:]

Safety assessments in the light of the accident at TEPCO's Fukushima Daiichi Nuclear Power Station

Undertake assessment of the safety vulnerabilities of nuclear power plants in the light of lessons learned to date from the accident

- Member States to promptly undertake a national assessment of the design of nuclear power plants against site specific extreme natural hazards and to implement the necessary corrective actions in a timely manner.

* * *

Emergency preparedness and response

Strengthen emergency preparedness and response

- Member States to conduct a prompt national review and thereafter regular reviews of their emergency preparedness and response arrangements and capabilities, with the IAEA Secretariat providing support and assistance through Emergency Preparedness Review (EPREV) missions, as requested.

- The IAEA Secretariat, Member States and relevant international organizations to review and strengthen the international emergency preparedness and response framework . . . .

* * *

National regulatory bodies

Strengthen the effectiveness of national regulatory bodies

- Member States to conduct a prompt national review and thereafter regular reviews of their regulatory bodies, including an assessment of their effective independence, adequacy of human and financial resources and the need for appropriate technical and scientific support, to fulfil their responsibilities.

* * *

International legal framework

Improve the effectiveness of the international legal framework

- States parties to explore mechanisms to enhance the effective implementation of the Convention on Nuclear Safety, the Joint Convention on the Safety of Spent Fuel Management and the Safety of Radioactive Waste Management, the Convention on the Early Notification of a Nuclear Accident and the Convention on Assistance in the Case of a Nuclear Accident or Radiological Emergency, and to consider proposals made to amend the Convention on Nuclear Safety and the Convention on the Early Notification of a Nuclear Accident.
- Member States to be encouraged to join and effectively implement these Conventions.
- Member States to work towards establishing a global nuclear liability regime that addresses the concerns of all States that might be affected by a nuclear accident with a view to providing appropriate compensation for nuclear damage. The IAEA International Expert Group on Nuclear Liability (INLEX) to recommend actions to facilitate achievement of such a global regime. Member States to give due consideration to the possibility of joining the international nuclear liability instruments as a step toward achieving such a global regime.

Member States planning to embark on a nuclear power programme

Facilitate the development of the infrastructure necessary for Member States embarking on a nuclear power programme

- Member States to create an appropriate nuclear infrastructure based on IAEA Safety Standards and other relevant guidance, and the IAEA Secretariat to provide assistance as may be requested.
- Member States to voluntarily host Integrated Nuclear Infrastructure Reviews (INIR) and relevant peer review missions, including site and design safety reviews, prior to commissioning the first nuclear power plant.

* * *

Protection of people and the environment from ionizing radiation

Ensure the on-going protection of people and the environment from ionizing radiation following a nuclear emergency

- Member States, the IAEA Secretariat and other relevant stakeholders to facilitate the use of available information, expertise and techniques for monitoring, decontamination and remediation both on and off nuclear sites and the IAEA Secretariat to consider strategies and programmes to improve knowledge and strengthen capabilities in these areas.
- Member States, the IAEA Secretariat and other relevant stakeholders to facilitate the use of available information, expertise and techniques regarding the removal of damaged nuclear fuel and the management and disposal of radioactive waste resulting from a nuclear emergency.
- Member States, the IAEA Secretariat and other relevant stakeholders to share information regarding the assessment of radiation doses and any associated impacts on people and the environment.

Communication and information dissemination

Enhance transparency and effectiveness of communication and improve dissemination of information

- Member States, with the assistance of the IAEA Secretariat, to strengthen the emergency notification system, and reporting and information sharing arrangements and capabilities.
- Member States, with the assistance of the IAEA Secretariat, to enhance the transparency and effectiveness of communication among operators, regulators and various international organizations, and strengthen the IAEA's coordinating role in this regard, underlining that the freest possible flow and wide dissemination of safety related technical and technological information enhances nuclear safety. * * *

3. 2015 Vienna Declaration on Nuclear Safety, CNS/DC/2015/2/Rev.1

THE CONTRACTING PARTIES TO THE CONVENTION ON NUCLEAR SAFETY

(i) *taking into account* the significant number of efforts and initiatives taken place after the accident at the Fukushima Daiichi Nuclear Power Plant on a national, regional and international level, to enhance nuclear safety;

(ii) *noting* changes adopted in the Guidance Documents INFCIRC/571, 572 and 573 to strengthen the review process of the Convention on Nuclear Safety (hereinafter referred to as CNS);

(iii) *recalling* the observations of the Contracting Parties of the CNS at the 2nd Extraordinary Meeting in 2012, confirmed at the 6th Review Meeting in 2014, that the displacement of people and the land contamination after a nuclear accident call for all national regulators to identify provisions to prevent and mitigate the potential for severe accidents with off-site consequences;

(iv) *reaffirming* the fundamental safety principles provided by the CNS and the commitment it entails to the continuous improvement of the implementation of these principles;

(v) *aware of* the world-wide Action Plan on Nuclear Safety endorsed by all Member States of the International Atomic Energy Agency in September 2011; and,

(vi) *having considered* the proposal by the Swiss Confederation to amend Article 18 of the CNS presented at the 6th Review Meeting of the CNS;

have adopted the following principles to guide them, as appropriate, in the implementation of the objective of the CNS to prevent accidents with radiological consequences and mitigate such consequences should they occur:

1. New nuclear power plants are to be designed, sited, and constructed, consistent with the objective of preventing accidents in the commissioning and operation and, should an accident occur, mitigating possible releases of radionuclides causing long-term off site contamination and avoiding early radioactive releases or radioactive releases large enough to require long-term protective measures and actions.

2. Comprehensive and systematic safety assessments are to be carried out periodically and regularly for existing installations throughout their lifetime in order to identify safety improvements that are oriented to meet the above objective. Reasonably practicable or achievable safety improvements are to be implemented in a timely manner.

3. National requirements and regulations for addressing this objective throughout the lifetime of nuclear power plants are to take into account the relevant IAEA Safety Standards and, as appropriate, other good practices as identified *inter alia* in the Review Meetings of the CNS.

The Contracting Parties to the CNS further decide that:

* * *

(2) With immediate effect, these principles should be reflected in the actions of Contracting Parties, in particular when preparing their reports on the implementation of the CNS, with special focus on Article 18 as well as other relevant Articles, including Articles 6, 14, 17 and 19, starting with the national reports to be submitted by Contracting Parties for consideration during the 7th Review Meeting of the CNS. * * *

4. IAEA Safety Standards: General Safety Requirements Part 1, No. GSR Part 1 (Rev. 1), Governmental, Legal and Regulatory Framework for Safety vii–viii (IAEA 2016)

Regulating safety is a national responsibility. However, radiation risks may transcend national borders, and international cooperation serves to promote and enhance safety globally by exchanging experience and by improving capabilities to control hazards, to prevent accidents, to respond to emergencies and to mitigate any harmful consequences.

States have an obligation of diligence and duty of care, and are expected to fulfil their national and international undertakings and obligations.

International safety standards provide support for States in meeting their obligations under general principles of international law, such as those relating to environmental protection. International safety standards also promote and assure confidence in safety and facilitate international commerce and trade.

A global nuclear safety regime is in place and is being continuously improved. IAEA safety standards, which support the implementation of binding international instruments and national safety infrastructures, are a cornerstone of this global regime. The IAEA safety standards constitute a useful tool for contracting parties to assess their performance under these international conventions.

* * *

The IAEA safety standards reflect an international consensus on what constitutes a high level of safety for protecting people and the environment from harmful effects of ionizing radiation. . . .

Requirement 3: Establishment of a regulatory body

The government, through the legal system, shall establish and maintain a regulatory body, and shall confer on it the legal authority and provide it with the competence and the resources necessary to fulfil its statutory obligation for the regulatory control of facilities and activities.

Requirement 4: Independence of the regulatory body

The government shall ensure that the regulatory body is effectively independent in its safety related decision making and that it has functional separation from entities having responsibilities or interests that could unduly influence its decision making.

2.7. An independent regulatory body will not be entirely separate from other governmental bodies. The government has the ultimate responsibility for involving those with legitimate and recognized interests in its decision making. However, the government shall ensure that the regulatory body is able to make decisions under its statutory obligation for the regulatory control of facilities and activities, and that it is able to perform its functions without undue pressure or constraint.

2.8. To be effectively independent from undue influences on its decision making, the regulatory body: (a) Shall have sufficient authority and sufficient competent staff; (b) Shall have access to sufficient financial resources for the proper and timely discharge of its assigned responsibilities; (c) Shall be able to make independent regulatory judgements and regulatory decisions, at all stages in the lifetime of facilities and the duration of activities until release from regulatory control, under operational states and in accidents; (d) Shall be free from any pressures associated with political circumstances or economic conditions, or pressures from government departments, authorized parties or other organizations; (e) Shall be able to give independent advice and provide reports to government departments and governmental bodies on matters relating to the safety of facilities and activities. This includes access to the highest levels of government; (f) Shall be able to liaise directly with regulatory bodies of other States and with international organizations to promote cooperation and the exchange of regulatory related information and experience. * * *

Requirement 17: Effective independence in the performance of regulatory functions

The regulatory body shall perform its functions in a manner that does not compromise its effective independence.

* * *

4.10. The regulatory body, consistent with its effective independence, shall exercise its authority to intervene in connection with any facilities or activities that present significant radiation risks, irrespective of the possible costs to the authorized party.

* * *

Requirement 31: Requiring of corrective action by authorized parties

In the event that risks are identified, including risks unforeseen in the authorization process, the regulatory body shall require corrective actions to be taken by authorized parties.

(b) Notification and Assistance

5. Edith Brown Weiss, Environmental Disasters in International Law, 1986 Ann. Jur. Interam. 141, 145–50 (1986)

A State in which a major environmental disaster occurs has the duty to minimize the damage to the human environment. At a minimum this requires that a State promptly notify countries that may be affected, provide available information about the course of the accident, and inform affected States of measures it is taking to reduce the damage. States must also take necessary and practicable steps to prevent or reduce injury to other States from the accident. They must do so for both natural and man-induced disasters, although the State may bear no responsibility for injury caused by the natural disaster. Those States potentially affected by an environmental disaster have an obligation to cooperate in minimizing the damage. The failure to do so on their own territory may be a defense available to the State in which the accident occurred, if claims for reparation are made against it. . . .

The duty to minimize damage from environmental disasters derives from the principle of State responsibility. Principle 21 of the Stockholm Declaration on the Human Environment . . . reflects customary international law. Support for it is contained in the resolution of earlier disputes, such as the Trail Smelter Arbitration, and in the multitude of international agreements which implement it. The U.S. Restatement on Foreign Relations Law confirms this obligation of States to "reduce and control" injury to the environment of other States and areas beyond national jurisdiction.

There are four aspects to the duty to minimize damage: the duty to notify promptly; the duty to provide information to potentially affected States; the duty to develop contingency plans; and the duty to cooperate in minimizing damage, as by providing emergency assistance.

6. Norbert Pelzer, Learning the Hard Way: Did the Lessons Taught by the Chernobyl Nuclear Accident Contribute to Improving Nuclear Law?, in International Nuclear Law in the Post-Chernobyl Period 78–83 (OECD 2006)

After the Chernobyl accident, the Soviet Union gave relevant information on the accident belatedly, if at all. Because of lack of information, affected states could not take timely measures to mitigate the radiological consequences. From a legal point of view, it was most difficult to identify an obligation of the Soviet Union to provide timely and appropriate information to other states. Under international custom, the principle of good neighbourliness could be a basis for requesting information but it is a vague concept which, in practice, requires readiness to co-operate. * * * [T]he 1941 Trail-Smelter-Arbitration principle that there is "the responsibility (of States) to ensure that activities under their jurisdiction or control do not cause damage to the environment of other States or areas beyond the limits of national jurisdiction" . . . is [also] too vague to serve as a legal basis for establishing a right on the notification of a nuclear accident.

The 1986 Convention on Early Notification of a Nuclear Accident aims at filling this gap in international law.

7. IAEA Convention on Early Notification of a Nuclear Accident, arts. 1, 2 & 5, Sept. 26, 1986, 1439 UNTS 275 (Basic Document 2.9)

Article 1 Scope of application

1. This Convention shall apply in the event of any accident involving [nuclear] facilities or activities of a State Party or of persons or legal entities under its jurisdiction or control . . . from which a release of radioactive material occurs or is likely to occur and which has resulted or may result in an international transboundary release that could be of radiological safety significance for another State.

* * *

Article 2 Notification and information

In the event of an accident specified in article 1 (hereinafter referred to as a "nuclear accident"), the State Party refeired to in that article shall:

(a) forthwith notify, directly or through the International Atomic Energy Agency (hereinafter referred to as the "Agency"), those States which are or may be physically affected as specified in article 1 and the Agency of the nuclear accident, its nature, the time of its occurrence and its exact location where appropriate; and

(b) promptly provide the States referred to in sub-paragraph (a), directly or through the Agency, and the Agency with such available information relevant to minimizing the radiological consequences in those States . . . .

8. Norbert Pelzer, Learning the Hard Way: Did the Lessons Taught by the Chernobyl Nuclear Accident Contribute to Improving Nuclear Law?, in International Nuclear Law in the Post-Chernobyl Period 78–83 (OECD 2006)

Mutual assistance is a more complex issue than early notification. It implies problems of state sovereignty, immunities and privileges, liability and last but not least of money. Consequently, it is not at all surprising that at the time of the Chernobyl accident there was no instrument on assistance available to be applied to the accident if assistance had been requested. The 1986 Convention [on Assistance in the Case of a Nuclear Accident or Radiological Emergency] therefore filled a gap that was perhaps more relevant and that was more difficult to close than the gap regarding early notification.

9. IAEA Convention on Assistance in the Case of a Nuclear Accident or Radiological Emergency, art. 2, Sept. 26, 1986, 1457 UNTS 133 (Basic Document 2.10)

Article 2 Provision of assistance

1. If a State Party needs assistance in the event of a nuclear accident or radiological emergency, whether or not such accident or emergency originates within its territory, jurisdiction or control, it may call for such assistance from any other State Party, directly or through the Agency, and from the Agency, or, where appropriate, from other international intergovernmental organizations (hereinafter referred to as "international organizations").

2. A State Party requesting assistance shall specify the scope and type of assistance required and, where practicable, provide the assisting party with such information as may be necessary for that party to determine the extent to which it is able to meet the request. In the event that it is not practicable for the requesting State Party to specify the scope and type of assistance required, the requesting State Party and the assisting party shall, in consultation, decide upon the scope and type of assistance required.

3. Each State Party to which a request for such assistance is directed shall promptly decide and notify the requesting State Party, directly or through the Agency, whether it is in a position to render the assistance requested, and the scope and terms of the assistance that might be rendered.

4. States Parties shall, within the limits of their capabilities, identify and notify the Agency of experts, equipment and materials which could be made available for the provision of assistance to other States Parties in the

event of a nuclear accident or radiological emergency as well as (he tc ms, especially financial, under which such assistance could be provided.

5. Any State Party may request assistance relating to medical treatment or temporary relocation into the territory of another State Party of people involved in a nuclear accident or radiological emergency.

6. The Agency shall respond, in accordance with its Statute and as provided for in this Convention, to a requesting State Party's or a Member State's request for assistance in the event of a nuclear accident or radiological emergency by:

(a) making available appropriate resources allocated for this purpose;

(b) transmitting promptly the request to other States and international organizations which, according to the Agency's information, may possess the necessary resources; and

(c) if so requested by the requesting State, co-ordinating the assistance at the international level which may thus become available.

(c) Liability and Compensation

10. Vienna Convention on Civil Liability for Nuclear Damage (as amended September 12, 1997), arts. I, II, III, IV, V, VII, & XI, 2241 UNTS 270 (Basic Document 2.12)

Article I

1. For the purposes of this Convention . . .

(a) "Person" means any individual, partnership, any private or public body whether corporate or not, any international organization enjoying legal personality under the law of the Installation State, and any State or any of its constituent sub-divisions.

* * *

(c) "Operator," in relation to a nuclear installation, means the person designated or recognized by the Installation State as the operator of that installation.

* * *

(e) "Law of the competent court" means the law of the court having jurisdiction under this Convention, including any rules of such law relating to conflict of laws.

* * *

(k) "Nuclear Damage" means—

(i) loss of life or personal injury;

(ii) loss of or damage to property;

and each of the following to the extent determined by the law of the competent court—

(iii) economic loss arising from loss or damage referred to in sub-paragraph (i) or (ii), insofar as not included in those sub-paragraphs, if incurred by a person entitled to claim in respect of such loss or damage;

(iv) the costs of measures of reinstatement of impaired environment, unless such impairment is insignificant, if such measures are actually taken or to be taken, and insofar as not included in sub-paragraph (ii);

(v) loss of income deriving from an economic interest in any use or enjoyment of the environment, incurred as a result of a significant impairment of that environment, and insofar as not included in sub- paragraph (ii);

(vi) the costs of preventive measures, and further loss or damage caused by such measures;

(vii) any other economic loss, other than any caused by the impairment of the environment, if permitted by the general law on civil liability of the competent court . . . .

(*l*) "Nuclear incident" means any occurrence or series of occurrences having the same origin which causes nuclear damage . . . .

* * *

Article II

1. The operator of a nuclear installation shall be liable for nuclear damage upon proof that such damage has been caused by a nuclear incident in his nuclear installation . . .

* * *

Article IV

1. The liability of the operator for nuclear damage under this Convention shall be absolute.

2. If the operator proves that the nuclear damage resulted wholly or partly either from the gross negligence of the person suffering the damage or from an act or omission of such person done with intent to cause damage, the competent court may, if its law so provides, relieve the operator wholly or partly from his obligation to pay compensation in respect of the damage suffered by such person.

3. No liability under this Convention shall attach to an operator if he proves that the nuclear damage is directly due to an act of armed conflict, hostilities, civil war or insurrection.

* * *

Article V

1. The liability of the operator may be limited by the Installation State for any one nuclear incident, either

(a) to not less than 300 million SDRs; or

(b) to not less than 150 million SDRs provided that in excess of that amount and up to at least 300 million SDRs public funds shall be made available by that State to compensate nuclear damage; or

(c) for a maximum of 15 years from the date of entry into force of this Protocol, to a transitional amount of not less than 100 million SDRs in respect of a nuclear incident occurring within that period. An amount lower than 100 million SDRs may be established, provided that public funds shall be made available by that State to compensate nuclear damage between that lesser amount and 100 million SDRs.

* * *

Article VII

1. (a) The operator shall be required to maintain insurance or other financial security covering his liability for nuclear damage in such amount, of such type and in such terms as the Installation State shall specify. The Installation State shall ensure the payment of claims for compensation for nuclear damage which have been established against the operator by providing the necessary funds to the extent that the yield of insurance or other financial security is inadequate to satisfy such claims, but not in excess of the limit, if any, established pursuant to Article V.

* * *

Article XI

1. Except as otherwise provided in this Article, jurisdiction over actions under Article II shall lie only with the courts of the Contracting Party within whose territory the nuclear incident occurred.

(d) State Responsibility

11. International Law Commission, Draft Articles on the Responsibility of States for Internationally Wrongful Acts, arts. 1–3 & 28–37, Aug. 3, 2001, Report on the Work of its Fifty-third Session, UN Doc A/56/10 and Corr 1, at 43–58 (2001) (Basic Document 1.15)

Article 1. Responsibility of a State for its internationally wrongful acts

Every internationally wrongful act of a State entails the international responsibility of that State.

Article 2. Elements of an internationally wrongful act of a State

There is an internationally wrongful act of a State when conduct consisting of an action or omission: (a) is attributable to the State under international law; and (b) constitutes a breach of an international obligation of the State.

Article 4. Conduct of organs of a State

1. The conduct of any State organ shall be considered an act of that State under international law, whether the organ exercises legislative, executive, judicial or any other functions, whatever position it holds in the organization of the State, and whatever its character as an organ of the central Government or of a territorial unit of the State.

2. An organ includes any person or entity which has that status in accordance with the internal law of the State.

Article 5. Conduct of persons or entities exercising elements of governmental authority

The conduct of a person or entity which is not an organ of the State under article 4 but which is empowered by the law of that State to exercise elements of the governmental authority shall be considered an act of the State under international law, provided the person or entity is acting in that capacity in the particular instance.

Article 8. Conduct directed or controlled by a State

The conduct of a person or group of persons shall be considered an act of a State under international law if the person or group of persons is in fact acting on the instructions of, or under the direction or control of, that State in carrying out the conduct.

Article 12. Existence of a breach of an international obligation

There is a breach of an international obligation by a State when an act of that State is not in conformity with what is required of it by that obligation, regardless of its origin or character.

12. International Law Commission, Draft Articles on the Prevention of Transboundary Harm From Hazardous Activities, art. 3, 11 May 2001, Report on the Work of its Fifty-third Session, UN Doc A/56/10 and Corr 1, at 370–76 (2001) (Basic Document 1.16)

Article 3

The State of origin shall take all appropriate measures to prevent significant transboundary harm or at any event to minimize the risk thereof.

13. Trail Smelter Arbitration (Chapter 3, section A, *supra*)

14. Alexandre Kiss, State Responsibility and Liability for Nuclear Damage, 35 Den. J. Int'l L. & Policy 67, 77–78 (2006)

Nuclear activities are included in the general obligation resulting from customary international law, which entails State responsibility "to ensure that activities within their [a State's] jurisdiction or control do not cause damage to the environment of other States or of areas beyond the limits of national jurisdiction." Whether the damage needs to be the consequence of a fault attributable to the State where the activities took place is the primary question to be determined.

Specific obligations resulting from treaties impose upon the contracting States the obligation to take the necessary measures through exercising due diligence in order to prevent such damage, either by prohibiting or by regulating such activities. The rule that the wrongful act should be attributable to the State is included in the customary law principle that the State has the responsibility to ensure that such activities do not cause damage. In addition, most of the previously discussed treaty provisions related to nuclear activities include specific obligations providing for State control on such activities: licensing, surveillance, or even prohibition if necessary. . . .

Articles 5 and 7 of the articles of the International Law Commission are quite clear that the conduct of a person or entity which is not an organ of the State but "which is empowered by the law of that State to exercise elements of the governmental authority shall be considered an act of the State under international law . . . even if it exceeds its authority or contravenes instructions." The same rule applies to persons or groups acting in fact on the instructions of, or under the direction or control, of a State.

While international responsibility is founded on fault imputable to the acting State, it is not necessary that a state intentionally or maliciously violates an international obligation to attribute responsibility. Fault exists if the actor fails to perform a duty or observe a standard, such as omitting to inform an organ designated by a treaty for surveying the implementation of the treaty. Generally, the applicable international rules and standards do not hold a state responsible when it has taken necessary and practicable measures, by exercising due diligence for the prevention of damage or for assisting the potential or real victims.

* * *

[O]ne of the main conclusions of this presentation is the importance of reinforcing the capacity of [IAEA] to control and ensure compliance with existing nuclear safety regulations and developing new compulsory rules in this field insisting on the responsibility and liability of States in this domain.

Other conclusions include the following: the determination that States are responsible under international law for any failure to exercise due diligence over the siting and operation of nuclear facilities and the transport and disposal of nuclear wastes; State parties are responsible for any failure to enforce the Paris and Vienna liability treaties; operators of nuclear facilities and shippers are strictly liable for any harm caused by their activities; and States are responsible for transfrontier harm at least when it results from negligence or intentional pollution and possibly even for harm resulting from accidents.

15. Antonia Layard, Nuclear Liability Damage Reform After Chernobyl, 5 Rev. Eur. Community & Int'l Envtl. L. (RECIEL) 222 (1996)

Even when nuclear power production is in private hands, the state retains residual responsibility. This principle was confirmed by the signatories to the 1994 Nuclear Safety Convention **[Basic Document 2.11]** who reaffirmed in a preambular paragraph that "responsibility for nuclear safety rests with the state having jurisdiction over a nuclear installation" confirming that they wish to promote "an effective nuclear safety culture" although prime responsibility rests with the operator. Consequently, while the liability regimes prohibit nationals of signatory states from bringing civil proceedings except under the terms of the conventions, the possibility of [states] pursuing claims for breach of state responsibility under public international law is expressly left open.

* * *

. . . Nevertheless, state practice provides little support for any one standard of responsibility and demonstrates the lack of consensus on the point. Indeed, Alan Boyle has argued that the failure to demand or offer compensation after Chernobyl points to the conclusion that responsibility is limited to a failure of due diligence and for causing avoidable loss only. Others, (such as Sands) consider that the failure to press a claim reflects a political desire to avoid establishing precedents.

16. Devereaux F. McClatchey, Chernobyl and Sandoz One Decade Later: The Evolution of State Responsibility for International Disasters, 1986–1996, 25 Ga. J. Int'l & Comp. L. 659, 673–75, 676–78, 680 (1996)

In two of the worst environmental catastrophes of all time, the Chernobyl explosion in the former Soviet Union and the Sandoz spill in Switzerland, neither of the offending states were held liable for failing to protect, assist, or otherwise notify any of their neighboring states. Both of these incidents took place in 1986, and both produced devastating consequences in the international community. * * *

[I]n revisiting the two disasters of 1986 and comparing the legal regimes which existed at the time with the current established standards which exist one decade later, the most glaring deficiency that remains today is the lack of firmly incorporated liability standards for transboundary harm.

In 1972, Principle 22 of the Stockholm Declaration **[Basic Document 1.21]** set forth a standard which has been followed over the course of the last two decades with frustrating repetition in innumerable conventions and treaties. It provides:

> States shall co-operate to develop further the international law regarding liability and compensation for the victims of pollution and other environmental damage caused by activities within the jurisdiction or control of such States to areas beyond their jurisdiction.

Even the recent Rio Declaration **[Basic Document 1.30]** . . . avoid[s] prescribing any specific standard of liability for transboundary harm. Principle 13 of the Rio Declaration copies, almost verbatim, the supplication enunciated in Stockholm 20 years earlier to "develop further international law regarding liability and compensation. . . ." . . .

Other important conventions and treaties have also elected to circumvent the issue of liability for transboundary harm. The Convention on Transboundary Effects of Industrial Accidents **[Basic Document 2.2]** sidesteps the issue when it states in Article 13, "The Parties shall support appropriate international efforts to elaborate rules, criteria and procedures in the field of responsibility and liability." Similarly, neither of the two Conventions which were created in the wake of the Chernobyl explosion, the Convention on Early Notification of a Nuclear Accident **[Basic Document 2.9]** and the Convention on Assistance in the Case of a Nuclear Accident **[Basic Document 2.10]**, contain any provisions which specifically address the issues of compensation or standards of liability. While the International Atomic Energy Agency (IAEA) has recognized the lack of global nuclear liability standards and has established a Standing

Committee on Liability for Nuclear Damage, the Committee has thus far made little practical progress in establishing nuclear liability standards.

* * *

One question that inevitably arises when the issue of liability is presented is the issue of whether a strict liability or a negligence standard should be applied. Many scholars point to Principle 21 of the Stockholm Declaration as evidence of strict liability for any type of transboundary harm. Principle 21 reads: "States have, in accordance with the Charter of the United Nations **[Basic Document 1.1]** and the principles of international law . . . the responsibility to ensure that activities within their jurisdiction or control do not cause damage to the environment of other states or of areas beyond the limits of national jurisdiction." While "damage" is not qualified by words like "substantial" or "significant," and while "activities" is not limited to activities within the state's control, the Principle nevertheless refrains from mentioning strict liability.

Some scholars believe that the spirit of the Principle endorses a strict liability standard, while others believe that the absence of the term "strict liability" indicates that the drafters of the declaration did not intend for strict liability to apply. Regardless of what the drafters intended, states in the international community have not usually recognized strict liability as the appropriate standard for state responsibility for transboundary harm. Only a small number of treaties have recognized strict liability as the appropriate standard of liability.

* * *

The previously-mentioned Trail Smelter Arbitration has been used by scholars in both camps of the strict liability/negligence debate. Those that endorse the strict liability standard focus on the part of the tribunal's decision which says, "Under the principles of international law, . . . no state has the right to use or permit the use of its territory in such a manner as to cause injury . . . in or to the territory of another or the properties of persons therein. . . ." These scholars hold fast to the Roman Law principle of *sic utere tuo ut alienum non laedas*, which means "One should use his own property in such a manner as not to injure that of another." However, other scholars who believe that Trail Smelter stands for a negligence standard of liability point out that both parties (the United States and Canada) had already agreed to a compromise which stipulated Canada's wrongdoing in the case, so fault was, in fact, a critical element of the decision.

* * *

Chernobyl and Sandoz highlight the critical role that politics play in determining a state's conduct in the wake of an international disaster. Because of strong diplomatic coercion from states which were harmed by the Sandoz spill, Switzerland agreed to take responsibility for the accident, and it made substantial concessions in subsequent negotiations. The Soviet Union, on the other hand, conceded nothing to the international community, in large part because the international community [did not] exert meaningful political pressure. . . .

(e) Nuclear Sabotage

17. Convention on the Suppression of Acts of Nuclear Terrorism, arts. 2 & 15, April 13, 2005, 2445 UNTS 89, reprinted in 44 ILM 815 (2005) (Basic Document 7.23)

Article 2

1. Any person commits an offence within the meaning of this Convention if that person unlawfully and intentionally: . . .

> (b) Uses in any way radioactive material or a device, or uses or damages a nuclear facility in a manner which releases or risks the release of radioactive material: (i) with the intent to cause death or serious bodily injury; or (ii) with the intent to cause substantial damage to property or to the environment; or (iii) with the intent to compel a natural or legal person, an international organization or a State to do or refrain from doing an act.

* * *

4. Any person also commits an offence if that person: . . .

> (b) Organizes or directs others to commit an offence as set forth in paragraph 1 . . . .

Article 11

1. The State Party in the territory of which the alleged offender is present shall . . . be obliged, without exception whatsoever and whether or not the offence was committed in its territory, to submit the case without undue delay to its competent authorities for the purpose of prosecution . . . .

Article 15

None of the offences set forth in Article 2 shall be regarded, for the purpose of extradition or mutual legal assistance, as a political offence . . . . Accordingly, a request for extradition or for mutual legal assistance based on such an offense may not be refused on the sole ground that it concerns a political offence or an offence connected with a political offence or an offence inspired by political motives.

18. Christopher C. Joyner and Alexander Ian Parkhouse, Nuclear Terrorism in a Globalizing World: Assessing the Threat and the Emerging Management Regime, 45 Stanford J. Int'l L. 203, 227–29 (2009)

As set out in Article 2 of the convention [on nuclear terrorism], a person who "unlawfully and intentionally" possesses radioactive materials or devices and intentionally aims to cause death or bodily injury or "substantial damage to property or the environment" commits an international criminal offense. An offense is also committed if a person threatens or damages a nuclear facility such that radioactive materials might be or are released with the intention of causing injury, death, or extensive damage to property or the environment, or if that person threatens or attempts by use of force to "demand unlawfully" any radioactive materials, a nuclear device, or a nuclear facility. A person who participates as an accomplice or "[o]rganizes or directs others" to commit an offense is likewise construed to be an offender. This provision lists actions done by individuals that amount to criminal acts. Put tersely, a person commits the unlawful act of nuclear terrorism if he or she acquires nuclear materials unlawfully, intentionally damages a nuclear facility, or participates in the planning or execution of such acts. . . .

. . . All state parties are bound by the legal principle of *aut dedere aut judicare*—their government must either extradite or prosecute persons detained for these crimes. Extradition can also be based on the principle of universal jurisdiction according to the CNT, which means any government may seize an accused offender anywhere and extradite or prosecute that person.

Section 5. Discussion Notes/Questions

1. Did Azykhstan violate international law relating to nuclear safety? If so, what law was violated: the Convention on Nuclear Safety? The IAEA standards? Something else?

Writing in 1989, Professor Alan Boyle noted that "nothing in the [IAEA] Statute confers any binding force on IAEA standards, or requires Member States to comply with them." But despite their "non-binding character," he concluded, "IAEA health and safety standards are a significant contribution to controlling the risks of nuclear energy." Alan Boyle, *Nuclear Energy and International Law: An Environmental Perspective,* 60 Brit. Y.B. Int'l L. 257, 261–265 (1989).

Has the situation changed? Should IAEA standards (such as those set out in Reading 4) be considered binding? Does the Convention on Nuclear Safety make them binding? If, as the IAEA says, its standards represent "an international consensus on what constitutes a high level of safety for protecting people and the environment," does this mean they have attained the status of international customary law? Do Readings 2 & 3 shed any light on that question?

2. Did Azykhstan have any customary law obligation to notify Osteuria of the nuclear accident? In Reading 5, Professor Brown Weiss argues that the state in which a nuclear accident occurs has several customary law duties toward other states, including the duty to provide notice and information about the accident and the duty to provide assistance in mitigating its impact. Professor Pelzer, on the other hand, says that the customary law principles upon which Professor Brown Weiss relies are too vague to serve as the basis for any legal claim against the accident State. (Readings 6 & 8). In support of his analysis, he observes that no state brought a claim against Russia arising from the Chernobyl accident.

What do you think? Much of the material that would support the existence of customary duties is presented in Chapters 3 and 4 of this coursebook. Do those materials support the existence of the duties suggested in Reading 5? Is the obligation to act clear enough to support a claim that a failure to act is a violation of international law for which reparation must be made?

If there is a customary obligation to provide assistance, would it obligate Osteuria to assist Azykhstan? Is this because Osteuria contributed to the accident through the actions of Igor Dahi? Or would Osteuria have an obligation to help even if it had nothing to do with the accident?

3. Did either Azykhstan or Osteuria violate their obligations under the Notification or Assistance Conventions (Readings 7 & 9)? Professor Pelzer says that the Notification Convention "establishes obligations for the willing only" because, under Article 1, accident states must provide notice only if they believe that a release of radioactive material poses a threat to another state. Do you see the language that creates this problem? Do you think it is a significant weakness in the notification scheme? How could the obligation to notify be defined to avoid giving this kind of discretion to the accident state?

Similarly, Article 2, paragraph 3 of the Assistance Convention says that the requested state "shall promptly decide" whether to grant assistance. Is the requested state's discretion absolute? Or does Article 2 impose any limits on that discretion? Does the general obligation to perform treaty obligations "in good faith" limit the requested state's discretion? (*See* art. 26, Vienna Convention on the Law of Treaties, Basic Document 1.14.) Can you think of any alternative way of handling this issue that would be workable?

4. Regardless of whether the Assistance Convention imposes any obligation to provide assistance, might it nonetheless have a purpose? Consider the following comment:

> Desirable as it may be, there is no obligation under international law for a State to provide assistance in the event of a major disaster, nuclear or otherwise. States may, of course, offer assistance on humanitarian grounds, as was the case after the Chernobyl accident. The provision of such assistance nevertheless raises certain legal

> questions. The most important relate to the direction and control of the assistance: the reimbursement of any costs incurred; the attribution of liability in the event of damage being suffered by the assisting State in the course of assistance: and the liability of the assisting State for damage it might cause during the course of assistance, including any privileges and immunities attaching to the assisting State. These questions require clear answers if the provision of assistance is to be encouraged.

Philippe Sands, Chernobyl: Law and Communication—Transboundary Nuclear Air Pollution—The Legal Materials 40–42, 44–47, 51 (1988). The Assistance Convention addresses each of the barriers to assistance that Sands identifies. *See* articles 3 & 7–10 of the Convention (Basic Document 2.10).

5. Under the terms of the Vienna Convention, are the Osteurian victims of the nuclear accident entitled to compensation from Elektrikon? If they were entitled to compensation, for what injuries could they recover? How about the Azyhtstani victims?

Assume that the accident was the result of the combined fault of Kernkraft, the Azyhkstani government, and Dahi. Under the terms of the Vienna Convention, could an Azyhkstani court permit a claim against any of those parties by the victims of the accident? If not, what is the policy rationale for precluding such claims?

Do either Article IV(2) or Article IV(3) of the Convention provide Electrikon with a viable defense to liability?

6. There are two central issues of State responsibility in this problem. First, does Azykhstan bear State responsibility for the harm done to Osteuria as a result of the accident at the Yadersk power plant. Second, does Osteuria bear State responsibility for the harm done to Azykhstan by Igor Dahi's actions.

State responsibility requires (a) an international wrong (b) that is attributable to a State. Notes 7 and 8 consider some of the complexities of the first issue with respect to Azyhkstan's potential State responsibility.

7. Undoubtedly, Azyhkstan has some obligation to prevent activities within its borders from causing significant transboundary harm. But what is the nature of this obligation? To put the point another way, what should be the standard of care for any obligation to avoid harmful transboundary radioactivity? The possibilities are fault (intention or negligence), strict liability (basically a *prima facie* liability with various defenses or qualifications), and absolute liability (for which there is no exculpation). *See* L. F.E. Goldie, *Liability for Damage and the Progressive Development of International Law,* 14 Int'l & Comp. L.Q. 1189, 1202–20 (1965) for an iconic discussion of the distinction between strict and absolute liability in the context of environmental damage. The dangers of nuclear activity probably mean that the standard of care should be a high one. The national laws of many countries have a standard of strict liability for ultra-hazardous activities.

How does the International Law Commission answer this question in Reading 12? Has Azyhkstan violated the standard set out in that document? What does "appropriate" mean? Can its meaning vary depending on the dangerousness of the particular activity authorized or allowed by a state?

8. If Azykhstan's simple failure to prevent transboundary harm from occurring is not alone sufficient to establish its responsibility, then its responsibility requires a finding that some other aspect of its conduct violated international law. Did any of the following acts by Azykhstan violate specific obligations Azykhstan has under either conventional or customary international law:

(a) authorizing the construction of the Yadersk nuclear power plant?

(b) allowing the plant to continue operation despite the discovery of cracks in its foundation?

(c) creating a regulatory structure in which the Office of Nuclear Safety was part of the Ministry of Energy?

(d) failing to report the accident to Osteuria for several hours?

(e) failing to provide Osteurian claimants with a judicial remedy against Elektrikon?

9. Professor Lakshman Guruswamy has observed that, despite the "considerable theoretical attention given to the concept of state responsibility," it has played little role in international environmental law (putting aside the *Trail Smelter* decision). He explains:

> The existence of a court or tribunal with compulsory jurisdiction is a pre-requisite for invoking state responsibility in an adjudicatory context. Public international law, with a few exceptions, does not encompass courts possessed of global and compulsory jurisdiction. The stubborn fact is that the legal machinery enabling compensation for the breach of international environmental wrongs has generally been deliberately neglected or omitted. Cases where compensation is obtained are the exceptions, not the rule, and the reluctance among states to develop adjudicatory regimes for implementing state responsibility, is yet another reason why judicial enforcement can prove elusive.

Lakshman Guruswamy, State Responsibility in Promoting Environmental Corporate Accountability, 21 Fordham Envtl. L. Rev. 209, 210–16, 221, 223–24, 227–28 (2010). On the other hand, he observes, states have been willing to develop civil liability regimes, where "the primary responsibility for environmental harm is . . . placed on the polluter and not the state." The Civil Liability Convention discussed in this problem is one example. Problem 6-3, *supra*, provides another example in the context of oil pollution damage.

10. Civil liability approaches can raise difficult issues related to the calculation of damage. For example, what value would be placed on the

destruction of the traditional Lapp way of life, alleged to be a casualty of the effect of radioactivity from Chernobyl on lichen which reindeer eat. States are unlikely to agree on any monetary value, given that it reflects a different set of cultural assumptions. One possible measure of damages would be the cost of making the environment whole. This approach finds support in traditional international law, which provides that "reparation must, as far as possible, wipe out all the consequences of the illegal act and establish the situation which would in all probability have existed if the act had not been committed." *Chorzow Factory Case* (Ger. v. Pol.), 1928 P.C.I.J. (ser. A) No. 17, at 47. But the cost of environmental restoration may be prohibitively high and, indeed, it may be impossible to achieve within a reasonable timeframe. Do the liability conventions allow this measure of damages?

Other consequences of a nuclear accident can be difficult to establish, especially with respect to proving damage and loss over the long term. How does the Vienna Convention on Civil Liability address this? What about the psychological impact of radioactive fallout on the state's people? Is this a recoverable element of damages? Gunther Handl, *Territorial Sovereignty and the Problem of Transnational Pollution*, 69 Am. J. Int'l L. 50 (1975). Suppose fear of radiation hurts the tourist trade, even though the fear was unfounded?

11. Where states agree to handle issues of transboundary environmental harm through treaties imposing civil liability on private actors who are responsible for such harm, the state takes on at least the obligation to establish the agreed civil-liability system. Presumably it would have State responsibility for any harm caused by its failure to do so. But if it establishes such a system, does that free it from all further responsibility with respect to the underlying harm? For example, if Azyykstan properly awards compensation under the Vienna Convention, is it free of State responsibility even if it is concluded that the nuclear accident was the result of its failure to perform its obligations under the Nuclear Safety Convention?

12. The 1972 Convention on International Liability for Damage Caused by Space Objects makes launching states responsible for space objects falling on the ground irrespective of fault. It has no ceiling or limit on possible compensation. In 1981, the USSR paid $3 million compensation in final settlement for damage incurred in locating and cleaning-up after the disintegration of a nuclear-powered satellite, Cosmos 954, on Canadian territory in 1978. In its statement of claim, Canada relied on Article 2 of the 1972 Convention and maintained that the principle of absolute liability applies to fields of activity having in common a high degree of risk in international law.

Should absolute liability without compensation limits be the standard for imposing liability on nuclear operators? Such a standard might make it impossible for operators to obtain financial security (insurance) coverage, and the lack of such coverage might mean the death knell of the nuclear power industry. Is that a problem?

13. The second State responsibility issue is whether acts that violate international law are attributable to the state that is charged with responsibility. Consider that issue in connection with Asykhstan's claim against Osteuria. If Igor Dahi's actions were unlawful under international law, was his violation attributable to Osteuria. Does it matter whether any high government official in Osteuria explicitly authorized those actions? Would it matter if Osteuria had policies in place that Dahi's actions violated?

14. Assume that the Osteurian military officer, Igor Dahi, deliberately arranged for Eletrikon's facilities to be infected with the computer worm that triggered the nuclear accident. Was this a violation of the Convention on Nuclear Terrorism? If not, was it a violation of other international law? (Perhaps Article 2(4) of the Charter of the United Nations **(Basic Document 1.1)**.)

15. What about the abolition of nuclear power altogether? Is this possible or desirable? *See, e.g.*, Richard Falk, *Nuclear Policy and World Order: Why Denuclearization*, 3 Alternatives—J. World Pol'y, 321 (1978). After Chernobyl, some countries abandoned plans for developing new nuclear power plants. Others looked at phasing-out nuclear power. However, concern over global climate change has led to a recent upsurge of interest in the expansion of nuclear power capacity. In contrast with power plants fired by fossil fuels (coal, oil, gas), nuclear power generation involves the release of negligible quantities of carbon dioxide, acidifying gases, and other air pollutants associated with fuel combustion. However, nuclear power plants have significant health, safety, and security risks of their own. And there are problems regarding the safe disposal of nuclear waste and the decommissioning of nuclear plants. But, given the potentially catastrophic consequences of continued reliance on fossil-fuel energy, does the world have any choice other than to support the rapid expansion of all non-carbon energy sources, including nuclear energy? For discussions, *see* Tanya Mortensen, *An Unattainable Wedge: Four Limiting Effects on the Expansion of Nuclear Power,* 5 Envt'l & Energy L. & Policy J. 60 (2010); Christopher E. Paine, *The Nuclear Fuel Cycle, Global Security, and Climate Change: Weighing the Costs and Benefits of Nuclear Power Expansion,* 44 U. Richmond L. Rev. 1047 (2010); Mariah Zebrowski, *Nuclear Power as Carbon-Free Energy: The Global Nuclear Energy Partnership,* 20 Col. J. Int'l Envtl. L. & Policy 391 (2009).

16. Finally, remember that Osteuria did not want Azykhstan to build the Yadersk nuclear power plant. Should neighboring states have a substantive right of veto or co-decision in respect of the development of a nuclear facility? Should the people and local authorities affected in the neighboring state have the same procedural rights as those enjoyed during a public inquiry by general public and local authorities in the constructing state? Should the constructing state be obliged to include the observations made by the affected people and local authorities of the neighboring state in its decision-making? Should the mere risk of a major accident be regarded as damage to the other state? What about the possible psychological effects of a nuclear power plant on the inhabitants of a region, or any effect on aesthetics and tourism? *See* Koen

Lenaerts, *Border Installations*, *in* Nuclear Energy Law After Chernobyl 49 (P. Cameron et al. eds., 1988). How can states decide what constitutes neighboring territories when distance does not always equate to danger of transboundary pollution? *See* Espoo Convention on Environmental Impact Assessment in a Transboundary Context **(Basic Document 1.38)**, discussed in Problem 5-1, *supra*.

CHAPTER ELEVEN

MANAGING THE GLOBAL COMMONS IN ANTARCTICA

■ ■ ■

Antarctica: a remote continent, unique in so many respects. It is necessary to introduce you to its special characteristics, as the wise application of law and policy to this area depends upon such knowledge. It is, in fact, a heightened awareness of this vast continent's unique qualities that is largely responsible for the increased attention that recently has been given to the legal safeguards needed to protect it. Today, there is considerable international law that relates to Antarctica, including a complex treaty system.

Following our description of the continent, we invite you to wrestle with two problems that we hope will engage and inform you relative to some of the more difficult legal issues that arise in relation to this vast realm. Our intent, through fictional scenarios that we believe are realistically capable of taking place in Antarctica, is to sensitize you, as student and potential advocate and policy-maker, to the ecological-legal challenge that Antarctica presents.

And make no mistake, the ecological-legal challenges are daunting, so fragile is the Antarctic environment. Oil spills, for example, of which there have been several in recent times, can affect the Antarctic ecosystem much more seriously than spills do in other parts of the world. Preservation of biodiversity in Antarctica also is key. While there is more aquatic life than might be expected—whales, seals, penguins, and birds—the history of human exploitation of some of these species has been at various times catastrophic. And now tourism poses fresh threats, with a potential for damage far beyond what so far has been experienced. Thus, the Antarctic environment requires the utmost professional as well as ecological sensitivity and acumen. However remote, Antarctica does not exist by itself, unconnected to the rest of the world. To the contrary, it exerts great influence upon the ecology and the climate of the entire world, and for this reason alone, requires to be taken into serious legal account.

Finally, throughout this chapter, we ask you to consider and recommend alternative norms, institutions, and/or procedures that you believe might do better than existing arrangements to contend with the situations posed by the problems presented. We ask you to think about the policy options available and imaginable for Antarctica's long-term governance. Questions about Antarctica's international legal regime are necessarily of the most fundamental sort: whether states claiming sovereignty over certain parts of Antarctica can and should have exclusive jurisdiction or legal control over the areas claimed; whether states not party to the treaties that constitute that Antarctic Treaty System (ATS) can and should be bound by the norms that flow from those treaties; whether the governance of Antarctica should be internationalized through the United Nations or some other multilateral agency or method; and so forth. In short, in addition to presenting an extraordinarily rich intersection of environmental and international law issues, Antarctica is a paradigmatic case of a global commons. It requires for its enlightened regulation and management over the long term the most fertile of imaginations—well trained in the art of the possible, but not necessarily insistent upon immediate feasibility of a chosen governance model.

And so, we wish you a pleasant legal journey around the coldest continent on Earth. Along the way, keep in mind that many of the issues of law and policy raised here apply also to other global and international environmental problems.

A. ANTARCTICA: A BRIEF PORTRAIT

A vast mountain continent, Antarctica has an awe-inspiring fascination no words can capture. It is a place of great grandeur and natural beauty. Also, it is a place where some of the most heroic deeds of modern-day exploration have taken place—which means that serious exploration on land has been possible only in the Twentieth Century, and even then in circumstances of great privation.

Two hundred million years ago, Antarctica was joined to Africa, Australia, India, New Zealand, and South America, forming the Gondwanaland supercontinent. Over millions of years, these continents drifted apart. As of 30 million years ago, they were almost in the same positions they are today (see Figure 6–1, infra). Antarctica drifted to a polar position and began to experience a winter of more than five months without sunlight.

Today, Antarctica is covered almost completely by ice. Without its ice cap, it covers an area of approximately 2.7 million square miles (or 699,297.3 million hectares). With its ice cap it covers an area larger than the United States (some 5.4 million square miles, or 1,398,594.6 million hectares), and boasts a diameter of about 2,800 miles (or 4,509 kilometers), making it the fifth largest continent. It also is the highest, driest, and coldest continent in the world. About ninety-eight percent of this expanse is buried beneath a thick ice sheet. Falling snow and ice crystals maintain

the depth of the ice sheet at an average of more than 7,000 feet (or 2,133.6 meters) and up to 13,450 feet (or 4,099.6 meters) thick in some places.

Figure 11-1

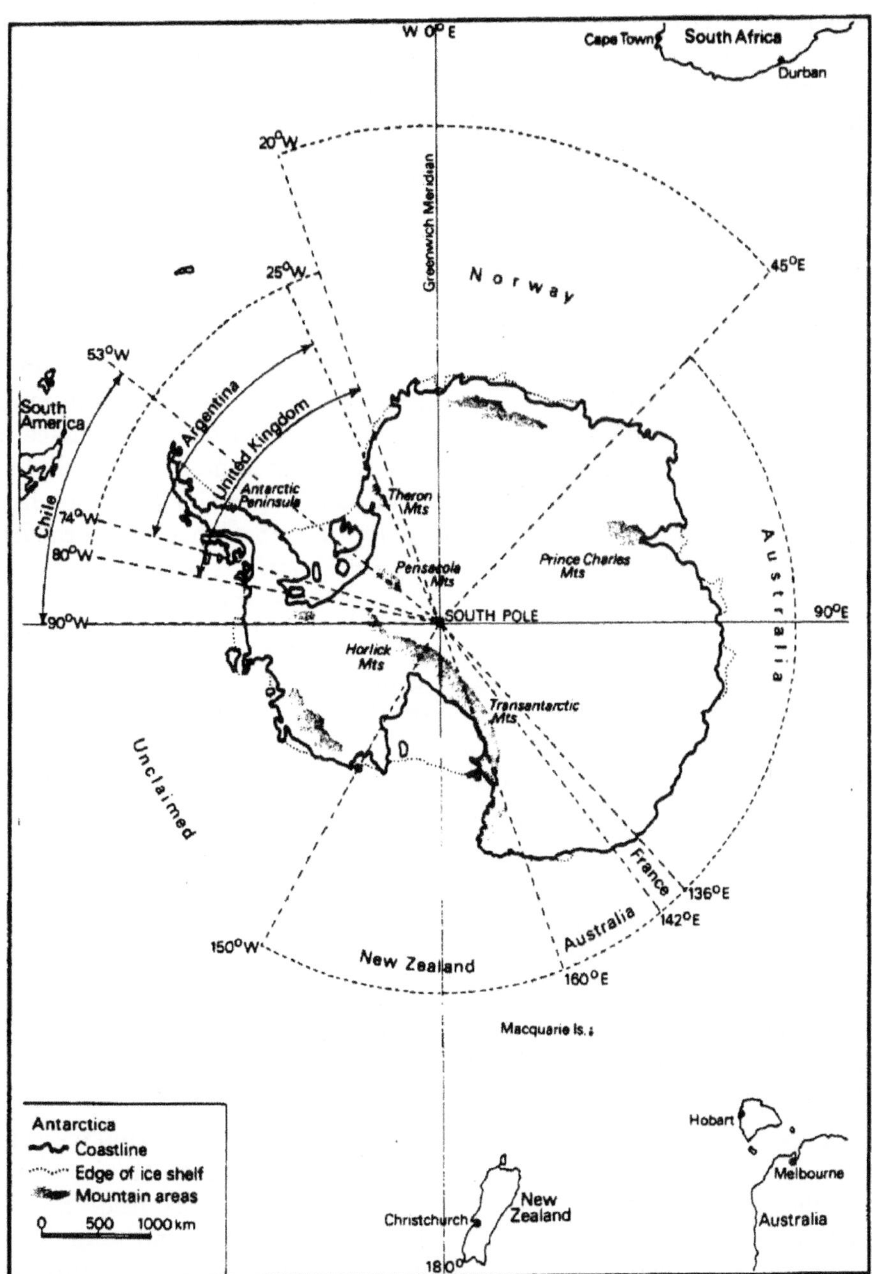

Figure 11-1. Map of national claims in Antarctica

The Antarctic ice sheet represents about 90 percent of the world's ice and 68 percent of the world's freshwater. Thus, it not only dominates the climate of the area, but also has an influence that extends to the equator and beyond in the form of cold air, cold water currents, and migratory bird and sea life. If all the ice were to melt, it would raise the levels of the world's oceans between 160 and 200 feet (or 48.8 and 60.9 meters). About one-third of the land that supports the ice sheet lies below the surface of the sea. The 2,400 mile (or 3,864.7 kilometers) long mountain ranges that subdivide the continent are some of the longest on Earth with many high peaks. As a consequence, the Antarctic has a mean height more than three times that of any other continent.

The main characteristic of the Antarctic climate is severe low temperatures. While the continent receives a surprising amount of sunlight in spite of its five- to six-months' "winter night" (more solar radiation reaches the South Pole during the Antarctic summer than is received at the equator in an equivalent period), the sunlight does not result in much surface heat because most of the sunlight is reflected back into space by the snow and sea ice. Thus, temperatures range in summer from slightly below freezing at the coast to an average of −36°F (or −37.7°C) on the high plateau. In the winter, the coasts and plateaus experience temperatures between −40°F and −90°F (or −40°C and −67.7°C). The world's lowest recorded temperature of −129.3°F (or −89.61°C) was measured at the base of Vostok in July 1983.

Antarctica is also a very dry continent, receiving just enough precipitation to allow snow to accumulate. The high winds in some parts of the continent whip this snow up, and the powdery blizzards can reduce visibility to zero. It is not unusual for these conditions to occur for up to two out of three days in August, which is the stormiest month.

Thus isolated, almost totally covered by ice, and having an exceedingly cold, dry climate, Antarctica has never been hospitable to colonization by plants, animals, or human beings. Ferns, freshwater fish, amphibians, and reptiles are found today only as fossils; and it is the only continent where humans are not indigenous and where civilizations have never developed. Indeed, Antarctica is the last continent to be explored. It remains the continent about which the least is known, especially in terms of its effect on global environmental processes.

Forms of life on the frozen continent have adapted in unusual ways for survival in the cold and the low humidity, and for living on the ice or the salty soils of the region. Only two percent of Antarctica is ice-free—mainly coastal areas—and this is where most life is found. Birds and seals breed and raise their young on the ice or land but depend on the rich resources of the ocean for their food. The sea—abounding with whales, fish, squid, and krill as important elements of the marine ecosystem—is rich with life.

However, terrestrial life is very limited and slow-growing in the cold, windy, dry conditions and long winter darkness. The largest land-based animal is a flightless midge 3 mm. long, and the vegetation is sparse, consisting of lichens, algae, mosses, fungi, microscopic plants, and two flowering species that grow at the northern tip of the Antarctic Peninsula. A variety of freshwater and saline lakes and ponds on the land contain a limited range of aquatic animals.

The coastal areas free of ice are where most human activities are concentrated—mainly scientific stations and field activities. Ground-level climate in the largest of these areas is warmer in the summer and considerably drier than surrounding areas. Once free of ice, they tend to stay free, partly because of the bare surfaces that soak up the heat and partly because snowfall is minimal and winds are strong. Many of the largest valleys, such as the "dry valleys" near McMurdo Sound, contain both salt and freshwater lakes.

Since 1957–58, the International Geophysical Year, Antarctica has been used by human beings primarily as a site for scientific research. The Antarctic Treaty **(Basic Document 6.1)**, a multilateral treaty entered into in 1959 by nations interested in Antarctica, established methods for international cooperation in scientific exploration and for preservation of Antarctica for peaceful purposes. In addition, state practice under the treaty has developed in ways designed to protect the fragile environment. Along with the oceans, the atmosphere, the moon, and other celestial bodies, Antarctica is now increasingly accepted as part of what has come to be known as "the global commons."

Antarctica's polar location, the vast bulk of its ice mass (90% of the total ice on the planet containing 70% of the earth's total fresh water), and the huge extent of the surrounding seas mean that the continent has a fundamental influence on the atmosphere, the oceans, and the biological conditions of the entire global system. In turn, the impact of human activities elsewhere on Earth is felt in Antarctica.

For these reasons, among others, the International Geosphere-Biosphere Programme uses Antarctica as part of its worldwide network of regional research centers and sites to gather data and analyze global change problems. A pristine laboratory within which, by examining the ice, changes in global pollution rates and world climates can be monitored, Antarctica is a natural resource in itself.

B. THE ANTARCTIC TREATY SYSTEM

While some of the sub-Antarctic islands were claimed by nations as their territory, there has never been a widely accepted framework of national sovereignty over the continent itself. Nor has any state effectively asserted its sovereign authority over any significant part of the continent.

A handful of countries have made claims of sovereignty over parts of Antarctica, but those claims have been widely rejected by other states. Furthermore, although there are many bases built in Antarctica for scientific research, there have never been any permanent inhabitants nor any successful effort to colonize any part of the continent. In short, no national government controls Antarctica.

In the absence of a national sovereign over the continent, Antarctica has been governed by a unique legal system consisting of a number of international treaties and various instruments and documents adopted pursuant to those treaties. Reliance exclusively on international law for the governance of Antarctica raises issues of considerable legal complexity for the resolution of disputes that may arise, particularly considering that many states are not parties to any of the treaties that make up the Antarctic Treaty System.

The foundational legal source for the System is the Antarctic Treaty, adopted in 1959. This unique agreement commits Member States to using Antarctica for peaceful purposes only. It sets aside the potential for disputes over territorial claims, and it focuses on scientific research and sharing findings with the rest of the world.

This agreement was forged during the Cold War when tensions between the USSR and the United States were at their height. The cooperation that began in the 1957 International Geophysical Year was the stimulant for the Treaty. Its essence can be captured by reading its first six articles.

THE ANTARCTIC TREATY

Adopted, October 15, 1959; Entered into force, June 23, 1961
402 U.N.T.S. 71 (Basic Document 6.1)

Article I

1. Antarctica shall be used for peaceful purposes only. There shall be prohibited, inter alia, any measure of a military nature, such as the establishment of military bases and fortifications, the carrying out of military manoeuvres, as well as the testing of any type of weapon.

2. The present Treaty shall not prevent the use of military personnel or equipment for scientific research or for any other peaceful purpose.

Article II

Freedom of scientific investigation in Antarctica and cooperation toward that end, as applied during the International Geophysical Year, shall continue, subject to the provisions of the present Treaty.

Article III

1. In order to promote international cooperation in scientific investigation in Antarctica, as provided for in Article II of the present Treaty, the Contracting Parties agree that, to the greatest extent feasible and practicable:

(a) information regarding plans for scientific programs in Antarctica shall be exchanged to permit maximum economy of and efficiency of operations;

(b) scientific personnel shall be exchanged in Antarctica between expeditions and stations;

(c) scientific observations and results from Antarctica shall be exchanged and made freely available.

2. In implementing this Article, every encouragement shall be given to the establishment of cooperative working relations with those Specialized Agencies of the United Nations and other technical organizations having a scientific or technical interest in Antarctica.

Article IV

1. Nothing contained in the present Treaty shall be interpreted as:

(a) a renunciation by any Contracting Party of previously asserted rights of or claims to territorial sovereignty in Antarctica;

(b) a renunciation or diminution by any Contracting Party of any basis of claim to territorial sovereignty in Antarctica which it may have whether as a result of its activities or those of its nationals in Antarctica, or otherwise;

(c) prejudicing the position of any Contracting Party as regards its recognition or non-recognition of any other State's rights of or claim or basis of claim to territorial sovereignty in Antarctica.

2. No acts or activities taking place while the present Treaty is in force shall constitute a basis for asserting, supporting or denying a claim to territorial sovereignty in Antarctica or create any rights of sovereignty in Antarctica. No new claim, or enlargement of an existing claim, to territorial sovereignty in Antarctica shall be asserted while the present Treaty is in force.

Article V

1. Any nuclear explosions in Antarctica and the disposal there of radioactive waste material shall be prohibited.

2. In the event of the conclusion of international agreements concerning the use of nuclear energy, including nuclear explosions and the disposal of

radioactive waste material, to which all of the Contracting Parties whose representatives are entitled to participate in the meetings provided for under Article IX are parties, the rules established under such agreements shall apply in Antarctica.

Article VI

The provisions of the present Treaty shall apply to the area south of 60° South Latitude, including all ice shelves, but nothing in the present Treaty shall prejudice or in any way affect the rights, or the exercise of the rights, of any State under international law with regard to the high seas within that area.

Four key elements of the Antarctic System are established by these and other provisions of the Antarctic Treaty.

First, Antarctica can only be used for peaceful purposes. Military activities cannot be carried out anywhere on the continent. Moreover, it is a nuclear-explosion-free area, and the Treaty may be understood as an arms control measure of continuing importance given that eight of the world's nuclear weapons states (China, France, India, North Korea, Pakistan, Russia, the United Kingdom and the United States) are parties to it. Indeed, the Treaty could be seen as something of a disarmament model for the world.

Second, the Antarctic Treaty imposes a standstill on territorial claims. Those claims are "put on ice," so to speak, and cannot be pursued by the Parties during the life of the Treaty. Prior to its adoption, seven countries (Argentina, Australia, Chile, France, New Zealand, Norway and the United Kingdom) claimed parts of the Antarctic as their own. Other countries, including the United States, asserted no territorial claim of their own and rejected the claims of sovereignty made by those seven states. The Treaty specifically puts all territorial claims in abeyance, providing both that nothing done in Antarctica while the Treaty endures can be used as a basis for asserting, supporting or denying a claim to territorial sovereignty there and that no new claim, or enlargement of an existing claim, to territorial sovereignty in Antarctica can be asserted while the Treaty is in force.

The result of these provisions is that there is no recognized sovereign that can exercise legislative, executive, and judicial functions in any part of Antarctica. Usually the authority of a nation state within its territory is absolute and exclusive. It is analogous to the property rights of an owner of fee simple estate in land, only greater. However, because states with territorial claims in Antarctica have agreed not to assert those claims, citizens of countries who visit Antarctica are generally not under the jurisdiction of any territorial sovereign and remain, at best, subject to the law of their nationality.

Third, the Treaty guarantees "freedom of scientific investigation in Antarctica" and, indeed, science is king on the continent. Significant scientific activity and research has occurred there for many years. As we learn more about climate change, interest in Antarctica is only growing. The impact of climate change on the extensive ice sheets and ice shelves of Antarctica is of enormous interest to scientists. More than 80 percent of the world's fresh water is captured in Antarctic ice formations, and that ice is melting in many parts of the continent, leading to flows of freshwater into the marine environment. How these flows will affect the behavior of the Southern Ocean, worldwide sea levels, and the Antarctic marine ecosystem is an important issue for the planet.

Fourth, the Antarctic Treaty establishes a unique (and sometimes controversial) governance system for the continent. Under article IX of the Treaty, decision-making concerning Antarctica is placed in the hands of the 12 states that originally negotiated the Treaty, with equal participatory rights given to any other Contracting Party to the Treaty that "demonstrates its interest in Antarctica by conducting substantial scientific research activity there." These Parties, referred to collectively as the Antarctic Treaty Consultative Parties (ATCPs), have the exclusive right under the treaty to participate in meetings of the Contracting Parties, to carry out inspections of facilities on Antarctica, and to formulate measures to carry out the principles of the Antarctic Treaty. Measures adopted by the ATCPs at their meetings become effective when approved by the governments of those Contracting Parties. Contracting Parties who do not have consultative status are bound by the Treaty, but lack any decision-making role. By 2018 there were 53 state parties to the Treaty, 29 of which were consultative parties and therefore enjoyed voting status.

From time to time, non-consultative Contracting Parties, and non-member nations generally, have viewed the ATCPs as forming a sort of club that controls Antarctica to the detriment of the rest of the world. This has led to occasional attempts to assert broader international control over Antarctica. Usually these attempts have taken the form of United Nations General Assembly Resolutions on "The Question of Antarctica." Those resolutions have called for detailed studies of the governance of Antarctica by the ATCPs, have asserted that activities in Antarctica are of significance "to the international community" as a whole, and have even demanded that Antarctica be established as a World Park under United Nations governance and control.[1] At present, however, the United Nations General Assembly seems content with governance by the ATCPs, especially as the ATCPs have worked to provide greater information about their activities

1 *See, e.g.,* G.A. Res. 44/124/B (on the question of Antarctica) (Dec. 15, 1989).

to the United Nations and have invited UNEP's Executive Director to attend ATCP meetings.[2]

Significant legal issues arise, however, in relation to nations that may assert some right in Antarctica but that are not treaty parties.

DISCUSSION NOTES/QUESTIONS

1. One of the important issues raised by current arrangements in Antarctica is how a commons area like Antarctica can be regulated when there is no single state authority that can exert the necessary power. Many states are, of course, party to the Antarctic Treaty and bound by its provisions. But many other states are not, and non-party states have, in fact, pursued activities on the continent. For example, Pakistan, which opposed the ATS in the United Nations, established a summer station in the area claimed by Norway in 1991. And Pakistan is not the only non-party state to have established a scientific base in Antarctica. India was the first and South Korea the second. (Both are now consultative parties.)

What if the activities of a non-party state were forbidden by the Treaty, or by some measure adopted by the Consultative Parties to the Treaty? Would the non-party state be bound by the Treaty? Could its provisions be enforced against that state or its nationals?

2. Article X of the Treaty provides that "Each of the Contracting Parties undertakes to exert appropriate efforts, consistent with the Charter of the United Nations, to the end that no one engages in any activity in Antarctica contrary to the principles or purpose of the present Treaty." This language raises several interpretive questions. First, does the reference to "no one" include states, or is enforcement authority limited to enforcement against individuals or business entities? Second, what are the enforceable "principles and purposes" of the Treaty, and do those "principles and purposes" include universal adherence to measures or recommendations adopted by the Consultative Parties? Third, what is the significance of the requirements that enforcement efforts must be "appropriate" and "consistent with the Charter of the United Nations?"

3. Would it be lawful for a state Party to the Antarctic Treaty to take action to enforce it against a non-party State? Article 34 of the Vienna Convention on the Law of Treaties **(Basic Document 1.14)**, restating the generally accepted customary law, provides that "a treaty does not create either obligations or rights for a third State without its consent." This understanding is also implicit in Article 38(1)(a) of the Statute of the International Court of Justice, which treats as binding law in ICJ cases "international conventions . . . establishing rules *expressly recognized* by the contesting states." Thus, even if one assumes that Article 10 is intended to give the Antarctic Treaty Parties some authority over third states, that intent,

---

2 *See* G.A. Res. 60/47 (on the Question of Antarctica) (Dec. 8, 2005).

without more, could not bind third states or make them subject to the rules of the Treaty.

4. Numerous efforts have been made to explain how the rules of the Antarctic Treaty system might apply to non-party states.

> One theory perceives art. 10 as a Janus-faced provision serving both as an *obligation inter partes* and as a *claim erga tertios.* Accordingly, the silence of third parties is not be be interpreted as disagreement because express consent to a treaty provision providing for obligations is lacking, but it must, on the contrary, be understood as acquiescence in the assertion of competences which lies behind art. 10.

Stefan Brunner, *Article 10 of the Antarctic Treaty Revisited,* in International Law for Antarctica 107 (Fracesco Francioni & Tullio Scovazzi eds. 1996).

A similar argument one might make is that the Antarctic Treaty System has become a part of customary international law or, at least, that the right of the ATCPs to govern Antarctica pursuant to the principles established in the Antarctic Treaty has become an accepted part of customary international law. Indeed, how else can one explain the General Assembly's failure in the past two decades to pursue the demands it made in the 1980s for broader participation in decisionmaking related to Antarctica?

Are you persuaded? Do the ATCPs have a kind of quasi-sovereignty over Antarctica?

5. One problem with treaty-based governance of Antarctica is that the governance mechanisms provided by the Treaty are rather clumsy and make it difficult to respond quickly to new challenges. The Antarctic Treaty Consultative Parties take three different kinds of actions, and the legal force of these actions is variable. Moreover, the adoption of binding measures ultimately requires consensus approval by home governments. Political scientist Christopher Joyner explains, in *Governing the Frozen Commons,* at 62–63 (1998):

> [T]he XIXth ATCM meeting in Seoul, Korea, in 1995 agreed to distinguish recommendations according to three categories. (1) Measures are texts approved by all ATCPs and intended to be legally binding as recommended for approval in accordance with Article IX of the Antarctic Treaty. The Measures category reflects the original intent of the term recommendations. . . . (2) Decisions concern internal organizational matters and become operative upon their adoption at an ATCM. . . . (3) Finally, there are "resolutions," which are nonbinding, hortatory texts adopted at ATCMs. Since 1995, nine resolutions have been adopted, largely dealing with logistical issues. Consensus agreement by the ATCPs is still required for the adoption of each new category of recommended text.
>
> Decisions [adopting "measures"] at ATCP meetings are only somewhat authoritative. While measures decided upon at ATCMs

require consensus approval of all present, they are considered to be only recommendations to governments. Those measures adopted do not become effective as official Antarctic Treaty policy, however, until all ATCP governments have approved them through their municipal procedures, either through ratification processes or domestic legislation.

Would you favor an amendment to the Treaty that allowed ATCP decisions to enter into force more easily? For example, some treaties allow various actions by the parties to enter into force for everyone upon approval by the home governments of a majority of the parties, but protect dissenters with an opportunity to opt out within a certain period of time.

6. In July 2001, the ACTPs decided to establish a Permanent Secretariat to the Antarctic Treaty. Notes Karen Scott, *Institutional Developments Within the Antarctic Treaty System*, Int'l & Comp. L.Q. 473–87 (2003):

> The key functions of the Secretariat are to manage the administrative side of the annual and intersessional meetings, facilitate contact between the Parties, maintain contacts with other international organizations, develop and maintain databases to the operation of the Treaty, and produce reports and publications.

What could be the impact of the Secretariat on the implementation of the Treaty? Can it realistically be seen to have any sort of policing function?

7. In recent times, nongovernmental organizations have had major influence in the shaping of policy about Antarctica. In particular, they have been instrumental in arousing public concern about the future of the continent, thereby shaping political attitudes and action. Greenpeace had an environmental and scientific program in Antarctica, dating from 1985 until 1992. Two facilities were used for this, the expedition ship *MV Gondawana* and World Park Base at Cape Evans, Ross Island. Its role in the Antarctic was largely as an environmental watchdog. Greenpeace conducted environmental inspections of Antarctic bases and field sites and published a report at the end of each season. The scientific program included collaborative research with a number of scientists from several nations. World Park Base was closed in 1992.

Today, the most influential nongovernmental organization in the region is the Antarctic and Southern Ocean Coalition (ASOC), which is a coalition of more than 100 environmental NGOs that is dedicated to preserving the Antarctic Treaty area as "the world's last unspoiled wilderness, a global commons for the heritage of future generations." Antarctic and Southern Ocean Coalition, http://www.asoc.org/about (2018).

8. The matter of policing Antarctica is addressed explicitly by the Antarctic Treaty in its provisions for on-site inspections by the Treaty parties. It is commonly recognized, however, that such monitoring does not take place on any great scale. There appears to be an unspoken policy that recognizes the mutual benefits of non-exercise of inspection provisions. There also is the

problem of non-parties to the Treaty. While non- parties cannot claim invasion of sovereign territory (a claim even Treaty parties cannot sustain), neither do they grant consent for inspection in the way that the Treaty parties do.

Greenpeace International acted unofficially to fill the Antarctic inspection gap from 1985 until it relinquished this role in 1992. Accordingly, it is now pertinent to consider who can best fulfill this important policing function. While the Antarctic Treaty System has been congratulated for its relatively conflict-free management, if this is to the detriment of environmental integrity a more internationalized intrusion in the form of monitoring and enforcement is arguably necessary. What body should serve this function? Is this an ideal situation for United Nations involvement? Could U.N. participation in Antarctica form part of a wider "environmental police force"? How much reliance can be placed on a body such as the Committee for Environmental Protection, provided for in the 1991 Protocol to The Antarctic Treaty on Environmental Protection? Should the recently created Antarctic Treaty Secretariat be assigned this role? Bear in mind that, during negotiations for the Minerals Convention, the Consultative Parties consistently rejected proposals for an independent Antarctic protection agency to play a monitoring role.

C. ENVIRONMENTAL PROTECTION IN ANTARCTICA

Over the years, efforts to protect the Antarctic environment have generated a web of complicated treaty and non-treaty arrangements that have continued to evolve in response to changes in the threats facing Antarctica and changes in internationally accepted principles related to environmental protection. Beginning with agreements on how to cope with particular environmental threats, the ATS now includes an agreement devoted to environmental protection broadly conceived and containing basic principles unknown in the early days of environmental protection, such as requirements for environmental impact assessment.

Antarctic Marine Living Resources and their Protection

In a climate as cold and forbidding as Antarctica's, it may be thought that life does not flourish. But that is not true. The convergence of cold Antarctic surface water and warmer waters from the north produces effects that support many varieties of marine life. Antarctic waters are rich in nutrients. With the arrival of spring and summer, phytoplankton develop and the wind can move them about. Krill, small shrimp-like creatures, eat the phytoplankton and, in turn, other creatures eat the abundant krill. Thriving populations of baleen whales, fish, birds, squid, penguins and seals can be found on the Antarctic coast and in the waters surrounding the continent.

It was the 1774 visit of the famous British explorer Captain James Cook to Antarctica that created the first human threat to this ecosystem. Captain Cook sailed around most of the continent. On the Island of South Georgia he found an abundant population of fur seals. Seal hunters soon followed and, in the unregulated environment, the seal population was nearly wiped out. By 1822, 1.2 million animals had been taken from the island, and hardly any seals were observed in the region from the mid-1800s until the 1920s.[3]

After the sealers came the whalers. The harsh Antarctic conditions meant that whaling was not a significant threat to Antarctic whaling populations in the days of wooden sailing vessels. But whaling activities increased with the development of steam navigation, factory ships and the harpoon gun. Whaling continued for many years and is still carried out by Japan. *See* Chapter One, *supra*. The stocks of some species of great whales such as the blue whale remain depleted.

In truth, however, environmental considerations were not perceived as important when the Antarctic Treaty was negotiated. The Treaty's only provisions dealing with environmental issues are those that prohibit nuclear explosions and the disposal of radioactive waste in Antarctica,[4] and one in which consultative meetings are given the task of recommending measures directed at, *inter alia*, the preservation and conservation of living resources in Antarctica.[5]

The first serious attempt to introduce some protective environmental measures occurred in 1964, with the adoption of the Agreed Measures for the Conservation of Antarctic Fauna and Flora. Pursuant thereto, the Antarctic Consultative Parties (ATCPs) declared that the Antarctic is a "Special Conservation Area" and they imposed restrictions on certain activities having the potential to harm the Antarctic environment. The Agreed Measures did not take effect until the early 1980s, however, because they were not ratified by all the states that negotiated them.

In 1972, the ATCPs negotiated the Convention for the Conservation of Antarctic Seals **(Basic Document 6.2)**. The Convention established permissible annual catches for three species found in the Southern Ocean, and forbade the killing or capturing of three other species. It also divided the year into a "Closed Season" and a "Sealing Season," provided that each "zone" is to be totally closed to all sealing operations for one year in six, and

---

[3] William N. Bonner "The Fur Seal of South Georgia," 56 British Antarctic Survey Scientific Reports 56 (1968).

[4] *See* art. V(1) & (2).

[5] *See* art. IX(1)(f).

established "Seal Reserves" to protect the main breeding areas of Antarctic seals. By the late 1970s, seal populations were recovering rapidly.[6]

In 1980, in the face of mounting pressures by distant-water fishing states (e.g., Japan) to exploit Antarctica's living resources, particularly krill, the Treaty parties adopted the Convention for the Conservation of Antarctic Marine Living Resources (CCAMLR) **(Basic Document 6.3)**. CCAMLR is significant for the fact that it introduces the "ecosystem concept" to the management of the marine resources of the Southern Ocean, with article II laying down conservation principles for any harvesting activities. The Convention is therefore a model for other treaty regimes aimed at protecting marine and other resources.

Other early measures bearing on the protection of the Antarctic environment include the 1975 Code of Conduct for Antarctic Expeditions and Station Activities (unpublished) and the 1979 rules for the guidance of visitors to the Antarctic (unpublished). These measures were agreed to under the structure of the Treaty itself.

The Fight Over Mineral Resources

Something of a crisis developed within the Antarctic Treaty System (ATS) in the last three decades of the twentieth century relative to environmental threats posed by the exploitation of mineral and other resources. Oil was believed to be present in significant quantities in some areas of Antarctica, particularly in the Ross Sea and Weddell Sea basins. In 1969, Texaco had asked the United States Department of State about prospecting for minerals in Antarctica but had been discouraged. Other governments had been approached about mining also. The ATCP meetings in 1970 and 1972 included discussions about these requests and about the possibility of exploration for minerals in Antarctica. In the meantime, a United States Government report suggested tens of millions of barrels were available, and a Gulf Oil representative thought the two seas might have 50 million barrels or more combined.[7] In response to these reports, an enormous diplomatic effort was made to open up Antarctica to mineral exploitation and, in 1981, the Consultative Parties agreed to elaborate a regime to govern mineral activity in the region.

On 2 June 1988, six years of negotiations culminated in adoption of the Convention on the Regulation of Antarctic Mineral Resources Activities (CRMRA). Although there were environmental protections contained in the proposed convention, it nonetheless faced heavy opposition from various countries and environmental NGOs concerned about the inherent risks of carrying out mining operations in such a fragile environment.

---

[6] M. Payne, "Growth of a Fur Seal Population," 279 Phil. Transactions of the Royal Soc'y of London 67 (1977).

[7] H. Spival, *The Energy Crisis Spurs Idea of Seeking Oil at the South Pole,* Wall Street J. Feb. 21, 1974.

Indeed, environmental groups had consistently urged the ATS Consultative Parties to set Antarctica aside as a world park, and those groups were at the heart of a diplomatic effort, running in parallel to the effort to open the continent to mineral activities, that was aimed precisely at preventing mineral resource activities in Antarctica. At the Second World Conference on National Parks held in 1972, some delegates began talking about the possibility of treating Antarctica as a "World Park." In 1975, at the eighth Antarctic Treaty Consultative Meeting, New Zealand informally offered a bold proposal to the other Consultative Parties: Antarctica should be declared a World Park, all mineral activity on the continent should be banned, the United Nations should take on administration of Antarctica, and all claimant states should renounce their territorial claims.

New Zealand's 1975 proposal failed for lack of support within the ATS. But by the time CRMRA was signed in 1988, the political situation had changed significantly. Environmental groups that had been active in advocating for a world park regime—Greenpeace International, the Environmental Defense Fund, the Cousteau Society, and the Antarctic and Southern Ocean Coalition—commanded substantial support in the public opinion of the countries comprising the ATS, and they began rallying that support against CRMRA.

In the meantime, the United Nations General Assembly adopted a resolution attacking the Consultative Parties for negotiating the Convention. The General Assembly advanced the idea that policy in Antarctica "must be for the benefit of mankind as a whole" and that any measures for the governance of Antarctica had to be negotiated "with the full participation of all members of the international community." The General Assembly urged all members of the international community to support efforts to ban prospecting and mining around Antarctica and to establish Antarctica as "a nature reserve or a world park."[8]

Thus, by the time the negotiating countries brought CRAMRA to their home governments for ratification, public opinion in many countries had moved against the possibility of exploiting minerals in Antarctica. Australia and France led the charge to set it aside, influenced strongly by NGOs opposed to the Convention.[9] In the end, the Convention never entered into force.

The Madrid Protocol

Arising from the ashes of CRAMRA came the rapidly negotiated Protocol on Environmental Protection to the Antarctic Treaty, agreed at Madrid in 1991 **(Basic Document 6.5)**. The Protocol applies to the same geographic area as the Antarctic Treaty itself: the land and fast ice areas

[8] G.A. Res. 44/124/B (on the question of Antarctica) (Dec. 15, 1989).

[9] Geoffrey Palmer, *Environmental Politics: a Greenprint for New Zealand* (1990).

south of 60° south latitude. It is composed of twenty-seven articles plus six annexes. Annexes I-IV—dealing with environmental impact assessment, conservation of fauna and flora, waste disposal, and marine pollution—were adopted together with the Protocol and entered into force when it entered into force, in 1998. Annex V, on protected areas, entered into force in 2002. Annex VI, on liability arising from environmental emergencies, has not yet entered into force. The Protocol commits its adherents to comprehensive protection of Antarctica and its ecosystems, and designates Antarctica as a natural reserve, devoted to peace and science. Articles 2 and 3 (reproduced below) set out the basic environmental principles to be applied in Antarctica.

Under the Protocol, all activities in Antarctica are subject to prior environmental evaluation. It establishes institutions—most notably a Committee for Environmental Protection—to ensure the safeguarding of environmental values, and it covers compliance, emergency response action, and dispute settlement. In addition, it includes an affirmative undertaking to "elaborate rules and procedures relating to liability for damage" for activities in the Antarctic Treaty area and, in article 7, prohibits mineral activities other than those for scientific research. Indeed, to take the minerals issue off the agenda, the Protocol cannot be reviewed for fifty years unless there is unanimous consent. After fifty years, any nation may call for a review; but a modification to allow mining requires agreement by a majority of the parties, including three-quarters of the consultative parties.

THE 1991 PROTOCOL ON ENVIRONMENTAL PROTECTION TO THE ANTARCTIC TREATY (THE MADRID PROTOCOL)

Adopted, October 4, 1991. Entered into force, January 14, 1998
2941 UNTS 1 (Basic Document 6.5)

Article 2. Objective and Designation

The Parties commit themselves to the comprehensive protection of the Antarctic environment and dependent and associated ecosystems and hereby designate Antarctica as a natural reserve, devoted to peace and science.

Article 3. Environmental Principles

1. The protection of the Antarctic environment and dependent and associated ecosystems and the intrinsic value of Antarctica, including its wilderness and aesthetic values and its value as an area for the conduct of scientific research, in particular research essential to understanding the global environment, shall be fundamental considerations in the planning and conduct of all activities in the Antarctic Treaty area. 2. To this end:

(a) activities in the Antarctic Treaty area shall be planned and conducted so as to limit adverse impacts on the Antarctic environment and dependent and associated ecosystems;

(b) activities in the Antarctic Treaty area shall be planned and conducted so as to avoid:

(i) adverse effects on climate or weather patterns;

(ii) significant adverse effects on air or water quality;

(iii) significant changes in the atmospheric, terrestrial (including aquatic), glacial or marine environments;

(iv) detrimental changes in the distribution, abundance or productivity of species or populations of species of fauna and flora;

(v) further jeopardy to endangered or threatened species or populations of such species; or (vi) degradation of, or substantial risk to, areas of biological, scientific, historic, aesthetic or wilderness significance;

(c) activities in the Antarctic Treaty area shall be planned and conducted on the basis of information sufficient to allow prior assessments of, and informed judgments about, their possible impacts on the Antarctic environment and dependent and associated ecosystems and on the value of Antarctica for the conduct of scientific research; such judgments shall take account of:

(i) the scope of the activity, including its area, duration and intensity;

(ii) the cumulative impacts of the activity, both by itself and in combination with other activities in the Antarctic Treaty area;

(iii) whether the activity will detrimentally affect any other activity in the Antarctic Treaty area;

(iv) whether technology and procedures are available to provide for environmentally safe operations;

(v) whether there exists the capacity to monitor key environmental parameters and ecosystem components so as to identify and provide early warning of any adverse effects of the activity and to provide for such modification of operating procedures as may be necessary in the light of the results of monitoring or increased knowledge of the Antarctic environment and dependent and associated ecosystems; and

(vi) whether there exists the capacity to respond promptly and effectively to accidents, particularly those with potential environmental effects;

(d) regular and effective monitoring shall take place to allow assessment of the impacts of ongoing activities, including the verification of predicted impacts;

(e) regular and effective monitoring shall take place to facilitate early detection of the possible unforeseen effects of activities carried on both within and outside the Antarctic Treaty area on the Antarctic environment and dependent and associated ecosystems.

3. Activities shall be planned and conducted in the Antarctic Treaty area so as to accord priority to scientific research and to preserve the value of Antarctica as an area for the conduct of such research, including research essential to understanding the global environment.

4. Activities undertaken in the Antarctic Treaty area pursuant to scientific research programmes, tourism and all other governmental and non-governmental activities in the Antarctic Treaty area for which advance notice is required in accordance with Article VII(5) of the Antarctic Treaty, including associated logistic support activities, shall:

(a) take place in a manner consistent with the principles in this Article; and

(b) be modified, suspended or cancelled if they result in or threaten to result in impacts upon the Antarctic environment or dependent or associated ecosystems inconsistent with those principles.

The Protocol was a powerful response to mounting public concern over environmental issues in Antarctica. However, a word of caution: in practice, the reality of environmental protection has not always corresponded with the claim of the Antarctic Treaty parties that the protection of the environment is their foremost concern. In some cases, there have been deliberate and knowing breaches of the letter and spirit of the Treaty. The state parties have been reluctant to criticize each other, probably because they perceived that such criticism would threaten the unity of the ATS itself.

Nonetheless, and recognizing that the future of Antarctica is not easy to predict, the Protocol appears to ensure that environmental protection will be a principal goal of the Antarctic Treaty System and a permanent concern of the Consultative Parties for many years to come.

The most recent development in protection of the Antarctic environment came in February 2017 with the adoption of a Marine Protected Area in the Ross Sea area by CCAMLR. Here is the media release announcing it:

CCAMLR to create world's largest Marine Protected Area[10]

The world's experts on Antarctic marine conservation have agreed to establish a marine protected area (MPA) in Antarctica's Ross Sea.

This week at the Meeting of the Commission for the Conservation of Antarctic Marine Living Resources (CCAMLR) in Hobart, Australia, all Member countries have agreed to a joint USA/New Zealand proposal to establish a 1.55 million km^2 area of the Ross Sea with special protection from human activities.

This new MPA, to come into force in December 2017, will limit, or entirely prohibit, certain activities in order to meet specific conservation, habitat protection, ecosystem monitoring and fisheries management objectives. Seventy-two percent of the MPA will be a 'no-take' zone, which forbids all fishing, while other sections will permit some harvesting of fish and krill for scientific research.

CCAMLR Executive Secretary, Andrew Wright, is excited by this achievement and acknowledges that the decision has been several years in the making.

"This has been an incredibly complex negotiation which has required a number of Member countries bringing their hopes and concerns to the table at six annual CCAMLR meetings as well as at intersessional workshops.

"A number of details regarding the MPA are yet to be finalised but the establishment of the protected zone is in no doubt and we are incredibly proud to have reached this point," said Mr. Wright.

CCAMLR's Scientific Committee first endorsed the scientific basis for proposals for the Ross Sea region put forward by the USA and New Zealand in 2011. It invited the Commission to consider the proposals and provide guidance on how they could be progressed. Each year from 2012 to 2015 the proposal was refined in terms of the scientific data to support the proposal as well as the specific details such as exact location of the boundaries of the MPA. Details of implementation of the MPA will be negotiated through the development of a specific monitoring and assessment plan. The delegations of New Zealand and the USA will facilitate this process.

This year's decision to establish a Ross Sea MPA follows CCAMLR's establishment, in 2009, of the world's first high-seas

[10] CCAMLR to Create World's Largest Marine Protected Area, Commission for the Conservation of Antarctic Marine Living Resources (24 Feb. 2017), https://www.ccamlr.org/en/news/2016/ccamlr-create-worlds-largest-marine-protected-area.

MPA, the South Orkney Islands southern shelf MPA, a region covering 94 000 km^2 in the south Atlantic.

"This decision represents an almost unprecedented level of International cooperation regarding a large marine ecosystem comprising important benthic and pelagic habitats," said Mr Wright.

"It has been well worth the wait because there is now agreement among all Members that this is the right thing to do and they will all work towards the MPA's successful implementation," he said.

MPAs aim to provide protection to marine species, biodiversity, habitat, foraging and nursery areas, as well as to preserve historical and cultural sites. MPAs can assist in rebuilding fish stocks, supporting ecosystem processes, monitoring ecosystem change and sustaining biological diversity.

Areas closed to fishing, or in which fishing activities are restricted, can be used by scientists to compare with areas that are open to fishing. This enables scientists to research the relative impacts of fishing and other changes, such as those arising from climate change. This can help our understanding of the range of variables affecting the overall status and health of marine ecosystem.

DISCUSSION NOTES/QUESTIONS

1. The Madrid Protocol is a framework agreement. It establishes basic principles and supplements them with annexes to address particular problems, along with agreed mechanisms for adopting new annexes as needed to address new problems. At the time the agreement was adopted, several annexes were also adopted to address particular problems (e.g., conservation of flora and fauna, waste disposal, and marine pollution). But some known challenges (e.g., the impact of tourism on Antarctica) were left for the future.

One perceived problem with the Protocol is that the provisions for adopting new annexes and modifying existing annexes incorporate the decision-making processes of Article IX of the Antarctic Treaty. This means that only the Consultative Parties can participate in making such decisions, that decisions will be made by consensus, and that any action taken will become effective only when approved by the home governments of *all* the Consultative Parties. This creates obvious barriers to the adoption of new annexes. Four annexes were adopted with the Protocol and entered into force with it. In 1991, shortly after the Protocol was adopted (but before it entered into force), an additional annex on protected areas was adopted. That annex entered into force in 2002. Since 1991, only one other annex has been adopted, and it has not yet entered into force.

2. One surprising gap in the protection of Antarctica's delicate ecosystem is the fact that none of the legal instruments pertaining to Antarctica prohibit the use of nuclear power. In the 1960s, the United States was the first to install nuclear equipment in Antarctica, a 1.8 megawatt pressurized water reactor located at the McMurdo base as an experiment with cheaper forms of power production. Production began in 1962 and continued for ten years. According to the United States, the only serious problem that arose during this ten-year period was a fire caused by the hydrogen by-product of the reactor. Greenpeace International contested these claims, contending instead that the ten-year period was characterized by shutdowns, fire damage, and radiation leakages. In 1972, a U.S. Navy cost-effectiveness study concluded that it was economically unjustified to overhaul and upgrade the power plant. Subsequently, the plant was closed down and demolished. Greenpeace claims that the demolition cost $1 million and that the reactor and large quantities of radioactive earth and rocks had to be shipped back to the United States. It was not until May 1979 that the site was released for unrestricted use and declared to be "decontaminated to levels as low as reasonably achievable." *See* John May, *The Greenpeace Book of Antarctica: A New View of the Seventh Continent* (1989).

Should the Consultative Parties seek to regulate the use of nuclear power in Antarctica, or is this a matter best left to individual nations (subject, of course, to their general obligations to protect the Antarctic environment)?

3. Shortly after the Environmental Protocol was adopted, one commentator offered the following thoughts on the Protocol's ban on mining:

> The most serious problem with the Protocol's approach to mining lies in the fact that the Protocol has created a legal vacuum and a dangerous situation for the Antarctic Treaty System as a whole. There can be little doubt that minerals are available in Antarctica, and it is therefore an artifice to attempt to ignore the issue. When minerals are eventually discovered, the Protocol will prove to be fundamentally unrealistic, and its chances of survival will be virtually nil. Worse yet, having dismissed CRAMRA, there will be no regulatory framework to deal with mineral resource activities. The Antarctic environment will be basically unprotected and the Antarctic Treaty System will face the greatest crisis of its lifetime.

Francisco Orrego Vicuña, *The Protocol on Environmental Protection to the Antarctic Treaty: Questions of Effectiveness,* 7 Geo. Int'l Envtl. L. Rev. 11–12 (1994). While CRAMRA sought to permit and regulate mining, Article 7 of the Protocol says simply that "any activity relating to mineral resources, other than scientific research, shall be prohibited." Is it fair to describe this as a "legal vacuum?"

It has been more than 25 years since the Protocol was adopted and, so far, no dispute over mining has emerged. Does that mean that Vicuña was wrong and the ban is working? Or is it simply that mining in Antarctic is uneconomical. An authority on these issues from the University of Aberdeen said in 2012:[11]

> The possibility of exploration in this area first came to the fore up to 70 years ago and was given further precedence in the media spotlight during the Falklands war, when there was speculation around areas of the Antarctica which fell adjacent to the Falkland islands.
>
> In truth, we actually still know very little about Antarctica and what could lie beneath the ice. What is happening here is what I call the Eldorado complex—the idea that unknown lands will be a treasure trove of resources.
>
> We are perhaps as humans, hard-wired to be optimistic and there is certainly a build up in public perception that there are vast oil resources hidden in this area of the world, but in actuality this location might be the least prospective continent due to its geology.
>
> What we know at the moment suggests that any oil and gas would either be under kilometres of ice, or in areas of the continental shelf that are constantly scoured by giant icebergs. The task of uncovering the resources would be mammoth and unlikely to be economically viable.
>
> At the moment there is a ban on searching beneath the Antarctic for oil and gas under the international Antarctic Treaty. I suggest this political protection is all very well, but a hard, sober and rational economic view should also dictate that oil exploration in this area is not a wise option.

If the economics of oil exploration (or other mineral resource activity) change, do you expect that the Protocol's ban will be sufficient to protect the continent? What if the efforts to exploit the resources are taken under the auspices of a nation that is not a party to either the Antarctic Treaty or the Madrid Protocol?

4. Article 8 of the Protocol requires prior assessment of the environmental impact of virtually any activity that is undertaken in Antarctica, including tourism and scientific research. Under the environmental assessment provisions of Annex I, an Initial Environmental Evaluation (IEE) must be done of all activities, unless it is determined that an activity will have "less than a minor or transitory impact." If the IEE concludes that the impact will be "minor or transitory," "the activity may proceed, provided that appropriate procedures, which may include monitory, are put in place to assess and verify the impact of the activity." (Annex I, art. 2). If the IEE concludes that the impact will be more than "minor or transitory," then a Comprehensive Environmental Evaluation (CEE) must be conducted. A draft CEE must be made public, provided to all Contracting Parties, and be circulated in time for discussion at the next Consultative Meeting. The final

---

[11] Professor David Macdonald, *quoted in* University of Aberdeen News, *Is there oil in Antarctica,* 14 May 2012, *see* www.abdn.ac.uk/news/4375/.

CEE must also be provided to the Contracting Parties, along with notice of any decisions that are made with regard to the proposed activity. (Annex I, art. 3)

Three criticisms have been made of this process. First, a Party that is planning an activity has no obligation to disclose information about its environmental assessment if it concludes that the activity has no more than a "minor or transitory impact." Second, the decision concerning the extent and seriousness of the impact of an activity is left entirely to the Party itself. Finally, even though Parties must be transparent about the content of any Comprehensive Environmental Assessment they prepare, they are under no obligation to take account of any concerns expressed by other Parties. The decision whether to proceed with an activity that has a significant environmental impact is a decision left exclusively to the judgment of the Party that is sponsoring the activity.

It is also worth noting that the 1991 Protocol makes exceptions for emergencies involving human safety or life, ships, aircraft, high value equipment, or protection of the environment.

5. The issue of whether and, if so, how the Committee on Environmental Protection (CEP) should consider Comprehensive Environmental Evaluations (CEEs) was raised at the CEP during the Antarctic Treaty Consultative Meeting (ATCM XXII) held in Norway, 25 May–5 June 1998. It arose during a discussion on the process for handling a United States CEE on a project to rebuild South Pole Station. This was the first CEE to come before the Committee following the ratification of the 1991 Protocol. There were major differences of opinion between the United States and almost all other Parties about the role of the CEP. The US maintained that the CEP's role was to advise on procedure only and not on issues of substance. The US argued that the CEP was not obliged to review every draft CEE submitted to the parties. Other delegations argued that the Protocol clearly instructed the CEP, as the committee of experts, to provide comprehensive advice to the ATCM and that this necessarily involved reviewing every CEE. As a result of this debate, there was no substantive discussion on the CEE for the South Pole Rebuild and the Committee did not provide advice to the ATCM on the CEE. In the report from the CEP's third meeting, it was stressed that the role of the CEP is to examine the adequacy of draft CEEs and to provide advice on draft CEEs to the ATCM.

6. As noted, another weakness of the environmental assessment scheme is the discretion left to countries promoting an activity. While requirements for publicity and exchange of documents may induce enlightened practices to some extent (such publicity is the ultimate sanction where an activity breaches objectives and principles), vested interests are likely to influence decisions as to what constitutes a "minor or transitory impact." Also problematic is the overlap of interests where a governmental agency is responsible for both the EIA and for promoting the proposed activity. There also is the problem of private operations whose management is left largely to individual countries.

7. How might some of these gaps be closed by modifications to the EIA provisions? In early 1993, in *Environmental Defense Fund, Inc. v. National*

Science Foundation, 986 F.2d 528 (D.C.Cir.1993), reversing *Environmental Defense Fund v. Massey*, 772 F.Supp. 1296 (D.D.C. 1991), a suit brought by the United States government during the administration of President George Bush, the United States Circuit Court of Appeals for the District of Columbia, ruled that the National Environmental Policy Act, which requires EIAs for all U.S. government projects, applied to two incinerators the U.S. National Science Foundation wanted to build in Antarctica. President Bill Clinton declined to appeal the ruling. This is a reminder that individual nations may adopt EIA requirements that are more stringent than those in the Environmental Protocol, at least for activities subject to their jurisdiction and control.

8. Should the Consultative Parties have been granted greater authority to restrict or prohibit activities with serious environmental impacts? Do the Protocol's provisions in this regard suggest that, in fact, the ATCPs do not "govern" Antarctica? If Parties are free to make unilateral decisions about whether to proceed with environmentally harmful activities, does that fact not imply that sovereign prerogative reigns supreme even here? If that is the case, then what claim do the ATCPs have to govern the activities of non-party states in Antarctica?

D. AN OVERVIEW OF ENVIRONMENTAL PROBLEMS IN ANTARCTICA

Today, people undertake a myriad of activities in the Antarctic region, whether on their own or with the sponsorship and approval of a particular government. Some of these activities create obvious risks for the Antarctic environment or for Antarctic marine resources. Other activities, while not necessarily posing any serious environmental danger, may be controversial in their own right (e.g., whaling) and create risks of international conflict in the region for that reason alone. In some cases, the activities in question are the subject of regulation, and the central problem is regulatory enforcement. In other cases, the activities may not be the subject of binding rules, and the problem is to develop new rules or to find a way to control the activity in the absence of such rules.

In this section, we briefly review some of the most significant environmental risks in Antarctica, with a (non-exclusive) focus on risks posed by human activities.

Tourism

Tourism began in the Antarctic in 1958 and is now a rapidly growing industry.

> From 1958 until 1987, an average of fewer than 1000 tourists visited Antarctica each season. In the 1993–1994 season, the tourists visiting Antarctica outnumbered the scientists for the first time. In recent years (1999–2003), between 13,000 and

15,000 tourists made landings in Antarctica, and during the last season (2003–2004) this number increased by 45 percent to more than 19,500. The estimate of total passengers for the 2003–2004 season, including those not landing, is over 27,000.

Kees Bastmeijer & Ricardo Roura, *Regulating Antarctic Tourism and the Precautionary Principle,* 98 Am. J. Int'l L. 763, 763–64 (2004).

These numbers have increased dramatically since then. Estimates for the 2017–2018 season put visitors to Antarctica at a record-breaking 45,808.[12] In addition to the increasing numbers of tourists, the size of the ships visiting Antarctica also has steadily increased. In 2006/07 a vessel carrying 3,700 people (more than the 2005 peak summer population for all Antarctic national programs) operated in Antarctic waters.[13]

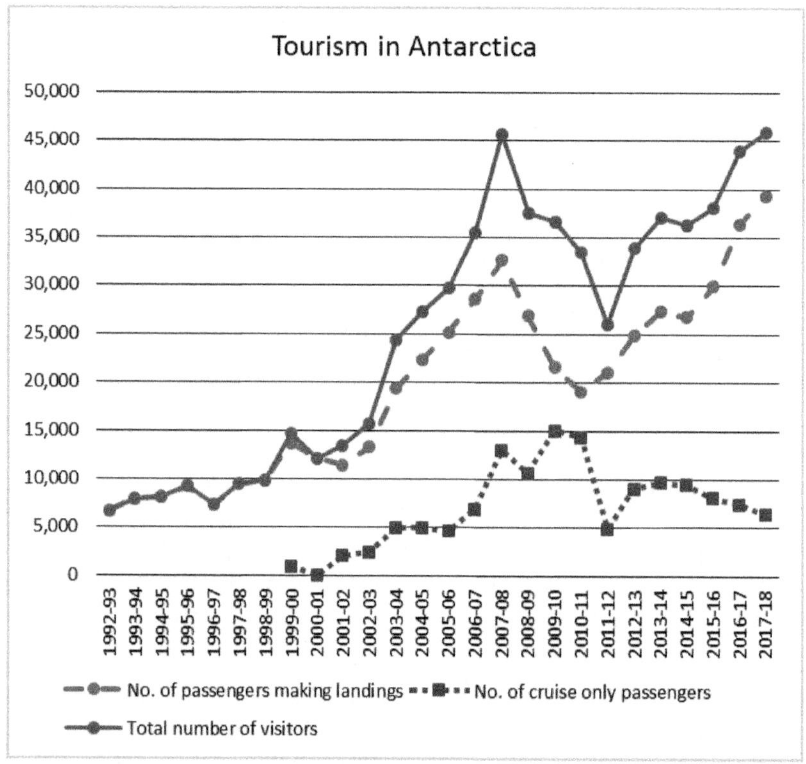

[Fig. 11-2] Graph derived from data in International Association of Antarctic Tour Operators, *IAATO Overview of Antarctic Tourism*, Informational Paper 163, XL Antarctic Treaty Consultative Meeting (Apr. 28 2017).

---

[12] *See* International Association of Antarctic Tour Operators, *IAATO Overview of Antarctic Tourism*, Informational Paper 163, XL Antarctic Treaty Consultative Meeting (Apr. 28 2017), https://iaato.org/current-iaato-information-papers.

[13] *See* Alan D. Hemmings, *Tourism and the Duty for ATCP Action*, Informational Paper 85, XXX Antarctic Treaty Consultative Meeting (2007), https://www.asoc.org/storage/documents/Meetings/ATCM/XXX/Tourism_and_the_Duty_for_ATCP_Action_-_XXX_ATCM_IP_85-2.pdf.

Increasing tourism poses many problems. First, there are the risks to the tourists themselves. There have been a number of serious tourist accidents in the Antarctic—tour ship groundings and sinkings (Southern Quest, MS Nordkapp, Lyubov Orlova, and MS Explorer), and serious air disasters (one on Mount Erebus). These accidents also create the risk of environmental harm, such as marine pollution and oil spills (as described below).

Second, there are problems connected with the sheer volume of tourist traffic in Antarctica, especially when the tourists land on the Antarctic coast.

> Tourism patterns since the early 1990s indicate a trend toward the concentration of visits in a relatively limited number of Antarctic sites and a parallel trend toward visiting new sites. All of those areas, which are often ice free, are usually biologically rich or otherwise have outstanding aesthetic, wilderness, historic, or scientific value, or a combination of those values, and are potentially susceptible to cumulative impacts. Furthermore, the tourism season, which usually extends from November to March, coincides with the peak of the breeding season for many Antarctic species.

Bastmeijer & Roura, *supra* p. 20, at 766. Even if the visit of an occasional careful tourist would have minimal impact, the visit of hundreds of tourists to the same sites can be devastating to the plant and animal life in the area, especially if the tourists behave less responsibly than one would like. Further, research is now showing that however careful people are, they leave behind more than footprints in the snow.

Most visitors to Antarctica take specialist clothing made of synthetic materials. Many take toiletries and medicines. Some take recreational drugs.

> We know this because a suite of surveys show that Antarctica is full of human litter. The sea bed in Terra Nova Bay is spotted with fragments of plastic including polyethylene, polypropylene and polystyrene. The shallow waters above swim with fragrance chemicals, chiefly amyl and hexyl salicylate, which are commonly used in soap, hair spray and fabric conditioner for their 'floral and herbal odour'. Meanwhile, the sea north of the Antarctic Peninsula, where the Larsen C iceberg could soon visit, is contaminated with drugs ranging from caffeine and ibuprofen to benzoylecgonine, a metabolite of cocaine. The strong circumpolar ocean currents around Antarctica normally seal the Southern Ocean off from the rest of the world's seas, so scientists think that most of these marine pollutants were released by visitors. One of the biggest sources is their clothing: a typical laundry load of

fleeces and specialist waterproofs can liberate more than 728,000 synthetic fibres.

Editorial, *New Antarctic Iceberg Echoes Old Problem*, 547 Nature 257 (2017).

These risks are compounded by the fact that tourism is not easily regulated. The International Association of Antarctic Tour Operations (IAATO) has for the past several decades implemented a system of industry self-regulation through a number of rules and regulations designed to ensure safe and environmentally friendly operations by its members. However, although IAATO does represent the majority of companies operating in the region, it is a voluntary organization and not every company conducting tourism activities in Antarctica is a member. It is ultimately the responsibility of the Antarctic Treaty Consultative Parties (ATCPs) to implement binding rules for activities in Antarctica, including tourism. The Antarctic Treaty Parties have adopted resolutions, recommendations, and guidelines designed to limit the impact of tourism, but these documents are not mandatory and, in any event, more than half the tourist ships visiting Antarctica are registered in non-Party states and are arguably not subject to any ATS rules.

Commercial tourism activities being carried out in the Antarctic include the operation of small boats, shore landings, Emperor Penguin colony visits and a number of 'deep field experiences' including kayaking, mountaineering, SCUBA diving, submersible diving, snorkeling, stand-up paddle boarding, skiing, snowboarding, camping (including short overnight stays), running events, helicopter operations, underwater Remote Operated Vehicles (ROVs) and Unmanned Aerial Vehicles (UAVs). These activities are undertaken in line with IAATO policies and guidelines. Most of these activities have taken place for the past decade, with some dating back to the beginning of Antarctic tourism in the late 1960s.

Finally, some countries have already sought to capitalize on the tourist boom by building facilities for tourists and taking other steps to support the tourism industry. Absent action by the Consultative Parties to stop it, the construction of more land-based tourist infrastructure is likely, with impacts similar or more severe than those attributed to science-oriented infrastructure. At the 29th meeting of the Consultative Parties in 2006, a draft resolution was proposed that would have encouraged Parties to refrain from authorizing any new permanent land-based facilities in Antarctica except for government-operated scientific facilities. The resolution was not adopted, and in 2007 New Zealand proposed that the Consultative Parties at least endorse the proposition that tourism and other non-governmental activities "should not proceed" if they would be likely to have "more than a minor or transitory impact upon the Antarctic environment." Environmental Impact of Tourism and Other Non-

Governmental Activities in the Antarctic Treaty Area, ATCM Agenda item 11/WP 13 (submitted by New Zealand). The Consultative Parties rejected that effort as well, adopting a resolution recommending that the Parties should "discourage any tourism activities which may substantially contribute to the long-term degradation of the Antarctic environment. . . ." The Antarctic Treaty Consultative Meeting, *Resolution 5* (2007), at ATCM XXX–EP X, New Delhi (2007).

More recently at the 40th meeting of the Consultative Parties in 2017 various working papers and issue papers were presented which focused on options for visitor management in the Antarctic or which set out possible strategic approaches to environmentally managed tourism. It is as yet unclear whether any of these recommendations have been adopted, but it highlights the ongoing issues arising from ever increasing tourism in the region.

There have been further discussions and measures adopted by the Treaty Parties to combat the environmental threat of tourism as the material relating to the tourism problem later in this chapter demonstrates, but they have not had sufficient effect in the views of many familiar with the problems in Antarctica.

Marine Pollution

In 1989, Argentina's supply ship, the *Bahia Paraiso*, grounded after a visit to Palmer Station.[14] The accident released approximately 170,000 gallons of diesel fuel, jet fuel, and lubricating oil into the marine environment, some of which was carried out to sea while much of the rest found its way onto the shores of nearby islands. Three hundred sixteen people were on board the ship at the time of the accident (most of them tourists), and they were taken to the nearby Palmer Station. The area is of interest, to scientists especially, because of its abundant wildlife.

Measures to prevent oil spilling from the damaged vessel were taken quickly. A Chilean navy oceanographic ship surrounded the vessel with a light boom. Staff from Palmer Station used their fleet of "zodiacs" (small inflatable boats) and the ship's lifeboats to recover drums, CNG cylinders, and other floating debris. In the United States, the National Science Foundation (which had invested a considerable sum in the research work at Palmer Station) assembled a team of experts and equipment to fly to Buenos Aires to join their research vessel RV Polar Duke. They arrived within about eight days, installed a heavier boom around the Bahia Paraiso, collected surface oil, and used chemical dispersants to break up patches of oil. Two Argentine vessels and a Chilean vessel assisted with

[14] Named after American explorer Nathaniel Palmer who, in 1820, discovered Palmer Peninsula, 60° West, without realizing that it was part of a continent.

the operations, including the sealing of the Bahia Paraiso to stop further leaking. The ship was eventually salvaged.

Soon after the grounding of the Bahia Paraiso, scientists found dead and dying krill washed up in tidal pools. Limpets, the main food source for kelp gulls, also were affected. Subsequently, skuas, penguins, and cormorants in a nearby colony were affected. Studies show that the animals most affected by the oil spill are those that regularly move in and out of the water.

The case of the Bahia Paraiso illustrates the possible effects and the difficulties that are associated with shipping accidents and marine pollution incidents in Antarctica. The Bahia Paraiso involved a relatively minor oil spill. What would be the likely consequences of an Exxon Valdez-type oil spill in Antarctica? The more human activity in Antarctica and the more ships that go there, the greater is the risk of accident leading to major marine pollution.

Add to that the increasing levels of pollution from plastics and chemicals, and a sad picture begins to emerge of an increasingly contaminated Antarctica.

Invasive species

As human activity increases in Antarctica, there is increasing risk of the introduction into the Antarctic environment of non-native species of plants or animals. Non-native species can pose a significant threat to indigenous flora and fauna, either directly or through competition for ecosystem space. A particular threat comes from ships visiting Antarctica, which frequently carry marine organisms in their ballast water. If ballast water from one biological region is discharged in a different biologically-distinct region, there is a possibility for transported species to colonize and multiply in the new region, with adverse effects for the local ecosystem. In 2006, the Consultative Parties sought to combat this threat by recommending that all ships visiting the Antarctic Treaty area follow a set of *Practical Guidelines for Ballast Water Exchange in the Antarctic Treaty Area* that are designed to minimize the risk of releases of invasive species. The Antarctic Treaty Consultative Meeting [ATCM], *Annex to Resolution 3: Practical Guidelines for Ballast Water Exchange in the Antarctic Treaty Area* (2006), at ATCM XXIX–CEP IX, Edinburgh (2006). The resolution adopting the *Practical Guidelines* is in the form of a non-binding recommendation.

Mining

Any future exploration and exploitation of mineral resources in Antarctica is likely to impact negatively on the Antarctic environment in two ways. First, there is the potential for damage to the marine ecosystem (as well as on shore from the operation of support facilities). The release of large amounts of crude oil into the Southern Ocean from tanker accidents and well blowouts, for example, could destroy the local ecosystem. Because oil takes much longer to degrade in the cold Antarctic temperatures than it does in the warmer climates, such mishaps would likely contaminate the krill (which form the bottom of the marine food chain) and thereby affect the well-being of both marine and land ecosystems. Second, a rise in particulate matter associated with oil and mineral development could alter the ability of Antarctica's ice cap to reflect the sun's heat, which in turn could cause the atmosphere to warm. Also, an increase in pollution could ruin Antarctica as a global laboratory for monitoring worldwide pollution levels.[15]

Despite the ban on mining in the Antarctic Protocol, there is reason to worry that mineral resource exploitation may become a live issue in Antarctica sooner rather than later. To date, the forbidding Antarctic environment has made mineral exploration hugely expensive and thus easy to ban. As global warming makes polar regions more accessible, this may change. States have recently begun asserting or re-asserting territorial claims in these regions. Russia recently claimed a major portion of the Arctic seabed as part of Russia's continental shelf.

In 2004, Australia filed a claim with the Commission on the Limits of the Continental Shelf, asserting sovereignty over areas of the Antarctic continental shelf. In 2006, New Zealand took a similar step, and Britain followed suit in 2007. Partially in response to Britain's action, Chile reiterated its own territorial claim to some of the same seabed areas. Although these states deny any intention to engage in mineral exploration or exploitation in these areas, environmental groups and others viewed their actions with alarm. They asserted that these sovereign claims showed the continued dangers of uncertainty about territorial authority in the Antarctic, the fragility of the Antarctic Treaty's freeze on territorial claims, the inadequacy of the Madrid Protocol as a long-term solution for environmental challenges in the region, and the need to resolve territorial claims in the Antarctic in favor of some definitive form of international ownership and control. As recently as 2016, however the Parties repeated their opposition to mining. At the 2016 ATCM, the 29 decision-making countries unanimously agreed to a resolution stating their "firm commitment to retain and continue to implement. . .as a matter of highest priority" the ban on mining activities in the Antarctic.

---

[15] *See* U.S. Department of State, Final Environmental Impact Statement on the Negotiation of an International Regime for Antarctic Mineral Resources (1982).

Icebergs

Antarctica has incredible fresh water reserves. What if someone decided to export icebergs to supply freshwater to water-short countries? Who has sovereignty over icebergs? What international law would apply to the activity? What international law should apply?

Bioprospecting

Bioprospecting is the study of the world's biological resources in plants, animals, and microorganisms. Before 1992, biological resources were considered a common heritage of mankind, which meant that scientists could take samples from anywhere in the world without any specific permission. In 1992, the Convention on Biological Diversity **(Basic Document 5.6)** was elaborated. This established sovereign national rights over biological resources.

As noted in a report by the United Nations University Institute of Advanced Studies, *The International Regime for Bioprospecting—Existing Policies and Emerging Issues for Antarctica*, 6–7 (2003):

> Bioprospecting activities in Antarctica tend to be carried out by consortia comprising a mixture of public and private bodies, making it difficult to draw a clear distinction between scientific research and commercial activities. In addition to public-private consortia, scientists on a strictly academic project may identify and exploit an organism's valuable use, thus blurring the line between scientific research and commercial activity.

Bioprospectors are interested in Antarctica for two reasons. First, the lack of knowledge surrounding Antarctica biota provides an opportunity to discover novel organisms of potential use to biotechnology. Second, Antarctica's environmental extremes, such as cold temperatures and extreme aridity and salinity, present conditions in which biota have evolved unique characteristics for survival. Thus, bioprospecting opportunities include, inter alia, the discovery of novel bioactives in species found in cold and dry lithic habitats, novel pigments found in hyper-saline lakes, and antifreezes in sea-lakes.

Amongst the many examples of commercially useful compounds discovered is a glycoprotein, which functions as the "antifreeze" that circulates in some Antarctic fish, preventing them from freezing in their sub-zero environment. The glycoprotein was discovered in the early 1970s by National Science Foundation (NSF) funded research conducted by Chi-Hing C Cheng and Liangbiao Cheng from the University of Illinois. The application of this glycoprotein in a range of processes is being considered, including increasing the freeze tolerance of commercial plants, improving farm-fish production in cold climates, extending the shelf life of frozen food, improving surgery involving the freezing of tissues, and enhancing the preservation of tissues to be transplanted. Attracted by such potentially useful discoveries, the private sector has started to include Antarctic flora and fauna in its product development programs.

Examples of companies' activities include a contract signed in 1995 between the Antarctic Cooperative Research Centre, University of Tasmania, Australia, and AMRAD Natural Products, an Australian pharmaceutical company. According to the contract, AMRAD is given the right to screen some 1,000 Antarctic microbial samples per year in search for natural antibiotics and other human pharmaceutical products. Genencor International, a global biotechnology company with more than $300 million in revenue in 1999 and over 3,000 owned and licensed patents and applications, also sources materials from Antarctica. One prominent Antarctic scientist estimated that the private sector has provided $1 million funding for Antarctic microbiology and biotechnology since 1997.

In some cases, these research activities have led to commercial applications. Patents are one indicator of the application of this research. Patents applied for or granted so far based on the bioprospecting of Antarctic biota are manifold. Preliminary investigation of the Database of the European Patent Office identified sixty-two patents that had relied upon Antarctic biodiversity. A preliminary examination of the US Patent Office Database identified over 300 references to Antarctica.

The major questions that arise in relation to bioprospecting in Antarctica include: What are the legal issues relating to the ownership and protection of these resources? Who owns the commercial products resulting from the resources? Is benefit-sharing feasible and, if so, with whom? Is bioprospecting contrary to Article III of the Antarctic Treaty?

IUU Fishing

Illegal, unreported, and unregulated fishing (IUU Fishing) is a huge problem in the Southern Ocean, as it is in other parts of the world. *See* Problem 10-2, *infra*. Fishing in the Southern Ocean is regulated by the parties to the Convention on the Conservation of Antarctic Marine Living Resources (CCAMLR) **(Basic Document 6.3)**. But fishing vessels flagged to those parties do not always comply with the regulations (illegal fishing) and fishing vessels from non-Party States are not bound by the regulations (unregulated fishing). The CCAMLR Commission estimated that IUU fishing has resulted in IUU catches in 2006 that were 10 times as large as legal catches in the Banzare Bank region. In addition, the Commission noted continued growth in IUU fishing through the Antarctic region, and a disturbing shift by fishing vessels from longline fishing to more environmentally destructive gillnet fishing. Available evidence indicates significant declines in stocks of key species, with little prospect for stock recovery in the near term. *See* CCAMLR Commission, *IUU Fishing in the Convention Area*, Report of the Twenty-Sixth Meeting of the Commission § 10 (2007).

Krill

As noted earlier in this chapter, krill are a key part of the Antarctic food chain. Global warming and ozone depletion are both blamed for declining numbers of krill, because both phenomena adversely impact the algae and plankton on which krill feed. In addition, however, there is a growing worldwide demand for krill because of its alleged health benefits and as food for commercial fish farms. At this point, the krill fishery does not appear by itself to be a significant threat to krill populations. But as fishing grows, there could be adverse impacts throughout Antarctica and especially on the penguins, whales, seals, and seabirds that depend on krill for a significant portion of their diets.

Ozone depletion

Antarctica's vulnerability to events elsewhere was revealed by the discovery, in 1985, of an ozone hole above it. This ozone hole—which first appears each year in September (when ozone levels plunge by over a third) and lasts until November—results in an increase in ultraviolet (UV) radiation exposure for Antarctic ecosystems. UV radiation has mutagenic and lethal effects on plant and animal cells, and experiments in Antarctica indicate diminished production of marine phytoplankton, including algae, with consequent declines in production of other marine life, including krill. See Mary Voyteck, *Addressing the Biological Effects of Decreased Ozone on the Antarctic Environment*, 19 Ambio 52 (1990).

Although recent studies do not indicate a catastrophic impact, they do clearly suggest a long-term, cumulative effect on the Antarctic food web, which will, in turn, have a major effect throughout the food chain and throughout the Southern Ocean ecosystem. For example, UV-induced food scarcity could have a significant effect on fish, seals, penguins, and whales. Indeed, stocks of certain whale species in the Southern Ocean are already depleted to the point where they may never recover. If food is limited because of increased competition, prey population reductions, or over-harvesting, increased UV impacts would further complicate recovery.

The discovery of the ozone hole led to rapid progress in the international legal regime now governing ozone depletion. The Montreal Protocol on Substances that Deplete the Ozone Layer **(Basic Document 2.8)**, was quickly negotiated in response to the discovery of the Antarctic ozone hole (*see* Chapter 5, *supra*) and the controls it imposed on chlorofluorocarbons (CFCs) were rapidly ratcheted up. *See* Joel Mintz, *Progress Toward a Healthy Sky*, 16 Yale J. Int'l L. 571 (1991). But despite the fact that significant steps to reduce ozone depletion have been taken (see Problem 5-2), full recovery of the ozone layer is not expected until 2050, and a significant ozone hole continues to appear over Antarctica every year.

Global Warming and Sea Level Rise

There is increasing evidence that global warming is having a profound impact in Antarctica. Although temperatures in the interior of the continent do not appear to have warmed (in fact, the interior may be cooling), changes in water temperature and wind patterns in the Southern Ocean have caused very rapid melting in western Antarctica, especially on the Antarctic Peninsula. Glaciers are receding, and major ice shelves collapsed in 2002 (Larson B ice shelf) and 2008 (Wilkins ice shelf). If this melting continues or accelerates, worldwide sea level rise from global warming could be significantly greater than previously estimated, as much as a 6.3 meter rise (over 19 feet) in Washington, D.C. if the West Antarctic Ice Sheet were to collapse. *See* Jerry X. Mitrovica et al., *The Sea-Level Fingerprint of West Antarctic Collapse*, 323 Science 753 (2009).

Science

Science has a major impact on the Antarctic environment. During the 1980s, often to satisfy more political than scientific motivations, the number of nations with scientific programs on the continent nearly doubled. Some stations are townships rather than small scientific bases (in the Antarctic summer season there are about 1,000 people at the United States stations), and typically involve the construction of bases and logistic support facilities, like airstrips, by different nations in close proximity to each other. All of which means greater environmental degradation.

For example, in May 1990, several thousand King penguins on a Macquarie Island breeding colony died, apparently in a stampede. The proximity of a large-supply aircraft flying at low altitude was consistent with the disturbance.

Also, Antarctic stations tend to disregard environmental protection agreements, like the Code of Conduct for Waste Disposal (unpublished) and the Agreed Measures. The legacy is one of pollution, with high levels of PCBs found in marine sediments, pesticide residues and other organochlorines in biological samples, and heavy metal contamination in soil. Few stations have containment facilities to prevent damage from fuel spills. What is more, Antarctic stations are turning to incineration to reduce volumes of waste. But this only transfers the impact of waste from soil and water to the air. Burning can result in new toxic products forming, the impact of which on the ecosystem is unknown.

DISCUSSION NOTES/QUESTIONS

1. As noted above, regulation of tourism in Antarctica is based largely on non-binding guidelines to which tourist operators voluntarily adhere (or not). Should the ATCPs take a more active regulatory role? If so, what should such regulations look like? Presumably, regulatory action could be taken by adopting a new annex to the Environmental Protocol, devoted entirely to tourism, or by amending existing annexes to deal with specific threats posed by tourism. Which approach would you recommend? What are the chances of securing unanimous approval by the ATCPs of your preferred approach?

2. Given the fragility of the Antarctic environment, should tourism be allowed at all? How could that be enforced? A dilemma is, of course, that tourists go home with a commitment to protecting Antarctica, thereby influencing the political climate on the future of Antarctica. Should tourism be regulated? For example, should tourists be limited to defined tourist areas? Should there be a restriction on numbers? How should that decision be made—on a country-by-country basis, or by some other method such as a ballot or an auction? Should there be a minimum standard that tourist operations must meet? Should there be comparable standards between government and non-government activities on the ice? Should there be regulation of aspects like safety, self-sufficiency, environmental impact, and emergency preparedness? Under what authority could any of this be done?

3. Should *individuals* have a duty under international law to protect the Antarctic environment? What if a tourist killed penguins? What if a vessel taking tourists to the site capsized, polluting the area and wiping out the penguins? What if a helicopter flight caused a stampede in a penguin colony during the breeding season, causing the deaths of a large number of chicks and breeding pairs, and thereby endangered the population? Who would be liable? On what authority?

4. One of the difficulties in establishing high environmental standards in Antarctica is that the governments that are the environmental watchdogs are also the sponsors (or passive supporters) of development activities in Antarctica, whether those activities consist of scientific research, tourism, or exploitation of living resources. Not surprisingly, development and operational priorities often take precedence over environmental planning and management.

Should a single body—perhaps the Antarctic Treaty Secretariat—be given responsibility for such matters as air safety, marine pollution and oil spill prevention, and contingency and emergency response planning in Antarctica? If the Consultative Parties decided to centralize control over activities in Antarctica in order to ensure those activities were conducted in accordance with the provisions of the Treaty and the Environmental Protocol, would their authority extend to controlling the activities of non-Party states and their nationals. Can the Antarctic environment possibly be protected without such centralized control? What other options exist?

5. Do you agree with the emphasis that the current regime in Antarctica puts on scientific research? Given the evidence of the serious environmental harm that can be caused by scientific stations, should we continue to encourage the expansion of research efforts in the area? Do scientists have any more right to intrude on the Antarctic ecosystem than tourists?

If you think scientific research in Antarctica justifies the resulting environmental harm, what do you consider to be the justification for that research? The discovery of glycoprotein antifreeze in Antarctica has a spin-off for stabilizing ice cream. Is this an adequate justification? If not, what would be an adequate justification? Climate change may well provide a strong argument in this respect. Antarctic ice can be used to gain a better understanding of past patterns of climate change.

What should be the limits of scientific investigation? Climate research but not bioprospecting? Climate research and bioprospecting, but not mineral prospecting? Others?

If greater regulation of scientific programs and operations is desirable, who should exercise that regulation and on what authoritative basis?

6. One reason that scientific research is likely to grow in Antarctica is that the structure of the ATS encourages such growth. In order to become a Consultative Party, and thus to have a significant voice in the governance of Antarctica, a Contracting Party to the Treaty must demonstrate "its interest in Antarctica by conducting substantial scientific research there, such as the establishment of a scientific station or the dispatch of a scientific expedition." Antarctic Treaty **(Basic Document 6.1)**, art. IX(2). It should be no surprise, therefore, that the number of nations conducting research in Antarctica is continually increasing. Would Antarctica be more appropriately governed if states that eschewed *all activities* in Antarctica (including research) had a voice in decision making?

E. TWO PROBLEMS ON THE ANTARCTIC ENVIRONMENT

Section 1. Facts

A. Unregulated Private Tourism

Andea is an economically nascent country with a small scientific research base in Antarctica located on the Saunders Coast, close to the Ross Dependency, in an area not claimed by any nation, but adjoining land claimed by New Zealand (*see* Figure 6–1, *supra*). A non-consultative party to the 1959 Antarctic Treaty **(Basic Document 6.1)**, Andea signed the 1991 Protocol on Environmental Protection **(Basic Document 6.5)** to the Antarctic Treaty just after it was negotiated in 1991. The nations present at the negotiations—both consultative and non-consultative parties—agreed in the Final Act that they all would ratify the Protocol quickly and that, until they did so, they all would act in accordance with the Protocol in so far as that was possible. But Andea was under pressure from a strong domestic environmental lobby. Thus, to secure favorable publicity that would help his government in an up-coming national election, Andea's Foreign Minister, His Excellency Enrique Carrasco, made the following press statement:

> On behalf of the Government of Andea, I welcome the Environmental Protection Protocol to the Antarctic Treaty.
>
> It is the general understanding of the parties to the Treaty contained in the Final Act that the Protocol will be ratified quickly and that, until ratification is complete, all nations will act in accordance with the Protocol as far as possible. Andea believes this most strongly.
>
> The Andean Cabinet has discussed the matter, and we give the following firm guarantee to our Antarctic Treaty partners: Andea will follow the provisions of the Protocol in every respect possible, and we will treat the Protocol as presently binding international law.

Sr. Carrasco went on to say, in conclusion: "I am sure that all of the nongovernmental organizations in Andea, which made such an impact on the fashioning of our Government's Antarctic policy, will be pleased with the position we have taken."

Copies of the foregoing statement were sent to all foreign embassies in Andea, and Andea's ambassadors were instructed to distribute copies to the foreign offices of all countries to which they were accredited.

Shortly thereafter, the incumbent government of Andea won the national election. Following the election, however, Sr. Carrasco and other Andean leaders focused their attention on domestic issues. The Protocol was put to one side and, to date, nothing has been done to ratify it. Andea's research station is more than big enough for Andea's national Antarctic program. In light of budgetary constraints and cuts to the funding for the program, it decided to use one of the buildings at the station for tourist accommodation. A private tour operator based in another country that is not party to the Antarctic Treaty or the Protocol was given the sole right to use the building under a contract between the Government of Andea and the corporation, Spectacular Adventure Tours Ltd., a company incorporated in Comros. After negotiations it was agreed that Spectacular Adventure Tours would lease the building from Andea for a term of 99 years. The company bulldozed land nearby to build an airstrip, and in so doing disturbed a large Adelie penguin colony. It also set up a windfarm with a large battery facility to provide the extra electrical power needed as a result of the increase in people in the area. The tour company promoted the site as an exclusive eco-retreat for wealthy tourists, with expansive views over Sulzberger Bay. No environmental impact assessment was completed or submitted to any party to the Protocol before the work took place.

Shortly after this work was done, there was an explosion at the wind farm caused by a battery malfunction. Burning debris from the wind turbine set fire to the research station, including storage sheds containing fuel and waste from the station as well as detergents varnishes, paints and sealants used in the upgrade of the building leased out as a tourist retreat. Efforts were made to fight the fire using chemical retardants, but the station burned to the ground. Debris from the buildings and a slick of chemical residue were released into the sea (which is within the CCAMLR area), and pushed by the wind into the waters off the Ross Dependency.

The fire forced an emergency evacuation of all people at the base. With the assistance of the *HMNZS Nelson*, a New Zealand naval vessel, the people were evacuated.

About three months ago, after a series of severe winter storms of great force, scientists and technicians appointed by the United Nations Environment Programme (UNEP) returned to the area to assess the damage. All penguins within ten miles were found to have perished and high levels of chemical residue were discovered to be present in the sea, with the result that krill, fish, seals, and whales in the area had died. A trail of greenish-black ooze had made its way along the ice shelf into the Ross Sea, causing serious pollution. Trash left over by tourists also littered the area, along with debris from the burnt station.

As a result of this environmental disaster, and because it became doubtful as to whether Andea would have the resources necessary to provide adequate cleanup, New Zealand (also a party to the 1959 Antarctic Treaty) took action to sequester all of Andea's assets within New Zealand's jurisdiction, condemning Andea's action as "in violation of international law" and requesting Andea to "cease and desist" from all operations in Antarctica "until such time as efforts are successful to restore the area to its former condition." Other States party to the 1959 Antarctic Treaty soon followed New Zealand's lead, citing, in addition, the 1989 Basel Convention on the Control of Transboundary Movements of Hazardous Wastes and Their Disposal **(Basic Document 4.7)**, another treaty to which Andea is a party.

Objecting to these actions by New Zealand and the other members of the Antarctic Treaty regime, Andea, invoking article XI(1) of the 1959 Treaty **(Basic Document 6.1)**, proposed a resolution of the dispute "by negotiation, inquiry, mediation conciliation, arbitration, judicial settlement, or other peaceful means." Desiring to establish firm legal precedent in their favor, however, New Zealand and its 1959 Treaty partners refused. After consulting with one another, and invoking article

XI(2) of the 1959 Treaty, they proposed, instead, to refer the dispute to the International Court of Justice. After much deliberation, Andea consented to this proposal, and the case is now awaiting argument at The Hague.

B. Polar Mineral Corporation Explores for Boron and Phosphorus

In the late Nineteenth Century, sealers and whalers from New Britain, a southern hemispheric nation, visited Antarctica and established huts along a relatively remote area of Antarctica's coast from which to conduct their harvesting operations during the summer season. In 1910, when interest in Antarctic exploration was at its zenith, the government of New Britain asserted a territorial claim of sovereignty over the area and has done so consistently ever since. Because of its remoteness, the area is seldom visited by scientific personnel and is well off the tourist track. However, New Britain did establish and continues to maintain a scientific research station in the area, which due to budgetary constraints is not permanently staffed.

Balaria, a medium-sized European nation, was once part of the old Soviet Union's sphere of influence and has a considerable mining industry. It jointed the Antarctic Treaty in 1998 and became a Consultative Party in 2000, but it is not a party to the Environmental Protocol.

Spurred on by recent mineral finds in Antarctica's Larsemann Hills, Balaria undertook research into the abundance of various minerals in Antarctica including boron and phosphorus. (Boron is a relatively rare element commonly used as a rocket fuel ignitor and in pyrotechnic flares, while phosphorus is increasingly difficult to find in concentration and is used most commonly in fertilizers.) Balaria reported that it had conducted ice-core sampling in the area claimed by New Britain, and a scientific survey of an area of the continental shelf for which New Britain has reserved the right to submit a claim to the Commission on the Limits of the Continental Shelf. The ice-coring and surveying was done by a private company, Polar Minerals Corporation (PMC), which is incorporated in a third State that is not party to the Antarctic Treaty or the Protocol.

A few months after this surveying was completed, a late-summer scientific expedition by the polar research institute of New Britain found evidence that the ostensibly scientific activities carried out by PMC on behalf of Balaria actually involved the removal of large quantities of boron and phosphorus minerals, including nodules from the sea floor. Evidence of this (including photographs) has been immediately reported to the New Britain government. The government of New Britain protested to Balaria and PMC on the grounds that the PMC's exploration violated the 1959 Antarctic Treaty, to which New Britain is a party, and, additionally, that it violated New Britain's claim of territorial sovereignty over the region in question. Under New Britain law, a license from the government of New

Britain is required to explore for minerals anywhere within New Britain's claimed territorial jurisdiction, and failure to secure one is an offense punishable by a fine of U.S. $100,000 for every day the activity continues. The legislation explicitly states that it extends to New Britain's Antarctic territory.

After consulting its legal counsel, Balaria and PMC served notice upon the government of New Britain that they considered PMC's operations to be lawful under the 1959 Treaty and, further, that New Britain's assertion of jurisdiction against PMC was invalid because "New Britain's territorial claim is not recognized by other nations." New Britain, having no ice breakers necessary to remove the mining equipment used by PMC to extract mineral nodules from the sea floor, called upon the United States for logistical support. After initial hesitation, the United States agreed that the equipment should be removed. The United States proceeded to remove the equipment, taking it into government custody and storing it at the U.S. Antarctica base at McMurdo Sound.

Soon after, PMC filed suit in the United States District Court for the District of Columbia praying for return of the equipment, compensation for its financial losses, and a declaratory judgment stating that its exploration activities in Antarctica were lawful. After bilateral negotiations between New Britain and the United States, it was agreed that New Britain would appear before the court to assert for itself its claim to sovereignty over the Antarctic territory in dispute. All procedural issues having been resolved and all issues of fact having been stipulated as above, the case now awaits legal argument.

Section 2. Questions Presented

There are many primary and secondary issues in both these problems that are *not* identified explicitly. Instead, trusting in your analytical talents, we leave these for you to determine—just as you would do, in fact, in the "real world" of every day legal practice. However, to facilitate clear analysis, we give you an assist; we arrange for your assistance reference to sources for each problem that should be consulted in order to define the legal issues and make the legal arguments. One problem or both can be addressed depending upon the preference of the instructor.

Section 3. Assignments

A. *Tourism*

There are a number of ways of using Problem A. The class could be divided into three. The first group would prepare a memorial for Andea. The second for New Zealand. The third would write the judgment of the Court. In order to save time, the memorial for each side could be prepared at the same time (not the case in the ICJ in real life) and the judgment a week later. Alternatively, oral argument could be heard from each side and a judgment of the court follow. This could take three class days in total.

B. Minerals

Here the issues are dealt with in a United States Court. And the assignment could include the preparation of written brief on each side and a judgment of the court.

Section 4. Readings

Possible relevant sources for Problem A (Tourism)

The following readings relate to the first scenario in this problem ("Unregulated Private Tourism").

1. Review Chapters 3 & 4, *supra*, for relevant rules and principles of customary international law

2. The Antarctic Treaty, arts. I, III, V, & X, Dec. 1, 1959, 402 U.N.T.S. 71(Basic Document 6.1)

3. Protocol on Environmental Protection to the Antarctic Treaty, arts. 2–4, 6–8, & Annexes I, III & VI, Oct. 4, 1991, 2941 U.N.T.S (Basic Document 6.5)

4. Basel Convention on the Control of Transboundary Movements of Hazardous Wastes and Their Disposal, arts. 1–4, 9, & 10, Mar. 22, 1989, 1673 U.N.T.S. 57 (Basic Document 4.7)

5. Nuclear Test Cases (New Zealand v. France), 1974 ICJ 253

[*Eds.* In 1973, Australia and New Zealand instituted proceedings before the International Court of Justice challenging the legality of French atmospheric nuclear tests in the South Pacific at France's Mururoa atoll. France denied the Court's competence and refused to appear. In the Judgment of the Court, from which the following excerpts are taken, the ICJ decided that a number of public statements made by France had rendered the case "moot" and that no decision on the merits of the legal issues was necessary.

20. Recently a number of authoritative statements have been made on behalf of the French Government [communicating its intention to cease the conduct of atmospheric nuclear tests in the South Pacific region]. . . .

46. It is well recognized that declarations made by way of unilateral acts, concerning legal or factual situations, may have the effect of creating legal obligations. Declarations of this kind may be, and often are, very specific. When it is the intention of the state making the declaration that it should become bound according to its terms, that intention confers on the declaration the character of a legal undertaking, the state being

thenceforth legally required to follow a course of conduct consistent with the declaration. An undertaking of this kind, if given publicly, and with an intent to be bound, even though not made within the context of international negotiations, is binding. In these circumstances, nothing in the nature of a *quid pro quo,* nor any subsequent acceptance of the declaration, nor even any reply or reaction from other states, is required for the declaration to take effect, since such a requirement would be inconsistent with the strictly unilateral nature of the juridical act by which the pronouncement by the state was made.

47. Of course, not all unilateral acts imply obligation; but a state may choose to take up a certain position in relation to a particular matter with the intention of being bound the intention is to be ascertained by interpretation of the act. When states make statements by which their freedom of action is to be limited, a restrictive interpretation is called for.

48. With regard to the question of form, it should be observed that this is not a domain in which international law imposes any special or strict requirements. Whether a statement is made orally or in writing makes no essential difference, for such statements made in particular circumstances may create commitments in international law, which does not require that they should be couched in written form. Thus the question of form is not decisive. As the Court said in its Judgment on the preliminary objections in the case concerning the *Temple of Preah Vihear:*

> "Where * * * as is generally the case in international law, which places the principal emphasis on the intention of the parties, the law prescribes no particular form, parties are free to choose what form they please provided their intention clearly results from it." (*I.C.J. Reports 1961,* p. 31.)

The Court further stated in the same case: " * * * the sole relevant question is whether the language employed in any given declaration does reveal a clear intention * * * " (*ibid.,* p. 32).

49. One of the basic principles governing the creation and performance of legal obligations, whatever their source, is the principle of good faith. Trust and confidence are inherent in international co-operation, in particular in an age when this co-operation in many fields is becoming increasingly essential. Just as the very rule of *pacta sunt servanda* in the law of treaties is based on good faith, so also is the binding character of an international obligation assumed by unilateral declaration. Thus interested states may take cognizance of unilateral declarations and place confidence in them, and are entitled to require that the obligation thus created be respected.

51. Of the statements by the French Government now before the Court, the most essential are clearly those made by the President of the Republic. There can be no doubt, in view of his functions, that his public

communications or statements, oral or written, as Head of State, are in international relations acts of the French State. His statements, and those of members of the French Government acting under his authority, up to the last statement made by the Minister of Defence (of 11 October 1974), constitute a whole. Thus, in whatever form these statements were expressed, they must be held to constitute an engagement of the state, having regard to their intention and to the circumstances in which they were made.

52. The unilateral statements of the French authorities were made outside the Court, publicly and *erga omnes,* even if some of them were communicated to the Government of New Zealand. As was observed above, to have legal effect, there was no need for these statements to be addressed to a particular state, nor was acceptance by any other state required. The general nature and characteristics of these statements are decisive for the evaluation of the legal implications, and it is to the interpretation of the statements that the Court must now proceed. . . .

53. In announcing that the 1974 series of atmospheric tests would be the last, the French Government conveyed to the world at large, including the Applicant, its intention effectively to terminate these tests. It was bound to assume that other states might take note of these statements and rely on their being effective. The validity of these statements and their legal consequences must be considered within the general framework of the security of international intercourse, and the confidence and trust which are so essential in the relations among states. It is from the actual substance of these statements and from the circumstances attending their making, that the legal implications of the unilateral act must be deduced. The objects of these statements are clear and they were addressed to the international community as a whole, and the Court holds that they constitute an undertaking possessing legal effect. The Court considers that the President of the Republic, in deciding upon the effective cessation of atmospheric tests, gave an undertaking to the international community to which his words were addressed. It is true that the French Government has consistently maintained that its nuclear experiments do not contravene any subsisting provision of international law, nor did France recognize that it was bound by any rule of international law to terminate its tests, but this does not affect the legal consequences of the statements examined above. The Court finds that the unilateral undertaking resulting from these statements cannot be interpreted as having been made in implicit reliance on an arbitrary power of reconsideration. The Court finds further that the French Government has undertaken an obligation the precise nature and limits of which must be understood in accordance with the actual terms in which they have been publicly expressed.

55. Thus the Court faces a situation in which the objective of the Applicant has in effect been accomplished, inasmuch as the Court finds

that France has undertaken the obligation to hold no further nuclear tests in the atmosphere in the South Pacific.

[The Judgment of the Court was, accordingly, for termination of the action with no decision on the merits of the legal issues raised by New Zealand and Australia.]

6. International Law Commission, Guiding Principles Applicable to Unilateral Declarations of States Capable of Creating Legal Obligations, 4 August 2006, Report on the Work of its Fifty-eighth Session, U.N. Doc. A/60/10 at 367 (2006) (Basic Document 1.18)

Possible Relevant Sources for Problem B (Minerals)

The following sources relate primarily but not exclusively to the second scenario in this problem ("Polar Minerals Corporation Explores for Boron and Phosphorus").

7. Charter of the United Nations, arts. 1–2, & 74, June 26, 1945, 1976 YBUN 1043, 59 Stat 1031, TS 993 (Basic Document 1.1)

8. The Antarctic Treaty, arts. I–XII, Dec. 1, 1959, 402 U.N.T.S. 71 (Basic Document 6.1)

9. Resolution on the Question of Antarctica, G.A. Res. 44/124, (Dec. 15, 1989) (Basic Document 6.4)

10. Protocol on Environmental Protection to the Antarctic Treaty, arts. 2–4, 6–8, & Annex I, Oct. 4, 1991, 2941 U.N.T.S. 3 (Basic Document 6.5)

11. United Nations Convention on the Law of the Sea (UNCLOS), arts. 192–96 & 207, Dec. 10, 1982, 1833 U.N.T.S. 3 (Basic Document 3.4)

Readings of relevance to both problems

The two documents that follow are Working Papers from the Antarctic Treaty Consultative Meeting in Beijing in 2017. The extracted text is presented exactly as it appears on the Antarctic Treaty Secretariat's website. These materials are included to provide students with assistance in consideration of the context in which both problems arise.

12. Russian Federation, Non-governmental activity in the Antarctic—current reality, requiring legal regulation, Working Paper No. 22, Fortieth Antarctic Treaty Consultative Meeting (ATCM XL), Beijing, China, 22 May–1 June 2017

The Antarctic Treaty of 1959 was signed by the delegations of governments of 12 countries, which took part in the expedition studies of the Antarctic during the period of holding the International Geophysical

Year 1957–58. Later on the governments of 41 states joined this Treaty. It is quite natural that all provisions of this act of the international law applied to the governmental activity in this region. At the same time, development of Antarctic tourism and other types of activity in this region, not related to scientific research and its logistical support, has determined appearance of a new type of activity, which was called the "non-government" activity. It was mentioned for the first time in the documents of the Antarctic Treaty Consultative Meetings (ATCMs) in Recommendation VI-7 (1970) *Effects of Tourists and Non-Government Expeditions to the Antarctic Treaty Area* at ATCM VI in Tokyo in 1970. In this document, by the non-government activity one meant missions to the Antarctic Treaty Area, not organized by any Treaty Party participating in ATCM. Later on, this notion was extended, which was connected with a significant increase of interest of the population in the Antarctic region. The sphere of these interests is often beyond the educational tourism, when different initiative groups plan to conduct yachting cruises, sports events, including adventure sport, trial of new transport types of non-industrial production, art exhibitions, public forums, concerts, amateur radio-sport expeditions, teleconferences, etc.

To be fair, it should be noted that the non-government organizations have been already successfully cooperating over a long time with the government Antarctic Programs, providing their activity with marine and air transport facilities, different types of logistical expedition support, etc. This activity can be performed both at the national and international level. As a rule, different foundations, business structures and public organizations act as sponsors of independent non-governmental projects in the Antarctic. In recent years such initiatives often attain an international character. These events are carried out with a purpose of extending business initiatives, advertising projects, support of achievements in adventure types of sport, etc. As a venue for such acts, one employs marine vessels, used for tourist operations under the programs coordinated with the International Association of Antarctica Tour Operators (IAATO), Antarctic stations and seasonal field bases, organized by government expeditions and special field camps, created by organizers for these purposes in the uninhabited regions of the Antarctic.

In the cases where organizers of non-governmental activity have legal addresses in the territory of the Consultative Parties, they aim to observe the existing national procedures for obtaining permits for activity in the Antarctic Treaty Area meeting all the requirements of the Madrid Protocol (naturally, if the Consultative Parties have such procedures).

A campaign of young Russian businessmen for testing methods of deployment of a seasonal field camp taking into account severe weather conditions in the Antarctic can serve as an example. It was held from 1 to 3 November 2016 at the Russian Antarctic Bellingshausen station by the

Leaders' Club for promotion of business initiatives. Using a chartered passenger vessel sailing under the flag of the Kingdom of the Netherlands, representatives of the Leaders' Club have delivered complexes of temporary inflatable service-living modules to Bellingshausen station with the necessary internal equipment for establishment of a temporary field camp. They held at its base their practical conference with participation of more than 100 representatives of the youth Russian business and organized a teleconference bridge via satellite with the leadership of the Russian Federation. The Initial Environmental Evaluation was prepared for all these operations and the Permit of Roshydromet No. P/2016/012 of 21 October 2016 was obtained.

Another example of organized non-governmental activity in the Antarctic is an annual field-and-track marathon race on King George Island (Waterloo) between the Antarctic stations of Uruguay, Russia, Chile and China. The formal role of organizer of this sports event was undertaken by the Canadian Tourist Company "One Ocean Expeditions" (the IAATO Member), which carries out this campaign in accordance with the national procedure, permitting activity in the Antarctic, adopted in Canada.

At the same time serious problems arise when a possibility of non-governmental activity in the Antarctic is considered in the case where such events are planned by the international associations without a clear legal address. An example of such activity is the Project "Antarctic Biennale," which was planned in the second part of March 2017 onboard the Russian vessel "Akademik Sergey Vavilov." This vessel was charted by several tourist companies for marine cruises to the area of the South Shetland Islands and the Antarctic Peninsula from the Argentine port of Ushuaia in the summer season 2016–17. A Permit No. R/2016/011 of 19 October 2016 for navigation in the aforesaid region until 31 March 2022 was granted by the authorized power body of the Russian Federation to the Russian ship-owner of the M/V "Akademik Sergey Vavilov." This Permit however was issued only for vessel navigation in Antarctic waters, rather than for the events, which organizers of the Project "Antarctic Biennale" planned to undertake at the Antarctic stations. This justification has not allowed the Russian side to conform to holding such event at the Russian Antarctic Bellingshausen station, the more so as the official request was received not from the organizing committee of the international project but from some of its Russian members.

In our opinion, the initiative of some non-government organizations to establish the Antarctic stations became a more serious problem. The first such practical example was a design and construction in the early 2000s of one of the new Antarctic stations by the initiative and using funds of the non-governmental foundation of one of the Consultative Parties. Later on, a contract was signed between this Foundation and the governmental organization responsible for the national Antarctic program of this country, for operating new station, which remained to be private property. In several years of successful operation of this Antarctic facility a legal dispute has arisen about the inappropriate use of funds from the state budget by the aforementioned foundation-operator of this station, resulting afterwards in two lawsuits. In the end, the judicial authorities of this state have permitted the governmental activity at this station only after repurchase of station permanent facilities by the government from the foundation. As a result, it was impossible to perform scientific studies of the national Antarctic Program during the past summer season. It is obvious that the government of any Consultative Party does not have available free financial resources to pay for station structures in the Antarctic in order to transfer them into its ownership. Similar situation also becomes real for similar projects of the Consultative Parties.

The Final Report of ATCM XXXV (Hobart, 2012), paragraph 227 reads: "the Russian Federation noted that non-governmental property in Antarctica could be mortgaged, leased, sold, and inherited. The new owner may be a citizen of a country which is not a Member of the Antarctic Treaty and the Protocol. In this case permanent structures may be used not for their initially intended purpose even if an EIA was available."

Although at that time the talk was about the permanent structures in the Antarctic for the purpose of Antarctic tourism, this viewpoint fully refers to other non-governmental activities in the region. The authors of this document are aware of some proposals about a possible legal transfer from the governmental organizations of facilities of the Antarctic expedition infrastructure, including operating Antarctic stations, under the management of non-governmental organizations with the aim of attracting additional financing sources for the national Antarctic programs.

In our opinion, current simplification of logistical possibility of access of different non-governmental including international organizations and private persons to the Antarctic on the one hand and appearance of new (including non-traditional) types of activity with non-predicted risks capable to significantly influence the activity of national Antarctic programs and the Antarctic environment, presents a new challenge to the effective Antarctic Treaty System.

For the purpose of working out one common approach to the aforesaid problem it is proposed to set up a permanent intersessional contact group at the ATCM forum, where participants could exchange opinions, discuss peculiarities and tendencies of development of the non-governmental activity in the Antarctic and prepare practical proposals to be considered at ATCM.

13. Norway and Belgium, Blue Ice Runway by Romnæsfjellet, Information Paper No. 66, Fortieth Antarctic Treaty Consultative Meeting (ATCM XL), Beijing, China, 22 May–1 June 2017

Summary

At ATCM XXXIX in Santiago, Chile, Norway and Belgium were tasked by the meeting to "conduct further inquiries on the development of the blue ice runway . . . and to report back to ATCM XL" (paragraph 282 of the final report). This document seeks to give an overview over the case, and summarise the facts pertaining to the development of the runway.

Background

Belgium introduced IP56 titled "*Developing a blue ice runway at Romnoes in Dronning Maud Land*" at ATCM XXXIX. As Parties will recall, the paper reported on the development of a blue ice runway by a private operator in the vicinity of Romnæsfjellet, near the Belgian Princess Elizabeth Station, in Dronning Maud Land. It noted that the operator had not submitted an IEE or CEE prior to commencing work on the runway. The meeting noted that there was a degree of confusion concerning responsibility for the activity. Norway and Belgium were tasked by the meeting to conduct further inquiries into the development of the blue ice runway, and to report to ATCM XL.

Result of inquiries

Norway and Belgium have reached out to the involved Parties and non-governmental actors (South Africa, Russia, IPF, and ALCI) to determine the course of events. It has been a challenging task to collect the necessary information due to the number of different actors involved, the complicated nuances of the case and the difficulties in identifying and therefore communicating appropriately with the key entities. In determining the course of events of this case, we sought answers to the following questions:

1. Who is the operator of the runway?
2. Who is responsible for the construction of the runway?
3. Is there any infrastructure present?
4. Has an EIA been submitted for establishment of runway, and has a permit been given for this activity?
5. Has an EIA been submitted for flights/use of the runway, and have any permits been given for this activity?

As far as we can verify, ALCI (Antarctic Logistics Centre International) is the operator in charge of construction and operation of the runway. There is no built infrastructure on the runway at present that we have been made aware of. From received documentation and as was visually confirmed during the inspection mission by Belgium and the Netherlands, there are containers, construction vehicles, building materials and other equipment present in the vicinity of the runway. There were concrete plans to erect infrastructure, but this work has been suspended.

In answering the questions relating to EIAs for the establishment of the runway, as far as we have been able to establish, plans for construction of the blue ice runway did commence before an IEE/CEE was submitted to an appropriate authority. We have, however, been notified that a draft IEE was made, and that this was sent to South African authorities for comments, but a final IEE/CEE was not submitted and an approval for the activity was not received.

An EIA has been submitted for flights to the runway. There was a test flight to the runway by Romnæsfjellet with an Ilyushin in 2015 with the aim of certifying the runway, and specialists of the Russian aeronautical authorities GOSNIIGA found the runway apt to receive IL 76 planes. This is required under Russian regulation before providing permits for flight activity. The information relating to the test-flight has been made available through EIES. Russia has conducted an IEE for flight activity, and plans to present this to the Meeting in Beijing. The impact assessment concerns flight activity, not the construction of the runway. ALCI has indicated that they have delivered an IEE to Russian authorities for the construction of the runway at Romnæsfjellet, and that Russian authorities are currently in the process of considering this IEE. It should be noted that Belgian authorities have not been given the opportunity to consider and provide input to this IEE even though the proposed runway is to be located close to the Belgian Princess Elisabeth Station.

There were plans to use the runway in a private expedition during the 16/17 season, but this did not come to fruition.

Conclusion

As far as we have been able to verify, the biggest issue in this case is that work on the runway was commissioned, equipment was transported into the location, and work on the runway was planned to begin before an EIA was in place, and before formal approval was given to the operator. ALCI should have submitted an EIA to the appropriate competent authority prior to planning or beginning work on the runway.

The establishment of a runway by Romnæsfjellet is not in itself problematic. The issue in this case was that the work began before an EIA was approved. The case does, however highlight the importance of proper procedure and clarity when multiple Parties are involved in Antarctic projects. When there are multiple Parties and private entities involved it is especially important that all parties are clear on what procedures need to be followed, and who is in charge of reporting activities to the appropriate authorities, and that all formalities are in order prior to commencing any work. In this context, it is important to emphasize the importance of Parties and private entities ensuring complete transparency with regard to their planned and intended activities in Antarctica, in the spirit of the Antarctic Treaty.

DISCUSSION NOTES/QUESTIONS

A. Tourism

1. First, review the facts of problem A ("Unregulated Private Tourism"). Is Andea bound by the Environmental Protocol **(Basic Document 6.5)** despite the fact that it has never ratified it? Andea's Foreign Minister pledged that Andea would abide by the Protocol. Is that pledge binding?

2. If Andea is bound to comply with the terms of the Environmental Protocol, did its conduct violate any provision of the Protocol? Did its conduct violate any provision of the Antarctic Treaty **(Basic Document 6.1)**? Did it violate any other treaty? Did it violate customary international law?

3. Were Andea's activities subject to environmental impact assessment? An initial environmental evaluation only? Or a comprehensive evaluation? *See* Annex I of the Environmental Protocol (**Basic Document 6.5**).

4. Did New Zealand and the other Antarctic Treaty parties violate Article XI of the Treaty when they refused to negotiate with Andea and insisted on judicial resolution of the dispute? As a general proposition, do you think negotiation or adjudication is a superior solution to conflicts in the Antarctic? Why?

5. Assuming the liability annex of the Environmental Protocol (Annex VI) is in force and binding on Andea, is Andea liable for the damage it has caused to the Antarctic environment? If the liability annex is not in force, is Andea liable under customary international law? Could anyone else be liable for the damage caused to the Antarctic environment?

6. Should the current governance structure in Antarctica be considered part of customary international law so that the rules adopted by the countries that participate in that structure are binding on the whole world? If not, then how can we protect the living resources in the Antarctic from over-exploitation?

B. Minerals

1. Did Polar Minerals' activities violate the provisions of the Antarctic Treaty **(Basic Document 6.1)**? Of the Environmental Protocol **(Basic Document 6.5)**? Were the activities peaceful? Could they be considered scientific research?

2. Do the provisions of the Antarctic Treaty or the Environmental Protocol even apply to Polar Minerals, a company incorporated in a state that is not a party to either of those agreements? What is the significance of Antarctic Treaty, art. X, and Environmental Protocol, article 13(2)?

3. Assuming that these treaty instruments do not apply to Polar Petroleum, is Polar Petroleum subject to New Britain's laws? Section 402 of the Restatement (Third) of The Foreign Relations Law of the United States (1987) purporting to reflect customary international law, says that:

> Subject to § 403, a state has jurisdiction to prescribe law with respect to:
>
> (1) (a) conduct that, wholly or in substantial part, takes place within its territory;
>
> (b) the status of persons, or interests in things, present within its territory;
>
> (c) conduct outside its territory that has or is intended to have substantial effect within its territory;
>
> (2) the activities, interests, status, or relations of its nationals outside as well as within its territory; and
>
> (3) certain conduct outside its territory by persons not its nationals that is directed against the security of the state or against a limited class of other state interests.

Jurisdiction to prescribe is "the authority of a state to make its law applicable to persons or activities." *Id.* at Introductory Note to Part IV. Section 403 further requires that the exercise of jurisdiction to prescribe (i.e., "the authority of a state to make its law applicable to persons or activities" to make binding rules) should be "reasonable."

4. Does New Britain have jurisdiction to prescribe rules for persons operating within the section of Antarctica which it claims? Within Antarctica generally? In the waters of the Antarctic coast? On what bases can it exercise such jurisdiction? In addition to the other materials cited, consider the United Nations Convention on the Law of the Sea **(Basic Document 3.4)**, articles 2–4, 89.

5. If New Britain does not have jurisdiction over Antarctica, then who does? Assuming the Antarctic Treaty parties claim some sort of "condominium jurisdiction," would it extend to the waters off the coast of Antarctica or to the seabed off the coast? *See* Antarctic Treaty, article VI and the UN Convention on the Law of the Sea, articles 1.1(1), 2, 76–77, 86–87, 136, 137, and 153.

6. Is mineral exploration in Antarctica forbidden by customary international law? Does New Britain have authority to enforce customary international law against Polar Petroleum?

C. Concluding Questions

7. As the two foregoing problems demonstrate, Antarctica provides a laboratory for international environmental law. However, since no state can claim sovereignty over it, must its problems be solved in the same way as other environmental problems? Are there approaches that might work for Antarctica that might not work for other global or regional environmental issues? Are

there approaches that might work for other global or regional environmental issues that will not work for Antarctica?

8. Perhaps the ultimate question is whether the Antarctic Treaty system can survive. With all its imperfections is it superior to any other system of governance that can be imagined for the continent? How could the current Antarctic regime, and the principles it adopts, be adapted with modifications designed to secure broader participation in the regime? Would you support an approach aimed at broader participation? Would it be harder or easier to adopt meaningful environmental protections if more countries were involved in decision making? What revisions to the decision-making process might overcome the barrier posed by the current requirement of unanimity among the Consultative Parties? Do you think such revisions would be politically feasible?

9. In 1968, the United Nations General Assembly declared the ocean seabed and its resources as the "common heritage of mankind."[16] That position was subsequently adopted in article 136 of the United Nations Convention on the Law of the Sea **(Basic Document 3.4)**. As implemented by UNCLOS, the principle of the "common heritage of mankind" (CHM) is strongly focused on the idea that benefits from the exploitation of seabed resources should be shared among all nations. Hence, UNCLOS declares that ownership of deep seabed resources is "vested in mankind as a whole," and that exploitation of those resources is only possible on terms established that the International Seabed Authority. The 1967 Outer Space Treaty similarly treats "the moon and other celestial bodies," as common property, providing that their "exploration and use . . . shall be carried out for the benefit and in the interests of all countries."[17] The 1979 Moon Agreement likewise provides that "the exploration and use of the moon shall be the province of all mankind and shall be carried out for the benefit and in the interests of all countries, irrespective of their degree of economic or scientific development."[18]

Should Antarctica be considered part of the "common heritage of mankind?" The CHM principle, as applied in international agreements, clearly contemplates the exploitation of the resources of heritage areas, albeit that exploitation is to occur in the interests of all. Thus, from the perspective of some environmentalists, application of the CHM principle to Antarctica would be inconsistent with the goals of forbidding mineral exploitation in Antarctica and preserving the continent as an ecological commons dedicated to nature preservation and scientific research. For a discussion of these issues, *see* Jem M. Spectar, *Saving the Ice Princess: NGOs, Antarctica & International Law in the New Millennium*, 23 Suffolk Transnat'l L. Rev. 57 (1999).

---

[16] G.A. Res. 2467 (1968).

[17] Treaty on Principles Governing the Activities of States in the Exploration and Use of Outer Space, including the Moon and Other Celestial Bodies, art. I, Oct. 10, 1987, 610 UNTS 205.

[18] Agreement Governing the Activities of States on the Moon and Other Celestial Bodies, art. 4, Dec. 5, 1979, 1363 UNTS 3.

On the other hand, one can see some benefits from the CHM principle—the undivided rights suggested by the notion of "common," for example, could refer to ownership rights (this precluding sovereign appropriation of the continent). The concept of "heritage" could imply transmission to future generations, in which case some regulation would be required to prevent resource destruction. The International Seabed Authority has been created by the parties to the UN Convention on the Law of the Sea to implement international policies and rules for the exploitation of the mineral resources of the deep seabed. Its rules and regulations include provisions designed to ensure that deep seabed mining does not harm the environment and that the financial benefits from exploitation of deep seabed mineral resources are shared globally. *See* International Seabed Authority, https://www.isa.org.jm, (2018). Would this be a better way to manage Antarctica than to ban resource exploitation altogether?

10. One unresolved issue is the extent to which the provisions of the United Nations Convention on the Law of the Sea **(Basic Document 3.4)** apply to the Antarctic maritime area, either by virtue of the Convention itself or by virtue of its provisions having become widely recognized as expression of international customary law. Some commentators argue that the failure of UNCLOS to directly address ocean areas within the scope of the Antarctic Treaty indicates an intention to exclude them from UNCLOS's coverage. Others observe that UNCLOS covers all ocean areas, including the Southern Ocean, and that "the exclusion of Antarctica from the ambit of the 1982 Convention's application would have required an express provision to that effect."[19]

The application of UNCLOS to Antarctica is not straightforward, however. The concept of a "coastal state" is central to the UNCLOS's system for governance of ocean spaces, and the standstill on territorial claims in Antarctica arguably precludes any state from asserting its authority as a coastal state in the region. More fundamentally, while the Antarctic claimant states would argue that they are, in fact, coastal states, the non-claimant states would, for the most part, dispute such assertions. In the absence of recognized coastal states in Antarctica, it is unclear who has the right to exercise the authority assigned to coastal states by UNCLOS to police fishing and enforce anti-pollution rules in the exclusive economic zone. For a discussion of these and related issues, *see* Davor Vidas, *The Antarctic Treaty System and the Law of the Sea: A New Dimension Introduced by the Protocol*, in Governing the Antarctic: The Effectiveness and Legitimacy of the Antarctic Treaty System 61 (Olav Schram Stokke & Davor Vidas eds., 1996).

11. Like Antarctica, the Arctic region has its share of sovereignty problems, albeit of a different sort. At least seven Arctic Ocean boundary disputes remain unresolved. Canada, for example, has formally claimed complete sovereignty over its waters while the United States, primarily for

[19] Francisco Orrego Vicuña, *The Law of the Sea and the Antarctic Treaty System: New Approaches to Offshore Jurisdiction*, *in* The Antarctic Legal Regime 101 (Christopher C. Joyner & Sudhir K. Chopra eds., 1988).

strategic military reasons, maintains that the Northwest Passage is an international strait subject to the right of transit passage. As global warming makes the Northwest Passage more accessible, this debate is likely to become more important. *See* Rob Huebert, *Climate Change and Canadian Sovereignty in the Northwest Passage,* 4 The Calgary Papers in Military and Strategic Studies (2011). *See also* Scott G. Borgerson, *Arctic Meltdown: The Economic and Security Implications of Global Warming,* 87 Foreign Aff. 63 (2008).

Despite the strategic military importance of the Arctic region, however, commentators have begun to record an increase in regional cooperation born of a growing awareness of Arctic ecosystem realities. The Arctic region, like Antarctica, plays a critical role in controlling global climate. Also, it offers in substantial proportions the hydrocarbon and mineral resources thought to exist in Antarctica. At the same time, however, the Arctic region, like Antarctica, is facing numerous pressures: pollution (particularly persistent organic pollutants, including pesticides, industrial compounds and combustion by-products), ozone depletion, and climate change, among others.

International attempts to respond to the issues facing the Arctic have resulted in an array of institutional arrangements created by a variety of actors. This has facilitated innovative experiments involving such matters as the participation of indigenous peoples' organizations in the Arctic Council, the creation of the Northern Forum as a league of subnational units of government, and the emergence of the North Atlantic Marine Mammal Commission as a body including both State and non-State actors among its members. However, the lack of a coherent, integrated system like the Antarctic Treaty System has led to criticisms that the institutional arrangements governing the Arctic are fragmented and weak. See David VanderZwaag et al., *The Arctic Environmental Protection Strategy, Arctic Council and Multilateral Environmental Initiatives: Tinkering While the Arctic Marine Environment Totters*, 30 Denver J. of Int'l L. & Pol. 131–71 (2002).

12. What lessons might be drawn from the two approaches to governance and management of the polar regions? Is one approach more desirable than the other? Antarctic history has been lauded for its relative harmony. Increased Arctic cooperation, however, perhaps provides lessons for Antarctica. Increased awareness of the systemic nature of environmental problems appears to create a more holistic perception of the area and therefore how it should be managed. Historical examples (e.g., driftnet fishing) show that public awareness of environmental issues can translate well into political awareness and legal action. How might such awareness be cultivated and exploited for effective Antarctic management?

CHAPTER TWELVE

PROTECTING AGAINST PARTICULAR HUMAN ENDEAVORS

■ ■ ■

Preceding chapters have identified transnational environmental problems with relation to particular earth-space environments—the atmosphere, the hydrosphere, the lithosphere, the biosphere, and Antarctica, or with respect to particular kinds of environmental threats (e.g., climate change or chemical pollution). But some human activities that create challenges to our ability to protect the environment cannot be so neatly categorized. We examine two such problems here—international trade and population growth.

International Trade. The pressures and incentives of international trade, like the desire for economic development generally, can contribute to the destruction of species and ecosystems when, for example, states pursue environmentally destructive practices to produce goods for export. At the same time, conditioning market access on a country's willingness to protect the environment could be a powerful means for enforcing environmental standards. The problem is, however, that the manipulation of trade barriers and market access, even if in the name of environmental protection, may run afoul of the rules and policies established by the General Agreement on Tariffs and Trade (GATT) **(Basic Document 7.1)** and other free trade agreements. Moreover, trade restrictions can lead to increased local production of goods that is more harmful to the environment than the foreign production it is replacing. Problem 12-1 raises important questions about the extent to which the GATT and it progeny prevent states from adopting environmentally motivated restrictions on international trade.

Population Growth. Population growth stretches environmental resources to their limits; unsustainable usage occurs as short-term human needs become paramount. To some extent, of course, population growth can be considered a natural phenomenon. On final analysis, however, human society is responsible for its control, and for this reason there is much debate about the true nature of the problem and about how it should be addressed. Some contend that there simply are too many people. Others argue that it is a problem essentially of resource distribution, or of the irresponsible exploitation of resources by environmentally destructive technology. Further, there are those who advocate increased population growth on the grounds that more people will compel better technological solutions. Often neglected in these debates, however, is the human rights dimension of the population problem, a neglect that some population theorists argue leads not only to gross abuses of such rights, but also to the continuation of the population problem itself. Human rights abuses certainly do exist relative to the curbing of population growth and consequently add complexity to the difficult issue of population control. Problem 12-2 addresses these issues.

PROBLEM 12-1: EUROPA IMPOSES ENVIRONMENTAL TRADE RESTRICTIONS ON BUKHARAN COTTON

Section 1. Facts

In the early 1960s, economic planners in the Soviet Union, pursuing an ambitious dream that dated to Joseph Stalin's Great Plan for the Transformation of Nature, decided to expand production of cotton by irrigating vast swaths of desert land in several Soviet republics in Central Asia. Soviet engineers built 45 dams, 85 reservoirs, and 20,000 miles of canals to divert and store the flow of two rivers—the Amu and the Syr—to provide water for cotton irrigation.

The plan worked. Soviet cotton production increased dramatically, the Soviet Union became a major cotton exporter, and "white gold" (i.e., cotton) brought economic development and a modicum of prosperity to a troubled region of the Soviet empire. After the breakup of the Soviet Union, the new nations in the region continued cotton production as before.

Unfortunately, this massive cotton irrigation system has had a devastating impact on the Aral Sea, once the world's fourth-largest body of inland water. The Aral Sea is fed primarily by the Amu and Syr rivers, and a significant inflow of water from those rivers is necessary for the sea to maintain itself. After construction of the Soviet cotton irrigation system, most of the flow of the Amu and Syr rivers was consumed in the irrigation of cotton plants. Very little water reached the Aral Sea, and the water that did get there was heavily polluted by agricultural runoff. Without a significant inflow of water from the Amu or the Syr, the Aral Sea steadily shrank. In 2010, the surface area of the sea was only 40% of its size in 1960, the sea had split into four separate bodies of water, and it had lost 80% of its total water volume. To put the loss in perspective: an amount of water equivalent to the *combined* water volume of two of North America's great lakes—Lake Erie and Lake Huron—has disappeared.

The consequences for the lake, and for the people living on or near it, have been devastating. Communities that were once thriving fishing ports or vacation resorts are now located on desert land many miles from the lake's shoreline. A fishing industry that employed 60,000 people at its height no longer exists. What water is left in the sea is so heavily polluted that few plants and animals can survive in it. As wind blows across the dried-out sea bed, it generates clouds of heavily polluted dirt and dust that impact communities as far as 150 miles away.

The Republic of Bukhara, one of the Central Asian states that was formed following the collapse of the Soviet Union in 1989, is a developing nation of 30 million people. It benefitted greatly from the Soviet Union's expansion of cotton production, and Bukhara, today, is the world's fourth leading cotton exporter. The Amu River flows through Bukhara, and, to support its vast state-controlled cotton industry, Bukhara continues to draw almost the entire flow of water from the river.

Bukhara has participated in discussions with neighboring nations about how to address the Aral Sea crisis, but it has resolutely refused to reduce its draw from the Amu River. However, Bukhara has promised to consider methods of using water more efficiently. Five years ago, it replaced a small part (about 5%) of its Soviet-era furrow irrigation system with a drip system, which proved to be more efficient than furrow irrigation. But Bukharan engineers determined that the cost of shifting to drip irrigation was prohibitively high and would price Bukharan cotton out of the world market, so that plan was abandoned.

At the same time that Bukhara was trying out new irrigation methods, it also planted about 10% of its cropland with a new genetically-modified (GM) cotton plant. Results from that experiment led Bukharan agronomists to conclude that the GM cotton used significantly less water and less fertilizer than other varieties of cotton yet still had higher yields. In response, many Bukharan cotton producers shifted to GM crops, although some continued to plant traditional crops. Today, 40% of Bukharan cotton is produced from GM cotton plants; 60% of Bukharan cotton production is still from non-genetically modified cotton plants.

Bukhara exports over 90% of its cotton crop. The majority of those exports, consisting of both cotton fiber and cotton seed oil, go to Europa, a large developed nation of 150 million people. These exports are vital to Bukhara's economy. Forty percent of Bukharan workers are employed in the agricultural sector, which accounts for 25% of Bukhara's GDP. Cotton production is responsible for nearly one-half of that income and employment.

Europa is one of the world's largest cotton-consuming countries. Most of that cotton is imported, except for a small amount of specialty "organic cotton" grown in a region of Europa that receives enough rainfall to allow cotton production without irrigation. No cotton grown in Europa is produced with GM seeds.

Two years ago, a documentary critical of the global cotton industry was televised in Europa. The documentary claimed that unsustainable cotton production was responsible for a wide variety of environmental and social ills in cotton-producing countries around the world. The documentary called special attention to the destruction of the Aral Sea in Central Asia. It also was highly critical of the widespread use of GM seeds in cotton production, pointing out that cotton is a significant food crop (cotton seed oil) as well as a source of fiber for textiles.

Large segments of Europa's population being highly concerned about the environment, the documentary generated great public interest just ahead of elections in Europa. The Green Party campaigned on promises to promote sustainable cotton production practices worldwide and to take steps to protect its population from imports of genetically-modified agricultural products. The Greens won sufficient representation to be invited into a coalition government following the elections, and thereafter the coalition promptly passed a Sustainable Cotton Import Act (SCIA).

The SCIA bans the importation of cotton or cotton products from any country where cotton is produced using irrigation—except in two instances. First, cotton can be imported if the exporting country can show that the total amount of water withdrawn from its groundwater or surface water sources (for all purposes) does not exceed the ability of the relevant water system to replenish itself. Second, the SCIA allows imports of cotton from any irrigating country if the exporter can demonstrate that the particular cotton in question was produced in a growing operation that used no irrigation and relied only on rainfall for its cotton production.

The SCIA also bans the import of any product derived from a genetically modified cotton plant.

Last year, Europa notified Bukhara that its cotton production methods were unsustainable and that no cotton or cotton seed oil would be imported from Bukhara unless the exporter could demonstrate that the cotton was produced without the use of irrigation water. Without irrigation, Bukhara cannot produce cotton, so this law will eliminate all Bukharan exports to Europa and will cripple the Bukharan cotton industry. Even if Europa backs down from its irrigation rule, the ban on products produced from genetically modified cotton plants will result in a loss to Bukhara of 40% of its cotton and cotton seed oil exports to Europa.

Bukhara and Europa are members of the World Trade Organization (WTO). After engaging in consultations with Europa, Bukhara filed a complaint with the WTO alleging that Europa's restrictions on cotton imports from Bukhara violate Articles III and XI of the General Agreement on Tariffs and Trade (GATT) **(Basic Document 7.1)**. Europa claims its actions are justified under Article XX. In addition to being WTO Members, Bukhara and Europa are also Parties to the 1992 Biodiversity Convention **(Basic Document 5.6)** and the Biosafety Protocol **(Basic Document 5.6a)**.

Section 2. Questions Presented

1. Do Europa's import restrictions on irrigated cotton violate Article III or Article XI of the GATT, and, if so, are the restrictions justified under Article XX?

2. Do Europa's import restrictions on GMO cotton violate Article III or Article XI of the GATT, and, if so, are the restrictions justified under Article XX?

Section 3. Assignments

A. Reading Assignment

Study the Readings presented in Section 4, *infra*, and the Discussion Notes/Questions that follow.

B. Recommended Writing Assignment

Prepare a comprehensive, logically sequenced, and *argumentative* brief in the form of an outline of the primary and subsidiary *legal* issues you see requiring resolution by the WTO dispute panel? Also, from the perspective of an independent objective judge, indicate which side ought to prevail on each issue and why. Retain a copy of your issue-outline/brief for class discussion.

C. Recommended Oral Assignment

Assume you are legal counsel for Bukhara or for Europa (as designated by your instructor); then, relying upon the Readings (and your issue-outline if prepared), present a 15–20 minute oral argument of your client's likely positions before the court.

D. Recommended Reflective Assignment

Consider (and recommend) alternative norms, institutions, and/or procedures that you believe might do better than existing world order arrangements to contend with situations of the kind posed by this problem. In so doing, but without insisting upon *immediate* feasibility, identify the particular transition steps that would be needed to make your alternatives a reality.

Section 4. Readings

1. Karst Kooistra, Rhiannon Pyburn, & Aad Termorshuizen, The Sustainability of Cotton: Consequences for Man and Environment, Report 223, Science Shop Wageningen University & Research Centre 6–9, 16–17, 33–34 (April 2006)

2.3.1 Irrigation

Cotton requires large amounts of water both for cultivation and processing. Irrigated cotton cultivation requires 550–950 l per square meter with an average production of 1600 kg raw cotton per hectare or 550 kg lint cotton per hectare. Otherwise stated, to produce 1 kg of cotton lint, 10,000–17,000 litres of water are needed. In areas where the normal precipitation quantity or pattern does not match the requirements of a cultivated crop, irrigation is applied. For this, rivers must be diverted, dams constructed, or soil water pumped up. Irrigation systems differ considerably in terms of efficiency, reliability and price. Irrigation is applied to 53% of the world's cotton fields, generating 73% of the world's cotton production because irrigated cotton on average results in higher yields per unit of area. It has been estimated that cotton cultivation accounts for 1–6% of world's total freshwater withdrawal. The major irrigation systems in use for cotton cultivation are described below:

- Flood-or-furrow irrigation. This is the most common type of irrigation. In this system, water is directed from a river or from deeper soil layers to the cotton field that is to be flooded. . . . The flood-or-furrow system is applied on approximately 95% of irrigated cotton fields in India, Uzbekistan, Australia, Mexico, the Yellow River region of China and the United States both on large and small scale farms. . . . The water efficiency (water that reaches the plant / water at source x 100%) of the flood-or-furrow system is approximately 40%, due to evaporation, see page losses and mismanagement, although water efficiencies as low as 20–50% have also been reported. . . .

- Mobile irrigation system. An overhead mobile irrigation system is usually made of aluminium piping with attached wheels that allow the system to be moved. This option has the ability to irrigate a very large area. Currently it is applied to only 2% of world's cotton areas. . . . The average water efficiency is high: 80–90%. It is a capital-intensive irrigation system . . . .

- Drip irrigation. A branched polypropylene pipe system doses the amount of water required by the plant and places the water exactly at the plant's root. Drip irrigation is being

> applied on less than 1% of the cotton fields. The technique is relatively expensive. . . . Drip irrigation can reduce the amount of water used by at least 16–30% compared to the most efficient flood-or-furrow systems, and is likely much higher when compared to many poorly functioning flood-or-furrow systems. The average water efficiency of drip irrigation is 90–98%.

* * *

Environmental impact

An estimated area as large as 108 (hundred million) hectares (representing 8% of the world's total arable land) is abandoned due to former use for intensive cultivation (especially cotton cultivation, although the share is not precisely known), soil salinisation being the main reason (FAO, 2002). . . .

In the twelve leading cotton producing countries an estimated 12–36% of the area under cotton cultivation is affected to some degree by salinisation. In Uzbekistan 44% of the land is now unproductive due to salinisation. Current estimates for salinisation-affected cotton areas are as follows: for India 27–60% of the irrigated land, for Pakistan 14%, Israel 13%, Australia 20%, China 15%, Iraq 50%, and Egypt 30%. . . . One-third of irrigated land is affected by salinity or is expected to become affected by salinity in the near future. This share will quite likely be higher for cotton since it tends to be cultivated in more sensitive regions. . . .

Apart from the direct effects of unsustainable water use on soil productivity there are additional significant side-effects. For large-scale irrigation projects, rivers are diverted and dammed, resulting in significant downstream effects, namely water shortages with significant effects on wildlife and water availability for human consumption. Surface water levels may drop as a result of overuse, a notable example being the Aral Sea area. . . .

Water use can be reduced by introducing more sustainable irrigation techniques, by breeding for cultivars with increased water use efficiency and, as mentioned above, increased tolerance to salinity. Shifting from flood-or-furrow irrigation to drip irrigation would significantly increase water efficiency for use in cotton production. These systems could be combined with 'irrigation-on-demand', using GPS-based techniques. However, due to the high investment costs required, these high-tech developments are not expected to be implemented in many cotton producing countries in the near future unless subsidies are provided. However, even furrow irrigation can be optimised through the use of conservation techniques, for example mulches.

* * *

2.3.7 Genetically modified cotton

One of the first plants to be modified genetically at a commercial scale was the cotton plant, mainly in an effort to reduce the quantity of pesticides used. A gene conferring resistance to glyphosate (an active ingredient in herbicides such as Roundup) was transferred into cotton for the first time in 1987. Monsanto introduced the Bt-cotton variety in 1989. The Bt-toxin-producing gene of *Bacillus thuringiensis* (Bt) was introduced into the plant's genome resulting in plant resistance against pests, notably the Bollworm. In 1996 Bt-cotton was first planted at a commercial scale in Australia and the USA. Since then, Bt and glyphosate-resistant cotton varieties have been planted in more than 20% of the area under cotton cultivation. 50% of the cotton cropped in Mexico and South Africa has been genetically modified, compared to 80% in the USA and 66% in China. Argentina, Australia, India, and Indonesia have also approved the commercial planting of genetically engineered cotton in recent years.

Since its release, Genetically Modified (GM) cotton has been the topic of considerable discussion. . . .

On the positive side genetically modified cotton is said to reduce pesticide use. . . . On the negative side, pests that are not sensitive to Bt have been observed . . . . Other negative features of Bt-cotton include that the farmer may have a higher economic risk due to the genetic homogeneity of the cotton, seed is more expensive, the farmer is more dependent on the seed producer, there is a possibility of outcrossing with wild relatives, environmental risks (the spread of GM genes to related wild species with unknown consequences), and the lack of clarity as to how the costs associated with expensive genetically modified crops will affect rural farming communities in developing countries.

* * *

. . . Lotz et al. (2000) concluded that the available literature does not indicate that cultivating glyphosate-resistant crops has major effects on the environment compared to conventional crops, though they also identified some important knowledge gaps.

IFOAM [International Federation for Organic Agriculture Movements] is opposed to genetic engineering in agriculture due to the 'unprecedented danger' it represents for the entire biosphere and the particular economic and environmental risks it poses for organic producers. IFOAM believes that genetic engineering in agriculture causes, or may cause:

a. negative and irreversible environmental impacts;

b. release of organisms which have never before existed in nature and which cannot be recalled;

c. pollution of the gene-pool of cultivated crops, micro-organisms and animals;

d. pollution of farm organisms;

e. denial of free choice, both for farmers and consumers;

f. violation of farmers' fundamental property rights and endangerment of their economic independence;

g. practices which are incompatible with the principles of sustainable agriculture;

h. unacceptable threats to human health.

2. Editors' Note: The Trade and Environment Debate

As the preceding reading illustrates, many environmental problems are caused by the manner in which products are produced. In addition, some products themselves pose or are believed to pose environmental or health risks. States (such as Europa in this problem) may seek to restrict the importation of such products either to avoid risks believed to be posed by the product itself or to discourage environmentally harmful production practices by denying market access to products produced in unsustainable ways.

The use of trade restrictions to promote environmental goals is both common and controversial. Trade restrictions are an accepted, and vital, part of international treaties regulating the disposal of hazardous waste (*see, e.g.,* Problem 8-1, *supra*), protecting endangered species (*see, e.g.,* Problem 7-2, *supra*), and controlling the use of dangerous chemicals (*see, e.g.,* Problem 8-2, *supra*). But trade restrictions are much less widely accepted when a state imposes them unilaterally. They can be a source of significant conflict and controversy, particularly when they are designed to coerce an exporting country to adopt environmental policies preferred by an importing country. Trade restrictions are also controversial when they are imposed on the basis of debatable claims about the environmental or health risks posed by the product being restricted.

Understanding the trade-environment debate requires some basic familiarity with the underlying assumptions and policy objectives of international trade law. The remainder of this note provides a necessarily brief introduction to this topic, and the readings that follow explore a few of the issues in greater depth.

Introduction to the GATT/WTO and International Trade Policy

As World War II was drawing to a close, American and British leaders began discussing the shape of the post-war world order. Many post-war planners were convinced that one of the causes of the war had been the economic turmoil of the 1930s and, in particular, the protectionist and mercantilist international economic policies that leading nations had pursued during that period. Accordingly, they resolved to create international institutions that would foster international economic openness and international economic cooperation.

The plan called for the creation of three international economic institutions, all designed to promote a liberal international economic order—i.e., an international economic order in which government intervention in the international economy was minimized, and goods and money were allowed to move across national borders with a minimum of government interference. As Gerald M. Meier put it in *The Bretton Woods Agreement—25 Years After*, 39 STAN. L. REV. 235, 245 (1971):

> [T]he IMF [International Monetary Fund] was intended to repair the disintegration that had befallen the international monetary system prior to the War, and the World Bank was designed to stimulate and support foreign investment, which had declined to insignificant amounts. . . . [The] GATT was intended to reverse the protectionist and discriminatory trade practices that had multiplied during the pre-war depression years.

The international planners were not *laissez faire* economists who opposed any government regulation of economic activity. To the contrary, both the American and British planners believed that government had a vital role to play in ensuring a vibrant economy, protecting against economic exploitation, and maintaining social safety nets for vulnerable groups. Their concern was to restrict the ability of governments to use so-called "beggar-thy-neighbor" international economic policies[1] in pursuit of domestic economic goals. Throughout the 1930s, many countries had attempted to export their economic problems to other countries through trade restrictions, manipulation of exchange rates, and preferential trade arrangements. The prevailing view was that these efforts had only made matters worse. The idea motivating the creation of the "Bretton Woods system" was that international institutions and policies could be developed that would protect future generations from the kinds of destructive restrictions on international commerce that had emerged during the 1930s and exacerbated the economic turmoil and political conflict of that decade.

The plan did not work out perfectly. Two of the institutions, the International Bank for Reconstruction and Development (IBRD), the original institution of the World Bank Group, and the International Monetary Fund (IMF), were created. A third institution, the International Trade Organization (ITO), failed to be established when it became clear

[1] A "beggar-thy-neighbor" economic policy is one that seeks to provide gains to one party at the expense of other parties. Proponents of such policies generally view international economic interaction as a zero-sum game in which one nation's benefit is another nation's loss. The framers of the post-WWII economic order saw international economic interaction as a positive-sum game in which nations would be able to enhance their overall welfare, both individually and as a group, by cooperating rather than competing in matters of economic policy.

that the U.S. Congress would not approve the Charter establishing an International Trade Organization (the Havana Charter). In place of the ITO was the General Agreement on Tariffs and Trade (GATT) **(Basic Document 7.1)**, negotiated simultaneously with the Havana Charter.

The GATT was intended to be only a short-term agreement on tariff reductions. The diplomats who negotiated the GATT assumed that it would be incorporated into the International Trade Organization, so they created only minimal rules for decision-making, dispute settlement, etc. No formal trade institution was created by the GATT, nor was it meant to be a permanent arrangement for governing trade relations. Indeed, the parties who signed the GATT agreed to apply it only provisionally.

When the ITO failed to receive U.S. congressional approval, the GATT was left as the only tool with which to pursue the dream of an international trade organization to manage international trade relations and promote trade liberalization. The international community made do with what they had been given. Despite the fact that the GATT was never intended as anything other than a temporary, provisional tariff-cutting agreement, it became the basis for the creation of a de facto international trade organization that lasted for over 40 years.

In 1994–95, after a decade of negotiations, the international community finally succeeded in achieving a formal agreement creating an international trade organization. This organization, called the World Trade Organization (WTO), was established to give formal legitimacy to the institutional structures that had grown up around the GATT and to provide a unified organizational structure for the many agreements about various trade issues that the GATT members had created over the years.

The Agreement Establishing the World Trade Organization (WTO) **(Basic Document 7.6)** is short—only a few pages. But attached to the Agreement as annexes are dozens of additional agreements (including an updated version of the original GATT). These additional agreements run into hundreds of pages, and most of them are binding on all WTO Members.[2] Many of the additional agreements reflect past practice under the GATT. But some agreements that became part of the WTO system addressed new issues not previously handled by GATT, such as trade in services and protection of intellectual property rights.

Despite the changes brought by the creation of the WTO, the original GATT agreement remains at the heart of the international trade system (renamed as GATT 1994 and slightly revised). The liberalizing rules it adopted remain at the foundation of nearly all other international trade law. The institutional structure provided by the WTO, and the new or expanded additional agreements that are part of the WTO system, have

[2] *See* Agreement Establishing the World Trade Organization **(Basic Document 7.6)**, Article II:2.

resulted in a more sophisticated and highly-developed body of law governing international trade. But the basic principles and rules of that legal system remain the principles and rules that were established by the GATT in 1948.

The preamble of the GATT states that its purpose is to create "arrangements directed to the substantial reduction of tariffs and other barriers to trade and to the elimination of discriminatory treatment in international commerce." The preamble to the WTO agreement repeats this goal and reaffirms the objective to strengthen the multilateral trading system and make "more viable and durable" the "results of past trade liberalization efforts." Trade liberalization and the protection of past agreements to reduce trade barriers are the centrals goal of the WTO/GATT legal system. The trade liberalization goal, however, is viewed as a means to achieve more fundamental goals, including "raising standards of living, ensuring full employment, . . . allowing for the optimal use of the world's resources in accordance with the objective of sustainable development," [and] enhancing the means to "protect and preserve the environment."[3]

The WTO's preamble reflects the views of many economists who argue that trade liberalization brings significant economic benefits to importing and exporting countries, that it promotes the efficient use of resources, and that it is likely to be less environmentally harmful than economic activity that occurs behind trade barriers. They also believe that the use of trade barriers to address environmental problems is, in many cases, only a second- or third-best alternative to meeting those problems head-on (e.g., through international environmental agreements or economic assistance to help exporting countries meet their environmental challenges). Indeed, the WTO Secretariat has argued that trade liberalization serves environmental goals by reducing poverty (and hence reducing the unsustainable natural resource exploitation that is common in very poor communities), fostering more efficient (i.e., less wasteful) use of resources, making environmental goods and services more widely available, and generally fostering international cooperation through ongoing multilateral interaction.[4]

An Overview of Some Environmental Arguments against Liberalized Trade

The privileging of free trade over environmental goals

The trade/environment conflict is partially a result of the historical and institutional differences in the way the world community has addressed trade and environmental issues. For over 70 years, the

---

[3] *Id.* preamble, ¶ 1.

[4] *See* WTO Secretariat, *Environmental Benefits of Removing Trade Restrictions and Distortions*, WTO Doc WT/CTE/W/67 (Nov. 7, 1997).

international community has accepted the need for international rules designed to promote a policy of liberal international trade and to discourage individual nations from departing from that policy. Moreover, the international community has created an institution that is charged with administering that policy and has given that institution important responsibilities.

By contrast, strong international action aimed at environmental protection is a relatively recent phenomenon. Moreover, environmental problems are addressed internationally on a piecemeal basis, through a patchwork quilt of international agreements administered by a dizzying array of independent organizations and secretariats, each of which has a limited mandate. There is no single, strong, institution charged with the responsibility for coordinating and managing the world's response to environmental problems. Nor are the principles and norms of international environmental law quite as definitive, clear, and strong as are the norms of international trade law.

This difference between the established international policies of liberalized trade and the emergent policies of environmental protection seems especially stark to environmental advocates when, as is often the case, disputes about environmentally motivated trade restrictions end up being adjudicated within the trade system's dispute settlement process; the international system, it often is argued, thus privileges the policies of liberalized international trade over environmental objectives.

The problem of externalities

Persons or firms that engage in economic activity do not always bear the full costs of that activity. Consider a cloth factory that creates a large amount of air pollution. In the absence of government regulation, the factory owners generally do not pay for polluting the air, nor are they likely to suffer the cost of the pollution (e.g., breathing polluted air)—typically they live away from the factory. The air pollution cost falls not on the factory owners, but "externally" on the people who live near the factory (or, in some cases, people who live thousands of miles away, *see* Problem 5-1, *supra*). And this cost might be significant: if, for example, the air pollution causes serious adverse health effects for the people who live around the factory, that will lead in turn to high health care costs. These are costs attributable to production of the cloth, but they won't be reflected in its price.

As long as the factory owners do not bear these "external costs," they are likely to continue manufacturing and selling cloth, even if the overall social value of the cloth is less than the social cost (direct costs of production plus external costs) incurred to produce it. If, however, the owners have to pay for the air pollution (e.g., by installing scrubbers to eliminate it or compensating the nearby residents for the damage caused to them by the pollution), they may decide that the profits from cloth production do not justify their incurring the costs of production. In that case, society would be better off without the cloth production because the costs it is imposing exceed the benefits it creates. In short, because environmental damage is often an "externality" from the point of view of persons engaged in economic production, there is a risk of too much economic production and not enough environmental protection.

In our current system of ecological governance, there are a number of possible ways to ensure that the environmental costs of various activities are taken into account by the people who engage in those activities. If this is done, the "externality" is turned into an "internality"—a cost the polluter must bear—so that the polluter will pollute only if the benefits from the activity exceed its costs (including the environmental costs). The polluter could be forced to "pay" through regulations requiring it to clean up the pollution, by allowing persons injured by the pollution to sue for damages, or in other ways. For example, a factory that generates hazardous waste could be required to bear the cost of disposing of the waste in a safe and effective manner.

There is a special problem with externalities that occur internationally. For example, if one country emits ozone-depleting substances or greenhouse gases that contribute to environmental problems that affect everyone—and that may, in fact, cause much greater harm to others than to the country where the emissions occur—there is not much that can be done absent an international government that can directly regulate the polluting country's activities. To put the point another way, the polluting country imposes "external costs" on other countries, and there is no international government that can force the polluter to internalize those costs absent its voluntary agreement to reduce pollution. Many environmental advocates believe that trade restrictions are an important tool that other countries can use to modify the offending country's behavior and force it to internalize the costs of its domestic production.

Richard Stewart identifies four kinds of international externalities that can be caused by a nation's environmental policies (or lack thereof):[5]

1. Pollution spillovers (pollution created by economic production in one nation is deposited in another);
2. Resource use externalities (a nation's overexploitation of a resource denies users in another nation of future access to the resource);
3. Preservation externalities—denial of non-use benefits (a nation's exploitation of a resource deprives individuals in

[5] Richard B. Stewart, *International Trade and Environment: Lessons from the Federal Experience*, 49 Wash. & Lee L. Rev. 1329 (1992).

another nation of "the value that comes from knowing of the existence of the resource," even if they don't intend to use it); and

4. Competitiveness externalities (a nation's lack of environmental regulations gives its firms a competitiveness advantage and imposes a corresponding disadvantage on others).

Restrictions on trade in the products of the offending nation are, in the view of many people, a legitimate tool for addressing externalities like these.

The "race to the bottom" argument

Stewart's "competitiveness externalities" reference the argument, frequently made, that free trade will encourage production in countries with the lowest environmental standards—i.e., where social costs of environmental harm are not imposed on the producer but are left to fall on society as a whole. As a result, some say, free trade will encourage all nations to lower their environmental standards so that their industries can remain competitive. At the very least, it is argued, free trade will chill the development of new environmental protections because industry groups will lobby against any regulations that will hurt their international competitiveness.

Some economists doubt that a race to the bottom actually occurs. As nations develop economically through free trade, according to the counter argument, they become better able to afford environmental protection and their consumers increasingly demand it. According to this view, a high level of environmental protection is a "luxury good" in the sense that people are willing to pay for it only after their more basic needs have been satisfied. Thus, it is said, rich nations will not lower standards to compete because rich nations will have a national preference for environmental protection. Poor countries, if allowed to grow, will eventually adopt adequate standards as well. Hence, a nation's tolerance for pollution should simply be seen as part of its (temporary) comparative advantage as a poor country.[6]

Ecological economics

Some environmentalists argue that the fundamental problem with free trade and free trade theory is that it is based on the notion that more is always better than less. Thus, economic analysis in general and free trade analysis in particular is oriented at determining how the economy can most efficiently exploit available resources. Moreover, free trade makes the whole world's resources available for exploitation by the globe's most

---

[6] *See* Jagdish Bhagwati & T.N. Srinivasan, *Trade and the Environment: Does Environmental Diversity Detract from the Case for Free Trade*, in 1 Fair Trade and Harmonization: Prerequisites for Free Trade?, ch. 4 (1996).

efficient producers (and most voracious consumers) regardless of where they live, thus allowing greater production with the same amount of resources.

Some people who object to this state of affairs argue for a fundamental change in the way we think about economic policy. If economic policy were truly environmentally friendly, it would be directed at reducing consumption and making it costly. Rather than strive constantly to grow our economies (which means, inevitably, to consume more natural resources in the production of more material goods), we should strive to conserve resources and to live on a smaller scale, in harmony with the ecological system. Stopping free trade and unregulated globalization would contribute to such a goal because it would force national economies to rely only on their own resources for their production. They would thus be forced to restrain their production now (because resources are limited) and to conserve their resources for the future (because they could not get them from elsewhere). From this perspective, free trade is bad for at least two reasons:

- an *ecological* reason: it allows nations to consume what they cannot themselves produce (e.g., imported oil, imported food) and encourages them to live beyond their ecological means; and
- a *social justice* reason: free trade allows rich nations to consume and destroy the natural resources of poor nations.

Moral considerations

In *Economics and the Environment: A Case of Ethical Neglect,* 26 Ecological Econ. 151, 153 (1998), Timothy N. Jenkins argues that

> it is inadequate to address ecological and social problems by relying entirely on pragmatic utilitarian moral attitudes in combination with scientific understanding of natural systems. Some form of "environmental reverence" is also required which requires a metaphysical grounding.

Jenkins goes on to suggest (at 159–62) that there is developing in the West a "postmodern land ethic . . . premised on the idea that an individual is a member of an interdependent [ecological] community" and that this ethic may lead to a "new benign postmodernism" to replace the "malign modernist model." For Jenkins, "environmental problems are a moral, rather than an institutional issue" and "their solution lies in changing personal moral values rather than in institutional action." The "main objective" of an environmental movement "should be to combat the current promotion of irresponsible technological civilisation inspired by an obsolete worldview . . . through a thorough programme of education and information." Trade restrictions imposed by "enlightened" nations to combat bad environmental practices by others, it may be argued, could be one way to promote the needed new outlook on production and consumption.

3. General Agreement on Tariffs and Trade (GATT), arts. I, III, XI, & XX, April 15, 1994, 1867 UNTS 243 (Basic Document 7.1)

Article I: General Most-Favoured-Nation Treatment

1. With respect to customs duties and charges of any kind imposed on or in connection with importation or exportation or imposed on the international transfer of payments for imports or exports, and with respect to the method of levying such duties and charges, and with respect to all rules and formalities in connection with importation and exportation, and with respect to all matters referred to in paragraphs 2 and 4 of Article III, any advantage, favour, privilege or immunity granted by any contracting party to any product originating in or destined for any other country shall be accorded immediately and unconditionally to the like product originating in or destined for the territories of all other contracting parties.

Article III: National Treatment on Internal Taxation and Regulation

1. The contracting parties recognize that internal taxes and other internal charges, and laws, regulations and requirements affecting the internal sale, offering for sale, purchase, transportation, distribution or use of products, and internal quantitative regulations requiring the mixture processing or use of products in specified amounts or proportions, should not be applied to imported or domestic products so as to afford protection to domestic production.

2. The products of the territory of any contracting party imported into the territory of any other contracting party shall not be subject, directly or indirectly, to internal taxes or other internal charges of any kind in excess of those applied, directly or indirectly, to like domestic products. Moreover, no contracting party shall otherwise apply internal taxes or other internal charges to imported or domestic products in a manner contrary to the principles set forth in paragraph 1.

3. With respect to any existing internal tax which is inconsistent with the provisions of paragraph 2, but which is specifically authorized under a trade agreement, in force on April 10, 1947, in which the import duty on the taxed product is bound against increase, the contracting party imposing the tax shall be free to postpone the application of the provisions of paragraph 2 to such tax until such time as it can obtain release from the obligations of such trade agreement in order to permit the increase of such duty to the extent necessary to compensate for the elimination of the protective element of the tax.

4. The products of the territory of any contracting party imported into the territory of any other contracting party shall be accorded treatment no less favourable than that accorded to like products of national origin in respect of all laws, regulations and requirements affecting their internal sale, offering for sale, purchase, transportation, distribution or use. The provisions of this paragraph shall not prevent the applications of differential internal transportation charges which are based exclusively on the economic operation of the means of transport and not on the nationality of the product.

Article XI: General Elimination of Quantitative Restrictions

1. No prohibitions or restrictions other than duties, taxes or other charges, whether made effective through quotas, import or export licences or other measures, shall be instituted or maintained by any contracting party on the importation of any product of the territory of any other contracting party or on the exportation or sale for export of any product destined for the territory of any other contracting party.

* * *

Article XX: General Exceptions

Subject to the requirement that such measures are not applied in a manner which would constitute a means of arbitrary or unjustifiable discrimination between countries where the same conditions prevail, or a disguised restriction on international trade, nothing in this Agreement shall be construed to prevent the adoption or enforcement by any contracting party of measures:

* * *

(b) necessary to protect human, animal or plant life or health;

* * *

(g) relating to the conservation of exhaustible natural resources if such measures are made effective in conjunction with restrictions on domestic production or consumption . . . .

4. Editors' Note

Articles I, III, and XI of the GATT are three of the most important rules in international trade law. Article I requires that all WTO Members treat imports from other WTO Members equally. Thus, if Europa imports cotton from Egypt and charges a 5% tariff rate, it may not charge a 25% tariff on cotton from Bukhara. Any "advantage, favour, privilege or immunity granted by" Europa to cotton originating in "shall be accorded

immediately and unconditionally to the like product originating in" Bukhara. This is called "most favoured nation" or MFN treatment.[7]

Article III of the GATT requires WTO Members to treat imported products exactly the same as they treat domestically produced "like products" with respect to "internal taxes" and "laws, regulations and requirements affecting the internal sale, offering for sale, purchase, transportation, distribution or use of products, and internal quantitative regulations." Thus, if Europa charges a 5% sales tax on cotton products produced in Europa, it may not charge a 10% sales tax on cotton products from Bukhara. If Europa allows cotton to be used in clothing made in Europa, it cannot insist that clothing made in Bukhara must be made from wool. This is called national treatment—once foreign-produced products are allowed in a country, they must be treated the same as domestically produced products.

Finally, Article XI of the GATT is designed to prohibit all forms of trade restrictions other than tariffs. Thus, Article XI says that no trade restrictions "other than duties, taxes or other charges" may be imposed on imported products. In particular, a WTO Member is not supposed to use quotas (limits on the quantity of goods that can be imported) or outright import bans. Any import restrictions should be in the form of tariffs only.

All these GATT rules are subject to exceptions of one sort or another. The most important exceptions, for our purposes, are the general exceptions in Article XX, which allow trade restrictions to be used in pursuit of certain specified environmental goals. In particular, trade restrictions can be used "when necessary to protect human, animal or plant life or health" (e.g., a restriction of agricultural imports from a country where a particularly dangerous food-borne disease was prevalent) or to conserve "exhaustible natural resources." Any restrictions imposed for these purposes must satisfy the requirements in the *chapeau* (the opening paragraph) of Article XX: they must not be applied in a manner that creates an "arbitrary or unjustifiable discrimination between countries where the same conditions prevail" and they must not amount to "a disguised restriction on international trade."

A number of legal issues have arisen in the interpretation of these GATT provisions, and the law in this area is very technical. One of the most important questions is what constitutes "like products" under Articles I and Article III. In particular, can products be differentiated on the basis of how they are produced? If, for example, cotton produced using irrigation is the same as (a "like product" to) cotton produced without irrigation, then discriminating against irrigated cotton may violate Article I (MFN) or

[7] There are exceptions to MFN treatment. In general, countries that are partners in a free trade area or customs union can give one another advantages that are not given to outsiders. In addition, preferential treatment can be given to the products of developing countries over those of more advanced countries.

Article III (National Treatment) or both. If, on the other hand, irrigated cotton is not a "like product" to non-irrigated cotton, then discrimination against irrigated cotton would not violate Articles I or III.

To date, the WTO decisions seem to support the view that "cotton is cotton"—that the way in which a particular product is produced is not relevant to whether it is "like" another product unless the production method changes the characteristics of the product in some way. To the extent that rule applies, then trade restrictions based on production methods of a product would need to be justified under Article XX of the GATT. But, of course, the line between production methods that change the "characteristics" of a product and those that do not is not always easy to draw. Is cotton produced from genetically modified seed the same as cotton produced from non-modified seed? What if the product is not cotton, but cotton seed oil?

5. United States-Import Prohibition of Certain Shrimp And Shrimp Products, WTO Doc. WT/DS58/AB/R (WTO Appellate Body Report, 12 October 1998)

[*Eds.*—The United States required domestic shrimp trawlers to equip their nets with turtle excluder devices (TEDs) to prevent the nets from entrapping sea turtles and drowning them. The United States also banned importation of shrimp from other states unless those states had similar requirements in place for their shrimp trawlers. The law imposing this import ban is referred to in the WTO decision as "Section 609."

India, Malaysia, Pakistan and Thailand filed a complaint alleging that the shrimp import restrictions violated GATT rules. The United States conceded a probable violation of GATT Article XI, but declined to discuss arguments that its law also violated Articles I and III of GATT. Instead, it argued that its actions were justified under GATT Article XX.

At the time of the decision, the WTO Appellate Body had developed a two-step approach to applying Article XX. First, it must be determined whether a trade restriction is "provisionally justified." This amounts to deciding whether the restriction falls within an Article XX exception. If a measure is provisionally justified, then it must be decided whether it satisfied the requirements of the *chapeau* (i.e. no arbitrary or unjustifiable discrimination and the measure is not a disguised restriction on international trade).

Excerpts from the Appellate Body's decision follow.]

114. [The meaning of any GATT provision must be ascertained by applying the "customary rules of interpretation of public international law." These rules of interpretation] call for an examination of the ordinary meaning of the words of a treaty, read in their context, and in the light of the object and purpose of the treaty involved. A treaty interpreter must

begin with, and focus upon, the text of the particular provision to be interpreted. It is in the words constituting that provision, read in their context, that the object and purpose of the states parties to the treaty must first be sought. Where the meaning imparted by the text itself is equivocal or inconclusive, or where confirmation of the correctness of the reading of the text itself is desired, light from the object and purpose of the treaty as a whole may usefully be sought.

* * *

Article XX(g): Provisional Justification of Section 609

125. In claiming justification for its measure, the United States primarily invokes Article XX(g). . . .

* * *

1. Exhaustible natural resources

127. We begin with the threshold question of whether Section 609 is a measure concerned with the conservation of "exhaustible natural resources" within the meaning of Article XX(g). . . . India, Pakistan and Thailand contended that a "reasonable interpretation" of the term "exhaustible" is that the term refers to "finite resources such as minerals, rather than biological or renewable resources." In their view, such finite resources were exhaustible "because there was a limited supply which could and would be depleted unit for unit as the resources were consumed." Moreover, they argued, if "all" natural resources were considered to be exhaustible, the term "exhaustible" would become superfluous. They also referred to the drafting history of Article XX(g), and, in particular, to the mention of minerals, such as manganese, in the context of arguments made by some delegations that "export restrictions" should be permitted for the preservation of scarce natural resources. For its part, Malaysia added that sea turtles, being living creatures, could only be considered under Article XX(b), since Article XX(g) was meant for "nonliving exhaustible natural resources." It followed, according to Malaysia, that the United States cannot invoke both the Article XX(b) and the Article XX(g) exceptions simultaneously.

128. We are not convinced by these arguments. Textually, Article XX(g) is not limited to the conservation of "mineral" or "non-living" natural resources. The complainants' principal argument is rooted in the notion that "living" natural resources are "renewable" and therefore cannot be "exhaustible" natural resources. We do not believe that "exhaustible" natural resources and "renewable" natural resources are mutually exclusive. One lesson that modern biological sciences teach us is that living species, though in principle, capable of reproduction and, in that sense, "renewable' " are in certain circumstances indeed susceptible of depletion, exhaustion and extinction, frequently because of human activities. Living

resources are just as "finite" as petroleum, iron ore and other non-living resources.

129. The words of Article XX(g), "exhaustible natural resources' " were actually crafted more than 50 years ago. They must be read by a treaty interpreter in the light of contemporary concerns of the community of nations about the protection and conservation of the environment. . . . The preamble of the WTO Agreement—which informs not only the GATT 1994, but also the other covered agreements—explicitly acknowledges "the objective of sustainable development" . . . .

130. From the perspective embodied in the preamble of the WTO Agreement, we note that the generic term "natural resources" in Article XX(g) is not "static" in its content or reference but is rather "by definition, evolutionary." It is, therefore, pertinent to note that modern international conventions and declarations make frequent references to natural resources as embracing both living and non-living resources. For instance, the 1982 United Nations Convention on the Law of the Sea ("UNCLOS"), in [Article 56, 61 and 62] repeatedly refers . . . to "living resources" in specifying rights and duties of states in their exclusive economic zones. The Convention on Biological Diversity uses the concept of "biological resources." Agenda 21 [Basic Document 1.31] speaks most broadly of "natural resources" and goes into detailed statements about "marine living resources." . . .

131. Given the recent acknowledgement by the international community of the importance of concerted bilateral or multilateral action to protect living natural resources, and recalling the explicit recognition by WTO Members of the objective of sustainable development in the preamble of the WTO Agreement, we believe it is too late in the day to suppose that Article XX(g) of the GATT 1994 may be read as referring only to the conservation of exhaustible mineral or other non-living natural resources. Moreover, two adopted GATT 1947 panel reports previously found fish to be an "exhaustible natural resource" within the meaning of Article XX(g). We hold that, in line with the principle of effectiveness in treaty interpretation, measures to conserve exhaustible natural re-sources, whether living or non-living, may fall within Article XX(g).

132. We turn next to the issue of whether the living natural re-sources sought to be conserved by the measure are "exhaustible" under Article XX(g). That this element is present in respect of the five species of sea turtles here involved appears to be conceded by all the participants and third participants in this case. The exhaustibility of sea turtles would in fact have been very difficult to controvert since all of the seven recognized species of sea turtles are today listed in Appendix 1 of the Convention on International Trade in Endangered Species of Wild Fauna and Flora

("CITES"). The list in Appendix 1 includes "all species threatened with extinction which are or may be affected by trade" (emphasis added).

133. Finally, we observe that sea turtles are highly migratory animals, passing in and out of waters subject to the rights of jurisdiction of various coastal states and the high seas. In the Panel Report, the Panel said:

> . . . Information brought to the attention of the Panel, including documented statements from the experts, tends to confirm the fact that sea turtles, in certain circumstances of their lives, migrate through the waters of several countries and the high sea. . . . (emphasis added)

The sea turtle species here at stake, i.e., covered by Section 609, are all known to occur in waters over which the United States exercises jurisdiction. Of course, it is not claimed that all populations of these species migrate to, or traverse, at one time or another, waters subject to United States jurisdiction. Neither the appellant nor any of the appellees claims any rights of exclusive ownership over the sea turtles, at least not while they are swimming freely in their natural habitat—the oceans. We do not pass upon the question of whether there is an implied jurisdictional limitation in Article XX(g), and if so, the nature or extent of that limitation. We note only that in the specific circumstances of the case before us, there is a sufficient nexus between the migratory and endangered marine populations involved and the United States for purposes of Article XX(g).

134. For all the foregoing reasons, we find that the sea turtles here involved constitute "exhaustible natural resources" for purposes of Article XX(g) of the GATT 1994.

2. *"Relating to the Conservation of [Exhaustible Natural Resources]"*

135. Article XX(g) requires that the measure sought to be justified be one which "relat[es] to" the conservation of exhaustible natural resources. In making this determination, the treaty interpreter essentially looks into the relationship between the measure at stake and the legitimate policy of conserving exhaustible natural resources. It is well to bear in mind that the policy of protecting and conserving the endangered sea turtles here involved is shared by all participants and third participants in this appeal, indeed, by the vast majority of the nations of the world. None of the parties to this dispute question the genuineness of the commitment of the others to that policy.

* * *

138. Section 609(b)(1) imposes an import ban on shrimp that have been harvested with commercial fishing technology which may adversely affect sea turtles. This provision is designed to influence countries to adopt national regulatory programs requiring the use of TEDs by their shrimp fishermen. . . . [Countries can avoid the ban by being "certified."]

139. There are two types of certification for countries under Section 609(b)(2). First, under Section 609(b)(2)(C), a country may be certified as having a fishing environment that does not pose a threat of incidental taking of sea turtles in the course of commercial shrimp trawl harvesting. [E.g., because no sea turtles live in the region where the fishing occurs.] There is no risk, or only a negligible risk, that sea turtles will be harmed by shrimp trawling in such an environment.

140. The second type of certification is provided by Section 609(b)(2)(A) and (B). Under these provisions, as further elaborated in the 1996 Guidelines, a country wishing to export shrimp to the United States is required to adopt a regulatory program that is comparable to that of the United States program and to have a rate of incidental take of sea turtles that is comparable to the average rate of United States' vessels. This is, essentially, a requirement that a country adopt a regulatory program requiring the use of TEDs by commercial shrimp trawling vessels in areas where there is a likelihood of intercepting sea turtles.

This requirement is, in our view, directly connected with the policy of conservation of sea turtles. It is undisputed among the participants, and recognized by the experts consulted by the Panel, that the harvesting of shrimp by commercial shrimp trawling vessels with mechanical retrieval devices in waters where shrimp and sea turtles coincide is a significant cause of sea turtle mortality. Moreover, the Panel did "not question . . . the fact generally acknowledged by the experts that TEDs, when properly installed and adapted to the local area, would be an effective tool for the preservation of sea turtles."

141. In its general design and structure, therefore, Section 609 is not a simple, blanket prohibition of the importation of shrimp imposed without regard to the consequences (or lack thereof) of the mode of harvesting employed upon the incidental capture and mortality of sea turtles. Focusing on the design of the measure here at stake, it appears to us that Section 609, cum implementing guidelines, is not disproportionately wide in its scope and reach in relation to the policy objective of protection and conservation of sea turtle species. The means are, in principle, reasonably related to the ends. The means and ends relationship between Section 609 and the legitimate policy of conserving an exhaustible, and, in fact, endangered species, is observably a close and real one. . . .

142. In our view, therefore, Section 609 is a measure "relating to" the conservation of an exhaustible natural resource within the meaning of Article XX(g) of the GATT 1994.

* * *

3. *"If Such Measures are Made Effective in conjunction with Restrictions on Domestic Production or Consumption"*

* * *

144. . . . [Regulations issued pursuant to the Endangered Species Act] require United States shrimp trawlers to use approved TEDs "in areas and at times when there is a likelihood of intercepting sea turtles' " with certain limited exceptions. . . .

145. Accordingly, we hold that Section 609 is a measure made effective in conjunction with the restrictions on domestic harvesting of shrimp, as required by Article XX(g).

The Introductory Clauses of Article XX: Characterizing Section 609 under the Chapeau's Standards

* * *

156. . . . . [T]he chapeau of Article XX . . . embodies the recognition on the part of WTO Members of the need to maintain a balance of rights and obligations between the right of a Member to invoke one or another of the exceptions of Article XX, specified in paragraphs (a) to (j), on the one hand, and the substantive rights of the other Members under the GATT 1994, on the other hand. Exercise by one Member of its right to invoke an exception, such as Article XX(g), if abused or misused, will, to that extent, erode or render naught the substantive treaty rights in, for example, Article XI:1, of other Members. Similarly, because the GATT 1994 itself makes available the exceptions of Article XX, in recognition of the legitimate nature of the policies and interests there embodied, the right to invoke one of those exceptions is not to be rendered illusory. . . .

* * *

159. The task of interpreting and applying the chapeau is, hence, essentially the delicate one of locating and marking out a line of equilibrium between the right of a Member to invoke an exception under Article XX and the rights of the other Members under varying substantive provisions (e.g., Article XI) of the GATT 1994, so that neither of the competing rights will cancel out the other and thereby distort and nullify or impair the balance of rights and obligations constructed by the Members themselves in that Agreement. The location of the line of equilibrium, as expressed in the chapeau, is not fixed and unchanging; the line moves as the kind and the shape of the measures at stake vary and as the facts making up specific cases differ.

160. With these general considerations in mind, we address now the issue of whether the application of the United States measure, although the measure itself falls within the terms of Article XX(g), nevertheless constitutes "a means of arbitrary or unjustifiable discrimination between

countries where the same conditions prevail" or "a disguised restriction on international trade." . . .

2. *"Unjustifiable Discrimination"*

* * *

163. The actual application of the [U.S. import restriction], through the implementation of the 1996 Guidelines and the regulatory practice of administrators, requires other WTO Members to adopt a regulatory program that is not merely comparable, but rather essentially the same, as that applied to the United States shrimp trawl vessels. Thus, the effect of the application of Section 609 is to establish a rigid and unbending standard by which United States officials determine whether or not countries will be certified, thus granting or refusing other countries the right to export shrimp to the United States. Other specific policies and measures that an exporting country may have adopted for the protection and conservation of sea turtles are not taken into account, in practice, by the administrators making the comparability determination.

164. We understand that the United States also applies a uniform standard throughout its territory, regardless of the particular conditions existing in certain parts of the country. The United States requires the use of approved TEDs at all times by domestic, commercial shrimp trawl vessels operating in waters where there is any likelihood that they may interact with sea turtles, regardless of the actual incidence of sea turtles in those waters, the species of those sea turtles, or other differences or disparities that may exist in different parts of the United States. It may be quite acceptable for a government, in adopting and implementing a domestic policy, to adopt a single standard applicable to all its citizens throughout that country. However, it is not acceptable, in international trade relations, for one WTO Member to use an economic embargo to require other Members to adopt essentially the same comprehensive regulatory program, to achieve a certain policy goal, as that in force within that Member's territory, without taking into consideration different conditions which may occur in the territories of those other Members.

165. Furthermore, when this dispute was before the Panel and before us, the United States did not permit imports of shrimp harvested by commercial shrimp trawl vessels using TEDs comparable in effectiveness to those required in the United States if those shrimp originated in waters of countries not certified under Section 609. In other words, shrimp caught using methods identical to those employed in the United States have been excluded from the United States market solely because they have been caught in waters of countries that have not been certified by the United States. The resulting situation is difficult to reconcile with the declared policy objective of protecting and conserving sea turtles. This suggests to us that this measure, in its application, is more concerned with effectively

influencing WTO Members to adopt essentially the same comprehensive regulatory regime as that applied by the United States to its domestic shrimp trawlers, even though many of those Members may be differently situated. We believe that discrimination results not only when countries in which the same conditions prevail are differently treated, but also when the application of the measure at issue does not allow for any inquiry into the appropriateness of the regulatory program for the conditions prevailing in those exporting countries.

166. Another aspect of the application of Section 609 that bears heavily in any appraisal of justifiable or unjustifiable discrimination is the failure of the United States to engage the appellees, as well as other Members exporting shrimp to the United States, in serious, across-the-board negotiations with the objective of concluding bilateral or multilateral agreements for the protection and conservation of sea turtles, before enforcing the import prohibition against the shrimp exports of those other Members. . . .

167. A propos this failure to have prior consistent recourse to diplomacy as an instrument of environmental protection policy, which produces discriminatory impacts on countries exporting shrimp to the United States with which no international agreements are reached or even seriously attempted, a number of points must be made. First, the Congress of the United States expressly recognized the importance of securing international agreements for the protection and conservation of the sea turtle species in enacting this law. . . .

168. Second, the protection and conservation of highly migratory species of sea turtles, that is, the very policy objective of the measure, demands concerted and cooperative efforts on the part of the many countries whose waters are traversed in the course of recurrent sea turtle migrations. The need for, and the appropriateness of, such efforts have been recognized in the WTO itself as well as in a significant number of other international instruments and declarations. As stated earlier, the Decision on Trade and Environment, which provided for the establishment of the CTE and set out its terms of reference, refers to both the Rio Declaration on Environment and Development and Agenda 21. Of particular relevance is Principle 12 of the Rio Declaration on Environment and Development, which states, in part:

> Unilateral actions to deal with environmental challenges outside the jurisdiction of the importing country should be avoided. Environmental measures addressing transboundary or global environmental problems should, as far as possible, be based on international consensus.

In almost identical language, paragraph 2.22(i) of Agenda 21 provides:

> Governments should encourage GATT, UNCTAD and other relevant international and regional economic institutions to examine, in accordance with their respective mandates and competences, the following propositions and principles: . . .
>
> (i) Avoid unilateral action to deal with environmental challenges out-side the jurisdiction of the importing country. Environmental measures addressing transborder problems should, as far as possible, be based on an international consensus.

Moreover, we note that Article 5 of the Convention on Biological Diversity states:

> . . . each contracting party shall, as far as possible and as appropriate, cooperate with other contracting parties directly or, where appropriate, through competent international organizations, in respect of areas beyond national jurisdiction and on other matters of mutual interest, for the conservation and sustainable use of biological diversity.

* * *

169. Third, the United States did negotiate and conclude one regional international agreement for the protection and conservation of sea turtles: The Inter-American Convention. . . .

* * *

171. The Inter-American Convention thus provides convincing demonstration that an alternative course of action was reasonably open to the United States for securing the legitimate policy goal of its measure, a course of action other than the unilateral and non-consensual procedures of the import prohibition under Section 609. It is relevant to observe that an import prohibition is, ordinarily, the heaviest "weapon" in a Member's armoury of trade measures. The record does not, however, show that serious efforts were made by the United States to negotiate similar agreements with any other country or group of countries before (and, as far as the record shows, after) Section 609 was enforced on a world-wide basis on 1 May 1996. Finally, the record also does not show that the appellant, the United States, attempted to have recourse to such international mechanisms as exist to achieve cooperative efforts to protect and conserve sea turtles before imposing the import ban.

172. Clearly, the United States negotiated seriously with some, but not with other Members (including the appellees), that export shrimp to the United States. The effect is plainly discriminatory and, in our view, unjustifiable. . . . As we have emphasized earlier, the policies relating to the necessity for use of particular kinds of TEDs in various maritime areas,

and the operating details of these policies, are all shaped by the Department of State, without the participation of the exporting Members. The system and processes of certification are established and administered by the United States agencies alone. The decision-making involved in the grant, denial or withdrawal of certification to the exporting Members, is, accordingly, also unilateral. The unilateral character of the application of Section 609 heightens the disruptive and discriminatory influence of the import prohibition and underscores its unjustifiability.

6. European Communities-Measures Affecting Asbestos and Asbestos-Containing Products, WTO Doc WT/DS135/AB/R (WTO Appellate Body Report, 12 March 2001)

[*Eds.*—France banned the manufacture, sale, and import of "all varieties of asbestos fibres" and of "any product containing asbestos fibres." It permitted limited and temporary exceptions for certain materials or products containing asbestos fibres when no substitute for those fibres was available that would pose a lesser risk to workers and would meet the safety requirements for the product in question.

Canada filed a complaint with the WTO, claiming that the French decree was inconsistent with the EC's obligations under Articles III and XI of the GATT 1994 and was not justified under Article XX. Canada complained, in particular, that the decree unfairly discriminated against cement products made with asbestos fibres (as opposed to cement products made with other types of fibres).

Excerpts from the Appellate Body's decision follow.]

C. Examining the "Likeness" of Products under Article III:4 of the GATT 1994

110. We turn to consideration of how a treaty interpreter should proceed in determining whether products are "like" under Article III:4. As in Article III:2, in this determination, "[n]o one approach . . . will be appropriate for all cases." Rather, an assessment utilizing "an unavoidable element of individual, discretionary judgement" has to be made on a case-by-case basis. The Report of the Working Party on Border Tax Adjustments outlined an approach for analyzing "likeness" that has been followed and developed since by several panels and the Appellate Body. This approach has, in the main, consisted of employing four general criteria in analyzing "likeness": (i) the properties, nature and quality of the products; (ii) the end-uses of the products; (iii) consumers' tastes and habits—more comprehensively termed consumers' perceptions and behaviour—in respect of the products; and (iv) the tariff classification of the products. We note that these four criteria comprise four categories of "characteristics" that the products involved might share: (i) the physical properties of the products; (ii) the extent to which the products are capable of serving the same or similar end-uses; (iii) the extent to which consumers perceive and

treat the products as alternative means of performing particular functions in order to satisfy a particular want or demand; and (iv) the international classification of the products for tariff purposes.

* * *

113. The European Communities argues that the inquiry into the physical properties of products must include a consideration of the risks posed by the product to human health. In examining the physical properties of the product at issue in this dispute, the Panel found that "it was not appropriate to apply the 'risk' criterion proposed by the EC." . . . [A]s we have said, in examining the "likeness" of products, panels must evaluate all of the relevant evidence. We are very much of the view that evidence relating to the health risks associated with a product may be pertinent in an examination of "likeness" under Article III:4 of the GATT 1994. We do not, however, consider that the evidence relating to the health risks associated with chrysotile asbestos fibres need be examined under a separate criterion, because we believe that this evidence can be evaluated under the existing criteria of physical properties, and of consumers' tastes and habits, to which we will come below.

114. Panels must examine fully the physical properties of products. In particular, panels must examine those physical properties of products that are likely to influence the competitive relationship between products in the marketplace. In the case of chrysotile asbestos fibres, their molecular structure, chemical composition, and fibrillation capacity are important because the microscopic particles and filaments of chrysotile asbestos fibres are carcinogenic in humans, following inhalation. . . .

This carcinogenicity, or toxicity, constitutes, as we see it, a defining aspect of the physical properties of chrysotile asbestos fibres. The evidence indicates that PCG fibres, in contrast, do not share these proper-ties, at least to the same extent. We do not see how this highly significant physical difference cannot be a consideration in examining the physical properties of a product as part of a determination of "likeness" under Article III:4 of the GATT 1994.

* * *

116. We, therefore, find that the Panel erred, in paragraph 8.132 of the Panel Report, in excluding the health risks associated with chrysotile asbestos fibres from its examination of the physical properties of that product.

* * *

3. Cement-based products containing chrysotile and PCG fibres

* * *

128. As the Panel said, the primary physical difference between cement-based products containing chrysotile asbestos fibres and cement-based products containing PCG fibres lies in the particular fibre incorporated into the product. This difference is important because, as we have said in our examination of fibres, we believe that the health risks associated with a product may be relevant to the inquiry into the physical properties of a product when making a determination of "likeness" under Article III:4 of the GATT 1994. This is also true for cement-based products containing the different fibres. In examining the physical properties of the two sets of cement-based products, it cannot be ignored that one set of products contains a fibre known to be highly carcinogenic, while the other does not. . . . We, therefore, reverse the Panel's finding, in paragraph 8.149 of the Panel Report, that these health risks are not relevant in examining the "likeness" of the cement-based products.

* * *

VII. Article XX(b) of the GATT 1994 and Article 11 of the DSU

155. Under Article XX(b) of the GATT 1994, the Panel examined . . . whether the measure at issue is "necessary to protect human . . . life or health." . . .

* * *

168. As to Canada's third argument, relating to the level of protection, we note that it is undisputed that WTO Members have the right to determine the level of protection of health that they consider appropriate in a given situation. France has determined, and the Panel accepted, that the chosen level of health protection by France is a "halt" to the spread of asbestos-related health risks. By prohibiting all forms of amphibole asbestos, and by severely restricting the use of chrysotile asbestos, the measure at issue is clearly designed and apt to achieve that level of health protection. Our conclusion is not altered by the fact that PCG fibres might pose a risk to health. The scientific evidence before the Panel indicated that the risk posed by the PCG fibres is, in any case, less than the risk posed by chrysotile asbestos fibres, although that evidence did not indicate that the risk posed by PCG fibres is non-existent. Accordingly, it seems to us perfectly legitimate for a Member to seek to halt the spread of a highly risky product while allowing the use of a less risky product in its place. In short, we do not agree with Canada's third argument.

169. In its fourth argument, Canada asserts that the Panel erred in finding that "controlled use" is not a reasonably available alternative to the Decree. This last argument is based on Canada's assertion that . . . an

alternative measure is only excluded as a "reasonably available" alternative if implementation of that measure is "impossible." . . .

170. Looking at this issue now, we believe that, in determining whether a suggested alternative measure is "reasonably available' " several factors must be taken into account, besides the difficulty of implementation. In Thailand-Restrictions on Importation of and Internal Taxes on Cigarettes, the panel made the following observations on the applicable standard for evaluating whether a measure is "necessary" under Article XX(b):

> The import restrictions imposed by Thailand could be considered to be "necessary" in terms of Article XX(b) only if there were no alternative measure consistent with the General Agreement, or less inconsistent with it, which Thailand could reasonably be expected to employ to achieve its health policy objectives. (emphasis added)

171. In our Report in Korea-Beef, we addressed the issue of "necessity" under Article XX(d) of the GATT 1994. In that appeal, we found that the panel was correct in following the standard set forth by the panel in United States-Section 337 of the Tariff Act of 1930:

> It was clear to the Panel that a contracting party cannot justify a measure inconsistent with another GATT provision as "necessary" in terms of Article XX(d) if an alternative measure which it could reasonably be expected to employ and which is not inconsistent with other GATT provisions is available to it. By the same token, in cases where a measure consistent with other GATT provisions is not reasonably available, a contracting party is bound to use, among the measures reasonably available to it, that which entails the least degree of inconsistency with other GATT provisions.

172. We indicated in Korea-Beef that one aspect of the "weighing and balancing process . . . comprehended in the determination of whether a WTO-consistent alternative measure" is reasonably available is the extent to which the alternative measure "contributes to the realization of the end pursued." In addition, we observed, in that case, that "[t]he more vital or important [the] common interests or values" pursued, the easier it would be to accept as "necessary" measures designed to achieve those ends. In this case, the objective pursued by the measure is the preservation of human life and health through the elimination, or reduction, of the well-known, and life-threatening, health risks posed by asbestos fibres. The value pursued is both vital and important in the highest degree. The remaining question, then, is whether there is an alternative measure that would achieve the same end and that is less restrictive of trade than a prohibition.

173. Canada asserts that "controlled use" represents a "reasonably available" measure that would serve the same end. The issue is, thus, whether France could reasonably be expected to employ "controlled use" practices to achieve its chosen level of health protection—a halt in the spread of asbestos-related health risks.

174. In our view, France could not reasonably be expected to employ any alternative measure if that measure would involve a continuation of the very risk that the Decree seeks to "halt." Such an alternative measure would, in effect, prevent France from achieving its chosen level of health protection. On the basis of the scientific evidence before it, the Panel found that, in general, the efficacy of "controlled use" remains to be demonstrated. Moreover, even in cases where "controlled use" practices are applied "with greater certainty" the scientific evidence suggests that the level of exposure can, in some circumstances, still be high enough for there to be a "significant residual risk of developing asbestos-related diseases." The Panel found too that the efficacy of "controlled use" is particularly doubtful for the building industry and for DIY enthusiasts, which are the most important users of cement-based products containing chrysotile asbestos. Given these factual findings by the Panel, we believe that "controlled use" would not allow France to achieve its chosen level of health protection by halting the spread of asbestos-related health risks. "Controlled use" would, thus, not be an alternative measure that would achieve the end sought by France.

7. Cartagena Protocol on Biosafety, arts. 1–4, 7–8 & 10, Jan. 29, 2000, 2226 UNTS 208 (Basic Document 5.6a)

Section 5. Discussion Notes/Questions

1. Does Europa's ban on imports of irrigated cotton violate the GATT **(Basic Document 7.1)**? Consider the following questions:

   a. Has Europa violated GATT Article III? Is irrigated cotton a "like product" to rain-fed cotton? Is the potentially adverse environmental impact of irrigation a basis upon which a lawful distinction between otherwise "like" products can be made under Article III?

   b. Does the ban on importation of irrigated cotton violate GATT Article XI?

   c. What GATT Article XX exceptions might apply to justify Europa's restriction on irrigated cotton?

   d. If Europa invokes Article XX(g), what issues arise? Is Europa's law related to "conservation of exhaustible natural resources"?

e. Is Europa entitled to impose trade restrictions to protect natural resources located wholly within other nations, or must it have some kind of territorial nexus with the resources being protected? Does Europa have a legitimate interest in seeking to protect water resources in other states? If Europa were beset by environmental refugees from states where water resources had been depleted, would this change the GATT analysis?

f. What additional facts do you need to know to determine whether Europa's action is "made effective in conjunction with restrictions on domestic production or consumption"?

2. What about Europa's ban on imports of GMO cotton?

a. Has Europa violated GATT Article III? Is GMO cotton a "like product" to conventional cotton?

b. Does the ban on importation of GMO cotton violate GATT Article XI?

c. What GATT Article XX exceptions might apply to justify Europa's restriction on irrigated cotton?

d. If Europa invokes both Articles XX(b) and XX(g), what issues arise? Is Europa's law "necessary" to protect human or plant life or health? Is a ban on GMO cotton related to "conservation of exhaustible natural resources"? Are there more facts you need to know?

e. If there is a dispute about the actual or potential risks of GMO cotton or cotton seed oil, what deference should be given to Europa's decision to ban importation? Should Europa's assessment of risk be given complete deference? If so, what is left of the requirement that trade restrictions be imposed only when "necessary." If a WTO decision-making body is entitled to determine whether there is a risk or not, what problems do you foresee?

For a thoughtful discussion of the challenges of requiring nations to justify trade restrictions with "scientific evidence" while still respecting each nation's sovereign right to determine for itself what safety and health risks are tolerable, *see* Alan O. Sykes, *Domestic Regulation, Sovereignty, and Scientific Evidence Requirements: A Pessimistic View,* 3 Chi. J. Int'l L. 353 (2002).

3. If Europa's restrictions on irrigated and GMO cotton are provisionally justified, what issues arise regarding application of the Article XX *chapeau* to evaluate Europa's law? Must Europa consider the steps Bukhara has taken to decrease its water usage? Must Europa consider Bukhara's economic need to export cotton? Must Europa seek to consult and negotiate with Bukhara before imposing a trade restriction (no irrigated cotton) designed to affect water conservation in Bukhara?

Is Principle 12 of the Rio Declaration relevant to the interpretation and application of Article XX of the GATT?

4. In *European Communities—Measures Affecting the Approval and Marketing of Biotech Products*, the United States, Canada, and Argentina challenged the European Union's processes for approving products that contain or are produced from genetically modified organisms. In a report that is more than 1000 pages long, a WTO Panel found that the EU rules violated certain aspects of the WTO Agreement on the Application of Sanitary and Phytosanitary Measures, but it specifically refused to consider "whether the biotech products at issue in this dispute are 'like' their conventional counterparts." *See* WTO Doc. WT/DS291/R at page 1067, para. 8.3. The dispute was settled without any review of the Panel Report by the WTO Appellate Body.

In the course of its lengthy report, the Panel offered this observation on whether discrimination between GMO products and non-GMO products violated the national treatment obligation of GATT Art. III:

> At any rate, even if it were the case that, as a result of the measures challenged by Argentina, the relevant imported biotech products cannot be marketed, while corresponding domestic nonbiotech products can be marketed, . . . this would not be sufficient, in and of itself, to raise a presumption that the European Communities accorded less favourable treatment to the group of like imported products than to the group of like domestic products. We note that Argentina does not assert that domestic biotech products have not been less favourably treated in the same way as imported biotech products, or that the like domestic non-biotech varieties have been more favourably treated than the like imported non-biotech varieties. In other words, Argentina is not alleging that the treatment of products has differed depending on their origin. In these circumstances, it is not self-evident that the alleged less favourable treatment of imported biotech products is explained by the foreign origin of these products rather than, for instance, a perceived difference between biotech products and non-biotech products in terms of their safety, etc. In our view, Argentina has not adduced argument and evidence sufficient to raise a presumption that the alleged less favourable treatment is explained by the foreign origin of the relevant biotech products.

Id. at para. 7.2514. Is the Panel correct in its suggestion that a violation of Article III requires proof that the less favourable treatment is "explained by the foreign origin" of the products? Doesn't Article III simply forbid different treatment of foreign products than of "like" domestic products, regardless of the reason for the different treatment? By insisting that the relevant comparison is between domestic GMO products and foreign GMO products, or domestic conventional products and foreign conventional products, isn't the Panel implicitly concluding that GMO products are not "like" conventional products?

5. There are other WTO Agreements that are relevant to the trade and environment debate. The most important such agreements are the Agreement on the Application of Sanitary and Phytosanitary Measures (SPS Agreement) and the Agreement on Technical Barriers to Trade (TBT Agreement). Because those agreements lay down very specific rules, trade and environment disputes are often resolved pursuant to the terms of those agreements without considering the applicability of the broader GATT rules. This is what the Panel did in the *Biotech Products* dispute. *See also* Report of the Appellate Body, *United States—Measures Concerning the Importation, Marketing and Sale of Tuna and Tuna Products,* WT/DS381/AB/R (May 16, 2012) (Panel resolved dispute on basis of TBT Agreement alone and did not consider alleged violations of GATT; Appellate Body criticized that approach but did not remand for further consideration or conduct its own evaluation of alleged GATT violations).

6. The Cartagena Protocol on Biosafety **(Basic Document 5.6a)** places some restrictions on the transboundary movement of genetically modified organisms. Does it cover the kinds of restrictions imposed by Europa in this problem? What is a "living modified organism"? Also, if the Cartagena Protocol were operative, how would it affect analysis of the GATT issues raised by restrictions on GMO imports? Could the two agreements be read consistently? In the event of a conflict, which would prevail?

7. As noted in Reading 2, several multilateral environmental agreements (MEAs) operate by imposing restrictions on trade or depend on trade restrictions for their enforcement. *See Matrix on Trade Measures Pursuant to Selected Multilateral Environmental Agreements—Note by the Secretariat,* WT/CTE/W/160/Rev.4 (Mar. 14, 2007). Although there has never been a trade dispute involving a trade restriction imposed pursuant to an MEA, there has been much commentary on the potential conflict between MEAs and the rules of the GATT/WTO system. *See, e.g.,* Miguel A. Elizalde Carranza, *MEAs with Trade Measures and the WTO: Aiming Toward Sustainable Development?,* 15 Buff. Envtl. L.J. 43 (2007–08). The WTO's Committee on Trade and Environment has addressed the topic, as has the OECD. *See, e.g.,* WTO Secretariat, *Background Paper on the Trade and Environment Debate* 35–43 (2004); Organization of Economic Cooperation and Development (OECD), Joint Working Party on Trade and Environment, *Trade Measures in Multilateral Environmental Agreements: Synthesis Report of Three Case Studies* (Feb. 12, 1999).

8. If the WTO system is too biased toward trade liberalization policies, are there other international forums that can decide issues involving a clash between GATT rules and environmental protection? Professor Lakshman Guruswamy argues in his article: *The Promise of the United Nations Convention on the Law of the Sea (UNCLOS): Justice in Trade and Environmental Disputes,* 25 Ecology L. Q. 189 at 191–93, 206–11 & 222–26 (1998), that GATT is not the exclusive forum for adjudicating environmental disputes with trade ramifications. He contends that tribunals established under the United Nations Convention on the Law of the Sea (UNCLOS), and

in specified circumstances even the International Court of Justice, are possessed of jurisdiction to hear such cases. *See also* Wen-chen Shih, *Conflicting Jurisdictions Over Disputes Arising from the Application of Trade-Related Environmental Measures,* 8 Rich. J. Global L. & Bus. 351 (2009).

9. The United Nations Environment Programme (UNEP) plays an important role in promoting global dialogue and action on environmental problems, but it does not have the power or authority of an organization like the WTO. The WTO administers and enforces several agreements that codify trade liberalization principles and rules. UNEP, by contrast, does not administer any treaties or enforce any binding code of rules on environmental protection, although it does host the secretariats of several multilateral environmental agreements. Do you think international environmental protection would be improved if there were a World Environmental Protection Organization (WEPO) operating in parallel to the WTO and applying an international environmental agreement codifying basic principles of international environmental law? *See* Commission on Environmental Law of the IUCN—The World Conservation Union & International Council of Environmental Law, *Draft International Covenant on Environment and Development,* Environmental Policy and Law Paper No. 31, Rev. 2 (3d ed. 2004). *See also* proposed Global Pact for the Environment, discussed in Chapter 4, part C, *supra.*

10. If consumers care about the environmental impact of the processes by which consumer goods are produced, then is it necessary to have mandatory government labeling programs or will voluntary programs work as well? So long as consumers can rely on the accuracy of labels (which may require some government regulation), won't producers pursue environmentally friendly production options if there is a market advantage to a product's being perceived as environmentally friendly? In fact, there are many voluntary programs aimed at promoting environmentally sound production processes, and there are many businesses that seek to improve the environmental dimensions of their production to secure the seal of approval of such programs. *See generally* Sean D. Murphy, *Taking Multinational Corporate Codes of Conduct to the Next Level,* 43 Colum. J. Transnat'l L. 389 (2005); David Wirth, *the International Organization for Standardization: Private Voluntary Standards as Swords and Shields,* 36 B.C. Envtl. Aff. L. Rev. 79 (2009). Sometimes, as in the case of the Forest Stewardship Council and the Sustainable Forestry Initiative, business groups and environmental groups may sponsor competing codes, which may make it difficult for consumers to determine the real meaning of a sustainability label. The impact of labels on consumer behavior is likely to vary from country to country. *See, e.g.,* J. L. Lusk, M. Jamal, L. Kurlander, M. Roucan, & L. Taulman, *A Meta-analysis of Genetically Modified Food Valuation Studies,* 30 J. Agric. & Resource Econ. 28 (2005). To the extent that government regulations support a labeling program (e.g., by specifying the conditions under which it can be applied), it will be subject to the TBT Agreement. *See* Report of the Appellate Body, *United States—Measures*

Concerning the Importation, Marketing and Sale of Tuna and Tuna Products, WT/DS381/AB/R (May 16, 2012).

PROBLEM 12-2: POPULATION CONTROL MEETS HUMAN RIGHTS IN SONGHAY

Section 1. Facts

Songhay is a landlocked nation of 20 million people in sub-Saharan Africa. It occupies an area just over 100,000 square miles, about the size of the U.S. state of Colorado. According to the International Monetary Fund, its per capita income in 2017 was $1884, placing it 171st out of the 187 countries in the ranking. Almost 80 percent of its population lives in rural areas, and its economy is dominated by agriculture. Despite economic growth rates averaging above 5 percent per year since the mid-1990s, Songhay's poverty rate has held steady at about 44 per cent of the population.

Songhay's population has doubled since 1994. The most recent data show that the population continues to grow at a rate of 3 per cent per year. The Government of Songhay has long believed that its rapidly growing population is lowering the standard of living and economic prosperity of its people. The Government is convinced that the finite natural resources available in Songhay, in particular the limited quantity of arable land, are necessarily strained by ever increasing demands resulting from exponentially growing populations.

Several years ago, the government decided that, as a matter of environmental and human integrity, it was necessary to implement policies to limit population growth. To this end, it established family planning clinics across the country that provided citizens with free access to a wide range of contraceptives (including oral contraceptives, long-term contraceptive implants, and barrier contraceptives such as condoms). In addition, health care professionals were trained to counsel all adult patients about family planning options, and comprehensive sexuality education was provided in schools. These programs were supported by funding from the United Nations Population Fund (UNFPA).[8] Songhay has pursued its voluntary family planning policy for nearly 20 years but has had only limited success in reducing its birth rate. According to the World Bank, the 2016 birth rate in the country was 5.4 births per woman, down only slightly from the 6.0 births per woman recorded in 1998, when Songhay's family planning program began.

[8] The United Nations Population Fund is generally known by the acronym UNFPA, which is derived from the original name of the organization: the United Nations Fund for Population Activities.

The primary reason for the relative lack of success of Songhay's family planning program is persistent resistance to the use of contraceptives, especially among the rural population of the country. The reasons for this resistance are both religious and cultural. Most of the country's population follow either Catholicism or Islam, and local religious leaders of both faiths preach that contraception is sinful. In addition, Songhay's social system is traditionally patriarchal, and married women are unlikely to seek or use contraceptives without their husband's consent, which they are reluctant to seek. Surveys suggest that men in Songhay have a negative view of contraception, believing that it will promote promiscuity and infidelity among their wives and daughters.

Frustrated by the persistently high birth rate in the country, the Government of Songhay recently adopted new laws aimed at strengthening the incentives for women to have fewer children. First, it embarked on a nationwide advertising campaign ("one is good, two are OK, three is too many") designed to encourage families to have fewer children. Second, it offered a payment equivalent to $100 to any woman of child-bearing age who agreed to receive a contraceptive implant that would prevent pregnancy for five years. Third, it adopted an array of economic incentives favoring smaller families, including rationing of public benefits. For example, free public education past the sixth grade would be provided only to the first two children in any family; women would have access to government-sponsored free pre-natal medical care only for their first two pregnancies; families with more than two children would be ineligible for government housing and food assistance; and families with four or more children are subject to a special "excess population tax" equal to 10 per cent of their annual income. The UNFPA continued to provide financial support for Songhay's family planning clinics and its family-planning counseling activities.

The UNFPA is maintained essentially by large Western countries, including a thirty percent contribution by the major industrialized country of the Federation of Columbia. The Federation of Columbia has been a member of UNFPA's Executive Board since 1994. The Executive Board provides support and encouragement for the work of UNFPA as well as supervision aimed at ensuring that UNFPA programs are responsive to the needs and interests of participating countries.

At the most recent meeting of the Executive Board, the representative of the Federation of Columbia (FC) expressed grave concern over Songhay's new policies. While she stated that FC's government believes that over-population in the developing world is a major problem, she also reiterated FC's longstanding view that population policies should conform to international human rights standards. She insists that both conventional and customary international law prohibit the kind of economically coercive policies being instituted by Songhay. She announced that the Federation of Columbia's support would be withdrawn from all UNFPA programs unless UNFPA agreed to stop providing funding to Songhay and to any other country that used "draconian methods to coerce men and women into using birth control in violation of their human rights." When asked what human rights Songhay had violated, she cited generally "rights enshrined in the 1948 Universal Declaration of Human Rights; the 1959 Declaration on the Rights of the Child; the 1966 International Covenant on Economic, Social and Cultural Rights; the 1966 International Covenant on Civil and Political Rights; the 1968 Proclamation of Teheran; the 1969 Declaration on Social Progress and Development; the 1979 Convention on the Elimination of All Forms of Discrimination Against Women; and the 1989 Convention on the Rights of the Child." The FC representative argued that these instruments were part of a pattern that established clear customary norms of international law on these matters and that Songhay was in breach of those norms.

Except for the 1948 Universal Declaration of Human Rights, Songhay has neither signed nor ratified any of the instruments in question. Along with the Federation of Columbia, however, it is a member of the United Nations, and at every international negotiation concerned with these human rights instruments—most of them sponsored by the United Nations—Songhay has vigorously argued that Western concepts of human rights have no application to Songhay. Such rights are at best aspirational, it contends, and always have been understood to be subject to national historical, social, economic, and cultural conditions. Songhay has been particularly adamant that such rights should not be used as a pretext for interfering in the internal affairs of any nation.

It came as no surprise, therefore, that the Government of Songhay saw the Federation of Columbia's ultimatum as directly attacking not only its policy, but also its sovereign right to regulate its own internal affairs. Songhayan representatives argued that the human rights provided by international law are not inviolable and that the general standard of living and environmental standards compromised by a burgeoning population must be weighed against individual rights. For the Federation of Columbia to attempt to stymie a governmental policy designed for the community good, was an infringement of state sovereignty. Songhay representatives also strongly argued that the unequal distribution of global wealth and power is what forces countries like Songhay to be so strict. Factors such as inadequate old age security and poorly funded education contribute greatly to population growth.

The conference erupted into a full-scale ideological debate. The Federation of Columbia stated that Songhay's drain on environmental resources was due to its increasing use of technologies and practices that are now well-known to be ecologically destructive. Songhay pointed out that the Federation of Columbia's per capita resource use was outrageously high and that it should be doing everything within its powers to address both that issue as well as aiding the developing world in its attempt to ensure economic and environmental security.

Since both countries had new leadership and there appeared to be no way that the countries could come together at the conference, wiser heads counseled that this unseemly diplomatic wrangle should not continue. On the third day, in a joint statement, both countries announced that they had decided to commence negotiations to sort out their differences. The statement said that they would attempt to agree on the international law applicable to the issues that sparked the debate, and then to act in accordance with that agreement.

Section 2. Questions Presented

1. Is Songhay in breach of any rule of international law in pursuing the population policies enumerated in the problem?

2. What policy arguments are available to enhance the position taken by each government?

Section 3. Assignments

A. Reading Assignment

Study the Readings presented in Section 4, *infra*, and the Discussion Notes/Questions that follow.

B. Recommended Writing Assignment

Prepare a comprehensive, logically sequenced, and argumentative brief in the form of an outline of the primary and subsidiary legal issues you see requiring resolution in the negotiations between Songhay and the Federation of Columbia. Also, from the perspective of an independent objective judge, indicate which side ought to prevail on each issue and why. Retain a copy of your issue-outline/brief for class discussion.

C. Recommended Oral Assignment

Assume you are legal counsel for Songhay, on the one hand, or the Federation of Columbia, on the other (as designated by your instructor); then, relying upon the Readings (and your issue-outline if prepared), present a 15–20 minute oral argument of your government's likely positions at the negotiating table where the diplomatic representatives from Songhay and the Federation of Columbia are meeting.

D. Recommended Reflective Assignment

Consider (and recommend) alternative norms, institutions, and/or procedures that you believe might do better than existing world order arrangements to contend with situations of the kind posed by this problem.

In so doing, but without insisting upon immediate feasibility, identify the particular transition steps that would be needed to make your alternatives a reality.

Section 4. Readings

1. Editors' Note: The Population Control Debate

In 1798, Thomas Malthus argued that gains in agricultural productivity would inevitably be offset by ever greater increases in population growth. He foresaw a world of continued struggle and hardship for the poorest members of society. In his analysis, unless steps were taken to limit population growth, a nation's population would increase until it reached the limits of that nation's capacity to support its people, effectively precluding real progress toward improved living standards. Among the various solutions he offered to the problem was a gradual end to the British poor-laws, which provided welfare assistance to poor families. Denied the prospect of such assistance, he reasoned, the poor would be less apt to have children, wages would rise as labor became more scarce, and the working poor would secure "a greater share of the produce of the country."[9] The "sheer cold-heartedness of Malthus' logic made him one of the most universally reviled figures in the annals of intellectual history."[10]

Malthus's most dire predictions did not come true. Population continued to increase in the United Kingdom and throughout Western Europe during the 19th and early 20th centuries. Yet living standards improved dramatically. The same was true in North America, where living standards increased despite the fact that local population growth was supplemented by the arrival of millions of immigrants. It appeared clear that, *contra* Malthus, technological innovation could lead to increases in productivity that could accommodate and surpass even substantial increases in population size.

The New Malthusians

150 years after Malthus originally raised his (false?) alarm about uncontrolled population growth, the subject re-emerged as a major public policy issue, this time on the international level:

> After World War II, there was growing concern with the unprecedented levels of population growth. A population-control movement developed, led by, among others, John D. Rockefeller III, whose main preoccupations were the growing imbalance between population and resource growth, and the potential for political instability given that most of the population growth was

[9] Thomas R. Malthus, An Essay on the Principle of Population, vol. II, ch. vii (6th ed. 1827).

[10] Hannes Bergthaller & Margarita Carretero Gonzalez, *Population, Ecology, and the Malthusian Imagination: An Introduction*, 9 Europ. J. Literature, Culture & Envt., No. 1 (2018).

concentrated in the poorest countries of the world. In 1952, Rockefeller founded the Population Council, aimed at providing research and technical assistance for population programs across the world. That same year, India started the first national population program, and in parallel, the International Planned Parenthood Federation was established. By the late 1950s, the "population question" was receiving the attention of the US government. A report by a Presidential Committee studying the United States Military Assistance Program (Draper 1959) devoted an entire chapter to the issue, ending with a recommendation that the government "assist those countries with which it is cooperating in economic aid programs, on request, in the formulation of their plans designed to deal with the problem of rapid population growth." By this time, private foundations including the Rockefeller and Ford Foundations were providing seed funding for research and planning programs, but it was in the mid-1960s that large-scale funding became available and the population planning movement really took off.[11]

In the 1960s, environmentalists joined the chorus of those advocating for population-control policies. For environmentalists, the concern was the stress that an ever-growing human population placed on the natural resources and "carrying capacity" of planet Earth. Kenneth Boulding noted that our global environment had built-in limits,[12] and Donella Meadows and her colleagues warned that our modern civilization was pushing those limits both because of unconstrained population growth and ever-rising *per capita* consumption.[13]

Paul Ehrlich made a similar assessment of the issue in a book he ominously titled *The Population Bomb.*[14] He reiterated the point twenty years later:

> The overriding reason to care about the population explosion is its contribution to the expanding scale of the human enterprise and thus to humanity's impact on the environmental systems that support civilization. The number of people (P), multiplied by per capita affluence (A) or consumption, in turn multiplied by an index of the environmental damage caused by the technologies employed to service the consumption (T), gives a measure of the

---

[11] Tiloka de Silva & Silvana Tenreyro, *Population Control Policies and Fertility Convergence,* 31 J. Econ. Persp. 305, 209–210 (2017).

[12] Kenneth Boulding, *The Economics of the Coming Spaceship Earth,* in Environmental Quality in a Growing Economy 3–14 (H.E. Jarrett, ed. 1966).

[13] Donella H. Meadows, Dennis L. Meadows, Jørgen Randers & William W. Behrens, The Limits to Growth: A Report for the Club of Rome (1972).

[14] Paul R. Ehrlich, The Population Bomb (1968).

> environmental impact (I) of a society. This is the basic I = P x A x T identity, often just called the "I = PAT equation." . . .
>
> Employing energy use as the standard, the scale of the human enterprise has grown about twenty-fold since 1850. During that time, per capita energy consumption has risen about five-fold globally, and the population has grown about four-fold. Roughly then, population growth can be considered to be responsible for about 45% of humanity's environmental peril: the combined risks accrued as a result of increasing worldwide environmental impacts. . . .[15]

An even more extreme view was advocated by proponents of the so-called "deep ecology" movement, who argued that slowing or stopping population growth was not enough; what was needed was, in fact, a "substantial reduction of the human population on the planet":

> [E]xcessive pressures on planetary life conditions stem from the human population explosion. The pressure stemming from industrial societies is a major factor, and population reduction must have a high priority in those societies, as well as in developing countries. Estimates of an optimal human population vary. Some quantitative estimates are 100 million, 500 million, and 1000 million, but it is recognized that there must be a long range, humane reduction through mild but tenacious political and economic measures. This will make possible, as a result of increased habitat, population growth for thousands of species which are now constrained by human pressures.[16]

The International Community Endorses Population Control

When the nations of the world met at Stockholm in 1972 for the first global conference on the environment, worries about population growth were firmly on the agenda and were reflected in the outcome document of the Conference, in which the participants "declared that":

> The natural growth of population continuously presents problems on the preservation of the environment, and adequate policies and measures should be adopted, as appropriate, to face these problems.[17]

---

[15] Paul R. Ehrlich & Anne H. Ehrlich, *The Population Explosion: Why We Should Care and What We Should Do About It*, 27 Envtl. L. 1187, 1188–90 (1997).

[16] Arne Naess, *The Deep Ecological Movement: Some Philosophical Aspects*, 8 Phil. Inquiry 12, 20–21(1986).

[17] Stockholm Declaration of the United Nations Conference on the Human Environment, paragraph 5, U.N. Doc. A/CONF.48/14/Rev., at 3 (June 16, 1972).

In Principle 16 of the Declaration, the participants left no doubt that population control was among the "adequate policies and measures" they had in mind as a tool of environmental protection:

> Demographic policies, which are without prejudice to basic human rights and which are deemed appropriate by Governments concerned, should be applied in those regions where the rate of population growth or excessive population concentrations are likely to have adverse effects on the environment or development, or where low population density may prevent improvement of the human environment and impede development.[18]

This post-WWII movement for population control reached its apex at the international level at the 1974 World Population Conference in Bucharest, Romania. The World Population Plan of Action adopted by the 135 participating countries strongly endorsed population control as a tool for economic development. The Plan began by noting that excessive population growth could "at certain stages of development, create[ ] additional difficulties for the achievement of sustained development." While the Plan acknowledged the "right of couples to have the number of children they desire," it added the important qualification that "individual reproductive behavior and the needs and aspirations of society should be reconciled," noting that "the desire of couples to achieve large families" resulted, in the view of some governments, "in excessive national population growth rates." The Plan noted that couples making decisions about the number and spacing of their children should take into account "their responsibilities towards the community," and it explicitly affirmed "the sovereign right of each nation" to formulate and implement population policies "in accordance with national objectives and needs <u>and without external interference</u>."[19]

Ten years later, the international community reiterated its support for national population control policies in crystal clear terms. The Mexico City Declaration on Population and Development, adopted by the 1984 International Conference on Population, "reaffirmed the full validity of the principles and objectives of the World Population Plan of Action" and emphasized that population growth continued to be a "great concern requiring immediate action." The Conferees then observed that "family planning programmes have been successful in reducing fertility at relatively low cost" and called upon "countries which consider that their

---

[18] *Id.*, principle 16.

[19] Report of the United Nations World Population Conference, 1974, at pages 4–5, UN Doc. E/CONF.60/19 (1975) (emphasis added). The UN General Assembly subsequently endorsed the plan and called for increased assistance the United Nations Fund for Population Activities in order to ensure the "proper implementation of the World Population Plan of Action." *See* GA Res 3344 (XXIX) (on the World Population Conference) (December 17, 1974).

population growth rate hinders their national development" to "adopt appropriate population policies and programmes."[20]

This population control movement was not without its critics. Some scholars argued that population control was both unnecessary and counterproductive. Population growth would stimulate technological innovation that would allow production to increase and living standards to rise.[21] Indeed, some said, the more people the better, as "larger populations would result in more brains that could be applied to solving any resource problems that might arise."[22]

However, the primary blow to the population-control movement came not from scholars, but from the brutality and excesses associated with the implementation of population-control policies in parts of the developing world. In the 1980s and 1990s, the news media was filled with graphic and disturbing accounts of female infanticide, forced sterilization, forced abortion, and other brutalities undertaken in the name of population control.[23] Although the governments involved protested that such practices were not part of government policy but were the result of unauthorized actions by over-zealous low-level officials, the reported abuses became a taint on population-control policies generally. In the United States, the Reagan Administration cut off support to the United Nations Population Fund in protest of UNFPA's support for family planning in China. Today, the questions whether the United States will support the UNFPA, in what amounts, and for what programs remain politically fraught issues.

The International Community Retreats

At the 1994 World Population Conference, the international community altered course. Although the Conference acknowledged the legitimacy of population-related policies, the principles adopted to guide implementation of such policies had a strong human-rights orientation. The "cornerstones" of effective population-related programs, the Conferees said, were: "gender equality and equity," the "empowerment of women," the "elimination of all kinds of violence against women," and the "ensuring [of] women's ability to control their own fertility." States were urged to "take all appropriate measures" to ensure access to "reproductive health care, which includes family planning and sexual health," with the admonition

[20] Report of the International Conference on Population, 1984, page 2, UN Doc. E/CONF.76/19 (1984).

[21] Ester Boserup, The Conditions of Agricultural Growth (1965).

[22] E. Wesley F. Peterson, *The Role of Population in Economic Growth*, SAGE Open 1, 9 (October-December 2017), doi: 10.1177/2158244017736094 (citing Julian Simon, The Ultimate Resource (1981)). *See also* Julian Simon, *The Population Debate: The Case for More People*, in Environmental Science: Action for a Sustainable Future 110 (D. Chira ed., 3d ed. 1991) ("The only constraint upon our capacity to enjoy unlimited raw materials at acceptable prices is knowledge. People generate that knowledge. The more people there are, the better off the world will be.").

[23] *See, e.g.*, Nicholas Kristof, *China's Crackdown on Births: A Stunning, and Harsh, Success*, N.Y. Times, May 24, 1993, at 1, cols. 4–5.

that "reproductive health-care programs" should not involve "any form of coercion. All couples and individuals have the basic right to decide freely and responsibly the number and spacing of their children . . . ."[24] This change in emphasis was the product of several factors, including the growing women's rights movement and strong empirical evidence that empowerment of women could lead to a rapid and substantial decline in a country's birth rate without the need for coercive population-control policies.

After 1994, population control received scant attention in international discussions. China maintained its one-child policy until very recently, and it was regularly criticized for doing so.[25] But apart from condemnations of human rights abuses associated with national population control policies, the international community was mostly silent on the issue. In its Millennium Declaration of 8 September 2000, the United Nations General Assembly identified development and poverty eradication as one of its primary objectives, yet not a word was said about population control as a tool to achieve that goal.[26] Similarly, the subsequently adopted Millennium Development Goals were conspicuously silent on the subject, despite its potential relevance to at least three of the eight goals: eradicating extreme poverty and hunger, achieving universal primary education, and ensuring environmental sustainability. No governmentally sponsored global population conference has been held since 1994.

Population Control Back on the Agenda?

In a 2012 report entitled *Population Matters for Sustainable Development,* the UNFPA made a strong case for the pursuit of population control policies, though it carefully avoided ever using the phrase "population control," preferring a euphemism—"policies that address population dynamics"—that can encompass policies that promote population growth as well as policies that suppress it. But the fundamental point of the Report is evident throughout it: sustainable development goals will be difficult, if not impossible, to achieve without limiting population growth. Hence, the Report aims to "restor[e] the relevance of population dynamics in the sustainable development agenda which has been lost over the past decades."

Despite UNFPA's call for action, the 2030 Agenda for Sustainable Development, adopted by the General Assembly in 2015, said nothing

[24] Programme of Action of the 1994 International Conference on Population and Development, principles 4 & 8, U.N. Doc. A/CONF.171/13/Rev.1 (1995).

[25] *See, e.g.,* United States Department of State, 2010 Country Reports on Human Rights Practices: China (April 8, 2011) (identifying China's "coercive birth limitation policy" as a "principal human rights problem" in China in 2010).

[26] United Nations Millennium Declaration, 8 September 2000, GA Res. 55/2, UN Doc. A/RES/55/2.

about population control. Indeed, there was no discussion whatsoever of the relevance of population growth to the achievement of development goals. The General Assembly simply noted that UN Members would "take account of population trends and projections in our national rural and urban development strategies and policies."[27]

Recently, expressions of concern about rapid population growth and the "slowly unfolding catastrophe" it is creating, especially in Africa, have begun to re-emerge in the popular media.[28] They are matched, as before, by those who argue that population control remains unnecessary: "human beings constantly find new and creative ways to take from the earth, increase the bounty for everyone and expand the number of seats at the table of plenty."[29]

As you review the following readings and the issues presented by this problem, ask yourself where you stand on population control. Among the questions to consider: Is it necessary? If not, is this because population stabilization will be the natural result of economic development and the expansion of human rights? Or is population stabilization simply not needed, given our proven ability (since the dawn of the industrial revolution at least) to expand production faster than population? Finally, you should consider whether the situation might be more complicated than any of these questions suggest—perhaps the consequences of population growth, and its impact on the human condition—depend on the particular circumstances in which that growth occurs.

Readings 2–6 address the human rights dimensions of coercive population-control policies. The remaining readings address population policy issues more broadly.

2. Reed Boland, The Environment, Population and Women's Human Rights, 27 Envtl. L. 1137, 1142–54 (1997)

. . . [P]opulation policies are [often] imposed as part of a strategy to lower the rate of population growth. As the world's population has increased dramatically since World War II, there has been growing acceptance of this strategy. High rates of population growth have been viewed as outstripping the ability of countries to sustain socioeconomic development, depleting the world's resources and causing major political

---

[27] Transforming Our World: the 2030 Agenda for Sustainable Development, para. 34, G.A. Res. 70/1 (Sept. 24, 2015).

[28] *See* Bill Marsh, *Overpopulated and Underfed: Countries Near a Breaking Point*, New York Times, June 15, 2017; Eugene Linden, *Remember the Population Bomb? It's Still Ticking*, New York Times, June 15, 2017; Damian Carrington, *Paul Ehrlich: 'Collapse of civilization is a near certainty within decades*, The Guardian, 22 March 2018; Derek Hoff, *A long fuse: 'The Population Bom' is still ticking 50 years after its publication*, July 20, 2018, The Conversation, https://theconversation.com/a-long-fuse-the-population-bomb-is-still-ticking-50-years-after-its-publication-96090; Fraces Kissling, Jotham Musinguzi & Peter Singer, *Talking about overpopulation is still taboo. That has to change.*, The Washington Post, June 18, 2018.

[29] William McGurn, *The Population Bomb Was a Dud*, Wall Street Journal, April 30, 2018.

instability. Stemming or reversing these rates has been judged to be the key to a sustainable and livable future. This strategy has gained widespread acceptance in the international population community, as well as in the planning departments of various governments.

One of the most consistent proponents of this approach has been the government of India, which recognized early in its history the problems associated with high rates of population growth and, in response, adopted one of the first major population policies. In the mid-1970s, the anxiety of the Indian government over the country's demographic prospects reached a fever pitch, leading it to adopt a highly coercive plan to lower the rate of population growth. One major component of the plan was the promotion of widespread sterilization of Indian citizens. To carry out these sterilizations, the Indian government established mass camps where sterilizations were performed in assembly line fashion under unsanitary conditions. At the height of the campaign, millions of people were sterilized within a six-month period. Many of these people were rounded up against their will and taken to the sterilization camps. In some cases, police were called upon to enforce the policy.

The most flagrant excesses of this plan were not long-lived. There was a public outcry over forced sterilizations and Prime Minister Indira Gandhi and her government, which had instituted the plan, were voted out of office in the next election. Nonetheless, the plan left lasting scars. First, it created a precedent for coercive action which has lasted until today. The Government still operates sterilization camps where conditions are unsanitary and women are pressured to be sterilized. Second, it created a population that mistrusts government efforts to deal with increasing population growth. This fact is particularly apparent in the negative reactions of male Indians to the plan. The sterilization program was largely directed at men who were induced to undergo vasectomies. Measures since then have been directed primarily at the sterilization of women, even though it is easier, safer, and more cost effective to perform a sterilization on a man than a woman.

The Chinese government has also engaged in major and well-publicized excesses in the execution of its population policy. The history of China's population policy has been one of broad fluctuations. After the takeover of the government by Communist forces in 1949, the new regime aggressively pursued a policy of encouraging births. . . . By the mid 1960s, however, China had largely reversed its policy. It began advocating the use of family planning, with a two child per family norm urged in some parts of the country. Despite this promotion of family planning and the continuing drop in the rate of population growth, by the end of the 1970s, the government tightened policy further. Alarmed by predictions that its population would exceed 1.2 billion before the end of the century and worried about the relative scarcity of domestic agricultural land to produce the food to sustain this population, the government adopted the one child per couple policy and instituted a series of strict measures to enforce it. Implicit or explicit threats of force were part of these measures that, on occasion, became real; persons who would not voluntarily comply with the policy were required to be sterilized or obtain an abortion.

Because of the secrecy of Chinese society and the government's denials of responsibility, the extent of the use of actual force is very difficult to gauge. Nonetheless, there are sufficient independent and unbiased reports to leave little doubt that coerced abortions and sterilizations have occurred, including evidence that mass sterilization campaigns have been carried out in various provinces. The government itself has acknowledged as much, although it places much of the blame for these excesses on overzealous local officials. Indeed, given a population of over one billion people that has never known a democratic regime and in which force has, in recent years, played a prominent role, to suggest otherwise would be, at the least, to ignore human fallibility. Such excesses and the hostility that they generated, particularly in the rural population, were responsible for a major relaxation of the one child policy in the mid to late 1980s. During this time many exceptions to that policy were established for rural couples, ethnic minorities, and various other groups, including families that had given birth only to girls. Moreover, enforcement of existing laws was less stringent than before. However, by the beginning of the [1990s], policy had once again shifted. Results of the 1990 census indicated that population targets had not been met, leading the government to tighten enforcement procedures once again.

C. Non-physical Forms of Coercion

Not all coercive activities carried out in the name of population control have been as obvious as forced sterilization, abortion, or forced motherhood. There are a number of more subtle ways in which governments have tried to enforce their will over citizens' reproductive behavior. One is through the use of incentives or disincentives. The incentives fall into two broad categories: incentives to individuals to adopt various forms of family planning. . . . India gave monetary rewards to persons who agreed to be sterilized, made the salary of officials contingent on their ability to recruit sterilization acceptors, and imposed fines and imprisonment upon those who failed to meet demographic targets. Since the emergency, India has continued to offer monetary incentives to both acceptors and recruiting officials and, relying heavily on sterilization to implement its policy, sets sterilization targets for villages.

Similarly, a constant feature of China's population policy has been the penalization of couples who have more than the allotted number of children. This has been done by denial of social benefits, demotion at work, and imposition of fines. In contrast, those who adhere to the one child per couple policy have been rewarded with improved housing, access to better medical and educational benefits, and promotion at work. Most recently, China has affirmed its belief in the efficacy of incentives by instituting a family planning responsibility system to enforce its population policy. Under this policy, local officials are given the responsibility for reaching contraception targets set by the national government. If they fail to do so, they are penalized. The use of such incentives has also been commonplace in the implementation of the population policies of a number of other countries, including Vietnam and Bangladesh.

Another coercive method of enforcing population policies is through the application of various psychological pressures to bring about desired conduct. The Chinese government relies extensively on this method. Friends, family members, co-workers, and local officials are all called upon to place pressure on women to use intra-uterine devices (IUDs) which they are forbidden to remove, to be sterilized after the birth of a second child, or to have an abortion if they become pregnant. In some areas, the contraceptive use and pregnancy status of women are now monitored by officials by means of periodic physical examinations, much like those carried out under the Ceaususcu regime. Often threats of more coercive measures accompany this pressure if the desired method of family planning is not adopted.

Pressure of a slightly different nature has been a continuing feature of the Indonesian population policy. "Safaris," caravans of medical personnel, officials, and members of the police or military who enter rural towns have applied this pressure. They gather the populace together, deliver lectures upon the benefits of contraception, usually one favored form, and, sometimes under implicit threat, sign up acceptors and dispense the particular contraceptive being promoted. Indonesia also has relied on a system of village group pressure under which officials and community leaders make efforts to persuade women to accept family planning. Meetings are held periodically at which the women of a village gather together to discuss family planning in terms that utilize collective pressure to strengthen compliance with national policy.

* * *

F. The Role of Law in Coercive Policies

One important point to emphasize, at least from the viewpoint of law, is that all of these population policies are or were supported by a carefully drafted series of laws. They are not simply informal policies implemented *sub rosa*, or as the government of China would try to convince the rest of the world, isolated excesses carried out by overzealous local officials. The governments sought to give legitimacy through the legal system to what otherwise might seem thoroughly illegitimate. . . . At the time of the most intense pressure to perform sterilizations in India, the state of

Maharashtra enacted legislation to justify its actions. The duty to practice family planning is enshrined in the Chinese constitution, which is one of only two constitutions in the world to contain such a provision. Local family planning laws spell out in detail the sorts of steps to be taken to fulfill this duty. In addition, many local laws make explicit what the government tries to deny—that coercion is endemic and, in fact, a key in the eyes of the government to population policy. Such laws often provide that excess pregnancies must be terminated and that persons who have exceeded targets must undergo operations or, in more euphemistic terms, "measures" must be adopted.

3. Universal Declaration of Human Rights, arts. 16(1) & 29, G.A. Res. 217A (Dec. 10, 1948) (Basic Document 7.10)

Article 16. (1) Men and women of full age . . . have the right to marry and to found a family. They are entitled to equal rights as to marriage, during marriage and at its dissolution.

Article 29. (1) Everyone has duties to the community in which alone the free and full development of his personality is possible.

(2) In the exercise of his rights and freedoms, everyone shall be subject only to such limitations as are determined by law solely for the purpose of securing due recognition and respect for the rights and freedoms of others and of meeting the just requirements of morality, public order and the general welfare in a democratic society.

(3) These rights and freedoms may in no case be exercised contrary to the purposes and principles of the United Nations.

4. International Covenant on Economic, Social and Cultural Rights, Dec. 19, 1966, 993 UNTS 3, (Basic Document 7.11)

Article 4. The States Parties to the present Covenant recognize that, in the enjoyment of those rights provided by the State in conformity with the present Covenant, the State may subject such rights only to such limitations as are determined by law only in so far as this may be compatible with the nature of these rights and solely for the purpose of promoting the general welfare in a democratic society.

Article 10. The States Parties to the present Covenant recognize that:

(1) The widest possible protection and assistance should be accorded to the family, which is the natural and fundamental group unit of society, particularly for its establishment and while it is responsible for the care and education of dependent children. Marriage must be entered into with the free consent of the intending spouses.

(2) Special protection should be accorded to mothers during a reasonable period before and after childbirth. . . .

(3) Special measures of protection and assistance should be taken on behalf of all children and young persons without any discrimination for reasons of parentage or other conditions. . . .

Article 11. (1) The States Parties to the present Covenant recognize the right of everyone to an adequate standard of living for himself and his family, including adequate food, clothing and housing, and to the continuous improvement of living conditions. The States Parties will take appropriate steps to ensure the realization of this right, recognizing to this effect the essential importance of international co-operation based on free consent.

5. International Covenant on Civil and Political Rights, arts. 23(1), 23(2) & 24(1), Dec. 16, 1966, 999 UNTS 171 (Basic Document 7.12)

Article 18. (1) Everyone shall have the right to freedom of thought, conscience and religion. This right shall include freedom to have or to adopt a religion or belief of his choice, and freedom, either individually or in community with others and in public or private, to manifest his religion or belief in worship, observance, practice and teaching.

(2) No one shall be subject to coercion which would impair his freedom to have or to adopt a religion or belief of his choice.

(3) Freedom to manifest one's religion or beliefs may be subject only to such limitations as are prescribed by law and are necessary to protect public safety, order, health, or morals or the fundamental rights and freedoms of others.

(4) The States Parties to the present Covenant undertake to have respect for the liberty of parents and, when applicable, legal guardians to ensure the religious and moral education of their children in conformity with their own convictions.

Article 23. (1) The family is the natural and fundamental group unit of society and is entitled to protection by society and the State.

(2) The right of men and women of marriageable age to marry and to found a family shall be recognized. . . .

Article 24. (1) Every child shall have, without any discrimination as to race, colour, sex, language, religion, national or social origin, property or birth, the right to such measures of protection as are required by his status as a minor, on the part of his family, society and the State.

6. Lisa B. Gregory, Examining the Economic Component of China's One-Child Family Policy Under International Law: Your Money or Life, 6 J. Chinese L. 45, 60–78 (1992)

The question of the legally binding nature of custom, resolutions and declarations, hardly a clear-cut subject under the best of circumstances, becomes even more complex with regard to the highly controversial area of international human rights. The Charter of the United Nations **[Basic Document 1.1]** specifically mandates "respect for, and observance of, human rights and fundamental freedoms."[30] It further provides that "[a]ll members pledge themselves to take joint and separate action in co-operation with the Organization for the achievement of [these] purposes[.]" The Charter is indisputably a treaty, legally binding upon all members of the United Nations, including China. However, even if one accepts the argument that "the legal duty to promote respect for human rights includes the legal duty to respect them,"[31] the scope of human rights is not defined within the Charter.

The Universal Declaration of Human Rights **[Basic Document 7.10]** represents the United Nations' first attempt to articulate this scope. Numerous subsequent United Nations resolutions, Final Acts and Covenants have reaffirmed the provisions of the Declaration, thus re-enforcing the view that "the Universal Declaration of Human Rights constitutes an authoritative interpretation of the Charter of the highest order, and has over the years become a part of customary international law."[32] Subsequent conventions and declarations have further elaborated specific types of "human rights" and how States should go about promoting and observing them.

A. *Family and Human Rights in the Universal Declaration of Human Rights*

Article 16 of the Universal Declaration of Human Rights seems concerned primarily with guaranteeing the freedom of individuals to enter into, maintain, and dissolve a conjugal union. Paragraphs (1) and (3) of Article 16 taken together suggest that the international community in 1948 regarded the family unit (i.e., the traditional model of husband-wife-child), rather than simply the spousal relationship, as the natural and desirable state of existence. Couples are guaranteed the right to attain the model status if they wish by bringing some number of children into their homes, either through procreation or adoption, and the State is exhorted to protect the resulting unit.

---

30 U.N. Charter, art. 55(c). It is interesting to observe that the tension between human rights and development is present even within this article, which states that the United Nations shall promote: "higher standards of living, full employment, and conditions of economic and social progress and development." *Id.* art. 55(a).

31 Hersch Lauterpacht, International Law and Human Rights 152 (1973).

32 Montreal Statement of the Assembly for Human Rights 2 (New York, 1968). This view is not undisputed. See Lauterpacht, *supra* note 17, at 408–17 for the proposition that the Universal Declaration is no more than "morally binding." Discussing the "grey zone" of legality in which the Universal Declaration exists, Henkin observes that: "[w]ith time, the Universal Declaration has itself acquired significant legal status . . . Few [States] claim that any state that violates any provision of the Declaration has violated international law. Almost all would agree that some violations of the Declaration are violations of international law." Louis Henkin, The Age of Rights 19 (1990).

The Universal Declaration may view the family as a fundamental building block, but does not conceive of it as an end unto itself. The "right" to found a family is expressed in language which suggests neither a mandate to procreate nor a guarantee that couples may have as many children as they wish. The Universal Declaration clearly places the individual and his rights within the broader context of society. Article 29 contemplates man living within a society, responsible to it for conducting his life in a communally non-detrimental manner. Individuals have "duties to the community"—namely that they must abide by the rule of law, respect the rights of others, and comply with the "just requirements" which promote the "general welfare." Article 29(3) suggests that the "just requirements" in Article 29(2) include the principle that no one shall exercise his rights to a degree which unreasonably harms others. In the Chinese context, it is possible to interpret the Universal Declaration to mean that parents have the right to *some* children under Article 16, but, according to Article 29, the number may be subject to legal limitations necessary to ensure the general welfare of the community.

Using the Universal Declaration as a skeletal frame upon which to build, many subsequent international instruments have specifically explored the connection between families, human rights and national development. While the language of these instruments is not identical, there are certain common elements which give the impression that these documents are cross-referential, and that collectively they may articulate an internationally recognized matrix of "laws" relating to familial rights and State duties. The following section will attempt to set forth the uniform aspects of these international instruments and to explore the significant distinctions between them, so that China's policy of economic incentives and disincentives may be measured against a concrete standard.

B. Articulating the "Law" of Procreative Rights and the Duty to Develop

The legal matrix of individual, familial and societal rights and duties appears to embrace the following principles: (1) the family is the natural and fundamental unit of society; (2) as such, it is entitled to some degree of State protection; (3) all children have, without distinction or discrimination, an explicit right to protection by the family and the State; (4) parents have the right to decide freely and responsibly the number and spacing of their children; (5) States have an affirmative duty to provide parents access to and education about family planning so that they may exercise this right; (6) every human being has the right to an adequate standard of living; and (8) by implication, in order to be successful, State policies may take precedence over certain individual and family rights.

C. *Variations Among the Instruments*

1. Principles 1 and 2: The Family Is the Fundamental Unit of Society and Therefore Entitled to Protection

The Universal Declaration's view that the family is the natural and fundamental unit of society and is therefore entitled to protection by society and the State[33] has been embraced unconditionally and with only slight linguistic variations by all subsequent instruments referring to the family. However, the instruments part company on the degree and character of protection a State must provide. Thus, the International Covenant on Economic, Social and Cultural Rights claims that the family should be afforded "[t]he widest possible protection and assistance" [in Article 10(1)]. The International Covenant on Civil and Political Rights states merely that the family is entitled to "protection" but identifies the source of this protection as "society and the State" [Article 23(1)]. The drafters of the Declaration on Social Progress and Development appear to have consciously steered a middle course by urging that the family should be "assisted and protected" [in Article 4]. Their approach was modified only slightly under the Convention on the Rights of the Child to provide that this assistance should be given as "necessary" [as stated in the preamble].

The issue of how much and what type of assistance and protection is afforded the family becomes important in the context of parental rights and State duties. If the locus of decision-making regarding number and spacing of children resides primarily with parents, their ability to make these decisions requires that the State assist with (or at least not hinder) access to contraceptive devices. Furthermore, because exercise of family rights is constrained by responsibilities to the community, protection may imply protection of all families collectively, rather than of each discrete family unit.

2. Principle 3: All Children Have the Right to Parental and State Protection without Distinction or Discrimination

International law appears to afford children heightened protection in certain areas, and to explicitly forbid differentiated treatment for children based upon birth order. The International Covenant on Economic, Social and Cultural Rights **[Basic Document 7.11]** provides that "special measures" should be taken on behalf of all children without discrimination "for reasons of parentage or other conditions" [Article 10(3)]. The International Covenant on Civil and Political Rights identifies the child's "family, society and the State" as the entities required to give protection and assistance without discrimination as to "birth" [Article 24(1)]. Both the

---

[33] It may also be entitled to protection by international organizations. The Proclamation of Teheran notes in Point 16 that "[t]he protection of the family and of the child remains the concern of the international community." U.N. Doc. A/CONF.32/41 (1968) [hereinafter Teheran Proclamation].

Declaration on the Rights of the Child[34] and the Convention on the Rights of the Child provide that States shall respect and ensure the rights of all children without discrimination on the basis of "birth or other status" [Declaration on the Rights of the Child Principle I], while the Convention on the Rights of the Child further insists that States shall protect the child from discrimination based upon the "status" or "activities" of the parents [Article 2(2)].

Economic policies which penalize a child solely on the basis of birth order appear to violate the international standard set forth above since they discriminate based upon a factor which is wholly outside the child's control. However, as will be discussed below, this standard is reactive, applying to the child once it is born, and should be distinguished from policies which are primarily aimed at discouraging prospective parents from conceiving and bearing the "additional" child.

3. Principle 4: Parents Have a Right to Decide the Number and Spacing of Their Children

The principle that parents have the right to decide the size of their family and therefore are entitled to access to information and means which will enable them to exercise this right also appears to have gained broad acceptance under international law. The General Assembly formally recognized the "sovereignty of nations in formulating and promoting their own population policies, with due regard to the principle that the size of the family should be the free choice of each individual family[.]"[35]

Yet, the relevant texts do not consistently express the degree to which these family rights are inviolable. The Proclamation of Teheran asserts that parents have a "basic right" to determine freely and responsibly the number and spacing of their children,[36] while the Declaration on Social Progress and Development states that this right is exclusive. The Convention on the Elimination of All Forms of Discrimination against Women does not qualify the right, but simply affirms that men and women shall have equal rights regarding decisions as to number and spacing of children.

* * *

4. Principle 5: Parents Have a Right to Practice Family Planning and States Have a Duty to Provide Information and Access

Over the years, family planning has gained the status of a "human right" and States have been assigned a certain degree of responsibility for

---

[34] G.A. Res. 1386 (XIV) (Nov. 20, 1959).

[35] Population Growth and Economic Development, G.A. Res. 2211, U.N. GAOR, 21st Sess. (1966), *reprinted in* 11 United Nations Resolutions, ser. I, Resolutions adopted by the General Assembly 1966–1968, at 157, 158 (D. Djonovich ed., 1975).

[36] Point 16 states that, "[p]arents have a basic right to determine freely and responsibly the number and spacing of their children." Teheran Proclamation, *supra* note 33.

ensuring this right. The Declaration on Population refers to family planning as a basic human right.[37] The Final Act of the International Conference on Human Rights claims that families have a right to adequate education and information to enable them to practice family planning.[38] The Declaration on Social Progress and Development requires States to formulate and establish, "as needed," population programs which shall include "education, training of personnel and the provision to families of the knowledge and means necessary" to enable them to exercise their rights regarding birth decisions [Article 22(6)]. The Convention on the Elimination of All Forms of Discrimination Against Women **[Basic Document 7.15]** provides that women shall have the same rights as men in the arena of family planning [Article 12].

Among these instruments, the Declaration on Social Progress and Development is most noteworthy because it moves beyond simply articulating the family's "rights," to requiring that States actively provide family planning information and means to their citizens. Among the drafters, the idea that national demographic policies and programs should include dissemination of knowledge, training and means necessary to ensure effective implementation proved as controversial as had the term "exclusive." In fact, a separate vote was taken on the words "and means."[39] General Assembly records indicate that the drafters' intent was to ensure individuals access to information about and means to exercise birth control. The issue of coercive birth control was not raised.

5. Principles 6, 7 and 8: Everyone Has the Right to an Adequate Standard of Living and the State Has a Duty to Formulate Policies Which Will Foster Realization of That Right, Even Though Such Policies May Intrude Upon Specific Family Rights

As was discussed above, the Universal Declaration conceives of the family as an *integrated* unit of society, and individual behavior as being subject to certain socially mandated limitations which will enhance "the general welfare" [Article 24(2)]. The International Covenant on Economic, Social and Cultural Rights calls upon States to "recognize the right of everyone to an adequate standard of living for himself and his family, including adequate food, clothing and housing, and to the continuous improvement of living conditions" [Article 11(1)]. Additionally, this Covenant requires that States placing limitations on specifically protected rights do so only in "so far as this may be compatible with the nature of these rights and solely for the purpose of promoting the general welfare in

[37] The Declaration was signed by 30 Heads of State on Human Rights Day, 10 December 1966. World Population Conference, Bucharest, U.N. Doc. E/Conf. 60/CBP/6, at n.7 (1974).

[38] *Human Rights Aspects of Family Planning*, International Conference on Human Rights, Res. XVIII, U.N. Sales No. E.68. XIV.2, at 14; *discussed in* the World Population Conference, Bucharest, U.N. Doc. E/Conf.60/CBP/5, at 3–4 (1974).

[39] It passed by 60 votes to 16, with 17 abstentions. U.N. GAOR 3rd Comm., 24th Sess., 1684th mtg., at 185, U.N. Doc. A/C/.3/SR.1684 (1969).

a democratic society" [Article 4]. However, without more, the Universal Declaration and the Covenants stop well short of addressing acceptable and unacceptable means of balancing procreative rights and community goals, let alone the specifics of the one-child-per-family policy.

The Proclamation of Teheran takes a step toward subordinating isolated parents' wishes to broader social authority by recognizing that "the widening gap between the economically developed and developing countries impedes the realization of human rights" and that it is "imperative for every nation, according to its capacities, to make the maximum possible effort to close this gap" [Point 12]. An examination of the United Nations records reveals that participants of the International Conference on Human Rights at which the Proclamation was drafted recognized that full realization of civil and political rights would be impossible without "sound and effective national and international policies of economic and social development."[40] The Conference ominously observed that unlimited population growth posed a serious threat to world health.

The Declaration on Social Progress and Development attempts to place "exclusive" parental rights within the broader context of communal and national concerns by affirming that each State has the "right and responsibility" to set its own goals and means for achieving social development, "without any external interference" [Article 3]. The family unit is to be protected "so that it may fully assume its responsibilities within the community" [Article 8]. Furthermore, the government is assigned "the primary role and ultimate responsibility of ensuring the social progress and well-being of its people," and of developing programs which bring these goals closer to realization [Article 8]. Lastly, the Declaration calls for the formulation of programs, "within the framework of national demographic policies," including education regarding and access to methods of birth control, which will enable families to exercise their rights [Article 22]. It appears that international human rights law leaves individual nations broad discretion with regard to internal demographic policies. Several international documents have explicitly stated that formation of a national demographic policy is an exercise of state sovereignty. However, State exercise of intrusive population control must be measured against other international standards, including human rights.

[40] Participants included representatives from the Food and Agricultural Organization (FAO) and the World Health Organization (WHO) as well as member states. Int'l Conf. on Hum. Rts., 1968 U.N.Y.B. 538 U.N. Sales No. E.70.I.1., 540.

7. Betsy Hartmann, Reproductive Rights and Wrongs: The Global Politics of Population Control and Contraceptive Choice 33 (1987)

The solution to the population problem lies not in the diminution of rights, but in their *expansion*. This is because the population problem is not really about a surplus of human numbers, but a lack of basic rights. Too many people have too little access to resources. Too many women have too little control over their own reproduction. Rapid population growth is not the cause of underdevelopment; it is a symptom of the slow pace of social reform.

Two basic sets of rights are at issue. First is the right of everyone on the earth today, not just in the future, to enjoy a decent standard of living through access to food, shelter, health care, education, employment, and social security. . . . Once people's physical survival is ensured and children are no longer their only source of security, history shows that population growth rates fall voluntarily. . . .

The right to a decent standard of living is necessary but not sufficient. The other critical right is the fundamental right of women to control their own reproduction. The expansion of reproductive choice, not population control, should be the goal of family planning programs and contraceptive research.

8. Elizabeth Spahn, Feeling Grounded: A Gendered View of Population Control, 27 Envtl. L. 1295, 1306–10 (1997)

A consensus developed at the 1994 United Nations International Conference on Population and Development (ICPD) is that the most effective approach to lowering female fertility involves empowering women rather than attempting to control them. . . .

There are four major factors . . . influencing a reduction in births. First, and statistically most significant to lowering female fertility rates, is the increase of secondary education for girls. Even just focusing on basic literacy helps significantly, but secondary education is preferable. Second, ensuring access to a full spectrum of reproductive health care, including family planning, but in particular treatment for reproductive tract infections, is a significant factor in the reduction of births. Third, providing economic opportunities, especially employment for which actual wages are paid directly to the women workers, and land rights directly held by women farmers instead of through male intermediaries, influences birth rates. Fourth, strengthening women's ability to make and implement their own decisions about their education, health, and economic lives (empowerment) in both the private and public aspects of their lives can reduce the number of births. Combining all four techniques is obviously the most effective approach to developing an environment, which will tend to encourage lower female fertility rates.

9. Program of Action of the International Conference on Population and Development, Sept. 13, 1994, Report of the International Conference on Population and Development, U.N. Conference on Population and Development, principles 4–11, U.N. Doc. A/CONF./171/13 (Annex) (1994)

Principle 4

Advancing gender equality and equity and the empowerment of women, and the elimination of all kinds of violence against women, and ensuring women's ability to control their own fertility, are cornerstones of population and development-related programmes. The human rights of women and the girl child are an inalienable, integral and indivisible part of universal human rights. The full and equal participation of women in civil, cultural, economic, political and social life, at the national, regional and international levels, and the eradication of all forms of discrimination on grounds of sex, are priority objectives of the international community.

Principle 5

Population-related goals and policies are integral parts of cultural, economic and social development, the principal aim of which is to improve the quality of life of all people.

Principle 6

Sustainable development as a means to ensure human well-being, equitably shared by all people today and in the future, requires that the interrelationships between population, resources, the environment and development should be fully recognized, properly managed and brought into harmonious, dynamic balance. To achieve sustainable development and a higher quality of life for all people, States should reduce and eliminate unsustainable patterns of production and consumption and promote appropriate policies, including population-related policies, in order to meet the needs of current generations without compromising the ability of future generations to meet their own needs.

Principle 7

All States and all people shall cooperate in the essential task of eradicating poverty as an indispensable requirement for sustainable development, in order to decrease the disparities in standards of living and better meet the needs of the majority of the people of the world. The special situation and needs of developing countries, particularly the least developed, shall be given special priority. Countries with economies in transition, as well as all other countries, need to be fully integrated into the world economy.

Principle 8

Everyone has the right to the enjoyment of the highest attainable standard of physical and mental health. States should take all appropriate measures to ensure, on a basis of equality of men and women, universal access to health-care services, including those related to reproductive health care, which includes family planning and sexual health. Reproductive health-care programmes should provide the widest range of services without any form of coercion. All couples and individuals have the basic right to decide freely and responsibly the number and spacing of their children and to have the information, education and means to do so.

Principle 9

The family is the basic unit of society and as such should be strengthened. It is entitled to receive comprehensive protection and support. In different cultural, political and social systems, various forms of the family exist. Marriage must be entered into with the free consent of the intending spouses, and husband and wife should be equal partners.

Principle 10

Everyone has the right to education, which shall be directed to the full development of human resources, and human dignity and potential, with particular attention to women and the girl child.

Education should be designed to strengthen respect for human rights and fundamental freedoms, including those relating to population and development. The best interests of the child shall be the guiding principle of those responsible for his or her education and guidance; that responsibility lies in the first place with the parents.

Principle 11

All States and families should give the highest possible priority to children. The child has the right to standards of living adequate for its well-being and the right to the highest attainable standards of health, and the right to education. The child has the right to be cared for, guided and supported by parents, families and society and to be protected by appropriate legislative, administrative, social and educational measures from all forms of physical or mental violence, injury or abuse, neglect or negligent treatment, maltreatment or exploitation, including sale, trafficking, sexual abuse, and trafficking in its organs.

10. The Laxenburg Declaration on Population and Sustainable Development, statement of a Global Expert Panel (October 2011) (excerpts)

Efforts to meet the legitimate needs and aspirations of rapidly growing populations in developing countries and to reduce poverty will entail higher consumption and production; if inappropriately managed, these efforts will further increase pressure on the natural environment. As well as increasing carbon emissions through fossil fuel combustion with current technologies, population growth also often contributes to depletion and degradation of essential life-support systems, including deforestation, depletion of aquatic resources, air pollution, loss of biodiversity and degradation of agricultural lands. It is important to reduce such negative impacts on the environment and the global climate in order to derive multiple benefits for local as well as global sustainable development.

Fertility decline in high-fertility countries, by slowing population growth, makes many environmental problems easier to solve and development easier to achieve. Some of these benefits operate through the changing age structure that declining fertility induces. If the number of children relative to the working-age population is reduced, the demographic dependency ratio falls, creating an opportunity to increase investments in health, education, infrastructure, and environmental protection.

11. Steven W. Sinding, Population, Poverty, and Economic Development, 364 Phil. Trans. R. Soc. B 3023, 3030 (2009)

Empirical studies increasingly support the idea that countries which have incorporated population policies and family planning programmes in their overall economic development strategies have achieved high and sustained rates of economic growth and that they have also managed significant reductions in poverty. Fertility reduction is by no means an economic development panacea and is certainly not a sufficient condition for economic growth, but it may well be a necessary condition, establishing conditions in which governments can invest more per capita in education and health, thus creating the human capital for sustained economic growth. Likewise, with fewer children to care for and raise, families can improve their prospects for escaping the poverty trap. . . .

Throughout the developing world, declining birth rates and rising living standards have gone hand in hand. The evidence suggests that the interrelationship between them represents a virtuous circle, whereby improvements in one reinforce and accelerate improvements in the other. The virtuous circle can be initiated either by investing in human development programmes such as healthcare and education or by investing in programmes to reduce fertility. But the example of the East Asian Tigers suggests that the best strategies have been those that do the two simultaneously.

12. United Nations Population Fund, Population Matters for Sustainable Development 10 (2012)

Efforts to promote sustainable development that do not address population dynamics have, and will continue to, fail.

* * *

[C]ountries have powerful instruments [for reducing population growth], which not only respect, but strengthen human rights and freedoms and support human development.

First, countries can direct individual choices and opportunities through incentives rather than controls, and can address population dynamics by enlarging, rather than restricting, individual choices and opportunities. . . .

Second, countries must empower women not only to decide on the number and timing of their children, by providing adequate access to sexual and reproductive health care, but also to promote their active participation in economic, social and political life. . . . Women who lack education and economic opportunities often have more children, and because they have more children many women lack education and economic opportunities. Such poverty traps must be broken through decisive policies. . . .

Third, countries must recognize, cultivate and seize the powerful potential of youth populations, be they small or large. . . .

Fourth, poverty constrains individual choices and opportunities, and countries should take active measures to combat poverty and develop human capabilities and functionings.

Section 5. Discussion Notes/Questions

1. In considering Songhay's population policy, is there any difference in the human rights analysis of the different methods it uses to encourage families to restrict the number of children they have? For instance, is required attendance at a family planning meeting a human rights violation? Provision of state-funded education only to one child? Required use of contraceptives? Denial of choice of contraceptives? Forced abortion? Are any of Songhay's techniques acceptable from a human rights perspective, or are all efforts to influence a woman's child-bearing decision a violation of fundamental reproductive rights?

Is a state's adoption of policies that encourage the use of contraception a violation of the religious rights of persons whose religious leaders preach against contraception? Does the provision of contraceptive education in public schools violate the rights of parents to control their children's religious education?

Principle 8 of the ICPD Programme of Action (Reading 9) states, in part, that "all couples and individuals have the basic right to decide freely and responsibly the number and spacing of their children . . . ." What is the significance of the phrase "and responsibly"? Does this mean that governments can discourage, or even punish, reproductive choices that are considered irresponsible? If not, what does it mean?

Do you think the policies mentioned in Reading 12 would, without more, be sufficient to reduce a country's population growth rate? Can poverty reduction occur without *first* reducing population growth?

2. President George W. Bush cut off funding to the United Nations Population Fund because, he said, "UNFPA's support of, and involvement in, China's population planning activities allows the Chinese government to implement more effectively its program of coercive abortion." UNFPA's executive director replied that "UNFPA does not support or promote abortion anywhere in the world. The services we promote reduce the incidence of abortion." *See* Sean D. Murphy, *U.S. Funding for the UN Population Fund*, 96 Am. J. Int'l L. 962–63 (2002). There is evidence, in fact, that the abortion rate in China is significantly lower than in the United States.

One factor in President Bush's decision may have been pressure from non-governmental organizations that are resolutely opposed to contraception and the kinds of family planning practices (not including abortion) encouraged by UNFPA. The Catholic Church believes that contraception is morally wrong, see *Humanae Vitae*, para. 14, Encyclical Letter of Pope Paul VI, and some NGOs closely allied with that church are actively involved in promoting the view that population control is unnecessary and that the UNFPA's activities are improper. *See* Population Research Institute, http://www.pop.org/about (visited on January 4, 2019).

Under the Obama Administration, U.S. funding for UNFPA increased considerably. Under the Trump Administration, U.S. policy again changed course. In April 2017, the State Department announced that it would cut all funding for the United Nations Population Fund on the grounds that UNFPA's partnership with China's National Health and Family Planning Commission created a risk that U.S. funds would "subsidize coercive abortion services." Members of Congress opposed to the decision stated that UNFPA has never supported or participated in any "coercive abortion or involuntary sterilization" programs. Mike Lillis, *Dems press Trump to restore family planning funding,* 2017 The Hill 328224, 2017 WL 1323553 (April 11, 2017).

3. Do we have too many people or too much consumption? Many people would say "both." If so, do policies focused on population control and/or reproductive choice address the problem if they do not also aim at reducing consumption? The evidence suggests that reductions in population spur economic growth and economic growth spurs population reduction. *See* David E. Bloom and David Canning, *Population, Poverty Reduction and the Cairo Agenda,* in Reproductive Health and Human Rights: The Way Forward 51 (Laura Reichenbach & Mindy Jane Roseman, ed. 2009). But doesn't this suggest that we are just replacing one problem (too many people) with another (ever growing consumption)? How can we address this?

4. Some commentators argue, in Malthusian fashion, that one solution to the population problem is for developed nations to adopt policies that make it more difficult for poorer nations to deal with their over-population problem. Thus, for example, Robert Hardaway argues that developed countries should adopt restrictive immigration policies:

> [A]s long as a country has the option of simply exporting humans in order to relieve population pressures within its boundaries, it will have no incentive to take on the Church or other groups which resist any kind of population or family planning policy. The export of excess humans, whom the country cannot feed or support, becomes the path of least resistance.
>
> Immigration reform in the developed countries of the world would force human-exporting countries to come to grips with their own population problems, including designing a system of family planning services and providing contraceptives to all of its citizens.

Robert M. Hardaway, *Environmental Malthusianism: Integrating Population and Environmental Policy*, 27 Envtl. L. 1209, 1241 (1997). Virginia Dean Abernethy similarly condemns "generous immigration policies and international economic development aid" on the ground that such practices

> send[ ] the message abroad that local constraints can be discounted because international wealth is abundant and opportunity is beckoning. If people believe that negative signals coming from their own environment and economy can be safely ignored, incentives to exercise marital and reproductive caution are overwhelmed. . . . The result of open-handed immigration and foreign assistance policies is almost sure to be continuing high fertility . . . .

On the other hand, she suggests, if people in the developing world know that international rescue is not coming, then they will understand that it is their responsibility to deal with their population problem themselves, and "one [can] proceed with confidence that worldwide fertility will swiftly fall." In this view, not all foreign aid is suspect (e.g., support for family planning programs is appropriate). What is disfavored is aid that helps a country cope with its problems of poverty and over-population without forcing it to develop solutions to those problems. Virginia Deane Abernethy, *Allowing Fertility Decline: 200 Years After Malthus's Essay on Population*, 27 Envtl. L. 1097 (1997).

Do you agree with these policy prescriptions? One problem with such analyses is that there isn't any empirical evidence to back them up: no studies of over-population suggest that helping a country improve its standard of living (e.g., by providing it with foreign aid or accepting immigrants or guest workers from that country) causes it to have higher birth rates than it would otherwise have. Indeed, the evidence suggests the contrary: fertility rates fall as states become economically better off. The countries with the highest fertility rates are also often the most desperately poor countries with the lowest prospects for economic development.

5. As populations age and birthrates decline in developed countries, a different kind of population problem emerges: a lack of a sufficiently large working age population to support the pension and health care needs of older citizens. *See* Wolfgang Lutz, Brian C. O'Neill, & Sergei Scherbov, *Europe's Population at a Turning Point,* 299 Science 1991 (2003). According to the United Nations, as of 2017, 83 countries had fertility rates below the level necessary for long-term replacement of the population.

Is the acceptance of substantial numbers of immigrants from over-populated countries a viable response to this problem? How about a policy of encouraging higher local birth rates? The United Nations reports that 28% of governments worldwide have policies in place to *raise* fertility rates. In Europe, two-thirds of governments pursue such policies. This compares with 42% of governments worldwide that are seeking to lower their fertility rates. *See* United Nations Department of Economic and Social Affairs—Population Division, *Population Facts,* no. 2017/10 (December 2017).

6. A fundamental assumption of the 1994 World Population Plan is that if given reproductive choice (e.g., through access to contraceptives) women will choose to have fewer children. This has the added bonus that the choice to have fewer children can empower women in other ways, including by giving them more economic opportunity. *See* Barbara Stark, *International Human Rights and Family Planning: A Modest Proposal,* 18 Den. J. Int'l L. & Pol'y 59, 78 (1989). So reproductive choice is celebrated as both a human right, a means to achieve lower population growth, and an economic-development tool.

But should reproductive choice include the choice to have as many children as one wishes, regardless of long-term social consequences? If it does include the freedom to have as many children as desired, should people who are denied the right to have two children be treated as human rights refugees? Three children? Four? Five? *See generally* Stefanie M. Duda, *Drawing the Interpretive Lines for Victims of Coercive Population Control: Why the Definition of 'Refugee' Should Include Spouses of Individuals Fleeing China's One-Child Policy,* 4 Seton Hall Circuit Rev. 409 (2008).

7. It is often suggested that educating women as to contraception is one of the best ways to address the population issue. It should be noted, however, that cultural constraints in the South limit the effectiveness of such programs. In some studies, male partner acceptance of contraceptive use is one of the greatest determinants of birth rates. *See* Lori L. Heise, *Freedom Close To Home,* 19 Populi No. 6, at 7 (1992). Such studies point to the cultural and other barriers (such as religion) that any international initiative is required to address. Should rights override cultural and religious norms? Would attempts to do so merely exacerbate the situation?

8. It has been denied by Chinese officials that coercion is part of official policy. However, the use of physical force was sufficiently documented to indicate its widespread use in the 1980s and 1990s. At one point, Chinese officials conceded that although "the Chinese Government does not condone forced abortions or sterilizations, . . . coercion, even though counter to official

policy, does occur in some instances." *See Is China's Birth Control Program Still Coercive?: Hearings Before the Senate Comm. on Foreign Relations*, 100th Cong., 1st Sess. (1987), *cited in* Note, *Coercive Population Control Policies: An Illustration of the Need for a Conscientious Objector Provision for Asylum Seekers*, 30 Va.J.Int'l L. 1007, 1012 (1990).

In 2016 China replaced its one-child policy with a two-child policy and, in 2018, began planning for further reforms including the possibility of a removal of the two-child limit. There is some speculation that China might begin encouraging or mandating larger families in order deal with the problem of a shrinking pool of young workers to support China's growing elderly population. Do you think policies to increase a country's birthrate are an appropriate response to the problems caused by an aging population?

9. In the developing world, environmental concerns and human rights are often perceived as a luxury, to be addressed after more pressing issues of human life and death are managed. Consider the following quote by Shen Guozian, director of publicity at China's Family Planning Commission: "If America had 1.1 billion people, then they would not be so concerned about this humanitarianism they talk about." *As quoted in* James Kynge, *China Steps Up Enforcement of 1-Child-Per-Family Law*, L.A. Times, May 6, 1990, at A4. On the other hand, human rights are generally perceived to be universal claims that are recognized as of right, not by love, grace, or charity. *See, e.g.*, Human Rights in the World Community: Issues and Action (Richard Pierre Claude & Burns H. Weston eds. and contribs., 3d ed., 2006). *See also* Myres S. McDougal, Harold Lasswell, & Lung-Chu Chen, Human Rights and World Public Order: The Basic Policies of an International Law of Human Dignity (1980).

10. What tests and/or mechanisms should be employed to recognize the more limited ability of the developing world to meet population limit standards? Should the developing world be allowed lower human rights or environmental standards at all? Does the developed world have an obligation in law to increase the ability of the developing world to meet standards?

11. There is an extensive literature analyzing the link between population and economic development, and it paints a much more complicated picture than that presented by Malthus or his critics. The evidence now suggests strongly that high population growth in low-income countries inhibits economic development, though it can be advantageous in some circumstances. *See* E. Wesley F. Peterson, *The Role of Population in Economic Growth,* SAGE Open, October-December 2017: 1–15 (2017) (and works cited therein). Empirical evidence also suggests that population-control policies in developing countries have caused a decline in fertility rates that would not have occurred otherwise and that those fertility-rate declines have contributed to rising standards of living in those countries. *See* John Bongaarts, *Development: Slow down population growth,* 530 Nature 409 (2016); Tiloka de Silva & Silvana Tenreyro, *Population Control Policies and Fertility Convergence,* 31 J. Econ. Persp. 205 (2017). *See also* Growth and Poverty in Sub-Saharan Africa (eds. Channing Arndt, Andy McKay & Finn Tarp, 2016); Andrey Korotayev, Jack A.

Soldstone & Julia Zinkina, *Phases of global demographic transition correlate with phases of the Great Divergence and Great Convergence,* 95 Tech. Forecasting & Soc. Change 163 (2015); Africa's Demographic Transition: Dividend or Disaster (eds. David Canning, Sangeeta Raja & Abdo S. Yazbeck, October 2015), https://doi.org/10.1596/978-1-4648-0489-2; O. Galor & D.N. Weil, *Population, Technology, and Growth: From Malthusian Stagnation to the Demographic Transition and Beyond,* 90 Am. Econ. Rev. 808 (2000).

INDEX

References are to Pages

INDEX

References are to Pages